ABNORMAL PSYCHOLOGY

CONTRASTING PERSPECTIVES

JONATHAN D.
RASKIN

RED GLOBE
PRESS

First published 2019 by
RED GLOBE PRESS

Red Globe Press in the UK is an imprint of Springer Nature Limited, registered in England, company number 785998, of 4 Crinan Street, London, N1 9XW.

Red Globe Press® is a registered trademark in the United States, the United Kingdom, Europe and other countries.

ISBN 978–1–137–54716–3 paperback

This book is printed on paper suitable for recycling and made from fully managed and sustained forest sources. Logging, pulping and manufacturing processes are expected to conform to the environmental regulations of the country of origin.

A catalogue record for this book is available from the British Library.

A catalog record for this book is available from the Library of Congress.

BRIEF CONTENTS

/////////////////////////////////////

TABLE OF CONTENTS

LIST OF FIGURES

///////////////////////////////

LIST OF TABLES

LIST OF DIAGNOSTIC BOXES

LIST OF FEATURES

TOUR OF THE BOOK

 LEARNING OBJECTIVES

After reading this chapter, you should be able to:

1. Explain why contradictory perspectives are common in abnormal psychology.
2. Define psychopathology, mental illness, harmful internal dysfunction, deviance, and social oppression.
3. Summarize common criteria of abnormality.
4. Describe historical perspectives on abnormality from the Stone Age to the present day.
5. Distinguish and explain the many types of quantitative and qualitative research perspectives.

LEARNING OUTCOMES

Structure your learning by focusing on the key points of understanding for this chapter.

Photo source: © Royalty-Free/Corbis

CASE EXAMPLES

Follow the developing stories of clients to keep the service-user at the forefront of your practice.

GETTING STARTED: HOW DO DEVELOPMENTAL ISSUES IMPACT BEHAVIOR?

Mark

Mark is a 9-year-old boy whose school has referred him for a psychological assessment because of his disruptive behavior in class. Mark has trouble staying in his seat and regularly interrupts his teacher. He bothers the other children, finds it difficult to pay attention to his work for more than a few minutes at a time, and often forgets to do his homework. Mark's parents aren't sure they see what the big deal is, although Mark seems to have some of the same problems at home—he forgets to complete his chores and is often loud and unruly. "Boys will be boys!" says his father. The school, however, is demanding that something be done.

CASE EXAMPLES

Source: © Royalty-Free/Corbis

CONTROVERSIAL QUESTION

Do Vaccines Cause Autism?

A 1998 study in the leading medical journal *The Lancet* found a link between receiving the measles-mumps-rubella (MMR) vaccine (typically administered between 12 and 15 months of age) and the development of autism symptoms (A. J. Wakefield et al., 1998). The study led to the widespread belief that the MMR vaccine can cause autism. However, most researchers and practicing doctors believe the study has been thoroughly debunked. How so? First, it's been refuted on scientific grounds, with study after study consistently finding no evidence that the MMR vaccine leads to autism (Ahearn, 2010; Demicheli, Rivetti, Debalini, & Di Pietrantonj, 2012; DeStefano, 2002; A. Jain et al., 2016; A. Jain et al., 2015; L. E. Taylor, Swerdfeger, & Eslick, 2014; Uchiyama, Kurosawa, & Inaba, 2007). Second, the study was retracted by *The Lancet* following allegations that the lead author of the paper, Dr. Andrew Wakefield, and several of his co-authors manipulated their data (T. S. S. Rao & Andrade, 2011; "Retraction—Ileal-lymphoid-nodular hyperplasia, non-specific colitis, and pervasive developmental disorder in children," 2010). It was also alleged that Wakefield had a financial conflict of interest because he received funding from a legal group seeking evidence that it could use to sue vaccine manufacturers (Deer, 2004; Godlee, Smith, & Marcovitch, 2011). In the aftermath of the controversy and his study's retraction, Wakefield's medical license was revoked by the U.K.'s General Medical Council (2010).

Despite the scandal and the consensus among most researchers that the MMR vaccine doesn't pose an autism risk, many parents continue to worry (Fischbach, Harris, Ballan, Fischbach, & Link, 2016). Because this can influence whether they have their children vaccinated, most health professionals warn that providing effective education about the safety of vaccines is critical—especially considering evidence that when vaccination rates go down, health and financial costs go up (K. F. Brown et al., 2012; Centers for Disease Control and Prevention, 2014; Demicheli et al., 2012; Godlee et al., 2011; C. King & Leask, 2017). The U.S. Centers for Disease Control and Prevention (2014) notes that before the measles vaccine, hundreds of children died every year from measles and that a 1964–65 outbreak of rubella (German measles) resulted in 12.5 million infections, 11,000 miscarriages, and the deaths of 2,000 babies.

Nonetheless, many people—including prominent celebrities such as Robert De Niro and Jenny McCarthy—continue to assert that the MMR vaccine contributes to autism and that further research on the topic is necessary (*Frontline*, 2015; H. Parry, 2016). Many research scientists have strongly pushed back, arguing that those who keep advocating the vaccine–autism link

Despite a large body of research evidence suggesting otherwise, many people still believe that vaccines can cause autism.
Source: BANANASTOCK

Photo source: © Getty Images/iStockphoto Thinkstock Images/bahri altay

CONTROVERSIAL QUESTION

Explore opposing perspectives on a "hot topic" currently bedevilling the field.

IN DEPTH

Ignorance and Abnormal Psychology

A 2015 *New York Times* opinion piece by Jamie Holmes advocates acknowledging that we often know less than we claim. In other words, ignorance is a lot more rampant than most of us wish to admit—even in academic subjects where we usually are told otherwise. Holmes describes how, in the 1980s, University of Arizona surgery professor Professor Marlys H. Witte created controversy when she began teaching a class called "Introduction to Medical and Other Ignorance." She wanted to include ignorance in her class because she believed we often ignore or minimize how little we know about many topics (Jamie Holmes, 2015). In Witte's view, textbooks often contribute to the problem. For example, she pointed out that surgery textbooks usually discuss pancreatic cancer without ever mentioning that our present understanding of it is extremely limited. Her goal? Helping students appreciate that questions are as important as answers (Jamie Holmes, 2015).

Some might deem it foolish of me to share Holmes' opinion piece at the very start of a textbook on abnormal psychology. Yet my experience teaching this course over the years fits nicely with Holmes' thesis. I once had a student who, several weeks into the class, said she was going back to being a math major. "At least in math, there are clear right answers," she exclaimed. "In abnormal psychology, there are so many conflicting viewpoints that it's hard to know what the right answer is." Admittedly, despite all the attempts at bringing rigorous research into an integrative perspective, all too often most abnormal psychology textbooks overstate how much we know. But acknowledging our ignorance up front potentially opens, rather than closes, possibilities. Holmes notes that we often think of ignorance as something to be eliminated, viewing it as simply lack of knowledge. Yet answers, Holmes (2015) notes, don't put an end to questions; they simply give rise to new questions! As you read this text, here's to the many questions you will hopefully begin to ask.

CRITICAL THINKING QUESTIONS

1. Do you think Witte's contention that ignorance is more rampant than we usually admit is applicable to abnormal psychology?
2. Does recognizing the limits of our knowledge about abnormality help us? If so, how?

Photo source: © PhotoDisc/Getty Images

IN DEPTH

Take a deep dive into a particular issue of interest.

THE LIVED EXPERIENCE

Two of Jill's TAT Stories

These are Jill's imagined responses to being shown the cards described below.

Card 3: Woman standing next to open door with hand to downcast face

Jill: "A woman woke up and her husband yelled at her for not cleaning up properly. Her kids were running around and making her crazy. The dog ran through and the kids spilled fruit punch. Her mail was full of bills. So, she called a babysitter, bought an airline ticket to Bermuda on her husband's credit card, and left. In Bermuda, she fell in love with a sexy Bermuda guy and never returned."

» HERO: woman
» OUTCOME: runs away to escape
» THEMES: responsibility, frustration, need to escape, familial relationships

Card 6: Young woman on sofa with older man smoking cigar behind her

Jill: "A 15-year old girl's father refuses to let her meet her boyfriend for a date because she isn't 16. The girl sneaks out of the house to meet him anyway. She has a wonderful time, but while kissing her boyfriend on the porch she is caught by her father. The father calls the boyfriend a cradle robber, then lectures the girl while smoking a cigar. The mother comes downstairs and tells the father to leave the girl alone because they were dating at her age. The mother also makes the father put out the cigar. The girl calls the boyfriend for a date the next night."

» HERO: the girl
» OUTCOME: positive; can see boyfriend, but without resolving father conflict
» THEMES: control, rebellion against authority, father–daughter relationship

For each card on the Thematic Apperception Test (TAT), the test-taker generates stories; common themes are often identified to understand client issues.
Source: Jonathan D. Raskin

Photo source: © PHOTOALTO

THE LIVED EXPERIENCE

Hear directly from clients and clinicians in these firsthand accounts.

Can My Smartphone Help Me Overcome an Eating Disorder?

TRY IT YOURSELF

If you can download an app onto your smartphone to help you keep track of your bank account, manage your exercise regimen, and keep tabs on the weather, why not an app to help you manage an eating disorder? One journal article provided a scholarly review of various smartphone apps designed for just that purpose, with special praise for those incorporating therapeutic features backed by research (Juarascio, Manasse, Goldstein, Forman, & Butryn, 2015). Below, two of the apps are described. Because they are free, you are encouraged to download one or both of them to your smartphone and check them out for yourself.

Smartphone apps have been developed to help people diagnosed with eating disorders.
Source: Getty Images/Image Source \ Image Source

» *Recovery Record* "allows users to set clinical goals, many of which are based on cognitive-behavioral strategies" (Juarascio et al., 2015, p. 6). This app contains various features consistent with empirically supported aspects of CBT-E and ACT, including providing users with information about in-the-moment and acceptance-based coping strategies. Users can also set goals for themselves, keep track of their food intake, and record their thoughts and emotions. This app is available in both Apple iOS and Google Android formats (Healthline, n.d.).

» *Rise Up + Recover* allows users to log what they eat, their corresponding feelings, and "target" behaviors such as bingeing and purging (R. Goldman, 2018). The app incorporates CBT-E coping skills (such as contacting friends during times of distress). It also contains "modules that include topics such as cultivating positive body image, building strong relationships with others, journaling, and mindfulness practice" (Juarascio et al., 2015, p. 6). This app is only available for Apple iOS (R. Goldman, 2018).

Photo source: © PhotoDisc/Getty Images

TRY IT YOURSELF

Complete a questionnaire or participate in a suggested real-life exercise to get a more personal perspective.

Diagnostic Box 15.2 Nonsuicidal Self Injury (NSSI)

Proposed DSM-5 Disorder
- Intentional self-inflicted damage to the surface of one's body during at least five days over the past year (e.g., cutting, burning, stabbing, hitting, excessive rubbing) without any intent of suicide.
- The self-injury is intended to accomplish at least one of these: (a) reduce negative thoughts and feelings; (b) address interpersonal conflict; (c) produce a state of positive feeling.
- The self-injury is related to at least one of these: (a) interpersonal conflicts or negative thoughts and feelings (e.g., depression, anxiety, tension, anger, self-criticism, or emotional upset) that occur immediately prior to the self-injury; (b) being preoccupied with the self-injurious behavior before doing it; (c) recurrent thoughts about the self-injury, whether acted on or not.
- The self-injury isn't socially approved (e.g., a tattoo, body piercing, or religious ritual) and is more serious than just picking a scab or biting one's nails.
- The behavior isn't due to delirium, psychosis, substance use, or substance withdrawal; it also isn't better explained by another disorder (e.g., autism spectrum disorder, stereotypic movement disorder, or hair-pulling disorder).

Based on American Psychiatric Association, 2013b, p. 803

ICD-11
- Intentional self-injury (e.g., cutting, scraping, burning, biting, or hitting).
- The self-injuring person expects no significant harm from the self-injury.

Based on https://icd.who.int/browse11/l-m/en

DIAGNOSTIC BOXES

DSM and *ICD* diagnoses summarized in clear, understandable language.

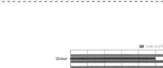

Figure 15.1 Proportion of all Violent De[aths]
Source: World Health Organization (2014, p. 23, ...

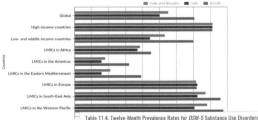

Table 11.4. Twelve-Month Prevalence Rates for *DSM-5* Substance Use Disorders

Disorder Type	Ages 12–17	Ages 18+	Men	Women
Alcohol Use Disorder	4.6%	8.5%	12.4%	4.9%
Cannabis Use Disorder	3.4%	1.5%	2.2%	0.8%
Phencyclidine Use Disorder	Unknown	Unknown	Unknown	Unknown
Other Hallucinogen-Use Disorder	0.5%	0.1%	0.2%	0.1%
Inhalant Use Disorder	0.4%	0.02%	0.02%	Close to 0%
Opioid Use Disorder	1.0%	0.37%	0.49%	0.26%
Sedative, Hypnotic, or Anxiolytic Use Disorder	0.3%	0.2%	0.3% (ages 18+); 0.2% (ages 12-17)	Slightly less than 0.3% (ages 18+); 0.4% (ages 12-17).

FIGURES AND TABLES

Discover important real-life data and anatomical diagrams.

KEY TERMS

Acceptance and commitment therapy (ACT)
Accommodation
Agoraphobia
Anterior cingulate cortex
Anxiety
Anxiolytics
Augmenting agents
Avoidance model of worry
Barbiturates
Beta blockers
Body dysmorphic disorder (BDD)
Buspirone
Catastrophic misinterpretation model of panic disorder
Compulsions
Corticostriatal pathophysiological models
Emotional dysregulation model
Excoriation (skin-picking disorder)
Existential anxiety

Existential givens
Fear
Generalized anxiety disorder (GAD)
Genome-wide association (GWA) study
Glutamate hypothesis of OCD
Group selection
Group selection theory of OCD
Gut-brain axis
Hoarding disorder
Imaginal exposure
In vivo exposure
Inhibitory learning
Insula
Intolerance of uncertainty model

Obsessions
Obsessive-compulsive disorder (OCD)
Panic attack
Panic disorder
Participant modeling
Prepared conditioning
Progressive relaxation
Rat Man
Relaxation training
Selective mutism
Separation anxiety disorder
Social anxiety disorder (social phobia)
Specific phobia
Striatum

In Vivo vs. Imaginal Exposure

Ideally, exposure therapies are done in real life with genuine exposure to the actual anxiety-provoking objects or situations. This is called *in vivo exposure*. However, real life exposure isn't always practical or possible. In such cases, clinicians use *imaginal exposure*, in which people are simply asked to imagine the feared scenario. The limitation of imaginal exposure is that it may not be as powerful as *in vivo* exposure. To counter this, clinicians have developed *virtual reality exposure*, which uses computer-generated virtual reality experiences to help clients face their fears. Evidence suggests that virtual reality exposure can be effective (Denney, Sullivan, & Thiry, 1977; D. Hughes, 1990).

KEY TERMS

Important terminology is highlighted as you encounter it and gathered in a handy checklist at the end of each chapter.

Immune system perspectives: Emphasize the importance of the immune system (the system of cells and biological processes used to fight off pathogens) in understanding psychopathology. (2)

In vivo exposure: Exposure technique in which client is exposed to the actual anxiety-provoking objects or situations in order to condition a new, non-anxious response to them. (6)

GLOSSARY

Vocabulary from the entire book alphabetically in one convenient location.

ONLINE LEARNING AND TEACHING RESOURCES

Accompanying this book is a full suite of supportive resources to help both students and lecturers get the most out of their learning and teaching.

Access the companion website here:

www.macmillanihe.com/raskin-abnormal-psych

Resources to help instructors teach with this book include:

- **Online test bank**: Multiple choice items to help instructors construct exams and quizzes.
- **Online instructor's manual**: Detailed lecture notes for each chapter.
- **Lecture slides**: MS® PowerPoint slides for instructors to use during class lectures.
- **Slides of diagnostic boxes, images, tables, and figures**: Visual information from chapters conveniently collected into one MS® PowerPoint file per chapter.
- **Online videos**: YouTube videos related to key topics from the book.

Students can benefit from the following resources to help their understanding of the key concepts and ideas in each chapter:

- **Online knowledge checks**: Test your comprehension using these brief online self-quizzes.
- **Online study guide**: Study questions to help students outline material from each chapter.
- **Online vocabulary lists**: Key terms and definitions all in one convenient online location.
- **Online flash cards**: An excellent study resource to help students master key concepts.

PREFACE

//////////////

THE CHALLENGE OF CONTRASTING PERSPECTIVES

When it comes to the discipline within psychology commonly referred to as "abnormal psychology," the one thing on which everyone can probably agree is that there isn't much agreement. On the contrary, abnormal psychology is a field filled with contrasting perspectives—different lenses that, when looked through, inevitably shape the definitions of abnormality arrived at, the research questions asked about it, and the clinical interventions undertaken to alleviate it. This makes sense because what counts as "abnormal" is inevitably a judgment call and the kinds of explanations offered to explain why people behave abnormally vary widely depending on one's point of view. Even when we do agree that particular ways of behaving are "abnormal," it doesn't necessarily mean we also agree on what causes such behavior. Is abnormal behavior mainly attributable to neurochemical imbalances or other brain disorders, genetic inheritance, immune system reactions to stress, evolutionary mismatches between our ancestral environments and modern society, unconscious conflicts, faulty attachment relationships, irrational thinking, conditioned learning, a failure to self-actualize, cultural differences, economic adversity, social oppression, or some combination thereof? To many students' dismay, the number of potential explanations can be dizzying!

To illustrate just how fractured the field of abnormal psychology can be, a couple of the reviewers who read this textbook while it was under development strongly advised that we not use "Abnormal Psychology" as our book's title. Why? Because to these reviewers, the term "abnormal" is stigmatizing and dismissive. It fails to appreciate or respect the many complex and diverse ways that human beings suffer emotionally. Thus, these reviewers recommended we adopt a less pathologizing title, such as "Mental Distress and Well-being." Their quite reasonable rationale was that labeling atypical or emotionally distressed people as "abnormal" is pejorative and inappropriate.

Yet despite these understandable objections, not everyone is troubled by the term "abnormal psychology." It is likely that many instructors and students would have been duly confused had we jettisoned the term as our book's title. For better or worse, the term "abnormal psychology" remains unquestioningly accepted in many (most?) professional and research domains—as evidenced by its continued and widespread use (with exceptions here and there) as a course title in undergraduate and graduate psychology programs around the globe. That some people view the term "abnormal psychology" as problematic while others take no issue with it at all is quite telling. It is a testament to divisions within the field—to the many contrasting perspectives this text endeavors to teach students about. As we shall see, those advancing these contrasting perspectives on "abnormal psychology" (or "mental distress and well-being," if you prefer) are often exceedingly passionate about their divergent outlooks.

This book tries to capture that passion by examining not simply the wide variety of perspectives on abnormal psychology, but also the ways that advocates of these perspectives often strongly and loudly disagree. The idea is to fully and thoroughly present these disagreements—but without being disagreeable! In order to accomplish this, the book adopts a *credulous approach* (Kelly, 1955/1991a), in which—rather than immediately judging the contrasting perspectives presented—students are encouraged to understand and appreciate each perspective in its own right. To that end, each perspective's theoretical rationale for viewing particular problems in certain ways is sympathetically discussed, along with how this gives rise to specific strategies for alleviating the problem. Then research on each perspective is examined to help students assess its current status. However, rather than me—as students' humble guide in this endeavor—declaring some perspectives as winners and others as losers, my goal is more modest: to provide necessary information, pose challenging questions, and then encourage students to draw their own conclusions.

Some might question this approach. "Aren't you the expert? Shouldn't you be informing students about which perspectives are most correct?" The trouble with offering definitive answers to students is that, in my experience of teaching abnormal psychology, different students inevitably draw different conclusions about the material they are learning, no matter how hard (or not) I advocate for some perspectives over others. This is so even when exposed to the same theories, research, and practice aspects of these perspectives. In many respects, this isn't surprising. Deciding what is "abnormal" and what to do about it is not simply a dry academic endeavor. It touches on people's core beliefs about what it means to be a person and to live a healthy and productive life. It also taps into students' ideas about themselves and their own personal problems. In this respect, student disagreements about what is or isn't abnormal, what should be done about it, and what the research recommends mirror fundamental disagreements in the field itself. Put simply, abnormal psychology is an arena where clear and definitive answers aren't always readily forthcoming. Thus, this book has a simple and exciting (if at times challenging) goal for students: after digesting the relevant information and trying to understand each perspective in a fair and open manner, students are encouraged to decide for themselves which perspectives they most agree with and why.

PEDAGOGICAL FEATURES

Accomplishing the goals outlined above is a difficult task! So, how does this book attempt to do so? Key features of the book are outlined below. Each feature is intended to help students as they go about the task of mastering the material, as well as to provide instructors with ways to guide and assist them along the way.

- **Learning Objectives**: Each chapter begins with a list of clearly defined learning objectives. By the time they finish studying each chapter, students should be able to fulfill these objectives.
- **Case Examples**: Each chapter presents one or more case examples to help illustrate the topics being explored. Typically introduced at the beginning of the chapter, these cases are regularly revisited to provide concrete instances of the theories and interventions discussed.
- **In Depth**: This feature zeros in on particular topics in order to provide students with a more detailed exploration of areas currently garnering attention. Going in depth on selected topics affords students the opportunity to gain a richer appreciation for the kinds of clinical and research explorations going on in the field.
- **Controversial Question**: Posing controversial questions allows students to grapple with some of the issues that researchers and clinicians often struggle to address. This feature is designed to expose students to prominent and ongoing debates within abnormal psychology.
- **The Lived Experience**: Abnormal psychology is not merely an academic pursuit. The material studied applies to many people's daily lives in unique and powerful ways. This feature brings topics to life by providing firsthand accounts from clients and clinicians alike of their lived experience in dealing with the many presenting problems the book explores.
- **Try It Yourself**: This feature offers activities in which students are invited to try out techniques and methods for themselves. The exercises and activities are intended to help students apply what they are learning in a more personal way.
- **Diagnostic Boxes**: Appearing in most chapters, these provide quick summary comparisons of *DSM-5*, *ICD-10*, and *ICD-11* definitions of disorders and help students grasp the similarities and differences across these three diagnostic schemes.
- **Key Terms**: Key terms are highlighted and defined in the text, listed together at the ends of chapters, and catalogued in the glossary, making it easy for students to master new vocabulary.
- **Glossary**: A comprehensive glossary is provided at the end of the book, with concise definitions of key terms. Glossary definitions also provide the number of the chapter where each term was first introduced in the book.

INFORMATION AND RESOURCES FOR INSTRUCTORS

- **A Perspectives Approach**: Chapters are organized by perspectives, allowing students to "try on" each way of looking at problems in the field. The perspectives typically covered in abnormal psychology texts (e.g., neurochemical, genetic, cognitive-behavioral, and classic psychoanalytic) are given extensive attention, but so are perspectives that often receive less consideration (e.g., immunological, evolutionary, modern psychodynamic, humanistic, social justice, cross-cultural, and systems). Further, rather than presenting traditional mental disorder categories as givens that other perspectives unquestioningly treat, they too are framed as perspectival products—hence the inclusion of *DSM* and *ICD* diagnostic perspectives. This subtle shift allows mental disorder categories to be explored more fully and fairly, without enshrining them as universally accepted (after all, the other perspectives covered have widely contrasting opinions about them). The idea is to place all perspectives side by side, so instructors may present them (as well as critiques lodged against them) in a dispassionate and even-handed manner. This allows instructors to help students understand each perspective's strengths and weaknesses while also encouraging them to develop their own educated points of view.

- **Numbered Sections**: Chapters are divided into numbered sections. Although it is recommended that instructors assign these sections in the order provided, they can easily be assigned in whatever order the instructor deems best. Further, for instructors who wish to spend more than one class on a chapter, specific numbered sections can easily be assigned for different class dates (e.g., "Read Chapter 1, Sections 1.1–1.3").

- **Online Test Bank**: Includes multiple choice questions. In devising the test bank, the goal was to create materials that target key ideas in the book. As a long-time instructor who is well aware of how often test banks disappoint, much effort was put into weeding out poor items and only maintaining those that effectively discriminate student understanding of key concepts.

- **Online Instructor's Manual**: This manual consists of detailed lecture notes for each chapter.

- **Lecture Slides**: MS® PowerPoint slides to accompany the chapter-by-chapter lecture notes in the instructor's manual are provided to use in class and/or to share with students as an additional course resource.

- **Slides of Diagnostic Boxes, Images, Tables, and Figures**: Instructors have access to an additional PowerPoint file per chapter that contains that chapter's diagnostic boxes, images, tables, and figures. Like the lecture slides, these can be used in class and/or shared with students as an additional course resource.

- **Online Videos**: Links to relevant YouTube videos for each chapter are provided. The videos can be assigned for students to view on their own or be shown by instructors in class.

RESOURCES FOR STUDENTS

- **Online Vocabulary Lists**: Chapter-by-chapter vocabulary lists are provided in two ways on the book's online companion website: with and without definitions. This provides students with maximum flexibility in how they use the lists to study.

- **Online Knowledge Checks**: Each chapter has an accompanying online "knowledge-check" quiz that students can complete to quickly assess their understanding; results can easily be sent to instructors.

- **Online Study Guide**: Each chapter includes a study guide, consisting of questions to help students develop study materials. By sketching answers to each of the study guide questions, students will be able to concisely summarize content from the chapters as they prepare for exams.

- **Online Flash Cards**: Students can use these flash cards to help them study for exams. They provide an excellent way for students to test themselves on key terms and concepts.

ABOUT THE AUTHOR

Jonathan D. Raskin earned his undergraduate degree in psychology from Vassar College and his Ph.D. from the APA-accredited counseling psychology program at the University of Florida. His doctoral training was completed with a one-year, APA-approved internship at Emory University's Counseling Center. Dr. Raskin has been in his current faculty position at the State University of New York at New Paltz since 1996. At SUNY New Paltz, Dr. Raskin teaches in the psychology undergraduate program and the counselor education graduate program. He began a term as chair of the Psychology Department in 2017. He also maintains an active private practice as a psychologist.

Source: Tessa E. Killian

In the course of his academic career, Dr. Raskin has authored or co-authored more than thirty journal articles, as well as twenty book chapters. Among the topics he has written about are constructions of abnormality, attitudes toward psychiatric diagnosis, and meaning-oriented approaches to counseling and psychotherapy. Dr. Raskin has co-edited six books: *Constructions of Disorder: Meaning-Making Frameworks for Psychotherapy* (published by the American Psychological Association) and all five volumes of the *Studies in Meaning* book series (published by Pace University Press). He holds appointments on several journal editorial boards and serves as managing editor for the *Journal of Constructivist Psychology.* A fellow of the American Psychological Association, Dr. Raskin has received the SUNY Chancellor's Award for Excellence in Scholarship and the Research and Scholarship Award from the SUNY Research Foundation.

AUTHOR ACKNOWLEDGMENTS

Writing a book is an enormous undertaking and I am indebted to so many people who helped me on the long and arduous journey of doing so. Although he is no longer at Red Globe Press, I wish to acknowledge my original commissioning editor Paul Stevens, whose excitement about and active interest in my textbook idea led me to signing with Red Globe Press. The next time Paul visits New York City, I owe him a black-and-white cookie. Of course, Paul's parting gift to me was to help hire his excellent replacement, Luke Block. Luke has made the transition from one editor to another seamless. When he next comes to New York City, I'll buy him a black-and-white cookie, too!

I also am deeply appreciative of the development editors who shepherded me through the writing and reviewing process. Lauren Zimmerman worked with me on the early chapters. Her kindness and support were extremely helpful as I got my sea legs and came to see that the project was doable. She was also really nice to my daughter, Noa, when we met for tea in London during the early stages of book development. For much of the time I was busily drafting chapters, my development editor was Tiiu Sarkijarvi. Tiiu was patient with my many questions and emails, all the while helping me sharpen the structure of chapters and refine my ideas. I wish her much luck now that she has left Red Globe Press to return to Finland, where (at least she believes) the weather is more pleasant. Niki Arulanandam saw the project to completion, providing me excellent feedback and working with me to polish the finished manuscript. She then turned things over to Sophiya Ali, who did a remarkable job chasing down permissions for material reproduced in the book—indulging my many requests for obscure photos and other hard-to-locate items! Finally, Amy Brownbridge ably steered me through the production process, while Ann Edmondson did a meticulous job copyediting the final manuscript. Thank you to all these folks!

In addition to Red Globe Press's London team, I'd also like to thank their New York counterparts, Iris Elam and Daniel DeBonis. Both showed earnest interest in the project when I met with them at the 2017 American Psychological Convention in Washington, DC. Besides Iris and Dan, a quick shout out to Kerri Russini, previously my campus' Macmillan book representative. Our discussions during her periodic visits to my office hours truly helped and encouraged me.

Professionally, there are too many colleagues to thank, so I'll just name a few. First and foremost, thanks to my doctoral advisor, Franz Epting. In many respects, this book is a culmination of his many years of mentorship. Thanks also to Sara Bridges, Mark Burrell, Don Domenici, Valerie Domenici, Jay Efran, Mike Gayle, Jack Kahn, Sarah Kamens, the late Chuck Lawe, Spencer McWilliams, Bob Neimeyer, Amberly Panepinto, Brent Dean Robbins, Donna Rockwell, Caroline Stanley (for her vital contributions to the test bank!), and my many colleagues at the State University of New York at New Paltz. I am also appreciative of the help of my students, including Caitlin Barrett, Nicole Hershkopf, Kelly Mahoney, Carol Majewski, Laura Scarimbolo, Cynthia Stewart, Hanna Zyshchuk, and especially Alexandria Perry and Ryan Ciuffetelli (for their assistance with supplementary materials).

Finally, I'd also like to thank the following people close to me (1) because their love and support has been invaluable and (2) just because: my daughters, Ari and Noa; my parents, Paula and Sherman; my brother, Daniel; my sister-in-law (and fellow psychologist), Kayoko Yokoyama; my nephew, Taro; my long-time friend, Mike Rozett; my partner's son, Liam Quinlan (you can have the basement back for D&D now); and my loving, kind, and exceptionally supportive partner, Tessa Killian. These people's patience and understanding while I wrote this book cannot be underestimated and I am deeply grateful to all of them.

Okay, now go read the book.

Jonathan D. Raskin

CHAPTER 1
CONCEPTUAL, HISTORICAL, AND RESEARCH PERSPECTIVES

1.1 OVERVIEW

LEARNING OBJECTIVES

After reading this chapter, you should be able to:

1. Explain why contradictory perspectives are common in abnormal psychology.
2. Define psychopathology, mental illness, harmful internal dysfunction, deviance, and social oppression.
3. Summarize common criteria of abnormality.
4. Describe historical perspectives on abnormality from the Stone Age to the present day.
5. Distinguish and explain the many types of quantitative and qualitative research perspectives.

GETTING STARTED: WHAT IS ABNORMAL?

Jim

Jim is a 20-year-old university student studying psychology. Though he is a good student with excellent grades, a few months before graduation Jim begins to behave erratically. He claims to hear voices, which tell him that his professors are spying on him. He insists that the university police have planted listening devices in his bedroom to monitor his activities. He stops bathing and combing his hair. His friends start to worry about him and so does one of his instructors, who alerts the campus health center. Jim is diagnosed with schizophrenia, sent home to his parents, and placed on antipsychotic drugs. After six months on the drugs, Jim gets a part-time job while living at home with his parents, but still does not feel ready to return to his university.

CASE EXAMPLES

Michelle

Michelle, a 14-year-old girl, has always been a bit outspoken, but recently she has become downright rebellious. She often initiates arguments with her mother and refuses to obey the eleven o'clock curfew set by her parents. In fact, Michelle stays out all night and when she comes home, she ignores her parents entirely or yells at them about how unfair they are to her. Exasperated, her parents take Michelle to a local psychiatrist, who diagnoses her with oppositional-defiant disorder. Michelle is briefly hospitalized and her behavior temporarily takes a turn for the better after she is released. However, within a month or so she returns to her rebellious ways, much to the chagrin of her overwhelmed parents.

HUMILIATION / DEFEAT

Sam

Sam is a 45-year-old successful businessman. Despite his success, he has always felt like a woman trapped inside a man's body. One summer he goes on vacation and, upon his return, begins to dress and live as a woman. He takes hormones to simulate a womanly appearance and, after some time, undergoes sex reassignment surgery to make him anatomically female. His friends are surprised when Sam becomes "Samantha." Many stop associating with him.

Mary

Mary is a 70-year-old grandmother of three. Her husband of thirty years, Phil, has recently passed away. Mary finds herself feeling isolated and depressed. She spends more and more time by herself in her apartment, has trouble sleeping, and loses her appetite. After several months, Mary tells her family doctor about her sadness and he writes her a prescription for antidepressants. Mary does not fill the prescription and instead seeks psychotherapy to talk about her loneliness and feelings of depression. The therapy raises her spirits some and she establishes a more active daily schedule and social life. However, though she is much happier than before therapy, her mood remains tinged with a hint of occasional sadness, as she continues to miss her husband. Her doctor keeps encouraging her to try the antidepressants, but she doesn't want to.

≣ **Jesse**
Jesse is a 37-year-old African-American man living in an urban area of the United States that has recently been rocked by racial tension over police profiling and mistreatment of minorities. Jesse goes to see a psychotherapist and states that he is worried that the police are monitoring his movements. "They're out to get me," he says. "I know they're watching me." Jesse's therapist, a white female, is unsure what to make of Jesse's assertions.

Abnormality in Everyday Life

The notion of abnormality is part of our everyday lives. Even if this is your first class in abnormal psychology, you regularly make determinations about what is or isn't abnormal behavior. When your roommate alphabetizes all the course books on his bookshelf by author and subject, you classify him as "neurotic." When your best friend repeatedly has difficulty committing to a romantic relationship, you informally diagnose him as having problems with commitment. When your sister repeatedly dates people who take advantage of and mistreat her, you suspect she has dependency issues. When your boss refuses to take airplanes for business trips because she is terrified of flying, you conclude that she suffers from a phobia, namely a fear of heights. See the "Try It Yourself" feature for an exercise intended to highlight your own judgments of abnormality.

TRY IT YOURSELF

Photo source: © PhotoDisc/Getty Images

Making Judgments about Abnormality

A major challenge for those embarking on a class in abnormal psychology is that people—including mental health professionals—often disagree with each other about what counts as abnormal. To demonstrate this, consider the case examples that opened the chapter. Take a few minutes to rate each of these cases on a scale of 1–10, with "1" being "not at all abnormal" and "10" being "extremely abnormal." Jot down one or two sentences explaining why you rated each case the way you did. After rating each case this way, you could even ask several of your friends and classmates to do the same thing. Afterwards, consider these questions:

1. How much agreement was there about the abnormality of these five people? What do you think accounts for this?

2. What kinds of reasons did you and those you asked offer for explaining their abnormality ratings? Which reasons seem convincing to you and which do not? Why?

3. When there was disagreement, by what means might you determine whose ratings should be better trusted?

4. Did you and those you asked about these cases have similar or different assumptions about what abnormality is? What are these assumptions and on what basis should we accept or reject them?

THE CHALLENGE FOR STUDENTS: EXPERTS DON'T ALWAYS AGREE

A common tendency among students taking abnormal psychology is to defer to the "experts" (usually their textbooks and instructor) about what abnormality truly is. However, as you progress through this book, you may occasionally find yourself scratching your head in confusion over the many different and often contradictory conceptualizations of abnormality. In other words, you will find that different experts define and treat abnormality in very different ways. This can prove frustrating to students, who often want concrete answers.

When it comes to what counts as abnormal and what should be done about it, people—including experts in the field—often disagree.
Source: Image Source \ Image Source/David Oxberry

An Example: What is "Mental Illness?"

It is common to equate abnormality with **mental illness**, although—as we will discuss shortly—abnormality isn't always (or even necessarily!) a product of bodily illness. Nonetheless, the idea of "mental illness" holds a central place in abnormal psychology. Yet its definition is hotly debated. For instance, the National Alliance on

Mental Illness (NAMI), an advocacy group that defines its mission as "building better lives for the millions of Americans affected by mental illness" (NAMI, n.d.), offers the following definition of mental illness:

> *Mental illnesses are medical conditions that disrupt a person's thinking, feeling, mood, ability to relate to others and daily functioning. Just as diabetes is a disorder of the pancreas, mental illnesses are medical conditions that often result in a diminished capacity for coping with the ordinary demands of life. Serious mental illnesses include major depression, schizophrenia, bipolar disorder, obsessive compulsive disorder (OCD), panic disorder, posttraumatic stress disorder (PTSD) and borderline personality disorder. The good news about mental illness is that recovery is possible. Mental illnesses can affect persons of any age, race, religion, or income. Mental illnesses are not the result of personal weakness, lack of character or poor upbringing. Mental illnesses are treatable. Most people diagnosed with a serious mental illness can experience relief from their symptoms by actively participating in an individual treatment plan. (NAMI Southern Arizona, n.d., para. 1–3)*

NAMI defines mental illnesses as *medical* conditions. This sounds pretty definitive and that may be comforting. The problem is that not all professionals agree with this view. Consider the perspective of the British Psychological Society (BPS), the professional association for psychology and psychologists in the United Kingdom. Like NAMI, the BPS also has expertise on the topic of abnormality. However, it takes a very different stance on mental illness, complaining about the tendency toward medicalization of people's everyday problems. Medicalization occurs when we inappropriately classify non-medical problems as medical. Here's what the BPS says about medicalization:

> *The Society is concerned that clients and the general public are negatively affected by the continued and continuous medicalisation of their natural and normal responses to their experiences; responses which undoubtedly have distressing consequences which demand helping responses, but which do not reflect illnesses so much as normal individual variation. … The Society recommends a revision of the way mental distress is thought about, starting with recognition of the overwhelming evidence that it is on a spectrum with "normal" experience, and that psychosocial factors such as poverty, unemployment and trauma are the most strongly-evidenced causal factors. (British Psychological Society, 2011, pp. 2–3)*

Contradictory Perspectives Are Common in Abnormal Psychology

What's going on here? We have two mainstream organizations taking completely different—and contradictory—positions on mental illness! One group says that mental illness is a medical condition. The other group says just the opposite, namely that many of the things we consider to be mental illnesses are instead reasonable responses to challenging life circumstances and oppressive social conditions—and that too often we are incorrectly classifying these things as medical problems.

At this point, I wouldn't be surprised to find you flipping a few pages ahead to figure out which view is the right one. Realizing that a definitive answer isn't provided, you might ask your instructor whether the NAMI or BPS viewpoint is correct. Even if your instructor offers an opinion, it only shows that he or she is partial to one perspective over the other. It doesn't resolve the fact that we have two prominent groups with extensive mental health expertise holding what appear to be irreconcilable views. While textbooks and professors can (and often do) offer their opinions, the truth is that on many issues in abnormal psychology, there simply is not clear consensus in the field. That is, there are many perspectives that often clash. What constitutes abnormality, how to best identify it, and how to deal with it effectively are important questions that receive different answers depending on who in the field you ask.

In other words, there are many contrasting perspectives on abnormality. Throughout this book, we will regularly revisit the three most influential ones: biological, psychological, and sociocultural. **Biological perspectives** see mental illnesses as medical conditions; they are diseases that afflict people. **Psychological perspectives**, by contrast, conceptualize abnormality in psychological terms as involving problematic thoughts, feelings, and behaviors; abnormality from a psychological view is due to psychological conflicts, not brain diseases. Finally, **sociocultural perspectives** attribute abnormality to social causes; factors such as socioeconomic conditions, cultural influences, and social oppression are the root causes of people's emotional upset. Your task is to figure out which perspectives on abnormality you most agree with and why.

Clear-cut answers aren't always found in abnormal psychology because it is an area concerned with forever-tricky questions about what it means to live a good and healthy life. This makes it difficult to agree on what is abnormal. Additionally, even when people agree that something is abnormal, its causes can be quite elusive. The causes emphasized often depend on the professional perspective adopted. Consequently, abnormal psychology is inevitably a messy subject. At the same time, its messiness and ambiguity also make it highly engaging because it is a subject that pushes students to form their own educated opinions. So, while you may not receive a "final answer" about what abnormality is and how best to remedy it, after reading this book you should be better able to articulate the different perspectives on abnormal psychology, and to identify their relative strengths and weaknesses. Let's just say that it's one of those cases where you may come to feel that the more you know, the less you know for sure. This is perhaps the most important thing to realize as you begin to study abnormal psychology. The "In Depth" feature further examines this perplexing conundrum.

IN DEPTH

Photo source: © PhotoDisc./Getty Images

Ignorance and Abnormal Psychology

A 2015 *New York Times* opinion piece by Jamie Holmes advocates acknowledging that we often know less than we claim. In other words, ignorance is a lot more rampant than most of us wish to admit—even in academic subjects where we usually are told otherwise. Holmes describes how, in the 1980s, University of Arizona surgery professor Professor Marlys H. Witte created controversy when she began teaching a class called "Introduction to Medical and Other Ignorance." She wanted to include ignorance in her class because she believed we often ignore or minimize how little we know about many topics (Jamie Holmes, 2015). In Witte's view, textbooks often contribute to the problem. For example, she pointed out that surgery textbooks usually discuss pancreatic cancer without ever mentioning that our present understanding of it is extremely limited. Her goal? Helping students appreciate that questions are as important as answers (Jamie Holmes, 2015).

Some might deem it foolish of me to share Holmes' opinion piece at the very start of a textbook on abnormal psychology. Yet my experience teaching this course over the years fits nicely with Holmes' thesis. I once had a student who, several weeks into the class, said she was going back to being a math major. "At least in math, there are clear right answers," she exclaimed. "In abnormal psychology, there are so many conflicting viewpoints that it's hard to know what the right answer is." Admittedly, despite all the attempts to combine rigorous research into an integrative perspective, all too often most abnormal psychology textbooks overstate how much we know. But acknowledging our ignorance up front potentially opens, rather than closes, possibilities. Holmes notes that we often think of ignorance as something to be eliminated, viewing it as simply lack of knowledge. Yet answers, Holmes (2015) notes, don't put an end to questions; they simply give rise to new questions! As you read this text, here's to the many questions you will hopefully begin to ask.

CRITICAL THINKING QUESTIONS

1. Do you think Witte's contention that ignorance is more rampant than we usually admit is applicable to abnormal psychology?
2. Does recognizing the limits of our knowledge about abnormality help us? If so, how?

HOW DOES THIS CHAPTER GET US STARTED?

This rest of this chapter introduces the contrasting perspectives approach to abnormal psychology by covering several distinct topics that are important to (and revisited regularly in) future chapters. First, the chapter defines basic terms common to the field. These terms (e.g., psychiatry, psychology, psychopathology, mental illness, mental disorder, and deviance) will be used throughout the text, so it is important to define them up front. Second, the chapter outlines common criteria used to determine what is or isn't abnormal. In discussing these criteria, it should become clear how challenging it can be to decide what's normal. Hopefully, reviewing these criteria, their strengths, and their limitations will help as you make your own judgments about what counts as abnormal. Third, the chapter reviews historical perspectives on abnormality in order to place current conceptions in historical context. We will revisit historical perspectives throughout the book to better ground our current understandings. Finally, the chapter summarizes research perspectives used in studying abnormal psychology. As we will regularly be referring to research in all subsequent chapters, it is important for students to understand how investigators study abnormality. Thus, while the chapter covers a variety of seemingly disparate topics, these topics have been chosen because they provide the grounding necessary to proceed.

1.2 BASIC TERMS

Some terms used in abnormal psychology are mainly descriptive. Others, however, have assumptions embedded within them that reflect broader perspectives. Below we introduce a variety of terms used throughout this text. Where appropriate, we discuss the implications of these terms for thinking about abnormality.

PSYCHIATRY VS. PSYCHOLOGY

Students are often confused about the difference between psychiatry and psychology, two of the major mental health professions. So, let's start by distinguishing between them. Psychiatry is a medical specialty concerned with mental disorders and their treatment. Psychiatrists, therefore, are physicians who have completed specialized training in psychiatry (American Psychiatric Association, n.d.-b). Not surprisingly, because they are medical doctors, psychiatrists generally adhere to a medical model of abnormality. The medical model sees psychiatric problems as categorical syndromes reflecting underlying biological illnesses that must, like all illnesses, be accurately diagnosed before they can be effectively treated (B. J. Deacon, 2013; Joyce, 1980; Kendler, 2005; Patil & Giordano, 2010).

Unlike psychiatrists, psychologists don't have medical degrees. Instead, they have graduate degrees (usually doctoral degrees) in psychology, a discipline that studies mental processes and behavior. The subspecialties in psychology that specifically focus on psychotherapy and abnormality are clinical psychology and counseling psychology. Clinical psychologists are typically trained to see abnormality as a dysfunction in the individual, usually of a psychological nature (G. J. Neimeyer, Taylor, Wear, & Buyukgoze-Kavas, 2011). In this regard, many but not all clinical psychologists are like psychiatrists in their tendency to adopt a medical model perspective. That is, clinical psychology's "alignment with the medical model, which places a premium on assessment, diagnosis, and treatment within a broad range of hospital and community contexts, reflects a coherent extension of the specialty across time" (G. J. Neimeyer et al., 2011, p. 44). Counseling psychologists differ from clinical psychologists in that their training tends to focus less on pathology and more on the everyday problems experienced by otherwise well-adjusted people (G. J. Neimeyer et al., 2011; Norcross, 2000; Society of Counseling Psychology, 2014).

In practice, clinical and counseling psychologists are often hired to do the same kinds of jobs, sometimes making it difficult to discern the difference between them (G. J. Neimeyer et al., 2011). Generally, counseling psychology focuses less on assessment and diagnosis of abnormality than clinical psychology and more on the emotional strengths and positive aspects of client functioning (G. J. Neimeyer et al., 2011; Norcross, 2000). Like clinical psychologists, counseling psychologists work in private practice and mental health agencies. They are somewhat less likely to work in hospital settings than clinical psychologists and more likely to be employed at university counseling centers and other sites where the client population is considered to be less seriously disturbed (G. J. Neimeyer et al., 2011).

PSYCHOPATHOLOGY

Psychopathology is a term suggesting that abnormality is the product of some kind of dysfunction or sickness within the person acting abnormally (Endleman, 1990). The pathology causing the problem might be biological or psychological, but it is clearly seen as coming from the person more than the person's surroundings. For example, a man who has suffered a traumatic brain injury and consequently finds it difficult to control his anger in social situations might be judged as suffering from psychopathology. Social factors are secondary to his brain damage in understanding his abnormally aggressive behavior. In this case, the man's psychopathology is primarily viewed via the medical model and thus seen as biologically based.

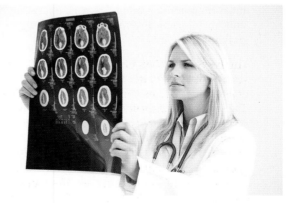

The term "psychopathology" sees abnormality as emanating from dysfunctions or illnesses inside the person.

The psychopathology perspective is readily identified in biological explanations of abnormality. For instance, when someone attributes depression to a chemical imbalance, the cause of the problem is thought to be a problem inside the person's brain. However, psychopathology can also be viewed as psychological rather than biological. For instance, a woman cheating on her husband feels extremely anxious, guilty, and depressed. Like the man with the brain injury, we might see her as suffering from psychopathology, but of a more psychological nature because we believe her problem is caused by conflicted feelings, not a biological malfunction. What both biological and psychological conceptions of psychopathology share is a view of the problem as a dysfunction originating inside the person.

MENTAL ILLNESS AND MENTAL DISORDER

As alluded to earlier, mental illness and mental disorder are terms rooted in the abnormality-as-psychopathology perspective. Both imply something wrong inside the person being diagnosed. However, distinguishing between these terms can prove difficult. In public discourse, mental illness usually has a somewhat more biological connotation than mental disorder. Recall NAMI's (n.d., para. 1) definition of mental illness as "a medical condition that disrupts a person's thinking, feeling, mood, ability to relate to others and daily functioning."

The American Psychiatric Association (APA), the professional organization of American psychiatry, uses the terms mental illness and mental disorder somewhat interchangeably on its website (www.psych. org/). However, it uses the term mental disorder in its *Diagnostic and Statistical Manual of Mental Disorders (DSM)*, a comprehensive book that lists and describes all APA-recognized disorders (and that we discuss in detail in Chapter 3). The *DSM* definition of mental disorder is a bit broader than NAMI's definition; it defines a mental disorder as "a syndrome characterized by clinically significant disturbance in an individual's cognition, emotion regulation, or behavior that reflects a dysfunction in the psychological, biological, or developmental processes underlying mental functioning" (American Psychiatric Association, 2013b, p. 20). Though this definition defines mental disorder as psychopathology (i.e., a dysfunction in the person), it leaves room for those who do not see all mental disorders as strictly brain diseases. However, as we shall see, even the broader *DSM* definition has sometimes proven controversial (Frances, 2013c; Paris, 2015). Next, we examine the idea of harmful internal dysfunction that is central to the psychopathology perspective in general and the *DSM* definition of mental disorder specifically.

HARMFUL INTERNAL DYSFUNCTION

The idea of abnormality as a harmful internal dysfunction has been most fully elaborated by Jerome Wakefield. To Wakefield (1992, 1999), a mental disorder is best viewed as having two components: (a) a mental mechanism that fails to operate according to its naturally designed function (i.e., an internal dysfunction), and (b) behavior society deems harmful that is caused by the internal dysfunction. Importantly, both harm and dysfunction are necessary conditions for something to be a disorder. As an example, Wakefield (1992) notes, "a dysfunction in one kidney often has no effect on the overall well-being of a person and so is not considered to be a disorder" (p. 384). At the same time, social deviance in the absence of internal dysfunction is also insufficient for something to qualify as a disorder. A biological or psychological mechanism inside the person must be malfunctioning—that is, operating in a way nature did not intend. Requiring both social judgment and an internal dysfunction protects us, in Wakefield's view, from incorrectly labeling social deviance as psychopathology:

> The requirement that a disorder must involve a dysfunction places severe constraints on which negative conditions can be considered disorders and thus protects against arbitrary labeling of socially disvalued conditions as disorders. … Diagnoses such as "drapetomania" (the "disorder" of runaway slaves), "childhood masturbation disorder," and "lack of vaginal orgasm" can be seen as unsound applications of a perfectly coherent concept that can be correctly applied to other conditions. … [T]he harmful dysfunction view allows us to reject these diagnoses on scientific grounds, namely, that the beliefs about natural functioning that underlie them—for example, that slaves are naturally designed to serve, that children are naturally designed to be nonsexual, and that women are naturally designed to have orgasms from vaginal stimulation in intercourse alone—are false. (J. C. Wakefield, 1992, p. 386)

Though Wakefield's model has been influential in *DSM* circles, it hasn't been explicitly incorporated into the *DSM* definition of mental disorder. Further, some mental health professionals have complained that it doesn't allow us to consistently identify disorder in everyday life (Lilienfeld & Marino, 1995, 1999). One reason offered for this is that it relies on social judgments about harmfulness. When these judgments change, so does what counts as a disorder (Sadler & Agich, 1995). Additionally, the concept of "mental mechanism" strikes some critics as fuzzy (Houts, 1996; D. Murphy & Woolfolk, 2000). These critics contend that Wakefield treats a mental mechanism as something biologically broken in the brain (G. R. Henriques, 2002), even though what is "mental" is by definition not physical and therefore can't literally be found in someone's brain. Something mental also cannot be scientifically observed or measured. If a mechanism is mental rather than physical, we can't see it. Consequently, we can never know whether mental mechanisms actually exist (Houts, 1996).

DEVIANCE

Not everyone subscribes to the internal dysfunction/psychopathology perspective. Some view abnormality as deviance instead. **Deviance**, a word often used by sociologists, is a term that tends to conceptualize abnormality as socially unacceptable behavior (Endleman, 1990). Deviant behavior is not necessarily believed to stem from pathology inside individuals. In fact, sociologist Thomas Scheff (1984) famously (and controversially) argued that abnormality is more a product of society labeling behavior as deviant than it is a product of internal psychopathology. From this viewpoint, the way different social groups define what is or is not a suitable way to act is central in determining who is considered abnormal. For example, in some conservative Muslim countries a woman who fails to veil her face in public may be acting in ways that are socially deviant, but most people would not consider her behavior to be a sign that something is pathologically wrong with her. Rather, her behavior would be deemed abnormal only if it violates social expectations and norms.

Not wearing a veil in certain Muslim countries is socially deviant, but most people wouldn't consider it a sign of psychopathology.
Source: © Royalty-Free/Corbis

SOCIAL OPPRESSION

Those adhering to a **social oppression** perspective believe that unjust societal conditions lead to troublesome behaviors and emotions. Some who stress the importance of social oppression believe that it leads to internal dysfunctions/psychopathology (i.e., prolonged exposure to economic inequality and discrimination produces ongoing stress, which produces illnesses inside people). However, others contend that ongoing oppression merely produces deviant behavior (i.e., oppressed people act out not because they are ill, but because they can no longer abide by the norms of a tyrannical society). The key point is that to those emphasizing social oppression, abnormal behavior originates in social conditions, not individuals. An example of this perspective can be found in the work of psychologist Isaac Prilleltensky, who argues that psychologists and other mental health professionals too often conceptualize abnormality as an individual, rather than social, problem:

> Oppression contributes to mental health problems in the form of depression, suicidal ideation, learned helplessness, surplus powerlessness, emotional isolation, and other difficulties. Although the link between oppressive societal conditions and psychological health may seem obvious to us now, this has not always been the case. Historically, psychology and psychiatry ascribed mental health problems to internal mechanisms that were thought to be quite independent from the social circumstances in which the person lived. (Prilleltensky, 1999, p. 107)

Those who emphasize social oppression sometimes reject the idea of internal dysfunction entirely. British clinical psychologist Peter Kinderman, for instance, challenges the idea of disorders as dysfunctions inside people. In his view,

> services should be based on the premise that the origins of distress are largely social. The guiding idea underpinning mental health services needs to change from assuming that our role is to treat "disease" to appreciating that our role is to help and support people who are distressed as a result of their life circumstances, and how they have made sense of and reacted to them. (Kinderman, 2014a, para. 14)

Others take a middle ground position in which internal dysfunctions are accepted as real, but are greatly impacted and influenced by social and cultural factors such as gender, race, and class (López & Guarnaccia, 2016; Winstead & Sanchez, 2016). The degree to which abnormality is caused by internal dysfunction versus social oppression is a question to which we will regularly return.

1.3 COMMON CRITERIA OF ABNORMALITY

It may be becoming apparent that abnormality is not something that comes readily labeled and identified for all to see. Rather, it is a distinction about human behavior that people make while interacting with one another. Below are some common criteria people use to distinguish normal from abnormal. Though many of these criteria have overlapping elements, each is important to consider on its own. Further, none of these criteria alone is necessary and sufficient in defining abnormality, even though each criterion is useful in judging what is abnormal. As you read about these criteria, consider the distinctions previously made between psychopathology, deviance, and social oppression. How do these criteria help us in determining when abnormal behavior is socially deviant versus when it is triggered by an internal dysfunction?

STATISTICAL DEVIATION

One way of defining what is abnormal is through statistical deviation, in which we identify what is atypical. We can do this by comparing people to statistical norms. For example, most of us live with other people, not by ourselves. Anyone who does live alone is, statistically speaking, abnormal. Of course, just because something is statistically deviant doesn't necessarily mean it's pathological. For instance, only a small percentage of people earn doctoral degrees. This makes doing so statistically abnormal, but few would argue that holding a doctorate is a sign of psychopathology!

Nevertheless, much of what gets labeled as abnormal is statistically atypical. Consider the *DSM*. It views statistical abnormality as an important aspect of mental disorders. In the *DSM*, prevalence and incidence estimates are listed for every mental disorder category, informing us about the statistical frequency of each diagnosis. Prevalence rates refer to the percentage of people in the population currently believed to have a specific disorder, while incidence rates are the number of new cases reported over a specified period (N. Pearce, 2012). A quick examination of research on prevalence and incidence rates for the *DSM* disorder of schizophrenia makes clear that mental disorders are statistically deviant. For example, the fifth edition of the *Diagnostic and Statistical Manual of Mental Disorders* (*DSM-5*) reports that schizophrenia has a lifetime prevalence rate between 0.3% and 0.7% of people (American Psychiatric Association, 2013b), whereas its annual incidence rate has been estimated to be anywhere between 14 and 42 out of every 100,000 people (Esan, Ojagbemi, & Gureje, 2012; McGrath, 2005). This means that a little less than 1% of the world's population is thought to have schizophrenia and that 14 to 42 people out of 100,000 are anticipated to develop it in any given year. So, while statistical deviance alone does not guarantee that something is abnormal, most of what mental health professionals consider disordered is statistically deviant.

VIOLATION OF SOCIAL NORMS AND VALUES

Sara and Brian

Sara and Brian seek couples counseling because their marriage is on the rocks. Brian was raised in a family where feelings were rarely discussed. Conflict was considered unpleasant and people's differences were usually ignored or minimized to maintain congenial relationships. Sara, by comparison, grew up in a home where people freely expressed emotions; even negative feelings were readily communicated, often with a great deal of yelling and screaming! As each proceeds to blame the other for their marital problems, it quickly becomes clear to their marriage counselor that Sara and Brian's different family norms and values lead them to see each other as abnormal.

CASE EXAMPLES

"Something's definitely wrong with him," Sara says of Brian. "He doesn't seem to have feelings. That's not normal, unless he's a robot!"

"It's not me, Doc," Brian retorts. "Sara's just out of control, always yelling or crying or getting upset. Last week she got so mad that she threw a stapler across the room at me. It's like she's a crazy person!"

Sara and Brian's assessments of one another demonstrate how violation of social norms and values plays into what people consider abnormal. Different people have different ideas about how others should behave, what is socially appropriate, and what is morally acceptable. Even though violation of social norms seems readily applicable to socially deviant behavior, we often infer internal pathology in those who consistently violate values we hold dear. Perhaps this is because across families and cultures, varied social norms and values influence what people deem out of the ordinary. Not surprisingly, this means that what mental health professionals consider abnormal is often controversial—and can change over time.

Sexuality is one of the most obvious areas where we can see the impact of changing social norms on perceptions of abnormality. Medical experts once considered masturbation and other forms of non-procreative sex to be clear indicators or causes of psychopathology (Bullough, 2002). The 18th-century Swiss physician S. A. D. Tissot labeled those who masturbate as having a mental disorder called onanism, which he defined as "all non-procreative sex" (Bullough, 2002). He described the dangers facing those suffering from it:

Onanism ... led to (1) cloudiness of ideas and sometimes even madness; (2) decay of bodily powers, resulting in coughs, fevers, and consumption; (3) acute pains in the head, rheumatic pains, and an aching numbness; (4) pimples on the face, suppurating blisters on the nose, breast, and thighs, and painful itchings; (5) eventual weakening of the power of generation as indicated by impotence, premature ejaculation, gonorrhea, priapism, and tumors in the bladder; and (6) disordering of the intestines, resulting in constipation, hemorrhoids, and so forth. (quoted in Bullough, 2002, p. 29)

While Tissot's 18th-century ideas about masturbation strike most people today as outdated, social norms about what constitutes abnormality continue to change, often quite rapidly. Until 1973, the *DSM* considered homosexuality to be a mental disorder (Drescher, 2012). However, as homosexuality became more socially acceptable, people began to question its deviant status and eventually the American Psychiatric Association stopped classifying it as a disorder (Drescher, 2012). Importantly, even when social norms change, it doesn't mean that everyone agrees. Though the American Psychiatric Association (1998, 2000) and American Psychological Association (2012) both formally reject homosexuality as a mental disorder and cite extensive research suggesting that therapies designed to convert homosexuals into heterosexuals are ineffective at best and damaging at worst, a small number of mental health professionals contend that homosexuality is pathological and can be successfully treated (Morrow & Beckstead, 2004). Social norms and values are one way of determining what is abnormal, but conflict always remains because people and cultures differ in what they see as socially acceptable and appropriate.

An important question to ask is whether at least some social norms and values are universal. For example, it can be argued that certain values cut across all people and cultures—such as taboos against murder and incest. Some people maintain that while many social values are relative to time, place, and culture, at least some norms are universal and that violating these is a clear indication of abnormality. In thinking about abnormality, you will need to decide for yourself whether you believe social values and norms are always culturally relative or at least sometimes universal.

BEHAVIOR THAT DISTURBS OTHERS

Behavior that disturbs others is often considered abnormal. For example, people riding in elevators usually face toward the doors. Next time you get on an elevator, see what happens when you face away from the doors—and toward those riding with you. Your fellow passengers will likely consider your actions strange and a significant number of them may feel uncomfortable. Behavior that disturbs others often violates social norms and values, too. Creating a scene in a restaurant, loitering on a street corner while talking to oneself, dressing in atypical fashion, and expressing emotions generally considered inappropriate to a situation (e.g., laughing during a funeral) violate social norms and, consequently, tend to disturb other people.

Our responses to people differ depending on how we interpret why they engage in disturbing or disruptive behavior. When we conclude that such behavior is a product of mental disorder, we often excuse it. In this line of thought, mentally disordered people are suffering from a form of internal psychopathology and therefore aren't accountable for their disturbing behavior. A contrary line of thinking holds that those engaging in disturbing behavior freely choose it, thus they are responsible for the consequences of their conduct. The "illness versus responsibility" debate occurs prominently in the legal arena because the legal system generally presumes that people are responsible for behaving in ways that are consistent with social norms and laws, whereas the mental health system contradicts this by arguing that sometimes disturbing or illegal behavior is a by-product of mental illness. More is said about this when we discuss issues of competency to stand trial and the insanity defense in Chapter 15.

Another difficult question arises: When someone else's behavior disturbs us, does this tell us more about us or them? For instance, protesters who engage in civil disobedience may disturb us by disrupting our routines and forcing us to examine issues we would rather ignore. However, this does not make them mentally disordered.

HARMFULNESS TO SELF OR OTHERS

Sue repeatedly cuts her arms with a razor blade. Jorge gambles away his life savings. Miwa overdoses on painkillers. Gerald beats his wife. These are all examples of behavior that appears maladaptive or causes **harmfulness to self or others**. People who act in such ways are commonly considered abnormal, often with the implicit assumption that their behavior indicates psychopathology (that is, their harmful behavior is caused by an internal dysfunction). So, we might diagnose Sue as suffering from borderline personality disorder (see Chapter 12), Jorge as having gambling disorder (see Chapter 11), Miwa as experiencing major depressive disorder (see Chapter 5), and Gerald as having intermittent-explosive disorder (see Chapter 13). Of course, there are also many cases in which harmful behavior might not be attributed to mental disorder. For example, Bill smokes cigarettes, Juanita eats fast food, Goran never puts on sunscreen, Isabella skydives, Cai drives fast on the freeway, and Gina likes to rock climb without safety gear. In these cases, there is clearly potential harm to self or others. However, are these people suffering from psychopathology?

Harmfulness to self or others as an indicator of abnormality seems most clear in those situations where there is widespread agreement that the potential harm in a behavior far outweighs any other benefits it might have. In psychology, this often applies to those circumstances where people are an imminent threat to themselves or others—such as in cases of attempted suicide, assault and battery, or attempted murder. Perhaps influenced by the previously discussed work of Jerome Wakefield, most mental disorders in the *DSM* explicitly include criteria indicating that impaired social, occupational, or other functioning is required before a disorder can be diagnosed (American Psychiatric Association, 2013b). That is, people's symptoms must somehow harm or interfere with their daily lives. In other words, harm to self or others is an important element of abnormality even though people sometimes disagree about what constitutes harm or how much harm is necessary before behavior is deemed abnormal.

Gambling away your life savings causes harm to self and others. Does doing so mean you suffer from psychopathology?
Source: PhotoDisc/ Getty Images

EMOTIONAL SUFFERING

Excessive **emotional suffering** and unhappiness are often considered abnormal. Consistently appearing depressed, anxious, angry, or ambivalent is both socially deviant and often thought to imply internal pathology of some kind. As with other criteria for abnormality, however, agreeing on how much emotional suffering is abnormal can prove challenging. Most of us would concur that a person who is suicidally depressed is suffering, but what about less extreme instances? For example, is it abnormal for someone to feel emotionally down for an extended period even if it does not affect work or relationships in any significant way? Further, do the reasons why someone is suffering emotionally matter?

Neil

Consider Neil, a successful businessman and husband who suddenly and inexplicably becomes extremely depressed. There appear to be no specific environmental triggers for Neil's sadness and only after he is briefly hospitalized and medicated does he begin to feel better. Neil is suffering, but for no apparent reason—which leads him and his doctors to view his suffering as due to an internal dysfunction rather than life circumstances.

CASE EXAMPLES

Sharon

Now compare Neil to Sharon, a middle-aged woman who feels extremely depressed, anxious, and angry after her 19-year-old son is killed while serving in the military. Sharon clearly is experiencing emotional suffering, but does having a good reason for it make it an expectable reaction to terrible life circumstances rather than a sign of mental disorder? Or is any extreme emotional suffering, even in response to difficult life events, a form of psychopathology?

This issue begs two important questions: namely, how do we decide what constitutes a good reason for suffering and how much suffering is appropriate for that reason? Further, how confident can we be in a case like Neil's that there is no reason for someone's suffering, as opposed to simply not being able to find the reason? It is not always easy to agree about when and whether suffering is an indicator of abnormality.

MISPERCEPTION OF REALITY

When Burt tells us that the CIA is monitoring all his actions via the fillings in his teeth, we are likely to feel he has lost touch with reality and therefore suffers from psychopathology of some kind. **Misperception of reality** is often attributed to faulty perceptions and interpretations. Those who misperceive reality are usually considered to be irrational or suffering from some sort of perceptual defect (Dryden & Ellis, 2001). The ability to accurately perceive reality is commonly thought to be quite important in thinking about abnormality. Conceptually, as with some of the other criteria we have been reviewing, misperception of reality as a criterion for abnormality is most useful in extreme cases. After all, few would question that Burt's perceptions do not match what is going on around him. But what about other situations where conflicting perceptions of reality are offered?

Sara and Brian

For example, let's return to the marriage counseling of Sara and Brian. Sara insists that her mother-in-law is "out to get her" by putting her down and manipulating Brian so that he spends more time with her than Sara. Brian sees no evidence of this, arguing that his mother only wants what is best for him and Sara. Whose perceptions of reality are correct? If we could determine whose perceptions are more correct, would it matter? Is the person whose perceptions are less correct more psychologically disturbed? Finally, who is the ultimate authority on reality? Is it Sara, Brian, Brian's mother, their therapist, or someone else altogether?

CASE EXAMPLES

CONTROVERSIAL QUESTION

Is Shortness a Disorder?

In 2003, an advisory panel for the Food and Drug Administration in the U.S. recommended genetically engineered human growth hormone be approved for use in otherwise-healthy children identified as being idiopathically short. *Idiopathic* illnesses are ones that arise unexpectedly without a known cause. Although these very short children were at the bottom of the normal growth curve, they showed no hormonal deficiencies (Angier, 2003). The FDA approved the advisory panel's recommendation and now growth hormone can be prescribed for children diagnosed with *idiopathic short stature* (*ISS*) (P. Cohen et al., 2008; M. Morrison, 2015). What is the rationale for this? American men under the average height of 5'9" are more likely to drop out of school, drink excessively, date sporadically, get sick, or experience depression (Angier, 2003). In other words, short men develop psychosocial problems more often than their taller friends—although whether they are at risk for more serious psychopathology remains unclear (P. Cohen et al., 2008).

Consider shortness in relation to the common criteria of abnormality discussed in this chapter. A case for shortness as abnormal, even pathological, can be made using four of the criteria: statistical deviance, violation of social norms and values, internal dysfunction, and emotional suffering:

» Shortness is *statistically deviant*: only a small percentage of men are under the 5'3" height targeted by the FDA.

» Shortness *violates social norms* requiring men to be imposing and strong. This perhaps explains why short men earn less money, date less often, and have a lot less luck getting elected to higher office (in U.S. presidential elections, for example, the shorter candidate almost always loses).

» Shortness is due to an *internal dysfunction*. Due to hormonal dysfunctions, what some medical specialists call a "growth failure" occurs.

» Shortness is associated with *emotional suffering*. As mentioned above, short men drink more, date less, get sick, and feel depressed more often than tall men.

Of course, the criteria used to discern shortness as abnormality can also be challenged:

» *Statistical deviance* is not always viewed negatively; LeBron James' extreme height is statistically deviant, but is generally credited with helping make him a spectacular basketball player. Singer Bruno Mars is quite short, but is often considered a sex symbol.

» *Social norms and values* change; sometimes they are foolish or shallow. In the past, social norms led people to see a lot of things as abnormal that today we do not. For instance, in the U.S. slaves who ran away from their masters were diagnosed as suffering from a disorder called **drapetomania** (Cartwright, 1851).

» The idea of shortness as *internal dysfunction* can be challenged, especially given the FDA's recommendation that short boys with no discernible growth hormone deficiency be medicated to cure their shortness. If there is no discernible hormone deficiency, what is the internal dysfunction? Maybe it's not that short people necessarily have an internal dysfunction, but rather that in Western cultures "short stature itself is often regarded as an inherently undesirable state" (M. Morrison, 2015, p. 310).

Almost everyone has something about their looks they don't like. How much emotional suffering must one experience about being short before it becomes a problem? Regardless of your opinion, the example of shortness highlights a fascinating aspect of abnormal psychology, namely that just about anything can be talked about in a way that makes it seem functional or dysfunctional. Criteria for abnormality can help us in thinking about what we consider normal or pathological, but these criteria can never resolve the issue once and for all.

Author disclaimer: I'm 5'3" tall. Check out this online list of short statured men (all better known than I am) who may or may not have suffered from idiopathic shortness: http://shortguycentral.com/gallery.php. For more general information and support for short people, see www.supportfortheshort.org.

CRITICAL THINKING QUESTIONS

1. Using the criteria for abnormality discussed in this chapter, do you believe that idiopathic short stature is a disorder? Why or why not?
2. Choose another physical difference between people besides shortness and apply the criteria for abnormality to it. Using the criteria as a guide, do you see this difference as a disorder or as normal human variation? Explain.

While assessing the degree to which someone misperceives reality can help us in making determinations about abnormality—especially in cases where someone's perceptions diverge extensively from most everyone else's—at times there is disagreement about how to make such determinations and who has the final say about which perceptions best reflect reality. See the "Controversial Question" feature for another example of how criteria for abnormality can be applied in different ways to make judgments about what is or isn't normal.

1.4 HISTORICAL PERSPECTIVES

HISTORICAL-CULTURAL VS. OBJECTIVE/UNIVERSAL/LEGAL VIEWS

Disagreement about what is abnormal psychology and what should be done about it is nothing new. Humans have tried to understand "madness" since the beginning of recorded history (R. Porter, 2002). However, studying the history of abnormal psychology can prove rather tricky. Obviously, any history is just a retelling, one that highlights some events while leaving out others as it tries to explain what happened and why it is important. In thinking about the history of abnormality, it is worth distinguishing historical-cultural views from objective/universal/legal views.

> *The Historical-Cultural view holds that certain lifestyles, behaviors, attitudes, perceptions, and thoughts might be deemed pathological in one historical-cultural context and not in another. The Objective/Universal/ Legal view holds that there are certain states of extreme withdrawal, states of disorientation, incoherent thoughts, and unconventional, disorganized behaviors, which will be universally considered the product of mental affliction, regardless of the attributed etiology. (Papiasvili & Mayers, 2013, pp. 16–17)*

Combining these views, even if some behaviors are deemed universally abnormal, our ideas about them may shift across historical eras. This makes telling an unbiased history extremely challenging, perhaps impossible! That said, the brief history that follows attempts to examine the origins of and influences on psychological, biological, and sociocultural perspectives in abnormal psychology.

STONE AGE PERSPECTIVES

The first evidence of people trying to manage those displaying abnormal behavior goes back to the Stone Age. Prehistoric skulls from all over the world show evidence of trepanation (also called *trephination*), a process by which holes were drilled in them (Sturges, 2013). Historians often view trepanation as evidence of the demonological perspective (also called the *supernatural perspective*), which views abnormal behavior as due to possession by evil spirits (Vadermeersch, 1994, p. 624). From a demonological perspective, drilling a hole in the skull allowed possessing spirits to escape (R. Porter, 2002). At the same time, trepanation has also been viewed as an early biological approach (Millon, 2004; Sturges, 2013). After all, drilling a hole in the skull constitutes a biological intervention. Trepanning continued to be used for many centuries. There is evidence of it during the Greek and Roman periods, the Middle Ages, and the Renaissance (Dreher, 2013; Missori et al., 2015; Weber & Czarnetzki, 2001). The rationales for it during these eras typically combined demonological and biological perspectives (Dreher, 2013). Though the idea of drilling holes in the skull strikes many students as primitive, keep in mind that the practice is sometimes still used today—not to treat abnormality, but as a method for treating subdural hematomas (which is when blood collects outside the brain, usually after a head injury) (Mondorf, Abu-Owaimer, Gaab, & Oertel, 2009).

GREEK AND ROMAN PERSPECTIVES

Hippocrates' (Mostly) Biological Perspective

Bodily Humors

The Greek physician Hippocrates (460–367 BCE) is considered to have been the founder of a scientific approach to medicine and neurology (Breitenfeld, Jurasic, & Breitenfeld, 2014). Many of his views about abnormality therefore reflect an early biological perspective (J. R. Matthews & Matthews, 2013; Millon, 2004). Ancient Greek thinkers such as Hippocrates believed that the world was made of four substances: earth, air, fire, and water. These elements were characterized by heat, cold, moisture, and dryness, which through a variety of factors (including the weather, heredity, and diet) combined inside each person to form bodily humors (J. R. Matthews & Matthews, 2013). Hippocrates believed there to be four bodily humors: *black bile* (combining cold and dryness), *yellow bile* (combining heat and dryness), *phlegm* (combining cold and moisture), and *blood* (combining heat and moisture). He maintained that abnormality occurred when these bodily humors were out of balance.

> For example, a person who had an excessive amount of yellow bile would be expected to exhibit symptoms of mania. Such a person would engage in a range of excessive and frenzied activities. However, a person who had an excessive amount of black bile in contrast to the other humors would be expected to exhibit symptoms of melancholia, or extreme sadness. (J. R. Matthews & Matthews, 2013, p. 2)

Hippocrates' effort to categorize different forms of madness based on bodily humor imbalances anticipates later attempts at diagnostic classification (Millon, 2004). In keeping with his rejection of supernatural explanations in favor of biological humors, many of the treatments that Hippocrates and other healers of the time used were medicinal, relying on various herbs to alleviate or ward off symptoms. Peppermint leaves were used to relieve depression, the herb St. John's wort was used to ward off evil spirits, and peony was worn around the neck to prevent epilepsy (J. R. Matthews & Matthews, 2013).

Hysteria and the Wandering Womb

Hippocrates' view of hysteria—a malady involving numerous psychological and physical symptoms that the Greeks diagnosed exclusively in women—also reflects a biological viewpoint in that he attributed it to a woman's uterus detaching from its natural location and wandering around her body (Ng, 1999; Palis, Rossopoulos, & Triarhou, 1985; Tasca, Rapetti, Carta, & Fadda, 2012). This explanation—the wandering womb theory—seems silly by today's standards, but it does represent an early effort to understand psychological distress in biological terms (as opposed to supernatural terms, in which evil spirits were thought to take possession of the person). Sociocultural theorists often argue that women from Hippocrates' days onward have often been unfairly diagnosed as hysterical and that how this longstanding diagnosis has been used over the centuries reflects changing cultural interpretations of women's roles—especially concerns about their power and sexuality (Tasca et al., 2012; Ussher, 2013).

Psychological Elements

Despite primarily employing a biological perspective, some aspects of Hippocrates' thinking had psychological elements. For instance, he saw people as possessing a life force that, despite operating according to physiological principles, produced dreams during sleep that were critical to understanding emotional problems. Further, he believed that careful observation of people's everyday behavior was necessary to grasp their difficulties. He also recommended various behavioral interventions. For instance, to treat hysteria he recommended "a regular schedule, a calm life situation, vigorous exercise, abstinence from all excessive behavior, and a mild diet (often vegetarian)" (J. R. Matthews & Matthews, 2013, p. 2).

Socrates, Plato, and Aristotle

Socrates and Plato

Whereas Hippocrates saw abnormal behavior as stemming primarily from brain processes, the philosopher Socrates (470–399 BCE) and his student Plato (429–347 BCE) focused less on the brain as the seat of abnormality and more on the soul. Their perspectives incorporate supernatural and biological elements, as well as psychological ones. Socrates believed that when human passions run amok, emotional distress results. His famous plea, "Know thyself," makes it clear that introspective self-knowledge is the key to overcoming our passions (Millon, 2004). Plato offered a similarly psychological perspective, arguing that abnormality originates when there is a problem in the part of the soul that controls reason (J. R. Matthews & Matthews, 2013). Interestingly, he distinguished madness instilled by the gods (which is desirable because it endows us with special abilities, such as being able to predict the future) from madness caused by disease (which isn't desirable and requires treatment) (J. R. Matthews & Matthews, 2013).

Aristotle

Plato's student Aristotle (384–322 BCE), like Hippocrates, adopted a more naturalistic perspective, although he saw the heart rather than the brain as the central organ responsible for mental functioning. Many view Aristotle as influencing today's cognitive-behavioral therapy (CBT) (defined in Chapter 2 and revisited throughout the book). His emphasis on using reason and logic to overcome emotional difficulties has a cognitive flavor (J. R. Matthews & Matthews, 2013), while his view of learning as the association of ideas seems to anticipate classical conditioning (described in detail in Chapter 2), in which learning results from repeatedly pairing stimuli so that they become associated with one another.

Galen's Perspective, Including Early Diagnostic Categories

Galenus Claudius (129–199 CE), usually known simply as Galen, was a Greek physician who served as the personal physician of the Roman emperor, Nero (J. R. Matthews & Matthews, 2013). Galen was interested in abnormal behavior and, in studying it, he built on the works of Hippocrates, Plato, and Aristotle (J. R. Matthews & Matthews, 2013; R. Porter, 2002). Like Hippocrates, Galen saw abnormal behavior as biologically caused (J. R. Matthews & Matthews, 2013; Millon, 2004). However, like Plato and Aristotle, he also emphasized the soul. He argued that the brain contained the rational soul, but that people also have an irrational subsoul—housed in the liver for women and the heart for men (J. R. Matthews & Matthews, 2013). Galen agreed with Hippocrates that abnormality has to do with imbalances in bodily humors and he expanded Hippocrates' classification system to eight categories: "anoia (reasoning problems), moria (retardation), phrenitis [delirium or frenzy], melancholia [depression and anxiety], mania, lethargus [lethargy], hysteria (found in both males & females), and epilepsy" (J. R. Matthews & Matthews, 2013, p. 7 [definitions in brackets added]). Galen's view is often interpreted as reflecting the primarily biological perspective we now attribute to the Greek and Roman era (Millon, 2004). However, our modern interpretations of this era may draw too firm a distinction among biological, psychological, and supernatural perspectives because the Greeks and Romans thought more holistically and didn't differentiate mind, body, and spirit as firmly we do today (R. Porter, 2002). This perhaps explains the wide variety of interventions they used to relieve abnormal symptoms, which included physical interventions (herbal drugs), psychological interventions (lifestyle changes that provided comfort), and supernatural interventions (use of magic) (J. R. Matthews & Matthews, 2013).

PERSPECTIVES DURING THE MIDDLE AGES

Avicenna's Biological Perspective and Early Hospitals

Avicenna

The Middle Ages roughly cover the period from the fall of the Western Roman Empire in 476 CE to Columbus' arrival in North America in 1492 (Papiasvili & Mayers, 2013). The scientific perspective of the Greeks flourished most fully in the Islamic Middle East, where the bodily humors theory maintained influence (Millon, 2004; Papiasvili & Mayers, 2013; R. Porter, 2002). The Islamic philosopher and physician Avicenna (980–1037 CE) described various symptoms of abnormality, including mania, melancholia, insomnia, and hallucinations (Papiasvili & Mayers, 2013). He adopted Hippocrates' biological perspective, hypothesizing that the middle part of the brain is responsible for intellectual dysfunction and the frontal areas control reason and common sense (Millon, 2004). Avicenna also noted a relationship between emotional states and health (Millon, 2004).

Early Hospitals

Hospitals were established in Baghdad, Cairo, Damascus, and Aleppo between the 8th and 13th centuries, providing services to those considered mad (Papiasvili & Mayers, 2013). During this period, a variety of psychological and biological treatments were developed. For instance, Cairo's Mansuri Hospital employed something that resembles today's bibliotherapy. Patients were encouraged to read books and discuss their emotional reactions in groups. Other techniques common in the era included hydrotherapy, music, and activities (Papiasvili & Mayers, 2013).

Demonological Perspectives in Europe

Malleus Maleficarum

In Christian Europe during much of the Middle Ages, Hippocrates' biological perspective held less sway than in the Islamic Middle East. Theological approaches to madness dominated, increasing the influence of demonological explanations. Christian theology saw madness as a moral struggle (Papiasvili & Mayers, 2013). Strategies for overcoming it often involved punishment for sinful behavior. Fasting, prayer, and various types of exorcism to expel the devil were employed. Many of those deemed possessed were labeled as witches. Two monks, Heinrich Kramer (1430–1505) and James Sprenger (~1435–1495), authored the *Malleus Maleficarum* (also known as the *Hammer of Witches*), a book in which they systematically examined witchcraft and demonic possession (Elkins, 2016; H. Kramer & Sprenger, n.d.; Papiasvili & Mayers, 2013; R. Porter, 2002).

Did Demonological Perspectives Lead to Persecution?

Some historians contend that during the Middle Ages it was common to accuse abnormal people of being witches and to punish them, often by killing them (Zilboorg, 1941). Other historians, however, cast doubt on this contention (Maher & Maher, 1982; S. M. Phillips, 2002; Schoeneman, 1984). Although they concede that many of those accused of witchcraft were women who didn't adhere to social norms, they challenge the idea (frequently presented in abnormal texts) that there was widespread persecution of abnormal people for being witches (Schoeneman, 1984). From this historical perspective, in Christian Europe during much of the Middle Ages, demonological explanations of abnormal behavior were common, but didn't result in widespread persecution. Nor did they wholly supplant biological perspectives. In fact, between the 11th and 13th centuries, many of the Islamic medical texts from the Middle East influenced some European approaches to abnormal behavior, with Hippocratic humoral theory a common means of understanding it (Papiasvili & Mayers, 2013).

The Influence of Cultural Context: Dancing Mania and Lycanthropy

Some of the syndromes identified during the Middle Ages strike us as strange today. For instance, **dancing mania** was a form of "mass madness" in which people would feel an unstoppable urge to dance. For instance,

> *dozens of mediaeval authors recount the terrible compulsion to dance that, in 1374, swept across western Germany, the Low Countries, and northeastern France. Chronicles agree that thousands of people danced in agony for days or weeks, screaming of terrible visions and imploring priests and monks to save their souls. ... On a far larger scale was the outbreak that struck the city of Strasbourg in 1518, consuming as many as 400 people. One chronicle states that it claimed, for a brief period at least, about 15 lives a day as men, women, and children danced in the punishing summer heat. (Waller, 2009, p. 624)*

Lycanthropy—the belief that one is possessed by or has been transformed into a wolf or other animal—was also widely reported during the Middle Ages. Reports of people suffering from it date back at least as far as the ancient Greeks (Poulakou-Rebelakou, Tsiamis, Panteleakos, & Ploumpidis, 2009), but continued on through the Middle Ages and into the Renaissance (Dreher, 2013). In medieval times, lycanthropy was explained both in terms of humoral imbalances and demonological possession (Poulakou-Rebelakou et al., 2009). Interestingly, although quite rare, it is still occasionally seen today—with eight cases being reported in Iraq over the past several decades, mainly in which people believed they had changed into a dog (Blom, 2014; Younis & Moselhy, 2009). The examples of dancing mania and lycanthropy can be used to bolster the idea that how people express abnormality is at least partly determined by historical context and culture (Waller, 2009).

RENAISSANCE PERSPECTIVES

The Renaissance as One of Europe's Most "Psychically Disturbed" Periods

The Renaissance in Europe, which lasted roughly from the late 15th until the early 18th century, is considered to have been a period of intense scientific and artistic achievement. However, the changes it brought resulted in substantial social upheaval. Consequently, some historians have argued that the Renaissance was one of Europe's most "psychically disturbed" periods, with **melancholia** (or *melancholy*, an early and somewhat more inclusive term for what today we might call depression) the condition warranting the most attention (Dreher, 2013). Long-established and new explanations of abnormality flourished, including those that attributed it to "the influence of the moon, the stars, weather, earwigs in the head, and an imbalanced life involving excessive or insufficient drink, diet, sleep, exercise, passions, and humors, along with witchcraft and the devil himself" (Dreher, 2013, p. 36). Treatments were as varied as the explanations: whipping, chaining, bloodletting, laxatives, exorcisms, herbal medicines, diets of various sorts, and even near-drowning were all employed as remedies for madness (Dreher, 2013).

Early Asylums in Europe

Geel

The Church often took on the task of caring for abnormal people, providing them with food and shelter. One of the best-known examples of humane religious treatment occurred in Geel, Belgium, where there were rumors of miraculous cures of madness (Aring, 1974; J. L. Goldstein & Godemont, 2003). Since at least the 13th century, pilgrims from all over Europe descended on the town to receive nine days of religious treatment. At the request of the church canons, area residents housed pilgrims before and after their treatments. To this day, Geel continues to offer community support services for those diagnosed with mental disorders—although no longer under the auspices of the Church (Aring, 1974; J. L. Goldstein & Godemont, 2003).

Bedlam

Not all Renaissance treatments for madness were as pleasant as those in Geel. Asylums for housing mad persons began to appear throughout Europe. Despite being founded in order to treat abnormality, these institutions usually wound up serving more of a custodial function, housing vagrants, criminals, sick people, homeless people, and people who today likely would be identified as psychotic or demented (Shorter, 1997). One of the more notorious asylums was Bethlehem Hospital in London. Begun as a Church institution, Bethlehem was acquired by the city of London in 1547. During the Renaissance and into the 1700s and 1800s, it was known for its deplorable conditions. Treatments included cold baths, bloodletting, and rotating patients in chairs for several hours at a time (often resulting in vomiting) (Devlin, 2014; Elkins, 2016). Many patients were kept in chains and displayed to sightseers visiting the gallery (J. C. Harris, 2003). In 1733, the artist William Hogarth famously portrayed these horrific conditions as part of his work, *A Rake's Progress* (J. C. Harris, 2003). Over time the hospital's nickname, "Bedlam," became synonymous with "a scene or state of wild uproar and confusion" (Dictionary.com, n.d.-b). Interestingly a modern version of the institution, now called Bethlehem Royal Hospital, remains an active psychiatric hospital, albeit in a different location and minus the notoriety. Although the harsh treatments typical of the early asylum era are generally condemned in most industrialized Western countries today, you might be surprised to learn that in some parts of the world, similarly harsh treatments can still be found (see the "In Depth" feature).

Plate 8 of William Hogarth's work "A Rake's Progress" portrays the chaos of Bedlam Hospital.
Source: © CORBIS/Corbis via Getty Images

IN DEPTH

Chaining the Inmates in West Africa

We think of chaining psychiatric inmates as an unpleasant and ill-informed practice of the past. However, in some parts of the world, chains are still used to deal with abnormal behavior. A *New York Times* article reported that in areas of West Africa where psychiatry is unknown, chains are often used to manage family members experiencing psychosis; religious retreats set up makeshift psychiatric wards in which the only intervention used is prayer (B. Carey, 2015a).

Such "prayer camps" have been established throughout West Africa, an area of the world that has been riddled with war for years and where standards of living remain low. At these prayer camps, local pastors take in people who easily meet the criteria for serious disorders such as schizophrenia. The inmates at these camps have often been brought there by distraught families ill-equipped to handle their abnormal behavior. The camps vary widely in exactly how they deal with patients, but typically they are chained and kept in conditions that would likely shock most Westerners. For instance, in one camp in Ghana, most of the residents were chained by their ankles to trees and had to sleep, urinate, and defecate while chained; no medical or mental health experts were employed (B. Carey, 2015a).

Importantly, the pastors don't see themselves as abusing the mentally ill. Harking back to a demonological perspective that is no longer adhered to in the West, they view themselves as helping people overcome spiritual crises or possession by evil spirits. For instance, Paul Noumonvi, the director of Jesus is the Solution (one of the larger camps in Ghana), believes that patients housed in the camp have had spells cast on them: that is, witchcraft causes their illness (B. Carey, 2015a). Interestingly, the *New York Times* article points out that West Africa isn't the only place where questionable practices are used in dealing with people who are deemed to be mentally ill. In the U.S. and other Western nations, hundreds of thousands of people with psychosis and other serious mental health diagnoses are placed in prisons; in Indonesia and elsewhere in Asia, shackles, wooden stocks, and cages are used to restrain patients (B. Carey, 2015a). So, while the practices in West Africa may shock and upset you, this area of the world is far from the only one that previously relied—or currently relies—on questionable methods for dealing with abnormal behavior.

CRITICAL THINKING QUESTIONS

1. The United Nations holds that involuntarily chaining people violates its disability rights convention, which countries such as Ghana, Nigeria, and Togo have approved. Should the United Nations do something to intervene and, if so, what should they do?

2. If we assume that the demonological model adopted by the pastors overseeing Prayer Camps is incorrect and that such camps where people are chained to trees are morally wrong, are we merely relying on modern science and ethics to inform our view? Or are we being culturally imperialistic and biased against a culture we don't understand?

PERSPECTIVES DURING THE 18TH AND 19TH CENTURIES

Moral Therapy

Alienists and the Development of Moral Therapy

Historical accounts of 18th- and 19th-century approaches to abnormality often focus on several interrelated themes: efforts toward more humane care, the development of biological and psychological perspectives, and the increasing reliance on asylums. In the late 18th and early 19th centuries, the first psychiatrists (known as alienists back then because they worked with people experiencing "mental alienation") began to see the asylum as critical to effective treatment (R. Porter, 2002). They generally viewed abnormality in biological terms, but many of their interventions had a psychological flavor. These interventions often involved talking to inmates about their difficulties and providing them a structured schedule and mild discipline within the confines of the asylum. So even though they hypothesized about biological causes of abnormality, these alienists were simultaneously contributing to the development of moral therapy (or *moral treatment*), which is often viewed as an early version of psychotherapy with an understandably psychological bent compared to more purely biological perspectives (Elkins, 2016; R. Porter, 2002). Moral therapy did away with physical coercion. Instead, patients became "part of a supportive social environment" in which they were treated kindly while being asked to participate in various activities (such as group discussions, chores/work, art, music, reading, and writing) that were "designed to enhance their physical, mental, and emotional well-being" (Elkins, 2016, p. 79).

Prominent Figures

Prominent figures associated with developing moral therapy treatments within asylum settings include Philippe Pinel (1745–1826) and Jean-Étienne-Dominique Esquirol (1772–1840) in France, Vincenzo Chiarugi (1759–1820) in Italy, William Battie (1703–1776) in England, and Johann Christian Reil (1759–1813) in Germany (Millon, 2004). Pinel is commonly credited with the compassionate act of unchaining the inmates at Bicêtre Hospital, though historians increasingly view the oft-repeated tale of his doing so as something of an "origin myth" (D. B. Weiner, 1994). Technically, it wasn't Pinel who unchained the inmates; it was his assistant. Further, Pinel stopped using chains but replaced them with straitjackets (R. Porter, 2002). Regardless, early alienists such as Pinel, Esquirol, Chiarugi, Battie, and Reil began viewing the asylum as a place where patients could be treated more gently than they had been previously so that effective therapy could occur. They advanced the then-radical notion "that institutions themselves could be made curative, that confinement in them, rather than merely removing a nuisance from the vexed family or the aggrieved village elders, could make the patient better" (R. Porter, 2002, p. 8).

Pinel categorized madness into four types: *melancholia*, *mania*, *idiocy*, and *dementia* (Telles-Correia & Marques, 2015). Porter (2002) contends that early alienists such as Pinel tried to balance biological and psychosocial models. Although these two contrasting approaches to abnormality frequently proved incompatible, moral treatment in these European hospital settings combined both biological and psychosocial aspects, despite the obvious tensions.

The York Retreat

The traditional asylum was not the only setting where moral therapy blossomed. Independently of Pinel and the other European asylum administrators, the English Quaker William Tuke (1732–1819) developed a version of moral therapy at the **York Retreat** that grew less from a biological perspective and more from a religious one—although it intermingled both (Charland, 2007). Tuke was not a doctor and the York Retreat was a very different kind of asylum, one that emphasized Quaker values (such as benevolence, charity, discipline, self-restraint, and temperance) more than medicine (Charland, 2007; Elkins, 2016). As Tuke himself wrote, "medicine, as yet, possesses very inadequate means to relieve the most grievous of human diseases" (Tuke, as cited in Charland, 2007, p. 66). Moral treatment spread throughout Europe and the United States. Unlike larger, more traditional institutions, asylums providing Tuke's version of moral therapy were typically small, rarely restrained patients, allowed them to wear their own clothes, and tried to foster a family-like atmosphere (J. Andrews, 2007; "Moral treatment in America's lunatic asylums," 1976). They also encouraged patient participation in activities such as arts and crafts, carpentry, domestic tasks, and farming—all consistent with the Quaker emphasis on living a healthy and meaningful life (Charland, 2007).

Critics of Moral Therapy

Historians generally view moral therapy as a benevolent movement that treated patients kindly and was a clear improvement upon previous practices (Bockoven, 1972; Charland, 2007; Elkins, 2016). However, in its day moral treatment did have its critics. Members of the Alleged Lunatics' Friends Society, a group concerned with the rights of those deemed mad, attacked moral treatment "as an imposition of society's values on the individual" and "expressed suspicion of the tranquility so frequently admired by the Commissioners in asylums," suggesting that "patients were first crushed, 'and then discharged to live a milk sop existence in society'" (Hervey, 1986, pp. 253–254). The issue of whether involuntary hospital treatment is an act of kindness or oppression isn't unique to thinking about moral treatment. It remains something we struggle with to this day (see Chapter 15). Critics during the 19th century notwithstanding, Elkins' (2016, p. 84) historical assessment is that "moral treatment was a new and more humane way of working with the insane."

Why Did Moral Therapy Decline?

The reasons for the decline of moral therapy in the second half of the 19th century have been hotly debated. Some historians argue that the movement spread too quickly. They contend that, in addition to suffering from uninspired leadership after its initial developers passed on (Bockoven, 1972), the moral treatment movement led to the rapid proliferation of asylums, resulting in overcrowding and staff shortages. Consequently, asylums lost the ability to offer the kind of personalized attention that moral treatment required. This problem was compounded in the United States, where immigration produced a more diverse population and the prejudices of those running the asylums interfered with their ability to provide compassionate care (Bockoven, 1972). Other historians assert that moral treatment failed because it simply wasn't effective enough. In this interpretation, many patients required more stringent, medically based interventions than moral therapy could provide. This contradicts historians who argue that moral treatment was highly successful (Bockoven, 1972), so much so that physicians turned against it because it showed how lay people could cure insanity better than doctors (Elkins, 2016). In this analysis, moral therapy disappeared because medical doctors reasserted their authority and instituted a more strictly medical model so that they would once again be the ultimate authorities on mental illness and its treatment (Elkins, 2016; Vatne & Holmes, 2006).

Larger Asylums and Their Reform

Custodial Care and the Reform Movement of Dorothea Dix

Regardless of which historical arguments you accept, what we can all agree on is that moral therapy all but disappeared in the late 19th century and was replaced by custodial care—warehousing patients for long periods of time without providing much in the way of treatment. As asylums became larger and more custodial in nature, the focus shifted from the question of best treatments to a more basic question: How do we insure inmates have adequate basic living conditions? Thus, the late 19th century was less about moral treatment and more about reforming oppressive conditions in asylums and other institutions such as jails and almshouses (charitable housing provided to the poor and indigent). The most famous asylum reformer was Massachusetts school-teacher Dorothea Lynde Dix (1802–1887), who for forty years investigated, reported upon, and tried to improve the settings where mad people were housed (T. J. Brown, 1998; Gollaher, 1995; Millon, 2004; M. S. Parry, 2006). In a petition she brought before the Massachusetts Legislature in 1843, Dix (1843/2006, p. 622) forcefully made her case: "I proceed, Gentlemen, briefly to call your attention to the present state of Insane Persons confined within this Commonwealth, in cages, closets, cellars, stalls, pens! Chained, naked, beaten with rods, and lashed into obedience!" Through her advocacy efforts in both the United States and Europe, more than 30 mental hospitals were founded or expanded during the latter half of the 19th century (M. S. Parry, 2006; Viney & Bartsch, 1984).

Nineteenth century asylum reformer Dorothea Dix.
Source: Fotosearch/Getty Images

Dix's Historical Standing

Dix's historical standing depends on whose accounts you read. She is often portrayed as a heroic social advocate whose 40-year crusade to build mental hospitals to house and care for the mentally ill marked a humane turning point in the history of abnormal psychology, even if the solutions she championed were unable to fully solve the longstanding problems of poverty and mental illness (Gollaher, 1995). However, some historians blame her for the rise of large, state-sponsored mental institutions that warehoused the mentally ill without providing sufficient treatment (Bockoven, 1972). Of course, pinning so much responsibility on Dix may be unreasonable. There were other social, economic, and political reasons behind the rise of large mental institutions, chief among them being the steadily growing population. These factors may have had at least as much influence as Dix over why mental hospitals grew so large during the late 19th and early 20th centuries and were ultimately unable to provide proper care (Viney & Bartsch, 1984).

PERSPECTIVES IN THE 20TH AND 21ST CENTURIES

Early 20th-Century Mental Hospitals

The first half of the 20th century saw an expansion in the size of mental hospitals in the U.S. and Europe—in part because housing patients together in a hospital was viewed as most effective and efficient, but also because families and communities welcomed having hospitals relieve their burden of care (Knapp, Beecham, McDaid, Matosevic, & Smith, 2011). In the U.S., for instance, more than 400,000 mental patients were institutionalized by 1940, mainly in large state psychiatric hospitals (Grob, 1994). Patients were often housed for long periods of time with little treatment provided. Funding was lacking, staff shortages were common, and the physical conditions of the hospitals were deteriorating (Grob, 1994).

Of the treatments that were used, some don't hold up very well to historical scrutiny, though they were used because they sometimes worked when few alternatives were available (Lieberman, 2015). Controversial 20th-century treatments include malarial therapy, convulsion therapy, and psychosurgery (Elkins, 2016). **Malarial therapy** was rooted in the assumption that a high fever improves symptoms of abnormality; thus, patients were injected with the malaria virus as a treatment for their ills (Elkins, 2016; Lieberman, 2015). **Convulsion therapy** was used to treat schizophrenia; to induce epileptic-like convulsions, patients were injected with insulin (**insulin coma therapy**) or administered an electric shock to their brains (**electroconvulsive therapy [ECT]**) (Endler, 1988; R. M. Kaplan, 2013; Lieberman, 2015; Shorter, 1997). Lastly, **psychosurgery** was used to sever connections between the prefrontal lobes and other parts of the brain; this was known as **lobotomy** (J. Johnson, 2014; Swayze, 1995). Except for ECT, these treatments are rarely (if ever) used anymore. Many of these interventions are revisited in future chapters, especially Chapter 4 (when we examine psychosis).

The Expansion of Contrasting Perspectives

The 20th and 21st centuries saw the continued expansion of competing perspectives on abnormality. However, despite ongoing critiques, the biological perspective has increasingly dominated psychiatry. The most famous 20th-century critic of the biological perspective was undoubtedly psychiatrist Thomas Szasz (1920–2012), whose writings include the seminal book, *The Myth of Mental Illness*. In this book Szasz argued that biological perspectives confuse mind and body (Szasz, 1974). He contended that *minds*, which are non-physical, couldn't be biologically diseased because only *brains* can be physically sick. This explains why the concept of a brain tumor makes sense, but a mind tumor doesn't; minds can't get tumors because minds aren't physical things! Therefore, in Szasz's view, the concept of "mental illness" (illnesses of the mind) makes no sense. Szasz was a longtime critic of biological psychiatry, arguing that mental disorder diagnoses describe objectionable behavior (i.e., social deviance), not brain diseases (Szasz, 1963, 1974, 1987, 1970/1991a). He believed that what we often call mental disorders are better conceptualized as problems in living. Szasz maintained that psychological upset due to problems in living—such as not having sufficient housing, being in an unhappy relationship, dealing with family problems, disliking one's job, or feeling dissatisfied in life—are part of human experience, not sicknesses. By calling them disorders, Szasz believed that we increasingly and incorrectly medicalize everyday life. Szasz's perspective was influential in the 1960s and 1970s and—as we will see in Chapter 15—it is important in thinking about how involuntary hospitalization is handled by the legal system. Critics of Szasz have countered that he overlooked compelling biological evidence of mental disorders (Vatz & Weinberg, 1983). However, Szasz's followers maintain that such critics fail to acknowledge Szasz's central thesis, namely that "mental illness" is an incoherent concept because minds cannot be physically ill (Vatz & Weinberg, 1983).

Deinstitutionalization

Partly due to the influence of thinkers like Szasz, who were opposed to involuntary commitment, the second half of the 20th century saw a large-scale deinstitutionalization movement at mental hospitals throughout North America and Europe (Dumont & Dumont, 2008; Grob, 1994; Hamlin & Oakes, 2008; Krieg, 2001; Torrey, 2014). Deinstitutionalization involves releasing people from mental hospitals and other institutional settings. The intent was to replace large public institutions with local community mental health care that provides an integrated array of outpatient services (medication management, therapy, family support, job training, etc.) to mental health service-users, often via government-funded programs. The reasons behind deinstitutionalization are numerous and ripe for debate. Among those most often given are (a) growing criticism of mental hospitals as ineffective institutions that dehumanized and mistreated mental patients, (b) the advent of psychotropic drugs that allowed many patients to be medicated and managed outside the confines of a hospital setting, and (c) economic pressures, mainly cuts in funding for mental health services that led to the closing of hospitals (usually without replacing them with community mental health centers). Critics have noted that oftentimes community mental health centers failed to replace large-scale mental hospitals because rather than providing services for the severely disturbed, they often wound up attending more to people with less serious problems (Grob, 1994). Torrey (2014), in his examination of the deinstitutionalization movement in the U.S., concludes that such a large-scale emptying of hospitals had not occurred at any other time. He argues that the enthusiasm over discharging inmates and shutting down institutions was never accompanied by a clear plan for how to fund and provide effective services once patients were released into the community. The U.K. and the rest of Europe have often experienced similar challenges, with deinstitutionalization generally taking priority over clear planning for how to provide sufficient services to released inmates (Emerson, 2004; Hans-Joachim & Wuld, 1999; B. Hudson, 1991; Stubnya, Nagy, Lammers, Rihmer, & Bitter, 2010).

Today many different perspectives compete with each another for influence. Some clinicians strongly advocate for biological perspectives, others for psychological and/or sociocultural perspectives. Yet others still try to integrate these perspectives. The history of abnormal psychology has often been about the ongoing struggle between these competing perspectives, a struggle that remains to this day.

> *Psychiatry has always been torn between two visions of mental illness. One vision stresses the neurosciences, with their interest in brain chemistry, brain anatomy, and medication, seeing the origin of psychic disturbance in the biology of the cerebral cortex. The other vision stresses the psychosocial side of patients' lives, attributing their symptoms to social problems or past personal stresses to which people may adjust imperfectly. … Yet even though psychiatrists may share both perspectives, when it comes to treating individual patients, the perspectives really are polar opposites, in that both cannot be true at the same time. Either one's depression is due to a biologically influenced imbalance in one's neurotransmitters, perhaps activated by stress, or it stems from some psychodynamic process in one's unconscious mind. … This bifurcation was present at the very beginning of the discipline's history. (R. Porter, 2002, pp. 26–27)*

1.5 RESEARCH PERSPECTIVES

One of the ways people try to distinguish which perspectives are best is through research. Understanding how researchers study abnormality is important because it provides a way to sift through all the conflicting perspectives to distinguish which are best. However, there are lots of different ways to conduct research. That is, just as there are many perspectives on what abnormality is and how best to remedy it, there are also competing research perspectives. Understanding different research perspectives is important if one hopes to comprehend, critique, and use research findings effectively.

Researchers typically rely on the scientific method in which they systematically collect data through various means of observation and measurement. Exactly which methods are used depends on the problem being studied and the perspective of the researcher. When using quantitative methods, the researcher uses mathematical statistics to test hypotheses (W. E. Martin & Bridgmon, 2012). Data is systematically collected and statistically analyzed, with the goal of discovering universal laws or truths. When using qualitative methods, on the other hand, the researcher gathers data about subjective experience or sociocultural phenomena, usually with the goal of comprehending the specific worldviews reflected in what is being studied. Qualitative researchers tend to see their findings as constructed understandings that are true within a particular context or time-period, but are not necessarily universal (N. Frost, 2011). Let's briefly review the quantitative and qualitative research perspectives that are commonly used in studying abnormality.

QUANTITATIVE RESEARCH PERSPECTIVES

Correlational Method

Positive and Negative Correlations

Correlational research looks at the relationship between two variables to see whether changes in one are systematically tied to changes in the other (D. T. Campbell & Stanley, 1963; W. E. Martin & Bridgmon, 2012; M. L. Smith & Glass, 1987). Variables are aspects of the world that can change; they must have two or more values (M. L. Smith & Glass, 1987). Gender, age, level of depression, and marital status are examples of variables. A correlation occurs when two variables are related (D. T. Campbell & Stanley, 1963; M. L. Smith & Glass, 1987). As one fluctuates, so does the other. As a hypothetical example, we might ask whether there is a relationship between how much time people spend on Facebook and their level of emotional well-being. We could gather data from people about how many hours a day they spend on Facebook and then ask them to complete an emotional well-being inventory. There are three possible results (M. L. Smith & Glass, 1987):

» The first possibility is a positive correlation. In such a correlation, as one score increases, so does the other. Look at the positive correlation in Figure 1.1. Note that as the number of hours on Facebook increases so does emotional well-being. If this were the data our correlational study yielded, we'd conclude that Facebook time is positively correlated with emotional well-being.

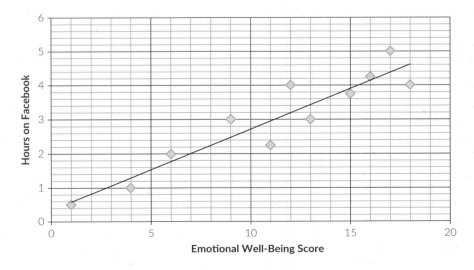

Figure 1.1 Positive Correlation

Positive correlations are indicated by a scatterplot of scores through which a line going upward to the right can be drawn. The stronger the correlation is, the steeper the line.

» The second possibility is a **negative correlation**. In this kind of correlation, as one score increases, the other decreases. In Figure 1.2, as the number of hours on Facebook increases, emotional well-being scores decrease. In this example, emotional well-being and time on Facebook are negatively correlated.

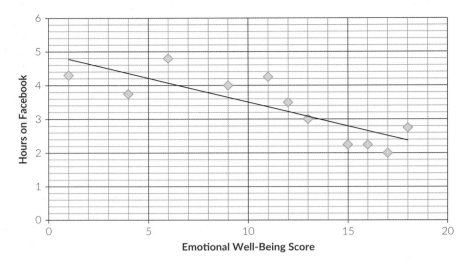

Figure 1.2 Negative Correlation

Negative correlations are indicated by a scatterplot of scores through which a line going downward to the right can be drawn. The stronger the correlation is, the steeper the line.

» The third possibility is **no correlation**. That is, we might find that the amount of daily time spent on Facebook is unrelated to emotional well-being scores. As you can see in Figure 1.3, there is no pattern to the scores. They show no signs of being related to one another and are therefore uncorrelated.

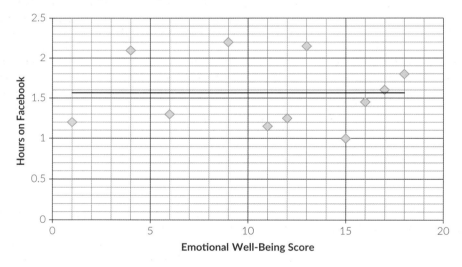

Figure 1.3 No Correlation

No correlation is indicated by a scatterplot of scores through which a horizontal line can be drawn. This shows there is no relationship between the variables.

Some variables are more strongly correlated than others. The strength of a correlation is expressed using a **correlation coefficient**, a statistically calculated number between –1.0 and +1.0 (M. L. Smith & Glass, 1987). Positive correlations are closer to +1.0, while negative correlations are closer to –1.0. When two variables are uncorrelated, the correlation coefficient hovers around 0. Correlation coefficients are symbolized by the letter *r*. So, from now on when you overhear instructors discussing *r*-values, you'll know they are talking about a correlation.

We made up the Facebook and emotional well-being data just to illustrate positive and negative correlations. But for the record, an interesting research study did find that frequent Facebook use is negatively correlated with self-esteem (Vogel, Rose, Roberts, & Eckles, 2014). That is, the more someone uses Facebook, the more likely they are to score low on measures of self-esteem. However, don't make the classic mistake of inferring that Facebook use causes low self-esteem! Correlations only tell us that there is a relationship between two variables. They don't tell us whether one variable causes the other (D. T. Campbell & Stanley, 1963). Sure, it's possible that using Facebook causes low self-esteem. Of course, it's also possible that low self-esteem causes Facebook use. However, there's another possibility, namely that neither of these things causes the other. A third variable could potentially explain the relationship between them. The same researchers who found the negative correlation between self-esteem and Facebook usage did a follow-up experiment, which showed that it is the kind of profiles looked at on Facebook that makes a difference in self-esteem; self-esteem only suffers if you are looking at profiles of people with whom you negatively compare yourself (Vogel et al., 2014). In this instance, a third variable does indeed help us make sense of the correlation between Facebook use and self-esteem! The take away message is: Correlational data merely tells us there is a relationship between two variables, not why such a relationship exists. If we want to infer cause, we need to do an experiment (discussed shortly).

Epidemiological Research

Correlational data is used in **epidemiological research**, which studies the prevalence and incidence of various disorders in a population (N. Pearce, 2012). As we discussed earlier, prevalence rates report the percentage of people in the population currently believed to have a given disorder, while incidence rates refer to the number of new cases reported over a specified period (N. Pearce, 2012). For example, one study examined prevalence rates for posttraumatic stress disorder (PTSD) in Uganda, a country that has long suffered from war and political violence. Results revealed an 11.8% overall prevalence rate—10.9% for women and 13.4% for men (Mugisha, Muyinda, Wandiembe, & Kinyanda, 2015). This means that 11.8% of the population qualifies for a PTSD diagnosis. Note that this data is correlational; there is a correlation between living in Uganda and meeting the criteria for PTSD, but no causal relationship can be inferred.

Another study looked at the relationship between social disorganization in neighborhoods and incident rates for psychotic disorders (that is, new cases reported during a given period) among people living in The Hague in the Netherlands (Veling, Susser, Selten, & Hoek, 2015). The study found a negative correlation between **socioeconomic status (SES)**—a measure of a person's social standing based on income, education, and employment (www.apa.org/topics/socioeconomic-status/)—and incident rates of psychosis; that is, as SES decreased, the likelihood of having a psychotic disorder increased. The study also found a positive correlation between residential mobility and incidence of psychosis. Those living in neighborhoods where people moved around a lot were at greater risk for developing psychosis. Once again, these results are correlational in nature (we don't know if social disorganization causes psychosis or vice versa or if there is another factor at play), but they do tell us there is a relationship between psychosis and social makeup of neighborhoods—one worth exploring, perhaps in future experimental research.

Experimental Method

Hypotheses and Variables

The goal of **experiments** is to uncover causal relationships among variables (D. T. Campbell & Stanley, 1963; Kennedy & Bush, 1985; W. E. Martin & Bridgmon, 2012; M. L. Smith & Glass, 1987). By carefully manipulating one variable, we can see its effect on another. For instance, let's imagine we are interested in knowing whether psychodynamic or cognitive-behavioral therapy (CBT) is more effective in alleviating depression. (These therapies are described in greater detail in Chapter 2.) We might design an experiment to find out. Type of therapy (psychodynamic or CBT) and level of depression are our variables. Once we settle on these variables, we need to develop a **hypothesis**, a prediction we make about how the variables will affect one another (Kennedy & Bush, 1985; M. L. Smith & Glass, 1987). We might hypothesize that psychodynamic therapy and CBT will be equally effective in reducing depression compared to no therapy at all.

Next, we need to design our study. This involves identifying the independent and dependent variables. The **independent variable** is the variable that we, as the researchers, control (Kennedy & Bush, 1985; M. L. Smith & Glass, 1987). In our hypothetical experiment, we control what kind of therapy participants receive (psychodynamic, CBT, or none). The **dependent variable** is the observed result (Kennedy & Bush, 1985; M. L. Smith & Glass, 1987)—in this case, how depressed our participants feel after undergoing psychodynamic or cognitive-behavioral therapy. For the dependent variable in our study, we might use participants' scores on the Beck Depression Inventory (BDI), a self-administered instrument used to measure levels of depression (see Chapters 3 and 5) (Dozios & Covin, 2004). If an experiment is constructed well, the outcome on the dependent variable will *depend* on the manipulation of the independent variable. In our study, the kind of therapy participants receive (the independent variable) should determine how much less depressed they are (the dependent variable).

Participants, Populations, and Sampling

Of course, before we can conduct our experiment, we need **participants** (also called *subjects*). The more participants we have, the more confident we can be in our results. In fact, in a perfect world we'd be able to include every depressed person out there—the entire **population** of depressed people (M. L. Smith & Glass, 1987). But that's obviously not feasible, so instead we select a **sample** of people to participate in our study (M. L. Smith & Glass, 1987). Ideally, we'd choose our sample from the population of all depressed people in the world, but in real-life circumstances researchers often have populations of convenience. In our case, maybe we have access to a large mental health clinic that provides outpatient psychotherapy. All the patients who go to this clinic who qualify for a *DSM* diagnosis of major depressive disorder (discussed in Chapter 5) would be our population for the study. Those we select as participants would be our sample. How should we choose our sample? Randomly! As its name implies, a **random sample** is chosen arbitrarily from the population (M. L. Smith & Glass, 1987). This gives us the best chance that the group of participants selected is representative of the larger population. If we choose people non-randomly, we are more likely to get a non-representative sample (based on whatever biases influence how we pick participants), and therefore our experiment's results might not reflect trends in the broader population.

Not only should we sample randomly, but we should also assign participants to different independent variable conditions randomly—a practice known as **random assignment** (Kennedy & Bush, 1985; M. L. Smith & Glass, 1987). Random assignment minimizes the chance that our respective treatment groups differ from one another in ways that could potentially influence our results. Any variable that interferes with our independent variable manipulation being responsible for results on our dependent variable is called a **confounding variable** (Kennedy & Bush, 1985; M. L. Smith & Glass, 1987). If, for example, we let our participants choose for themselves whether to receive psychodynamic therapy, CBT, or no therapy, we might wind up with skewed results; maybe people who choose CBT are different in some way from those who choose psychodynamic therapy and this factor, not the kind of therapy they receive, is what determines how much less depressed they feel after treatment. Using random sampling (to select participants) and random assignment (to decide which treatment participants receive) are critical to limiting the potential effects of confounding variables on experimental results.

Control Groups

Did you notice that in our proposed experiment, we included a group that doesn't get any therapy at all? This is a **control group**, a group of participants who do not receive the treatment. A control group gives us something to compare our treatment groups to (M. L. Smith & Glass, 1987). Without a control group, it would be hard to know whether our treatments are effective. In our experiment, we want to compare psychodynamic therapy and CBT to each other, but we also want to know if these therapies are more helpful than no therapy. That's what a control group is for. Of course, if our control group does nothing and winds up more depressed than either of our treatment groups after the experiment, it will be difficult to tell whether it is therapy or simply engaging in a weekly activity that determined how depressed participants were. Therefore, we might implement a **placebo control group** instead of a traditional control group. A placebo control group gets an activity that is comparable to the treatment, but not the treatment (Chiodo, Tolle, & Bevan, 2000; M. L. Smith & Glass, 1987; Vickers & de Craen, 2000). In our therapy study, we might have control group participants do something that takes the same amount of time as therapy, but isn't therapy. For instance, our placebo control participants might simply play cards with a friendly adult for an hour each week. We would then compare these participants' levels of depression to those of the treatment participants who received either psychodynamic or cognitive-behavioral therapy.

Placebo control groups are commonly used in studies testing antidepressants and other psychotropic drugs (which are discussed in many chapters throughout the book). In these studies, the placebo control group is given a sugar pill (rather than no pill at all) and compared to the experimental group that is given the antidepressant. This way the researchers control for whether it is the antidepressant drug itself or simply knowing you are taking a pill that is responsible for the results. Interestingly, taking a placebo pill (or being in a placebo control group of any kind) often results in improvement on its own. This is called a **placebo effect** (Kirsch, 2010, 2014; F. G. Miller & Rosenstein, 2006; M. L. Smith & Glass, 1987). For a treatment to be considered effective, experimental research must show that its effectiveness goes above and beyond any placebo effect.

Internal and External Validity

We want our experiment to have high internal validity. **Internal validity** involves the degree to which results are caused by the manipulation of the independent variable (M. L. Smith & Glass, 1987). Random assignment and use of control groups both help to insure internal validity. However, researchers sometimes control for other variables that they think might influence their results. In our imaginary experiment gender, socioeconomic status, and being on antidepressants are all variables we might wish to control for. In doing so, we improve the likelihood that it is the type of therapy participants receive, and not these extraneous variables, that determines our results. Researchers also like to conduct **double-blind studies** to improve internal validity. In a double-blind study, neither the participants nor researchers testing them know which treatment group participants belong to (M. L. Smith & Glass, 1987). In drug trial studies, for example, participants typically don't know whether they are receiving the experimental drug or a placebo pill. Further, those evaluating the degree to which participant symptoms improve aren't privy to this information either. To keep our participants blind, we would not inform them about what kind of therapy they are receiving. To insure the experiment is double-blind, we would also keep the researcher who administers the Beck Depression Inventory in the dark about which therapy group participants belong to. In doing so, we hope to neutralize any biases in how the inventory is administered so that internal validity is insured.

We also want our experiment to have high external validity. **External validity** is the extent to which we can generalize our results to everyday life (M. L. Smith & Glass, 1987). Researchers must balance the demands of internal and external validity. A study in a tightly controlled environment where the experimenter can control potentially confounding variables is high in internal validity. However, the cost may be a study that has so little resemblance to everyday life that its results may not generalize beyond the laboratory. Psychology students often have a sense of this issue when they are asked to be participants in research themselves (something most of them are asked to do given how hard it can be for psychology professors to round up participants for their experiments!). I have often heard psychology students complain that the tasks they are asked to do in psychology experiments (such as memorizing nonsense syllables or clicking a button whenever they see a dot on a screen) are so far removed from activities people do in the real world that whatever results are found couldn't possibly generalize beyond the laboratory. When students make complaints like this, they are raising issues of external validity. If the way that psychodynamic and cognitive-behavioral therapies are administered in our experiment doesn't reflect how these therapies are conducted in daily life, we might have an external validity problem. By the way, overreliance on undergraduate psychology students as experimental participants is one of the most common threats to external validity. After all, can we really generalize to the wider population based on how undergraduate students respond?

Randomized Controlled Trials

Mental and physical health researchers often conduct a certain kind of experiment called a **randomized controlled trial (RCT)**, in which participants are randomly assigned to different treatments, whose efficacy is then compared (Hollon, 2006; MacGill, 2016; Sibbald & Roland, 1998). RCTs are commonly used to evaluate the effectiveness of different psychotherapies in treating specific presenting problems. The experiment in which we wanted to compare psychodynamic and cognitive-behavioral therapies is an example of a randomized controlled trial. One RCT that is quite like our hypothetical experiment compared the effectiveness of cognitive-behavioral and interpersonal therapies for depression (Lemmens et al., 2015). The researchers randomly assigned patients diagnosed with major depression to receive either CBT or interpersonal therapy. They also used a control group, but not a placebo control group (control group participants didn't receive a comparable activity; they simply remained on a wait-list for therapy). Using scores on the Beck Depression Inventory-II as the dependent measure, the study found both CBT and interpersonal therapy to be more effective than no therapy but equally effective compared to one another.

Because they ostensibly reveal cause and effect relationships, randomized controlled trials are considered the "gold standard" by many psychotherapy researchers (Nezu & Nezu, 2008). **Empirically supported treatments (ESTs)** are those that have been found to be effective for specific presenting problems in randomized controlled trials (Norcross, Beutler, & Levant, 2006). Some clinicians argue that it is ethically questionable to use any therapy that hasn't been shown to be effective in RCT research (T. B. Baker, McFall, & Shoham, 2008). Other researchers strongly disagree, arguing that RCTs don't always capture the nuances of therapy (T. A. Carey & Stiles, 2015), focusing too much on treatments and not enough on the relationship between therapist and client (Wampold & Imel, 2015). As we will see in upcoming chapters, therapists from cognitive-behavioral and biological perspectives have generally been more supportive of RCTs than those from psychodynamic and humanistic perspectives. This makes sense, given some of the traditional theoretical commitments that adherents of these perspectives hold.

Quasi-Experiments

Sometimes abnormal psychology researchers are unable to randomly assign participants to groups. For example, imagine we want to follow up on the previously mentioned correlational research and study how prolonged living in a war zone affects psychological functioning. We can't randomly assign participants to live in a war zone, insist they remain there, and keep the area in a state of sustained battle. Doing so wouldn't be practical or ethical! So, we simply need to find participants who have lived in a war zone for a long time and compare them to those who haven't. This kind of experimental design, one without random assignment, is called a **quasi-experiment** (D. T. Campbell & Stanley, 1963; M. L. Smith & Glass, 1987). The problem is that without random assignment, quasi-experiments increase the risk of confounding variables affecting the results. People unable to escape a war zone might be poorer, less educated, and more likely to belong to ethnic groups that other countries don't want as immigrants—and it's possible that our experimental results are due to these factors, not prolonged exposure to a war zone. To compensate for this, quasi-experiments often employ **matched control groups**, in which people comparable to experimental group participants along various confounding variables (such as age, sex, socioeconomic status, ethnicity, etc.) are chosen to be in the control group (M. L. Smith & Glass, 1987).

Analogue Experiments

Sometimes we can't conduct certain abnormal psychology experiments because they are too expensive, impractical, or unethical. In such cases, experimenters often rely on analogue experiments. An **analogue experiment** is one in which researchers create laboratory scenarios that are similar (or *analogous*) to those they want to study and use them to draw inferences about the situation they are interested in but can't practically study (Abramowitz et al., 2014; B. G. Cook & Rumrill, 2005). Sticking with a previous example, we can't simulate prolonged exposure to war, but we can create an analogous laboratory experience. Perhaps participants watch a documentary about surviving a war or play a realistic video game in which they are exposed to the horrors of war. We could measure participants' stress levels while they are watching the documentary or playing the video game. The advantage of analogue experiments is that they usually have good internal validity because the experimenter has tight control over the laboratory environment. However, external validity can be an issue. Remember earlier when we discussed your experiences as a research participant in studies that seemed to bear little resemblance to everyday life? Many of those studies are analogue experiments. So, the advantage of analogue studies is strong internal validity and the weakness is the potential for poor external validity.

Animal studies can be used to study many things in abnormal psychology—including the effectiveness of experimental new drug treatments.
Source: Getty Images/iStockphoto Thinkstock Images\Vit Kovalcik

Animal studies are one of the best-known examples of analogue studies. In animal studies, the animal participants serve as analogues for human beings (Abramowitz et al., 2014). Many drug studies use animals as human analogues. These studies test the effectiveness of experimental drugs by giving them to animal subjects. For example, recent studies testing treatments for Alzheimer's disease (examined in Chapter 14) are analogue studies that use mice and rats as subjects (Faivre & Hölscher, 2013; Long-Smith et al., 2013; Talbot & Wang, 2014; Y. Yang et al., 2013).

Animal studies aren't limited to drug testing. Behavioral researchers have long used animal research to study human learning processes. In a series of classic studies, psychologist Martin Seligman used dogs to test the hypothesis that learned helplessness (see Chapter 5) is a central component of depression (Overmier & Seligman, 1967; M. E. Seligman & Maier, 1967; M. E. Seligman, Maier, & Geer, 1968). The dogs were placed in an experimental situation in which they were unable to avoid an electric shock. After a while, the dogs stopped trying to avoid the shock because they learned they couldn't. Once the dogs learned this, they gave up trying to avoid the shock, even when the situation changed and escape was again possible. The idea that depression is partly about learning to feel helpless and ineffective has been generalized from dogs to humans and used to advance cognitive-behavioral therapy techniques in which attributions that produce helplessness can be challenged and modified. As you can see from these examples, animal studies often provide important information about human functioning. Still, there are people who object to animal research, seeing it as cruel to the animals. Defenders insist that animal research is necessary and that without it we would be hard-pressed to make advances in abnormal psychology and other areas of scientific inquiry.

Single-Subject Experiments

Finally, sometimes experiments are conducted on just one person. These are called **single-subject experiments** (D. T. Campbell & Stanley, 1963; M. L. Smith & Glass, 1987). They are experiments because they involve actively manipulating an independent variable to determine its effect on a dependent variable. However, only one subject is tested. The most common type of single-subject experiment is probably an **ABAB design** (also called a *reversal design*). We might use such a design when we are testing a new therapy for the first time and don't think the expense of an RCT is justified yet. We might also use an ABAB design when an RCT is untenable because we don't have access to a lot of participants. For example, let's imagine that we wanted to use this kind of design to test the effectiveness of a new technique to treat the rare problem of lycanthropy (discussed earlier when reviewing historical perspectives). We would alternate between A and B options, as follows:

 » *A*: Measure our single subject's symptoms over a period of two weeks to establish baseline symptom levels.
 » *B*: Have our participant practice our new therapy technique each day for two more weeks and measure symptom levels daily.
 » *A*: Have our participant stop using our new technique for an additional two weeks while continuing to measure daily symptom levels.
 » *B*: Reinstate the participant's use of the new technique for a final two weeks while still measuring symptoms each day.

Using this ABAB design, we can examine whether symptoms of lycanthropy decrease during the initial use of the new technique, increase again when the technique is stopped, and return to lower levels when the new technique is reinstituted. Despite not having access to lots of participants, an ABAB design lets us infer causal relations between the independent variable (in this example whether the participant is practicing our new therapy technique) and the dependent variable (symptoms of lycanthropy). Internal validity can be an issue in ABAB designs because we can't always know if the changes we observe are due to our intervention or due to other factors, such as time passing, the subject maturing, and the subject being tested repeatedly (D. T. Campbell & Stanley, 1963; M. L. Smith & Glass, 1987). An ABAB design can also lack external validity because it is hard to generalize from one participant to larger populations. Our single lycanthropy client might do well with our new therapy technique, but others with the same symptoms might not. Further, sometimes we can't use an ABAB design because once we go from A to B we can't always go back. If we were testing the effectiveness of a new antibiotic drug on infections, the subject might no longer have an infection after initially receiving the drug. Therefore, we'd be unable to return to the baseline condition.

QUALITATIVE RESEARCH PERSPECTIVES

Most psychology texts still don't include qualitative methods so it isn't surprising that students are often unfamiliar with qualitative research perspectives. Compared to quantitative approaches, qualitative methods constitute a fundamentally different "way of knowing." Whereas quantitative methods test objective theories using statistical analyses to infer relationships among variables, qualitative methods focus more on studying people's subjective experiences, aiming to explore and understand "the meaning individuals or groups ascribe to a social or human problem" (Creswell, 2011, p. 4). Whether one uses quantitative or qualitative methods depends on the research question being asked because some questions lend themselves better to one approach or the other.

For instance, the question, "Does being exposed to television violence result in higher levels of aggression in people diagnosed with schizophrenia?" is clearly best answered using quantitative methods. Doing so, we might expose people with and without schizophrenia (discussed in Chapter 4) to a violent or non-violent program and then objectively measure their level of aggression using a standardized aggression scale. Our goal at the end of the study is to be able to make general statements about the effect of violence on aggression in those diagnosed with schizophrenia. Now consider another research question: "What is it like to experience auditory hallucinations?" This is a different kind of question entirely. Rather than looking to uncover universally true causal relationships among variables, this question asks about the subjective experience of hallucinations. As such, it lends itself to qualitative inquiry. Approaching this research question qualitatively, we might ask people with schizophrenia about their hallucinatory experiences to understand what these experiences are subjectively like for them—and in doing so we might learn about what sorts of experiences are common among those who hallucinate.

Unfortunately, one of the challenges in reviewing qualitative methods is that there are many approaches that operate from somewhat different theoretical assumptions. However, Giorgi (1997, p. 245) notes that all qualitative methods require the following steps: "(1) collection of verbal data, (2) reading of the data, (3) breaking of the data into some kind of parts, (4) organization and expression of the data from a disciplinary perspective, and (5) synthesis or summary of the data for purposes of communication to the scholarly community." There are many different qualitative methods, including case studies, grounded theory methods, phenomenological analysis, discursive methods, and narrative methods. Herein, we briefly review the first three of these methods.

Case Studies

Because most abnormal psychology texts don't review qualitative methods, case studies (which generate qualitative data) are usually discussed alongside quantitative methods. When presented in this way, case studies are often portrayed as precursors to experimental studies. At the same time, despite yielding qualitative data, case studies—perhaps because they go back a long way and originated independently of other qualitative methods—are often overlooked in texts about qualitative research (Yin, 2014). Thus, in many ways case studies are caught betwixt and between quantitative and qualitative approaches, not quite fitting easily within either approach. This has led one prominent case study researcher to comment on "the separateness of case study research from other social science research methods" (Yin, 2014, p. 210). Despite this separateness, case studies are presented here because the qualitative (as opposed to quantitative) data they provide is often highly valuable.

In a **case study**, a specific instance of something is examined in depth, often using a theoretical perspective to organize the data gathered and to generalize to other instances (Yin, 2014). The subject of a case study can vary widely. Its focus can be on a person, a small group, an organization, a partnership, a community, a relationship, a decision, or a project (Yin, 2014). For instance, an organizational case study might scrutinize a particular psychiatric unit in depth to examine common issues faced by such units. As another example, a community case study might look at the specific neighborhood street where a community mental health center has recently been established to document the responses of residents. Most familiarly, an individual case study would focus on a given individual in depth—examining his or her upbringing, education, career, personal relationships, and current situation.

Various sources of data can be used in constructing a case study (Yin, 2014):

» *Documents* (using letters, e-mails, diaries, calendars, minutes of meetings, news clippings, administrative documents, etc.);

» *Archival records* (using census data, organizational records, maps and charts of the geography of a place, etc.);

» *Interviews* (speaking directly with the subjects of case studies or others in their lives);

» *Direct observation* (observing meetings, activities, classrooms, therapy sessions, etc.);

» *Participant observation* (participating in the situation being studied; for example, moving to the street where the community mental health center has been established as a way of learning firsthand what the experience is like).

Case studies have the advantage of being rich, providing a thorough examination of the situation or person being studied. One of the most famous individual case studies in abnormal psychology is that of Phineas Gage, an American railroad worker who suffered a terrible injury in 1848 when an explosion sent a tamping iron through his skull, taking a large portion of his brain's frontal lobe with it (Yin, 2014, p. 210). Gage survived, but reportedly underwent a noticeable personality change. Whereas before his injury he was responsible, cordial, and an excellent worker, afterwards he was irreverent, temperamental, and stubborn (J. M. Harlow, 1848). Gage was a perfect subject for a case study. Where else could someone with this kind of brain damage be studied?

The case of Phineas Gage is but one famous case study in abnormal psychology. Sigmund Freud relied almost exclusively on case studies in developing psychoanalytic theory (see Chapter 2). For example, his case study of Little Hans served as an illustration of how unresolved Oedipal feelings in children can produce phobias (Rolls, 2015). Though perhaps most often associated with case studies, psychoanalysis isn't the only theoretical perspective to have made use of them. John Watson's infamous work teaching **Little Albert** to fear a white rat served as a powerful case study of classically conditioned fear (Rolls, 2015; J. B. Watson & Rayner, 1920)—so powerful, in fact, that it has been argued that the strength of its findings are often exaggerated in the behavioral literature (B. Harris, 1979). We discuss Little Albert and classical conditioning further in Chapter 2.

As noted, quantitative researchers often see case studies as limited due to their inability to infer causal relationships between variables. In this view, case studies best serve as a means for generating more formal hypotheses that can then be tested using experimental methods. That is, although qualitative in nature (they don't usually involve statistically analyzing data), case studies have often been treated as precursors to quantitative research. However, case study researchers frequently object to the view of case studies as hierarchically below experiments, arguing that case studies are different from, but not inferior to, quantitative methods for understanding abnormality (Yin, 2014).

In the (in)famous Little Albert case study, psychologist John Watson conditioned fear in an infant.

Grounded Theory Methods

Grounded theory methods help researchers develop conceptual theoretical models of the topics they study that are *grounded* in the data collected. This is very different from what occurs in quantitative experiments, where the researcher begins with a theory and then tests it to see if it withstands scrutiny. In contrast, grounded theory researchers build their theories from the ground up while conducting their research. Many variations on grounded theory have been developed. Some are more *positivist-postpositivist* in assuming grounded theory allows researchers to build theories that approximate objective reality, while other approaches are more *constructivist* in maintaining that grounded theories are human constructions that help us understand something from a specific perspective at a given juncture in time (Charmaz, 2014; Morrow, Castañeda-Sound, & Abrams, 2012).

There are numerous steps in conducting a grounded theory research project. The process begins by developing a research question. Using an example relevant to abnormal psychology, Singh (2003, 2004) used a grounded theory method to examine the question, "How do mothers and fathers experience parenting boys diagnosed with attention deficit hyperactivity disorder (ADHD)?" This question in part was devised using the grounded theory technique of **theoretical sensitivity** in which the researcher's knowledge and experience inform the question being asked. In this case, Singh (2004) had extensive experience with ADHD (a topic examined in Chapter 13)—including attending ADHD conferences and support groups, following how ADHD is portrayed in the scientific literature and by the media, observing clinical evaluations for ADHD, and talking to people affected by ADHD. She used this experience to formulate her research question.

Once a question is posed, a grounded theory researcher begins gathering data. This can be done in a number of ways: through *participant observation*, conducting *interviews*, and examining *documents and archives* (N. Frost, 2011). In Singh's (2003, 2004) work, she interviewed 39 mothers and 22 fathers of boys diagnosed with ADHD. Grounded theory often relies on **theoretical sampling**, which entails devising and revising strategies for recruiting participants as the research project goes along; the tactics used may change as the researcher learns more about the topic being studied and figures out what kinds of additional data are needed (Charmaz, 2014; N. Frost, 2011; Morrow et al., 2012). Participants in Singh's research were recruited using **purposive sampling**, in which people are asked to participate because they have characteristics that allow the research question to be examined in depth (N. Frost, 2011). Sometimes purposive sampling is supplemented with **snowball sampling**, where initial participants are asked if they know anyone else with similar experiences (N. Frost, 2011). Thus, a researcher interviewing parents of boys with ADHD might locate additional interviewees by asking participants if they know of other parents who also have boys with ADHD.

Once participants are recruited, they can be interviewed and any data gathered can be used to refine and further focus the research question. For instance, Singh (2003, 2004) initiated interviews by having participants look at magazine materials related to ADHD. Their reactions were used to begin a conversation with them. She then asked participants how they felt about using stimulant medications to treat ADHD (again, see Chapter 13). Singh used data from these early interviews to refine and further focus her research question. Her resulting understanding helped her to better focus later interviews on emerging concepts and hypotheses. As hopefully is becoming clear, this is a key feature of grounded theory research: the researcher tacks back and forth between data collection and analysis, using budding hypotheses about existing data to determine what additional information needs to be obtained.

In analyzing data, the grounded theory researcher uses several techniques (Charmaz, 2014; N. Frost, 2011; Levitt, 2016). Coding involves going through data (e.g., interview transcripts or archival documents) line by line, jotting down relevant phrases and codes; the goal is to distill key ideas. Categorizing is when the researcher examines the codes created and looks for links among them, eventually sorting them into categories that seem to best fit. Throughout the entire research process, the grounded theory researcher also utilizes memo writing, in which analytical reactions to the data are written down to help shape the researcher's evolving understanding of the topic. Codes, categories, and memos are examined to devise a theoretical coding, where latent links among them are sought and an integrated conception of the topic being studied starts to materialize. Theoretical coding and categorizing are often arrived at using the method of constant comparison, which involves comparing instances highlighted in various codes, categories, and memos. That is, "the researcher continually moves from comparing data to other data in the early stages, data to emerging codes, codes to codes, codes to categories, and back again" (Morrow et al., 2012, p. 100).

For example, as Singh used constant comparison throughout the process of her research, she began to realize that mothers and fathers experienced their sons' ADHD quite differently. Mothers tended to endorse the ADHD diagnosis as a medical explanation that relieved them of blame for their sons' problems. Fathers, by comparison, were generally skeptical (if often quietly tolerant) of medical explanations and treatments of ADHD, identifying with many of their sons' symptomatic behaviors (I. Singh, 2003, 2004).

Phenomenological Analysis

Phenomenological methods are rooted in the phenomenological philosophical tradition, which can be traced back at least as far as the work of philosopher Edmund Husserl. The idea is to describe the essence of something by setting aside our biases and preconceptions in order to "study conscious experience" in its most basic form and identify "the building blocks of subjectivity" (Levitt, 2016, p. 340). Conscious experience is characterized by intentionality, the idea that mental events always refer to or "intend" something in the world (Morrow et al., 2012). Thus, by setting aside our biases and carefully studying conscious experience, we can describe the essences of things in the world and (more interestingly for psychologists) subjective experiences. Numerous phenomenological research approaches have been developed. Here we briefly summarize Amedeo Giorgi's version as a representative example. Giorgi (1997) breaks down the phenomenological method into three steps.

The Phenomenological Reduction

The first step is the phenomenological reduction, which consists of two parts. First, the researcher must bracket his or her preconceptions. Bracketing involves laying aside one's taken-for-granted beliefs about what is being studied (Z. C. Y. Chan, Fung, & Chien, 2013; Tufford & Newman, 2012). For instance, if we were to conduct a phenomenological study of the experience of hallucinations, bracketing would require us as the researchers to set aside any previous beliefs about the phenomenon of hallucinations (e.g., they are only experienced by "crazy" people and are meaningless by-products of neurochemistry). While some question whether researchers can ever fully bracket their experience, the idea is to let the thing being studied (instead of our biases and preexisting mindsets about it) influence our results. The second component of the phenomenological reduction can be a bit difficult for newcomers to grasp, but it basically is about shifting from the view that our understandings accurately mirror the world to the view that objects in the world "present" themselves to us and we must interpretively make sense of them. Another way to think about this is that we shouldn't naïvely accept the commonplace belief that our experience shows us the world as it is. Thus, in our phenomenological study, the assumption that our everyday experience reflects what hallucinations really are must be bracketed and replaced with the idea that hallucinations present themselves to us for us to interpret and understand.

Description

The second step involves description, in which the researcher obtains descriptions of what is being studied from the participants. As with grounded theory, we likely use purposive sampling in which we seek and select individuals who are experiencing hallucinations to be our participants. In our study, we solicit vivid and detailed descriptions from these participants of what the experience of hallucinations is like. Bracketing our biases, we record these descriptions and attempt to understand the participants' experiences as best we can.

The Search for Essences

The third step involves the **search for essences**. The researcher breaks participants' descriptions down into meaningful units, looking for commonalities across participants. The results constitute the essence of the experience of hallucinating. Phenomenological analysis is a challenging method to learn because it requires a lot of the researcher. However, its emphasis on understanding lived experience makes it an interesting approach for understanding what it is like to experience psychological distress.

Trustworthiness, Mixed Methods, and the Status of Qualitative Methods

Postpositivist qualitative researchers, who use qualitative methods to generate accounts approximating external reality as accurately as possible, tend to view validity similarly to how quantitative experimental researchers view it (Morrow, 2005). They judge their research based on how well it controls for biases and answers the question "Do results accurately reflect the world as it is?" More constructivist qualitative researchers, by comparison, argue that because subjective bias can't be eliminated, it is important for researchers to acknowledge it by highlighting (rather than obscuring) their role in the research process (Charmaz, 2014). These qualitative researchers shift how they judge the validity of their studies. They examine the **trustworthiness** of qualitative research—evaluating it by looking at its social validity, whether it acknowledges its biases, and whether it provides adequate data (evaluated using criteria such as number of participants, variety of data sources, richness of analysis, and adequate searching for disconfirming evidence) (Morrow, 2005).

Although tensions between qualitative and quantitative research perspectives remain unresolved, many researchers are increasingly emphasizing **mixed methods**, in which quantitative and qualitative work is combined in studying a specific issue (Creswell, 2011; Fetters, Curry, & Creswell, 2013; Heyvaert, Maes, & Onghena, 2013). Whether you ultimately decide it is a good thing or not, it is fair to say that qualitative methods have not gained parity with quantitative methods and that philosophical differences between these approaches remain (M. R. Jackson, 2015). However, abnormal psychology is an area where both quantitative and qualitative methods are often used. The research cited throughout the rest of this text draws on both these research traditions. Should you go on to a research career in abnormal psychology, familiarity with both quantitative and qualitative methods will likely be a necessity.

The remaining chapters of this text regularly cite research on various kinds of abnormal behavior. An adequate understanding of different research methods is critical if you wish to evaluate for yourself the results of the studies presented. Don't simply take it for granted that whenever this books states "Research suggests ..." that what follows is necessarily something you should accept at face value. Being a good consumer of research requires you to continually improve your ability to read and evaluate research studies so that you can determine for yourself whether the findings being presented are convincing. That is one of the ongoing challenges any good student faces in learning about abnormal psychology and the many perspectives that claim to define, explain, and treat it.

1.6 CLOSING THOUGHTS: CAVEATS BEFORE PROCEEDING

Having a basic grasp of conceptual, historical, and research perspectives provides the foundation for discussions throughout this text. In ensuing chapters, we continually revisit major perspectives on abnormality as they relate to different **presenting problems**—the issues that people present when they enter a clinical setting. As you read the chapters that follow, bear several things in mind. First, not every perspective speaks as fully to every possible problem, so depending on the presenting problem, some perspectives may receive more attention than others. Second, it is common for various perspectives to be used in conjunction with one another. For instance, diagnostic perspectives are often, though not always, combined with various other perspectives in working to address presenting problems. When this happens, efforts are made to differentiate each perspective's contribution and to make clear the ways in which the perspectives complement and contradict one another. Third, disagreement is common. The perspectives presented sometimes fit together nicely, but just as often are at odds; one of the goals of this introductory chapter has been to highlight how abnormal psychology is characterized by clashing perspectives that often are difficult to reconcile. Fourth, even though this text endeavors to give each perspective a fair and evenhanded hearing, biases are inevitable. It is impossible not to privilege some perspectives over others sometimes, so you are encouraged to look at what is being presented with a skeptical eye. What are the author's biases, blind spots, and theoretical preferences? How might the material have been organized and presented differently? Might conveying the information in other ways change reader reactions to it? If so, how? You are encouraged to reflect on what you see as the strengths and limitations of the text as you read it.

Finally, you should remain aware that it's very common (we might even dare to say, normal!) for students reading an abnormal psychology textbook like this one to start feeling like everything they are reading about applies to them, their families, and their friends. "Oh no! That's me!" is a common refrain as students learn about various presenting problems, which they then worry that they might have. When not seeing themselves as suffering from every syndrome reviewed throughout the text, some students start engaging in the unfortunate habit of diagnosing friends and family—who don't always appreciate the free consultation. The good news is that learning about abnormal psychology can encourage people to reflect on their own experience and, in some cases, seek help for their problems. The bad news is that it's common for students to worry they have problems that they probably don't. Regardless, appropriate self-awareness about whether you need help is never something to dismiss. Should anything you read about in the text raise concerns, talk to your instructor or seek therapy. After all, a class in abnormal psychology often places us face to face with concerns many of us have encountered in our own lives. That is what makes it both challenging and interesting.

KEY TERMS

ABAB design
Alienists
Analogue experiment
Animal studies
Asylums
Behavior that disturbs others
Bibliotherapy
Biological perspectives
Bodily humors
Bracketing
Case study
Categorizing
Clinical psychologists
Coding
Community mental health care
Confounding variable
Constant comparison
Control group
Convulsion therapy
Correlation
Correlation coefficient
Correlational research
Counseling psychologists
Dancing mania
Deinstitutionalization
Demonological perspective
Dependent variable
Description
Deviance
Diagnostic and Statistical Manual of Mental Disorders (DSM)
Double-blind studies
Drapetomania
Electroconvulsive therapy (ECT)
Emotional suffering
Empirically supported treatments (ESTs)
Epidemiological research

Experiments
External validity
Grounded theory methods
Harmful internal dysfunction
Harmfulness to self or others
Historical-cultural views
Hypothesis
Hysteria
Incidence
Independent variable
Insulin coma therapy
Intentionality
Internal validity
Little Albert
Lobotomy
Lycanthropy
Malarial therapy
Malleus Maleficarum
Matched control groups
Medical model
Medicalization
Melancholia
Memo writing
Mental disorder
Mental illness
Misperception of reality
Mixed methods
Moral therapy
Negative correlation
No correlation
Objective/universal/legal views
Onanism
Participants
Phenomenological methods
Phenomenological reduction
Placebo control group
Placebo effect

Population
Positive correlation
Presenting problems
Prevalence
Problems in living
Psychiatrists
Psychological perspectives
Psychologists
Psychopathology
Psychosurgery
Psychotherapy
Purposive sampling
Qualitative methods
Quantitative methods
Quasi-experiment
Random assignment
Random sample
Randomized controlled trial (RCT)
Sample
Scientific method
Search for essences
Single-subject experiments
Snowball sampling
Social oppression
Sociocultural perspectives
Socioeconomic status (SES)
Statistical deviation
Theoretical coding
Theoretical sampling
Theoretical sensitivity
Trepanation
Trustworthiness
Variables
Violation of social norms and values
Wandering womb theory
York Retreat

Full definitions of the terms listed above can be found in the end-of-book glossary on p. 533.

 Go to the companion website, www.macmillanihe.com/raskin-abnormal-psych, to access a study guide, multiple choice and flashcard quizzes for this chapter, and other useful learning aids.

CHAPTER 2
THEORETICAL PERSPECTIVES

2.1 OVERVIEW

LEARNING OBJECTIVES

After reading this chapter, you should be able to:

1. Describe biological perspectives on psychopathology that emphasize brain chemistry, brain structure, genetics, evolutionary theory, and the immune system.
2. Summarize biological perspective assumptions and evaluate the strengths and weaknesses of the biological perspective.
3. Describe the following psychological perspectives on abnormality: psychoanalytic/psychodynamic, cognitive-behavioral, and humanistic.
4. Summarize the assumptions of psychodynamic, behavioral, cognitive, and humanistic perspectives and evaluate their respective strengths and weaknesses.
5. Describe the following sociocultural perspectives on abnormality: multicultural and social justice perspectives, consumer and service-user perspectives, and systems perspectives.
6. Summarize sociocultural perspective assumptions and evaluate the strengths and weaknesses of the sociocultural perspective.

GETTING STARTED: THE IMPORTANCE OF THEORETICAL PERSPECTIVES

Seth and Lillian

Seth is a 21-year old university student who seeks therapy, complaining about angry outbursts that keep getting him into trouble. He has a long history of getting into fights. In his view, people purposely provoke and disrespect him, although he doesn't know why. Seth has had a string of girlfriends, all of whom he eventually loses interest in right before they break up with him. Seth's current girlfriend, Lillian, a 20-year old student attending the same university, reports that their relationship has been deteriorating. Seth and Lillian have been arguing a lot lately because Lillian suspects Seth has a crush on her best friend, Abigail. Seth says problems in the relationship have led Lillian to become quite depressed recently; she hasn't been eating or sleeping and seems tearful much of the time. The precipitating event that led Seth to seek therapy occurred when he was arrested for assaulting Jorge, a fellow student, in the library after an argument about who was first in line to use the copy machine. Seth reports a reasonably normal childhood, although his parents always argued a lot and were quite strict with him and his younger brother. These days, he often argues with his father, who doesn't understand why Seth is studying art rather than accounting. His father has been threatening to stop paying for Seth's education unless Seth reconsiders his "poor choices."

CASE EXAMPLES

Perspectives as Frameworks for Understanding People's Problems

What makes Seth and Lillian behave as they do? What is the cause of their problems and how can we best help them? The answers to these questions depend on one's theoretical perspective. This chapter reviews the main theoretical perspectives in abnormal psychology, dividing them into those that primarily emphasize biological, psychological, or sociocultural explanations. Of course, just because a perspective emphasizes one of these three kinds of explanations doesn't mean it necessarily ignores the other two. Many psychological perspectives acknowledge roles for biological and sociocultural factors; likewise, biological perspectives often acknowledge psychological and sociocultural factors, while sociocultural perspectives often take psychological and biological factors into account.

2.2 BIOLOGICAL PERSPECTIVES

When we look at abnormality using biological perspectives, we view it through a medical model lens as being caused by physiological malfunctions; the medical model organizes presenting problems into categories that are thought to reflect underlying biological illnesses. Patients are viewed as sick, just as one might be sick with cancer or diabetes. Consider this provocative quote advocating the biological perspective over social and environmental explanations:

> It has become fashionable periodically to ascribe much psychopathology to the evils of modern society, and the resurgence of this notion from time to time reflects the popularity of the simple. Often imbued with political overtones, and rarely aspiring to scientific insights, such a view of the pathogenesis of psychiatric illness ignores the long tradition of both the recognition of patterns of psychopathology and successful treatment by somatic therapies. Further, it does not take into account the obvious fact that humanity's biological heritage extends back many millions of years. (Trimble & George, 2010, p. 1)

Researchers and clinicians look to four basic kinds of explanations when using a biological perspective to understand and treat abnormal behavior: those pertaining to brain chemistry, brain structure, genetics and evolution, and viral infections. One thing that is very important to keep in mind is that these explanations aren't mutually exclusive. Genetics, for example, can influence brain structures and brain chemistry, just as viruses and a compromised immune system can impact how genes are expressed. Different biological factors are interrelated in ways we are only beginning to comprehend. See Table 2.1 for a summary of biological perspective assumptions.

Table 2.1 Five Biological Assumptions

1. Human experience can be reduced to and explained in biological terms.	Thoughts, feelings, and behaviors are ultimately best understood as mental illnesses caused by underlying biological processes.
2. Many mental disorders are brain diseases.	Because human experience can be reduced to and explained in terms of underlying biological processes, many of the problems identified as mental disorders will eventually be revealed to be brain diseases.
3. Scientifically studying the brain will yield an understanding of mental illness.	Our understanding of the human brain is in its infancy. As we learn more about how the brain works, we will begin to discover the biological causes of mental illness.
4. Biological processes are central in understanding mental illness, but social and contextual factors have a secondary influence.	While life experiences and environmental circumstances may affect the course of mental illnesses, their primary cause is rooted in biological processes (e.g., from a biological perspective, posttraumatic stress disorder is triggered by events in the environment, but will only occur if the person suffering a tragedy is biologically predisposed to it).
5. Mental disorders can be caused by malfunctions in brain chemistry, brain structures, genetics, and even viruses.	Sometimes more than one of these explanations must be used to explain a disorder; a person's genetic makeup may make one susceptible to brain chemistry, brain structure, or viral causes of mental illness.

BRAIN CHEMISTRY PERSPECTIVES

The most common biological treatment of abnormality is the use of prescription drugs. These drugs typically affect brain chemistry. Thus, **brain chemistry perspectives** emphasize how brain chemistry (and the psychiatric drugs we develop to alter it) influences cognition, emotion, and behavior. How does brain chemistry work? Well, the brain consists of billions of cells called **neurons**, which communicate with one another both electrically and chemically (see Figures 2.1 and 2.2). When a neuron is at rest, its inside has a negative electrical charge (usually around −70 millivolts) compared to its outside. It also has receptors at the end of its dendrites, the tree-like branches that extend out from its cell body. These dendrites are responsive to various **neurotransmitters**—brain chemicals involved in neural communication. A neuron "fires" when enough neurotransmitter chemicals released by other neurons bind with the receptors on its dendrites. This chemical bonding rapidly shifts the neuron's electrical charge from negative to positive. When this happens, an **action potential** occurs in which an electrical (or neural) impulse is sent along the neuron's axon (see Figure 2.1). This causes the neuron to release neurotransmitters from its axon terminals into the synapses (open spaces) between it and surrounding neurons (see Figure 2.2). When these neurotransmitters bond with receptors on the dendrites of other nearby neurons, they potentially trigger similar electrical reactions in those neurons. Neural transmission involves neurons firing and triggering other neurons to fire in rapid succession.

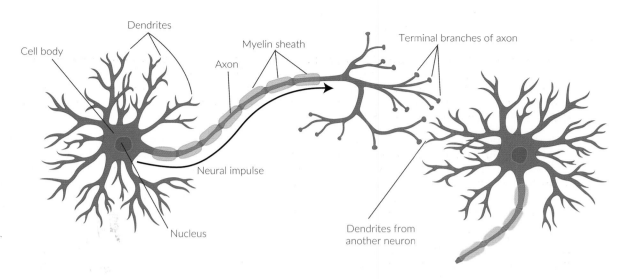

Figure 2.1 Parts of a Neuron

The brain consists of billions of neurons, cells that communicate electrically and chemically. When an electrical impulse travels along the axon to the terminal branches, neurotransmitters are released that trigger surrounding neurons to fire.

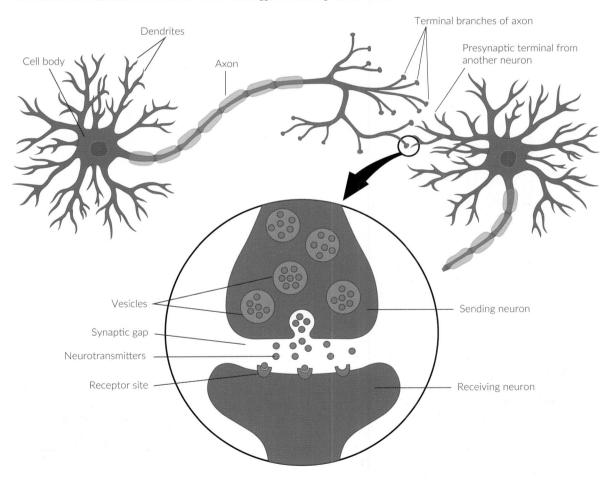

Figure 2.2 Neurotransmission Across a Synapse

Upon firing, a neuron releases neurotransmitters from its terminal branches into the synaptic gap between it and surrounding neurons. When the released neurotransmitters bind with the receptors on surrounding neurons, these neurons fire.

There are a few important things to remember. First, action potentials are all-or-none; a neuron either fires or it doesn't. Second, some neurotransmitters send excitatory signals while others send inhibitory ones; the former stimulate the brain (causing surrounding neurons to fire) and the latter calm it (preventing surrounding neurons from firing). **Gamma-aminobutyric acid (GABA)** is the brain's primary inhibitory neurotransmitter, while **glutamate** is its main excitatory neurotransmitter (Littrell, 2015). Third, extra neurotransmitter chemicals remaining in the synapse after neurons fire are either broken down or reabsorbed by the neurons that released them. Some prescription drugs work by affecting the reabsorption process. For instance, selective serotonin reuptake inhibitors (SSRIs), one of the most common classes of antidepressant drugs, work by preventing the reuptake of the neurotransmitter serotonin (i.e., they keep serotonin from being reabsorbed, making more of it available). We discuss SSRIs in Chapter 5 when examining mood issues.

There are many neurotransmitters—so many, actually, that we haven't discovered them all yet (Valenstein, 1998). Neurotransmitters are significant in thinking about abnormality because they play important roles in mood and cognition. A few examples are: **norepinephrine** (an excitatory neurotransmitter) and **serotonin** (an inhibitory neurotransmitter) are associated with depression and anxiety; too much **dopamine** (an inhibitory neurotransmitter implicated in memory, motivation, and rewards/pleasure) with psychosis; and too little GABA with fear and anxiety (Itoi & Sugimoto, 2010; Littrell, 2015; Möhler, 2013). Many of the prescription drugs used to alleviate depression, psychosis, and anxiety affect these neurotransmitters. However, because we do not currently have the ability to directly measure neurotransmitter levels in people's brains, we prescribe these drugs based on people's reported moods rather than tests of neurotransmitter levels (Valenstein, 1998).

Certain neurotransmitters are grouped together due to their chemical similarities. GABA and glutamate are **amino acids** (chemical compounds consisting of carbon, hydrogen, nitrogen, and oxygen), whereas norepinephrine, serotonin, and dopamine are **monoamines** (chemical compounds derived from ammonia). The monoamines can be further divided into **catecholamines** (dopamine and norepinephrine) and **indolamines** (serotonin).

Seth and Lillian

In the case of Seth and Lillian, a psychiatrist might assess them and diagnose Seth with intermittent explosive disorder (see Chapter 13) and Lillian with persistent depressive disorder (see Chapter 5). Both disorders are often treated using antidepressant drugs. The psychiatrist might prescribe selective serotonin reuptake inhibitors (SSRIs) for each of them.

CASE EXAMPLES

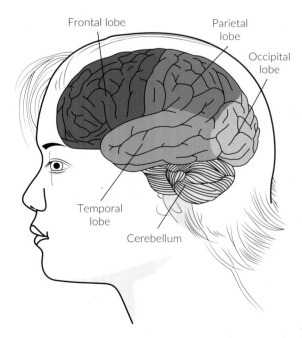

Figure 2.3 The Cerebrum and Cerebellum

The cerebrum is the upper area of the brain consisting of four lobes, each associated with certain functions: *frontal* (executive functioning, problem solving, judgment, memory, language, sexual behavior), *parietal* (sensory processing, visual and spatial perception, language and math processing), *occipital* (visual reception and processing), *temporal* (language comprehension, memory, hearing). The cerebellum, the lower area of the brain behind the brain stem, is responsible for movement, coordination, and balance.

BRAIN STRUCTURE AND FUNCTION PERSPECTIVES

Brain structure and function perspectives examine how the functioning (or malfunctioning) of different areas in the brain influences abnormal behavior. Let's briefly introduce a few of the most relevant brain structures. Many of them will be revisited when discussing specific presenting problems in later chapters, along with additional structures not mentioned below.

The **brain stem** connects the brain to the spinal cord. It plays a role in many involuntary activities, such as breathing, heart rate, digestion, blood pressure, body temperature, perspiration, and sleeping. Then we have the cerebellum and the cerebrum, which can get confused because of their similar sounding names. The **cerebellum** is the lower area of the brain behind the brain stem that is critical in voluntary movement, balance, and reflexes. By contrast, the **cerebrum** is the upper area of the brain that consists of two hemispheres (or halves) that are connected and communicate via a bundle of nerves known as the **corpus callosum**. The cerebrum is notable for being the largest portion of the brain. It consists of four lobes: the occipital, frontal, parietal, and temporal lobes. The cerebrum is important in many psychological functions—including speech, vision, hearing, movement, sensation, and intelligence. The cerebrum and cerebellum are presented visually in Figure 2.3.

The **limbic system** is a brain region beneath the cerebrum that is especially relevant in discussions of psychopathology. Researchers believe that the limbic system developed early in human evolution (MacLean, 1985; Ploog, 2003). It is associated with motivation, emotional regulation, and long-term memory.

The limbic system contains several structures of interest to biologically oriented clinicians. One such structure is the **amygdala**, an almond-sized area deep in the brain that has been linked to basic emotions such as fear and anger. Research suggests that excessive activity in the amygdala is correlated with depression (Hamilton, 2015; Kanner, 2004; Sharpley, 2010; Sheline, 2003). The **hippocampus** is another limbic system structure that lies deep within the brain. It appears to play an important role in memory, as decreased hippocampal volume has been tied to Alzheimer's disease and other forms of dementia (see Chapter 14) (Brigola et al., 2015; Hill et al., 2014; Marlatt & Lucassen, 2010; Wolz et al., 2014). The hippocampus has also been connected to depression (Sheline, 2003), posttraumatic stress disorder (Bremner, 2001; Childress et al., 2013; Horner & Hamner, 2002; Liberzon & Phan, 2003), and schizophrenia (Boyer, Phillips, Rousseau, & Ilivitsky, 2007; Schmajuk, 2001; Siekmeier & vanMaanen, 2014). Additional limbic structures worth mentioning are the **entorhinal cortex**, also associated with memory; the **orbitofrontal cortex**, which plays a role in decision-making; and the **nucleus accumbens**, which has been implicated in addictive behavior (see Chapter 11).

Remember that brain structure and brain chemistry explanations are deeply interrelated. For instance, the neurons making up the amygdala, hippocampus, and other areas of the limbic system send and receive messages through the electrical and chemical processes described earlier. Neural communication also occurs throughout the cerebrum. Because such communication occurs within and between different parts of the brain, it means that whenever we refer to a structure of the brain that is suspected of malfunctioning, we are also talking about potential problems with neural communication in these areas.

GENETIC AND EVOLUTIONARY PERSPECTIVES
Genetic Perspectives

Structural and chemical problems in the brain are often related to genetic inheritance. **Genetic perspectives** focus on the role of genes in explaining the origins of presenting problems. Unfortunately, it's common for people to discuss the role of genetics in abnormal behavior without having a basic understanding of what genes are or how they work. **Genes** can be thought of as biological instructions for building a person. The complete set of genetic information for each human (its **genome**) consists of 23 sets of **chromosomes**, which are made out of **DNA (deoxyribonucleic acid)** (C. Baker, 2004). DNA consists of four chemical compounds (*adenine, cytosine, guanine,* and *thymine*) known as **nucleotides**. The sequences of nucleotides influence a person's development; they are instructions for how you will mature over time. DNA nucleotides are coiled up inside each cell's nucleus in the well-known *double helix* shape. The DNA's blueprint for development gets copied into **RNA (ribonucleic acid)**. RNA consists of three of the same four nucleotides as DNA (*adenine, cytosine,* and *guanine*), along with a fourth nucleotide (*uracil*). RNA carries out DNA's genetic instructions (C. Baker, 2004). Figure 2.4 illustrates the structure of DNA and RNA.

Genes can be found at random intervals on a chromosome's DNA. The human genome has been estimated to contain roughly 30,000 genes (C. Baker, 2004), though some suspect the number may be as low as 19,000 (Ezkurdia et al., 2014). We have two versions of every gene, each one called an **allele**. For every gene, we inherit one allele from our mother and one from our father. Usually one or the other allele in a pair is dominant. *Dominant alleles* take priority in influencing how particular characteristics genetically unfold, while *recessive alleles* only influence development when a person inherits two of them (one from each parent). The presence of

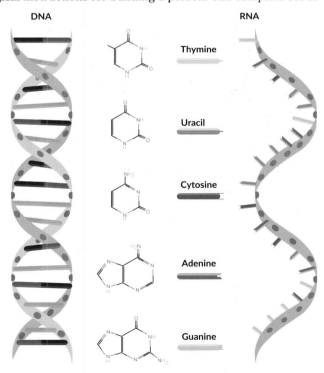

Figure 2.4 Structure of DNA and RNA

Chromosomes are made of DNA, which consists of four nucleotides (chemical compounds) called adenine, cytosine, guanine, and thymine. DNA gets copied into RNA, which carries out its instructions for building a person. RNA is made of three of the four DNA nucleotides (adenine, cytosine, and guanine) plus a fourth nucleotide called uracil.

dominant or recessive alleles means that gene expression depends on many factors. Recessive alleles are carried from generation to generation, but are only displayed in the rare instances in which a person inherits two of them.

Genes provide complex instructions that cells use to manufacture proteins. Simply put, cells use these proteins to communicate and to build the human body. Cells both influence and are influenced by genes (C. Baker, 2004). While genes have the potential to express themselves in different ways, only some of the information contained in genes visibly displays itself in the organism. A person's **genotype** is his or her entire genetic makeup; it includes all alleles, even non-dominant ones that aren't reflected in the individual's physical and psychological makeup. In contrast, a person's **phenotype** consists of a person's actual properties, the physical and psychological traits a person has developed because of genetic and environmental influences.

Whether and how various genetic instructions are expressed can also be influenced by environmental factors. This becomes very important in thinking about abnormality. **Heritability** refers to the percentage of phenotypic variation that can be attributed to genes, as opposed to environment (C. Baker, 2004). When it comes to studying abnormality, researchers often conduct heritability studies to estimate how much a given psychological trait or disorder is influenced by genetic, rather than environmental, factors. These studies yield **heritability estimates**, scores from 0.0 to 1.0. For example, research on autism (see Chapter 13) has yielded heritability estimates as high as 0.90 (Bailey, Le Couteur, Gottesman, & Bolton, 1995). To correct a common misconception, this doesn't mean that any given individual's autism is 90% caused by genes and 10% by environment. It just means that 90% of phenotypic variation across the entire population of people with autism is estimated to be influenced by differences in genes. Importantly, heritability estimates remain controversial. Some researchers, for instance, have argued that autism heritability is grossly inflated and should really only be estimated as 37% (Joseph, 2012). They have even questioned whether heritability estimates are useful at all, arguing that genes and environment mutually influence each other in ways that heritability estimates can't tease apart (Joseph, 2012).

Debates over heritability make clear that biological processes alone don't entirely determine gene expression. The environment plays a role too. That fern you own that you always forget to water and place in the sunlight looks quite different from the one that your botany major friend meticulously tends. These two plants may be genetically the same (they have the same genotype), but their different environments trigger whether and how their genes express themselves, thus influencing what each of the ferns actually looks like (its phenotype). To further complicate things, gene expression isn't just influenced by the environment. It is also **polygenic** (C. Baker, 2004; Bouchard & McGue, 1981; Lisik, 2014). This means that multiple genes are implicated. In other words, under certain conditions, combinations of genes work together to produce a trait or disorder. Only when environmental conditions and multiple gene expression align does a psychological problem such as schizophrenia or autism result. This kind of complicated causality makes it very difficult to predict when a specific phenotype will be expressed.

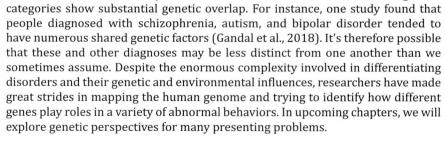

Lillian
Lillian may have a genetic predisposition toward depression, but her life circumstances are what could have caused it to emerge. Had she grown up under different environmental circumstances, the multiple genes responsible for depression might simply never have been "triggered."

CASE EXAMPLES

Genetic inheritance is a lot more complicated and nuanced than we are often taught to believe. Separating genetic from environmental influences can be incredibly difficult. Further, some mental disorder diagnostic categories show substantial genetic overlap. For instance, one study found that people diagnosed with schizophrenia, autism, and bipolar disorder tended to have numerous shared genetic factors (Gandal et al., 2018). It's therefore possible that these and other diagnoses may be less distinct from one another than we sometimes assume. Despite the enormous complexity involved in differentiating disorders and their genetic and environmental influences, researchers have made great strides in mapping the human genome and trying to identify how different genes play roles in a variety of abnormal behaviors. In upcoming chapters, we will explore genetic perspectives for many presenting problems.

Charles Darwin (1809–1882)
Source: Getty Images/iStockphoto
Thinkstock Images \ pictore

Evolutionary Perspectives

Evolutionary perspectives use Charles Darwin's (1839/2008) evolutionary theory to explain how and why different presenting problems evolved. Evolutionary theory maintains that whether an organism survives and reproduces (therefore passing on its genes) depends on its fitness. An organism's **fitness** reflects how well it is adapted to its environment. Fish are adapted to their environment (i.e., they are fit) because their gills allow them to extract oxygen from the water in which they live. However, what counts as fitness always depends on the environment. If a lake were to dry up, the fish would die off because they no longer would be biologically adapted to their surroundings. Thus, the term **survival of the fittest** refers to the idea that only those organisms well suited to an environment reproduce and keep their species alive. Of course, different organisms are fit in different environments. As environments change, those species that can adapt are the ones that survive, reproduce, and pass on their genes. Those that can't adapt die off. Evolutionary changes in species are slow, occurring over many millions of years. Further, sometimes people mistakenly assume that evolution is taking people on a path toward becoming more "advanced" and "higher evolved." This isn't so. Evolution has no direction or purpose. It has no endpoint. How organisms evolve is purely a matter of whatever is adaptive at a given time within a given environment.

Evolutionary perspectives of abnormality apply evolutionary principles to understanding psychological problems (Adriaens & De Block, 2010; MacLean, 1985). Some evolutionary perspectives posit that traits that were once adaptive in our early ancestors' environments no longer work well in modern society. For instance, today very few people are killed by poisonous spiders or falling from great heights. In fact, many more people die in car accidents. However, our evolutionary heritage makes us much more likely to develop a phobia of spiders or heights than of automobiles. That is, evolution has biologically prepared us to easily develop conditioned fears to certain kinds of things (such as spiders and heights), even though these are no longer as threatening as other things in our environment (such as Fords and Hondas). According to evolutionary perspectives, behaviors we consider disordered—such as psychosis (Burns, 2006), depression (Allen & Badcock, 2006), and obsessive-compulsive rituals (Feygin, Swain, & Leckman, 2006)—may also have origins in what was previously adaptive behavior within ancestral environments.

IMMUNE SYSTEM PERSPECTIVES

Immune system perspectives have been rapidly gaining attention when it comes to understanding psychopathology. The immune system is the system of cells and biological processes used to fight off **pathogens** (foreign bodies that cause disease, such as viruses, bacteria, parasites, and cancer cells). As we will see in many future chapters (especially Chapter 8), research consistently shows that prolonged stress has an extremely powerful—and usually negative—impact on physical health and emotional wellbeing (Dhabhar, 2014; Glaser, 2005). Because psychological factors clearly influence immune functioning and physical health, those wishing to understand abnormality must attend to the complex relationship between them.

Viral theories are immune-system approaches that hypothesize that psychological disorders can be caused by viral infections. One of the earliest and most successful instances of the immunological perspective in action can be found in the **viral explanation of general paresis** (Wallis, 2012). What is **general paresis**? It is a syndrome in which individuals show progressive decline in mental functioning. In its later stages, people with general paresis exhibit mania, psychotic delusions, physical deterioration, and eventually death. It turns out that the cause of general paresis is the syphilis virus (Wallis, 2012). Once the syphilis is treated using antibiotics, the symptoms disappear. General paresis is the best example of abnormality being explained entirely in biological terms. It would be silly to try to recondition paretic patients' behavior, dispute their irrational beliefs, or inquire about their childhoods because their psychological symptoms are most effectively treated biologically. The viral theory of general paresis helped launch the medical model view that abnormality could, in many instances, be explained entirely in biological terms.

Inspired by the success of the viral explanation of general paresis, biological researchers have developed viral theories for other presenting problems. For example, the viral theory of schizophrenia (see Chapter 4) holds that mothers who contract viral infections during pregnancy are more likely to have children who develop schizophrenia. This theory emerged from evidence suggesting that children born in winter months are more likely to be diagnosed with schizophrenia in adulthood (Fatemi, Folsom et al., 2012; Kneeland & Fatemi, 2013). A viral theory of autism similar to the one for schizophrenia has also been posited (see Chapter 13) (Jiang et al., 2016). Broadly speaking, the relationship between immune system functioning and emotional distress is examined for many of the presenting problems reviewed elsewhere in this book because immune system explanations are increasingly garnering interest from researchers and clinicians alike.

EVALUATING BIOLOGICAL PERSPECTIVES

Biological models are viewed as having the following strengths:

1. *Mental phenomena explained in terms of biological processes.* The biological perspective holds out promise that complex and elusive behaviors can be explained in physiological terms.

2. *Scientific.* The biological perspective has generated an enormous amount of research into the relationship between physical and mental functioning.

3. *Development of psychiatric drugs and other biological interventions.* Biological researchers have developed many psychiatric drugs and related interventions for problems ranging from depression to psychosis to anxiety.

Biological models also are prone to the following criticisms:

1. *Reductionistic.* Some critics—particularly humanists—complain that complex psychological phenomena cannot be explained in purely biological terms.

2. *Everyday problems become "medicalized."* Critics also argue that some presenting problems aren't illnesses and that the biological perspective errs by conceptualizing too many daily life problems as brain diseases. Medicalization occurs when non-medical problems are inappropriately classified as medical (Pridmore, 2011).

3. *Overreliance on psychiatric drugs.* A common criticism of the biological perspective is that its view of abnormality as illness has resulted in the over prescription of psychiatric drugs.

2.3 PSYCHOLOGICAL PERSPECTIVES

Psychological perspectives stress thoughts, feelings, and behaviors in explaining abnormality. Although they sometimes (but by no means always) endorse a medical model that frames abnormality as the manifestation of disorders, the interventions they offer are psychological in nature—such as discussing and processing upsetting feelings, analyzing and changing troublesome thoughts, and teaching new and more adaptive behaviors to replace problematic ones. Psychological perspectives often advance psychotherapy to alleviate emotional distress. Psychotherapy relies on conversation between a professional helper (the therapist) and the person being helped (the client or patient, depending on the preferred term). Although lots of people seek therapy, myths about it remain widespread (see "In Depth: Myths about Therapy"). To help dispel common misconceptions, "The Lived Experience" feature provides explanations from three psychotherapists about what the first session of therapy is like. Of course, not all forms of therapy are the same. Despite a shared grounding in psychology, different types of psychotherapy vary greatly in how they conceptualize and remedy presenting problems. Below we review the most common psychological perspectives.

IN DEPTH

Myths about Therapy

Students taking abnormal psychology inevitably apply a lot of what they learn to themselves, their friends, and their family. Thus, some consider seeking therapy, but—perhaps ironically—often cling to common myths about it. Here's a list of such myths from Helpguide.org (www.helpguide.org/articles/emotional-health/finding-a-therapist-who-can-help-you-heal.htm):

1. **I don't need a therapist. I'm smart enough to solve my own problems.** We all have our blind spots. Intelligence has nothing to do with it. A good therapist doesn't tell you what to do or how to live your life. He or she will give you an experienced outside perspective and help you gain insight into yourself so you can make better choices.

2. **Therapy is for crazy people.** Therapy is for people who have enough self-awareness to realize they need a helping hand, and want to learn tools and techniques to become more self-confident and emotionally balanced.

3. **All therapists want to talk about is my parents.** While exploring family relationships can sometimes clarify thoughts and behaviors later in life, that is not the sole focus of therapy. The primary focus is what you need to change unhealthy patterns and symptoms in your life. Therapy is not about blaming your parents or dwelling on the past.

4. **Therapy is self-indulgent. It's for whiners and complainers.** Therapy is hard work. Complaining won't get you very far. Improvement in therapy comes from taking a hard look at yourself and your life, and taking responsibility for your own actions. Your therapist will help you, but ultimately you're the one who must do the work.

CRITICAL THINKING QUESTIONS

1. How many of these myths have you adhered to?

2. How many of these myths have your friends and families adhered to?

3. Should we try to debunk these myths and, if so, how?

THE LIVED EXPERIENCE

CHAPTER 2

What Will Happen in My First Therapy Session?

Many people who have never participated in a therapy session wonder what it will be like. Will the therapist ask you a lot of questions about your feelings? Will you be asked to discuss your fears? Will you have to talk about your childhood? The truth is that different therapists handle their first therapy sessions differently. They may even encourage you to ask them questions about their lives, training, or experiences in the first session. Three therapists explain below what goes on in their first sessions with new clients.

Valerie Domenici, Ph.D.

In our first meeting, I have two goals. First, I'd like to get to know you, hear about the kinds of things you'd like help with, and to decide if I can be helpful with those things. Second, I'd like you to get to know me, so that you can decide if I'm the kind of person you'd be comfortable working on those things with. To accomplish these goals, I will start by making you as comfortable as possible. I will explain how our conversation is confidential, and also describe the exceptions to that rule. You will get some paperwork ahead of time that explains all of this, but we'll go over it again so that you have the opportunity to ask any questions that you may have about it. You can also ask me anything about me or my practice that would make you more comfortable sharing about yourself. If you want to know whether I've worked with a particular problem before, or how many years I've been in practice, or what my feelings are on a particular issue, I'll invite you to do that right up front. Often, people feel a bit more at ease when they know something about the person they are speaking with, and I'm happy to help.

Valerie Domenici
Source: Simply Well/Eric Klinedinst

In getting to know you, I like to get to a few different areas. First, what is the current problem, feeling, or situation that brings you to therapy? Second, what is the history of that problem? For example, how long has it been going on? What has made the problem better or worse? And third, it can be extremely helpful to gather some family history. Sometimes we can get through all of this in one session, but often it takes two or three. It's okay if this all comes out in a jumbled mess. It's part of my job to help you put it all together in a way that makes sense. I will repeat back to you what I've heard you say, to make sure I have it right, and ask questions to fill in any blanks in my understanding of the situation.

You will likely get to know some things about me by the questions that I ask, or the way that I react to what you've said. I will also describe for you what my typical approach to therapy is like, and how that might apply to the specific issues you want to work on. I will ask you what you hope therapy will be like, and how you would not want it to be. If you've had any experience with therapy before, I can describe how my approach might be similar to or different than that one.

By the end of our first meeting (or after several), I will either say "yes, I think I can be helpful!" or I will suggest another colleague or type of service that might better fit your needs. Sometimes, I can give you a sense of how long therapy might take to address your concern, but often this is unpredictable. I will make a recommendation about how often to meet, which is usually based on the severity of the problem. Hopefully, at this point, you have a good sense of how comfortable you feel with me and my office, and it's up to you to decide whether to move forward with therapy!

Jonathan Rust, Ph.D., NCC

When you first contact me, I will schedule a brief, 10- to 20-minute phone consultation with you. During this consultation, I'll ask you to tell me a little about yourself, what your major concerns are, and how long you've been experiencing these issues. I'll also ask how you heard about me and what may be your main goal or expectation for therapy. Finally, I will explain my fee structure and payment options. I find these brief phone interactions to be extremely helpful for myself and you as a potential client, as I'm able to determine (with your help) if we may be a good fit to work together. If we both decide that we'd like to proceed, I will schedule an initial appointment with you, which is usually an hour in length.

Jonathan Rust
Source: SUNY New Paltz

When you arrive for the initial appointment, I'll meet you in the waiting area with an "informed consent" form, which explains in writing what you can expect from therapy. This document explains how long our sessions will be, our respective roles as therapist and client, my fee and cancellation policies, and your rights as a client—especially privacy, confidentiality, and their limits.

After you've read and signed the informed consent, I'll ask you to come into my office and I'll answer any questions or concerns you may have about the information on the form. After this, I'll invite you to again begin telling me about yourself and your concerns, with no particular instructions or directions on what to talk about. As I listen, I may ask questions or make comments to encourage you to tell me more about yourself and to make you feel comfortable with the therapy process.

The purpose of the intake session is to gather as much relevant information about you as possible—including your current issues and their history—to assist me in understanding you. Usually we will just brush the surface in terms of relevant information, but we will form the basis of a productive working relationship. At the end of the intake, I will ask if you have any questions or concerns and how you felt about the session. If we both feel we can work together, I'll schedule another session for you. Then, I'll give you an "Intake" form to complete before our next session. The reason I give the intake form to you at this point is to save you time filling it out if you did not want to continue working with me. The intake form gives me supplemental information that may not come out initially in our work together. If either of us feels it would be better for you to work with someone else, I will do my best to find an appropriate referral for you.

Jay S. Efran, Ph.D.

When you first arrive, I would ask the question: "What can I do for you?" Your answer would help me understand why you are there and what you hope to get out of our meetings. Even if you could not give a very specific answer—and many individuals cannot—the question helps determine an appropriate starting point, including what I might need to explain about the therapy process and our work together.

Usually, I also want to know about "the final straw" that motivated you to pick up the phone and make an appointment. People often suffer for a long time before asking for help. Knowing why they are now ready to take action often provides important insights into the nature of the problem. Similarly, it helps to hear about any steps you previously took to solve the problem or reduce your distress. Even partially successful solutions can provide clues to useful approaches, and past failures may suggest approaches that might best be avoided.

Jay S. Efran

Obviously, during this first session, I want to learn many details about what is bothering you. This is important information for me to have, but such exchanges can also increase your confidence that your situation is being understood. During this first meeting, I will check to see if we agree on an initial set of goals as well as the criteria we will use to determine if we are achieving those goals. We can add or subtract goals later, but it is important that we have at least a preliminary working agreement. Also in this first session, we will attempt to identify some fundamental beliefs about yourself that may be getting in your way and keeping you stuck. It will be part of my job to propose some alternatives to those ways of looking at the world.

Printed with permission of Valerie Domenici, Jonathan Rust and Jay S. Efran.

PSYCHODYNAMIC PERSPECTIVES

Psychodynamic perspectives originate in the work of Viennese neurologist Sigmund Freud (1856–1939). Many different psychodynamic approaches grew out of Freud's theorizing. Freud's original psychodynamic approach is known as **psychoanalysis**. Thus, "classic" Freudian approaches are commonly referred to as psychoanalytic theories, while later approaches that trace their origins back to Freud but diverge from some of Freud's core assertions are called psychodynamic theories. Admittedly, despite the terms "psychoanalytic" and "psychodynamic" providing a nice distinction, authors often use them interchangeably. Let's begin with Freud's original psychoanalytic theory and then discuss offshoot psychodynamic approaches. Table 2.2 provides a useful summary of the core assumptions of psychodynamic perspectives.

Sigmund Freud (1856–1939)
Source: © Hulton-Deutsch Collection/ CORBIS/ Corbis via Getty Images

Table 2.2 Five Psychodynamic Assumptions

Psychodynamic theories uphold all or most of these assumptions (Grzywacz, Almeida, Neupert, & Ettner, 2004; Schmidt & Lerew, 1998; Williams, Yu, Jackson, & Anderson, 1997):	
1. *The centrality of the unconscious.*	The *unconscious* can be defined as mental experiences that a person is unaware of and can't easily make conscious.
2. *The importance of early life experiences in shaping personality and psychopathology.*	What happens in childhood is very important in both normal and abnormal psychological development.
3. *Every mental event is caused.*	Freud referred to this as *psychic determinism*. Psychological experiences never happen by accident and often have multiple causes.
4. *The importance of defense mechanisms.*	Defense mechanisms are partly unconscious strategies people use to avoid anxiety and cope with emotionally upsetting experiences.
5. *The ability of the therapeutic relationship to address and resolve unconscious conflicts.*	Psychodynamic therapists use their relationships with patients to make them aware of how their unconscious conflicts lead to problematic ways of dealing with others; in the process, patients come to learn new relational patterns.

Freud's Original Psychoanalytic Theory

Drive Theory

Psychoanalytic theory is a *drive theory* (Bornstein, Denckla, & Chung, 2013; Eagle, 2011). Drive theories see people as psychologically motivated (i.e., driven) to think, feel, and act in certain ways. Freud conceptualized human psychology as a kind of energy system. He said that each person was born with a set amount of **psychic energy**, which must be expressed. Some of this energy takes the form of **libido**, or sexual instinct (S. Freud, 1923/1960), which can be framed more broadly as a drive to seek pleasure and avoid pain (Miller, 2015).

Importantly, Freud's drive theory roots human psychology in biological instincts. Freud was trained as a medical doctor, so it's understandable that he emphasized instinctual drives. He also endorsed **psychic determinism**, the idea that all mental events are caused. In psychoanalytic theory, every mental event originates from psychic drives building up and then being expressed. Mental actions aren't freely chosen; they always have underlying (often multiple) causes that are rooted in the relationships among psychoanalytic theory's three psychic structures: id, ego, and superego. Put simply, the **id** is the unconscious part of the personality from which aggressive and self-serving drives originate; the **ego** is the part of the personality that must express id impulses in acceptable ways; and the **superego** houses the person's moral beliefs. The relationships among id, ego, and superego determine mental events. Definitions of id, ego, and superego are further fleshed out below.

Seth
From a psychoanalytic perspective Seth's fights are caused by angry id impulses that are regularly triggered when other people challenge him. His ego expresses these impulses by getting into physical altercations with others, while his superego causes him to feel guilty for hurting other people. His anger and guilt aren't freely chosen. They are psychically determined.

CASE EXAMPLES

Topographic and Structural Models

An emphasis on both conscious and (especially) unconscious experience is central to psychoanalytic theory. Over the course of his more than 40-year career, Freud shifted the way he talked about such experiences. His early **topographic model** conceived the unconscious and conscious as locations in the mind where memories are stored (S. Freud, 1900/1965a). The **conscious** constitutes the rational and adult part of the mind that the person is cognizant of, whereas the **unconscious** is the childish and irrational part that is out of awareness but influences how the person thinks, feels, and behaves. While today we take the idea of unconscious determinants of behavior for granted, in Freud's day his emphasis on the unconscious was both controversial and revolutionary. The conscious mind pushes unacceptable ideas and feelings out of awareness and into the unconscious through the psychological process of **repression**. Repressed memories are prevented from entering conscious awareness. Of course, not everything out of awareness is unconscious (i.e., repressed). The topographic model also includes the **preconscious**, where unrepressed memories not currently in consciousness are stored. Preconscious memories (e.g., that time you had fun at the beach with a friend) may not be conscious at a given moment, but can easily be made conscious if focused on. Unconscious memories (e.g., parental abuse that a person is unable to recall) can't be made conscious because they are repressed.

Late in his career, Freud shifted to a **structural model** of mind (S. Freud, 1923/1960), which both extended and subtly altered some of his earlier ideas. It was in his structural model that Freud fully incorporated the three previously mentioned psychic structures of id, ego, and superego. The combined topographic and structural models of mind are often visualized as an iceberg (see Figure 2.5). Freud never fully clarified discrepancies between the models because he was actively refining his theory up until he died (Bornstein et al., 2013; Marmer, 2003).

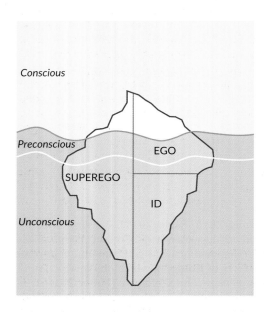

Figure 2.5 Freud's Iceberg Model of Mind
Freud's psychoanalytic theory envisions the mind as an iceberg. Everything below the water line is unconscious. Note how the id is fully unconscious, while the ego and superego have both conscious and unconscious parts.

Psychosexual Stages

Freud's (1923/1960, 1905/1962) *psychosexual stages* stirred a lot of controversy in Freud's day and still do today. They accentuate the importance of early childhood development, holding that personality is formed during the first five or so years of life. It's worth noting that Freud's psychosexual stages combine both nature (in the form of instinctual drives that must be expressed) and nurture (the effect of child-rearing on personality development). What happens during the first five years of life determines how psychic energy distributes itself across id, ego, and superego.

The first stage is the **oral stage** (from birth to roughly 1½ years old). At birth, all psychic energy is contained in the id. In fact, you could say that newborns are "pure id"—no egos or superegos just yet! Expanding on our earlier definition, the id is the unconscious part of the personality consisting of all the infant's aggressive, selfish, and sexual desires. It is ruled by what Freud called the **pleasure principle**—the desire to experience pleasure and avoid pain. During the oral stage, psychic energy is most easily expressed through oral activities (those involving the mouth). Oral activities are the focus because instinctually, newborns rely on the sucking reflex to nurse and to engage their surroundings. By sucking on anything they can get into their mouths, infants not only feed but also learn—depending on the effectiveness of their caregivers— how well the world responds to their needs.

Effective caregivers attend to their babies and provide them the optimal amount of oral gratification. If their infants are hungry or curious about the world, they provide them sufficient oral gratification; too much or too little leads to **fixation**, or getting stuck at the stage. A fixated child who doesn't receive adequate oral gratification can't successfully move on to the next stage. Freud believed that children who get fixated at the oral stage develop issues around *autonomy* and *dependence*. With too much oral gratification, some children feel smothered and wind up feeling overwhelmed by people, but others come to expect people to overindulge them and feel needy and demanding when this doesn't occur. On the other hand, with too little oral gratification, some children become desperate or clingy in efforts to obtain the nurturing that hasn't been provided; others learn that people can't be depended on and become emotionally distant. As adults, therefore, orally fixated individuals are ambivalent about how much they wish to rely on people. Some feel overwhelmed by people and desire distance from them, while others become clingy and dependent.

The second stage is the **anal stage** (roughly 1½–3 years old), during which toilet training serves as the basis for ego development. The ego, as already noted, is the partly conscious/partly unconscious component of the personality that monitors the constraints and demands of the environment. It is ruled by the **reality principle**, the need to consider the requirements of the external world when expressing id impulses. The ego emerges primarily during toilet training because such training requires **delay of gratification**—postponing the expression of id impulses until circumstances best allow it. Toilet training is about learning to express the id impulse to "let go" in ways that are appropriate to the situation (e.g., using the toilet when given permission by one's teacher as opposed to going in one's pants in the middle of class!). Learning to delay gratification during toilet training eventually generalizes to all situations where it is necessary to take external demands into account in deciding when and how id impulses should be expressed.

CHAPTER 2

If caregiving is too lax or strict during toilet training, the child can become fixated at the anal stage in one of two ways. **Anal-retentive** individuals are overly ego-regulated, priding themselves on their ability to delay gratification. They are extremely rigid, neat, stingy, stubborn, and highly organized (think of that student you know who organizes her bookshelf alphabetically by author and doesn't let anyone touch any of her books). **Anal-expulsive** individuals, on the other hand, rebel against demands to delay gratification. They are unregulated, messy, reckless, disobedient, and disorganized (think of that roommate you had who was a huge slob, overwhelming you with his mess). Importantly, both anal-retentive and anal-expulsive people have issues with control; the former wants to exert control over the environment, while the latter refuses to be controlled by it.

The third stage is the **phallic stage** (roughly 3–5 years old), famous for Freud's controversial Oedipus complex (boys) and Electra complex (girls), which results in the development of the partly conscious/partly unconscious superego—the personality component that houses moral beliefs. The Oedipus and Electra complexes differ because in psychoanalytic theory *anatomy is destiny*, by which Freud meant that having or lacking a penis affects superego development. In the **Oedipus complex**, the little boy desires mom for himself and wishes to get rid of dad. These feelings persist for some time, until the boy starts worrying that if dad discovers his desires, dad will become so angry that he might castrate the boy. This *castration anxiety* is so terrifying that the little boy represses his Oedipal feelings for his mother and—to avoid being found out—identifies with his father. The identification with father results in the boy internalizing his father's moral beliefs. When this occurs, the superego is formed and the entire Oedipus experience repressed (which is why adult males don't recall it). For girls, the **Electra complex** goes a bit differently. Freud said it begins with castration anxiety. Once a girl realizes she has nothing to castrate, she experiences *penis envy*. According to classic psychoanalytic theory, little girls develop weaker superegos because their castration anxiety isn't as powerful as that experienced by boys. Consequently, they don't identify as strongly with their mothers as boys do with their fathers—and this leads to weaker internalization of same-sex parent moral beliefs. (Not surprisingly, Freud's Electra complex has been widely criticized as sexist.) Children who get fixated at the phallic stage may be narcissistic, proud, competitive, and vain. They also may be overly sexualized in how they deal with others.

By the end of the phallic stage, the structure of the child's personality is in place. It consists of the ego trying to balance the demands of three harsh taskmasters: the id (unconscious self-serving drives), the superego (moral beliefs about acceptable behavior), and external reality (the constraints and consequences the world can impose) (S. Freud, 1933/1965b). As Freud (1933/1965b, p. 69) put it, "the poor ego ... serves three severe masters and does what it can to bring their claims and demands into harmony with one another." Sometimes people mistakenly think of the ego as opposing the id, but this is not so. The ego serves the id; it must find outlets for id impulses, but in a manner which satisfies the often-conflicting demands of the superego and external reality. This is a difficult task, one most of us struggle with at times. **Neurosis** is the term Freud used to identify instances when the ego feels overwhelmed in balancing the conflicting demands of its three harsh taskmasters.

Seth

Seth finds himself sexually attracted to his girlfriend Lillian's best friend, Abigail. From a psychoanalytic perspective, Seth's ego must find a way to express this id impulse. However, both social norms and Seth's superego object to cheating on one's girlfriend—especially with her best friend! Seth experiences neurosis when his ego struggles to balance the need to express his sexual attraction to Abigail while keeping his superego and girlfriend Lillian at bay.

CASE EXAMPLES

After the phallic stage, there are two more stages. The fourth stage is the **latency stage** (6 years old to pre-adolescence), a period of relative calm and quiet. The fifth stage is the **genital stage** (adolescence onward), during which any fixations at the first three stages fully emerge. When conflicts created at the first three stages surface during adulthood, Freud believed psychoanalysis was often necessary to successfully uncover and resolve them.

Psychoanalysis

Psychoanalysis, Freud's brand of psychotherapy, maintains that the basic structure of personality can, through laborious and intense work, be restructured in healthier ways (S. Freud, 1900/1965, 1933/1965). In psychoanalysis, patients attend hourly sessions with their analysts 3–5 times per week. They lie on a couch facing away from their analysts, who rely on two main techniques to help bring unconscious conflicts to the fore.

The first technique is **free association**, during which patients are instructed to say whatever comes to mind without censoring themselves. The goal is to have unconscious conflicts leak out, often through **slips of the tongue** (also called *Freudian slips*) in which the person accidentally uses wrong words and, in so doing, expresses unconscious feelings or thoughts (S. Freud, 1914). For example, "soon after the adulterous Tiger Woods complained of a neck injury, a female reporter blurted that the golfer withdrew from the 2010 Players tournament due to 'a bulging di**' in his back" (Pincott, 2012, para. 5).

The second psychoanalytic technique is **dream analysis**. During dream analysis, patients share their dreams and the analyst analyzes them. Freud believed that every dream contains a **wish fulfillment**, an unconscious desire that is often disguised by the ego to satisfy superego and external reality constraints (S. Freud, 1900/1965).

Seth

When it comes to Seth's repressed sexual wish to have sex with his girlfriend Lillian's best friend Abigail, his ego may disguise this wish and allow it to be expressed in a dream about sex with a famous movie star—who reminds him of (and is a stand-in for) Abigail.

CASE EXAMPLES

According to Freud's psychoanalytic theory, every dream contains an unconscious (sometimes disguised) wish.
Source: Image Source\Image Source/DIRK LINDNER

Another important element of psychoanalysis is analyzing transference. **Transference** occurs when patients transfer feelings about important people in their lives onto their analysts. For instance, a patient who feels hostile toward her father may come to interact with and treat her analyst the same way. Another patient who feels deferent and weak when dealing with his mother may start feeling that way with his analyst, too. Transference provides analysts with helpful information for understanding patients' repressed conflicts. Psychoanalysis encourages transference by having patients lie facing away from their analysts during sessions. The idea is that with the analyst out of sight, transference is more likely. The logic here is that feelings about others (say, your mother or father) are more easily transferred onto the analyst when the analyst sits outside your line of vision.

Seth

Imagine Seth sees a psychoanalytic therapist. Over the course of the first few sessions, transference would be expected to develop, in which Seth would feel the same kind of anger toward his therapist that he feels toward his father. "You're just like my dad!" Seth might exclaim in session. "You don't respect my choices and you don't understand me!"

CASE EXAMPLES

Unlike transference, **countertransference** isn't desired. Countertransference occurs when analysts project their own feelings onto patients. This interferes with analysts' grasp of patient behavior. To minimize countertransference, psychoanalytic trainees undergo their own analysis to work through any issues that are likely to interfere with their ability to accurately read patients.

Seth

Imagine that Seth's psychoanalyst is a middle-aged woman with a teenage son. She might notice herself starting to feel the same frustration with Seth that she sometimes feels toward her son. To address this, she would hopefully seek consultation with another therapist, who could help her work through these countertransference feelings.

CASE EXAMPLES

Through free association, dream analysis, and examination of transference, analysts eventually come to understand the repressed conflicts behind their patients' symptoms. They then begin offering interpretations, with the goal of bringing the repressed conflict into their patients' consciousness. **Resistance** often occurs initially, with patients rejecting their analysts' interpretations and relying on **defense mechanisms** (partly unconscious mental processes used to ward off or reduce anxiety). Although it is common to attribute psychoanalytic defense mechanisms to Sigmund Freud, it was his daughter Anna Freud who fully articulated them (Bornstein et al., 2013; A. Freud, 1937/1966; Miller, 2015). The ego employs defense mechanisms in response to id impulses that aren't easily reconciled with the superego and/or external constraints. Some of the more common defense mechanisms are shown in Table 2.3. However, if all goes well in treatment, patients eventually overcome their resistance and accept the analysts' interpretations, consciously re-experiencing previously repressed conflicts. When their conflicts fully enter consciousness, patients experience **catharsis**, a strong emotional release of the pent-up feelings associated with unconscious conflict. Psychoanalysis doesn't end with catharsis. Once unconscious conflicts enter consciousness there is a long **working through** period, during which patients integrate what's been uncovered into their lives and slowly begin engaging others in new ways. Psychoanalysis is a long-term project that often takes many years.

Table 2.3 "The Best Offense is a Good Defense!"—Defense Mechanisms

Defense	Defined	In Action
Denial	Refusing to acknowledge an impulse or desire.	Bill insists he doesn't have a crush on Hillary, even though he clearly does.
Displacement	Redirecting one's feelings for one person toward someone else.	Pedro is mad at his boss, so he goes home and kicks his cat.
Identification	Becoming like someone else by incorporating their beliefs into one's own sense of self.	Donald starts dressing and acting like his professor, whom he admires very much.
Intellectualization	Logic and reason are used to minimize powerful emotions resulting from upsetting events.	After barely surviving a violent battle, a soldier describes it in emotionally detached terms as "a necessary evil" and "not a big deal."
Projection	Attributing one's own unacceptable feelings and thoughts to others.	Aparna feels a colleague dislikes her, even though it is she who dislikes her colleague.
Rationalization	Logic and reason are used to justify or explain away one's own behavior.	Sidney plagiarizes her term paper; when confronted about it she shrugs and remarks how "everyone does it."
Reaction formation	Transforming one's underlying feelings into their opposite.	A preacher who rails against homosexuality is discovered having gay sex.
Regression	Reverting to an earlier stage of behavior and development.	Sally coos and whines like a 5-year old when her partner isn't attentive.
Repression	Keeping unacceptable impulses unconscious.	Someone sexually abused in childhood has no recollection of it.
Sublimation	Directing aggressive and unacceptable impulses in socially approved ways.	Steven's aggressive impulses are channeled into football, where he becomes a celebrated player.

Psychodynamic Theories

There are many psychodynamic perspectives emerging from Freud's original work. They are variously grouped together under such headings as neo-Freudian, ego psychology, object relations theory, interpersonal theory, and self-psychology (Eagle, 2011; Elliott, 2015). There are too many versions of psychodynamic therapy to cover them all here. Below we focus on two popular psychodynamic approaches, both of which stress relationships over instinctual drives.

Object Relations Therapy

Object relations therapy refers to a loose cluster of psychodynamic perspectives that emphasize how early attachment relationships with caregivers lead to psychologically internalized expectations, which result in recurring patterns of interacting with others later in life (Caligor & Clarkin, 2010). The term "object" often strikes students as odd and confusing. Object relations therapists define an **object** as any person or thing for which an infant develops an *introjection*, or internal mental representation; this introjection may contain actual or imagined elements (Cashdan, 1988; Elliott, 2015; Klein, Heimann, Isaacs, & Riviere, 1952). Your internal representation of your mother may or may not be an accurate representation of your mother, but you use it in relating to her and to others who remind you of her. Early childhood relationships with caregivers are critical in developing internal object representations. When infants experience anger toward their caregivers, those whose caregivers provide consistent love and nurturing deal with it in a healthy way by learning that both they and their caregivers have positive and negative qualities. However, infants whose caregivers respond inconsistently or in a rejecting manner learn that their feelings of hostility aren't acceptable. Therefore, they isolate and repress these feelings in a process that object relations theorists call **splitting**, whereby the offending object is divided into "good" and "bad" parts (Cashdan, 1988; Elliott, 2015; Klein et al., 1952). Psychopathology develops when the relational patterns learned in childhood—including splitting off unacceptable feelings—impact relationships in adolescence and adulthood. People who rely on splitting are unable to experience the good and bad aspects of others simultaneously. They alternate between seeing others as all good or all bad, leading to relational difficulties.

Just as they do with other people in their lives, patients often project unwanted and split-off feelings about themselves onto their therapists; object relations therapists call this **projective identification** (Cashdan, 1988; Klein et al., 1952). For instance, a projective identification of *dependency* occurs when patients project onto their therapists their longstanding feelings of helplessness (initially learned in childhood relationships with caregivers), perhaps by repeatedly asking their therapists to tell them what to do (Cashdan, 1988). A *power* projective identification, on the other hand, results in patients recreating a relational pattern where they dominate and control others to avoid being hurt (Cashdan, 1988). Object relations therapists uncover their patients' projective identifications by examining countertransference feelings—distinguishing "good" from "bad" countertransference. The "bad" kind is the type Freud spoke of: therapists transferring their own issues onto patients. This is to be avoided. The "good" kind occurs when therapists are induced to act and feel certain ways because of their patients' behavior. According to object relations therapists, this sort of countertransference is "good" because it becomes the mechanism by which therapists come to understand patients' projective identifications. The therapist who feels helpless with patients who project power or bossy with patients who project dependency can use these feelings to inform the therapy. By talking with patients about their projective identifications and refusing to abide by them, object relations therapists provide a **corrective emotional experience** (Alexander & French, 1946)—a new kind of relationship in which patients learn to assess others more realistically so that they no longer must rely on projective identifications.

Seth

Consider what might happen were Seth to work with an object relations therapist. After a few sessions, the therapist might feel intimidated by Seth and fear doing anything to provoke his anger. She would eventually begin sharing these feelings with Seth. By processing Seth's projective identification and conveying caring toward him while also refusing to tiptoe around him as others do, Seth would have a corrective emotional experience in which he explores what it's like to interact with his therapist without resorting to the familiar pattern of browbeating her into submission to avoid emotional injury. After developing this new way of relating to his therapist, Seth would hopefully start to generalize it to others in his life, as well.

CASE EXAMPLES

Time-Limited Dynamic Psychotherapy (TLDP)

Time-limited dynamic psychotherapy (TLDP) is a briefer, contemporary form of psychodynamic therapy (Levenson, 2017). It shares the object relations emphasis on using therapy to identify and revise problematic interpersonal patterns, but— by establishing clear therapeutic goals and addressing them in 20–25 sessions—it accommodates modern contexts that don't permit long-term therapy. TLDP combines aspects of the **attachment theory** of John Bowlby (1907–1990) and the interpersonal/psychodynamic therapy of Harry Stack Sullivan (1892–1949), the latter having much in common with object relations therapy. Bowlby and Sullivan both believed that people develop internal working models of relationships based on their initial experiences with caregivers (Levenson, 2017). From a TLDP perspective, children develop interpersonal patterns through their relationships with their parents. They typically continue to rely on these patterns in adult relationships, even when doing so is counterproductive. In TLDP, the therapist uses the therapy interaction to identify the client's **cyclical maladaptive pattern**, the problematic interpersonal pattern reproduced in relationship after relationship (Levenson, 2017). Just as in object relations therapy, TLDP provides clients with a corrective emotional experience.

Seth

A time-limited dynamic therapist beginning work with Seth would notice how he tends to behave in assertive and intimidating ways with others, eliciting deference from them. This keeps him from being taken advantage of by others, but prevents him from experiencing intimacy; hence, his long string of girlfriends who have broken up with him because they found him bossy and hard to talk to. After all, who wants to confide in someone intimidating? The TLDP therapist would see Seth's cyclical maladaptive pattern as involving relating to others in intimidating ways that keep them deferent and at a distance. TLDP with Seth would aim to identify this pattern, which inevitably would get reproduced in Seth's interactions with the therapist. The therapeutic relationship would be used to help Seth develop more effective ways of relating to others.

CASE EXAMPLES

CHAPTER 2

Evaluating Psychodynamic Perspectives

The following are often cited as strengths of psychodynamic perspectives:

1. *Clinically rich and engaging.* Freud and later psychodynamic therapists offered many compelling case studies to illustrate their ideas. The psychodynamic perspective's rich clinical descriptions of intriguing cases continue to attract newcomers to this perspective.

2. *Emphasis on childhood origins of psychopathology.* We often take the importance of early life events for granted today, in large part due to Freud's influence. While some question whether early experiences are as important as psychodynamic theorists claim (Efran & Fauber, 2015), an emphasis on childhood remains central to many theories of abnormality.

3. *Attention to irrational and unconscious aspects of human functioning.* When it comes to abnormality, the psychoanalytic approach reminds us that sometimes reason has less influence over our behavior than irrational emotions and drives that we aren't aware of.

4. *Psychoanalysis as the first fully articulated form of psychotherapy.* Dubbed the "talking cure" by an early patient (Breur & Freud, 1893–1895/2013), psychoanalysis legitimized the idea that discussing one's problems with a trained professional can be helpful.

Psychodynamic theories are also commonly criticized on the following grounds:

1. *Not very scientific.* Freud relied almost exclusively on case studies rather than controlled experiments. Also, many of Freud's concepts don't lend themselves to traditional scientific inquiry. Scientific psychology usually demands that concepts be readily observable, but much of what Freud stressed was unconscious material that can't be directly observed. However, in recent times psychodynamic therapists have undertaken more rigorous research on the effectiveness of their approach, with some promising results (Steinert, Munder, Rabung, Hoyer, & Leichsenring, 2017).

2. *Sexist and culture-biased.* Freud's views on female psychology have been widely criticized (Balsam, 2013; Horney, 1924; Mead, 1974). Early psychoanalysis also denied the reality of patient reports of sex abuse, arguing that they were merely "projected fantasies" (Masson, 1984). Finally, the psychosexual stages, in assuming a traditional nuclear family, have been criticized as culture-biased—although there have been efforts to think about how psychosexual development occurs in non-nuclear family environments (Parsons, 1970).

3. *Deterministic view of people.* Not everyone likes Freud's notion of psychic determinism, the idea that every mental event is caused. Theorists who emphasize choice and free will are especially critical of psychodynamic determinism.

4. *Overly pathologizing.* Some critics complain that psychoanalytic theory tends to see pathology in everything. Of course, psychoanalysts view this as a strength, not a weakness. Freud (1914) did, after all, write a book called *The Psychopathology of Everyday Life*. Nonetheless, his notion that everyone is a bit neurotic and that every little thing a person does potentially betrays some underlying unconscious conflict rubs some people the wrong way. To these critics, sometimes a cigar is just a cigar!

COGNITIVE-BEHAVIORAL PERSPECTIVES

Cognitive-behavioral therapy (CBT), mentioned in Chapter 1, combines elements of two distinct perspectives that are often blended together in clinical practice: cognitive perspectives and behavioral perspectives. Because behavioral perspectives developed first, we begin there, then move on to cognitive perspectives, and finish with ways cognitive and behavioral perspectives have been combined.

Behavioral Perspectives

Whereas Freud endorsed psychic determinism, behavioral perspectives embrace a different kind of determinism, one in which environmental conditioning shapes abnormal behavior. Students and practitioners often fail to fully grasp that behaviorists—at least old time *radical behaviorists*—don't see psychopathology as residing inside people. To them, any speculation about disorders inside people is unnecessary and unscientific (Andersson & Ghaderi, 2006). Instead we should stick to what we can observe. To them, abnormality isn't something we "have." It's something we do. It consists of undesirable behaviors we learn through environmental conditioning. In the behavioral perspective, simply change the environment to recondition behavior—and voilà! Problem solved. See Table 2.4 for a summary of behavioral assumptions.

Table 2.4 Five Behavioral Assumptions

1. *Psychology as the scientific study of observable behavior.*	To be scientific, psychology must rely on empirical observation. It should limit its focus only to what can be directly observed; mental concepts that can't be observed (e.g., id, self, mind, cognitions) aren't scientific and therefore have no place in a scientific psychology.
2. *Behavior as determined by conditioning.*	The environment conditions human behavior, mainly through classical and operant conditioning.
3. *Most behavior is learned.*	While people are born into the world with some basic emotions, most human behavior is learned through conditioning; people are mostly *blank slates* when they're born.
4. *Abnormal behavior as conditioned behavior.*	The environment has conditioned behaviors deemed abnormal; thus, we can use conditioning to replace these undesirable behaviors with more desirable ones.
5. *We can learn a lot about abnormality in humans by studying non-human animals.*	Conditioning processes are the same for humans and non-human animals; therefore, studying the latter can provide insight into human abnormality.

Classical Conditioning

The most important early behaviorist was John B. Watson (1878–1958). Watson drew heavily on the work of Russian physiologist Ivan Pavlov (1849–1936) in developing **classical conditioning**. As mentioned in Chapter 1, in classical conditioning an unconditioned stimulus is paired repeatedly with a neutral stimulus in order to turn the latter into a conditioned stimulus that elicits the same response as the unconditioned stimulus (Craske, 2017). Let's unpack this a bit further. Pavlov gave his dogs food and they began salivating. The food was an **unconditioned stimulus (US)** and the salivation an **unconditioned response (UR)**. Neither required learning; dogs just instinctually salivate in response to food. After Pavlov repeatedly rang a bell every time he fed his dogs, he found that the bell elicited the same response as the food—even when no food was given. The bell had become a **conditioned stimulus (CS)**, now capable of evoking the same salivation response as food. Salivating after the bell rang was a **conditioned response (CR)**; the dogs had learned to associate food with the sound of a bell.

Watson and the early behaviorists quickly realized that the principles of classical conditioning could be used to explain abnormal behavior. Recall from Chapter 1 that Watson notoriously tried to illustrate this by classically conditioning fear in an 18-month-old infant known as Little Albert (Watson & Rayner, 1920). By clanging loud steel bars behind Albert whenever Watson presented him with a white rat, he taught Albert to fear the rat. Rather than seeing phobias as symptoms of deeply repressed internal conflicts (as psychoanalysts do), behaviorists see them as classically conditioned behaviors.

Operant Conditioning

Operant conditioning is most readily associated with the radical behaviorist B. F. Skinner (1904–1990). It emphasizes how reinforcement and punishment influence future behavior (Bolling, Terry, & Kohlneberg, 2006). Whereas classical conditioning focuses on the conditioned stimuli that precede a behavior, operant conditioning focuses on the consequences that follow a behavior. **Reinforcers** are consequences that increase the future likelihood of behaviors, while **punishers** are consequences that decrease that likelihood (Bolling et al., 2006). There are two ways to reinforce and two ways to punish (McConnell, 1990):

» **Positive reinforcement** is when something desirable is added after a behavior. A teacher who praises a student for speaking in class is positively reinforcing the student; something desirable (praise) is added that makes it more likely the student will speak again next class.

» **Negative reinforcement** is when something undesirable is removed after a behavior. Taking aspirin for a headache is negatively reinforced if the headache goes away; something undesirable (a headache) is eliminated, making it more likely you will take an aspirin again the next time your head hurts.

» **Positive punishment** is when something undesirable is added after a behavior. Parents who smack their children for misbehaving at the grocery store are positively punishing them; by adding something undesirable (a smack), they are making it less likely the children will misbehave during the next grocery store visit.

» **Negative punishment** is when something desirable is removed after a behavior. Parents who take away their children's Internet access for rudely talking back are negatively reinforcing them; by removing something desirable (time on the Internet), they are making it less likely the children will be rude the next time.

Students often mistake negative reinforcement as a form of punishment because they incorrectly equate "positive" and "negative" with "good" and "bad" rather than with "adding" or "subtracting." When we remove something undesirable (negative reinforcement) we are providing a reward that makes behavior more likely—that's why, for instance, removing stress by completing your homework reinforces doing homework! Remember that reinforcement (positive or negative) always increases the likelihood of the behaviors it follows, while punishment (positive or negative) always decreases the likelihood of the behaviors it follows (McConnell, 1990).

Seth

A behavioral therapist would note how Seth has often received reinforcement for behaving aggressively. By getting angry with people, he usually gets what he wants. Others have inadvertently rewarded him by backing down when he becomes belligerent. His recent arrest for assaulting Jorge is the first time that Seth recalls receiving any kind of serious punishment for his angry behavior.

CASE EXAMPLES

Social Learning

Not all behavior is conditioned directly. **Social learning theory** holds that a great deal of learning occurs through observation and modeling. Observation involves watching others and modeling occurs when others behave in ways we can imitate. In a series of famous studies, psychologist Albert Bandura (b. 1925) showed how children who watched a movie in which an adult acted aggressively towards an inflatable "Bobo" doll later imitated what they saw (Bandura, Ross, & Ross, 1961, 1963a, 1963b, 1963c). Interestingly, they were less likely to imitate what they observed if the adult in the movie was punished. However, even when the adult was punished, observational learning still occurred: the children didn't tend to spontaneously imitate the adult, but were quite able to when given a reward for doing so (Bandura, 1965)!

Observation and modeling both play key roles in social learning theory.
Source: Photodisc/ Getty Images

Seth

Now let's imagine Seth working with a behavioral therapist steeped in social learning theory. In this therapy steeped in social learning theory, Seth might recall seeing his father get in fights while Seth was growing up. This earned his father the respect of his male friends who worked with him at the loading dock, but resulted in Seth's mother becoming increasingly fed up with Seth's father for losing his temper too often. Seth and his therapist could discuss what Seth may have learned from observing his father model aggressive behavior.

CASE EXAMPLES

Behavior Therapy

Behavior therapy applies the principles of classical and operant conditioning, as well as social learning, to alter behavior deemed abnormal. There are many behavior therapy techniques, which will be discussed at various points throughout later chapters. Classical conditioning techniques often involve exposure that leads to extinction of the conditioned response (Craske, 2017). **Extinction** works by no longer pairing the unconditioned and conditioned stimuli; consequently, the conditioned stimulus loses its ability to evoke a conditioned response. Extinction would occur with Pavlov's dogs if we stopped ringing the bell before presenting the dogs with food. Over time, the bell would stop eliciting salivation as its association with food weakens. In **exposure therapies**, the client is placed in the presence of the conditioned stimulus to extinguish the old response and condition a new one (Zalta & Foa, 2012). Exposure plus response prevention and systematic desensitization are both examples of exposure techniques. In **exposure plus response prevention** (also called *flooding and response prevention*), the client is thrust into contact with the conditioned stimulus that evokes the problematic response and is prevented from leaving the situation (Baum, 1970; Craske, 2017; van Bilsen, 2013). Therefore, the client learns that nothing bad happens when in contact with the stimulus. For example, if we were reconditioning Little Albert, we might place a white rat in his lap. Assuming nothing bad happens when we do this, Albert will stop associating the rat with fear and instead associate it with being calm. Unfortunately, sometimes flooding backfires because the person has a negative response to being immediately placed in close contact with the conditioned stimulus. Thus, a subtler exposure technique called systematic desensitization is often used. **Systematic desensitization** involves gradually exposing the client to the conditioned stimulus while the client is in a relaxed state, with the goal of conditioning a new response (Wolpe, 1958).

Evaluating Behavioral Perspectives

The following are often cited as strengths of behavioral perspectives:

1. *Scientific.* Behaviorists have done extensive research testing their approach. Many studies on behavioral interventions for various presenting problems have been conducted over the years, and these support the behavioral perspective.

2. *No speculation about hard-to-prove mental entities.* By focusing exclusively on behavior, speculation about processes inside the person that we can't directly observe becomes unnecessary.

3. *Highly practical therapy approach.* Reconditioning behavior is straightforward and easy for clients to understand. It has also been shown to help with many behavioral problems.

4. *Optimistic.* By seeing abnormality as caused by an environment with which we can intervene, behaviorists paint an optimistic picture of abnormality as learned behavior that can be reconditioned.

At the same time, behavioral perspectives have been criticized for several reasons:

1. *Too deterministic.* Its insistence that people are little more than conditioned responses to the environment is sometimes seen as limited and simplistic; humanistic critics, for instance, argue that people have some say in how they behave.

2. *Internal processes ignored.* While supporters like behaviorism's exclusion of unobservable mental concepts, critics see an impoverished view of the person; just because scientists can't directly observe internal processes by which people interpret and respond to the world doesn't mean that they don't exist or we should give up studying them.

3. *Biological influences minimized.* Because they see almost all behavior as learned, behaviorists are often accused of ignoring or minimizing the importance of biology; critics complain that some forms of abnormality—such as schizophrenia—may be best seen as caused by brain disease, not conditioning.

4. *Animals are limited in what they teach us about human abnormality.* This criticism is often put forward by those who believe people are mentally much more complex than the non-human animals used in behavioral research. These critics feel that drawing conclusions about human abnormality based on animal research is limited in what it can teach us. They argue that rats and dogs can only tell us so much about people.

Cognitive Perspectives

Cognitive perspectives emerged during the 1950s and emphasize thoughts and beliefs as the root causes of abnormal behavior. Early cognitive therapists were intrigued by advances in computer technology and began conceptualizing people as sophisticated information processors. Unlike psychodynamic approaches (which give primacy to irrational feelings) and behavioral approaches (which focus almost exclusively on environmental conditioning), cognitive approaches stress **cognitive restructuring**—techniques designed to help people overcome their problems by thinking more rationally (Leahy & Rego, 2012; van Bilsen, 2013). Cognitive theory builds on the tradition of Stoic philosophers such as Epictetus, who famously quipped, "What upsets people is not things themselves but their judgments about the things. ... So when we are thwarted or upset or distressed, let us never blame someone else but rather ourselves, that is, our own judgments" (Epictetus, as cited in Reinecke & Freeman, 2003, p. 225). Cognitive therapy and rational emotive behavior therapy quintessentially exemplify the cognitive perspective. Assumptions made by cognitive therapists are presented in Table 2.5.

Table 2.5 Five Cognitive Assumptions

These assumptions are inspired by Reinecke and Freeman (2003):	
1. *How people interpret events influences how they feel or behave.*	Events don't determine our responses; what we think of them does.
2. *People actively interpret events.*	We are always actively making sense of events.
3. *People develop their own unique belief systems.*	We not only develop unique belief systems; we then selectively attend to events in ways that fit with these belief systems. We become sensitive to specific stressors based on our beliefs about them.

| 4. *People become functionally impaired when they respond to stressors based on problematic belief systems.* | Stressors we believe to be important lead us to respond to situations in maladaptive and sometimes self-fulfilling ways: "the person who believes . . . that 'the freeway is horribly dangerous' might drive in such a timid manner ... that he causes an accident, thus strengthening his belief in the danger of freeways" (Reinecke & Freeman, 2003, p. 229). |
| 5. *Mental disorders can be distinguished based on their specific cognitive content and processes.* | This is known as the **cognitive specificity hypothesis** and it basically holds that each disorder has a unique way in which its sufferers cognitively interpret events. |

Cognitive Therapy

Psychiatrist Aaron Beck (b. 1921) founded **cognitive therapy**. It is based on a rather straightforward assumption, namely that all psychological difficulties involve dysfunctional thinking (J. S. Beck, 2011). Successful treatment of abnormality involves getting people to evaluate their beliefs and think more realistically and adaptively. Cognitive theorists identify four levels of cognition: automatic thoughts, intermediate beliefs, core beliefs, and schemas (J. S. Beck, 2011).

1. **Automatic thoughts** are the spontaneous thoughts that occur to us throughout daily life (e.g., "I'm not good enough to win the race," "I'm hungry for ice cream," "Why am I always the one who has to take care of everything?"). It's our automatic thoughts, not events themselves, which trigger our emotional responses.

Seth and Lillian
Seth is waiting to make copies in the library and Jorge cuts in front of him. Seth has the automatic thought "I'm being disrespected!" and, consequently, he feels angry. In response to his anger, he yells at Lillian, who has the automatic thought, "I wound up with the sort of boyfriend I deserve" and feels sad.

2. **Intermediate beliefs** are general rules and beliefs that influence automatic thoughts. Problems arise when intermediate beliefs become rigid.

Seth and Lillian
Seth's intermediate belief, "Deferring to others in social situations is a way of showing them respect," helps us understand why he thinks Jorge's line cutting is disrespecting him. Lillian, on the other hand, maintains the intermediate belief that "Only valuable people deserve to be well treated."

3. **Core beliefs** are basic philosophies or mindsets we hold about ourselves that influence intermediate beliefs and automatic thoughts.

Seth and Lillian
One of Seth's core beliefs is "I may not be good enough to warrant respect," whereas one of Lillian's may be "I am not valuable to others."

4. **Schemas** are the mental structures we use to organize information. Broader than core beliefs, schemas are generalized scripts about how the world works that we use to anticipate what will happen in different situations (Reinecke & Freeman, 2003). We have schemas for mundane events such as what to expect when we go to a restaurant, but we also have schemas for relationships. When our relational schemas are negative or rigid, we get into psychological trouble. Schemas influence how we interpret events because we often attend to information that confirms them and overlook information that doesn't (Reinecke & Freeman, 2003).

Seth and Lillian
One of Seth's schemas holds that "I may not be good enough to warrant respect, but to ensure I get it I must stand up for myself and demand that others treat me properly. When they don't, the only way to win is to get angry." Lillian maintains a very different schema: "I am unimportant, unattractive, and invisible. Other people know this and will eventually come to ignore and mistreat me. Life will be a series of disappointments in which I won't get what I want or need."

Cognitive therapy involves client and therapist working together to examine the client's belief system, which is often riddled with **cognitive distortions** (see Table 2.6). Many strategies for doing this have been developed. One of the earliest techniques, developed by Beck himself, is to have clients complete the **Daily Record of Dysfunctional Thoughts (DRDT)**, a form on which they keep track of events, their emotional reactions to these events, their automatic thoughts about these events, how they responded to these events, and the outcomes of the events; the goal is to identify errors in logic in their automatic thoughts (A. T. Beck, Rush, Shaw,

& Emery, 1979; J. S. Beck, 2011; Leahy & Rego, 2012; van Bilsen, 2013). Therapy focuses on challenging the illogic of automatic thoughts and replacing them with more reasonable thoughts and responses.

Table 2.6 "You Don't Really Believe That, Do You?"—Common Cognitive Distortions

Distortion	Defined	In Action
All-or-nothing thinking	Interpreting everything as either "all good" or "all bad" with no middle ground.	"If I don't do this perfectly, then I am a complete failure."
Catastrophizing	Expecting the worst to always come true even though it is unlikely.	"I have a headache. It's probably a brain tumor."
Emotional reasoning	Relying on feelings to make judgments, even when they aren't supported by evidence.	"I feel unattractive, therefore I must be unattractive."
Filtering	Focusing exclusively on negative events and discounting positive ones.	"When I won the game it was due to luck; when I lost it was because I'm dumb."
Jumping to conclusions	Reaching a conclusion despite little evidence for doing so.	"They haven't replied to the job application I submitted last week; they definitely aren't going to."
Magnification	Overemphasizing negative events.	"This pimple is hideous! Nobody is going to talk to me until it goes away."
Mind reading	Assuming one knows what others are thinking.	"He didn't return my text. He must not like me."
Minimization	Underemphasizing positive events.	"Sure I got an 'A' this time, but usually I don't."
Overgeneralization	Taking one instance and applying it too broadly to explain other instances.	"She rejected me for a date. Nobody will ever date me!"
Personalization	Assuming others' behavior is necessarily about you.	"When the professor said in class that some students ask too many questions, she had to mean me."

Albert Ellis (1913–2007)
Source: Bettman/Getty Images

Rational Emotive Behavior Therapy (REBT)

Psychologist Albert Ellis (1913–2007) developed **rational emotive behavior therapy (REBT),** which—like cognitive therapy—builds on the idea that it is our beliefs that determine our emotions and behavior (Craske, 2017; Dryden & Ellis, 2001). In REBT, eliminating irrational thinking is the way to remedy psychological dysfunction. REBT relies on the five-step **ABCDE model** for conceptualizing how psychological problems originate and how best to fix them (Dryden & Ellis, 2001; Trower, Casey, & Dryden, 1988). In this model, "A" is an *a̲ctivating event* that occurs in a person's life, "B" is a *b̲elief* that determines how the person interprets the event, and "C" is the *emotional c̲onsequence* that results from the belief.

Lillian

Perhaps Lillian receives a reprimand from her professor for not doing the math homework assignment correctly. This is an a̲ctivating event, which triggers a specific b̲elief ("I'm incompetent"). The emotional c̲onsequence is that Lillian feels depressed about her ability to succeed at school.

CASE EXAMPLES

Rational emotive behavior therapists engage clients therapeutically at "D" by *disputing irrational beliefs* and at "E" by helping them replace irrational beliefs with *effective new beliefs.*

Lillian

An REBT therapist might ask Lillian to examine whether her belief system is supported by evidence. If it isn't, then the therapist would dispute Lillian's illogical beliefs. For example, he might help her replace her irrational belief ("I'm incompetent") with a more realistic and effective belief ("I may not always do everything well at school, but I am able to learn and improve my performance").

 CASE EXAMPLES

Even if it turns out to be true that Lillian is bad at math, the rational emotive therapist will work to prevent **awfulizing**, the irrational tendency to interpret things as more awful than they truly are (Dryden & Ellis, 2001).

Lillian

If Lillian isn't competent at math, an REBT therapist might ask her, "What's the absolute worst thing that could happen?" Perhaps she'd have to pursue a degree in something besides math—and while that might not be ideal in Lillian's view, it wouldn't be the end of the world or as awful as she thinks.

 CASE EXAMPLES

Therapy with Lillian might also stress her **musterbating**, Ellis' humorously named term for the irrational belief that things must be a certain way or life can't go on (Dryden & Ellis, 2001).

Lillian

Lillian might be thinking she must succeed in math class or life will be awful. This isn't true; Lillian's life after dropping a class she isn't good at could be quite enjoyable in ways she can't yet fully appreciate. After dropping math, she might take a literature class and find that she's quite good at writing poetry.

 CASE EXAMPLES

The REBT therapist challenges whether events—even those we don't like—are as bad as they seem. By changing our irrational beliefs about events, we can change our responses to them.

Evaluating Cognitive Perspectives

Cognitive perspectives are viewed as having several strengths:

1. *Scientific.* Like the behavioral perspective, the cognitive perspective is well grounded in empirical science. Many research studies on the effectiveness of cognitive therapy for problems such as depression and anxiety have been conducted. Cognitive approaches are judged to have substantial empirical support.

2. *Straightforward and intuitive.* Compared to psychodynamic theories, which are often criticized for overly complex explanations of problems, cognitive therapies are frequently praised for offering logical and intuitive solutions to problems. Clinicians can learn how to do cognitive therapy easily because—compared to psychodynamic and humanistic therapies—it offers concrete procedures; its well-defined therapy techniques are intuitive, clear, and broken into discrete steps.

3. *Adaptable.* Cognitive therapies are adaptable enough that they can readily be combined with other approaches. As you will see below, cognitive therapies are most often combined with behavioral approaches.

Cognitive perspectives have been criticized on the following grounds:

1. *Logic and reason overemphasized.* Critics believe the cognitive perspective overemphasizes logic and reason. Psychodynamic and humanistic theorists complain that the mind-as-computer metaphor overlooks the importance of emotion.

2. *Biology minimized and mind–body dualism instituted.* From a biological perspective, cognitive therapists minimize physiological influences, such as brain chemistry and reinstitute a kind of mind–body dualism that distinguishes thinking as a psychological product of mind rather than a biological product of brain.

3. *Mentalistic explanations.* From a behavioral perspective, cognitive approaches are no better than psychodynamic and humanistic approaches because they rely on speculation about mental entities that cannot be scientifically observed (Skinner, 1985, 1987, 1990).

Combining Cognitive and Behavioral Perspectives

Despite objections from old-time radical behaviorists like Skinner, cognitive and behavioral therapies are so often combined that cognitive-behavioral therapy (CBT) is commonly viewed as its own distinct perspective. Obviously, CBT is less theoretically "pure" than either behavioral or cognitive perspectives alone. In many ways, combining these approaches exemplifies the move toward integrating theoretical perspectives. In CBT, how people think and how they are conditioned by their environments are both stressed. Due to a shared emphasis on concrete and direct interventions that can be studied using the methods of objective science, behavioral and cognitive perspectives fit nicely together. Throughout the text many additional CBT approaches that are used to address a variety of presenting problems will be introduced. The CBT therapies discussed in upcoming chapters include stress inoculation training, eye movement desensitization and reprocessing (EMDR), mindfulness and acceptance therapies, and dialectical behavior therapy (DBT).

HUMANISTIC PERSPECTIVES

In this text, **humanistic perspectives** refer to approaches that place personal meaning front and center. This includes humanistic, existential, and constructivist therapies. These therapies maintain that people are proactive meaning-makers who strive to develop their full potential. Psychological problems result when they are prevented from doing so. Humanistic theorists—building on the work of humanistic pioneers such as Abraham Maslow (1968) and Carl Rogers (1959)—advance a positive view of human nature; people are seen as naturally moving in constructive and growth-oriented directions when provided with a supportive environment for doing so. Existential and constructivist theorists tend to be less overtly optimistic about human nature. They see no inherent meaning or purpose in life, but hold people responsible for inventing and living by their own meanings. Humanistic perspectives reject **reductionism**, the idea that we can break complex human experience into component parts—such as thoughts, behaviors, and drives (when theorizing psychologically) or genes, neurochemicals, and brain parts (when theorizing biologically). They are skeptical of attempts to reduce complex human difficulties to a set of mental disorder categories that, in their view, fail to adequately attend to client meanings. Instead, humanistic approaches emphasize studying the whole person. They also reject the assumption that all human behavior is caused, believing instead that people have free will. Five humanistic assumptions are presented in Table 2.7.

Table 2.7 Five Humanistic Assumptions

These assumptions are inspired by Reinecke and Freeman (2003):	
1. *People as growth-oriented.*	Humanistic approaches stress *self-actualization*, the process of developing one's full potential. Existential and constructivist approaches don't speak of actualization, but do stress how people develop as they invent the meanings by which they live.
2. *People as meaning-makers.*	Humanistic perspectives see people as meaning-makers. In a humanistic approach, this meaning making is in the service of self-actualization. Existentially, there is no inherent meaning or purpose in life; people must invent and be responsible for their own meanings. Constructivists also see people as imbuing meaningfulness into life by inventing ways of understanding and then committing to them.
3. *People as in process.*	Humanistic theorists see people as forever changing and growing as they actualize. Existentialists stress *existence over essence*. People change as they make choices; they can't be reduced to static qualities: *Human existence is irreducible to a set of essential components. That is, even if I could list every one of your essential qualities—for instance, your level of extraversion, your 'Intelligence Quotient', the neurochemicals passing through your brain—I would still not be describing* you*, because the actual, concrete* you *that you are is more than all these essential components put together. (Cooper, 2017, p. 15)*
4. *People as free.*	Humanistic and existential theorists believe people have free will. They reject the idea that abnormal behavior is *entirely* caused by things like internal drives, environmental conditioning, irrational thinking, or biological processes. Constructivists also emphasize human agency, though some of them say our psychological and physical structures both limit and inform human meaning making.
5. *"Psychopathology" as self-inconsistency.*	Humanistic-existential theorists see psychological difficulties as arising from a failure to be true to one's self. Humanists tend to explain this in terms of interference with the self-actualizing process, while existentialists focus on people lying to themselves about certain human truths and denying responsibility for their choices. Constructivists say that "psychopathology" results from a failure to revise one's meanings, even when there is a lot of evidence that they are no longer working very well.

Rogers' Person-Centered Therapy

Carl Rogers' (1902–1987) **person-centered therapy** (also known as *client-centered therapy*) integrates a theory of personality with an approach to therapy (Cain, 2010; Murphy & Joseph, 2016; Rogers, 1951, 1959, 1961). Person-centered therapy starts from the humanistic assumption that people are born with an **actualizing tendency**, an innate motivation to fulfill their full potential—to be all they can be, which humanists call **self-actualization**. When provided with love, support, and understanding from others, people naturally develop in ways that are consistent with their actualizing tendency. To help them actualize, people rely on what Rogers called the **organismic valuing process**. Through this process, people seek experiences that enhance their personal growth and avoid those that don't.

In addition to having an innate need to actualize our potential, we also have a need for acceptance and love from others—what Rogers called positive regard. There are two ways to obtain positive regard: unconditionally or conditionally. When others provide **unconditional positive regard**, they love us as we are, even when we

Carl Rogers (1902–1987)
Source: Bettman/Getty Images

behave in ways they don't like. This allows us to stay true to our actualizing tendency because we know there aren't any conditions we must meet to maintain others' affection. When your best friend still conveys acceptance and approval for you as a person despite the two of you disagreeing about whom to vote for in the next election, that's unconditional positive regard. Unfortunately, sometimes people don't accept us unconditionally. Instead, they only love and support us if we abide by certain conditions—that is, they provide **conditional positive regard**. A good example would be those teenagers at school who only liked you if you dressed a certain way and listened to certain music. Psychopathology occurs when there is a conflict between our need for positive regard and our need for **congruence** (i.e., *self-consistency*, the need to be true to our actualizing tendency). When positive regard is conditional, people lose touch with their organismic valuing process and have a difficult time knowing whether they are doing something because it enhances them or because it allows them to sustain conditional positive regard. When people behave in self-inconsistent ways to maintain conditional positive regard, they are in a state of psychological **incongruence**.

When it came to therapy, Rogers disliked the medical model of abnormality; he preferred the term "client" to "patient" because he didn't see the people he worked with as ill. His therapeutic goal was to help clients reconnect with their organismic valuing process to return them to a self-actualizing path. In person-centered therapy, this is accomplished by providing clients with three **core conditions for change**: unconditional positive regard, empathy, and genuineness. The first condition, unconditional positive regard, allows clients to feel safe and be themselves in therapy; providing unconditional positive regard means being warm and caring toward clients and accepting them no matter what. The second condition, **empathy**, involves understanding clients; it requires therapists to actively listen to what clients say and reflect what is heard back to clients. This insures that therapists correctly grasp each client's unique experience. The third condition is **genuineness**; therapists must be self-consistent (i.e., congruent) if they expect their clients to be, too.

When therapists provide the core conditions, clients reconnect with their actualizing tendency. Person-centered therapy is non-directive in that it assumes that therapists shouldn't tell clients what to talk about or what to do because, quite frankly, they don't know what is right for clients. Instead, therapists simply need to provide the core conditions. When they do, clients will get back in touch with the actualizing tendency and figure things out for themselves.

Lillian

A person-centered therapist working with Lillian would aim to provide her the core conditions necessary for change. When Lillian says that she feels undeserving of a nice boyfriend and feels inept at math, the therapist would endeavor to empathically understand her perspective by nonjudgmentally reflecting her thoughts and feelings back to her to make sure he comprehends them correctly. He would also convey unconditional positive regard by continuing to be kind and caring toward Lillian, even when she expresses negative feelings about herself. Lastly, he would behave genuinely; when Lillian puts herself down, he would let her know that it is difficult for him to hear her talk that way about herself. From a person-centered perspective, a safe and supportive therapeutic environment in which she is listened to and accepted would allow Lillian to rediscover what future directions might be best for her. She would begin reconnecting with her own organismic valuing process and actualizing tendency. Consequently, Lillian might realize that she doesn't want to date Seth anymore. She might also start feeling like she wants to drop math class; she was only taking it because her parents wanted her to anyhow.

CASE
EXAMPLES

Existential Therapy

There are numerous **existential psychotherapies**—such as logotherapy, daisenanalysis, American humanistic-existential therapy, and British existential therapy (Cooper, 2017). Without delving into the specifics of each, let's review commonalities across these approaches. Existential therapies view people as free to make choices. At the same time, human freedom has its limits. From an existential vantage point, life is inherently meaningless and full of givens we can't control—things like death, suffering, guilt, and anxiety (Cooper, 2017). Each of us is thrown into the world at a certain time and place with a unique combination of physical and cultural characteristics over which we have no say. You don't get to choose your family, ethnic background, or hat size! However, how you fashion a life for yourself within the constraints of these givens is utterly up to you. Bearing the responsibility of meaningfully creating a life from the lot you are given constitutes the crux of the existential dilemma. Psychological problems develop when people become overwhelmed by the existential anxiety that accompanies this kind of burdensome responsibility. In the words of the famous existential philosopher Jean-Paul Sartre: "Man is condemned to be free: condemned, because he did not create himself, yet nonetheless free, because once cast into the world, he is responsible for everything he does" (Sartre, 1947/2007, p. 29). Because the burden of being responsible for our lives often provokes anxiety, we sometimes lie to ourselves and act as if we have no say over our behavior.

Seth

What might happen if Seth worked with an existential therapist? In discussing the violent outbursts that repeatedly land him in trouble, Seth might claim "I had to punch Jorge in the face because he disrespected me." The existential therapist would likely challenge Seth on whether punching Jorge was something he "had" to do or something he "chose" to do.

CASE EXAMPLES

Seth's statement exemplifies **inauthenticity**, the denial of responsibility for one's choices. Seth didn't "have" to punch anyone, but by convincing himself he was forced to behave a certain way by circumstances, he avoids taking responsibility for his actions. The existential therapist sees psychological maladjustment as a product of inauthentic living: "Inauthenticity is illness, is our living in distorted relation to our true being" (Bugental, 1987, p. 246). By contrast, **authenticity** involves awareness of one's responsibility for creating meaning and living by it. In other words, "authentic living is about being able to make clear and well-informed choices in accordance with the values one recognizes as worth committing oneself to" (van Deurzen, 2012, p. 61). Existential therapy focuses on helping people gain awareness of themselves and their experience so they can live more authentic lives.

Constructivist Perspectives

Although sometimes considered a variant of the cognitive perspective, **constructivist perspectives** are included here as humanistic-existential approaches because they emphasize people as active meaning-makers who are responsible for the meanings they create. There are numerous constructivist perspectives, such as *personal construct theory* (Kelly, 1955/1991a, 1955/1991b), *radical constructivism* (Glasersfeld, 1995), and *narrative therapy* (White & Epston, 1990). All focus on how people create meaningful ways of understanding themselves, their world, and their relationships, which they then use to guide their lives. From a constructivist perspective, difficulties occur when people mistake their constructed meanings for reality itself and get locked into meanings that no longer work well (Chiari & Nuzzo, 2010; Neimeyer, 2009; Neimeyer & Mahoney, 1995; Neimeyer & Raskin, 2000; Raskin & Bridges, 2008). Therapy attempts to help people revise their constructed meanings to generate new possibilities.

Narrative therapy is a particularly popular constructivist perspective, one that emphasizes the stories (or narratives) that we construct to account for and understand our experiences (Madigan, 2011; Monk, Winslade, Crocket, & Epston, 1997; White & Epston, 1990). Although creating meaningful stories to live by is necessary, sometimes the stories we tell ourselves limit us and lead to unhappiness. Narrative therapists argue that in the Western world, we tend to tell stories that are highly individualistic and which locate problems inside people. To counter this, narrative therapists use a technique called **externalizing the problem**, in which they ask their clients to talk about their problems as distinct from themselves rather than as internal defects (Madigan, 2011; White & Epston, 1990). In so doing, clients begin to tell a different kind of story about the problem, one in which it is viewed as something separate from them that sometimes gets the best of them (rather than a disorder they "have"). Externalizing problems allows clients to look for exceptions—times when the problem was resisted successfully. This helps clients to stop relying on problem-saturated narratives in which they see themselves as disordered or defective. Instead they start telling new stories in which they can resist their problems' influence.

CHAPTER 2

> ### Seth
> *Now let's think about what might happen if Seth sought narrative therapy. Seth lives by the narrative that he was born with a bad temper; he considers himself an inherently angry and explosive person. However, his narrative therapist would challenge this story. She might ask Seth to externalize his temper by talking about it as something distinct from him that sometimes gets the best of him. In doing so, Seth would start to map his temper's influence. He'd learn that his temper often gains sway when others criticize him, which is when he tends to lash out angrily. Seth's therapist would encourage him to recall exceptions, times when his temper didn't get the best of him. Seth might remember several exceptions—times when his temper didn't goad him into getting into altercations with others—and realize that when he surrounds himself with supportive friends he can resist temper's invitations to attack those who criticize him. Seth therefore would begin to revise his narrative, shifting it from "I am an inherently temperamental and angry person" to "I am someone able to resist the influence of my temper by making sure I seek out people to support and care for me during challenging times in my life."*

CASE EXAMPLES

Evaluating Humanistic Perspectives

The following are often viewed as strengths of humanistic perspectives:

1. *Emphasis on the whole person as free and responsible.* The humanistic-existential emphasis on people as free agents who make choices places it in stark contrast with perspectives that view abnormality as reducible to biology, conditioning, irrational thinking, or social factors. This can seem highly refreshing, especially compared to approaches that see people as ill or as victims of circumstance.

2. *Emphasis on people as unique.* Humanistic-existential approaches see each person as unique. Careful attention to each person's problems and a strong disinclination to lump people together into diagnostic categories are often viewed as strengths of the humanistic-existential viewpoint.

3. *Impact on therapy.* Person-centered and narrative therapies have been enormously influential. The former's early use of face-to-face weekly sessions quickly eclipsed the psychoanalytic practice of daily sessions with patients on the couch. Most therapy approaches have adopted Rogers' emphasis on providing a supportive and safe environment for clients to explore their issues.

Criticisms of humanistic perspectives include:

1. *Unscientific.* Critics decry the humanistic emphasis on free will because it runs counter to scientific determinism. Because people are active agents, humanists argue that psychology must develop human science methods to effectively study them (Giorgi, 1970). However, critics lament that throughout its history the humanistic-existential perspective has rejected subjecting its ideas to proper scientific inquiry.

2. *Inadequate for treating serious disorders.* Some critics see humanistic-existential approaches as fine when working with everyday problems-in-living, but inadequate for conceptualizing and treating serious mental disorders such as schizophrenia and bipolar disorder (Cain, 2010).

3. *Too individualistic.* Humanistic perspectives have been critiqued for overemphasizing individualism in a way that inadvertently encourages self-absorption and ethnocentrism (Cain, 2010). Some complain that humanistic approaches reflect Western biases. The goal of helping people fulfill their full potential even when it conflicts with social expectations fits the individualistic emphasis of Western cultures, but may be inappropriate or counterproductive when working with clients from more communal cultures.

2.4 SOCIOCULTURAL PERSPECTIVES

Sociocultural perspectives focus on how social and cultural factors influence psychological functioning. These perspectives view social, familial, and cultural factors as affecting the development of people's presenting problems. Some sociocultural theorists accept the idea that abnormal behavior stems from biologically or psychologically based mental disorders, but look at cultural variations in how people express symptoms; other sociocultural theorists go farther, arguing against biological and psychological perspectives that view abnormal behavior as reflecting defects inside people (Bassett & Baker, 2015). A more purely sociocultural orientation reframes our understanding of human suffering almost entirely in social terms.

There are, of course, different kinds of sociocultural perspectives. We will discuss three: multicultural/social justice perspectives, consumer/service-user perspectives, and systems perspectives. Multicultural and social justice perspectives argue that emotional distress is the product of culture and social oppression, not biological disease. Adherents of such perspectives believe that intervening at the broader social level, rather than sticking solely to interventions at the individual level, is the key to relieving emotional distress (Aldarondo, 2007; Chung & Bemak, 2012; Prilleltensky, Dokecki, Frieden, & Ota Wang, 2007). From a somewhat different vantage point, consumer and service-user perspectives focus on the experiences of those who receive services for emotional distress; they highlight the ways in which society and the mental health professions treat those diagnosed as mentally ill. Finally, systems perspectives shift from working primarily with individuals to working mainly with "systems" (i.e., groups, communities, and families). They maintain a focus on therapy, but differ from psychological perspectives by locating dysfunction within systems, not individuals.

Importantly, despite a shared emphasis on environment, sociocultural theorists move beyond what they see as the behaviorists' narrow focus on conditioning and instead stress broader factors such as social norms, cultural customs, family dynamics, economic disparities, racism, sexism, and social oppression in trying to understand abnormality. Therapeutically, sociocultural approaches often emphasize community mental health care, which provides patients with support, guidance, and in some cases housing (see history section of Chapter 1). Common assumptions of the sociocultural perspective are found in Table 2.8.

Table 2.8 Five Sociocultural Assumptions

1. *Abnormality is primarily explainable in familial and social terms.*	Thoughts, feelings, and behaviors are ultimately best understood as caused by family dynamics, cultural influences, and social factors such as racism, sexism, and economic inequality.
2. *What we call mental disorders are actually social, cultural, and family problems.*	Many of the problems we usually attribute to mental disorder are better understood as social problems.
3. *Changing family dynamics or broader social systems is the key to remediating emotional suffering.*	Clinicians need to rely less on adjusting people to their situations and more on helping them to redress oppressive family dynamics and social conditions.
4. *Move beyond working with individuals.*	Family systems therapists work with families, rather than individuals because they see abnormality as emerging primarily from recurrent family patterns, not individual pathology. Social justice therapists believe in social action as a supplement to individual therapy.
5. *Therapists should be advocates for social change.*	A social justice perspective maintains that it is not enough to work with individual clients; instead, advocating social change is essential.

MULTICULTURAL AND SOCIAL JUSTICE PERSPECTIVES

Multicultural Perspectives

Multicultural perspectives hold that culture is critical in shaping our understanding of abnormality. **Culture** can be defined as the values, beliefs, and practices of any ethnic or cultural group (López & Guarnaccia, 2016). In keeping with this definition, multicultural perspectives maintain that human behavior (and our judgments about it) always take place within a cultural context in which communal values play a major role. Therefore "psychopathology should be examined within the context of culturally embedded worldviews, norms, and practices (taking into account the level of cultural assimilation of the individual[s])" (Krigbaum, 2013, p. 234). When working from a multicultural perspective, clinicians must attend to cultural differences because these differences impact client behavior and clinician understanding of it (Causadias, 2013; Fields, 2010; Krigbaum, 2013; López & Guarnaccia, 2016). Consequently, multicultural perspectives often hesitate to evaluate patients from minority cultures using research and interventions developed within the dominant culture. That is, "some authors advocate that mental health providers avoid the tendency to infer diagnoses and psychopathology based on a unilateral cultural understanding or use of psychometric assessments normed outside of the clients'/patients' culture" because doing so "can distort the clinical facts" and risk finding "too much or too little psychopathology" (Krigbaum, 2013, p. 236).

Thus, multicultural perspectives often view mental disorders not as culturally universal (true across times and cultures), but as culture-bound (true within a given historical time and context) (Bassett & Baker, 2015). **Culture-bound syndromes** reflect shared cultural values (Isaac, 2013; Stanley & Raskin, 2002). For example, rather than seeing "dependent personality disorder" (see Chapter 12) as a universal affliction that cuts across time and place, multicultural theorists might reframe it as reflecting Western culture's view that people should be autonomous and independent; those who aren't are considered disordered. However, in a different historical and cultural context, the same behavior might not be deemed abnormal. Hence, a dependent personality diagnosis—in being historically tied to a specific set of social norms and values—can be viewed as culture-bound.

As noted, not all multicultural theorists reframe psychopathology entirely in social terms. Some see psychopathology as biologically and psychologically based, but influenced in course, development, and expression by social factors (Bassett & Baker, 2015; López & Guarnaccia, 2016). These theorists are extremely interested in cross-cultural data that looks at differences in incidence and prevalence of disorders (see Chapter 1) in various countries and cultures, as well as in distinctive ways of effectively remediating mental disorders across cultural contexts (López & Guarnaccia, 2016). Other multicultural theorists endorse a more fully social view, arguing that most of what we call mental disorders are better reframed from being internal mental disorders people "have" to being forms of understandable emotional distress with primarily cultural and social origins (Kinderman, 2014b, 2017). Such theorists often view ideas about abnormality as socially constructed. A **social construction** is any socially shared way of defining, talking about, and understanding something that influences how people come to experience it (Burr, 2015; Gergen, 2015). From a social constructionist viewpoint, mental disorders are not universal things, but socially invented and context-dependent ways of talking about people (Gergen & McNamee, 2000; Maddux, Gosselin, & Winstead, 2016; Stanley & Raskin, 2002). As such, behavior that is socially understood to be disordered in one culture may not even raise eyebrows in another.

Social Justice Perspectives

Social justice perspectives build on multicultural perspectives, viewing abnormality as the product of social inequalities. From a social justice vantage point, the problems people have aren't explicable primarily in terms of disorders inside people or even recurrent family patterns (discussed later), but by economic inequality, racism, sexism, and other forms of social oppression (Aldarondo, 2007; Chung & Bemak, 2012). From a social justice perspective:

> Structural features of society are seen as systematically marginalising and disempowering some people and not others; and psychology itself is viewed as part of an ideological dimension which shapes how we think and feel about ourselves. Importantly, this includes what is regarded as acceptable or deviant behaviour, such as what is seen as mental "ill health." In fact, the very notion of psychological experience as indicative of a state of "health" is a pervasive and questionable assumption. (McClelland, 2014, p. 121)

For instance, leaders of the British Psychological Society's (BPS) Division of Clinical Psychology (2014) take a social justice perspective on schizophrenia and other psychotic experiences. Despite acknowledging that genetics, neurochemistry, and brain structure all play a role, they maintain that traumatic life events, relational stressors, and social factors such as inequality, poverty, and economic disadvantage better explain schizophrenia. They point to evidence that people who hear voices are more likely to have been sexually abused in childhood. They also cite research suggesting that being poor and living in densely populated urban areas constitute major risk factors for developing psychosis. Therapy involves helping those diagnosed with psychosis and/or schizophrenia to gain insight into how their psychotic symptoms are meaningful responses to extremely difficult and stressful social circumstances—and then altering those circumstances through social reform (Division of Clinical Psychology, 2014).

Feminist therapy is an excellent example of a social justice perspective. Feminist therapy holds that *patriarchy* (the structuring of society so that men are in charge) is the root cause of many problems commonly labeled as mental disorders. In a feminist conception, individuals aren't sick; society is. As prominent feminist therapist Laura Brown remarked, "the first and foremost important 'client' of feminist therapy is the culture in which it takes place; the first and foremost commitment of feminist therapists is to radical social transformation" (Brown, 1994, p. 17). A famous phrase used to exemplify the feminist stance is that "the personal is political" (Hanisch, 1969), meaning that individual problems always occur in a social context. Instead of viewing people as "having" mental illnesses that are primarily attributed to individual psychology and biology, feminist and other social justice therapists view people as reacting in understandable ways to social injustices such as trauma, socioeconomic disadvantage, and sexism. Therapy is reconceptualized from a treatment that fixes disturbed individuals to a collaborative relationship between therapist and client, one in which both work for social reform. Feminist theorist Carol Hanisch put it this way in critiquing the traditional therapy-as-individual-treatment approach:

The very word "therapy" is obviously a misnomer if carried to its logical conclusion. Therapy assumes that someone is sick and that there is a cure, e.g., a personal solution. I am greatly offended that I or any other woman is thought to need therapy in the first place. Women are messed over, not messed up! We need to change the objective conditions, not adjust to them. Therapy is adjusting to your bad personal alternative. (Hanisch, 1969, para. 2)

One of the impediments to social reform, according to feminist and other social justice therapists, is that therapy clients often live in a state of **false consciousness**. When living in such a state, oppressed people fail "to recognize their own economic and political interests by internalizing the values of their oppressors" (Perkins & Cross, 2014, p. 98).

Lillian and Seth

Lillian has internalized the unfair idea that as a female she must defer to men in positions of power. A social justice view maintains that holding this attitude keeps Lillian oppressed. Similarly, Seth opposes increased government taxation even though it would help fund his university education. From a social justice vantage point, he has internalized an anti-tax perspective that is false and not in his own best economic interests.

CASE EXAMPLES

Social justice therapies focus on **consciousness-raising,** which involves educating clients about racism, sexism, and other economic and social inequalities that they have unwittingly accepted and which lead to emotional distress (Goodman et al., 2004; Morrow, Hawxhurst, Montes de Vegas, Abousleman, & Castañeda, 2006; Toporek & Williams, 2006). Clients are encouraged to challenge the status quo and work toward a more just world, often with their therapists' assistance. Social justice therapists often step outside the therapy room and into the social world where they actively advocate for their clients because, from their perspective, traditional therapies too often adjust clients to oppressive social conditions rather than helping them fight for a more just society (Prilleltensky et al., 2007). From a social justice orientation, the most direct way to alleviate human suffering is not to change people but to change society.

From a social justice perspective, psychological distress is mainly attributable to economic inequality, racism, and sexism.
Source: PHOTOALTO

Lillian

Lillian grew up in a poor family. Her parents held very traditional ideas about the role of women in a family. If she were to see a therapist adopting a social justice perspective, the therapist might employ consciousness-raising by encouraging Lillian to examine social and cultural factors that have given rise to her current difficulties—specifically the detrimental effects of having been born into a male-dominated society and having been raised in a socioeconomically poor family that espoused traditional gender roles. As her consciousness is raised regarding ways she's been oppressed, Lillian might begin to stand up for herself more as she starts to question the attitudes she was taught about male and female roles by her parents and by the wider culture. She might begin to view her deference to Seth as due to her having internalized traditional gender roles. As therapy progresses, she might eventually break up with Seth. Her therapist would potentially encourage Lillian to become politically involved. Lillian might do so and gain further self-confidence as she fights for economic justice and equal treatment for women.

CASE EXAMPLES

CONSUMER AND SERVICE-USER PERSPECTIVES

So far, we have focused almost exclusively on conceptual models used by professionals to understand those they view as abnormal. This overlooks the experience of "abnormal people" themselves. In the broadest sense, **consumer and service-user perspectives** focus on "what it is like to be on the receiving end of the mental health system" (Campbell, 2013, p. 141). However, there are important differences between the consumer movement in general and the service-user/survivor movement specifically. Much of the **consumer movement** accepts psychiatric views of mental disorder and often finds traditional treatments helpful (Adame, 2014; Forbes & Sashidharan, 1997; Hölling, 2001). The movement's activism is "largely directed toward reducing the stigma of mental illness, reform of policy and practices, and generating more treatment choices within the mental health field" (Adame, 2014, p. 458). **Stigma** can be defined as society's negative and often hostile responses to people carrying certain marks or labels, in this case those related to mental disorder (Corrigan & Kleinlein, 2005). The consumer movement's goal is to better understand the needs and experiences of those stigmatized by mental disorders, thereby allowing professionals and the wider society to deal with them more compassionately and effectively. The consumer movement aims to rectify problematic social attitudes and practices to improve traditional psychiatric practice. Two of the most well-known consumer groups are the National Alliance on Mental Illness (NAMI) in the U.S. (mentioned in Chapter 1) and the Mental Health Foundation in the U.K.

By contrast, the **service-user/survivor movement** (also called the *psychiatric survivor movement*) rejects mainstream psychiatric perspectives, contending that many interventions—especially prescription drugs and involuntary treatments—are often inhumane, abusive, and fail to take into consideration the desires of the people forced to endure them (Bassman, 2001; Campbell, 2013; Crossley, 2004; Oaks, 2006). Like others advancing sociocultural perspectives, those who identify as psychiatric survivors frequently argue that the problems identified by psychiatry as mental disorders are better viewed as psychosocially caused problems in living. Therefore, they critically challenge and deconstruct medical model psychiatric perspectives. For instance, consider the experience of Matthew, a psychiatric survivor who ultimately rejected both his diagnosis and the mental health system that assigned it to him. Interviewed as part of a study exploring the experience of psychiatric survivors, Matthew described the professionals he encountered:

> It was just like they had all bought into this pathologizing model of mental illness. And they tried to inculcate you with that. And you were made to feel as if you were irreparably damaged inside your brain. And that you couldn't trust yourself anymore because you might become ill again. That was the message. And it was extremely damaging. (Adame, 2014, p. 460)

Many psychiatric survivor groups openly defy psychiatric authority. Herein, we mention two of them. The Hearing Voices Network (HVN) advances a psychosocial (rather than medical) view of auditory hallucinations (www.hearing-voices.org). Present in more than 20 countries, HVN advocates for "an alternative approach to coping with emotional distress that is empowering and useful to people, and does not start from the assumption that they have a chronic illness" (www.hearingvoicesusa.org). Another survivor group, MindFreedom International, identifies itself as an "independent nonprofit that unites 100 grassroots groups and thousands of members to peacefully take action for human rights in the mental health system" (www.mindfreedom.org/mfi-faq). Most of its members "identify themselves as 'psychiatric survivors,' that is, individuals who have personally experienced human rights violations in the mental health system" (www.mindfreedom.org/mfi-faq).

Not surprisingly, the relationship between the psychiatric survivor movement and professional psychiatry is uneasy at best. According to critics of the survivor movement, "organized psychiatry has found it difficult to have a constructive dialogue with" survivor groups because they see such groups as opposing psychiatry and as spreading "disinformation on the use of involuntary commitment, electroconvulsive therapy, stimulants and antidepressants among children, and neuroleptics among adults" (Rissmiller & Rissmiller, 2006, p. 866). However, survivor groups see things differently, contending that critics of the survivor movement unfairly dismiss "all public education efforts" that question the validity of psychiatric diagnosis and treatment; in their view psychiatry is defensive, having "generally refused our repeated invitations for conversation" (Oaks, 2006, p. 1212).

SYSTEMS PERSPECTIVES

Systems perspectives look at how individuals are influenced by and function within "systems" of relationships. What constitutes a **system** varies, ranging "from small groups such as the family to the largest, called civilization" (von Bertalanffy, 1969, p. 44). The main idea in systems perspectives is that individuals—ever-changing systems themselves—combine into larger systems that establish recurring patterns. How given individuals function is therefore best understood within the dynamic context of the broader system of relationships in which they exist. Because "systems are integrated wholes whose properties cannot be reduced to those of smaller units," systems theories tend to locate dysfunction and abnormality not in individuals, but in systemic patterns of relationships (Mitchell, 2015, para. 4).

One system of great interest to mental health professionals is the family. **Family systems therapy** looks at couple and family dynamics in trying to understand and remediate psychological issues. There are many different family systems theories, but all place recurring family patterns front and center in trying to understand abnormal behavior. From a family systems viewpoint, problems exist within a family's dynamics, not within its individual members (Dallos & Stedmon, 2014). Whoever in the family is the **identified patient** (the family member outwardly displaying symptoms) simply bears the burden of "carrying" the family's pathology. Instead of seeing individual family members as disordered, the family itself is diagnosed as dysfunctional in its propagation of problematic relationship patterns. Let's briefly examine two systemic approaches to get a feel for how family systems theories shift the locus of pathology from the person to the family.

Minuchin's Structural Family Therapy

Salvador Minuchin's (1921–2017) **structural family therapy** focuses on how unspoken **family rules** influence family members' behaviors (Minuchin, 1974). Structural family therapists posit that in many families, there are problems with **boundaries** between members—for instance, in **enmeshed families** the boundaries between members are blurred. Dysfunctional families also often form **coalitions**, in which some members are aligned with one another against other members. This can lead to problematic **power hierarchies** in which some coalitions dominate others in detrimental ways. The key to helping the family becomes establishing appropriate boundaries, addressing unspoken rules, and helping the family to communicate better so it can be more flexible in adapting to external demands.

Family systems therapy focuses on dysfunctional family dynamics, not disordered individuals. Perhaps the problem isn't you, but longstanding patterns in your family!
Source: PHOTOALTO

Bowen's Multigenerational Family Therapy

Murray Bowen's (1913–1990) **multigenerational family therapy** focuses on what he dubbed the **multigenerational transmission process**, in which families pass down their dysfunctional patterns from generation to generation (Bowen, 1978). Such families engage in a variety of problematic behaviors such as **triangulation**, in which two family members deal with conflict between them by pulling a third family member into the mix. The inevitable "two versus one" interaction that results only serves to create further family conflict. **Emotional cutoff** is another hallmark of dysfunctional families. It occurs when family members place emotional or physical distance between one another to avoid conflict. Bowen maintained that to overcome family dysfunction, **differentiation** must occur. That is, family members must distinguish their own thoughts and feelings from others in the family so that they can resist and eliminate problematic family patterns.

Seth

In Seth's family, his parents were often aligned against Seth and his younger brother. This sort of familial power hierarchy made it rare for Seth and his younger brother to have their feelings and opinions listened to or considered. Seth's younger brother spent a lot of time during childhood with his friends and away from the family; he eventually moved to California to get away from his controlling parents—an example of emotional cutoff. When it came to Seth, his parents often identified him as the family "troublemaker" with the "explosive temper." Thus, Seth became the identified patient even though his parents often displayed angry outbursts too, as did Seth's grandparents before them. From a family systems perspective, Seth's angry behavior could be accounted for by longstanding family patterns that had been passed down via a multigenerational transmission process. Were Seth to undergo family systems therapy, he might start to differentiate his own thoughts and feelings from those espoused by his parents. If effective, he'd begin thinking and behaving in new ways that are less influenced by past family patterns.

CASE EXAMPLES

EVALUATING SOCIOCULTURAL PERSPECTIVES

Strengths of sociocultural perspectives include:

1. *Social, cultural, and familial factors highlighted.* With its focus on the mental processes of the individual, psychology has often overlooked social, cultural, and family influences. Sociocultural perspectives counter this.

2. *Cultural differences accounted for.* Social justice perspectives emerged from the multicultural psychology movement, which emphasizes attending to how cultural assumptions play a strong role in what kinds of issues cause emotional distress and how people express that distress.

3. *Social change encouraged by attributing human suffering to oppressive social systems rather than unfairly blaming individuals.* Social justice perspectives avoid blaming individuals for their problems. Instead, they see family patterns, cultural norms, and unfair social conditions as the things that must be changed in order to alleviate psychological distress.

4. *The experience of people diagnosed with mental disorders is highlighted.* Most of the perspectives discussed in an abnormal psychology course are those advanced by mental health professionals. Consumer and service-user/survivor approaches encourage us to pay attention to the voices of those experiencing psychological distress.

Noted weaknesses of sociocultural perspectives include:

1. *Difficulty establishing causal connection between abnormality and social factors.* Those who see mental disorders as individual afflictions contend that social factors such as poverty and racism are correlated with emotional suffering, but whether they cause such suffering remains unclear. Critics tend to see social and cultural factors as exacerbating mental disorders, but not their primary cause.

2. *Familial and social conditions don't always produce abnormality.* Two different people facing the same oppressive familial and social conditions may respond quite differently, with one developing symptoms of abnormality and the other not. Sociocultural perspectives cannot account for this. Biological critics argue that sociocultural factors can only exacerbate or trigger individual disorders, but cannot explain them in their entirety.

3. *Tied to a specific political agenda.* Critics argue that social justice perspectives impose a left-wing political ideology on clients by objecting to the status quo of Western capitalism and demanding that clients and therapists adopt progressive positions on fair trade, unions, prison reform, education reform, environmental issues, and the minimum wage (Johnson, 2001; Raskin, 2014; Smith, Reynolds, & Rovnak, 2009).

4. *Consumer and service-user perspectives are either too extreme or not extreme enough.* Psychiatric survivor groups are often considered extreme in their antipsychiatry views. On the other hand, consumer groups may be too wedded to traditional medical model views of mental illness and, consequently, fail to see how traditional approaches can sometimes have damaging consequences for patients.

2.5 CLOSING THOUGHTS: SO MANY PERSPECTIVES!

The perspectives discussed in this chapter make different assumptions about what abnormality is, where it originates from, and what to do about it. However, many clinicians rely on and integrate multiple perspectives when working with people. This makes sense. Consider the relationship between psychological and biological perspectives. Clearly early childhood experiences, failure to self-actualize, irrational thinking, and environmental conditioning can all influence a person's biology—and vice versa! Thus, biological and psychological factors mutually influence one another, making biological and psychological perspectives incomplete on their own.

The same is true of psychological and sociocultural perspectives. Our sociocultural ideas about what it means to be a person—highly individualized in the Western world (where most of this book's ideas about abnormality originate)—surely affect the kinds of psychological theories that make sense to us. Freud, Skinner, Beck, Rogers, and most of the other theorists discussed in this chapter developed their theories within a Western social context. However, their ideas haven't simply emerged from this context, but also have had an unmistakable impact on it. Just as biological and psychological theories are mutually influential, so are sociocultural and psychological ones.

Lastly, biological and sociocultural perspectives are also interconnected. For example, researchers increasingly combine social and biological perspectives in looking at the relationship between social circumstances and physical health. They find that people under socially stressful circumstances are at higher risk of experiencing physical illness. Racism, socioeconomic and educational disadvantage, and undergoing military training have all been correlated with both physical illness and psychological distress (Grzywacz et al., 2004; Schmidt & Lerew, 1998; Williams et al., 1997). Biological and social factors undoubtedly influence one another when it comes to psychological maladjustment.

The point is that taking all perspectives on abnormality into account contributes to an integrative understanding of presenting problems. That said, just because perspectives are combined doesn't mean that the different assumptions they make about abnormality disappear. Sure, early childhood experiences likely influence brain development, but this doesn't make the psychodynamic perspective automatically adopt the same basic assumptions as the biological perspective. Yes, stress affects emotional well-being and physical health, but this doesn't change the fact that—at their core—biological and sociocultural perspectives hold fundamentally different views about abnormal behavior. The challenge for students of abnormal psychology is to balance efforts to understand each of the perspectives on its own with equally important efforts to combine them. That is what we will try to do throughout the rest of this book as we use psychological, biological, and sociocultural perspectives to understand a vast array of presenting problems. The "Controversial Question" feature asks how (or whether!) different theories should be combined in clinical practice.

CONTROVERSIAL QUESTION

Is Theoretical Integration a Good Idea?

As seen in this chapter, there are many compelling theories of abnormality. You may find it hard to choose among them because there are things about each that you like and dislike. You might even ask, "Can't I simply combine the best elements of each theory as I see fit?" Asking such a question means you've stumbled into an ongoing and complex debate that has long plagued the psychotherapy field—namely, whether theoretical integration is a good idea.

What is Psychotherapy Integration?

Numerous definitions of **psychotherapy integration** have been offered. In the broadest sense, integrating different psychotherapy approaches involves "ongoing rapprochement, convergence, and complementarity not only at the conceptual level but also at the clinical and empirical level" (Fernández-Álvarez, Consoli, & Gómez, 2016, p. 820). That's a fancy way of saying that links among different theories are identified and used together to develop effective therapy interventions. There are many reasons why integration is a contentious topic. Below we briefly identify two of them.

How Important Are Common Factors?

One of the more well-known integrationist positions is the **common factors** perspective. Common factor advocates argue that all effective therapies share certain features—such as a supportive and caring client–therapist relationship; they contend that these "common factors" are much more important in predicting therapy outcomes than specific interventions (Wampold & Imel, 2015). Thus, from a common factors standpoint, identifying what all effective therapies share is key to theoretical integration. The power of common factors is compelling—and consistent with humanistic therapies such as Carl Rogers' person-centered approach, which holds that core conditions are all that is necessary and sufficient for transformative change. However, critics of the common factors approach argue that it overlooks differences in the kinds of problems people bring to therapy. To these critics, specific interventions must be tailored to particular presenting problems (T. B. Baker, McFall, & Shoham, 2008). Many of the less relationally oriented therapies (such as CBT) hew toward the view that different clinical strategies—organized into empirically supported treatments (ESTs) consisting of a concrete series of standardized steps—must be devised depending on the presenting problem at hand (for more on ESTs, revisit Chapter 1). Debate over whether psychotherapy effectiveness studies best support common factors or ESTs continues to rage within the field (T. B. Baker et al., 2008; Wampold & Imel, 2015).

Does Integrating Theories Lead to a Theoretical Mess?

Even if there are common factors that cut across all effective therapies, when we combine different theories rooted in different assumptions, do we risk producing theoretical muddle? Unless attention is paid to the theoretical challenges integration produces, some critics think so. Such critics argue that **technical eclecticism** (combining the use of whatever techniques are shown to work) results in therapist confusion (Fernández-Álvarez et al., 2016). Without a clear theoretical base to guide decision-making, how does the technically eclectic therapist know what counts as a good outcome? To these critics, theoretical integration must be done carefully; when different ideas from different therapies are used together, it is necessary to think through the implications of combining them (Fernández-Álvarez et al., 2016). Along these lines, advocates of **assimilative integration** argue that when therapists operating from one theoretical perspective incorporate a technique from another theoretical perspective, they must be careful to think about how the theory they are using and the theory from which they are co-opting a technique are both changed (Messer, 2001). However, to the technically eclectic therapist, the only thing one needs worry about is whether a technique works in practice.

CRITICAL THINKING QUESTIONS

1. What risks and benefits do you see in psychotherapy integration?
2. Do you believe common factors that cut across all therapies are the most important in therapy outcomes? Or, are specific ESTs necessary to address different problems? If unsure, what evidence would you need to seek out to answer these questions?
3. Do you have a preference for technical eclecticism or assimilative integration? Why?

The thorny issue of theoretical integration notwithstanding, before forging ahead you might wish to spend some time thinking through your own emerging theoretical orientation. To that end, the "Try It Yourself" feature allows you to assess your current theoretical preferences. Feel free to return to this test periodically to see if your preferences change as you read subsequent chapters.

Theoretical Evaluation Self-Test

**TRY IT
YOURSELF**

Theoretical Evaluation Self-Test
CIRCLE the number which best reflects your agreement or disagreement with each item.

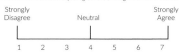

	Strongly Disagree			Neutral			Strongly Agree
	1	2	3	4	5	6	7

Statement	Rating
1. One central therapeutic factor is the symbolic recreation of a nurturing caretaker relationship with the therapist.	1 2 3 4 5 6 7
2. The therapist should educate the client about the relationship of patterns of cognition and many mental health problems.	1 2 3 4 5 6 7
3. The therapist's unconditional positive regard for the client is a crucial therapeutic factor.	1 2 3 4 5 6 7
4. It is important for therapists to see clients together with their families.	1 2 3 4 5 6 7
5. The therapeutic alliance is important primarily to provide a foundation for collaborative case management.	1 2 3 4 5 6 7
6. Human behavior is shaped by patterns of reinforcements and punishments in the environment.	1 2 3 4 5 6 7
7. Change occurs in therapy because of the therapist's empathic, non-judgmental, positive attitude towards the client.	1 2 3 4 5 6 7
8. Psychoeducation about the benefits and side effects of medications is an important part of treatment.	1 2 3 4 5 6 7
9. Dreams discussed in therapy can uncover significant unconscious wishes, conflicts and feelings.	1 2 3 4 5 6 7
10. Most psychotherapy theories are distractions from the central task of solving the client's problems.	1 2 3 4 5 6 7
11. Advocacy with other providers on behalf of clients is a central role of the therapist.	1 2 3 4 5 6 7
12. It is important for the therapist to respond to clients with spontaneous, genuine affect.	1 2 3 4 5 6 7
13. Primary emphasis should be placed on the client's interactions with his or her family.	1 2 3 4 5 6 7
14. The role of the therapist is to advise and guide the client.	1 2 3 4 5 6 7
15. Client's problems are often caused by negative patterns of thinking.	1 2 3 4 5 6 7
16. Psychological problems vary with the culture of the client.	1 2 3 4 5 6 7
17. Many mental health problems are effectively treated with medication.	1 2 3 4 5 6 7
18. The therapist should be active, directive and goal-oriented.	1 2 3 4 5 6 7
19. Client's problems are often contributed to by social problems and gaps in the social service system.	1 2 3 4 5 6 7
20. It is important to attend to what the client is projecting onto the therapist.	1 2 3 4 5 6 7
21. The therapist should teach clients techniques to address problem areas.	1 2 3 4 5 6 7
22. When one person in a family is experiencing problems, it is usually the expression of family communication and relationship problems.	1 2 3 4 5 6 7
23. Many clients can benefit from psychiatric medication.	1 2 3 4 5 6 7
24. It is important to assess not only the person seeking services, but his or her environment as well.	1 2 3 4 5 6 7
25. Change occurs in therapy through restoring healthy family structures.	1 2 3 4 5 6 7
26. It is essential for therapists to be aware of the values and worldview of their own culture and how they might affect clients.	1 2 3 4 5 6 7
27. Change occurs in therapy because of the client's insight into characteristic ways of relating with others set in early childhood.	1 2 3 4 5 6 7
28. It is helpful to ask questions to lead the client to realize their mistakes or misperceptions.	1 2 3 4 5 6 7
29. There is evidence that most mental health problems have biological causes.	1 2 3 4 5 6 7
30. Denial, repression, intellectualization and other defense mechanisms are important to understanding psychology.	1 2 3 4 5 6 7

CHAPTER 2

Scoring

SUBSCALE	YOUR SCORE	SAMPLE OF 130 mean / standard deviation
Psychodynamic Sum totals for Items 1, 9, 20, 27, and 30 and divide by 5		26.2 / 5.2
Biological Sum totals for Items 8, 17, 23, and 29 and divide by 4		14.6 / 4.0
Family Sum totals for Items 4, 13, 22, and 25 and divide by 4		18.2 / 4.0
Ecosystems Sum totals for Items 16, 19, 24, and 26 and divide by 4		24.2 / 2.6
Cognitive Sum totals for Items 2, 6, 15, 21, and 28 and divide by 5		25 / 4.5
Pragmatic Sum totals for Items 5, 10, 11, 14, and 18 and divide by 5		20.1 / 5.7
Humanistic Sum totals for Items 3, 7, and 12 and divide by 3		10.4 / 2.4

INTERPRETING YOUR SCORE: The reliability of the scale is adequate to discriminate group differences, but not individual differences. These scores should be used to stimulate reflection, but not as precise measurements of individual theoretical orientation.

© Coleman, D. (2004). *Theoretical Evaluation Self-Test (TEST): A preliminary validation study*, Social Work Research, 28(2), 117–127. doi:10.1093/swr/28.2.117. Reprinted with permission of Oxford University Press.

KEY TERMS

ABCDE model
Action potential
Actualizing tendency
Allele
Amino acids
Amygdala
Anal stage
Anal-expulsive
Anal-retentive
Assimilative integration
Attachment theory
Authenticity
Automatic thoughts
Awfulizing
Behavior therapy
Boundaries
Brain chemistry perspectives
Brain stem
Brain structure and function
   perspectives
Catecholamines
Catharsis
Cerebellum
Cerebrum
Chromosomes
Classical conditioning
Coalitions
Cognitive distortions
Cognitive perspectives
Cognitive restructuring
Cognitive specificity hypothesis
Cognitive therapy
Cognitive-behavioral therapy (CBT)
Common factors
Conditional positive regard
Conditioned response (CR)
Conditioned stimulus (CS)
Congruence
Conscious
Consciousness-raising
Constructivist perspectives
Consumer and service-user
   perspectives
Consumer movement
Core beliefs
Core conditions for change
Corpus callosum
Corrective emotional experience
Countertransference
Culture
Culture-bound syndromes
Cyclical maladaptive pattern
Daily Record of Dysfunctional
   Thoughts (DRDT)
Defense mechanisms
Delay of gratification
Differentiation
DNA (deoxyribonucleic acid)
Dopamine
Dream analysis

Ego
Electra complex
Emotional cutoff
Empathy
Enmeshed families
Entorhinal cortex
Evolutionary perspectives
Existential psychotherapies
Exposure plus response prevention
Exposure therapies
Externalizing the problem
Extinction
False consciousness
Family rules
Family systems therapy
Feminist therapy
Fitness
Fixation
Free association
Gamma-aminobutyric acid (GABA)
General paresis
Genes
Genetic perspectives
Genital stage
Genome
Genotype
Genuineness
Glutamate
Heritability
Heritability estimate
Hippocampus
Humanistic perspectives
Id
Identified patient
Immune system perspectives
Inauthenticity
Incongruence
Indolamines
Intermediate beliefs
Latency stage
Libido
Limbic system
Monoamines
Multicultural perspectives
Multigenerational family therapy
Multigenerational transmission process
Musterbating
Narrative therapy
Negative punishment
Negative reinforcement
Neurons
Neurosis
Neurotransmitters
Norepinephrine
Nucleotides
Nucleus accumbens
Object
Object relations therapy
Oedipus complex
Operant conditioning

Oral stage
Orbitofrontal cortex
Organismic valuing process
Pathogens
Person-centered therapy
Phallic stage
Phenotype
Pleasure principle
Polygenic
Positive punishment
Positive reinforcement
Power hierarchies
Preconscious
Projective identification
Psychic determinism
Psychic energy
Psychoanalysis
Psychodynamic perspectives
Psychotherapy integration
Punishers
Rational emotive
   behavior therapy
   (REBT)
Reality principle
Reductionism
Reinforcers
Repression
Resistance
RNA (ribonucleic acid)
Schemas
Self-actualization
Serotonin
Service-user/survivor movement
Slips of the tongue
Social construction
Social justice perspectives
Social learning theory
Splitting
Stigma
Structural family therapy
Structural model
Superego
Survival of the fittest
System
Systematic desensitization
Systems perspectives
Technical eclecticism
Time-limited dynamic
   psychotherapy (TLDP)
Topographic model
Transference
Triangulation
Unconditional positive regard
Unconditioned response (UR)
Unconditioned stimulus (US)
Unconscious
Viral explanation of general paresis
Viral theories
Wish fulfillment
Working through

Full definitions of the terms listed above can be found in the end-of-book glossary on p. 533.

Go to the companion website, www.macmillanihe.com/raskin-abnormal-psych, to access a study guide, multiple choice and flashcard quizzes for this chapter, and other useful learning aids.

CHAPTER 3
DIAGNOSIS, FORMULATION, AND ASSESSMENT

3.1 OVERVIEW

LEARNING OBJECTIVES

After reading this chapter, you should be able to:

1. Explain the origins of the term "diagnosis" and distinguish medical and non-medical ways of using the term.
2. Name the organizations that author the *Diagnostic and Statistical Manual of Mental Disorders (DSM)* and *International Classification of Diseases (ICD)*, and describe the historical antecedents of both manuals.
3. Identify the current editions of the *DSM* and *ICD*, recite their respective definitions of mental disorder, and define diagnostic guidelines, diagnostic criteria, and diagnostic codes.
4. Explain what reliability and validity are, and explain their importance in evaluating the *DSM* and *ICD*.
5. Describe the success and influence of the *DSM* and *ICD*, summarize the advantages and criticisms of these manuals, and identify trends for these manuals' future development.
6. Define what formulation is, outline two types of formulation, and evaluate the strengths and weaknesses typically ascribed to formulation.
7. Explain and evaluate these approaches to diagnosis: *Psychodynamic Diagnostic Manual (PDM)*, Research Domain Criteria (RDoC), and Hierarchical Taxonomy of Psychopathology (HiTOP).
8. Summarize the following forms of assessment: clinical interviews (unstructured and structured), personality tests (objective and projective), cognitive and behavioral forms of assessment, humanistic forms of assessment, intelligence tests, neuropsychological tests, and neurological tests.
9. Define what culture bias is, and explain how awareness of it is important in thinking about diagnosis, formulation, and assessment.

Photo source: © Royalty-Free/Corbis

GETTING STARTED: DEFINING DIAGNOSIS

Jill

Jill is a 20-year-old student who arrives in therapy feeling anxious and lacking the motivation to complete her schoolwork. She is studying medicine, something her parents always wanted her to do. However, she complains that she cannot focus on her work and regularly feels fidgety and short-tempered. In addition, she reports difficulty sleeping, daily stomachaches, and occasional shortness of breath. Growing up, Jill danced ballet. However, she gave up dancing because her parents were concerned that it interfered with her medical studies. Jill appears touchy and tense during her first session, as well as a bit sad and helpless over her situation.

CASE EXAMPLES

Perspectives on Diagnosis

Before we can assist someone like Jill, we need to evaluate the situation and identify the problem. In a nutshell, this is what diagnosis, formulation, and assessment are about. The challenge for students is that mental health professionals hold contrasting opinions about them and, consequently, go about them in a variety of ways. This chapter introduces some of the main approaches to diagnosis, formulation, and assessment.

The word "diagnosis" came into modern use in the late 17th century. It is a Latin application of the Ancient Greek words *dia* ("through") and *gignoskein* ("to know"). In modern phrasing, it simply means "to know thoroughly" or to "discern or distinguish" (Online Etymology Dictionary, n.d.). What confuses abnormal psychology students is that some mental health professionals adopt a definition that defines **diagnosis** as a medical procedure for determining the "nature and circumstances of a diseased condition" (Dictionary.com, n.d.-c). However, others opt for an alternative, non-medical definition, viewing diagnosis as merely seeking "the cause or nature of a problem or situation" (Dictionary.com, n.d.-c). This means that the term "diagnosis" can be (and often is!) used in a variety of ways.

Of course, how we use the term diagnosis influences how we understand problems we consider abnormal.

Jill

Let's revisit the case of Jill. If we think of diagnosis in medical terms, we might diagnose Jill as suffering from an underlying mental disorder such as generalized anxiety disorder (discussed shortly); if we think about diagnosis in psychological terms instead, we might diagnose Jill as failing to self-actualize or as engaging in overly negative and irrational thinking; and if we switch to a sociocultural definition, we shift away from diagnosing the problem as something medically or psychologically wrong inside Jill and instead might diagnose her difficulties as due to deficits in her surroundings, such as insufficient social support to succeed in her studies. All three "diagnoses" posit a cause of Jill's presenting problem, but in very different terms (as mental disorder, illogical thinking, or lack of social support).

CASE EXAMPLES

This illustrates that abnormal psychology has a number of competing diagnostic **nomenclatures**—a term that refers to any system of names used in a field of study (Merriam-Webster Dictionary, n.d.). We now turn to some of the more influential ones.

3.2 PSYCHIATRIC DIAGNOSIS: *DSM* AND *ICD* PERSPECTIVES

When it comes to diagnosing emotional distress, the *Diagnostic and Statistical Manual of Mental Disorders (DSM)* (introduced in Chapter 1) and the mental, behavioral, and neurodevelopmental disorders section of the ***International Classification of Diseases (ICD)*** are the two most prevalent diagnostic systems. They are generally referred to as forms of **psychiatric diagnosis** because even though every kind of mental health practitioner uses them, primarily psychiatrists develop them. Given that psychiatrists are medical doctors, it should come as no surprise that both the *DSM* and *ICD* use a medical model in which clusters of symptoms are organized into distinct **syndromes** consisting of **symptoms** (presenting complaints) and **signs** (physical changes) (Kawa & Giordano, 2012; Paris, 2015). In this respect, they utilize **categorical diagnosis**, where similar patterns of symptoms and signs are grouped into categories and distinguished as distinct disorders.

By grouping observable symptoms and signs into categories, the *DSM* and *ICD* also exemplify **descriptive psychopathology**, in which diagnoses are made using descriptions of how people think, feel, and act rather than measures of underlying **etiology** (a medical term for "cause") (Zachar, 2009). Why are *DSM* and *ICD* diagnoses merely descriptive when the medical model assumes disorders reflect dysfunctions (i.e., psychopathology) inside people? Because, despite all the research being done, we currently still don't know the underlying etiology of *DSM* and *ICD* disorders. We therefore lack the ability to make diagnoses based on underlying causes (Paris, 2015). Descriptive psychopathology is currently the best we can do!

Familiarity with the *DSM* and *ICD* is essential in studying abnormal psychology because they are the diagnostic systems most often employed in clinical practice. Both manuals are used all over the world. In the United States, the *DSM* remains dominant, though the *ICD* is making inroads (Goodheart, 2014; "ICD vs. DSM," 2009). Regardless of which is used, in the U.S. these manuals play a central role in getting mental health services covered by health insurance (Goodheart, 2014). Given their dominance in clinical practice, it is important to understand how the *DSM* and *ICD* are used to conceptualize and diagnose abnormality.

WHO WRITES THEM?

ICD

The *ICD* is an international classification system authored by the World Health Organization (WHO), which is part of the United Nations (G. M. Reed, 2010). Its scope is broader than simply mental health. The *ICD* catalogs all internationally recognized "diseases, disorders, injuries, and related health problems" (Goodheart, 2014, p. 13). Currently, 194 WHO member countries have signed an international treaty that commits them to using the *ICD*'s coding system for reporting health information (Goodheart, 2014; G. M. Reed, 2010; M. C. Roberts & Evans, 2013). To many people, this makes the *ICD* "the clinical and research standard for the world, for both physical and mental disorders" (Goodheart, 2014, p. 13; M. C. Roberts & Evans, 2013). In abnormal psychology, we focus almost exclusively on just one part of the *ICD*: the classification of mental, behavioral, and neurodevelopmental disorders section (World Health Organization, 1992, 2018a). This section is overseen by an advisory committee consisting primarily of academics with affiliations mostly in psychiatry departments (World Health Organization, 2015).

DSM

While the *ICD* is developed internationally under the auspices of the U.N.'s World Health Organization, the *DSM* is a purely American product. Despite being an American rather than international undertaking, some consider the *DSM* (rather than the *ICD*) the standard for research and practice throughout the world (Paris, 2015). It is written and published by the American Psychiatric Association, the professional organization of American psychiatry. In other words, psychiatrists (not psychologists) author it. So even though psychologists and other mental health professionals use it, psychiatrists publish it, making it the official diagnostic system of American psychiatry—a medical specialty with a medical identity (Kawa & Giordano, 2012).

Besides the *ICD* being international and the *DSM* being American, another important difference between them is that the *ICD-10* and *ICD-11* are available for free and can be accessed online (World Health Organization, 1992, 2018a), whereas the *DSM-5* must be purchased. As of 2018, the *DSM-5*'s list price is $128 (eBook), $160 (paperback), or $210 (hardcover) in the U.S. and £118 (paperback) or £156 (hardcover) in the U.K. In the European Union, prices of translated editions vary by country, ranging roughly between €123 and €169. An abridged desk reference and an app for phones and tablets are also available and sell for less.

HISTORICAL PERSPECTIVES

ICD

The *ICD*'s origins predate the WHO. In 1893, the International Statistical Institute developed the first edition of the *International List of Causes of Death*. This manual went through numerous revisions over the years. When the WHO was established in 1948, it was charged with overseeing the manual, its name now changed to the *International Classification of Diseases, Injuries, and Causes of Death*. That year, *ICD-6* was published and it included a section on mental disorders—although technically mental disorders first appeared in *ICD-5* even though there wasn't a clearly demarcated section for them (Halter, Rolin-Kenny, & Grund, 2013). There have been six versions of the *ICD* since the WHO began overseeing it and these days its name has been shortened to the simpler *International Classification of Diseases*. At the time of writing (2018), the version used in most countries is the *ICD-10*, which was completed in 1992. The *ICD-11* was released in June 2018 and will go into effect in January 2022, giving WHO member countries time to plan their transition to it (A. Stewart, 2018). WHO nations will continue to use the *ICD-10* until they each formally review and adopt the *ICD-11*. Thus, the *ICD-10* will remain in use while countries—each at their own pace—transition to the *ICD-11*. This is why we cover both *ICD-10* and *ICD-11* diagnoses throughout the rest of the book.

DSM

Modern *DSM* diagnosis is heavily influenced by the work of the late 19th-century German psychiatrist Emil Kraepelin (1856–1926), who was among the first to catalog psychological disorders (Decker, 2013; Halter et al., 2013). Kraepelin examined groups of symptoms and organized them into categories of disorder in the hope that eventually their causes would be uncovered; this goal is similar to the current *DSM* system (Decker, 2013; Kirk & Kutchins, 1992).

In the U.S., the first efforts at diagnostic classification were related to a very practical purpose, namely counting abnormal people for the census (Halter et al., 2013; Kawa & Giordano, 2012; Kirk & Kutchins, 1992). The first time this was done, during the 1840 census, there was only one category (idiocy) that included people considered insane; by 1880, the census included seven categories: mania, melancholia, paresis, monomania, dementia, epilepsy, and dipsomania (Kirk & Kutchins, 1992). Census goals were no longer the focus by 1918 when the American Medico-Psychological Association (a precursor to today's American Psychiatric Association) developed a standardized diagnostic system, the *Statistical Manual for the Use of Institutions for the Insane*, which included 22 diagnostic categories. By 1942, this manual had gone through ten different editions (Kawa & Giordano, 2012; Kirk & Kutchins, 1992). It is generally considered to be the forerunner of today's *DSM* system. The 1918 version is available online (https://archive.org/details/statisticalmanu00assogoog). Because this early manual focused on serious disorders found mostly in inpatient settings, its utility in addressing concerns more typical of the general population was limited. Therefore, during the Second World War, the U.S.

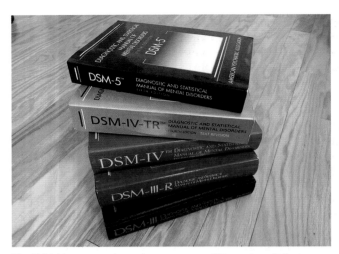

The DSM *has gone through numerous editions since it first appeared in 1952. The most recent edition, DSM-5, was published in 2013.*
Source: Jonathan D. Raskin

Army and Surgeon General developed **Medical 203**, a classification system that also included less acute problems common in soldiers and veterans (Halter et al., 2013). Medical 203 is often seen as the immediate predecessor to the *DSM* (Halter et al., 2013).

The American Psychiatric Association published *DSM-I*, with 106 categories, in 1952; the 182-category *DSM-II* appeared in 1968 (Decker, 2013). Neither was especially influential (Shorter, 2013). The *DSM-II*, in particular, was seen as having a psychoanalytic bent (Shorter, 2013). It was the *DSM-III* in 1980 that really changed psychiatric diagnosis (Decker, 2013; Kawa & Giordano, 2012; Kirk & Kutchins, 1992; Paris, 2015). Heralded as a triumph of "science over ideology" (Kawa & Giordano, 2012), the *DSM-III* tried to rely on scientific data more than previous editions had done to determine what belonged in the manual. Importantly, its 265 categories contained two features now considered essential to *DSM* diagnosis: diagnostic criteria and diagnostic codes (both discussed below). The *DSM-III-R* ("R" for "revised"), with 292 categories, appeared in 1987 and the *DSM-IV*, with 297 categories, debuted in 1994. In 2000, the *DSM-IV* was republished in slightly revised form as *DSM-IV-TR* ("TR" for "text revision"), but without changes to *DSM-IV* diagnostic categories (Kawa & Giordano, 2012; Paris, 2015).

CURRENT VERSIONS

ICD

After the *ICD-10* was completed in 1992, many WHO member countries adopted it within a decade or so and continue to use it (Bohnett, 2013). Remarkably, the United States trailed behind the rest of the world in this regard (Bohnett, 2013). The U.S. didn't shift to *ICD-10* until October 2015. Some of the delay was because the U.S. modifies the *ICD* to make it easier to use for insurance reimbursement and statistical recording purposes. The process of switching from the *ICD-9-CM* (with CM standing for the U.S.'s "clinical modification" of the manual) to *ICD-10-CM* was delayed several times due to resistance from U.S. doctors and the healthcare industry, who were concerned that the change would produce too many errors in insurance claims submissions (Friedan, 2015; Kirkner, 2015). It will be interesting to see how long it takes WHO member nations to transition to the *ICD-11*; they will begin doing so in 2022 (A. Stewart, 2018).

DSM

The current version of the manual, *DSM-5*, was published in 2013 and includes 541 categories (Paris, 2015). It is organized into three sections. Section I is "*DSM-5* Basics," which introduces the manual and reviews how to use it. Section II is "Diagnostic Criteria and Codes." It contains criteria, codes, and additional information for all officially recognized mental disorders. Importantly, Section II also constitutes the bulk of the *DSM-5*. Section III is "Emerging Measures and Models," which includes various assessment measures, cultural information, an alternative proposal for personality disorders, and conditions for further study; this section contains proposals for new measures and new disorders that are not yet officially recognized. Every edition of the *DSM* since *DSM-III* has been highly influential and used extensively in research and practice (Kawa & Giordano, 2012). The *DSM-5* promises to continue this trend.

DEFINITION OF DISORDER

ICD

The *ICD-10* acknowledges that "disorder" is an inexact term, but prefers it to terms such as "disease" and "illness," which it says are problematic (although it doesn't explain why). The **ICD definition of mental disorder**—roughly comparable in both the *ICD-10* and *ICD-11* but expanded somewhat in the latter (World Health Organization, 1992, 2018a)—defines a disorder as an underlying dysfunction in psychological, biological, or developmental processes that affects cognition, emotional regulation, and behavior. According to the *ICD*, social deviance and conflict alone aren't sufficient for something to be a mental disorder. In other words, being socially rebellious or disagreeable isn't disordered; there must also be "personal dysfunction" (World Health Organization, 1992), which implies something malfunctioning within the person.

DSM

The **DSM-5 definition of mental disorder** also locates disorders inside people, defining a disorder as "a syndrome characterized by clinically significant disturbance in an individual's cognition, emotion regulation, or behavior that reflects a dysfunction in the psychological, biological, or developmental processes underlying mental functioning" (American Psychiatric Association, 2013b, p. 20). According to this definition, disorders are internal dysfunctions within us that impact how we think, feel, and behave. Despite the *DSM* using a medical model in which disorders constitute something broken inside people, what is broken isn't necessarily biological—as with the *ICD*, dysfunctions viewed as psychological or developmental count too. Because the *DSM* only considers itself a descriptive manual, it takes no official position on what causes the disorders it contains. It merely specifies that mental disorders typically disrupt social, occupational, or other functioning. Importantly, like the *ICD*, the *DSM* distinguishes social deviance from mental disorder. It doesn't consider civil disobedience (during which people may violate social norms) or culturally expected responses to everyday stressors (such as mourning the death of a loved one) to be mental disorders (American Psychiatric Association, 2013b).

GUIDELINES, CRITERIA, AND CODES
Diagnostic Guidelines

The *ICD* provides **diagnostic guidelines** to help clinicians make diagnoses. Diagnostic guidelines are sets of descriptors used to gauge whether a patient qualifies for a diagnosis. Although the goal is to provide clear and agreed upon sets of symptoms, the *ICD-10* purposely worded its guidelines to provide diagnostic flexibility and allow clinicians to use their own judgment in determining when specific guidelines apply (WHO, 1992). As such, the *ICD-10*'s diagnostic guidelines utilize a **prototype model** in which general guidelines describe a syndrome and clinicians are expected to impressionistically use the descriptive guidelines to decide whether a patient's presentation approximates (or looks enough like) the disorder at hand (Maj, 2015; Paris, 2015; D. J. Stein, Lund, & Nesse, 2013). Table 3.1 contains an example of *ICD-10* diagnostic guidelines, in this case for generalized anxiety disorder (GAD), exemplified by excessive and consistent worry that is global rather than specific (and discussed further in Chapter 6). The guidelines for the *ICD-11* (see Table 3.2) are a bit more structured than those in *ICD-10*. Although not finalized, lists of "essential features" are being developed, which specify in greater detail the symptoms required for a diagnosis, as well as their minimum duration (First, Reed, Hyman, & Saxena, 2015).

Table 3.1 *ICD-10* Diagnostic Guidelines for Generalized Anxiety Disorder

The sufferer must have primary symptoms of anxiety most days for at least several weeks at a time, and usually for several months. These symptoms should usually involve elements of:

a. apprehension (worries about future misfortunes, feeling "on edge", difficulty in concentrating, etc.);

b. motor tension (restless fidgeting, tension headaches, trembling, inability to relax); and

c. autonomic overactivity (lightheadedness, sweating, tachycardia or tachypnoea, epigastric discomfort, dizziness, dry mouth, etc.).

In children, frequent need for reassurance and recurrent somatic complaints may be prominent.

The transient appearance (for a few days at a time) of other symptoms, particularly depression, does not rule out generalized anxiety disorder as a main diagnosis, but the sufferer must not meet the full criteria for depressive episode (F32.-), phobic anxiety disorder (F40.-), panic disorder (F41.0), or obsessive-compulsive disorder (F42.-).

Includes: anxiety neurosis anxiety reaction anxiety state

Excludes: neurasthenia (F48.0)

Source: Reproduced from World Health Organization (1992, p. 116).

Table 3.2 *ICD-11* Diagnostic Guidelines for Generalized Anxiety Disorder

- Marked symptoms of anxiety that persist for at least several months, for more days than not, manifested by either:
  - general apprehensiveness that is not restricted to any particular environmental circumstance (i.e., "free-floating anxiety"); or
  - excessive worry (apprehensive expectation) about negative events occurring in several different aspects of everyday life (e.g., work, finances, health, family).

- Anxiety and general apprehensiveness or worry are accompanied by characteristic additional symptoms, such as:
  - muscle tension or motor restlessness;
  - sympathetic autonomic overactivity as evidenced by frequent gastrointestinal symptoms such as nausea and/or abdominal distress, heart palpitations, sweating, trembling, shaking, and/or dry mouth;
  - subjective experience of nervousness, restlessness, or being "on edge";
  - difficulties maintaining concentration;
  - irritability;
  - sleep disturbances (difficulty falling or staying asleep, or restless, unsatisfying sleep).

- The symptoms are not transient and persist for at least several months, for more days than not.

- The symptoms are not a manifestation of another health condition (e.g., hyperthyroidism), are not due to the effect of a substance or medication on the central nervous system (e.g., coffee, cocaine), including withdrawal effects (e.g., alcohol, benzodiazepines), and are not better accounted for by another mental and behavioural disorder (e.g., a depressive disorder).

- The symptoms are sufficiently severe to result in significant distress about experiencing persistent anxiety symptoms or result in significant impairment in personal, family, social, educational, occupational, or other important areas of functioning.

Source: Reproduced from https://gcp.network/en/private/icd-11-guidelines/categories/disorder/trastorno-de-ansiedad-generalizada

Diagnostic Criteria

The *DSM* uses **diagnostic criteria** instead of diagnostic guidelines. They are like diagnostic guidelines, but more strict and precise in specifying the number of symptoms a patient needs and how long these symptoms must be present. In this respect, *DSM* diagnostic criteria employ an **algorithmic model**, in which clinicians are asked to observe countable criteria (Paris, 2015). Diagnostic criteria were first added to the *DSM* in 1980's revolutionary *DSM-III*, but each revision since then has aimed for greater specificity in operationalizing its criteria (Kawa & Giordano, 2012).

Table 3.3 shows the *DSM-5* diagnostic criteria for generalized anxiety disorder. Compare these to the *ICD* guidelines in Tables 3.1 and 3.2, then think about what kind of information you might need to determine if Jill (the case study introduced at the start of this chapter) qualifies for a diagnosis. Note how the *DSM* criteria—in being more precise in specifying what is needed to make a diagnosis—leave less room for clinical judgment than the *ICD* criteria. In the case of generalized anxiety disorder, the *DSM* is more specific about how many symptoms are required (three of six) and how long these symptoms must be present (six months, as opposed to "several months" in the *ICD*). With their specificity, diagnostic criteria are intended to reduce errors in clinician judgment and enhance diagnostic reliability (discussed more below).

Table 3.3 *DSM-5* Diagnostic Criteria for Generalized Anxiety Disorder

A. Excessive anxiety and worry (apprehensive expectation), occurring more days than not for at least 6 months, about a number of events or activities (such as work or school performance).

B. The individual finds it difficult to control the worry.

C. The anxiety and worry are associated with three (or more) of the following six symptoms (with at least some symptoms having been present for more days than not for the past 6 months). Note: Only one item is required in children.

  1. Restlessness or feeling keyed up or on edge.

> 2. Being easily fatigued.
>
> 3. Difficulty concentrating or mind going blank.
>
> 4. Irritability.
>
> 5. Muscle tension.
>
> 6. Sleep disturbance (difficulty falling or staying asleep, or restless, unsatisfying sleep).
>
> D. The anxiety, worry, or physical symptoms cause clinically significant distress or impairment in social, occupational, or other important areas of functioning.
>
> E. The disturbance is not attributable to the direct physiological effects of a substance (e.g., a drug of abuse, a medication) or a general medical condition (e.g., hyperthyroidism).
>
> F. The disturbance is not better explained by another mental disorder (e.g., anxiety or worry about having panic attacks in panic disorder, negative evaluation in social anxiety disorder [social phobia], contamination or other obsessions in obsessive-compulsive disorder, separation from attachment figures in separation anxiety disorder, reminders of traumatic events in posttraumatic stress disorder, gaining weight in anorexia nervosa, physical complaints in somatic symptom disorder, perceived appearance flaws in body dysmorphic disorder, having a serious illness in illness anxiety disorder, or the content of delusional beliefs in schizophrenia or delusional disorder).

Source: Reprinted with permission from the *Diagnostic and Statistical Manual of Mental Disorders*, Fifth Edition, (Copyright ©2013). American Psychiatric Association. All Rights Reserved.

Diagnostic Codes

Every diagnostic category in the *ICD* has a unique diagnostic code. A **diagnostic code** is an alphanumeric key assigned to each disorder (O'Malley et al., 2005). For instance, the diagnostic code for generalized anxiety disorder is F41.1 in the *ICD-10* and 6A70 in the *ICD-11* (World Health Organization, 1992, 2018a). Diagnostic codes are useful for record-keeping purposes, making it easier to track things such as incidence and prevalence rates in various populations (incidence and prevalence are defined in Chapter 1). Importantly, diagnostic codes originate in the *ICD*, not the *DSM* (Goodheart, 2014; O'Malley et al., 2005). However, the *DSM* appropriates and uses *ICD* codes (O'Malley et al., 2005). This allows for "harmonization" across the *ICD* and *DSM*, with the goal of the *ICD* and *DSM* authors being to make the manuals as consistent and similar as possible (American Psychiatric Association, 2013b; Goodheart, 2014). Results of this harmonization are mixed (Blashfield, Keeley, Flanagan, & Miles, 2014; McGuffin & Farmer, 2014). Differences between *ICD* and *DSM* remain—a situation made more complicated because, as previously noted, the U.S. only recently adopted *ICD-10* while the WHO is shifting attention to the *ICD-11* (Blashfield et al., 2014).

Including *ICD* diagnostic codes in the *DSM* is important for a very practical reason. As previously mentioned, in the U.S. these codes are used for insurance billing (O'Malley et al., 2005). To collect payments from insurance companies for services provided, American clinicians need to assign each patient a reimbursable diagnostic code. As they have become increasingly aware that the codes in the *DSM* are taken directly from the *ICD*, some American mental health professionals have begun to question whether purchasing and using the *DSM* is necessary at all (Gornall, 2013). After all, the same codes (and very similar "harmonized" diagnoses) are freely available online by downloading the mental health disorders section of the *ICD-10* (World Health Organization, 1992).

RELIABILITY
What is Diagnostic Reliability?

Because diagnostic guidelines and diagnostic criteria provide standardized rules for deciding whether someone qualifies for a diagnosis, they potentially enhance **reliability**. Reliable measures yield similar results each time. Diagnostic guidelines and diagnostic criteria help with a type of reliability called **interrater reliability**. A diagnostic category has good interrater reliability when different raters using the same diagnostic criteria or guidelines reach the same diagnosis much of the time. Without diagnostic criteria and guidelines, clinicians trying to decide whether someone should be diagnosed with a disorder must decide for themselves whether specific behaviors count. This potentially yields poor reliability, with different clinicians assigning different diagnoses for the same presenting problem. You can probably see why this is bad. If one psychologist diagnoses a client with generalized anxiety disorder, a second diagnoses bipolar disorder, and a third diagnoses narcissistic personality disorder, this clearly will create confusion. *DSM-5* Task Force member Helena Kraemer, in an interview with *Psychiatric News*, explained the problem of poor diagnostic reliability quite simply:

> *If two clinicians give a patient two different diagnoses, you know at least one of them has to be wrong. ... And the clinician who was wrong may have given the patient a treatment that was unnecessary for a condition the patient didn't have. (Moran, 2012, para. 3)*

Diagnostic criteria and guidelines try to prevent this by having all raters use the same rules for defining what counts as a symptom when making diagnoses.

Diagnostic Criteria and Reliability

The *DSM*'s more specific and algorithmic diagnostic criteria potentially should yield even better reliability than the *ICD*'s prototype-oriented diagnostic guidelines because they leave less room for interpretation (Paris, 2015). Thus, it has been observed that

> *high reliability is now accepted as a prerequisite for research and this could in part explain why since DSM-III the American Psychiatric Association's criteria have overtaken ICD as the more favoured system of classification used in research papers around the world. (McGuffin & Farmer, 2014, p. 195)*

A clinician consulting the *DSM-5* knows that a client must display at least three of six symptoms for a minimum of six months before being diagnosed with generalized anxiety disorder. The more specific the guidelines are, the more agreement we are likely to get when clinicians make diagnoses. However, some clinicians believe that making criteria too specific prevents them from exercising clinical judgment—this despite some provocative research suggesting that clinicians often overestimate the accuracy of their clinical judgment (Garb, Lilienfeld, & Fowler, 2016). The goal in using diagnostic criteria and guidelines is to reduce variations in clinical judgment and enhance diagnostic reliability.

Reliability and *DSM-5*

When the *DSM-III* was published in 1980, it was hailed for improving diagnostic reliability (American Psychiatric Association, 2013b; Decker, 2013; Kirk & Kutchins, 1992). All versions of *DSM* since have generally had a good reputation when it comes to reliability and a solid body of research suggests that some *DSM-5* categories—such as posttraumatic stress disorder, schizophrenia, autism spectrum disorder, and bipolar disorder—can be diagnosed quite reliably (Clarke et al., 2013; Freedman et al., 2013; Narrow et al., 2013; Regier et al., 2013). However, the research also shows mediocre to poor reliability for other *DSM-5* categories—including widely used diagnoses such as major depression and generalized anxiety disorder (Freedman et al., 2013). Critics contend that the *DSM-5* has lowered standards for what counts as reliable (K. D. Jones, 2012; Spitzer, Williams, & Endicott, 2012; Vanheule et al., 2014) and that the manual's reputation for reliability is unwarranted (Lacasse, 2014; Obiols, 2012). However, those responsible for the *DSM-5* contend that such criticisms are unfair and that the *DSM* has paid greater attention to reliability than other medical specialties have (H. C. Kraemer, Kupfer, Clarke, Narrow, & Regier, 2012; Moran, 2012). We revisit the controversial yet important issue of diagnostic reliability throughout this text as we discuss different *ICD* and *DSM* disorders.

VALIDITY
What is Diagnostic Validity?

Diagnostic **validity** is concerned with whether a diagnostic measure is accurate in measuring what it is supposed to (Paris, 2015). There are various kinds of validity relevant to diagnosis: *descriptive validity* (does a diagnosis accurately describe what is being observed?), *face validity* (on the face of it, does a diagnosis seem accurate?), *predictive validity* (does a diagnosis allow us to predict outcomes?), *construct validity* (does a diagnosis correlate with other measures that we think are getting at the same thing?), and *concurrent validity* (is the diagnosis consistent with other measures assessing the same disorder and given concurrently—that is, at the same time?). Each of these types of validity is important in thinking about the diagnostic validity of *ICD* and *DSM* categories.

Validity for mental disorders has generally proven rather elusive because there isn't agreement in the field about what a mental disorder is. Without a widely accepted definition, it is hard to know what is or isn't a disorder (Kirk & Kutchins, 1992; Paris, 2015). This may explain why the *DSM* has often focused more on reliability than validity (Kirk & Kutchins, 1992). However, reliable measures aren't always valid. Despite more overall attention to reliability, ongoing efforts to address validity in psychiatric diagnosis go back a long way.

In a classic paper, psychiatrists Eli Robins and Samuel Guze (1970) proposed five criteria for establishing diagnostic validity. They argued that valid diagnoses should (a) provide precise clinical descriptions, (b) have measurable biological lab tests, (c) clearly distinguish disorders from one another, (d) have good construct validity to help distinguish disorders, and (e) be supported by genetic evidence. This is a tall order!

Validity of the *DSM* and *ICD*

The problem for *DSM* and *ICD* is that Robins and Guze's criteria remain aspirational (Paris, 2015). We haven't been able to establish whether they are the best criteria for validity and this is, in good measure, because we still do not have biological lab tests and genetic evidence that allow us to clearly distinguish mental disorders from one another (Kirk & Kutchins, 1992; Obiols, 2012; Paris, 2015). Even with disorders judged to have good diagnostic reliability, **comorbidity** (multiple disorders co-occurring, or being diagnosed at the same time) remains a problem. Another way of saying this is that the boundaries between disorders often remain fuzzy (Paris, 2015). Therefore, critics contend that *DSM* and *ICD* have yet to solve the validity problem (Kirk & Kutchins, 1992; Obiols, 2012).

The challenge of validity is reflected in the fact that the *DSM* definition of mental disorder is rarely invoked when debating what to include in each revision of the manual (J. C. Wakefield & First, 2013). It is easier to develop criteria and teach clinicians how to use them reliably than it is to establish whether the criteria being used are valid in the first place. This perhaps explains why the *DSM-5* field trials studied reliability, but didn't examine validity (K. D. Jones, 2012; Welch, Klassen, Borisova, & Clothier, 2013). To effectively address Robins and Guze's criteria for validity, critics argue that the *DSM* would need to define disorder in clear, measurable, and etiological (causal) terms. Even the authors of the *DSM* acknowledge that validity is a challenge and that diagnostic reliability doesn't necessarily solve the problem: "Although the use of explicit 'operational criteria' is essential for obtaining reliable clinical assessments, the reliability of such criteria does not guarantee that they are the most valid representation of an underlying pathological process" (Regier et al., 2013, p. 59). We revisit the issue of validity when we discuss various *DSM* and *ICD* disorders throughout the rest of the book. For now, simply be aware that the consensus in the field is that, despite our best efforts, *ICD* and *DSM* categories still have questionable validity. For an interesting "classic study" of diagnostic validity, see the "In Depth" feature for a discussion of the psychologist David Rosenhan's famous pseudopatient study.

IN DEPTH

Sane People, Insane Places

In the early 1970s, psychologist David Rosenhan (1973) conducted his famous **pseudopatient study** on the validity of psychiatric diagnosis. Eight people (three women, five men—including Rosenhan) with no history of mental illness posed as *pseudopatients* and presented at 12 different psychiatric hospitals in the United States. The pseudopatients were instructed to feign auditory hallucinations, telling hospital staff that they heard voices saying "empty," "hollow," and "thud." Rosenhan wondered how many of the pseudopatients would be correctly turned away as imposters. None were. All were hospitalized. Seven were diagnosed with schizophrenia and one with manic-depressive psychosis.

Once admitted, the pseudopatients behaved normally to see how long it would take for the staff to realize they were impostors. The staff never did. In fact, staff members interpreted the pseudopatients' note taking (done to record data for the study) as symptomatic of their psychopathology—at least this was Rosenhan's interpretation. Though the staff never caught on, the other patients did. During the first three pseudopatient hospitalizations, 35 of 119 patients commented that the pseudopatients didn't belong there. Some were quite emphatic, making comments like "You're not crazy! You're a journalist, or a professor [referring to the continual note taking]" (Rosenhan, 1973, p. 252). In the end, pseudopatient hospital stays ranged from 7 to 52 days, with an average of 19 days. When released, the pseudopatients weren't identified as fakers, but as "in remission," leading Rosenhan to conclude that diagnostic labels have a permanently stigmatizing "stickiness."

Upon hearing of the pseudopatient study, staff at one research and teaching hospital doubted Rosenhan's results and assured him that pseudopatients would not likely go unnoticed at their facility. To test this, Rosenhan informed the hospital that he might be sending pseudopatients to seek psychiatric admission. Dutifully, the staff began identifying potential pseudopatients—41 of 193 patients were alleged to be impostors by at least one staff member. The twist? Rosenhan never sent any pseudopatients. This confirmed Rosenhan's suspicion that mental health professionals are often unable to reliably distinguish "sane" from "insane."

Rosenhan's study has long been cited by psychiatry's critics as an example of the poor validity and reliability of psychiatric diagnosis. The study is often covered in abnormal psychology textbooks, but usually without discussing its limitations (Bartels & Peters, 2017). We try to avoid that pitfall here by noting that Rosenhan's research was not without detractors at the time of its publication (D. A. Davis, 1976; Spitzer, 1975, 1976; B. Weiner, 1975). Chief among them was Robert Spitzer, principal architect of the *DSM-III*. He argued that Rosenhan incorrectly assumed that if "pseudopatients" can fake symptoms successfully, then diagnosis is invalid. However, what about a patient who drinks a quart of blood, then goes to the hospital complaining of stomach pain? Would it be any surprise for such a patient to be diagnosed with a stomach ulcer and—if so—would that invalidate the entire enterprise of medical diagnosis (Spitzer, 1975)? Further, Spitzer (1976) pointed out that an "in remission" diagnosis for psychiatric patients is rare. To Spitzer, this meant that the hospital staff correctly realized the pseudopatients weren't symptomatic, leading them to adjust their diagnoses accordingly. Whether identifying pseudopatients as "in remission" is the same as revealing them as fakers remains an ongoing area of disagreement among those debating the significance of Rosenhan's research.

Another objection to Rosenhan's study focuses on research methods. Rosenhan only sent pseudopatients to the hospital. There was no control group, so there was no systematic test comparing how professionals distinguish the "sane" from the "insane." Had a group of pseudopatients, along with a matched control group of people diagnosed with schizophrenia, been placed together in a hospital setting, could staff have told them apart? (See Chapter 1 for a refresher on matched control groups). The answer remains unknown, but it's been suggested that doing the study this way would have been more methodologically sound (B. Weiner, 1975).

Finally, do Rosenhan's 1973 results still apply today? His study was conducted prior to 1980's *DSM-III*, which added diagnostic criteria to help clinicians diagnose more reliably. Therefore, might Rosenhan's results no longer be relevant because diagnosis today is supposed to be conducted in a more systematic and objective way? Again, the answer remains unclear.

Despite all the criticisms, Rosenhan's study is among the most famous in abnormal psychology. It is still discussed because it speaks to questions that remain hotly debated in the field. Foremost among those questions: Are psychiatric diagnoses reliable and valid and what is their impact on those to whom they are assigned?

CRITICAL THINKING QUESTIONS

1. Do the results of Rosenhan's study tell us anything important about psychiatric diagnosis or not? Your response may tell you something about your own emerging perspective on abnormal psychology.

2. Are critiques of Rosenhan's study compelling? Do you think these critiques undermine Rosenhan's conclusions? Explain your view.

3. Do you think the same results would be found if this study was done today? Why or why not?

4. Can you design a study to test the hypothesis that mental health professionals are unable to reliably distinguish people with mental disorders from those without them? How might your study improve on the limitations of Rosenhan's classic study?

EVALUATING THE *DSM* AND *ICD*

Success and Influence

In many respects, the *DSM* and *ICD* have been remarkably successful. These manuals have introduced into psychiatric diagnosis two major innovations that we now take for granted: diagnostic criteria and diagnostic codes (Decker, 2013; Kirk & Kutchins, 1992; Paris, 2015). They have also tackled the challenging issue of diagnostic reliability (Regier et al., 2013). The phenomenal success of these manuals is reflected in their widespread use. Although the *ICD* is free, the *DSM* and the many supplemental books published alongside it sell large numbers of copies and have a mass readership (R. Cook, 2014; Halter et al., 2013)—an impressive feat for a dry and technical manual ostensibly aimed at clinicians and researchers. For most of the past 40 years or so, the *DSM*'s influence has extended to both practice settings (where clinicians are often required to use it for clinical and insurance reimbursement purposes) and research settings (where many grant agencies, journals, and medical schools have required mastery of and use of its diagnoses) (Halter et al., 2013; Kawa & Giordano, 2012; Paris, 2015; Shorter, 2013).

Advantages

Supporters of the *DSM* and *ICD* see these manuals as having numerous advantages:

» **DSM and ICD provide a common language for communication among professionals.** One of the biggest advantages people see in the *ICD* and *DSM* systems is that they provide a common language for professionals (J. L. Sanders, 2011). The goal is to facilitate easy and quick communication. A diagnosis potentially allows a great deal of information to be conveyed readily and efficiently. Instead of having to explain all the details of a patient's situation, the clinician or researcher can economically communicate the gist of things by simply naming the patient's diagnosis.

» **DSM and ICD are important in getting people treatment.** Without a diagnosis, it can be hard to know how to help someone. A *DSM* or *ICD* diagnosis is often seen as the first step in determining the best course of action. How a clinician treats someone often depends on the diagnosis assigned. It shouldn't come as a surprise that clinicians are likely to treat patients diagnosed with social anxiety disorder differently than those diagnosed with schizophrenia. Put another way, when operating within a medical model of abnormality, accurate diagnosis is critical to getting people the correct treatment. In addition to helping guide clinicians in their choice of treatment, a *DSM* or *ICD* diagnosis is usually a practical necessity because many agencies and insurance companies simply won't cover services without one. Diagnoses are often required for patients to be eligible for treatment.

» **DSM and ICD help advance scientific understanding of mental disorders.** Having a shared language allows researchers to examine the underlying causes of and effective treatments for *DSM* and *ICD* disorders. For example, having shared *DSM* criteria for schizophrenia provides a way for researchers to diagnose and then study the underlying causes of schizophrenia, as well as effective treatments for it. Therefore, many people argue that these manuals, despite any flaws identified by critics, have overall helped improve our understanding and treatment of mental disorders (Decker, 2013).

» **DSM and ICD give patients names for their problems and lessen the stigma of mental disorder.** The issue of stigma is an important one in abnormal psychology; those diagnosed as abnormal often face a great deal of social stigma (Corrigan, 2005). Supporters of the *ICD* and *DSM* contend that diagnoses are ways to bring mental illness out of the shadows. *ICD* and *DSM* diagnoses allow people to attach names to their problems, permitting them to (a) better understand what is happening to them, (b) receive effective treatment, (c) find a community of fellow-sufferers who share their experience, and (d) reduce stigma by seeing themselves as having an illness from which recovery is possible (Angell, Cooke, & Kovac, 2005).

Disadvantages

Despite (and perhaps because of) their success and widespread use, the *ICD* and *DSM* have received substantial criticism. Detractors see these manuals as having numerous disadvantages. Common objections are:

» **DSM and ICD have reliability and validity problems.** We have reviewed how the *DSM* and *ICD* have been criticized for not adequately addressing reliability and validity issues. Critics contend that these issues are reflected in high levels of comorbidity, in which a client qualifies for multiple diagnoses (Widiger, 2016). According to critics, if a client fits numerous categories, then it is uncertain whether we are reliably or validly identifying distinct disorders.

» **DSM and ICD "medicalize" everyday problems.** Whereas supporters believe *ICD* and *DSM* diagnoses reduce stigma by conceptualizing problems as illnesses rather than personality flaws, critics often see these same diagnoses as dehumanizing. These critics worry that recasting personal life problems as illnesses is dangerous because it incorrectly recasts everyday human struggles as diseases (A. Frances, 2013b; Gambrill, 2014; Johnstone, 2014b; Kinderman, 2014b, 2017). Thus, they believe *DSM* and *ICD* encourage medicalization—inappropriately classifying non-medical problems as medical (see Chapter 2). For example, when the *DSM-5* was being developed, some critics complained about one of its new categories—disruptive mood dysregulation disorder (DMDD), which is characterized by "severe recurrent temper outbursts" (see Chapter 5) (American Psychiatric Association, 2013b). To critics, this category dubiously turns an everyday problem (children having temper tantrums) into a medical disorder (Frances, 2012a, 2013c). *DSM-5* also stirred controversy by revising criteria for disorders such as attention-deficit hyperactivity disorder (ADHD) (characterized by difficulty sustaining attention, being revved-up and full of excessive energy, and impulsive behavior; see Chapter 13). Critics worry that revised criteria for several disorders inappropriately qualify too many additional people for diagnoses (Frances, 2013c; Kamens, Elkins, & Robbins, 2017; Paris, 2015). Whether the authors of the *DSM-5* are guilty of **lowering of diagnostic thresholds** (and therefore medicalizing too many presenting problems) has been an ongoing area of disagreement and debate (Frances, 2013c; Kamens et al., 2017; Kinderman & Cooke, 2017; Paris, 2015; Robbins, Kamens, & Elkins, 2017). The *DSM-5* did lower diagnostic thresholds for some disorders, allowing more people to meet the criteria for a diagnosis. Some argue this is a bad thing, continuing the *DSM* trend of pathologizing normal behavioral variations. Others contend that when more people qualify for diagnoses, more people become eligible for much-needed treatment. Table 3.4 summarizes some instances where thresholds have been lowered from *DSM-IV-TR* to *DSM-5* and compares the criteria for those categories. *DSM-5* defenders say these revised criteria simply capture more people who warrant a diagnosis. What do you think?

Table 3.4 *DSM-5* and the Lowering of Diagnostic Thresholds

Disorder	DSM-IV-TR	DSM-5
Attention-deficit hyperactivity disorder (ADHD)	Symptoms must be present before age 7.	Symptoms must be present before age 12.
Major depressive disorder	Not diagnosed for symptoms lasting less than 2 months following the death of a loved one (i.e., the bereavement exclusion).	Bereavement exclusion eliminated; someone grieving death of a loved one can be diagnosed if clinician deems it appropriate.
Agoraphobia, specific phobia, and social anxiety disorder (social phobia)	Individuals over 18 must recognize their anxiety is excessive.	Individuals over 18 no longer need to recognize their anxiety is excessive.
Bulimia nervosa	Frequency of binge eating and inappropriate compensatory behavior: at least twice weekly.	Frequency of binge eating and inappropriate compensatory behavior: at least once weekly.
Oppositional defiant disorder	Must exclude conduct disorder in making a diagnosis.	Exclusion criterion for conduct disorder eliminated.
Intermittent-explosive disorder	Physical aggression required.	Physical aggression or verbal aggression and non-destructive/non-injurious physical aggression required.

» **DSM and ICD's descriptive-based symptom approach has led to increased use of pharmacological interventions.** Critics who accuse the *DSM* and *ICD* of too much medicalization maintain that using descriptive, symptom-based criteria has resulted in significant increases in the number of prescriptions being written (Frances, 2013c). Of course, whether this is a bad or good thing depends in large measure on whether you see the problems listed in these manuals as medical disorders or everyday problems in living. Critics tend to see them as the latter, while supporters of the *DSM* and *ICD* see them as the former.

» **DSM and ICD have been unable to uncover the etiology of disorders.** That is, the manuals remain descriptive rather than etiological. Efforts to identify **biomarkers** (biological measures that can be used to make diagnoses) are ongoing, but mental disorders are still diagnosed using behaviors rather than underlying biological indicators (Paris, 2015). The validity of *DSM* and *ICD* categories therefore remains uncertain, something critics see as a major problem.

» **DSM and ICD not only rely more on political consensus than science, but are also culturally imperious.** Ever since homosexuality was removed from the *DSM-III* based on a vote by the American Psychiatric Association membership (see "In Depth" in Chapter 10 for a detailed account), critics have complained that decisions about the *DSM* and *ICD* are often determined less by science and more by political considerations (Decker, 2013; Kirk & Kutchins, 1992). Additionally, critics complain that these manuals are culturally imperious, imposing a Western view of mental disorder on the rest of the world. To these critics, the authors of the *DSM* and *ICD* forget that their understanding of disorder is influenced by their cultural assumptions and may not translate well when applied to other cultures (Nadkarni & Santhouse, 2012). The *DSM-5* has tried to address this by including a **cultural formulation interview (CFI)** in the diagnostic process. Table 3.5 lists the *DSM-5* guidelines for conducting a CFI, in which clinicians inquire about cultural factors potentially impacting the presenting problem. The *DSM-5* stipulates that "information

Has the medical model approach of the DSM and ICD led to increased use of pharmacological interventions? If so, do you think this is good or bad? Why?
Source: Corbis

obtained from the CFI should be integrated with all other available clinical material into a comprehensive clinical and contextual evaluation" (American Psychiatric Association, 2013b, p. 751). However, the issue of whether the disorders in the *DSM* are culture-bound syndromes (see Chapter 2) remains hotly debated. We examine this further in the "Controversial Question" feature.

Table 3.5 *DSM-5*'s Cultural Formulation Interview

The CFI assesses four domains (American Psychiatric Association, 2013b, pp. 751–754):

1. **Cultural definition of the problem** (3 questions); sample question: "Sometimes people have different ways of describing their problem to their family, friends, or others in their community. How would you describe your problem to them?"

2. **Cultural perceptions of cause, context, and support** (7 questions); sample question: "Are there any aspects of your background or identity that make a difference to your [PROBLEM]?"

3. **Cultural factors affecting self-coping and past help seeking** (3 questions); sample question: "Often, people look for help from many different sources, including different kinds of doctors, helpers, or healers. In the past, what kinds of treatment, help, advice, or healing have you sought for your [PROBLEM]?"

4. **Cultural factors affecting current help seeking** (3 questions); sample question: "Sometimes doctors and patients misunderstand each other because they come from different backgrounds or have different expectations. Have you been concerned about this and is there anything we can do to provide you with the care you need?"

CONTROVERSIAL QUESTION

Is the *DSM* Culture-Bound?

Despite its efforts to incorporate culture into assessment, the *DSM* has been accused of assuming its categories are *culturally universal* rather than *culture-bound* (a distinction introduced in Chapter 2). In a letter to the editor of the *Asian Journal of Psychiatry*, psychiatrists Abhijit Nadkarni and Alastair Santhouse (2012) ask pointedly whether, despite being used globally, "could DSM itself be seen as a 'culture bound' document" (p. 118)? They continue:

Culture-bound syndromes were first introduced into the DSM in its fourth edition. These illnesses have been seen largely as curiosities occurring outside Western concepts of mental health, and imply that the Western classification of diseases is the reference point, with any experiences outside its domain being culture bound. (p. 118)

From this perspective, gathering cultural information in making a diagnosis isn't sufficient because incorporating cultural information gathered from patients doesn't address whether the very diagnostic categories being used are—in and of themselves—biased entities that shouldn't be assumed to be cross-culturally valid. Nadkarni and Santhouse (2012) conclude that

the cross-cultural portability of diagnoses is limited, and any expansion of these will have effects not just on overdiagnosis and misdiagnosis, but even more worryingly will have economic implications. ... It is now time for a renewed debate about the use of DSM outside the country of its origin. (p. 118)

CRITICAL THINKING QUESTIONS

1. How important is culture bias in diagnosis, formulation, and assessment?

2. How can culture bias best be reduced?

3. Does the *DSM-5*'s inclusion of the cultural diagnostic formulation interview (see Table 3.5) adequately address concerns about culture bias? If so, how? If not, what more needs to be done?

4. Do you agree with Nadkarni and Santhouse that there needs to be discussion about whether *DSM* categories should be used outside the United States? Explain your position.

Trends and Future

The *DSM* and *ICD* are always changing as new research is done and ideas about diagnosis evolve. Here are some *DSM* and *ICD* trends worth noting.

» **More frequent updates.** Students often ask why the *DSM* switched from Roman numerals (*DSM-II, III,* and *IV*) to Arabic numbers (*DSM-5*). The reason is a wholly practical one. Before *DSM-5*, revisions of the manual were done all at once. However, shifting to Arabic numbers allows the *DSM* to publish incremental updates as evidence calls for them without having to revamp the entire manual. It's not that different than when your smartphone does regular small updates between total overhauls of its operating system. Therefore, in the future we may have *DSM-5.1*, *DSM-5.2*, *DSM-5.3* (and so on) prior to *DSM-6* (American Psychiatric Association, n.d.-a). As part of this "continuous improvement model," guidelines for evaluating proposed revisions to the *DSM-5* have been developed (First, Kendler, & Leibenluft, 2017). Using these guidelines, interested parties can submit revision proposals online via the *DSM-5* website (www.psychiatry.org/psychiatrists/practice/dsm), though the *DSM-5* committee ultimately makes revision decisions.

» **Move toward dimensional diagnosis.** One of the biggest changes in the *DSM-5* was a long-anticipated shift away from categorical diagnosis (organizing disorders into discrete and mutually exclusive categories) and toward **dimensional diagnosis** (charting degrees of severity for different symptoms rather than dividing disorders into discrete categories) (Blashfield et al., 2014; Helzer, Kraemer, & Krueger, 2006; Widiger, 2016). The idea behind this shift is that people don't always come in discrete categories; sometimes their pathology comes in degrees. For instance, dimensions allow us to chart the degree of a person's depression, anxiety, and overall dysfunction. Rather than sticking solely with all-or-none categories, the *DSM-5* tries to incorporate dimensions with many disorders. For example, in *DSM-IV* there were distinct categories for substance abuse and substance dependence, but in *DSM-5* these disorders have been combined into a single dimensional category, substance use disorder (American Psychiatric Association, 2013b; Paris, 2015). Someone with substance use disorder can be diagnosed as having mild, moderate, or severe versions of it (see Chapter 11). There was also an attempt—ultimately placed in Section III for later consideration and discussed further in Chapter 12—to recast personality disorders in a dimensional way (American Psychiatric Association, 2013b; Widiger, 2016). Perhaps the most controversial example of the shift toward dimensional ways of thinking about diagnosis is the *DSM-5*'s combining of *DSM-IV*'s autism and Asperger's categories into a single autism spectrum disorder diagnosis. Many people objected to this change; it is reviewed in greater detail in Chapter 13.

» **The search for biomarkers.** One of the reasons why *DSM-5* has shifted toward dimensional diagnosis is because of research suggesting there may be commonalities in the biology behind various disorders (Halter et al., 2013). This could mean that many disorders we see as distinct from one another are instead variations on a theme with shared underlying causes. This may also shed light on the *DSM-5*'s subtle shift toward a more implicitly biological view of mental disorders. *DSM-III* through *IV-TR* all strongly claimed to be "atheoretical" regarding etiology (American Psychiatric Association, 1980). That is, they didn't take an official position on the causes of disorders, but merely described them. *DSM-5* remains a descriptive manual, but no longer claims to be atheoretical about causes of disorders. During its development, the *DSM-5* more explicitly aspired to incorporate biomarkers to make diagnoses instead of merely observing behaviors, thoughts, and feelings (Carroll, 2013). However, as mentioned before, biomarkers for making diagnoses remain elusive despite research suggesting biological correlates of many mental disorders (Paris, 2015). Thus, biomarkers aren't used in *DSM-5, ICD-10*, or *ICD-11*.

» **Rise of the *ICD* in the United States.** Clinicians in the United States overwhelmingly use the *DSM*, but after all the controversy over changes to the *DSM-5*, they have begun to take an interest in the *ICD-10-CM*. According to Carol Goodheart (2014), past president of the American Psychological Association, American clinicians will increasingly be trained to use both the *DSM* and the *ICD* and eventually "these practitioners will outnumber those who are only familiar with the DSM system" (p. 15). In comparing the *DSM* and *ICD*, the American Psychological Association has noted that "there is little justification for maintaining the DSM as a separate diagnostic system from the ICD in the long run, particularly given the U.S. government's substantial engagement with WHO in the area of classification systems" ("ICD vs. DSM," 2009, para. 6). The U.S. government, like all countries that belong to WHO, is required to use *ICD* codes, so even though most American clinicians still use the *DSM*, technically "the official U.S. diagnostic system for mental illness is the *ICD*" (M. C. Roberts & Evans, 2013, p. 72). In places where *DSM* diagnoses do not correspond directly with *ICD* diagnoses (and sometimes they don't, as not all categories are perfectly "harmonized" across the manuals), the "*DSM* diagnoses must be recoded or translated via computerized 'crosswalks' into *ICD* codes" (M. C. Roberts & Evans, 2013, p. 72). This explains why some mental health professionals are starting to see the *DSM* as redundant ("ICD vs. DSM," 2009). However, even if the *ICD* does at some point eclipse the *DSM* in the U.S. (and it isn't certain it will!), many believe that a role remains for the *DSM* because it contains a lot more information and detail than the *ICD* ("ICD vs. DSM," 2009). How and whether the *ICD-11* will impact the influence of the *DSM* remains to be seen.

» **Ongoing controversy but sustained influence.** The *DSM-5* revision process was rife with controversy (Blashfield et al., 2014). Critics were unhappy with the process and the decisions made, leading one of them to sarcastically decry the manual as psychiatry's misguided "Book of Woe" (G. Greenberg, 2013). Meanwhile, the *ICD-11* is a potential alternative (Goodheart, 2014). Time will tell if its mental disorder section comes in for less criticism than the *DSM-5*. Nonetheless, despite controversies over and disagreements in preference for the *DSM* and *ICD*, these two manuals remain the preeminent systems for diagnosis in abnormal psychology. In fact, it is common to hear people refer to the *DSM* in particular as the "psychiatric bible" (Decker, 2013). This nickname, which not everyone appreciates (R. Friedman, 2013), fits because the *DSM* is arguably the most influential diagnostic system today (Paris, 2015). In thinking about its tremendous impact, *DSM* historian Hannah Decker (2013, p. 330) perhaps put it best, remarking that it's "not completely unthinkable to call it a Bible for the millions it affects, an actual holy book, whose verses guide professional authorities in many fields." Amen.

3.3 OTHER DIAGNOSTIC APPROACHES/ALTERNATIVES TO DIAGNOSIS

While the *DSM* and *ICD* are widely used, clinicians rely on other diagnostic approaches, too. Some clinicians see these approaches as nicely complementing their use of the *DSM* and *ICD*, while others see them as alternatives to be used instead of the *DSM* and *ICD*—although practically speaking this often isn't possible because agencies and insurers usually require clinicians to use *DSM* or *ICD* regardless of their theoretical preferences. Below we review five diagnostic alternatives: formulation, the *Psychodynamic Diagnostic Manual*, the Research Domain Criteria (RDoC), the Hierarchical Taxonomy of Psychopathology (HiTOP), and the Power Threat Meaning Framework (PTM).

FORMULATION
Distinguishing Formulation from Diagnosis

A **formulation** is a *"hypothesis about a person's difficulties*, which *draws from psychological theory"* (Johnstone & Dallos, 2014b, p. 5 [italics in original]). In Chapter 2 we reviewed prominent psychological perspectives and sociocultural perspectives in abnormal psychology—such as psychodynamic, cognitive-behavioral, humanistic, social justice, and family systems. Quite simply, a formulation is when a practitioner uses concepts and ideas from one of these perspectives to **conceptualize** (i.e., think about in the theory's terms) what is happening with a client and then uses this conceptualization to plan what to do about it (Bolton, 2014; Eels, 2015; R. N. Goldman & Greenberg, 2015a; Johnstone & Dallos, 2014a). Formulation differs from psychiatric diagnosis in that it relies on psychological and sociocultural theories, not medical model disorder categories. While a *DSM* or *ICD* diagnosis can be used in conjunction with formulation (Eels, 2015), not all psychologists support doing so (Johnstone, 2014b). Regardless of whether one incorporates psychiatric diagnosis or not, it's important to realize that formulation doesn't require such a diagnosis because built into any formulation is a hypothesis about what is going wrong with the client—and such a hypothesis stands on its own, with or without an accompanying diagnosis. For instance, in psychoanalysis, formulations frame client problems in terms of underlying unconscious conflicts; in cognitive-behavioral therapy (CBT), formulations posit issues with how the client interprets information; in person-centered therapy, formulations emphasize disruptions in the self-actualizing process; and in social justice perspectives, formulations tie emotional distress to socioeconomic inequality, discrimination, and other forms of societal oppression.

Thus, a formulation can be made using any theoretical perspective without necessitating the use of *DSM* or *ICD* diagnoses because each formulation has its own built-in theory of psychological function and dysfunction. In other words, every theory used in formulation has its own internal conception of abnormality. However, formulations share core features. All formulations: (a) summarize the client's central problem; (b) draw on psychological theory to understand how the client's issues are interrelated; (c) use psychological theory to explain why the client has developed these issues; (d) develop a plan for alleviating the difficulties that is rooted in the psychological theory applied; and (e) must be revised and updated as needed (Johnstone & Dallos, 2014b).

Two Examples of Formulation

Integrative Evidence-Based Case Formulation

As noted, clinicians often combine the use of formulation and psychiatric diagnosis (Eels, 2015). For some, this is because they work in settings where psychiatric diagnoses are required. For others, it is because they find that psychiatric diagnoses complement their use of formulation. Regardless of why they do so, many clinicians rely on both psychiatric diagnosis and formulation. **Integrative evidence-based case formulation** provides a representative example of what formulation that incorporates psychiatric diagnosis can look like in clinical practice (Eels, 2015). The four steps of this model are as follows (Eels, 2015):

» *Step 1: Create a Problem List.* Problems are defined as discrepancies between perceived and desired states. Four kinds of problems are distinguished: *red flags* (problems demanding immediate attention, such as substance use issues, dangerousness to self or others, and neglect), *self-functioning* (problems involving troublesome behavior, problematic ways of thinking, upsetting moods, physical illnesses, or existential issues), *social/interpersonal functioning* (difficulties in relationships or getting along with others), and *societal functioning* (legal, financial, or employment problems). The first thing a clinician must do with new clients is to work with them to identify relevant problems they wish to address.

» *Step 2: Diagnose.* DSM diagnoses are made, but with the caveat that any diagnosis is a social construction that "does not 'exist' in the sense that some general medical conditions exist" (Eels, 2015, p. 103; see Chapter 2 for a definition of social constructions). Thus, diagnostic categories are viewed as merely one source of useful information that helps clients and clinicians better formulate understandings of client problems. Diagnoses aren't treated as medical entities to be taken literally, nor are they viewed as explanations for why clients behave as they do.

» *Step 3: Develop an Explanatory Hypothesis.* In this step, theories (e.g., psychodynamic, CBT, humanistic) and evidence (e.g., assessment data, observations of the client, research on therapy effectiveness) are used to arrive at explanatory *core hypotheses* of clients' presenting problems. Core hypotheses might explain client difficulties in psychodynamic or humanistic terms as due to having desires accompanied by feared negative consequences (e.g., a client wants to establish social connections but fears rejection). However, they might also offer cognitive or behavioral explanations (e.g., a client relies on cognitive distortions in making assessments about job prospects or is negatively reinforced for avoiding social situations because avoiding them reduces anxiety). The idea is that whatever the explanation, it is theoretically grounded and rooted in evidence.

» *Step 4: Plan Treatment.* This involves working with clients to develop shared goals and then employing psychotherapy techniques from whatever theoretical approaches were used in earlier steps to achieve these goals (Eels, 2015).

Formulation In Lieu of Diagnosis

As mentioned, not all systems for devising formulations incorporate *DSM* or *ICD* diagnoses. The **4P model of case formulation** typically excludes such diagnoses, rejecting them as static and unhelpful labels. Why are such labels viewed as static and unhelpful? Because, in the view of 4P formulation advocates, "the act of giving a diagnosis conveys a sense of finality"—in direct contrast to the theoretically grounded act of developing a provisional (and thus revisable) formulation (Bolton, 2014, p. 182). In other words:

> *Diagnosis encourages the clinician to see the person or the person's problem as a type of problem; formulation encourages the clinician to see the person or problem as something unique, complex, and situated. Diagnosis is a label; formulation is a map. It is a map of the extensions and connections of a problem and a map for action. (Bolton, 2014, p. 181)*

There are four areas of the 4P model that clinicians must consider in devising a formulation. Each begins with the letter "P" (hence, the name of the model). The four areas (and the questions they generate) are (Bolton, 2014; S. W. Henderson & Martin, 2014):

» *Preconditions*: What preconditions made the client vulnerable to the current presenting problem? Depending on the theoretical perspective(s) being used in the formulation, what biological, psychological, and sociocultural factors contributed to or were required for the development of the problem? Was the person genetically vulnerable to the problem? Did past relationships or learned ways of thinking and behaving influence the problem? Are there social conditions—poverty, discrimination, social norms—that have made the problem possible?

» *Precipitating factors*: What events or factors specifically triggered the current problem or led the client to seek help with the problem now? Emotional upset, developing physical symptoms, getting arrested, being unable to pay the rent, or being served with divorce papers are examples of precipitating factors. Knowing what elicited the problem or prompted the request for assistance is extremely important in understanding the problem in context.

» *Perpetuating factors*: What factors maintain the problem and prevent it from being resolved? Are there things keeping the person from getting help or being able to effectively address the problem? Understanding such factors is critical to conceptualizing the case because without addressing these factors, improvement is unlikely.

» *Protective factors*: What factors have prevented the problem from being worse? What strengths does the client have that have kept the problem from having an even more detrimental impact? Identifying client strengths (e.g., emotional resilience, physical health, social resources) can provide a foundation for building potential solutions to the problem.

Evaluating Formulation

The integrative and 4P models are just two ways of conducting a formulation. However, they provide a general idea of how formulation uses psychological theories to conceptualize and remedy clients' presenting problems. Table 3.6 presents humanistic, cognitive-behavioral, and narrative formulations for the case of Jill. In examining these formulations, you may wish to review the humanistic, cognitive-behavioral, and narrative perspectives in Chapter 2.

Table 3.6 Three Formulations of Jill's Presenting Problem

Humanistic Formulation

Jill is experiencing psychological *incongruence* because her parents haven't provided her with *unconditional positive regard*. Because Jill's parents only have provided *conditional positive regard*, she has lost touch with her *actualizing tendency*. Therapy should provide Jill with the core conditions for change—*empathy, genuineness,* and *unconditional positive regard*. Once provided, Jill should begin to reconnect with her actualizing tendency, become more *self-consistent*, and begin figuring out what future course is right for her.

Cognitive-Behavioral (CBT) Formulation

Jill's *self-schema* is one in which she sees herself as requiring guidance to make decisions and as only being likable if she defers. She employs cognitive distortions such as *mind reading* ("Others will disapprove if I pursue ballet over medical school."); *"should" statement* ("I should study medicine so as not to disappoint others."), and *catastrophizing* ("If I don't study medicine, it will be the end of the world."). Further, Jill's deferent behavior has been negatively reinforced; when behaving deferentially, she experiences relief from anxiety about displeasing others. Therapy should focus on challenging Jill's cognitive distortions and changing her self-schemas, as well as helping her have new experiences that reinforce less deferential behavior.

Narrative Formulation

Jill has internalized a *problem-saturated narrative* in which she has come to see herself as suffering from anxiety, sadness, and lack of motivation. Therapy should *externalize the problem* by talking about "anxiety," "sadness," and "lack of motivation" as external entities that influence her, rather than internal maladies she "has." Through externalizing the problem, Jill may start to identify *sparkling moments* when "anxiety" and "lack of motivation" failed to get the best of her. This will help Jill start telling a new story about who she is and what she wants from life.

While many clinicians are attracted to the nuanced and individualized conceptualizations of each client that formulation provides, debate continues over whether diagnostic categories should be retained in case formulation. Those who think they should say diagnosis provides a shared professional language that allows for efficient communication among clinicians. To these supporters, "diagnosis helps with treatment selection since an enormous amount of treatment research has been conducted on the basis of selecting individuals according to diagnostic categories" (Eels, 2015, p. 100). Others vociferously disagree. To them, incorporating diagnosis is theoretically inconsistent with formulation because "it introduces an extra layer of confusion to use *medical/psychiatric* concepts in order to describe something that is actually being conceptualised in *psychological terms*" (Johnstone, 2014b, p. 273 [italics in original]). On a more practical level, when formulation doesn't include traditional psychiatric diagnosis, real-world difficulties can arise. For example, American clinicians must make *DSM* or *ICD* diagnoses if they wish to be reimbursed for their services by their clients' insurance companies. Thus, even clinicians who see diagnosis as inconsistent with formulation may include a diagnosis in their formulation process if for no other reason than to get paid.

PSYCHODYNAMIC DIAGNOSTIC MANUAL (PDM)

Psychodynamic clinicians often conceptualize diagnosis in explicitly theoretical terms using psychodynamic theory. This contrasts with the *DSM* and *ICD* approach, which—while adopting a medical model by dividing diagnoses into disorder categories—is theoretically more neutral about the underlying causes of disorders. This is not so of psychodynamic diagnostic systems, such as the *Psychodynamic Diagnostic Manual (PDM)* and *Operational Psychodynamic Diagnosis (OPD)* (OPD Task Force, 2007; Lingiardi & McWilliams, 2017). Below we examine one of these systems, the *PDM*.

Distinguishing *PDM* from *DSM* and *ICD*

Clinicians operating primarily from psychodynamic perspectives (see Chapter 2) have developed their own diagnostic nomenclature—the **Psychodynamic Diagnostic Manual (PDM)**, now in its second edition, *PDM-2* (Lingiardi & McWilliams, 2017). The *PDM-2*'s goal is to help clinicians make psychodynamic diagnostic formulations. Its authors have criticized the *DSM* and *ICD*'s descriptive, categorical approach. To them, the *DSM* and *ICD* don't sufficiently attend to clients' underlying psychological processes (American Psychoanalytic Association, 2006; Bornstein, 2011; Huprich, 2011; Lingiardi & McWilliams, 2017; McWilliams, 2011; Wallerstein, 2011). They feel that *DSM* and *ICD* categories encourage too much emphasis on symptom reduction rather than on understanding clients' psychological dynamics. The *PDM-2*'s introduction outlines how it is different from the *DSM* and *ICD*. Discussing the *DSM* specifically, the *PDM-2* asserts that

> The DSM system is intended to be noninferential: It is constructed to put symptoms and attributes that people have in common into the same diagnostic compartments, without imputation of underlying mental processes or meaning. In fact, the intent of the framers of recent editions of DSM ... was to be atheoretical—that is, to describe phenomena without assuming any overarching theory of mental functioning. (Lingiardi & McWilliams, 2017, p. 68)

By contrast, the *PDM-2* classification system "is geared toward individualized case formulation and treatment planning for therapies that address the full range and depth of a person's psychological experience" (Lingiardi & McWilliams, 2017, p. 69). As the *PDM-2* states:

> Our intent, in the various dimensions that constitute our nosological array, is to describe human problems dimensionally and to infer meanings, as best we can discern them, of observed phenomena: symptoms, behaviors, traits, affects, attitudes, thoughts, fantasies, and so on—the full human range of mental functioning. (Lingiardi & McWilliams, 2017, p. 69)

PDM Axes

PDM diagnoses are made along three axes. Different versions of these axes are tailored to adults, children, adolescents, and the elderly. The first axis is the **P-Axis (Personality Syndromes)**. It is used to map healthy and disordered personality functioning. The *PDM* defines **personality** as "relatively stable ways of thinking, feeling, behaving, and relating to others" (Lingiardi & McWilliams, 2017, p. 71). When using the P-Axis, clinicians first assess the client's *level of personality organization* using a dimensional scale; then they identify specific *personality syndromes* the client may exhibit (see Table 3.7). Regardless of whether a client's problems are severe enough for a personality disorder diagnosis, the clinician briefly summarizes the underlying psychodynamics of the client's personality according to six areas of functioning: *contributing constitutional-maturational patterns* (basic temperament—such as shy, aggressive, irritable, etc.); *central tension/preoccupation*; *central affects* (**affect** is a clinical word for emotion); *characteristic pathogenic belief about the self*; *characteristic pathogenic belief about others*; and *central ways of defending* (i.e., defense mechanisms used; see Chapter 2). Three of these six areas of functioning are included in Table 3.7. We revisit the P-Axis when discussing personality disorders in Chapter 12.

Table 3.7 The P-Axis in *PDM-2*

Levels of Personality Organization (1–10 scale, with 1 most pathological and 10 least pathological)

Psychotic level (1–2): Break with reality; poor sense of identity; highly defensive; difficulty distinguishing fantasy and reality.

Borderline level (3–5): Have difficulty with emotional regulation; often overwhelmed by intense depression, anxiety, and rage.

Neurotic level (6–8): Respond to certain stressors with rigidity, despite having many functional capacities overall.

Healthy level (9–10): Have preferred coping style, but it is flexible enough to accommodate challenges of everyday life.

Source: Gordon, R. M., & Bornstein, R. F. (2018). Construct validity of the Psychodiagnostic Chart: A transdiagnostic measure of personality organization, personality syndromes, mental functioning, and symptomatology. *Psychoanalytic Psychology*, 35(2), 280–288. doi:10.1037/pap0000142

Personality Syndromes

Syndrome	Tension/Preoccupation	Central Affects	Pathogenic Belief about Self	Pathogenic Belief about Others
Depressive	Self-critical, self-punishing, overly concerned with relatedness and/or loss	Sadness, guilt, shame	"I am bad or inadequate" or "Something I need for well-being has been lost."	"Others will reject me once they get to know me."

Dependent	Maintaining relationships	---	"I'm inadequate, ineffective, and need others."	"I need powerful others to care for me, but I resent it."
Anxious-avoidant and phobic	Staying safe vs. avoiding danger	---	"I am always in danger and must keep myself safe."	"Others are dangerous or able to protect me."
Obsessive-compulsive	Submitting to vs. rebelling against the control or authority of others.	Anger, guilt, shame, fear	"Feelings are dangerous, so I must control them."	"Others are less careful and controlled than I am, so I must control them and resist them controlling me."
Schizoid	Fearing intimacy vs. wanting intimacy	Emotional upset when overstimulated; emotions so strong they must be repressed.	"It is dangerous to depend on or love others."	"Others overwhelm me, impinge on me, and engulf me."
Somatizing	Integrity vs. fragmentation of the physical body	General distress; implied anger or rage; difficulty identifying and acknowledging emotions	"I am fragile and in physical danger of dying."	"Others are powerful and healthy but indifferent to me."
Hysteric-histrionic	Unconscious devaluing of own gender while being envious and fearful of opposite gender	Fear, shame, guilt	"My gender and its meaning are somehow problematic."	"Others are best understood in terms of gender binaries and conflicts."
Narcissistic	Inflating vs. deflating self-esteem	Shame, humiliation, contempt, envy	"I must be perfect to be okay."	"Others are okay and have good things; I must have more of those things to feel better."
Paranoid	Attacking vs. being attacked by others	Fear, rage, shame, contempt	"I am always in danger."	"Others will attack and use me."
Psychopathic	Manipulating others vs. being manipulated by them	Rage and envy	"Anything I want to do, I can do."	"Others are selfish and weak and are going to try to manipulate me."
Sadistic	Suffering humiliation vs. imposing humiliation	Hatred, contempt, sadistic pleasure	"I am permitted to humiliate and hurt others."	"Others are there for me to dominate."
Borderline	Coherent vs. fragmented sense of self; enmeshed attachment vs. despair at abandonment	Intense and shifting emotions, especially rage, shame, and fear.	"I am unsure who I am; I have many disconnected emotional states rather than an integrated sense of self."	"Others are defined only by their effect on me, rather than as complex individuals with their own unique psychological features."

Source: Lingiardi, V., & McWilliams, N. (Eds.) *Psychodynamic Diagnostic Manual* (2nd ed.). New York, NY: Guilford Press (2017). Adapted with permission of Guilford Press.

PDM's second axis is the **M-Axis (Profile of Mental Functioning)**, along which the clinician evaluates and describes 12 categories of basic mental functioning that assess four basic areas: *cognitive and emotional processes, identity and relationships, defenses and coping,* and *self-awareness and self-direction.* The M-Axis evaluates aspects of functioning that may lie outside of conscious awareness but nonetheless affect clients (Etzi, 2014). The *PDM* lists numerous established assessment instruments that clinicians can use to help make M-Axis appraisals. The third and final axis of a *PDM-2* diagnosis is the **S-Axis (Subjective Experience)**. The S-Axis places common symptom patterns into diagnostic categories. It takes the major *DSM* disorders and describes, in psychodynamic terms, what it is like to have them. The *PDM* provides diagnostic codes for each of its S-Axis symptom patterns. Table 3.8 shows Jill's *PDM* diagnosis.

Table 3.8 Jill's *PDM* Diagnosis

P-Axis

Levels of Personality Organization 1–10 scale (with 1–2 psychotic level, 3–5 borderline level, 6–8 neurotic level, and 9–10 healthy level)	Rating = 5 (high functioning end of borderline level)
P-Axis Select from 12 personality syndromes	Anxious-Avoidant and Somatizing

Source: adapted from Gordon, R. M., & Bornstein, R. F. (2018). Construct validity of the Psychodiagnostic Chart: A transdiagnostic measure of personality organization, personality syndromes, mental functioning, and symptomatology. *Psychoanalytic Psychology*, 35(2), 280–288. doi:10.1037/pap0000142

M-Axis

Rate each of the 12 mental functions on this 1–5 scale:
1 (severe deficit), 2 (major impairment), 3 (moderate impairment), 4 (mild impairment), 5 (healthy)

Cognitive and Affective Processes	
Capacity for regulation, attention, and learning	4
Capacity for affective range, communication, and understanding	4
Capacity for mentalization and reflective functioning	3
Identity and Relationships	
Capacity for differentiation and integration (identity)	3
Capacity for relationships and intimacy	3
Self-esteem regulation and quality of internal experience	3
Defense and Coping	
Impulse control and regulation	4
Defensive functioning	3
Adaptation, resiliency, strength	3
Self-Awareness and Self-Direction	
Self-observing capacities (psychological mindedness)	3
Capacity to construct and use internal standards and ideals	3
Meaning and purpose	3
TOTAL	35

Healthy functioning (54–60), appropriate functioning with some difficulties (47–53), mild impairments (40–46), moderate impairments (33–39), major impairments (26–32), significant impairments (19–25), severe impairments (12–18)

S-Axis

S41.1. Adjustment disorder (*DSM-5* diagnosis: Adjustment disorder with mixed anxiety and depressed mood; *ICD-10* code F43.23)

Source: Lingiardi, V., & McWilliams, N. (Eds.) *Psychodynamic Diagnostic Manual* (2nd ed.). New York, NY: Guilford Press (2017). Adapted with permission of Guilford Press.

Evaluating the *PDM*

The *PDM* has been praised for providing a diagnostic system that maps the internal meaning systems of clients (Bornstein, 2011; Etzi, 2014; McWilliams, 2011)—something the *DSM* and *ICD*, in sticking to objective descriptions of disorders, don't do. Many psychodynamic psychotherapists believe that the *PDM* can nicely supplement the *DSM* (E. B. Davis & Strawn, 2010; McWilliams, 2011; Wallerstein, 2011). Others have criticized it for adopting the style and language of the *DSM* in a manner that *reifies* diagnosis (**reification** is when we start to treat our invented categories as if they are real) and oversimplifies psychodynamic theories by homogenizing them into a single diagnostic system (I. Z. Hoffman, 2009; McWilliams, 2011). These critics prefer psychodynamic formulations for clients without relying on diagnostic categories, even *PDM*-style diagnostic categories.

Unlike *ICD* codes, *PDM* codes aren't widely accepted for health insurance reimbursement in most countries—although in New Zealand, governmental authorities that pay for treatment now accept a *PDM* diagnosis (Lingiardi & McWilliams, 2017). Despite its generally psychodynamic nature, research suggests that both psychodynamic and non-psychodynamic psychologists approve of the *PDM* (R. M. Gordon, 2009). Thus, in developing the *PDM-2*, some "suggested that it would be more accurate, and would stimulate wider interest in the book, to have called it the *Psychological* Diagnostic Manual, thus clearly distinguishing it from psychiatric, disease-model taxonomies" (McWilliams, 2011, p. 120 [italics in original]). However, having already established a "brand," the name "*Psychodynamic Diagnostic Manual*" was retained for *PDM-2* (Lingiardi & McWilliams, 2017). What has the overall impact of the *PDM* been? It's had a significant impact on some clinicians, yet remains virtually unknown among others (Lingiardi, McWilliams, Bornstein, Gazzillo, & Gordon, 2015). Those who like it see it as a psychodynamically oriented psychological alternative (or supplement) to the *DSM* and *ICD*.

RESEARCH DOMAIN CRITERIA (RDoC)

Toward a Diagnostic System Based on Biomarkers

The **Research Domain Criteria (RDoC)** project is an initiative by the U.S.'s National Institute of Mental Health (NIMH) to devise a diagnostic system that uses biological measures (i.e., biomarkers), rather than observable behaviors, to diagnose mental disorders. It is rooted in three assumptions: (a) mental illnesses are brain disorders that "can be addressed as disorders of brain circuits," (b) "dysfunction in neural circuits can be identified with the tools of clinical neuroscience," and (c) "data from genetics and clinical neuroscience will yield biosignatures" that can be used to diagnose and treat disorders (Insel et al., 2010, p. 749). When it comes to searching for the biological bases of abnormal behavior, RDoC's developers reject *DSM* and *ICD* diagnostic categories for being unhelpful in advancing research due to their questionable validity. Consequently, the NIMH is no longer funding studies that rely exclusively on such categories. Instead it is asking investigators to focus on five biological *domains* related to different presenting symptoms.

RDoC's Five Domains

RDoC's five domains are:

a) *Negative valence systems* (such as fear, anxiety, threat, loss, and frustration);

b) *Positive valence systems* (response to rewards, learning, and habit creation);

c) *Cognitive systems* (attention, perception, memory, and language skills);

d) *Systems for social processes* (emphasizing development of attachment, social communication skills, and understandings of self and others); and

e) *Regulatory systems* (concerned with arousal, emotional regulation, and sleep–wake cycles).

The goal is to start from scratch by identifying brain mechanisms, mapping their functions, and seeing which behavioral domains they affect. RDoC researchers contend that only once this is done can valid mental disorder categories—diagnosable via measurable dysfunctions in the biological domains underlying them—be devised. Thus, the RDoC project is about developing a biomarker-based diagnostic scheme from the ground up.

RDoC has been surrounded by confusion over whether it is a research initiative or a diagnostic system. It currently considers itself a research initiative, with the eventual goal of developing into a thoroughgoing diagnostic system based on biological ways of assessing the five domains. Bruce Cuthbert of the NIMH explains RDoC's present status nicely:

> *What does RDoC involve? The official statement of the RDoC goal—"Develop, for research purposes, new ways of classifying mental disorders..."—could be inferred to mean that NIMH has created a fully-fledged new nosology that is now ready for field trials. This is misleading. In fact, the goal of RDoC is to foster research to validate dimensions defined by neurobiology and behavioral measures that cut across current disorder categories, and that can inform future revisions of our diagnostic systems. In other words, RDoC is intended to support research toward a new classification system, but does not claim to be a completed system at the current time. (Cuthbert, 2014, p. 29)*

Evaluating RDoC

Reactions to the RDoC initiative vary widely. Critics say RDoC mistakenly assumes that mental disorder can be reduced entirely to brain function even though emotional difficulties are often meaningful psychological, situational, or spiritual conflicts as much as they are biological issues (Maj, 2015; McLaren, 2011). Others complain that the NIMH is dictating how it will fund research based on an undeveloped system that faces as many or more validity challenges as the *DSM* system it wishes to supplant (Peterson, 2015). Nonetheless, RDoC has garnered significant attention. Thomas Insel, former Director of the U.S. Institute for Mental Health, hopes that RDoC yields biological means for identifying "precise diagnostic groups within what we now call mental disorders. Such a tectonic shift could ultimately improve the lives of many millions of people" (Insel, 2015). Time will tell whether RDoC succeeds, but it constitutes the latest effort to define, diagnose, and treat mental disorders primarily in biological terms.

HIERARCHICAL TAXONOMY OF PSYCHOPATHOLOGY (HiTOP)

Defining HiTOP and Distinguishing it from *DSM* and *ICD*

The **Hierarchical Taxonomy of Psychopathology (HiTOP)** is an emerging approach to diagnosis that eventually (with further development and refinement) aims to give the *DSM* and *ICD* a run for their money (Gambini, 2017; Kotov et al., 2017). It breaks with the *DSM* and *ICD* by rejecting their long-standing practice of dividing problems into discrete diagnostic categories—noting that the supposedly discrete categories these manuals contain all too often overlap (reflecting the problem of comorbidity, described earlier) (American Psychological Association, 2017; Gambini, 2017; Kotov et al., 2017). Instead, the HiTOP system offers a dimensional and hierarchical approach to diagnosis. HiTOP is dimensional in that instead of dividing pathology into all-or-none categories, it plots it in degrees along dimensions of severity; it is hierarchical in that its dimensions are divided into different levels, with those that are strongly correlated (suggesting they measure overlapping aspects of mental functioning) linked in the hierarchy (American Psychological Association, 2017; Gambini, 2017; Kotov et al., 2017). For a visual representation of HiTOP's empirically based hierarchical dimensional system, see Figure 3.1.

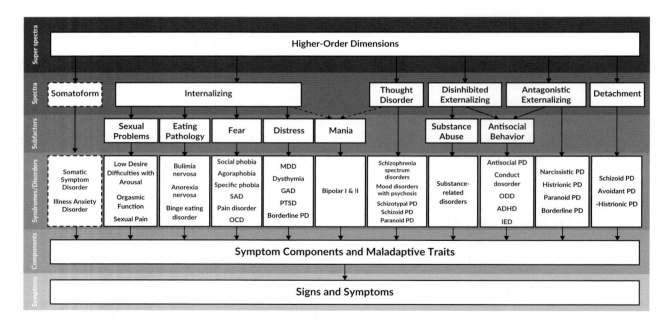

Figure 3.1 The Hierarchical Taxonomy of Psychopathology (HiTOP)

Note: HiTOP contains six hierarchical levels of dimensions that are used to diagnose psychopathology. The *super spectra* level is the *general dimension of psycholopathology (p)*. The *spectra* level beneath the super spectra level contains six basic dimensions of psychopathology (detachment, anatagonistic externalizing, disinhibited externalizing, thought disorder, internalizing, and somatoform). Directly below that are *subfactors*, additional dimensions that measure different aspects of the spectra above them in the hierarchy. Below subfactors are *syndromes/disorders*, clusters of comorbid *DSM* disorders that represent different ways of displaying subfactor and spectra dimensions. Below syndromes/disorders are *components*, or maladaptive traits. Each disorder, subfactor, and spectra consists of certain common co-occurring trait components. Finally, below components are *symptoms*, which are the presenting behaviors and experiences that constitute a patient's presenting problem. All presenting problems consist of specific combinations of components, subfactors, and spectra. Dashed lines refer to provisional aspects of the model that require more research; the minus sign next to histrionic highlights that histrionic is negatively associated with the detachment spectrum.

Source: Figure 2 reproduced from: Kotov, R., Krueger, R. F., Watson, D., Achenbach, T. M., Althoff, R. R., Bagby, R. M., ... Zimmerman, M. (2017). The Hierarchical Taxonomy of Psychopathology (HiTOP): A dimensional alternative to traditional nosologies. *Journal of Abnormal Psychology*, *126*(4), 454–477. Published by APA and reprinted with permission.

HiTOP supporters boldly assert that "unlike *DSM-5*, the HiTOP project adheres to the most up-to-date scientific evidence, rather than relying on expert opinion" (American Psychological Association, 2017, para. 12). Thus, HiTOP constitutes a direct challenge to the scientific status and authority of the long dominant *DSM* and *ICD* categorical systems: "HiTOP's guiding spirit is correcting the shortcomings of DSM-5 and other similar classification schemes, like the World Health Organization's International Classification of Diseases (ICD), by changing the way mental disorders are classified and diagnosed" (Gambini, 2017, para. 5). As Roman Kotov, the psychologist behind the HiTOP system, pointedly put it, "this is about moving the science forward" rather than about "selling books"—a swipe at the *DSM-5*'s large profit margin and, in Kotov's view, its scientific limitations (MacLellan, 2017, para. 18).

HiTOP and RDoC

Besides challenging the *DSM-5*, HiTOP also distinguishes itself from RDoC and its heavy focus on neurobiology (American Psychological Association, 2017). Compared to RDoC, HiTOP has a broader and more inclusively psychological flavor. Further, unlike RDoC—which is currently just a research initiative—practicing clinicians can already use HiTOP to make diagnoses, even if it remains an emerging approach that hasn't yet developed sufficiently to supplant the *DSM-5* (Kotov et al., 2017; MacLellan, 2017). Differences notwithstanding, however, HiTOP's creators hope that when RDoC eventually develops diagnostic applications, the two systems can complement each another (Kotov et al., 2017).

HiTOP's Six Spectra Dimensions

HiTOP can initially seem confusing, mainly because most of us are so accustomed to a categorical as opposed to dimensional way of thinking about psychopathology. The basic gist is that, at the second level of its hierarchy, HiTOP divides psychopathology into six essential dimensions, or **HiTOP spectra** (again, see Figure 3.1). These spectra dimensions, which HiTOP indicates can be assessed using a variety of scientifically validated assessment measures, are as follows:

1. *Internalizing* (or *negative affectivity*) *spectrum*, characterized by negative emotions inside the person, such as social withdrawal, loneliness, depression, anxiety, and difficulty concentrating.

2. *Thought disorder spectrum,* which ranges from eccentric thinking to florid *psychosis* (a broad term used to describe people whose thoughts, behaviors, and perceptions are so strange that they appear to have lost contact with reality; psychosis is more fully defined and discussed in Chapter 4).

3. *Disinhibited externalizing spectrum*, which assesses acting out behaviors attributed to inability to control oneself (e.g., impulsivity, irresponsibility, risk taking, substance use).

4. *Antagonistic externalizing spectrum*, which assesses acting out behaviors attributed to antagonizing others (e.g., callousness, deceitfulness, rudeness, physical aggression).

5. *Detachment spectrum*, entailing disengagement from others (e.g., intimacy avoidance, interpersonal passivity, withdrawal).

6. *Somatoform spectrum*, characterized by displaying physical symptoms (e.g., headaches, gastrointestinal complaints, converting psychological stress into physical symptoms); unlike the other five, the somatoform spectrum is considered "provisional" because there is currently only weak evidence for it.

Interestingly, HiTOP locates familiar *DSM* and *ICD* categories below the level of spectra in the hierarchy. While HiTOP admits that these categories are recognizable and handy ways of naming presenting problems, it views those grouped together under the same spectra not as discrete disorders (as *DSM* does, despite comorbidity issues), but as merely diverse expressions of the spectra above them in the hierarchy. Looking at Figure 3.1, for example, generalized anxiety disorder (GAD) and major depressive disorder (MDD) are nothing more than two ways of exhibiting pathology along the internalizing spectrum dimension. Should HiTOP succeed in supplanting the *DSM*, it might eliminate *DSM* categories from its diagnostic hierarchy entirely and instead rely exclusively on its six spectra and the lower-level traits that constitute them.

Evaluating HiTOP

At the time of writing, HiTOP is brand new, so there is little or no published debate over its relative merits. Its authors point to several possible strengths of the HiTOP system (Kotov et al., 2017). Citing twin, family, and even some genetic marker studies, they point to evidence suggesting that HiTOP's research-derived spectra may have common genetic and environmental risk factors, as well as shared neurobiological correlates. They also argue that HiTOP is more *parsimonious* than *DSM* and *ICD*—meaning that it accounts for psychopathology equally as well or better than *DSM* and *ICD* while relying on far fewer concepts; six basic spectra complemented by several other hierarchical dimensions offer a much leaner assessment system compared to the many hundreds of *DSM* and *ICD* categories. Finally, HiTOP's authors suggest that their diagnostic system may explain why the same treatments (such as SSRIs) often work for many different *DSM* and *ICD* diagnoses. How so? Well, in the HiTOP system, supposedly discrete *DSM* and *ICD* disorders that inexplicably respond to the same treatment are reframed as simply different expressions of dysfunction along the same spectra. This makes their similar responsiveness to treatment totally understandable.

Speculating about weaknesses, the HiTOP system remains new and requires further study. Its somatoform spectrum, especially, lacks adequate research support (Kotov et al., 2017). More practically, as in formulation, abandoning discrete diagnostic categories (and, perhaps more importantly, the codes that accompany them) makes the everyday cataloging of psychopathology much more difficult. Quick communication about presenting problems—to track incidence and prevalence patterns or grease the wheels of insurance reimbursement—remains a real-world issue that HiTOP will need to address if it hopes to become widely utilized. For better or worse, diagnostic systems not only must be scientifically reliable and valid. They also need to meet the administrative demands of everyday practice. Diagnostic categories, for all their limitations, do this quite well. Whether HiTOP can match this practical requirement necessary for widespread adoption remains to be seen.

POWER THREAT MEANING (PTM) FRAMEWORK

A Psychosocial Framework for Identifying Patterns in Human Distress

Clinical psychologists from the British Psychological Society (BPS) have recently introduced the **Power Threat Meaning (PTM) Framework** as a more psychosocial alternative to the medical-model orientation of *DSM* and *ICD* (Johnstone & Boyle, 2018). The PTM Framework rejects the use of psychiatric diagnostic categories that attribute psychological distress to biologically based diseases. Instead, it holds that such distress originates in economic and social injustices that affect psychosocial functioning. These injustices limit the ability of caregivers to provide their children with the secure relationships they need to be able to cope with future adversity. Difficulty coping with adversity, in turn, leads to emotional distress and the development of problematic and counterproductive behaviors. The PTM Framework maintains that this cycle is perpetuated as long as the original economic and social injustices remain unaddressed. Instead of assuming something is "wrong" with clients, the PTM Framework assesses three intertwined constructs—*power*, *threat*, and *meaning*:

» *Power* emphasizes what has happened to people. When considering the role of power, clinicians look at social circumstances clients have faced that have impacted them—such as coercive power (e.g., war, assault, bullying), legal power (e.g., arrest, imprisonment, hospitalization), economic and material power (e.g., lack of access to employment, housing, medical care), ideological power (socially dominant ways of understanding the world that may disadvantage clients), interpersonal power (e.g., being abandoned or not cared for by others), and biological power (being treated in certain ways based on one's physical and intellectual attributes).

» *Threat* focuses on people's responses to the ways power impacts them. People respond in an infinite number of ways to what happens to them, but certain responses are common. Table 3.9 presents common threat responses identified by the PTM Framework.

» *Meaning* concerns itself with how people make sense of what happens to them. It includes people's feelings, bodily reactions, and thoughts, all of which arise within wider social discourses about acceptable ways of responding. Does a client who has faced economic discrimination make sense of her situation in a way that leads her to feel hopeless, alienated, outraged, ashamed, isolated, defeated, and so on? The PTM Framework maintains it is essential to understand client meanings to fully comprehend their emotional distress.

Table 3.9 The *PTM* Framework's Functional Groupings of Threat Responses

Regulating overwhelming feelings	E.g. by dissociation, self-injury, memory fragmentation, bingeing and purging, differential memory encoding, carrying out rituals, intellectualisation, 'high' mood, low mood, hearing voices, use of alcohol and drugs, compulsive activity of various kinds, overeating, denial, projection, splitting, derealisation, somatic sensations, bodily numbing
Protection from physical danger	E.g. by hypervigilance, insomnia, flashbacks, nightmares, fight/flight/freeze, suspicious thoughts, isolation, aggression.
Maintaining a sense of control	E.g. by self-starvation, rituals, violence, dominance in relationships

Seeking attachments	E.g. by idealisation, appeasement, seeking care and emotional responses, use of sexuality
Protection against attachment loss, hurt and abandonment	E.g. by rejection of others, distrust, seeking care and emotional responses, submission, self-blame, interpersonal violence, hoarding, appeasement, self-silencing, self-punishment
Preserving identity, self- image and self-esteem	E.g. by grandiosity, unusual beliefs, feeling entitled, perfectionism, striving, dominance, hostility, aggression
Preserving a place within the social group	E.g. by striving, competitiveness, appeasement, self-silencing, self-blame
Meeting emotional needs/self-soothing	E.g. by rocking, self-harm, skin-picking, bingeing, alcohol use, over-eating, compulsive sexuality
Communication about distress, elicit care	E.g. by self-injury, unusual beliefs, voice-hearing, self-starvation
Finding meaning and purpose	E.g. by unusual beliefs, overwork, high moods

Source: Reproduced from Johnstone and Boyle (2018) with permission of the British Psychological Society through PLSclear.

Although the PTM Framework eschews diagnostic categories, it does describe general patterns of threat response to common social and economic inequalities—including common ways clients react to rejection, entrapment, and invalidation; disrupted attachment relationships and adversity in childhood; separation and identity confusion; defeat, disconnection and loss; social exclusion, shame, and coercive power; and single threatening events (e.g., natural disasters, accidents, assaults, bereavement, medical issues). Importantly, the PTM Framework sees these general patterns as not only common, but as expected and reasonable responses to troublesome social circumstances. As an example, consider the PTM Framework's description of common responses to *surviving or witnessing domestic abuse as a child/young person*:

> *These children may be particularly likely, especially if boys, to pass on violence (cruelty to animals, aggression and temper outbursts, delinquency, fighting, bullying, threatening, poor peer relationships, disrespect for women, domestic abuse as an adult). This may involve a process of "identifying with the aggressor." Alternatively they (mainly girls) may resort to compliance, withdrawal, and feel great responsibility for the abused parent, as shown in high levels of guilt, anxiety, and separation anxiety. Later, adolescents and adults may seek affection through risky and indiscriminate sexual behaviour. The worse the violence in the home, the more severely children are affected. (Johnstone & Boyle, 2018, p. 229)*

Evaluating the PTM Framework

As with HiTOP, the PTM Framework is new and research on it is in the early stages. The PTM Framework is highly consistent with formulation in that, unlike the purely descriptive *DSM* and *ICD* approach, it aims to provide a psychosocial explanation for clients' presenting problems. Consistent with the RDoC approach, the PTM Framework is skeptical of existing diagnostic categories. However, unlike RDoC, it does not seek to identify underlying biological markers for presenting problems because—in direct contrast to RDoC—it sees psychological distress as originating first and foremost from social conditions, not brain diseases. Social and economic disparities, not biomarkers, are privileged in the PTM Framework's conception of presenting problems. Thus, your preference for RDoC, HiTOP, or the PTM Framework may tell you something about your implicit assumptions about the origins of (and therefore the best way to evaluate and identify) emotional distress.

3.4 ASSESSMENT

To devise a formulation or arrive at a diagnosis (*DSM*, *ICD*, *PDM*, or perhaps—someday—RDoC or HiTOP), clinicians rely on a variety of assessment techniques. To assess something is to appraise or evaluate it (Dictionary.com, n.d.-a). Therefore, **assessment** involves gathering information to understand or diagnose a person's difficulties. The main kinds of assessments in clinical practice are clinical interviews, personality tests, intelligence tests, neuropsychological tests, and neurological tests (all discussed below). Most, but not all, assessment involves **standardization**, in which clearly defined rules for how to administer and interpret a test instrument are developed. Standardization insures that the instrument is used in the same way regardless of who is administering it. As with diagnosis, reliability and validity are important in thinking about assessment.

Reliable assessment measures yield similar results each time they are administered, whereas valid measures measure what they are supposed to. In thinking about the validity of assessment, keep in mind that—as with diagnosis (discussed earlier)—various types of validity are relevant, including *descriptive validity* (does an assessment accurately describe the individual?), *face validity* (on the face of it, does the assessment seem accurate and sensible?), *predictive validity* (does an assessment allow us to predict future behavior?), and *concurrent validity* (are the assessment results consistent with other assessments measuring the same thing and given concurrently—that is, at the same time?). We discuss different types of assessment below, but before proceeding, check out the "Try It Yourself" feature for a link to PsychCentral's online collection of self-assessments, most of which are rooted in scientific research.

TRY IT YOURSELF

Free Online Self-Assessments

The PsychCentral website (https://psychcentral.com) offers a wide selection of online self-assessments, most of which it says are rooted in scientific research. These assessments can be used to learn more about many of the presenting problems discussed throughout this book. While they may provide you with insights into yourself, in rare instances students become upset with what these online tests tell them. If you have concerns, consult your professor or seek professional help.

Quizzes available online at https://psychcentral.com/quizzes/

CLINICAL INTERVIEWS

In a **clinical interview**, the clinician talks to the client about the problem. Interviews are useful in learning the client's history; they also allow for direct observation of behavior—observing the client's demeanor, style of speech, and mannerisms can provide useful insights (Anastasi & Urbina, 1997; K. D. Jones, 2010).

Unstructured Interviews

The degree of structure in an interview varies. In an **unstructured interview** the clinician asks the client open-ended questions. Because there is no clear script, the information gleaned depends on what a clinician chooses to ask.

Jill

An unstructured interview with Jill might involve the clinician inquiring about what brings her to therapy. The direction the interview takes depends on Jill's responses and the clinician's follow-up questions.

CASE EXAMPLES

The advantage of unstructured interviews is that they are open-ended, allowing clients the chance to share what they deem important. The disadvantage is that such interviews lack standardization and important areas may get overlooked (Anastasi & Urbina, 1997). Vital questions may not get asked and reliability and validity may suffer.

Structured Interviews

In a **structured interview** the clinician employs a clear set of questions. These interviews vary from *semi-structured* (where clinicians retain some latitude in how they respond) to *highly structured* (where the interview is akin to a questionnaire administered verbally). When conducting a structured interview, the clinician often asks a scripted set of questions in precise order. This guarantees that everyone undergoing such an interview receives the exact same questions. Spontaneity is removed, but greater reliability and validity are potentially gained.

One very well-known structured interview is the **mental status exam**, the goal of which is to assess the client's current functioning. When conducting a mental status exam, the clinician observes and inquires about the client's *appearance, attitude, and activity*; *mood and affect*; *speech and language*; *thought processes, thought*

Interviews can be unstructured or structured. Here a clinician conducts a highly structured interview with a scripted set of questions.
Source: PHOTODISC

content, and perception; cognition; and *insight and judgment* (K. D. Jones, 2010). Compared to an unstructured interview, a mental status exam has a definite focus regardless of who is administering it. The areas assessed are clear, unambiguous, and generally asked about in a standardized manner.

Jill

A mental status exam with Jill reveals that she appears neat and well groomed, seems lethargic but also deferent to the assessor, talks slowly and methodically, thinks clearly for the most part except when discussing family and career issues, and lacks insight into why she has been feeling anxious.

CASE EXAMPLES

Using Interviews in Diagnosis and Formulation

Interviews can be used to assist in making *DSM, ICD,* or *PDM* diagnoses. They can also be used to assist clinicians in developing formulations. Some research suggests that when making *DSM* diagnoses, unstructured interviews are less accurate than more structured ones (R. W. Baker & Trzepacz, 2013). Therefore, many clinicians use procedures such as the **Structured Clinical Interview for *DSM* Disorders (SCID)**, a well-known semi-structured interview for making *DSM* diagnoses (K. D. Jones, 2010). A clinician administering the SCID asks a series of structured questions and then—depending on the client's responses—uses decision-trees to ask follow-up questions and arrive at a *DSM* diagnosis. The SCID-5 was published in 2015 and is based on *DSM-5* categories. A SCID interview might help a clinician arrive at a generalized anxiety disorder diagnosis for Jill.

PERSONALITY TESTS

A **personality test** can be broadly defined as a test that measures emotions, interpersonal relationship patterns, levels of motivation and interest, and attitudes (First & Gibbon, 2004). Personality tests are often used to understand abnormal behavior. There are many kinds of personality tests. Self-report inventories and projective tests are the most common personality assessments, but other approaches to personality assessment are also used.

Self-Report Personality Inventories

Self-report personality inventories are examples of objective tests. An **objective test** uses standardized items with limited response choices (e.g., multiple choice, "true/false," or "yes/no") (Anastasi & Urbina, 1997). Self-report inventories are usually quite easy to administer and score because they have clear answer choices and scoring schemes. However, by limiting responses, important issues that the test doesn't ask about may be overlooked. Additionally, test-takers can minimize their concerns or interpret items in ways the test-constructors did not intend.

The best-known self-report inventory in abnormal psychology is the **Minnesota Multiphasic Personality Inventory (MMPI)**—currently in its second edition, the MMPI-2. It consists of 567 statements to which respondents can answer "true," "false," or "cannot say." The test's norms—the data used to determine how to score test items—were established by seeking responses to many true–false sample statements from people with different mental disorder diagnoses; the 567 statements that most reliably distinguished people in the different diagnostic groups from one another were retained and became the MMPI-2. There are ten clinical scales on the MMPI-2, as well as validity scales that try to pick up whether test-takers are *faking bad* or *faking good* (trying to appear more or less troubled than they truly are) (D. L. Segal & Coolidge, 2004). The ten clinical scales are: *hypochondriasis, depression, hysteria, psychopathic deviate, masculinity-femininity, paranoia, psychasthenia* (symptoms such as phobias, obsessions, compulsions, and anxiety), *schizophrenia, mania,* and *social introversion* (J. R. Graham, 2011). Subscales have been developed to measure a variety of things, including anxiety, depression, social discomfort, antisocial practices, and family discord (Butcher, Atlas, & Hahn, 2004; J. R. Graham, 2011). Figure 3.2 shows Jill's MMPI-2 profile.

Another of the many established personality inventories is the **Sixteen Personality Factor (16PF) Questionnaire**. The 16PF consists of 185 multiple-choice items and yields scores on 16 primary personality factors (*warmth, reasoning, emotional stability, dominance, liveliness, rule-consciousness, social boldness, sensitivity, vigilance, abstractedness, privateness, apprehension, openness to change, self-reliance, perfectionism,* and *tension*), as well as on the **Big Five** global personality traits (*extraversion, anxiety* [*neuroticism*], *tough-mindedness* [*openness*], *independence* [*agreeableness*], and *self-control* [*conscientiousness*]) (Butcher et al., 2004). The 16PF has fewer items than the MMPI-2, so it doesn't take as long to complete.

Some inventories assess an aspect of abnormal functioning rather than trying to evaluate the entire personality. The most famous example of this kind of assessment is the **Beck Depression Inventory (BDI)**, a 21-item self-administered inventory for measuring depression that was originally developed by cognitive therapist Aaron

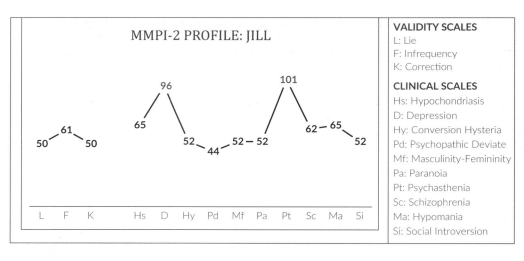

VALIDITY SCALES
L: Lie
F: Infrequency
K: Correction

CLINICAL SCALES
Hs: Hypochondriasis
D: Depression
Hy: Conversion Hysteria
Pd: Psychopathic Deviate
Mf: Masculinity-Femininity
Pa: Paranoia
Pt: Psychasthenia
Sc: Schizophrenia
Ma: Hypomania
Si: Social Introversion

Figure 3.2 Jill's MMPI-2 Profile

Note: Jill's two highest scores are on the *Depression* (D) and *Psychasthenia* (Pt) scales. People who score this way are thought to be highly anxious, high-strung, and jumpy. They have a high need for achievement, but are often passive and dependent in relationships with others (J. R. Graham, 2011). Source: MMPI®-2 Profile for Jill adapted from the MMPI®-2 (Minnesota Multiphasic Personality Inventory®-2) Manual for Administration, Scoring, and Interpretation, Revised Edition. Copyright © 2001 by the Regents of the University of Minnesota. All rights reserved. Used by permission of the University of Minnesota Press. "MMPI" and "Minnesota Multiphasic Personality Inventory" are registered trademarks owned by the Regents of the University of Minnesota.

Beck (Cattell, 2004). Other examples of inventories intended to assess a specific area of functioning are the *Child Abuse Potential (CAP) Inventory* (Dozios & Covin, 2004), the *State-Trait Anxiety Inventory (STAI)*, and the *State-Trait Anger Expression Inventory (STAXI)* (J. S. Miller, 2004).

Projective Tests

When taking a **projective test**, the individual engages in some form of artistic representation that is used to infer aspects of psychological functioning (Spielberger & Reheiser, 2004). Whereas objective tests require discrete answers, projective assessments are more ambiguous and open-ended (Leichtman, 2004). Many but not all projective tests have psychodynamic origins. There are many projective tests; two well-known ones are discussed here.

Rorschach Inkblot Method (RIM)

The **Rorschach Inkblot Method (RIM)** is perhaps the best-known projective test. Originally developed by Hermann Rorschach in 1921, it consists of 10 inkblots on 6¾ by 9¾-inch cards (Leichtman, 2004). Numerous procedures for administering it have been devised—often employing psychodynamic perspectives (I. B. Weiner, 2004). John Exner has developed the *Comprehensive System (CS)*, the most popular Rorschach procedure in recent years—perhaps because Exner *normed* the test. Just as the builders of the MMPI-2 did in constructing that measure, Exner administered Rorschach tests to many people from different diagnostic groups and identified which kinds of responses differentiated them from one another. These norms have since been used to inform how the Rorschach is scored when using the Comprehensive System. In the CS, test-takers are presented with each card and asked what it might be. Responses are coded based on what is seen, whether the entire blot or specific areas of it are incorporated into the response,

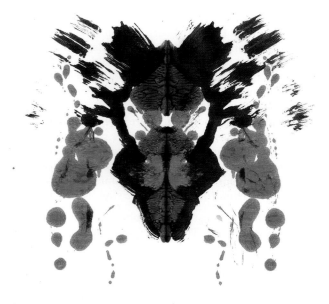

Figure 3.3 An Inkblot like the ones used in the Rorschach Test

Note: A sample inkblot is shown to protect real Rorschach cards from exposure outside of an assessment setting.
Source: iStock.com/spxChrome

and how the test-taker uses features of the blot such as form, color, and texture in explaining what makes it look that way to them (Lerner, 1998). Based on the norms (the most common answers given by each diagnostic group), Rorschach response patterns have been identified that can be used to make *DSM* diagnoses. Figure 3.3 shows an inkblot like those used in the Rorschach test.

Critics of the Rorschach complain that it is difficult to administer and score. They also have challenged Exner's research, arguing that the Comprehensive System isn't valid (I. B. Weiner, 2004). However, some critics concur with research showing the CS to be useful in identifying cognitive ability and impairment (Lilienfeld, Wood, & Garb, 2000; J. M. Wood & Lilienfeld, 1999; J. M. Wood et al., 2010; J. M. Wood, Nezworski, Garb, & Lilienfeld, 2001). Regardless, the Rorschach remains controversial. It is widely used in some settings and not at all in others.

Thematic Apperception Test (TAT)

The **Thematic Apperception Test (TAT)** is another projective technique. It contains 30 cards, all of which contain illustrations of vague scenes—except for one that is blank (Mihura, Meyer, Dumitrascu, & Bombel, 2013; J. M. Wood, Garb, Nezworski, Lilienfeld, & Duke, 2015). Depending on age and gender, test-takers are presented with 20 of the cards, usually in two separate 50-minute sessions (Moretti & Rossini, 2004). For each card, test-takers are asked to tell a story with a beginning, middle, and end. Though many TAT administrators find scoring and analyzing test-takers' stories for thematic content or psychodynamic and narrative themes clinically useful (Moretti & Rossini, 2004), critics complain that the TAT lacks standardization and that administrators use different scoring systems—or sometimes none at all, instead relying on their own subjective interpretations (Cramer, 1999). However, some TAT supporters counter that clinical interpretations are often more valid and useful than reliance on strict scoring schemes (Garb, 1998; Lilienfeld et al., 2000). In-depth coverage of the TAT is no longer part of many clinical training programs, but it remains popular in some circles (Karon, 2000; Rossini & Moretti, 1997). See the "The Lived Experience" feature for two of Jill's TAT stories, along with an analysis of their thematic content.

**THE LIVED
EXPERIENCE**

Two of Jill's TAT Stories

These are Jill's imagined responses to being shown the cards described below.

Card 3: Woman standing next to open door with hand to downcast face

Jill: "A woman woke up and her husband yelled at her for not cleaning up properly. Her kids were running around and making her crazy. The dog ran through and the kids spilled fruit punch. Her mail was full of bills. So, she called a babysitter, bought an airline ticket to Bermuda on her husband's credit card, and left. In Bermuda, she fell in love with a sexy Bermuda guy and never returned."

» HERO: woman
» OUTCOME: runs away to escape
» THEMES: responsibility, frustration, need to escape, familial relationships

Card 6: Young woman on sofa with older man smoking cigar behind her

Jill: "A 15-year old girl's father refuses to let her meet her boyfriend for a date because she isn't 16. The girl sneaks out of the house to meet him anyway. She has a wonderful time, but while kissing her boyfriend on the porch she is caught by her father. The father calls the boyfriend a cradle robber, then lectures the girl while smoking a cigar. The mother comes downstairs and tells the father to leave the girl alone because they were dating at her age. The mother also makes the father put out the cigar. The girl calls the boyfriend for a date the next night."

» HERO: the girl
» OUTCOME: positive; can see boyfriend, but without resolving father conflict
» THEMES: control, rebellion against authority, father–daughter relationship

For each card on the Thematic Apperception Test (TAT), the test-taker generates stories; common themes are often identified to understand client issues.
Source: Jonathan D. Raskin

EXAMPLES OF PERSONALITY ASSESSMENT FROM OTHER PERSPECTIVES

Cognitive-Behavioral Assessment

Behavioral Assessment

Because purely behavioral perspectives reject speculation about processes inside people, their understanding of abnormality almost exclusively emphasizes how the environment influences behavior (Hadaway & Brue, 2016; Heiby & Haynes, 2004; Ollendick, Alvarez, & Greene, 2004). Therefore, **behavioral assessment** focuses on identifying conditions in the environment that sustain undesirable behaviors (Hadaway & Brue, 2016; Haynes, 1998; Heiby & Haynes, 2004; Strosahl & Linehan, 1986). Once these conditions are understood, the environment can be altered accordingly to encourage preferred behaviors. Behavioral assessment uses a variety of techniques—including *behavioral observation*, *clinical interviews*, and *self-reports*—to arrive at a **functional analysis**, which consists of judgments about relationships between environmental conditions and client behavior, along with estimates of how these relationships might be modified (Hadaway & Brue, 2016; Ollendick et al., 2004). Let's briefly examine several behavioral assessment techniques.

Behavioral observation is just what it sounds like: direct observation of behavior. For instance, the behavioral observation method known as **ABC recording** involves directly observing and recording client behaviors ("B"), while also writing down their antecedents (what comes before them, or "A") and their consequences (what comes after them, or "C") (Gable, Quinn, Rutherford, Howell, & Hoffman, 1999; Lanovaz, Argumedes, Roy, Duquette, & Watkins, 2013; R. H. Thompson & Borrero, 2011). By doing this, the clinician identifies reinforcement patterns that maintain undesired behaviors. Sometimes ABC recording is conducted using a *narrative method* in which the observer provides a running description (i.e., a narrative) of the patient's behavior (Lanovaz et al., 2013; R. H. Thompson & Borrero, 2011). Other times ABC recording is done using a *checklist method*. This involves having the observer mark a list of antecedents and consequences, checking them off each time they occur (Lanovaz et al., 2013; R. H. Thompson & Borrero, 2011).

Jill

A behavior therapist employing ABC recording might observe Jill during a day at school while narratively recording her behavior. This would allow the therapist to gather data that reveals patterns among Jill's behavior, its antecedents, and its consequences. In so doing, the behavior therapist might identify how Jill displays more anxiety during and after pre-med classes and less anxiety during and after dance classes.

Another form of behavioral observation is the **scatterplot** method, in which the client's behavior in a specific environment is continuously observed over time to identify temporal patterns (Gable et al., 1999; R. H. Thompson & Borrero, 2011). In scatterplot assessment, no antecedents or consequences are recorded; only the behavior of interest is logged. The data is then used to chart changes during the day in the frequency of the target behavior. Once this is known, alterations to the environment can be made during identified times of day to change the target behavior's frequency.

Because it might not be practical to follow Jill around to conduct an ABC recording or a scatterplot assessment, a behavior analyst might employ yet another form of direct observation known as an **analogue behavioral observation** (Haynes, 1998). In an analogue observation, people are interviewed about their problem or observed in a setting analogous to the one suspected of causing difficulties. As with the ABC method and scatterplot assessment, the goal is to identify environmental patterns that may be sustaining undesired behaviors.

Jill

If a behavior therapist employed analogue behavioral observation with Jill, he might interview Jill and her parents or ask them to have dinner together in an environment in which they could be naturally observed. The clinician would then evaluate the behavior of Jill and her parents and look for functional relationships that sustain and reinforce problematic patterns.

Of course, it's not always feasible to directly observe behavior. Therefore, indirect forms of behavioral assessment are often used instead. Some indirect behavioral assessments rely on clinical interviews. For example, the **functional analysis interview (FAI)** is a structured interview method in which the interviewer gathers information from the client about the behavior of interest, its antecedents, its consequences, and circumstances and strategies that seem to increase or decrease the behavior (Kelley, LaRue, Roane, & Gadaire, 2011). Self-reports are another means of indirect behavioral assessment. The **Problem Behavior Questionnaire (PBQ)** and the **Questions About Behavioral Function (QABF)** checklist are two prominent behavioral self-report measures. The PBQ is a 15-item scale that asks questions about the target behavior;

people completing it rate the percentage of the time the behavior occurs (never, 10%, 25%, 50%, 75%, 90%, or always) (Kelley et al., 2011; T. J. Lewis, Scott, & Sugai, 1994). The QABF is a 25-item inventory that assesses the extent to which behaviors are reinforced by providing social attention, escape from undesirable situations, tangible rewards, a way of coping with physical discomfort, or a way to entertain or pacify oneself in nonsocial situations (Kelley et al., 2011; Matson, Tureck, & Rieske, 2012; Paclawskyj, Matson, Rush, Smalls, & Vollmer, 2000). Self-report measures offer a quick and easy alternative to more labor-intensive behavioral assessments.

The goal of all these behavioral assessments—direct or indirect—is to identify the functional relations between environment and behavior. Once these relationships are understood, the environment can be altered to condition desired behaviors and discourage or eliminate undesired ones. While critics complain that behavioral assessment fails to get at underlying meanings that may not be readily observable, its main appeal is that by limiting itself to observable behaviors, it locates the source of problems in the environment rather than in individuals. Of course, not all clinicians conducting behavioral assessment limit themselves solely to observable behaviors. Sometimes behavioral assessments are complemented by cognitive assessments, discussed next.

Cognitive Assessment

Cognitive-behaviorists (as opposed to pure behaviorists) incorporate cognitive data into their behavioral assessments. However, as soon as they do so, they are no longer adhering to the strictly behavioral strategy of avoiding speculation about internal processes. Assessment measures rooted in cognitive perspectives evaluate clients' ways of thinking about things. For example, self-report measures have been developed that allow clinicians to quickly assess their clients' **self-efficacy** (their cognitive estimates of how likely they are to succeed in performing tasks) (Luszczynska, Scholz, & Schwarzer, 2005; Scholz, Doña, Sud, & Schwarzer, 2002; Sherer et al., 1982). This sort of data can be helpful in evaluating how a client's cognitive attributions influence their psychological functioning.

Most cognitive assessments focus on measuring negative thinking or cognitive distortions. Two well-known examples of such assessments are the Daily Record of Dysfunctional Thoughts (DRDT) (see Chapter 2) and the Beck Depression Inventory (BDI) (discussed earlier in this chapter). The DRDT is a form with five columns. In these columns, the client records the situation, any accompanying emotions, automatic thoughts the situation triggers, a more rational response, and the outcome of the situation (A. T. Beck, 1979; J. S. Beck, 2011; van Bilsen, 2013). The idea is for client and therapist to gather data allowing them to identify and revise the client's negative automatic thoughts. The DRDT and the BDI are both used to assess problematic thoughts, in keeping with the cognitive emphasis on psychopathology as a product of dysfunctional thinking.

Humanistic Assessment

Humanistic perspectives on assessment emphasize the underlying meanings that clients assign to their symptoms, as well as having clinicians describe client experience using everyday (rather than diagnostic) language. Rather than arriving at a static categorical diagnosis, they aim to understand the problem in terms of the client's ever-changing experience. Below we provide two examples of humanistic assessment: the Q-sort and the role construct repertory test.

Q-sort

The **Q-sort** is a person-centered assessment procedure that uses everyday descriptors to understand psychological functioning (Heyman & Smith Slep, 2004). In the *California Q-sort*, test administrators sort 100 cards, each with a descriptor on it, into nine sets containing 5, 8, 12, 16, 18, 16, 12, 8, and 5 cards. This is done using their clinical impressions of the client. In the first set, assessors place the 5 cards most descriptive of the person; in the second set, they place the 8 cards next most descriptive of the person; and so on until reaching the last 5 cards, which are least descriptive of the person. Different descriptors can be used with different populations (e.g., adults, children, parents) (Block, 2008). Three examples of descriptors used with adults are "Is fastidious, meticulous, careful and precise," "Initiates humor; makes spontaneous funny remarks," and "Feels cheated and victimized by life; self-pitying; feels sorry for self" (Block, 2008). The idea is to describe personality in terms of everyday descriptions rather than *DSM* or *ICD* diagnostic categories. Multiple assessors can complete sorts for a client and their results can be compared. Q-sort researchers have tried to identify sorting patterns that reflect things like paranoia, hysteria, ego-resiliency, and optimal functioning. While the Q-sort has been criticized for assuming all assessors interpret descriptors similarly and for forcing assessors to sort cards into nine predetermined piles, the test is interesting in its humanistic effort to understand clients using everyday language (Block, 2008). Some humanistic therapists don't sort the cards themselves. Instead, they have clients do it. This provides therapists with a sense of how clients understand themselves.

Role Construct Repertory Test

The **role construct repertory test (rep test)** emerges from George Kelly's (1955/1991a, 1955/1991b) personal construct theory (mentioned in Chapter 2). When using the rep test, clients are provided with a list containing sets of three people in their lives. For each set, they must identify how two of the people are similar and different from the third (Fromm, 1995/2004). Each result constitutes a *personal construct*.

Jill

For instance, Jill might be asked about her mother, best friend, and favorite professor. She indicates that her mother and favorite professor are "powerful," while her best friend is "influenced by others." "Powerful vs. influenced by others" is one of Jill's personal constructs, which she uses to make sense of events.

CASE EXAMPLES

Analyses can be done to map the relationships among a client's personal constructs. While this can be time consuming, personal construct therapists argue that the personal constructs elicited during a rep test help clinicians understand presenting problems in terms of the client's meanings rather than the clinician's diagnostic categories.

INTELLIGENCE TESTS

Intelligence can be defined as "cognition comprising sensory, perceptual, associative, and relational knowledge" (Sas, 2004, p. 5). Most theorists see intelligence as generally stable over time, even though they disagree about how many different abilities intelligence consists of. Psychologists have devised many different **intelligence tests**—a difficult task because intelligence is not something that can be observed directly, but something that must be inferred from performance. Another challenge is distinguishing intelligence from achievement. Whereas intelligence is often assumed to consist of innate abilities, **achievement** describes successful performance following learning. Intelligence and achievement are clearly related, but are not one and the same (Benson, 2003). Performance on intelligence tests often correlates with academic performance.

Among the most popular intelligence tests are the *Weschler Adult Intelligence Scales (WAIS)* and the *Weschler Intelligence Scales for Children (WISC)* (M. C. Ramsay & Reynolds, 2004). Both can be used to calculate an **intelligence quotient (IQ)**, which is calculated by taking one's *mental age* (a score reflecting level of performance on an intelligence test), dividing it by one's *chronological age* (how old one is), and multiplying it by 100. An IQ of 130–145 is considered gifted; 120–129, superior; 110–119, high average, 90–110, average; 80–89, low average; and 70–79, borderline (School Psychologist Files, n.d.). Scores lower than 70 may indicate an intellectual disability (see Chapter 14) (Bhaumik et al., 2016). IQ is a popular, but relatively crude, means for communicating something as complex as intelligence, which is often seen as consisting of many different abilities. Still, intelligence tests are commonly considered to be one of professional psychology's greatest achievements and are widely used to predict school performance and diagnose intellectual and learning disabilities (J. Zhu, Weiss, Prifitera, & Coalson, 2004). We discuss intellectual and learning difficulties further in Chapter 14.

NEUROPSYCHOLOGICAL AND NEUROLOGICAL TESTS

The medical model assumes that abnormality is tied to underlying brain function. Two kinds of tests designed to assess brain functioning have been devised: neuropsychological tests and neurological tests. **Neuropsychological tests** are psychological tests in which someone completes a variety of perceptual, cognitive, and motor tasks designed to assess things like *memory*, *visuospatial skills* (ability to understand spatial relationships among objects), *sensorimotor skills* (ability to receive sensory messages and produce an appropriate motor response) and **executive functioning** (cognitive processes involving attention, planning, decision-making, and goal-directed behavior). Based on performance, hypotheses about potential brain dysfunction are inferred. In contrast, **neurological tests** are physiological tests that measure brain functioning directly. To further clarify, let's discuss a few examples of neuropsychological and neurological tests.

Neuropsychological Tests

The **Bender Visual Motor Gestalt Test** is a commonly used neuropsychological test consisting of nine cards with geometrical designs printed on them. Test-takers are asked to examine the designs and then draw them from memory. Difficulty doing so is viewed as an indicator of brain damage. One of the weaknesses of tests like the Bender Gestalt is that they only assess one area of neuropsychological functioning. Consequently, several different tests must be combined in order to assess the full range of functioning. However, these tests are typically not designed to be used together and often duplicate measurement of some functions while leaving out others (Benson, 2003; Martínez, White, Jochim, & Nellis, 2012). To counter this drawback, standardized

test batteries consisting of various tasks intended to assess the full range of neuropsychological functioning have been developed.

Two examples of neuropsychological test batteries are the **Halstead-Reitan Neuropsychological Test Battery (HRB)** and the **Luria-Nebraska Neuropsychological Battery (LNNB)**. The HRB consists of eight tests that combine to assess the following domains: visual, auditory, and tactile functioning; verbal communication; spatial and sequential perception; ability to analyze information; motor ability; and attention, concentration, and memory ("Halstead-Reitan Battery," n.d.). It is used to assess brain damage, as well as to hypothesize about causes of lost function (e.g., stroke, Alzheimer's disease, alcohol use, and head injury) (Anastasi & Urbina, 1997). The LNNB is a 269-item inventory that takes less time to complete than the HRB. It has 11 clinical scales assessing areas such as reading, writing, math, memory, language, and motor function ("Luria-Nebraska Neuropsychological Battery," n.d.; Reitan & Wolfson, 2004). Both the HRB and LNNB have versions for use with children (Golden, 2004; "Luria-Nebraska Neuropsychological Battery," n.d.).

Neurological Tests

Among the neurological tests, psychologists commonly use the **electroencephalogram (EEG)**, a device that records the electrical activity of neurons firing, known as **brain waves**. The EEG is one way of measuring brain activity. **Neuroimaging techniques** are more advanced (and expensive!) neurological measures that photograph brain activity.

Positron emission topography (PET scan) is a powerful neuroimaging technique in which radioactive isotopes are placed into the bloodstream (Portnow, Vaillancourt, & Okun, 2013; Weingarten & Strauman, 2015). The PET scan detects the location of these isotopes using gamma rays and generates images reflecting changes in cerebral blood flow. Areas with increased blood flow are more active, so if we ask someone to complete a task and take a PET scan, we can see which brain areas "light up" during the task.

Magnetic resonance imaging (MRI) is another neuroimaging technique, which creates an x-ray-like picture of the brain using the magnetic activity of hydrogen atoms (Weingarten & Strauman, 2015). One kind of MRI, *functional magnetic resonance imaging (fMRI)*, is of interest in abnormal psychology because it can be used to measure blood flow in various brain areas while the person is thinking, feeling, or completing a task. The fMRI maps brain blood-flow activity by tracking the amount of oxygen in the brain's hemoglobin (Weingarten & Strauman, 2015). From fMRI data, researchers can infer which areas of the brain are associated with different psychological experiences. The fMRI has eclipsed the PET scan in abnormal psychology, though both are still used.

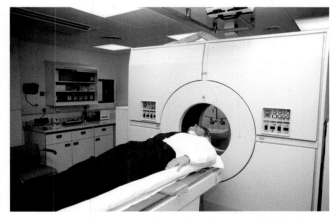

Although neurological measures have advanced immeasurably over the last few decades, even their supporters agree that they remain in their infancy (Anastasi & Urbina, 1997; Leark, 2004). Mental disorders cannot yet be diagnosed using neurological tests, leading some to argue that current neurological tests are only capable of

Neuroimaging techniques such as the PET scan and MRI allow clinicians and researchers to photograph brain activity.
Source: PhotoDisc/ Getty Images

assessing lower-level aspects of brain functioning (such as brain blood flow), while neuropsychological tests remain at this time the "only rigorous and objective method of assessing higher-level aspects of brain functions" (Reitan & Wolfson, 2004, p. 107). Regardless of whether you agree with this sentiment, diagnosing underlying brain pathology suspected to cause abnormality remains an elusive if widely sought-after goal (think RDoC) that neuropsychological and neurological assessments aim to reach (Reitan & Wolfson, 2004).

3.5 CLOSING THOUGHTS: BEWARE OF CULTURE BIAS

As discussed in this chapter's "Controversial Question" feature, clinicians increasingly emphasize how diagnostic and assessment tools are always developed within a cultural context. Therefore, many researchers warn against **culture bias**, which occurs when diagnostic, formulation, or assessment approaches reflect the cultural assumptions of those devising them and, consequently, provide misleading results that place members of certain groups at a disadvantage. Assessment tests, for example, might be biased in their construct validity, content validity, or predictive validity.

» *Construct validity bias* occurs when a test fails to measure what it purports to; for instance, an intelligence test that uses English words unfamiliar to those from certain cultures may be measuring language skills, not intellectual ability.

» *Content validity bias* occurs when members of some cultural groups don't perform as well on a test because they (a) haven't been exposed to necessary information, (b) give answers that make sense from their cultural perspective but are considered "wrong" by the test developers, or (c) are asked questions in a manner that culturally doesn't make sense to them. For instance, some old intelligence tests used to ask people to match a cup with a saucer; those who did not scored lower on intelligence. However, people who were lower in socioeconomic status (SES) or from cultural groups where they had never seen a saucer before didn't know to match cup with saucer. Thus, the test developers' lack of cultural sensitivity led them to devise a test that was biased against members of certain groups—and in so doing, yielded inaccurate assessments of intelligence!

» *Predictive validity bias* occurs when a test fails to predict outcomes for members of a certain culture; an "unbiased" test should predict outcomes for different groups equally well. While culture bias can probably never be avoided entirely (no measure can ever truly be "culture free"), attending to it allows clinicians and researchers to minimize its impact as much as possible. In the example of cups and saucers, test-takers from cultural groups unfamiliar with saucers would score lower on intelligence and therefore the test might not accurately predict their future academic success as well as it could if it were more culturally sensitive.

The approaches to diagnosis, formulation, and assessment discussed in this chapter are revisited throughout the rest of the book as we discuss various presenting problems. Keep in mind that the choices clinicians make about which approaches to use both reflect and shape their perspective. Every diagnostic and assessment strategy has advantages and disadvantages. Hopefully these will become clearer as we discuss them in subsequent chapters.

KEY TERMS

4P model of case formulation
ABC recording
Achievement
Affect
Algorithmic model
Analogue behavioral observation
Assessment
Beck Depression Inventory (BDI)
Behavioral assessment
Bender Visual Motor Gestalt Test
Big Five
Biomarkers
Brain waves
Categorical diagnosis
Clinical interview
Comorbidity
Conceptualize
Cultural formulation interview (CFI)
Culture bias
Descriptive psychopathology
Diagnosis
Diagnostic code
Diagnostic criteria
Diagnostic guidelines
Dimensional diagnosis
DSM-5 definition of mental disorder
Electroencephalogram (EEG)
Etiology
Executive functioning
Formulation
Functional analysis
Functional analysis interview (FAI)

Halstead-Reitan Neuropsychological
   Test Battery (HRB)
Hierarchical Taxonomy of
   Psychopathology (HiTOP)
HiTOP spectra
ICD definition of mental disorder
Integrative evidence-based case
   formulation
Intelligence
Intelligence quotient (IQ)
Intelligence tests
International Classification of Diseases
   (ICD)
Interrater reliability
Lowering of diagnostic thresholds
Luria-Nebraska Neuropsychological
   Battery (LNNB)
M-Axis (Profile of Mental Functioning)
Magnetic resonance imaging (MRI)
Medical 203
Mental status exam
Minnesota Multiphasic Personality
   Inventory (MMPI)
Neuroimaging techniques
Neurological tests
Neuropsychological tests
Nomenclature
Objective test
P-Axis (Personality Syndromes)
Personality
Personality test
Positron emission topography (PET scan)
Power Threat Meaning (PTM) Framework

Problem Behavior Questionnaire (PBQ)
Projective test
Prototype model
Pseudopatient study
Psychiatric diagnosis
*Psychodynamic Diagnostic Manual
   (PDM)*
Q-sort
Questions About Behavioral Function
   (QABF)
Reification
Reliability
Research Domain Criteria (RDoC)
Role construct repertory test (rep test)
Rorschach Inkblot Method (RIM)
S-Axis (Subjective Experience)
Scatterplot
Self-efficacy
Self-report personality inventories
Signs
Sixteen Personality Factor (16PF)
   Questionnaire
Standardization
Structured Clinical Interview for *DSM*
   Disorders (SCID)
Structured interview
Symptoms
Syndromes
Test batteries
Thematic Apperception Test (TAT)
Unstructured interview
Validity

Full definitions of the terms listed above can be found in the end-of-book glossary on p. 533.

Go to the companion website, www.macmillanihe.com/raskin-abnormal-psych, to access a study guide, multiple choice and flashcard quizzes for this chapter, and other useful learning aids.

CHAPTER 4
PSYCHOSIS

4.1 OVERVIEW

 LEARNING OBJECTIVES

After reading this chapter, you should be able to:

1. Define psychosis and describe its five symptoms.
2. Differentiate these *DSM* and *ICD* diagnoses and evaluate their scientific status: schizophrenia, delusional disorder, brief psychotic disorder, schizophreniform disorder, schizoaffective disorder, and schizotypal disorder.
3. Summarize the history of the schizophrenia diagnosis and describe historical treatments for schizophrenia.
4. Discuss and evaluate biological perspectives on psychosis—including the dopamine and glutamate hypotheses, the use of antipsychotics, research on ventricle size and brain volume, genetic and evolutionary explanations, and immune system accounts.
5. Explain and critique psychodynamic, cognitive-behavioral, and humanistic approaches to psychosis.
6. Describe and assess sociocultural perspectives on psychosis—including cross-cultural and social justice perspectives, consumer and service-user perspectives, and community care and family systems perspectives.

Photo source: © Royalty-Free/Corbis

GETTING STARTED: WHAT IS PSYCHOSIS?

CASE EXAMPLES

Luke

Luke is a 21-year-old university student studying chemistry. He has always been a strong student academically and seemed to do reasonably well socially. However, a noticeable change occurred in Luke as he approached graduation. He became increasingly focused on how the university administration was intruding into student privacy. He often spoke about university officials monitoring student email accounts and placing security cameras around campus to keep an eye on what students were doing. Eventually, he started complaining that the government was spying on him via a radar device secretly implanted in fillings in his teeth. He also reported hearing voices telling him that he would soon be revealed to the world as the next Messiah and that he needed to go around campus blessing his fellow students. Luke's personal hygiene deteriorated and his speech became hard to follow; he began using made up words others didn't understand and sometimes strung together words in a way that simply made no sense to others. These days Luke has stopped going to class and spends long periods of time alone in his room. When he does go out, he walks around town alone muttering to himself or trying to bless those he encounters. The university has recently placed Luke on leave and has contacted his family to request that they come take him home.

Psychosis and Reality Contact

This chapter examines **psychosis**, a broad term used to describe people who appear to have lost contact with reality. Those identified as psychotic tend to think and perceive in ways that strike the rest of us as grossly inappropriate or strange. Their manner of talking, thinking, and communicating seems bizarre or off the mark. Individuals labeled psychotic are those whose behavior often seems the most extremely and stereotypically "mad" or "insane" in everyday life (Beer, 1996; Lobel, 2013). Psychosis evokes strong reactions from others (including clinicians and researchers), and there are many perspectives on it. As you read the chapter, notice how sometimes different perspectives appear at odds, yet other times they are combined in integrative efforts to comprehend psychosis.

4.2 *DSM* AND *ICD* PERSPECTIVES

FIVE SYMPTOMS OF PSYCHOTIC DISORDERS

The *DSM-5* defines psychotic disorders as involving one or more of the following symptoms: delusions, hallucinations, disorganized thinking and speech, abnormal motor behavior, and negative symptoms. Let's examine these symptoms one at a time. Also, see the "Try It Yourself" feature for links to several online self-tests for psychosis.

TRY IT YOURSELF

Photo source: © PhotoDisc/Getty Images

Online Screenings for Psychosis and Schizophrenia

Check out these links to several online self-tests from reputable professional and advocacy groups. These tests aim to screen for psychosis and schizophrenia. Note that some of these tests are more thoroughly researched and validated than others. Can you tell which from reading the websites?

Test	Source	Web Address
Psychosis Test	Mental Health in America	www.mentalhealthamerica.net/mental-health-screen/psychosis-screen
Schizophrenia Test and Early Psychosis Indicator	Counseling Resource	http://counsellingresource.com/quizzes/misc-tests/schizophrenia-test/
Schizophrenia Screening Test	PsychCentral	https://psychcentral.com/quizzes/schizophrenia.htm
Reality Check	Mindcheck.ca	https://mindcheck.ca/reality-check/reality-check
Yale University PRIME Screening Test	Schizophrenia.com	www.schizophrenia.com/sztest/

Importantly, the websites containing these tests typically warn people that these are just screening tests. People shouldn't use them to diagnose themselves or others. Individuals who score high on these self-tests are merely encouraged to consult a mental health professional. How do you feel about people using these tests to determine whether they might be experiencing psychosis? What benefits and hazards do you think such tests may have?

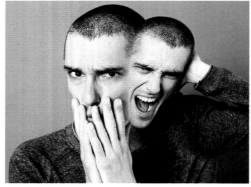

People labeled as psychotic often experience delusions, hallucinations, disorganized thinking and speech, abnormal motor behavior, and negative symptoms.
Source: iStock.com/STUDIOGRANDOUEST

Delusions

Delusions are false beliefs that the person won't give up, despite overwhelming evidence against them. Some delusions are **non-bizarre delusions**. These kinds of delusions don't seem especially outlandish; they just seem false. In contrast, **bizarre delusions** are unrealistic and, to be blunt, just plain odd.

Luke

In Luke's case, an example of a non-bizarre delusion occurs when Luke thinks the university is spying on him even though there is absolutely no evidence of this. An example of a bizarre delusion is when Luke believes that the university is monitoring him via radio waves broadcast through the fillings in his teeth. This belief isn't simply false; it's downright strange and all-but impossible.

CASE EXAMPLES

Still other delusions are grandiose. In **grandiose delusions**, people view themselves as important or special in some way. Grandiose delusions can be non-bizarre or bizarre.

Luke

If Luke thinks the university is spying on him because he alone fully understands the degree of its corruption, this would be a non-bizarre but grandiose delusion. If Luke believes the university is monitoring him because he will soon be revealed as the Messiah, this would be a bizarre grandiose delusion. Note that in both these delusions, not only is Luke special (which is what makes the delusion grandiose), but he is also being persecuted (for knowing about university corruption or being the Messiah). These are therefore not just grandiose delusions. They are also persecutory delusions (sometimes called paranoid delusions) because they include the idea that Luke is being unfairly treated or pursued by others.

CASE EXAMPLES

The tricky part with non-bizarre delusions is that it isn't always easy to tell when they're false. Are those conspiracy theories you keep reading about on the Internet true or the product of delusional thinking? Being arbiters of what is or isn't a false belief can often prove challenging!

Hallucinations

Whereas delusions involve thinking, hallucinations involve perceiving. Quite simply, hallucinations are sensory experiences in the absence of sensory stimulation.

Luke
An example in Luke's case is when he hears voices that nobody else hears instructing him, as the Messiah, to bless his fellow students. This is an example of an auditory hallucination because it involves the auditory system (i.e., hearing). Although auditory hallucinations are most common in psychosis, hallucinations can also be visual (seeing things that aren't there), olfactory (smelling things that aren't there), gustatory (tasting things that aren't there), or tactile (feeling things touching you that aren't there). Hallucinations and delusions often occur together. In Luke's case, his belief that he is the Messiah is a delusion, while hearing voices telling him to bless people is a hallucination.

The way to avoid confusing delusions and hallucinations is to always remember that delusions contain false beliefs while hallucinations involve false sensory perceptions.

Disorganized Thinking and Speech

Disorganized thinking—which the *DSM-5* also refers to as *formal thought disorder*—can't be observed directly. It must be inferred from how people talk and what they say. People whose thinking is disorganized tend to display loose associations in which they regularly leap from topic to topic during everyday conversation. Their responses to questions tend to be *tangential*, or unrelated to what was asked. Sometimes their language use is so incoherent and hard to follow that their speech simply seems like a jumble of random words—a phenomenon known as word salad.

Luke
When Luke does this, other people simply are unable to understand him and therefore experience him as strange and frightening.

The *DSM* and *ICD* assume that by listening for word salad and other peculiarities in speech, we can infer oddities in thought.

Abnormal Motor Behavior

Abnormal motor behavior can be reflected in physical agitation or restlessness, difficulties performing daily activities, and—in some cases—catatonia. Catatonia is characterized by a decreased responsiveness to one's surroundings. Sometimes this involves reduced movement, holding oneself in a rigid posture, or ceasing to respond at all either verbally or physically.

Luke
Luke, for instance, might remain completely still and not speak at all. This would be an example of a catatonic *stupor.*

However, catatonia can also involve agitated or extreme movement. The person might stare, scowl, or verbally imitate what has just been said. The tendency to repeat what's just been said is called echolalia.

Luke
If Luke engaged in it, we might ask him "Why do you think the university is monitoring your email?" and he would repeat back verbatim "Why do you think the university is monitoring your email?"

In the *DSM* and *ICD*, catatonia is associated primarily with schizophrenia diagnoses, but is also diagnosable in other psychotic disorders.

Negative Symptoms

The symptoms described so far are chiefly positive symptoms. Positive symptoms (also known as *Type I symptoms*) are additions to the personality. Hallucinations and delusions, for example, are added to the personality in psychosis. So are disordered thought and speech. Negative symptoms, on the other hand, are things detracted from the personality. Avolition is a common negative symptom in schizophrenia. It

Avolition and anhedonia are negative symptoms of psychosis; the former involves decreased motivation, while the latter involves lack of pleasure from previously enjoyed activities.
Source: Corbis

is a fancy term for decreased motivation; such a person stops initiating goal-directed behavior. Another negative symptom is diminished emotional expression. DSM-5 also identifies algoia, anhedonia, and asociality as negative symptoms. Algoia involves reduction in speech; the individual just doesn't say much. Anhedonia is when a person gets little pleasure from previously entertaining activities. Finally, asociality refers to a lack of interest in social contact.

Luke

Luke might sit for long periods doing nothing and showing little interest in work, school, or social activities. Luke might display flattened affect in which he speaks in an unemotional voice with few inflections and little expressive body language. Over time, Luke speaks less and less. Maybe Luke used to love going to the theater, but now he seems to get little enjoyment out of it. Luke wants to sit in his room and declines invitations from visitors.

CASE EXAMPLES

Notice how all these negative symptoms involve the diminishment of the personality? Positive and negative symptoms are most commonly referenced regarding schizophrenia, but the *DSM-5* cautions that they can also be seen in other psychotic disorders.

SPECIFIC PSYCHOTIC DISORDERS IN *DSM-5* AND *ICD-10*

The *DSM-5* contains five major categories of psychosis, which correspond to a similar (but not identical) set of *ICD-10* diagnoses that use the same diagnostic codes. The *ICD-11* uses an entirely different set of updated diagnostic codes, but compared to the much older (though still commonly used) *ICD-10*, the actual diagnostic categories in *ICD-11* are more like those in the *DSM-5*. Below we briefly distinguish the *DSM-5*'s five main psychotic disorders and review differences between them and those found in *ICD-10*.

Schizophrenia

Schizophrenia is the most well-known and severe psychotic disorder listed in the *DSM-5*, *ICD-10*, and *ICD-11*. To meet the *DSM-5* diagnostic criteria for schizophrenia, a patient must actively display at least two of the five major symptoms of psychosis (discussed above) for at least one month, with at least one of the symptoms being hallucinations, delusions, or disorganized speech. There must also be ongoing signs of the disorder for six months or more, which means that even if overt positive symptoms such as hallucinations and delusions are only present for one month, over a six-month or longer period there is evidence of negative symptoms or borderline positive symptoms (such as odd thinking and perceiving, which don't quite rise to the level of positive symptoms).

ICD-10's diagnostic guidelines don't require that hallucinations, delusions, or disorganized speech be present. Instead, the patient must simply display two of the five major symptoms of psychosis for at least one month. Additionally, the *ICD-10* specifies that a patient can qualify for a schizophrenia diagnosis with only one symptom (either hallucinations or delusions) if that symptom is extremely clear. Lastly, the *ICD-10* doesn't include the *DSM-5* requirement that in addition to showing overt symptoms for one month, the disorder must also be evident for at least six months—a "major difference" between *DSM* and *ICD* that remains in *ICD-11* (Gaebel, Zielasek, & Cleveland, 2012). Overall, however, the *ICD-11* guidelines (compared to those in *ICD-10*) are a bit more like *DSM-5* criteria in requiring that one of the five symptoms be delusions, hallucinations, disorganized thinking, or feeling influenced or controlled by one's thoughts (Gaebel, Zielasek, & Falkai, 2015). See Diagnostic Box 4.1 for more on *DSM-5* criteria and *ICD-10* guidelines for schizophrenia.

Diagnostic Box 4.1 Schizophrenia

DSM-5
- Two or more of these symptoms for one month, with at least one being (1), (2), or (3): (1) delusions, (2) hallucinations, (3) disorganized speech, (4) disorganized or catatonic behavior, (5) negative symptoms.
- Level of functioning at work, in interpersonal relationships, or in self-care has declined.
- Additional signs of disturbance for at least six months (negative symptoms or milder symptoms such as odd thinking and perceiving).

Based on American Psychiatric Association, 2013b, pp. 99–100

ICD-10
- Minimum of one very clear symptom: (1) hallucinations or (2) delusions; or, if symptoms less clear, two of these: (1) thought disorder, (2) delusions, (3) hallucinations, (4) catatonic behavior, (5) negative symptoms.
- Symptoms typically last for at least one month.

Based on World Health Organization, 1992, pp. 78–79

ICD-11
- Two or more of these symptoms, with at least one being (1), (2), (3), or (4): (1) delusions, (2) hallucinations, (3) disorganized thinking, (4) feeling as if one's thoughts or actions were being controlled from outside oneself, (5) negative symptoms, (6) disorganized behavior, (7) psychomotor disturbances.
- Symptoms typically last for at least one month.

Based on https://gcp.network/en/private/icd-11-guidelines/grouping

There is one other major difference between *DSM-5* and *ICD-10* regarding schizophrenia: the *DSM-5* eliminates the classic subtypes found in the *ICD-10*. This reflects the recent shift away from subtypes because of difficulty with reliably distinguishing them (Braff, Ryan, Rissling, & Carpenter, 2013; W. T. Carpenter & Tandon, 2013; Gaebel et al., 2015; Heckers et al., 2013; Tandon et al., 2013). The new *ICD-11* is following *DSM-5*'s lead and also excluding subtypes (Gaebel et al., 2015). Nevertheless, these subtypes (paranoid, hebephrenic, catatonic, undifferentiated, residual, simple) are still commonly referred to, so they are summarized for your convenience in Table 4.1.

Table 4.1 *ICD-10* Subtypes of Schizophrenia

The *DSM-5* and *ICD-11* have done away with schizophrenia subtypes, but in the *ICD-10* (as well as in everyday life), subtypes are still often invoked. Here are the *ICD-10* subtypes (World Health Organization, 1992).

Subtype	Defining Characteristics
Paranoid schizophrenia	Includes persecutory delusions; auditory hallucinations that threaten the patient or give commands also common.
Hebephrenic schizophrenia	Includes fleeting hallucinations and delusions, but mainly inappropriate affect.
Catatonic schizophrenia	Psychomotor disturbances are central; can range from or alternate between catatonic stupor and physically agitated.
Undifferentiated schizophrenia	Reserved for patients who don't easily fit into any of the other schizophrenia subtypes.
Residual schizophrenia	Reserved for patients who may have previously displayed positive symptoms, but now display primarily negative symptoms.
Simple schizophrenia	No delusions or hallucinations; only loss of interest, aimlessness, idleness, self-absorption, and social withdrawal. Symptoms must last one year.

DSM-5 estimates lifetime prevalence rates for schizophrenia to be between 0.3% and 0.7%. This means there is a 0.3% to 0.7% chance of developing it during one's lifetime. The manual also notes that onset of schizophrenia is most common between the teen years and age 30. Onset tends to be later in women (Moldin, 2000); males are most likely to develop it in their early to mid-20s; females in their later 20s. Once diagnosed, the prognosis is not terribly good. Only 20% show a favorable prognosis, with few patients recovering completely. Most cases of schizophrenia are chronic; many people with a diagnosis need ongoing assistance with daily living. Because schizophrenia is the most commonly researched and discussed psychotic disorder, we spend more time discussing it than other psychotic disorders.

Delusional Disorder

Delusional disorder is diagnosed when symptoms are limited to delusions (see Diagnostic Box 4.2). In the *DSM-5* these delusions must last one month or more and the person can't ever have been diagnosed with schizophrenia. In the *ICD-10* (and the *ICD-11*), the delusions must persist a bit longer; the diagnosis is only made if the symptoms have lasted at least three months. Given the shorter duration required, we'd expect more people to qualify for a delusional disorder diagnosis if we use *DSM-5* criteria rather than *ICD-10* or *ICD-11* guidelines. *DSM-5* also specifies different types of delusions that people with this disorder might display. We have already discussed grandiose and persecutory delusions. Both these types of delusions can occur in people diagnosed with delusional disorder. However, other delusions are also possible, including **erotomanic delusions** (incorrectly insisting that a person is in love with you), **jealous delusions** (preoccupation with the idea that your partner is cheating despite no evidence of this), and **somatic delusions** (falsely believing that you have a disease).

The *DSM-5* warns clinicians that delusional disorder needs to be distinguished from obsessive-compulsive disorder and body dysmorphic disorder. The manual also indicates a 0.2% prevalence rate for the disorder and says that the persecutory type is the most common. Delusional disorder is diagnosed about equally in males and females.

Diagnostic Box 4.2 Delusional Disorder

DSM-5
- One or more delusions, lasting at least one month.
- Has never met criteria for schizophrenia.
- Besides the delusion, functioning not seriously impaired; behavior not bizarre or odd.

Based on American Psychiatric Association, 2013b, pp. 90–91

ICD-10
- Delusions lasting at least three months.
- Depressive symptoms or even a full-blown depressive episode may periodically occur, but delusions persist even when depressive symptoms lift.
- No evidence of brain disease.

Based on World Health Organization, 1992, pp. 84–85

ICD-11
- Delusions lasting at least three months, usually longer.
- No clear hallucinations, but in some instances hallucinations related to the delusion may occur.
- No negative symptoms or feeling as if one's thoughts or actions were being controlled from outside oneself.

Based on https://gcp.network/en/private/icd-11-guidelines/grouping

Brief Psychotic Disorder

In the *DSM-5*, **brief psychotic disorder** is diagnosed in people whose psychotic symptoms only last a short time. It applies to those who experience delusions, hallucinations, or disorganized speech for at least a day but no more than a month. Disorganized or catatonic behavior is also possible. The *ICD-10* and *ICD-11* don't use the name "brief psychotic disorder" (Gaebel et al., 2012; Gaebel et al., 2015). Instead, they speak of **acute and transient psychotic disorder (ATPD)**. The *ICD-10* identifies six types of acute and transient psychotic disorder, distinguishing them primarily on whether symptoms of schizophrenia are present.

To qualify for this diagnosis, symptoms must abate by the one-month (*DSM-5*) or three-month (*ICD-10* and *ICD-11*) time limit. If symptoms last longer than that, the diagnosis is changed to a different psychotic disorder (exactly which one depends on the combination of symptoms presented). The *DSM-5* indicates that 9% of first-onset psychoses are classifiable as brief psychotic disorder. Interestingly, brief psychotic disorder is twice as common in women as it is in men. Like schizophrenia, it often first appears in the teens or twenties, with average onset by the mid-thirties. See Diagnostic Box 4.3 for a summary of *DSM* criteria and *ICD* guidelines.

Diagnostic Box 4.3 Brief Psychotic Disorder/Acute and Transient Psychotic Disorder

DSM-5: Brief Psychotic Disorder
- One or more of the following, with at least one being (1), (2), or (3): (1) delusions, (2) hallucinations, (3) disorganized speech, (4) disorganized or catatonic behavior.
- Duration of one day to less than one month, with eventual return to regular functioning.

Based on American Psychiatric Association, 2013b, p. 94

ICD-10: Acute and Transient Psychotic Disorder
- Acute onset of psychosis (from nonpsychotic state to psychotic state within two weeks or less).
- The *ICD-10* includes multiple acute and transient psychotic disorder diagnoses, some with and some without symptoms of schizophrenia.

Based on World Health Organization, 1992, pp. 85–86

ICD-11: Acute and Transient Psychotic Disorder
- Acute onset of psychosis (from nonpsychotic state to psychotic state within two weeks or less) that can include (1) delusions, (2) hallucinations, (3) disorganized thinking, (4) feeling as if one's thoughts or actions were being controlled from outside oneself, and (5) psychomotor disturbances.
- Duration of one day to three months, but one day to one month is most common.

Based on https://gcp.network/en/private/icd-11-guidelines/grouping

Schizophreniform Disorder

Schizophreniform disorder shows the same basic symptom pattern as schizophrenia, but doesn't last as long (see Diagnostic Box 4.4). As with schizophrenia, *DSM-5* specifies that to receive a schizophreniform disorder diagnosis, a person must experience two of the five major psychotic symptoms for at least one month, with at least one of the symptoms being delusions, hallucinations, or disorganized speech. As with schizophrenia, there must also be other indications of the disorder, typically negative symptoms. However, in schizophreniform disorder these additional symptoms last less than six months, while in schizophrenia they last six months or more. The *ICD-10* and *ICD-11* don't include schizophreniform disorder, although a diagnostic code for it has been added to the U.S. modification of the *ICD*, the *ICD-10-CM* (Centers for Disease Control and Prevention, 2017).

The onset of schizophreniform disorder is like schizophrenia, with symptoms usually appearing between the teens and twenties. A person can be diagnosed with schizophreniform disorder and then, if the symptoms last longer than six months, the diagnosis can be changed to schizophrenia. The *DSM-5* notes that about one-third of people diagnosed with schizophreniform disorder recover within six months, but most of the remaining two-thirds wind up with a schizophrenia or schizoaffective diagnosis.

Diagnostic Box 4.4 Schizophreniform Disorder

DSM-5
- Two or more of the following for one month, with at least one being (1), (2), or (3): (1) delusions, (2) hallucinations, (3) disorganized speech, (4) grossly disorganized or catatonic behavior, (5) negative symptoms.
- An episode lasts at least one month but less than six months.
- Schizoaffective disorder and depressive or bipolar disorder with psychotic features ruled out.

Based on American Psychiatric Association, 2013b, pp. 96–97

ICD-10 and ICD-11
- There is no schizophreniform disorder in *ICD-10* and *ICD-11*.
- There is a *schizotypal disorder* in the *ICD-10* psychotic disorders section, but because that disorder is considered to be a personality disorder in the *DSM-5* (where it is called *schizotypal personality disorder*), we cover it in Chapter 12 rather than here.

Schizoaffective Disorder

Schizoaffective disorder combines elements of psychosis and depression (see Diagnostic Box 4.5). This mix of symptoms is sometimes seen as making schizoaffective disorder a somewhat fuzzy category that can be difficult to discern and diagnose (Jonathan, Chee, & Ng, 2013). As with schizophrenia, people diagnosed with schizoaffective disorder using *DSM-5* criteria must display two of the five psychotic symptoms for at least one month and at least one of the symptoms must be hallucinations, delusions, or disorganized speech. However, the person must also concurrently experience a manic or depressive *mood episode* (both discussed in Chapter 5). When the mood episode subsides, hallucinations or delusions must persist for at least two weeks. The *ICD-10* guidelines are roughly similar, but patients shouldn't fully qualify for either schizophrenia or a depressive or manic mood episode. This is a bit different from *DSM-5*, which says the person must meet the full criteria for a depressive or manic episode. The *ICD-11* guidelines are more like the *DSM-5* criteria, requiring the patient to meet guidelines for a schizophrenia diagnosis and for a mood episode. Diagnostic subtleties across *DSM-5*, *ICD-10*, and *ICD-11* notwithstanding, the main point is that schizophrenic and depressive symptoms must occur simultaneously for a schizoaffective disorder diagnosis.

The *DSM-5* notes that lifetime prevalence for schizoaffective disorder is 0.3%, but that the incidence rate is higher for females, probably because depressive disorders are more common in women. The *DSM-5* also says that age of onset is usually in early adulthood, but the disorder can occur anytime from adolescence until old age. In terms of symptom pattern, the *DSM-5* also notes that psychotic symptoms tend to occur for approximately the first two months, concurrent psychotic and depressive symptoms for roughly the next three months, and psychotic symptoms alone again for the final month or so. Because of the depressive symptoms, there is a higher risk of suicide than with other psychotic disorders.

Diagnostic Box 4.5 Schizoaffective Disorder

DSM-5
- Two or more for one month, with at least one being (1), (2), or (3): (1) delusions, (2) hallucinations, (3) disorganized speech, (4) grossly disorganized or catatonic behavior, (5) negative symptoms.
- Major mood episode (depressive or manic) concurrent with the above for most of the time symptoms present.
- Delusions or hallucinations for two or more weeks when there is no major mood episode.

Based on American Psychiatric Association, 2013b, pp. 105–106

ICD-10
- Diagnosed when schizophrenic and affective symptoms occur simultaneously (or at least within a few days of each other).
- Criteria for either schizophrenia or a depressive or manic episode are not met.

Based on World Health Organization, 1992, pp. 89–91

ICD-11
- Diagnosed when criteria for schizophrenia are met at the same time as mood criteria for a depressive, manic, or mixed episode.
- Psychotic and mood episodes develop at the same time or within a few days of each other.
- Symptoms last at least one month.

Based on https://gcp.network/en/private/icd-11-guidelines/grouping

Schizotypal Disorder

ICD-10 and *ICD-11* include one additional psychotic disorder known as schizoptypal disorder. It is characterized by a long-standing pattern of odd and eccentric ways of talking, perceiving, and behaving that don't rise to the level of schizophrenia, schizoaffective disorder, or delusional disorder. Because of its milder and more enduring nature, the *DSM-5* classifies this disorder not as a psychotic disorder, but as a personality disorder. We don't discuss schizoptypal disorder—called *schizotypal personality disorder (STPD)* in the *DSM-5*—any further in this chapter. Instead, we examine it when reviewing personality disorders in Chapter 12.

EVALUATING *DSM* AND *ICD* PERSPECTIVES

Categorical vs. Dimensional Diagnosis

Researchers who conducted the *DSM-5* field trials report that the revised criteria for schizophrenia (the most well-known psychosis category) yielded good test-retest reliability (the degree to which a test yields similar results each time) (Regier et al., 2013). Nonetheless, the *DSM-5* has been criticized for sticking with a categorical diagnostic approach to psychosis rather than shifting toward a more dimensional model (Reininghaus, Priebe, & Bentall, 2013). In a categorical approach, psychosis is broken into distinct categories (such as the *DSM* and *ICD* categories described above). By contrast, in a dimensional approach, various symptoms of psychosis are identified and patients are evaluated along each dimension without bothering to place them into categories at all. Some critics—including those adopting a Research Domain Criteria (RDoC) perspective (introduced in Chapter 3 and discussed again later in this chapter)—have argued that the *DSM-5*'s continued use of questionable diagnostic categories interferes with efforts to identify presumed biological mechanisms behind individual psychotic symptoms. That is, people lumped together in a category such as schizophrenia often vary widely in their specific symptoms and these specific symptoms might be better understood in terms of their individual causes—without any need to assume they are part of the broader schizophrenic diagnostic category. One schizophrenia researcher summarizes the concern about traditional *ICD* and *DSM* diagnostic categories this way:

> *Despite sustained effort, the mechanism of schizophrenia has remained elusive. There is increasing evidence that the categorical diagnosis of schizophrenia and other psychotic disorders contributes to this lack of progress. ... The current diagnoses do not accurately capture the considerable variability of symptom profile, response to treatment, and most importantly, social function and outcome. As a result, there is increasing pressure to change the structure of psychiatric nosology, in order to accelerate better treatment, prevention, and ultimately cure. ... The 5th edition of the DSM does not represent such a paradigm shift. (Heckers et al., 2013, p. 11)*

Postmodern vs. Medical Views

Critics of the *DSM-5* can be divided into two kinds (N. Ghaemi, 2014). Some take a *postmodern view*. They argue that mental disorder categories aren't medically and scientifically established diseases, but social constructions (socially shared ways of defining, talking about, and understanding behavior identified as "abnormal," which influence how people come to experience it). Postmodern critics throw "into doubt the biological and scientific validity of diagnoses such as manic-depressive illness and sometimes even schizophrenia" (N. Ghaemi, 2014, p. 78). They support a less medical orientation toward psychotic disorders given what they see as a lack of evidence that ever-changing *DSM* and *ICD* categories are biologically based. By contrast, other critics adopt a *medical view*, complaining that the *DSM-5* makes decisions about what to include or exclude based on pragmatic and political motives (what's best for clinicians, insurers, and drug companies) rather than scientific evidence (N. Ghaemi, 2014). Such critics want to see the *DSM* and *ICD* move in a more medical direction in which diagnoses can eventually be made using biological markers. Again, the RDoC approach fits here. It can be helpful to keep the postmodern and medical views in mind as you read the rest of this chapter, with an eye toward thinking about whether adherents of the various biological, psychological, and sociocultural perspectives we discuss are more likely to endorse one of these views or the other. As a final example of the controversy over *DSM* and *ICD* conceptions of psychotic disorders, see the "Controversial Question" feature for a discussion of the intense debate over a proposed new *DSM-5* psychotic disorder, attenuated psychosis syndrome (APS).

CONTROVERSIAL QUESTION

CHAPTER 4

Should Attenuated Psychosis Syndrome Be in the *DSM-5*?

During the development of the *DSM-5*, intense controversy surrounded a proposed new category called attenuated psychosis syndrome (APS). The syndrome is "characterized by psychotic-like symptoms that are below a threshold for full psychosis" (American Psychiatric Association, 2013b, p. 122). In other words, attenuated psychosis syndrome is a diagnosis for people whose behavior is odd or eccentric and might eventually develop into full-blown psychosis—but doesn't yet technically qualify. Advocates for including attenuated psychosis syndrome in the *DSM-5* have argued that doing so would allow clinicians to provide early treatment (most likely antipsychotic drugs) for high-risk patients, hence preventing full-blown psychosis from ever occurring (W. T. Carpenter & van Os, 2011; Tsuang et al., 2013; Yung et al., 2012). The logic behind this is that all too often treatment for psychotic disorders is initiated too late, when the prognosis is not as good. The argument for adding APS to the *DSM* holds that "the best hope for secondary prevention of the often devastating course of psychotic disorders resides in early detection and intervention when individuals first develop symptoms" (W. T. Carpenter & van Os, 2011, p. 460).

DSM-5 critics, however, have expressed concern over prescribing powerful antipsychotics to people before they ever display a clear set of psychotic symptoms (Frances, 2013b; Kamens, Elkins, & Robbins, 2017). To these critics, this is just another example of the *DSM-5* pathologizing normal human variations. Their argument is that being odd or eccentric doesn't make one mentally ill. At the very least, it is difficult to know which patients who meet the diagnostic criteria for attenuated psychosis syndrome will eventually develop full-blown psychosis (Fusar-Poli & Yung, 2012; Nelson, 2014; A. E. Simon, Riecher-Rössler, Lang, & Borgwardt, 2013). This view was somewhat supported by *DSM-5* diagnostic trials showing that clinicians were unable to reliably diagnose APS (Yung et al., 2012). This isn't surprising; any diagnosis with mild and subtle symptoms is likely to be difficult to consistently spot. Because of its poor showing in reliability trials and concerns that adding a psychotic diagnosis for people with mild symptoms could be unnecessarily stigmatizing, APS was relegated to Section III of the *DSM-5* (where proposed but not officially accepted disorders in need of further study are placed) (Tsuang et al., 2013; Yung et al., 2012).

However, the controversy doesn't end there. It turns out that even though attenuated psychosis syndrome isn't an officially approved *DSM-5* disorder, it was "slipped" back into the *DSM-5* under the awkwardly named *other specified schizophrenia spectrum disorder and other psychotic disorder* (Frances, 2013b; Kamens, 2013; A. E. Simon et al., 2013). The *DSM-5* encourages clinicians to use this diagnosis for patients whose symptoms don't meet the criteria for any other psychotic disorder but who nonetheless are believed to be psychotic—including those thought to be suffering from attenuated psychosis syndrome! Thus, despite the controversy surrounding it and its technically not being an officially endorsed disorder, the *DSM-5* instructs clinicians to diagnose attenuated psychosis syndrome using the "other psychotic disorder" category. *DSM-5* authors defended this decision by claiming that no reasonable person examining the *DSM-5* closely could conclude that APS was anything other than a disorder for further study (W. T. Carpenter, Regier, & Tandon, 2014). However, *DSM-IV* chair turned *DSM-5* critic Allen Frances (2013b) expressed outrage over allowing clinicians to diagnose APS using the "other psychotic disorder" diagnosis, arguing that it could result in a large number of teens and young adults who won't ever develop schizophrenia being improperly told they have a scientifically suspect "other specified" form of it. Still, advocates contend that the ability to diagnose and treat APS will get many people the early intervention they need to avoid long-term problems (W. T. Carpenter et al., 2014; W. T. Carpenter & van Os, 2011). Whether attenuated psychosis syndrome eventually becomes an official diagnosis in a future revision of the *DSM* remains to be seen. Until then, debate over its merits as a diagnosis is likely to continue.

CRITICAL THINKING QUESTIONS

1. Do you think attenuated psychosis syndrome is a sound proposal for a new *DSM* disorder? Why or why not?

2. What do you see as the risks and benefits of adding attenuated psychosis syndrome to the *DSM*?

3. Should attenuated psychosis syndrome be added to the next version of *DSM*? If yes, why? If not, why not?

4. Did the *DSM* do something improper by allowing clinicians to diagnose attenuated psychosis syndrome using the "other psychotic disorder" category? Explain your reasoning.

4.3 HISTORICAL PERSPECTIVES

DEMENTIA PRAECOX

The Greek origins of the word psychosis mean "an abnormal psyche, or mind" (Lobel, 2013, p. 15). Although descriptions of extreme madness can be traced all the way back to the Ancient Greeks, the concept of schizophrenia (the most well-known form of psychosis) is relatively new, arising after 1800 (Tueth, 1995). The French psychiatrist Bénédict-Augustin Morel (1809–1873) is credited with first describing what we now call schizophrenia. He used the term dementia praecox, which means "premature dementia." Morel defined dementia praecox as involving "mental degeneration with acute episodes of 'madness' that begin in the young"; such a definition "is central in subsequent accounts of what we now call 'schizophrenia'" (M. D. Hunter & Woodruff, 2005, p. 2).

Emil Kraepelin (1856–1926), an early developer of psychiatric diagnosis (see Chapter 3), included Morel's dementia praecox category in his classification system. However, he expanded it to include symptoms of catatonia, hebephrenia, and paranoia (revisit Table 4.1) (M. D. Hunter & Woodruff, 2005; Tsoi, Hunter, & Woodruff, 2008). Kraepelin also distinguished dementia praecox from manic-depressive psychosis (Lavretsky, 2008). Importantly, he identified dementia praecox as an endogenous disorder, meaning he thought it originated within the body. That is, he suspected it had a physical cause (Beer, 1996; Lavretsky, 2008). Kraepelin's views on dementia praecox "profoundly influenced European and American psychiatry. These diagnostic categories continue to guide our clinical practice and research in the twenty-first century, despite the fact that Kraepelin himself recognized their limitations" (Lavretsky, 2008, p. 4).

BLEULER COINS THE TERM "SCHIZOPHRENIA"

The term "schizophrenia" originated with the Swiss psychiatrist Eugene Bleuler (1857–1939) in 1911. Bleuler thought of schizophrenia in more psychological terms than Kraepelin and the name he chose for the disorder literally means "a mind that is torn asunder" (Lavretsky, 2008, p. 4). Unfortunately, because the term has also been interpreted as "split mind," many people incorrectly assume that people with schizophrenia have multiple personalities—but talk of multiple personalities belongs in discussions of dissociative identity disorder, an entirely different presenting problem discussed in Chapter 8. Although the criteria for schizophrenia used in the *ICD* and *DSM* have become narrower and more fully operationalized in the days since Bleuler first coined the term, the basic concept is similar (Lavretsky, 2008).

EARLY 20TH-CENTURY TREATMENTS

Early 20th-century treatments for schizophrenia (many of which were introduced in Chapter 1) are often considered odd and/or abusive from today's vantage point, though the alternative to these treatments was generally long-term incarceration in a hospital setting (A. Gibson, 2014). Among the treatments used were hydrotherapy, insulin coma, electroconvulsive therapy, and lobotomy (Lavretsky, 2008; Lobel, 2013; Shorter, 1997; Tueth, 1995). There were numerous forms of hydrotherapy, but it often involved leaving patients voluntarily or involuntarily wrapped in wet sheets of varied temperatures for several hours at a time; the goal was to alleviate toxic impurities in the body that were thought to influence psychotic symptoms (Lobel, 2013). In insulin coma therapy, insulin injections were used to bring patients in and out of comas daily over several weeks (R. M. Kaplan, 2013; Lobel, 2013; Shorter, 1997; Tueth, 1995); this reduced the symptoms of schizophrenia, though nobody quite knows why. Eventually electroconvulsive therapy (ECT) overtook insulin coma as a treatment; the idea was that schizophrenia and epilepsy are incompatible so inducing an epileptic-like seizure by administering an electric shock to the brain could potentially neutralize psychotic symptoms (Endler, 1988; Lobel, 2013; Tueth, 1995). More modern forms of ECT are sometimes still used with schizophrenia patients (Flamarique et al., 2015; Haack, Borghesani, Green, Neumaier, & Shyn, 2014; Kristensen, Hageman, Bauer, Jørgensen, & Correll, 2013; S. Park & Lee, 2014; Petrides et al., 2015; Xiang et al., 2015). Lastly, the psychosurgery technique known as lobotomy (also called *leucotomy*) involved disconnecting the prefrontal cortex

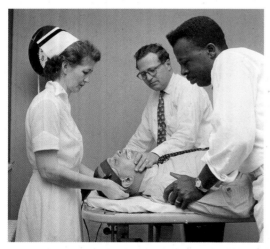

During the mid-20th century, electroconvulsive therapy (ECT) overtook insulin coma as a treatment for schizophrenia; modern forms of ECT are still sometimes used today for schizophrenia.
Source: Carl Purcell/Three Lions/Getty Images

from the rest of the brain; it decreased aggression but seriously impaired cognitive and emotional functioning (Johnson, 2014; Lobel, 2013; Swayze, 1995; Tueth, 1995). All of these historical treatments for schizophrenia enjoyed popularity prior to the advent of antipsychotic drugs in the 1950s, after which they generally fell into disrepute and stopped being used (Lavretsky, 2008). The take-home message is that there have been many treatments for psychosis, most of which seem archaic in retrospect. Although today's treatments seem eminently reasonable to us now, only time will tell how well they stand up to the retrospective gaze of history.

4.4 BIOLOGICAL PERSPECTIVES

Biological perspectives on psychosis have dominated both research and treatment in recent decades. Adopting a medical model (see Chapters 1–3), they conceptualize schizophrenia and related psychoses as bodily diseases. Researchers are exploring many different biological explanations of psychotic disorders—neurochemical, structural, genetic, and viral/immunological. They are also looking for linkages between the various biological explanations—such as how genetics might make people more susceptible to neurochemical brain imbalances associated with schizophrenia. Keep in mind that despite many promising research avenues, the primary biological intervention for psychosis these days remains neurochemical, namely the use of prescription drugs.

BRAIN CHEMISTRY PERSPECTIVES
Dopamine Hypothesis of Schizophrenia

Since the late 1960s and early 1970s, the dopamine hypothesis of schizophrenia has been the most influential brain chemistry perspective on schizophrenia. In its most basic form, the dopamine hypothesis holds that schizophrenia and other forms of psychosis result from too much of the brain neurotransmitter dopamine (Kendler & Schaffner, 2011; Keshavan, Tandon, Boutros, & Nasrallah, 2008). Antipsychotics (also called *neuroleptics* or *major tranquilizers*) are prescribed to treat psychosis. This is consistent with the dopamine hypothesis because antipsychotic drugs decrease dopamine receptivity. Yet students are often surprised to learn that these drugs were in use before the dopamine hypothesis was formulated (Kendler & Schaffner, 2011). The dopamine hypothesis emerged in response to these drugs' efficacy in reducing positive symptoms of schizophrenia.

Distinguishing the Dopamine Hypothesis from Antipsychotic Use

Because antipsychotic drugs were developed first and then efforts to explain how they work came afterwards, it can be helpful to distinguish the clinical use of antipsychotics from research into the dopamine hypothesis of schizophrenia. Regardless of whether we accept the dopamine hypothesis, there is evidence that antipsychotic drugs can reduce positive symptoms such as hallucinations and delusions in many psychotic patients (Tandon, Nasrallah, & Keshavan, 2010). Unfortunately, the consensus among researchers is that the evidence supporting the dopamine hypothesis itself (which potentially explains why these drugs help) is far less conclusive (O. D. Howes, McCutcheon, & Stone, 2015; Kendler & Schaffner, 2011; Keshavan et al., 2008; Moncrieff, 2009). This may be because our ability to measure dopamine levels is limited; we can only measure them indirectly via neuroimaging techniques, analyzing a patient's brain after death, or measuring metabolites that remain in cerebrospinal fluid after the body breaks down dopamine. While some recent imaging and postmortem studies have found evidence of excessive dopamine production in the brains of patients with schizophrenia (O. D. Howes et al., 2015), other researchers contend that the results of these studies are confounded by the fact that most of the subjects in them were on antipsychotic medications for much of their lives and this could account for the results (Kendler & Schaffner, 2011).

Dopamine Hypothesis and Amphetamine Psychosis

Some argue that the most compelling evidence to date for the dopamine hypothesis comes from studies looking at the relationship between amphetamines and psychosis (Kendler & Schaffner, 2011). In large doses amphetamines induce psychotic symptoms. This is called amphetamine psychosis. The fact that amphetamines can cause psychosis is important for the dopamine hypothesis because we know that amphetamines increase dopamine levels. We also know that antipsychotic drugs relieve symptoms of amphetamine psychosis. Therefore, it's reasonable to infer that psychosis results from abnormally high dopamine levels. Research studies looking at the effect of amphetamines on psychosis have provided some support for the dopamine hypothesis, but the fact that amphetamines affect other neurotransmitters besides dopamine makes it difficult to conclude with certainty that excess dopamine is the sole cause of psychotic symptoms (Howes et al., 2015). Given the mixed research support, the overall trend has been towards a more skeptical view of the dopamine hypothesis, with many biological researchers now questioning whether the dopamine hypothesis alone is sufficient to explain schizophrenia and other psychotic disorders (Howes et al., 2015; Kendler & Schaffner, 2011).

Aberrant Salience

Considering evidence that excessive dopamine alone may not explain psychosis, some researchers now view dopamine as fueling the experience of psychosis rather than being its sole cause (Howes & Nour, 2016; Kapur, 2003, 2004; Kapur, Mizrahi, & Li, 2005). These researchers have proposed the **aberrant salience hypothesis**, which starts with the observation that dopamine is important in making attributions of salience. When something is experienced as salient, it is viewed as important or noticeable; thus, attributing salience to something is "a process whereby events and thoughts come to grab attention, drive action, and influence goal-directed behavior because of their association with reward or punishment" (Kapur, 2003, p. 14). The aberrant salience hypothesis holds that psychosis results when the mesolimbic dopamine pathway is overactive, leading to excessive dopamine. The mesolimbic dopamine pathway is a dopamine-mediated brain circuit implicated in rewards and pleasure (we discuss it further when examining addiction in Chapter 11). Why does psychosis result from an overactive mesolimbic dopamine pathway? Because, according to the aberrant salience hypothesis, excess dopamine leads to over-attributing meaning (i.e., salience) to extraneous and irrelevant events. This provides an explanation for delusions and hallucinations: Delusions reflect efforts to interpret and make sense of the experience of salience, while hallucinations constitute responses to abnormally salient perceptions and memories that are treated as externally generated rather than internally generated phenomena (Howes & Nour, 2016; Kapur, 2003, 2004). While there is evidence that people diagnosed with schizophrenia exhibit aberrant salience (Kapur et al., 2005; Roiser et al., 2009), the aberrant salience hypothesis is difficult to test because our ability to directly measure dopamine activity remains limited and the patients studied are typically on antipsychotic drugs that affect dopamine transmission (Howes & Nour, 2016; Roiser et al., 2009). Because a direct link between excessive dopamine activity and aberrant salience has yet to be established, the hypothesis remains tantalizing but speculative (Howes & Nour, 2016).

Dopamine and Antipsychotic Drugs

First-Generation Antipsychotics

Despite problems with the dopamine hypothesis, antipsychotic drugs almost exclusively target dopamine. They tend to be effective in reducing positive symptoms, but are less helpful at alleviating negative symptoms (Dunlop & Brandon, 2015). The development of the original **first-generation antipsychotics**—known as *phenothiazines*—was accidental, but once their efficacy in reducing positive symptoms was established they became the primary biological treatment for psychosis. Early phenothiazines were developed as industrial dyes and later used as antihistamines (Frankenburg & Baldessarini, 2008). *Chlorpromazine* (sold under the trade name *Thorazine*) was the first phenothiazine employed to treat psychosis. It was first synthesized in 1950 and initially used as a sedative (Frankenburg & Baldessarini, 2008). However, it was soon found to help relieve hallucinations, delusions, and mania. Consequently, it began to be prescribed as a treatment for schizophrenia (W. T. Carpenter, Jr. & Davis, 2012; Frankenburg & Baldessarini, 2008). Chlorpromazine and other common first-generation antipsychotics are listed in Table 4.2.

Table 4.2 Common First- and Second-Generation Antipsychotic Drugs

First-Generation (common trade names in parentheses)

- Chlorpromazine (Thorazine, Largactil)
- Fluphenazine (Prolixin, Permitil)
- Haloperidol (Haldol, Peridol)
- Thiothixene (Navane)
- Trifluoperazine (Stelazine)

Second-Generation/Atypical Antipsychotics (common trade names in parentheses)

- Clozapine (Clorazil, Denzapine)
- Aripiprazole (Abilify, Aristada)
- Olanzapine (Zyprexa)
- Paliperidone (Invega)
- Quetiapine (Seroquel)
- Risperidone (Risperdal)
- Ziprasidone (Geodon)

Despite the mixed performance of the dopamine hypothesis in research studies, we do know that antipsychotic drugs decrease dopamine receptivity. They do this mainly by binding to neurons' dopamine receptors, preventing dopamine from doing so. When dopamine doesn't bind to these receptors, the neurons don't fire. Brain researchers have located five different kinds of dopamine receptors in the brain. Antipsychotic drugs seem to have the greatest impact on a type of dopamine receptor known as *D2 receptors* (O. D. Howes et al., 2015; Keshavan et al., 2008; M. V. Seeman & Seeman, 2014; P. Seeman, 2011, 2013). In the view of many researchers, what remains unclear is whether people who suffer from psychotic symptoms have too many D2 receptors, whether their D2 receptors are too sensitive, or whether their brains simply produce too much dopamine (O. D. Howes et al., 2015; Kendler & Schaffner, 2011; P. Seeman, 2011).

The first-generation antipsychotics are still used today, but less often because they have very severe side effects (Ling Young, Taylor, & Lawrie, 2015). These side effects, known as extrapyramidal side effects, produce symptoms like Parkinson's disease that include muscle tremors, a shuffling gait, and drooling. Patients sometimes experience muscle-rigidity (*dystonia*), involuntary muscle movements that affect the legs, lips, and fingers (*dyskinesia*), and a tendency to fidget and have a difficult time remaining still (*akasthesia*). When antipsychotic drugs are taken for many years, these symptoms can develop into an irreversible syndrome known as tardive dyskinesia, which involves repetitive and involuntary muscle movements. Other symptoms include lip smacking, tongue wagging, and repeated eye blinking.

Second-Generation Antipsychotics

The last quarter century has seen the development of second-generation antipsychotics. Because of their unique chemical makeup and different side effects (they have less likelihood of causing extrapyramidal side effects), they are also referred to as atypical antipsychotics. *Clozapine* was the first of these second-generation antipsychotics; it is frequently used in treatment-resistant cases where other antipsychotics don't help (Mortimer, Singh, Shepherd, & Puthiryackal, 2010). Clozapine does affect dopamine, but it also affects serotonin (a neurotransmitter implicated in depression). Clozapine may bind more loosely to D2 dopamine receptors. Thus, its less powerful impact on dopamine may explain why it has fewer extra-pyramidal side effects. However, clozapine's looser binding to D2 receptors combined with its effect on serotonin may also undermine the dopamine hypothesis itself. At the very least, it makes it hard to know for sure whether it is dopamine, serotonin, or some other factor that leads clozapine to reduce psychotic symptoms (Moncrieff, 2009).

Clozapine and other commonly prescribed atypical antipsychotics are listed in Table 4.2. Although the data is not always equivocal, second-generation antipsychotics are often deemed equally or more effective than first-generation drugs, especially in (a) improving cognitive functions such as memory and attention (Buchanan, Freedman, Javitt, Abi-Dargham, & Lieberman, 2007; S. K. Hill, Bishop, Palumbo, & Sweeney, 2010), and (b) alleviating negative symptoms (W. T. Carpenter, Jr. & Davis, 2012; Mortimer et al., 2010)—two areas where older antipsychotics clearly aren't very helpful. Despite optimism about atypical antipsychotics, some researchers contend that the newer drugs are overall no more effective than the older ones (Cheng & Jones, 2013; Lin, Rosenheck, Sugar, & Zbrozek, 2015; Nielsen, Jensen, Friis, Valentin, & Correll, 2015; Rosenheck, 2013). This has led to arguments about whether the increased cost of second-generation drugs is justified, especially if evidence continues to show that first-generation drugs perform similarly (L. M. Davies et al., 2007; Nielsen et al., 2015).

While atypical antipsychotics are usually viewed as less likely to cause extra-pyramidal side effects (Lin et al., 2015), it is noteworthy that the U.S. Food and Drug Administration hasn't allowed pharmaceutical companies to remove warnings about tardive dyskinesia from the labels of second-generation antipsychotics (Rosenheck, 2013). Additionally, the newer drugs have their own set of unpleasant side effects, such as weight gain and increased diabetes risk (Ling Young et al., 2015). Given the serious side effects of first- and second-generation antipsychotics, it should come as little surprise that many patients stop taking them—and often experience *discontinuation symptoms* that resemble drug withdrawal (a topic revisited in Chapter 5 when discussing antidepressants) (C. Salomon & Hamilton, 2014; Stonecipher, Galang, & Black, 2006). It's worth remembering that even if first- and second-generation antipsychotic drugs are currently the best available, they remain less than perfect. By some estimates, they lead to full remission of symptoms in less than 35% of patients (Papanastasiou, Stone, & Shergill, 2013) and have little to no effect at all in nearly one-third of patients (Mortimer et al., 2010; J. M. Stone, 2011).

Luke

A psychiatrist at the university health center initially sees Luke. The psychiatrist places Luke on the antipsychotic drug Risperdal. He also arranges for Luke to withdraw from his courses and go home to his family. When Luke arrives home he sees a local psychiatrist who, after a few months, decides that the Risperdal isn't helping to sufficiently relieve Luke's psychotic symptoms. He takes Luke off the Risperdal and prescribes Clozapine instead.

CASE EXAMPLES

CHAPTER 4

Glutamate Hypothesis

The mixed research support for the dopamine hypothesis has led researchers to wonder about the roles of glutamate and serotonin in psychosis, as well as to consider whether schizophrenia isn't due to excessive dopamine activity in the brain's striatum but underactivity in its frontal cortex (Guillin, Abi-Dargham, & Laruelle, 2007). Increased uncertainty about the dopamine hypothesis has fueled the rise in recent years of another brain chemistry hypothesis. The glutamate hypothesis of schizophrenia holds that a lack of the neurotransmitter glutamate is behind many symptoms of schizophrenia (Dunlop & Brandon, 2015; O. D. Howes et al., 2015; Pomerantz, 2007; P. Seeman, 2009; J. M. Stone, Morrison, & Pilowsky, 2007). The same kinds of evidence sought to support the dopamine hypothesis are now also being sought for the glutamate hypothesis. But measuring glutamate is just as challenging as measuring dopamine. Researchers are looking at the brains of deceased schizophrenia patients for evidence suggesting deficient glutamate. They are also looking for glutamate metabolites in cerebrospinal fluid. Currently there are no glutamate-focused antipsychotic drugs, but researchers hold out hope that such drugs will eventually be developed (Buchanan et al., 2007; Dunlop & Brandon, 2015; Papanastasiou et al., 2013). If such drugs are successfully devised, they will be the first antipsychotics whose primary focus is on a neurotransmitter besides dopamine.

BRAIN STRUCTURE AND FUNCTION PERSPECTIVES

Whereas dopamine is associated with positive symptoms, brain structure abnormalities are often seen as related to negative symptoms (Asami et al., 2014). When it comes to schizophrenia, brain structure and function perspectives tend to emphasize the roles of brain ventricle size and brain volume. These factors seem potentially to be related to one another in thinking about schizophrenia.

Ventricle Size

Human brains have four ventricles, which are empty spaces filled with cerebrospinal fluid. This fluid serves as a pathway to remove waste material and transport hormones; it also protects the brain by cushioning it (Juuhl-Langseth et al., 2015). Research has consistently found a correlation between schizophrenia and enlargement of these four brain ventricles, especially the third ventricle (Haijma et al., 2013; Juuhl-Langseth et al., 2015; Rosa et al., 2010; Sayo, Jennings, & Van Horn, 2012; van Erp et al., 2014). Having larger ventricles suggests that schizophrenia patients have fewer brain cells. That is, their overall brain volume is decreased, leaving more ventricle space. Why this is remains unclear.

Decreased Brain Volume

Given that larger ventricles imply less brain matter, it makes sense that other brain structure research has found decreased volume and additional abnormalities in brain regions such as the prefrontal cortex and areas in and around the temporal cortex—including the hippocampus (important in memory), amygdala (implicated in basic emotions like fear and rage), and caudate nucleus (important in goal-directed activity) (Cahn et al., 2009; Collin et al., 2012; Ebdrup et al., 2010; El-Sayed et al., 2010; Haijma et al., 2013; S. W. Lewis & Buchanan, 2002; Niznikiewicz, Kubicki, & Shenton, 2003; Radulescu et al., 2014; Rais et al., 2012; Sugranyes et al., 2015; van Erp et al., 2014; Veijola et al., 2014; Yüksel et al., 2012). The prefrontal cortex is important in decision-making, emotional regulation, goal-oriented behavior, and speech, whereas the temporal cortex plays a part in language, emotion, and memory. Thus, decreased brain volume in these areas could influence the deficits in speech, emotion, and planning that are common in schizophrenia.

The challenge with brain volume studies is their correlational nature. It is difficult to know for certain whether decreased brain volume and larger ventricles are caused by schizophrenia or by other factors. Research studies have found a number of additional factors associated with changes in brain volume and schizophrenia, including childhood trauma (Brown, 2011), cannabis use (Koenders et al., 2015; Malchow et al., 2013; Rapp et al., 2013), socioeconomic status (SES) (A. S. Brown, 2011), and being on antipsychotic medication (Borgwardt, Smieskova, Fusar-Poli, Bendfeldt, & Riecher-Rössler, 2009; Fusar-Poli et al., 2013; D. A. Lewis, 2009, 2011). However, even when accounting for these factors, there does still appear to be a relationship between volume in various brain regions and schizophrenia. We just don't know exactly what the relationship is.

GENETIC AND EVOLUTIONARY PERSPECTIVES

Genetic Perspectives

It is common to hear people say that schizophrenia is genetic. However, because this statement is insufficiently nuanced, students sometimes are given the false impression that schizophrenia can be attributed solely to genes. This isn't so. Like most of the presenting problems in this book, genes and environment both play important roles.

There are a variety of genetic perspective studies that look at the degree to which susceptibility to schizophrenia is inherited. Twin studies, family studies, and adoption studies all try to estimate the overall degree of heritability (see Chapter 2) for schizophrenia, but don't focus on specific genes. Genetic marker studies, on the other hand, do focus on specific genes; these studies try to identify chromosome defects associated with schizophrenia. Let's examine twin studies, family studies, adoption studies, and genetic marker studies one at a time.

Twin Studies

Twin studies examine concordance rates in twins—the percentage of the time that both twins in a twin pair are diagnosed with schizophrenia. These studies typically compare concordance rates of identical twins to those of fraternal twins. Identical twins are monozygotic twins. Having come from a single fertilized egg that split in two, monozygotic twins share all the same genes. In contrast, fraternal twins are dizygotic twins—they come from

(a)

(b)

Are these identical twin brothers who share all their genes more likely to both develop schizophrenia than these sisters who share only half their genes?

Sources: (a) PhotoDisc/Getty Images; (b) Jonathan D. Raskin

separate fertilized eggs, making them siblings who share only half their genes despite being in utero at the same time. Twin studies are rooted in the assumption that schizophrenia must have a genetic influence if pairs of genetically identical monozygotic twins develop schizophrenia at higher rates than pairs of genetically different dizygotic twins.

Averaging across studies, the concordance rate for schizophrenia is typically estimated to be between 0.45 and 0.50 for identical twins and 0.10 and 0.15 for fraternal twins (Glatt, 2008; Gottesman, 1991; M. F. Green, 2001; Levinson & Mowry, 2000; S. W. Lewis & Buchanan, 2002; Prescott & Gottesman, 1993). A concordance rate between 0.45 and 0.50 means that 45%–50% of the time when one twin is diagnosed with schizophrenia, the other one is too. From this, we might conclude that identical twins both wind up having schizophrenia approximately 45%–50% of the time compared to only 10%–15% of the time for non-identical twins. This suggests a genetic influence on the development of schizophrenia—or at least a genetic vulnerability to it. Thus, twin studies are often used to argue that some people have a genetic susceptibility to schizophrenia, which the environment may or may not elicit (Glatt, 2008; Gottesman, 1991; M. F. Green, 2001; S. W. Lewis & Buchanan, 2002; Shean, 2004).

While the evidence does suggest genes play a role in schizophrenia, it is important to remember that an identical twin concordance rate of 45%–50% means that 50%–55% of the time when one identical twin develops schizophrenia, the other one doesn't. This is at least half the time, often more! So even if schizophrenia is partly genetic (which the higher concordance for identical twins compared to fraternal twins suggests it is), the environment matters as much as or more than genes. In other words, even if genes tell part of the story, they don't tell the whole story. Genes may predispose some people to schizophrenia, but environmental influences clearly play a role in how and whether genes are expressed (T. Karl & Arnold, 2014).

Critics of twin studies point out a variety of problems with them. First, many of these studies are quite old, having been done in the mid-20th century when the criteria for diagnosing schizophrenia were not standardized across studies or based on the same definitions of the disorder that we use today. These older studies are often viewed as overestimating schizophrenia concordance rates (Shean, 2004).

Second, some critics argue that all concordance rates for schizophrenia, not just those from the older studies, are inflated. Concordance rates of 45%–50% for identical twins and 10%–15% for fraternal twins are often arrived at by averaging concordance rates from many different twin studies (Shean, 2004). However, this can be misleading because (a) concordance rates vary widely from study to study, and (b) averaging them doesn't adequately account for methodological differences across studies—such as how schizophrenia diagnoses were made, how participants were recruited, and how concordance was calculated (J. Joseph, 2004; Shean,

2004). More conservative estimates suggest concordance rates around 28% for monozygotic twins and 6% for dizygotic twins (Torrey, 1992). This still implies a genetic influence on schizophrenia, but far less of one.

Third, environment is a confounding variable in twin studies; these studies assume that identical twins aren't treated more similarly to one another than non-identical twins. That is, twin studies make the equal environments assumption that the environments of monozygotic twins and dizygotic twins are identical (C. A. Ross, 2014). Critics of twin studies challenge this assumption, arguing that it is quite likely that identical twins receive more similar treatment than non-identical twins and this is potentially why they have higher concordance rates for schizophrenia (J. Joseph, 2004; C. A. Ross, 2014).

Family Studies

Family studies look at how often relatives of those with schizophrenia are also diagnosed with schizophrenia. These studies assume that the closer you are genetically to someone with schizophrenia, the more likely you are to develop schizophrenia too. Many studies seem to support this hypothesis (Gottesman, 1991; Gottesman, Laursen, Bertelsen, & Mortensen, 2010; M. F. Green, 2001; Shean, 2004). In his seminal review of the genetics of schizophrenia, Gottesman (1991) concluded that first-degree relatives of those with schizophrenia were much more likely to be diagnosed with the disorder than second- or third-degree relatives. Even among the first-degree relatives, the closer someone was genetically to the schizophrenic patient, the more likely that person was to receive a schizophrenia diagnosis. For instance, an identical twin (who shares all the genes of the person with schizophrenia) was estimated to have a 48% chance of developing schizophrenia, but a fraternal twin (who only shares half the genes of the person with schizophrenia) was estimated to have merely a 17% chance of developing schizophrenia (Gottesman, 1991). Non-twin siblings developed schizophrenia just 9% of the time and parents only 6% of the time (Gottesman, 1991). These findings suggest a role for genes in making people susceptible to schizophrenia.

Despite their tantalizing results, family studies are usually viewed as limited in what they can tell us. For one thing, lots of schizophrenia patients have no close relatives with schizophrenia. In Gottesman's review of family studies, it turned out that 89% of those diagnosed with schizophrenia didn't have a parent with schizophrenia and 65% didn't have any first- or second-degree relatives who suffered from it either (Gottesman, 1991; Shean, 2004). For another thing, it is very difficult to determine the relative influence of genetics versus the environment in family studies. Genetically close relatives (e.g., siblings and their parents) are more likely to share similar environments compared to less genetically close relatives (e.g., aunts, uncles, and cousins) (J. Joseph, 2004). The former usually live together, the latter don't. Thus, it could be shared environment, as much or more than genetics, that accounts for some of what is found in family studies. In looking at family studies, researchers often warn us to be careful before concluding that genes explain the results:

> Schizophrenia may run in families, but not all traits that run in families are genetic. Drinking red wine runs in Italian families, but it takes considerable mental acrobatics to attribute this behavior to anything other than environmental influences. In searching for explanations for this behavior we do not feel compelled to invoke a red-wine-drinking gene that lurks in the Italian blood. We have a much simpler explanation: If you are raised with red wine at dinner, odds are good that you will maintain this custom when you get older. (M. F. Green, 2001, p. 54)

Because family studies suggest genetic influences but are limited in what they can tell us, twin and adoption studies are often relied on instead (M. F. Green, 2001; Shean, 2004).

Adoption Studies

Adoption studies look at rates of schizophrenia among siblings adopted early in life and reared in separate environments. The idea is to control for environmental influences. If siblings raised in different environments develop schizophrenia, then it is reasonable to attribute the cause to genes rather than environment. A number of adoption studies have been done in Scandinavian countries because these countries maintain nationwide health records and have populations that are less mobile than many other countries (Shean, 2004).

One Danish study found that 8.7% of biological relatives of adoptees with schizophrenia were diagnosed along the schizophrenia spectrum compared to only 1.9% of the relatives of adoptees without schizophrenia—although when "schizoid" and "inadequate" personality disorders were excluded from the schizophrenia spectrum, the percentage of biological relatives of adoptees diagnosed along the schizophrenia spectrum dropped slightly to 7.9% (Kety, 1988). Another study by Heston (1966) looked at the adopted offspring of 47 women diagnosed with schizophrenia during the 1930s and found that five of their offspring were also diagnosed with schizophrenia. By comparison, none of the adopted children of 50 control subjects was ever diagnosed with schizophrenia.

Some adoption studies have gone even further in trying to tease out gene–environment interactions. Wender and colleagues compared children whose biological parents had schizophrenia but whose adoptive parents didn't to children whose adoptive parents had schizophrenia but whose biological parents didn't. They found the former more likely to develop a schizophrenia spectrum disorder (18.8% of the time) than the latter (only 4.8% of the time) (Wender, Rosenthal, Kety, Schulsinger, & Welner, 1974). A more recent Finnish adoption study looked at whether being raised in a high-risk (dysfunctional) adoptive family was associated with greater likelihood of schizophrenia (Tienari, Wahlberg, & Wynne, 2006). This study confirmed previous findings that adopted children of biological parents with schizophrenia are at higher risk for developing schizophrenia themselves. However, it also found that adopted children whose biological mothers had schizophrenia were at much greater risk when their adoptive family was dysfunctional; being raised in an emotionally healthy family seemed to protect genetically vulnerable children from developing schizophrenia. This supports the idea that, when it comes to schizophrenia, genes and environment interact (Tienari et al., 2006).

Critics contend that adoption studies too often use overly broad criteria for diagnosing schizophrenia (such as including anyone along the "schizophrenia spectrum" and relying on questionable diagnoses such as "inadequate" personality) and this artificially inflates results (Fleming & Martin, 2011). Another common criticism of adoption studies is that they can't use random assignment (see Chapter 1) to place children with adoptive families. This creates confounding variables, such as potential differences between families that adopt children whose biological parents had schizophrenia and those that adopt children whose parents didn't (J. Joseph, 2004). Moreover, adoption studies also can't account for the fact that children are rarely adopted immediately after birth. Regardless of whether a child is adopted six months, two years, or four years after birth, we are faced with another confounding variable—namely that the child was raised by the biological parents for at least some period (J. Joseph, 2004). Events during this pre-adoption time with their biological parents might affect whether the children in adoption studies later develop schizophrenia.

Genetic Marker Studies

Rather than investigating the degree to which schizophrenia runs in families, **genetic marker studies** look for specific genetic indicators associated with schizophrenia (Guang et al., 2014; Levinson & Mowry, 2000; Müller, 2014; Ripke et al., 2013; Shibata et al., 2013). A genetic marker is "a DNA sequence with a known physical location on a chromosome" (www.genome.gov/Glossary/index.cfm?id=86). The idea is that DNA sequences on specific chromosomes (see Chapter 2) may correlate with psychosis. The list of genes with possible markers for schizophrenia is long (for examples, see Table 4.3), but the exact roles they play remain unclear because (a) these studies are correlational in nature, (b) many of the genes implicated are also associated with other mental disorders, and (c) findings have proven difficult to consistently replicate (Guang et al., 2014; Ripke et al., 2013; C. A. Ross, 2013a; van Os et al., 2014). A relationship of some kind between the identified genes and schizophrenia is suspected, but we currently can't stipulate what it is—not surprising given how schizophrenia consists of complex behavioral symptoms tied to many genes. Importantly, gene expression is apt to be significantly impacted by the environment (P. J. Harrison, 2015; van Os et al., 2014). Consequently, identifying gene–environment interactions is becoming an important goal for researchers as they move forward with genetic research (Husted, Ahmed, Chow, Brzustowicz, & Bassett, 2012; Karl & Arnold, 2014; van Os et al., 2014). Table 4.3 lists some of the many candidate genes that have been identified as potentially important in schizophrenia.

Table 4.3 Schizophrenia Candidate Genes

Disrupted in schizophrenia 1 (DISC1)
Catechol-o-methyl transferase (COMT)
Dopamine transporter (DRD2)
Neuregulin1 (NRG1)
Transcription factor 4 (TCF4)
MicroRNA-137 (MIR137)
Calcium Voltage-Gated Channel Subunit Alpha1 C (CACNA1C)
Zinc finger protein 804A (ZNF804A)
Neurogranin (NRGN)
Neurexin-1-alpha (NRXN1)
RAC-alpha serine/threonine-protein kinase (AKT1)
Glycogen synthase kinase 3 beta (GSK3B)
Protein Phosphatase 1 Regulatory Inhibitor Subunit 1B (PPP1R1B)

Source: This non-exhaustive list draws on the works of: Elder, B. L., & Mosack, V. (2011). Genetics of depression: An overview of the current science. *Issues in Mental Health Nursing, 32*(4), 192–202. doi:10.3109/01612840.2010.541588; and Harrison, P. J. (2015). Recent genetic findings in schizophrenia and their therapeutic relevance. *Journal of Psychopharmacology, 29*(2), 85–96. doi:10.1177/0269881114553647

Evolutionary Perspectives

Why Have Schizophrenia and Psychosis Been Retained by Evolution?

Evolutionary perspectives often ask why schizophrenia and other psychoses have been retained by evolution, despite their obvious disadvantages (Adriaens, 2008; Crow, 2000; Kelleher, Jenner, & Cannon, 2010). This has led many researchers to posit that schizophrenia confers certain evolutionary benefits that allow it to keep being passed down genetically (Nichols, 2009). Not everyone agrees with this; the data on whether schizophrenia provides a reproductive advantage or disadvantage is mixed across both gender and culture (Adriaens, 2008; Nichols, 2009). Further, like many evolutionary hypotheses, explanations proposing that schizophrenia has evolutionary benefits are difficult—if not impossible—to empirically verify. They are mostly theoretical speculation. Still, we present examples of such theorizing below because they are compelling, generate a lot of attention from investigators, and provide a good sense of how and why certain theorists believe psychosis is evolutionarily maintained.

Psychosis as Beneficial When It Accompanies Creativity and Charisma

Some evolutionary psychiatrists and psychologists contend that people who display psychotic behaviors are more likely to be creative and to engage in short-term sexual relationships (Del Giudice, 2014). From this perspective, creative types (artists, musicians, authors, performers, etc.) who also display psychosis will—because creativity is evolutionarily desirable—be able to attract mates, allowing them to successfully pass on their genes. Therefore, some evolutionary theorists view psychotic behaviors as a high-risk mating strategy whose downside is full-blown schizophrenia or other psychotic disorders (Del Giudice, 2014).

In a similar vein, it's also been theorized that many psychotic people are charismatic leaders—often becoming inspirational politicians or religious figures. Consequently, they attract and inspire others in a manner that fosters social unity. This benefits the group by enhancing its chances of survival (Brüne, 2004; Burns, 2006; Nichols, 2009). If charismatic leaders also run a higher risk for psychosis, then psychosis may get transmitted (rather than eliminated) by evolution because it accompanies the compelling traits that foster social cohesiveness and survival (Brüne, 2004; Burns, 2006; Nichols, 2009). Critics see this sort of theorizing as highly speculative and wonder whether the charismatic leaders described are truly schizophrenic or if they merely show certain schizophrenia-like features (Nichols, 2009). They also question whether the social benefits conferred by charismatic but psychotic leaders necessarily translate into reproductive success for those leaders; psychotic religious or political figures may help the groups they lead, but may not be more likely themselves to reproduce (Burns, 2006). Objections notwithstanding, the idea that psychosis might be maintained by evolution because it provides a reproductive advantage remains intriguing.

Psychosis as Evolved Perceptual Sensitivity to Threats

Some theorists believe that psychosis results from an excessively hypersensitive perceptual system that lets people identify and eliminate threats in their environment. In this conception, the hypervigilance that often accompanies psychosis is adaptive to the extent that being perceptually sensitive to threats helps people avoid being taken by surprise (Dodgson & Gordon, 2009). However, when this usually adaptive perceptual hypersensitivity becomes too extreme, it morphs into something dysfunctional, namely full-blown psychosis. For instance, it's been hypothesized that hallucinations are a pathological by-product of this extremely sensitive, evolutionarily adaptive perceptual system. Thus, when some people face highly stressful situations, their auditory perceptual sensitivity may lead them to hear things that aren't there. When this becomes habitual, such people are diagnosed as psychotic. Though one recent study lent empirical support to this explanation of schizophrenia (Dudley et al., 2014), it remains mostly theoretical and could benefit from additional research support.

Schizophrenia and Theory of Mind

In one interesting line of research rooted in evolutionary theory, schizophrenia and other forms of psychosis are conceptualized as problems with theory of mind—the evolved human ability to view the world through others' eyes and generate interpretations of why others behave as they do, as well as to infer and comprehend one's own mental states and behavior (Brüne, 2005; Frith, 2004). From an evolutionary standpoint, having strong theory of mind skills is highly adaptive; theory of mind likely evolved as a way for us to effectively predict other people's behavior based on being able to place ourselves in their shoes. Therefore, schizophrenia can be viewed as reflecting impaired theory of mind skills. In this vein, people identified as psychotic struggle with theory of mind and other aspects of social cognition, leading them to act in ways that seem strange or disconnected from reality (Bora, Yucel, & Pantelis, 2009; Brüne, 2005; Brüne & Brüne-Cohrs, 2006; Frith, 2004; Frith & Corcoran, 1996; Pickup & Frith, 2001; Popolo et al., 2016). Importantly, according to theory of mind researcher Chris Frith (2004), it's not that patients with schizophrenia have failed to develop any theory of mind skills. Such patients do, after all, attribute intentions to themselves and other people. However, they do so badly. That is, the intentions they attribute to themselves or others are often wrong.

While there isn't always agreement among researchers about precisely what kinds of theory of mind impairments occur in psychosis, many interesting hypotheses have been advanced and explored. Let's examine a few of them. Some researchers propose that psychotic patients' mind-reading skills are especially lacking in *affective empathy* (the ability to perceive others' feelings) (Bonfils, Lysaker, Minor, & Salyers, 2016; Frith, 2004). Thus, these patients' responses to people come across as odd and confusing because they aren't informed by an empathic understanding of those around them. Other researchers theorize that schizophrenia involves difficulty in discerning what information is socially relevant (thus extraneous stimuli are often mistakenly attended to, leading to bizarre behavior that befuddles others) (Brüne, 2005). Finally, it's been hypothesized that theory of mind impairments reflect difficulties with *subjective representations*; that is, many people diagnosed with schizophrenia mistake their subjective experiences for reality itself, resulting in false beliefs that manifest as deeply held delusions (Brüne, 2005).

Luke
Luke, for instance, mistakes his subjective worry that others may harm him as a feature of the objective world, thereby coming to believe that the government is monitoring him.

Interestingly, theory of mind difficulties may vary depending on which psychotic symptoms are most prominent in an individual. Researchers have found that patients displaying mainly negative symptoms show the largest overall theory of mind deficits (Frith & Corcoran, 1996; U. M. Mehta, Thirthalli, Kumar, Kumar, & Gangadhar, 2014). Of all patients with schizophrenia, they perform most poorly on theory of mind tasks, consistent with the emotional withdrawal and social disengagement that characterize negative symptoms. By comparison, patients who show positive symptoms—especially paranoid delusions—perform better (but still worse than non-psychotic people) on theory of mind tasks (Frith, 2004; Pickup & Frith, 2001); however, although they impart feelings and intentions to others, the attributions they make are frequently incorrect (Frith & Corcoran, 1996). Some have even suggested that for positive symptoms, theory of mind may be overdeveloped, not underdeveloped—resulting in patients over-interpreting things and attributing intentions to themselves and others that simply aren't true. This leads to wildly delusional inferences that don't stand up to scrutiny and result in behavior that appears out of touch with reality. Consistent with this, the cliff-edge fitness theory of psychosis holds that some people cross the line, shifting from being exceedingly sensitive in reading others to simply over-interpreting their behaviors. This subtle shift may explain the difference between highly attuned social sensitivity and psychosis: "It is only one step further, over the cliff's edge of psychotic cognition, as it were, to finding secret meanings and evidence for conspiracies in other people's most casual gestures, to believing idiosyncratic grand theories and religions, and to thinking that others are controlling your thoughts" (Nesse, 2004, p. 862).

IMMUNE SYSTEM PERSPECTIVES
Viral Theory of Schizophrenia

The **viral theory of schizophrenia** (introduced briefly in Chapter 2) holds that people whose mothers had a virus while pregnant with them are at higher risk for schizophrenia (Boksa, 2008; A. S. Brown & Derkits, 2010; Crow, 1988; Kneeland & Fatemi, 2013; Meyer, 2013; Murray & Lewis, 1987; Weinberger, 1987). Such explanations initially developed in response to correlational data showing that people with schizophrenia diagnoses were more likely to have been born during the winter months when their mothers stood a greater chance of contracting the flu. Viral theory research examines a variety of maternal immune system disruptions during pregnancy—such as exposure to influenza, the herpes simplex 2 virus, the toxoplasma gondii parasite, or an excess of cytokines (soluble peptides in the immune system whose presence suggests past viruses and infections) (A. S. Brown & Derkits, 2010; Torrey, Simmons, & Yolken, 2015). The resulting prenatal inflammation caused by these agents is hypothesized to influence fetal development and increase an infant's chances of later developing schizophrenia. Viral theory evidence is obviously correlational in human studies (it would be unethical to conduct experiments in which we give pregnant women viruses to see if doing so induces schizophrenia in their children). However, experimental animal studies in rats and mice indicate that maternal viral infections affect offspring in ways that may be relevant to thinking about schizophrenia (Boksa, 2008; A. S. Brown, 2011; A. S. Brown & Derkits, 2010; Kneeland & Fatemi, 2013; Meyer, 2013; B. J. Miller, Culpepper, Rapaport, & Buckley, 2013; Moreno et al., 2011).

Inflammation and Schizophrenia

Consistent with the maternal virus theory, a growing body of research has found that many patients diagnosed with schizophrenia show immune system inflammation themselves (Feigenson, Kusnecov, & Silverstein, 2014; P. D. Harvey, 2017; Leboyer, Oliveira, Tamouza, & Groc, 2016; B. J. Miller, Buckley, Seabolt, Mellor, & Kirkpatrick, 2011; B. J. Miller,

Gassama, Sebastian, Buckley, & Mellor, 2013; Mondelli & Howes, 2014; Tomasik, Rahmoune, Guest, & Bahn, 2016). This is consistent with the inflammatory hypothesis, which theorizes that immune system inflammation is associated not just with psychosis, but with many psychiatric disorders. When it comes to psychosis specifically, it's possible that the inflammation is traceable to maternal infection—with pro-inflammatory cytokines crossing the placenta and blood brain barrier during pregnancy (Chaves, Zuardi, & Hallak, 2015). However, there are likely to be other immune system-related factors at play, with studies often finding psychosis positively correlated with autoimmune diseases, gastrointestinal disorders, and infections following hospitalization (Benros et al., 2011; Severance, Yolken, & Eaton, 2016). Regardless of origins, elevated levels of inflammatory cytokines are found in many patients with schizophrenia (Harvey, 2017; B. J. Miller et al., 2011; Mondelli & Howes, 2014; Potvin et al., 2008).

Figuring out exactly how inflammation and psychosis are related poses challenges. For one thing, elevated cytokines are also associated with other presenting problems—most commonly depression (an issue revisited when discussing mood problems in Chapter 5). Teasing apart the potential interrelationships among elevated cytokines, psychosis, and depression can be tricky. Attempting to do so, a notable study compared non-depressed patients with schizophrenia to a control group of people with no psychiatric diagnosis (E. E. Lee, Hong, Martin, Eyler, & Jeste, 2017). It found that cytokines were higher among the non-depressed people with schizophrenia—suggesting that elevated cytokines in psychosis aren't always attributable to comorbid depression. As evidence for a psychosis–inflammation relationship accrues, some researchers are theorizing that one way antipsychotic drugs relieve symptoms of psychosis is by reducing inflammation (Leza et al., 2015; Mondelli & Howes, 2014). Still, additional research on the relationship between inflammation and psychosis is needed to draw firmer conclusions.

Of course, research tying psychosis to inflammation is correlational, so inferring a direct causal link between the two isn't appropriate based on existing studies. Nonetheless, inflammatory hypotheses of numerous presenting problems are gaining increasing traction in the field. We revisit them often when discussing other problems in later chapters. Interestingly, given that inflammation is associated not just with physical illnesses but also with environmental stressors, immune system hypotheses of presenting problems may help bridge biological and sociocultural perspectives—with immune system dysfunction and social adversity (a topic discussed later) mutually influencing one another in fostering emotional distress (in this case psychosis) (Harvey, 2017).

EVALUATING BIOLOGICAL PERSPECTIVES

Although biological perspectives on schizophrenia and psychosis are currently the most influential, they do have detractors. Some critics complain that biologically based research still tends to treat schizophrenia as a single disorder even though many researchers increasingly view the schizophrenia category as an unfortunate catch-all for people with a variety of severe but not-always-similar psychological and behavioral symptoms. In keeping with this view, the Research Domain Criteria (RDoC) movement is changing the way researchers study psychoses by discouraging them from taking traditional diagnostic categories for granted and then casting about for evidence of their biological bases (Fanous, 2015; Shepard, 2014). Instead, RDoC argues that we must begin with basic biological research that uncovers underlying mechanisms behind psychotic symptoms (W. T. Carpenter, 2013; Insel, 2013). Only then can we construct valid disorder categories capable of being diagnosed via biological tests (Insel, 2013). The RDoC approach fits with the growing belief among many researchers that what we now call schizophrenia will ultimately turn out to be many different disorders (Fanous, 2015). Along these lines, a recent genetic study suggested that schizophrenia isn't just one disorder, but eight distinct disorders, each with its own cluster of unique genetic markers (Arnedo et al., 2015). If schizophrenia is multiple disorders that we still can't clearly differentiate, it makes sense that no single biological explanation has yet been found for it.

Other critics feel that the search for biological markers is ultimately a dead end. They question whether the concepts of psychosis and schizophrenia are scientifically valid, reliable, and best thought of in biological terms (M. Boyle, 2002; Read, 2013; Szasz, 1976/2004; Whitaker, 2002). In so doing, they challenge the assumption that schizophrenia is indisputably a brain disease by pointedly reminding us that it is diagnosed behaviorally, not biologically (Szasz, 1976/2004; S. E. Wong, 2014). Why isn't schizophrenia diagnosed biologically? Because we have yet to identify any specific biological mechanism that reliably lets us do so. To biological perspective opponents, this implies that the "schizophrenia-as-proven-brain-disease" position is typically asserted more conclusively than the evidence justifies (Bentall, 2013). According to these detractors, by privileging the biological perspective we unfairly overlook alternative explanations focused on psychological and sociocultural factors (S. E. Wong, 2014)—and consequently lean too much on drug treatments and not enough on psychological and social interventions (L. Mosher, Gosden, & Beder, 2013; Whitaker, 2002).

Of course, not all critics take such a strong stance against the biological model. Many simply argue for a more integrated biopsychosocial model that sees biological, psychological, and social factors all contributing to schizophrenia (Corradi, 2011; Kotsiubinskii, 2002; Zipursky, Reilly, & Murray, 2013)—an idea introduced previously and revisited periodically through the rest of the chapter. Nonetheless, the biological view has clearly taken precedence over psychological and social explanations in recent decades (Read & Dillon, 2013; Whitaker, 2002; Zipursky et al., 2013). Whether this is defensible depends on your perspective. Regardless of whether you ultimately conclude that psychological and sociocultural explanations have been marginalized in discussions of psychosis, it is to those explanations that we turn next.

4.5 PSYCHOLOGICAL PERSPECTIVES

Because drug therapy is often considered the first line of attack in battling schizophrenia, psychological perspectives are often seen as supportive but secondary treatments to antipsychotics. Thus, one reviewer concluded "all effective individual psychotherapies" see schizophrenia "as a biologically based disorder that can be partially managed by learned and practiced coping strategies" such as those taught in psychotherapy (Fenton, 2000, p. 60). Some psychotherapists endorse this view. Others don't. Consider one clinician's lament:

> *Currently ... individual psychotherapy—therapeutic listening, understanding, and talking by a psychiatrist— has little currency in the treatment of schizophrenic patients. A confluence of forces has contributed to this: the emphasis on schizophrenia as simply a brain disease for which any form of psychotherapy is irrelevant; a managed care model of treatment in which the psychiatrist's role is limited to diagnosis and medication management; and the Diagnostic and Statistical Manual's ... focus on a symptom checklist that limits the appreciation of the complex human dimensions of schizophrenia and fosters drug-targeting of symptoms. (Corradi, 2011, p. 718)*

Advocates for placing psychotherapy on more equal footing with drug treatments received a boost from a study funded by the U.S. National Institute of Mental Health (NIMH) suggesting that psychotherapy and other community interventions are effective at treating early onset schizophrenia (Kane et al., 2016). You'll need to decide for yourself whether you think psychotherapeutic approaches to schizophrenia and other psychoses are unfairly marginalized or correctly treated as supplements to more essential biological interventions. What you decide may hinge on whether you believe that schizophrenia is primarily a form of organic brain pathology or a psychologically understandable mental condition (Alanen, 2009). To make sure your beliefs about this issue are sufficiently informed, let's review some of the main psychotherapeutic approaches to schizophrenia and psychosis.

PSYCHODYNAMIC PERSPECTIVES
Classic Psychoanalytic and Psychodynamic Views of Schizophrenia

Freud: Ego Turned Inward

Sigmund Freud (1924/1959) believed psychosis occurs when the ego is overwhelmed by the id and turns inward, away from the external world. Recall that the ego is motivated by the reality principle, the idea that what is practical and possible must be considered when satisfying unconscious id impulses. If a person regresses to a pre-ego state, then there is minimal contact with the practical realities of the conscious world. Consequently, the person seems to be out of touch with reality—that is, psychotic. Freud saw the psychotic patient's efforts to reestablish ego control and reengage the social world as generally ineffective, merely exacerbating psychotic symptoms. Psychotic patients often rely on the defense mechanism of projection, in which they project a lot of their confused and unacceptable feelings out onto the world—hence, symptoms such as paranoia (A. J. Lewis, 2009). Freud was not optimistic that psychosis could easily be treated using psychoanalysis.

Interpersonal View: Relational Origins of Psychosis

More interpersonally oriented psychodynamic thinkers such as Frieda Fromm-Reichmann and Harry Stack Sullivan were more optimistic than Freud regarding psychosis. They saw schizophrenia as having relational origins and believed it could be effectively treated using psychotherapy (Fromm-Reichmann, 1939, 1954; Silver & Stedman, 2009; H. S. Sullivan, 1962). Sullivan viewed schizophrenia as an extreme anxiety response to difficult relationships in infancy and childhood. Fromm-Reichmann also emphasized the importance of early relationships. She described schizophrenogenic mothers as cold, demanding, and domineering, and believed that this fostered schizophrenia in their children (Fromm-Reichmann, 1948). Sullivan and Fromm-Reichmann were both skilled therapists who saw the therapeutic relationship as a means for understanding and treating schizophrenia (Fromm-Reichmann, 1939; H. S. Sullivan, 1962). Their view that schizophrenia emerges from emotionally traumatic childhood relationships is like the view adopted in object relations therapy (see Chapter 2), which treats early parent–child interactions as critical to later schizophrenia (M. Jackson, 2009; Shean, 2004). However, as biological perspectives gained influence, interpersonal and object relations approaches to schizophrenia became increasingly seen as misguided (Vahia & Cohen, 2008). Fromm-Reichmann's notion of schizophrenogenic mothers has received particularly strong criticism on the grounds that it not only overlooks the role of biology (Willick, 2001), but is also sexist in erroneously blaming mothers for their children's schizophrenia (Hartwell, 1996).

Modern Psychodynamic Therapy for Schizophrenia

Although modern psychodynamic approaches to schizophrenia continue to take a back seat to the predominant medical model view, these approaches still have advocates (Koehler & Silver, 2009). Today's psychodynamic therapies vary somewhat in how they conceptualize and work with patients diagnosed with schizophrenia. In general, however, psychodynamic approaches continue to argue that biological perspectives err by insisting that schizophrenic symptoms are little more than meaningless by-products of underlying disease processes (Koehler & Silver, 2009). Even when they recommend an integrated approach that relies on both drugs and therapy (Larsen, 2009), psychodynamic therapists tend to see schizophrenic symptoms as personally meaningful ways of expressing anxiety and terror reactions in response to extreme mistreatment (often early in life) that interferes with the ability to form attachment relationships (Hertz, 2016; Karon, 2003, 2008a; Koehler, Silver, & Karon, 2013; Searles, 2013; Shean, 2004). From a psychodynamic perspective, "too often, mental health professionals attend minimally to the content of a client's psychotic processes, not recognizing that they may be internally logical and rational to the client" (Hertz, 2016, pp. 345–346). In other words, the psychodynamic clinician sees psychotic symptoms as meaningful defenses against overwhelming anxiety:

> For people with schizophrenia, the heavy reliance on *denial, projection, introjection, and* externalization *helps to manage chaotic and intrusive thoughts, and to avoid the experience of unbearable loss and frightening contact with others. These defenses are attempts at a solution, and on some level "work"—but at an enormous price. Painful thoughts and feelings are disavowed, but reality becomes distorted. (Hertz, 2016, p. 349)*

Psychodynamic therapists believe that exploring transference feelings in the therapeutic relationship (see Chapter 2) is essential to successfully helping patients work through their past traumas and establish more effective ways of relating to other people without becoming emotionally overwhelmed and withdrawing from reality contact (R. Horowitz, 2002; Karon, 2003, 2008a, 2008b; Searles, 2013).

Luke
A psychodynamic therapist working with Luke would try to understand Luke's psychotic symptoms as meaningful defenses against overwhelming terror.

CASE EXAMPLES

Perhaps the therapist would uncover something similar to what psychodynamic therapist Bertram Karon did when working with a patient diagnosed with schizophrenia who stuttered and spoke in Latin:

> The patient's terrible stutter was ... revealed to have an extraordinary cause. In the middle of his stutter there were words in Latin. When asked if he had been an altar boy, he said, "You swallow a snake, and then you stutter. You mustn't let anyone know." He was extremely ashamed and guilty. Apparently, he had performed fellatio on a priest. (1992, p. 201)

In this instance, a seemingly meaningless psychotic symptom—odd and incoherent speech—turned out to be a meaningful response to an intensely terrifying and abusive experience.

Although psychodynamic therapists contend that their approach to schizophrenia is supported by their research (Karon, 1992, 2003; Koehler et al., 2013), others have challenged this claim on the grounds of poor methodology and few randomized controlled trials (RCTs) (Strupp, 1986; Summers & Rosenbaum, 2013). Nonetheless, a couple of studies do suggest that psychodynamic therapy in addition to drug treatment may be more helpful than drugs alone (Duggins & Veitch, 2013; Rosenbaum et al., 2012). Regardless, most clinicians today don't use a psychodynamic approach with schizophrenia. Some see it as blaming parents, others as being clinically vague and confusing. However, psychodynamic theorists counter that drug treatments for schizophrenia often don't help and that, even in non-psychodynamic research into schizophrenia's causes, environmental factors—including upbringing—are implicated (Larsen, 2009; Tienari & Wynne, 1994). Thus, in some instances psychodynamic therapy for psychosis and schizophrenia continues to be used as an alternative to relying exclusively on antipsychotics.

COGNITIVE-BEHAVIORAL PERSPECTIVES

Cognitive Perspectives

From cognitive perspectives, psychosis involves problematic thinking that leads to abnormal perceptions (A. T. Beck & Rector, 2000). One cognitive therapist put it this way: "Negative beliefs about the self, the world, and other people ... are associated with psychosis" (A. P. Morrison, 2001, p. 226). Indeed, there is evidence that cognitive misinterpretations play a role in psychotic experience. For example, people diagnosed with paranoid schizophrenia are especially attuned to threat-related stimuli, while those with auditory hallucinations are more likely to misinterpret printed words and garbled sounds as voices (A. T. Beck & Rector, 2000). Other evidence suggests that social adversity and negative beliefs about others may lead to paranoid thinking (O. D. Howes & Murray, 2014; A. P. Morrison et al., 2015) and that paranoid people tend to attribute negative events to others rather than themselves or their surroundings (A. T. Beck & Rector, 2000; S. Sullivan, Bentall, Fernyhough, Pearson, & Zammit, 2013). Thus, the main assumption of a cognitive approach is that cognitive processes influence psychotic symptoms.

Behavioral Perspectives

Behavioral perspectives conceptualize psychosis as learned behavior. Behavioral research has historically maintained that often-subtle reinforcement contingencies produce and maintain psychotic symptoms and that behavior therapy can be used to recondition more appropriate responses (Lindsley, 1956, 1960; Rutherford, 2003; Skinner, 1954; S. E. Wong, 2006). Psychosis, then, becomes about lack of reinforcement of appropriate social behavior so that the psychotic individual no longer attends to typical social cues and instead receives attention from people for bizarre behavior and other psychotic symptoms. To the lament of some behaviorists (S. E. Wong, 2006; Wyatt & Midkiff, 2006), a strictly behavioral view of psychosis is typically rejected today in favor of biological perspectives (J. C. Wakefield, 2006). However, combined cognitive-behavioral therapies are widely used, usually as a supplement to drug treatment. Yet tension remains in the CBT approach to psychosis, with some practitioners more comfortable with the biological perspective than others.

Syndrome vs. Symptom Approaches

Syndrome Approach

Cognitive-behavioral therapy for psychosis (CBTp) combines cognitive and behavioral perspectives. It looks at how thought processes and behavioral conditioning influence psychotic behavior. The current tension in CBTp is between syndrome and symptom approaches. In the *syndrome approach*, schizophrenia and other psychoses are viewed as bodily diseases for which CBTp serves as a secondary treatment to antipsychotics (Brockman & Murrell, 2015). The syndrome approach often employs a stress-vulnerability-coping skills model in which a biological vulnerability to psychosis is triggered by environmental stress; the degree to which someone has sufficient cognitive coping skills then influences whether stress triggers the biological vulnerability or, once triggered, allows the resulting psychotic symptoms to be dealt with effectively (Muesser, 1998). From a stress-vulnerability-coping skills perspective, combining drug treatment with cognitive-behavioral interventions makes a lot of sense. There is also substantial research support to justify doing so. Research reviews consistently conclude that adding CBT to drug treatment for psychosis is more effective than drug treatment alone (Dickerson, 2000, 2004; Dickerson & Lehman, 2011). Some practitioners even use CBT as a way to improve medication compliance (Sudak, 2011). Notably, the American Psychiatric Association, the United Kingdom's National Health Service, and the German Association of Psychiatry, Psychotherapy, and Psychosomatics all recommend CBTp as an evidence-based psychosocial treatment for schizophrenia (Brockman & Murrell, 2015; Dixon, Perkins, & Calmes, 2009; Heibach, Brabban, & Lincoln, 2014)—although reviewers of the research literature have argued that while CBTp is helpful, it isn't necessarily more effective than other psychological therapies (C. Jones, Hacker, Cormac, Meaden, & Irving, 2012). To sum it up, the syndrome perspective views CBTp as a supplementary intervention for psychotic illness to be used in conjunction with drug treatment.

Symptom Approach

The *symptom approach*, on the other hand, questions the wisdom of looking at psychosis using traditional medical model diagnostic categories such as schizophrenia. Rather than trying to figure out which *ICD* or *DSM* psychotic syndrome someone suffers from, the symptom perspective prefers to take each individual patient's symptoms one at a time and figure out how best to address them (Brockman & Murrell, 2015). Importantly, those advocating a symptom perspective don't reject biological aspects of psychosis. They agree that some people may be biologically predisposed to cognitively interpret events in psychotic ways (Bentall, 2013). However, they also maintain that assigning psychotic people to stigmatizing diagnostic categories that they feel are of dubious scientific validity isn't especially helpful (Bentall, 2013; Bentall, Jackson, & Pilgrim, 1988). From a symptom perspective, rather than relying on global categories of mental disorder that are often hard to reliably distinguish, individualized CBTp interventions tailored to address each patient's specific symptoms are the best way to manage psychosis.

Common Strategies Used in CBTp

CBTp appears to work better for positive symptoms than negative ones (Lincoln et al., 2012), possibly because people with negative symptoms have a hard time forming a strong therapeutic alliance with their therapists (Jung, Wiesjahn, & Lincoln, 2014). However, while some practitioners use CBTp to try to reduce positive and negative symptoms of schizophrenia, others prefer to use it to help people manage the emotional distress such symptoms cause (Brockman & Murrell, 2015; A. P. Morrison, 2001). Many different CBT techniques can be employed when working with psychotic clients. Here we review just a few to give you a sense of these kinds of techniques and how they are used.

In Socratic questioning, the therapist asks questions designed to help therapists and clients better understand the client's experiences (Padesky, 1993). With psychosis, Socratic questioning might be used to gently call into question the client's hallucinatory perceptions and delusional beliefs. Evidential analysis involves client and therapist generating a list of evidence for and against the client's psychotic beliefs (A. P. Morrison, 2001). Normalization is when the therapist explains that what the client is experiencing is more common than the client thinks. For example, psychotic clients are usually unaware of the fact that in the U.S. alone nearly 15 million people hear voices, but many of them go about their lives just fine and never receive psychiatric services (A. P. Morrison, 2001). Finally, therapists often invite clients experiencing psychosis to engage in behavioral experiments in which they test the reality of their delusional beliefs. Table 4.4 presents illustrations of how some CBT techniques could be used with Luke.

Table 4.4 CBTp for Psychosis with Luke

Socratic Questioning

Luke: The government is spying on me by using radar signals sent through the fillings in my teeth.
Therapist: How long have they been doing this?
Luke: Since last May.
Therapist: Why are they doing this?
Luke: Because they are afraid of me. I may be revealed soon as the next Messiah.
Therapist: How do you know they are doing this?
Luke: The voices told me. Sometimes my teeth hurt.
Therapist: Is there any other reason your teeth might hurt?
Luke: I guess I could have a cavity.

Evidential Analysis

Evidence for "The government is spying on me by using radar signals sent through the fillings in my teeth."
- The voices tell me it is true.
- The government has spied on other people before.
- My teeth hurt sometimes and that could be from the radar device implanted in them.

Evidence against "The government is spying on me by using radar signals sent through the fillings in my teeth."
- The voices could be wrong.
- The government hasn't moved against me; nobody's been sent to arrest me.
- I might have a cavity and that's why my tooth hurts.

Behavioral Experiment

Luke's therapist asks him to go to the dentist to see if the radar device in his teeth can be found and removed. Luke is skeptical and says he might not be able to trust just any dentist. He only agrees if he can go to his family's long-time dentist, who Luke believes the government would be unlikely to corrupt. After giving Luke a thorough check-up, the dentist tells Luke that there is no radar device in his teeth. Luke remains skeptical but agrees to discuss the issue further with his therapist during their next session.

When undergoing social skills training, people diagnosed with schizophrenia are taught how to interact in various social situations, such as ordering food in a restaurant.
Source: ImageSource

In addition to the techniques above, social skills training is often used to help people suffering from schizophrenia to interact with others more effectively in social situations. In social skills training, complicated social scenarios—such as making friends, dating, ordering food in a restaurant, or going on a job interview—are broken down into discrete steps and taught to clients (Tenhula & Bellack, 2008). Various behavioral techniques are used to assist clients in the process, including modeling of appropriate behavior by the therapist and behavioral rehearsal in which the client role-plays how to act in specific social situations. During social skills training, "participants are first taught to perform the elements of the skill, then gradually learn to combine them smoothly through repeated practice, shaping, and reinforcement of successive approximations" (Tenhula & Bellack, 2008, p. 242). Some research has found social skills training to be effective, but other research is less encouraging (Kern, Glynn, Horan, & Marder, 2009).

Luke

As Luke improves, he begins to think about finding a job. Luke's therapist could use social skills training to help Luke develop job interview skills. If so, the therapist would model how to behave during a job interview, then Luke would practice job interviewing in role-plays. Concrete behaviors such as dressing professionally, giving the interviewer a firm handshake, making eye contact with the interviewer, and smiling at appropriate moments would be practiced individually. Once mastered, these individual skills could be integrated into a broader role-play experience.

CASE EXAMPLES

HUMANISTIC PERSPECTIVES

A variety of humanistic approaches to psychosis and schizophrenia have been advanced, even though—as with psychodynamic approaches—they are often dismissed by biologically oriented practitioners (Torrey, 2013). Humanistic perspectives view the retreat into psychosis as a meaningful effort to maintain a sense of self or identity in the face of overwhelming invalidation and mistreatment by others. Along these lines, Carl Rogers (1967)—through the prism of person-centered therapy—saw psychosis as due to an extreme case of incongruence and invalidation that could be addressed by providing psychotic clients with a secure and supportive relationship consisting of empathy, genuineness, and unconditional positive regard. Rogers' more existential colleague, psychiatrist R. D. Laing, saw schizophrenia as a sane response to an insane world. Laing (1965, 1967) didn't see schizophrenia as a disease, but as the person's best efforts to respond to exceedingly pathological family and social conditions. His position, like the humanistic perspective more broadly, has been strongly criticized for adopting an anti-medical view of psychosis (Torrey, 2013), but humanistic therapists maintain that the medical model of psychiatry reduces psychotic symptoms to by-products of brain disease when they should be viewed as meaningful responses to extremely difficult life circumstances. Let's examine two examples of humanistic ways of thinking about and working with psychosis: pre-therapy and narrative therapy.

Pre-therapy

Back in the 1960s, Carl Rogers and his colleagues were optimistic that client-centered therapy could help those with schizophrenia, but their study of its effectiveness provided only middling results (Prouty, 2002; Rogers, 1967). However, Garry Prouty (1994) developed something called **pre-therapy,** a version of client-centered therapy specifically for use with psychotic individuals. The logic of pre-therapy is that before people experiencing psychosis can engage in full-fledged psychotherapy, their therapists must make *psychological contact* with them, which Prouty feels traditional client-centered therapy doesn't always do, given how hard it is to establish psychological contact with someone in a psychotic state. In pre-therapy, the therapist makes contact by reflecting the client's experiences in a variety of very concrete ways such as restating the client's bizarre language word for word, describing what the client is doing in the moment, reflecting the client's emotions, and imitating the client's body language and facial expressions (Barker, 2015; Prouty, 1994, 2002). Once contact is established, genuine therapy can begin in which client and therapist begin to explore the meaning behind the client's psychotic symptoms.

Luke

Imagine Luke is brought to the hospital during a psychotic episode. He keeps insisting that the government is spying on him via the fillings in his teeth and that he can feel the fillings monitoring him because they are vibrating. The psychiatric nurse admitting him might use pre-therapy to help Luke reestablish reality contact. When Luke cowers in the corner, points to his jaw, and screams "They're watching me!" the nurse—in keeping with the active listening approach of pre-therapy—simply reflects what she observes: "You're here at the hospital. You're in the corner, pointing at your jaw, and screaming." When Luke turns toward the wall and yells "Must hide! Can't let them get me!" the nurse again offers a concrete reflection, stating "You're facing the wall and trying to hide." Luke responds in a tearful voice, "I had to hide." "You had to hide," reflects the nurse. "Yes," says Luke, turning toward the nurse and looking her right in the eye for the first time while tears stream down his face. "My teacher hurt me. He hurt me!" The nurse embraces Luke while he sobs. Psychological contact has been made.

CASE EXAMPLES

Prouty (2002) cites a variety of small research studies suggesting that pre-therapy can be helpful in working with psychosis. However, a lot of this research consists of pilot studies with few participants. More quantitative and qualitative research on pre-therapy might help us better ascertain its effectiveness.

Narrative Therapy

Externalizing Schizophrenia

Narrative therapy (described in Chapter 2) encourages clients to question the dominant social narrative in which they are "afflicted by" psychosis. In this pathologizing narrative, psychosis is a part of them. Thus, their essential identity is that they "are" psychotic. Instead, by using the narrative technique of externalizing the problem (defined in Chapter 2), clients are encouraged to view psychosis as something separate from them that negatively influences their lives (Hewson, 2015). Once externalized, questions can be asked to help map the influence of psychosis, such as: "How does psychosis get the best of you?" "When does psychosis have the most influence over you?" "Are there times when you are able to neutralize psychosis?" The goal is to encourage clients to view schizophrenia as something distinct from them (rather than a disorder inside them that they "have"). Ideally, externalizing psychosis helps clients devise new life narratives that highlight *exceptions*— times they did not give in to schizophrenia's influence. Clarifying exceptions provides clients with clear ideas about how best to behave to avoid letting psychosis get the best of them (Hewson, 2015).

Luke

CASE EXAMPLES

Were Luke to work with a narrative therapist, the therapist might ask him to "externalize" schizophrenia by talking about it not as a disease he "has" but as a separate entity that often gets the best of him. In so doing, Luke might realize that schizophrenia has the firmest grip on him when he is alone and has nothing to do. However, Luke might also identify several exceptions—times when schizophrenia and the voices it uses against him aren't as powerful. As he identifies these exceptions, an alternative narrative might be developed in which schizophrenia loses much of its influence over Luke when he is busy with other people (e.g., on a lunch date, at a movie, or playing Dungeons and Dragons at the local community center). Luke might find that, when he becomes engaged in social activities, the voices are quieter and Luke's urge to obey them is weaker. Luke might begin to adopt this new, less pathologizing narrative about himself—coming to view himself not as a "schizophrenic" but as a person distinct from schizophrenia with the tools to evade its influence over him when he plans accordingly.

Impoverished Narratives and Difficulty with Metacognition

Paul Lysaker and colleagues have developed a variation of the narrative approach in which they conceptualize schizophrenia as occurring when biological and environmental conditions combine in ways that lead people to have impoverished personal narratives and difficulty with reflecting on their own thinking (Lysaker et al., 2013; Lysaker, Glynn, Wilkniss, & Silverstein, 2010; Lysaker & Lysaker, 2006). From this perspective, people with schizophrenia have trouble constructing meaningful stories about their lives—hence the assertion that they have impoverished narratives (Lysaker et al., 2013; Lysaker, Lysaker, & Lysaker, 2001). They also struggle with metacognition, the ability to think about their thinking. Thus, they aren't very adept at reflecting on their own thought processes or the thought processes of others (Lysaker et al., 2013). Lysaker's narrative therapy for schizophrenia helps clients to focus on the stories they live by and revise or replace them as needed. This is accomplished through the therapeutic relationship. Clients are encouraged to not only pay attention to their own and their therapists' thinking (as they might in cognitive therapy), but also to reflect on their personal narratives. Where did these narratives originate? What purposes do they serve? Are there other (more helpful) stories? Lysaker has developed rating scales that clinicians can use to measure the coherence of client narratives (Lysaker, Clements, Plascak-Hallberg, Knipscheer, & Wright, 2002; Lysaker, Wickett, Campbell, & Buck, 2003). He notes that the next step is to generate a concrete and empirically testable narrative therapy for schizophrenia (Lysaker et al., 2010).

If Paul Lysaker's narrative therapy for psychosis helps this woman experiencing psychosis, she will come to construct a more coherent and meaningful personal narrative.
Source: Photodisc

EVALUATING PSYCHOLOGICAL PERSPECTIVES

As noted, because schizophrenia and other psychoses are so often viewed through the prism of the biological illness model, psychological perspectives have often been relegated to the sidelines—an afterthought to supplement the effects of antipsychotic drugs. Early psychodynamic therapies for schizophrenia didn't perform well in clinical research trials and for a long time afterwards therapy was generally viewed as ineffective

(Hamm, Hasson-Ohayon, Kukla, & Lysaker, 2013; Lysaker et al., 2010). However, advocates of psychotherapeutic approaches contend that there has been a significant shift in recent years, with psychotherapy again being looked at as a viable way to help people with schizophrenia. Much of the shift has been due to the limitations of antipsychotic drugs (they often don't work, have unpleasant side effects, and patients often stop taking them), which has led people to seek other interventions. The shift can also be attributed to the emergence of a recovery-oriented approach in which schizophrenia is viewed as something from which people can successfully recover (Hamm et al., 2013; Lysaker et al., 2010). A growing body of research suggests that psychotherapy, rehabilitation, and other psychosocial interventions are effective in addressing psychosis (Bargenquast & Schweitzer, 2014; L. W. Davis et al., 2015; Dickerson & Lehman, 2011; Lincoln et al., 2012)—especially during early onset (Armando, Pontillo, & Vicari, 2015; Goldsmith, Lewis, Dunn, & Bentall, 2015; Kane et al., 2015). Some researchers are even looking at how psychotherapy might biologically alter brain processes associated with schizophrenia and other psychoses (Bomba & Cichocki, 2009). In other words, biological and psychological approaches to schizophrenia are increasingly being integrated.

Efforts at integration notwithstanding, psychoses are still usually seen as brain diseases for which psychotherapy is only marginally helpful. For instance, there are many critics of CBTp who contend that research showing its effectiveness overstates its case. Various studies and *meta-analyses* (in which data from many previous studies are combined and analyzed) have concluded that CBTp is either not effective for psychosis or only slightly helpful (Garety et al., 2008; Jauhar et al., 2014; Lynch, Laws, & McKenna, 2010; McKenna & Kingdon, 2014). A challenge those studying CBTp and other therapies for psychosis face is that how therapy is conducted often varies depending on client and clinician characteristics (N. Thomas, 2015). Building on this observation, CBTp has also been criticized on the grounds that even if it works, it requires highly trained clinicians—consequently, in many settings there are few people able to competently deliver it (N. Thomas, 2015). Obviously, more training is needed to conduct psychotherapy than dispense medication. While therapists who are eager for psychosis to be managed using fewer drugs and more psychotherapy may be enthusiastic about CBTp and other therapies, they undoubtedly will need to (a) undertake more research showing that their strategies are effective and (b) find ways to train enough clinicians to administer these therapies.

4.6 SOCIOCULTURAL PERSPECTIVES
CROSS-CULTURAL AND SOCIAL JUSTICE PERSPECTIVES
Inequality and Adversity

Those coming from social justice perspectives point out that psychosis is often strongly correlated with social inequality and adversity. For one thing, those who experience psychosis are much more likely to have been physically or sexually abused as children (DeRosse, Nitzburg, Kompancaril, & Malhotra, 2014; H. L. Fisher et al., 2010; Longden, Madill, & Waterman, 2012)—suggesting that even if there is a genetic predisposition to psychosis, environmental and genetic factors often interact to elicit it (Husted, Ahmed, Chow, Brzustowicz, & Bassett, 2010; Husted et al., 2012; Karl & Arnold, 2014; van Os et al., 2014). Other sociocultural factors frequently associated with psychosis and schizophrenia are cannabis use, low socioeconomic status, and living in an urban environment (A. S. Brown, 2011; Keshavan, Nasrallah, & Tandon, 2011; Tandon, Keshavan, & Nasrallah, 2008). Because the data on sociocultural factors is correlational (just as it is with a lot of the biological research), we can't conclude that social factors such as abuse and neglect cause psychosis. However, we do know that they are important variables that can be used to predict who is most at risk.

Ethnic and Racial Factors

Ethnic and racial factors are also important. Research spanning the U.S., Canada, and Europe has found that belonging to an ethnic or racial minority group and experiencing perceived discrimination places one at higher risk for psychosis (D. M. Anglin, Lighty, Greenspoon, & Ellman, 2014; Berg et al., 2011; C. Cooper et al., 2008; Oh, Yang, Anglin, & DeVylder, 2014; Reininghaus et al., 2010; M. V. Seeman, 2011a). Given this, it isn't surprising that immigrants and those living in neighborhoods where they are a clear minority are more likely to be diagnosed as psychotic (DeVylder et al., 2013; Veling & Susser, 2011). These findings suggest that being from an ethnic or racial minority group can result in extreme psychological stress that increases the chances of psychosis. On the other hand, there is also evidence that members of ethnic and racial minority groups are often viewed as more disturbed than other people. This implies that higher rates of psychotic disorders may be due—at least in part—to culture bias in diagnosis. In the United States, for instance, African Americans in both inpatient and outpatient settings are much more likely to be diagnosed with schizophrenia than members of other ethnic groups (A. Barnes, 2004, 2008; Blow et al., 2004; Lawson, 2008). Is this because of racial bias in diagnosis or because African Americans often face emotionally stressful environmental conditions such as poverty and discrimination, which predispose them to psychosis? It may turn out to be a bit of both.

CONSUMER AND SERVICE-USER PERSPECTIVES

Stigma of Psychosis

Consumer and service-user perspectives stress how psychosis has a significant impact on people's lives. Recent qualitative research studies identified various things that people with schizophrenia commonly experience (Gumber & Stein, 2013; Howe, Tickle, & Brown, 2014; Jansen, Wøldike, Haahr, & Simonsen, 2015). First, they experience a change in social roles; their work, social, and family relationships are impacted. Many things they could do before their symptoms developed are no longer easy for them (S. Gibson, Brand, Burt, Boden, & Benson, 2013). Second, they think of themselves differently, needing to incorporate "schizophrenia" into their sense of self (Gumber & Stein, 2013; Howe et al., 2014; Jansen et al., 2015). Some do this by coming to see themselves as suffering from a chronic illness, while others resist the medicalization of their difficulties. One patient who came to accept the schizophrenia diagnosis commented: "It was like a relief in a way that at least they knew now what I already knew, that I'd got this schizophrenia" (Howe et al., 2014, p. 157). Third, they often must deal with the challenges of hospitalization and taking antipsychotic drugs. Drug side effects are unpleasant and patients often grapple with whether the tradeoffs are worth it. As one patient described it:

> Because of the side effects, I gained nearly 80 pounds, developed severe acne, and tried to fight the involuntary jaw movements and painful oculogyral reactions brought on by the medications. These side effects added to the visible stigma of having a mental illness and consequently contributed to the ostracism by my peers at school. (Bjorkland, as cited in Gumber & Stein, 2013, p. 190)

Finally, people diagnosed with schizophrenia encounter a great deal of social stigma (Howe et al., 2014), which often leads them and their caregivers to avoid seeking services (Dockery et al., 2015). For instance, one patient remarked, "I couldn't tell anyone what was happening [related to my illness] because I was so afraid of being labeled as 'crazy'" (Jordan, as cited in Gumber & Stein, 2013, p. 190). Stigma is commonly accompanied by discrimination, with patients simultaneously dealing with their own feelings of shame and the unfair treatment they receive from others. Another patient stated:

> You're just kind of afraid of being stigmatised by other people ... you just know there are prejudices about all these things; I used to be like that myself ... and so in order to avoid that people were thinking badly of me, I thought I'd better put on a façade. (Jansen et al., 2015, p. 90)

Overcoming stigma is an important achievement. According to one patient, "Though I still plan to keep a low profile as far as my psychosis goes, I will never again allow stigma to guide my life, at least not to a significant extent" (BGW, as cited in Gumber & Stein, 2013, p. 190). Coping with psychosis clearly requires not just dealing with the experience of psychosis itself, but also with the stigma that accompanies it.

Consumer Groups vs. Survivor Groups

Consumer Groups

Consumer groups such as the Mental Health Foundation and the National Alliance on Mental Illness (NAMI) campaign against stigma and try to educate the public. For instance, the Mental Health Foundation contends that "there is more media misinformation about schizophrenia than about any other type of mental health problem. ... Sensational stories ... tend to present people with schizophrenia as dangerous, even though most people diagnosed with schizophrenia don't commit violent crimes" (www.mentalhealth.org.uk/our-work/policy/schizophrenia-policy/). NAMI advocates a medical model perspective that sees schizophrenia as a treatable illness. See "The Lived Experience" feature for a personal story about recovering from schizophrenia, adapted from the NAMI website.

THE LIVED EXPERIENCE

Recovering from Schizophrenia

I started to hear voices. The voices were degrading. The radio started talking to me. I thought that people were conspiring against me.

I was perplexed and disturbed. I was isolated and unable to function. I experienced a nervous breakdown and was hospitalized.

The hospital was an unfamiliar, restricted environment. My symptoms persisted and my anxiety sparked. Treatment included medications with adverse side effects.

I was discharged with a diagnosis of schizophrenia. It seemed that my goals and dreams were shattered. I didn't want to admit that I had schizophrenia.

I was involuntarily committed to outpatient treatment. I had no control over my choices or my illness. I was discouraged and I felt isolated.

Trying to run away from Schizophrenia was futile.

Outpatient treatment educated me about schizophrenia and helped me accept what I could and couldn't change.

Acceptance came easier when I learned that recovery is possible.

NAMI, The National Alliance on Mental Illness, offered support groups where I knew I was not alone. I learned that mental illness is nothing to be ashamed of, which was essential for my accepting it.

I had a stellar support system, which also included my mother and friends.

Treatment required a trusting relationship between me and the therapists, as it was a collaboration and teamwork. Treatment also required patience and stamina. Medications had negative side effects and the process for finding the one that was therapeutic was arduous. Cognitive therapy, such as counseling, entailed much practice and it was very trying.

Eventually, I found a medication that alleviated my symptoms. Coping skills learned from cognitive therapy helped manage symptoms, such as voices, radio signals and people conspiring against me. With cognitive therapy, I became accustomed to recognizing and dismissing the symptoms, and I later experienced a reduction in paranoia.

Treatment also included goal planning and community integration. Goal planning was person centered, in that it was based on my unique strengths and will. Goal planning helped me achieve a quality life. Community integration helped me integrate into society after isolation.

Support groups have been essential in my treatment. They have provided social integration and I have also learned a treasure trove of coping skills from other members of the group.

In addition to my treatment, I have found that a positive attitude makes the difference between discouragement and perseverance. I have been blessed with a great support system and I have found that exercise is important. Humor is great medicine and spirituality has given me much peace and strength as well.

I later graduated from high school. Another milestone was completing a college education, where I majored in communications.

Being a support group facilitator has been rewarding. In addition, I write to educate people about mental illness and to serve as an advocate for others with disabilities. I am a speaker about mental illness and I am on committees that advocate for ethical treatment and rights for people with disabilities.

People with mental illness and their therapists work incredibly hard to recover. One must persevere and never give up. Success is possible.

Reproduced with permission of NAMI. Original article available at:
www.nami.org/Personal-Stories/Recovering-from-Schizophrenia

Survivor Groups

Whereas consumer groups such as NAMI and the Mental Health Foundation try to reduce stigma and enhance services while supporting a medical model perspective, service-user/survivor groups such as the Hearing Voices Network (HVN) actively resist traditional psychiatric treatments for psychosis. They contend that instead of seeing psychotic symptoms as meaningless by-products of brain disease, these symptoms are better viewed as meaningful strategies for dealing with underlying conflicts, life problems, and oppressive social circumstances. Survivor groups often maintain that with insight and understanding, many patients can learn to cope with their voices. "The Lived Experience" feature on "The Schizophrenist" provides a personal account of someone who rejected the medical model.

THE LIVED EXPERIENCE

Photo source: © PHOTOALTO

"The Schizophrenist"

Reshma Valliappan (also known as Val Resh) is an artist and mental health activist from India. She is the subject of the award-winning documentary film, A Drop of Sunshine, *which recounts her controversial recovery from schizophrenia without taking psychiatric drugs. Her autobiographical book,* Fallen, Standing: My Life as a Schizophrenist, *provides further insights into her experiences as someone who recovered from schizophrenia while rejecting the medical model. In this brief piece, she explains what she means when she refers to herself as "The Schizophrenist."*

My story of psychosis revolved around bad vampires trying to kill me because I was the prophesized good vampire who needs to save the world. The voices told me "If you are true, change will happen." I was obsessed with trying to decode the messages I received from the radio and television. I would make journal entries dated to every second and in mirrored writings. I felt I was living in a mirror, stuck and cursed to be inside forever. Thus, when I was told I had schizophrenia, I agreed that I was indeed mad. My life had reached a roadblock and there was no turning back or moving forward. It was the end; a really frightening place to be.

Reshma Valliappan
Source: Val Resh

My adult mind was experiencing something horribly wrong (so it appears). It was reflecting the reality of the adults around me through voices and visions because I couldn't accept that people could be dishonest, cruel, and greedy. I was scared of people, including my parents. Stepping beyond my room was not a possibility because another set of commanding voices sat in my living room, urging me to do things I didn't want to do. There were dead people lined up outside my house looking in all the time. When they saw me, their hands would extend towards my windows and they would try to grab me. And so, I would yell and tell my family members to shut all the windows. Over the next few years, life wasn't worth living. Doctors told me there were no known cases of people with schizophrenia returning to "normalcy." They said I would have to be on medications my entire life, with no guarantee of recovery. In other words, "no hope, lost case, live with it."

The medications failed to work for me after a while. At 14 pills a day, I was still hearing voices and seeing people, but the drugs prevented me from responding or reacting to them. This kept everyone else happy and comfortable, but not me. The socio-bio-political world considered this recovery. I did not.

I soon figured the problem wasn't with me or this thing called schizophrenia. I didn't survive my schizophrenia; I survived the mockery, labelling, insults, humiliations, and degradation of a psychiatric system and a world that thinks it knows what schizophrenia is without experiencing it. My "cure?" I learnt to live with my schizophrenia.

The concept of recovery that has been laid out by Western constructs of normalcy has also influenced the concept of surviving, of healing, of creating balance in one's life. Those know-it-all authorities who "treated" me told me not to listen to the voices in my head. They wanted me to listen to them instead, so they numbed me and told me what to do, how to live, what to say, how to behave, what to eat and read, and whom to sleep with. What a paradox!

Schizophrenia to me is a communication of the visions and voices I hear while interpreting the metaphors and symbols I experience. I have learnt to experience the visions and voices with confidence. My "symptoms" haven't changed, but my reaction to them and my ability to translate them for others has—through my writing, art, and public speaking engagements. Such is the way of the world. Until we learn to say things in a way that others can understand, we remain mad. The schizophrenia label has made my life difficult at every stage, even after carving my own way out of it through artistic pursuits and my own spiritual practices.

Hi, I'm Ganesh. I have BIG EARS because I need to HEAR billions of VOICES who need my blessings everyday. My father had a PANIC ATTACK after cutting my human head in anger. So he replaced it with that of an Elephant's.

I have a Big Belly cause I carry the WHOLE UNIVERSE in it.

My rat is my vehicle. He takes me all over the world.

thegodsarecrazy(c)ValResh 2014

Lord Ganesh from Val Resh's The Gods Are Crazy *series.*
Source: ©Val Resh 2014

Today people see my "schizophrenic" experiences as normal because, being from India, I tell them I'm the spiritual daughter of an Aghora (a Hindu ascetic), whose tantric mysticism was practiced by my biological father, his father, and his father's father. So, when I now present my story of vampirism as the worship of the Goddess Kali, it is accepted and admired. People don't tell me to consult shamans anymore after I tell them I've received my initiation in the path.

Most people call my experience schizophrenia; I call it waking up to life's many uncertainties. When they pray to gods and goddesses and believe in a person long dead who commands their spiritual evolution, they consider it personal growth; when I hear voices in my head, they consider it a mental sickness. While they market my metaphors under the label of "schizophrenia," I practice the art of what I call "schizophrenistry," which involves challenging stereotypes about madness and misconceptions about atypical life experiences like mine. So, I call myself "The Schizophrenist" and my job is to demystify "madness" by reframing it as a way some people absorb meaning from the world using all their different senses.

In my religion of Hinduism, there is a God named Lord Ganesh, who is easily identifiable by his elephant head and pot-belly. Ganesh is a God who helps people remove life's obstacles. I try to do the same. However, because I do not possess male genitalia, an elephant head, or a pot-belly, I am reduced to a mental disorder. I do wonder who truly are the mad ones. *wink

By Reshma Valliappan. Printed with permission.

You may be confused because "The Lived Experience" features in this chapter endorse utterly contradictory viewpoints on psychosis—with one author endorsing a medical model perspective and the other a psychosocial one. Yet both claim to have overcome their psychosis! The idea that different people find different solutions to the same presenting problems to be helpful can foster uncertainty among students about which perspectives to accept. However, students aren't alone in grappling with this issue. The tension between psychosocial and medical models is something community care perspectives, to which we turn next, also struggle to balance.

SYSTEMS PERSPECTIVES

Systems perspectives view psychosis as occurring within a social context. Community mental health care approaches (introduced in Chapters 1 and 2) attempt to integrate people experiencing psychosis into the social environment, often by housing them in group homes or other shared living situations; community care also emphasizes continuity of care, encouraging independence, and advocacy that insures patients receive necessary services and are treated properly (Bowl, 1996; Thornicroft, 1994). Family systems perspectives stress how psychosis impacts (and is impacted by) family dynamics. We discuss community care and family systems perspectives below.

Community Care Approaches

The Soteria Model

The Soteria model is a community-based approach to schizophrenia that applies humanistic-existential ideas to therapeutic communities for people diagnosed with schizophrenia. Recalling historical material from Chapter 1, the Soteria model owes a lot to the moral therapy movement of the 19th century (Elkins, 2016). Consistent with moral therapy, "Soteria" derives from a Greek term meaning "salvation" or "deliverance" (L. R. Mosher, 1999). In the Soteria model, people with schizophrenia are housed in a small and supportive environment with minimal or no use of antipsychotic drugs and a staff of mainly non-professionals (L. R. Mosher, 1991, 1999; Prouty, 2002). In keeping with humanistic principles, the Soteria model is skeptical of the brain disease view of schizophrenia. Instead, schizophrenia is conceptualized as a meaningful existential crisis that is best overcome in a caring, reassuring environment. In keeping with the humanistic tradition, "the primary focus is on growth, development and learning" (L. R. Mosher, 1991, p. 54). The Soteria model is named after the original but now-defunct Soteria House founded by the psychiatrist Loren Mosher in the San Francisco area during the 1970s. Several therapeutic communities based on the Soteria model currently exist in Europe. There is also a relatively new Soteria House in Alaska, USA.

Mosher and his colleagues have conducted research on the effectiveness of the Soteria model, concluding that it is equally or more effective than traditional medical treatment for people experiencing their first psychotic episode (Bola et al., 2006; Bola & Mosher, 2003; Calton, Ferriter, Huband, & Spandler, 2008; Lindgren, Hogstedt, & Cullberg, 2006; L. R. Mosher, Menn, & Matthews, 1975; L. R. Mosher, Vallone, & Menn, 1995). However, critics argue that the Soteria model is misguided in its hostility toward antipsychotics and its refusal to see schizophrenia as a brain disease (W. T. Carpenter, Jr. & Buchanan, 2002). Defenders contend that the medical establishment purposely sabotaged the original Soteria House because it threatened to show that psychosis could be effectively treated outside of medical settings without so much reliance on drugs (Bola & Mosher, 2003; Whitaker, 2002). The debate over Soteria is ongoing. The mainstream healthcare system continues to view it with suspicion, but humanistic clinicians celebrate it as a notable achievement (Elkins, 2016).

Assertive Community Treatment (ACT)

First developed during the 1970s, assertive community treatment (ACT) is not considered a treatment itself, but rather a way to organize services for those diagnosed with schizophrenia and other severe psychological disorders (DeLuca, Moser, & Bond, 2008). The ACT model works in conjunction with a medical model view of schizophrenia as a manageable illness. In the ACT model, team members from a variety of professions work together to coordinate services for outpatients with schizophrenia and other chronic mental disorder diagnoses. They conduct home visits, work to encourage medication compliance, and focus on everyday problems that patients encounter. The service is long term, provided consistently over many years to those who need it. The program seeks to reduce homelessness, substance abuse, incarceration, and hospitalizations of patients while improving drug compliance (DeLuca et al., 2008). Although there is substantial empirical support for ACT (DeLuca et al., 2008; Karow et al., 2012), one research review notes that not all studies have found it to be effective (C. C. Lee et al., 2015). Still, numerous agencies and organizations—including NAMI—have classified ACT as an evidence-based program for chronic mental illness (Ellenhorn, 2015).

Open Dialogue

A less well-known alternative to ACT is Open Dialogue, developed in Finland during the 1990s by Jaakko Seikkula and colleagues. Open Dialogue is a community care approach rooted in narrative and dialogical theories (Seikkula, Alakare, & Aaltonen, 2001a; Seikkula & Olson, 2003; Van Rensburg, 2015). The basic idea is to quickly create a support network that can intervene and assist the person experiencing psychosis. The support network consists of the patient, various mental health professionals, and significant people in the patient's life that the patient and team agree have roles to play (friends, relatives, romantic partners, employers, etc.). Treatment meetings include all members of the support network, with one of the goals being to have participants engage one another in dialogue that fosters decisions about how best to help the patient. Medication is sometimes used, but the idea is to rely less on drugs and more on the relational network to help the patient recover from the psychotic episode in ways that frame it more relationally and less medically. Seikkula and colleagues have conducted numerous studies providing support for the Open Dialogue Approach (Aaltonen, Seikkula, & Lehtinen, 2011; Seikkula et al., 2006; Seikkula, Alakare, & Aaltonen, 2001b, 2011). Open Dialogue is beginning to spread around the globe—including programs in New York City and the U.K. (Sykes, 2015). Continued efforts to study its effectiveness will hopefully show whether it can work outside of Finland (S. P. Thomas, 2011).

At Open Dialogue treatment meetings, the patient, mental health professionals, and significant people in the patient's life meet to discuss best strategies for helping the patient.
Source: Getty Images/iStockphoto Thinkstock Images \ monkeybusinessimage

The NAVIGATE Program

Another promising community intervention for first episode psychosis is the relatively new NAVIGATE program, a product of the U.S. National Institute of Mental Health's "Recovery After an Initial Psychotic Episode" (RAISE) initiative. NAVIGATE is a team-based approach that stresses four areas of intervention: individualized medication management (intended to keep doses of antipsychotics as low as possible), psychoeducation about psychosis (to educate patients and their families about psychosis, encourage medication adherence, and assist with problems with which the patient and family must cope), resilience-focused psychotherapy, and employment training (Kane et al., 2015; Mueser et al., 2014). The treatment team consists of (a) the director, who leads the team and provides the psychoeducation program; (b) the prescriber, who handles personalized drug treatment; (c) two clinicians who conduct the resilience-focused therapy; and (d) an education specialist who provides the supported employment training (Mueser et al., 2014). A randomized controlled clinical trial found NAVIGATE to be a more effective intervention for first episode psychosis than the usual more drug-focused approach (Kane et al., 2015). Clinicians and the media have argued that this study provides long-overdue evidence that the best way to handle psychosis is to limit the role of antipsychotic drugs and instead provide more psychotherapy, psychoeducation, skills training, and family interventions (B. Carey, 2015b). Importantly, although the NAVIGATE program focuses on providing the lowest dose of drugs possible, the randomized clinical trial didn't control for drug dosage—so we don't know if the NAVIGATE participants received lower dosages than control participants (B. Carey, 2015b; Kane et al., 2015). Future studies should control for this. For now, the most we can conclude is that adding psychosocial interventions to traditional drug treatments appears to improve outcomes for psychosis.

Family Systems and Psychosis

Double Binds

Family systems therapists are interested in the relationship between family dynamics and psychosis. One early family-oriented theory was Gregory Bateson and colleagues' *double bind theory of schizophrenia*. A double bind occurs when someone is placed in a situation where there are two contradictory demands, neither of which can be satisfied or avoided (Bateson, Jackson, Haley, & Weakland, 1956). Bateson and his colleagues theorized that children who grow up in families where double binds are the norm are at higher risk for developing schizophrenia.

Luke

In therapy, Luke discusses his parents, who mean well but have long sent him two contradictory messages: "You cannot succeed on your own" and "Why don't you grow up already and leave us alone?" In addition, his parents make it difficult for him to avoid this contradictory dilemma because they also tell him "We're not going to let you move away from us because you need us to keep a roof over your head." Thus, from a very early age, Luke has been in a double bind that has proven quite difficult to escape.

CASE EXAMPLES

The double bind theory has been criticized for blaming parents and for lacking sufficient research support (Koopmans, 2001; Ringuette, 1982; Schuham, 1967). However, its supporters argue that those who use it to blame families for their children's schizophrenia are "less skilled theorists, given to dull and reductive readings of complex work" (Gibney, 2006, p. 51). More recent efforts have attempted to update the double bind theory and integrate it with the vulnerability stress model, wherein biological factors play a role in how susceptible people are to double bind family dynamics (Koopmans, 2001).

Expressed Emotion

Perhaps influenced by Bateson's double bind work, extensive research has been conducted showing that the amount of **expressed emotion** in the family often is related to outcomes in cases of schizophrenia. Expressed emotion is defined as the degree to which family members respond to a person diagnosed with schizophrenia in hostile, critical, or emotionally overinvolved ways (Kymalainen & Weisman de Mamani, 2008). There is substantial research showing that the more expressed emotion there is in a family, the worse the outcome in cases of schizophrenia (Breitborde, López, & Nuechterlein, 2010; Cechnicki, Bielańska, Hanuszkiewicz, & Daren, 2013; Hashemi & Cochrane, 1999; Kohler, Walker, Martin, Healey, & Moberg, 2010; Kymalainen & Weisman de Mamani, 2008; Meneghelli et al., 2011; von Polier et al., 2014; Wasserman, de Mamani, & Suro, 2012). Research has also found that the form of expressed emotion often varies by culture (Hashemi & Cochrane, 1999) and that more of it tends to be expressed when the individual with schizophrenia consistently violates the family's cultural norms and expectations (Kymalainen & Weisman de Mamani, 2008). Problems associated with expressed emotion in families may be compounded by research also showing that those diagnosed with schizophrenia are not very good at perceiving others' emotions (Kohler et al., 2010). The takeaway message here is that how families respond to a family member diagnosed with schizophrenia seems to matter quite a bit in how well that family member fares over time.

EVALUATING SOCIOCULTURAL PERSPECTIVES

Vespia (2009) nicely summarizes research evidence that sociocultural factors influence the development and course of psychosis. It is generally agreed that people in developing nations tend to have a better chance of recovery from schizophrenia than those in developed nations. Further, women fare better in dealing with the disorder than men. Additionally, symptoms are displayed somewhat differently across cultures and socioeconomic status and this is highly relevant in thinking about outcomes. Although there is social drift among those diagnosed with schizophrenia (they tend to slide down the socioeconomic ladder, which makes sense given how their symptoms impede their ability to function and earn a living), this doesn't account for the fact that low socioeconomic status places people at higher risk for schizophrenia in the first place. Taken in combination with the fact that family dynamics are also associated with course and outcome, it is reasonable to conclude that all in all, the evidence that sociocultural factors have a strong influence on psychosis is strong (Vespia, 2009).

That said, many argue that psychosis can't be understood in terms of sociocultural factors alone. Just as not everyone who is genetically vulnerable to psychosis develops it, it can similarly be argued that not everyone at social risk develops symptoms either. In fact, most people at social risk don't ever become psychotic. This suggests that the biological perspective emphasis on physiological susceptibility to psychosis is at least as important as sociocultural factors—and that in many ways, these two seemingly contradictory ways of understanding psychosis ultimately need to be more thoroughly integrated. As noted at various points throughout the chapter, the difficulty is in figuring out what the relative biological, psychological, and sociocultural contributions to psychosis might be. Recent efforts to integrate biological, cognitive, and sociocultural perspectives have led to an integrated sociodevelopmental-cognitive model of schizophrenia, examined in the "In Depth" feature. Sociocultural perspectives nonetheless force us to attend to the ways in which our Western cultural biases and presumptions inform the often-taken-for-granted ways that we conceptualize what psychosis is and how best to understand and manage it.

IN DEPTH

The Integrated Sociodevelopmental-Cognitive Model of Schizophrenia

Should biological, cognitive, and sociocultural perspectives be combined into an integrated model of schizophrenia? Researchers Oliver D. Howes and Robin M. Murray (2014) believe so and have proposed just such a model. Their model views schizophrenia as a neurodevelopmental disorder, one that typically develops in early adulthood. It integrates the following independent lines of research evidence previously discussed in this chapter:

» Dopamine dysregulation is commonly correlated with psychosis and schizophrenia.

» Vulnerability to schizophrenia seems to have a genetic component.

» Schizophrenia is associated with progressive neurodevelopmental brain deterioration, as evidenced by decreased brain volume.

» Psychosis is characterized by cognitive impairments, most notably problems with aberrant salience (attributing meaning to irrelevant events)—a problem believed to be related to dopamine dysregulation.

» Social disadvantage (e.g., being a minority group member, being an immigrant, being low in socioeconomic status) and social adversity (e.g., being physically or sexually abused in childhood or experiencing parental neglect) are predictors of psychosis and schizophrenia.

The integrated sociodevelopmental-cognitive model of schizophrenia assimilates these research findings into a multifactorial explanation of how schizophrenia develops and persists. It asserts that schizophrenia only emerges when a genetic vulnerability combines with social disadvantage and/or adversity to elicit problems with dopamine transmission in the brain. The resulting dopamine dysregulation leads to excessive dopamine, which yields cognitive difficulties—the over-attribution of meaning posited by aberrant salience theory. This, in turn, produces psychological stress, which further amplifies dopamine dysregulation by causing more dopamine to be released. A vicious cycle ensues. As more dopamine is released in response to stress, aberrant salience continues or worsens, leading to increasingly paranoid and psychotic cognitive processing and further stress—and so on and so on. Continuing symptoms of schizophrenia, therefore, occur due to a repetitive and self-perpetuating sequence of mutually influencing genetic, social, and cognitive factors. Figure 4.1 portrays this ongoing circular process visually.

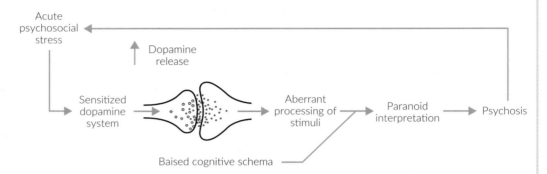

Figure 4.1 The Onset of Psychosis in the Integrative Sociocultural-Cognitive Model

Note: The integrative sociocultural model posits that biological factors (sensitized dopamine system), cognitive factors (aberrant processing of stimuli), and social factors (acute psychosocial stress) interact with one another to foster psychosis. Source: Figure 3 from: Howes, O. D., & Murray, R. M. (2014). Schizophrenia: An integrated sociodevelopmental-cognitive model. *The Lancet, 383*(9929), 1677–1687. doi:10.1016/S0140-6736(13)62036-X

The strength of Howes and Robin's model is that there is already substantial research on the genetic, neurodevelopmental, neurochemical, and sociocultural components that the model integrates. However, the proposed dynamic relationship between social disadvantage/adversity and dopamine dysregulation remains somewhat speculative (especially in humans) and it's not clear how much neurodevelopmental changes in the brain (such as decreased brain volume) are due to stress versus ongoing treatment with antipsychotic drugs. Nevertheless, the integrative sociocultural-cognitive model is noteworthy for trying to account for what often seem like contradictory findings. It entertains the audacious (and increasingly commonsensical) idea that psychosis—rather than being singularly biological, cognitive, or sociocultural—is a complex phenomenon that materializes from the mutual interaction of all three factors.

CRITICAL THINKING QUESTIONS

1. Do you think Howes and Robins' model overcomes long-standing disagreements about whether schizophrenia and other forms of psychosis are mainly biological, cognitive, or sociocultural problems?

2. What research studies might you design to further test Howes and Robins' model?

3. Are there factors that you believe Howes and Robins have not accounted for in their model? If so, what are they?

4.7 CLOSING THOUGHTS: CARING FOR THOSE EXPERIENCING PSYCHOSIS

Caring for seriously impaired people suffering from psychoses such as schizophrenia is costly and difficult. Theoretically, the advent of antipsychotic drugs has allowed for the deinstitutionalization of many psychotic patients, which involves releasing them from psychiatric hospitals and placing them in community care settings—something that would generally be celebrated except for the fact that funding for community care has traditionally been lacking (Torrey, 2014). This has often led to wide-scale homelessness and lack of support for many people experiencing psychosis, especially those low on the socioeconomic ladder. How to care for those with severe psychosis is a sociopolitical issue that requires thoughtful deliberation and careful planning.

CHAPTER 4

This is complicated by the simple fact that professionals often differ in how they define psychosis and what they think is the best way to address it. Should we primarily rely on medication, therapy, or social change to deal with it? Even if we take an integrated path and combine these approaches, the question of which should take precedence remains. Though the biological perspective emphasis on schizophrenia as a brain disease treatable with drugs remains the dominant viewpoint, we still diagnose the disorder behaviorally. To be honest, it is unclear when, if ever, we will be able to diagnose it biologically. Given this difficulty, it isn't surprising that researchers and clinicians continue to debate whether schizophrenia is a single disorder or a catch-all category for people who act the most "mad." Such debates matter because the stigma of schizophrenia remains significant—so much so that some researchers have suggested that Bleuler's now 100-year-old name "schizophrenia" should be retired in favor of something more modest such as "salience syndrome" or "psychosis susceptibility syndrome" (George & Klijn, 2013; van Os, 2009a, 2009b). These researchers note that the term "schizophrenia" has already been changed in Japan to something deemed less stigmatizing. Their argument for other countries to follow suit is based on their belief that our knowledge remains modest at best and that the term "schizophrenia" misleads us into thinking there is a singularly agreed-upon disorder that we understand more fully than is truly the case:

> The complicated, albeit ultimately meaningless, greek [sic] term suggests that schizophrenia really is a "thing", i.e. a "brain disease" that exists as such in Nature. This is a false suggestion, however, as schizophrenia refers to a syndrome of symptom dimensions that for unknown reasons cluster together in different combinations in different people with different contributions of known risk factors and dramatically different outcomes and response to treatment; no knowledge exists that may help decide to what degree schizophrenia, for example, reflects a single or 20 different underlying diseases—or none at all. Nevertheless, the way mental health professionals use the medical diagnosis of schizophrenia in clinical practice and communication inevitably results in its "reification"—or becoming a "thing." (van Os, 2009b, p. 368)

Regardless of whether you agree with this quote or not, it illustrates how—when it comes to categorizing, comprehending, and treating psychosis—many different and competing perspectives remain in play. As is often the case with abnormal psychology, psychosis is an area where—despite noble efforts to integrate contrasting perspectives—we still have many more questions than we have answers.

KEY TERMS

Aberrant salience hypothesis
Abnormal motor behavior
Acute and transient psychotic disorder (ATPD)
Adoption studies
Algoia
Amphetamine psychosis
Anhedonia
Antipsychotics
Asociality
Assertive community treatment (ACT)
Attenuated psychosis syndrome (APS)
Atypical antipsychotics
Avolition
Behavioral experiments
Behavioral rehearsal
Biopsychosocial model
Bizarre delusions
Brief psychotic disorder
Catatonia
Caudate nucleus
Cliff-edge fitness theory
Cognitive-behavioral therapy for psychosis (CBTp)
Community care
Concordance rates
Cytokines
Delusional disorder
Delusions

Dementia praecox
Diminished emotional expression
Disorganized thinking
Dizygotic twins
Dopamine hypothesis of schizophrenia
Double bind
Echolalia
Equal environments assumption
Erotomanic delusions
Evidential analysis
Expressed emotion
Extrapyramidal side effects
Family studies
First-generation antipsychotics
Genetic marker studies
Glutamate hypothesis of schizophrenia
Grandiose delusions
Hallucinations
Hydrotherapy
Inflammatory hypothesis
Integrated sociodevelopmental-cognitive model of schizophrenia
Jealous delusions
Loose associations
Mesolimbic dopamine pathway
Metacognition
Modeling
Monozygotic twins
Negative symptoms

Non-bizarre delusions
Normalization
Open Dialogue
Persecutory delusions
Positive symptoms
Pre-therapy
Prefrontal cortex
Psychoeducation
Psychosis
Schizoaffective disorder
Schizophrenia
Schizophreniform disorder
Schizophrenogenic mothers
Schizotypal disorder
Second-generation antipsychotics
Social drift
Social skills training
Socratic questioning
Somatic delusions
Soteria model
Stress-vulnerability-coping skills model
Tardive dyskinesia
Temporal cortex
Test-retest reliability
Theory of mind
Twin studies
Ventricles
Viral theory of schizophrenia
Word salad

Full definitions of the terms listed above can be found in the end-of-book glossary on p. 533.

Go to the companion website, www.macmillanihe.com/raskin-abnormal-psych, to access a study guide, multiple choice and flashcard quizzes for this chapter, and other useful learning aids.

CHAPTER 5
MOOD PROBLEMS

5.1 OVERVIEW

LEARNING OBJECTIVES

After reading this chapter, you should be able to:

1. Differentiate depression from mania, as well as endogenous from exogenous depression.
2. Distinguish types of mood episodes, define the depressive and bipolar disorders in *DSM* and *ICD*, and summarize critiques of these disorders.
3. Outline historical antecedents of modern mood problems, including defining melancholia, acedia, and neurasthenia.
4. Review and appraise biological perspectives on mood problems—including the monoamine and glutamate hypotheses, the use of antidepressants and mood stabilizers, the brain structures implicated, non-drug biological treatments, genetic and evolutionary perspectives, and the role of inflammation.
5. Discuss and critique the following psychological perspectives on mood problems: psychodynamic, cognitive-behavioral, and humanistic approaches.
6. Explain and evaluate sociocultural perspectives stressing the following issues in understanding and alleviating mood problems: socioeconomic inequality, gender issues, relationship problems, expressed emotion, and systems conceptualizations and interventions.

GETTING STARTED: THE HIGHS AND LOWS OF MOOD

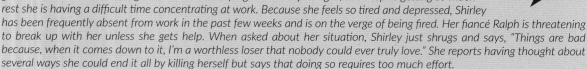

Shirley

Shirley, a 34-year-old accountant, comes to therapy feeling extremely depressed. Depression is not something new for her. She has had bouts of sadness before. However, this time the feelings came on abruptly and out of the blue. Shirley says that for the last six weeks she has felt despondent, having to fight back tears throughout the day. She also reports feeling listless and tired, with almost no energy to get out of bed in the morning. She has been sleeping 14 hours per night, but despite getting so much rest she is having a difficult time concentrating at work. Because she feels so tired and depressed, Shirley has been frequently absent from work in the past few weeks and is on the verge of being fired. Her fiancé Ralph is threatening to break up with her unless she gets help. When asked about her situation, Shirley just shrugs and says, "Things are bad because, when it comes down to it, I'm a worthless loser that nobody could ever truly love." She reports having thought about several ways she could end it all by killing herself but says that doing so requires too much effort.

CASE EXAMPLES

Don

Don is a 25-year-old freelance writer with a history of depression who comes to therapy after being arrested for drunk driving. He doesn't believe he needs help because, for the past two weeks, he has felt highly energetic and excited about life—so inspired, in fact, that he has been working non-stop on the "greatest novel of this decade." When asked when he last slept, Don waves his hand dismissively and notes that he has little need for sleep or food. Instead, he has been staying up 22 hours per day working on his novel. The night he was arrested Don went on a shopping spree for the new wardrobe he would need now that he is going to be an acclaimed author. Afterwards, he went to a bar to celebrate. Don was pulled over on the way home for driving erratically and at high speeds. A breath test showed him to be legally intoxicated. The judge mandated that Don seek treatment immediately. Don thinks it's all a plot to sabotage his budding career as a novelist. "They always undermine the truly great ones," he quips as he rambles on incessantly during his first session.

Depression and Mania

This chapter explores presenting problems pertaining to mood, namely depression and mania. **Depression** involves feelings of intense and often debilitating sadness and melancholy, along with a generally pessimistic

138

worldview and loss of interest in previously enjoyed activities. **Mania** is quite the opposite, characterized by euphoric mood, boundless energy, and a sometimes-distorted sense of one's capabilities. These sorts of disturbed moods are something to which abnormal psychology students can usually relate because everyone has experienced emotional ups and downs in life. This makes us all rather opinionated on the subject. Take depression, for instance. How often is it okay to feel depressed? How long is it acceptable to feel that way? What are justifiable reasons for depression? What causes it? Different perspectives address these questions differently, each offering its own take on why people experience extreme sadness.

Endogenous vs. Exogenous Depression

Clinicians and researchers have often distinguished endogenous from exogenous depression. **Endogenous depression** (historically often called *melancholia*) refers to depression believed to originate inside the person via faulty physiological processes (Shorter, 2007). Biological perspectives, with their emphasis on depression as an anatomically based disorder, are especially oriented toward an endogenous view of depression. On the other hand, **exogenous depression** is a term used to describe depression seen as originating outside the person (S. N. Ghaemi & Vöhringer, 2011)—in external circumstances such as poverty, racism, and sexism; or situational factors such as job or marital dissatisfaction. Psychosocial perspectives (sociocultural ones particularly) tend to emphasize exogenous explanations of depression. Unfortunately, even if there are two discrete kinds of depression (exogenous vs. endogenous), the distinction between them is more easily made in theory than in practice because, quite honestly, there is no clinical test that can tell us whether someone's depression is due to internal or external causes. Some argue that the classic endogenous–exogenous distinction no longer is useful because all forms of depression originate from both biological and psychosocial causes (S. N. Ghaemi & Vöhringer, 2011). When it comes to mood disturbances like depression, debate about their origins and which perspectives best explain and treat them can be especially intense. This chapter maps the current terrain by introducing various perspectives on mood-related presenting problems.

CHAPTER 5

5.2 *DSM* AND *ICD* PERSPECTIVES

MOOD EPISODES DEFINED

Depressive Episodes

The *DSM* and *ICD* conceptualize depression and mania as occurring in discrete *episodes*. In *DSM-5* and *ICD-11*, a **depressive episode** involves either (a) intense sadness and depressed mood or (b) loss of interest in daily activities; these symptoms must last two weeks or more. *ICD-10* also indicates two weeks but allows for a shorter duration if the symptoms appear abruptly or are especially severe. Other behaviors used to diagnose a depressive episode in all three manuals are changes in appetite (with associated weight gain or loss), changes in sleep habits (sleeping more or having trouble sleeping), tiredness and fatigue, indecisiveness and trouble concentrating, feelings of worthlessness, physical lethargy or restless, and suicidal feelings or overtures (see Diagnostic Box 5.1). In considering these symptoms, it becomes clear that depressive episodes are intense and debilitating forms of depression. Functioning is usually noticeably impaired during them. The person might stop going to work, stay in bed all day, give up leisure activities, be consistently teary-eyed and weepy, display very low energy levels, and seem generally sluggish and unmotivated.

Mood or bipolar disorder diagnoses are distinguished by the exact combination of depressive, manic, and/or hypomanic episodes.
Source: PhotoDisc/ Getty Images

 Shirley
Shirley, our first case study client, meets the criteria for depressive episodes.

 CASE EXAMPLES

Diagnostic Box 5.1 Depressive Episodes

DSM-5

- One of these two symptoms: (1) depressed mood almost every day for most of the day (feels sad or hopeless), (2) loss of interest or pleasure in all or nearly all activities.
- Depending on whether one or both of the above symptoms are present, three or four of these additional symptoms: (1) increased or decreased appetite or noticeable weight change, (2) insomnia or hypersomnia (difficulty sleeping or excessive sleep), (3) physically agitated/restless or lethargic, (4) tiredness or reduced energy, (5) feeling worthless or guilty without reason, (6) hard time concentrating or making decisions, (7) focus on death or a suicidal plan/attempt.
- Clinical judgment in diagnosing depressive episodes should be used if the person is experiencing bereavement.
- Duration of at least two weeks.

Based on American Psychiatric Association, 2013b, p. 125

ICD-10

- Depressed mood, decreased interest and enjoyment, and loss of energy leading to tiredness and diminished activity.
- Other symptoms include (1) trouble concentrating/paying attention, (2) low self-esteem and self-confidence, (3) feeling guilty and unworthy, (4) pessimism about the future, (5) thoughts/acts of suicide/self-harm, (6) sleep disruptions, (7) poor appetite.
- Duration typically two weeks but can be less if symptoms are severe or onset is rapid.

Based on World Health Organization, 1992, pp. 99–100

ICD-11

- One of these two symptoms: (1) depressed mood (as reported by the patient or observed by others), (2) loss of pleasure in activities, especially those typically enjoyed.
- Depending on whether one or both of the above symptoms are present, three or four of these additional symptoms: (1) trouble concentrating or difficulty making decisions, (2) feelings of low self-worth or excessive guilt, (3) hopelessness, (4) focus on death or a suicidal plan/attempt, (5) disrupted or excessive sleep, (6) increased or decreased appetite or noticeable weight change, (7) physically agitated/restless or lethargic, (8) tiredness or reduced energy.
- Duration of two weeks.
- Symptoms not better explained as due to bereavement.

Based on https://gcp.network/en/private/icd-11-guidelines/grouping

Manic, Hypomanic, and Mixed Episodes

Whereas depression entails intense sadness and loss of interest in things, a **manic episode** is characterized by one week or more of persistently elevated mood accompanied by high energy and intense goal-directed activity (see Diagnostic Box 5.2). Manic episodes often involve inflated self-esteem or **grandiosity** (the idea that one is very important), decreased need for sleep, extreme talkativeness, racing thoughts, distractibility, and impulsive or risky behavior (e.g., shopping sprees, poor financial choices, unsafe or indiscrete sexual activity, drug abuse). Extreme cases of mania can include distortions in thinking and perceiving that cross the line into psychosis (see Chapter 4).

Don
Don, the client in our second case study, appears to be experiencing a manic episode.

CASE EXAMPLES

A **hypomanic episode** constitutes a shorter version of a manic episode. In *DSM-5*, symptoms must occur for at least four days but not a full week. *ICD-10* and *ICD-11* merely indicate that symptoms last several days (see Diagnostic Box 5.2). The *ICD* also includes a **mixed episode**, in which manic and depressive symptoms rapidly alternate or co-occur for at least two weeks. However, the *DSM-5* no longer includes mixed episodes; instead, it has clinicians specify "with mixed features" when diagnosing bipolar and depressive disorders. Differentiating depressive, manic, hypomanic, and (if using *ICD*) mixed mood episodes is crucial in distinguishing the specific *DSM* and *ICD* categories discussed next.

Diagnostic Box 5.2 Manic, Hypomanic, and Mixed Episodes

DSM-5

- Inflated or irritable mood with extremely intensified energy and activity levels.
- At least three of these symptoms (four if mood only irritable): (1) exaggerated self-esteem or grandiosity, (2) diminished need for sleep, (3) talkativeness or urge to talk, (4) rapidly fluctuating ideas or racing thoughts, (5) easily distractible, (6) excessive activity (goal-directed or unfocused), (7) risky, impulsive, or dangerous behavior.

- *Manic*: Duration of at least one week.
- *Hypomanic*: Duration of at least four days but less than one week.
- *Mixed*: No longer a mood episode in *DSM-5*; used as a specifier for mood and bipolar disorders instead.

Based on American Psychiatric Association, 2013b, p. 124

ICD-10

- Elevated mood and an increase in the quantity and speed of physical and mental activity.
- *Manic*: Duration of at least one week.
- *Hypomanic*: Duration of several days but less than one week.
- *Mixed*: For at least two weeks, rapid shifting (often within several hours) among depressive, manic, and hypomanic symptoms.

Based on World Health Organization, 1992, pp. 94–95, 108

ICD-11

- Euphoric, irritable, inflated, or rapidly changing mood with amplified energy and activity levels.
- Several of these symptoms: (1) talkativeness or urge to talk, (2) rapidly fluctuating ideas or racing thoughts, (3) exaggerated self-esteem or grandiosity, (4) diminished need for sleep, (5) easily distractible, (6) risky, impulsive, or dangerous behavior, (7) enhanced sexual desire, feelings of sociability, or goal-oriented behavior.
- *Manic*: Duration of at least one week.
- *Hypomanic*: Duration of several days but less than one week.
- *Mixed*: For at least two weeks, rapid shifting (often within several hours) among depressive, manic, and hypomanic symptoms.

Based on https://gcp.network/en/private/icd-11-guidelines/grouping

MAJOR DEPRESSION AND BIPOLAR DISORDERS

Major Depressive Disorder

Using the *DSM-5*, **major depressive disorder (MDD)** (also called *major depression*) is diagnosed in those who suffer one or more depressive episodes. People who only experience one depressive episode are diagnosed with *major depressive disorder, single episode*. Those who have more than one episode are diagnosed with *major depressive disorder, recurrent*. The *ICD-10* and *ICD-11* don't use the term "major depressive disorder." Instead, they distinguish **single episode depressive disorder** from **recurrent depressive disorder**, with the former being roughly equivalent to *DSM-5*'s *major depressive disorder, single episode* and the latter to *major depressive disorder, recurrent*. See Diagnostic Box 5.3 for *DSM-5* criteria and *ICD-10* and *ICD-11* guidelines. Importantly, to qualify for major depression in either the *DSM* or *ICD*, there can't be any history of manic or hypomanic episodes. If these are present, then the most appropriate form of bipolar disorder is diagnosed instead.

Diagnostic Box 5.3 Major Depressive Disorder

DSM-5

- One or more major depressive episodes.
- There has never been a manic or hypomanic episode.

Based on American Psychiatric Association, 2013b, pp. 160–161

ICD-10

- In *ICD-10*, called "single depressive episode" if only one depressive episode and "recurrent depressive disorder" if more than one depressive episode.
- No history of manic, hypomanic, or mixed episodes.

Based on World Health Organization, 1992, pp. 99–100

ICD-11

- In *ICD-11*, called "single episode depressive disorder" if only one depressive episode and "recurrent depressive disorder" if more than one depressive episode.
- Repeated episodes of depression without any history of manic, hypomanic, or mixed episodes.

Based on https://gcp.network/en/private/icd-11-guidelines/grouping

The *DSM-5* indicates that during a twelve-month period, the prevalence rate for major depression in the U.S. is 7%. World Health Organization research has estimated twelve-month U.S. prevalence rates at 8.3%, notably greater than many other developed countries such as France (5.9%), Belgium (5.5%), Israel (6.1%), Germany (3%), Italy (3%), and Japan (2.2%) (Kessler et al., 2010). Compared to developed countries, twelve-month prevalence rates are generally a bit higher in developing countries, with Brazil having the highest rates (10.4%) and Mexico the lowest (4%) (Kessler et al., 2010).

The *DSM-5* notes that when it comes to depression, there are big differences by age group. Depressive episodes can first occur at any age, though those in their teens or 20s are at greatest risk. In fact, 18–29 year olds have three times the risk as those over 60. There are gender differences, too. Starting in early adolescence, women are one-and-a-half to three times more likely to be diagnosed than men. There is also a lot of variability in the course of symptoms, with some people having long breaks between depressive episodes and others being almost continually depressed. However, it is common for depressive episodes to spontaneously begin lifting within three months of onset even without intervention. The more time since a depressive episode, the less the likelihood of having another one.

Bipolar Disorder and Cyclothymic Disorder

The *DSM-5* divides bipolar disorder (sometimes still called by its older name, *manic depression*) into two basic kinds. **Bipolar I disorder** is diagnosed in anyone who has ever had a full-blown manic episode. People who meet the criteria for bipolar I disorder may also experience hypomanic and depressive episodes, but these aren't required for a diagnosis. **Bipolar II disorder**, on the other hand, is considered less severe than bipolar I. It is diagnosed in people who have experienced both hypomanic and depressive episodes but have never had a manic episode. If someone diagnosed with bipolar II undergoes a full-scale manic episode, then the diagnosis is changed to bipolar I. The *ICD-10* doesn't make the bipolar I–bipolar II distinction, but the *ICD-11* is adopting it for the first time. Using the term **bipolar affective disorder**, the *ICD-10* instead contains numerous subtypes such as *bipolar affective disorder, current episode hypomanic* and *bipolar affective disorder, current episode mild or moderate depression*.

Cyclothymic disorder is a category reserved for people who consistently have hypomanic and depressive symptoms, neither of which rise to the level of a hypomanic or depressive episode. These symptoms must be present for at least half the time over two years for a *DSM-5* or *ICD-11* diagnosis; no minimum duration is specified in the *ICD-10*. The *DSM-5* reports twelve-month U.S. prevalence rates of 0.6% for bipolar I disorder, 0.3% for bipolar II disorder, and 0.4%–1% for cyclothymic disorder. These rates are similar to the twelve-month bipolar I and bipolar II prevalence rates found in countries such as Brazil (0.6% and 0.2%), Mexico (0.5% and 0.1%), and New Zealand (0.6% and 0.5%); Japan and Columbia, however, have noticeably lower twelve-month prevalence rates (Merikangas et al., 2011). Diagnostic Boxes 5.4 and 5.5 list criteria and guidelines for bipolar disorder and cyclothymic disorder, respectively.

Diagnostic Box 5.4 Bipolar Disorder

DSM-5
- **Bipolar I disorder**
  - At least one lifetime manic episode: Required.
  - Hypomanic and depressive episodes: Common but not required.
- **Bipolar II disorder**
  - At least one lifetime hypomanic episode: Required.
  - At least one lifetime major depressive episode: Required.
  - There has never been a manic episode.

Based on American Psychiatric Association, 2013b, pp. 123–126 and 132–135

ICD-10
- **Bipolar affective disorder**
  - At least two mood episodes where mood and activity levels are disrupted.
  - On some occasions, mania or hypomania; on other occasions, depression.

Based on World Health Organization, 1992, p. 97

ICD-11
- **Bipolar I disorder**
  - At least one lifetime manic or mixed episode: Required.
  - Hypomanic and depressive episodes: Common but not required.
- **Bipolar II disorder**
  - At least one lifetime hypomanic episode: Required.
  - At least one lifetime major depressive episode: Required.
  - There has never been a manic episode.

Based on https://gcp.network/en/private/icd-11-guidelines/grouping

Diagnostic Box 5.5 Cyclothymic Disorder

DSM-5
- Hypomanic symptoms that don't meet criteria for a hypomanic episode.
- Depressive symptoms that don't meet criteria for a depressive episode.
- Symptoms present at least half the time for last two years (one year in children and adolescents) and symptoms never absent for more than two months.
- There has never been a full-blown depressive, manic, or hypomanic episode.

Based on American Psychiatric Association, 2013b, pp. 139–140

ICD-10
- Persistent instability of mood, involving numerous periods of mild depression and elation.
- Mood states are milder than depressive or manic episodes, so don't qualify for bipolar affective disorder or recurrent depressive disorder.

Based on World Health Organization, 1992, p. 107

ICD-11
- Hypomanic symptoms that may or may not meet criteria for hypomanic episode.
- Depressive symptoms that don't meet criteria for a depressive episode.
- Symptoms present often for at least two years.
- No manic or mixed episodes.

Based on https://gcp.network/en/private/icd-11-guidelines/grouping

CHAPTER 5

OTHER DEPRESSIVE DISORDERS

Persistent Depressive Disorder (Dysthymia)

Prior to the *DSM-5*, both *ICD* and *DSM* used the term **dysthymia** (or *dysthymic disorder*) to describe ongoing depression that is milder than major depression. However, in *DSM-5* the term dysthymia has been changed to **persistent depressive disorder (PDD)** and the symptoms broadened to encompass cases of chronic depression whether or not they meet the criteria for a full-blown major depressive episode. The same kinds of depressive symptoms found in major depression occur—changes in appetite and sleep, decreased energy level, difficulty concentrating, low self-esteem, and feelings of hopelessness. However, they are considered chronic because they last for a minimum of two years (one year for children and adolescents) and never remit for more than two months at a time (see Diagnostic Box 5.6). When making a PDD diagnosis, clinicians indicate whether symptom severity rises to the level of a major depressive episode. If yes, then the diagnosis is given a "with major depression" specifier. If no, then the diagnosis is given a "with dysthymia" specifier.

In contrast to *DSM-5*, the *ICD-10* still uses the name "dysthymia" instead of persistent depression (with the *ICD-11* adopting the more formal name, "dysthymic disorder"). Both *ICD-10* and *ICD-11* generally adhere to the more classic definition of a milder, long-term depression. *ICD-10* describes it as a chronic depression that doesn't meet the guidelines for recurrent depressive disorder. *ICD-11* is less definitive. It moves somewhat closer to the *DSM-5* by permitting dysthymic disorder to include depression that rises to the level of a depressive episode, but only after a milder depression has lasted for at least two years. These differences notwithstanding, *DSM-5*, *ICD-10*, and *ICD-11* all agree that there can never be a manic or hypomanic episode in persistent depression/dysthymia. If there is, then the person should be diagnosed with the most appropriate form of bipolar disorder.

Diagnostic Box 5.6 Persistent Depressive Disorder (Dysthymia)

DSM-5
- Major or mild depression for at least two years, with symptoms never absent for more than two months.
- Two or more of these symptoms: (1) change in appetite, (2) change in sleep habits, (3) tiredness or reduced energy, (4) decreased self-esteem, (5) trouble with concentration or decision-making, (6) feels hopeless.
- There has never been a manic episode, hypomanic episode, or cyclothymic disorder.
- Specify: *with pure dysthymic syndrome* (major depressive episode criteria not met in last two years), *with persistent major depressive episode* (major depressive episode criteria met throughout last two years), *with intermittent major depressive episodes, with current episode* (major depressive episode criteria currently met, but they haven't been met in at least eight weeks during last two years), or *with intermittent major depressive episodes, without current episode* (major depressive episode criteria not currently met, but there has been at least one major depressive episode during last two years).

Based on American Psychiatric Association, 2013b, pp. 168–169

ICD-10
- Ongoing and long-term depression that rarely, if ever, qualifies as recurrent depressive disorder.
- Typically starts early in life and persists for many years; when onset is late in life, it usually follows a depressive episode and is often tied to bereavement or other life stress.

Based on World Health Organization, 1992, pp. 107–108

ICD-11
- Persistently depressed mood most days for at least two years.
- For at least the first two years, symptoms not severe enough to qualify for a depressive episode.
- Symptoms such as: (1) loss of pleasure in activities, (2) tiredness or reduced energy, (3) trouble with concentration or decision-making, (4) feeling guilty and unworthy, (5) suicidal thoughts, (6) change in sleep habits, (7) change in appetite, (8) physically agitated/restless or lethargic.
- No history of manic, hypomanic, or mixed episodes.

Based on https://gcp.network/en/private/icd-11-guidelines/grouping

DSM-5 reports a 1.5% U.S. prevalence rate for PDD with major depressive episodes, but only a 0.5% prevalence rate for PDD without them. It also indicates that PDD tends to start in childhood, adolescence, or young adulthood and often shows comorbidity with personality disorders and substance use. The *DSM-5* lists childhood separation from or loss of parents as a risk factor. Prevalence rates for other countries are unclear because PDD is a new *DSM-5* diagnosis. However, twelve-month prevalence rates for the somewhat similar *ICD-10* diagnosis of dysthymia are comparable to the U.S. rates for PDD: 1.1% across Belgium, France, Germany, Italy, the Netherlands and Spain (Alonso et al., 2004).

Premenstrual Dysphoric Disorder and Disruptive Mood Dysregulation Disorder

The *DSM-5* added two new depressive disorders, premenstrual dysphoric disorder and disruptive mood dysregulation disorder (see Diagnostic Boxes 5.7 and 5.8). **Premenstrual dysphoric disorder (PMDD)** is diagnosed in women who consistently show depressive symptoms during the week before their menstrual periods. **Disruptive mood dysregulation disorder (DMDD)** (mentioned briefly in Chapter 3) is a diagnosis reserved for children and adolescents who show depressive symptoms combined with temper outbursts. While neither PMDD nor DMDD is listed in the *ICD-10*, PMDD has been added to the new *ICD-11*—but in the section on diseases affecting the genital organs rather than in the section on mental disorders. Additionally, the *ICD-11* indicates that those wishing to diagnose DMDD can code it as a form of oppositional defiant disorder (see Chapter 13). PMDD and DMDD diagnoses have been surrounded by extensive criticism and controversy, discussed further below.

Diagnostic Box 5.7 Premenstrual Dysphoric Disorder (PMDD)

DSM-5
- During menstrual cycles for the last year, at least five symptoms.
- At least one symptom must be: (1) mood swings, (2) touchiness, anger, relational conflicts, (3) sadness, hopelessness, self-denigrating thoughts, (4) anxiety, tension, edginess.
- At least one symptom must be (1) loss of interest in activities, (2) feeling distracted, (3) tiredness or low energy, (4) changes in appetite, (5) insomnia or hypersomnia, (6) sense of being overwhelmed, (7) physical symptoms (tender breasts, muscle pain, bloating, gaining weight).

Based on American Psychiatric Association, 2013b, pp. 171–172

ICD-11
- During most menstrual cycles, mood symptoms (e.g., depressed, anxious, irritable), physical symptoms (e.g., joint pain, fatigue, overeating, sleeping excessively), and cognitive symptoms (e.g., trouble concentrating).

Based on https://icd.who.int/browse11/l-m/en

Diagnostic Box 5.8 Disruptive Mood Dysregulation Disorder

DSM-5
- Verbal and behavioral temper outbursts roughly three times per week that are developmentally inappropriate.
- Consistently irritable mood most days.
- Symptoms last at least a year and are never absent for three or more months.
- Onset before age 10; shouldn't be diagnosed before age 6 or after age 18.

Based on American Psychiatric Association, 2013b, p. 156

ICD
- Not in *ICD-10* or *ICD-11*, but can be coded as "oppositional defiant disorder with chronic irritability-anger" in *ICD-11*.

Postpartum Depression and Seasonal Affective Disorder

Postpartum depression is depression that develops in women who are pregnant or have given birth within the last four weeks. **Seasonal affective disorder (SAD)** describes depression which occurs during the winter months when there are fewer hours of daylight. Neither is formally recognized in the *DSM* or *ICD* as a stand-alone diagnosis. However, when diagnosing major depressive disorder or persistent depressive disorder using the *DSM-5*, a clinician can specify "with peripartum onset" or "with seasonal pattern." Postpartum depression and SAD can also be diagnosed in *DSM-5* as either *other specified depressive disorder* or *unspecified depressive disorder*—categories reserved for symptom patterns (postpartum depression and SAD patterns included) that either don't fit into or don't meet the full criteria for any other depressive disorder. "Other specified" is used when the clinician wishes

Depression during the winter months when there are fewer hours of daylight is called seasonal affective disorder, though it is not currently a stand-alone DSM *or* ICD *diagnosis.*
Source: Getty Images/Cultura RF \ Lars Forsstedt

to explain the uniqueness of the symptom pattern; "unspecified" is used when the clinician doesn't explain this, perhaps due to a shortage of information.

While *ICD-10* and *ICD-11* also lack stand-alone categories for postpartum depression and SAD, they code them a bit differently than *DSM-5*. Postpartum depression is coded as a "mental and behavioural disorder associated with pregnancy, childbirth and the puerperium, not elsewhere classified"—*puerperium* being a technical term for the six-week period after birth when a woman's reproductive system fully returns to a nonpregnant condition. SAD is simply diagnosed in *ICD-10* and *ICD-11* as a type of recurrent depressive disorder.

EVALUATING *DSM* AND *ICD* PERSPECTIVES

The *ICD-10* appeared more than twenty years ago, so most current concerns expressed about diagnostic perspectives on depression and mania refer to the *DSM-5*, which was published in 2013. Interestingly, while the *ICD-11* was in development, its authors were warned by critics not to repeat the *DSM-5*'s perceived mistakes (Frances & Nardo, 2013). What kinds of problems have been highlighted? Comorbidity, threshold problems, and competing classification system conflicts have all been identified as troublesome issues when it comes to diagnosing depression and mania (Bebbington, 2013).

» *Comorbidity* involves the fact that many patients <u>meet the criteria for more than one mood disorder</u>. Mood disorders are also highly comorbid with other presenting problems—notably <u>anxiety, posttraumatic stress, substance use, and impulse-control issues</u> (all discussed in future chapters) (Cummings, Caporino, & Kendall, 2014; R. M. A. Hirschfeld, 2001; Horesh et al., 2017; Kessler et al., 2003; Kessler et al., 2010; Klein Hofmeijer-Sevink et al., 2012; Stander, Thomsen, & Highfill-McRoy, 2014). Some critics see this as evidence that <u>*DSM* and *ICD* are conceptually flawed because they can't</u> clearly distinguish different disorders. Others feel this is unfair and argue that <u>depression isn't merely comorbid with other mental disorders</u>, but also with many <u>physical disorders</u>—including cancer, stroke, and coronary issues (H.-J. Kang et al., 2015).

» *Threshold problems* refer to uncertainty about how <u>severe mood symptoms must be before they rise</u> to the <u>level of disorder.</u> We have already mentioned how difficult it is for laypeople to agree about this. Those creating *DSM* and *ICD* haven't always been able to, either.

» *Competing classification system conflicts* reflect the fact that when it c<u>omes to mood problems, *DSM* and *ICD*</u> <u>aren't always on the same page</u>—despite ongoing efforts to harmonize them (Maj, 2013).

Next let's review several questions specifically raised about the recently revised *DSM-5* sections on depressive and bipolar disorders.

Are the *DSM-5* Depressive and Bipolar Categories Reliable?

Somewhat surprisingly given how common a diagnosis it is, major depressive disorder showed questionable diagnostic reliability in the *DSM-5* field trials—meaning that clinicians didn't consistently agree on which patients warranted a major depression diagnosis (Regier et al., 2013). Bipolar I disorder fared better in these trials. However, disruptive mood dysregulation disorder fared much worse (Regier et al., 2013). Thus, for several *DSM-5* depressive disorder diagnoses, reliability is a concern. Why might reliability for depressive disorders be low? One possible explanation is that depression is a *heterogeneous* diagnosis—meaning that people assigned to it often have somewhat dissimilar symptoms and circumstances (Ghaemi & Vöhringer, 2011; Lieblich et al., 2015). Thus, clinicians are unclear about what counts as depression and who should receive a diagnosis, as evidenced by the fact that in *DSM-5* field trials "highly trained specialist psychiatrists under study conditions were only able to agree that a patient has depression between 4 and 15% of the time" (Lieblich et al., 2015, p. e5). Without reliable diagnostic categories, it is extremely difficult to determine which treatments for depression are helpful (Lieblich et al., 2015).

Are Persistent Depression and Major Depression Distinct Disorders?

Building on the issue of diagnostic reliability, *DSM-5*'s PDD diagnosis has been criticized for blurring the line between milder chronic depression (dysthymia in *ICD* and previous *DSM*s) and more acute but less long-lasting major depression (Uher, Payne, Pavlova, & Perlis, 2014). As some critics put it, PDD "is intended to encompass both dysthymia and chronic depression, but its relationship to MDD is ambiguous with conflicting statements on whether the two diagnoses should be concurrent if both sets of criteria are fulfilled" (Uher et al., 2014, p. 459). However, others have countered that because such a firm distinction between persistent depression and major depression is scientifically suspect, the *DSM-5* had to loosen the boundaries between PDD and MDD (Gotlib & LeMoult, 2014). This debate highlights how taken-for-granted boundaries between diagnostic categories may be less certain than assumed.

Should the Bereavement Exclusion Have Been Maintained?

The **bereavement exclusion** was a criterion in *DSM-IV* that discouraged clinicians from diagnosing major depression in people grieving the loss of a loved one (A. V. Horwitz & Wakefield, 2007). The exclusion's logic was that bereavement looks like major depression but is really an expectable and normal reaction to grief. Yet those who wanted to eliminate the exclusion asked why we should make a special case for bereavement when other situations such as divorce or job loss don't exclude people from a major depression diagnosis (Iglewicz, Seay, Vigeant, Jouhal, & Zisook, 2013; Karam, Tabet, & Itani, 2013; Pies, 2014). They argued that depression is depression regardless of circumstances. However, critics didn't budge. They saw removing the bereavement exclusion as pathologizing normal human sadness in response to loss (Frances & Nardo, 2013; J. C. Wakefield, 2013a; J. C. Wakefield & First, 2012). In the end, the *DSM-5* removed the bereavement exclusion, indicating that clinicians should use their own judgment in diagnosing bereaved people with major depression. This means that if you go to a therapist while grieving, whether you get diagnosed with major depression will depend on whether the clinician supports or opposes the bereavement exclusion. Not a great way to maintain diagnostic reliability, according to *DSM-5* critics.

Why Was Premenstrual Dysphoric Disorder (PMDD) Added?

Critics have loudly criticized the *DSM-5* and *ICD-11* for including PMDD as a new disorder. PMDD has a long history. Several earlier versions of the *DSM* only listed it as a proposed disorder warranting further study, but it was promoted to an officially recognized disorder in *DSM-5*, a step also taken by the *ICD-11*. Critics complain that PMDD is a sexist category that pathologizes women by reinforcing stereotypes about them being emotionally unstable during menstruation (Caplan, 1995; Offman & Kleinplatz, 2004; J. C. Wakefield, 2013b). In contrast, supporters argue that PMDD is a legitimate disorder that should only be diagnosed in extreme cases requiring treatment (American Psychiatric Association, 2013b; Gotlib & LeMoult, 2014).

Why Was Disruptive Mood Dysregulation Disorder (DMDD) Added?

DMDD was added to *DSM-5* despite a rather poor performance in diagnostic reliability trials (Regier et al., 2013). Supporters hope the addition of DMDD will counter the alarming trend of diagnosing children with "childhood bipolar" (a disorder not found in either the *DSM* or *ICD*) and placing them on powerful antipsychotic drugs (Margulies, Weintraub, Basile, Grover, & Carlson, 2012; A. K. Roy, Lopes, & Klein, 2014; Stebbins & Corcoran, 2015). They contend that adding DMDD provides a diagnosis that clinicians can use instead of childhood bipolar, one that potentially discourages use of strong antipsychotic drugs (Margulies et al., 2012; A. K. Roy et al., 2014; Stebbins & Corcoran, 2015). Critics, on the other hand, see DMDD as turning a normal part of childhood—temper tantrums—into a mental disorder. From their point of view, this diagnosis clearly encourages the continued and inappropriate use of antipsychotics and other medications in young children (R. Cook, 2014; Frances, 2012a; Raven & Parry, 2012). For more on the "childhood bipolar" controversy, see the "In Depth" feature.

IN DEPTH

Childhood Bipolar, Antipsychotics, and Drugging Our Children

Bipolar disorder has traditionally been diagnosed almost exclusively in adults—although discussion of its occurrence in children has been debated on and off since the early 20th century (Carlson & Glovinsky, 2009). However, starting in the 1990s, there was an explosion of diagnoses in American children. By some estimates, the number of children diagnosed with childhood bipolar disorder increased forty-fold between 1994–1995 and 2002–2003 (C. Moreno et al., 2007; Parens & Johnston, 2010). This has been contentious for the following reasons.

1. Not everyone believes that there is such a thing as "childhood bipolar." Critics see it as the product of bad science and good marketing by doctors and pharmaceutical companies (S. L. Kaplan, 2011).

2. When childhood bipolar first started gaining in popularity, it wasn't even listed in the *DSM* or *ICD* as a diagnosis for children. Further, the symptoms don't necessarily correspond to those seen in adults. Some researchers contend that the primary symptom of childhood bipolar is aggression, while others say it is grandiosity (Kaplan, 2011). The criteria for childhood bipolar remain unclear.

3. Many people question how it's possible for the number of cases to have increased forty-fold in such a short time. Supporters of the diagnosis argue that the rates only increased exponentially because so few cases were being identified before the mid-1990s; in other words, we were overlooking the disorder entirely and now we no longer are (Parens & Johnston, 2010). However, opponents of the diagnosis say the huge increase constitutes a false epidemic. In their view, most or all of the children being diagnosed do not warrant the diagnosis (Kaplan, 2011).

4. The large increase in childhood bipolar diagnoses has occurred almost entirely in the United States. Why this is remains unclear. Some say this shows greater levels of misdiagnosis in the U.S., whereas others speculate that childhood bipolar simply takes a more aggressive course in American children (Post et al., 2014). At the very least, the issue of culture bias in diagnosis warrants further discussion.

5. There has been a backlash against the use of mood stabilizers and antipsychotics to treat children diagnosed as bipolar. Lithium, valproate, and risperidone are all commonly prescribed even though the long-term effects of giving such strong drugs to children aren't clear (Whitaker, 2012). The side effects of these drugs are significant. Atypical antipsychotics such as risperidone may cause movement disorders, weight gain, and endocrine dysfunction in the children who take them (Whitaker, 2012).

6. Rather than relying so heavily on drugging children whose behavior is challenging, some critics argue that what is really needed is social change to help parents better take care of their children—the provision of affordable day care and housing, paid parental leave, a living wage, adequate public schools, flex time at work, and social services that teach effective parenting skills (Olfman, 2012). These things would provide more effective solutions to severe behavior problems in children than the overuse of powerful and dangerous drugs, according to critics.

Some hope that the recent addition of disruptive mood dysregulation disorder (DMDD) will replace the diagnosis of childhood bipolar. However, the jury is still out on this question (Margulies et al., 2012) and the DMDD diagnosis itself also remains controversial. Debate over childhood bipolar disorder is likely to continue for some time.

CRITICAL THINKING QUESTIONS

1. Do you think childhood bipolar is a legitimate diagnosis? Why or why not?

2. Why do you think the rates of childhood bipolar increased so rapidly? If you're unsure, what evidence would you need to help you answer this question?

3. Are we drugging our kids too much? Is childhood bipolar better seen as a medical problem in need of drugs or a social problem best rectified by social changes?

CHAPTER 5

Photo source: © PhotoDisc/Getty Images

5.3 HISTORICAL PERSPECTIVES

MELANCHOLIA IN ANCIENT GREECE

Today's *ICD* and *DSM* conceptions of depression and mania can be traced back through the history of abnormal psychology, as these problems have been recognized throughout the ages (Baldessarini, Pérez, Salmtore, Trede, & Maggini, 2015). Ancient Greek medicine divided madness into three kinds: *frenzy*, *mania*, and *melancholy* (Lawlor, 2012). Its definitions of mania and melancholy don't map precisely onto our current sense of these terms (Lawlor, 2012). For instance, melancholy—or melancholia—was broader than what today we call depression. It involved not just seemingly baseless sadness and fear, but sometimes included other symptoms such as hallucinations (Lawlor, 2012). Ancient Greek humoral theory blamed melancholia on imbalances in (and sometimes overheating of) black bile, one of the four bodily humors (see Chapter 1) (Azzone, 2013; Lawlor, 2012). Melancholia was also often attributed to unrequited love (Lawlor, 2012). Treatments for mania and melancholia included bloodletting and leeching, intended to correct the humoral imbalances (Lawlor, 2012).

ACEDIA AND MELANCHOLIA IN THE EARLY CHRISTIAN ERA AND RENAISSANCE

Later, during the early Christian era, the term **acedia** was used to describe the low mood, boredom, and longing found among isolated monks living in the Egyptian desert during the fourth century (Azzone, 2013; Lawlor, 2012). Acedia also involved despair arising from pressure to avoid temptation. These elements of acedia became incorporated into Western conceptions of melancholia.

During the Renaissance, melancholia was perhaps the most prevalent form of madness (Dreher, 2013). However, it was a noticeably broader category than today's depression. Symptoms included

> *overwhelming anxiety, fearfulness, sadness, and gloom, restlessness, dissatisfaction, emotional instability, suspicion, weeping, complaining, ill-tempered and aggressive behavior, withdrawal from social life, disturbed sexual relations, torpor, the inability to feel pleasure, lethargy, oppression with a sense of guilt and unworthiness, inability to sleep, delusions, hallucinations, profound weariness with life, and suicidal tendencies. (Dreher, 2013, p. 41)*

Renaissance thinkers attributed melancholy to a variety of factors, including supernatural causes (e.g., God or the devil), natural causes (e.g., astrological influences or biological factors such as imbalances in the digestive system), and external causes (e.g., conflicted interpersonal relations with others or unfortunate life circumstances such as financial loss, poverty, or grieving) (Dreher, 2013). These kinds of explanations anticipate the biological, psychological, and sociocultural perspectives outlined later in this chapter. Importantly, the Renaissance also introduced the romanticizing of melancholy, with feelings of sadness and despair often seen as natural accompaniments of genius—a view sometimes still held today (Lawlor, 2012).

INDUSTRIALIZATION, DEPLETED NERVOUS SYSTEMS, AND NEURASTHENIA

During the late 19th and early 20th centuries in Europe and North America, melancholy was often associated with the oppressive consequences of industrialization (Lawlor, 2012). Interestingly, some of the language we use today to describe depression can be traced back to the industrial era's emphasis on harnessing energy (for instance, the *DSM* and *ICD* cite loss of energy as a key symptom). When the energy-system comparison was applied to understanding people's psychological states, the idea of depression and mania as due to extreme variations in energy (or overly stimulated or depleted nervous systems) emerged and influenced a host of important thinkers, including Emil Kraepelin (1856–1926; see Chapter 4) and Sigmund Freud (1856–1939; see Chapter 2) (Lawlor, 2012).

Can the hustle and bustle of city life make you sad? In the late 19th and early 20th centuries, doctors thought so, calling the condition "neurasthenia"
Source: Getty Images \ Xavier Arnau

Sticking with the energy metaphor, **neurasthenia** was another popular diagnosis during the later 19th and early 20th centuries. It was given to sad and anxious people whose nervous systems were thought to be exhausted (J. Beck, 2016). Interestingly, neurasthenia was often attributed to social causes such as the "fast pace of entrepreneurial urban life" (Lawlor, 2012, p. 130), especially among the lower classes (J. Beck, 2016). It was also often seen as an affliction accompanying genius (as melancholia had been during the Renaissance). Although it is no longer used as a diagnostic category in many countries and is not listed in the *DSM-5*, neurasthenia was retained in the *ICD-10* for those who still found it a useful diagnosis. However, it isn't in the *ICD-11* (Creed & Gureje, 2012; "References for intention not to retain Neurasthenia for ICD-11," 2015). Still, in many respects neurasthenia represents a historical leftover that bridges ancient conceptions of melancholia and modern notions of depression (Lawlor, 2012).

KRAEPELIN AND THE MANIC-DEPRESSIVE ILLNESS CONTINUUM

Coming from a biological orientation, early diagnostician Emil Kraepelin placed depression and mania along a manic-depressive illness continuum—greatly influencing modern understandings (Baldessarini et al., 2015). Mania involved overactivity and the flight of ideas, while depression involved feelings of sadness accompanied by slowed down physiology and cognition (Lawlor, 2012). Kraepelin's perspective was complemented by (if also at odds with) Freud's concurrent view, which saw melancholy as anger directed at the self. In early object relations therapy (refer to Chapter 2), clinicians shared the psychoanalytic view of depression as traceable to childhood; they attributed it to conflicts over loss and separation originating in the mother–infant relationship (Lawlor, 2012). We revisit this later when discussing psychodynamic approaches.

FROM MELANCHOLIA TO DEPRESSION

Adolf Meyer (1866–1950), a psychiatrist who influenced the first *DSM*, found both Kraepelinian and Freudian perspectives valuable. He advocated eliminating the overly broad construct of melancholia and replacing it with the more focused term "depression" (Lawlor, 2012). This was a precursor to the more Kraepelinian biological model definitions currently found in the *DSM* and *ICD*. Both manuals emphasize dysphoric (i.e., sad) and euphoric (i.e., elevated) moods as primary characteristics of depression and mania. However, despite the great influence of biological perspectives today, other approaches—including cognitive, behavioral, interpersonal, and sociocultural—compete for influence, just as they did in times past. Keeping historical perspectives in mind, we now turn to current models of depression and mania.

5.4 BIOLOGICAL PERSPECTIVES

As with psychosis, the most commonly used biological intervention for depression is prescription drugs. However, many different biological theories of depression and mania have been advanced in recent years—so many, in fact, that it can be difficult to easily summarize them. Below we review some of the better-known biological approaches.

BRAIN CHEMISTRY PERSPECTIVES

Monoamine Hypothesis of Depression and Antidepressants

The **monoamine hypothesis** holds that depression is due to a shortage of the monoamine neurotransmitters serotonin, norepinephrine, and dopamine (Di Benedetto, Rupprecht, & Rammes, 2010; Hillhouse & Porter, 2015). Just as the dopamine hypothesis was devised after the fact to explain why antipsychotics reduce schizophrenia symptoms (see Chapter 4), the monoamine hypothesis was developed in the 1960s after early antidepressant drugs were found to alleviate depression. The earliest antidepressant drugs were the MAO inhibitors and the tricyclics. In more recent decades, the SSRIs and SNRIs have become popular. All work in ways consistent with the monoamine hypothesis. Let's examine them more closely.

MAO Inhibitors and Tricyclics

As with antipsychotics, the first **antidepressants** were discovered serendipitously (Di Benedetto et al., 2010; Hillhouse & Porter, 2015; S. Hyman, 2014). *Iproniazid*, a drug originally developed to treat tuberculosis, became the first successful antidepressant during the 1950s when it was accidentally found to reduce depressive symptoms (France, Lysaker, & Robinson, 2007; Hillhouse & Porter, 2015; Shorter, 2009). It is an **MAO inhibitor (MAOI)**, a class of drugs that does exactly what its name suggests: inhibit **monoamine oxidase (MAO)**, a brain enzyme that breaks down excess monoamine neurotransmitters in the synapses between neurons. Inhibiting the action of monoamine oxidase leaves more serotonin, norepinephrine, and dopamine available, thus increasing the chances these neurotransmitters will bind with surrounding neurons and cause them to fire. Around the same time, researchers developed another class of antidepressants, the **tricyclics**, which mainly affect norepinephrine and serotonin (usually with more impact on norepinephrine) (Di Benedetto et al., 2010; Hillhouse & Porter, 2015). The tricyclics work by inhibiting the synaptic reabsorption of serotonin and norepinephrine, leaving more available to trigger neuronal firing. One of the first tricyclic drugs was *imipramine* (France et al., 2007). Table 5.1 lists common antidepressants.

Table 5.1 Common Antidepressants

MAO Inhibitors (trade names in parentheses)
• Isocarboxazid (Marplan)
• Phenelzine (Nardil)
• Selegiline (Emsam)
• Tranylcypromine (Parnate)

Tricyclics (trade names in parentheses)

- Amitriptyline (Vanatrip, Elavil, Endep)
- Amoxapine (Asendin, Asendis, Defanyl, Demolox)
- Desipramine (Norpramin)
- Doxepin (Deptran and Sinequan)
- Imipramine (Tofranil)
- Nortriptyline (Pamelor)
- Protriptyline (Vivactil)
- Trimipramine (Surmontil)

SSRIs (trade names in parentheses)

- Citalopram (Celexa, Cipramil)
- Escitalopram (Lexapro)
- Fluoxetine (Prozac)
- Paroxetine (Paxil, Pexeva, Seroxat)
- Sertraline (Zoloft, Lustral)

SNRIs (trade names in parentheses)

- Duloxetine (Cymbalta)
- Venlafaxine (Effexor XR)
- Desvenlafaxine (Pristiq)

MAOIs and tricyclics are not used much today because they have a host of unpleasant side effects such as dry mouth, constipation, weight gain, and drowsiness. Those taking MAOIs must avoid cheese and other dairy products or they run the risk of increased heart rate, sweating, and high blood pressure that can culminate in a hypertensive crisis that damages internal organs (Bauer et al., 2013; Hillhouse & Porter, 2015). Additional side effects of tricyclics include dizziness and memory problems (Bauer et al., 2013; Hillhouse & Porter, 2015).

SSRIs and SNRIs

The 1980s and 1990s saw the rise of a new class of antidepressants, the **selective serotonin reuptake inhibitors (SSRIs)**. As with the MAOIs, the name of the SSRIs nicely describes how they work. SSRIs selectively block the reuptake of serotonin. The term "selective" is used to make clear that the SSRIs affect only serotonin. Because their effect is more focused, they are commonly seen as having fewer side effects than MAOIs and tricyclics. The most famous SSRI is probably *fluoxetine* (often sold under the trade name *Prozac*), but many others have been developed (see Table 5.1).

An early advertisement for Prozac.

Starting in the 1990s, **serotonin and norepinephrine reuptake inhibitors (SNRIs)** began appearing on the market. These drugs work similarly to SSRIs except instead of only targeting serotonin, they prevent the reuptake of both serotonin and norepinephrine. *Venlafaxine* (trade name *Effexor*) is one of the better-known SNRIs. See Table 5.1 for others.

The Rapid Rise in Antidepressant Usage

The advent of SSRIs and SNRIs coincided with a sharp increase in the number of people taking antidepressants. Simply put, these drugs are very popular. Depressed U.S. outpatients who received antidepressants increased from 37.3% in 1987 to 74.5% by 1998—with three-quarters being given SSRIs (Shorter, 2009). Since then, the prevalence of antidepressant usage in the U.S.—for both depression and other presenting problems—has increased substantially (Medco, 2010; Pratt, Brody, & Gu, 2017). By 2011–2014, 12.7% of Americans over age 12 reported having taken antidepressants in the last month, up from 7.7% between 1999–2002; this constitutes a 65% increase (Pratt et al., 2017). Of the 12.7% of people taking these drugs, there were roughly twice as many females (16.5%) as males (8.6%). For many of them, antidepressant use was a long-term affair: 68% of users over age 12 indicated they had been taking antidepressants for more than two years, with 21.4% of men and 27.2% of women saying they had been on these drugs for a decade or more (Pratt et al., 2017). Further, the older one was, the more likely one was to be taking antidepressants (Pratt et al., 2017). See Figures 5.1 and 5.2 for graphic illustrations of these startling increases.

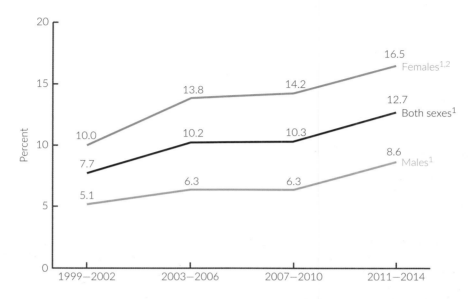

Figure 5.1 Trends in Antidepressant Use Among Persons Aged 12 and Over, by Sex: United States, 1999–2014

[1]Significant increasing trend.
[2]Significantly higher than males for all years.
Note: Antidepressant use in the U.S. has consistently increased over the years for both males and females, with a higher percentage of females taking antidepressants than males.
Source: Figure 4 from: Pratt, L. A., Brody, D. J., & Gu Q. (2017). Antidepressant use among persons aged 12 and over: United States, 2011–2014. *NCHS Data Brief*, No. 283. Hyattsville, MD: National Center for Health Statistics.

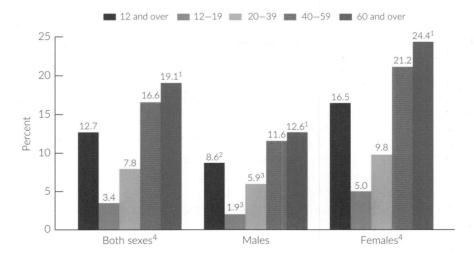

Figure 5.2 Percentage of Persons Aged 12 and Over who Took Antidepressant Medication in the Past Month, by Age and Sex: United States, 2011–2014

[1]Statistically significant trend by age.
[2]Significantly lower than females in all age groups.
[3]Significantly lower than the older age groups.
[4]Each age group is significantly different from all other age groups.
Note: U.S. data suggests that the older one gets, the more likely one is to be taking an antidepressant.
Source: Figure 1 from: Pratt, L. A., Brody, D. J., & Gu Q. (2017). Antidepressant use among persons aged 12 and over: United States, 2011–2014. *NCHS Data Brief*, No. 283. Hyattsville, MD: National Center for Health Statistics.

While the U.S. leads the way, the rise in antidepressant usage isn't just an American phenomenon. Across the European Union antidepressant consumption is believed to have increased 80% between 2002 and 2012 (Organisation for Economic Co-operation and Development, 2012). In the U.K., one report estimated that the number of people prescribed antidepressants rose by 165% between 1998 and 2012 (Spence, Roberts, Ariti, & Bardsley, 2014). Further, a 2013 survey reported high antidepressant usage rates among developed countries, with Iceland, Australia, and Portugal consuming the most antidepressants (T. Hale, 2015). This survey didn't include the U.S. but, based on 2013 data, the U.S. would be second behind Iceland. See Figure 5.3.

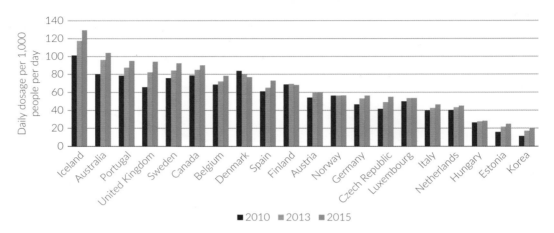

Figure 5.3 Antidepressant Use Around the Globe

Note: The chances of being on an antidepressant vary, depending on country. This figure doesn't include the U.S., where antidepressant consumption rates are estimated at 100 per 1,000 people. This would place the U.S. second behind Iceland in antidepressant use, based on 2013 data (Hale, 2015).

Source: Based on data from Organisation for Economic Co-operation and Development (2015), *Health at a Glance 2015: OECD Indicators*, OECD Publishing, Paris. http://dx.doi.org/10.1787/health_glance-2015-en

Effectiveness of Antidepressants

Despite their widespread use, how often antidepressants help is a matter of debate. Researchers generally conclude that antidepressants are effective (A. Cipriani et al., 2018), working somewhere between 50% and 75% of the time (Bauer et al., 2013; Rush et al., 2006). However, others warn that antidepressants are less effective than often believed because many who initially respond to them later redevelop symptoms (Ghaemi, Vohringer, & Whitham, 2013). One study of antidepressant use in everyday practice indicated that only 28% of depressed people experienced full remission of depressive symptoms (S. Hyman, 2014; Trivedi et al., 2006). Overall, it's been estimated that between 33% and 50% of depressed people are resistant to the effects of antidepressants (N. J. Wolf & Hopko, 2008). Additionally, side effects lead many people to stop taking their drugs (Ghaemi et al., 2013; Hotopf, Hardy, & Lewis, 1997; Keller & Boland, 1998; Settle, 1998). Although SSRIs and SNRIs are deemed easier to tolerate than the older antidepressants, they still have adverse effects—including nausea, dizziness, headaches, drowsiness, and reduced sexual desire and/or performance (Settle, 1998; Stahl, Grady, Moret, & Briley, 2005). SSRIs sometimes also cause nervousness, insomnia, and weight gain, while SNRIs can lead to dry mouth, sweating, and constipation.

Shirley

Shirley discusses her depressed mood with her family physician. He prescribes Zoloft, an SSRI. Several weeks after starting on Zoloft, Shirley reports feeling less depressed. However, she also complains about trouble sleeping and lack of interest in sex.

CASE EXAMPLES

Black Box Warning on Antidepressants

Controversy surrounds the issue of whether antidepressants raise the risk of suicide in adolescents. This has led the U.S. government to include an intensely debated **black box warning** on antidepressants. A black box warning informs people that a drug may have hazardous consequences. The U.S. black box warning on antidepressants says that the drugs may increase suicidal tendencies in teens. Some applaud this warning as warranted (Leon, 2007), especially in a culture they feel overprescribes to children and adolescents (Sparks & Duncan, 2013). Others lament this warning, arguing that the benefits of giving depressed teens antidepressants clearly outweigh any risks (R. A. Friedman, 2014; Nagar, Mehta, Bhatara, & Aparasu, 2010).

Discontinuation Syndrome

Those on SSRIs and SNRIs for any length of time often encounter **discontinuation syndrome** when they stop taking them. Discontinuation can induce flu-like symptoms, dizziness, insomnia, nausea, diarrhea, irritability, nightmares, and depressive symptoms due to stopping the drug (rather than a return of the depression that precipitated drug use in the first place) (Fava, Gatti, Belaise, Guidi, & Offidani, 2015; B. H. Harvey & Slabbert, 2014; Himei & Okamura, 2006). Given the severity of discontinuation symptoms and the difficulty many people have getting off antidepressants, it has been argued—albeit controversially within psychiatry—that "discontinuation syndrome" should be renamed "withdrawal syndrome" (Fava et al., 2015). Discontinuation symptoms, side effects, and large numbers of people who don't respond to the drugs notwithstanding, antidepressants are recommended as an effective frontline treatment by the World Federation of Biological Psychiatry and are commonly prescribed (Bauer et al., 2013; Bauer et al., 2015). The "Controversial Question" box outlines a provocative (and oft-disputed) alternative view by asking if antidepressant mood improvements are merely a placebo effect.

CONTROVERSIAL QUESTION

Antidepressants as Placebo?

Recall from our research methods discussion in Chapter 1 that when researchers study a drug's effectiveness, they often compare it to a placebo pill. Placebo pills typically cause improvement on their own due to patient expectations that they will get better. For a drug to be considered effective, it needs to improve symptoms more than a placebo pill does.

To study the placebo effect in the treatment of depression, psychologist Irving Kirsch (2010, 2014) used meta-analysis (the statistical technique that pools results of many studies to see what the overall effects are). Kirsch reached a controversial conclusion, namely that antidepressants aren't noticeably more effective than placebo pills! This finding rocked the psychiatric establishment. Kirsch wound up being interviewed repeatedly in the media about his shocking finding. After all, given the billions of dollars that pharmaceutical companies generate selling antidepressants, could it be possible that they are no more effective than sugar pills?

Critics—and even Kirsch himself—note that there does seem to be a small effect for antidepressants compared to placebo pills. However, upon conducting further meta-analyses, Kirsch (2010, 2014) concluded that this difference probably has a lot to do with whether subjects can guess if they are getting the antidepressant or the placebo pill. Being able to figure this out is called *breaking blind*. Participants who break blind and realize they are getting the real drug improve more than those who get the real drug but don't know it; think of this as a placebo effect on top of the drug effect. Oddly, one of the ways participants break blind is by identifying drug side effects. If they experience side effects, then they must be getting the real drug! If they don't, they're probably taking the placebo pill. Kirsch found that some studies account for this by using active, as opposed to passive, placebos. An active placebo is designed to cause side effects, making it harder to break blind. In studies where an active placebo was used, Kirsch found no difference between antidepressants and placebos. Based on his research, all the money spent on antidepressants is for naught; a sugar pill each day might work just as well.

Not everyone buys Kirsch's conclusions. Psychiatrist Peter Kramer (2011) argues that a lot of research shows antidepressants to be helpful and that many of the studies Kirsch looked at were sloppily done and included too many people who didn't really qualify for a depression diagnosis, thereby potentially washing out any effect of the drugs. Kramer (2011) also points to evidence that taking antidepressants can be helpful in a variety of specific situations—including recovering from a stroke, dealing with depression due to neurological problems, and alleviating anxiety in children. To Kramer, Kirsch's conclusion that antidepressants are mainly placebos is dangerous because it encourages people to stop taking drugs that Kramer believes can help them.

But Kirsch isn't convinced and stands by his findings. He notes that meta-analyses on therapy, antidepressants alone, antidepressants with therapy, and alternative treatments such as acupuncture all show equal effectiveness in alleviating depression. Kirsch concludes: "There is a strong therapeutic response to antidepressant medication. But the response to placebo is almost as strong;" therefore, if antidepressants "are to be used at all, it should be as a last resort, when depression is extremely severe and all other treatment alternatives have been tried and failed" (Kirsch, 2014, p. 132).

CRITICAL THINKING QUESTIONS

1. How is it that Kirsch and Kramer draw such different conclusions about the effectiveness of antidepressants?

2. Are you more sympathetic to Kirsch's or Kramer's view of antidepressants? Why?

3. Antidepressants currently are dispensed quite readily and are used more often than psychotherapy to treat depression. Do you agree with Kirsch that these drugs should only be used as a last resort? Why or why not?

CHAPTER 5

Shortcomings of the Monoamine Hypothesis

The monoamine hypothesis has several shortcomings. First, antidepressants impact monoamine levels quickly, but their effect on mood doesn't appear until people have been taking them for between two and four weeks (Hashimoto, 2009; Malhi, Hitching et al., 2013; Nair & Sharma, 1989). Why this is remains a mystery. Some hypothesize that antidepressants stimulate the growth of new dendrites and synaptic connections, but this takes time (Di Benedetto et al., 2010). Second, there is evidence from an analogue experiment on rats that long-term SSRI use lowers rather than raises serotonin levels; the proposed explanation for this is that the brain compensates for increased availability of serotonin by synthesizing less of it (Bosker et al., 2010). Third, not all drugs that enhance monoamine levels—such as cocaine and amphetamines—are effective as antidepressants (Di Benedetto et al., 2010; Nair & Sharma, 1989). Fourth, monoamine levels can't be measured directly. Only indirect measures such as metabolite levels in urine are currently possible (Nair & Sharma, 1989; Valenstein, 1998). Fifth, depleting monoamine levels in non-depressed people doesn't induce depression, so depression can't be about depleted monoamines alone (Hillhouse & Porter, 2015; R. M. Salomon, Miller, Krystal, Heninger, & Charney, 1997). Based on these challenges, many researchers have begun to think that depression can't be fully explained via the monoamine hypothesis. Instead, biological model researchers now often hypothesize that low monoamine levels interact with other neurobiological systems in triggering depression (Di Benedetto et al., 2010; Hillhouse & Porter, 2015).

Glutamate Hypothesis of Depression

The **glutamate hypothesis of depression** proposes that depression is associated with high levels of glutamate, the brain's main excitatory neurotransmitter (Hashimoto, 2009; Sanacora, Treccani, & Popoli, 2012; Tokita, Yamaji, & Hashimoto, 2012). In a variety of studies examining the glutamate hypothesis, **ketamine**—an anesthetic drug with antidepressant effects—has been found to inhibit glutamate receptors, which decreases glutamate levels (Hashimoto, 2011; Krystal, Sanacora, & Duman, 2013; Musazzi, Treccani, & Popoli, 2012; Skolnick, Popik, & Trullas, 2009). Excitement about the potential of the glutamate hypothesis centers around the fact that glutamate-inhibiting substances such as ketamine tend to take effect within 24 hours, which is much faster than the 2–4 weeks it takes monoamine antidepressants (Dutta, McKie, & Deakin, 2015; Kavalali & Monteggia, 2015; Musazzi et al., 2012). However, their impact also wears off more quickly and it remains unclear whether or not their negative properties will ultimately make them unusable for long-term treatment of depression (Miller, Moran, & Hall, 2016). A big downside of ketamine, for instance, is that it has hallucinatory properties and is considered a drug of abuse. It is sold illegally as the street drug "Special K" and—as just one example of its widespread misuse—it's reportedly the second most abused drug in Hong Kong, behind only heroin (a drug discussed in Chapter 11) (Hillhouse & Porter, 2015). Potential obstacles notwithstanding, researchers remain cautiously optimistic about developing glutamate-inhibiting antidepressants (Dutta et al., 2015; Kavalali & Monteggia, 2015; Krystal et al., 2013; Pilc, Wierońska, & Skolnick, 2013; Sanacora et al., 2017; Skolnick et al., 2009; Zanos et al., 2015). However, at this time these drugs remain in the development stage and a thorough review concluded that evidence for glutamate drugs as effective antidepressants is limited—even for the most promising drug, ketamine (Caddy et al., 2015). A task force of the American Psychiatric Association (APA) recently recommended that although ketamine shows promise as an antidepressant, it shouldn't be prescribed outside of tightly controlled research settings until further research is conducted on its safety and effectiveness (Sanacora et al., 2017).

Herbal Remedies for Depression

Despite much skepticism in mainstream medicine, herbal remedies for depression—most notably **St. John's wort** and **Rhodiola rosea**—have garnered significant attention over the last few decades. The active ingredients in St. John's wort, a plant found in parts of Europe and Asia, are *hyperforin* and *hypericin*. It's not fully understood how St. John's wort reduces depressed mood. However, it's suspected that, like many traditional antidepressants, it fosters serotonin transmission. Rhodiola rosea's active ingredients are *rosavin*, *rosin* and *rosarian*. It has long been used as an herbal remedy in Scandinavia and Russia. Like St. John's wort, it's mechanism of action isn't fully understood, but it may impact serotonin and glutamate (Panossian, Hamm, Wikman, & Efferth, 2014). Research on the use of St. John's wort and Rhodiola rosea is mixed, with numerous studies finding them helpful at reducing mild and moderate depression, but others finding little or no effect (Deltito & Beyer, 1998; Gahlsdorf, Krause, & Beal, 2007; Hypericum Depression Trial Study, 2002; Linde, Berner, Egger, & Mulrow, 2005; Mao et al., 2015; Pilkington, Boshnakova, & Richardson, 2006; Qureshi & Al-Bedah, 2013; Randløv et al., 2006; Ravindran et al., 2016). Although these herbal treatments don't always perform as well as traditional antidepressants in research trials, they do have fewer side effects (Brattström, 2009). Thus, they may be a viable alternative to antidepressants in mild and moderate cases of depression, according

(a)   (b)

(a) St. John's wort and (b) Rhodiola rosea are herbal remedies for depressed mood; their exact mechanisms of action are unknown.
Sources: (a) Bildagentur-online/UIG via Getty Images; (b) DeAgostini/Getty Images

to herbal medicine advocates. However, it's probably wise to only take these herbs under the supervision of a doctor because they can interact with other medications one is taking; special caution is warranted when already taking antidepressants because adding herbal supplements to antidepressant treatment can produce excessive serotonin levels, resulting in a life-threatening condition called *serotonin syndrome* (Deltito & Beyer, 1998; National Center for Complementary and Integrative Health, 2013). Although we don't mention them much in future chapters, keep in mind that St. John's wort and Rhiodiola rosea are used not just for depression. Herbal remedy supporters also recommend them for many other mental health problems. However, such remedies aren't typically approved by government testing agencies as sanctioned treatments for depression and other presenting problems (National Center for Complementary and Integrative Health, 2013).

Mood Stabilizers and Bipolar Disorder

Types of Mood Stabilizers

The drugs used to treat the manic symptoms of bipolar disorder are called **mood stabilizers**. The term "mood stabilizer" is broad and doesn't specify the exact mechanism by which these drugs work—which is why this term applies to several different classes of drugs (Hirschowitz, Kolevzon, & Garakani, 2010). The best-known mood stabilizer is **lithium**, a metallic mineral salt that can reduce mania (G. Curran & Ravindran, 2014; Gao, Wu, Grunze, & Calabrese, 2015; Hirschowitz et al., 2010; Keck, McElroy, & Yildiz, 2015; A. H. Young & Hammond, 2007). How lithium works is unknown, but researchers have hypothesized various reasons for its effectiveness, including its potential impact on second-messenger neurotransmitter systems and circadian rhythms (discussed later) (Geddes & Miklowitz, 2013; Malhi, Tanious, Das, Coulston, & Berk, 2013). The genetics of lithium response are also being studied (Schulze et al., 2010). Besides lithium, three other kinds of drugs are used as mood stabilizers: **anticonvulsants** (initially developed to treat seizures), **benzodiazepines** (more often considered anti-anxiety drugs, but also used to stabilize mood), and antipsychotics (because, as previously mentioned, mania can include psychotic symptoms). As with lithium, exactly why these drugs stabilize mood remains unclear. Table 5.2 lists common mood stabilizers.

Table 5.2 Common Mood Stabilizers

Lithium
Anticonvulsants (trade names in parentheses)

◦   Valproic acid (Depakote)
    ◦   Lamotrigne (Lamictal)
    ◦   Carbamazepine (Tegretol)

First-Generation Antipsychotics (trade name in parentheses)
◦   Haloperidol (Haldol)

Second-Generation (Atypical) Antipsychotics (trade names in parentheses)

- Apriprazole (Abilify)
- Asenapine (Saphris)
- Loxapine (Adasuve or Loxapine)
- Lurasidone (Latuda)
- Olanzapine (Zyprexa)
- Quetiapine fumarate (Seroquel)
- Risperidone (Risperdal)
- Ziprasidone (Geodon)

Benzodiazepines (trade names in parentheses)

- Alprozolam (Xanax)
- Clonazepam (Klonopin)
- Diazepam (Valium)
- Lorazepam (Ativan)

Side Effects of Mood Stabilizers

Lithium levels must be closely monitored via regular blood tests. If doses are too low, then there is no effect. If they are too high, then lithium poisoning can occur—as evidenced by symptoms such as nausea, vomiting, tremors, kidney malfunction, and (in extreme cases) death. Lithium is also associated with weight gain, cognitive difficulties, tremors, and feelings of sedation (Keck et al., 2015; Mago, Borra, & Mahajan, 2014). Long-term lithium use (20 or more years) puts people at risk for renal failure (Werneke, Ott, Renberg, Taylor, & Stegmayr, 2012). Anticonvulsants can also have serious side effects, causing a variety of stomach, liver, or kidney problems. As for antipsychotics, they have extrapyramidal side effects such as muscle tremors, shuffling gait, and drooling (discussed in detail in Chapter 4). Side effects from mood stabilizers may partly explain why somewhere between 23% and 68% of patients stop taking their drugs (Mago et al., 2014).

Effectiveness of Mood Stabilizers

Although most research concludes that lithium is the gold standard drug for bipolar disorder, there is evidence that its use has declined somewhat, while the use of anticonvulsants and antipsychotics has increased (Mondimore, Fuller, & DePaulo, 2003; Werneke et al., 2012; A. H. Young & Hammond, 2007). This may be because lithium use needs to be monitored so closely to avoid lithium poisoning. When it comes to effectiveness, about half the people given mood stabilizers show improvement, but this also means a lot of people don't respond (Hauser, n.d.). Further, it's been estimated that 75%–85% of patients taking mood stabilizers relapse within five years (Hunsely, Elliott, & Therrien, 2013). Some contend that efficacy increases when more than one mood stabilizer is used (McIntyre & Konarski, 2005). Mood stabilizers are also sometimes combined with antidepressants because mood stabilizers don't always help bipolar patients with their depressive episodes (Baldessarini, Vieta, Calabrese, Tohen, & Bowden, 2010). Mixing mood stabilizers and antidepressants can be complicated, as it is not always clear how each drug contributes to symptom improvements (Geddes & Miklowitz, 2013). Further, findings are mixed regarding which mood stabilizers are best for long-term maintenance (Coryell, 2009; G. Curran & Ravindran, 2014; Gigante, Lafer, & Yatham, 2012; Hirschowitz et al., 2010; Mondimore et al., 2003). This sheds light on the fact that mood stabilizers—like antidepressants—are a way to manage bipolar symptoms over the long term, rather than a cure.

Don

After a judge mandates treatment following his drunk driving arrest, Don sees a psychiatrist who diagnoses him with bipolar disorder and prescribes him two mood stabilizers: Latuda (an antipsychotic approved to treat bipolar disorder) and Depakote (an anti-seizure drug also approved for bipolar disorder). Don begins taking these drugs. Although he complains the drugs make him feel dizzy, within a week or two his wild mood swings appear to level off. However, Don says he feels "out of it" when taking the drugs and he isn't sure he wishes to take them for an extended period.

CASE EXAMPLES

BRAIN STRUCTURE AND FUNCTION PERSPECTIVES

Reviewing brain studies on depression is challenging because so many different brain regions have been implicated and findings aren't always consistent. As psychiatrist Steven Hyman (2014, p. 190) put it: "Depression is difficult to study: it is hard to find features of the brain to focus on." Biological researchers sometimes explain their divergent findings by noting that what we currently classify as depression and mania may ultimately prove to be many different brain disorders—a view consistent with the Research Domain Criteria (RDoC) emphasis on finding symptom-related biomarkers independent of *ICD* and *DSM* categories (refer to Chapter 3 for a refresher on biomarkers and RDoC). That said, several brain regions have been linked with depression and bipolar disorder. We'll focus specifically on the hippocampus, the amygdala, the prefrontal cortex, and the hypothalamic-pituitary-adrenal (HPA) axis.

Hippocampus

The hippocampus is a limbic structure involved in forming memories. Research on the hippocampus' role in major depression has yielded divergent results. Many depressed patients show decreased hippocampal volume—that is, the physical size of this brain area is smaller and takes up less space (Arnone, McIntosh, Ebmeier, Munafò, & Anderson, 2012; Lener & Iosifescu, 2015; Treadway & Pizzagalli, 2014). However, others show enlarged volume or no difference in volume compared to non-depressed people (Lorenzetti, Allen, Fornito, & Yücel, 2009). Why the inconsistent results? It's possible that depression involves different volume changes in different parts of the hippocampus (Malykhin & Coupland, 2015). Interestingly, decreased overall volume is most common among the chronically depressed, suggesting that hippocampal volume loss is somehow related to having multiple depressive episodes (Lorenzetti et al., 2009; Treadway & Pizzagalli, 2014). Gender differences further complicate matters, with women sometimes showing larger hippocampal volumes during first episodes of depression than men (Lorenzetti et al., 2009). Additionally, women who respond to antidepressants often have larger hippocampal volumes compared to those who don't. This suggests antidepressants may help prevent hippocampal volume from shrinking (Lorenzetti et al., 2009; Malykhin & Coupland, 2015). While research has generated important hypotheses about the hippocampus and depression, no clear conclusions can yet be drawn (Lorenzetti et al., 2009).

Hippocampal research on bipolar disorder provides similarly mixed results. Some studies haven't found volume changes in people diagnosed as bipolar. However, other research shows reduced volume early in the course of the disorder and increases in volume as the disorder progresses (M. R. Schneider, DelBello, McNamara, Strakowski, & Adler, 2012).

Amygdala

The amygdala, which plays a role in the regulation of basic emotions, has been implicated in depression. Research consistently shows increased amygdala activity in depressed and anxious individuals (J. R. Swartz, Knodt, Radtke, & Hariri, 2015). Further, depression is often associated with decreased amygdala volume (Lener & Iosifescu, 2015; Sacher et al., 2012). However, findings vary. Some research suggests that those in the early stages of depression show increased amygdala volume while those with recurrent depression show decreased volume (Lorenzetti et al., 2009; Sacher et al., 2012). Still other research has found essentially the opposite: less amygdala gray matter among first-time patients compared to chronic patients (Bora, Fornito, Pantelis, & Yücel, 2012). Amygdala volume in depression is clearly important, but not fully understood.

Regarding bipolar disorder, some but not all studies have shown increased amygdala responsiveness in those diagnosed with mania (Maletic & Raison, 2014; M. R. Schneider et al., 2012). Further, research suggests that the amygdala volumes of people diagnosed as bipolar are smaller in children and teens, but larger in adults (Garrett & Chang, 2008; Maletic & Raison, 2014; M. R. Schneider et al., 2012). This implies that changes to the amygdala may occur after the onset of bipolar symptoms. Further research is necessary to clarify the amygdala's exact role.

Frontal Lobe

The **frontal lobe** is another brain region tied to depression. It is central in helping people execute behavior. Severely depressed people tend to show reduced frontal lobe volume, but mildly depressed people do not (Lorenzetti et al., 2009). The frontal lobe's prefrontal cortex plays a role in mood, attention, decision-making, and immunity. In some studies of depressed people, it shows decreased activity, but in other studies it shows increased activity (Lemogne, Delaveau, Freton, Guionnet, & Fossati, 2012; Lemogne et al., 2010; Vialou et al., 2014). Thus, as with the hippocampus and amygdala, research into the frontal lobe suggests it is involved in depression, but exactly how remains unclear.

Volume loss is a problem in bipolar disorder, too. Prefrontal cortex volumes are often decreased in children and adolescents diagnosed as bipolar (Schneider et al., 2012). Volume loss in the prefrontal cortex seems to be tied to decreased synaptic connections to other brain areas, with decreased connectivity patterns differing for manic versus depressive individuals (Maletic & Raison, 2014).

Hypothalamic-Pituitary-Adrenal (HPA) Axis

In addition to looking at individual brain areas, researchers also look at how interconnected brain structures contribute to depression and mania. The **hypothalamic-pituitary-adrenal (HPA) axis**, which plays a role in managing stress as people respond to physical and psychosocial changes in their environments, appears to be overactive in depressed people (H. M. Burke, Davis, Otte, & Mohr, 2005). The HPA axis is integral in the release of **cortisol**, the primary stress hormone (**hormones** are chemical messengers in the **endocrine system**, a collection of glands important in regulating things like sexual functioning, sleep, mood, and metabolism). Cortisol counters bodily substances that cause physical inflammation. Depression has been correlated with high levels of cortisol. Thus, it's possible that a malfunctioning HPA axis results in too much cortisol, which leads to depressed mood (H. M. Burke et al., 2005; Dedovic & Ngiam, 2015; Lamers et al., 2013; Varghese & Brown, 2001). It's also possible that prolonged stress negatively impacts the HPA axis and leads to excessive cortisol production, resulting in depression (H. M. Burke et al., 2005). Although not studied as often in bipolar patients, there is evidence that the HPA axis and elevated cortisol levels are also implicated in mania (Bauer & Dinan, 2015). An overactive HPA axis leading to high cortisol levels may reflect the body's attempt to reduce inflammation, which—as we will see shortly when discussing immune system perspectives—is also associated with depression.

Non-Drug Brain Treatments for Depression

Electroconvulsive Therapy (ECT)

Antidepressants are by far the most common biological intervention, but there are other biological treatments for depression. Electroconvulsive therapy (ECT) is sometimes used, especially when antidepressants don't work (Lisanby, 2007). In this controversial treatment (introduced in Chapter 1), 70–130 volts of electricity are delivered to patients' brains, inducing a seizure. ECT is typically administered 2–3 times per week for seven weeks. In the early days of ECT, the current was sent bilaterally through the entire brain without anesthesia. However, today anesthesia is used, the shocks are more localized, and current is delivered only through the non-dominant hemisphere. There are many theories of why ECT alleviates depression, but none have much research support (Fink, 2009). The best we can say is that we don't really know how or why ECT works. Despite its immediate effectiveness, many people who receive ECT eventually become depressed again (McClintock, Brandon, Husain, & Jarrett, 2011). By one estimate, relapse rates are 37% within six months and 51% within a year (Jelovac, Kolshus, & McLoughlin, 2013). Consequently, some severely depressed patients undergo ECT repeatedly over many years.

ECT is seen as especially helpful in cases of psychotic depression (Fink, 2009). It is also sometimes used for bipolar disorder (C. H. Kellner & Fink, 2015; Liebman, Ahle, Briggs, & Kellner, 2015) and postpartum depression (Gressier, Rotenberg, Cazas, & Hardy, 2015). ECT's main side effects are confusion and memory loss—even in newer forms of ECT where only the non-dominant hemisphere is shocked (Breggin, 2007; Fink, 2009). Given its impact on memory and the fact that we don't really know why it works, ECT is controversial (Cleare & Rane, 2013). Its supporters argue that it is a scientifically proven treatment for chronic and intense depression (Fink, 2009), but its detractors contend that it is brutal, imprecise, and damages the brain (Breggin, 2007, 2009, 2010).

Transcranial Magnetic Stimulation (TMS)

Transcranial magnetic stimulation (TMS) is another technique used with depressed (and sometimes bipolar) patients who are unresponsive to drug treatments and psychotherapy (Berlim, van den Eynde, Tovar-Perdomo, & Daskalakis, 2014; Yip & Carpenter, 2010). In TMS, magnetic energy is sent through the brain via electromagnetic coils placed on the scalp. As with ECT, we don't know why TMS works (Janicak & Carpenter, 2014). However, a recent meta-analysis indicated that TMS is more effective than a placebo treatment, with 29.3% of depressed patients responding to it and 18.6% showing a remission of symptoms (Berlim et al., 2014). Some research suggests that TMS can be used as a maintenance treatment for ECT instead of administering additional ECT (Cristancho, Helmer, Connolly, Cristancho, & O'Reardon, 2013; Janicak & Carpenter, 2014; Pridmore, 2000). TMS does have side effects (including headaches, lightheadedness, face tingling, and in rare cases seizures) (Mayo Clinic, n.d.-b), but they are less severe than those associated with ECT (Janicak & Carpenter, 2014). Still, TMS is generally found to be less effective and more labor intensive to deliver than ECT, so it isn't used as often (Cleare & Rane, 2013).

Deep Brain Stimulation (DBS)

Finally, **deep brain stimulation (DBS)** is another technique being explored as a treatment for chronic depression that doesn't respond to antidepressants (Giacobbe & Kennedy, 2006; Mayberg et al., 2005). It is an already established treatment for movement disorders such as Parkinson's disease (Blomstedt, Sjöberg, Hansson, Bodlund, & Hariz, 2011; Mayo Clinic, n.d.-a). In DBS, electrodes are permanently implanted in the brain and then low levels of electrical current are sent to these electrodes using a transmitter the person wears. The evidence for DBS's effectiveness in depression is mixed and it is currently considered an experimental treatment (R. J. Anderson et al., 2012; Morishita, Fayad, Higuchi, Nestor, & Foote, 2014; Mosley, Marsh, & Carter, 2015; Schlaepfer, Bewernick, Kayser, Mädler, & Coenen, 2013). However, research refining it and further testing its effectiveness continues.

GENETIC AND EVOLUTIONARY PERSPECTIVES

Genetic Perspectives

Genetic perspectives emphasize that depression and mania are common in many families. Family studies reveal that individuals diagnosed with major depression run three times the risk of having a first-degree relative who is also depressed (E. C. Dunn et al., 2015). There is also evidence that bipolar symptoms recur in families (Perlis, 2015). Of course, whether these findings are due to genetics or shared environment remains somewhat unclear.

Reviews of twin studies have yielded heritability estimates in the 0.37–0.38 range for major depression (B. L. Elder & Mosack, 2011; Lohoff, 2010). This means that 37%–38% of phenotypic variation among people diagnosed with major depression can be attributed to genetic factors. Heritability estimates for bipolar disorders are considerably higher: 73% for bipolar I disorder, 56% for bipolar II disorder, and 71% for cyclothymic disorder (Edvardsen et al., 2008). As discussed in Chapter 2, heritability estimates can be controversial and difficult to interpret, especially because they don't always account for gene–environment interactions (J. Joseph, 2012). Nonetheless, genetics researchers remain confident that depression and mania are heritable disorders, with bipolar being more heritable than major depression.

In addition to examining heritability, researchers have also been trying to locate specific genes associated with depression and mania. In **candidate gene studies**, allele frequencies on genes of interest are statistically analyzed to see if some allele variations are present more often among case subjects compared to controls (Lohoff, 2010). Case subjects in this instance would be those with either depressive or bipolar diagnoses (depending on which we are studying). Controls would be those with no history of depressive or manic symptoms. Candidate gene studies have placed several genes on researchers' radar as important in depression and mania—including genes tied to serotonin, dopamine, and glutamate (all of which we discussed previously as being implicated in mood problems). Table 5.3 lists some of these genes.

Table 5.3 Depression and Bipolar Candidate Genes

Depression Candidate Genes	Bipolar Candidate Genes
Serotonin transporter (5HTT/SLC6A4)	Serotonin transporter (5HTT/SLC6A4)
Brain-derived neurotrophic factor (BDNF)	Brain-derived neurotrophic factor (BDNF)
Catechol-o-methyl transferase (COMT)	Catechol-o- methyl transferase (COMT)
Dopamine transporter (DAT1)	Dopamine transporter (SLC6A3)
Tryptophan Hydroxylase (TPH)	Tryptophan hydroxylase-2 (TPH2)
Hydroxytryptamine (HTT)	Disrupted in schizophrenia 1 (DISC1)
	NMDA glutamate receptor, subunit 2 B (GRIN2B)
	D-amino-acid oxidase activator (DAOA, a.k.a. G72)
	Peroxisome proliferators-activated receptor delta (PPARD)
	Neuregulin1 (NRG1)

Source: This table has been compiled using information from Elder, B. L., & Mosack, V. (2011). Genetics of depression: An overview of the current science. *Issues in Mental Health Nursing*, 32(4), 192–202. doi:10.3109/01612840.2010.541588; and Barnett, J. H., & Smoller, J. W. (2009). The genetics of bipolar disorder. *Neuroscience*, 164(1), 331–343. doi:http://dx.doi.org/10.1016/j.neuroscience.2009.03.080

It's hard to say with certainty which candidate genes are most important because although many have been identified, researchers sometimes have trouble replicating past findings (Crow, 2011; Flint & Kendler, 2014). When it comes to major depression, for instance, candidate gene studies "have generated many publications but few robust findings" (Flint & Kendler, 2014, p. 486). Consequently, depression and bipolar disorder can't currently be diagnosed using genetic biomarkers. Nonetheless, most researchers remain optimistic, believing we are on the verge of major breakthroughs in identifying genes for depression and bipolar disorder. Others contend that we will never uncover such genes because the array of behaviors that depression and bipolar disorder diagnoses classify are simply too complex and psychosocial in origin to be reduced mainly to genetics (J. Joseph, 2012). In the end, genes and environment are both important; mood problems inevitably emerge from interactions between them (Benjamin & Taylor, 2010). Regardless of whether you place greater emphasis on genes or environment, we can all agree that nature–nurture debates over the genetics of depression and mania will likely continue for some time.

Evolutionary Perspectives

Depression as Evolved Adaptation

Evolutionary perspectives emphasize how human emotions evolved to help people survive and reproduce. According to **adaptationist models**, depression may be adaptive for several reasons. It can help people avoid social risks, minimize losses, ruminate about problems they need to address, fight infection and recover from sickness, conserve energy, give in when socially defeated, and solicit resources by encouraging others to help them (N. B. Allen & Badcock, 2006; Anders, Tanaka, & Kinney, 2013; P. W. Andrews & Thomson, 2009; Durisko, Mulsant, & Andrews, 2015; Nesse, 2000; P. J. Watson & Andrews, 2002). Controversially, advocates of adaptationist models sometimes contend that if their perspective is correct even part of the time, then wide-scale antidepressant use is questionable because it interferes with depressed feelings that lead people to ruminate about and resolve problems that need fixing (P. W. Andrews & Thomson, 2009; Durisko et al., 2015). Instead, some adaptationists argue that we should use psychotherapy to help people address life situations that give rise to depression (Durisko et al., 2015). Not surprisingly, others have challenged the evolutionary adaptation explanation and its inference that antidepressants should be withheld (McLoughlin, 2002; Sinyor, 2012). According to one critic: "Even if it has adaptive underpinnings, depression is clearly a source of true suffering and its theoretically adaptive value is an insufficient argument for withholding antidepressants or other treatments that may provide relief" (Sinyor, 2012, p. 336). Of course, the adaptationist counterargument is that antidepressants prevent people from experiencing the adaptive feelings necessary to help them remedy pressing life problems.

Shirley

Imagine Shirley goes to a psychotherapist who adopts an adaptationist evolutionary perspective. He might question whether she needs to be on Zoloft, noting that Shirley became depressed after losing a power struggle with a work colleague, which resulted in Shirley getting demoted. The therapist could view Shirley's depression as an adaptive strategy that serves two purposes. First, it is a way of socially giving in after being defeated by her colleague. Second, it is a signal to herself that she needs to think about what her next steps should be professionally, as her current job situation is untenable.

CASE EXAMPLES

Importantly, not all evolutionary psychologists endorse the adaptationist view. Some propose **dysregulation models**, which hold that the adaptive mechanism behind normal sadness is broken and runs amok in severe and recurrent cases of depression (Nettle, 2004). The main difference between adaptationist and dysregulation models is that the former see depression as a normal and evolutionarily adaptive response to trying circumstances, whereas the latter view it as caused by the malfunctioning of evolved mechanisms that handle feelings of sadness and loss (Nettle, 2004). The main criticism of the "broken adaptive mechanism" view is that it is purely speculative. As of now, no specific "adaptive mechanism" has been identified.

Circadian Rhythms and Bipolar Disorder

One intriguing but still minimally researched hypothesis of bipolar disorder is that it evolved among people living in cold climates as an adaptation to extreme changes in light and dark throughout the year (Sherman, 2001, 2012). This is consistent with findings of circadian rhythm disruptions in people diagnosed as bipolar (Abreu & Bragança, 2015; Tal & Primeau, 2015). **Circadian rhythms** are mental and behavioral changes in alertness and energy that people experience throughout the day that are tied to levels of light and dark in the environment (National Institute of General Medical Sciences, 2015). The theory that bipolar disorder is a circadian rhythm disorder that developed in people living in cold climates is similar to theories attempting to explain seasonal affective disorder (SAD) (Abreu & Bragança, 2015). **Light therapy**, in which a person sits next to a box that projects bright light, is often used to treat SAD. If bipolar disorder is also tied to light levels, then combinations of light therapy and **dark therapy** (in which the patient is kept in the dark for several hours) may be helpful for stabilizing circadian rhythms (Tal & Primeau, 2015)—although this remains a preliminary hypothesis without much research support (Abreu & Bragança, 2015).

IMMUNE SYSTEM PERSPECTIVES

The inflammatory hypothesis (introduced in Chapter 4) postulates that—like various other psychiatric disorders—depression and bipolar disorder may be tied to immune system inflammation (Iwata, Ota, & Duman, 2013; R. H. B. Mitchell & Goldstein, 2014; Rosenblat et al., 2015; J. J. Young, Bruno, & Pomara, 2014). In testing this hypothesis, cytokine levels are often measured. Cytokines (mentioned in Chapter 4) are small proteins produced by immune system cells; they are important in healing, but large amounts of them can cause swelling. Studies have found elevated cytokine levels in depressed people, suggesting that their immune systems are highly active (Felger & Lotrich, 2013). There is also evidence that immune system inflammation is associated with cognitive impairment in bipolar patients (Rosenblat et al., 2015). As the data is correlational, we can't specify the precise relationship between cytokines, depression, and bipolar disorder. Immunological stress might lead to depression and mania, but depression and mania might also trigger the immune system. Regardless, if immune system inflammation is involved in mood problems, then one potential treatment is to prescribe anti-inflammatory drugs—especially to the 30%–40% of depressed people who don't respond to antidepressants (J. J. Young et al., 2014). Researchers are currently studying the use of **nonsteroidal anti-inflammatory drugs (NSAIDs)** for depression; NSAIDS are pain relieving drugs such as *aspirin*, *ibuprofen* (trade names *Advil*, *Motrin*, and *Nuprin*), and *naproxen* (trade names *Aleve* and *Naprosyn*). One recent meta-analysis found NSAIDs reduced depressive symptoms (O. Köhler et al., 2014), but there are concerns about serious side effects such as dyspepsia and gastrointestinal bleeding when taken along with SSRIs (Anglin, Moayyedi, & Leontiadis, 2015). NSAIDs are still being studied and aren't regularly used to treat depression.

EVALUATING BIOLOGICAL PERSPECTIVES

Biological approaches to depression and mania have been criticized on several grounds. One of the main criticisms is that even though biological model researchers consider depression and mania to be physical illnesses and are busy studying many possible biomarkers, these problems still cannot be diagnosed using physical measures (Strawbridge, Young, & Cleare, 2017). Quite simply, despite all the research, we remain unclear on the biological bases of depression and mania despite regularly invoking medical metaphors to describe it (Patten, 2015). Even when antidepressants or mood stabilizers are prescribed to depressed or manic people, this is not done based on biological tests that show the mood disturbance has an anatomical origin. This is because no lab tests for depressed or manic moods exist, so diagnoses can't be based on underlying biological defects or chemical imbalances.

This doesn't mean that biological interventions don't help. It just means that even when they do help, their helpfulness isn't sufficient to conclude that an underlying disease-state is being corrected. For instance, a person responding to antidepressants doesn't prove that depression is a disease. Consider a comparative example. People often feel calm after smoking marijuana, but this doesn't mean they were pathologically anxious in the first place! Similarly, feeling better after taking a mood-altering drug doesn't necessarily prove that the original mood was caused by an underlying chemical imbalance. Discussing depression, France et al. (2007, p. 412) humorously illustrate the logical fallacy behind the "if they respond to antidepressants, then it was a chemical imbalance" view, noting that

> response to antidepressants is not by itself proof that an imbalance of brain chemicals causes depression. Psychotherapy can alleviate depression ... therefore (using the above logic), a deficiency of psychotherapy causes depression (of course, we are unaware of any serious assertions to this effect).

Furthering this critique, Alan Horwitz and Jerome Wakefield note that "the most serious conceptual problem with the neurochemical deficiency hypothesis ... is that no adequate contextually grounded standard exists for normal versus disordered levels of serotonin or other amines" (Horwitz & Wakefield, 2007, p. 169). Not only are we unable to directly measure monoamine levels, but we also have no idea what constitutes "normal" amounts of these neurotransmitters—just as we don't know how active one's amygdala, hippocampus, or frontal lobe should ideally be or what the "healthiest" constellation of mood-related genes truly is. More broadly, Horwitz and Wakefield argue that the biological model's endless quest to subsume more and more mood problems under its aegis has resulted in the loss of normal sadness (Horwitz & Wakefield, 2007). According to their critique, by recasting every possible mood variation as a physical illness, the biological perspective inappropriately pathologizes ordinary grief and melancholy. This leads us to no longer see them as customary and expected experiences that, to greater or lesser degrees, play a role in every single person's life. Consequently, normal forms of sadness and loss get inappropriately "treated" with drugs and other medical interventions. Unless depression and mania can eventually not only be treated—but also diagnosed—physiologically, the biological perspective will remain speculative and in competition with the psychological and sociocultural models that we turn to next.

CHAPTER 5

5.5 PSYCHOLOGICAL PERSPECTIVES

Psychological perspectives view mood problems as arising from psychological processes. They typically advance psychotherapy as an intervention for depression, noting that therapy more than holds its own against antidepressants. For mania, therapy tends to be viewed as a secondary intervention to drugs that often serves the purpose of psychoeducation—teaching people about their disorder and how to manage it (Miklowitz, 2008). Nonetheless, therapy for those diagnosed as bipolar has been found to reduce relapse rates and improve functioning and quality of life (Hunsely et al., 2013; Schöttle, Huber, Bock, & Meyer, 2011). Still, psychotherapy has traditionally focused more on depression than mania. When it comes to depression, cognitive-behavioral therapy (CBT) is typically considered the main psychotherapeutic alternative to antidepressants. However, psychodynamic and humanistic practitioners have also developed therapies for mood problems, which often compare favorably to CBT approaches.

PSYCHODYNAMIC PERSPECTIVES

Because CBT has been the most researched approach to depression (Dekker et al., 2014), psychodynamic clinicians sometimes feel overshadowed by it. They note that psychodynamic perspectives are increasingly supported by research and shouldn't play second fiddle to CBT (Lemma, Target, & Fonagy, 2013; Steinert, Munder, Rabung, Hoyer, & Leichsenring, 2017). Recent psychodynamic efforts in treating depression have focused on both providing empirical support for psychodynamic therapies and integrating psychodynamic and cognitive-behavioral approaches. Below we discuss classic and modern psychodynamic perspectives on depression and mania.

Classic Psychoanalytic and Attachment Perspectives

Classic Psychoanalytic Perspectives

Early in his career, Freud (1917/1953) saw depression as tied to grief and loss. He believed real losses (such as the death of a loved one) or symbolic losses (such as failing at work or in a relationship) both trigger depression. In his model, the difference between simple grief and depression is that depressed people redirect the repressed anger they have for the lost object onto themselves—hence the psychoanalytic idea of depression as anger turned inward. Freud (1917/1953) said that mania, on the other hand, is caused by the ego asserting itself as a way to counter depression; feelings of grandiosity and inflated sense of self are defenses against internally directed anger. In his later writings, Freud (1923/1960) attributed depression less to loss and grief and more to an overly stern superego. Nonetheless, the psychodynamic perspective overall retains an emphasis on the roles of attachment and loss in depression and mania.

Attachment Perspectives

The psychodynamic emphasis on loss of attachment and its relevance to mood problems has ample research support. In his famous studies of *contact comfort*, psychologist Harry Harlow raised baby monkeys in an environment where their biological mothers were replaced with fake surrogate mothers made of wire, foam, and terry cloth. The baby monkeys formed strong attachments to the surrogate mothers and became alarmed and depressed when separated from them (Harlow, 1958; Harlow & Suomi, 1974). Additional support for the role of attachment can be found in John Bowlby's attachment theory (introduced in Chapter 2)—an approach both compatible with and influenced by psychodynamic theory. Attachment theory emphasizes how early childhood relationships affect later psychological functioning (Ainsworth, Blehar, Waters, & Wall, 1978; Bowlby, 1980, 1988). It holds that children of attentive and emotionally responsive parents develop *secure attachments*; they become emotionally hardy, see themselves in a positive light, and can safely establish relationships with others (Ainsworth et al., 1978). By comparison, children of parents who are inconsistently attentive and emotionally unresponsive develop *insecure attachments*. Consequently, they experience others as untrustworthy and undependable; they worry about being abandoned and struggle to regulate negative emotions in relationships with others (Ainsworth et al., 1978). Research on attachment theory has found that insecurely attached infants are at increased risk for later emotional upset—including moodiness and depression (Blatt & Homann, 1992; Fonagy, 2001). In the past, the term **anaclitic depression** was used to describe depression in young children caused by separation from their caregivers. In more recent times anaclitic depression refers to attachment-related depression in adults who are clingy, helpless, dependent, and fear abandonment (Reis & Grenyer, 2002).

Short-Term Interpersonal and Psychodynamic Therapies for Depression

Interpersonal therapy (IPT)

Interpersonal therapy (IPT) for depression, originally developed by psychiatrist Gerald Klerman and colleagues, is a modern-day short-term relational therapy influenced by the works of early interpersonal therapists such as Harry Stack Sullivan, Frieda Fromm-Reichmann, and Karen Horney (Klerman, Weissman, Rounsaville, & Chevron, 1984). IPT has four potential areas of focus, all of which stress improving interpersonal relationships to alleviate depression (Klerman et al., 1984; Law, 2011; Markowitz, 2013). Client and therapist might work on *interpersonal role transitions, interpersonal role disputes, grief,* or *interpersonal sensitivity.* The goal is to help clients build the relational skills necessary to deepen existing relationships and develop new ones. Research has consistently shown IPT to be as or nearly as effective as CBT, usually considered the "gold standard" therapy for depression (Cuijpers, Berking, et al., 2013; de Mello, de Jesus Mari, Bacaltchuk, Verdeli, & Neugebauer, 2005; Hollon & Ponniah, 2010; Luty et al., 2007).

Short-Term Psychodynamic Therapies

IPT has received criticism for being less theoretically elaborated than it could be (Law, 2011). Some have even said it is insufficiently psychodynamic in its theoretical focus (de Jonghe et al., 2013; Lemma, Target, & Fonagy, 2010). As alternatives to IPT, psychotherapies with a more explicit psychodynamic focus have been developed. In **dynamic interpersonal therapy (DIT)**, client and therapist work to uncover and remedy one major unconscious interpersonal pattern that contributes to the client's depression. Similarly, **short-term psychoanalytic supportive therapy (SPST)** emphasizes helping depressed people revise *intrapersonal relationships (IPRs)*, the internalized relational patterns that people project onto others. IPRs are like what in Chapter 2 we called cyclical maladaptive patterns. Both DIT and SPST are short-term therapies (by psychodynamic standards), lasting 16 sessions. Initial research suggests that DIT is effective in reducing depression, but randomized controlled trials haven't yet been conducted (Lemma et al., 2010; Lemma, Target, & Fonagy, 2011; Lemma et al., 2013; D. Wright & Abrahams, 2015). SPST, on the other hand, has been shown to be effective in several randomized controlled trials (de Jonghe et al., 2013; Dekker et al., 2014).

Shirley

If Shirley sought short-term supportive psychodynamic therapy (SPST) for her depression, her therapist would focus on how Shirley keeps projecting certain attributes onto her fiancé, Ralph—seeing him as critical and rejecting. Therapy might reveal that she has felt this way with a lot of men, including her father. The therapist would try to help Shirley gain insight into how projecting criticality onto others contributes to her depression. Therapy would serve as a place for Shirley to explore new patterns of relating.

CASE EXAMPLES

Interpersonal and Social Rhythm Therapy for Mania

Questions about its psychodynamic bona fides notwithstanding, a version of interpersonal therapy may be beneficial in treating bipolar disorders. **Interpersonal and social rhythm therapy (IPSRT)** uses IPT's interpersonal problem-solving techniques to help clients regulate their sleep habits. The idea is to manage disrupted circadian rhythms suspected of playing a part in bipolar symptoms (Reilly-Harrington, Roberts, & Sylvia, 2015). IPSRT also uses interpersonal therapy techniques to help clients identify mood states, regulate levels of stimulation, minimize emotional ups and downs, manage grandiosity, and attend to risks of drug abuse (H. A. Swartz, Levenson, & Frank, 2012). Some researchers have concluded that IPSRT appears effective as an adjunct to mood stabilizers (Geddes & Miklowitz, 2013; Inder et al., 2015; Reilly-Harrington et al., 2015; Rizvi & Zaretsky, 2007; H. A. Swartz et al., 2012), although others believe that results are inconclusive and further research is needed (Geller & Goldberg, 2007; Hollon & Ponniah, 2010; Miziou et al., 2015; Reinares, Sánchez-Moreno, & Fountoulakis, 2014). Interestingly, one study found IPSRT helpful on its own when given to bipolar II disorder patients not on mood stabilizers (H. A. Swartz, Frank, Frankel, Novick, & Houck, 2009).

Interpersonal and social rhythm therapy (IPSRT) uses interpersonal problem-solving techniques to help clients regulate sleep habits.
Source: ImageSource

CHAPTER 5

COGNITIVE-BEHAVIORAL PERSPECTIVES

CBT perspectives combine cognitive and behavioral interventions in trying to alleviate depression. The cognitive therapy side stresses how negative thinking leads to depression. The focus is on changing people's thought processes to alter their moods. The behavior therapy side accentuates the role of environmental conditioning in depression, with an emphasis on eliminating depression-related behaviors. Aaron Beck's cognitive therapy and Martin Seligman's theory of learned helplessness, both discussed next, have contributed much to the CBT approach.

Beck's Cognitive Theory of Depression

The Cognitive Triad

Aaron Beck's cognitive theory holds that depression results from negative thinking. Beck famously proposed the **cognitive triad**—a thought pattern consisting of three kinds of negative beliefs that cognitive therapists believe lead to depression (A. T. Beck, Rush, Shaw, & Emery, 1979; A. J. Rush & Beck, 1978). The cognitive triad consists of negative beliefs about *self*, *experience*, and *future*:

» *Negative beliefs about the self* involve seeing oneself as unworthy and as lacking the attributes necessary for happiness.

» *Negative beliefs about experience* emphasize how current, ongoing life circumstances are negative and unpleasant.

» *Negative beliefs about the future* assume that the future will continue to be bleak.

It isn't hard to see how negative thinking about self, experience, and future produces depression.

Shirley

» *Shirley thinks she is unlikable and incapable of being valued and loved by others at work or home. These negative beliefs about self are why she thinks she was demoted at work and why her fiancé Ralph has threatened to leave her.*

» *When Shirley laments how awful and unbearable her current employment and personal situations are, she is focusing on negative beliefs about experience.*

» *Shirley's insistence that she will be stuck in her current dead-end job forever and that her relationship with her fiancé Ralph is doomed exemplify negative thinking about the future.*

If Shirley believes that she (a) is unlikable and lacks the personal qualities to succeed, (b) faces terrible ongoing circumstances, and (c) will continue to be unhappy indefinitely, then how could we expect her to feel anything but depressed?

Schemas and Cognitive Distortions

In addition to emphasizing the importance of the cognitive triad in depression, Beck's approach also stresses the role of cognitive schemas. Recall from Chapter 2 that schemas are mental structures we use to organize information—scripts we rely on as guides to help us navigate everyday interactions.

Shirley

Shirley's schema for relationships might go something like this: "The more people know about me, the less they will like me. Therefore, I shouldn't open myself up emotionally—even with those I wish to be closest to. Of course, keeping quiet and avoiding intimacy will only delay the inevitable because eventually everyone realizes just how unlovable I am and they leave me. Thus, working too hard to preserve a relationship is pointless."

Unfortunately, when people hold negative schemas like this, they tend to distort information to fit their expectations. They engage in faulty information processing, which reinforces negative schemas and fosters depression. Said another way, depressed individuals often fall prey to common cognitive distortions (see Table 2.6 in Chapter 2) such as *absolutistic thinking*, *arbitrary inference*, *magnification*, *minimization*, *overgeneralization*, *personalization*, and *selective abstraction* (A. T. Beck et al., 1979).

Criticisms of Cognitive Therapy

Critics contend that Beck's approach privileges logical thinking over emotional experience by assuming people must change how they think to change how they feel. These critics question whether irrational feelings are best altered via logic and reason, while also wondering whether what is deemed "logical" often reflects unexamined social norms (Gipps, 2013; Kantrowitz & Ballou, 1992). However, advocates of cognitive perspectives maintain that interventions at the level of thinking are indeed essential for emotional transformation and point to a large body of research support for their approach (A. C. Butler, Chapman, Forman, & Beck, 2006; Hofmann, Asnaani, Vonk, Sawyer, & Fang, 2012; Tolin, 2010). See Table 5.4 for examples of how cognitive distortions contribute to Shirley's depression.

Table 5.4 Shirley's Depression-Producing Cognitive Distortions

Distortion	Defined	In Action with Shirley
Absolutistic thinking	Dividing experience into one of two opposite categories; like "all or nothing" thinking from Chapter 2.	"I must be perfect at work or else I am a complete failure."
Arbitrary inference	Drawing a specific conclusion without sufficient evidence; like "jumping to conclusions" from Chapter 2.	"My fiancé doesn't like seeing me sad, which must mean he wants to break up with me."
Magnification	Overemphasizing negative events.	"Losing that power struggle at work tells me everything I need to know about my ability to advance in my profession."
Minimization	Underemphasizing positive events.	"Yes, I have previously succeeded at work, but that was a fluke."
Overgeneralization	Taking one instance and applying it too broadly to explain other instances.	"I was demoted at work. I'll never succeed at my job again."
Personalization	Assuming others' behavior is necessarily about you.	"The secretary at work didn't say hello this morning. She did that on purpose to let me know she dislikes me."
Selective abstraction	Taking a detail out of context and ignoring other more relevant aspects of the situation.	"Ralph has complained about me being depressed, which—even though he recently proposed and keeps buying me wedding planning magazines—must mean he wants to break up."

Source: Categories of cognitive distortion listed in the first column are derived from the work of A. T. Beck et al. (1979).

Learned Helplessness

Seligman's Original Theory

Martin Seligman's original work on **learned helplessness** was introduced when discussing research methods in Chapter 1 (as an example of analogue studies with animals). Learned helplessness results when operant conditioning teaches an organism that its behavior has no effect on its surroundings. In Seligman's initial research, he created learned helplessness in dogs by shocking them repeatedly and not allowing them to escape the shock. After a while, the dogs didn't even bother trying to avoid getting shocked—even when the situation was altered so that they could escape (Overmier & Seligman, 1967; M. E. Seligman & Maier, 1967; M. E. Seligman, Maier, & Geer, 1968). Seligman analogized learned helplessness in dogs to depression in people, arguing that depression is about learning to feel helpless. Thus, learned helplessness is a behavioral way to understand depression, one that contends people learn to be depressed when their behavior has little or no effect on their surroundings. For instance, people in abusive situations they can't escape learn that their actions are irrelevant. They therefore become depressed due to learned helplessness and stop trying to get out of their situation—even overlooking opportunities to do so when circumstances change.

 Shirley
Shirley, for instance, might not look for a new job because she has learned her actions have no effect on her current job.

Attribution Style and Hopelessness Theory

Despite its behavioral origins, researchers have extensively studied the cognitive aspects of learned helplessness. Their main research question has been, "What kinds of cognitive attributions contribute to learned helplessness?" By attributions, we mean, "How do people explain their behavior and experiences?" **Hopelessness theory** predicts that depressed people tend to make attributions that are *stable*, *global*, and *internal* (Abramson, Metalsky, & Alloy, 1989; Abramson, Seligman, & Teasdale, 1978; T. Hu, Zhang, & Yang, 2015). Stable attributions don't change; global attributions apply globally across most or all situations; and internal attributions assign responsibility for an outcome to oneself. When people make negative stable, global, and internal attributions, they typically feel depressed. The opposite of stable, global, and internal attributions are unstable, specific, and external attributions—which hopelessness theory posits don't produce depression when applied to negative events. Table 5.5 maps Shirley's attribution style and provides examples of stable-unstable, global-specific, and internal-external attributions.

Table 5.5 Learned Helplessness and Shirley's Attribution Style

Attributions Leading to Depression	Potential Alternative Attributions
Stable: "My job situation will never change."	*Unstable*: "It's possible there are better jobs out there."
Global: "The work world is terrible no matter where you work."	*Specific*: "Working here stinks, but it might be better elsewhere."
Internal: "My problems at work are my own fault; I'll be dissatisfied no matter where I work."	*External*: "My problems at work are because my workplace is toxic; I'll be more satisfied in a different job."

A meta-analysis of past studies found a positive correlation between negative attribution style and depression—with global and stable attributions moderately correlated with depression, but internal attributions only weakly associated with it (T. Hu et al., 2015). The meta-analysis also found differences for age and gender (T. Hu et al., 2015). Global attributions were only correlated with depression in adults, not children or adolescents. Further, all three attributions—stable, global, and internal—showed a significantly stronger correlation with depression among females compared to males. This may mean that men who make negative attributions don't become depressed as often as women who make negative attributions. If so, this is consistent with research showing that women are at greater risk for depression than men. More is said about this later when discussing sociocultural perspectives.

Criticisms of Learned Helplessness

The learned helplessness model of depression has been criticized for relying too extensively on animal research; this is partly what led to hopelessness theory's emphasis on attributions over conditioning (Abramson et al., 1978). Because it isn't clear that animals make cognitive attributions in the same way as people, generalizing from Seligman's dogs to human beings is questionable. Most people's everyday life circumstances and meaning-making capabilities are much more complex than the experiences of a shocked dog in a controlled lab setting.

Learned helplessness theory has also been chastised for attributing too much importance to individual attributions in depression while insufficiently attending to the role of socially constructed societal norms (Stam, 1987). Overlooking how social norms shape ideas about depression—including failing to challenge the assumption that depression emerges mainly from individuals making attributions rather than from social structures imposed on those individuals—may unwittingly encourage people to bring their attributions into sync with dominant social norms rather than challenge those norms.

Shirley
Maybe Shirley's learned helplessness is less about her making unrealistic negative attributions and more due to ongoing societal discrimination against women in the workplace.

CASE EXAMPLES

Whether hopelessness theory inappropriately encourages people to accept social limits by viewing attributions that don't fit dominant social norms as "unrealistic" is an argument that those who don't care for learned helplessness theory will find compelling, but those who like it will probably dismiss.

CBT Assessment and Therapy for Depression

Beck Depression Inventory (BDI)

The cognitive part of CBT assesses and then works to change how people think about things. It focuses on helping people examine the negative beliefs, schemas, and cognitive distortions that lead them to feel depressed (Power, 2013). Clients might be administered the Beck Depression Inventory (BDI), introduced in Chapter 3. Currently in its second version, the BDI-II is a 21-item self-administered scale that measures depression by assessing thinking patterns. Items ask respondents to rate aspects of their experience over the past two weeks using 4-point scales. For instance, one item asks about guilty feelings, and the response choices are "I don't feel particularly guilty (0)," "I feel guilty over many things I have done or should have done (1)," "I feel guilty most of the time (2)," and "I feel guilty all of the time (3)" (Dozios & Covin, 2004, p. 51). Scores range from 0 to 63, with scores of 14–19 deemed "mild depression," 20–28 "moderate depression," and 29–63 "severe depression" (Dozios & Covin, 2004). The BDI can be completed in 5–10 minutes. Many clinicians view it as an efficient way to quickly assess depressive feelings. Its advocates point to strong evidence of the BDI's validity (specifically its good *convergent validity*, the degree to which BDI scores correlate positively with other depression measures) and reliability (especially its strong *internal consistency reliability*, the extent to which BDI items highly correlate with each other) (Dozios & Covin, 2004). Good internal consistency suggests that BDI items are measuring the same variable, in this case depression. Nonetheless, BDI scores are unstable over time; that is, there may be issues with test-retest reliability (the degree to which a test yields similar results each time) (Dozios & Covin, 2004). One reason results may change over time is that the person retaking the BDI no longer feels depressed. The BDI's developers warn that a depression diagnosis shouldn't be made based on a BDI score alone. It has also been noted that women often score higher than men (Dozios & Covin, 2004). It remains unclear whether this means the test is gender biased, women are more depressed than men, or women simply are more willing to report feeling depressed.

Daily Record of Dysfunctional Thoughts (DRDT)

After taking the BDI-II, clients might be asked to complete a Daily Record of Dysfunctional Thoughts (DRDT) (described in Chapter 2) in which they chart events, their thoughts, their emotional reactions, their behavioral responses, and their errors in logic. (See "Try It Yourself" to complete your own record of dysfunctional thoughts.) In therapy, client and therapist then examine dysfunctional thinking patterns and errors in logic. Beck's cognitive therapy or Ellis' rational emotive behavior therapy (REBT) might be used to revise and replace depression-related beliefs (A. T. Beck et al., 1979; J. S. Beck, 2011; Dryden & Ellis, 2001; A. Ellis & Ellis, 2011; Power, 2013).

TRY IT YOURSELF

CBT Thought Record

CBT Thought Record

Situation	Emotion or feeling	Negative automatic thought	Evidence that supports the thought	Evidence that does not support the thought	Alternative thought	Emotion or feeling
Describe what was happening: Who, what, when where?	Emotions can be described with one word: e.g. angry, sad, scared Rate 0-100%	Identify one thought to work on: What thoughts were going through your mind? What memories or images were in my mind?	What facts support the truthfulness of this thought or image?	What experiences indicate that this thought is not completely true all of the time? If my best friend had this thought what would I tell them? Are there any small experiences which contradict this thought?	Write a new thought which takes into account the evidence for and against the original thought	How do you feel about the situation now? Rate 0 - 100%

PSYCHOLOGY**TOOLS**   http://psychologytools.com

From https://psychologytools.com/worksheets/free/english_us/cbt_thought_record_free_en-us.pdf

Behavioral Activation, Exercise, and Problem-Solving Therapy

The behavioral component of CBT supplements the cognitive part by actively changing what people do (Power, 2013). One of the most common behavior-based techniques in CBT is **behavioral activation**, which involves asking clients to schedule particular activities—such as taking a walk or calling a friend (Martell, Dimidjian, &

Herman-Dunn, 2010). The idea is to get clients to engage in behaviors that will bring them positive reinforcement. Depressed people have usually stopped participating regularly in these kinds of behaviors. Behavioral activation seeks to counter this by assigning such behaviors as homework. There is ample evidence from a variety of research reviews that behavioral activation helps reduce depression (Bell & D'Zurilla, 2009; Mazzucchelli, Kane, & Rees, 2009; Sturmey, 2009). It seems counterintuitive when you are depressed to go out and do something. However, getting out into the world and partaking in activities is a straightforward and proven technique for reducing depression. Behavioral activation can be used on its own or in combination with other types of cognitive therapy—including **problem-solving therapy**, an empirically supported CBT approach in which the therapist helps the client to define specific problems the client faces and then generate concrete solutions the client can implement (Bell & D'Zurilla, 2009; Cuijpers, van Straten, & Warmerdam, 2007; Martell et al., 2010).

One specific behavior that many therapists encourage in their depressed clients is physical exercise. Consistent with this, a comprehensive review of existing research found that people who exercised regularly experienced a moderate decrease in depression (Cooney et al., 2013). However, the only randomized controlled trial (RCT) examining exercise and depression found no significant effect (Chalder et al., 2012). Despite this somewhat surprising finding, many clients report that moderate exercise improves their mood. Nonetheless, more research is needed.

Shirley

Here's what combining various CBT assessment and therapy techniques might look like with Shirley:

CASE EXAMPLES

In therapy, Shirley's therapist could employ cognitive-behavioral therapy techniques. Cognitively, he might assess Shirley's level of depression by administering the Beck Depression Inventory, which would likely reveal her to be quite depressed. He could then help map Shirley's negative thought processes by asking her to complete a dysfunctional thought record between sessions. Behaviorally, he might use behavioral activation. He could ask Shirley what things she likes to do when not feeling depressed. If she says she likes to go to the movies with friends and go to the gym, the therapist might assign these behaviors as homework between sessions.

Later sessions with Shirley would involve more directly challenging her irrational beliefs and cognitive distortions:

Imagine Shirley tells her therapist that she is unlovable, everyone eventually leaves her, and she will never be happy. Working cognitively, the therapist might ask what evidence she has that happiness isn't possible. Regarding work, he could point out that Shirley has had many past successes and her recent demotion is an aberration. He also might note that Shirley's fiancé, Ralph, wants to salvage his relationship with her despite her insistence that he is bound to leave her. By pointing out cognitive distortions and negative attributions, the therapist would be encouraging Shirley to think about how she thinks about things—and to evaluate how her thought processes contribute to her sadness. Over a dozen sessions or so, Shirley would hopefully revise her negative beliefs, thereby improving her mood.

CBT Effectiveness

CBT is perhaps the most studied therapeutic approach to depression, with extensive research showing its effectiveness (Cuijpers, Berking, et al., 2013). For instance, research reviews suggest that CBT for depression is helpful with adults (Cuijpers, Berking, et al., 2013), adolescents (N. Singh & Reece, 2014), postpartum women (Sockol, 2015), older adults with cognitive deficits (S. S. Simon, Cordás, & Bottino, 2015), and those whose depression doesn't respond to antidepressants (Wiles et al., 2016). Given its effectiveness, one of the big debates in abnormal psychology is how CBT compares to antidepressants. Much research indicates CBT is equally as effective as antidepressants (DeRubeis, Siegle, & Hollon, 2008; Roshanaei-Moghaddam et al., 2011; N. Singh & Reece, 2014), but other research suggests combining CBT with antidepressants is the most effective approach (Cuijpers, Berking, et al., 2013; S. Köhler et al., 2013). There is evidence that the effect of CBT is more long-lasting than antidepressants (DeRubeis et al., 2008), although other research suggests antidepressants are somewhat better than CBT for treating dysthymia (Cuijpers, Sijbrandij, et al., 2013). Still, some therapists feel that when drugs and therapy are equivalent, it is better to go with therapy because it lacks side effects (Elkins, 2016).

Mindfulness

One recent variation on CBT is **mindfulness-based cognitive therapy (MBCT)**, which combines cognitive therapy with mindfulness training (Z. V. Segal, Teasdale, & Williams, 2004; Teasdale, 2004). In **mindfulness training**, influenced by Zen Buddhist traditions, people are taught to simply observe and be aware of their thoughts (as opposed to trying to stop or change them) (Baer, 2003; Langer, 1989). The logic of MBCT is that learning to observe our depressive thoughts alters our relationship to them, often decreasing their influence (Z. V. Segal, Williams, & Teasdale, 2013). Rather than getting upset about being depressed, mindfulness encourages simple acceptance of feelings. By not resisting depressed feelings, the idea is that they will run their course and dissipate on their own rather than become more intense as we ruminate about them. MBCT has been shown to be effective in preventing the recurrence of depression (Hollon & Ponniah, 2010). Researchers found it to be more effective than psychoeducation in reducing depression among people who were unresponsive to antidepressants, though the sample size was small and more studies are needed to draw firmer conclusions (Chiesa et al., 2015; Chiesa, Mandelli, & Serretti, 2012). Nevertheless, mindfulness shows promise as a treatment for depression. Additional research is underway to see if MBCT is also helpful in reducing bipolar symptoms (Lahera et al., 2014).

CBT and Mania

While mostly used for depression, CBT has also been adapted to treat mania. It is often used in conjunction with drug treatments as a way to increase medication adherence (Popovic, Scott, & Colom, 2015). However, it can also be used to

Mindfulness training—which often includes mindfulness meditation—teaches people to observe, rather than try to stop, their thoughts.
Source: Getty Images/iStockphoto \ f9photos

help change the irrational thinking patterns that are common during mania. The logic behind CBT for mania holds that manic individuals suffer from overly optimistic thinking and CBT can be used to correct this (Geddes & Miklowitz, 2013). Therapy revolves around helping manic individuals monitor and reality-test their irrationally optimistic beliefs (Schwannauer, 2013). Studies examining the effectiveness of CBT for addressing mania are inconclusive (Geddes & Miklowitz, 2013; Miziou et al., 2015). Some researchers conclude that CBT can help as an addendum to mood stabilizers, but others feel that CBT shows little or no effect (Bond & Anderson, 2015; Geddes & Miklowitz, 2013; Geller & Goldberg, 2007; S. Jones, 2004; Miziou et al., 2015; Schwannauer, 2013).

Don

Once he begins taking mood stabilizers, Don also seeks psychotherapy. The therapist might use CBT techniques to challenge Don's contention that he needs little or no sleep. In CBT, Don's belief that he is writing the greatest novel of this decade would be explored—especially how Don's grandiose expectations in this regard have made it difficult for him to accept feedback from others about his writing. Of course, CBT might prove more helpful once Don has been taking mood stabilizers for a while and has become calmer, more coherent, and more rational.

CASE EXAMPLES

HUMANISTIC PERSPECTIVES
Person-Centered Therapy

Humanistic perspectives are typically skeptical of the medical model view of depression associated with diagnostic and biological perspectives. Rather than seeing depression as a diseased state, humanists tend to view it as a meaningful response to life circumstances. Classic person-centered therapy sees depression as arising from the failure to receive empathy, unconditional positive regard, and genuineness from key relationships. Sadness results because the person is in a state of incongruence, behaving in self-inconsistent ways to maintain love from others. By providing core conditions for change in therapy, the person-centered therapist provides a space for the client to reestablish self-consistency and move toward self-actualization. As this occurs, depression lifts.

Emotion-Focused Therapy (EFT)

More recent humanistic approaches to depression have had to accommodate the trend toward brief, evidence-based therapies. One approach that has done so is **emotion-focused therapy (EFT)**, a short-term (8–20 sessions) humanistic psychotherapy that combines person-centered, Gestalt, and constructivist ideas (Goldman & Greenberg, 2015b; L. S. Greenberg & Goldman, 2006). EFT has proven helpful for depression. Importantly, emotion-focused therapists emphasize *process diagnosis*, not *person diagnosis*, when diagnosing depression. The former stresses understanding how the client makes sense of experience in ways that produce depressed mood, while the latter is more about assigning people to depressive disorder diagnostic categories and seeing them as mentally ill (a practice humanistic therapists generally don't like) (Goldman & Greenberg, 2015b; Greenberg & Goldman, 2006).

Emotion-focused therapists question the primacy that cognitive therapists give to thinking's role in depression (L. S. Greenberg & Watson, 2006). Instead, EFT stresses emotion as more central. EFT holds that depressed people often experienced unsupportive environments growing up—especially in their teens, when they may not have felt liked, attractive, or athletically competent. They also may have lacked peer and/or parental support. In adulthood, the feelings of inadequacy they developed as teenagers often become supplemented with feelings of shame for not being able to deal more effectively with negative social interactions (L. S. Greenberg & Watson, 2006). Thus, in the adult EFT model of depression, disappointing life events activate primary emotions of sadness and disappointment. In response to these primary emotions the person feels fear and shame and then concludes, "I'm weak, worthless, and unable to cope." This in turn triggers hopelessness. Out of this hopelessness comes depressive behavior and thinking that makes the person even more vulnerable to experiencing future events as disappointing. In the EFT model, feelings take precedence over thoughts in generating depression, with the emotional organization of the self being critical to how vulnerable someone is to depression (L. S. Greenberg & Watson, 2006).

Shirley

If she were working with an emotion-focused therapist, Shirley would be encouraged to share and process her feelings. The therapist would listen intently and empathize with Shirley's plight. As Shirley trusted the therapist more and more, he would steer the conversation toward Shirley's feelings about herself. Shirley often felt unsupported and ridiculed growing up. Now, as an adult, she feels ashamed whenever social interactions don't go well. EFT would endeavor to explore her feelings of disappointment, shame, and hopelessness about how things have gone recently at work and in her relationship with her fiancé. Shirley would be encouraged to experience her negative emotions to better get in touch with them. Her therapist would help her transform these negative feelings into more positive, productive ones by processing his relationship with her so she has a new relational experience that is different from past unsupportive relationships. EFT would help Shirley identify her needs and goals, while encouraging her to construct new ways of understanding herself that lead to different and more positive emotions.

CASE EXAMPLES

EVALUATING PSYCHOLOGICAL PERSPECTIVES

As noted, psychological therapies are often considered as effective as drugs in alleviating depression, but without the side effects (Elkins, 2016). However, while psychological perspectives are often praised for being as good as biological approaches for depression, they are usually seen as inadequate on their own for managing mania. Thus, they are typically talked about as a secondary—albeit often effective—treatment for bipolar disorder (Salcedo et al., 2016). As mentioned earlier, many psychotherapies incorporate psychoeducation to teach patients about their disorder and how to manage it (Bond & Anderson, 2015; S. Jones, 2004; Miklowitz, 2008; Miziou et al., 2015; Otto & Miklowitz, 2004; Reinares et al., 2014). Although psychoeducation is a psychological intervention, it often accepts bipolar disorder as a biological illness and then uses therapy techniques to teach this to clients.

Despite doing about as well as drug interventions for depression, psychological approaches do have their limits. Roughly half of those who improve in response to psychotherapy become depressed again within a year or two (Steinert, Hofmann, Kruse, & Leichsenring, 2014). Further, even though research suggests that up to 62% of people with major depression no longer meet diagnostic criteria for the disorder following therapy, neither do 43% of control patients who don't receive therapy (Cuijpers et al., 2014). This implies that while therapy can help, depression often lifts on its own with the simple passage of time.

Given that drugs and therapy both have their limits, it makes sense that they are often combined. Even when combined, however, not everyone with a mood problem improves. What might these approaches be overlooking? As one possible answer, we turn to sociocultural perspectives, which contend that biological and psychological perspectives often minimize the importance of context and culture in the development and maintenance of mood difficulties.

5.6 SOCIOCULTURAL PERSPECTIVES

Sociocultural perspectives, in their purest theoretical form, stress how depression and mania are traceable to social, cultural, and environmental factors. For example, a growing research literature has found a relationship between materialism and depression (Azibo, 2013; Claes et al., 2010; A. Mueller et al., 2011; Otero-López & Villardefrancos, 2013; D. C. Watson, 2015), suggesting that capitalist culture and its emphasis on compulsive buying over social interest may play a role in generating depressive experience (Richardson & Manaster, 2003). This sort of analysis—where social influences are placed front and center in trying to understand mood disturbances—is typical of sociocultural approaches. Rather than seeing people as biologically sick, a purely sociocultural viewpoint views mood disturbances as originating in social oppression, family dynamics, cultural factors, and environmental conditions. However, most sociocultural perspectives take a somewhat integrative view. They acknowledge the relevance of biological and psychological processes but see sociocultural factors as critical in eliciting and shaping the course of these processes (R. A. Gordon, 2010).

CROSS-CULTURAL AND SOCIAL JUSTICE PERSPECTIVES

Socioeconomic Inequality and Depression

People advancing social justice perspectives argue that depression doesn't occur in a vacuum. It is tied to, and perhaps caused by, social conditions. Many, but not all, studies find depression correlated with lower earnings and socioeconomic status (SES) (Andersen, Thielen, Nygaard, & Diderichsen, 2009; Fryers, Melzer, Jenkins, & Brugha, 2005; D. Levinson et al., 2010). One British study, for example, found living in a poor neighborhood was associated with anxiety and depression, especially when the neighborhood lacked social cohesion (Fone et al., 2014). This is correlational data, so it isn't fully clear whether economic adversity leads to depression or vice versa. However, several researchers have argued that social policies addressing economic equality should be implemented in an attempt to remedy the higher rates of depression in those facing economic hardship (Butterworth, Olesen, & Leach, 2012). It's even been proposed that depression is a "disease of civilization" (TedX Talks, 2013). This view combines sociocultural and evolutionary perspectives in contending that depression is a response to a fast-paced, high-stress industrialized society to which people aren't evolutionarily adapted.

Gender and Depression

Gender Differences in Diagnosis and Treatment

In addition to socioeconomic factors, research consistently reveals gender differences when it comes to depression. Women are much more likely than men to be diagnosed with depression—perhaps twice as often (Norman, 2004; Ussher, 2011). They are also far more likely to receive antidepressants. Although the total number of prescriptions is on the rise for both men and women, men take antidepressants almost half as often as women. A 2010 U.S. report found that "21 percent of women ages 20 and older were using an antidepressant" and that "from 2001 to 2010 the number of women on an antidepressant grew 29 percent" (Medco, 2011, p. 3). It is unclear to what extent these gender differences are because (a) women truly are more depressed, (b) there is a great deal of gender bias in diagnosis, or (c) men are socialized to exhibit depression through displays of irritability, hostility, and acting out rather than sadness (Jack & Ali, 2010b; Norman, 2004; Ogrodniczuk & Oliffe, 2011; Ussher, 2011; Wilhelm, 2009).

Socioeconomic inequality and gender differences play important roles in depression, according to sociocultural theorists.
Source: © Royalty-Free/Corbis

Those stressing gender bias note that women are socialized to show vulnerable emotions more openly than men. As noted, depressed men often present with anger and behavior problems, not sadness (Ogrodniczuk & Oliffe, 2011; Wilhelm, 2009). Thus, socialized gender differences in expressing depression could lead to women being more readily diagnosed than men (Norman, 2004). Women also face certain social barriers more frequently than men—such as higher poverty rates, domestic violence, unequal pay, being denied educational opportunities, and disproportionate household responsibilities (Astbury, 2010; Ussher, 2011). Such obstacles could lead to higher rates of depression. Thus, gender differences in depression may be attributable to cultural and social factors. From a social justice perspective, therefore, women aren't necessarily more inherently predisposed to depression. Rather, they become or are identified as depressed more than men primarily due to gender bias and inequality. Social justice therapists cite evidence showing that "women who experience frequent sexism, or who perceive themselves to be subjected to personal discrimination, report higher levels of depression than those who experience little sexism or low levels of discrimination" (Ussher, 2011, p. 38).

Silencing the Self Theory

Silencing the self (STS) theory proposes that depression in women is a product of deeply rooted cultural assumptions that direct women to silence or suppress certain thoughts and feelings to satisfy the demands of a male-centered world (Jack, 1991; Jack & Ali, 2010a). STS theory holds that women are raised in a society that repeatedly tells them they must be pleasing, unselfish, and loving. This leads them to be compliant and deferent in ways that result in them silencing themselves, which often leads to depression (Jack, 1991; Jack & Ali, 2010a).

STS theory implies that when medicalization occurs and we think about depression as a disorder, depressed women become seen as sick individuals suffering from brain diseases rather than oppressed individuals responding emotionally to ongoing social subjugation in expectable ways. This model is suspicious of antidepressants, worrying that they too-often become a form of social control, further silencing women by accommodating them to social conditions that they should be upset by and resist. That is, "medication both subdues and pathologizes women's complaints" (Sparks, 2002, p. 30). This view argues that therapists should "resist the pull to steer clients automatically toward diagnosis and medication" (Sparks, 2002, p. 36). Instead, "a rightful role for therapy and therapists might be to do whatever it takes to encourage the agency, voice, and connection that allow client knowledge and resources preeminence in solving even the most daunting dilemmas" (Sparks, 2002, p. 36).

ROAD Program

Social justice approaches contend that it is not enough to simply intervene on an individual level with depressed women because their depression isn't about them being biologically or psychologically broken. It is about them being socially oppressed. Thus, interventions must go beyond the traditional 50-minute therapy hour and target the wider social system in working to reduce social inequality (L. A. Goodman, Pugach, Skolnik, & Smith, 2013; L. A. Goodman, Smyth, & Banyard, 2010). For instance, although now defunct due to lack of funding (a common problem for

Is this woman depressed because she feels pressure to please others while suppressing her own thoughts and feelings? Quite possibly, according to silencing the self (STS) theory.
Source: IMAGESOURCE

nontraditional intervention programs), the **Reaching Out About Depression (ROAD)** program in Cambridge, Massachusetts was an excellent example of a community action social justice approach. Like other social justice based community programs, the rationale behind ROAD was that "instead of imposing diagnostic labels on women's emotional distress, feminist relational advocates, like feminist therapists, work to understand its roots in social conditions" (L. A. Goodman, Glenn, Bohlig, Banyard, & Borges, 2009, p. 855).

ROAD was developed to assist low-income women experiencing depression and consisted of two components, the *Supportive Action Workshop Series* and the *Resource Advocacy Team*. The first component was a 12-session workshop series intended to educate participants about the relationship between depression and poverty. The workshop series also covered topics such as self-confidence, motherhood, healthy relationships, self-care, financial problems, and effective communication ("ROAD," n.d.; "ROAD* Reaching out about depression," n.d.). At the end of the workshop series, participants took part in a "social action event, such as advocating for specific pieces of state legislation or conducting a workshop for mental health providers on poverty and mental health" (L. A. Goodman et al., 2009, p. 852). The second component of ROAD was an advocacy program in which participants were paired with law or counseling students who worked with them one on one in meetings that occurred outside the traditional therapy setting—often at the participants' homes or at relevant service-related agencies. The goal was to develop a shared plan that addressed participants' needs and helped them identify and make use of relevant social services (L. A. Goodman, n.d.; L. A. Goodman et al., 2007). Qualitative research revealed that participants found the ROAD program helpful in overcoming obstacles contributing to their depression (e.g., getting their heat turned on, getting approved for disability services), while also improving their self-worth and their ability to advocate for themselves (L. A. Goodman et al., 2009). However, if the program is ever refunded and revived, more controlled research could help further evaluate its effectiveness.

CONSUMER AND SERVICE-USER PERSPECTIVES
The Experience of Depression

The experience of depression itself can be extremely intense for people regardless of whether clinicians diagnose the depression as mild or severe. One patient described depression this way: "I was in a terrible state ... I would simply break down and cry and you know feel absolutely useless and it's hard to describe really but you just—something inside of you which just starts to eat—to eat away" (Louch, Goodman, & Greenhalgh, 2005, p. 113). Another depressed person stated bluntly: "Personally I can say that in my experience being depressed is worse than knowing that I will die of cancer" (M. Deacon, 2015, p. 458). As these quotes illustrate, outlining the symptoms of depression doesn't fully convey the intensity of it. See the "The Lived Experience" feature for three additional accounts of what it's like to be depressed.

THE LIVED EXPERIENCE

Feeling Depressed

What's it like to be depressed? Here are three people's first-hand experiences.

Douglas Cootey, Author of "The Splintered Mind" Blog

Often [depression] is simply an undertone of sadness that plays throughout my day, like a radio station signal that comes and goes.

At the worst, depression is a cacophony of low tones that throb and blare over everything in my life, like bass from the car next to you when you are stuck at a traffic light. During those times, I feel as if my chest is weighted down from within. Simple things like changing the channel on the TV seem incredibly exhausting, never mind getting up and moving. My heart feels burdened with sadness, and my sense of self-worth sinks. It is a bad time to make decisions, yet years ago — before I trained myself to act otherwise — many foolish decisions were made while I hated myself stuck there on the couch.

Lisa Keith, Special Education Professor

Depression is like being eaten to death from the inside out. First, you think "I just don't feel well ... it'll pass" ... but it doesn't.

Then you think, "What have I got to be sad about? Nothing." So, you try and fake it.

Next, your limbs become heavy as though they were encased in cement. Everything becomes an overwhelming effort. So you think "If I just eat the right thing, take the right pill, get enough sleep," but nothing is ever enough.

Then, the pain starts. The real physical pain. Deep in your chest and no matter how deep the sobs come, it won't abate. And everything becomes a blur: time, people, memories. And the self-hatred, shame, and guilt get stronger and stronger.

Soon, you rationalize your demise as doing everyone a favor because you've become a burden. You stop eating, bathing, and even though you can't sleep, you lie in bed, listless, with your face covered by the blankets ..."

Ruth C. White, Mental Health Activist and Social Worker

Sometimes I ache all over. It is frustrating because my life is good and so to feel no control over feelings of overwhelming sadness that makes me want to cry, makes me feel helpless. I want to stay under the covers because every thought and every movement requires immense amounts of energy.

Some days just trying to get to the kitchen to eat seems like an impossible task. And without food the energy loss deepens. My lifeline is my smartphone through which I can stay in touch with the world, even though, sometimes, even texting is exhausting. But I can answer emails and watch Netflix, though, sometimes I can't even focus enough to watch television so I lie in bed like an empty shell because depression takes me away from myself.

And then it lifts and it's like it didn't happen and yet I live knowing that the cloud can come back and dump on me again and rob me of my very active and social life and my career as an intellectual.

Stigma

As with most presenting problems, those experiencing mood disturbances often face stigma and discrimination (Aromaa, Tolvanen, Tuulari, & Wahlbeck, 2011; Louch et al., 2005). One interesting qualitative study in which almost 70% of participants were diagnosed with a depressive or bipolar disorder found that 38% of participants believed that discrimination led to their feeling suicidal and 20% felt it contributed to an actual suicide attempt (Farrelly et al., 2015). Another qualitative study found that, when it comes to treatment, many depressed people worry about getting caught in a "drug loop" that makes it difficult to get off medication (Bayliss & Holttum, 2015). They appreciate antidepressants when in a crisis, but once the crisis is over they are often ambivalent about remaining on the drugs long-term (Bayliss & Holttum, 2015).

SYSTEMS PERSPECTIVES
Relationship Problems and Expressed Emotion

Depression and mania are both strongly associated with relationship problems. Divorce, for instance, can place people at higher risk for depression and suicide (Hiyoshi, Fall, Netuveli, & Montgomery, 2015; Sbarra, Emery, Beam, & Ocker, 2014; S. Stack & Scourfield, 2015). Of course, although bad relationships may lead to mood problems, people with mood problems may also have a harder time sustaining effective relationships. That is, mood problems likely both lead to and result in relational and family difficulties.

Shirley

Shirley's depression is negatively impacting her fiancé, Ralph. He has increasingly taken on responsibility for paying bills, doing household chores, and taking care of Spot (the dog they co-own) because Shirley has been too depressed to attend to these issues. Further, as Shirley has sunk into depression, their sex life has deteriorated and conflict between them increased. This, in turn, has led to Ralph also feeling depressed.

CASE EXAMPLES

Couple and family therapists often try to reduce expressed emotion from partners and relatives of clients presenting with mood problems. Recall from Chapter 4 that expressed emotion involves the extent to which partners or family members express hostility and criticism toward the identified patient—in this case the person displaying depression or mania. There is evidence that high expressed emotion in families of people diagnosed with mood problems correlates with worse outcomes (Division of Clinical Psychology, 2010). This may be because high levels of expressed emotion provoke dysfunctional thinking that is counterproductive when it comes to improving the identified patient's mood difficulties (Bodenmann & Randall, 2013; K. Wright, 2013).

Family Therapies

Couple and family therapies often use **family-focused therapy (FFT)** with depression and mania. FFT is a 21-session, nine-month treatment program emphasizing psychoeducation, improving communication skills, and problem solving (Reilly-Harrington et al., 2015). The goal is to help patients, their partners, and their family members to communicate and support one another more effectively. Family-focused therapy seems to be helpful for depression and mania (Reilly-Harrington et al., 2015), but some research has found it no more helpful than less time-intensive psychoeducation programs for bipolar disorder (Miklowitz et al., 2014; H. A. Swartz, 2014). Another approach that has shown promise is **attachment-based family therapy**, which integrates attachment theory into family therapy to help strengthen parent–child attachment relationships in depressed and suicidal adolescents (Diamond, 2014; Ewing, Diamond, & Levy, 2015).

Couple and family approaches do seem to be helpful for mood disturbances, with the best predictor of long-term outcomes being the degree to which levels of expressed emotion are reduced (Bodenmann & Randall, 2013; K. Wright, 2013). Although couple and family approaches are often used in conjunction with prescription drugs, conceptually they expand our understanding of mood difficulties beyond the biological to the relational realm. They contend that depression and mania do not simply emerge from within broken individuals; they emerge systemically from a network of problematic relationships.

EVALUATING SOCIOCULTURAL PERSPECTIVES

Sociocultural perspectives highlight the importance of social factors in mood problems, yet social factors alone don't always account for why some people become depressed or manic. Many people living under oppressive social conditions or in dysfunctional family environments don't develop mood difficulties, while many others from advantaged backgrounds and "happy" families do. Thus, social conditions alone can't explain all cases of depression and mania. For instance, biologically oriented researchers and clinicians contend that sex differences in depression are rooted in physiological differences between men and women; to them, although social considerations are important, disorders such as major depression and premenstrual dysphoric disorder are equally if not more influenced by genetic, neurochemical, hormonal, and immunological factors (Altemus, 2006; Altemus, Sarvaiya, & Epperson, 2014; Pérez-López, Chedraui, Pérez-Roncero, López-Baena, & Cuadros-López, 2009). That said, sociocultural perspectives provide a strong counterweight to the individualistic emphasis of biological and psychological viewpoints, which—in conceptualizing mood problems as disorders inside people—tend to ignore or downplay the importance of social factors in human distress. When mood issues are portrayed as originating mainly inside the broken biology or psychology of individuals, social reform takes a backseat and we risk using psychiatric drugs and psychotherapy to adjust people to oppressive social conditions.

Of course, agreeing on which social conditions are oppressive and how they should be changed is not always obvious or easy. Some critics of social justice approaches worry about mental health professionals imposing their political views about what is or isn't a just society on clients and the public (S. Johnson, 2001; Raskin, 2014; S. D. Smith, Reynolds, & Rovnak, 2009). Of course, just because determining what is socially just is difficult doesn't mean we shouldn't try. All in all, sociocultural approaches that intervene at family and social levels remain an important component of helping those with mood problems.

5.7 CLOSING THOUGHTS: THE WIDE-RANGING RELEVANCE OF MOOD

Chapters on depression and mania often include a discussion of *suicide*, the act of intentionally ending one's own life. After all, people who experience mood disturbances are at substantially increased risk for killing themselves (Costa et al., 2015; World Health Organization, 2014). The lifetime risk of suicide is 4% in those diagnosed with a depressive disorder and 8% in those diagnosed with a bipolar disorder (World Health Organization, 2014). However, suicide shouldn't be linked exclusively to mood problems—people with substance abuse issues or schizophrenia have a greater risk of suicide than depressed people (World Health Organization, 2014). In discussing depression, one researcher poignantly noted how "many people who complete suicide or attempt suicide are not depressed and the overwhelming majority of depressed people will not attempt or complete suicide" (A. K. MacLeod, 2013, p. 413). Suicide is an important issue not just when discussing mood disturbances, but in abnormal psychology more generally. It will be considered further in Chapter 15 when we examine ethics, law, and suicide.

We will revisit mood disturbances throughout the rest of the text because they accompany many of the other presenting problems we examine. This makes sense, even though it is often talked about as something surprising—with technical terms such as "comorbidity" invoked to indicate that depression is regularly diagnosed simultaneously with other *DSM* and *ICD* disorders. However, this should come as little surprise. If you are having a hard time with eating issues, trauma, obsessions and compulsions, drug abuse, or sexual performance, then there is a good chance you will also feel depressed. So, while the conclusion of this chapter officially marks the end of our formal discussion of mood disturbances, altered mood reappears regularly in later chapters given its role in so many of the presenting problems discussed.

CHAPTER 5

KEY TERMS

Acedia
Adaptationist models
Anaclitic depression
Anticonvulsants
Antidepressants
Attachment-based family therapy
Behavioral activation
Benzodiazepines
Bereavement exclusion
Bipolar affective disorder
Bipolar I disorder
Bipolar II disorder
Black box warning
Candidate gene studies
Circadian rhythms
Cognitive triad
Cortisol
Cyclothymic disorder
Dark therapy
Deep brain stimulation (DBS)
Depression
Depressive episode
Discontinuation syndrome
Disruptive mood dysregulation disorder (DMDD)
Dynamic interpersonal therapy (DIT)
Dysregulation models
Dysthymia

Emotion-focused therapy (EFT)
Endocrine system
Endogenous depression
Exogenous depression
Family-focused therapy (FFT)
Frontal lobe
Glutamate hypothesis of depression
Grandiosity
Hopelessness theory
Hormones
Hypomanic episode
Hypothalamic-pituitary-adrenal (HPA) axis
Interpersonal and social rhythm therapy (IPSRT)
Interpersonal therapy (IPT)
Ketamine
Learned helplessness
Light therapy
Lithium
Major depressive disorder (MDD)
Mania
Manic episode
MAO inhibitors (MAOIs)
Mindfulness training
Mindfulness-based cognitive therapy (MBCT)
Mixed episode

Monoamine hypothesis
Monoamine oxidase (MAO)
Mood stabilizers
Neurasthenia
Nonsteroidal anti-inflammatory drugs (NSAIDs)
Persistent depressive disorder (PDD)
Postpartum depression
Premenstrual dysphoric disorder (PMDD)
Problem-solving therapy
Reaching Out About Depression (ROAD)
Recurrent depressive disorder
Rhodiola rosea
Seasonal affective disorder (SAD)
Selective serotonin reuptake inhibitors (SSRIs)
Serotonin and norepinephrine reuptake inhibitors (SNRIs)
Short-term psychoanalytic supportive therapy (SPST)
Silencing the self (STS) theory
Single episode depressive disorder
St. John's wort
Transcranial magnetic stimulation (TMS)
Tricyclics

Full definitions of the terms listed above can be found in the end-of-book glossary on p. 533.

 Go to the companion website, www.macmillanihe.com/raskin-abnormal-psych, to access a study guide, multiple choice and flashcard quizzes for this chapter, and other useful learning aids.

CHAPTER 6
ANXIETY, OBSESSIONS, AND COMPULSIONS

6.1 OVERVIEW

 LEARNING OBJECTIVES

After reading this chapter, you should be able to:

1. Distinguish anxiety from fear and obsessions from compulsions.
2. Define and critique the major anxiety and obsessive-compulsive disorders contained in the *DSM* and *ICD*.
3. Summarize historical perspectives on anxiety, obsessions, and compulsions.
4. Outline and appraise biological perspectives on anxiety, obsessions, and compulsions—including neurochemical conceptions and interventions, brain structure hypotheses, genetic and evolutionary explanations, and the suspected roles of inflammation and the gut.
5. Distinguish and evaluate psychodynamic, cognitive-behavioral, and humanistic approaches to anxiety, obsessions, and compulsions.
6. Explain and critique sociocultural accounts of and interventions for anxiety, obsessions, and compulsions—including the roles of culture, economics, gender, stigma, expressed emotion, accommodation, and family systems.

GETTING STARTED: ANXIETY, FEAR, OBSESSIONS, AND COMPULSIONS

CASE EXAMPLES

The Steadman family consists of Theresa, 35; her husband Gary, 36; and their daughter Tammy, 8.

Theresa Steadman

Theresa has a long history of worrying about things. She feels anxious almost every day, but usually can't pinpoint specific concerns that worry her. In addition to feeling generally anxious most of the time, Theresa has recently become nervous about speaking in front of groups—a real problem for her given that she is a pharmaceutical representative who often gives presentations to health professionals about new drugs on the market.

Tammy Steadman

Theresa and Gary's 8-year-old daughter, Tammy, also has been experiencing a lot of anxiety of late. Over the last few months, she has begun to fret whenever her parents leave for work, often crying and expressing worry about when she will get to see them again. She often gets so emotionally upset that her parents let her miss school and instead take her to work with them.

Gary Steadman

Finally, Gary is facing challenges these days, too. He has a lot of little rituals that he needs to complete before leaving the house in the morning—such as repeatedly making sure the gas on the stove is turned off and the security alarm on the house is properly programmed. If he doesn't sufficiently attend to these tasks, he feels extremely anxious and cannot stop worrying. He also is highly anxious about dirt and repeatedly washes his hands throughout the day. Gary's rituals have been taking up more and more of his time lately, to such an extent that his boss is complaining about how often Gary is late for work.

Gary and Theresa decide that maybe it is time for them and Tammy to seek professional help for their problems.

Defining Anxiety, Fear, Obsessions, and Compulsions

Anxiety and Fear

This chapter focuses on anxiety, obsessions, and compulsions. The American Psychological Association defines anxiety as "an emotion characterized by feelings of tension, worried thoughts and physical changes like increased blood pressure" (American Psychological Association, n.d.-a, para. 1). Those experiencing anxiety worry a lot and feel fear, uneasiness, or dread (A. A. Shah & Han, 2015). While everyone worries sometimes, those experiencing intense anxiety find it very difficult to function.

Theresa and Tammy
Theresa and her daughter Tammy are both facing debilitating feelings of anxiety.

CASE EXAMPLES

To what extent is anxiety a unitary thing versus something that should be divided into different types? This question has long been debated, as "some researchers emphasize the similarities of all anxieties and postulate the unity of all anxiety disorders. Others stress the differences between different kinds of anxiety, positing several distinct disorders, each with its own etiology, phenomenology, and treatment" (I. M. Marks & Nesse, 1994, p. 249). In keeping with the latter view, many clinicians and researchers distinguish anxiety from fear. Fear is defined as a basic emotion in response to something perceived as dangerous; it has distinct physiological symptoms that are universal, automatic, and brief. Anxiety, by contrast, is viewed as involving cognitive appraisals related to more basic fear responses. To better illustrate this, phobias are often viewed as fear-based problems (there's something specific that causes an immediate fear reaction) compared to generalized anxiety (in which the person's thoughts about a variety of life situations lead to pervasive and global feelings of unease). Because they involve thinking and reflection, anxiety reactions are often considered less biologically "hard-wired" than fear reactions (Hofmann, Moscovitch, & Heinrichs, 2002).

CHAPTER 6

Obsessions and Compulsions

Sometimes fear and anxiety are accompanied by obsessions and compulsions. Obsessions are persistent thoughts, images, or urges that are hard to dismiss or stop thinking about. Compulsions, on the other hand, are behaviors or mental acts that a person feels driven to perform, often in response to obsessions. One way to keep the difference between them straight is to remember that obsessions are thoughts and compulsions are actions.

Gary
Gary's endless ruminating about whether the stove is off or the security system is properly programmed exemplify obsessional thinking. His repeated checking the stove and reprograming the security keypad constitute compulsive behavior.

CASE EXAMPLES

Most of us know what it's like to experience anxiety or to occasionally obsess or get compulsive about certain issues. After all, anxiety is highly common in the Western world. In fact, one estimate contends that nearly 30 million Americans will meet the diagnostic criteria for an anxiety disorder at some point in their lives (A. A. Shah & Han, 2015). However, as with all the presenting problems discussed in this text, there are many perspectives on anxiety, obsessions, and compulsions. This chapter reviews some of them.

A Caveat: We All Feel Anxious Sometimes

Given how many people qualify for a diagnosis, it suffices to say that anxiety is a common human response to challenging circumstances. We all have experienced it and know that it can motivate us. Without anxiety, you might not have read this chapter by the date your instructor told you to! You also might not work so hard to do well in your exams without anxiety to spur you on. Yet how much anxiety is too much? When does it become a problem? Is it primarily due to biological, psychological, or sociocultural causes? Because anxiety is so prevalent a problem in the modern world, answering these questions definitively remains a challenge. Before we delve into these issues, check out the "Try It Yourself" box for information on several self-assessments for anxiety.

Repetitive handwashing associated with an irresistible urge to wash one's hands is an example of a compulsion.
Source: Getty

TRY IT YOURSELF

How Anxious Are You?

Many self-assessments have been developed to assess levels of anxiety (Julian, 2011). Most of these instruments can be completed and scored quickly. Some are even free to complete online. While anxiety self-assessments shouldn't be used to make diagnoses (Julian, 2011), people scoring as highly anxious on these scales might consider whether professional help could be beneficial. Below we identify three of the more well-known anxiety self-assessments.

» **Zung Self-Rating Anxiety Scale (SAS):** This scale, first published in the early 1970s, remains widely used today (Zung, 1971). An auto-scoring version is available online at https://psychology-tools.com/zung-anxiety-scale/

» **Generalized Anxiety Disorder Assessment (GAD-7):** This scale was developed by *DSM-III* editor Robert Spitzer and colleagues to assess generalized anxiety symptoms (Spitzer, Kroenke, Williams, & Löwe, 2006). An auto-scoring version is available online at https://patient.info/doctor/generalised-anxiety-disorder-assessment-gad-7

» **Beck Anxiety Inventory (BAI):** This 21-scale inventory was developed by Aaron Beck and colleagues in the 1980s (A. T. Beck, Epstein, Brown, & Steer, 1988). This inventory isn't available for free online, but you can learn a lot about it by doing an online search.

6.2 *DSM* AND *ICD* PERSPECTIVES

The *DSM-5* contains separate chapters titled "Anxiety Disorders" and "Obsessive-Compulsive and Related Disorders." The *ICD-11* is similarly organized, with sections on "Anxiety and Fear-Related Disorders" and "Obsessive-Compulsive or Related Disorders." By comparison, the *ICD-10* includes anxiety and obsessive-compulsive disorders under the broader heading of "Anxiety, Dissociative, Stress-Related, Somatoform and other Nonpsychotic Mental Disorders."

ANXIETY DISORDERS

Specific Phobia

When most of us use the word "phobia," we are describing what *DSM-5*, *ICD-10*, and *ICD-11* categorize as **specific phobia**, namely fear associated with a given object or situation (see Diagnostic Box 6.1). The fear is focused, with the phobic individual afraid of something in particular—such as heights, flying, enclosed spaces, a kind of animal, getting an injection, or going to the dentist. The feared object or situation is actively avoided and provokes immediate anxiety, but when the person isn't near the phobic object, anxiety isn't present.

Diagnostic Box 6.1 Specific Phobia

DSM-5
- Disproportionate fear and avoidance of a specific object or situation that occurs upon exposure to it.
- The phobic response persists for at least six months.

Based on American Psychiatric Association, 2013b, pp. 197–198

ICD-10
- Fear and avoidance of a specific object or situation that occurs upon exposure to it.
- Symptoms are expressions of anxiety, which is restricted to the phobic object or situation.

Based on World Health Organization, 1992, p. 114

ICD-11
- Disproportionate fear and avoidance of a specific object or situation that occurs upon exposure to it.
- The phobic response persists for at least several months.

Based on https://gcp.network/en/private/icd-11-guidelines/grouping

The *DSM-5* estimates prevalence rates between 6%–9% in the U.S. and Europe, but only 2%–4% in Asia, Africa, and Latin America. Females are two times as likely as males to experience specific phobias. Teens have the highest prevalence (16%) and older people the lowest (only 3%–5%). Specific phobias often show comorbidity (i.e., co-occur) with various other anxiety disorders. Older adults with specific phobias are also often diagnosed with depression (see Chapter 5), which is consistently comorbid with anxiety and related problems.

Social Anxiety Disorder (Social Phobia)

Social anxiety disorder (social phobia) is diagnosed in people who become anxious and fear embarrassing or humiliating themselves in social situations where they might be scrutinized—such as when meeting people, having social conversations, eating in a restaurant, asking someone on a date, or making a speech. *ICD-10* still uses the term social phobia, but the *DSM-5* and *ICD-11* changed the name to social anxiety disorder. For more on diagnosing this disorder, see Diagnostic Box 6.2.

DSM-5 reports that prevalence rates are higher in younger people and, geographically, are notably higher in the U.S. (7%) than Europe (2.3%) and the rest of the world. Women tend to experience social anxiety more than men, although in clinical samples (those diagnosed with other mental disorders) this trend disappears or reverses. Social anxiety disorder diagnoses tend to be comorbid with depression, substance use, and various other anxiety disorders.

People diagnosed with social anxiety disorder (social phobia) become extremely anxious in social situations where they might be scrutinized—such as making a speech.
Source: © Stockbyte Royalty Free Photos

CHAPTER 6

Diagnostic Box 6.2 Social Anxiety Disorder (Social Phobia)

DSM-5
- Disproportionate fear and avoidance of social situation(s) where the person might be scrutinized.
- Overly concerned about behaving anxiously and being evaluated negatively for it.
- Symptoms last at least six months.

Based on American Psychiatric Association, 2013b, pp. 202–203

ICD-10
- Disproportionate fear and avoidance of small groups (rather than crowds) where the person might be scrutinized.
- Symptoms are expressions of anxiety, which is restricted to the social situation.

Based on World Health Organization, 1992, pp. 113–114

ICD-11
- Disproportionate fear and avoidance of social situation(s) where the person might be scrutinized.
- Overly concerned about behaving anxiously and being evaluated negatively for it.
- Symptoms last at least several months.

Based on https://gcp.network/en/private/icd-11-guidelines/grouping

Panic Disorder

Panic disorder is characterized by recurrent and unexpected panic attacks. A **panic attack** is an intense anxiety reaction that comes on abruptly. Its symptoms include things like a pounding heart, trembling, shortness of breath, chest pain, nausea, dizziness, feeling chilled or hot, tingling sensations, and detachment from oneself or the world. Those experiencing panic attacks often feel like they are dying; therefore it isn't surprising that panic attacks can be mistaken as heart attacks, strokes, or other sudden life-ending events. Unfortunately, the term "panic attack" has entered our everyday vocabulary in a way that doesn't fit with the *DSM* and *ICD* definitions of the term. It is common to hear students describe mild anxiety using the term "panic attack," but a genuine panic attack is more than just run of the mill worry. It is severe, debilitating, and terrifying.

It's worth noting that panic attacks can occur in people who don't qualify for a panic disorder diagnosis. Sometimes people have panic attacks in response to very specific and known events. For example, an intense specific phobia reaction could develop into a full-blown panic attack. Only when the attacks are recurrent (they happen repeatedly) and unexpected (the person has no idea when or why they occur) is panic disorder diagnosed. Further, to be diagnosed with panic disorder there must be persistent worry (at least a month, according to *DSM-5*) about having more panic attacks, during which behavior is changed and situations avoided to prevent further attacks (see Diagnostic Box 6.3).

Diagnostic Box 6.3 Panic Disorder

DSM-5
- Regular and unanticipated panic attacks.
- Following one or more of these attacks, either or both these symptoms: (a) one month or longer of worrying about further panic attacks, or (b) dysfunctional alteration of behavior in response to the attacks (e.g., avoiding novel situations).

Based on American Psychiatric Association, 2013b, pp. 208–209

ICD-10
- Severe and unpredictable panic not tied to specific circumstances or situations.
- Within roughly one month, panic attacks in random situations where there is no danger.
- No anxiety between attacks, other than worry about additional attacks.

Based on World Health Organization, 1992, p. 115

ICD-11
- Regular and unanticipated panic attacks.
- Following one or more of these attacks, either or both these symptoms: (a) worry about further panic attacks or their potentially negative significance, or (b) attempts to avoid additional attacks (e.g., only going out if accompanied by a friend).

Based on https://gcp.network/en/private/icd-11-guidelines/grouping

According to *DSM-5*, panic disorder prevalence rates in the U.S. and Europe are about 2%–3%, but only 0.1%–0.8% in Asia, Africa, and Latin America. As with specific phobia, females get diagnosed twice as often as males. Onset usually occurs in the early- to mid-20s. Anywhere between 10%–65% of people diagnosed with panic disorder also receive a depression diagnosis.

Agoraphobia

Agoraphobia literally means "fear of the marketplace" and in the *DSM* and *ICD* refers to a diagnosis given to people who dread being in situations where they may have an intense and embarrassing fear reaction and won't be able to escape. Those with agoraphobia may worry about using public transportation, going to the movies, or being in a crowd because they might experience anxiety or a panic attack and be unable to flee the situation easily or without feeling humiliated. Because panic attacks often occur in people with agoraphobia, panic disorder and agoraphobia are often diagnosed simultaneously. The *ICD-10* includes specific diagnostic codes for agoraphobia without panic disorder and agoraphobia with panic disorder. *DSM-5* and *ICD-11* don't include these codes and instead instruct clinicians to simply diagnose panic disorder and agoraphobia separately in those who fit both diagnoses (see Diagnostic Box 6.4).

Diagnostic Box 6.4 Diagnosing Agoraphobia

DSM-5
- Disproportionate fear and avoidance of two of these: (1) public transportation, (2) open spaces like parking lots, public markets, and bridges, (3) enclosed spaces like theaters or stores, (4) crowds or lines, (5) being away from home by oneself.
- These situations are feared or avoided because escape might not be possible and panic or other embarrassing anxiety symptoms might ensue.
- Feared situations typically provoke fear and anxiety and are avoided or anxiously tolerated.
- Symptoms last at least six months.

Based on American Psychiatric Association, 2013b, pp. 217–218

ICD-10
- Disproportionate fear and avoidance of at least two of these: open or public spaces, crowds, travelling by oneself, or being away from home.
- Avoidance of the feared situations is a main feature; symptoms are expressions of anxiety.

Based on World Health Organization, 1992, pp. 112–113

ICD-11
- Disproportionate fear and avoidance of: (1) public transportation, (2) open spaces like parking lots, public markets, and bridges, (3) enclosed spaces like theaters or stores, (4) crowds or lines, (5) being away from home by oneself.
- These situations are feared or avoided because escape might not be possible and panic or other embarrassing anxiety symptoms might ensue.
- Feared situations typically provoke fear and anxiety and are avoided or anxiously tolerated.
- Symptoms last at least several months.

Based on https://gcp.network/en/private/icd-11-guidelines/grouping

DSM-5 indicates that approximately 1.7% of adolescents and adults meet criteria for agoraphobia, with females twice as likely to receive a diagnosis as males. There don't seem to be cultural differences in prevalence rates. The diagnosis is rare in older adults, with only 0.4% estimated to qualify. Other anxiety disorders, depression, posttraumatic stress, and alcohol use problems often co-occur among people diagnosed with agoraphobia.

Agoraphobia is diagnosed in people who dread having an embarrassing fear reaction in public. Thus, they often avoid public spaces.
Source: iStock.com/martin-dm

Generalized Anxiety Disorder

Whereas specific phobias and social anxiety disorder involve focused anxiety that occurs in very particular circumstances, generalized anxiety disorder (GAD) is exemplified by excessive and consistent worry that is global rather than specific. People who qualify for this diagnosis experience persistent anxiety that isn't associated with anything in particular; they are just continually anxious in general (see Diagnostic Box 6.5 or full criteria/guidelines in Chapter 3). *ICD-10* and *ICD-11* simply indicate that symptoms must continue for several months, but *DSM-5* stipulates a minimum of six months before a diagnosis can be made.

The *DSM-5* reports U.S. prevalence rates of 0.9% among teens and 2.9% among adults. By comparison, it estimates prevalence rates in the rest of the world range from 0.4% to 3.6%. As with many of the other anxiety disorders, generalized anxiety disorder is twice as common in females compared to males.

Diagnostic Box 6.5 Generalized Anxiety Disorder

DSM-5
- Undue, hard to control, and ongoing anxiety and worry that occurs almost every day.
- Three or more of these symptoms: (1) restlessness, (2) easily tired, (3) trouble concentrating, (4) irritability, (5) muscle tension, (6) sleep difficulties.
- Symptoms last at least six months.

Based on American Psychiatric Association, 2013b, p. 222

ICD-10
- Anxiety, apprehension, tension, and physiological indicators (gastrointestinal problems, heart racing, sweating, trembling, dry mouth) most days.
- Symptoms last for a few weeks at a time and typically for several months.

Based on World Health Organization, 1992, pp. 115–116

ICD-11
- General worry or "free floating" anxiety about several areas of life that is not restricted to specific situations.
- Three or more of these symptoms: (1) restlessness, (2) physiological indicators (gastrointestinal problems, heart racing, sweating, trembling, dry mouth), (3) trouble concentrating, (4) irritability, (5) muscle tension, (6) sleep difficulties.
- Symptoms last for at least several months.

Based on https://gcp.network/en/private/icd-11-guidelines/grouping

Separation Anxiety Disorder

Those diagnosed with separation anxiety disorder show excessive anxiety about potentially being separated from people they are attached to. The *DSM-5* and *ICD-11* no longer limit this disorder to children, but the *ICD-10* does—calling it "separation anxiety disorder of childhood." Regardless, *DSM-5* notes that prevalence of this presenting problem is much higher in children (roughly 4%) than in teens (1.6%) and adults (0.9%–1.9%). Specific phobia and generalized anxiety are often comorbid with separation anxiety. See Diagnostic Box 6.6 for criteria and guidelines.

Diagnostic Box 6.6 Separation Anxiety Disorder

DSM-5
- Disproportionate worry about being separated from or losing important attachment figures—usually parents or close relatives in children and significant others or children in adults.
- Symptoms last at least four weeks in children and usually six months in adults.

Based on American Psychiatric Association, 2013b, pp. 190–191

ICD-10
- Called "separation anxiety disorder of childhood."
- Disproportionate worry about being separated from or losing important attachment figures, usually parents or close relatives.

Based on World Health Organization, 1992, pp. 214–215

ICD-11
- Disproportionate worry about being separated from or losing important attachment figures—usually parents or close relatives in children and significant others or children in adults.
- Symptoms last at least several months.

Based on https://gcp.network/en/private/icd-11-guidelines/grouping

Selective Mutism

Selective mutism is diagnosed mainly in children who consistently fail to speak in social situations where doing so is expected (see Diagnostic Box 6.7). It used to be called *elective mutism* (a name still listed in the *ICD-10*), which implied choice in refusing to speak. By comparison, the name "selective mutism" (used in both *DSM-5* and *ICD-11*) doesn't assume the child purposely chooses not to speak, but instead merely indicates that the child fails to speak in certain situations. Note, however, that the failure to speak is not due to inability. For example, the child might speak at home to parents and grandparents, but not in school or with strangers. *DSM-5* notes that few prevalence studies have been done, but that selective mutism is quite rare, occurring in just 0.03% to 1% of children. Both *DSM-5* and *ICD-10* indicate selective mutism occurs about equally in boys and girls.

Diagnostic Box 6.7 Diagnosing Selective Mutism

DSM-5 and ICD-11
- Not speaking when socially expected, even though speaks in other situations.
- Failure to speak not due to inability or lack of comfort speaking the language required.
- Interferes with achievement at school or work.
- Symptoms last at least one month (excluding the first month of school).

Based on American Psychiatric Association, 2013b, p. 195; and https://gcp.network/en/private/icd-11-guidelines/grouping

ICD-10
- Called "elective mutism," and indicates this includes "selective mutism."
- Selective speaking based on emotional response to situation; child speaks in some situations, not others.

Based on World Health Organization, 1992, p. 218

OBSESSIVE-COMPULSIVE AND RELATED DISORDERS

Obsessive-Compulsive Disorder

Obsessive-compulsive disorder (OCD) is marked by the presence of obsessions and compulsions. People with an OCD diagnosis spend inordinate amounts of time engaging in obsessive thinking and compulsive behavior. While for most disorders the *DSM-5* lists how long symptoms must last, it doesn't for OCD. Neither does the *ICD-11*. However, the *ICD-10*, which often relies on clinician judgment over specific symptom durations, specifies that symptoms must be present for at least two weeks. For more, see Diagnostic Box 6.8.

Diagnostic Box 6.8 Obsessive-Compulsive Disorder

DSM-5
- Obsessions and/or compulsions.
  - *Obsessions* are persistent, distressing, invasive, and unwelcome thoughts, impulses, or images that are difficult to ignore or eliminate; they are often counteracted by engaging in compulsions.
  - *Compulsions* are recurring behaviors or mental acts that the person feels compelled to engage in to decrease anxiety associated with obsessions (even though doing so has no effect).
- The obsessions and compulsions take up enormous amounts of time.

Based on American Psychiatric Association, 2013b, p. 237

ICD-10
- Obsessional thoughts and/or compulsive acts.
  - *Obsessional thoughts* are ideas, urges, or images that repeatedly run through the individual's mind.
  - *Compulsive acts* are ritualistic behaviors the person feels driven to engage in to ward off harm, though the person does not especially enjoy the acts and usually realizes they have no effect.
- Obsessive thoughts and compulsive acts must be present most days for at least two weeks.

Based on World Health Organization, 1992, p. 117

ICD-11
- Obsessions or compulsions, usually both.
  - *Obsessions* are repeated and recurring thoughts, impulses, or images that are unwanted, intrusive, and associated with anxiety; they are often counteracted by engaging in compulsions.
  - *Compulsions* are recurring behaviors or mental acts that the person feels compelled to engage in to decrease anxiety associated with obsessions (even though doing so has no effect).
- The obsessions and compulsions take up enormous amounts of time.

Based on https://gcp.network/en/private/icd-11-guidelines/grouping

DSM-5 estimates that 1.2% of people in the U.S. meet criteria for OCD; it gives a prevalence range of 1.1%– 1.8% for the rest of the world. Females are believed to develop OCD symptoms slightly more often than males, but males develop OCD in childhood more than females. Average age of onset in the U.S. is thought to be 19.5 years old, but almost 25% of male cases develop before age 10. OCD is highly comorbid with anxiety disorders, mood disorders, and eating disorders. Many people with OCD (up to 30%) also qualify for a tic disorder (see Chapter 14).

Other Obsessive-Compulsive Related Disorders

DSM-5 and *ICD-11* list several other OCD-related diagnostic categories. *ICD-10* includes most of these problems too, though not necessarily as their own distinct disorders or as OCD-related diagnoses. People diagnosed with **body dysmorphic disorder (BDD)** display obsessional preoccupation with one or more perceived physical flaws in their appearance. As examples, they might think their nose is too big, their ears are lopsided, their chin is shaped funny, or their hips are too wide. Some people even worry about not being muscular enough, a form of BDD for which the *DSM-5* uses the specifier "with muscle dysmorphia." Unlike the *DSM-5* and *ICD-11*, which include BDD as a type of obsessive-compulsive disorder, the *ICD-10* lists BDD as a variant of hypochondriasis, which the *DSM-5* now calls illness anxiety disorder; for more on hypochondriasis and illness anxiety disorder, see Chapter 8.

Hoarding disorder is a *DSM-5* and *ICD-11* diagnosis given to people who have a hard time giving up possessions, even when they have too many or the possessions are no longer useful or valuable. As a result, living space becomes cluttered and congested. Hoarding disorder has no equivalent in the *ICD-10*. Thus, even though *DSM-5* lists it as a stand-alone disorder, it is currently coded in *DSM-5* using the *ICD-10* code for OCD— so clinicians diagnosing it are technically diagnosing OCD. In the revamped *ICD-11* coding system, hoarding disorder has its very own code for the first time.

Trichotillomania (hair-pulling disorder) describes those who compulsively pull out their own hair. It is considered an impulse-control disorder in *ICD-10*, but as an OCD-related disorder in *DSM-5* and *ICD-11*. Finally, **excoriation (skin-picking disorder)** involves compulsive picking at the skin, resulting in lesions. *DSM-5* and *ICD-11* classify it as an OCD-related disorder, but in *ICD-10* "neurotic excoriation" is merely listed under "other disorders of skin and subcutaneous tissue, not elsewhere classified." See Diagnostic Box 6.9 for details about other OCD-related disorders.

When obsessions and compulsions focus on one or more perceived physical flaws, body dysmorphic disorder (BDD) may be diagnosed.
Source: ImageSource

CHAPTER 6

Diagnostic Box 6.9 Other Obsessive-Compulsive Related Disorders

Body dysmorphic disorder (BDD)
- **DSM-5**: Excessive focus on at least one perceived physical defect or flaw that is not noticeable or significant. Includes (a) repetitive behaviors like checking appearance, grooming excessively, picking at skin, or asking to be reassured, or (b) mental acts like comparing appearance to others.
Based on American Psychiatric Association, 2013b, pp. 242–243
- **ICD-10**: Listed as a type of *hypochondriacal disorder*.
Based on World Health Organization, 1992, p. 131
- **ICD-11**: Excessive focus on at least one perceived physical defect or flaw that is not noticeable or significant. Characterized by self-consciousness and concern about being judged. Person repeatedly checks appearance, tries to hide perceived flaws, or avoids social situations.
Based on https://icd.who.int/browse11/l-m/en

Hoarding disorder
- **DSM-5**: Anxiety and worry about disposing of possessions, even ones no longer of value; results in accumulating possessions that clutter living space.
Based on American Psychiatric Association, 2013b, p. 247
- **ICD-10**: No hoarding disorder in *ICD-10*.
- **ICD-11**: Excessive collection of possessions and distress over getting rid of them due to their emotional, not monetary, value; leads to cluttered and/or dangerous living space.
Based on https://icd.who.int/browse11/l-m/en

Trichotillomania (hair-pulling disorder)
- **DSM-5**: Frequent pulling out of one's own hair (causing hair loss) with ongoing efforts to stop.
Based on American Psychiatric Association, 2013b, p. 251
- **ICD-10**: Hair loss due to failure to resist urge to pull out hairs; feelings of tension before hair-pulling, followed by relief or satisfaction afterwards.
Based on World Health Organization, 1992, pp. 167–168
- **ICD-11**: Regular pulling of one's own hair, leading to hair loss; there are unsuccessful attempts to stop.
Based on https://icd.who.int/browse11/l-m/en

Excoriation (skin-picking disorder)
- **DSM-5**: Frequent skin picking leading to injuries accompanied by ongoing efforts to stop.
Based on American Psychiatric Association, 2013b, p. 254
- **ICD-10**: Listed as "neurotic excoriation" under "other disorders of skin and subcutaneous tissue, not elsewhere classified."
Based on World Health Organization, 1992, p. 235
- **ICD-11**: Regular picking at one's skin, leading to injuries; one specific subtype focuses on recurrent picking at acne pimples.
Based on https://icd.who.int/browse11/l-m/en

EVALUATING *DSM* AND *ICD* PERSPECTIVES

Diagnostic Reliability

The *DSM-5* diagnostic reliability trials found questionable reliability for generalized anxiety disorder (Regier et al., 2013). This result suggests that clinicians have a hard time agreeing when someone should be diagnosed with generalized anxiety. This shouldn't be surprising, as generalized anxiety is (by its very definition) somewhat broad; getting people to agree on how much amorphous anxiety is too much has proved challenging. The field trials also found unacceptable reliability for a proposed new diagnosis called mixed anxiety and depressive disorder, reserved for people who display symptoms of both depression and anxiety for two weeks or more, but whose symptoms don't qualify them for other mood or anxiety disorders. This disorder wasn't included in the *DSM-5* due to its poor showing in reliability trials—clinicians couldn't reliably distinguish it from major depressive disorder (MDD) or generalized anxiety disorder (Regier et al., 2013). However, mixed anxiety and depressive disorder does appear in *ICD-11* (as a mood, not anxiety, disorder). Difficulties distinguishing anxiety from depression are revisited throughout the chapter. Meanwhile, several other *DSM-5* controversies are worth mentioning.

Changes to Anxiety Disorders

A variety of changes were made to the anxiety disorders in *DSM-5* and *ICD-11*. Some engendered controversy. A few examples are:

» In *DSM-5*, the anxiety disorders section was reorganized, with several disorders relocated elsewhere. Posttraumatic stress disorder (PTSD) and acute stress disorder (see Chapter 7) were moved to a new "trauma and stressor-related disorders" section, while OCD was moved to the "obsessive-compulsive and related disorders" section. Some objected to this, arguing that there was insufficient evidence for the reorganization given that anxiety is central to all these disorders (Abramowitz & Jacoby, 2014; L. A. Zoellner, Rothbaum, & Feeny, 2011). However, a similar reorganization was incorporated into *ICD-11*.

» Panic disorder and agoraphobia are separated in *DSM-5* and *ICD-11*, whereas in *ICD-10* and the now defunct *DSM-IV* "agoraphobia with panic disorder" constitutes its own diagnostic category. Some believe that separating these disorders makes it easier to meet the criteria for either one (Asmundson, Taylor, & Smits, 2014). The potential advantage is that more people will qualify for services, while the disadvantage is that people with mild symptoms may be diagnosed unnecessarily. Concern over inflated diagnostic rates is somewhat offset because *DSM-5*'s agoraphobia criteria now require that symptoms last for six months (Asmundson et al., 2014). The *ICD-11* is less specific, merely requiring symptoms to last "several" months.

» Comorbidity is a challenge facing diagnoses such as generalized anxiety disorder, OCD, and hoarding disorder (Abramowitz & Jacoby, 2014; R. O. Frost, Steketee, & Tolin, 2011; D. Nutt, Argyropoulos, Hood, & Potokar, 2006; Pertusa et al., 2008). While it is possible that these diagnoses are distinct from those with which they co-occur, too much comorbidity can raise reliability and validity concerns.

One proposed *DSM-5* change that wasn't made would have shortened the minimum duration of symptoms for generalized anxiety disorder from six months to three months. This potential revision was hotly debated (G. Andrews & Hobbs, 2010), but ultimately rejected. The hullabaloo over it highlights a major concern of critics, who felt that *DSM-5* authors were trying to lower diagnostic thresholds to qualify more people for diagnoses (Kamens, Elkins, & Robbins, 2017). The *ICD-11* leaves more to clinician judgment, merely indicating that GAD symptoms must last "at least several months" (World Health Organization, 2018a).

6.3 HISTORICAL PERSPECTIVES

Although anxiety has been talked about throughout history, it is only over the past 40–50 years that such a firm distinction between anxiety and other presenting issues—depression, in particular—has been drawn (A. V. Horwitz, 2013). Before that, it was common for anxiety and depression to be considered as different aspects of the same problem (Gee, Hood, & Antony, 2013). The complex relationship between anxiety and depression, already mentioned when discussing their diagnostic comorbidity, is a recurring theme in this chapter.

ANCIENT GREECE THROUGH THE RENAISSANCE

As with many forms of emotional distress, the ancient Greeks attributed anxiety to imbalances in bodily humors (Gee et al., 2013; A. V. Horwitz, 2013). This early physiological view remained influential until the Renaissance (Gee et al., 2013). Courage (as opposed to fear and anxiety) was considered a moral virtue among the Greeks and its development was instilled, but only in men: "Men act bravely, not because they are compelled to but because it is noble for them to do so and they have developed this nobility. Women were of such low social status that such considerations did not apply to them" (A. V. Horwitz, 2013, p. 31). This nicely illustrates how attitudes about anxiety have been influenced by gender biases throughout history.

During the middle ages, humoral theory remained influential, but with the rise of Christianity, more spiritual explanations of anxiety became prominent. Faith in the teachings of Jesus were seen as a remedy, but Christian dogma could also produce a great deal of anxiety: "Fear of perpetual damnation in the afterlife was a particular source of terror that persisted through the Reformation in the sixteenth century" (A. V. Horwitz, 2013, p. 37). Spiritual and medical explanations of anxiety existed side by side throughout this period. As alluded to above, while anxiety was discussed from ancient Greek times through the middle ages, Renaissance, and into the 19th century, it was not usually considered its own distinct disorder (M. H. Stone, 2010): "Before the 19th century, symptoms of anxiety were grouped with the melancholic states (e.g., depression) or considered to be the cause of other mental disorders, including insanity; however, rarely was anxiety considered a disease in its own right" (Gee et al., 2013, p. 31).

18TH THROUGH 20TH CENTURIES

The view of anxiety as a form of depression began to change over the course of the 18th century as it increasingly was distinguished from melancholia (a historical precursor to modern notions of depression; see Chapter 5) and identified as a key component of the "nervous disorders" (A. V. Horwitz, 2013; M. H. Stone, 2010). This trend continued into the 19th century, with the medical model of anxiety eclipsing moral and religious perspectives. However, depression and anxiety still were more interconnected in 19th-century diagnostic categories than they are today. Neurasthenia (previously discussed in Chapter 5) was commonly diagnosed in people exhibiting both sadness and anxiety. This diagnosis was much broader than today's more focused *DSM* and *ICD* anxiety disorders (M. H. Stone, 2010):

> *Neurasthenics complained of numerous yet amorphous physical pains, including headache, stomachache, back pain, fatigue, skin rashes, insomnia, asthma, and poor general health. ... Although symptoms of anxiety were not among the most prominent aspects of neurasthenia, irrational concerns, various phobias, and fears of contamination were explicitly part of this condition. (A. V. Horwitz, 2013, p. 65)*

As the 19th and early 20th centuries unfolded, anxiety continued to slowly become more clearly distinguished in its own right—even though the somewhat vague neurasthenia remained a popular catch-all diagnosis (A. V. Horwitz, 2013; R. B. Miller, 2015; M. H. Stone, 2010). For example, while obsessions and compulsions have been discussed for centuries, it wasn't until the 1830s that Jean-Étienne-Dominique Esquirol (the early French alienist whose role in the development of moral therapy was discussed in Chapter 1) provided the first detailed clinical descriptions of patients who today would be diagnosed with OCD: "Esquirol described a 34-year-old woman who feared retaining money in her hands when giving change to a customer, and who would vigorously shake her hands despite not having touched anything, in order to make sure nothing remained on her hands" (Gee et al., 2013). Later, the French neurologist Edouard Brissaud (1852–1909) described "paroxystic anxiety," which today we would call a panic attack. Similarly, in 1901 another Frenchman—the psychiatrist Paul Hartenberg (1871–1949)—offered an early account of social phobia (Gee et al., 2013). He observed "how the presence of other humans precipitated in some people feelings of intense anguish, sweating, and heart palpitations" (A. V. Horwitz, 2013, p. 70). As one last example, German psychiatrist and neurologist Karl Friedrich Otto Westphal (1833–1890) coined the term "agoraphobia" to describe his male patients who "feared and avoided being alone in wide streets and open space" (Gee et al., 2013, p. 35). He was also the first to distinguish obsessions (recurrent thoughts) from delusions (demonstrably false thoughts) (W. K. Goodman, Grice, Lapidus, & Coffey, 2014).

In the 20th century, the *DSM* eventually reflected the move to distinguish anxiety from other presenting problems. *DSM-I* and *DSM-II* both used the word neurosis, a psychodynamic term with anxiety at its center. However, it was with the appearance of *DSM-III* in 1980—with its strong emphasis on descriptive categories that were diagnostically distinct and aimed for high interrater reliability (refer to Chapter 3)—that anxiety disorders as we now know them became fully differentiated from depression and other issues (A. V. Horwitz, 2013). Some historians and theorists have begun suggesting that this firm cleavage between anxiety and depression might be unwise, as these experiences are often interrelated (A. V. Horwitz, 2013; R. B. Miller, 2015). This perhaps explains the above-mentioned efforts by *DSM-5* and *ICD-11* to develop a mixed anxiety and depression diagnosis (Fawcett, Cameron, & Schatzberg, 2010). Due to poor diagnostic reliability this diagnosis ultimately wasn't added to the *DSM-5* (Regier et al., 2013), but it is in the *ICD-11*. Whether we will eventually return to an approach where anxiety, depression, anger, and other emotions are less differentiated as separate disorders remains unclear, but it seems unlikely in an era that stresses diagnostically discrete categories that can be reliably discerned (A. V. Horwitz, 2013).

6.4 BIOLOGICAL PERSPECTIVES
BRAIN CHEMISTRY PERSPECTIVES
Neurotransmitters and Prescription Drugs for Anxiety

Benzodiazepines and GABA

With their emphasis on neurochemistry, brain chemistry perspectives are intertwined with the use of psychiatric drugs. The drugs used to relieve anxiety are called anxiolytics. Benzodiazepines (introduced in Chapter 5) are probably the most well-known anxiolytic drugs, although antidepressants are used more often to relieve anxiety. Benzodiazepines enhance the ability of gamma-aminobutyric acid (GABA) (the brain's primary inhibitory neurotransmitter; see Chapter 2) to bind with GABA-A receptors in the brain. This slows or stops neurons from firing and is believed to reduce anxiety ("Benzodiazepine Drug Information," n.d.; C. Taylor & Nutt, 2004). Thus, it is sometimes hypothesized that a problem with GABA or its receptors is involved in anxiety disorders (Nuss, 2015). The problem with this theory is that we don't know whether GABA inactivity leads to anxiety or anxiety leads to GABA inactivity. This theory also doesn't account for the role of other neurotransmitters in anxiety. Regardless, benzodiazepines enhance GABA activity.

Benzodiazepines were first introduced in the late 1950s as a safer and less addictive alternative to barbiturates, which we discuss in greater detail in Chapter 11 (A. V. Horwitz, 2013; López-Muñoz, Álamo, & García-García, 2011). Marketed as minor tranquilizers—as opposed to major tranquilizers, another name for antipsychotics (discussed in Chapter 4)—benzodiazepines immediately became very popular, peaking at more than 103 million prescriptions in 1975 (A. V. Horwitz, 2013). Since then, their use has decreased because of concerns that they might be habit forming. Some research suggests that one-fifth to one-quarter of people on them for extended periods show signs of dependency (C. Taylor & Nutt, 2004). Further, when people stop taking them, anxiety often rebounds (Hearon & Otto, 2012). Such findings have resulted in much tighter regulation of the benzodiazepines—the United Nations Commission on Narcotic Drugs, at the request of the World Health Organization, declared them controlled substances in 1984 (López-Muñoz et al., 2011). While some clinicians feel an unfair media campaign was waged against the benzodiazepines (López-Muñoz et al., 2011), the current consensus seems to be that these drugs do pose an addiction risk with some patients—usually those with a history of drug abuse (Hearon & Otto, 2012; Nash & Nutt, 2007; K. R. Tan, Rudolph, & Lüscher, 2011). Additional side effects include memory loss, drowsiness, and impaired balance (C. Taylor & Nutt, 2004). The people who are most likely to receive benzodiazepines today are those diagnosed with generalized anxiety disorder, panic disorder, and social anxiety disorder (Griebel & Holmes, 2013). However, to avoid the potential for dependency, clinicians are advised to only keep patients on these drugs for short periods of time when anxiety is highly intense (C. Taylor & Nutt, 2004). Table 6.1 lists common benzodiazepines.

Table 6.1 Common Benzodiazepines

• Alprazolam (Xanax)	• Flurazepam (Dalmane)
• Bromazepam (Lectopam, Lexotan)	• Lorazepam (Ativan)
• Chlordiazepoxide (Librium)	• Oxazepam (Serax, Serapax)
• Clonazepam (Klonopin, Rivotril)	• Temazepam (Restoril)
• Clorazepate (Tranxene)	• Triazolam (Halcion)
• Diazepam (Valium)	

Antidepressants and Monoamine Neurotransmitters

Antidepressants have overtaken benzodiazepines as the drugs of choice for anxiety. The rationale for prescribing antidepressants is that the same monoamine neurotransmitters implicated in depression (primarily norepinephrine and serotonin) are also associated with anxiety (Nash & Nutt, 2007; A. A. Shah & Han, 2015). SSRI and SNRI antidepressants are considered first-line drug treatments for anxiety, though other antidepressants (tricyclics and MAOIs) are sometimes used too (Griebel & Holmes, 2013; Nash & Nutt, 2007; A. A. Shah & Han, 2015). As discussed in Chapter 5, antidepressants have a variety of unpleasant side effects including impaired sexual performance, weight gain, nausea, and withdrawal-like symptoms when drug use ends (Nash & Nutt, 2007). Therefore, many patients stop taking them. Further, as also noted in Chapter 5, some parents are hesitant to give their children SSRIs due to controversial black box warnings about possible suicidal behavior (R. A. Friedman, 2014; Sparks & Duncan, 2013); this can influence whether children receive SSRIs for anxiety problems such as selective mutism and separation anxiety.

Other Drugs Prescribed as Anxiolytics

Several other drugs are used to relieve anxiety. Buspirone is an anxiolytic drug that affects serotonin levels; it partially inhibits serotonin activity, but overall results in increased serotonin availabilty (Egger & Hebert, 2011). Buspirone doesn't appear to be habit forming like the benzodiazepines, but it takes several weeks to take effect. Further, it doesn't always work that well in patients who previously took benzodiazepines (Nash & Nutt, 2007). In addition to buspirone, numerous other drugs are occasionally used to address anxiety. Antipsychotics (which affect not only dopamine, but also serotonin), beta blockers (blood pressure reducing drugs that block norepinephrine receptors), and anticonvulsants (which enhance GABA activity) are all sometimes prescribed as anxiolytics—though evidence for their effectiveness is mixed or lacking and so they are usually deemed secondary treatments (Nash & Nutt, 2007; C. Taylor & Nutt, 2004).

In addition to the monoamines and the inhibitory neurotransmitter GABA, the excitatory neurotransmitter glutamate is drawing increased attention for its potential role in anxiety (Griebel & Holmes, 2013; A. A. Shah & Han, 2015). The anesthetic drug ketamine (which reduces glutamate levels; see Chapter 5) is being researched as a potential drug treatment for anxiety—just as it is for depression (Griebel & Holmes, 2013). However, its short-lasting effects and its potential as a drug of abuse make ketamine's prospects as a widely prescribed anxiolytic questionable. Despite ongoing research on glutamate's role in anxiety, antidepressants and benzodiazepines remain the main drugs used for anxiety reduction.

Obsessions and Compulsions

SSRIs and Serotonin

Prior to the mid-1970s, OCD was typically considered unresponsive to drug interventions (W. K. Goodman et al., 2014). However, trial-and-error use of antidepressants found them to be helpful in many cases. Therefore, researchers began to hypothesize that serotonin (which is made more available by antidepressants) is implicated in OCD and related disorders (W. K. Goodman et al., 2014). SSRIs are the most common antidepressants used to ameliorate obsessive-compulsive symptoms (Bandelow, Reitt, & Wedekind, 2012; Pittenger & Bloch, 2014; M. T. Williams, Davis, Powers, & Weissflog, 2014). The SSRIs fluvoxamine (Luvox), fluoxetine (Prozac), sertraline (Zoloft), and paroxetine (Paxil) are frequently prescribed (M. T. Williams et al., 2014). SSRIs are also used for OCD-related problems such as body dysmorphia and hair pulling (Chamberlain, Odlaug, Boulougouris, Fineberg, & Grant, 2009; Fang, Matheny, & Wilhelm, 2014). Interestingly, when used for OCD (compared to major depression), SSRIs take a longer time to fully impact symptoms (8–12 weeks) and usually require high doses; why this is so isn't known (Pittenger & Bloch, 2014).

While research has found SSRIs to be better than placebos for reducing obsessions and compulsions (W. K. Goodman et al., 2014; W. K. Goodman et al., 1989), they are not cure-alls. When used for OCD, SSRI antidepressants often don't work. One research study appraised them as effective only about half the time (Griebel & Holmes, 2013) and another estimated that 25%–60% of people prescribed them for OCD show little or no response (M. T. Williams et al., 2014). While antidepressants alone do reduce symptoms of OCD in many cases, their effectiveness compared to cognitive-behavioral therapy (CBT) (discussed below) isn't clear. One meta-analysis found medication to be less effective than CBT; it also found CBT alone to be as effective as CBT plus antidepressants (Öst, Havnen, Hansen, & Kvale, 2015). Still, those who are helped by antidepressants are encouraged to remain on them for at least a year and preferably indefinitely because 80%–90% of those who stop taking them relapse (M. T. Williams et al., 2014). However, convincing people to stay on these drugs can be difficult because (as previously noted) SSRIs have a variety of unpleasant side effects.

When the initial SSRI a person is given for OCD doesn't help, usually two or three other SSRIs are tried; if those also don't work, sometimes a tricyclic antidepressant (typically *clomipramine*) is prescribed (M. T. Williams et al., 2014). Clomipramine is considered roughly as effective as SSRIs for OCD symptoms, but its side effects are more severe due to it being an older, tricyclic type of antidepressant (Pittenger & Bloch, 2014; M. T. Williams et al., 2014). Therefore, it's usually only tried after SSRIs have proven ineffective.

Augmenting Agents

Because SSRIs alone are often not very helpful, OCD patients are sometimes given other drugs at the same time. Secondary drugs used to improve the impact of primary drugs are known as **augmenting agents**. Benzodiazepines, mood stabilizers (such as lithium), and atypical antipsychotics (such as risperidone [Risperdal], olanzapine [Zyprexa], and quetiapine [Seroquel]) are all used as augmenting agents intended to improve the effect of SSRIs for OCD (Pittenger & Bloch, 2014; M. T. Williams et al., 2014). One study found that, once stabilized, patients have a 40% chance of responding to the medication they are on for five years (Peselow, Pizano, & IsHak, 2015). This means that 60% of patients wind up not responding over the long term. Not everyone believes augmenting agents are the best secondary treatment for OCD. Some researchers argue that adjunctive therapy (often CBT) is as good or better than placing patients on a second drug; for instance, CBT ritual and response prevention has fared better than risperidone as a secondary treatment for OCD (Simpson et al., 2008).

Glutamate Hypothesis of OCD

Given the limitations of SSRIs and augmenting drugs, it isn't surprising that, as with anxiety, glutamate has increasingly gained attention for its possible role in obsessions and compulsions (W. K. Goodman et al., 2014; Pittenger, Bloch, & Williams, 2011). The **glutamate hypothesis of OCD** is like the glutamate hypothesis of depression in contending that OCD may be the result of excess glutamate. Researchers are presently conducting research into glutamate's role and are investigating the potential of glutamate inhibiting drugs such as *riluzole* (a glutamate blocking agent also used to manage symptoms of amyotrophic lateral sclerosis [ALS], a degenerative disease that leads to muscle degeneration) (Pittenger & Bloch, 2014; Pittenger et al., 2011; K. Wu, Hanna, Rosenberg, & Arnold, 2012). Glutamate-based drug treatments for OCD are mainly in the exploratory stage, but early trials suggest that riluzole may help up to half of OCD patients for whom it is prescribed (Ting & Feng, 2008; K. Wu et al., 2012).

Gary
Gary is prescribed Zoloft for his OCD. He remains on it for a few months, but it doesn't relieve his symptoms. His doctor switches him to Prozac and eventually—when that doesn't help either—to Luvox. The Luvox does improve Gary's symptoms, but only after he has taken it for about 10 weeks. Had the Luvox not worked, the doctor's next plan would have been to augment it with a benzodiazepine or switch to the tricyclic antidepressant clomiprazine.

BRAIN STRUCTURE AND FUNCTION PERSPECTIVES

Anxiety and Fear

Recall that the amygdala is a brain structure important in emotional memory. In Chapter 5, we noted that the amygdala tends to be highly active in depressed people (J. R. Swartz, Knodt, Radtke, & Hariri, 2015). The same is true for anxiety and fear. The amygdala has been identified as the most central structure in the brain's *fear circuit*; it's the brain location where fear-related classically conditioned associations are stored (LeDoux, 2015). Consistent with this, research using brain scans has repeatedly found anxiety correlated with high levels of amygdala activity (M. G. Newman, Llera, Erickson, Przeworski, & Castonguay, 2013); it is also tied to activity in the insula, a small area deep within the cerebral cortex that appears to play a role in basic emotions, sense of self, awareness of desires, and awareness of bodily states (Brühl, Delsignore, Komossa, & Weidt, 2014; Etkin & Wager, 2007). Thus, one theory of anxiety disorders is that they result from excessive reactivity of the amygdala and insula (Etkin, 2012; Etkin & Wager, 2007; M. G. Newman et al., 2013). The relationship between amygdala/insula hyperactivity and heightened anxiety was discovered by meta-analyzing imaging studies of people diagnosed with specific phobia, social anxiety disorder (SAD), and posttraumatic stress disorder (PTSD) and comparing the results to imaging studies of healthy controls undergoing fear conditioning.

> *Strikingly, all three disorders, despite differing levels of severity and generalization, resulted in hyperactivation of the amygdala and insula in patients, a pattern also observed during fear conditioning in healthy subjects. As such, the "fear" component of these disorders appears to be mapped to excessive amygdala and insula reactivity. (Etkin, 2012, p. 356)*

Note that PTSD, one of the three disorders included in the meta-analysis, is no longer categorized as an anxiety disorder in *DSM-5*—even though people diagnosed with it show similar brain patterns as those diagnosed with specific phobia and SAD. This highlights an important disagreement between investigators relying on *DSM-5* or *ICD-11* categories and those adopting an RDoC approach. RDoC, as you recall from Chapter 3, is the U.S. National Institute of Mental Health (NIMH) initiative to devise a diagnostic system that uses biological measures to diagnose mental disorders. RDoC researchers are skeptical of existing diagnostic demarcations that divide anxiety into discrete categories such as PTSD, SAD, and specific phobia. Wishing to move beyond *DSM*'s behavioral diagnostic criteria, they focus on locating common biological mechanisms that cut across people assigned these diagnoses (Craske, 2012; Simpson, 2012). While the *DSM-5* and *ICD-11* may no longer consider PTSD (discussed further in Chapter 7) an anxiety disorder, RDoC-oriented biological research suggests that many disorders involving anxiety may ultimately turn out to have similar biological etiologies. Though this potentially makes many existing *DSM* and *ICD* distinctions somewhat suspect, admittedly it remains hard to talk about anxiety and other presenting problems without relying on these long-dominant diagnostic categories.

Obsessions and Compulsions

When it comes to OCD and related disorders, many different brain regions have been implicated—mostly through PET scan and MRI studies—but findings have not always been consistent (Friedlander & Desrocher, 2006; B. J. Harrison et al., 2009). Because compulsions constitute problems with impulse control, some studies have examined the role of various parts of the brain involved in executive functioning and goal-directed behavior—including the prefrontal cortex, caudate nucleus, anterior cingulate cortex (important in decision-making, anticipating rewards, emotion, and impulse control), thalamus (a midbrain region that relays sensory information), and striatum (part of the brain's reward system) (Del Casale et al., 2011; Friedlander & Desrocher, 2006; Gillan et al., 2015; W. K. Goodman et al., 2014; van den Heuvel et al., 2011; Whiteside, Port, & Abramowitz, 2004). In many instances, excessive activity or changes in volume in one or more of these regions (or others, such as the hippocampus and amygdala) have been correlated with obsessive-compulsive symptoms in OCD and related disorders such as hair-pulling disorder (Atmaca et al., 2008; Banca et al., 2015; Chamberlain et al., 2009; Del Casale et al., 2011; Friedlander & Desrocher, 2006; Gillan et al., 2015; van den Heuvel et al., 2011). This has led to the development of corticostriatal pathophysiological models, which hold that OCD is explicable in terms of the complex circuitry by which these various brain regions communicate with one another (Del Casale et al., 2011; B. J. Harrison et al., 2009).

While research on which brain structures play a role in OCD and related disorders is promising, it does have limitations. For one thing, study results are often inconsistent. If we continue to get inconsistent findings, then perhaps OCD is not best understood in terms of brain structure abnormalities. That is, "non-replicated and inconsistent findings … may in fact reflect the null hypothesis that there is no consistent structural abnormality in OCD and that cognitive impairments are not underpinned by structural abnormalities identifiable by MRI" (Menzies et al., 2008, p. 542).

However, there may be reasons for the inconsistent findings that don't discredit the idea of OCD as tied to brain structure. In keeping with the RDoC model, perhaps what we call "OCD" isn't one disorder, but numerous disorders—each with its own pattern of brain pathology (Mataix-Cols, 2006). If so, then "different symptom dimensions, e.g., contamination/washing versus symmetry/ordering, may have distinct neural substrates … which may lead to inconsistent findings in groups of patients with differing symptom profiles" (Menzies et al., 2008, p. 539). Specifically, it has been proposed that there are three different types of symptom patterns in OCD, each with its own biological correlates—people with "symmetry/ordering," "contamination/washing," and "harm/checking" types of OCD all show distinct patterns of brain structure activity and volume (van den Heuvel et al., 2009). With any luck, future research will clarify our current understanding of how different parts of the brain relate to obsessive and compulsive symptoms.

GENETIC AND EVOLUTIONARY PERSPECTIVES
Genetic Perspectives

Anxiety

Anxiety appears to run in families, perhaps because some people are genetically predisposed to an anxious temperament (S. Taylor, Abramowitz, McKay, & Asmundson, 2010). Meta-analyses have consistently found that first-degree relatives of people with generalized anxiety disorder, panic disorder, specific phobia, social phobia, and agoraphobia are at increased risk of being diagnosed with these same problems (Hettema, Neale, & Kendler, 2001; Schumacher et al., 2011; Shimada-Sugimoto, Otowa, & Hettema, 2015). Likewise, twin studies also suggest a genetic influence on anxiety (M. N. Davies et al., 2015; Skre, Onstad, Torgersen, Lygren, & Kringlen, 1993; Torgersen, 1983). Such studies have generated heritability estimates for anxiety disorders between 0.30 and 0.40 (Shimada-Sugimoto et al., 2015). This means that 30%–40% of phenotypic variation is thought to be due to genetic influences. These estimates are numerically comparable to those for major depression and are often taken as showing that anxiety is partly attributable to genetic factors. Of course, as we have seen in previous chapters, there is debate over how much heritability estimates can be trusted and how they should be interpreted (J. Joseph, 2012).

When it comes to identifying specific genes that are implicated in anxiety disorders, candidate gene studies have yielded mixed results, making it difficult to draw clear conclusions (Shimada-Sugimoto et al., 2015). The largest number of candidate gene studies have been done on panic disorder, but one comprehensive review of these studies laments that most results have been "inconsistent, negative, or not clearly replicated" (Maron, Hettema, & Shlik, 2010, p. 681). To counteract this, another kind of genetic study called a genome-wide association (GWA) study has been used to identify genes associated with panic disorder. The difference between candidate gene studies and GWA studies is that the former specifically focus on a small number of genes already suspected of being related to panic (hence the term "candidate genes"), while the latter include all the genes in the genome. GWA studies are hard to conduct because they require analysis of the entire genome (quite a big undertaking!), but they have the advantage of potentially uncovering new candidate genes. GWA studies have identified numerous possible genetic risk markers for panic disorder, but the results must be looked at tentatively because the studies lack the very large sample sizes necessary to generate significant results (Maron et al., 2010; Shimada-Sugimoto et al., 2015).

Obsessions and Compulsions

Like anxiety disorders, OCD and related disorders are also suspected of having a genetic influence. Many family studies provide support for this. One review reports that 12% of first-degree relatives of those with an OCD diagnosis also meet the criteria for the disorder, compared to only 2% among relatives of normal controls (Nicolini, Arnold, Nestadt, Lanzagorta, & Kennedy, 2009). Another review found that 6.7% to 15% of first-degree relatives of children diagnosed with OCD also had it (Mundo, Zanoni, & Altamura, 2006). Of course, not all family studies have found a familial connection for OCD (Rasmussen, 1993). However, some studies that look more broadly suggest that those with OCD are—at the very least—more likely to have related symptoms or diagnoses, such as anxiety or depression (Rasmussen, 1993). Given this, it shouldn't surprise us that one review found family members of those with OCD are not only at increased risk of being diagnosed with OCD, but are also more likely to be diagnosed with generalized anxiety disorder, separation anxiety disorder, panic disorder, and agoraphobia (Nicolini et al., 2009). While family studies don't control for shared environment, they are still commonly believed to provide imperfect evidence that people with similar genetic backgrounds may be predisposed to obsessive-compulsive symptoms and other forms of anxiety.

Many but not all twin studies on OCD also suggest a genetic contribution (Browne, Gair, Scharf, & Grice, 2014; Nicolini et al., 2009; Pauls, 2012; Rasmussen, 1993; Torgersen, 1983; M. Wolff, Alsobrook, & Pauls, 2000). One review concluded that concordance rates in OCD twin studies range from 62% to 87% (M. Wolff et al., 2000). However, a more recent review noted that many twin studies (especially older ones) suffer from serious methodological limitations—especially small sample sizes (Pauls, 2012). This more conservative analysis highlighted studies showing identical twin concordance rates ranging anywhere from 18% to 87%. This means that somewhere between 18% and 87% of the time when one twin has OCD symptoms so does the other. Yes, this is a large range. However, heritability estimates run between 0.45 and 0.65—therefore, 45% to 65% of variance is estimated as due to genetics (Pauls, 2012). Such results are usually interpreted as implying a genetic predisposition toward obsessions and compulsions, but with the recognition that environmental factors also have a significant influence (Rasmussen, 1993).

Given that serotonin, norepinephrine, and glutamate are implicated in OCD and related disorders, it is not surprising that candidate genes that are important in the functioning of these neurotransmitters have been identified as possibly contributing to the development of obsessions and compulsions (Grünblatt, Hauser, & Walitza, 2014). When it comes to the serotonergic system, a region of the serotonin transporter (5-HTT) gene known as 5-HTTLPR has garnered a lot of attention for its potential role in OCD. Like all genes, the 5-HTTLPR gene has two alleles—usually an S-allele and an L-allele. Some studies suggest that the S-allele is associated with OCD (Grünblatt et al., 2014; S. Taylor, 2013), but other studies haven't always found this. One meta-analysis, for example, concluded that the S-allele might be associated with OCD in females (results didn't reach statistical significance, but there was a trend in this direction) (Mak, Streiner, & Steiner, 2015). However, the S-allele didn't appear to be related to OCD in males (Mak et al., 2015). For males, another meta-analysis found that an allele important in norepinephrine regulation (the Met allele on the COMT gene) is correlated with OCD; yet this finding didn't hold for females (S. Taylor, 2013). Finally, a variety of genes related to glutamate transmission have also been implicated in OCD; because these candidate genes are the only ones whose associations with OCD have been replicated in a variety of studies, the glutamatergic system is currently receiving a lot of attention from genetic researchers studying obsessions and compulsions (Grünblatt et al., 2014).

The broader conclusion to be taken from candidate gene research on OCD is that although many potentially relevant genes have been identified, OCD can't currently be understood exclusively in genetic inheritance terms (Mak et al., 2015; Rasmussen, 1993). One likely reason for this is that OCD, like many mental disorder categories, involves a complex set of behaviors, cognitions, and feelings. Thus, many different genes likely make one susceptible to it. Trying to locate a single "OCD" gene may be unrealistic. Not only are multiple genes probably involved, but the environment inevitably also makes an important contribution. One group of OCD genetic researchers summed it up quite nicely:

> It is important to note that a heterogeneous disorder such as OCD cannot fully be explained by a simple one-gene cause and effect model. This lends support to not only a polygenic [multiple gene] model but also to the possible role of environment–gene interactions. (Mak et al., 2015, p. 440)

Evolutionary Perspectives

From evolutionary perspectives, "fear and anxiety are commonly experienced by all human beings and are part of an elaborate menu of defensive, adaptive processes that have evolved over millions of years in us humans and our mammalian ancestors" (S. G. Hofmann et al., 2002, p. 317). Fear and anxiety are adaptive in alerting people to dangers in their environment, which enhances their chances of surviving and reproducing. However, these emotions turn maladaptive when people decide they have become too intense in duration or interfere with daily living; this is when anxiety disorders are diagnosed. Said another way, "everyone recognizes that anxiety is a useful trait that has been shaped by natural selection. Even good things, however, cease to be good when they become excessive" (I. M. Marks & Nesse, 1994, p. 247).

Prepared Conditioning

Evolutionary psychologists have directly challenged behavioral perspectives that view fear and anxiety reactions as resulting almost exclusively from environmental conditioning. Along these lines, researchers studying

Although this spider is far less dangerous to you than an automobile, evolutionary theory suggests you are biologically predisposed to develop a fear of it rather than your Honda.
Source: Getty Images \ Freder

prepared conditioning have found that some phobias are a lot easier to condition than others (S. G. Hofmann et al., 2002; Mineka & Öhman, 2002; Zafiropoulou & Pappa, 2002). Psychologist Martin Seligman (1971) first established that people seem more physiologically predisposed to develop phobias of situations or objects that have signaled danger to humans since the dawn of the species—things like heights, rats, bugs, and blood. Even though other things are potentially more dangerous to people in modern society—cars and planes, for example—phobias of them are less likely because people aren't biologically primed to develop such fears. As noted in Chapter 2, lots of people are phobic of bugs, but very few of Hondas.

Malfunctioning Mental Mechanisms

More broadly, evolutionary theorists contend that problems with anxiety, obsessions, and compulsions occur when evolved mental mechanisms (or *adaptations*) that are meant to keep people safe malfunction (Feygin, Swain, & Leckman, 2006; Glass, 2012; S. G. Hofmann et al., 2002; I. M. Marks & Nesse, 1994; D. J. Stein & Bouwer, 1997; D. J. Stein & Nesse, 2011). For example, Marks and Nesse (1994) argue that *escape or avoidance* responses are often highly adaptive because they help people elude threatening situations. However, an overly responsive escape or avoidance mechanism leads to problems such as generalized anxiety, phobias, and social anxiety. Similarly, they argue that *freezing/immobility* responses evolved to let people conceal themselves and assess dangerous situations. Yet if the apparatus behind such responses becomes maladaptive, then it provokes so much inhibition that one can't engage the world—as happens in cases of selective mutism, for example. Finally, Marks and Nesse (1994) note that *submission/appeasement* is also adaptive, especially in helping people get along peaceably with others in their own social group. However, like freezing/immobility, submission and appeasement can lead to too much inhibition: problems like social anxiety and selective mutism may result.

Group Selection

Regarding OCD, one intriguing evolutionary perspective maintains that OCD is the product of **group selection**, a hypothesized process by which different members of a species or social group evolve specialized functions that benefit the larger community (Polimeni, Reiss, & Sareen, 2005). Among honeybees, for example, we find workers, drones, and a queen—each with distinct and important jobs that contribute to and strengthen the hive. The **group selection theory of OCD** in humans proposes that behaviors such as checking, cleaning, and hoarding are adaptive and important, but also time consuming (Polimeni et al., 2005). If everyone did them it would place too many members of the group at risk. However, by having specific individuals focused on these vital tasks, the entire group benefits without everyone needing to expend energy on them. Unfortunately, inheriting a tendency toward a specialized focus on checking, cleaning, and hoarding may not be adaptive in modern society; those who have it may be diagnosed with OCD.

Criticisms of Evolutionary Perspectives

A common criticism of evolutionary perspectives is their reliance on the idea of evolved mental mechanisms, or adaptations. Detractors maintain that such mechanisms are assumed, not proven (Chrisler & Erchull, 2011; Gannon, 2002; Peters, 2013; Raskin, 2013). That is, we can't directly observe the mental mechanisms that supposedly control human anxiety responses—which makes evolutionary accounts hypothetical and impossible to test (Feygin et al., 2006). Further, to critics the notion of evolutionary mechanisms provides something of a circular argument: people behave anxiously because these mechanisms exist and we know these mechanisms exist because people behave anxiously. Nonetheless, the evolutionary perspective is compelling in many respects and continues to exert an influence on how we think about anxiety, obsessions, and compulsions—even if it doesn't necessarily have a direct impact on how we treat such problems.

IMMUNE SYSTEM PERSPECTIVES

Inflammation

In Chapters 4 and 5, we examined how immune system inflammation has been positively correlated with psychosis and mood problems. Similarly, it has also been correlated with anxiety, obsessions, and compulsions—although research results haven't always confirmed this (Furtado & Katzman, 2015; Marazziti, Mucci, Lombardi, Falaschi, & Dell'Osso, 2015; Najjar, Pearlman, Alper, Najjar, & Devinsky, 2013). As with psychosis and mood problems, inflammatory cytokines—the small immune-system-produced proteins that aid healing but cause swelling in large amounts—are often increased among people diagnosed with anxiety and obsessive-compulsive disorders (Fluitman et al., 2010; Furtado & Katzman, 2015; Hou et al., 2017; Marazziti et al., 2015; Najjar et al., 2013; N. P. Rao et al., 2015; Uddin & Diwadkar, 2014). Altered levels of cortisol (sometimes increased, sometimes decreased) have also been found at times, occasionally with gender differences (Furtado & Katzman, 2015; Hou & Baldwin, 2012; Kluge et al., 2007; Yousry Elnazer & Baldwin, 2014; Zorn et al., 2017). As cortisol is the body's main stress hormone, these mixed results imply that in some instances anxiety may produce an upsurge in the release of cortisol stress hormone (after all, anxiety is stressful), but in other instances may result in physiological adjustment and habituation to anxiety (resulting in lower cortisol levels) (Furtado & Katzman, 2015).

The Gut

One immune-related area of interest to anxiety/OCD researchers specifically (but increasingly being looked at in terms of its relationship to psychological problems more generally) is the **gut-brain axis**, the system of biochemical connections between the gut and brain (Crumeyrolle-Arias et al., 2014; Foster & McVey Neufeld, 2013; Turna, Grosman Kaplan, Anglin, & Van Ameringen, 2016). The *gut* (or *gastrointestinal tract*) is the tube extending from the mouth to the anus through which food is taken in and digested. The gut contains *bacteria* (also known as *gut microbiome*) necessary for digestion and health (P. Ho & Ross, 2017; Turna et al., 2016). Gut microbiome help absorb nutrients, prevent bad bacteria from accumulating, and are considered important in the release of cytokines. Thus, they are intimately tied to inflammation and immune system function (P. Ho & Ross, 2017). Researchers are busy exploring the relationship between anxiety/OCD symptoms and imbalances in gut microbiome (Foster & McVey Neufeld, 2013). Depression, autism, and psychosis (see Chapters 5, 13, and 4, respectively) have also been targeted in studies looking at the gut (Burokas et al., 2017; Foster & McVey Neufeld, 2013; P. Ho & Ross, 2017; Turna et al., 2016).

Despite the promise that gut–brain research holds for understanding anxiety and other presenting problems, the exact relationship among the gut, the immune system, neurotransmitters, and brain circuitry when it comes to anxiety remains under investigation (Turna et al., 2016). To date, the research on gut microbiome and psychiatric problems has been intriguing, but inconclusive. Some researchers strongly suspect that dietary supplements containing healthy gut bacteria can reduce anxiety and depression, though the evidence base for this remains modest (Burokas et al., 2017; Foster & McVey Neufeld, 2013; MacQueen, Surette, & Moayyedi, 2017). More studies in this area will hopefully help us better grasp gut–brain connections in anxiety, mood, and related presenting problems. Still, this emerging area of research may ultimately shed light on why anxious people often report feeling worry and fear in their stomachs. Perhaps those butterflies in your tummy before a big exam will indeed turn out to have a biological basis, after all!

EVALUATING BIOLOGICAL PERSPECTIVES

Students are occasionally surprised to hear that antidepressants are so frequently prescribed for anxiety, obsessions, and compulsions. However, once it is understood that these symptoms are highly comorbid with depression, the widespread use of antidepressants becomes more understandable. Consider, for instance, that 90% of people diagnosed with OCD are thought to have another comorbid mental disorder—with 40% suspected of having a depressive disorder and 75% an anxiety disorder (M. T. Williams et al., 2014). Yet do these high levels of comorbidity mean that people are truly suffering from distinct anatomical disorders, or does it merely reflect that our ability to distinguish various problems at a biological level is currently lacking? Critics of biological models of anxiety contend it is the latter. In their view, the fact that the same drugs are used for all these problems suggests that our knowledge of what is going on biochemically across various presenting problems remains somewhat basic and undifferentiated.

While numerous brain structures and genes have been implicated in anxiety, problems with replicating findings, combined with the fact that most of this research is correlational, provide ample reason to pause before concluding that anxiety can be explained primarily in biological terms. Critics contend that biological approaches to anxiety, obsessions, and compulsions sometimes minimize the important roles of psychological and sociocultural factors—especially considering evidence that therapy may be as or more effective for such issues (Bandelow, Reitt, et al., 2015; Öst et al., 2015). We next turn to psychological and sociocultural conceptions of anxiety.

6.5 PSYCHOLOGICAL PERSPECTIVES
PSYCHODYNAMIC PERSPECTIVES

One of the challenges facing psychodynamic therapies is that, unlike CBT, they are "traditionally not tailored to single mental disorders or specific symptoms" (Leichsenring & Salzer, 2014, p. 226). Instead, psychodynamic perspectives focus "on core underlying processes" that cut across all disorders (Leichsenring & Salzer, 2014, p. 226). Thus, psychodynamic perspectives tend to see all presenting problems generally—and various anxiety disorder categories specifically—as having similar origins in unconscious conflicts.

Classic Freudian Case Studies

The psychodynamic interest in unconscious meanings can be traced all the way back to Freud himself. His cases of Little Hans and the Rat Man provide vivid examples of a psychoanalytic approach to anxiety, obsessions, and compulsions (S. Freud, 1909/1955a, 1909/1955b).

Little Hans was a 5-year-old boy who developed an intense fear of horses, worrying that one might fall on him or bite him. Hans' father asked Freud for advice in understanding this peculiar phobia. Freud (1909/1955a) hypothesized that Hans' phobia reflected an unresolved Oedipus complex (see Chapter 2), with Hans displacing Oedipal-anger toward his father (including his fear of being castrated by him) onto horses. Thus, Hans' phobia symbolically expressed castration anxiety. By helping Hans gain insight into this unconscious conflict, his phobia of horses was eliminated.

The Rat Man was an attorney in his late 20s whose main symptom was fear that something terrible might befall his father and fiancée—even though his father was already dead. More specifically, the Rat Man experienced obsessions about rats boring into the anuses of his father and fiancée. He also felt a compulsion to slit his own throat with a razor. Freud (1909/1955b) traced these symptoms back to childhood sexual experiences the Rat Man had with his governesses. The Rat Man worried about his father finding out about these experiences and unconsciously developed a conflict that Freud described this way: "If I have this wish to see a woman naked, my father will be bound to die" (S. Freud, 1909/1955b, p. 163). When he became an adult with a fiancée he was attracted to, this unconscious conflict reemerged. Freud's nearly year-long psychoanalysis with the Rat Man successfully resolved this conflict, eliminating the obsessions and compulsions.

Unconscious Impulses and Anxiety

Even if you don't accept all the tenets of classic psychoanalysis, the important psychodynamic idea illustrated by these two cases is that anxiety is due to more than just behavioral conditioning, illogical thinking, or biological brain dysfunction. Psychodynamically speaking, anxiety is symptomatic of meaningful internal conflicts. While modern psychodynamic treatments sometimes differ in their specific conceptualizations of anxiety, they all share Freud's emphasis on anxiety as representing underlying psychological conflicts: "psychodynamic models conceptualize anxiety disorders as developing from wishes, feelings, and fantasies, often unconscious, that are experienced as frightening or intolerable" (Busch, Milrod, & Shear, 2010, p. 125). For example, today's psychodynamic therapists often maintain that chronic worry emerges from either unacceptable repressed wishes or inconsistent parenting in early life. In the former case, powerful but problematic unconscious impulses overwhelm the person, resulting in an "ongoing threat and struggle with unacceptable feelings and fantasies"—hence the emergence of anxiety (Busch & Milrod, 2015, p. 155). In the latter case, the anxious person lacks secure attachments in childhood. Inconsistent parenting leads to "perceptions that the child will be rejected by the parent, cannot depend on the parent for care, or must take care of a fragile or incompetent parent" and this "chronic fear of disruption in attachments" exacerbates prolonged worry (Busch & Milrod, 2015, p. 155). For a refresher on the importance of attachment in psychodynamic approaches, see Chapter 5.

INSECURE ATTACHMENTS AND OCD

Problematic attachment relationships are also implicated in psychodynamic notions of obsessive-compulsive disorder. Psychodynamic therapists argue that people are at risk for OCD when intrusive thoughts threaten "core perceptions of the self" (Doron, Mikulincer, Kyrios, & Sar-Ei, 2015, p. 202). In this psychodynamic interpretation, OCD develops in someone whose parents are emotionally ambivalent or superficially supportive but subtly rejecting. As a result, the person lacks secure attachment to others and becomes extremely sensitive and self-doubting about things such as job and school performance, morality, and relationship success. Intrusive thoughts or events related to these areas negatively affect feelings of self-worth and trigger efforts to compensate for or correct such feelings—often in the form of compulsive behaviors. Ironically, the compulsive behaviors often produce more intrusive negative thoughts, which only worsen the original problem.

Gary

Gary Steadman's parents were often subtly critical and rejecting of Gary's interests and responses to things, although outwardly they claimed to be and appeared supportive of their son. As he grew up, Gary increasingly felt unsure of himself and his abilities. Despite succeeding in his career, he experienced himself as borderline incompetent; many of his obsessions and compulsions centered on his uncertainty about whether he had done something correctly ("I can't trust myself to remember to turn off the stove, set the thermostat, or meet my boss's expectations"). He also worried he wasn't smart or attractive enough for his wife, Theresa—and often found himself obsessing about whether he belonged with her. If Gary pursued psychodynamic therapy, it would focus on addressing his self-doubt and insecure attachments to significant people in his life.

CASE EXAMPLES

CHAPTER 6

Unified Psychodynamic Protocol for Anxiety Disorders (UPP-ANXIETY)

An important challenge facing modern psychodynamic approaches to anxiety, obsessions, and compulsions is the widespread impression that they aren't supported by empirical research. However, psychodynamic therapists note that they have increasingly utilized randomized controlled trials (RCTs) to test their techniques. As one example, German psychodynamic therapist Falk Leichsenring and colleagues have proposed a **unified psychodynamic protocol for anxiety disorders (UPP-ANXIETY)**, which they developed from the results of randomized controlled trials of psychodynamic therapy (Leichsenring, Abbass, Luyten, Hilsenroth, & Rabung, 2013; Leichsenring, Leweke, Klein, & Steinert, 2015; Leichsenring & Salzer, 2014; Leichsenring et al., 2014; Leichsenring et al., 2009). Essentially, after being socialized into therapy, treatment goals are set and relationships explored with the objective of mapping the underlying core conflicts that produce anxiety. Ways in which patients ward off anxiety are also examined. Helping clients obtain insight into their conflicts and the ways they defend against them allows them to alter long-standing relational patterns and overcome their anxiety. Because the therapy is divided into concrete steps, or "modules"—which have strong empirical support and can be tailored to each patient—Leichsenring sees his approach as an effective psychodynamic method for treating anxiety (Leichsenring & Salzer, 2014). Critics still generally view cognitive-behavioral therapy (discussed shortly) as more effective and having a stronger evidence base than psychodynamic therapy (Bandelow, Lichte, Rudolf, Wiltink, & Beutel, 2014; Bandelow, Reitt, et al., 2015; A. A. Shah & Han, 2015). However, there are indeed psychodynamic therapists trying to test how well their approach works with anxiety.

Theresa

If Theresa underwent psychodynamic therapy, she would be encouraged to talk about past relationships. During these conversations, she might reveal that while growing up, she had a younger sister who had many emotional and behavioral problems that consumed her parents' attention. Thus, Theresa came to believe that she could make her parents' lives less stressful by not causing them any additional grief beyond what they had to deal with from her sister. Doing well in school and being a well-behaved and compliant high achiever prevented her parents from having to face further stress. However, this also placed a lot of pressure on Theresa. Any time she didn't live up to her high standards, she felt like she was hurting her parents. Further, she lost track of what mattered to her. In psychodynamic therapy, the unconscious conflict likely to emerge would be "I must always succeed to spare others stress—regardless of my own feelings about what I'm doing." This would explain why, when she was recently promoted at work and asked to do a lot more public speaking (something she didn't especially want to do), she began experiencing intense social anxiety. The promotion triggered an internal conflict in which she either had to succeed at an unwanted task (public speaking) or feel like she had massively disappointed others who—like her parents when she was young—she felt had more important problems to worry about. Psychodynamic therapy would help Theresa understand this unconscious conflict, its origins, and the strategies she has relied on to keep it at bay. Consequently, it would be expected that her anxiety (both about public speaking and in general) would resolve. She eventually might even speak to her boss about a career trajectory more in keeping with her interests.

CASE EXAMPLES

COGNITIVE-BEHAVIORAL PERSPECTIVES

Cognitive-behavioral therapy (CBT) approaches to anxiety, obsessions, and compulsions stress conditioning, modeling, and irrational thinking as central to these problems. While most CBT practitioners do typically utilize *DSM* and *ICD* diagnostic categories as frameworks for thinking about anxiety, obsessions, and compulsions, in its purest theoretical form CBT has no need for these categories (for a provocative argument on this front, see the Controversial Question feature, "Can We Diagnose Anxiety Using Everyday Language?"). Regardless of whether they favor using diagnostic categories or not, CBT approaches see learning and thinking as central to anxiety and obsessive-compulsive problems. Let's examine CBT approaches more closely.

CONTROVERSIAL QUESTION

Can We Diagnose Anxiety Using Everyday Language?

Dr. S. Lloyd Williams is a psychologist who challenges *DSM* and *ICD* conceptions of anxiety and obsessive-compulsive disorders. As he provocatively argues, "people's mental problems are painfully real, but mental disorders and psychopathology are scientific illusions" (S. L. Williams, 2016, p. 141). To him, *DSM* and *ICD* categories lead us astray by encouraging us to mistake behavior problems as illnesses. Williams' skepticism about the medical model recalls the radical behaviorist view of abnormality discussed in Chapter 2. In a purely behavioral model, abnormality equals undesirable behaviors we can objectively measure, not presumed internal disorders we can't directly observe. From such a perspective, we are better off (and more scientifically justified) recasting "mental disorders" as psychosocial problems defined in terms of observable behaviors and understood using everyday language.

In keeping with this view, Williams reframes anxiety and obsessive-compulsive disorders as psychosocial problems describable in terms of thoughts, feelings, and behaviors. That is, abnormality isn't a disorder one "has." It is a set of behaviors one does, accompanied by various thoughts and feelings. Thus, instead of talking about social anxiety disorder, specific phobia, and generalized anxiety disorder, Williams says we should speak of anxiety and fear responses—things like *feelings* of subjective anxiety, *thoughts* that bad things will happen, and *behaviors* like panicking. Similarly, obsessive-compulsive disorder should be recast as merely experiencing troubling thoughts and compulsive behaviors. As two further examples: Williams maintains that people don't "have" hair-pulling disorder; they simply find it hard not to engage in hair pulling behavior. Neither do they "have" hoarding disorder; they just experience difficulty with collecting useless paraphernalia and feel anxious about getting rid of it.

Rather than diagnosing anxiety and obsessive-compulsive disorders using *DSM* and *ICD* categories, Williams says clinicians are better off diagnosing the extent to which clients struggle with the following psychosocial problems: *phobic behavior, compulsive behavior, troubling thoughts,* and *anxiety/fear*. Williams notes that every client exhibits these problems in a unique constellation and, once the ways each of these problems affect a client are understood, therapeutic interventions designed to remedy them can be implemented. Again, in many respects this echoes the old behaviorist emphasis on conducting a functional analysis of behavior, in which the specific psychosocial influences on a person's problem are measured and then a specific treatment is tailored to that client's needs (see Chapter 2). Biologically minded clinicians are likely to critique Williams for not recognizing that many problems in abnormal psychology are indeed medical disorders rather than psychosocial problems. Williams respectfully disagrees. While his perspective isn't the dominant one in most circles today, it highlights the ongoing tension between more biologically oriented and psychosocially oriented approaches in the field.

CRITICAL THINKING QUESTIONS

1. Do you agree with Williams that mental disorders are best recast as psychosocial problems? Why or why not?
2. Does Williams' approach imply that medications shouldn't be used because psychosocial problems are best addressed via psychosocial interventions?
3. What do you see as the main advantages and disadvantages of Williams' approach? How do these compare to what you see as the main advantages and disadvantages of the *DSM*?

CBT Conceptualizations of Anxiety and Panic

Behavioral Conditioning of Anxiety

According to strictly behavioral perspectives, anxiety is the product of environmental conditioning. A phobia, for example, is an anxiety response formed through classical conditioning. Recall the case study of Little Albert from Chapter 2, in which John Watson and Rosalie Rayner (1920) took a white rat (a neutral stimulus that

18-month old Albert wasn't initially scared of) and repeatedly paired it with a loud noise—an unconditioned stimulus (US) that naturally evoked fear. After the white rat was associated with the loud noise, it became a conditioned stimulus (CS) that caused anxiety on its own. Consequently, Albert began showing a phobic response to the rat—even though initially it hadn't frightened him. Behaviorists contend that all anxiety reactions are conditioned in this manner.

Although anxiety responses are often conceptualized as classically conditioned, operant conditioning plays an important role in sustaining them. Because their anxiety decreases when they steer clear of situations that scare them, people receive negative reinforcement (defined in Chapter 2) for avoiding anxiety-producing situations (Mowrer, 1939, 1947). Given that they avoid rather than test their fears, anxious people don't have an opportunity to learn that their fears aren't as bad as they think. Thus, the anxiety is never extinguished.

Of course, anxiety doesn't have to develop from firsthand experience. According to social learning theory (discussed in Chapter 2), when it comes to learning what to be anxious about, people often take their cues from others. Observational learning—in which people learn behavioral and emotional reactions by watching other people model responses to situations—is integral to this process.

Theresa and Gary

Theresa and Gary, the parents in our case study, have modeled many anxiety reactions for their daughter, Tammy. Tammy has observed her father Gary's anxiety when he calls his wife Theresa at work and she fails to answer her phone. Gary becomes very agitated, breaks out in a sweat, and frantically dials Theresa again and again until he reaches her. In so doing, Gary has inadvertently modeled anxious behavior, which Tammy— through the process of observational learning—repeats when her parents leave for work.

CASE EXAMPLES

CHAPTER 6

Cognitive Explanations of Anxiety

Cognitive perspectives stress the centrality of thought processes in understanding and alleviating fear and anxiety. In his cognitive model, Albert Ellis (1998) attributed anxiety to irrational thinking. More recent models build on this idea. For instance, numerous cognitive models of generalized anxiety have been proposed (Mowrer, 1939, 1947). Here are four examples:

» The avoidance model of worry maintains that people often are anxious about negative events potentially befalling them in the future (Behar, DiMarco, Hekler, Mohlman, & Staples, 2009; P. L. Fisher & Wells, 2011). Because the events haven't happened yet, fight or flight responses aren't possible. The only alternative is to worry, which is negatively reinforced because thinking about anxiety-provoking possibilities is less stressful than experiencing more intense physiological symptoms of anxiety.

» The intolerance of uncertainty model posits just what its name implies: ongoing anxiety occurs in those who have a difficult time handling uncertainty (Borkovec, Alcaine, & Behar, 2004; Sibrava & Borkovec, 2006). Such people tend to have a negative problem orientation, seeing challenges as threatening and insurmountable—thus, problems are often avoided. They also hold positive beliefs about worry, viewing it as essential in motivating problem-solving.

» The metacognitive model focuses on how people think about worrying (Dugas, Freeston, & Ladouceur, 1997; Dugas, Gagnon, Ladouceur, & Freeston, 1998; Dugas & Koerner, 2005; Dugas, Marchand, & Ladouceur, 2005). It hypothesizes that people hold both positive and negative beliefs about worry. Examples of positive beliefs are "worrying helps me to cope" and "worry helps me to deal with problems more effectively" (A. Wells, 1995, 2010). Negative beliefs portray worry as uncontrollable and harmful; when such beliefs become powerful, there is a tendency to begin worrying about how much one is worrying.

» The emotional dysregulation model contends that anxious people have difficulty regulating their emotions and therefore find strong emotions highly aversive (P. L. Fisher & Wells, 2011, p. 129). They experience their emotions more intensely than others and have a difficult time identifying and understanding their feelings. Consequently, they respond poorly to their own emotions and attribute negative consequences to experiencing them.

Cognitive Explanations of Panic and Agoraphobia

From a cognitive standpoint, people susceptible to panic disorder and agoraphobia tend to be extremely sensitive and attuned to subtle physiological variations—such as increased heart rate, altered blood pressure, or fluctuations in breathing rate. The catastrophic misinterpretation model of panic disorder holds that people prone to recurrent, unexpected panic attacks catastrophically misinterpret certain bodily sensations

A client who expects to have a panic attack in an elevator likely avoids elevators. Through behavioral activation, the client tests (and hopefully disconfirms) this expectation.
Source: iStock.com/erwo1

(D. W. Austin & Richards, 2001; D. M. Clark, 1986; D. M. Clark & Ehlers, 1993). The more they interpret sensations in an anxious way, the stronger the sensations become—eventually resulting in a full-blown panic attack.

> *The sensations which are misinterpreted are mainly those which are involved in normal anxiety responses (e.g. palpitations, breathlessness, dizziness etc.) but also include some other bodily sensations. The catastrophic misinterpretation involves perceiving these sensations as much more dangerous than they really are. Examples of catastrophic misinterpretations would be a healthy individual perceiving palpitations as evidence of impending heart attack; perceiving a slight feeling of breathlessness as evidence of impending cessation of breathing and consequent death; or perceiving a shaky feeling as evidence of impending loss of control and insanity. (D. M. Clark, 1986, p. 462)*

Research studies have generally supported the catastrophic misinterpretation model (D. W. Austin & Richards, 2006; Hermans et al., 2010; Schniering & Rapee, 1997; Teachman, Marker, & Clerkin, 2010). Cognitive therapy for panic disorder focuses on changing clients' interpretations of bodily events (Roy-Byrne, Craske, & Stein, 2006; Salkovskis, 2007). Psychoeducation is employed to teach clients about their tendency to catastrophically misinterpret bodily feedback; this is often combined with cognitive interventions intended to help people correct faulty beliefs about panic symptoms. Behavioral activation (introduced when discussing depression in Chapter 5) is also used to disconfirm client predictions that certain situations will produce panic attacks. A client who avoids elevators because she thinks they will make her panic might be taken on an elevator ride by her therapist. When panic doesn't occur, the client's previous predictions are disconfirmed and her beliefs about elevators are apt to change. Finally, the therapist might use exposure therapies (discussed more below) in which bodily changes such as dizziness, heart palpitations, and shortness of breath are induced to show clients that these events don't necessarily lead to panic attacks.

CBT Conceptualizations of Obsessions and Compulsions

Behavioral Conditioning

Behavioral perspectives generally focus more on compulsions than obsessions, which isn't surprising given that compulsions are observable behaviors and behaviorists like to stress that which is observable. Like other problems where anxiety is central, behaviorists contend that compulsions are classically conditioned responses. Neutral stimuli become associated with threatening objects or events, which conditions them to evoke anxiety and fear. Understandably, people generally avoid anxiety-provoking stimuli, but those who get diagnosed with OCD rely on rituals as their strategy for doing so (Fresco, Mennin, Heimberg, & Ritter, 2013; Mennin, 2004). These rituals—what we have been calling compulsions—bring temporary relief from anxiety. This reinforces them (M. E. Franklin, Goss, & March, 2012).

Gary
Gary repeatedly checks whether the gas stove is on and the home security system is off. From a behavioral standpoint, these compulsive rituals are negatively reinforced because when Gary does them his anxiety is temporarily relieved. Gary's compulsive behavior is maintained by the ongoing, if temporary, reinforcement he receives.

Cognitive Explanations

Cognitive perspectives pay greater attention to obsessions—again, not surprising given that obsessions are thoughts and cognitive theorists place thoughts front and center. From a cognitive perspective, people diagnosed with OCD tend to have negative automatic thoughts (see Chapter 2) in response to intrusive, obsessional thoughts (Mowrer, 1939). Like those experiencing generalized anxiety, they tend to see negative beliefs as dangerous and uncontrollable. However, compared to generalized anxiety clients, those with an OCD diagnosis tend to excessively reflect on their own cognitive processes (Salkovskis, 1985). Further, they feel shame about the thoughts they have when obsessing and they automatically infer that they are bad people who are responsible for these terrible thoughts (Janeck, Calamari, Riemann, & Heffelfinger, 2003). This provokes intense anxiety, which these clients try to reduce through their compulsions. By neutralizing their obsessive thoughts through compulsive rituals, they decrease their sense of responsibility for having these thoughts in the first place (M. E. Franklin et al., 2012; Weingarden & Renshaw, 2015).

CBT Interventions

A variety of CBT interventions address anxiety, obsessions, and compulsions. Some of these are cognitively oriented, while many others are more strictly behavioral. Let's examine some of the more common cognitive and behavioral interventions.

Exposure Plus Response Prevention

Behaviorally, exposure therapies are often used and are typically considered first-line interventions for anxiety and OCD issues. As discussed in Chapter 2, exposure therapies involve placing a client in the presence of a conditioned stimulus to extinguish the old response and condition a new one. These treatments are commonly used with a wide array of anxiety problems. One kind of exposure therapy used in cases of anxiety (and previously introduced in Chapter 2) is exposure plus response prevention (also called flooding and response prevention) (Foa & Kozak, 1986; M. E. Franklin et al., 2012). The client is placed into direct contact with the anxiety-provoking stimulus and prevented from leaving the situation (Baum, 1970). Recall from Chapter 2 our hypothetical description of flooding with Little Albert. After a white rat is placed in his lap and nothing bad happens, Albert calms down and comes to form a new association between the rat and feeling calm. Flooding and response prevention are often used to address anxiety, obsessions, and compulsions.

Gary   **CASE EXAMPLES**

Imagine a behavior therapist uses flooding and response prevention with Gary. Gary would be placed in the heart of an anxiety-provoking situation—for instance, getting ready for work in the morning. While getting ready, he would inevitably feel compelled to check the stove and the house alarm, but would be prevented from doing so. At first, this might cause Gary's anxiety to increase, but after a few minutes he would realize that nothing bad has happened even though he hasn't gone through his lengthy checking rituals. Gary would therefore begin to calm down. After numerous sessions of flooding and response prevention, Gary would feel calm rather than anxious while preparing for work, even when he doesn't compulsively check. Why? Because a new emotional response has been conditioned!

Systematic Desensitization

The danger in flooding is that sometimes the person being flooded panics rather than calms down when placed in the heart of the feared situation and this merely strengthens the original association between anxiety and the feared object. To avoid this risk, many behavior therapists instead use systematic desensitization (introduced in Chapter 2) (Wolpe, 1961). Systematic desensitization consists of two parts: a *fear hierarchy* and **relaxation training** (M. E. Franklin et al., 2012). Client and counselor work together to develop a fear hierarchy, in which they identify potential experiences with the feared object or situation and rank them from least to most scary. The client also undergoes relaxation training. The most commonly used relaxation training is **progressive relaxation**, wherein the client is taught to alternately relax and tense each muscle in the body. This training teaches the client how to become completely relaxed. Systematic desensitization involves going through each step of the fear hierarchy while the client is in a state of progressive relaxation. Note that anxiety is conceptualized in purely behavioral terms: tense muscles constitute anxiety, while relaxed muscles equal calmness. The idea is that one cannot be tense and relaxed simultaneously. When the client reaches the top of the fear hierarchy and can stay calm when exposed to the dreaded object or situation, the anxiety is extinguished.

In progressive relaxation, clients learn to alternately tense and relax their muscles; this form of relaxation plays a major role in the behavioral technique of systematic desensitization.
Source: Jonathan D. Raskin

CHAPTER 6

Theresa

Theresa's fear of speaking in front of groups could be addressed using systematic desensitization. If so, her therapist would help her develop a fear hierarchy related to public speaking—with sitting on stage in front of a group (but not talking) at the bottom of the hierarchy and standing at a lectern giving a prepared speech to her colleagues at the top of the hierarchy. Theresa would be taught progressive relaxation and asked to practice it while role-playing each step of her fear hierarchy. After a few sessions, she would hopefully be able to stay relaxed even while standing at the lectern and giving a speech to an audience.

Modeling

Modeling (introduced in Chapter 4) is an indirect form of exposure in which the therapist models the aversive behavior for the client, demonstrating that the fear is unjustified. A client who fears dogs might observe his therapist petting a Labrador. Or, a client phobic of heights might watch on a webcam as her therapist rides an elevator to the top story of a skyscraper. Sometimes participant modeling is used, wherein the client is invited to partake in the anxiety-provoking activity with the therapist (Wolpe, 1958).

Theresa and Gary

If Theresa's therapist were to use modeling to help her overcome her social anxiety about speaking in front of a crowd, he might invite her to come with him to a nearby conference where he is scheduled to give a presentation. Similarly, Gary's therapist could model getting her hands dirty but not immediately washing them. She might then encourage Gary to join her in the activity and if—after initial reluctance—he did so, he might be surprised when his anxiety about having dirty hands starts to dissipate.

In Vivo vs. Imaginal Exposure

Ideally, exposure therapies are done in real life with genuine exposure to the actual anxiety-provoking objects or situations. This is called *in vivo* exposure. However, real life exposure isn't always practical or possible. In such cases, clinicians use imaginal exposure, in which people are simply asked to imagine the feared scenario. The limitation of imaginal exposure is that it may not be as powerful as *in vivo* exposure. To counter this, clinicians have developed virtual reality exposure, which uses computer-generated virtual reality experiences to help clients face their fears. Evidence suggests that virtual reality exposure can be effective (Denney, Sullivan, & Thiry, 1977; D. Hughes, 1990).

Thought Stopping

Thought stopping is a CBT technique in which clients are taught to stop their thoughts, often by saying or thinking "Stop!" whenever an intrusive thought occurs (J. S. Kaplan & Tolin, 2011). It is often used to reduce anxiety, obsessions, and compulsions (Bakker, 2009; Wolpe, 1958). However, some CBT practitioners—especially those emphasizing a mindfulness approach (see below) in which clients are encouraged to accept rather than resist upsetting thoughts—are skeptical of any approach they see as encouraging thought suppression (Bakker, 2009; Lombardo & Turner, 1979; D. M. Ross, 1984). In their view, resisting unwanted thoughts only makes them stronger. Yet some CBT clinicians counter that thought stopping isn't the same as thought suppression. Rather, it is a cognitive self-control technique for overcoming dysfunctional thinking (Bakker, 2009). Both critics and supporters of thought stopping may have a point because research evidence suggests that the technique is helpful when anxiety is in response to concrete stimuli (as commonly occurs in phobias), but may be contraindicated when anxiety is in response to thoughts themselves (as in OCD and sometimes in social phobia) (Bakker, 2009).

Mindfulness and Acceptance Cognitive Therapies

Given their apprehension about thought stopping, some cognitive therapists instead emphasize mindfulness and acceptance-oriented approaches to anxiety. Thus, CBT approaches increasingly incorporate mindfulness training (see Chapter 5), in which clients are taught to observe and accept upsetting thoughts and feelings without trying to squelch or eliminate them. Some types of mindfulness training involve teaching clients *meditation techniques*, in which they consciously focus on observing their mind's processes and thoughts; other types encourage more informal means of nonjudgmentally observing and accepting thoughts and feelings (Norton, Abbott, Norberg, & Hunt, 2015).

Two examples of mindfulness-oriented approaches are mindfulness-based cognitive therapy (MBCT) and acceptance and commitment therapy (ACT). As discussed in Chapter 5, MBCT combines cognitive therapy with mindfulness meditation techniques, helping clients observe and acknowledge anxiety-provoking thoughts (Z. V. Segal, Teasdale, & Williams, 2004; Teasdale, 2004). The idea is that calmly observing thoughts changes clients' relationship to them, reducing the thoughts' negative emotional impact. In a similar vein, ACT emphasizes accepting, rather than banishing or taking literally, stressful cognitions that lead to anxiety (Hayes, 2004). As with MBCT (and in contrast to traditional cognitive therapies), ACT doesn't try to change client thoughts. Rather, it assumes that accepting those thoughts as they occur in the moment decreases their power and negative influence. Consequently, the thoughts cause less anxiety. Although exposure therapies generally remain the first-line intervention for these problems in the eyes of most researchers, studies of MBCT and ACT usually (but not always) find it to be as or more beneficial than traditional cognitive approaches (Arch et al., 2012; Bandelow, Lichte, Rudolf, Wiltink, & Beutel, 2015; Bluett, Homan, Morrison, Levin, & Twohig, 2014; Faucher, Koszycki, Bradwejn, Merali, & Bielajew, 2016; Goldin et al., 2016; L. Hale, Strauss, & Taylor, 2013; Hjeltnes et al., 2017; Hoge et al., 2015; Hoge et al., 2017; Key, Rowa, Bieling, McCabe, & Pawluk, 2017; Kocovski, Fleming, Hawley, Huta, & Antony, 2013; Koszycki et al., 2016; Raftery-Helmer, Moore, Coyne, & Reed, 2016; Sguazzin, Key, Rowa, Bieling, & McCabe, 2017; S. Y. S. Wong et al., 2016). Even so, more studies have been called for (Khusid & Vythilingam, 2016; Norton et al., 2015).

Effectiveness of CBT

Research on CBT has found it to be effective in addressing anxiety, obsessions, and compulsions. Exposure therapies, especially, are championed for having an extensive evidence base as treatments for anxiety and OCD; thus, as noted, they are often recommended as first-line interventions (Kaczkurkin & Foa, 2015). As with many presenting problems, CBT is often used in conjunction with drug treatments—although evidence suggests that certain anti-anxiety drugs may detract from exposure therapy's effectiveness (M. T. Williams et al., 2014). When it comes to anxiety, mindfulness/acceptance approaches and CBT are both considered effective (Bandelow et al., 2014; Bandelow, Reitt, et al., 2015). There is also evidence that they help reduce obsessions and compulsions (Bluett et al., 2014; Key et al., 2017; Olatunji, Davis, Powers, & Smits, 2013; Sguazzin et al., 2017). As noted when discussing biological perspectives, a meta-analysis found CBT more effective for OCD than antidepressants (Öst et al., 2015). Interestingly, when it comes to CBT interventions, there are many nuances in how to administer them for maximum effectiveness. For instance, recent research suggests that incorporating inhibitory learning into exposure therapy can greatly enhance its impact—an issue explored more fully in the "In Depth" feature.

IN DEPTH

Using Inhibitory Learning to Maximize Exposure Therapy

Psychologist Michelle Craske and colleagues have explored how inhibitory learning can be used to enhance exposure therapy (Craske, Treanor, Conway, Zbozinek, & Vervliet, 2014). To grasp what inhibitory learning is, it's helpful to recall (from Chapter 2) how classical conditioning works. In classical conditioning, an unconditioned stimulus (US) is repeatedly paired with a neutral stimulus until the neutral stimulus becomes a conditioned stimulus (CS) that now evokes the same response as the unconditioned stimulus. Thus, in the case of Little Albert, a neutral stimulus (a white rat) was repeatedly paired with an unconditioned stimulus (a loud noise) that evoked an unconditioned response (UR) (fear). Consequently, the neutral stimulus (the rat) became a conditioned stimulus—it eventually evoked a conditioned response (CR) (fear) all on its own.

Inhibitory learning happens during the process of extinction. Extinction, as you remember, occurs when the conditioned stimulus is no longer paired with the unconditioned stimulus. As a result, the conditioned stimulus stops eliciting a conditioned response. For example, had John Watson tried to extinguish Little Albert's fear of rats (which, unfortunately, he never did!), he would have repeatedly presented the white rat without making a loud noise. Eventually, inhibitory learning would have occurred, in which Albert learned that the white rat no longer predicted the loud noise. Why is this inhibitory learning? Because it's not that the earlier conditioning somehow goes away or is eliminated. Rather, it's just that additional conditioning occurs that inhibits the previously learned conditioned response. In other words, "the original CS-US association learned during fear conditioning is not erased during extinction, but rather is left intact as new, secondary inhibitory learning about the CS-US develops—specifically, that the CS no longer predicts the US" (Craske et al., 2014, p. 11).

Craske and colleagues maintain that to enhance exposure therapy's effectiveness, we must maximize inhibitory learning. Otherwise, the original conditioning is likely to reassert itself. They offer various strategies for maximizing inhibitory learning (Craske et al., 2014). Let's discuss three of them, using Little Albert to illustrate how these strategies could be implemented with him were he alive today.

1. *Expectancy violation*: One way that exposure therapy works is by violating expectancies—the cognitive predictions of how unpleasant a situation's outcome will be. If we were doing exposure therapy with Little Albert, our failure to pair the white rat with a scary noise would violate Albert's expectancies. Research finds that making sure expectancies are reduced to 5% or less improves the effectiveness of exposure therapy (Craske et al., 2014). This incorporates a cognitive component (expectancies) into the otherwise behavioral process of exposure therapy. Instead of simply stopping exposure at the first signs that the fearful behaviors are eliminated, it is continued until the expectancy of the

conditioned stimulus evoking fear reaches 5% or less. The idea is that inhibitory learning is stronger when expectancies (not just behaviors) are altered through consistently and intensely violating them.

2. *Occasional reinforced extinction*: This is counterintuitive because it involves periodically repairing the CS and US; thus, during exposure therapy we would occasionally make a loud noise when presenting Albert with the white rat. Why would this help? Because "the participant is less likely to expect the *next* CS presentation to predict the US because CS-US pairings have been associated with both further CS-US pairings *and* CS-no US pairings" (Craske et al., 2014, p. 13). Albert would learn that even though encounters with rats periodically evoke fear, usually they don't. Thus, his original fear expectancies would be challenged.

3. *Multiple contexts*: Fear responses that have been extinguished in one context often reappear in others. It might not be enough to simply use exposure therapy with Albert in a laboratory setting. For exposure therapy to be most effective, inhibitory learning should occur in a variety of situations in which Albert might encounter a rat (e.g., at home, at work, at a pet store, or while riding the London Underground).

CRITICAL THINKING QUESTIONS

1. If inhibitory learning is always in addition to the original conditioning, does this mean that once people are conditioned to be fearful of something, they are always at risk of the fear reemerging—even after therapy has eliminated it?

2. If exposure therapy is strengthened by incorporating attention to violating people's fear-related expectations, is it better to consider it a cognitive-behavioral, rather than purely behavioral, intervention?

3. Can you think of a time when your own expectations were violated and previous learning was weakened? Did the previous learning ever reassert itself? Why do you think it did or didn't?

HUMANISTIC PERSPECTIVES

Person-Centered Therapy

A traditional person-centered perspective sees anxiety as caused by incongruence. When people can only obtain positive regard from others by behaving in ways that are inconsistent with their true selves, then anxiety and other emotional difficulties result (Cain, 2010; R. Elliott, 2013; D. Murphy & Joseph, 2016; C. R. Rogers, 1951, 1959). In other words, "psychological distress in general and anxiety in particular derives from discrepancies between different aspects of self, variously referred to as 'actual/organismic,' 'perceived,' and 'ideal' or 'ought' selves" (R. Elliott, 2013, p. 20). Person-centered therapy for anxiety is no different than for any other presenting problem: the therapist avoids what person-centered theory views as stigmatizing, medical-model diagnostic labels while providing a safe and supportive environment containing Rogers' core conditions for change (empathy, genuineness, and unconditional positive regard). Doing so offers the conditions necessary for clients to reconnect with their self-actualizing tendencies. Once they are more in touch with their true selves, they will start behaving in more psychologically congruent ways and their anxiety should lift (R. Elliott, 2013).

Tammy

If eight-year-old Tammy Steadman worked with a person-centered therapist, he would provide Tammy with a safe therapeutic environment, one in which he would empathize with Tammy's concerns and accept her unconditionally—even when Tammy gets extremely anxious. Over time, Tammy could be expected to share that her parents like it when she performs before others. She might even recount how they made her sing in the third-grade talent show, although she told them she didn't want to. Tammy would also likely confide that she prefers to draw or do math puzzles in a workbook they have at school. The therapist would reflect Tammy's feelings back to her. He would also keep paper, pencil, and puzzles in his office and encourage Tammy to use them whenever she wants during sessions. Over several months, Tammy would hopefully become less and less anxious, especially in therapy. Tammy and her therapist might discuss inviting her parents to a future session so Tammy could share her feelings with them about what kinds of activities she enjoys most.

CASE EXAMPLES

Existential Perspectives

Existential Therapy

Existential psychotherapies (see Chapter 2) contend that although anxiety is often seen as a "medico-psychological problem," it is also a "metaphysical and spiritual problem" (Costello, 2011, p. 65). Existential therapists distinguish existential anxiety from neurotic anxiety. **Existential anxiety** is a normal and expected part of human existence. It emerges from four basic **existential givens** that none of us can avoid or escape (Yalom, 1980). These givens are:

» *Death*: We are all going to die—a fact none of us can avoid, but one that understandably causes us anxiety.

» *Freedom*: While we usually think of freedom as a good thing, it is often terrifying because it means that we are responsible for our own choices. Yet we often don't want to bear the responsibility of making choices. Sometimes we deny our freedom and act as if the way we are living our lives has been foisted upon us and we have no say in the matter.

» *Isolation*: We are all ultimately alone in the world, trapped inside our bodies and never fully able to move beyond that fact. While we may seek out social relations and connections with others, our aloneness is an inevitable and unavoidable fact of existence.

» *Meaninglessness*: There is no inherent meaning in life. The only meaning it has is whatever meaning we imbue in it. A lot of our existential anxiety stems from our struggle to invest life with meaning, which we must create ourselves.

Although not always pleasant, existential anxiety is healthy and adaptive. Awareness of their mortality and need for connection motivates people to take responsibility for constructing meaningful and rich lives for themselves. However, sometimes people experience **neurotic anxiety**, which occurs when they refuse to acknowledge existential givens that demand they invest their lives with meaning.

Logotherapy

A nice example of the existential approach to anxiety is found in the work of psychiatrist and psychotherapist Victor Frankl (1959, 1968), a Holocaust survivor who was able to find meaning within the horrible circumstances he faced in a Nazi concentration camp at Auschwitz. This led him to develop an existential treatment method that he called **logotherapy**. Frankl's approach stresses how failure to make meaning can lead to a variety of symptoms—including anxiety, obsessions, and compulsions. For Frankl, when people don't face their responsibility to make meaning in an inherently meaningless world, they run the risk of developing neurotic anxiety. To cope with the overwhelming anxiety caused by their lack of meaning, they disproportionately focus on insignificant things:

> *The phobic focuses on some object that has caused him concern in the past; the agoraphobic sees her anxiety as coming from the world outside her door; the patient with stage fright or speech anxiety focuses on the stage or the podium. The anxiety neurotic thus makes sense of his or her discomfort with life. (Boeree, 2006)*

Frankl (1968) explained OCD similarly. He argued that, in the absence of having constructed personal meaning, people who experience obsessions and compulsions demand perfect certainty about minor details, something that is ultimately impossible. In logotherapy, clients with anxiety neuroses are taught not only to accept uncertainty, but also encouraged to find meaning in life because only by doing so can they overcome anxiety. Finding meaning in relationships, work, and even through accepting one's own suffering are all ways to overcome neurotic anxiety (Frankl, 1959, 1968). The evidence base for existential therapies is relatively small—there simply hasn't been that much research conducted (S.-Y. Tan & Wong, 2012). The research that has been done is usually interpreted as providing encouraging but limited support (Shumaker, 2012; S.-Y. Tan & Wong, 2012; Vos, Craig, & Cooper, 2015; M. J. M. Wood, Molassiotis, & Payne, 2011).

Gary

Gary regularly obsesses about whether he properly programmed the security system in his house. By preoccupying himself with such an insignificant event, he avoids the larger existential questions behind his obsessive-compulsive anxiety. If a logotherapist were to work with Gary, the goal would be to help Gary gain awareness of his neurotic anxiety. Consequently, Gary might realize that he has been unwilling to risk taking a leave of absence from his job as an accountant so that he can pursue an interest in creative writing. Logotherapy would try to help Gary see how he has rationalized this decision as something beyond his control by telling himself "I need to earn a living for my family" and "There's always tomorrow." If logotherapy was effective, Gary would begin accepting responsibility for creating his own future—a future that might involve him incorporating creative writing into his life in meaningful and rewarding ways. As a result, his obsessions and compulsions would be expected to recede.

CASE EXAMPLES

Emotion-Focused Therapy (EFT)

Although humanistic-existential therapies can often be helpful, recent reviews suggest they are somewhat less effective for relieving anxiety than more directive approaches such as CBT (R. Elliott, Greenberg, Watson, Timulak, & Freire, 2013). The possible exception to this appears to be emotion-focused therapy (EFT), a more modern humanistic psychotherapy that we previously discussed as an empirically supported treatment (EST) for depression (see Chapter 5). EFT has also shown promise in relieving social anxiety and generalized anxiety (R. Elliott, 2013; R. MacLeod & Elliott, 2012; R. MacLeod, Elliott, & Rodgers, 2012; Priest, 2013; Shahar et al., 2012). As you may recall, EFT theorizes that addressing emotional conflicts (rather than reconditioning behavior or learning to think logically) is at the heart of resolving psychological problems. According to EFT, emotional conflicts originate in difficult or painful past experiences. For instance, the EFT formulation of social anxiety holds that socially anxious people experience shame due to "repeated experiences of being bullied, criticized, rejected, or neglected" (Shahar, 2014, p. 538). Socially anxious situations are those that elicit these feelings of shame. Similarly, people experiencing generalized anxiety feel as if they are under constant threat because almost all situations trigger painful past emotions for them (Timulak & McElvaney, 2016).

Emotion-focused therapy aims to help anxious clients gain awareness of the emotional conflicts that cause them to be fretful or avoidant in everyday interactions. The goal is to provide a supportive therapeutic environment in which they can learn to tolerate and accept (rather than fear and avoid) painful and difficult feelings. Reducing avoidance allows clients to face and resolve emotional conflicts, which ultimately frees them to better identify their own needs and cope more effectively in situations that previously caused anxiety. The evidence base for EFT's effectiveness is not quite as clear for anxiety as it is for depression. However, initial efforts to develop and test EFT as a therapy for anxiety problems have shown promise (R. MacLeod & Elliott, 2012; R. MacLeod et al., 2012; A. L. Robinson, McCague, & Whissell, 2014). A recent study testing the effectiveness of EFT for social anxiety concluded that EFT significantly reduced symptoms and self-criticism; while such results are encouraging, the sample size was small and additional studies are necessary to draw firmer conclusions (Shahar, Bar-Kalifa, & Alon, 2017).

EVALUATING PSYCHOLOGICAL PERSPECTIVES

The most common psychotherapeutic approach used to address anxiety is 10–20 sessions of CBT (A. A. Shah & Han, 2015). This is probably because CBT has the most established evidence base showing it to be effective (Cuijpers, Sijbrandij et al., 2014). One set of treatment guidelines developed in Germany recommends CBT as the first-line psychotherapy for social anxiety disorder, generalized anxiety disorder, panic disorder, and agoraphobia (Bandelow, Reitt, et al., 2015). However, these guidelines advise clinicians to use CBT in conjunction with drug treatments for these disorders. The only anxiety disorder they say should be treated with CBT alone is specific phobia. Psychodynamic therapies are usually considered a second-line therapy if CBT doesn't work. Interestingly, psychotherapy—even when combined with prescription drugs—is estimated to be effective only 45%–65% of the time (Bandelow, Reitt, et al., 2015). This means a lot of people don't benefit from available therapy approaches. Therapy can be helpful for anxiety, but it often isn't.

CBT is also the main type of therapy recommended for OCD and related disorders. Recent reviews and meta-analyses conclude that CBT is quite effective at reducing obsessions and compulsions (M. E. Franklin et al., 2012; Lewin, Wu, McGuire, & Storch, 2014; Olatunji et al., 2013; Öst et al., 2015). Additionally, CBT has not only proven effective for addressing hoarding (Tolin, Frost, Steketee, & Muroff, 2015), but is also encouraged for compulsive skin-picking and hair-pulling (Keuthen et al., 2015). In fact, the authors of one recent meta-analysis contend that CBT is the only therapy with a clear evidence base for OCD (Öst et al., 2015). Their results imply that when it comes to OCD, CBT fares better than antidepressants. Perhaps even more striking is their finding that adding CBT to antidepressant treatment improves outcomes, but adding antidepressants to CBT does not (Öst et al., 2015). This suggests that CBT may be a slightly more effective way of alleviating obsessions and compulsions than antidepressants. That said, many people with OCD and related disorders don't respond to therapy; further additional research is needed to better understand whether the improvements CBT provides for OCD symptoms last over the long run (Olatunji et al., 2013).

6.6 SOCIOCULTURAL PERSPECTIVES
CROSS-CULTURAL AND SOCIAL JUSTICE PERSPECTIVES
Cultural Differences in the Expression of Anxiety

Sociocultural perspectives tend to view presenting problems through a cultural lens, believing that mental disorders are culture-bound syndromes that inevitably emerge and are defined within social contexts (D. J. Stein & Williams, 2010). In keeping with this idea, research consistently shows that cultural background influences how people exhibit anxiety. For example, a small but compelling body of evidence suggests that symptoms of panic attacks vary by culture—with higher rates of dizziness in Asian cultures, burning or skin-pricking sensations among African Americans, trembling in Caribbean Latinos, and fears of death in

African American and Arab populations (Lewis-Fernández et al., 2010). Similarly, some Chinese and Japanese patients diagnosed with social anxiety disorder don't avoid social situations because they are concerned about embarrassing themselves (as the *DSM* and *ICD* suggest). Instead, they worry about embarrassing or offending others—a form of social anxiety referred to in Japan as *taijin kyofusho* (TKS) (Hofmann, Asnaani, & Hinton, 2010; Lewis-Fernández et al., 2010; X. Zhu et al., 2014). Of course, there are many other ways that anxiety looks different cross-culturally. Three additional examples are:

» Social anxiety is far less prevalent in Asian countries, especially compared to the U.S. and Russia (where it seems to occur most) (Hofmann et al., 2010). In some rural areas of Russia, nearly 50% of people show signs of social anxiety (Hofmann & Hinton, 2014)!

» In non-Western societies, generalized anxiety is much more likely to involve somatic (physical) complaints (Lewis-Fernández et al., 2010). For example, in Cambodian culture it is common to believe that an internal air-like substance called *khyâl* flows through the limbs and body. Thus, physical symptoms such as sore necks, weak or cold limbs, and panic attacks about neck pain or gastrointestinal symptoms are common ways of displaying anxiety (Hofmann & Hinton, 2014).

» *Ataques de nervios* is a culturally specific syndrome found in Puerto Rico and the Dominican Republic (Hofmann & Hinton, 2014). In addition to fear and anger, an *ataque* often includes tightness in the chest, feeling one is losing control, sensations of heat in the body, feeling faint, heart palpitations, and shaking that affects the arms and legs. Patients often feel like they are dying or fret that their impending loss of control could lead to hurting themselves or others (Hofmann & Hinton, 2014).

It's important for therapists to be aware of how anxiety presents differently across cultural contexts. Without such awareness, cultural misunderstandings that lead to ineffective or harmful interventions may result. Of course, as noted when reviewing historical perspectives, notions of anxiety have evolved through history, which is why some theorists see them as social constructions—socially shared ways of defining, talking about, and understanding the experience we collectively label as "anxiety" (Dowbiggin, 2009; K. J. Gergen & McNamee, 2000; Stanley & Raskin, 2002). You must decide the extent to which you believe anxiety is a universal experience across cultures versus an experience constituted by culture and context.

Economic Conditions and Anxiety

Since the middle of the 20th century, when the poet W. H. Auden published a poem of the same name, it has been common for social critics to contend that we live in an "age of anxiety" (Dowbiggin, 2009). The term refers to our ever-present awareness of the perils of modern times. The age of anxiety has continued for six decades now, as we continually worry about a myriad of terrible things—including environmental destruction, nuclear waste, drug addiction, pornography, violence, religious fanaticism, terrorist attacks, and loss of privacy in an Internet age (D. Smith, 2012). The idea that we live in an age of anxiety is consistent with perspectives that see anxiety as emerging from sociocultural factors such as socioeconomic, gender, and racial inequality. Along these lines, many studies have found anxiety and depression correlate with lower socioeconomic status (SES) and current financial strain (Dijkstra-Kersten, Biesheuvel-Leliefeld, van der Wouden, Penninx, & van Marwijk, 2015; Lahelma, Laaksonen, Martikainen, Rahkonen, & Sarlio-Lähteenkorva, 2006; G. Lewis et al., 2003; McLaughlin et al., 2011; Pulkki-Råback et al., 2012; Stansfeld, Clark, Rodger, Caldwell, & Power, 2008). Further, low levels of parental education (a measure closely associated with SES) effectively predict severity of anxiety and depression in adulthood (McLaughlin et al., 2011). This suggests that economic disadvantage—lacking the means to manage life's challenges—makes it more difficult to harness the resources necessary to ward off anxiety and depression.

A notable drawback of many of these studies is their failure to differentiate anxiety from depression. One study that did make such a distinction unearthed an interesting age-related difference, namely that the likelihood of anxiety decreases with age while the likelihood of depression increases (M. J. Green & Benzeval, 2011). However, SES amplified this pattern across the lifespan: the anxiety of lower SES individuals decreased more slowly with age, but their depression increased more rapidly. This finding supports one of the main premises of social justice perspectives, namely that lack of economic resources exacerbates psychological distress—in this case, economic inequality places older people without financial means in "double jeopardy" when it comes to anxiety and depression (M. J. Green & Benzeval, 2011, p. 72).

Gender and Anxiety

When it comes to gender, studies consistently find that for most anxiety disorders women are diagnosed more often than men—in many cases, twice as often (American Psychiatric Association, 2013b; MacKinaw-Koons & Vasey, 2000; Vesga-López et al., 2008). Women also seem to be more burdened by anxiety, as indicated by more doctor visits and missed days from work (C. P. McLean, Asnaani, Litz, & Hofmann, 2011; Vesga-López et al., 2008). Reasons for gender differences in the rates and intensity of anxiety are passionately debated, with some arguing that genetic, neurochemical, and hormonal differences between men and women make women more biologically vulnerable to anxiety difficulties (Altemus, 2006; Altemus, Sarvaiya, & Epperson, 2014; Ginsberg, 2004; Kinrys & Wygant, 2005; McHenry, Carrier, Hull, & Kabbaj, 2014). However, others counter that women face social disadvantages that men don't and this better explains higher rates of female anxiety. For instance, research has found that physical abuse, sexual abuse, and trauma place women at greater risk for anxiety issues (Ranta, Kaltiala-Heino, Pelkonen, & Marttunen, 2009; Ussher, 2011). Further, studies of people (mostly women) diagnosed with anxiety disorders have found that having been overtly or covertly bullied, teased, and victimized by peers during childhood is associated with experiencing anxiety problems in adolescence and adulthood (Ginsberg, 2004; McCabe, Miller, Laugesen, Antony, & Young, 2010; Ranta et al., 2009).

Somewhat controversially, women are more likely than men to be prescribed drugs for their anxiety. This is a long-standing pattern, especially in the United States. In 1975, 20% of all U.S. women (but only 8% of men) reported having taken benzodiazepines (A. V. Horwitz, 2013). A quarter of a century later in 2001–2002, U.S. epidemiological data showed that among those diagnosed with social anxiety disorder, 12.39% of women but only 8.76% of men had taken medication for it (Y. Xu et al., 2012). A 2010 report posted on the World Health Organization's website indicated that the percentage of middle-aged American women taking anti-anxiety drugs was estimated to be 11%, nearly twice the 5.7% rate for middle-aged men (Medco, 2011). This gender gap is not as great everywhere, but it also occurs elsewhere—an Australian study found that 5.7% of women, but only 3.6% of men, had taken anxiolytic drugs in the two weeks prior to being surveyed (M. G. Harris et al., 2011). Similarly, a U.K. study found females both more likely to be diagnosed with anxiety disorders and to be on anxiolytics than males (John et al., 2015). Given this data, feminist critics contend that mainstream mental

Feminist therapists have critiqued pharmaceutical ads marketing anti-anxiety drugs to women. This ad is from 1967.
Source: © Pfizer
Disclaimer: This advertisement is being used to represent the general attitudes of this era in relation to anxiety drugs and gender and is not in any way representative of the current views or attitudes of Pfizer.

health care too often conceptualizes women's emotional difficulties as due to mental illnesses rather than deeply ingrained societal discrimination and consequently is too quick to prescribe drugs. These critics argue that the real solution is not to medicate women into submission, but to reform social institutions that oppress women and produce their anxiety in the first place (Ussher, 2011). From a social justice perspective, addressing women's emotional distress at the individual level is best accomplished by political reform at the societal level. This involves a shift away from individual treatment and towards community action. Social justice psychologist Isaac Prilleltensky provides an example from the state of Kerala in India:

> [W]omen in this poor state began to organize into social movements that demanded tenant protection, nutrition programs for children, land reform, and community development. Through the organizing process women experienced a psychological sense of empowerment. But solidarity resulted not only in enhanced personal control and a sense of mastery; it also led to meaningful social change. Public health indices such as literacy, infant mortality, and longevity have been higher in Kerala than in the rest of India for many years. (Prilleltensky, Dokecki, Frieden, & Ota Wang, 2007, p. 24)

CONSUMER AND SERVICE-USER PERSPECTIVES

What is the consumer's experience of being diagnosed with anxiety? Much of the mainstream research literature on anxiety, obsessions, and compulsions focuses on the problems of stigma and insuring that people who need treatment receive it. Even though the public views anxiety less negatively than depression or schizophrenia, being labeled with anxiety still carries significant stigma; in particular, it is common for people to blame those with anxiety for their problems (L. Wood, Birtel, Alsawy, Pyle, & Morrison, 2014). Further, one study found that simply describing someone as experiencing social anxiety was just as stigmatizing as identifying someone as mentally ill (K. N. Anderson, Jeon, Blenner, Wiener, & Hope, 2015). In both cases, stigma occurred when the person described was evaluated as dangerous or having an embarrassing problem—and this led to not wanting to be near the person. Importantly, as is often so with other stigmatizing psychological problems, people who have personally faced anxiety or know others who have experienced it are less likely to hold negative attitudes towards anxious individuals (Alonso et al., 2008; Batterham, Griffiths, Barney, & Parsons, 2013). Thus, many researchers advocate educating people about anxiety problems by exposing people directly or indirectly (e.g., via the media) to those diagnosed with anxiety disorders (Batterham et al., 2013; L. Wood et al., 2014).

OCD and related disorders also carry with them significant stigma (Fang et al., 2014; Fennell & Boyd, 2014; Fennell & Liberato, 2007; Simonds & Thorpe, 2003). A survey of psychiatrists found that even though they reported having a compassionate attitude toward those with OCD, they also "thought that OCD patients talk too much, waste a lot of time, and need more patience when compared with other psychiatric disorder sufferers" (Kusalaruk, Saipanish, & Hiranyatheb, 2015, p. 1703). Interestingly, stigma toward those with OCD varies based on the types of obsessions and compulsions. In a study examining different types of OCD, patients with obsessions and compulsions that focused on harming self or others were regarded most negatively, followed by those whose obsessions and compulsions involved handwashing; the least stigmatized obsessions and compulsions concerned compulsive checking (Fang et al., 2014; Fennell & Boyd, 2014; Fennell & Liberato, 2007; Simonds & Thorpe, 2003).

Consumers of mental health services must overcome the stigma associated with anxiety to recognize their problem and seek help for it. It is important for service providers to keep this in mind. "The Lived Experience" feature provides one service-user's story of how she overcame her OCD.

THE LIVED EXPERIENCE

A True Story of Living with Obsessive-Compulsive Disorder

The underlying reasons why I have to repeatedly re-zip things, blink a certain way, count to an odd number, check behind my shower curtain to ensure no one is hiding to plot my abduction, make sure that computer cords are not rat tails, etc., will never be clear to me. Is it the result of a poor reaction to the anesthesiology that was administered during my wisdom teeth extraction? These aggravating thoughts and compulsions began immediately after the procedure. Or is it related to PANDAS (Pediatric Autoimmune Neuropsychiatric Disorder Associated with Streptococcal infection) which is a proposed theory connoting a strange relationship between group A beta-hemolytic streptococcal infection with rapidly developing symptoms of obsessive-compulsive disorder in the basal ganglia? Is it simply a hereditary by-product of my genetic makeup associated with my nervous personality? Or is it a defense tactic I developed through having an overly concerned mother?

The Consequences Associated with My OCD

Growing up with mild, in fact dormant, obsessive-compulsive disorder, I would have never proposed such bizarre questions until 2002, when an exacerbated overnight onset of severe OCD mentally paralyzed me. I'd just had my wisdom teeth removed and was immediately bombarded with incessant and intrusive unwanted thoughts, ranging from a fear of being gay to questioning if I was truly seeing the sky as blue. I'm sure similar thoughts had passed through my mind before; however, they must have been filtered out of my conscious, as I never had such incapacitating ideas enter my train of thought before. During the summer of 2002, not one thought was left unfiltered from my conscious. Thoughts that didn't even matter and held no significance were debilitating; they prevented me from accomplishing the simplest, most mundane tasks. Tying my shoe only to untie it repetitively, continuously being tardy for work and school, spending long hours in a bathroom engaging in compulsive rituals such as tapping inanimate objects endlessly with no resolution, and finally medically withdrawing from college, eventually to drop out completely not once but twice, were just a few of the consequences I endured.

Seeking Help

After seeing a medical specialist for OCD, I had tried a mixed cocktail of medications over a 10-year span, including escitalopram (Lexapro), fluoxetine (Prozac), risperidone (Risperdal), aripiprazole (Abilify), sertraline (Zoloft), clomipramine (Anafranil), lamotrigine (Lamictal), and finally, after a recent bipolar disorder II diagnosis, lurasidone (Latuda). The only medication that has remotely curbed my intrusive thoughts and repetitive compulsions is lurasidone, giving me approximately 60 to 70 percent relief from my symptoms.

Many psychologists and psychiatrists would argue that a combination of cognitive behavioral therapy (CBT) and pharmacological management might be the only successful treatment approach for an individual plagued with OCD. If an individual is brave enough to undergo exposure and response prevention therapy (ERP), a type of CBT that has been shown to relieve symptoms of OCD and anxiety through desensitization and habituation, then my hat is off to them. ... In the majority of cases of severe OCD, I believe pharmacological management is a must.

How I Conquered My OCD

So, what does a person incapacitated with OCD do? If, as a person with severe OCD, I truly had an answer, I would probably leave my house more often, take a risk once in a while, and live freely without fearing the mundane nuances associated with public places. It's been my experience with OCD to take everything one second at a time and remain grateful for those good seconds. If I were to take OCD one day at a time, well, too many millions of internal battles would be lost in this 24-hour period. I have learned to live with my OCD through writing and performing as a spoken word artist. I have taken the time to explore my pain and transmute it into an art form which has allowed me to explore the topic of pain as an interesting and beneficial subject matter. I am the last person to attempt to tell any individuals with OCD what the best therapy approach is for them, but I will encourage each and every individual to explore their own pain, and believe that manageability can come in many forms, from classic techniques to intricate art forms, in order for healing to begin.

By Tiffany Dawn Hasse in collaboration with Kristen Fuller, MD. Reprinted with permission. This is Tiffany's personal story.

SYSTEMS PERSPECTIVES

Expressed Emotion and Accommodation

Family context plays a role in anxiety, obsessions, and compulsions. Among people diagnosed with such disorders, interpersonal relationships are often strained—especially with parents and significant others. The problem is often circular: "The considerable burden of living with a person with a severe anxiety disorder may strain relationships, but relationship dysfunction, in turn, plays a role in exacerbation of anxiety problems and affects response to treatment" (Chambless, 2012, p. 548). Higher levels of expressed emotion—relatives and significant others being hostile, critical, or emotionally overinvolved—are associated with worse treatment outcomes (Chambless, Bryan, Aiken, Steketee, & Hooley, 2001; Chambless, Floyd, Rodebaugh, & Steketee, 2007; De Berardis et al., 2008; Ozkiris, Essizoglu, Gulec, & Aksaray, 2015; Przeworski et al., 2012; Steketee & Chambless, 2001). We saw that this was true for both psychosis and mood issues (see Chapters 4 and 5) and it is also true for anxiety; having significant people in your life who are critical or hostile in response to your difficulties simply makes matters worse.

Theresa and Gary

When Theresa gets angry with her husband Gary for having to repeatedly check the stove and is contemptuous and critical about it, she hampers his recovery. Couples therapy might help Theresa better understand how this kind of strong expressed emotion is counterproductive in helping Gary overcome his obsessive-compulsive issues.

CASE EXAMPLES

~~Accommodation~~—the process by which patients' relatives or significant others collude with them to help them avoid anxiety-provoking situations or repeatedly reassure them that everything is okay—also correlates with poorer outcomes (Albert et al., 2010; Boeding et al., 2013; Chambless, 2012; Cherian, Pandian, Math, Kandavel, & Janardhan Reddy, 2014; Lebowitz, Panza, Su, & Bloch, 2012; Peris, Sugar, et al., 2012; Peris, Yadegar, Asarnow, & Piacentini, 2012; B. M. Rudy, Storch, & Lewin, 2015; Strauss, Hale, & Stobie, 2015; Thompson-Hollands, Edson, Tompson, & Comer, 2014). This makes sense because accommodating anxious family members simply allows them to continue their problematic behavior patterns.

Tammy

Eight-year-old Tammy repeatedly seeks reassurance from her parents that everything will be okay if she goes to school. She also regularly asks them if she can stay home from school; when they accommodate her in this way to prevent her from feeling anxious, they inadvertently encourage her anxious behavior.

CASE EXAMPLES

In cases of OCD, some family members are so accommodating that they end up performing rituals on the patient's behalf.

Theresa and Gary

When Theresa, at her husband Gary's request, checks whether the stove is off, she accommodates his obsessive-compulsive tendencies. Besides allowing him to perpetuate his problematic behavior patterns, it also leads Theresa to feel put upon and, over time, resentful and angry. This, in turn, generates more expressed emotion from her. Her accommodating behavior, combined with the resulting expressed emotion, only hampers Gary's recovery.

CASE EXAMPLES

CHAPTER 6

A main goal of family therapy in such cases is to help significant others and relatives better understand the ways that expressed emotion and accommodation interfere with their loved one's improvement. Changing these family dynamics ostensibly enhances treatment outcomes. Educating family members about better ways to respond to their anxious loved ones, as well as helping them gain insight into the problematic family dynamics that perpetuate the problem, become the focus of many family interventions.

Structural Family Therapy for Generalized Anxiety

Bowen's structural family therapy, which has long viewed anxiety as a problem in family and couple relationships (K. G. Baker, 2015; M. Bowen, 1978), has recently been adapted to address generalized anxiety specifically (Priest, 2015). This adapted model nicely exemplifies how family systems perspectives can be used to conceptualize anxiety. It contends that people with generalized anxiety often experience high levels of tension in their romantic relationships because their ability to effectively differentiate is poor. Recall from Chapter 2 that differentiation is the ability to distinguish one's own thoughts and feelings from others'. From a structural family therapy perspective, anxious people—due to trauma or abuse in their families of origin—have a hard time with differentiation. When anxious, they either fuse with other people in order to gain comfort and reassurance or they emotionally cut themselves off from others as a form of self-protection. Their relational boundaries therefore become too loose or too rigid and they

Structural family therapists contend that people who experienced trauma or abuse in their families of origin often have difficulty regulating boundaries in adult relationships.
Source: Getty Images/iStockphoto \ stockvisual

often respond to significant others in emotionally impulsive and defensive ways. Not surprisingly then, their romantic relationships suffer. Structural family therapy aims to work with couples to help them develop more differentiated boundaries, allowing for more effective communication and support (K. G. Baker, 2015; M. Bowen, 1978). Research is needed to determine how effective such an approach is for alleviating generalized anxiety in particular, but a broader review recently concluded that systemic therapies have generally proven effective for anxiety issues (Carr, 2014). Regardless, systemic conceptualizations constitute a compelling family systems way of thinking about GAD.

Theresa and Gary

Were Theresa and Gary to seek structural family couples therapy, the therapist would work to help them better understand the dynamics of their relationship. Over time, it would become clear that whenever Gary inquires about Theresa's ongoing anxiety, Theresa emotionally withdraws. In response, Gary becomes more solicitous of Theresa, which in turn only elicits further emotional distance from her. Structural family couples therapy would try to help Theresa gain insight into how her family dynamics while growing up are relevant to how she deals with Gary. Her parents always fussed over her when she felt anxious, which only made Theresa feel like she couldn't handle things. Today, when Gary asks about Theresa's anxiety, it elicits self-doubt and withdrawal. Couples therapy would aim to teach Theresa and Gary to understand how patterns in their respective families of origin often recur in destructive ways in their marriage. As they come to better understand these dynamics, they would hopefully begin to change their communication patterns and improve their relationship.

CASE EXAMPLES

EVALUATING SOCIOCULTURAL PERSPECTIVES

Sociocultural perspectives emphasize family, social, and cultural influences on anxiety. Their main advantage is that they remind us how human emotions such as anxiety are shaped by context. Family perspectives have been shown to be helpful at reducing expressed emotion and accommodation, while also helping people to alter family patterns to minimize anxiety. Social justice perspectives stress not simply treating anxiety as an individual problem, but addressing economic, racial, and gender inequality. The question is whether social justice perspectives alone can account for anxiety issues. Not everyone who faces challenging social circumstances experiences anxiety, leading many to conclude that biological and psychological approaches are needed to supplement a sociocultural viewpoint.

6.7 CLOSING THOUGHTS: ANXIETY AND FEAR AS UNIQUELY HUMAN

Joseph LeDoux is a neuroscientist who has conducted groundbreaking research on the underlying fear circuitry of the brain. His work has been essential in identifying the amygdala as a key component of the brain's fear circuit (discussed earlier). However, despite his neuroscience underpinnings, LeDoux (2015) is skeptical of a strictly biological account of anxiety and fear. On the contrary, he has provocatively argued that anxiety and fear are uniquely human emotions that emerge from, but can't be fully reduced to, brain processes. His ideas provide a nice way of trying to integrate biological, psychological, and sociocultural perspectives as we bring this chapter to a close. Let's briefly discuss why.

LeDoux (2015) believes he made a mistake when he called the brain circuitry implicated in fear and anxiety the "fear circuit." In reflecting on this error, LeDoux explains that "the mistake I made was a semantic one—the mistake was to label the amygdala as part of the 'fear circuit.' And that has led to all kinds of bad consequences in the field" (Schwartz, 2015, para. 9). Why? Because by calling it this, people erroneously concluded that anxiety and fear arise directly from this circuit being activated. But this is incorrect, contends LeDoux. What happens is that the fear circuit (which LeDoux now thinks he should have named the "threat detection circuit") is activated whenever people sense a threat to their safety (LeDoux, 2015; Schwartz, 2015). Anxiety and fear, as emotional experiences, only occur in response to actively interpreting threat detection system activity:

> *In other words, fear and anxiety are not wired into the brain as basic responses to the world around us—rather, the responses that lead to them are, and they only coalesce into fear when the brain interprets them as such. (Schwartz, 2015, para. 7)*

Thus, anxiety and fear are uniquely human emotions because humans are thought to be alone among animals in being able to interpret their own bodily sensations. Other animals experience threat when the fear circuit is activated, but because they can't reflect on it and interpret what it means, they never truly experience the more complex emotions of anxiety or fear. Besides nicely highlighting the integrative aspects of complex emotions such as anxiety and fear (they are, in this conception, a combined product of basic brain circuitry and psychological reflection influenced by socially shared definitions and understandings of various emotions),

LeDoux's ideas have therapeutic implications. When we express disappointment that psychiatric drugs for anxiety are limited in their helpfulness, LeDoux (2015) points out that they are merely doing what we designed them to do, namely target and subdue threat detection circuitry. However, because anxiety and fear aren't reducible to that circuitry (cognitive interpretation is necessary before people feel these emotions), drugs alone are unlikely to fully eliminate them. Thus, LeDoux—a neuroscientist—is ultimately arguing that talk therapy may be essential in remediating anxiety and fear.

As we move on to discussions of other presenting problems, it may be helpful to keep in mind LeDoux's contention that complex human emotions are attributable to a combination of biological, psychological, and sociocultural processes. While there are indeed many perspectives in abnormal psychology and while these perspectives are each enlightening in their own ways when adopted, they can also blind us to alternative possibilities. In such instances, any anxiety we feel may provide highly useful information. It may be a way of telling ourselves that a larger, more integrative frame is necessary for a fuller grasp of the presenting problem at hand.

KEY TERMS

Acceptance and commitment therapy (ACT)
Accommodation
Agoraphobia
Anterior cingulate cortex
Anxiety
Anxiolytics
Augmenting agents
Avoidance model of worry
Barbiturates
Beta blockers
Body dysmorphic disorder (BDD)
Buspirone
Catastrophic misinterpretation model of panic disorder
Compulsions
Corticostriatal pathophysiological models
Emotional dysregulation model
Excoriation (skin-picking disorder)
Existential anxiety

Existential givens
Fear
Generalized anxiety disorder (GAD)
Genome-wide association (GWA) study
Glutamate hypothesis of OCD
Group selection
Group selection theory of OCD
Gut-brain axis
Hoarding disorder
Imaginal exposure
In vivo exposure
Inhibitory learning
Insula
Intolerance of uncertainty model
Little Hans
Logotherapy
Metacognitive model
Minor tranquilizers
Mixed anxiety and depressive disorder
Neurotic anxiety
Observational learning

Obsessions
Obsessive-compulsive disorder (OCD)
Panic attack
Panic disorder
Participant modeling
Prepared conditioning
Progressive relaxation
Rat Man
Relaxation training
Selective mutism
Separation anxiety disorder
Social anxiety disorder (social phobia)
Specific phobia
Striatum
Thalamus
Thought stopping
Trichotillomania (hair-pulling disorder)
Unified psychodynamic therapy protocol for anxiety disorders (UPP-ANXIETY)
Virtual reality exposure

Full definitions of the terms listed above can be found in the end-of-book glossary on p. 533.

 Go to the companion website, www.macmillanihe.com/raskin-abnormal-psych, to access a study guide, multiple choice and flashcard quizzes for this chapter, and other useful learning aids.

CHAPTER 6

CHAPTER 7
TRAUMA, STRESS, AND LOSS

7.1 OVERVIEW

 LEARNING OBJECTIVES

After reading this chapter, you should be able to:

1. Define trauma, stress, bereavement, grief, and dissociation.
2. Describe and evaluate *DSM* and *ICD* conceptualizations of posttraumatic and acute stress, adjustment disorder, and persistent complex bereavement/prolonged grief.
3. Explain historical perspectives on trauma.
4. Summarize and critique biological perspectives on trauma, stress, and loss—including neurochemical theories and treatments, brain structures implicated, genetic and evolutionary theories, and immune system explanations.
5. Review and assess psychodynamic, cognitive-behavioral, and humanistic approaches to trauma, stress, and loss.
6. Discuss and evaluate sociocultural approaches to trauma, loss, and stress that emphasize the importance of gender, culture, socioeconomic status, stigma, and expressed emotion; explain group interventions and couple/family system therapies.

 Photo source: © Royalty-Free/Corbis

GETTING STARTED: THE IMPACT OF TRAUMA, STRESS, AND LOSS

Joe

Joe is a 30-year-old single man who recently survived an earthquake. The apartment complex where he lives was severely damaged in the quake and the roof collapsed, killing neighbors in several adjacent apartments. Joe himself was trapped in the rubble for six hours until rescuers could get him out safely. Miraculously, Joe escaped the building unharmed. Still, he has been having a difficult time psychologically in the six months since the event. Joe feels emotionally anxious and keeps having nightmares about the roof collapsing on him. He also complains about not being able to concentrate at work or in social situations. When asked about this he merely replies, "I'm not quite myself lately." Joe also finds many things remind him of the quake. His office is near a metro station and whenever a train rumbles by, he gets anxious and jumpy because the sound is like the loud noise the apartment roof made just before crashing down. When asked what it was like to be trapped in the debris after the roof collapsed he says, "It was like I was outside my own body watching it happen to someone else." Despite feeling grateful he survived the event, Joe is not getting much sleep, is worried about another earthquake, feels guilty that he survived while others perished, and can't seem to move past the incident. His relationships with others—especially with his girlfriend Carol—are starting to suffer, so he decides to seek professional help.

CASE EXAMPLES

Marigold

Marigold is a 55-year old woman whose husband Harry passed away three years ago. Since that time, she has had a difficult time functioning. She feels sad and weepy much of the time; she even complains that time seems slower since Harry's death and food hasn't tasted the same to her since he died. She desperately yearns to be reunited with her deceased husband and thinks about him much of the time. Reminders of Harry, however, rarely produce positive feelings of reminiscence and appreciation. Instead, they usually result in Marigold becoming tearful, upset, or angry over the loss. Marigold reports feeling emotionally numb and says she has lost interest in many things that she used to enjoy. For instance, her work as an attorney—which she used to love—now holds little interest for her and instead feels like a chore. Marigold has cut herself off from most of the friends and family with whom she and Harry used to associate. She is in a great deal of emotional pain and decides to seek out a psychotherapist.

Defining Trauma, Stress, Bereavement, Grief, and Dissociation

Trauma, stress, and loss are common presenting problems. They are so common, in fact, that a lot of the words that clinicians use when talking about them—terms such as trauma, stress, bereavement, grief, and dissociation—are used in everyday life by non-professionals, but often imprecisely. Therefore, before proceeding it seems important to define how clinicians and researchers typically use these terms.

Trauma

Let's start with **trauma**. Just like "panic attack" (discussed in Chapter 6), the term "trauma" is used much more loosely in casual conversation than it is by most helping professionals. It's common to hear non-professionals identify events such as taking a difficult exam or having a favorite sports team lose a key game as "traumatic." This watered-down use of the term causes confusion because in clinical situations a "traumatic event" is typically limited to something severe, life threatening, and intense. For example, the *DSM-5* defines a trauma as involving "exposure to actual or threatened death, serious injury, or sexual violence" (American Psychiatric Association,

According to the DSM and ICD, natural disasters are traumatic events when they involve being exposed to actual or perceived harm, death, or severe injury.
Source: The Asahi Shimbun via Getty Images

CHAPTER 7

2013b, p. 271). Taking a difficult exam clearly doesn't qualify! Events that do qualify include things like a "natural or man-made disaster, combat, serious accident, witnessing the violent death of others, or being the victim of torture, terrorism, rape, or other crime" (World Health Organization, 1992, p. 120). Less disruptive events may be upsetting and cause for concern, but don't fit the clinical definition of trauma.

Joe

Joe's life-threatening experience surviving a deadly earthquake constitutes a traumatic event.

CASE EXAMPLES

Stress

Stress is another term we often use imprecisely, probably "because it is such a highly subjective phenomenon that it defies definition" (American Institute of Stress, n.d., para. 1). The American Psychological Association (n.d.-b, para. 1) defines stress in exceedingly broad terms as "a feeling of being overwhelmed, worried or run-down." Hans Selye, the father of stress research, borrowed the term from physics (Burrows, 2015; M. Jackson, 2014). In physics, it refers to "the force that produces strain on a physical body" (Centre for Studies on Human Stress, n.d., para. 1). Selye famously developed his ideas about stress in his **general adaptation syndrome (GAS)**. In the GAS, Selye (1950) defined stress in terms of three stages: *alarm* (the immediate fight or flight reaction to a stressor), *resistance* (the way the organism adapts physically and psychologically to the stressor), and *exhaustion* (the effects of long-term stress on physical and emotional well-being). Selye's GAS is general in the sense that it applies broadly to a wide variety of stressors—being attacked by a bear is an obvious example, but ongoing pressure and hard-to-meet deadlines at work count too. Importantly, although prolonged stress tends to have deleterious effects, stress in and of itself isn't always a bad thing. Selye pointed out that stress is an unavoidable part of life and isn't only associated with negative events such as trauma and bereavement; it also accompanies events we usually construe positively (graduation, marriage, having a baby). Nonetheless, in abnormal psychology we usually focus on the undesirable impact of stress, despite vagueness in how we often use the term. The "Try it Yourself" feature contains an inventory you can use to assess your own current level of stress.

TRY IT YOURSELF

How Stressed Are You?

Perceived Stress Scale (PSS)

The questions in this scale ask you about your feelings and thoughts during the last month. In each case, please circle how often you felt or thought a certain way.

0 = never   1 = almost never   2 = sometimes   3 = fairly often   4 = very often

1. In the last month, how often have you been upset because of something that happened unexpectedly?	0 1 2 3 4
2. In the last month, how often have you felt that you were unable to control the important things in your life?	0 1 2 3 4
3. In the last month, how often have you felt nervous and "stressed"?	0 1 2 3 4
4. In the last month, how often have you felt confident about your ability to handle your personal problems?	0 1 2 3 4
5. In the last month, how often have you felt that things were going your way?	0 1 2 3 4
6. In the last month, how often have you found that you could not cope with all the things that you had to do?	0 1 2 3 4
7. In the last month, how often have you been able to control irritations in your life?	0 1 2 3 4
8. In the last month, how often have you felt that you were on top of things?	0 1 2 3 4
9. In the last month, how often have you been angered because of things that were outside of your control?	0 1 2 3 4
10. In the last month, how often have you felt difficulties were piling up so high that you could not overcome them?	0 1 2 3 4

Scoring

PSS scores are obtained by reversing responses (e.g., 0 = 4, 1 = 3, 2 = 2, 3 = 1 & 4 = 0) to the four positively stated items (items 4, 5, 7, & 8) and then summing across all scale items.

The PSS Scale is reprinted with permission of the American Sociological Association, from Cohen, S., Kamarck, T., and Mermelstein, R. (1983). A Global Measure of Perceived Stress. Journal of Health and Social Behavior, 24, 385–396.

Photo source: © PhotoDisc/Getty Images

Bereavement and Grief

One common stressor people face is **bereavement**, defined as "the situation of having recently lost a significant person through death" (M. Stroebe, Schut, & Stroebe, 2007, p. 1960). Given that death is a part of life, everyone experiences bereavement at some point. Of course, bereavement is more likely as one gets older. As evidence, only 3%–4% of children age 18 and under have lost a parent, but 45% of women and 15% of men over age 65 have faced the death of a spouse (M. Stroebe et al., 2007). Bereaved individuals often undergo intense suffering and are vulnerable to emotional problems and physical illnesses (M. Stroebe et al., 2007).

Grief is the primary emotional response to bereavement, consisting of both emotional and physical reactions (M. Stroebe et al., 2007). The grieving process is often conceptualized as occurring in discrete stages. The psychologist Elisabeth Kübler Ross developed the most famous stage theory of grief. She proposed a **five-stage theory of grief** in which a mourner progresses through stages of *denial, anger, bargaining, depression,* and *acceptance* (Kübler-Ross, 1970; Kübler-Ross, Wessler, & Avioli, 1972). While stage theories of grief have enjoyed widespread popularity, they have also been criticized for many reasons—including being simplistic, assuming people neatly move from one stage to the next in an orderly fashion, overlooking cultural differences, and lacking research support (M. Stroebe,

We all experience grief and bereavement during our lives. When, if ever, do they shift from normal and expected reactions to psychopathology?
Source: iStock.com/KatarzynaBialasiewicz

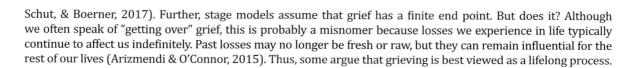

Schut, & Boerner, 2017). Further, stage models assume that grief has a finite end point. But does it? Although we often speak of "getting over" grief, this is probably a misnomer because losses we experience in life typically continue to affect us indefinitely. Past losses may no longer be fresh or raw, but they can remain influential for the rest of our lives (Arizmendi & O'Connor, 2015). Thus, some argue that grieving is best viewed as a lifelong process.

Dissociation in Response to Trauma, Stress, and Bereavement

In response to upsetting events such as trauma, stress, and bereavement people sometimes dissociate. **Dissociation** is difficult to explain because the experience of it isn't logical or easily conveyed in words. Even clinical researchers often disagree on the particulars, with many definitions having been offered—including ones that stress narrowed consciousness, altered consciousness, and disengagement or separation from aspects of everyday experience (Nijenhuis & van der Hart, 2011). Despite some differences in emphasis, most definitions hold that dissociation involves detaching from experience, usually by separating, or *compartmentalizing*, emotions from one another so that when experiencing one emotion, other emotions are out of awareness (Nijenhuis & van der Hart, 2011). For example, when feeling extremely angry with your best friend, it is difficult to recall positive feelings you also have about this person; such feelings are, in that moment, dissociated. Two commonly discussed aspects of dissociation are derealization and depersonalization (E. A. Holmes et al., 2005). In **derealization** the world seems remote, altered, or unreal.

Marigold
Examples of derealization are Marigold's complaints that since her husband's death food hasn't tasted the same and time has slowed down. To Marigold, it's as if her physical surroundings have changed since her loss.

CASE EXAMPLES

In contrast, in **depersonalization** the self (rather than the world) seems unreal or changed. Those who are depersonalizing disconnect from themselves and their emotions.

Joe
Joe's recollection that "It was like I was outside my own body watching it happen to someone else" is a good example of depersonalization; he feels detached from his own experience.

CASE EXAMPLES

In addition to depersonalization and derealization, people who are dissociating sometimes also experience **amnesia** (memory gaps), especially about emotionally charged issues (E. A. Holmes et al., 2005). For instance, someone who has been sexually assaulted may not be able to recall the event later.

The terms discussed above obviously are interrelated. Trauma and bereavement, for instance, can cause stress and dissociation. The presenting problems examined in this chapter and Chapter 8 focus most explicitly on trauma, stress, loss, and dissociation. However, other presenting problems (depression, anxiety, and psychosis, among others) often involve these issues too, but without them necessarily being the prime focus of clinical attention. That is, problems like anxiety, depression, and psychosis often are associated with a history of trauma (DeRosse, Nitzburg, Kompancaril, & Malhotra, 2014; H. L. Fisher et al., 2010; Kinderman, Schwannauer, Pontin, & Tai, 2013)—something that the sociocultural sections of chapters on these problems explore in greater detail.

7.2 *DSM* AND *ICD* PERSPECTIVES

There are numerous differences in how *DSM-5*, *ICD-10*, and *ICD-11* catalog trauma and stress disorders. In its "Trauma and Stressor-Related Disorders" chapter, the *DSM-5* includes posttraumatic stress disorder (PTSD), acute stress disorder, and adjustment disorders. The *ICD-10* includes comparable versions of these same diagnostic categories in its "Anxiety, Dissociative, Stress-Related, Somatoform and other Nonpsychotic Mental Disorders" section (the same section that contains the anxiety and obsessive-compulsive disorders reviewed in Chapter 6). The *ICD-11*'s "Disorders Specifically Associated with Stress" section diverges a bit from both *ICD-10* and *DSM-5*. It doesn't consider acute stress to be a disorder and has added new complex PTSD and prolonged grief diagnoses. The *DSM-5* doesn't contain a complex PTSD diagnosis and its equivalent of prolonged grief remains in the proposal stage. The *ICD-10* doesn't include either complex PTSD or a bereavement-focused disorder.

TRAUMA AND STRESS DISORDERS
Posttraumatic Stress Disorder (PTSD)

To receive a diagnosis of **posttraumatic stress disorder (PTSD)**, a person must have experienced a traumatic event (traumatic in the clinical sense, as described above). This makes PTSD "distinctive among psychiatric disorders in the requirement of exposure to a stressful event as a precondition" (Pai, Suris, & North, 2017, p. 2). However, trauma alone isn't sufficient for a PTSD diagnosis. The disorder is only diagnosed in people who experience significant psychological difficulty after the traumatic occurrence. Symptoms include distressing and intrusive memories of the incident, intense emotional upset about what happened, avoidance of things that remind them of the event, and reliving the event through bad dreams and flashbacks (experiences in which a person feels and acts as if the traumatic event is happening again). Ongoing and exaggerated anxiety is common, as is a tendency to dissociate. (Note that although *DSM-5* classifies PTSD as a trauma- and stressor-related disorder, it includes dissociative elements.) To qualify for a diagnosis, the *DSM-5* requires that symptoms last one month or longer. The *ICD-10* is less clear about duration. However, both *DSM-5* and *ICD-10* note that there can be up to a six-month delay from the time of the trauma to when symptoms first appear. In *DSM-5* reliability field trials, PTSD was among the most reliable diagnoses (Freedman et al., 2013).

Joe
Our case study client, Joe, qualifies for a PTSD diagnosis.

Some worry that PTSD, as defined in *DSM-5*, has become too broad (Andreasen, 2010; S. A. Baldwin, Williams, & Houts, 2004; DiMauro, Carter, Folk, & Kashdan, 2014). In response, the *ICD-11* has made significant changes. It divided the disorder into two separate diagnoses: PTSD and complex PTSD (Maercker, Brewin, Bryant, Cloitre, Reed, et al., 2013; Maercker, Brewin, Bryant, Cloitre, van Ommeren, et al., 2013; M. W. Miller, Wolf, & Keane, 2014). The *ICD-11* guidelines for PTSD define it much more narrowly than in the past. It is now limited to three core symptoms that persist for at least several weeks: re-experiencing the trauma, avoiding reminders of the event, and a sense of heightened threat and arousal. The newly added complex PTSD, on the other hand, is a somewhat broader diagnosis (Herman, 2015). It involves the three core symptoms of PTSD plus additional symptoms such as difficulty managing emotion; the belief that one is worthless plus feelings of shame, guilt, or failure; and trouble maintaining relationships. By dividing PTSD into basic and complex types, *ICD-11* diverges significantly from the *DSM-5*, where a single PTSD category is used regardless of whether one displays these additional symptoms. Diagnostic Box 7.1 spells out these differences in greater detail.

Diagnostic Box 7.1 Posttraumatic Stress Disorder (PTSD)

DSM-5
- Exposure to a traumatic event (actual or threatened death, physical injury, or sexual violation that is experienced, witnessed, or happened to a close friend or family member).
- At least one *intrusive symptom*: (1) invasive and upsetting recollections of the event, (2) dreams related to the event, (3) dissociative re-experiencing of the event (like flashbacks), (4) psychological or physical distress when reminded of the event.
- Avoids thoughts, feelings, memories, and reminders of the event.
- Has altered thoughts and feelings about the event (e.g., struggles to recall it, has distorted beliefs about it, blames self for it, feels negative emotions, loses interest in important activities, feels alienated from people, is unable to feel positive emotions).
- Regularly feels aroused and reactive (e.g., feels irritable and angry, engages in irresponsible and self-destructive actions, is easily alarmed or startled, has trouble concentrating and/or sleeping).
- Symptoms last more than one month and can develop up to six months after the event.

Based on American Psychiatric Association, 2013b, pp. 271–274

ICD-10
- Response to an extremely threatening or catastrophic event (disaster; war; serious accident; witnessing someone die; being tortured, raped, assaulted, etc.).
- Relives the trauma through recollections, dreams, and flashbacks. Symptoms such as reliving the trauma in memories, dreams, flashbacks, numbness, flattened emotions, feeling detached and disengaged, and feeling depressed or anxious.
- Avoids reminders of the event and is easily aroused or startled.
- No minimum duration, but symptoms can develop up to six months after the event.

Based on World Health Organization, 1992, pp. 120–121

ICD-11
- Response to an extremely threatening or catastrophic event (disaster; war; serious accident; witnessing someone die; being tortured, raped, assaulted, etc.).
- Displays three core symptoms: (1) re-experiences the trauma through memories, flashbacks, and dreams accompanied by strong emotions, (2) intentionally avoids reminders of the event, (3) experiences an ongoing sense of exaggerated threat.
- Symptoms last at least several weeks.
- *Complex PTSD*: Diagnosed instead of PTSD if the person also displays (1) difficulties regulating emotions, (2) the belief that one is worthless plus feelings of shame, guilt, or failure, (3) impaired interpersonal relationships.

Based on https://gcp.network/en/private/icd-11-guidelines/grouping

The *DSM-5* reports higher 12-month prevalence rates for PTSD in the U.S. (3.5%) compared to European, Asian, African, and Latin American countries (0.5%–1.0%). This seems counterintuitive, right? Wouldn't we expect the highest rates of PTSD to be found among people from poor countries—where poverty, malnutrition, and civil war run rampant? Common sense says yes, but recent research says no (Dückers, Alisic, & Brewin, 2016; Dückers & Brewin, 2016; Dückers & Olff, 2017). That is, research has found that countries that are better able to protect their citizens from trauma (e.g., Australia, Canada, the Netherlands, New Zealand, and the U.S.) tend to have much higher PTSD prevalence rates than countries that are less equipped to do so (e.g., Columbia, Israel, Lebanon, Mexico, and South Africa); in the former countries, lifetime PTSD prevalence was 7.4%, while in the latter countries it was just 2.1% (Dückers et al., 2016)! The researchers explain these unexpected findings by positing a **vulnerability paradox**, the idea that people from wealthier and more sheltered countries tend to believe that the world is a safe place. When they do face a trauma this belief is shattered, placing them at greater risk for PTSD (Dückers et al., 2016). By comparison, those living in more vulnerable countries have no expectation of safety. Because they realize—often through painful firsthand experience—that the world can be quite dangerous, they are cognitively less susceptible to a posttraumatic stress response to life-threatening events. Thus, it appears that prevalence rates for PTSD, while clearly correlated with exposure to trauma, are indeed higher in wealthier and more privileged nations.

Variations by country notwithstanding, the *DSM-5* notes that the highest rates of PTSD are found among people who have faced unbearable traumas such as rape, imprisonment, or war. *DSM* reports that prevalence is lower for older adults and children, but this may be because previous diagnostic criteria for young people weren't very clear and because older people's symptoms, even when debilitating, aren't always severe enough to qualify them for a diagnosis. Further, those who have experienced prior psychological difficulties are at higher risk for PTSD, which makes sense given that the less well-adjusted one is the more difficult it will be to deal with a traumatic event. Childhood adversity, lack of social support, being of lower socioeconomic status, and belonging to minority racial or ethnic groups are also associated with developing PTSD. What all these factors have in common is that they involve social hardships that can make it more difficult to cope with something traumatic.

Why are childhood adversity, lack of social support, lower SES, and being from a minority racial or ethnic group positively correlated with posttraumatic stress?
Source: Getty Images/iStockphoto/Thinkstock\Karen Low Phillips

Acute Stress

The *DSM-5* and *ICD-10* both use the term "acute stress" to describe PTSD-like symptoms that don't last long enough to constitute full-blown PTSD. However, the *DSM-5* and *ICD-10* differ notably regarding symptom duration. According to *DSM-5* criteria, **acute stress disorder (ASD)** is diagnosed if symptoms last between three days and one month following a traumatic event. By comparison, the *ICD-10* guidelines for **acute stress reaction** stipulate a much shorter period of time—a few minutes to three days after the trauma. Thus, even though the *DSM-5* and *ICD-10* both use the same diagnostic code for acute stress, their definitions of it are pretty different when it comes to how long symptoms must last.

The *ICD-11* calls acute stress a "reaction" rather than a disorder. Although it lists acute stress reaction (along with a corresponding diagnostic code), it does not consider it a mental disorder. Instead, it indicates that acute stress reaction is a normal response to a traumatic event. This change responds to criticism that by including acute stress as a disorder, any reaction to trauma—even a brief and expected one—is unfairly deemed abnormal. The *ICD-11* guidelines for acute stress reaction are similar to those in the *ICD-10*; symptoms typically last a few hours to a few days after the trauma. However, they can last up to a month if the traumatic stressor is ongoing. Diagnostic Box 7.2 outlines *DSM* criteria and *ICD* guidelines.

Diagnostic Box 7.2 Acute Stress Disorder/Acute Stress Reaction

DSM-5: Acute Stress Disorder
- Exposure to a traumatic event (actual or threatened death, physical injury, or sexual violation that is experienced, witnessed, or happened to a close friend or family member).
- Symptoms of intrusion, negative mood, dissociation, avoidance, and arousal like those found in PTSD.
- Symptoms usually occur right after the trauma and persist for three days to one month.

Based on American Psychiatric Association, 2013b, pp. 280–281

ICD-10: Acute Stress Reaction
- Response to an extremely threatening or catastrophic event.
- Person may appear dazed, anxious, depressed, angry, despairing, overactive, or withdrawn following the event.
- Symptoms occur within minutes of the event and last no more than two or three days.

Based on World Health Organization, 1992, pp. 120–121

ICD-11: Acute Stress Reaction
- Normal and expected response to an extremely threatening or catastrophic event (disaster; war; serious accident; witnessing someone die; being tortured, raped, assaulted, etc.); not considered a disorder, but still can be diagnosed.
- Person may appear dazed, anxious, depressed, angry, despairing, overactive, or withdrawn—all symptoms considered normal given the intensity of the event.
- Symptoms occur within minutes of the event and last no more than a few days; when stressor or event continues, symptoms usually decrease within one month.

Based on https://gcp.network/en/private/icd-11-guidelines/grouping

Because of its shorter duration, it's understandable that more people encounter acute stress than PTSD following a traumatic event. Consistent with this, the *DSM-5* reports that half of people with PTSD previously experienced acute stress. *DSM-5* authors also note that acute stress is most likely among those who have been assaulted, raped, or witnessed a mass shooting. They estimate that, across both U.S. and non-U.S. populations, acute stress occurs "in less than 20% of cases following traumatic events that do not involve interpersonal assault; 13%–21% of motor vehicle accidents, 14% of mild traumatic brain injury, 19% of assault, 10% of severe burns, and 6%–21% of industrial accidents" (American Psychiatric Association, 2013b, p. 284).

Adjustment Disorders

Whereas PTSD and acute stress are responses to intense, often life threatening, traumatic events, **adjustment disorders** are emotional reactions to milder life circumstances. People who receive adjustment disorder diagnoses are having a hard time coping with stressful life events—things like breaking up with someone, starting a new job, getting married, moving to a new home, starting a new business, retirement, or dealing with an ongoing health situation (the list is endless, really). It's common for such experiences to affect conduct and mood as long as the stressful situation is ongoing. Adjustment disorders are often used as catch-all categories for people who are facing continuing life stress but otherwise aren't considered especially disturbed and don't meet the criteria for any other major mental disorder (Grubaugh, 2014; Strain & Diefenbacher, 2008). This allows clinicians to use adjustment disorder codes to diagnose people in a relatively non-stigmatizing way. Diagnostic Box 7.3 contains criteria and guidelines for adjustment disorders.

Diagnostic Box 7.3 Adjustment Disorders

DSM-5
- Emotional and behavioral symptoms due to one or more life stressors.
- Disproportionate distress and/or impaired functioning.
- Symptoms not due to bereavement or another mental disorder.
- Symptoms develop within one month of the stressor, but once the stressor is eliminated symptoms resolve within six months.
- Specific types of adjustment disorder are diagnosed depending on whether the main symptoms are depression, anxiety, disruptive conduct, or some combination thereof.

Based on American Psychiatric Association, 2013b, pp. 286–287

ICD-10
- Emotional distress due to major life changes or stressful circumstances.
- Symptoms not due to bereavement or another mental disorder.
- Occurs within one month of the stressful event and symptoms do not typically last more than six months.
- Specific types of adjustment disorder are diagnosed depending on whether the main symptoms are depression, anxiety, disruptive conduct, or some combination thereof.

Based on World Health Organization, 1992, pp. 121–122

ICD-11
- Emotional distress due to major life changes or stressful circumstances (e.g., divorce or break-up, job loss, receiving an illness diagnosis, work conflicts, family conflicts).
- The person is preoccupied with the stressor and worries excessively about it.
- Symptoms develop within one month of the stressor, but once the stressor is eliminated symptoms resolve within six months.

Based on https://gcp.network/en/private/icd-11-guidelines/grouping

Persistent Complex Bereavement/Prolonged Grief

The *DSM-5*'s Section III contains a proposed new diagnostic category for people who have a difficult time getting over the loss of a loved one. Recall from Chapter 3 that Section III includes disorders that the *DSM* doesn't officially recognize, but is considering for future editions. The anticipated new diagnosis, **persistent complex bereavement disorder** (also called *persistent grief*, *complicated grief*, *prolonged grief*, or *pathological grief*), applies to clients who feel intense grief for an extended period of time and have difficulty moving on with their lives. These clients yearn for and seem preoccupied with the lost loved one, feel intense sorrow, and experience a great deal of emotional distress over the loss that interferes with their daily functioning. The *DSM-5* estimates the prevalence of this disorder at 2.4%–4.8% of people, also noting that it is more common in women. The proposal to add persistent complex bereavement to the *DSM* has been intensely debated and for now it remains an unofficial diagnosis, although the *DSM-5* notes that clinicians who wish to diagnose it can do so using the diagnostic code for "Other Specified Trauma- and Stressor-Related Disorder." Despite controversy over it, this diagnosis has been included in the *ICD-11* as **prolonged grief disorder** (one of the alternative names mentioned above). Diagnostic Box 7.4 shows how *DSM-5* and *ICD-11* conceptualize this disorder.

Diagnostic Box 7.4 Persistent Complex Bereavement/Prolonged Grief

DSM-5: Persistent Complex Bereavement Disorder [proposed disorder for further study]
- After the death of someone close, one or more of the following: (1) yearning for the lost person, (2) immense grief and emotional upset over the loss, (3) fixation on the lost person, (4) overly focused on how the person died.
- Experiences both (1) *reactive distress* (e.g., trouble accepting the death, incredulity about the loss, difficulty reminiscing positively, angry or bitter feelings, avoids reminders of the loss); and (2) *social/identity disruption* (e.g., wants to die and be reunited with dead person, doesn't trust others, feels detached, feels life is meaningless without the lost person, lack of interest in planning for the future).
- Reactive distress and social/identity disruption last at least 12 months (six months in children).

Based on American Psychiatric Association, 2013b, pp. 789–790

ICD-10
- Not included in *ICD-10*.

ICD-11
- Ongoing and extensive grief response involving longing for and fixation on the lost person, intense emotional upset (e.g., anger, guilt, denial, blame, numbness), and trouble participating in social interactions.
- Symptoms last at least six months, though cultural differences should be considered in making a diagnosis.

Based on https://gcp.network/en/private/icd-11-guidelines/grouping

EVALUATING *DSM* AND *ICD* PERSPECTIVES

Various concerns and controversies have surrounded the *DSM* and *ICD* approaches to PTSD, ASD, and adjustment disorders. A few of these are highlighted below.

Creating a New Trauma- and Stressor-Related Disorders Chapter in *DSM-5*

DSM-5 provoked controversy by creating a new "Trauma- and Stressor-Related Disorders" chapter and placing PTSD, ASD, and adjustment disorders within it (Pai et al., 2017). Regarding PTSD specifically, there has long been discussion about where best to locate it in the *DSM-5*. It was classified as an anxiety disorder for more than 30 years, from its first appearance in *DSM-III* through *DSM-IV-TR*. However, even when PTSD was grouped with the anxiety disorders, some wondered whether it might better be placed elsewhere—as a dissociative disorder, for instance (R. D. Marshall, Spitzer, & Liebowitz, 1999). When *DSM-5* moved PTSD to the newly devised trauma- and stressor-related disorders section, critics worried that this shift would undermine researchers working to identify PTSD's underlying fear mechanisms (L. A. Zoellner, Rothbaum, & Feeny, 2011). However, others dismissed this concern, arguing that PTSD's location in the manual wouldn't significantly affect how researchers and clinicians conceptualize it (M. W. Miller et al., 2014). Consistent with this conclusion, the *ICD-11* (like the *DSM-5*) groups PTSD, acute stress, and adjustment disorder together as "stress" disorders. The takeaway message is that PTSD—with its mix of anxiety, fear, and dissociation—has similarities to a variety of other presenting problems. This may be why figuring out where to house it in the *DSM* and *ICD* has proven so controversial.

PTSD as an Expectable Reaction, Not a Disorder

Beyond debates about where it should be grouped within *DSM* and *ICD*, PTSD has also been criticized for something more serious: violating the very definition of mental disorder. How so? Well, many consider the symptoms of PTSD—even if they last notably longer than acute stress reactions—to be reasonable reactions to unreasonable and understandably traumatizing events (Burstow, 2005; M. Thompson, 2011). That is, we expect many or most people will struggle psychologically after being raped, surviving an accident, or returning from war. Even the *ICD-10* and *ICD-11* note that PTSD is a response to horrible or catastrophic events "likely to cause pervasive distress in almost anyone" (World Health Organization, 1992, p. 120). If such distress is expected in practically everyone, then how is PTSD a disorder? After all, according to the *DSM-5*, a mental disorder cannot be an "expectable or culturally approved response to a common stressor or loss" (American Psychiatric Association, 2013b, p. 20). Thus, critics maintain that we are on shaky ground when we classify PTSD as a disorder. Along these lines, some military veterans have argued that in order to stop incorrectly pathologizing those who have faced the horrors of war, we should drop the "D" in PTSD and simply speak of *posttraumatic stress* or *posttraumatic stress injury (PTSI)* (Ochberg, 2014; M. Thompson, 2011). The *DSM* and *ICD*, however, continue to use the term PTSD.

Adjustment Disorder as a "Waste-Basket" Diagnosis

Adjustment disorders have been criticized for being nebulous, perhaps because they were purposely devised to lack specific symptoms that must be present for a diagnosis (Strain & Friedman, 2011). The reason for this ambiguity appears to be so that anyone experiencing ongoing stress who doesn't quite meet the criteria for more serious mental disorder categories such as depression or anxiety can be diagnosed and receive services (Casey & Bailey, 2011). Because of its open-endedness and lack of clear criteria, critics have long complained that "adjustment disorder is one of the most ill-defined mental disorders, often described as the 'waste-basket' of the psychiatric classification scheme" (Maercker, Brewin, Bryant, Cloitre, van Ommeren, et al., 2013, p. 198). Perhaps even more than PTSD and ASD, adjustment disorders have been criticized for improperly turning expectable forms of everyday emotional distress into mental disorders (Casey & Bailey, 2011). However, despite conceptual disagreement over whether they are "real" disorders, including adjustment disorders in *DSM* and *ICD* serves a highly practical purpose, at least in the U.S. where a mental disorder diagnosis is required for health insurance to pay for services; without adjustment disorder diagnostic codes, many people who don't meet the criteria for any other disorder couldn't afford psychotherapy (Casey & Bailey, 2011). Whether this practical goal justifies considering adjustment disorders as mental disorders depends on how much concern you have over the medicalization of emotional distress.

Should Prolonged Grief Be a Disorder?

As you may recall from Chapter 5, there was heated debate over the *DSM-5*'s elimination of the bereavement exclusion, which discouraged clinicians from diagnosing bereaved people with major depression. The issue of including prolonged grief in the *DSM-5* has spurred similar controversy. Supporters of officially adding persistent complex bereavement to the *DSM-5* say that it is a clearly identifiable problem that research shows can, in most cases, be readily distinguished from normal bereavement (Dillen, Fontaine, & Verhofstadt-Denève, 2008). Further, many prolonged grief clients approve the inclusion of persistent grief in the *ICD-11* and also want to see persistent complex bereavement added to the *DSM* because such actions formally recognize their problem. Critics, however, strongly object to adding prolonged grief to the *DSM*. They argue that complicated grief researchers are inconsistent. On the one hand, these researchers claim that every grief experience is unique and there isn't a "normal" way to mourn a loss; on the other hand, they maintain that "normal" grief can be differentiated from pathological grief (Breen & O'Connor, 2007). Critics contend that adding persistent bereavement to the *DSM* would unnecessarily turn long-lasting grief into a mental disorder. As one critic put it, "the medicalization of grief narrows the criteria of what is considered 'appropriate grief,' both in the duration and magnitude of depressive feelings, turning much of normal grief into a psychiatric disorder in need of treatment" (Bandini, 2015, p. 351). So how long is it okay to grieve before doing so should be considered a disorder? According to the thought-provoking "The Lived Experience" box, grief isn't a disorder; it's a lifelong process.

THE LIVED EXPERIENCE

Grief 10 Years Later

This September, it will be ten years since my mother died of cancer. It seems as if it were a lifetime ago and it seems as if it were yesterday. That is the nature of grief; it has its own rhythm. It is both present and in the past and it appears that it continues to stay that way no matter how much time has gone by.

A few years ago when my friend Meghan O'Rourke and I published a series of articles on grief and loss in *Slate* magazine, some criticized the findings because some of the respondents had experienced a loss many years before taking the survey. In psychology we call this phenomenon "recall bias," where people filling out surveys wrongly or incompletely remember experiences from the past.

Memory is certainly pliable, and it is possible that people made errors in recalling what their grief was really like for them. Methodologically and intuitively that makes sense, but as a griever, I am not so sure.

The idea that the more years have passed since a loss, the less likely someone is to recall their grief rests on the assumption that grief is a static event in time that will eventually fade. This view is aligned with what many researchers in the field of psychology and psychiatry believe: that grief has a starting point, a middle point, and an end point. The heated debates in the media and in the field about when grief becomes pathological rest on the assumption that at some point, grief becomes "too much" and needs to be treated with medication or a mental health professional. If grief is a static event in time, then it certainly makes sense that it would be hard for people to remember what their experience was like five or ten years after a loss.

Having spent years studying grief, and being a griever myself now entering her tenth year of loss, I know that grief does not work this way. It is not an event in time. It is not even just an emotional response to a loss. It is a process that changes us permanently but also constantly as we ourselves change and grow. In this sense, grief is just like love. It is not something that happens once and goes away—it is something that evolves, expands and contracts, and changes in shape, depth, and intensity as time goes on.

Grief is a lifelong, ever-changing companion. It is both in the present and in the past. Moments of intense yearning and pain for the deceased can come and go even 10 or 20 or 30 years after a person we love has died. It is cliché to say it, but it is also true: grief is the price we pay for love. Grief is still with me because my mother is still with me. To deny one is inevitably to deny the other.

Interestingly, between mothers and children, there is a biological correlate to "the being with and in each other" called fetal microchimerism. It is an amazing phenomenon where fetal cells from the baby make their way into their mother's bodies and vice versa, mother's cells become intertwined into the baby's body. In other words, my mother is literally part of me biologically and emotionally and my cells were with, and in her when she died.

To be sure, microchimerism is just a metaphor—this being with and part of each other is not just for biological mothers and children. It is for everyone who has loved and lost. When I present my professional work, I often say I am a grief researcher, but actually, grief is just a stand in for what I am really studying—love and attachment. One cannot come without the other. Just like love, grief is an experience that evolves and changes with time; but one thing is for sure, it is not forgettable, because it never goes away.

By Leeat Granek, Ph.D. Reprinted with permission.

7.3 HISTORICAL PERSPECTIVES

EARLY CLINICAL DESCRIPTIONS OF TRAUMA

In this section, we limit our historical discussion to trauma specifically. Accounts of what today we call posttraumatic stress can be found throughout history. For example, six months after surviving the 1666 Great Fire of London, renowned diarist Samuel Pepys reported ongoing emotional symptoms, including panic and nightmares (Tehrani, 2004). Some of the earliest clinical descriptions of posttraumatic stress can be traced back to the U.S. Civil War, when soldiers experienced heart palpitations, exhaustion, and excessive alcohol and tobacco use. Their condition was alternately referred to as *disordered palpitation of the heart*, *irritable heart*, or *soldier's heart* (DiMauro et al., 2014; van der Kolk, 2007). Combatants exhibiting these symptoms were often stigmatized and viewed negatively as either having a constitutional weakness or simply being malingerers (DiMauro et al., 2014).

TRAUMATIC NEUROSIS

By the 1880s, the German neurologist Herman Oppenheim had coined the term **traumatic neurosis** and argued that it had an organic cause originating in the central nervous system (Tehrani, 2004; van der Kolk, 2007). In the U.K., the idea of traumatic neurosis was applied to people who experienced emotional difficulties following railway accidents, a condition known as *railway spine* (E. Jones & Wessely, 2007; van der Kolk, 2007). Oppenheim's emphasis on physiology anticipated current biological theories of PTSD. However, not everyone shared his biological perspective. Those coming from a more psychological orientation saw trauma and stress—including sexual abuse—as central to cases of *hysterical neurosis* (a broad diagnostic category reserved for people who displayed a variety of physical and psychological symptoms). Jean-Martin Charcot, Pierre Janet, and later Sigmund Freud all gravitated toward this more psychological way of understanding trauma. Yet they weren't always accurate in their assessments. Freud, for instance, incorrectly predicted that soldiers' war neuroses would disappear when the fighting ended (van der Kolk, 2007); he also focused too much on patient's projected fantasies, downplaying the psychological impact of real traumas such as actual sexual abuse (Tehrani, 2004). However, in connecting posttraumatic stress to repression and avoidance of painful memories, Freud and his colleagues planted the seeds for a psychodynamic model of trauma that remains influential to this day (van der Kolk, 2007).

WAR NEURASTHENIA AND SHELL SHOCK

If this First World War soldier exhibited signs of trauma upon returning from the front, he might have been diagnosed with "shell shock".
Source: Superstock

Diagnostically, the term **war neurasthenia** became popular in the late 19th and early 20th centuries. It constituted a variation on neurasthenia, the diagnosis given to sad and anxious people (see Chapters 5 and 6). War neurasthenia was a vague disorder attributed to a weak nervous system that was deemed unable to handle the challenges of combat (DiMauro et al., 2014). During the First World War, war neurasthenia gave way to **shell shock**, another somewhat broad diagnosis that—like soldier's heart before it—included symptoms such as "chest pain, heart palpitations, tremors, fatigue, and even paralysis" (DiMauro et al., 2014, p. 777). The condition was called shell shock because it was thought to originate from repeated exposure to exploding artillery shells (Andreasen, 2010).

After the First World War, psychoanalyst Abram Kardiner wrote extensively about shell shock (Kardiner & Spiegel, 1947). Kardiner preferred Oppenheim's term traumatic neurosis, which makes sense given that he combined Oppenheim's biologically based explanations with Freud's emphasis on repressing traumatic memories (E. Jones & Wessely, 2007; van der Kolk, 2007). In describing traumatic neurosis, Kardiner noted that many soldiers exhibited exaggerated startle responses, irritability and aggression, nightmares, and a fixation on the trauma—all symptoms today considered part of PTSD. Given how well he anticipated current understandings, it has been argued that "more than anyone else, Kardiner defined PTSD for the remainder of the 20th century" (van der Kolk, 2007, p. 26). However, his impact wasn't immediate. At the start of the Second World War, many of Kardiner's insights went unheeded and had to be learned anew as many soldiers began displaying signs of trauma (van der Kolk, 2007). Yet by the end of the war awareness was much greater, with one study predicting that 98% of surviving soldiers would suffer from emotional exhaustion, anxiety, and depression (E. Jones & Wessely, 2007).

THE EMERGENCE OF PTSD AS A DIAGNOSIS

Both before and after the Second World War, a variety of other diagnostic names went in and out of fashion before clinicians settled on PTSD. Besides *traumatic war neurosis*, other common diagnoses for combat-induced posttraumatic stress included *combat fatigue*, *battle stress*, and *gross stress reaction* (Andreasen, 2010). Gross stress reaction was the term found in 1952's *DSM-I* (American Psychiatric Association, 1952). It was a much milder and more general diagnosis than today's PTSD. Its symptoms were conceptualized as temporary reactions to exceptional mental or physical stress (DiMauro et al., 2014). Surprisingly, gross stress reaction was removed from 1968's *DSM-II*. Some historians attribute this omission to the fact that *DSM-II* was developed during a period of relative peace when few soldiers were returning from war in a damaged emotional state (Andreasen, 2010). Regardless of why, from 1968 until 1980 the *DSM* contained no diagnosis specifically for trauma.

Posttraumatic stress disorder—originally developed using names like *post-Vietnam syndrome* and *delayed stress syndrome*—debuted as a diagnosis in 1980's *DSM-III* (Jones & Wessely, 2007). The category was added mainly in response to Vietnam War veteran groups, which lobbied to have it recognized as a disorder. However, although the proposal for PTSD was originally intended for veterans, it soon broadened to encompass similar symptoms in response to other threatening life events (S. A. Baldwin et al., 2004). For instance, researchers studying what was then informally called **rape trauma syndrome** (Burgess, 1983; Burgess & Holmstrom, 1974)—a reaction to being sexually assaulted characterized by symptoms similar to those displayed by returning war veterans—began using the PTSD diagnosis, as well. In the end, PTSD came to include not just trauma from war and rape, but also from accidents, natural disasters, physical assaults, terrorism, and genocide.

Regardless of whether one sees PTSD as having become too inclusive, an important point in thinking about its history is that—despite its preeminence today—PTSD is a relatively recent diagnosis and our ways of understanding and talking about it continue to change with the times. Considering that the *ICD-11* has recently revised "classic" PTSD, added complex PTSD, and removed acute stress as a disorder, it is easy to see how in just a few short years our historical perspective on PTSD is likely to be different. As one PTSD historian warned, "research on mental disorders reflects the historical period and associated cultural values in which the research is conducted" and therefore "what we today call PTSD is quite different from both what started out as PTSD and from previous war-related problems" (S. A. Baldwin et al., 2004, para. 30). Some historians believe this

Research on "post-Vietnam syndrome," as well as lobbying by veterans who wanted their suffering recognized, preceded PTSD being added to the DSM-III in 1980.
Source: PhotoDisc/ Getty Images

makes PTSD a culture-bound syndrome that mirrors current societal ways of defining and responding to trauma (E. Jones & Wessely, 2006). From a historical perspective, evolving understandings of PTSD reflect how ideas about abnormality shift and transform across time.

7.4 BIOLOGICAL PERSPECTIVES
BRAIN CHEMISTRY PERSPECTIVES
Posttraumatic Stress

Although the roles of various neurotransmitters in posttraumatic stress have been studied, defects in norepinephrine and serotonin transmission are often highlighted (Bryant et al., 2010; Pietrzak et al., 2013; Southwick et al., 1999). Consistent with this, antidepressants that increase serotonin transmission (i.e., SSRIs) are usually considered the most effective drugs for people diagnosed with PTSD and are often prescribed to those having difficulty in the aftermath of trauma (Benedek, Friedman, Zatzick, & Ursano, 2009; Wallace & Cooper, 2015). Although there is debate over which SSRIs are best (Benedek et al., 2009), *paroxetine* (trade name *Paxil*), *sertraline* (trade name *Zoloft*) and *fluoxetine* (trade name *Prozac*) are generally identified as helpful in alleviating posttraumatic stress, along with the norepinephrine and serotonin enhancing SNRI *venlafaxine* (Effexor) (M. J. Friedman & Davidson, 2014; Hoskins et al., 2015; Ipser & Stein, 2012; Jeffreys, Capehart, & Friedman, 2012). Tricyclic and MAOI antidepressants are not usually recommended. While some researchers maintain that these older antidepressants may be equally or more effective than SSRIs, they haven't received much attention in recent years because (a) they have more serious side effects and (b) drug companies have few economic incentives to further research and market them (J. Davidson, 2015; M. J. Friedman & Davidson, 2014).

Beyond antidepressants, the atypical antipsychotic *risperidone* (Risperdol) has shown promise in some studies (Ipser & Stein, 2012; Krishnamurthy, Garabadu, & Joy, 2013). Nevertheless, the consensus seems to be that antipsychotics aren't well supported in alleviating posttraumatic stress (Hoskins et al., 2015; Management of Post-Traumatic Stress Working Group, 2010; National Collaborating Centre for Mental Health, 2005; Wallace & Cooper, 2015). When it comes to benzodiazepines and anticonvulsants, such drugs are still given to people diagnosed with PTSD even though clinical researchers don't typically recommend them (Benedek et al., 2009; Jeffreys et al., 2012; Lund, Abrams, Bernardy, Alexander, & Friedman, 2013; Management of Post-Traumatic Stress Working Group, 2010; Wallace & Cooper, 2015). One drug that researchers often do recommend is the high-blood-pressure medicine *prazosin* (an alpha-adrenergic drug, which blocks norepinephrine at alpha receptors), especially in cases where the goal is reducing nightmares and improving sleep (Benedek et al., 2009; Ipser & Stein, 2012; Jeffreys et al., 2012). Prazosin's utility isn't surprising given research suggesting elevated levels of norepinephrine among PTSD patients (Wimalawansa, 2014).

The main takeaway regarding drugs for posttraumatic stress is that even though a variety of them are prescribed, they are generally considered inferior to psychological therapies (Forbes et al., 2007; Forbes, Wolfgang, Cooper, Creamer, & Barton, 2009; Freeman, 2006; Hoskins et al., 2015; Jeffreys et al., 2012; Management of Post-Traumatic Stress Working Group, 2010; National Collaborating Centre for Mental Health, 2005). Whether or not they should be used for combat-related PTSD remains controversial (Steckler & Risbrough, 2012). So, while SSRIs are the

CHAPTER 7

most highly regarded drug for posttraumatic stress, they aren't considered a first-line treatment. One review put it rather succinctly, concluding that "pharmacological interventions for PTSD can be effective, but the magnitude of effect unfortunately is small, and the clinical relevance of this small effect is unclear" (Hoskins et al., 2015, p. 98). When it comes to PTSD, drugs are a second-line treatment after psychological therapy.

Joe
In the first few months after the earthquake, when Joe's posttraumatic stress symptoms were at their worst, his family physician prescribed him the antidepressant paroxetine (Paxil). Joe took it for six months or so, despite his girlfriend Carol's misgivings. Eventually, however, Joe weaned himself off the paroxetine. He thinks taking it helped him somewhat, but feels that seeking psychotherapy to come to terms with what happened will ultimately prove to be more important in the end.

CASE EXAMPLES

Stress and Adjustment

Given that adjustment disorder is diagnosed in generally well-adjusted people dealing with ongoing life stress, it makes sense that research on brain chemistry has not been very extensive. Nonetheless, in clinical practice people experiencing adjustment difficulties in response to stress are sometimes prescribed benzodiazepines to help them cope with sleep difficulties, panic, and anxiety (P. Casey & Bailey, 2011). Antidepressants are also prescribed in many cases and though there is some evidence for their utility, they are not always recommended (Bisson & Sakhuja, 2006; Carta, Balestrieri, Murru, & Hardoy, 2009; P. Casey & Bailey, 2011; Hameed, Schwartz, Malhotra, West, & Bertone, 2005; Strain & Diefenbacher, 2008). This may be because adjustment problems are by definition attributed to stressful life circumstances rather than underlying brain chemistry imbalances. Therefore, short-term psychotherapy, not drugs, is usually considered the best form of intervention (Carta et al., 2009; P. Casey & Bailey, 2011). One of the challenges in both diagnosing and treating adjustment difficulties using drugs is that clinicians aren't always able to reliably distinguish adjustment issues from depression (Carta et al., 2009). However, use of antidepressants suggests that in practice adjustment problems are often viewed as mild forms of depression and anxiety, making prescribing benzodiazepines and antidepressants understandable even to those who do not support their use.

Prolonged Grief

When it comes to prolonged grief, psychotherapy has received a lot more attention than medication. Only a small number of studies have examined the use of drugs and many of these studies suffer from small sample sizes (Bui, Nadal-Vicens, & Simon, 2012; A. H. Jordan & Litz, 2014; N. M. Simon, 2013). What evidence there is suggests that antidepressants—both SSRIs and tricyclics—can reduce signs of bereavement-related depression (Bui et al., 2012). However, many researchers draw a distinction between bereavement-related depression and complicated grief. Research on the latter diagnosis provides some evidence that SSRIs may be effective. Studies on *paroxetine* (Paxil) and *escitalopram* (Lexapro) suggest they can be helpful, especially when combined with talk therapy (Bui et al., 2012; A. H. Jordan & Litz, 2014; Mancini, Griffin, & Bonanno, 2012; Shear & Mulhare, 2008; N. M. Simon, 2013). Until further studies are done, the use of drugs for complicated grief remains unclear (A. H. Jordan & Litz, 2014). Critics of prescribing drugs remain wary that doing so simply reflects the inappropriate trend toward medicalizing grief (Bandini, 2015). Of course, supporters of using medications counter that when grief goes on for a long period of time, prescribing drugs potentially provides much needed assistance.

BRAIN STRUCTURE AND FUNCTION PERSPECTIVES

A lot of research has examined different brain structures that are important in how people respond to trauma. Much of this research concerns the limbic system, a term referring to several interrelated brain areas that, among other things, play important roles in regulating basic emotions such as fear and anger—especially as they relate to survival. Various components of the limbic system have been implicated in posttraumatic stress responses. Herein we discuss two limbic areas, the hippocampus and amygdala, and an area that has many neural connections to these limbic structures, the medial prefrontal cortex.

Hippocampus

The hippocampus was previously discussed in relation to both mood and anxiety issues (see Chapters 5 and 6). It is a limbic structure involved in storing and recalling long-term memories. When it comes to long-term memories, people diagnosed with PTSD encounter a variety of symptoms. They ruminate about the trauma, relive it through flashbacks, and have trouble recalling it. Researchers suspect the hippocampus plays a significant role in these symptoms because of its importance in long-term memory storage. Many studies have found that hippocampal volume is reduced in people diagnosed with PTSD (J. A. Andrews & Neises, 2012; Bremner, 1999; Karl et al., 2006; Sala et al., 2004; Sapolsky, 2000; Shin, Rauch, & Pitman, 2006; Villarreal et al., 2002; Woon, Sood, & Hedges, 2010). This means that people with PTSD have less hippocampal brain matter. It has even been hypothesized that SSRIs might help address the issue of hippocampal shrinkage, though evidence has yet to bear this out (L. L. Davis, Frazier, Williford, & Newell, 2006). Another issue that hasn't been resolved is whether smaller hippocampal volume makes people vulnerable to posttraumatic stress or whether posttraumatic stress leads to reduced hippocampal volume (Gilbertson et al., 2002; Sherin & Nemeroff, 2011; Wignall et al., 2004; Woon et al., 2010). The existing research suggests it may be both: smaller hippocampal volume may place one at risk for PTSD, but trauma may also affect the size of the hippocampus.

Amygdala and Medial Prefrontal Cortex

Two other limbic structures that appear relevant to posttraumatic stress are the amygdala and the medial prefrontal cortex. As we saw in Chapter 5, the amygdala (which is involved in emotional memory) is often extremely active in depressed people. It is also very active in acute and posttraumatic stress (Aupperle, Melrose, Stein, & Paulus, 2012; Jorge, 2015; Reynaud et al., 2015; Shin et al., 2006). While the amygdala appears to be overresponsive, the **medial prefrontal cortex** (important in memory and decision-making) appears underresponsive in PTSD patients (Shin et al., 2006; Shin et al., 2005). Because different limbic structures often affect each other, it's been hypothesized that the underactive medial prefrontal cortex and hippocampus fail to inhibit the amygdala and this explains the amygdala's hyperactivity (Koenigs & Grafman, 2009). In addition to examining activity levels, researchers are also exploring whether the amygdala and medial prefrontal cortex have decreased volumes in those diagnosed with PTSD. Existing evidence is mixed, but does suggest that posttraumatic stress may be associated with smaller volumes in these two brain regions (Garfinkel & Liberzon, 2009; L. Li et al., 2014; R. A. Morey et al., 2012; Shin et al., 2006).

Autonomic Nervous System and HPA Axis

It makes sense that the limbic system is implicated in posttraumatic stress because it is critical to the functioning of the **autonomic nervous system (ANS)**. The ANS is responsible for regulating automatic biological functions affected by prolonged stress—such as heart rate, blood pressure, and emotional arousal. The ANS has two branches: the sympathetic and parasympathetic nervous systems. The **sympathetic nervous system (SNS)** is activated when a person is under stress, causing physiological changes such as increased breathing and heart rates, pupil dilation, inhibition of appetite, and higher blood pressure. The **parasympathetic nervous system (PNS)** counters the SNS, slowing down breathing and heart rates, normalizing pupils, reestablishing hunger, and lowering blood pressure. Thus, the **fight or flight response** (in which an organism decides whether to flee from danger, engage it, or freeze) is controlled by the sympathetic nervous system. People experiencing posttraumatic stress often appear to be in a perpetual "fight or flight" state. One hypothesized reason for this is underactivity of the medial prefrontal cortex, which plays a role in suppressing the sympathetic nervous system (J. B. Williamson, Heilman, Porges, Lamb, & Porges, 2013).

The **hypothalamus**, a limbic system region that regulates **homeostasis** (the process of maintaining the status quo for things like body temperature, body weight, fluid balances, and heart rate), plays an important part in communicating with and directing the autonomic nervous system. Particularly noteworthy to PTSD researchers (just as it was to depression researchers in Chapter 5) has been the hypothalamic-pituitary-adrenal (HPA) axis. The HPA axis consists of the hypothalamus as well as the pituitary and adrenal glands. It is involved in stress, immunity, mood regulation, and sex drive. Recall from Chapter 5 that one of the things the HPA axis oversees is production of the anti-inflammatory stress hormone cortisol. It is suspected that in cases of posttraumatic stress the HPA axis first becomes hypersensitive and then inhibited due to a negative feedback loop that, in response to the hypersensitivity, instructs the HPA axis to slow down (Ironson, Cruess, & Kumar, 2007). The inhibited HPA axis functioning results in lower cortisol levels. However, research on cortisol levels has provided mixed results, with some studies showing less cortisol in PTSD patients but others not finding this or occasionally even finding more (de Kloet et al., 2006; Ironson et al., 2007; Olff, Güzelcan, de Vries, Assies, & Gersons, 2006; Pace & Heim, 2011; Santa Ana et al., 2006). These results illustrate that while the HPA axis and cortisol levels are associated with posttraumatic stress, our precise understanding of their roles still requires clarification. Nonetheless, some researchers have been experimenting with administering low doses of *hydrocortisone* (an anti-inflammatory drug that replicates the effect of cortisol) as an early intervention for posttraumatic stress (Amos, Stein, & Ipser, 2014).

CHAPTER 7

GENETIC AND EVOLUTIONARY PERSPECTIVES

Genetic Perspectives

Heritability of Trauma and Stress

Genetic perspectives research finds that only 20%–30% of those exposed to trauma develop full-blown posttraumatic stress; when it comes to PTSD risk, heritability accounts for 30%–40% of the variance (Almli, Fani, Smith, & Ressler, 2014). This suggests a genetic predisposition to having difficulty following trauma. That is, genetic studies on posttraumatic stress have repeatedly found that inheritance matters. However, given that PTSD is essentially a response to an environmental (rather than genetic) event, most researchers seem to believe that it is best understood in terms of gene–environment interactions. In this way of thinking, genetic predispositions make people vulnerable to PTSD following traumatic occurrences (Koenen, Amstadter, & Nugent, 2009; D. Mehta & Binder, 2012). This potential for interaction between genes and environment highlights a major challenge faced by PTSD genetics researchers, namely that it is difficult to know whether biological differences (things such as smaller hippocampal volume, discussed earlier) are primarily the result of trauma itself or inherited predispositions that make people vulnerable to PTSD. A previously cited study on hippocampal volume suggests it could be the latter; in identical twins discordant for PTSD (meaning one was exposed to combat trauma and the other wasn't), both twins generally showed decreased hippocampal volume (Gilbertson et al., 2002). While confounds (such as alcohol use by both twins) make it hard to draw firm conclusions from this finding, future twin studies might help us discern whether lower hippocampal volume makes one vulnerable to posttraumatic stress or is a result of it (Kremen, Koenen, Afari, & Lyons, 2012).

Candidate Genes in Trauma and Stress

Candidate gene studies have identified a number of specific genes that seem to correlate with stress, trauma, and depression. Given that impaired serotonin transmission is thought to play a role in posttraumatic stress, it makes sense that much attention has focused on *polymorphisms* (common variations) within the serotonin transporter (5-HTTPLR) gene. The 5-HTTPLR gene has short and long alleles and some (but not all) studies have found a relationship between having the shorter allele and being at higher risk for suicide and depression following stressful life events (Bryant et al., 2010; Caspi et al., 2003; McGuffin, Alsabban, & Uher, 2011). More specific to posttraumatic stress, researchers have started examining whether variations in the glutamate transporter gene (SLC1A1) predict PTSD; one study found preliminary evidence that allele variations along the SLC1A1 gene correlate with posttraumatic stress, but more research is needed to replicate this finding (Zhang et al., 2014). Genes related to the dopamine system and the HPA axis have also been implicated in PTSD (G. Young, 2014). Although a variety of specific genes have drawn interest as potentially correlating with PTSD, genome-wide association (GWA) studies have provided mixed and inconsistent results (Duncan et al., 2018; M. B. Stein et al., 2016), possibly because such studies require many subjects to generate significant findings.

Bereavement

There isn't a lot of research on genetic correlates of persistent complex bereavement. One small pilot study found that having the longer allele on the *monoamine oxidase gene* (MAO-A) is related to increased likelihood of complicated grief (Kersting et al., 2007). Other research has examined genes related to inflammation in response to stress. One recent study found that for some bereaved people, certain genetic markers correlate with higher levels of inflammation (Schultze-Florey et al., 2012). However, these markers did not predict a complicated grief diagnosis. More research needs to be done to tease apart any relationships between genes, grief, and inflammatory responses to stress.

Evolutionary Perspectives

Trauma and Stress

Evolutionary perspectives look at how responses to trauma and stress may serve adaptive purposes that help people survive and reproduce. Importantly, evolved stress reactions differ from person to person and are often products of complex gene–environment interactions (B. J. Ellis, Jackson, & Boyce, 2006). When it comes to identifying psychopathology, fight or flight responses are viewed as evolved mechanisms that help people to cope most effectively with stress and danger (D. V. Baldwin, 2013). When these mechanisms become hypersensitive or malfunction, ongoing difficulties with trauma and stress result (D. V. Baldwin, 2013; Christopher, 2004).

From an evolutionary vantage point, PTSD symptoms reflect the malfunctioning of biologically evolved survival mechanisms. The evolutionary viewpoint can be used to argue that when evolved traumatic stress mechanisms are operating properly, initial emotional upset is expected and normal. In most cases it eventually yields to personal growth—an idea surprisingly consistent with the humanistic view discussed later. The end result is greater emotional resilience, deeper and more intimate relationships with others, and a transformed philosophy of life (e.g., changed priorities, enhanced personal meaning, and a heightened appreciation for what life has to offer) (Christopher, 2004). PTSD only results when there is "a failure to adequately modulate the normal adaptive trauma response, resulting in symptoms that include severe dissociation,

Social support is often considered critical to trauma recovery, perhaps because it allows trauma survivors to make sense of what they have been through.
Source: Getty Images/Lightwavemedia\Wavebreakmedia Ltd

intrusive re-experiencing of events, extreme avoidance, severe hyperarousal, debilitating anxiety, severe depression, problematic substance use, and even psychotic breaks with reality" (Christopher, 2004, p. 86). Because people have evolved as social animals with advanced cognitive abilities, providing those experiencing posttraumatic stress with social support and opportunities to transform their interpretations of the traumatic event are the best ways to help them (Christopher, 2004). Evolutionary theories of trauma and stress are compelling, but clear empirical support for them can be hard to come by.

Bereavement and Grief

What about evolution and grief? According to evolutionary psychologist John Archer, grief doesn't appear especially adaptive because it decreases fitness (the likelihood of reproducing and passing on one's genes; see Chapter 2). He argues that the emotional and physical health deficits that bereaved individuals encounter may make them less likely to attract a mate (Archer, 2001). Yet he also points out how grief may be adaptive in a different way by reflecting a strong ability to form attachments to others. This ability in turn increases social cohesion, which enhances survival rates of all group members. That is, being part of a socially cohesive group bound by strong attachments provides safety and protection, making survival and reproduction more likely. In this conception, grief is the downside of an evolved tendency to form strong, mutually supportive attachments with others (Archer, 2001). Unfortunately, while this is a compelling argument, there isn't clear empirical evidence that grief negatively affects fitness or is explainable in terms of an evolved need for attachment relationships (Nesse, 2005a). In fact, one evolutionary psychology study seemed to contradict the idea that grief decreases fitness. In this study, it was found that strong grief responses signal an ability to form strong attachments (Reynolds, Winegard, Baumeister, & Maner, 2015). Thus, high grievers were judged as trustworthy, loyal, and nice—all qualities that might actually enhance their fitness. What to conclude from all this? Despite theoretical disagreements, evolutionary psychologists remain focused on exploring the adaptive functions of grief.

IMMUNE SYSTEM PERSPECTIVES

Just like many other presenting problems, difficulties with trauma, stress, and loss are often associated with inflammation in the immune system. Numerous researchers have found evidence of inflammation in those diagnosed with PTSD (J. M. Gill, Saligan, Woods, & Page, 2009; J. M. Gill & Szanton, 2011; Michopoulos & Jovanovic, 2015; Passos et al., 2015). Research has also found a link between immune response and grief, with inflammation and (as previously noted) cortisol levels often higher in recently bereaved people (M. Cohen, Granger, & Fuller-Thomson, 2015). Interestingly, inflammation appears only related to recent bereavement, not prolonged grief (J. M. Holland et al., 2014). The fact that inflammation is correlated with many other presenting problems (and not just trauma, stress, and loss) raises questions about the extent to which all adverse psychological experience taxes the immune system. One reasonable hypothesis is that all psychological difficulties cause stress that impacts immunity and potentially compromises physical health. Nonetheless, it isn't surprising that survivors of trauma and loss—both highly stressful events—are at increased risk for illness and death (Jankowski, 2016; Klest, Freyd, Hampson, & Dubanoski, 2013; Schultze-Florey et al., 2012; M. Stroebe et al., 2007).

EVALUATING BIOLOGICAL PERSPECTIVES

The main challenge for biological researchers studying the physiological underpinnings of trauma, stress, and loss is that there are many biological hypotheses, but the evidence for them is often contradictory or inconclusive. For instance, PTSD is often attributed to low cortisol levels, but research support for this hypothesis isn't clear. That is, "variability of cortisol findings within and among patients ... appears to be the norm" (G. M. Rosen & Lilienfeld, 2008, p. 848). Similarly, it was previously noted that lower hippocampal volumes are associated with PTSD. However, because studies linking hippocampal volume to PTSD are examples of correlational research, it remains to be clarified whether PTSD causes hippocampal deterioration or whether a smaller hippocampus places one at greater risk for PTSD (G. M. Rosen & Lilienfeld, 2008). Until these kinds of questions can be answered, biological perspectives have a long way to go.

More broadly, from the perspective of RDoC (the research initiative to build a diagnostic system from the ground up by studying basic biological and psychological processes; discussed most fully in Chapter 3), biological research on trauma, loss, and stress falls into the same trap that negatively affects much psychiatric research: it adopts a syndrome-based rather than symptom-based approach (Cuthbert, 2014; Insel et al., 2010; Peterson, 2015; U. Schmidt, 2015). That is, it starts with what RDoC considers to be scientifically questionable *DSM* and *ICD* categories such as PTSD, acute stress disorder, and persistent complex bereavement and then casts about trying to uncover the biological bases of these empirically suspect disorders. This is backwards. The RDoC perspective urges us to stop using existing diagnostic categories as the departure point for biological brain research. Instead we should begin by trying to understand normal physiological responses to trauma, stress, and loss. Not until we understand such responses can we begin mapping what happens psychologically and behaviorally when these responses go awry (U. Schmidt, 2015). Only at that point can we begin constructing diagnostic categories tied to measurable biological markers.

7.5 PSYCHOLOGICAL PERSPECTIVES

Are there psychological factors that make certain people more likely to respond poorly to trauma? Yes. Research consistently finds that people who display a lot of **negative emotionality (NEM)**—the tendency toward negative moods such as anger, anxiety, and depression—are more likely to struggle with posttraumatic stress (Jakšić, Brajković, Ivezić, Topić, & Jakovljević, 2012; M. W. Miller, 2003; M. W. Miller et al., 2012; J. S. Robinson, Larson, & Cahill, 2014). However, negative emotions aren't the only factors correlated with PTSD. Being interpersonally cold and domineering are good predictors of chronic PTSD; the hypothesized reason for this is that a cold and domineering style prevents people from obtaining the necessary social support for coping with their posttraumatic stress, thus it lingers (K. M. Thomas et al., 2014). These findings are relevant in thinking about the psychological perspectives presented next: cognitive-behavioral approaches might decrease negative emotionality by changing PTSD clients' belief systems, while psychodynamic and humanistic therapies might make PTSD clients more aware of how their interpersonal patterns prevent them from getting much needed social support.

You may notice that we only touch on adjustment issues periodically when discussing psychological perspectives (and throughout the rest of the chapter). This is because there isn't a great deal of work on specific psychotherapies for adjustment disorder—probably because it is a broad diagnostic category usually reserved for reasonably well-adjusted people managing a large and incredibly disparate array of everyday stressors (Carta et al., 2009). For example, how a therapist approaches one adjustment disorder client whose mother-in-law is constantly berating him versus another whose pet dog just died versus another who is about to be fired from her job may be quite different. Said another way, the broad generality of the adjustment disorder diagnosis—that is, its aforementioned use as a "waste-basket" diagnosis for all mild and situation-specific complaints—means that therapists typically use whatever their favored approach happens to be. Studying what works best for such a heterogeneous (i.e., varied) group of clients assigned this vague diagnosis is difficult for the simple reason that these clients differ so much from one another. The mildness of the diagnosis in most instances, combined with its variability from case to case, has resulted in clinicians and researchers showing minimal interest in systematically studying it. Thus, there simply isn't a lot to say about it from this point forward.

PSYCHODYNAMIC PERSPECTIVES

Sigmund Freud and Josef Breuer's early psychoanalytic work in the late 19th century is notable because, more fully than most perspectives at the time, it pointed to past trauma, stress, and loss as the primary causes of psychological disturbance. Freud and Breuer maintained that having patients recall past traumatic and stressful events while also re-experiencing the emotions that accompanied them led to the disappearance of symptoms (Breur & Freud, 1893–1895/2013; Kudler, Krupnick, Blank, Herman, & Horowitz, 2009). Today's psychodynamic perspectives continue to uphold the view that psychological symptoms reflect underlying emotional conflicts originating in past experiences of trauma, stress, and loss. Given that there are many different psychodynamic and interpersonal perspectives for conceptualizing and conducting psychotherapy with people experiencing trauma and stress, it is helpful to consider what they all share. In the broadest sense:

> *Psychodynamic treatment seeks to reengage normal mechanisms of adaptation by addressing what is unconscious and, in tolerable doses, making it conscious. The psychological meaning of a traumatic event is progressively understood within the context of the survivor's unique history, constitution, and aspirations. … The therapist-patient relationship itself is a crucial factor in the patient's response. (Kudler et al., 2009, p. 364)*

Posttraumatic Stress

Psychoanalyst Mardi Horowitz developed a **short-term dynamic therapy of stress syndromes** for posttraumatic stress (M. J. Horowitz, 1973, 1991; Horowitz, Wilner, Kaltreider, & Alvarez, 1980; Horowitz, Wilner, Marmar, & Krupnick, 1980). According to this approach, posttraumatic stress reactions result when people have a hard time successfully navigating the phases that everyone must face when dealing with a trauma: (a) *initial outcry* and awareness that the traumatic event has occurred; (b) *denial and numbness*, including dissociation from self and world; (c) *intrusive thoughts and feelings* about what has happened; (d) *working through* the trauma, so that thoughts and feelings about it are integrated into the self, and (e) *completion* of the process, in which the person comes to terms with the trauma and is able to move past it (Brewin & Holmes, 2003; M. J. Horowitz, 1973, 1991). Horowitz's 12-session short-term dynamic therapy focuses on helping trauma victims reach the completion phase. The first four sessions establish trusting relationships between therapists and patients so that patients can recount what they have been through at their own pace in a safe and nonjudgmental atmosphere (M. J. Horowitz, 1991; Krupnick, 2002). The next four sessions constitute a "working through" phase in which the emphasis turns to patients' unconscious conflicts, maladaptive interpersonal patterns, and problematic beliefs about relationships that interfere with their ability to put the trauma or loss behind them (Horowitz, 1991; Krupnick, 2002). Underlying emotional conflicts and counterproductive patterns of relating to others are examined: "For example, individuals who place great value on being able to control their emotions and their capacity to endure life's adversity might see themselves as weak and vulnerable when they cannot control their tears after a violent assault" (Krupnick, 2002, p. 923). Helping patients use the therapeutic relationship to experiment with more effective ways of relating to others is a main goal during this stage of therapy. Building on the previous example, those who feel ashamed of being emotionally vulnerable might undergo a corrective emotional experience (see Chapter 2) with their therapists, one in which they share vulnerable feelings about the trauma or loss without being judged or critiqued. Based on this positive experience, these patients might generalize being more vulnerable to their interactions with significant people outside the therapy room. The final four sessions help patients integrate the strides they have made during the therapy and process feelings about therapy coming to an end (Horowitz, 1991; Krupnick, 2002).

Horowitz and others have invested considerable energy in conducting research that they feel illustrates that the psychodynamic approach works. However, critics complain that studies on the effectiveness of psychodynamic therapies for PTSD are currently inconclusive (Ehlers et al., 2010). Psychodynamic researchers seem especially sensitive to concerns that their research fails to meet the strict methodological standards of randomized controlled trials (RCTs) (Kudler et al., 2009). In response, they counter that RCTs are less than optimal for investigating the nuances of psychodynamic therapy. In their view, the complex relational process that unfolds between patient and therapist in psychodynamic therapy cannot be broken down and measured as easily as the more concrete techniques used in cognitive-behavioral approaches (discussed shortly) (Kudler et al., 2009; Spermon, Darlington, & Gibney, 2010). Still, psychodynamic researchers might benefit from moving beyond their strong reliance on case studies and instead undertaking more controlled experiments. Along these lines, one recent randomized controlled trial found a 14-week interpersonal therapy for PTSD to be just as effective as exposure therapy and relaxation training; the therapy helped patients improve interpersonal coping skills as a way to overcome trust issues in the aftermath of trauma (Markowitz et al., 2015). Additional studies like this one would help bolster the case for psychodynamic and interpersonal therapies for trauma and stress.

Bereavement

In his classic paper, "Mourning and Melancholia," Freud (1917/1953) argued that grieving requires **decathexis**, the process of divesting psychic energy from the lost love. This is a fancy way of saying that id energy must be withdrawn from memories of the loved one before it can be redirected towards others. In even simpler terms, we must detach from the deceased person before we can move forward (Berzoff, 2003; G. Hagman,

2001). This classic Freudian view framed grief as a restorative process, one that plays out in a person's private psychological experience rather than in relationships with others (G. Hagman, 2001).

More recent psychodynamic approaches tackle the problem of prolonged grief. Horowitz's (2014) short-term brief psychodynamic therapy was designed not only for trauma, but for persistent complex bereavement too. The same phases discussed previously—initial outcry, denial and avoidance, intrusive feelings and thoughts, "working through," and completion—apply not just to trauma, but also to grief. People who successfully move through these phases and complete the mourning process incorporate the loss into their identities and become able to form new attachments. However, those who experience prolonged grief get stuck and are unable to reach the completion phase (M. J. Horowitz, 2014). Short-term dynamic therapy for grief involves discussing patients' underlying (often unacknowledged) feelings about the loss and challenging interpersonal ways of coping that prevent them from successfully navigating the mourning process.

Marigold

If a therapist decided to use short-term dynamic therapy to help Marigold with her prolonged grief, he would be especially attentive to the fact that Marigold avoids reminders of her late husband because she finds them too painful and upsetting. He'd also note that, at the same time, Marigold cannot stop thinking about her husband. Marigold's therapist would therefore work to form a strong interpersonal relationship with her. As she comes to trust him more, he would gently encourage her to share her memories of her husband. Although Marigold might initially find this difficult, she eventually would feel safe enough within therapy to do so. In sharing more of her memories, she would likely find herself less preoccupied with thoughts of her husband between sessions. She would have begun successfully "working through" her grief.

CASE EXAMPLES

COGNITIVE-BEHAVIORAL PERSPECTIVES

Cognitive-behavioral therapy (CBT) approaches to trauma, stress, and loss focus on the roles of conditioning and illogical thinking. Behaviorally, symptoms are viewed in terms of classical conditioning. As such, environmental stimuli become strongly associated with—and therefore evoke—anxiety and other negative emotions (S. P. Cahill, Rothbaum, Resick, & Follette, 2009). Cognitively, the individual makes irrational attributions that overestimate the level of danger, lead to being preoccupied with the loss, and produce exaggerated levels of psychological arousal. As with many other presenting problems, there is a large research literature devoted to CBT interventions for trauma, stress, and loss. A variety of CBT-oriented therapies have large evidence bases. We briefly discuss behavioral, cognitive, and combined CBT approaches.

Behavioral Perspectives

Exposure Therapies for Posttraumatic Stress

Recall from Chapter 6 that exposure therapies are often used to alleviate environmentally conditioned anxiety. Exposure therapies include behavioral techniques such as exposure plus response prevention, systematic desensitization, and modeling (all discussed in previous chapters). In these procedures people are exposed

Exposure therapy that incorporates virtual reality technology can simulate traumatic events that cannot be recreated—in this case the hurricane that destroyed this woman's home.
Source: Digital Vision \ Sally Anscombe

to anxiety-provoking stimuli to condition new, non-anxious emotional responses to them. Because anxiety is an important element of posttraumatic stress, exposure therapies are used for it too. In fact, exposure therapies are well supported by research and typically recommended as a first-line intervention for posttraumatic stress (S. P. Cahill et al., 2009; S. A. M. Rauch, Eftekhari, & Ruzek, 2012). One provocative study even implied that exposure therapy may "normalize" amygdala and prefrontal cortex brain functioning in PTSD patients (Roy, Costanzo, Blair, & Rizzo, 2014). Exposure therapy for PTSD is often done using imaginal exposure or virtual reality exposure (see Chapter 6) (Botella, Serrano, Baños, & Garcia-Palacios, 2015; Gonçalves, Pedrozo, Coutinho, Figueira, & Ventura, 2012; S. A. M. Rauch et al., 2012). This makes sense because it is often impractical, impossible, or unethical to recreate traumatic situations *in vivo* (in real life). Thus, *in vivo* exposure isn't always doable when it comes to re-experiencing traumas like accidents, wars, and natural disasters; imaginal and virtual reality exposure are often the only options.

Interestingly, research has found that therapists don't widely use exposure therapies with PTSD clients despite strong evidence of their effectiveness (C. B. Becker, Zayfert, & Anderson, 2004; van Minnen, Hendriks, & Olff, 2010). When asked why, therapists commonly express worry that doing so might backfire and re-traumatize clients—especially those who are suicidal, homicidal, or psychotic (C. B. Becker et al., 2004; Jaeger, Echiverri, Zoellner, Post, & Feeny, 2010; van Minnen et al., 2010). Given these concerns, it isn't surprising that therapists often assume clients are reluctant to try exposure therapies. However, evidence suggests that clients who believe that talking about problems is an important and necessary part of therapy are actually quite willing to undergo exposure therapies (Jaeger et al., 2010). Thus, exposure therapy advocates encourage clinicians to overcome their hesitance about using it, especially considering its demonstrated effectiveness.

Joe

If exposure techniques were used to help Joe overcome his posttraumatic stress, his therapist might begin by using imaginal exposure, in which Joe would be asked to practice relaxation techniques while recalling the earthquake and building collapse. Then, Joe and his therapist could move on to in vivo exposure. They would slowly expose him to increasingly anxiety-provoking situations related to the trauma. For instance, at one point Joe's therapist might accompany him to the location of the building collapse—a part of town that Joe has actively avoided since the quake. Joe would initially feel distressed and panicked, but after a few minutes these feelings could be expected to dissipate as he realizes that nothing bad is likely to happen. Joe's anxiety would decrease as he is gradually exposed to reminders of the trauma.

CASE EXAMPLES

Exposure Therapies for Prolonged Grief

Exposure therapies have been used not just for trauma, but also for prolonged grief. In fact, exposure has been deemed a "key intervention" for those diagnosed with persistent complex bereavement (Boelen, van den Hout, & van den Bout, 2013, p. 226). When using exposure for prolonged grief, the client gradually confronts the loss by focusing on the most painful parts of the loved one's passing (Boelen et al., 2013). Thus, exposure therapies aim to stop people from avoiding their feelings about the loss and instead face its reality (Boelen, de Keijser, van den Hout, & van den Bout, 2007). It's worth noting that exposure for prolonged grief differs from exposure for PTSD in that instead of eliminating fear and anxiety, the focus is on reducing feelings of longing and sadness (N. M. Simon, 2013). There is evidence that exposure is helpful for prolonged grief, with one study finding it to be more effective than either cognitive restructuring or supportive counseling (Boelen et al., 2007).

Behavioral Activation for Posttraumatic Stress

Due to concerns that exposure therapies are often impractical in real-world settings, interest remains strong in other behaviorally oriented approaches to trauma. For example, behavioral activation (previously discussed in Chapters 5 and 6) is often used for PTSD. As with depressed clients, those experiencing posttraumatic stress often stop engaging in many previously enjoyed activities and become increasingly isolated. In behavioral activation, they are instructed to engage in activities that they will likely find rewarding. The reinforcement they receive helps them overcome patterns of avoidance and social isolation that are central symptoms of their PTSD (Cukor, Spitalnick, Difede, Rizzo, & Rothbaum, 2009; Jakupcak, Wagner, Paulson, Varra, & McFall, 2010).

Cognitive and CBT Perspectives on Posttraumatic Stress

A variety of cognitive perspectives are regularly used to address posttraumatic stress. Cognitive therapies generally focus on educating clients about typical responses to trauma while also using cognitive restructuring (see Chapter 2), a process that involves helping clients to challenge and revise their automatic thoughts about the event (Chard, Ricksecker, Healy, Karlin, & Resick, 2012; Foa, Hearst-Ikeda, & Perry, 1995; A. G. Harvey, Bryant, & Tarrier, 2003). Research has found cognitive approaches to be effective, though they are often combined with exposure and other behavioral techniques and called CBT (Chard et al., 2012; Ehlers et al., 2014; A. G. Harvey et al., 2003). Let's review several cognitive/CBT approaches to trauma.

Emotional Processing Theory

Although exposure therapies reflect behavioral perspectives by emphasizing the environmental conditioning of trauma responses, researchers utilizing cognitive perspectives argue that exposure is most effective when attention is paid to client beliefs. For example, **emotional processing theory** is a cognitive theory

CHAPTER 7

that attributes posttraumatic stress (as well as other fear and anxiety responses) to dysfunctional *fear structures* (Foa, Huppert, & Cahill, 2006; Foa & Kozak, 1991; S. Rauch & Foa, 2006; S. A. M. Rauch et al., 2012). A fear structure is best thought of as closely associated thoughts, feelings, beliefs, and behaviors that are simultaneously elicited when faced with a threatening event.

> *For instance, a fear structure may include a gun as a stimulus element. This would be connected to various behavioral and physiological response elements (i.e., running away, hiding, heart racing, sweating, etc.). In addition, it would be connected to various meaning elements (i.e., "I am going to die"). When something in the environment matches one or more of the fear structure elements, it is activated and the activation spreads throughout the network. (S. Rauch & Foa, 2006, p. 61)*

According to emotional processing theory, the fear structures of clients experiencing posttraumatic stress are characterized by two dysfunctional beliefs, namely that: (a) the world isn't safe; and (b) their symptoms prove that they are crazy and incapable of managing their distress. Emotional processing theorists rely on exposure therapy as their primary intervention for PTSD (Foa et al., 2006; Foa & Kozak, 1991; S. Rauch & Foa, 2006; S. A. M. Rauch et al., 2012). However, they argue that exposure therapy works best when clients' underlying fear structures are elicited. That is, clients' dysfunctional beliefs, feelings, and meanings must be activated, causing them to experience distress during the exposure training. This is accomplished by repeatedly exposing clients imaginally to memories of the trauma and *in vivo* to reminders of the trauma (places, objects, and even people associated with the traumatic event). By so doing, clients come to realize that their beliefs about the trauma are irrational and incorrect. In other words, "these exposures present patients with information that disconfirms the pathological elements of the fear structure, thereby ameliorating PTSD symptoms" (S. Rauch & Foa, 2006, p. 62). Emotional processing theory approaches to posttraumatic stress have shown promise, but additional research is needed to tease apart the precise role of emotional processing in exposure therapies (S. Rauch & Foa, 2006; S. A. M. Rauch et al., 2012).

Dual Representation Theory

Dual representation theory (DRT) offers a somewhat different cognitive perspective on PTSD. Its notion of "dual representations" refers to the theory's central premise that people cognitively encode trauma memories in two ways: through *verbally accessible memories (VAMs)*, which can be actively remembered and expressed in words; and *situationally accessible memories (SAMs)*, which aren't consciously available and are only elicited by stimuli that remind the person of the trauma (Brewin & Holmes, 2003). VAMs are believed to be tied to memory recall activities of the hippocampus, but SAMs are linked to emotion-based brain structures like the amygdala (Brewin, Gregory, Lipton, & Burgess, 2010; Brewin & Holmes, 2003). An example of a VAM is a trauma client recalling a physical assault and describing what happened, while an example of a SAM is a client returning to the scene of the assault and experiencing a flashback (detailed recollections and emotions that otherwise can't be recalled).

The unconscious nature of SAMs makes them difficult to treat because the thoughts and feelings associated with them can't readily be accessed. Thus, dual representation theory contends that "PTSD is a hybrid disorder that potentially incorporates two separate pathological processes, one involving the resolution of negative beliefs and their accompanying emotions and one involving the management of flashbacks" (Brewin & Holmes, 2003, p. 357). The key to trying to address SAMs is to turn them into VAMs by encouraging PTSD clients to focus on them when elicited (rather than avoid them, which is what they typically do). Focusing on SAMs allows clients to verbalize them, thereby transforming them into VAMs. In an updated version of dual representation theory, VAMs have been renamed *contextual memories* (to acknowledge that they aren't simply verbal, but also include abstract thoughts and context-bound recollections that can easily be conveyed in words), while SAMs are now called *sensation-based memories* (to highlight that they are elicited nonverbally when specific stimuli are encountered) (Brewin et al., 2010). This updated version of dual representation theory has been critiqued on the grounds that sensation-based memories may change each time they are recalled—meaning that they are reconstructed rather than literally remembered as encoded. If so, then verbal and contextual information can affect and influence sensation-based memories, making the dual representations less separate than dual representation theory proposes (Pearson, 2012; Pearson, Ross, & Webster, 2012). Debate over this is ongoing (Brewin & Burgess, 2014; Pearson, 2014).

Cognitive Processing Therapy (CPT)

Cognitive processing therapy (CPT) is similar to emotional processing theory in that it sees cognitive change as critical to effective exposure therapy. CPT is a specific cognitive therapy for PTSD that was originally developed for working with rape survivors. It combines exposure with a more primary focus on having clients examine and revise their cognitions about the traumatic event (Resick & Schnicke, 1992). It diverges somewhat from emotional processing theory by placing less emphasis on fear structures. Instead, CPT says that problematic cognitions associated with posttraumatic stress are often about issues besides danger and safety—beliefs about things like self-esteem, competence, or emotional intimacy. The traumatic event violates or conflicts with such beliefs and this is what produces psychological upset (Resick & Schnicke, 1992). To help clients overcome their distress, CPT focuses on helping them reduce their tendency to overgeneralize beliefs about the traumatic event to other situations, while also teaching them to challenge cognitions that result in self-blame and avoidance. The exposure component involves writing a narrative of the event and reading it aloud at home and in the therapy room (S. P. Cahill et al., 2009). A review of research on CPT for posttraumatic stress found low to moderate quality evidence of its effectiveness; whether it's more effective than exposure and other PTSD therapies remains uncertain (Tran, Moulton, Santesso, & Rabb, 2016).

Joe

Imagine Joe's therapist used CPT to help challenge some of the automatic thoughts that cause Joe to feel anxious and avoid certain situations. Recall that Joe finds himself worrying whenever he is indoors that another earthquake might occur and he will again be trapped inside a collapsing building. A cognitive therapist would educate Joe that it is common for people who have survived a natural disaster to worry about it happening again. However, the therapist would also help Joe realize that the probability of his being caught inside a collapsed building again is very low and that life is inherently risky. She might point out that no matter how many precautions Joe takes, it is impossible to guarantee one's safety at all times. Joe would hopefully become more aware of his automatic negative thoughts and get better at catching himself when he thinks this way. He'd replace irrational thoughts (e.g., "I can't tolerate the fear that this building may collapse") with more logical ones (e.g., "While it's possible the building could collapse in an earthquake, the chances of it are low and spending a lot of time worrying about such an unlikely event interferes with my ability to enjoy my job"). Joe would be asked to write a story describing what happened to him during the earthquake, which he would then read aloud to himself at home and to his therapist during a session. As therapy progressed, the expectation would be for Joe to become better able to effectively resist the anxiety provoked by his automatic thoughts.

CASE EXAMPLES

Negative Appraisals Theory

Negative appraisals theory hypothesizes that people **develop** symptoms of **posttraumatic stress** when they process past traumatic events in a manner that produces an ongoing sense of threat. They interpret the external world as dangerous and come to see themselves as damaged and no longer able to function effectively (Ehlers & Clark, 2000). Examples of such negative appraisals are beliefs like "Nowhere is safe," "I attract disaster," "I deserve the bad things that happen to me," "I'll never be able to relate to people again," and "I will never be able to lead a normal life again" (Ehlers & Clark, 2000, p. 322). So, what occurs during negative appraisals-based cognitive therapy? The approach has three goals (Ehlers, Clark, Hackmann, McManus, & Fennell, 2005):

1. *Alter negative appraisals of the trauma.* For example, a client who was deeply traumatized following a rape found herself regularly reacting emotionally to having been called ugly by her assailant. After the attack, she developed negative appraisals of herself as unattractive and undesirable. Consequently, she began engaging in casual sex to try to convince herself otherwise (Ehlers et al., 2005). Cognitive therapy helped her develop an alternative interpretation, namely that the man who raped her targeted her because she was attractive and told her she was ugly because he could only get aroused by abusing women (Ehlers et al., 2005).

2. *Reduce re-experiencing of the trauma by elaborating memories of it and identifying triggers.* Negative appraisals theory assumes that clients often haven't fully articulated a narrative of what happened to them. Clients accomplish this in therapy by writing a detailed narrative of the event, imaginally reliving the experience, and revisiting the scene of the trauma. These activities allow them to construct a more coherent story about what happened to them and make clear to themselves that the event is in the past. To further distinguish "now" from "then," clients are also taught to identify triggers that provoke intrusive thoughts and feelings about the trauma. For example, a man traumatized by a past nighttime car accident came to realize that bright lights (like the headlights he recalled from the wreck) triggered upsetting memories of the event. However, "once this became clear, the patient discriminated between 'then' and 'now' ... by telling himself that he was reacting to a past meaning of the light" (Ehlers et al., 2005, p. 418).

3. *Eliminate dysfunctional cognitive and behavioral strategies.* Certain strategies used by trauma survivors are beneficial in the short term, but have long-term negative consequences. For instance, avoiding reminders of the trauma or refusing to discuss it may prevent immediate upset, but interferes with the ability to challenge negative appraisals and construct a coherent narrative that places the event squarely in the past. Therefore, negative appraisals-focused therapy often begins by talking to clients about the harmful consequences of avoidance strategies (Ehlers et al., 2005).

CHAPTER 7

There is evidence that cognitive therapy for PTSD rooted in negative appraisals theory reduces posttraumatic stress (Ehlers et al., 2005; Ehlers et al., 2014). A randomized controlled trial found that 73%–77% of PTSD clients provided it recovered (Ehlers et al., 2014). Comparatively, only 43% of clients who underwent supportive therapy recovered, while just 7% of clients who didn't receive any therapy recovered (Ehlers et al., 2014). Interestingly, the principles of negative appraisals-based cognitive therapy for PTSD have also been applied to clients experiencing persistent grief (Ehlers, 2006).

Stress Inoculation Training (SIT)

Stress inoculation training (SIT) combines a variety of CBT techniques to decrease avoidance and anxiety related to the trauma. The idea, as the therapy's name implies, is to inoculate the client against the destructive consequences of stress. CBT techniques used in SIT include "education, muscle relaxation training, breathing retraining, role playing, covert modeling, guided self-dialogue, graduated *in vivo* exposure, and thought stopping" (S. P. Cahill et al., 2009, p. 144). The evidence for SIT is not as robust as it is for some of the other CBT approaches, but it can help in many cases (S. P. Cahill et al., 2009).

Mindfulness and Acceptance Approaches

Mindfulness-based cognitive therapy (MBCT) (introduced in Chapter 5 and revisited in Chapter 6) and acceptance and commitment therapy (ACT) (introduced in Chapter 6) are additional CBT interventions that train PTSD clients to stay focused on and in touch with the present moment (rather than being preoccupied with memories of past traumatic events). The idea is to accept one's present reactions without letting them become overwhelming. Mindfulness meditation training, for instance, teaches clients how to observe their experience in the moment without being emotionally triggered by it (Mulick, Landes, & Kanter, 2011; Orsillo & Batten, 2005). The assumption is that being more mindful and accepting one's feelings—however unpleasant it seems—goes a long way toward helping people cope better with the emotions that accompany posttraumatic stress. As the old saying goes, "What we resist persists." In other words, acknowledging rather than avoiding anxious feelings about traumatic events weakens the power these feelings have over us. The research base for ACT is currently modest, but inquiries into its effectiveness for reducing posttraumatic stress are ongoing (S. P. Cahill et al., 2009). That said, one caveat to consider is that even though mindfulness-based interventions may help in some cases of posttraumatic stress, in other instances they may trigger negative reactions (Hanley, Abell, Osborn, Roehrig, & Canto, 2016; Lustyk, Chawla, Nolan, & Marlatt, 2009). It's not known why this is, but one hypothesis is that by discouraging the avoidance of unpleasant thoughts and feelings associated with traumatic events, mindfulness may inadvertently re-traumatize certain PTSD clients (Lustyk et al., 2009). Thus, it should be used with caution when working with trauma survivors. Of course, concern over potentially re-traumatizing clients by having them revisit past traumas is something all CBT approaches must attend to, without losing sight of the central CBT idea that exposure, rather than avoidance, is ultimately preferable for most clients.

Eye Movement Desensitization and Reprocessing (EMDR)

Eye movement desensitization and reprocessing (EMDR) is a technique combining elements from cognitive, behavioral, and neuroscience perspectives. It is used for a variety of anxiety-related problems. However, its strongest research support is for PTSD. EMDR for PTSD involves asking clients to imagine the traumatic event while engaging in **bilateral stimulation**, which involves rhythmically exposing people to alternating stimulation on their left and right sides. The most common form of bilateral stimulation is visually moving a stimulus in front of clients' faces so their eyes move back and forth—hence the "eye movement" part of EMDR. However, bilateral stimulation can also be auditory (alternating sounds between left and right ears) or tactile (back and forth tapping of the right and left sides of the body). Still, the most common way of conducting EMDR involves bilateral visual stimulation. Therapists gently move their fingers back and forth. Clients are then asked to visually track the movement of their therapists' fingers while recounting a traumatic event. Before and after each set of eye movements, clients rate how anxious they are on a scale of 1–10. They also rate positive and negative statements about the trauma. When EMDR is working, anxiety ratings rapidly decrease with each set of bilateral eye movements. The following case example illustrates the use of EMDR in the case of a mother mourning the death of her infant daughter:

> A baby was killed in the Oklahoma City bombing. The mother was not allowed to see the remains, but was told that the baby had died of a head wound. For the next two months, the only image the mother had of her child was an imagined one of her baby with a severe head wound. She had no access to other memories. Further, this negative image was easily triggered and disrupted her ability to function. Two months later, after an hour

assessment, EMDR was provided. The negative vicarious image of the baby was targeted. After the first set of eye movements, a memory of the baby with her husband came to mind. With further sets of eye movements, more memories came to mind—the baby with her, family interactions, and finally the memory of handing her baby to the daycare worker and saying "Good-bye" and "I love you." At that moment, she wanted to stop the EMDR because she felt a sense of peace and closure. This memory was then installed by having her keep the positive image and feelings in mind during sets of eye movements. (Solomon & Rando, 2007, pp. 111–112)

A large body of research has been conducted showing that EMDR is effective in reducing posttraumatic stress (M. S. K. Ho & Lee, 2012; McGuire, Lee, & Drummond, 2014; Natha & Daiches, 2014; E. Shapiro, 2012; F. Shapiro, 2012). Nonetheless, EMDR has been surrounded by debate and controversy, probably because the exact reasons it works aren't known. Several researchers have proposed psychological and/or neurobiological explanations for why eye movements help people integrate and resolve traumatic memories (Elofsson, von Schèele, Theorell, & Söndergaard, 2008; R. W. Gunter & Bodner, 2008; Oren & Solomon, 2012). However, others remain skeptical of these accounts. Critics contend that EMDR too-often employs unreliable verbal reports from clients about whether they feel less anxious (J. M. Lohr, Lilienfeld, Tolin, & Herbert, 1999; J. M. Lohr, Tolin, & Lilienfeld, 1998; Sikes & Sikes, 2003). Further, critics maintain that even if EMDR works it isn't due to bilateral stimulation, but because of overlooked commonalities with exposure therapies (Herbert et al., 2000; J. M. Lohr et al., 1999). EMDR advocates counter by arguing that research has shown eye movements to be essential to EMDR's effectiveness (Jeffries & Davis, 2013). They also maintain that critics have misinterpreted the research and unfairly reject EMDR despite much evidence supporting it (Lipke, 1999; Oren & Solomon, 2012; B. R. Perkins & Rouanzoin, 2002). Its effectiveness notwithstanding, debate over EMDR is likely to continue given ongoing disagreement about the precise role of bilateral stimulation in helping people process trauma. Though its strongest research support is for PTSD, EMDR has also been adapted for use in addressing grief and bereavement. The goal is to help clients reprocess their grief in a way that fosters more productive cognitions and coping strategies.

This EMDR client is recalling a traumatic memory while undergoing bilateral stimulation.
Source: Jonathan D. Raskin

HUMANISTIC PERSPECTIVES

Posttraumatic Growth

According to the old saying, "what doesn't kill us makes us stronger." This nicely captures the spirit of humanistic perspectives on trauma and loss. Although people who have undergone traumatic crises usually would undo what has happened if they could, many nevertheless report that having to cope with the event transformed them in unexpected ways. That is, many people experience what humanistic practitioners call **posttraumatic growth (PTG)**—positive changes following crises, traumas, losses, and other stressful events (Calhoun & Tedeschi, 2006; Tedeschi & Calhoun, 2004).

Posttraumatic growth describes the experience of individuals whose development, at least in some areas, has surpassed what was present before the struggle with crises occurred. The individual has not only survived, but has experienced changes that are viewed as important, and that go beyond what was the previous status quo. Posttraumatic growth is not simply a return to baseline—it is an experience of improvement that for some persons is extremely profound. (Tedeschi & Calhoun, 2004, p. 4)

Researchers have developed a variety of ways to measure posttraumatic growth, including the 21-item *Posttraumatic Growth Inventory (PTGI)*, the 50-item *Stress-Related Growth Scale (SRGS)*, and the 13-item *Benefit Finding Scale (BFS)* (Antoni et al., 2001; C. L. Park, Cohen, & Murch, 1996; C. L. Park & Lechner, 2006; Tedeschi & Calhoun, 1996). These inventories assess how much respondents have changed and grown in the aftermath of a traumatic event. They have been used widely in research examining characteristics of people most inclined toward posttraumatic growth. Results of this burgeoning literature suggest that being extraverted, open to experience, and optimistic often predict posttraumatic growth; having a strong social support system helps too (Tedeschi & Calhoun, 2004; T. Zoellner & Maercker, 2006b). Interestingly, posttraumatic growth is also

CHAPTER 7

associated with the propensity to think a lot about the traumatic event—that is, to ruminate about it (Tedeschi & Calhoun, 2004; T. Zoellner & Maercker, 2006b). This is notable because ruminating about something is often viewed negatively and taken as a sign of abnormality. However, PTG research implies that being preoccupied for a while after experiencing a traumatic event may be essential to the growth process. The "symptoms" people display sometimes turn out to be beneficial. Psychotherapy within a posttraumatic growth framework assumes that those who have encountered trauma and loss have had their previous worldviews shattered. Humanistic therapies guide trauma and loss survivors through the arduous process of devising new understanding of themselves and the world in light of what they have been through (S. Joseph & Linley, 2006; R. A. Neimeyer, 2001b; T. Zoellner & Maercker, 2006a).

The study of posttraumatic growth is relatively new and many questions remain unanswered. Critics note that research on rumination fails to clearly distinguish between intentional and deliberate thinking about the trauma or loss versus intrusive and obsessional thinking that the person can't control (T. Zoellner & Maercker, 2006b). They also point out that researchers have encountered difficulty generating reliable and valid measures of PTG (C. L. Park & Lechner, 2006; T. Zoellner & Maercker, 2006b). Finally, it isn't clear whether posttraumatic growth is related to adjustment; it's also unclear whether those who score high on measures of PTG are necessarily wiser or have successfully attached meaning to what they have been through (T. Zoellner & Maercker, 2006b). Future research should try to address these issues so that we have a better grasp of how people grow and develop in response to traumatic experiences.

Joe

Although Joe has encountered many challenges since surviving the building collapse, he also feels he has grown in unexpected ways. "I appreciate things much more since the quake," he says, "because I am much more attuned to how precious life is." He no longer allows little things to bother him, is closer to and more open with loved ones, and feels wiser and more mature than he did before. "If I could undo what happened, I would," he observes during a therapy session, "but in lots of ways I've become a more patient, understanding, and kind person."

CASE EXAMPLES

Meaning Reconstruction following Trauma and Loss

Recall from Chapter 2 that constructivist perspectives are humanistic approaches that emphasize how people invent (i.e., "construct") meaningful ways of understanding themselves and their worlds, which they then use to navigate and make sense of events in their lives (Chiari & Nuzzo, 2010; R. A. Neimeyer, 2009; R. A. Neimeyer & Mahoney, 1995; R. A. Neimeyer & Raskin, 2000). Constructivist psychotherapists have been especially interested in trauma and loss because these events often invalidate people's core assumptions about the world, requiring them to revise their understandings in order to move forward effectively (R. A. Neimeyer, 2001b). Thought of another way, trauma and loss can destroy the personal stories—or *self-narratives*—by which people live (R. A. Neimeyer, 2001a, 2005; R. A. Neimeyer, Klass, & Dennis, 2014). Thus, from a constructivist perspective, posttraumatic stress and complicated grief occur when people have difficulty "constructing a plausible account of important events, a story that has the ring of narrative truth, regardless of whether it corresponds to a historical truth that would be endorsed by a disinterested observer" (R. A. Neimeyer, 2001a, p. 263).

The distinction between historical truth and narrative truth is important because in a constructivist approach it is less important whether the stories we tell ourselves are objectively correct (something constructivist theorists say we might never be able to discern anyway; after all, who is to say what's the "best" or "right" way to make sense of a traumatic event or a tragic loss?). Rather, what matters most is whether the narratives we construct in the face of trauma and loss are internally coherent, personally meaningful, and capable of permitting us to move forward with our lives. Although constructivist therapies have been criticized for sometimes being too theoretical without sufficient attention to practical applications of their ideas, efforts to outline concrete techniques for working with people facing posttraumatic stress and loss are continuing (R. A. Neimeyer, 2001a, 2005; R. A. Neimeyer et al., 2014; Sewell & Williams, 2001).

EVALUATING PSYCHOLOGICAL PERSPECTIVES

Evaluating psychological interventions for grief is difficult because "loss is universal and permanent" and the grief that results rarely fully resolves (N. M. Simon, 2013, p. 419). The things we generally assume are essential to help people overcome grief may not be. For example, it isn't clear that emotional disclosure necessarily helps people experiencing normal bereavement (W. Stroebe, Schut, & Stroebe, 2005). Regarding complicated grief specifically, the lack of an official diagnostic category in the *DSM* or *ICD* has made it difficult for researchers to know which clients to include in therapy effectiveness studies (A. H. Jordan & Litz, 2014). Nevertheless, there is some evidence that cognitive-behavioral therapies and other grief-specific therapies are more effective than more general interventions (A. H. Jordan & Litz, 2014; N. M. Simon, 2013; Wittouck, Van Autreve, De Jaegere, Portzky, & van Heeringen, 2011). However, the research on therapy effectiveness for prolonged grief remains in its early stages.

When it comes to posttraumatic stress it is clear that psychotherapy is effective, but disagreement remains over which types of therapy are best. Exposure, EMDR, and trauma-focused cognitive interventions are usually viewed as having the strongest evidence base compared to other therapies (Ehlers et al., 2010; N. P. Roberts, Roberts, Jones, & Bisson, 2015; Steenkamp, Litz, Hoge, & Marmar, 2015; Wallace & Cooper, 2015). However, not everyone shares this view. One meta-analysis concluded that all bona fide therapies for PTSD are more or less equally effective (Benish, Imel, & Wampold, 2008). Others have vigorously disagreed with this conclusion, countering that most meta-analyses consistently find that treatments focused specifically on having people face their trauma memories (e.g., exposure therapies, EMDR, and trauma-focused CBT) are clearly more effective than those that don't (Ehlers et al., 2010). Two recent investigations have confirmed that exposure and cognitive processing therapy are highly effective (Haagen, Smid, Knipscheer, & Kleber, 2015; Steenkamp et al., 2015). In fact, these studies concluded that these approaches are more effective than EMDR and stress-management techniques. However, another study contradicted this, finding EMDR equally as effective as trauma-focused CBT and more effective for co-occurring depression (M. S. K. Ho & Lee, 2012). The most reasonable conclusions are that (a) trauma-focused therapies such as exposure, EMDR, and cognitive therapy clearly appear to be effective (even if we disagree about which of them is best and why), and (b) passionate debate over the effectiveness of other therapeutic approaches continues. The "In Depth" feature brings our discussion of therapy effectiveness to a close by discussing **critical incident stress debriefing (CISD)**, a formerly popular but now controversial PTSD treatment that researchers and practitioners increasingly agree does not work, and comparing it to a newer approach called **psychological first aid (PFA)**.

IN DEPTH

Critical Incident Stress Debriefing vs. Psychological First Aid

Critical incident stress debriefing (CISD) is an extended single-session post-trauma intervention during which trauma victims are asked to recall the event in vivid detail shortly after it occurs (A. M. Mitchell, Sakraida, & Kameg, 2003; J. T. Mitchell, 1983). It was originally developed in 1983 to help workers in high-risk occupations (such as firefighters and police officers) cope with trauma; over time its use has expanded to anyone exposed to a traumatic event (A. M. Mitchell et al., 2003; J. T. Mitchell, 1983). CISD is based on the rationale that actively and aggressively intervening as quickly as possible with trauma survivors (ideally within 24–72 hours after the event) hastens the recovery process. CISD is typically delivered as a structured group session lasting between one-and-a-half and three hours, during which trauma survivors are (a) asked to describe their experience of the traumatic event and process their feelings about it, (b) provided psychoeducation about normal and expected trauma responses, and (c) encouraged to return to their regular routines.

Although initially popular, controversy engulfed CISD when various researchers found it to be ineffective and possibly even harmful (Bisson, McFarlane, Rose, Ruzek, & Watson, 2009; B. T. Litz, Gray, Bryant, & Adler, 2002; Rose, Bisson, & Churchill, 2002; van Emmerik, Kamphuis, Hulsbosch, & Emmelkamp, 2002). Critics assert that CISD coerces trauma victims to process what has happened to them even if they prefer not to and this can be psychologically damaging. These critics also complain that CISD incorrectly assumes that most trauma survivors will have difficulty handling the event and consequently require a preventative intervention. However, a lot of research suggests that most people are fairly resilient in the face of trauma and therefore it is questionable to impose a treatment on them when they haven't shown clear signs of psychological distress. CISD advocates counter that the evidence for it isn't as negative as critics say, but rather it is mixed—with some studies finding it helpful and others not (A. M. Mitchell et al., 2003; Pack, 2013). Supporters also maintain that in instances where CISD proved harmful it wasn't being used as intended. They argue that when CISD is generalized beyond homogenous groups, used with individuals, or used with people who haven't been screened for previous trauma issues, it is being implemented improperly in a manner inconsistent with its theoretical underpinnings (Aucott & Soni, 2016). The counterarguments of supporters notwithstanding, the consensus in the field seems to be that CISD is potentially harmful and shouldn't be used.

An alternative to CISD is psychological first aid (PFA), a less invasive intervention that builds on research showing that most people are resilient in the face of traumas (Brymer et al., 2006; Vernberg et al., 2008). Thus, contact and engagement with trauma survivors is handled in a non-intrusive but compassionate manner; unlike CISD, it is not pushed on those who aren't interested or ready. Broad goals of PFA include "(a) promoting sense of safety, (b) promoting calming, (c) promoting sense of self- and community efficacy, (d) promoting connectedness, and (e) instilling hope" (Vernberg et al., 2008, p. 383). PFA is a relatively new intervention and therefore the evidence base for it remains preliminary; in this regard, it has been deemed "evidence-informed" rather than "evidence-derived" (Kantor & Beckert, 2011). Still, PFA attempts to avoid the problems associated with CISD. After all, the first rule for all interventions is to do no harm!

CHAPTER 7

CRITICAL THINKING QUESTIONS

1. Do you agree with critics of CISD that it should be avoided because it can harm vulnerable people? Or do you concur with those who believe people are more resilient than CISD critics claim?

2. We know that avoidance is not an especially effective strategy for dealing with trauma, but we also have evidence that pushing people to talk when they aren't ready can be counterproductive. How can we best address this in clinical practice?

7.6 SOCIOCULTURAL PERSPECTIVES

Cultural norms, social standards, and socioeconomic factors all play important roles in how well people handle trying circumstances. In the most general sense, people who lack social support simply don't handle trauma, stress, and loss as well as those who do have such support (Bonanno, Galea, Bucciarelli, & Vlahov, 2007; Brewin, Andrews, & Valentine, 2000; Neria, Nandi, & Galea, 2008; J. Platt, Keyes, & Koenen, 2014; Xue et al., 2015). This is understandable. Family, friends, and community provide much-needed assistance to those going through difficult times; without them, even the most resilient person won't fare as well. At the same time, constant exposure to aversive social conditions—whether they rise to the level of trauma or not—is consistently associated with emotional difficulties (Kinderman et al., 2013). Below we examine various sociocultural perspectives on trauma, stress, and loss.

CROSS-CULTURAL AND SOCIAL JUSTICE PERSPECTIVES
Sociocultural Factors and Posttraumatic Stress

Gender

Women are diagnosed with PTSD two to three times more often than men, even though men have a higher lifetime risk for trauma exposure than women (Dückers & Olff, 2017; Kimerling, Weitlauf, Iverson, Karpenko, & Jain, 2014; Seedat, Stein, & Carey, 2005). How can this be so? One explanation posits that even though women encounter fewer traumas than men, the traumas that they do face more than men (such as sexual assault and child sexual abuse) are not only socially stigmatized, but also highly correlated with increased risk of posttraumatic stress (Kimerling et al., 2014; Tolin & Foa, 2008). It's also been hypothesized that the traumas women experience often occur within a **traumatic context**—a set of circumstances in which there is prolonged and intense exposure to trauma. Spending a lot of time in such a context makes developing PTSD more likely (Kaysen, Resick, & Wise, 2003; Kimerling et al., 2014). As examples, think again about sexual assault and child abuse. These traumas often occur within the ongoing traumatic context of an abusive home. Thus, when it comes to gender differences in PTSD "some of what appears to be excess vulnerability among women" may be "partially a function of chronicity and context" (Kimerling et al., 2014, p. 317). From the standpoint of social justice perspectives, future research should further explore gender differences in PTSD, with special attention to how socially embedded gender norms affect diagnosis and treatment.

Race, Ethnicity, and Socioeconomic Status

Race, ethnicity, and socioeconomic status (SES) are also extremely relevant when it comes to posttraumatic stress. Being poor or belonging to certain ethnic or racial minority groups is associated with higher rates of PTSD (Bonanno et al., 2007; T. D. Davis et al., 2012; Klest, 2012; Klest, Freyd, & Foynes, 2013; Klest, Freyd, Hampson, et al., 2013; Pole, Best, Metzler, & Marmar, 2005; T. Weiss et al., 2011; Xue et al., 2015). Teasing apart exactly how much of the increased risk is due to poverty as opposed to racial and ethnic discrimination is challenging, but at the very least it appears these factors influence one another and together enhance the likelihood of posttraumatic stress following trauma. In some respects, research pointing to poverty and racial/ethnic minority status as predictors of heightened PTSD risk recalls our earlier discussion about the connection between low social support and PTSD. Poor people and members of minority groups often lack access to necessary social support and services that help prevent or minimize posttraumatic stress. In many cases they may face ongoing racial discrimination too, which some believe makes them more susceptible to posttraumatic stress (see the Controversial Question Box for more).

CONTROVERSIAL QUESTION

Can Racism Cause Posttraumatic Stress?

Can racism cause posttraumatic stress? This question is being posed by some prominent mental health professionals, who argue that it can (Butts, 2002; Carter, 2007; Corley, 2015; Helms, Nicolas, & Green, 2012). They maintain that individual and institutional discrimination are too often overlooked as triggers that lead to posttraumatic stress. Psychologist Robert Carter (2007), for example, has proposed that *race-based traumatic stress injury* be used as a non-pathologizing diagnosis to help clinicians better identify and understand the traumatizing impact of racism on members of minority groups. As an example, he presents the following vignette, adapted from psychiatrist Hugh F. Butts, who has also argued that racism can lead to PTSD:

> A light-skinned Hispanic male was treated courteously when he made [an] application for an apartment in New York City. However, when he returned with his African-American wife, the renting agent became aloof and informed them that the apartment was rented. In response to the denial of the apartment, the wife immediately became depressed, insomniac, and hypervigilant. She had repeated nightmares. At the time of the alleged discrimination, she noticed that her hair had begun to fall out, that her skin was dry, and she was constipated. There were no hallucinations, delusions or ideas of reference, and there was a mild paranoid trend. All of her symptoms were causally related to the discrimination. (Butts, 2002, p. 338)

Building on this, psychologist Janet Helms identified three kinds of racially charged events that potentially lead to trauma (Helms et al., 2012):

1. *Direct cataclysmic racial or ethnic cultural events* involve threatened death or injury that is due to or impacted by racial discrimination. An overtly race-based incident such as a hate crime qualifies, but so do things like natural disasters and wars when their effects are made worse by racism.

2. *Vicarious or witnessed cataclysmic events* are events where someone is witness to discrimination or violence directed at others who share the same or a similar racial or ethnic background. For example, seeing videos on television of police shooting young African Americans may be vicariously traumatic for many African Americans.

3. *Racial and cultural microaggressions* are casual experiences of degradation and discrimination that elicit memories of past individual or group traumas; "examples include being called a racial slur or being followed around a department store by a sales clerk" (Helms et al., 2012, p. 68). Because microaggressions don't involve as direct a threat to physical safety and integrity as cataclysmic events, not everyone responds to them as traumatic events—only those whose past trauma histories are triggered.

The *DSM* and *ICD* define trauma more narrowly than psychologists such as Carter and Helms, making it less likely that clinicians using these manuals will diagnose victims of discrimination with PTSD (Corley, 2015). However, social justice advocates argue that the definition of trauma needs to account for the overt and subtle impacts of racial oppression. Helms and colleagues go so far as to contend that, in some instances, Western society's emphasis on individual rights fosters and tolerates trauma-inducing racism. With examples such as rallies by the Ku Klux Klan and Neo-Nazis in mind, they argue "it is often the case that social policies (e.g., freedom of speech) legitimize the rights of the perpetrators while disregarding the possible mental health consequences to the victims" (Helms et al., 2012, p. 68). Their argument that free speech rights should be curtailed in an effort to curb trauma-inducing racism is fascinating and bound to provoke intense discussion from supporters and detractors alike. Regardless, the question of whether mental health professionals should accept the notion of race-induced trauma remains one worthy of further theorizing and research. As Helms and colleagues conclude:

> Failure to recognize or acknowledge the mental health relevance of the sociopolitical, racial, and cultural factors that intersect with trauma experiences for the survivors of trauma as well as for the service-providers will greatly inhibit one's ability to provide effective treatment programs or to conduct meaningful trauma research. (Helms et al., 2012, p. 72)

CRITICAL THINKING QUESTIONS

1. Should the experience of racism be considered a form of trauma, akin to natural and human-made disasters? Why or why not?
2. Does research on racism as a traumatic stressor suggest that our definition of trauma is too narrow? Explain your reasoning.
3. Should the free speech rights of hate groups be restricted to protect members of racial and ethnic minority groups from being traumatized, as Helms argues?
4. How might we research the question of whether racism can induce trauma?

CHAPTER 7

Cultural awareness is critical in effectively helping those experiencing posttraumatic stress. Along these lines, some mental health professionals have advocated that it is often necessary to make **cultural adaptations** to empirically supported trauma interventions (Mattar, 2011). Such adaptations modify the treatment to account for cultural differences. Because interventions developed within one ethnic, racial, or cultural context may not work in another, "trauma education and training must integrate cultural considerations in order to remain relevant for demographically and culturally diverse groups" (Mattar, 2011, p. 263).

Cross-Cultural Differences in Bereavement

From a cross-cultural perspective bereavement research has too often overlooked the powerful role of culture in shaping the experience of grief, thinking of mourning mainly in terms of individual deficits distinct from social context. However, in some circles this is changing. According to one culturally focused researcher, although the bereavement field "continues to develop a substantial literature that is oblivious to culture … it also is developing a substantial literature about the connections of culture and grief" (Rosenblatt, 2008, p. 207). In the mental health professions, conceptions of healthy grief are often shaped by distinctly Western ideas about when life ends, how long it is okay to grieve, how one should properly express grief, and what the goal of grieving is (Rosenblatt, 2008). Yet when it comes to mourning there are extensive differences cross-culturally in death rituals, customs, gender expectations, and spiritual/religious beliefs (Morgan, Laungani, & Palmer, 2009). As one example, Chinese and American grievers show certain differences in how they mourn. Chinese bereaved often display more intense grief immediately after the loss but recover from it more quickly, while the grief of American bereaved tends to be less acute initially, but lasts longer (Bonanno, Papa, Lalande, Zhang, & Noll, 2005; Pressman & Bonanno, 2007). So, even though some aspects of grief may be universal, culture and context clearly influence the experience. In other words, "the context (relational, social, cultural) in which the loss and subsequent mourning behaviors occur will impact the type and amount of grief processing engaged in by bereaved individuals" (Pressman & Bonanno, 2007, p. 730). It is important for mental health practitioners to be aware of cultural differences in bereavement patterns so that they don't improperly pathologize people from other backgrounds whose ways of grieving differ from their own.

Cultural factors may explain why researchers have found that Chinese and American grievers tend to mourn differently.
Source: PhotoDisc/ Getty Images

CONSUMER AND SERVICE-USER PERSPECTIVES
Posttraumatic Stress

Part of the original impetus for adding PTSD to the *DSM* was to bring attention to the plight of combat veterans who encountered difficulties upon returning home. PTSD's inclusion in 1980's *DSM-III* was influenced by the political lobbying of service-users and service-providers during the Vietnam War, when "activists began to note the inequity created by sending men to war without recognizing the psychiatric consequences and the need to provide adequate treatment for them" (Andreasen, 2010, p. 68). Some have gone so far as to provocatively argue that many who advocated the addition of PTSD to the *DSM-III* were motivated by an anti-war political agenda. According to this line of thinking, authenticating PTSD was a means of

> *undermining the US government's pursuit of the war. If it could be shown that the conflict caused long-term and widespread psychological injury to US servicemen, then this was further reason to call the campaign to a close. Hence … PTSD was one of the few politically driven psychiatric diagnoses. (E. Jones & Wessely, 2007, p. 171)*

Obviously, not everyone accepts this interpretation. Regardless, while recognizing PTSD as a mental disorder certainly raised awareness about the need to provide combat veterans with mental health services, the potential stigma associated with the diagnosis sometimes discourages veterans from taking advantage of these services (Blais & Renshaw, 2014). Research with U.K. and U.S. veterans returning from combat reveals that soldiers seeking treatment for posttraumatic stress—especially men—hold a lot of stereotypes about PTSD and worry about being labeled as "dangerous/violent" or "crazy" (Mittal et al., 2013; Osório, Jones, Fertout, & Greenberg,

2013). Overcoming internal stigma is a daunting obstacle these soldiers must overcome before they seek help (D. Murphy, Hunt, Luzon, & Greenberg, 2014).

Stigma research potentially explains why, as mentioned previously, some veterans have strongly advocated against the idea of PTSD as a disorder. In the words of U.S. Staff Sergeant and Medal of Honor winner Ty Carter, "If you just call it stress, what it really is, it explains the fact that it's a natural reaction to a traumatic experience. … It's our body's and mind's natural reaction to try and remember and avoid those situations" (Timm, 2013, para. 2). In keeping with this sentiment, a consumer-based movement to change the name of PTSD to PTSI (posttraumatic stress injury) is currently underway (Ochberg, 2014). Just as in the 1970s when political pressure helped get PTSD added to the *DSM*, the consumer initiative to rename PTSD as PTSI may again influence how we talk and think about posttraumatic stress. In the words of one psychiatrist, if a name change occurs it will be "because our patients, our potential patients, and their advocates have convinced us that this is accurate and honorable and hopeful" (Ochberg, 2014, p. 99). Whether or not you support this prospective change, the fact that it is getting so much attention illustrates that when service-users speak up, they can have a significant impact.

Adjustment Issues

What should service-users know about stigma associated with adjustment disorders? In keeping with its reputation as a generic "waste-basket" diagnosis, adjustment disorders are usually considered fairly non-stigmatizing. For instance, one study found that 55% of child psychiatrists reported diagnosing patients with adjustment disorders (as opposed to something more serious) as a way to avoid stigmatizing them (Setterberg et al., 1991). Other research bears out the finding that people with adjustment disorders don't suffer from significant stigmatization. A study of labor outcomes found that, unlike people with other mental disorder diagnoses, employment rates for people diagnosed with adjustment disorders are no different than for people with no mental disorder diagnosis (M. L. Baldwin & Marcus, 2007). The reason offered for this is that "adjustment disorders are typically time-limited, stress-related disorders occurring in otherwise normally functioning individuals. These would be expected to confer relatively little long-term impairment in productivity, and also relatively little stigma" (M. L. Baldwin & Marcus, 2007, p. 506). Still, any diagnosis carries the risk of stigma and the fact that there simply isn't very much research on adjustment disorder and stigma warrants caution.

Prolonged Grief

When it comes to stigma and grief, concerns have been raised about possible negative effects of adding persistent complex bereavement to the *DSM* (Bandini, 2015). Yet grief sometimes carries stigma even without a new *DSM* diagnosis. One study concluded that the more severe one's grief symptoms, the more negative the reaction of others (J. G. Johnson et al., 2009). However, this same study also found that over 90% of people experiencing severe grief would be relieved to know there is a psychiatric diagnosis to account for their difficulties. This suggests that clients struggling with ongoing grief are inclined to add a prolonged grief diagnosis to the *DSM*. Clinicians also tentatively support the idea, despite lingering reservations about potentially pathologizing grief (S. P. Ogden & Simmonds, 2014). In light of the research, prominent grief researchers have concluded that "the potential benefit of creating a new diagnosis in order to identify individuals who require clinical attention appears to outweigh the potential harm as long as the diagnosis is applied appropriately" (Shear et al., 2011, p. 107). It appears that many consumers agree with this conclusion and support a prolonged grief diagnosis—as does the *ICD-11*, which officially includes it.

Marigold

Marigold reads about a new proposed diagnosis called persistent complex bereavement. "That describes me!" she exclaims. Awareness of this new diagnosis might help Marigold realize that she isn't the only person who has ever had difficulty dealing with the death of a close loved one.

CASE EXAMPLES

SYSTEMS PERSPECTIVES
Group Therapy for Posttraumatic Stress

Posttraumatic stress is often treated using group therapy (Shea, McDevitt-Murphy, Ready, & Schnurr, 2009). In fact, many clinicians consider group therapy to be the "treatment of choice for trauma survivors" (Harney & Harvey, 1999, p. 1). Lots of group interventions have been developed, several of which are mentioned here. **Psychodynamic PTSD groups** aim to make members' traumatic memories conscious so feelings about them can be worked through in the group setting. Similarly, **interpersonal PTSD groups** and **PTSD process groups** emphasize helping group members gain awareness of their feelings and patterns of relating to others; the group setting provides an excellent forum for members to give one another interpersonal feedback. **Supportive PTSD groups** focus more broadly on having group members provide each other with emotional support and encouragement; the idea is that by fostering supportive relationships, those coping with trauma can assist one another. Psychodynamic, interpersonal, process, and supportive groups are usually less structured than **trauma-focused cognitive-behavioral groups**, which stress educating group members about trauma and using various exposure and relaxation techniques to address their anxiety. Given that there are many different ways people become traumatized, groups with different foci have been developed irrespective of theoretical emphasis—including groups for combat veterans, substance users, disaster workers, automobile-accident survivors, sexual assault survivors, child-abuse survivors, and disaster survivors (B. H. Young & Blake, 1999).

Joe

Let's envision Joe joining a supportive therapy group for trauma survivors led by a local therapist. The group would likely consist of around eight trauma survivors and meet once a week for 90 minutes. Members would share their stories and support one another as they all try to cope with their posttraumatic stress. In session, Joe might share that he has been feeling especially anxious and jittery at work. In response, other members would empathize with Joe and share similar difficulties that they have had. As a result, Joe would come to feel that others understand what he is going through. Several members of the group would likely talk about strategies they have used to overcome their difficulties at work and Joe, listening intently, would be encouraged to think about how he could adopt similar strategies himself.

CASE EXAMPLES

Although group therapy is often a "go to" treatment for trauma, especially in agency settings, the evidence base for it is inconclusive. Research does suggest that cognitive-behavioral, interpersonal, and process-oriented group therapies can be effective (Bisson et al., 2007; Ehlers et al., 2014; Harney & Harvey, 1999; Shea et al., 2009). However, few large randomized controlled studies have been conducted and it isn't clear which trauma-focused group interventions are best (J. G. Beck & Sloan, 2014; Harney & Harvey, 1999; Shea et al., 2009; Sloan, Bovin, & Schnurr, 2012). Many of the studies done have small sample sizes, lack control groups (or only include a wait-list control group), find group interventions to be roughly equal in effectiveness, or have focused too much on CBT groups at the expense of other approaches (J. G. Beck & Sloan, 2014; Campanini et al., 2010; Classen et al., 2011; Harney & Harvey, 1999; Shea et al., 2009; Sloan et al., 2012). It also isn't known whether trauma-specific groups are superior to individual treatment or to groups that only offer psychoeducation and support (Shea et al., 2009; Sloan et al., 2012)—though one study did find a trauma-focused CBT group superior to supportive group therapy (Ehlers et al., 2014). More generally, few studies have tested the assumption that groups improve interpersonal functioning by providing social support; additionally, while groups are often seen as cost effective, research on this issue is also lacking (Sloan et al., 2012). Finally, discerning gender and cultural differences in response to group interventions has proven challenging (J. G. Beck & Sloan, 2014). So, although groups are used often to treat posttraumatic stress, there is much that we don't know about their effectiveness (J. G. Beck & Sloan, 2014). This doesn't mean groups don't help; it merely means that more research is needed because currently, "given the limitations of the research literature, there is little evidence to guide clinicians on what group treatments for PTSD should be used and when they should be applied" (Sloan et al., 2012, p. 698).

Group therapy is considered a "go to" treatment for trauma, but the evidence base for it remains mixed.
Source: iStock.com/KatarzynaBialasiewicz

Couples and Family Therapy Approaches

Posttraumatic Stress

As is true for many presenting problems (see earlier chapters on psychosis, mood problems, and anxiety), expressed emotion by family members is associated with poorer PTSD outcomes. Posttraumatic stress clients with hostile and critical family members simply don't respond to treatment as well as those whose families are emotionally supportive (Barrowclough, Gregg, & Tarrier, 2008; Tarrier, Sommerfield, & Pilgrim, 1999). Thus, couples and family therapies often aim to improve interpersonal relationships by improving family communication and reducing expressed emotion.

As with group therapies, many different couple and family therapies have been developed for posttraumatic stress. For example, when it comes to working with combat-induced PTSD, one review highlighted six distinct family therapy approaches (Sensiba & Franklin, 2015): (a) **cognitive-behavioral conjoint therapy (CBCT)**, a 15-session *manualized treatment* (i.e., a highly structured treatment intended to ensure uniformity of administration across different therapists) in which cognitive therapy techniques are used to teach conflict management (Monson, Macdonald, Fredman, Schumm, & Taft, 2014); (b) **integrative behavioral couples therapy**, which teaches emotional acceptance while also employing exposure techniques to eliminate interpersonal avoidance; (c) **strategic approach therapy (SAT)**, a 10-session manualized therapy in which stress inoculation and other coping skills are taught (Monson et al., 2014); (d) **family systems therapy for PTSD** to address dysfunctional family patterns; (e) **multifamily group psychoeducation**, in which families are brought together in a group format to share stories and provide one another with support; and (f) **parent management training** to teach PTSD patients and their partners effective parenting techniques. An additional couples approach that has shown promise is **emotion-focused couple therapy (EFCT) for trauma**, a 10-20 session approach that—like other emotion-focused interventions—stresses processing emotions in an effort to help the couple identify and eliminate negative relational interaction patterns (Monson et al., 2014). Three elements that tend to cut across these different approaches are psychoeducation, *in vivo* exposure, and improving interpersonal communication (Sensiba & Franklin, 2015). There is some evidence for effectiveness (especially for CBCT, SAT, and EFCT), but in general a lot less research has been done on couple and family treatments for trauma compared to individual treatments (Monson et al., 2014). Future research should tease out how effective these different family interventions are in diminishing posttraumatic stress.

Grief and Loss

One noteworthy example of a family approach to bereavement is the 10-session **family focused grief therapy** (Kissane & Lichtenthal, 2008; Kissane et al., 2006). This therapy model distinguishes five different styles of family interaction that affect how families handle grief. Two family styles are considered functional. *Supportive families* are cohesive, emotionally expressive, lack conflict, and are good at comforting one another; *conflict resolving families* are less cohesive and have more conflict, but are still able to talk through and resolve their issues in a supportive way. Two other family styles are considered dysfunctional. *Hostile families* have a lot of conflict, lack cohesion, and aren't good at constructively expressing feelings; *sullen families* display muted anger, poor cohesiveness, moderate conflict, and high levels of depression. Finally, *intermediate families* are somewhere in between functional and dysfunctional; they are moderately cohesive, have members who display lots of anxiety and depression, and don't function that well but show potential to do so. The 10-session group treatment teaches families to communicate and share emotions more effectively to assist members with the mourning process. A randomized controlled study found evidence of improvement (albeit modest) among families who underwent family focused grief therapy; sullen families appeared to benefit the most (Kissane & Lichtenthal, 2008; Kissane et al., 2006). More research is called for. In the meantime, the originators of this approach urge us to think about grief not as an individual affliction, but as a family problem (Kissane & Lichtenthal, 2008).

EVALUATING SOCIOCULTURAL PERSPECTIVES

Trauma, stress, and loss are problems especially intertwined with the social world. When people present with such problems, the emotional upset they experience is directly attributable to events in their social surroundings. Wars, disasters, and death—as well as less dramatic, more run-of-the-mill everyday stressors—exemplify the kinds of external, socially embedded events that produce posttraumatic stress, persistent complex bereavement, and adjustment issues. Yet even though sociocultural factors set off these problems and influence how we define and treat them, such factors alone can't fully explain these experiences. Not everyone who faces trauma, stress, and loss responds in the same way; individual differences inevitably interact with social context in shaping our reactions to these kinds of events. Nonetheless, sociocultural perspectives maintain that mental health professionals tend to disproportionately attribute human distress to individual dysfunctions at the expense of social influences. Trauma, stress, and loss remind us that people's psychological difficulties are often deeply connected to what their culturally embedded surroundings expose them to.

7.7 CLOSING THOUGHTS: ERASE TRAUMA, LOSS, AND GRIEF?

Memories related to trauma, stress, and loss are unpleasant. Nobody enjoys experiencing them and most of us wouldn't mind forgetting them. So, what if we could simply erase such memories? Numerous researchers have begun exploring precisely this possibility (Lu, 2015). Analogue experiments using rodents and snails

CHAPTER 7

have met with some success in eradicating conditioned memories (Clem & Huganir, 2010; J. Hu et al., 2017; Meloni, Gillis, Manoukian, & Kaufman, 2014; Redondo et al., 2014). One promising way to accomplish this is by blocking specific molecules related to an enzyme essential for long-term memory, *protein kinase M (PKM)* (J. Hu et al., 2017). According to the snail study's lead author, "memory erasure has the potential to alleviate PTSD and anxiety disorders by removing the non-associative memory that causes the maladaptive physiological response" (Columbia University Medical Center, 2017, para. 11). The hope is to isolate "the exact molecules that maintain non-associative memory" in order to "develop drugs that can treat anxiety without affecting the patient's normal memory of past events" (Columbia University Medical Center, 2017, para. 11). We can't yet delete bad memories in people, but one day we might be able to.

If we do develop the ability to eliminate or change traumatic or distressing memories, should we? Every one of us will face stress and loss at some point in our lives and almost all of us will be touched—directly or indirectly—by trauma, too. To this point in our species' history, these arduous experiences have simply been part of being human. The ongoing challenge for researchers, clinicians, and service-users has been determining how much upset over these events is called for, when intervention is necessary, and whether what people gain from such experiences is worth the sacrifice of what is lost. When (if ever) might it be appropriate to erase grief over a loved one's death or preoccupation with surviving a rape, assault, war, accident, or natural disaster? Would altering memory through psychiatric drugs be any better or worse than altering it through cognitive-behavioral therapy? Does erasing painful memories impede personal development by preventing posttraumatic growth? These are questions you will have to answer for yourself. Regardless of what you conclude, hopefully the material in this chapter has helped you better grasp current perspectives on the difficult issues of trauma, loss, and stress.

KEY TERMS

Acute stress disorder (ASD)
Acute stress reaction
Adjustment disorders
Amnesia
Autonomic nervous system (ANS)
Bereavement
Bilateral stimulation
Cognitive processing therapy (CPT)
Cognitive-behavioral conjoint therapy (CBCT)
Complex PTSD
Critical incident stress debriefing (CISD)
Cultural adaptations
Decathexis
Depersonalization
Derealization
Dissociation
Dual representation theory (DRT)
Emotion-focused couple therapy (EFCT) for trauma
Emotional processing theory

Eye movement desensitization and reprocessing (EMDR)
Family focused grief therapy
Family systems therapy for PTSD
Fight or flight response
Five-stage theory of grief
Flashbacks
General adaptation syndrome (GAS)
Grief
Homeostasis
Hypothalamus
Integrative behavioral couples therapy
Interpersonal PTSD groups/PTSD process groups
Medial prefrontal cortex
Multifamily group psychoeducation
Negative appraisals theory
Negative emotionality (NEM)
Parasympathetic nervous system (PNS)
Parent management training
Persistent complex bereavement disorder

Posttraumatic Growth (PTG)
Posttraumatic stress disorder (PTSD)
Prolonged grief disorder
Psychodynamic PTSD groups
Psychological first aid (PFA)
Rape trauma syndrome
Shell shock
Short-term dynamic therapy of stress syndromes
Strategic approach therapy (SAT)
Stress
Stress inoculation training (SIT)
Supportive PTSD groups
Sympathetic nervous system (SNS)
Trauma
Trauma-focused cognitive-behavioral groups
Traumatic context
Traumatic neurosis
Vulnerability paradox
War neurasthenia

Full definitions of the terms listed above can be found in the end-of-book glossary on p. 533.

 Go to the companion website, www.macmillanihe.com/raskin-abnormal-psych, to access a study guide, multiple choice and flashcard quizzes for this chapter, and other useful learning aids.

CHAPTER 8

DISSOCIATION AND SOMATIC COMPLAINTS

8.1 OVERVIEW

LEARNING OBJECTIVES

After reading this chapter, you should be able to:

1. Define dissociation, somatic complaints, and the posttraumatic model commonly used to explain them.
2. Describe *DSM* and *ICD* dissociative and somatic symptom diagnostic categories, as well as discuss debates about these categories.
3. Recall historical antecedents of dissociative and somatic symptom complaints.
4. Discuss biological perspectives on dissociation and somatic symptom complaints, including those looking at brain chemistry, brain structure, genes, evolution, and the immune system.
5. Distinguish psychodynamic, cognitive-behavioral, and humanistic perspectives on dissociative and somatic complaints.
6. Describe the sociocognitive model of dissociative identity disorder, the false memories debate, the role of stigma in dissociation and somatic symptoms, and family systems perspectives on dissociation and somatic symptoms.

Photo source: © Royalty-Free/Corbis

CHAPTER 8

GETTING STARTED: DISSOCIATION, SOMATIC SYMPTOMS, AND STRESS

Lauren

Lauren is a 25-year-old woman who seeks therapy at a local health clinic. Meek and quiet in demeanor, her primary complaint concerns gaps in her memory. She reports periods of several days (including the previous two) that she simply can't recall and is befuddled as to why. She knows that she must be doing something during these times because she finds her food eaten and her clothes in the laundry. Although her childhood memories are also spotty, Lauren recollects being raised in a poor family that moved around a lot. When asked about how her parents treated her, her body language and demeanor shift abruptly; she now speaks in a louder and more aggressive voice, with a distinctly different accent. She tells the therapist her name is "Bix" and that she doesn't want to talk about Lauren's family, but does know what has been going on the last two days. She reports going to a local bar and picking up a man, whom she took to a hotel for a one-night stand. When asked about Lauren, it becomes clear that Bix sees Lauren as a distinctly different person. "She doesn't know about me," Bix says, "but I look out for her."

CASE EXAMPLES

Paul

Paul, a 35-year-old man, is referred to psychotherapy after seeking treatment for a thyroid condition. "I don't know why the doctor sent me to you," Paul tells the therapist. "I just need her to figure out what's wrong with my thyroid." It turns out that Paul has a long and complicated medical history. He has previously been treated for a variety of digestive issues, ongoing headaches, and arthritic-like pain in his hands. His doctors haven't identified the precise biological origins of Paul's complaints, but in the past he has received medical treatments to help address his various and sometimes changing symptoms.

Tiiu

Tiiu is a military pilot who has run more than 100 bombing missions. She has won numerous commendations and is well respected by her peers and superiors. Recently, however, Tiiu has started experiencing numbness in her hands. This has resulted in her being grounded from flying. Oddly, all physical exams conducted to date have found no medical reason for her hand numbness. Because Tiiu has been grounded, her commanding officer recently decided to reassign her to a base near her home and family. Tiiu seems rather calm about it all. "They'll just have to run more tests and figure it out," she says unemotionally to her co-pilot just before being sent home.

Isabel

Isabel is a 39-year-old businesswoman who works at a large investment firm. She works long hours and is expected by her boss to bring in new business for the company. The pressure at work has started taking a toll on Isabel's health. At her last doctor's visit, she was told she has high blood pressure. Isabel isn't surprised. "If you had my job, you'd have high blood pressure, too!" she exclaims. In addition to blood pressure medication, Isabel seeks psychotherapy to help her cope with the stress she feels at work and at home.

The Posttraumatic Model

As we saw in Chapter 7, environmental stressors such as trauma and loss often result in psychological suffering. Yet posttraumatic stress, adjustment difficulties, and prolonged grief aren't the only presenting problems commonly attributed to external stressors. This chapter discusses dissociation and somatic symptoms, two other kinds of psychological problems linked to stressful life events. Given this link, it isn't surprising that many perspectives on dissociation and somatic symptoms adhere to a **posttraumatic model** (also called the *traumagenic position*). This model holds that somatic and dissociative issues are usually tied to stressful or traumatizing life events (S. J. Lynn et al., 2016; Reinders, 2008), and it will be discussed throughout the chapter.

Defining Dissociation and Somatic Complaints

Although dissociation and somatic complaints differ—with the former involving disconnection from experience and the latter physical symptoms with some underlying psychological connection—both are responses to stress that involve detaching from psychological upset emotionally or physically. Thus, despite the *DSM-5* doing so, not all clinicians make a firm distinction between dissociation and somatization; the boundary between them can sometimes appear arbitrary and artificial (Lewis-Fernández, Martínez-Taboas, Sar, Patel, & Boatin, 2007; C. A. Ross, 2008). Although we often distinguish them, in many cases dissociative and somatic symptoms strongly correlate with one another (Lewis-Fernández et al., 2007). Perhaps it is best to think about them as slightly different but interrelated ways of avoiding emotional anguish—by disconnecting from it, expressing it in physical terms, or both.

Dissociation

Recall from Chapter 7 that dissociation involves disconnecting from feelings and experiences or separating (i.e., *compartmentalizing*) different feelings from one another (Nijenhuis & van der Hart, 2011). A dissociating individual might feel nothing during an emotionally charged situation. Or, if in a state of extreme anger, the person might be unable to simultaneously experience other feelings because dissociation often involves separating different feeling states so that while experiencing one, others aren't consciously accessible. Everyone dissociates sometimes, but—as discussed in Chapter 7—severe dissociation often produces a sense of disconnection from or unreality about self (depersonalization) and/or world (derealization) (Şar, 2014). Dissociation can also result in amnesia (memory loss) about upsetting events. In cases where the dissociative compartmentalization of experience is very extreme, **identity confusion** and **identity alteration** may even occur (Şar, 2014). In the former the person is confused about and/or has a hard time recalling his or her identity, while in the latter the person establishes a new identity in lieu of the old one.

Identity confusion and alteration are less common aspects of dissociation, but depersonalization, derealization, and amnesia are common. For example, during an intense argument with a friend, depersonalization occurs when you feel like you're watching the proceedings from outside your own body. The experience of derealization, by contrast, happens when reality appears altered—for instance, in the midst of the argument, time seems like it's standing still. Finally, you encounter amnesia to the extent that, after the argument, you have difficulty recalling precisely who said what to whom!

Dissociation can seem strange and dramatic, but keep in mind that most dissociation is mild and mundane (R. J. Brown, 2006; L. D. Butler, 2004). Losing track of time due to getting absorbed in a task can be viewed as a minor form of dissociation. So can daydreaming, fantasizing, and **highway hypnosis** (in which people drive long distances without paying conscious attention to what they're doing) (Barlow & Freyd, 2009; Cerezuela, Tejero, Chóliz, Chisvert, & Monteagudo, 2004). These examples are all generally considered "normal" forms of dissociation. They are distinguished from the more "pathological" forms mentioned above (derealization, depersonalization, amnesia, and identity confusion). Besides being more severe, dissociation deemed to be pathological is commonly (and, as we shall see, controversially!) viewed as a response to highly traumatic events such as assault or abuse (Barlow & Freyd, 2009). Given this trauma-oriented perspective on dissociation, it's no wonder that distressing events such as wars, natural disasters, and sexual assaults are believed to produce it. This explains why dissociation is a criterion for posttraumatic stress disorder (PTSD) (see Chapter 7). However, dissociation is only one of various prominent PTSD symptoms, perhaps explaining why *ICD* and *DSM* don't classify PTSD as a dissociative disorder. In this chapter, we focus on presenting problems in which dissociation itself is identified as the primary issue.

Ever driven somewhere and, when you get there, realized you weren't paying conscious attention to your driving for much of the trip? Researchers call this highway hypnosis.
Source: PhotoDisc/ Getty Images

Somatic Complaints

A **somatic complaint** involves experiencing or worrying about physical symptoms. Having a stomachache, feeling pain in one's chest, and spells of dizziness are all somatic complaints. Over the last few decades (until the *DSM-5* appeared in 2013), somatic complaints were often distinguished using the terms *psychosomatic* and *somatization*. According to this distinction, a complaint is **psychosomatic** (or *psychophysiological*) when prolonged psychological stress results in or exacerbates a real medical condition (R. Kellner, 1994; J. Stone, Colyer, Feltbower, Carson, & Sharpe, 2004).

Isabel

For example, someone like Isabel, who is under a lot of pressure at work, develops high blood pressure. The high blood pressure is physiologically real, but caused or made worse by ongoing psychological tension.

CASE EXAMPLES

Somatization, on the other hand, traditionally refers to the process of expressing psychological problems in physical terms (Rohlof, Knipscheer, & Kleber, 2014). In this classic definition, somaticized symptoms are medically unexplained—they are viewed as excessive and/or suspected of being physical representations of underlying emotional conflicts (De Gucht & Fischler, 2002; R. Kellner, 1994).

Tiiu

An example of somatization would be Tiiu, our army pilot who develops medically inexplicable hand numbness and can no longer fly bombing missions. The numbness in her hands appears to be a way of conveying her psychological conflict about dropping bombs on people; she is experiencing emotional distress and expressing it in a physical symptom, but her hand numbness can't be explained by any known physical impairment.

CASE EXAMPLES

Although the psychosomatic–somatization distinction goes back a long way, it isn't always firmly adhered to. Nowhere is this clearer than in the *DSM-5*'s somatic symptom disorders chapter, which includes various diagnoses that combine or blur the line between psychosomatic and somatization problems. This blurring can sometimes make it difficult to differentiate various kinds of somatic symptom complaints.

8.2 *DSM* AND *ICD* PERSPECTIVES

The *DSM-5* contains discrete chapters on "Dissociative Disorders" and "Somatic Symptom and Related Disorders." Similarly, *ICD-10* has sections devoted to "Dissociative (Conversion) Disorders" and "Somatoform Disorders" (somatoform being an older term related to somatization that *DSM-5* no longer uses), which it includes under the broader heading of "Anxiety, Dissociative, Stress-Related, Somatoform and other Nonpsychotic Mental Disorders." The *ICD-11* has a "Dissociative Disorders" section, but its closest equivalent to the *DSM-5*'s somatic symptom disorders chapter is titled "Disorders of Bodily Distress or Experience." The *DSM* and *ICD* disorders in these variously titled sections have gone by many names. Table 8.1 is intended to help you keep the names straight.

Table 8.1 The Many Names of Dissociative and Somatic Symptom Disorders

DSM-5	Closest ICD-10 Equivalent	Closest ICD-11 Equivalent	Also Known As
Dissociative amnesia (with or without dissociative fugue)	Dissociative amnesia and dissociative fugue (considered distinct diagnoses)	Dissociative amnesia (with or without dissociative fugue)	—
Depersonalization/ derealization disorder	Depersonalization/ derealization syndrome	Depersonalization/ derealization disorder	—
Dissociative identity disorder	Multiple personality disorder	Dissociative identity disorder	—
Somatic symptom disorder	Somatization disorder	Bodily distress disorder	Briquet's syndrome
Conversion disorder	Dissociative disorders of movement and sensation	Dissociative neurological symptom disorder	Psychogenic movement disorders
Illness anxiety disorder	Hypochondriacal disorder	Hypochondriasis	Hypochondria
Psychological factors affecting other medical condition	Psychological and behavioral factors associated with disorders or diseases classified elsewhere	Psychological and behavioral factors associated with disorders or diseases classified elsewhere	Psychosomatic illness
Factitious disorder (distinguish if imposed on self or imposed on another)	Intentional production or feigning of symptoms or disabilities, either physical or psychological (factitious disorder)	Factitious disorder (distinguish if imposed on self or imposed on another)	Munchausen syndrome (if imposed on another, called Munchausen syndrome by proxy)

DISSOCIATIVE DISORDERS

Dissociative Amnesia and Dissociative Fugue

People diagnosed with **dissociative amnesia** have difficulty recalling important autobiographical information. The information that can't be remembered is usually of a traumatic nature and isn't attributable to simple forgetting. For example, a person who survived a violent sexual assault later reports no memory of the attack and doesn't recall being hospitalized afterwards or attending the trial at which the perpetrator was acquitted.

In some cases, a person experiencing dissociative amnesia leaves home, travels to a new location, and establishes a new identity. This is called **dissociative fugue**. A change included in both the *DSM-5* and *ICD-11* is that dissociative fugue is now considered a subtype of dissociative amnesia. Therefore, both manuals now use the terms "dissociative amnesia without dissociative fugue" and "dissociative amnesia with dissociative fugue." The *ICD-10* system treats "dissociative amnesia" and "dissociative fugue" as distinct diagnoses. Diagnostic Box 8.1 presents condensed criteria and guidelines.

Diagnostic Box 8.1 Dissociative Amnesia

DSM-5 and ICD-11
- Unable to recall information about oneself and one's life.
- Forgotten information is typically associated with trauma or stress and is more than just everyday forgetfulness.
- Diagnose *with fugue or without fugue*; fugue involves intentional travel or confused wandering from home.
Based on American Psychiatric Association, 2013b, p. 298 and from https://icd.who.int/browse11/l-m/en

ICD-10
- Divided into two disorders in *ICD-10*:
  o **Dissociative amnesia:** Inability to recall recent traumatic or stressful events; not due to a brain disorder, drunkenness, or exhaustion.
  o **Dissociative fugue:** Dissociative amnesia plus intentional travel from home.
Based on World Health Organization, 1992, pp. 123–125

Prevalence rates for dissociative amnesia and dissociative fugue are hard to come by. The *DSM-5* simply notes that the 12-month prevalence rate for dissociative amnesia among adults in a U.S. community study was 1.8% (American Psychiatric Association, 2013b). The *DSM-5* reports 1% prevalence for males and 2.6% for females, even though other research suggests prevalence across sexes is roughly equal (Staniloiu & Markowitsch, 2014). Dissociative amnesia prevalence estimates for other countries range between 0.2% and 7.3% (Staniloiu & Markowitsch, 2014). Data for dissociative fugue is even scarcer. One study from China estimated prevalence at 1.3%; another from Turkey at 0.2% (Şar, Akyüz, & Doğan, 2007; Staniloiu & Markowitsch, 2014).

Depersonalization/Derealization

The *DSM-5* and *ICD-11* both contain a diagnosis called **depersonalization/derealization disorder**, which the *ICD-10* refers to as *depersonalization/derealization syndrome*. As its name implies, this diagnosis is given to people who **experience depersonalization, derealization, or both**. The *DSM-5* reports that 12-month U.S. prevalence rates aren't available, but estimates lifetime prevalence at 2%. This is comparable to rates in the U.K. (1.2 to 1.7%) and Canada (2.4%) (E. C. M. Hunter, Sierra, & David, 2004). Notably, prevalence is much higher in clinical populations—30% of PTSD war veterans, 60% of people with **major depressive disorder** (MDD), and between 7.8% and 82.6% of those with panic disorder qualify for a depersonalization/derealization diagnosis (E. C. M. Hunter et al., 2004). This nicely illustrates how dissociation is part of many presenting problems. See Diagnostic Box 8.2 for details on depersonalization/derealization disorder.

Diagnostic Box 8.2 Depersonalization/Derealization Disorder

Criteria/guidelines roughly similar across *DSM-5*, *ICD-10*, and *ICD-11*.
- Repeated depersonalization, derealization, or both.
- *Depersonalization*: Feeling disconnected from or outside one's thoughts, emotions, and behavior; one's experience seems altered or unreal.
- *Derealization*: Feeling disconnected from or outside one's environment; world seems altered or unreal.
- Called "depersonalization/derealization syndrome" (rather than disorder) in *ICD-10*.

Based on American Psychiatric Association, 2013b, p. 302, World Health Organization, 1992, pp. 135–136, and from https://icd.who.int/browse11/l-m/en

 CHAPTER 8

Dissociative Identity Disorder

Dissociative identity disorder (DID) is one of the more controversial *DSM-5* and *ICD-11* categories. In the *ICD-10* it is called by its better-known but older name, **multiple personality disorder**. The hallmark of DID is having two or more distinct "personalities," with only one being present at any given time. Patients diagnosed with DID experience amnesia and can't recall personal information or past trauma. When one personality (or **alter**) is in conscious control, the person may not remember information about the other personalities—or even be cognizant of their existence at all. People with this diagnosis vary in how aware they are of their multiple identities. Many of them minimize their amnesias even though they often experience quite odd things—such as not remembering their names, their family, what happened yesterday, or how they arrived at a given location. Despite its seemingly dramatic symptoms, personality shifts can be subtle and patients often don't know of their various alters, making DID hard to detect. Symptoms typically persist for 5–12 years before a diagnosis is made (Spiegel et al., 2013). "The Lived Experience" box illustrates what it's like to have dissociative identities and how challenging it can be for therapists to recognize them. See Diagnostic Box 8.3 for diagnostic details.

 Lauren
Lauren, who appears to have several distinct "personalities," would likely be diagnosed with DID.

CASE EXAMPLES

Photo source: © PHOTOALTO

THE LIVED EXPERIENCE

Living with Dissociative Identity Disorder

Rachel took a deep breath and grabbed her coffee cup to prevent herself from going into a full-blown panic attack, hoping that it would quiet the overwhelming surge of voices in her head, all fighting to be heard. Dr. Jones, sensing her distress, said encouragingly, "You can share anything here and it will be kept strictly confidential. I know it's hard to open up, but I really want to hear your story." That reassurance seemed to be exactly what Rachel needed.

"Well, I guess I'm here because I don't know what to do anymore. I've been dealing with some really difficult things for a long time. Lately, things have just started to unravel. Weird things have been happening to me and I feel like I'm losing control of my life. I just don't know how to handle things anymore. My doctor recently diagnosed me with depression and anxiety and put me on medication for that, but it's not really helping all that much. I kind of feel like I'm at the end of my rope."

"You mentioned weird things happening recently," Dr. Jones commented. "Can you tell me more?"

Rachel's heart started racing, and she began gulping in deep breaths. Peering up at her doctor's kind face, she quickly looked back down. *I can do this. I have to tell her! I can't do this on my own anymore.* Without looking up, Rachel began speaking very quietly, voice shaking.

"Sometimes ... I can be talking to someone and all of a sudden I get this really weird far away and foggy feeling ... like I am way back in my head somewhere ... The next thing I know I'll 'come back,' but things just aren't right. For instance, I'll be in the house doing housework, then the next thing I know I'm back in the house but three hours have passed and there are grocery bags on the counter, but I don't remember going to the store. One time I all of a sudden was sitting on my couch and I realized my ankle was hurting like crazy and I looked down and I had a cast on it! But I couldn't remember getting hurt.

"I'll get this odd sensation like I'm in my body, but I'm not 'me' ... like I'm behind someone looking through their eyes, or I'll look at my hands touching something and know that it's me, but it's someone else's hands that are touching the object. Or I'll hear myself having a conversation with someone but I don't know how because I'm not talking.

"I have nightmares and flashbacks. Sometimes I see pictures of things in my head that are familiar yet I don't know what they are or where they are from. Other times, sights, sounds, smells, they'll send me into a panic and scare me silly, but I don't know why. They always seem familiar but again, for no reason. And sometimes, and I know this will make me sound completely nuts, but sometimes I'll hear voices, two, three ... having a conversation and I'm listening to it ... only the voices are having a conversation *inside* my head, but I'm not a part of it.

"Stuff like this, well, it's been happening my whole life. And up until a while ago I managed to cope with it pretty well, you know, I developed ways to cover up dealing with people who knew me that I didn't seem to know, and I managed to create explanations for why I suddenly had groceries or a new item of clothing that I couldn't remember buying. I just faked my way through life, you know?"

Rachel finally looked up, tears streaming down her face. "Can you please help me understand what's happening to me? Am I crazy? Please tell me honestly, because I'd rather know and deal with it than continue living my life like this. I just can't do it anymore. For the first time I can remember, I'm really scared. I don't know what to do anymore."

Dr. Jones looked compassionately at Rachel and spoke very gently, "I'm so sorry to hear about how much you've been struggling. You must have felt so alone." Rachel nodded shakily as Dr. Jones continued, "Thank you for your courage to be honest with me, Rachel. I don't want you to feel alone dealing with these symptoms, so I'm glad you've told me what's going on for you so I can help you. And no, you're not crazy, I have a feeling your mind is trying very hard to deal with trauma that's happened in your life, and it's just coping the best way it can right now."

At the word "trauma," Rachel stiffened and a visible shudder ran through her body. The tears continued streaming down her face, and that was when it happened, one of those weird things Rachel had hoped wouldn't happen while she was here with her doctor. As Dr. Jones was asking her questions Rachel felt the like the room was getting more and more distant ... things were fading and her head felt fuzzy and distant ....

"Daddy says we can't talk about dat cause I could get a whoopin'. He says bad men will take me away from him cause Mommy went to heaven so I can't say nuthin'." Right before Dr. Jones' eyes, Rachel slumped back into the couch and sat cross legged. She started to nervously pick at the sore on her arm, scratching as she talked.

As she continued talking in a high-pitched lisp, Dr. Jones reached for a squeeze ball on her desk and handed it to Rachel, who took it and started playing with it. "Rachel," she coaxed gently, "Rachel, please come back. Listen to the sound of my voice, and feel the squeeze ball in your hand. Feel the rubbery spikes on the ball and just let my voice bring you back."

Rachel found herself coming out of the fog that had enveloped her brain so suddenly. The distant feeling she had had the moment before was fading and she again was able to focus on the fact that she was sitting in the doctor's office. For some reason though, she couldn't remember anything that she and Dr. Jones had been talking about before her space-out happened. Even more startling to her was the realization that she was holding a squeeze toy in her hands, and she couldn't remember how it got there.

Panic rose up inside of her and she caught her breath ... not this again! Not here! With hands that shook slightly, Rachel reached over and put the squeeze toy on the therapist's desk. "I'm sorry," Rachel said, "Um, I seem to have forgotten your question. Would you mind repeating it?"

The therapist took a deep breath herself and carefully considered how to explain her diagnosis. "Rachel, have you ever heard of *Dissociative Identity Disorder*?"

Diagnostic Box 8.3 Dissociative Identity Disorder

DSM-5
- Presence of two or more discrete personality states; in some cultures, may be described as an experience of possession.
- Difficulty remembering daily events, personal information, or past traumas that are more than simple forgetfulness.

Based on American Psychiatric Association, 2013b, p. 292

ICD-10
- Called "multiple personality disorder."
- Two or more discrete personalities, with only one evident at a time.
- Rare and may be iatrogenic or culture-specific.

Based on World Health Organization, 1992, pp. 120–121

ICD-11
- Presence of two or more discrete or not-fully integrated personality states that alternately take control of the person's functioning.
- NOTE: *ICD-11* includes two new disorders not discussed in this chapter, but which should be distinguished from DID; these are *trance disorder* (in which identity is lost and awareness narrowed) and *possession trance disorder* (in which identity is lost and the person feels influenced by a spirit, deity, or higher power).

Based on https://icd.who.int/browse11/l-m/en

Prevalence rates for DID are difficult to assess, in part because the disorder is controversial and many clinicians don't believe in it (Gleaves, May, & Cardeña, 2001). The *DSM-5* reports 12-month U.S. prevalence rates at 1.5%, based on a small community study (J. G. Johnson, Cohen, Kasen, & Brook, 2006). However, U.S. rates have been estimated as high as 3.1% (C. A. Ross, 1991). Turkish studies have found prevalence rates ranging from 0.4% to 1.1% (Akyüz, Doğan, Şar, Yargiç, & Tutkun, 1999; Sar, 2011; Şar et al., 2007). However, in countries such as the Netherlands, Switzerland, Germany, Japan, and India prevalence is much lower (Adityanjee, Raju, & Khandelwal, 1989; Friedl & Draijer, 2000; Fujii, Suzuki, Sato, Murakami, & Takahashi, 1998; Modestin, 1992; Sar, 2011). Not surprisingly, DID rates are significantly higher among people with other mental disorders (Sar, 2011; Sar, Önder, Kilincaslan, Zoroglu, & Alyanak, 2014). This may be because DID is associated with trauma—and those who have faced extensive trauma may lack the emotional resources to cope with additional adversity, making them more susceptible to anxiety, sadness, and other presenting problems.

CHAPTER 8

SOMATIC SYMPTOM AND RELATED DISORDERS

Somatic Symptom Disorder, Somatization Disorder, and Bodily Distress Disorder

For many years, both the *DSM* and *ICD* contained a diagnosis called **somatization disorder**, characterized by multiple changing and frequent physical symptoms that lacked adequate physical explanations. The often-unspoken assumption was that the medical complaints weren't biologically based but rather ways of expressing psychological conflict. For instance, a person who was upset about a romantic partner breaking up with her might develop various physical symptoms to convey her distress, none with a clear medical origin.

Somatization disorder remains an *ICD-10* category, but the *DSM-5* replaced it with a new diagnosis called **somatic symptom disorder (SSD).** Somatic symptom disorder is diagnosed in people who have one or more somatic symptoms that they think and worry about excessively. Unlike somatization disorder, somatic symptom disorder criteria don't require that symptoms lack a physiological basis. They might be biologically based, but they also might not be. This reflects the *DSM-5*'s move away from assuming that somatic symptoms are necessarily all in people's heads. The *ICD-11* is following the *DSM-5*'s lead in this regard. However, because the word "somatic" has come to have negative connotations (implying physical symptoms that aren't real), the *ICD-11* is banishing the term "somatic" entirely and calling its version of this disorder **bodily distress disorder** (Gureje & Reed, 2016).

Because it's a new diagnosis, prevalence of somatic symptom/bodily distress disorder isn't known. *DSM-5* estimates 5%–7% of the adult population might have it. A U.K. study revealed 0.5% prevalence for the older somatization disorder (de Waal, Arnold, Eekhof, & van Hemert, 2004). See Diagnostic Box 8.4 for details about *DSM-5*'s somatic symptom disorder, *ICD-10*'s somatization disorder, and *ICD-11*'s bodily distress disorder.

Paul
The case of Paul describes someone who might receive one of these three diagnoses, depending on whether the clinician he saw was using DSM-5, ICD-10, or ICD-11.

CASE EXAMPLES

Diagnostic Box 8.4 Somatic Symptom Disorder, Somatization Disorder, and Bodily Distress Disorder

DSM-5: Somatic Symptom Disorder
- One or more upsetting and disruptive somatic symptoms.
- At least one of these symptoms: (1) ongoing and excessive thinking about the symptom(s); (2) extreme anxiety about the symptom(s) or one's health; (3) lots of time and attention focused on the symptom(s) or one's health.
- Continuous symptoms of some kind persist, usually for six months or more.

Based on American Psychiatric Association, 2013b, p. 311

ICD-10: Somatization Disorder
- At least two years of multiple and varied physical symptoms for which no adequate physical explanation has been found.
- For at least two years, many physical symptoms that can't be adequately explained.
- Reassurance by doctors that the symptoms lack a physical basis is not accepted.
- The physical symptoms impair family and social functioning to some extent.

Based on World Health Organization, 1992, pp. 120–121

ICD-11: Bodily Distress Disorder
- Physical symptoms that the person finds distressing and pays excessive attention to.
- Even when the symptoms have a physical explanation, worry about them is excessive and the person cannot be reassured, even by doctors.
- The physical symptoms are present for several months or more.

Based on https://icd.who.int/browse11/l-m/en

Conversion Disorder

DSM-5's **conversion disorder** (less commonly referred to as *functional neurological symptom disorder*) involves loss or alteration of physical symptoms for which there is no known neurological or medical explanation (see Diagnostic Box 8.5). In other words, someone with conversion disorder literally converts psychological conflict into a physical symptom. Such a person displays symptoms related to *motor functioning* (e.g., weak limbs, paralysis, physical tremors) or *sensory loss* (e.g., blindness, hearing impairment), but these symptoms aren't easily explained medically and seem to be related to stressors in the person's life. The *ICD-11* calls conversion disorder **dissociative neurological symptom disorder**, while the *ICD-10* groups several diagnoses together as **dissociative disorders of movement and sensation**. *ICD-10* and *ICD-11*'s use of the term "dissociation" when referring to conversion highlights how the *ICD* doesn't differentiate somatization from dissociation as much as the *DSM* does. The *DSM-5* says that the exact prevalence of conversion disorder isn't known; one British study estimated it at 0.5% (de Waal et al., 2004).

Diagnostic Box 8.5 Conversion Disorder, Dissociative Disorders of Movement and Sensation, and Dissociative Neurological Symptom Disorder

DSM-5: Conversion Disorder (Functional Neurological Symptom Disorder)
- One or more physical symptom involving lost or altered motor or sensory functioning.
- Incompatibility between the symptom(s) and known neurological/medical conditions.
- Subtypes: *with weakness or paralysis; with abnormal movement; with swallowing or speech symptoms; with attacks or seizures; with anesthesia, sensory loss, or special sensory symptoms; with mixed symptoms.*
- Specify *acute* (less than six months) or *persistent* (more than six months); specify *with psychological stressor* or *without psychological stressor.*

Based on American Psychiatric Association, 2013b, pp. 318–319

ICD-10: Dissociative Disorders of Movement and Sensation
- Loss or altered functioning affecting motor or sensory function, but with no evidence of physical disorder.
- Evidence of social and/or relational issues that justify the diagnosis.
- Specific dissociative disorders and movement and sensation: *dissociative motor disorders; dissociative convulsions; dissociative anesthesia and sensory loss; mixed dissociation (conversion) disorders; other dissociative (conversion) disorders.*

Based on World Health Organization, 1992, pp. 126–128

ICD-11: Dissociative Neurological Symptom Disorder
- Lost or altered sensory, motor, or cognitive functioning inconsistent with any known disease or health condition.
- Subtypes: *with seizures or convulsions; with weakness or paralysis; with alteration of sensation; with symptoms of movement disorder; with symptoms of gait disorder; with cognitive symptoms; with alteration of consciousness; with visual symptoms; with swallowing symptoms; with auditory symptoms; with dizziness; with symptoms of speech production.*

Based on https://icd.who.int/browse11/l-m/en

Illness Anxiety Disorder and Hypochondriacal Disorder

The *ICD-10* and *ICD-11* still use the terms "hypochondriasis" and "hypochondriacal" but the *DSM-5* doesn't. **Hypochondriasis** involves excessive worry about being physically ill, traditionally with the assumption that there is little or no basis for such concern. Thus, the *ICD-11*'s hypochondriasis (called *hypochondriacal disorder* in *ICD-10*) is diagnosed in people who worry about having one or more physical illnesses and can't be reassured that they don't—even though there is nothing medically wrong with them. The *DSM-5*'s **illness anxiety disorder** is similar, except for one very significant difference: it doesn't insist that those diagnosed with illness anxiety aren't sick. In this respect, illness anxiety disorder is like somatic symptom disorder in not requiring that patients' complaints lack a physical basis. The *DSM-5* estimates the prevalence of illness anxiety at somewhere between 1.3% and 10%. Prevalence of hypochondriasis in a U.K. sample was 1.1% to 1.4%, roughly comparable to the low end of the *DSM-5* estimate (de Waal et al., 2004).

Interestingly, while the *ICD-10* lists hypochondriacal disorder as a somatoform disorder and the *DSM-5* classifies illness anxiety disorder as a somatic symptom disorder, the *ICD-11* categorizes hypochondriasis as an obsessive-compulsive disorder. The logic behind this shift is that, unlike somatoform/somatic symptom disorders, hypochondriasis involves few or no physical symptoms; further, the excessive concern about the symptoms involves obsessive thinking and compulsive checking (van den Heuvel, Veale, & Stein, 2014). Thus, hypochondriasis best fits as an obsessive-compulsive type of disorder. The differences between *DSM-5*'s illness anxiety disorder and the *ICD-10* and *ICD-11* versions of hypochondriasis are summarized in Diagnostic Box 8.6.

Diagnostic Box 8.6 Illness Anxiety Disorder and Hypochondriasis

DSM-5: Illness Anxiety Disorder
- For six months or more, excessively concerned about being or becoming ill.
- No physical symptoms or mild physical symptoms; if ill, disproportionate concern about it.
- Easily and excessively worried about health.
- Checks symptoms constantly or avoids doctors and hospitals.
- Classified as a "somatic symptom and related disorder."
Based on American Psychiatric Association, 2013b, p. 315

ICD-10: Hypochondriacal Disorder
- Consistent belief that one is ill, despite medical exams having found nothing; or, consistent concern that one is deformed or disfigured.
- Cannot be reassured by doctors that no illness is present.
- Includes body dysmorphic disorder (*DSM-5* and *ICD-11* list body dysmorphic disorder as a separate diagnosis and classify it as a type of obsessive-compulsive disorder).
- Classified as a "somatoform disorder."
Based on World Health Organization, 1992, pp. 131–132

ICD-11: Hypochondriasis
- Consistent preoccupation with having one more serious illnesses.
- Catastrophically misinterprets bodily feedback as indicating illness.
- Checks symptoms constantly or avoids doctors and hospitals.
- Cannot be reassured by doctors that no illness is present.
- Classified as an "obsessive-compulsive and related disorder."
Based on https://icd.who.int/browse11/l-m/en

Psychological Factors Affecting Other Medical Conditions

Psychological factors affecting other medical conditions is the *DSM-5* diagnosis for people who have a known medical symptom that is brought on or made worse by ongoing psychological stress. The *ICD-10* and *ICD-11* use the even wordier name, **psychological and behavioral factors associated with disorders or diseases classified elsewhere**. The *DSM* and *ICD* versions of this diagnosis can be viewed as psychosomatic problems because they involve real medical conditions impacted by emotional conflict. However, in including "psychological factors affecting other medical conditions" in the same chapter as somatic symptom and conversion disorders, the *DSM-5* has purposely challenged the traditional psychosomatic versus somatization distinction. This change—not found in the *ICD-11*, which doesn't group this disorder with any others—has generated much debate and receives more attention below. According to the *DSM-5*, prevalence rates for psychological factors affecting other medical conditions aren't clear. See Diagnostic Box 8.7 for concise criteria and guidelines.

 Isabel
Isabel, our emotionally stressed case example client with high blood pressure, may qualify for a diagnosis of psychological factors affecting other medical conditions.

Diagnostic Box 8.7 Disorders in which Psychological Factors Impact Medical Conditions

DSM-5: Psychological Factors Affecting other Medical Conditions
- The patient has a medical condition (besides a mental disorder).
- Psychological factors adversely impact the medical condition by influencing its course or treatment, endangering the person's health, or making the symptoms worse.

Based on American Psychiatric Association, 2013b, p. 322

ICD-10: Psychological and Behavioral Factors Associated with Disorders or Diseases Classified Elsewhere
- Psychological or behavioral factors influence a physical disorder.
- Mild but ongoing worry and emotional upset influence a non-mental disorder medical condition.

Based on World Health Organization, 1992, pp. 131–132

ICD-11: Psychological and Behavioral Factors Associated with Disorders or Diseases Classified Elsewhere
- Psychological or behavioral factors influence a physical disorder.
- Psychological factors adversely impact the medical condition by influencing its course or treatment, endangering the person's health, or making the symptoms worse.

Based on https://icd.who.int/browse11/l-m/en

Factitious Disorder

Factitious disorder is an *ICD* and *DSM* diagnosis that isn't easily classified as either psychosomatic or somaticizing, which may explain why it was included in its own chapter in *DSM-IV-TR* before being moved to the broader somatic symptom disorders chapter of *DSM-5*. It is a diagnosis reserved for those who physically tamper with themselves or otherwise exaggerate or simulate symptoms in order to produce signs of illness and convince others they are sick (see Diagnostic Box 8.8). The goal is to get medical attention. Factitious disorder is usually distinguished from **malingering**, a fancy word for "just faking"—although the dividing line between them can be difficult to discern (Bass & Halligan, 2014). One common way of differentiating them is to see the malingerer as faking in order to gain something, such as disability insurance payments or being relieved of burdensome responsibilities at work. The factitious disorder patient, by comparison, has a deep psychological need for medical attention (McCullumsmith & Ford, 2011).

DSM-5 distinguishes *factitious disorder imposed on self* from *factitious disorder imposed on another* (previously called *factitious disorder by proxy*). In the former, the person focuses on his or her own health; in the latter, the person interferes with the health of someone else—often by surreptitiously doing things to spouses or children to make them ill, such as slipping toxins into their food. Factitious disorder is also sometimes known as **Munchausen syndrome**. Because of the deceptiveness involved in this disorder, *DSM-5* notes that prevalence rates are hard to determine.

Diagnostic Box 8.8 Factitious Disorder

DSM-5
- Deceptively falsifying physical or psychological signs or symptoms, or purposely tampering with self or others to produce injury or illness.
- Individual misleadingly presents to others as sick, damaged, or hurt despite no obvious rewards or incentives for doing so.
- The individual is not delusional or psychotic.
- If imposed of self, then diagnose *factitious disorder imposed on self*; if imposed on someone else, then diagnose *factitious disorder imposed on another* (previously called *factitious disorder by proxy*).

Based on American Psychiatric Association, 2013b, pp. 324–325

ICD-10
- Also called "intentional production or feigning of symptoms or disabilities, either physical or psychological."
- The individual continually and regularly fakes symptoms of mental or physical disorders.
- May purposely self-inflict injuries or tamper with self to cause signs and symptoms of illness.
- Reasons for inducing symptoms unclear, but there is a desire to imitate illness and inhabit the role of sick person.
- Different from malingering, which is motivated by external rewards.

Based on World Health Organization, 1992, p. 174

ICD-11
- Regularly faking, falsifying, or tampering with self to produce physical or psychological disorders or injuries.
- Individual misleadingly presents to others as sick, damaged, or hurt despite no obvious rewards or incentives for doing so.
- Even when illness is present, symptoms are exaggerated, fabricated, or made worse.

Based on https://icd.who.int/browse11/l-m/en

EVALUATING *DSM* AND *ICD* PERSPECTIVES

Doubts About Dissociation and Dissociative Identity Disorder

Dissociation has been criticized for being an overly broad concept that is imprecisely defined (Nijenhuis & van der Hart, 2011). According to some research, many clinicians are skeptical of dissociation and aren't convinced that dissociative disorders should be unquestioningly accepted as legitimate diagnoses (Lalonde, Hudson, Gigante, & Pope, 2001; Pope, Barry, Bodkin, & Hudson, 2006; Pope, Oliva, Hudson, Bodkin, & Gruber, 1999). Part of the issue is that, like the Freudian notion of repression, dissociation can't be scientifically observed. After all, if an experience is compartmentalized and out of awareness, by definition it isn't overtly visible. This means we must rely on abstract theoretical definitions. Consequently, many scientists and practitioners doubt whether dissociation is scientifically testable, leading them to challenge its validity.

Although all the dissociative disorders come in for such criticism, the debate gets especially intense when it comes to dissociative identity disorder. Psychiatrists critical of DID don't believe it exists, seeing it as a "fad" diagnosis propagated by misguided mental health professionals (Paris, 2012; Pope et al., 2006). They have called for its removal from *DSM* and *ICD*, arguing that it is an iatrogenic condition—meaning that mental health professionals who believe in it subtly encourage their patients to see themselves as having multiple personalities and that, in response, these patients start acting as if they do because they don't wish to displease their therapists (Piper & Merskey, 2004a, 2004b). This argument isn't out of the mainstream; even the *ICD-10* says that multiple personality disorder may be an iatrogenic condition (Lalonde et al., 2001; World Health Organization, 1992). But critics go further, arguing that not only is DID scientifically suspect, but that there are no randomized controlled trials (RCTs) of effective therapies for DID and that so-called treatments actually make patients worse (Paris, 2012; Piper & Merskey, 2004a, 2004b). Defenders counter that critics ignore data showing that DID can be reliably diagnosed using assessment methods such as the *Structured Clinical Interview for Dissociative Disorders (SCID-D)* (Dorahy et al., 2014). They also contend that DID is a genuine disorder found throughout the world and that critics ignore a large research literature that has established its scientific legitimacy (Brand, Loewenstein, & Spiegel, 2013; Brand, Loewenstein, & Spiegel, 2014; C. A. Ross, 2009, 2013b). Other key aspects of the debate over DID—especially disagreement about whether child abuse causes it—are examined later in the chapter. For now, the main takeaway message is that dissociation and DID are highly controversial concepts.

Debate Over Somatic Symptom Disorders in *DSM-5*

Some clinicians have roundly criticized the new somatic symptom disorders chapter of *DSM-5*. They feel that replacing somatization disorder with somatic symptom disorder was a mistake because the latter, in downplaying the inexplicability of physical symptoms, is now too broad and will result in overdiagnosis. *DSM-IV* chair Allen Frances has been among the most vocal critics of somatic symptom disorder, arguing that it unnecessarily pathologizes normal worry about being physically sick (Frances, 2012b, 2013a; Frances & Chapman, 2013). He laments:

> There are serious risks attached to over-psychologizing somatic symptoms and mislabeling the normal reactions to being sick—especially when the judgments are based on vague wording that can't possibly lead to reliable diagnosis. DSM-5 as it now stands will add to the suffering of those already burdened with all the cares of having a medical illness. (Frances & Chapman, 2013, p. 484)

Those in favor of somatic symptom disorder challenge Frances' contention that it is an unreliable diagnosis, pointing to research trials showing it to have good interrater reliability (a concept introduced in Chapter 3) (Dimsdale et al., 2013). Additionally, SSD supporters argue that older diagnoses like somatization disorder and hypochondriasis were stigmatizing in falsely suggesting that nothing was wrong with patients, implying their suffering wasn't justified or legitimate. By contrast, advocates of the new somatic symptom disorder believe it will reduce stigma because "it offers greater acknowledgement of patients' suffering and avoids questioning the validity of their somatic symptoms" (Dimsdale et al., 2013, p. 227). While downplaying medically unexplained symptoms may avoid stigma, it is easy to see how—for better or worse—taking a more neutral stance on whether somatic symptoms are truly without a medical basis blurs the old psychosomatic–somatization distinction and, in so doing, may make determining what constitutes somatic symptom disorder confusing to clinicians and patients alike.

CHAPTER 8

8.3 HISTORICAL PERSPECTIVES

HYSTERIA AND THE WANDERING WOMB

The *ICD-10* notes how issues identified as dissociative and somatoform originate in the classic term hysteria, which is no longer used in the *ICD* or *DSM*. In Chapter 1, we traced the concept of hysteria all the way back to ancient times. Throughout much of history, it was a broadly defined diagnosis that included symptoms such as emotionality, nervousness, and physical complaints. It was diagnosed almost exclusively in women in ancient Egypt and Greece, as well as during later eras (da Mota Gomes & Engelhardt, 2014; Tasca, Rapetti, Carta, & Fadda, 2012). In addition to ancient Greek humoral imbalance theories, recall from Chapter 1 that the wandering womb theory, an early and memorable biological theory that continued to exert influence until the 19th century, attributed hysteria to a wandering uterus (da Mota Gomes & Engelhardt, 2014; van der Feltz-Cornelis & van Dyck, 1997). The famous Greek philosopher Plato, for instance, vividly referred to the womb of the typical hysterical patient as a "sexually and socially frustrated animal" (van der Feltz-Cornelis & van Dyck, 1997, p. 119). Some historians have interpreted the tendency to see hysteria as caused by disordered female anatomy as evidence that people diagnosed with it—particularly women—have often been (and perhaps continue to be!) those whose behavior challenges traditional notions of gender and sexuality (Dmytriw, 2015).

SYDENHAM, BRIQUET, AND CHARCOT ON HYSTERIA

Sydenham, Briquet, and Briquet's Syndrome

The wandering uterus theory finally began losing influence between the 17th and 19th centuries. The famous British physician Thomas Syndenham (1624–1689) felt that hysteria was best understood as a disease of the nervous system that occurred in men as well as women (Boss, 1979; da Mota Gomes & Engelhardt, 2014; Lamberty, 2007). Two centuries later, the French physician Paul Briquet (1796–1881) shared Sydenham's view that men could have hysteria, even though his research found it much more prevalent in women (Mai & Merskey, 1980). Briquet's greatest contribution to modern understandings of hysteria may have been to destroy once and for all "its historical association with physical pathology of the female genitalia" (Mai, 1983, p. 420). In his 1859 treatise on the subject, Briquet described hysteria in detail and attributed it not to sexual pathology, but to brain dysfunction (Mai, 1983; Mai & Merskey, 1980, 1981). He wasn't able to specify precisely where in the brain the dysfunction was, except to say that "affective" rather than "intellectual" brain regions were impacted (Mai, 1983). Briquet's work greatly influenced later conceptions of somatoform disorders. In the early 1970s, what the *DSM* and *ICD* later began to call somatization disorder was even named after Briquet (Guze, Woodruff, & Clayton, 1972). To this day, somatization disorder is still sometimes referred to as Briquet's syndrome (for the many different somatic symptom diagnostic names, refer back to Table 8.1).

Charcot, La Belle Indifférence, and Hypnosis

Jean-Martin Charcot (1825–1893), a neurologist at the Salpêtrière Hospital in Paris during the latter half of the 19th century, was a seminal figure in the history of dissociative and somatic symptom problems. As noted in Chapter 7, Charcot worked with patients who were diagnosed with hysteria. These patients often displayed medically unexplainable symptoms. Nonetheless, Charcot believed that hysteria had biological origins, even though precisely what the ailment was remained a mystery. He did, however, also hypothesize that in addition to a constitutional susceptibility, hysteria usually requires the experience of trauma (Havens, 1966)—clearly adding a psychological aspect to his conceptualization. One of the interesting observations Charcot made about his hysterical patients was that they seemed unconcerned about their symptoms (the French term for this is **la belle indifférence**) (J. Stone, Smyth,

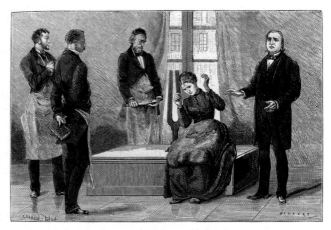

At the Salpêtrière Hospital in Paris, Dr. Jean-Martin Charcot (far right) used hypnosis to treat patients diagnosed with hysteria.
Source: Stefano Bianchetti/Corbis via Getty Images

Carson, Warlow, & Sharpe, 2006). Being indifferent to symptoms implies they serve a psychological purpose for hysterical patients.

Charcot used **hypnosis** to treat hysteria (Havens, 1966; Teive, Germiniani, Munhoz, & de Paola, 2014). Hypnosis is best understood as combining deep relaxation (what often is referred to as a *trance* state) with suggestion (requests that hypnotic subjects can follow if they wish to). Because hypnosis was considered scientifically suspect in Charcot's day, he was heavily criticized by his colleagues for using it (Teive et al., 2014). However, his work did deeply influence Sigmund Freud, who later developed the term "conversion disorder" to explain hysterical symptoms (Nydegger, 2013).

JANET AND DISSOCIATION

The modern concept of dissociation can be traced to one of Charcot's protégées, Pierre Janet (1859–1947) (Dorahy & van der Hart, 2006; Heim & Bühler, 2006; Janet, 1886; LeBlanc, 2001; van der Hart & Horst, 1989). Like Charcot, Janet employed hypnosis to study hysteria. With a case study participant named Lucie, Janet used **post-hypnotic suggestion**—wherein a suggestion made during hypnosis is obeyed while no longer hypnotized (Janet, 1886; LeBlanc, 2001; van der Hart & Horst, 1989). Janet gave Lucie the post-hypnotic suggestion that she would be able to write down things he said while simultaneously talking to others and not consciously paying attention to him. She was able to do so, even though she couldn't recall Janet asking her to write anything. Janet took this as evidence of "double consciousness," the idea that people could have separate and distinct conscious experiences that were split off from one another (LeBlanc, 2001; van der Hart & Horst, 1989). In 1887 he began calling this phenomenon dissociation (LeBlanc, 2001). He argued that dissociation could be used to understand hysteria, which he believed was caused by dissociated memories of traumatic events (Heim & Bühler, 2006). Thus, "in working out his solution to the problem of post-hypnotic suggestion, Janet had arrived at the ideas of the traumatic memory and, in a rudimentary way, the cathartic cure" (LeBlanc, 2001, p. 62). Many current ideas (and controversies) about dissociation are directly traceable to Janet's pioneering work.

8.4 BIOLOGICAL PERSPECTIVES
BRAIN CHEMISTRY PERSPECTIVES
Dissociation

Pharmacotherapy

Antidepressants, anxiolytics, and even antipsychotics are all sometimes prescribed for dissociative symptoms (Gentile, Dillon, & Gillig, 2013). However, these drugs don't appear to have much direct effect on dissociation itself (Maldonado & Spiegel, 2014). Rather, they are typically used to address accompanying depression, anxiety, psychosis, and PTSD symptoms (Gentile et al., 2013; Loewenstein, 2005). The International Society for the Study of Trauma and Dissociation (2011) indicates that "psychotropic medication is not a primary treatment for dissociative processes, and specific recommendations for pharmacotherapy for most dissociative symptoms await systematic research" (p. 205). It notes that, despite minimal evidence, medication remains a common treatment for DID.

Glutamate and Opioid Antagonists

The excitatory neurotransmitter glutamate has been implicated in dissociation, although its exact role appears complicated and currently remains unclear (Loewenstein, 2005; Packard & Teather, 1999). There is also some preliminary evidence for using opioid antagonists to treat dissociation (Brand, Lanius, Vermetten, Loewenstein, & Spiegel, 2012; Gentile et al., 2013). **Opioid antagonists** are drugs traditionally used to treat substance addiction; they bond to opioid receptors, preventing other opioid substances (such as heroin) from doing the same (see Chapter 11). Research on the opioid antagonist **naltrexone** suggests it may reduce dissociation (Gentile et al., 2013). The rationale for why it works is that certain dissociative symptoms—such as depersonalization and **stress-induced analgesia** (pain suppression that occurs when exposed to frightening or possibly traumatizing situations)—appear to be mediated by the body's kappa and mu opioid systems, respectively (Brand et al., 2012). Giving dissociative clients opioid antagonists may interfere with opioid system activity, thereby reducing dissociation. However, as we will see in Chapter 11, such drugs are controversial because of their potential for abuse (Rosenblum, Marsch, Joseph, & Portenoy, 2008). Additional research should continue to examine the roles of glutamate and opioid antagonists in dissociative symptoms.

Lauren

In addition to psychotherapy, what might happen were Lauren—our case example client experiencing dissociative identities—referred to a psychiatrist for medication? There is a good chance she'd be prescribed an SSRI antidepressant. This might reduce some of her mood symptoms, but it probably wouldn't have much effect on her multiple personalities. If the SSRI alone didn't prove helpful, naltrexone might also be prescribed. Lauren might find that these two drugs help her to some extent, but she also might view them mainly as supplements to weekly psychotherapy sessions.

CASE EXAMPLES

Somatic Symptoms

A variety of drugs are given to people with somatic symptoms—including antidepressants, antipsychotics, anticonvulsants, and herbal remedies such as St. John's Wort (Somashekar, Jainer, & Wuntakal, 2013). However, antidepressants are the most common drugs used (Somashekar et al., 2013). Unfortunately, research on the effectiveness of drug treatments for somatic symptoms is meager (Kroenke, 2007; Somashekar et al., 2013). A small amount of research has found a correlation between somatization and decreased serotonin levels (Bresch et al., 2016; Rief et al., 2004). This fits with evidence that antidepressants, which increase serotonin, reduce somatic symptoms (Fallon, 2004; Kroenke, 2007). All kinds of antidepressants appear beneficial, with SSRIs (which impact only serotonin) preferred for hypochondriasis and SNRIs (which impact norepinephrine and serotonin) for pain symptoms (Sumathipala, 2007). Beyond traditional antidepressants, a limited number of studies point to St. John's Wort as a potentially effective herbal remedy for somatization (Sumathipala, 2007). Finally, the few studies that have been done on antipsychotics and anticonvulsants have found these drugs reduce somatic and pain symptoms, respectively (Sumathipala, 2007). Looking at the overall picture, there isn't sufficient research on somatic symptom drug treatments to draw any firm conclusions. Consequently, doctors must employ a trial-and-error approach to finding drugs that work for particular patients.

BRAIN STRUCTURE AND FUNCTION PERSPECTIVES

Dissociation

People prone to dissociation show enhanced activity of the hippocampus and the posterior parietal cortex, which are associated with encoding and recall of negative information (de Ruiter, Veltman, Phaf, & van Dyck, 2007). Dissociation has also been connected to reduced parietal lobe activity, as well as decreased volume of the hippocampus (important in memory) and amygdala (important in basic emotions) (García-Campayoa, Fayed, Serrano-Blanco, & Roca, 2009; Reinders, 2008; Vermetten, Schmahl, Lindner, Loewenstein, & Bremner, 2006). It has also been linked to dysfunction along the hypothalamic-pituitary-adrenal (HPA) axis (Chalavi et al., 2015). Recall from Chapters 5 and 7 that the HPA axis is also implicated in depression and posttraumatic stress, both problems in which dissociation is common. Given the HPA axis' role in stress responses, it makes sense that cortisol, the primary stress hormone, has also been implicated in dissociation (Nijenhuis & den Boer, 2009). As with PTSD, there is disagreement among researchers about whether cortisol levels are increased or decreased among trauma survivors who dissociate (Nijenhuis & den Boer, 2009).

Other brain regions are also being studied for possible roles in dissociation. Decreased hippocampal and amygdalar volumes have been correlated with dissociative identity disorder (Chalavi et al., 2015; Vermetten et al., 2006). So has decreased blood flow to orbitofrontal and superior frontal regions, which are important in cognitive functioning, decision-making, and self-awareness (Sar, Unal, & Ozturk, 2007). Consistent with this finding, some suspect that orbitofrontal development is negatively impacted by early traumatic abuse (Forrest, 2001). Keep in mind that neuroimaging studies of dissociation are still relatively new. Because they are generally correlational, causal inferences can't be made.

Somatic Symptoms

Broadly speaking, the brains of people diagnosed with various somatoform disorders show increased limbic system and frontal lobe activity (D. A. Nowak & Fink, 2009), while also having decreased gray matter density (Browning, Paul Fletcher, & Sharpe, 2011). Research results on brain structures involved in somatic symptoms can appear inconclusive because the number of subjects is often small, data is correlational, and the exact brain regions involved vary depending on the somatic problem at hand (D. A. Nowak & Fink, 2009). Regarding the quantity of research, there have been many investigations of somatic symptoms related to pain, but fewer on conversion and fatigue symptoms (Browning et al., 2011). Studies have found decreased blood flow to several brain areas in people diagnosed with somatization disorders—including frontal, prefrontal, cerebellar, and temporoparietal regions (the latter being an area where the temporal and parietal lobes meet) (García-Campayoa et al., 2009). Decreased prefrontal cortical activity appears to be related to greater difficulty handling intense pain (García-Campayoa et al., 2009).

While conversion is tied to activity in the left **dorsolateral prefrontal cortex** (important in decision-making, working memory, and planning), malingering and factitious symptoms are both associated with activity in the **right anterior prefrontal cortex** (suspected of helping people perform tasks related to one goal while simultaneously keeping information about a different goal in working memory) (Chahine, Diekhof, Tinnermann, & Gruber, 2015; Kaufer, 2007; Leong, Tham, Scamvougeras, & Vila-Rodriguez, 2015; Ramnani & Owen, 2004). This difference may help distinguish genuine cases of conversion from malingering and factitious disorder (de Lange, Toni, & Roelofs, 2010; D. A. Nowak & Fink, 2009). Conversion symptoms have also been tied to increased blood flow to the *left inferior frontal gyrus* (important in language comprehension) and the left insula (Czarnecki, Jones, Burnett, Mullan, & Matsumoto, 2011).

Transcranial magnetic stimulation (TMS) (in which magnetic energy is sent through the brain; see Chapter 5) has shown promise as a treatment for **psychogenic movement disorders** (another term for conversion cases in which there is medically unexplained difficulty moving a limb or body part). It is hypothesized that TMS works by stimulating motor areas of the brain that have been inhibited, perhaps in response to limbic activity (D. A. Nowak & Fink, 2009). The number of patients in TMS studies has been small and results remain preliminary. The controversial technique of electroconvulsive therapy (ECT) (previously discussed in Chapters 1, 4, and 5) is also occasionally used to treat somatic symptom disorders, with researchers theorizing that it fosters long-term changes to the limbic system and prefrontal cortex (Leong et al., 2015)—a claim in need of further study.

GENETIC AND EVOLUTIONARY PERSPECTIVES
Genetics of Dissociation

Adoption and Twin Studies

There aren't many studies on the genetics of dissociative experience, but genetic perspectives maintain that the tendency to dissociate is innate and not dependent on trauma to bring it out (Dorahy, 2006). A notable study comparing biological siblings to adopted siblings concluded that there is a considerable genetic influence on dissociation, even if environmental factors are also relevant (Becker-Blease et al., 2004). Earlier twin studies also found strong genetic influences on dissociation (Jang, Paris, Zweig-Frank, & Livesley, 1998). Agreement isn't universal, however. Investigators examining twin data in another study concluded that dissociation is almost exclusively tied to environmental events (N. G. Waller & Ross, 1997). When it comes to the influence of genes versus environment on dissociation, researchers disagree.

Genetic Marker Research

Turning to genetic marker studies for dissociation, some evidence points toward the 5-HTT (serotonin) gene. One interesting study found that the presence of the S/S allele on the 5-HTT gene predicted higher levels of dissociation among people diagnosed with obsessive-compulsive disorder (OCD) (Lochner et al., 2007). However, environmental neglect also predicted dissociation (Lochner et al., 2007). One twin study suggested a gene–environment interaction. In this study, the SS allele on the 5-HTT gene predicted greater levels of dissociation. However, environmental factors were critical too, explaining over half (55%) the variation in dissociative symptoms (Pieper, Out, Bakermans-Kranenburg, & van Ijzendoorn, 2011). It seems as if both genetic and environmental factors contribute to dissociative experiences.

Beyond the 5-HTT gene, a recent genome-wide association (GWA) study identified two genes worthy of further attention when it comes to dissociation: ADCY8 and DPP6 (E. J. Wolf et al., 2014). Unfortunately, the study's results didn't quite reach statistical significance. Whether this is because large sample sizes are needed to obtain significant results in genome-wide association studies or because these two genes don't play a role in dissociation is something future research should address.

CHAPTER 8

Genetics of Somatic Symptoms

Family, Adoption, and Twin Studies

A classic U.S. family study concluded that somatization runs in families (Guze, Cloninger, Martin, & Clayton, 1986). However, family studies can't always account for environmental versus genetic influences. To address this, a Swedish adoption study tried to tease apart gene–environment interactions in somatization. It attributed an association between frequent somatization and alcohol abuse to genetic inheritance, noting that the male biological relatives of adopted women with somatic symptoms were more likely to abuse alcohol and commit violent crimes (Bohman, Cloninger, von Knorring, & Sigvardsson, 1984). However, in some cases the adoptive environment was also extremely relevant; the adopted fathers of daughters with somatic symptoms were more likely to be unskilled workers, petty criminals, and alcohol abusers (Bohman et al., 1984). Family environment seems to matter. In further studies, children of parents who reported frequent somatic symptoms were more likely to show somatic symptoms themselves (T. K. J. Craig, Cox, & Klein, 2002; Gilleland, Suveg, Jacob, & Thomassin, 2009).

It appears that both environment and genes influence somatic symptoms—but in what proportions? The renowned psychiatric geneticist Kenneth Kendler concluded that somatization is mainly genetic, with family and environmental factors having little influence (Kendler et al., 1995). Yet this conclusion wasn't borne out in a Norwegian twin study that found concordance rates for somatoform disorders to be only 29% for monozygotic twins (identical twins) (Torgersen, 1986). Although this was higher than the 10% concordance rate for dizygotic twins (non-identical twins) and therefore suggests some genetic influence, it still meant that more than 70% of the time only one sibling among identical twins developed somatoform issues (signifying a large role for environment). Further, even in twin pairs where both twins developed somatic symptoms, there was evidence that family environment was important (Torgersen, 1986). A somewhat more recent Australian study found both genetic and environmental influences on somatoform issues (Gillespie, Zhu, Heath, Hickie, & Martin, 2000). So did a Norwegian twin study, which concluded that somatic complaints were moderately heritable but also influenced by environment (Vassend, Røysamb, & Nielsen, 2012). Debate about the relative contributions of genes and environment to somatic symptom complaints will likely continue for some time.

Genetic Marker Research

As already mentioned, low serotonin levels are suspected of playing a part in somatization (just as they are with depression). In light of this, it isn't surprising that genetic marker research has focused on various serotonin-related gene pathways. British researchers have correlated somatic symptoms with a serotonin receptor gene (HTR2A) and a tryptophan hydroxylase (TPH2) gene (important in synthesizing serotonin) (Holliday et al., 2010). A Korean study found a similar association between the TPH1 gene (also important in synthesizing serotonin) and somatoform symptoms (Koh, Choi, Lee, & Han, 2011). However, the Korean investigators found no other correlations between serotonin-related genes and somatic symptoms, suggesting that most serotonin gene variations may not place people at higher risk for somatoform problems. Again, genetic marker research is correlational, so we can't infer that genes cause somatic symptoms.

Evolutionary Explanations of Dissociation

Dissociation as Adaptive

Although we tend to think of dissociation negatively, evolutionary perspectives counter that dissociation "may be an evolutionarily adaptive mechanism designed to prevent overwhelming flooding of consciousness at the time of trauma" (Leigh, 2015, p. 260). For example, feeling too much strong emotion in the midst of a stressful situation such as a house fire may not be helpful. It's probably better to temporarily disconnect from that emotion in order to calmly determine the best way to escape the flames. Therefore, a little bit of dissociation may be adaptive. Dissociation only becomes pathological from an evolutionary standpoint when overgeneralized to too many non-traumatic situations (J. G. Allen & Smith, 1993; Leigh, 2015).

Dissociative Identity Disorder

Beahrs (1994) offered an evolutionary explanation of dissociative identity disorder. This explanation holds that people displaying multiple personalities avoid further trauma by convincing others they are ill. In order to successfully pull this off, however, they themselves must believe their own symptoms. In other words, successful DID patients not only convince others that their symptoms are real; they deceive themselves, as well. (Beahrs, 1994). Beahrs' perspective is intriguing and could be used to counter concerns about DID being merely an iatrogenic condition. However, research evidence for this perspective is lacking.

Evolutionary Explanations of Somatic Symptoms

Unexplained Somatic Symptoms

When it comes to unexplained somatic symptoms such as pain, evolutionary theorists speak of ways in which pain can be adaptive. For instance, studies have found that shared pain brings people together and fosters social cooperation; thus, going through something painful with others can actually enhance group survival by serving as a "social glue" that promotes group cohesion (Bastian, Jetten, & Ferris, 2014). Other research finds that displaying pain to others elicits empathy and assistance from them; in this way, pain serves as an evolutionarily based form of communication designed to help the individual obtain assistance from others (Hadjistavropoulos et al., 2011). Perhaps, then, people with inexplicable medical symptoms are, like chronic dissociators, overgeneralizing the use of an otherwise evolutionarily adaptive behavior. This hypothesis is somewhat speculative, but is understandably inferred from research on the social benefits of conveying pain to others. An important factor that shouldn't be overlooked is that how people express pain is influenced by cultural, as well as individual, differences; failing to keep this in mind can lead to racial and ethnic stereotypes that negatively affect how we respond to people's chronic pain (Tait & Chibnall, 2014).

Psychophysiological Disorders

At the core of psychosomatic (psychophysiological) disorders is the idea that when individuals feel run down and tired, they are more likely to get sick. Importantly, all people don't come down with the same illness. Rather, how people get sick depends on the particular biological vulnerabilities they inherited. Whether you develop acne, backaches, stomach issues, ulcers, high blood pressure or something else entirely is contingent on where you are constitutionally the weakest. In other words, from the standpoint of evolution, people break down where they are most susceptible. This is consistent with the **diathesis-stress model of psychosomatic illness**, which maintains that psychosomatic illnesses emerge from a combination of *diathesis*—a "predisposing organic or psychological condition" (Flor, Birbaumer, Schugens, & Lutzenberger, 1992, p. 452)—and *stress*. The stress slowly takes a toll on the predisposing organic susceptibility, eventually resulting in illness. Diathesis-stress models have been used to understand a variety of psychophysiological issues, including hypertension (high blood pressure) and chronic pain (Coulon, 2015; Flor et al., 1992; Flor, Birbaumer, & Turk, 1990; Flor & Turk, 1989).

IMMUNE SYSTEM PERSPECTIVES
Psychoneuroimmunology, Stress, and Vulnerability to Illness

There is evidence that prolonged stress weakens immune system functioning. If so, then it makes sense that people who experience trauma and dissociation are also more likely to experience somatic symptoms because their depleted immune systems are less able to combat illness. Understanding psychosomatic disorders, in particular, therefore requires a grasp of how stress can compromise the immune system. A substantial amount of psychoneuroimmunology research has been done on the relationship between stress and vulnerability to illness. **Psychoneuroimmunology (PNI)** is the field that studies how psychological stress influences the central nervous system, endocrine system, and immune system (R. Glaser, 2005). PNI research has consistently identified a relationship between psychological stress and physical health. As just a few examples, research has shown that people experiencing less anxiety respond more quickly to Hepatitis-B vaccines and that women caregiving a spouse (a stressful and emotionally

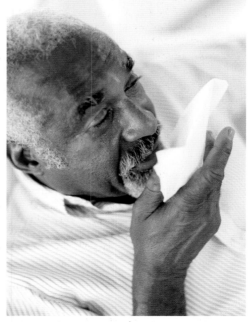

Chronically stressed? If so, you may be more susceptible to catching a cold.
Source: BANANASTOCK

CHAPTER 8

draining activity) heal more slowly than non-caregivers (R. Glaser, 2005). PNI research has also found that not only is there a relationship between chronic stress and susceptibility to catching colds (S. Cohen et al., 1998), but also that ongoing stress makes it more difficult for people to fight off cancer progression (Kemeny & Schedlowski, 2007). The relationship between stress and health that psychoneuroimmunology studies is complex. See the "Controversial Question" box for a discussion of whether your basic temperament—that is, your core personality traits—can increase your risk of high blood pressure and coronary heart disease.

CONTROVERSIAL QUESTION

Can Your Personality Give You a Heart Attack?

There's a good chance you've heard about the **Type A personality**—that driven, impatient, and competitive style with which some people aggressively engage the world. Type A individuals are highly achievement-oriented, want recognition for their accomplishments, and have a heightened sense of time urgency (i.e., they like to get things done quickly) (M. Friedman & Rosenman, 1959). The Type A behavior pattern is usually contrasted with the **Type B personality** (the opposite of Type A: easygoing folks who lack drive, ambition, and urgency) and the **Type C personality** (people who seem Type B, but are anxious and insecure) (M. Friedman & Rosenman, 1959). It's common to hear that being Type A makes you more likely to have a heart attack. Where did that idea come from? And is it true? Well, let's discuss where it came from, along with several perspectives on how true it is.

The Type A style first came to widespread attention in the late 1950s and early 1960s, when cardiologists Meyer Friedman and Ray H. Rosenman conducted research suggesting a positive correlation between Type A behavior and coronary heart disease (M. Friedman, 1977; M. Friedman & Rosenman, 1959; Rosenman & Friedman, 1961). Being too intense, it appeared, might literally place you at higher risk of having a heart attack! Friedman and Rosenman's work was an early effort to link psychological stress with physical health. It garnered so much attention that everyday people often take it for granted that being Type A is bad for your health.

But is it? While research between the 1950s and 1970s generally found a relationship between coronary disease and Type A behavior, later studies have often found little or no relationship (Khayyam-Nekouei, Neshatdoost, Yousefy, Sadeghi, & Manshaee, 2013; Šmigelskas, Žemaitienė, Julkunen, & Kauhanen, 2015). Why the inconsistent results over time? Some researchers argue that personality style is enormously difficult to measure, making Type A research extremely challenging (Šmigelskas et al., 2015). This line of thinking maintains that because it's so hard to measure personality style, what we call the Type A personality contains a variety of traits—only some of which predict heart disease. Thus, since the 1990s it has become increasingly common to hear investigators say that being Type A alone doesn't place one at risk for heart disease. What poses the risk, these researchers argue, is something that some (but not all!) Type A individuals display: *hostility*. Angry, hostile, time-urgent, and stressed people are the ones more likely to have coronary issues (R. J. Burke, 1985; Khayyam-Nekouei et al., 2013; Šmigelskas et al., 2015). Being driven, ambitious, and competitive as you move through life is fine, so long as these characteristics aren't accompanied by hostility. While this argument may come as a relief to all you non-hostile Type A individuals out there, some researchers still contend that Type A behavior is something to watch for as a coronary heart disease risk (Rosenman, 1991).

To further complicate matters, one study found that a Type A style predicts better outcomes in diabetes treatment! In this study, people who were Type A had less immune system inflammation and better diabetes treatment outcome than other people (Chauvet-Gélinier et al., 2016). Beyond Type A research, investigators have begun examining the **Type D personality**, characterized by emotional negativity and social inhibition. Like the Type A research before it, this new research has found that being Type D appears correlated with heart and other health problems (Condén, Ekselius, & Åslund, 2013; S. Howard & Hughes, 2013; Oliva et al., 2016; Staniute et al., 2015). This may be because Type D individuals are highly stressed. It may also be because their negativity and hostility place them at greater health risk. As with the Type A personality, whether or not it is Type D broadly or some specific factor associated with Type D that places people at risk remains unclear.

Rather than relying on Type A–D personality types, some investigators prefer to research the relationship between physical health and the Big Five personality traits (introduced in Chapter 3). For example, when it comes to coronary heart disease, people who score high on neuroticism (characterized by mood swings and negative emotions) appear to be at increased risk (Armon, 2014; Čukić & Bates, 2015). Compared to others, they tend to have lower levels of "good" cholesterol (high-density lipoprotein cholesterol [HDL], a fat-like substance found in body cells) and higher levels of triglycerides (fat in the bloodstream)—two crucial factors associated with coronary heart disease (Armon, 2014). Neuroticism doesn't only predict coronary heart risk, however. Individuals high in neuroticism (and, in some cases, low in conscientiousness) show increased rates of psychosocial health problems in general (Hengartner, Kawohl, Haker, Rössler, & Ajdacic-Gross, 2016). Interestingly, while neuroticism predicts coronary heart disease, extraversion (another Big Five trait) is often predictive of stroke risk (Jokela,

Pulkki-Råback, Elovainio, & Kivimäki, 2014). Thus, researchers increasingly have taken interest in how Big Five personality traits can assist doctors in predicting coronary heart problems specifically and other health problems more broadly.

Of course, all this talk of personality style as a predictor of heart disease potentially overlooks the fact that people's behavior patterns are highly responsive to their environmental circumstances. Some researchers suggest that *environmental stressors* interact with personality in fostering heart disease and other health problems. Along these lines, there is evidence that low socioeconomic status, lack of social support, and stress tied to work and family all predict coronary heart disease (Albus, 2010). Therefore, when we focus so heavily on biological aspects of personality, do we overlook the impact of social conditions on physical health? Although it is clear that psychological, biological, and social factors all play a role in who does or doesn't experience coronary issues, sorting out the exact relationships can be quite challenging!

CRITICAL THINKING QUESTIONS

1. To what extent do you think personality style impacts physical health? Explain.
2. When it comes to coronary heart disease and other health issues, what is the relative contribution of personality style and environmental stressors?
3. What future research do you think needs to be done to clarify the influence of personality style on physical health? What methodological challenges do researchers who are interested in this topic face?

The Negative Effect of Stress on Lymphocytes

How does psychological stress compromise the immune system? Various types of **lymphocytes** (white blood cells important in fighting off illness) appear to be affected by stress. For instance, early PNI research found that people experiencing stressful life events and loneliness lack **natural killer (NK) cells** (a lymphocyte important in fighting off viral infections and tumors) (R. Glaser, 2005). This fits with the previously mentioned studies suggesting that stress negatively affects our ability to combat viruses and cancer. Other lymphocytes known as B cells and T cells also are impacted by stress. **B cells** produce *antibodies* that attack invading viruses and bacteria to stop them from entering cells, while various kinds of **T cells** work to kill viruses and bacteria once they have entered cells (O'Leary, 1990). Some T cells produce cytokines (previously mentioned in Chapters 4 and 5), small proteins important in healing that can also cause inflammation. Research over the past few decades has repeatedly found that lymphocyte number and functioning can be negatively affected by stress (Coe & Laudenslager, 2007; Dhabhar, 2014; Esterling, Kiecolt-Glaser, Bodnar, & Glaser, 1994; R. Glaser, 2005; Kemeny & Schedlowski, 2007; Kiecolt-Glaser & Glaser, 1992; Moynihan & Santiago, 2007; O'Leary, 1990; Segerstrom & Miller, 2004; E. V. Yang & Glaser, 2002; Zakowski, McAllister, Deal, & Baum, 1992).

Although in many instances stress tends to negatively impact the immune system, its exact influence depends on the circumstances. Acute but short-lasting stress actually boosts immune system functioning (an adaptive feature that, evolutionarily speaking, enhances survival), but chronic stress depletes it (Segerstrom & Miller, 2004). As mentioned earlier when discussing dissociation, the hypothalamic-pituitary-adrenal (HPA) axis plays a role in immune system responsiveness to stress, mainly through releasing steroid stress hormones such as cortisol and non-steroid stress hormones such as adrenaline and dopamine (yes, the brain neurotransmitter dopamine also serves as a hormone in the endocrine system). Thus, there is a clear link between brain structures such as the HPA axis and immune system responsiveness to stress. Although many questions about the complex intricacies of how the immune system responds to stress remain, PNI investigations of psychosomatic illnesses constitute one of the more thoroughly researched areas related to somatic symptoms.

EVALUATING BIOLOGICAL PERSPECTIVES

Compared to some other presenting problems we have discussed (e.g., psychosis, mood issues, posttraumatic stress), there is generally less biologically oriented research on dissociative and somatic symptoms—with the possible exception of research on the immune system and psychosomatic illnesses. Many different medications are prescribed on a trial-and-error basis, mainly because there is not much consensus on the biochemistry of dissociative and somatic symptoms. Serotonin is suspected of being involved, but the evidence remains sketchy. Numerous brain areas are implicated in dissociative and somatic symptoms but, again, the research is meager compared to that on other presenting problems, and results remain preliminary. Genetic and evolutionary explanations are intriguing, but also still in need of additional research.

As is true of most of the biological research discussed in this text, its correlational nature makes it impossible to infer causal relationships. For example, we don't know if low serotonin leads to dissociation and somatic symptoms, if somatic and dissociative symptoms negatively impact serotonin production, or if there is some other as-yet-undiscovered relationship between these symptoms and serotonin. Regardless of the often-correlational nature of biological investigations, clearly the best researched topic among those reviewed herein pertains to psychoneuroimmunology—with studies repeatedly pointing to a powerful relationship between psychological stress and immune system functioning. Future investigations will hopefully continue to make advances in PNI research, as well as flesh out the burgeoning research on biological correlates of dissociative and somatization symptoms.

8.5 PSYCHOLOGICAL PERSPECTIVES

PSYCHODYNAMIC PERSPECTIVES

Psychodynamic perspectives conceptualize dissociative and somatic symptoms as expressions of unconscious conflicts, often of a traumatic or upsetting nature (M. J. Kaplan, 2014; Kluft, 2000; Sinason & Silver, 2008; W. C. Tomlinson, 2006). In other words, they adhere to the previously mentioned posttraumatic model (Lynn et al., 2016; Reinders, 2008). The psychodynamic emphasis on unconscious memories of trauma is traceable to Breuer and Freud's (1893–1895/2013) early psychodynamic work on hysteria. Below we discuss how a psychodynamic approach can be used to conceptualize dissociation and somatic symptoms.

Primary vs. Secondary Gain

Before proceeding, let's clarify the psychodynamic distinction between primary and secondary gain. **Primary gain** is the reason for a symptom; it's the central (or primary) conflict the symptom is intended to address (Fishbain, 1994; van Egmond, 2003). The primary gain to be had from a dissociative or somatic symptom is to manage an unconscious conflict and prevent it from entering awareness. **Secondary gain** involves any other advantages the symptom provides (Fishbain, 1994; van Egmond, 2003). A secondary gain isn't the original unconscious conflict that the symptom expresses. It's the other good stuff the patient gets from having the symptom (hence it is secondary to the original conflict).

Tiiu

The primary gain that Tiiu the fighter pilot obtains from her hand numbness is that she avoids and remains oblivious to her conflicted feelings about dropping bombs on people. Getting shipped home and being near her family are the secondary gains she receives. These are additional benefits of being symptomatic, but they aren't the reason she developed hand numbness in the first place.

One way to distinguish malingerers from people with legitimate (if unexplained) somatic symptoms is that for the malingerer there is no primary gain. Why? Because for malingerers, there is no underlying psychological conflict that their deliberately feigned symptoms express. Instead, the entire goal is secondary gain; for malingerers, such gain is actually what's primary. That's why they fake their symptoms.

Tiiu

Our case study client Tiiu isn't a malingerer. She really has an involuntary somatic symptom that represents her emotional upset about bombing people. By contrast, a malingerer is pretending to have a somatic symptom; he wants to go home, so he feigns hand numbness to trick his superiors into sending him. What constitutes a secondary gain for Tiiu is actually the primary goal of the malingerer.

Can you recall that time from childhood when you faked having the flu so you could stay home from school? You didn't have a somatic symptom problem. You were just malingering (how sneaky!).

Dissociation as Response to Trauma

Dissociation and Splitting

At the heart of the psychodynamic approach is the idea that people often cope with trauma by repressing it or disconnecting from their memories of it. In this respect, dissociation involves psychologically splitting off painful memories and emotions by compartmentalizing them in ways that keep them out of conscious awareness, thereby muting their impact. That is, "dissociation is a defensive response to severe physical, sexual, or emotional abuse and/or other highly aversive events that often date to childhood" (Lynn et al., 2016, p. 307). Psychodynamic explanations of dissociative amnesia, dissociative fugue, conversion disorder, and dissociative identity disorder are therefore rooted in a posttraumatic model. There is evidence for such a model, with one study finding that people who dissociate often are more likely to have experienced past traumas (Dalenberg et al., 2012). Critics, however, point to other research suggesting that the link between trauma and dissociation may not be as strong as many people believe (Lynn et al., 2016).

Reintegrating Dissociated Experiences into Awareness

Traditional psychodynamic therapies for dissociation focus on helping patients make unconscious conflicts conscious so that dissociated feelings and memories can be reintegrated into awareness. However, more recent psychodynamic approaches sometimes conceptualize dissociated experiences not as repressed, but as *unformulated* (D. B. Stern, 2009). In this way of thinking, dissociation isn't about placing clearly formed memories out of awareness. Rather, it is about failing to coherently articulate (usually in words) perceptions about a traumatic event. Until the trauma is properly articulated, it is difficult for the person to integrate it into his or her life. Consequently, dissociative perceptions of what happened unconsciously influence behavior. Psychodynamic therapy in this context involves assisting patients to verbally articulate their experiences in order to raise awareness of and make sense of them.

The goal in psychodynamic approaches—regardless of the type of dissociative disorder being treated—is to use the therapeutic relationship to help patients gain insight into their unconscious conflicts and integrate the various dissociated parts of the personality. As noted, critics skeptical of psychodynamic theory question the idea that traumatic memories can be dissociated from awareness (Lynn et al., 2016). These critics not only doubt recovered memories of past trauma, but—as already mentioned—they also contend that dissociation itself is a dubious concept. However, supporters of the psychodynamic perspective counter that traumas really do occur, people often defensively respond to them by dissociating, and that effective psychotherapy must help people gain insight into feelings about these past traumas.

Self-Hypnosis and Dissociative Identity Disorder

In keeping with the posttraumatic model, psychodynamic approaches generally conceive of DID as occurring in people who have been severely abused as children and who are very susceptible to hypnosis. Patients diagnosed with DID are thought to be especially good at self-hypnosis, the ability to enter a hypnotic trance on their own without guidance from others (Kihlstrom, Glisky, & Angiulo, 1994; Loewenstein & Ross, 1992). Self-hypnosis can be thought of as dissociative because it involves mentally going elsewhere while facing highly stressful and traumatic circumstances. Psychodynamically speaking, people who develop DID are highly creative and use self-hypnosis to invent a variety of alternate "personalities" that offer a psychological escape from the terrible abuse they have endured (Kihlstrom et al., 1994; Loewenstein & Ross, 1992).

CHAPTER 8

Somatic Symptoms Due to Unconscious Conflicts

Sometimes people dissociate in response to upsetting or traumatic events by isolating their negative feelings somatically. According to psychodynamic theorists, when this occurs the unconscious conflict is set aside and expressed indirectly as a physical symptom.

Tiiu
Recall Tiiu, whose hand numbness prevents her from running bombing missions. If medical exams reveal nothing wrong with her nervous system, a psychodynamic therapist might conclude that the numbness represents an unconscious conflict about dropping bombs on innocent civilians.

CASE EXAMPLES

Besides some of the same objections mentioned previously when discussing dissociation (especially doubt that past trauma leads to unconscious conflicts) (Lynn et al., 2016), critics caution against dismissing legitimate medical concerns by incorrectly attributing them to psychological conflicts (Dimsdale et al., 2013). Casting aside such criticism, psychodynamic therapy operates from the assumption that eliminating a conversion symptom (or any other somatic symptom caused by unconscious conflict) requires bringing its underlying meaning into conscious awareness. Once this is accomplished, the goal becomes helping the patient to work through the resulting emotions. There are few randomized controlled trials on psychodynamic therapy for somatic symptoms, but those that have been done suggest it can be effective (Sumathipala, 2007). See the "In Depth" feature for an example of psychodynamic therapy for conversion.

IN DEPTH

Psychodynamic Therapy for a Case of Conversion

M. J. Kaplan (2014) presents the case of "Mr. A," a 28-year-old man who was having tonic clonic seizures in which he would lose consciousness and have rapid muscle convulsions. A thorough medical examination at an epilepsy-monitoring unit revealed no biological basis for the seizures, so Mr. A. was referred for psychodynamic psychotherapy. Although Mr. A told the therapist that he often felt depressed as a child, he denied ever having been physically or sexually abused. After two sessions, Mr. A's mother contacted the therapist and told him that Mr. A had been a normal and happy child until age 7, when he developed *encopresis* (involuntary defecation; see Chapter 14). At age 8, Mr. A made his first suicide attempt; after the third attempt, he was admitted to a psychiatric unit, where he admitted to having been bullied by other children because of his involuntary defecation problems. The therapist asked Mr. A about this in the next session, which led to a discussion in which Mr. A tearfully recalled having been repeatedly sexually abused as a child by his older cousin in the loft of the family barn. The abuse only stopped after Mr. A began attempting suicide, probably because at that point the cousin worried about the abuse being discovered. Mr. A never told anyone about the abuse because he didn't think his family would believe him or respond sympathetically.

Soon after telling the therapist about the abuse, Mr. A had a seizure in church. In the next session, the therapist wondered aloud whether "if having had to hold all this pain and anger inside all these years, and having no way to ever express the bad feelings meant it could only come out this way, through the seizures" (M. J. Kaplan, 2014, p. 605). This interpretation resonated with Mr. A, who shortly thereafter told his parents about the abuse. To Mr. A's surprise and relief, they responded supportively. As of a year later, no additional seizures had occurred. Kaplan (2014, p. 609) concludes:

> When previously well-functioning individuals develop conversion symptoms, it is safe to assume that an old conflict related to childhood traumatic experience has been revived by more recent trauma that cannot be addressed with conscious thought. ... With help from a psychotherapist to develop a narrative about one's life experiences and the current experience of an old conflict, the conversion symptom is no longer necessary and forward development is again possible, albeit with the acceptance and mourning necessary for progress in any form of psychoanalytic psychotherapy.

Obviously, this quote reflects commitment to psychodynamic principles. The assumption is that conversion symptoms are a way of expressing an underlying unconscious conflict. Once Mr. A gains insight into the conflict and works through his feelings about it, his conversion symptoms disappear. Those who question psychodynamic theory are likely to be skeptical of the therapeutic outcome described above, but supporters of psychodynamic approaches will inevitably appreciate the emphasis on unconscious meanings behind symptoms.

CRITICAL THINKING QUESTIONS

1. Do you agree with the psychodynamic assumption that Mr. A's seizures stopped because he gained conscious insight into his past abuse? Explain.

2. How confident should doctors be before assuming that someone like Mr. A's symptoms are better explained psychologically than medically? What sort of evidence is required?

A psychodynamic approach could be also be used with our case example client Paul, who qualifies for a *DSM-5* diagnosis of somatic symptom disorder.

Paul

If Paul—who is experiencing somatic symptoms—sought psychodynamic therapy, the focus would likely be on his childhood. His parents rarely talked about their feelings, but Paul's father often lost his temper and became violent. Throughout his childhood, Paul was unable to express his fear about his father's temper directly lest he risk angering his father. It was during this time that he began to first make somatic complaints, with his mother often taking him to the doctor. Psychodynamic therapy would try to help Paul make connections between his childhood pattern of somaticizing his anxiety by expressing it physically and his current tendency to do the same thing. Instead of focusing so much time and attention on his physical symptoms, Paul and his therapist would examine what is going on in Paul's life. While initially it might be difficult for Paul to identify or express how he feels about this, over time he would hopefully become better at accessing previously unacknowledged feelings. A psychodynamic perspective assumes that if Paul becomes more in touch with unconscious feelings, his somatic complaints will decrease.

CASE EXAMPLES

COGNITIVE-BEHAVIORAL PERSPECTIVES

Cognitive and Behavioral Perspectives on Dissociation

Dissociation as Conditioned Response

According to behavioral perspectives, dissociation is learned through classical and operant conditioning (P. Casey, 2001; C. V. Ford & Folks, 1985; Nijenhuis & van der Hart, 2011). According to a classical conditioning perspective, dissociation involves internal and external stimuli that become conditioned to evoke not just physical, but also mental, avoidance responses (Nijenhuis & den Boer, 2009). From an operant conditioning perspective, forgetting painful and traumatic memories provides emotional relief—hence doing so is encouraged and maintained via negative reinforcement. The research literature on behavioral approaches to dissociation is relatively small and much of it goes back 30–40 years (R. Barr & Abernethy, 1977; C. V. Ford & Folks, 1985). Today cognitive perspectives typically supplement the behavioral view.

Dissociation as Difficulty with Cognitive Encoding

One way of thinking about dissociation cognitively is to see it as "a *failure to integratively* encode, consolidate and store processed information" (Dorahy, 2006, p. 32 [italics in original]). In explaining this cognitive model, Dorahy (2006) offers the example of Mr. X, an emergency services worker in Belfast, Ireland who was haunted by memories of one particularly horrible auto accident scene. His visual memory of the event was vivid. He recalled the exact positions of the dead bodies and destroyed cars. However, he was unable to remember any of the onlookers or the smell of burning blood; this information had not been encoded alongside aspects of the event that he recalled. Cognitively speaking then, dissociation occurs when multiple streams of sensory information fail to be combined into an integrated memory. Instead they are recalled separately under different circumstances. The

Could the dissociative experiences of Mr. X, an emergency worker haunted by memories of a horrible auto accident, be due to his difficulty cognitively integrating multiple streams of sensory information?
Source: PhotoDisc/ Getty Images

idea that dissociation affects cognitive retrieval processes can help us understand various dissociative processes. People with amnesia, for instance, are unable to retrieve certain memories, while those having flashbacks (see Chapter 7) struggle with involuntary memory retrieval—they can't stop painful memories from intruding into awareness at inopportune moments (Dorahy, 2006).

Dissociation and State-Dependent Learning

A related cognitive-behavioral explanation of dissociation suggests it results from **state-dependent learning**—the idea that people's ability to recall something is affected by their psychological or emotional state. Studies with both rats and humans have found that recall can be affected by the state in which learning occurs (Arkhipov, 1999; G. Bower, 1994; G. H. Bower, 1981; J. H. Gill, DeWitt, & Nielson, 1986; Lowe, 1983; Oberling, Rocha, di Scala, & Sandner, 1993). In humans, for example, memories encoded while angry may be easier to recall when angry, while those encoded while frightened may be easier to recall when frightened. This potentially explains dissociated memories. Multiple personalities—perhaps the most severe and dramatic example of dissociation—may reflect an extreme form of state-dependent learning in which, when emotional states shift, the "personality" and its specific memories shift too (G. Bower, 1994; E. K. Silberman, Putnam, Weingartner, Braun, & Post, 1985).

Cognitive Therapy for Dissociation

When it comes to cognitive therapy for dissociation, Kennerley (1996) discusses several interesting techniques. *Managing trigger events* (occurrences that trigger dissociation by reminding the person of the traumatic event) can help people use *planned avoidance* to steer clear of environments or situations that

CHAPTER 8

lead to dissociative reactions. Cognitive therapy can also teach people to *manage the dissociative reaction* by *distracting* themselves from traumatic triggers; this is accomplished by focusing on other aspects of the environment besides the traumatic trigger. Perhaps most importantly, cognitive restructuring can be used to help clients overcome irrational beliefs that upset them and lead to dissociation. Along these lines, Kennerley (1996) describes Linda, a rape survivor who dissociated in the presence of unfamiliar men. Cognitive restructuring enabled Linda to revise one of her automatic thoughts from "all men are rapists" to "some men are safe and decent." This helped her overcome the tendency to dissociate when encountering men whom she hadn't met before.

Cognitive and Behavioral Perspectives on Somatic Symptoms/Bodily Distress

Behavioral Conditioning and Cognitive Misinterpretation

From a cognitive-behavioral therapy (CBT) perspective, somatic symptom problems often involve both behavioral conditioning and cognitive misinterpretations of bodily symptoms. Behaviorally speaking, somatic symptoms are reinforced. People with illness anxiety concerns, for instance, receive negative reinforcement for seeking assurance that they are okay because their worry temporarily decreases when others tell them that they aren't sick; carrying out safety behaviors is also reinforced because it temporarily reduces worrying (T. K. Bouman, 2014). Cognitively speaking, people prone to somatic symptoms interpret bodily changes erroneously, misreading minor aches and pains in catastrophic ways that lead to symptoms or excessive worry about becoming ill (T. K. Bouman, 2014). There is substantial research support for the CBT view that cognitive and behavioral factors contribute to illness anxiety (D. K. Marcus, Gurley, Marchi, & Bauer, 2007), as well as to unexplained somatic symptoms (Witthöft, Basfeld, Steinhoff, & Gerlach, 2012).

Cognitive and Behavioral Therapy Techniques for Somatic Symptoms

Behaviorally, CBT practitioners often use techniques such as relaxation training (in which clients are taught how to calm themselves) and exposure plus response prevention (first introduced in Chapter 2). For instance, teaching people relaxation techniques is often effective in assisting them to reduce high blood pressure (Yen, Patrick, & Chie, 1996). Similarly, exposing hypochondriacal individuals to illness-related stimuli and preventing avoidance also appears to work (S. Visser & Bouman, 2001).

Cognitively, CBT interventions for somatic issues typically employ cognitive therapy to help people identify and change their tendency to catastrophically misinterpret minor physical changes in ways that lead to or exacerbate physical symptoms (or anxiety associated with these symptoms). For example, stress inoculation training (SIT)—previously discussed in Chapter 7—assists with pain management by helping people eliminate negative thoughts that make pain harder to handle (Milling & Breen, 2003; Milling, Levine, & Meunier, 2003; M. J. Ross & Berger, 1996). Mindfulness-based stress reduction (MBSR)—a version of mindfulness-based cognitive therapy (see Chapters 5, 6, and 7)—facilitates maintaining awareness of one's thoughts without trying to influence or stop them. It has been used to reduce stress associated with psychosomatic illness (Grossman, Niemann, Schmidt, & Walach, 2004). SIT and MBSR are excellent examples of how CBT techniques are used to change people's cognitive responses to somatic symptoms.

CBT techniques such as cognitive therapy, relaxation training, and exposure plus response prevention have all been shown to be somewhat or substantially effective with problems like illness anxiety, somatization, and psychosomatic complaints (L. A. Allen & Woolfolk, 2010; Bleichhardt, Timmer, & Rief, 2004; T. K. Bouman, 2014; Buwalda, Bouman, & van Duijn, 2007; Greeven et al., 2009; Gropalis, Bleichhardt, Hiller, & Witthöft, 2013; D. K. Marcus et al., 2007; Neng & Weck, 2015; Olatunji et al., 2014; Schröder, Heider, Zaby, & Göllner, 2013; S. Visser & Bouman, 2001; Woolfolk & Allen, 2012). There has been minimal research on the effectiveness of

Learning relaxation techniques might be able to help you reduce high blood pressure and alleviate other somatic symptoms.
Source: ImageSource

CBT interventions for conversion symptoms (L. A. Allen & Woolfolk, 2010; Woolfolk & Allen, 2012). However, overall CBT approaches are considered reasonably effective with somatic complaints.

Paul

If Paul pursued CBT for his unexplained somatic complaints, cognitive interventions would focus on helping him reinterpret bodily feedback more realistically. Instead of thinking about his symptoms in overly negative ways ("My thyroid symptoms are unbearable and mean I am severely ill!"), he would be taught more reasonable interpretations ("My symptoms are uncomfortable but I can manage them; the doctor and I will figure out what's wrong and take care of it"). To supplement cognitive interventions, the behavioral technique of exposure plus response prevention might also be used. Paul would be exposed to educational information about thyroid issues, which ordinarily would upset him and lead to his repetitively checking his symptoms. However, he would be prevented from checking his symptoms and, as a result, eventually realize that doing so isn't necessary or helpful. Finally, Paul would be taught relaxation training so he would be able to relax in situations where he ordinarily becomes anxious.

CASE EXAMPLES

Biofeedback for Psychosomatic Illnesses

Biofeedback is a behavioral intervention often used with people suffering from psychosomatic illnesses. In this technique, patients are hooked up to a machine that measures one or more biological functions (e.g., heart rate, breathing rate, muscle tension, or temperature). Patients are reinforced for desired changes to these biological functions—for instance, lowering the heart rate line on the biofeedback monitor. Thus, biofeedback rewards patients (through positive reinforcement) for altering biological functions that they typically assume they have little control over. It can be quite effective at reducing biological symptoms caused or made worse by ongoing psychological stress. Biofeedback is used with a variety of psychosomatic complaints, such as hypertension (high blood pressure), migraine headaches, tension headaches, asthma, ulcers, and irritable bowel syndrome (Khazan, 2013). Evidence suggests it is especially helpful with headaches and hypertension (Nanke & Rief, 2004; J. B. Newman, 2013).

Isabel

Biofeedback training could be used to help Isabel manage her hypertension (high blood pressure). Isabel would be taught a deep breathing relaxation technique. She would then be attached to a monitoring device that measures her blood pressure. A tone would sound more often as Isabel's blood pressure rose and less often as it dropped. Isabel would be instructed to use deep breathing to decrease the frequency of the tone. In operant conditioning terms, this reinforces her for lowering her blood pressure. After several sessions of biofeedback, Isabel would hopefully learn how to practice deep breathing and lower her own blood pressure.

CASE EXAMPLES

CHAPTER 8

HUMANISTIC PERSPECTIVES

Dissociation as Meaningful and Adaptive Strategy

Although those coming from humanistic perspectives have not devoted that much attention to dissociation, when they have their focus has often been on its positive aspects (Krycka, 2010; Richards, 1990). This is very much in keeping with the humanistic emphasis on adjustment, meaning-making, and personal growth. One qualitative humanistic study found that when asked to reflect on their bodily experience, people who dissociate a lot found dissociation to be quite meaningful:

> *Meaning is freshly made from dissociative experiences when the bodily felt sense process is invited. Even when emotions of fear, confusion, or excitement accompany it, new meaning begins to form, ushering in a multiplicity of new engagements and reflections. This very human activity frees up dissociation to be one in which the capacity to further the lives of those experiencing it is possible. (Krycka, 2010, p. 153)*

Despite highlighting the adaptive aspects of dissociation, humanistic therapists have otherwise generally adhered to the same posttraumatic model of severe dissociation espoused by their psychodynamic peers (Humphreys, Rubin, Knudson, & Stiles, 2005; Warner, 1998). Psychotherapist Margaret Warner (1998) advocated a person-centered therapy approach to dissociation (particularly DID), one in which clients are provided person-centered theory's core conditions necessary for change—empathy, genuineness, and unconditional positive regard (see Chapter 2). From a person-centered standpoint, when such conditions are provided clients naturally reconnect with their own dissociated experiences and slowly share them with their therapists. Through this process, clients become more aware of their own dissociated "parts" and the trauma responsible for them. As awareness grows, the need to dissociate decreases. Person-centered therapy's nondirectedness may be advantageous in working with DID clients because it avoids the pitfall of pressuring clients into accepting that they have multiple personalities (Warner, 1998). Consequently, a person-centered approach may be less likely to iatrogenically induce DID. There is little experimental research support for the humanistic approach to DID, but its emphasis on empathy and not actively trying to convince clients that they have DID seem like intuitive advantages worthy of further study.

Somatic Symptoms and the Need to Integrate Bodily Awareness

Practitioners who employ body-oriented psychotherapies challenge the traditional mind–body distinction that sometimes ensnares our thinking about somatic symptoms (Marlock & Weiss, 2015). They contend that our physical and psychological states are deeply interconnected; understanding the whole person (a goal in humanistic approaches) requires overcoming the artificial division of mind and body (Criswell & Serlin, 2015). Body-oriented therapies incorporate dance, meditation, martial arts, yoga, and awareness through movement techniques into the therapeutic encounter (Criswell & Serlin, 2015; Marlock & Weiss, 2015). Their origins are often traced to clinicians such as Wilhelm Reich (1945) and Alexander Lowen (1971). Reich (1945), for instance, held that people often establish character armor (or *body armor*), the physical postures they adopt—including how they walk, talk, breathe, and carry themselves (Moss, 2015). A person's body armor tells us a great deal about his or her psychological functioning.

Although used for a variety of presenting problems, it is easy to see the relevance of body-oriented therapies for somatic symptoms. People who somaticize express their emotional conflicts physically because they experience alexithymia—difficulty in expressing emotions verbally; consequently, "they use body language (symptoms) instead of talking about problems" (Röhricht, 2009, p. 144). Body-oriented psychotherapies aim to help people get back in touch with their emotions by reintegrating awareness of bodily sensations (Ben-Shahar, 2014; Criswell & Serlin, 2015; Marlock & Weiss, 2015). While the evidence base for body-oriented therapies isn't especially large because many practitioners work outside of academic institutions where research can be more readily conducted (Röhricht, 2009), one noteworthy randomized controlled trial did show that bioenergetics exercises (breathing and other exercises intended to enhance bodily awareness) were effective in reducing chronic somatoform symptoms (Nickel et al., 2006). Additional studies offer evidence that functional relaxation can reduce psychosomatic symptoms associated with asthma, tension headaches, and irritable bowel syndrome (Lahmann et al., 2009; Lahmann et al., 2010; Loew, Sohn, Martus, Tritt, & Rechlin, 2000; Röhricht, 2009, 2015). Functional relaxation is a body-oriented technique to increase body awareness; it is similar to progressive relaxation in that the muscles of the body are systematically relaxed.

EVALUATING PSYCHOLOGICAL PERSPECTIVES

At this point in time, there have been no randomized controlled trials testing treatments for dissociative disorders (Brand, 2012; Brand, Classen, McNary, & Zaveri, 2009). The absence of RCTs has been blamed on lack of funding and the complexity of studying something as elusive as dissociation (Brand, 2012). Existing research is limited to case studies, *naturalistic observations* (observing people in their natural environment), and *nonrandomized studies without control groups*. Such studies have found psychodynamic, cognitive-behavioral, and various other therapies to be effective in reducing dissociation (Brand, 2012; Brand et al., 2009). They also point to establishing a strong therapeutic alliance between patient and therapist as especially important (Cronin, Brand, & Mattanah, 2014)—not surprising if dissociation results from abuse that leaves people lacking trust in others. Without RCTs to confirm these findings, however, many researchers remain skeptical of them.

There has been a bit more research on therapy effectiveness with somatic symptoms, although the total number of studies is still relatively small. A meta-analysis of ten randomized and six nonrandomized trials found that psychotherapy had a large effect on reducing physical symptoms and a medium effect on improving health, life satisfaction, interpersonal problems, and maladaptive cognitions and behavior (Koelen et al., 2014). However, therapy didn't have much effect on reducing psychological symptoms such as depression, anger, and anxiety (Koelen et al., 2014). As already noted, CBT and exposure plus response prevention have been found especially helpful when it comes to reducing illness anxiety/hypochondriasis (T. K. Bouman, 2014; Buwalda et al., 2007; Greeven et al., 2009; Gropalis et al., 2013; D. K. Marcus et al., 2007; Neng & Weck, 2015; Olatunji et al., 2014; S. Visser & Bouman, 2001; Weck, Gropalis, Hiller, & Bleichhardt, 2015). There is some evidence for psychodynamic therapies, as well (Sumathipala, 2007). Finally, when it comes to psychosomatic illnesses, supplementing physical treatments with psychotherapy is often helpful (R. Kellner, 1994; Matheny, Brack, McCarthy, & Penick, 1996). A variety of psychotherapeutic strategies—including relaxation, hypnosis, exercise, classical conditioning, biofeedback, self-disclosure, cognitive-behavioral therapy, mindfulness and other forms of meditation, and exposure techniques—have been used to help people better manage psychological stress and relieve psychosomatic illnesses (Grossman et al., 2004; Kiecolt-Glaser & Glaser, 1992; J. B. Newman, 2013; G. Tan et al., 2015).

8.6 SOCIOCULTURAL PERSPECTIVES
CROSS-CULTURAL AND SOCIAL JUSTICE PERSPECTIVES
Cross-Cultural Differences and the Risk of Culture Bias

The precise boundaries of dissociation and somatization vary cross-culturally (Janca, Isaac, Bennett, & Tacchini, 1995; Lewis-Fernández et al., 2007; Sirri & Fava, 2014). For instance, U.S. clinicians make a stronger distinction between dissociation and somatization than do their European and Turkish counterparts (Lewis-Fernández et al., 2007). Interestingly, they also more firmly differentiate psychosis from dissociation—even though dissociation and psychosis are both associated with trauma and can involve auditory hallucinations and delusions of control (Lewis-Fernández et al., 2007).

Given that conceptualizations of dissociation and somatization vary by country, it makes sense that people display symptoms differently across cultures. As a somatic symptom-related example, a classic cross-cultural research study found that Chinese patients are more likely than Westerners to present with somatic complaints than with psychological complaints (Kleinman, 1977). Recent research suggests it may not be that Chinese people experience somatic symptoms more often. Rather, cultural norms make them more likely to present psychological concerns somatically (Zaroff, Davis, Chio, & Madhavan, 2012). More broadly, from a sociocultural standpoint, somatization is not so much a disorder as it is a socially and culturally influenced means of communicating psychological distress (Lipowski, 1987).

Turning to a dissociation-based example of cultural differences in symptom expression, in many non-Western countries people diagnosed with dissociative identity disorder experience themselves as being possessed by spirits or supernatural beings rather than as having multiple personalities (Dorahy et al., 2014). This has led to disagreement about whether symptoms of spirit possession are merely a cultural variation on DID, or something completely distinct from it (American Psychiatric Association, 2013b; Dorahy et al., 2014). At the heart of discussions about culture's role in dissociative and somatic symptoms lies a fundamental disagreement: Are *DSM* and *ICD* categories like dissociative identity disorder universal, occurring in all countries and cultures—just as diseases such as diabetes and cancer do? Or, are they are culture-bound syndromes that reflect culture-specific beliefs and values about how to (a) best live life, and (b) appropriately express emotional suffering? It is important to keep this debate in mind because when we overlook our cultural biases, we run the risk of treating clients in socially unjust ways.

The Sociocognitive Model of Dissociative Identity Disorder

The **sociocognitive model** of dissociative identity disorder (sometimes also referred to as the *fantasy model* or *iatrogenic position*) stands in direct opposition to the previously discussed posttraumatic model (Lynn, Lilienfeld, Merckelbach, Giesbrecht, & van der Kloet, 2012; Reinders, 2008). It maintains that there is no such thing as DID because DID is a purely social invention—a false diagnosis made up by society and then imposed on patients by misguided but well-meaning psychotherapists who hold questionable cultural assumptions about personality and the effect of abuse on memory (Lilienfeld et al., 1999; Lynn, Knox, Fassler, Lilienfeld, & Loftus, 2004; Lynn et al., 2012; Lynn et al., 2016). Sociocognitive theorists argue that DID's popularity is spread by media accounts that incorrectly portray it as real. Therapists who accept these accounts then iatrogenically induce DID in their fantasy-prone patients through various suggestive means, encouraging these patients to reinterpret their symptoms as evidence of multiple personalities (Lynn et al., 2012; Lynn et al., 2016). Perhaps the most controversial aspect of the sociocognitive model is its doubt about the suspected child abuse (especially sexual) that the posttraumatic model holds to be at the root of most dissociative problems. From a sociocognitive perspective, therapists often use techniques such as hypnosis, dream analysis, guided imagery, interpreting symptoms, and self-help books to persuade patients that abuse actually happened (Lynn et al., 2004).

Lauren
Sociocognitive theorists would argue that Lauren (our DID case client) began attributing her difficulties to multiple personalities only after being induced into doing so by previous therapists.

CASE EXAMPLES

CHAPTER 8

Sociocognitive theorists would also say that trying to convince people of past abuse is problematic because there is substantial research (much of it by renowned memory researcher Elizabeth Loftus) showing that people's memories are malleable and that encouraging them to remember past sexual abuse or see themselves as having DID may be creating self-fulfilling prophecies, not to mention false memories of abuse (Loftus & Ketcham, 1994). Sociocognitive theorists argue that when these false memories become accusations of sexual abuse lodged against family members, social injustice results (Lindsay, 1998; Loftus, 2011).

Dissociation and the Reality of Child Sexual Abuse

Opponents of the sociocognitive model also make strong social justice claims. They argue that the only way to obtain justice for child sex abuse victims is to acknowledge such abuse and bring it out of the shadows. They also cite research supporting their hypothesis that dissociation is caused by trauma, not fantasy-proneness (Dalenberg et al., 2012). From their point of view, the sociocognitive model improperly impugns the integrity of therapists who believe in dissociated memories of abuse by insisting that such therapists uncritically encourage false memories (Dell, 2013; Gleaves, 1996). To its detractors, the sociocognitive model also makes the "startling … claim that an extremely debilitating, chronic disorder such as DID … can be caused by mere exposure to media portrayals of the disorder" (Dell, 2013, p. 438). Countering those who question the reality of child sexual abuse, feminist psychologist Laura S. Brown (1997) has argued that good therapists must be open to the possibility their clients were really abused. Rather than disbelieve their clients, ethical therapists should validate them while remaining careful not to suggest or plant memories.

Lauren
From this perspective, if Lauren began recalling past abuse during therapy sessions, her emerging recollections should be believed.

CASE EXAMPLES

To Brown and others who agree with her, the problem with questioning the reality of recovered memories is that in doubting abuse, they sustain power hierarchies that oppress the abused. From this perspective, social justice demands that clients be believed when they re-experience previously dissociated memories of past abuse.

CONSUMER AND SERVICE-USER PERSPECTIVES

The false memory debate isn't only important to clinicians coming from a social justice perspective. It is also significant to consumers and service-users. Service-users who believe they have been abused clearly fall on one side of this debate, while those who feel they are being falsely accused of abuse fall on the other. However, in addition to the false memory debate, consumers and service-users are also deeply concerned about potential stigma that accompanies dissociative and somatic symptom diagnoses. We turn to that issue next.

Dissociation, Abuse, and Stigma

While there has been little examination of the connection between dissociation and stigma, research bears out the intuitive notion that child abuse (the presumed trigger for dissociation, according to the posttraumatic model) is strongly stigmatized. Survivors of childhood sexual abuse dissociate more than others and experience extensive stigma over what happened to them—especially feelings of shame and self-blame (Feiring, Cleland, & Simon, 2010). This isn't surprising, given that many cultures tend to blame abuse victims for what happened to them and unfairly view them as "damaged goods" (Follette, La Bash, & Sewell, 2010). The resulting stigma can make it much more difficult for survivors to come to terms with the abuse and disclose it to others (Follette et al., 2010). Avoiding what happened because of stigma only encourages continued dissociation of traumatic memories.

Somatic Symptoms as Less Stigmatizing than Psychological Symptoms

Having somatic symptoms actually carries less stigma than displaying psychological concerns directly. Recall the previously cited finding that Chinese patients present psychological issues somatically more than their Western peers. One potential explanation for this is that presenting somatically avoids the stigma associated in Chinese culture with having a psychological problem (Zaroff et al., 2012). Other research has found a similar pattern in India, where somatic symptoms were less stigmatizing because of their similarity to typical illnesses that everyone occasionally encounters (Raguram & Weiss, 2004; Raguram, Weiss, Channabasavanna, & Devins, 1996). To put it bluntly, better "sick" than "crazy!"

This doesn't mean that somatic symptom issues are stigma-free. One noteworthy study with English- and French-speaking Canadian participants found greater levels of stigma associated with medically unexplained somatic syndromes (fibromyalgia, chronic fatigue syndrome, and irritable bowel syndrome) than with comparable medically explained conditions (rheumatoid arthritis, multiple sclerosis, and inflammatory bowel disease) (Looper & Kirmayer, 2004). Experiencing unexplained somatic symptoms does indeed carry stigma, just not as much as having more transparently psychological concerns.

SYSTEMS PERSPECTIVES

Family Systems Perspectives on Dissociation

Caution Before Using Family Therapy for Dissociation

Clinicians operating from a posttraumatic model urge caution before using family therapy for dissociation. They encourage therapists to keep in mind the reported history of abuse in the family and consider whether the dissociative client is ready to handle a family session in which an abusive relative is present (Pais, 2009). At the same time, sessions with members of the client's family who weren't part of past abuse can help educate them about the client's dissociative issues (Pais, 2009).

Internal Family Systems Therapy (IFS)

Internal family systems therapy (IFS) applies a systemic approach to thinking about the internal psychological functioning of individuals facing various presenting problems, including dissociation. IFS conceptualizes human personality as a series of "parts" that relate to one another (Sweezy & Ziskind, 2013). The idea is that just as each family has different members who play specific roles in maintaining long-standing family patterns, each individual has different parts (or subpersonalities) that play specific roles in maintaining how the individual functions. The goal of therapy is not to eliminate these parts, but to help them communicate and work together. Three particularly common parts are exiles, managers, and firefighters (Pais, 2009; Sweezy & Ziskind, 2013; Twombly, 2013). *Exiles* are "young" parts that have experienced trauma; they are often separated from other parts in order to avoid the terror and other negative emotions they experienced in response to the trauma. *Managers* direct daily activities; they try to control situations and ward off trouble. Finally, *firefighters* work to extinguish the emotional pain of exiles; for instance, they might push the individual to take drugs, impulsively shop, binge eat, or pursue sexual activities in response to exile distress.

(a) "Exile" (isolates itself to protect against terror)

(b) "Manager" (directs everyday affairs)

(c) "Firefighter" (tries to extinguish the pain of the exile)
Internal family systems theory sees trauma survivors as commonly having three "parts" to their personality.
Sources: (a) JGI/Jamie Grill; (b) Getty Images/Cultura RF \ Monty Rakusen; (c) Getty Images/Cultura RF \ Array

IFS therapists hold that the parts of people prone to extreme dissociation are especially isolated from one another. As it does for other presenting problems, IFS therapy for dissociative disorders aims to get the various parts to communicate and cooperate (Twombly, 2013). As cooperation increases, traumatic memories can be processed. Once this occurs, the trauma becomes less influential in the individual's life and the various parts of the personality work together more effectively (Twombly, 2013). The relevance of IFS for thinking about dissociation in general and DID in particular is obvious—multiple personalities are parts that don't communicate and they all have their own ways of dealing with (or avoiding) past traumas. Despite the compelling nature of IFS, it has mainly been described theoretically and in case vignettes without much in the way of experimental evidence of its effectiveness.

Family Systems Perspectives on Somatic Symptoms

Systems perspectives on somatic complaints focus on how family dynamics foster or exacerbate somatic symptoms. Research points to lack of family coherence and parental criticism as familial predictors of childhood somatization (Bafiti, 2001; B. N. Horwitz et al., 2015). Conversion symptoms specifically correlate with lack of psychological sophistication, low socioeconomic status, lack of education, and living in a rural setting (Scher, Knudsen, & Leamon, 2014).

Structural Family Therapy

Salvador Minuchin's structural family therapy (see Chapter 2) offers one example of a family systems approach to psychosomatic complaints. In keeping with a systems perspective, it views psychosomatic and related symptoms—including asthma, diabetes, and eating disorders (see Chapter 9)—as emerging from dysfunctional family patterns (Minuchin et al., 1975). Structural family therapy speaks of **psychosomatogenic families** in which there is a great deal of *enmeshment* (blurred boundaries between family members), *rigidity*, *overprotectiveness*, and *difficulty with conflict* resolution (Kog, Vandereycken, & Vertommen, 1985; Minuchin et al., 1975; S. Rousseau et al., 2014). In such families, somatic symptoms are believed to be much more likely. To address somatic symptoms, structural family therapists work with the entire family to help members strengthen boundaries, reduce rigidity and overprotectiveness, and learn to resolve conflicts.

Critics have argued that structural family therapy concepts such as enmeshment, rigidity, and overprotectiveness are poorly defined (Kog et al., 1985). Recent research has updated Minuchin's original conceptualizations and identified five types of families: *chaotic families, insecure families, families with few functioning problems, families with average functioning problems*, and *families with high support but communication problems* (S. Rousseau et al., 2014). Interestingly, none of these family types alone appears necessary or sufficient in predicting somatic symptoms. However, adolescents from chaotic families and families with average functioning problems display significantly more somatic symptoms than those from families with few functioning problems. This may be because marital problems and poor parental functioning are more common in chaotic and average functioning families—and these two factors are particularly good predictors of somatic symptoms (Rousseau et al., 2014).

Isabel, Anna, and Malcolm

CASE EXAMPLES

In addition to her own somatic symptom problems with high blood pressure, Isabel's 9-year-old daughter, Anna, sometimes experiences asthma attacks. What might structural family therapy for Isabel, her husband Malcolm, and her daughter Anna look like? Initially, we might expect Isabel to be annoyed that the therapist is interpreting Anna's asthma as "all in her head" and "due to Malcolm and I being bad parents." During family therapy sessions, it might become clear that Isabel and Malcolm have a great deal of conflict in their marriage. They also do a poor job of communicating with one another and with Anna. Of particular note would be the fact that Isabel and Malcolm often do Anna's homework for her ("We have to!" we can imagine Isabel exclaiming. "In today's world children need every last bit of help possible to insure they get ahead."). The therapist would work with the family to improve communication and strengthen boundaries—including differentiating rigid overprotectiveness from supportive help when it comes to issues such as Anna's homework. As boundaries are firmed up and family communication improves, Anna would ideally experience fewer and milder asthma attacks.

Family Resistance to Psychological Aspects of Somatic Symptoms

One of the challenges in working with families is that they are sometimes understandably resistant to the idea that their members' somatic symptoms are in any way psychological (Kozlowska, English, & Savage, 2013). Given that people often develop somatic symptoms as a way to avoid psychological issues, this lack of insight into psychological factors isn't really that surprising. However, it's extremely important to make sure that all medical explanations of symptoms are fully investigated before concluding that medically unexplained symptoms are primarily psychological (Kozlowska et al., 2013). Otherwise, there is a risk of dismissing legitimate medical concerns and denying patients essential treatments. For instance, research shows that doctors are less likely to take women's medical complaints seriously and more likely to attribute them to psychological causes compared to men's complaints (Colameco, Becker, & Simpson, 1983; Daniel, Burn, & Horarik, 1999; Ruiz & Verbrugge, 1997). Thus, clinicians should exercise caution because the last thing they want is to discourage patients from obtaining medical attention due to mistakenly attributing their problems to psychological causes.

EVALUATING SOCIOCULTURAL PERSPECTIVES

Just as with trauma, stress, and loss, presenting problems involving dissociation and somatic symptoms are deeply tied to social factors. Research supports aspects of both posttraumatic and sociocognitive theories of dissociation, but debate over the reality of child sexual abuse remains an area of simmering disagreement in professional circles, with both sides claiming the mantle of social justice. Family systems perspectives for both dissociation and somatic symptoms are interesting and have generated a lot of case studies, but little in the way of experiments (Sumathipala, 2007). Future research should further explore the effectiveness of family systems therapies, try to find middle ground between posttraumatic and sociocognitive theories of dissociation, and continue to unpack the important role of culture in how people experience and display dissociative and somatic symptoms.

Doctors often take women's complaints less seriously than men's, which can result in women not receiving necessary treatments.
Source: © Royalty-Free/CORBIS

CHAPTER 8

8.7 CLOSING THOUGHTS: DISSOCIATION AND SOMATIC SYMPTOMS AS ELUSIVE YET INTRIGUING

Complaints pertaining to dissociation and somatic symptoms are among the more controversial topics discussed in this book. In good measure, this is because they are difficult to define and differentiate from other issues. That is, dissociation and somatic symptoms typically accompany (i.e., show comorbidity with) anxiety, depression, and posttraumatic stress (J. G. Allen & Smith, 1993; Bozkurt, Mutluer, Kose, & Zoroglu, 2015; Kroenke, 2003; Spiegel et al., 2013). To further complicate matters, some clinicians have doubts about the scientific legitimacy of concepts like dissociation, thus research studies on dissociation and dissociation-related somatic symptom issues are fewer compared to other presenting problems. Ongoing debate over the reality of dissociation is unlikely to be resolved any time soon.

One of the biggest challenges going forward will be how the extensively revamped *DSM-5* and *ICD-11* will affect our understanding of dissociation and somatic symptoms. This is especially true for somatic symptoms because the *DSM-5* and *ICD-11* substantially overhauled these diagnoses. Consequently, it is no longer assumed that somatic complaints lack a physical basis. What this will mean for how clinicians use and think about these diagnoses remains unknown.

Finally, dissociative and somatic symptom issues highlight the power of the mind–body relationship. When something upsets us psychologically, it frequently affects our physical health. Further, when we dissociate from the pain of traumatic events, we often express the conflict in physical ways. The relationships among psychological stress, dissociation, and physical health are complex and we still often have a tenuous grasp of them. Even in our own lives, we often fail to make the connection between physical and psychological well-being. We close with a "Try It Yourself" exercise, a scale developed specifically for university students that asks you to consider the potential impact of life stressors that influence physical and emotional health more than we often realize. The elusive (and at times controversial) nature of dissociation and somatic symptom problems is in part why so many of us find them thoroughly intriguing.

**TRY IT
YOURSELF**

Is Stress at School Affecting Your Physical and Emotional Well-Being?

The University Stress Scale

How often have each of the following caused you stress over the past month? If any are not applicable to you, tick *Not at all*.

	Not at all	Sometimes	Frequently	Constantly
	0	1	2	3
1. Academic/coursework demands				
2. Procrastination				
3. University/college environment				
4. Finances and money problems				
5. Housing/accommodation				
6. Transport				
7. Mental health problems				
8. Physical health problems				
9. Parenting issues				
10. Childcare				
11. Family relationships				
12. Friendships				
13. Romantic relationships				
14. Relationship breakdown				
15. Work				
16. Parental expectations				
17. Study/life balance				
18. Discrimination				
19. Sexual orientation issues				
20. Language/cultural issues				
21. Other demands				

Scoring

Problem score = Number of items endorsed > 0 (Problem scores range from 0 to 21.)
Extent score = Sum of all items (Extent scores range from 0 to 63.)

Source: University Stress Scale (Stallman, 2008).

This scale was developed in Australia as a screening tool for use with university students (Stallman & Hurst, 2016). Research by its developers found higher extent scores (greater than 13) correlated with poorer physical and emotional well-being (Stallman & Hurst, 2016). If you scored 13 or higher, you're not alone. More than half (59.7%) of the university students who completed the scale as part of its development scored above 13 (Stallman & Hurst, 2016). This suggests that today's university students are, in general, pretty stressed.

Importantly, the scale is provided here simply to get you thinking about the relationship between stress and health, not to provide a definitive assessment of your own illness risk (or to add to any stress you are already experiencing!). People have different degrees of illness vulnerability and some of us cope with stress better than others. Thus, scores should be interpreted cautiously. That said, if you believe that stress is currently creating challenges for you, please speak to your instructor or seek help from your university health/counseling service or another mental health professional.

KEY TERMS

Alexithymia
Alter
B cells
Bioenergetics exercises
Biofeedback
Bodily distress disorder
Body-oriented psychotherapies
Character armor
Conversion disorder
Depersonalization/derealization
  disorder
Diathesis-stress model of
  psychosomatic illness
Dissociative amnesia
Dissociative disorders of movement
  and sensation
Dissociative fugue
Dissociative identity disorder (DID)
Dissociative neurological symptom
  disorder
Dorsolateral prefrontal cortex
Factitious disorder
Functional relaxation

Highway hypnosis
Hypnosis
Hypochondriasis
Iatrogenic condition
Identity alteration
Identity confusion
Illness anxiety disorder
Internal family systems therapy (IFS)
La belle indifférence
Lymphocytes
Malingering
Mindfulness-based stress reduction
  (MBSR)
Multiple personality disorder
Munchausen syndrome
Naltrexone
Natural killer (NK) cells
Opioid antagonists
Parietal cortex
Post-hypnotic suggestion
Posttraumatic model
Primary gain
Psychogenic movement disorders

Psychological and behavioral factors
  associated with disorders or diseases
  classified elsewhere
Psychological factors affecting other
  medical conditions
Psychoneuroimmunology (PNI)
Psychosomatic
Psychosomatogenic families
Right anterior prefrontal cortex
Secondary gain
Self-hypnosis
Sociocognitive model
Somatic complaint
Somatic symptom disorder (SSD)
Somatization
Somatization disorder
State-dependent learning
Stress-induced analgesia
T cells
Type A personality
Type B personality
Type C personality
Type D personality

Full definitions of the terms listed above can be found in the end-of-book glossary on p. 533.

Go to the companion website, www.macmillanihe.com/raskin-abnormal-psych, to access a study guide, multiple choice and flashcard quizzes for this chapter, and other useful learning aids.

CHAPTER 8

CHAPTER 9
FEEDING AND EATING PROBLEMS

9.1 OVERVIEW

 LEARNING OBJECTIVES

After reading this chapter, you should be able to:

1. Distinguish feeding from eating problems, describe *DSM* and *ICD* eating and feeding disorder diagnostic categories, and discuss debates about these categories.
2. Describe historical ways of conceptualizing eating problems.
3. Explain biological perspectives on feeding and eating problems, including those emphasizing brain chemistry, brain structure, genes, evolution, and the immune system.
4. Differentiate psychodynamic, cognitive-behavioral, and humanistic approaches to feeding and eating problems.
5. Discuss the roles of culture, ethnicity, gender, and education on the development of eating problems.
6. Explain the role of the family in eating problems and outline structural family therapy and family-based treatment (FBT) approaches to addressing them.

Photo source: © Royalty-Free/Corbis

GETTING STARTED: FEEDING VS. EATING PROBLEMS

Marta
Marta, a 16-year-old female, is extremely underweight due to continuous dieting and a refusal to eat enough. Since she was 14, Marta has consistently complained about being "too fat." She goes to the gym for intense daily workouts and is exceedingly careful about what she eats—often skipping lunch entirely and limiting her dinner to a single piece of toast, three pieces of lettuce without salad dressing, and a glass of water. Occasionally, when she thinks she's eaten too much, Marta forces herself to throw up. Marta's friends and teachers have become increasingly alarmed at how dangerously thin she is. When they ask her about it, she dismisses their concerns. Marta, a champion on her school debate team, recently passed out during a tournament. Apparently, she hadn't eaten anything all day. Her doctor repeatedly warns her that she must eat enough to have sufficient energy. He tells Marta that not getting her period in recent months is a symptom of starvation.

CASE EXAMPLES

Zayna
Zayna is a 24-year-old woman who comes to therapy at the request of her live-in boyfriend, Emmanuel. "He's unnecessarily worried about my eating," Zayna tells the therapist with a roll of her eyes. Emmanuel complains that Zayna often secretly locks herself in the bedroom for several hours and eats large stashes of food that she's hidden throughout their apartment. Zayna denies this, though she admits that Emmanuel has periodically found evidence that she has thrown up what she has eaten, or—in at least one case—that she drank large amounts of laxative in order to clear her system. "It's not a big deal," Zayna says. "Everyone overeats sometimes." The rest of the time, Zayna is quite careful about what she eats, avoiding junk food while exercising regularly. Zayna is of average weight for her height and build, but complains that she doesn't like her body shape: "I look like a bloated pear!" Ashamed and embarrassed, Zayna only reluctantly shares that she has had eating and body image issues on and off since she was a teen.

Daemyn
Daemyn is a 22-year-old male computer programmer who is extremely overweight. He seeks therapy because he is unhappy with his weight and wants to do something about it. Daemyn admits that he sometimes feels compelled to eat large amounts of food. Several times per week he gathers numerous boxes of his favorite cookies, a pint of chocolate ice cream, and whatever other sweets he finds around the house and eats them all in one sitting. This has been going on for a few years now. Daemyn is distressed and ashamed about his eating and weight and wants to address them because he is starting to have associated health problems as a result.

Wendy

Wendy is an 8-year-old girl who is an extremely picky eater. Other than the occasional dessert, Wendy has restricted her diet to essentially two foods: fried chicken fingers and plain pasta. She refuses to eat anything else. When asked why, she says that she doesn't like the taste of other foods or "how they feel in my mouth." Her parents are frustrated because they feel obligated to always make Wendy a different meal from what everyone else in the family is eating. They also worry that Wendy's restricted diet may prevent her from growing and developing properly.

Alastair

Alastair, a 6-year-old boy, is taken for medical attention by his parents because he keeps eating things that aren't food. First, it was the chalk from his chalkboard set. Then, it was soap from the bathtub. Most recently, Alastair began eating pebbles from the driveway outside his home. Alastair has previously been diagnosed with an intellectual disability and his parents wonder if that has anything to do with his odd feeding habits.

Simone

Simone is a 13-year-old girl whose parents are concerned because she brings up food she has previously eaten and then re-chews and re-swallows it. Like Alastair, she has also been diagnosed with an intellectual disability. Simone's parents want her to stop engaging in regurgitating and re-chewing food because they find it disgusting. Simone says it is a harmless, if bad, habit that she finds comforting.

Can We Distinguish Feeding from Eating Problems?

In abnormal psychology, it is common to distinguish *feeding* from *eating* problems. What is the difference? **Feeding problems** are discussed much less often than eating problems (C. Howard, 2016). Traditionally, feeding problems have been defined as being about food preferences. Most often diagnosed in children, they typically involve fussy or faddish eating habits in which certain foods are avoided or refused because of taste, texture, or a basic dislike for them (C. Howard, 2016; Uher & Rutter, 2012). However, feeding disorders can also involve eating inappropriate, non-food substances such as dirt, chalk, paper, clay, coins, or paint chips (C. Howard, 2016; Mishori & McHale, 2014); or regurgitating and re-chewing one's food (Bryant-Waugh, Markham, Kreipe, & Walsh, 2010; A. S. Hartmann, Becker, Hampton, & Bryant-Waugh, 2012). Many, but not all, people with feeding problems also suffer from developmental disabilities (American Psychiatric Association, 2013c; Bryant-Waugh et al., 2010; A. S. Hartmann et al., 2012).

Eating problems, on the other hand, are usually characterized by disturbed body image. They often involve concerns about being overweight or experiencing one's body negatively or in ways that appear distorted (C. Howard, 2016; Uher & Rutter, 2012). Eating problems are more commonly diagnosed in adolescents and adults. Unfortunately, the distinction between feeding and eating problems is a fuzzy one at best. Many of the eating problems identified in adolescents and adults are predated by feeding issues in childhood, which means that dividing presenting problems into feeding versus eating problems may not always be valid or useful (Uher & Rutter, 2012).

This boy refuses to eat broccoli and other vegetables, complaining about their taste and texture. Does this make him a fussy or faddish eater?
Source: © Royalty-Free/Corbis

9.2 *DSM* AND *ICD* PERSPECTIVES

Perhaps reflecting the difficulties in distinguishing feeding from eating problems, both the *DSM-5* and *ICD-11* include combined sections on "Feeding and Eating Disorders." The *DSM-5* section contains six feeding and eating diagnoses: anorexia nervosa, bulimia nervosa, binge-eating disorder, pica, avoidant/restrictive food intake disorder, and rumination disorder. The *ICD-11* also includes a diagnosis called *cyclic vomiting syndrome*, which involves recurrent episodes of vomiting and nausea (Hermus et al., 2016); because it is grouped with headache disorders rather than eating disorders, cyclic vomiting isn't discussed further in this text. The *ICD-10* is organized slightly differently. It classifies anorexia and bulimia as eating disorders (under the broader heading of "behavioural syndromes associated with physiological disturbances and physical factors"). However, it lists versions of pica and rumination disorder (often considered feeding disorders) elsewhere, as "other behavioural and emotional disorders with onset usually occurring in childhood and adolescence." *ICD-10* doesn't include binge-eating disorder or avoidant/restrictive food intake disorder; these are new categories that debuted in *DSM-5*. Although *ICD-10* doesn't combine feeding and eating disorders into one section of the manual, the *ICD-11* has taken after the *DSM-5* and done so (Uher & Rutter, 2012).

DISORDERS GENERALLY IDENTIFIED AS EATING DISORDERS

Anorexia and Bulimia

By far the two most well-known eating disorder diagnoses are anorexia and bulimia. Because these two diagnoses are often confused with one another, it is helpful to discuss them together as a way of clarifying their similarities and differences.

Anorexia

The key element of **anorexia nervosa** in both the *ICD* and *DSM* is significantly low body weight due to restricted food intake. People diagnosed with anorexia have an intense fear of gaining weight. They also have a distorted sense of their own body shape, which negatively affects how they feel about themselves. Perhaps most alarmingly, anorexic clients don't recognize that they are extremely underweight or the health risks that this poses. So, the key aspect of anorexia is a *failure to maintain minimum body weight.*

People with anorexia nervosa diagnoses fail to maintain minimum body weight.
Source: Getty Images/Tetra images RF \ Tetra Images

Marta

CASE EXAMPLES

Our first case example, Marta, would probably be diagnosed with anorexia.

Diagnostic Box 9.1 contains diagnostic criteria and guidelines, while "The Lived Experience" box provides a vivid firsthand account of what it's like to struggle with anorexia.

Diagnostic Box 9.1 Anorexia Nervosa

DSM-5
- Limits food intake, resulting in extremely low body weight (less than minimally normal or expected).
- Fears gaining weight or becoming fat, or regular behavior that prevents weight gain even though notably underweight.
- Has a distorted sense of one's own body shape, body weight or shape excessively influences sense of self, or low body weight not acknowledged as a serious problem.
- Subtypes: *restricting type* (no binge eating or purging during last three months); *binge-eating/purging type* (recurrent binge eating or purging during last three months).
- Specify: *mild* (BMI ≥ 17), *moderate* (BMI = 16–16.99), *severe* (BMI < 15).
- Use the "other specified feeding or eating disorder" code for "atypical anorexia," in which weight loss criterion not met.

Based on American Psychiatric Association, 2013b, pp. 338–339

ICD-10
- Body weight at least 15% below what is expected, or BMI less than 17.5.
- Avoids foods deemed fattening and one of these present: self-induced vomiting; self-induced purging; excessive exercise; use of appetite suppressants and/or diuretics.
- Distorted body-image, fear of fatness, and low weight expectations imposed on self.
- Amenorrhea (loss of period) in women; loss of sexual interest/performance in men.
- If occurs before puberty, puberty is delayed or impeded.
- Can diagnose "atypical anorexia" when one or more of the central features is absent.

Based on World Health Organization, 1992, pp. 138–139

ICD-11
- Exceedingly low body weight (BMI < 18 for adults; or below fifth percentile for weight in children and teens); physical signs of starvation evident.
- Recurrent behaviors to lose weight (e.g., fasting; eating little or slowly; hiding or spitting out food; forced vomiting; use of laxatives, diuretics, or enemas; excessive exercise).
- Overvalues being thin or has a distorted sense of own body weight and shape.

Based on https://gcp.network/en/private/icd-11-guidelines/grouping

THE LIVED EXPERIENCE

Brenda's Story: My Battle and Recovery from Anorexia

When I was in 6th grade, my life changed forever with one comment from my dance teacher, whom I truly adored and admired. Yes, I probably had the genetic predisposition to developing an eating disorder, but the environment in which I found my passion was not the most conducive to preventing its onset. It all began when I was not accepted at a summer dance camp. I was accepted at four others but could not understand why I had been denied admission to that one in particular. When I discussed my summer camp options with my dance teacher, she stated that I was going to have a tough time in the years to come because I would continuously battle with my body weight, size, and shape. According to her, since my father was overweight I was destined to be overweight as well and would never be as successful as other dancers who had the "ideal dancer's body."

I wanted my dance teacher to see me in a different light. I wanted her see me as the perfect dancer I desired to be. So, for nearly five years, 7th through 12th grade, I followed the same daily routine as I dressed for ballet class: use the restroom (to purge if necessary), tape blisters, carefully put on seamed pink tights and a black leotard, pull my hair tightly and perfectly into a bun, sit and slip on pointe shoes, swallow two extra-strength painkillers, and snap on a tummy belt. ... The dance studio became my second home. Every part of my being loved dancing because it was my way of expressing myself and releasing any emotion that occupied my mind. Others recognized my talent and my passion, and I embraced the identity of a dancer and a person with an eating disorder. For me the two were inseparable.

As part of this identity, I was not allowed to make a mistake, experience physical pain, or expose my self-hatred. I was supposed to be "perfect." Fighting against hunger and denying myself food were expressions of my effort to become perfect. I was striving to live up to the expectations I had of myself—to be the perfect dancer, the perfect student, the perfect daughter, the perfect sister, and the perfect friend.

Even though I had many friends and a family who clearly thought I was lovable, I believed that being thin would make me more perfect and, therefore, more lovable. The thinner I was, the more love I could and would receive—or so I believed.

My eating disorder voice told me that being thin was the key to being loved, but in my journey to recovery I came to realize that this was not true. In reality, it was a lie my eating disorder loved to tell me.

When I entered college I began to get frustrated with my struggle. Unfortunately, my belief that if I quit dancing my eating disorder would go away also turned out to be untrue. Rather, when I stopped dancing I became involved in NCAA Division I rowing. I signed up for 20+ hours of training and my eating disorder fully supported that commitment. Before I knew it, I was exercising up to four hours per day, counting every calorie that entered my mouth, and isolating myself from my closest friends in an effort to hide what I knew was not normal behavior. Once again I was striving for perfection. I wanted to be the fastest, strongest, and leanest person on my team. We practiced indoors using rowing machines, and for me, each practice was a fight for my seat in the top boat—until I collapsed after a practice race and needed medical attention.

"Dehydration" was the diagnosis, but fluids were not the only thing I received from this event. My coach and the Athletic Department forced me to enter therapy and see a physician every week. I would have to be cleared by a psychologist and physician before I could return to regular practices with the team. While I was not yet ready to begin recovery, I had to face my eating disorder and began to entertain the idea of seeking help.

Over the years, my eating disorder placed me in a wrist cast from falling while running, in a walking cast from a stress fracture due to over-exercise, on crutches from a sprained ankle, and finally in therapy to address my eating disorder, in a doctor's office for medical clearance, checkups, and blood work, and in the hospital to replace fluids that I'd lost through restricting and purging. Most important to me, however, was the emotional pain that my family and closest friends had endured as a result of my eating disorder. At that point, I did not want to find out where or what the next stop on the path of self-destruction might be.

My journey to recovery has not been easy or smooth, but it has been memorable. It took many hours of therapy, nutrition counseling, journaling, attending support groups, and a strong willingness to choose recovery with each new day. There were many times when I wanted to throw in the towel and give up because the fight seemed like too much for me to handle. But fortunately, my support system and treatment team were there to help me at every wrong turn and obstacle I encountered.

I now live my life free from the grips of an eating disorder. I wake up and go through my day without having to weigh myself or my worth. I eat without having to know how many calories are in the food. I shop for clothing and walk out with full shopping bags! Admittedly, there are still days when I find myself being critical of my body weight, size and/or shape, but I no longer allow those negative thoughts to determine my mood or how I will interact with others. Rather, I let them pass and do not allow them to ruin my day.

Each day I make the choice to continue walking the path towards being "recovered." I have learned that this path is as much about discovery as it is about recovery. Each new day I am blessed to experience is another day I choose to put my best foot forward and work to maintain my recovery. Never would I have thought I would be saying this, but I offer you these words: recovery is possible and worth it!

Adapted and reprinted with permission of The Alliance for Eating Disorders Awareness. Original article available at: www.allianceforeatingdisorders.com/portal/brendas-story

CHAPTER 9

Bulimia

Compared to anorexia, both *ICD* and *DSM* characterize **bulimia nervosa** as involving binge eating followed by compensatory behavior. **Binge eating** is a form of overeating in which a person eats a huge amount of food in a single sitting—much more than most people would eat during a comparable period. During a binge, there is a sense of being unable to control or limit how much one eats. **Compensatory behavior** is behavior a person engages in to counteract having binged. People often equate compensatory behavior with **purging**, in which the person who has binged actively removes the food from his or her body through self-induced vomiting or misuse of laxatives, diuretics, or other drugs. However, while purging is a type of compensatory behavior, compensatory behavior is broader than just purging. It can also involve behaviors that don't involve removing the food from one's system, but which are still meant to counteract having binged. Fasting and excessive exercise are non-purging compensatory behaviors. Importantly, people with bulimia diagnoses—such as Zayna, one of the cases presented at the start of the chapter—aren't excessively underweight. Unlike anorexic clients, they don't appear strikingly thin. Keep this in mind as we discuss distinguishing anorexia from bulimia. Diagnostic Box 9.2 outlines bulimia criteria and guidelines.

When case study client Zayna binge eats, she gathers an enormous amount of food and then eats it all in one sitting.
Source: PhotoDisc/ Getty Images

Distinguishing Anorexia from Bulimia

There are two subtypes of anorexia in the *DSM-5*: the restricting type and the *binge-eating/purging type*. Restricting types lose weight

Diagnostic Box 9.2 Bulimia Nervosa

DSM-5

- Regular binge eating (eats more food in a distinct period than most others would and feels unable to control the eating).
- Regular compensatory behavior (e.g., forces self to vomit; takes laxatives, diuretics, or other drugs; fasts, or exercises excessively).
- Binging and compensatory activities occur once a week or more for three months.
- Self-assessments are disproportionately based on body shape and weight.
- Does not occur only when experiencing symptoms of anorexia.
- Specify: *mild* (compensatory behavior 1–3 times weekly), *moderate* (compensatory behavior 4–7 times weekly), *severe* (compensatory behavior 8–13 times weekly), *extreme* (compensatory behavior more than 14 times weekly).
- If some or none of the symptoms are no longer present for an extended time, can specify "in partial remission" or "in remission."

Based on American Psychiatric Association, 2013b, p. 345

ICD-10

- Preoccupation with and craving for food; lots of food eaten in a short time-period.
- After eating a lot of food, the person does at least one of these: forces self to vomit; misuses purgatives; fasts; takes appetite suppressants, thyroid drugs, or diuretics.
- Dreads idea of being overweight; sets ideal weight well below what is healthy.
- In many cases, a previous episode of anorexia.
- Can diagnose "atypical bulimia nervosa" if the person doesn't meet full diagnostic guidelines.

Based on World Health Organization, 1992, pp. 139–141

ICD-11

- Regular binge eating (e.g., once a week or more for one month or more).
- Regular compensatory behavior (e.g., once a week or more for one month or more); forced vomiting most common compensatory behavior, but may also use laxatives or enemas, take diuretics, fast, or exercise excessively).
- Overly attentive to weight and body shape.

Based on https://gcp.network/en/private/icd-11-guidelines/grouping

mainly by dieting, fasting, and exercising excessively, but they don't binge or purge. Bing-eating/purging types, on the other hand, do engage in bingeing and purging; they binge and then make themselves vomit or use laxatives or diuretics to rid their bodies of what they've eaten. Sometimes students get confused distinguishing the binge/purge subtype of anorexia from bulimia—especially cases of bulimia in which the diagnosed person compensates for bingeing with non-purging behaviors. This is bewildering because it means that there are some cases of anorexia in which the person binges and purges while at the same time there are cases of bulimia in which bingeing is followed only by non-purging compensatory behaviors. The key to distinguishing anorexia from bulimia is to not worry so much whether there is bingeing or purging and instead to focus on body weight. *If the person isn't maintaining minimal body weight, then the diagnosis must be anorexia.* In fact, if someone with a bulimia diagnosis becomes excessively thin and refuses to maintain body weight, the diagnosis is changed to anorexia.

According to the *DSM-5*, the 12-month prevalence of anorexia in females is roughly 0.4%. The 12-month prevalence of bulimia in females is higher, between 1% and 1.5%. Anorexia and bulimia are much less common in males, although the exact male prevalence rates aren't known. The *DSM-5* estimates that bulimia occurs in females ten times more often than in males. Cross-culturally, anorexia and bulimia are much more common in Western industrialized countries, although rates in non-Western countries have been increasing (Makino, Tsuboi, & Dennerstein, 2004; Qian et al., 2013). Within the U.S., prevalence is substantially lower among African Americans, Latinos, and Asian Americans—although *DSM-5* cautions that this may be because people from these groups are less likely to seek services and thus don't always come to clinical attention.

Binge-Eating Disorder (BED)

The *DSM-5* and *ICD-11* have both added **binge-eating disorder (BED)** as a freestanding diagnostic category. BED is characterized by **recurrent binge-eating episodes**. These episodes must occur **at least once a week for three months** or more in *DSM-5* and for **one month or more** in *ICD-11*. Binge-eating disorder **differs from bulimia** in that there is **no compensatory behavior to counteract having binged**. Thus, it shouldn't surprise you that people who seek treatment for binge eating are **often overweight or obese**.

Daemyn
One of our case examples—Daemyn—probably qualifies for a BED diagnosis.

CASE EXAMPLES

BED was previously diagnosed in *DSM-IV-TR* using the unspecified eating disorder category. While there is an *ICD-10* category called "overeating associated with other psychological disturbances" that can be used to diagnose obese clients who overeat, BED itself isn't included in *ICD-10*. However, as has been anticipated for a number of years (Uher & Rutter, 2012), it has been added to the *ICD-11*. *DSM-5* estimates prevalence of BED among adults to be 1.6% for females and 0.8% for males. Men experience binge-eating issues less often than women, but the ratio of males to females diagnosed with BED is more even than the 10:1 female to male ratio found for bulimia. Prevalence rates are considered roughly equal across Western industrialized countries. In contrast to anorexia and bulimia, the *DSM-5* says that prevalence rates in the U.S. for Latinos, African Americans, and Asian Americans are comparable to whites. See Diagnostic Box 9.3 for diagnostic information.

Diagnostic Box 9.3 Binge-Eating Disorder (BED)

DSM-5
- Regular binge eating (eats more food in a distinct period than most others would and feels unable to control the eating).
- Binge eating involves at least three of these: (1) eats much faster than usual; (2) eats until overly full; (3) eats a lot even if not hungry; (4) eats alone due to shame about amount being eaten; (5) feels revolted, despondent, or remorseful after bingeing.
- Experiences great distress about bingeing.
- Bingeing occurs approximately once a week for at least three months.
- Does not occur only when experiencing symptoms of anorexia or bulimia.
- No compensatory behaviors.

Based on American Psychiatric Association, 2013b, p. 350

ICD-10
- Binge-eating disorder is not in *ICD-10*.

ICD-11
- Regular binge eating (e.g., once a week or more for one month or more); eats more than usually does and feels like can't stop.
- Person may eat alone because embarrassed about bingeing, or may eat foods not usually eaten.
- No compensatory behaviors.

Based on https://gcp.network/en/private/icd-11-guidelines/grouping

Avoidant/Restrictive Food Intake Disorder (ARFID)

Avoidant/restrictive food intake disorder (ARFID) is another new diagnosis in both *DSM-5* and *ICD-11*, one reserved for extremely picky eaters who fail to eat enough to meet basic nutritional requirements. People given this diagnosis tend to suffer from malnutrition and often must rely on dietary supplements (or in extreme cases,

CHAPTER 9

a feeding tube) to compensate for their poor eating habits. ARFID can technically be viewed as a refinement and extension of the *ICD-10*'s **feeding disorder of infancy and early childhood**. ARFID focuses exclusively on fussy eating and refusal to eat, while feeding disorder of infancy and childhood also applies to instances of rumination (see below). Further, ARFID differs from feeding disorder of infancy and childhood by including cases that persist into adulthood. According to the *DSM-5*, ARFID is equally common in males and females. It is believed to show comorbidity with anxiety disorders, obsessive-compulsive disorder (OCD), autism (especially in males), attention-deficit/hyperactivity disorder, and intellectual disability (the latter three diagnoses are discussed in Chapters 13 and 14). Criteria and guidelines are in Diagnostic Box 9.4.

Wendy
Our case example client, Wendy, is a likely candidate for an ARFID diagnosis.

CASE EXAMPLES

Diagnostic Box 9.4 Avoidant/Restrictive Food Intake Disorder (ARFID)

DSM-5
- Disinterested in eating or food; avoids food due to sensory characteristics; concern about unpleasant consequences of eating.
- Doesn't meet nutritional needs, with one or more of the following: (1) substantial weight loss (fails to meet expected weight gain goals or reduced growth in children); (2) inadequate nutrition; (3) requires a feeding tube or nutritional supplements; (4) psychosocial functioning negatively impacted.
- Not due to lack of food or cultural practices.
- Does not experience body weight and shape in a distorted manner.
- Does not occur only when experiencing symptoms of anorexia or bulimia.

Based on American Psychiatric Association, 2013b, p. 334

ICD-10
- No "avoidant/restrictive food intake disorder" in *ICD-10*, but there is a similar category called "feeding disorder of infancy and childhood."
- Refuses food and is very fussy about eating.
- The child's eating difficulties are unmistakably beyond what is normal, the child does not gain weight, or the child loses weight for at least one month.

Based on World Health Organization, 1992, pp. 225–226

ICD-11
- Does not eat enough to meet nutritional requirements.
- Weight loss, failure to gain weight, inadequate nutrition, requires nutritional supplements, or negatively impacts health.
- Does not experience body weight and shape in a distorted manner and is not preoccupied with body weight and shape.

Based on https://gcp.network/en/private/icd-11-guidelines/grouping

DISORDERS GENERALLY IDENTIFIED AS FEEDING DISORDERS

Pica

Pica is diagnosed in people who consistently eat nonfood substances. Such substances include things like "paper, soap, cloth, hair, string, wool, soil, chalk, talcum powder, paint, gum, metal, pebbles, charcoal or coal, ash, clay, starch, or ice" (American Psychiatric Association, 2013b, p. 330). Pica is most commonly diagnosed in children (the *ICD-10* name for it is even "pica of infancy and childhood"), but it can be diagnosed in adults too (using a different diagnostic code). Prevalence rates for pica are unknown. However, it is more common in people with intellectual disabilities—such as our case study client, Alastair. See Diagnostic Box 9.5 for diagnostic information.

Diagnostic Box 9.5 Pica

DSM-5
- For at least one month, regularly eats non-nutritious substances that are not food.
- The behavior is developmentally inappropriate and is not due to cultural or other social norms.

Based on American Psychiatric Association, 2013b, pp. 329–330

ICD-10
- Called "pica of early infancy and childhood."
- Regularly eats non-nutritious substances (e.g., dirt, paint chips).
- Common in children with intellectual disabilities.

Based on World Health Organization, 1992, p. 225

Rumination Disorder

Rumination disorder describes those who regularly re-chew, re-swallow, or spit out food after intentionally regurgitating it. They don't find this disgusting or nausea-inducing. Instead, they tend to experience it as an uncontrollable habit. In *ICD-10*, rumination disorder is included under the feeding disorder of infancy and childhood diagnosis, but *DSM-5* notes it can also occur in adolescence or adulthood. As with pica, prevalence rates for rumination disorder aren't known, but it is more common in those with intellectual disabilities.

 Simone

Simone, the last of our case examples, meets guidelines for rumination disorder.

CASE EXAMPLES

Diagnostic Box 9.6 lists diagnostic information. Note that this disorder goes by a slightly different name in *ICD-11*, where it is listed as *rumination-regurgitation disorder.*

Diagnostic Box 9.6 Rumination Disorder

DSM-5
- For at least one month, habitually regurgitates food; may re-chew food or spit it out.
- Not due to a gastrointestinal or other medical condition.
- Does not occur only when experiencing symptoms of anorexia, bulimia, binge-eating disorder, or ARFID.
- If symptoms are no longer present for an extended time, can specify "in remission."

Based on American Psychiatric Association, 2013b, p. 332

ICD-10
- Rumination disorder is diagnosed as a specific type of "feeding disorder of infancy and childhood" category.
- Habitually regurgitates food.
- No signs of nausea or gastrointestinal illness.

Based on World Health Organization, 1992, pp. 225–226

ICD-11
- Called "rumination-regurgitation disorder."
- Purposely brings swallowed food back up into mouth (regurgitation), then either re-chews and re-swallows it (rumination) or spits it out.
- Occurs at least several times per week for at least several weeks.
- Not due to a medical condition.

Based on https://gcp.network/en/private/icd-11-guidelines/grouping

CHAPTER 9

EVALUATING *DSM* AND *ICD* PERSPECTIVES

Impact of Revised Anorexia and Bulimia Criteria on Prevalence

Are the *DSM-5* anorexia and bulimia criteria too inclusive? For anorexia, two criteria have been revised in a way that could lead to more people being diagnosed. First, anorexia patients no longer must weigh 85% or less than what is expected for their height and build. Second, amenorrhea (loss of period) from lack of nutrition is no longer an anorexia criterion, allowing both females who are still menstruating and males to more easily be diagnosed (American Psychiatric Association, 2013c; Attia & Roberto, 2009). For bulimia, more people might get diagnosed because the minimum frequency of binge eating and compensatory behavior has been changed from twice to only once per week (American Psychiatric Association, 2013c).

Researchers who favor the revised criteria point to evidence that even though *DSM-5* changes have increased prevalence rates for anorexia and bulimia, they have also yielded fewer diagnoses of other specified feeding or eating disorder (the *DSM-5* category for those who don't meet full criteria for any other feeding or eating disorder diagnosis) (C. Call, Walsh, & Attia, 2013; Flament et al., 2015; Ornstein et al., 2013; J. J. Thomas et al., 2015; Trace et al., 2012). To further allay concerns when it comes to anorexia, *DSM-5* defenders note that a measure known as body mass index (BMI) can be used in place of the now defunct 85% or less weight criterion (American Psychiatric Association, 2013b; T. A. Brown, Holland, & Keel, 2014). BMI is a weight by height index used to measure whether people are underweight, normal, or overweight; it's calculated by taking the person's weight in kilograms and dividing it by the square of the person's height in meters. BMI scores can be used to limit anorexia diagnoses to extremely underweight clients. Thus, despite increased prevalence rates, many researchers don't appear overly worried about *DSM-5* revisions leading to excessive anorexia and bulimia diagnoses.

Is Binge-Eating Disorder a Good Addition to the *DSM-5* and *ICD-11*?

Binge-eating disorder has been one of the most discussed additions to *DSM-5* and *ICD-11*. The consensus seems to be that its inclusion was overdue (Attia et al., 2013; C. Call et al., 2013; L. L. Myers & Wiman, 2014; Striegel-Moore & Franko, 2008). However, there have been complaints that it pathologizes normal variations in eating and may lead to widespread overdiagnosis (Frances & Widiger, 2012; Paris, 2015). These concerns notwithstanding, *DSM-5* field trials concluded that BED has good interrater reliability (a concept introduced in Chapter 3) (L. L. Myers & Wiman, 2014; Regier et al., 2013). One of the remaining areas of disagreement concerns what should count as a binge (an issue for the bulimia diagnosis too). Some researchers want the definition to focus on lack of control over eating more than how much is eaten (L. L. Myers & Wiman, 2014). Further, ongoing discussion surrounds similarities and differences between BED and

Should obesity be added to the DSM *and* ICD *as a mental disorder?*
Source: Getty Images/Hemera /Thinkstock\Tomasz Caderek

obesity, defined by the World Health Organization as an extremely high body mass index (greater than 30) (www. who.int/mediacentre/factsheets/fs311/en/). Many BED patients are obese, but not all obese individuals meet BED criteria. Hopefully future research will clarify the differences between obese patients who binge and those who don't (J. J. Thomas et al., 2014). Perhaps most provocatively, some have argued that obesity itself should be added to *ICD* and *DSM* as a mental disorder—especially given its high comorbidity with and suspected underlying biological similarities to depression (Attia et al., 2013; Bühren et al., 2014; Rossetti, Halfon, & Boutrel, 2014).

Concerns about Misuse of the "Other Specified Feeding and Eating Disorder" Diagnosis

As noted, *DSM-5* includes a category called "other specified feeding and eating disorder" for cases that "do not meet the full criteria for any of the disorders in the feeding and eating disorders diagnostic class" (American Psychiatric Association, 2013b, p. 353). *DSM-5* explicitly indicates that clinicians should use the "other specified" diagnosis for cases of purging disorder (where someone recurrently purges but doesn't binge) and night eating syndrome (in which a person wakes up during the night and eats excessively). Clinicians are also encouraged to use it for instances of "atypical" anorexia and bulimia. Atypical anorexia nervosa is diagnosed in cases where significant weight loss doesn't occur but the person meets all other criteria for anorexia; atypical bulimia nervosa is diagnosed when bingeing and compensatory behaviors occur less than once a week and/or for fewer than 3 months. Whether these two atypical "other specified" diagnoses exemplify the improper lowering of diagnostic thresholds or simply allow clinicians to diagnose and treat people who don't quite meet the stringent criteria for anorexia and bulimia is a matter of ongoing debate.

Should Orthorexia be Added to the *DSM* and *ICD*?

Over the last several years, there has been increasing interest in a potential new eating disorder for people who display an "obsessional preoccupation with eating 'healthy foods'" (T. M. Dunn & Bratman, 2016, p. 13). This would-be disorder, dubbed orthorexia nervosa, is not currently recognized by either the *DSM* or *ICD*. It was first proposed in the late 1990s by Dr. Steven Bratman (1997), who argued that orthorexia begins with an admirable goal, namely the "desire to overcome chronic illness or to improve general health" (para. 23). However, as people struggle to develop healthy dietary habits, "what they eat, how much, and the consequences of dietary indiscretion come to occupy a greater and greater proportion of the orthorexic's day" (Bratman, 1997, para. 23). This results in behavioral symptoms such as eating a nutritionally unbalanced diet, excessive worry and guilt about eating unhealthy foods, rigid avoidance of foods considered unhealthy, inordinate time and money spent on researching and thinking about eating healthily, and intolerance of other people's dietary habits (Dunn & Bratman, 2016; Koven & Abry, 2015).

Is orthorexia a valid new disorder and should it be added to the *DSM* and *ICD*? This issue is currently being debated. Some mental health professionals caution that orthorexia overlaps (i.e., is comorbid) with anorexia and bulimia, as well as with obsessive-compulsive disorders (Brytek-Matera, 2012; Koven & Abry, 2015). Thus, they worry that we are fostering future diagnostic reliability problems by prematurely creating an orthorexia diagnosis, and that this could lead to difficulty in distinguishing orthorexia from the various other disorders with which it is comorbid. Along these lines, research suggests that anorexia, bulimia, and orthorexia are similar in that people with these diagnoses tend to score high on perfectionism while also displaying body image and attachment issues (Barnes & Caltabiano, 2017). Other professionals, however, counter that orthorexia is distinct enough from anorexia, bulimia, and obsessive-compulsive disorders to warrant further research and/or the establishment of a separate diagnostic category—one that can alert clinicians to the pathology of clients disproportionately concerned with maintaining a healthy diet (Bratman, 1997, 2014; Dunn & Bratman, 2016; Koven & Abry, 2015). Only time will tell whether the *DSM* and *ICD* decide to include orthorexia as a mental disorder. If they do add it, then it will be the latest evolution in the long history of ideas about eating and feeding problems—a topic examined next.

Orthorexia nervosa is a proposed diagnosis for people considered obsessively preoccupied with eating healthy foods. It is not currently in the DSM *or* ICD.
Source: Getty

9.3 HISTORICAL PERSPECTIVES
ANOREXIA, BULIMIA, AND BINGE-EATING

Reports of disturbed eating and self-starvation are found throughout Western history—from ancient Greece to the Roman Empire to the Middle Ages to the Renaissance (J. M. S. Pearce, 2004; Shafter, 1989). It has been posited that numerous historical figures suffered from anorexia—including Saint Catherine of Siena and Joan of Arc (Moncrieff-Boyd, 2016). However, labeling such cases as anorexia or bulimia is problematic because "instances of self-starvation and food abstinence are essentially culture-bound and cannot be separated from their sociocultural context" (Moncrieff-Boyd, 2016, p. 115). Applying present-day eating disorder diagnoses to historical figures is tricky because these diagnoses reflect today's worldview rather than the worldviews of past eras.

Perhaps the first medical account of something resembling our modern notion of anorexia was provided in 1689 by the British physician Richard Morton (1637–1698) (Caparrotta & Ghaffari, 2006; J. M. S. Pearce, 2004). Morton observed that symptoms included "a want of appetite, and a bad digestion, upon which there follows a languishing weakness of nature, and a falling away of the flesh every day more and more" (Morton, as cited in J. M. S. Pearce, 2004, pp. 191–192). Some years afterwards, in 1764, Scottish physician Robert Whytt (1714–1766) provided additional descriptions of patients who today would probably be considered anorexic or bulimic (Silverman, 1987). In 1859, nearly a century later, the French doctor Louis-Victor Marcé (1828–1864) offered even more detailed portrayals of anorexia-like behavior (Blewett & Bottéro, 1995; Silverman, 1989). He described

> *young girls, who at the period of puberty and after a precocious physical development, become subject to inappetency carried to the utmost limits. Whatever the duration of their abstinence they experience a distaste for food, which the most pressing of want is unable to overcome. (Marcé, as cited in Silverman, 1989, p. 833)*

The term "anorexia" has Greek origins and means "without appetite" (Moncrieff-Boyd, 2016). It was first applied to patients in 1873 by two physicians—Britain's Sir William Gull (1816–1890) and France's Charles Lasègue (1816–1883) (Caparrotta & Ghaffari, 2006; Gull, 1874/1954; Lock & Kirz, 2008; Moncrieff-Boyd, 2016; Soh, Walter, Robertson, & Malhi, 2010; Vandereycken & Van Deth, 1990). Gull (1874/1954) described anorexia as a "disease occurring mostly in young women, and characterized by extreme emaciation" (p. 173). Because it was considered a variant of hysteria, Gull called the condition "anorexia hysterical," while Lasègue used the term "anorexia hystérique" (Lock & Kirz, 2008).

By 1914, the German pathologist Morris Simmonds (1855–1925) offered a purely medical account of anorexia, attributing it to underactive pituitary glands—a hypothesis that was refuted after the Second World War (Caparrotta & Ghaffari, 2006; Lock & Kirz, 2008; J. M. S. Pearce, 2004). Early psychodynamic theories (discussed later) conceptualized anorexia and bulimia as related to **oral impregnation**—the unconscious

Oedipal wish to become pregnant by oral means (Caparrotta & Ghaffari, 2006; Lock & Kirz, 2008; Zerbe, 2010). These psychodynamic explanations notwithstanding, it wasn't until the 1960s and 1970s that anorexia began truly receiving extensive attention (Lock & Kirz, 2008), in part due to the groundbreaking work of psychiatrist and psychoanalyst Hilde Bruch (1904–1984). Bruch outlined many of the characteristics of anorexia discussed elsewhere in this chapter—in particular distorted perceptions about body image and problematic family dynamics (Bruch, 1962, 1963, 1971, 1978/2001).

Bulimia first received widespread attention in the late 1970s—although American psychiatrist Albert Stunkard (1922–2014) described symptoms resembling binge eating as early as the 1950s. However, the binge/compensate pattern of bulimia nervosa wasn't formally recognized as a disorder until 1979 when British psychiatrist Gerald Russell (b. 1928) coined the term (Russell, 1979, 2004). Thus, despite eating problems being seen throughout history, current notions of anorexia, bulimia, and binge-eating disorder are relatively recent historical developments. This becomes clear in recalling that while anorexia has been in the *DSM* since 1952, bulimia didn't appear until 1980 and binge-eating disorder wasn't added until 2013.

PICA

Pica has been documented throughout history, although depending on the time and place "it has been regarded as a psychiatric disease, a culturally sanctioned practice or a sequel to poverty and famine" (Woywodt & Kiss, 2002, p. 143). Between the 16th and 20th centuries, it was often considered to be a symptom of other disorders more often than a disorder unto itself (Parry-Jones & Parry-Jones, 1992). The most commonly identified type of pica in historical descriptions is geophagia, the intentional eating of dirt, soil, or clay (Mishori & McHale, 2014; Woywodt & Kiss, 2002). There have been accounts of geophagia in ancient Greece (provided by Hippocrates himself), the Roman Empire, 6th century Turkey, the Middle Ages, and throughout the 16th through 19th centuries (Woywodt & Kiss, 2002).

RUMINATION

Although rumination in animals—especially regurgitation and re-chewing of food by cows ("chewing the cud")—has been written about since ancient Greece, the first historical attention to it in humans didn't occur until the 17th century (Parry-Jones, 1994). The Italian anatomist Fabricius ab Aquapendente (1537–1619) believed that human ruminators were somehow descended from cows; that is, they had some sort of bovine ancestry (Parry-Jones, 1994). By the 18th century, mercyism (another name for rumination in humans) was beginning to be studied as a digestive disorder (Parry-Jones, 1994). Medical accounts of mercyism expanded in the 19th century; some of the patients described used their ruminating abilities to get out of military service or earn a living by performing in side shows and circuses (Parry-Jones, 1994). By the 20th century, discussions of rumination focused increasingly on its high rate of occurrence in infants and adults with intellectual disabilities; however, it was recognized that some anorexics or bulimics also ruminated (Parry-Jones, 1994). Interestingly, the term "rumination"—which emphasized obsessional regurgitating, re-chewing, and re-swallowing of food—also came to refer to obsessional mental reflection, an issue seen in past versions of the *ICD* that classified rumination as both an aspect of obsessive-compulsive disorder (OCD) and as a somatic disorder of digestive origins (Parry-Jones, 1994).

9.4 BIOLOGICAL PERSPECTIVES

BRAIN CHEMISTRY PERSPECTIVES

Monoamine Neurotransmitters

A variety of neurotransmitters important in regulating mood, emotion, memory, and anxiety are also relevant when it comes to weight and feeding—including the monoamine neurotransmitters (dopamine, norepinephrine, and serotonin), the inhibitory neurotransmitter gamma-aminobutyric acid (GABA), and the excitatory neurotransmitter glutamate (Haleem, 2012; McElroy, Guerdjikova, O'Melia, Mori, & Keck, 2010). Here we focus mainly on the monoamine neurotransmitters. The current consensus is that when it comes to anorexia, both dopamine and serotonin are implicated (Hildebrandt & Downey, 2013). However, for bulimia many view the main culprit as serotonin (Hildebrandt & Downey, 2013), although dopamine plays a notable role in binge eating (Bello & Hajnal, 2010). Because it is a new *DSM* diagnosis, there is little or no research on the neurochemistry of ARFID (J. Steinglass, Mayer, & Attia, 2016).

Serotonin

A lot of anorexia and bulimia research has focused on serotonin. Some but not all of this research suggests that serotonin levels are decreased in people with active symptoms of bulimia (Jimerson et al., 1997; W. Kaye, 2008; W. H. Kaye, Gendall, & Strober, 1998). Decreased serotonin levels are also found (even more consistently than in bulimia) among active anorexics (Haleem, 2012; Hildebrandt & Downey, 2013; W. H. Kaye et al., 2005; W. H. Kaye, Fudge, & Paulus, 2009; W. H. Kaye, Wierenga, Bailer, Simmons, & Bischoff-Grethe, 2013). However, serotonin deficiencies may be the result of anorexia and bulimia rather than their cause. Here's why: when people don't eat, they fail to take in an essential amino acid obtained from food called **tryptophan** (Haleem, 2012; W. Kaye, 2008). The body requires tryptophan to make serotonin. Therefore, someone who isn't eating properly lacks enough tryptophan to make serotonin. Consequently, serotonin levels drop (Haleem, 2012; W. Kaye, 2008). This may explain why recovering anorexics and bulimics whose eating returns to normal show surges in serotonin levels (Hildebrandt & Downey, 2013). They finally have sufficient tryptophan to produce serotonin again. Thus, many patients show decreased serotonin levels while in the midst of anorexia or bulimia, but increased serotonin levels once recovered (W. Kaye, 2008; W. H. Kaye et al., 2005; W. H. Kaye, Gwirtsman, George, & Ebert, 1991; Phillipou, Rossell, & Castle, 2014).

While this suggests that low serotonin levels result from (rather than cause) eating disorders, additional research on anorexia and bulimia implies that dysregulation of the serotonin system may predispose people to developing symptoms in the first place. For instance, anorexia research has found that the binding potential of serotonin receptors in various brain areas is increased among non-recovered anorexics, but decreased among recovered anorexics (Haleem, 2012; Hildebrandt & Downey, 2013; Phillipou et al., 2014). Exactly which neurons in which brain regions show increased or decreased binding potential remains unclear, with research offering contradictory results. Nonetheless, the working hypothesis is that serotonin receptor dysregulation combined with a predisposition to have high amounts of extracellular serotonin (serotonin between neurons) increases susceptibility to anorexia (Hildebrandt & Downey, 2013; Phillipou et al., 2014).

Dopamine

Like serotonin, dopamine—a neurotransmitter important to both appetite and reward—appears to play a part in eating problems, especially anorexia. Past research suggests that dopamine levels are lower than normal in non-recovered anorexic patients, but—as with serotonin—they increase in recovered patients (Brambilla, Bellodi, Arancio, Ronchi, & Limonta, 2001; W. H. Kaye, Ebert, Gwirtsman, & Weiss, 1984; W. H. Kaye, Ebert, Raleigh, & Lake, 1984; Phillipou et al., 2014). However, more recent investigations have found that dopamine levels increase only among anorexics diagnosed with the binge-purge subtype, not those with the restricting subtype (W. H. Kaye, Frank, & McConaha, 1999; Phillipou et al., 2014). In addition to dopamine levels, it is suspected that dopamine receptor sensitivity may be decreased among anorexic patients (Hildebrandt & Downey, 2013; Phillipou et al., 2014). Although both dopamine and serotonin are implicated in anorexia, any interrelationship of these two neurotransmitter systems hasn't been explored (Hildebrandt & Downey, 2013).

Those diagnosed with the binge-purge subtype of anorexia show increased dopamine levels, but those with the restricting subtype generally don't.
Source: iStock/KatSnowden

Dopamine has also been implicated in binge-eating disorder and bulimia, though neuroimaging studies remain limited (Bello & Hajnal, 2010). It is thought that binge-eaters may be hyper-responsive to rewards and that this is tied to excessive amounts of extracellular dopamine (C. Davis et al., 2012). Alternating between eating highly enjoyable foods and limiting calories via strict dieting may impact the dopamine system (Bello & Hajnal, 2010). Along these lines, some findings indicate that people with a BED diagnosis have a greater density of D2 dopamine receptors (C. Davis et al., 2012). Unfortunately, one of the problems with research on dopamine as it relates to binge eating is that the notion of "rewards" is often poorly defined. Does it refer to motivation to eat, enjoyment of eating, or reinforcement of eating (Salamone & Correa, 2013)? While its exact role remains unclear, dopamine appears important in understanding bingeing due to its involvement in eating behavior, decision-making, and emotional response to "rewards" (W. Kaye, 2008).

CHAPTER 9

Psychopharmacology for Eating Problems

Antidepressants

Many different drugs are prescribed to people with eating problems. Given the suspected role of serotonin and the fact that eating disorders are often comorbid with other presenting problems in which serotonin is implicated (most notably depression and obsessive-compulsive disorder), it makes sense that people experiencing eating issues are often prescribed SSRI antidepressants (discussed in Chapter 5) (McElroy et al., 2010). Unfortunately, SSRIs have not been found to be especially effective for anorexia (Bodell & Keel, 2010; Flament, Bissada, & Spettigue, 2012; A. S. Kaplan & Howlett, 2010; Lock & Kirz, 2008; Powers & Bruty, 2009; Rossi et al., 2007; K. J. Steffen, Roerig, & Mitchell, 2014; J. Steinglass et al., 2016). This may be because starving anorexics lack the tryptophan necessary to produce serotonin. SSRIs can only block the reuptake of serotonin if there is serotonin available (Powers & Bruty, 2009). Therefore, SSRIs can only be helpful in conjunction with interventions that get patients eating enough to have sufficient tryptophan available for serotonin production (Powers & Bruty, 2009). Because eating must improve before SSRIs can be helpful, SSRIs can be viewed as less useful for changing eating habits and more useful in reducing co-occurring depression and anxiety.

CASE EXAMPLES

Marta

If our anorexic client Marta consulted with a psychiatrist, there is a good chance she might be prescribed an SSRI. However, for the drug to help her, Marta would first need to improve her eating sufficiently to insure she had enough tryptophan in her system. Therefore, other interventions—such as psychotherapy or, under dire circumstances, forced feeding—might be necessary prior to beginning SSRIs. Even so, because SSRIs aren't especially effective for anorexia, there is a reasonable chance they won't prove helpful for Marta.

Whereas little evidence favors prescribing antidepressants for anorexia, there is somewhat more evidence for using these drugs with bulimia. Numerous types of antidepressants (SSRIs, SNRIs, tricyclics, and MAO inhibitors; all discussed in Chapter 5) have been found to reduce symptoms of bulimia (McElroy et al., 2010; Powers & Bruty, 2009). The SSRI fluoxetine (known by the trade names Prozac and Sarafem) is generally considered the "gold standard" drug for bulimia (Broft, Berner, & Walsh, 2010; J. R. Shapiro et al., 2007). Other SSRIs (such as fluvoxamine [Luvox] and citalopram [Celexa]) are also considered effective (Broft et al., 2010; J. R. Shapiro et al., 2007). However, there are some important caveats. First, SSRI dosages usually need to be higher for bulimia than for other problems (Powers & Bruty, 2009). Consequently, side effects—although less than those produced by MAO inhibitors and tricyclics (Flament et al., 2012)—are often an issue and many patients stop taking their drugs (J. E. Mitchell, Roerig, & Steffen, 2013). Second, although SSRIs and other antidepressants do appear to be more effective than placebos, full remission of bulimia symptoms is rare and in many cases, patients don't even show a 50% improvement rate (McElroy et al., 2010; J. E. Mitchell et al., 2013). Third, relapse after antidepressants is higher than relapse after cognitive-behavioral therapy, suggesting therapy has more long-lasting effects than medication (Craighead & Smith, 2008). Fourth, in the U.S., where there are black box warnings on SSRIs due to concerns they may increase suicide risk (see Chapter 5), additional consultation with and approval from parents is necessary before antidepressants can be prescribed to children and teens (Powers & Bruty, 2009).

Like bulimia, BED is also often treated with antidepressants—under the assumption that BED and bulimia, which share the same bingeing symptoms, are related. SSRIs, SNRIs, and tricyclics are commonly used with BED and the limited evidence available suggests these drugs may be helpful even though they rarely result in full remission of symptoms (Bodell & Devlin, 2010; Flament et al., 2012; Goracci et al., 2015; J. E. Mitchell, Agras, & Wonderlich, 2007). *Bupropion*, a **norepinephrine-dopamine reuptake inhibitor (NDRI)**—a drug that blocks reuptake of norepinephrine and dopamine, leaving more available—is also occasionally prescribed for BED, though the body of research on its utility remains small (Goracci et al., 2015; McElroy et al., 2010). Some researchers actively warn against using bupropion because in some instances it has induced unexplained seizures (Flament et al., 2012; J. E. Mitchell et al., 2013)—certainly a concerning side effect!

Finally, SSRIs are also prescribed for ARFID. However, at this time there aren't any randomized controlled trials (RCTs) on whether doing so is effective (J. Steinglass et al., 2016). This is probably because ARFID is such a new diagnosis and there is not much research on it yet.

Antipsychotics

In addition to antidepressants, antipsychotics—which typically target dopamine—are also prescribed for eating problems. Anorexic patients are periodically given atypical antipsychotics; *olanzapine* is the most researched and prescribed, but *risperidone, quetiapine, aripiprazole,* and *ziprasadone* are sometimes used too (A. S. Kaplan & Howlett, 2010; McElroy et al., 2010; Powers & Bruty, 2009; J. Steinglass et al., 2016). These drugs are often given because they induce weight gain, something obviously desirable with anorexia (though an adverse side effect when prescribed for problems like psychosis). However, research on whether atypical antipsychotics reduce anorexic symptoms and yield weight gain are mixed; as such, there is disagreement about the wisdom of giving patients such powerful drugs with significant side effects (Dold, Aigner, Klabunde, Treasure, & Kasper, 2015; J. Hagman et al., 2011; Halmi, 2013; Kishi, Kafantaris, Sunday, Sheridan, & Correll, 2012; McElroy et al., 2010; Newman-Toker, 2000; Powers & Bruty, 2009; J. Steinglass et al., 2016). In some instances antipsychotics and antidepressants are actually prescribed together for anorexic patients—although there isn't a lot of research on the effectiveness of doing so (McElroy et al., 2010).

Marta

If the goal was weight gain, our anorexic case study client Marta might be prescribed an antipsychotic such as olanzapine. The antipsychotic would be instead of or in addition to any SSRI she was taking. Of course, Marta would need to pay attention for potential side effects. Ideally, the antipsychotic would help her regain lost weight, though it isn't guaranteed to work.

CASE EXAMPLES

There is little to no research on using antipsychotics for bulimia, BED, or ARFID. Such drugs aren't usually prescribed to people diagnosed with bulimia or BED. In fact, atypical antipsychotics may actually be contraindicated in such cases because they can make bingeing worse (McElroy et al., 2010). When it comes to ARFID, antipsychotics haven't yet been studied (J. Steinglass et al., 2016); thus, their use in such cases isn't supported by evidence.

Other Drugs

Besides antidepressants and antipsychotics, a variety of other drugs are given to people experiencing eating problems. Here we focus just on three types of these drugs: mood stabilizers, anticonvulsants, and benzodiazepines. Mood stabilizers such as lithium (see Chapter 5) are sometimes prescribed for eating problems, though there is currently minimal evidence that they are effective (Bodell & Keel, 2010; A. S. Kaplan & Howlett, 2010; Powers & Bruty, 2009; Rossi et al., 2007). Anticonvulsants such as *topiramate* (a GABA/glutamate receptor antagonist) are also used (Bodell & Devlin, 2010; Broft et al., 2010). Topiramate requires further study, but some researchers believe it shows promise for eating problems—especially binge eating (Flament et al., 2012; Goracci et al., 2015; Halmi, 2013; Leombruni, Lavagnino, & Fassino, 2009; McElroy et al., 2010; J. E. Mitchell et al., 2007; Powers & Bruty, 2009). Finally, benzodiazepines (anti-anxiety drugs that enhance activity of the inhibitory neurotransmitter GABA; see Chapter 6) are occasionally prescribed to help people with eating issues such as anorexia and ARFID deal with the apprehension they experience before meals; however, there isn't much evidence that benzodiazepines reduce pre-meal anxiety (J. Steinglass et al., 2016).

Psychopharmacology for Feeding Problems

The causes of pica and rumination are not clear. There are almost no randomized controlled trials on how to treat these problems (A. S. Hartmann et al., 2012). As a result, there aren't any widely agreed-upon drug treatments. However, a variety of drugs are occasionally prescribed. Numerous antidepressants—mainly SSRIs, but sometimes tricyclics and bupropion—have all been used to treat pica (Baheretibeb, Law, & Pain, 2008; Bhatia & Gupta, 2009; Ginsberg, 2006; Gundogar, Demir, & Eren, 2003; Hergüner, Özyıldırım, & Tanıdır, 2008; Schreier, 1990). This is probably because some clinicians conceptualize pica as a variant of obsessive-compulsive disorder—and OCD is often treated with antidepressants (see Chapter 6) (Gundogar et al., 2003; Hergüner et al., 2008; Schreier, 1990). There is very little published work on drug interventions for rumination. However, it can be misdiagnosed in patients who are taking benzodiazepines and antipsychotics because these drugs sometimes interfere with swallowing (Fredericks, Carr, & Larry Williams, 1998; B. Rogers, Stratton, Victor, Kennedy, & Andres, 1992).

Alastair

Our pica client, Alastair, might be given an SSRI in an effort to prevent him from eating things he isn't supposed to. It isn't clear whether it would help. Whether it would be recommended would be wholly at the discretion of the doctor, who would have little research on which to base her decision.

CASE EXAMPLES

BRAIN STRUCTURE AND FUNCTION PERSPECTIVES

The Hypothalamus and the HPA Axis

As you may remember from Chapter 7, the hypothalamus regulates numerous involuntary functions of the autonomic nervous system. One of the things the hypothalamus regulates is the sensation of hunger. The hypothalamus consists of the lateral hypothalamus and the ventromedial hypothalamus. The former

CHAPTER 9

is responsible for making people feel hungry (Jennings, Rizzi, Stamatakis, Ung, & Stuber, 2013), while the latter induces feelings of satiation and leads people to stop eating (Krasne, 1962). Because the hypothalamus regulates hunger, it is important in setting the body's weight set point—the weight your body tries to maintain (Keesey & Hirvonen, 1997). One of the reasons it is often hard to gain or lose weight is that the body works hard to stay at its established weight set point—a frustrating predicament to which anyone who has ever dieted can attest!

Given its importance in hunger regulation, the hypothalamus is thought to play a major role in eating problems. More broadly, the hypothalamus is part of the hypothalamic-pituitary-adrenal (HPA) axis (mentioned in several previous chapters). Recall from these earlier chapters that the HPA axis produces cortisol, an anti-inflammatory stress hormone. More precisely, the hypothalamus produces *corticotrophin-releasing hormone (CRH)*, which in turn triggers the pituitary gland to secrete *adrenocorticotropic hormone (ACTH)*, which then stimulates the release of cortisol by the adrenal gland (Lo Sauro, Ravaldi, Cabras, Faravelli, & Ricca, 2008). Research has examined the roles of the HPA axis and cortisol in eating issues. People with anorexia often show elevated cortisol levels, suggesting hyperactivity of the HPA axis (Connan et al., 2007; Hildebrandt & Downey, 2013; Licinio, Wong, & Gold, 1996; Lo Sauro et al., 2008). Increased cortisol may also occur in bulimia, but probably less so compared to anorexia (Lo Sauro et al., 2008).

Whereas the HPA axis appears more responsive in anorexia and bulimia, it seems less responsive in cases of binge eating (Rosenberg et al., 2013). One possible explanation for this is that binge-eaters may experience chronic stress. This is important because while short-term stress is correlated with increased HPA axis activity and higher cortisol levels, chronic stress results in decreased HPA activity and lower cortisol levels (an idea discussed in Chapter 7 when discussing posttraumatic stress). Thus, lower cortisol levels suggest that binge eating could be a response to chronic stress. Therefore, it isn't surprising that eating disorders and posttraumatic stress disorder (PTSD) are often comorbid (Brewerton, 2007). Perhaps eating issues are one way of responding to posttraumatic stress?

Regardless of the exact role of the HPA axis in eating problems, keep in mind that existing research is correlational. We don't know the exact relationship among stress, eating, and the HPA axis. Does stress lead to altered eating, which then impacts the HPA axis? Or does HPA axis dysfunction lead to stress, which then yields altered eating? Hopefully, future research will shed some light on these questions. For now, suffice to say that brain researchers suspect that the HPA axis is important in eating problems and continue to explore its precise role.

Reward Pathway Disturbances

Some researchers suspect that eating problems are a type of addiction. The thinking behind this hypothesis holds that the same brain systems affected by substance abuse (see Chapter 11) are also impacted in cases of anorexia, bulimia, and BED—with anorexics being unresponsive to rewards, and bulimics, binge-eaters, and obese individuals being too responsive to rewards (W. H. Kaye, Wierenga, Bailer, Simmons, Wagner, et al., 2013; O'Hara, Campbell, & Schmidt, 2015; R. J. Park, Godier, & Cowdrey, 2014; Schreiber, Odlaug, & Grant, 2013; D. G. Smith & Robbins, 2013; Volkow, Wang, Tomasi, & Baler, 2013; R. A. Wise, 2013).

We previously discussed the suspected role of dopamine in eating problems. One brain system in which dopamine plays a crucial part is the brain's mesolimbic pathway, also known as the *reward pathway* (again, see Chapter 11). In cases of binge eating and obesity, it has been proposed that a dysfunction in dopamine transmission along the mesolimbic pathway literally causes people to become addicted to food (D. G. Smith & Robbins, 2013; Volkow et al., 2013). Precisely what goes wrong in the mesolimbic pathway continues to receive extensive research attention.

Other Brain Correlates

Ventricle Size and Brain Volume

There are many changes in the brains of people suffering from eating problems, making it difficult to assess the significance of these changes (Hildebrandt & Downey, 2013). Symptomatic anorexic patients often have larger brain ventricles (cavities containing cerebrospinal fluid), as well as less gray and white matter; such findings indicate brain volume reduction (Bär, de la Cruz, Berger, Schultz, & Wagner, 2015; Friederich et al., 2012; Fujisawa et al., 2015; Hildebrandt & Downey, 2013; Phillipou et al., 2014; Suchan et al., 2010; Titova, Hjorth, Schiöth, & Brooks, 2013). When it comes to brain volume, it is generally believed that most (but not all) volume reductions reverse as patients regain weight (Friederich et al., 2012; Hildebrandt & Downey, 2013; Lambe, Katzman, Mikulis, Kennedy, & Zipursky, 1997; Roberto et al., 2011).

Compared to anorexia, overall gray matter volume doesn't appear to decrease as much in bulimia. Nevertheless, research has found gray matter differences in specific brain areas among bulimics and binge-eaters (A. Schäfer, Vaitl, & Schienle, 2010). For example, in bulimia there appears to be a correlation between enlarged gray matter in the nucleus accumbens (important in reward-based behavior) and frequency of purging (A. Schäfer et al., 2010). Bulimics also seem to have less gray matter in the caudate nucleus (mentioned in Chapter 6 and important in goal-directed activity) (Amianto et al., 2013). Unfortunately, firm conclusions can't be drawn because so many different brain areas are implicated and research on how much gray matter bulimics have is correlational.

The Anterior Insula

Although many brain regions have been implicated in eating problems, the anterior insula—which links a variety of brain areas and is important in regulating autonomic activities such as hunger—may be key (Hildebrandt & Downey, 2013). Research has found a correlation between anterior insula activity and feelings of disgust among anorexics, which may explain their lack of interest in food (Aharoni & Hertz, 2012; Hildebrandt & Downey, 2013). Whereas anterior insula impairment is hypothesized to keep anorexics from identifying when they're hungry, it is suspected of providing too strong a hunger signal in cases of bulimia and BED (Oberndorfer et al., 2013). Promising research notwithstanding, the anterior insula's exact role in eating problems remains debatable and additional research is needed (W. H. Kaye, Wierenga, Bailer, Simmons, Wagner, et al., 2013; Vicario, 2013).

GENETIC AND EVOLUTIONARY PERSPECTIVES
Genetic Perspectives

Family and Twin Studies

Family studies find that relatives of people diagnosed with anorexia or bulimia are more likely to develop their own eating issues (J. L. Hudson, Pope, Jonas, Yurgelun-Todd, & Frankenburg, 1987; Lilenfeld et al., 1998; Mazzeo & Bulik, 2009; Stein et al., 1999; Strober, Freeman, Lampert, Diamond, & Kaye, 2000). However, it is difficult to infer how much such findings are influenced by genes (as opposed to environment). This is because family studies don't control for shared surroundings very well. People with eating problems may have inherited problematic eating habits, been raised in a way that fostered such habits, or both.

Twin studies suggest that eating issues are indeed influenced by genetics (Fairweather-Schmidt & Wade, 2015; Javaras et al., 2008; Kendler et al., 1991; Klump, Miller, Keel, McGue, & Iacono, 2001; Mazzeo & Bulik, 2009; Munn-Chernoff et al., 2013; T. L. Root et al., 2010; Wade et al., 2008). However, the extent of this influence is disputed, with some researchers warning that twin and other genetic studies overrate the role of genes (Bulik, Sullivan, Wade, & Kendler, 2000; C. A. Ross, 2006). This possibly explains the wide variation in heritability estimates for eating disorders—anywhere between 48% and 88% for anorexia and 28% and 83% for bulimia (Becker, Keel, Anderson-Fye, & Thomas, 2004; Hinney & Volckmar, 2013). Despite this wide variation, many researchers settle on heritability estimates in the low to mid 50% range for anorexia, bulimia, and BED (Bulik et al., 2006; Culbert, Racine, & Klump, 2015; Javaras et al., 2008). If such estimates are accepted, it means that a little more than 50% of differences in anorexia, bulimia, and binge-eating respectively can be attributed to genes. The remaining differences would be due to environment. Given the wide range of heritability estimates, many researchers simply conclude that genes and environment interact in complex ways to shape the development of eating problems, with the precise contribution of each unclear at this time (Becker et al., 2004; Culbert et al., 2015; Fairweather-Schmidt & Wade, 2015; Mazzeo & Bulik, 2009).

Genetic Marker Research

In genetic marker studies, many different gene indicators have been correlated with eating problems (Klump & Culbert, 2007; Peñas-Lledó et al., 2012; Slof-Op 't Landt et al., 2011; Slof-Op 't Landt et al., 2014; Slof-Op 't Landt et al., 2013; Wade et al., 2013). Given the suspected importance of serotonin and dopamine in disordered eating, it isn't surprising that serotonergic and dopaminergic genes have been the focus of candidate gene studies (first discussed in Chapter 5), which test whether specific genes correlate with particular disorders

CHAPTER 9

or symptoms (Munn-Chernoff & Baker, 2016). Some serotonergic and dopaminergic candidate gene studies have yielded significant findings (Y. Lee & Lin, 2010; Munn-Chernoff & Baker, 2016). However, the results of candidate gene studies to date are considered inconsistent and inconclusive (Brandys, de Kovel, Kas, van Elburg, & Adan, 2015; Munn-Chernoff & Baker, 2016; Munn-Chernoff et al., 2012; Trace, Baker, Peñas-Lledó, & Bulik, 2013).

The same is true of genome-wide association (GWA) studies (introduced in Chapter 6), which include all the genes of the genome rather than only candidate genes suspected of being relevant to a given disorder (Munn-Chernoff & Baker, 2016). Because they are testing every possible gene there is, GWA studies require an enormous number of participants to find significant results. Not surprisingly then, GWA studies of eating problems haven't produced any significant results yet, but they have identified some promising genes worthy of future attention (Boraska et al., 2012; Boraska et al., 2014; Brandys et al., 2015; Munn-Chernoff & Baker, 2016). Based on the inconclusive findings of candidate gene and GWA studies, it is hard to infer which genes are most important in eating problems.

Despite the uncertainty, it is easy to see why genetic marker and GWA studies hold great appeal. In one intriguing study, the Met allele on the COMT gene was associated with symptoms of bulimia (Donofry et al., 2014). This is noteworthy because, as you may recall from Chapter 6, the Met allele has also been associated with obsessive-compulsive disorder (OCD) in females (S. Taylor, 2013). This suggests that OCD and eating problems could have similar biological origins. Even though a lot more research is needed to test such a hypothesis, the idea that we might find common genetic underpinnings for different disorders is precisely the kind of thing that motivates Research Domain Criteria (RDoC) researchers who are interested in building a diagnostic system based on biological markers (such as genes!) rather than behavioral symptoms. It is also what makes genetic marker and GWA studies appealing. Still, it is important to keep in mind the correlational (rather than causal) nature of these studies. Just because a gene is associated with a particular disorder doesn't mean that it causes that disorder.

Evolutionary Perspectives

Sexual Competition Hypothesis

The **sexual competition hypothesis** proposes that eating problems like anorexia and bulimia emerge because women must compete with one another to attract men (Abed, 1998; Faer, Hendriks, Abed, & Figueredo, 2005; Mealey, 2000). This evolutionary hypothesis claims that one way women attract men is by maintaining a desirable body shape—the "nubile" hour-glass shape with a low waist to hip ratio (Abed, 1998; Kardum, Gračanin, & Hudek-Knežević, 2008). Anorexia and bulimia, with their focus on thinness, help females achieve this sort of body shape. Not only does the sexual competition hypothesis argue that eating problems are caused by female competition to be thin and attract mates, but it also tries to explain the increase in eating disorders in industrialized societies by pointing out how—in industrial (compared to preindustrial) societies—families are less involved in helping their daughters obtain mates. Without things like dowries and prearranged marriages, women are required to secure mates on their own without much family assistance. This places extra pressure on women to maintain a desirably thin shape so they can successfully attract men. There are several drawbacks of the sexual competition hypothesis: (a) it assumes there are universal ideals of female attractiveness (mainly, being thin); (b) it doesn't explain what specific events trigger eating disorders; and (c) it doesn't account for eating disorders in men (Abed, 1998; Kardum et al., 2008).

Reproductive Suppression Hypothesis

The **reproductive suppression hypothesis** was first developed to explain animal mating behavior, but was later used to understand anorexia in women (Condit, 1990; Kardum et al., 2008; Salmon & Crawford, 2012; Salmon, Crawford, Dane, & Zuberbier, 2008; Voland & Voland, 1989; Wasser & Barash, 1983). It holds that anorexia is a female strategy for maximizing long-term reproductive success. According to this hypothesis, anorexic behaviors, which shut down a woman's reproductive capacity, are adaptive when current conditions aren't optimal for having babies. How so? Research suggests that girls who reach sexual maturity sooner are more likely to marry early, have children early, and be of lower socioeconomic status (SES) (probably because rather than going to school and gaining the education necessary to improve their economic standing, they are raising babies) (Condit, 1990). Teenage girls who hit puberty sooner may benefit from anorexia because the loss of menstruation that often accompanies it prevents them from carrying a baby to term. The reproductive suppression hypothesis predicts that anorexic behaviors will decrease later in life as anorexic girls grow into economically secure women who are now in a better situation to have and raise children.

While compelling in some ways, this hypothesis has been criticized for not explaining why (a) anorexics experience distorted body image and hyperactivity; (b) less costly means for inducing amenorrhea didn't evolve instead; (c) anorexia disproportionately affects wealthy girls at low risk for economic problems; and (d) men and postmenopausal women sometimes develop anorexia (Guisinger, 2003; Kardum et al., 2008).

Adapted to Flee Famine Hypothesis

The **adapted to flee famine hypothesis** argues that anorexia evolved to assist those facing famine (Guisinger, 2003). It hypothesizes that anorexia's symptoms are adaptive because they lead people to feel energetic and restless (i.e., "hyperactive") while remaining in denial about their extreme weight loss. This makes it easier for them to migrate to new locations in search of food. The main drawback of this explanation is that it while it might account for anorexic behaviors under famine conditions, it doesn't really explain why anorexics refuse to eat when plenty of food is available (Kardum et al., 2008).

Evolution and Binge Eating

When it comes to binge eating and obesity, evolutionary explanations contend that ancestral humans didn't have as much access to food as we do today. Therefore, eating as much as possible was adaptive because it wasn't known when food would next be available (Kardum et al., 2008; Pinel, Assanand, & Lehman, 2000). Today we still eat as if such scarcity exists, even when there is plenty of food. Further, the snacks we eat today (e.g., energy drinks, granola bars) have a lot more calories in them than the snacks ancient humans ate (e.g., wild berries and seeds), but people don't naturally take this into account by adjusting their non-snack food intake (de Graaf, 2006). This therefore fosters overeating and obesity.

Could anorexia have evolved in past historical eras as a strategy for coping with famine?
Source: Image Source\Image Source/Javier Perini CM

Critique of Evolutionary Perspectives

Evolutionary explanations of eating problems are intriguing. However, they are difficult to study because they rely on theoretical assumptions about what ancestral life was like for humans. Further, critics contend that they don't account for sociocultural factors very well. Sociologists have complained that evolutionary psychology "offers an impoverished view of culture" (S. Jackson & Rees, 2007, p. 920). How so? By reducing "the entirety of human social life … to the heterosexual, reproductive imperative: the drive to pass on our genes to the next generation" (S. Jackson & Rees, 2007, p. 918). According to such critics, complex human problems like eating and feeding difficulties are better explained sociologically and cannot be understood exclusively in evolutionary terms. Whether you find this critique sensible or not likely reflects the extent to which you are sympathetic to evolutionary psychological perspectives.

IMMUNE SYSTEM PERSPECTIVES

Recall that cytokines are small proteins produced by the immune system—and that elevated cytokine levels are often found in depressed people (Felger & Lotrich, 2013). That's relevant because, according to some studies, people with anorexia and bulimia also have increased cytokine levels (R. F. Brown, Bartrop, & Birmingham, 2008; Corcos et al., 2003; Marcos, 1997; Nova, Samartín, Gómez, Morandé, & Marcos, 2002). This is an intriguing finding given that cytokines—as part of the immune system's reaction to invading foreign bodies—produce not only fever, but also decreased appetite and food intake (Marcos, 2000). Additionally, because eating problems often co-occur with depression, it is noteworthy that both depression and eating problems involve immune system inflammation. However, just as with depression, the relationship between cytokines and eating problems is correlational. It isn't clear whether increased cytokines cause or are caused by eating problems. When eating returns to normal, so do cytokine levels (Corcos et al., 2003).

Another remarkable immune system-related finding is that people diagnosed with anorexia and bulimia are surprisingly free of viral infections (R. F. Brown et al., 2008; Marcos, 2000; Marcos, Nova, & Montero, 2003). However, they have a harder time fighting off bacterial infections (R. F. Brown et al., 2008). As one last observation about immune functioning, one study found that people diagnosed with anorexia, bulimia, or BED were at increased risk of various autoimmune diseases (Raevuori et al., 2014). All these findings suggest that the immune system is important in eating issues, even if there is a lot we still don't understand.

EVALUATING BIOLOGICAL PERSPECTIVES

As is the case for other presenting problems, biological research on eating issues has mostly been correlational. Thus, we must be careful not to incorrectly make causal inferences. All we know at this time is that certain biological differences are related to problematic eating. Precisely how requires further investigation.

Biological explanations focus mainly on physiological aspects of eating problems, such as understanding the brain's role in hunger. This makes them helpful in identifying neurotransmitters and brain structures implicated in appetite and eating behavior. However, biological perspectives have little to say about the psychological components of eating problems. For instance, why do people with anorexia and bulimia experience distorted body image issues? Why are they so fearful about becoming overweight? For such questions, we may need to look beyond biological explanations.

Finally, biological perspectives frequently minimize or overlook sociocultural factors. Yet eating habits always develop within a cultural context. Many researchers feel that the wider culture is equally or more important than biology in shaping problematic and non-problematic eating habits and how people experience their bodies—especially in Western industrialized societies that place extraordinary value on thinness.

9.5 PSYCHOLOGICAL PERSPECTIVES

Unsurprisingly, many (though not all!) psychological perspectives stress the importance of personality factors in eating issues. For example, *perfectionism* and *negative emotionality* (frequently experiencing anxiety, sadness, stress, and anger) strongly correlate with all eating disorders (Farstad, McGeown, & von Ranson, 2016; Franco-Paredes, Mancilla-Díaz, Vázquez-Arévalo, López-Aguilar, & Álvarez-Rayón, 2005). *Impulsivity*, in contrast, is specifically associated with binge-eating (Culbert et al., 2015; Farstad et al., 2016). Reducing perfectionism can be difficult, but some researchers have found that it can be done using cognitive-behavioral therapy (CBT) (discussed further below)—although doing so may only minimally improve problematic eating behaviors (M. Goldstein, Peters, Thornton, & Touyz, 2014; S. Lloyd, Schmidt, Khondoker, & Tchanturia, 2015). Below we examine psychological approaches to eating and feeding problems.

PSYCHODYNAMIC PERSPECTIVES

Early Psychoanalytic Conceptualizations of Anorexia

Classic psychoanalysis traced anorexia back to oral stage conflicts. The anorexic patient was viewed as having a weak ego that was unable to manage strong oral id impulses—especially the unconscious desire for oral impregnation (defined earlier as yearning to become pregnant by oral means) (Caparrotta & Ghaffari, 2006; Lock & Kirz, 2008). Anorexic eating behaviors were seen as a way to manage unacceptable oral impregnation wishes and reassert control (Zerbe, 2010). By starving themselves and keeping their bodies from developing and becoming sexualized, anorexic girls were thought to reject these inappropriate impulses (McIntosh, Bulik, McKenzie, Luty, & Jordan, 2000). Oral impregnation is no longer an accepted psychoanalytic explanation; it strikes many people today as both sexist and outdated. However, the idea of anorexia as a way to exert control over frightening and overwhelming feelings—sexual or otherwise—remains central to more modern psychodynamic conceptualizations (Winston, 2012).

Early psychodynamic explanations also often portrayed anorexia as a type of hysteria (Zerbe, 2010). So even though the *DSM-5* distinguishes eating disorders from somatic symptom disorders (discussed in Chapter 8), psychodynamic perspectives don't always strictly abide by this distinction. They often view eating disorders as specific types of somatic symptom disorders. This makes sense. After all, problems like anorexia and bulimia involve somatic symptoms related to eating.

Modern Psychodynamic Approaches

More recent psychodynamic perspectives shift from classic psychoanalytic drive theory to more relationship-focused explanations of eating problems. There are various psychodynamic approaches used with eating issues, many of them rooted in object relations therapy and attachment theory (see Chapter 2). What today's psychodynamic perspectives generally share is the view that eating problems can be traced back to early parent–child interactions. Specifically, eating issues arise when caregivers resist their children's attempts to establish independence and autonomy (Bruch, 1978/2001; Zerbe, 2010). Instead of providing the necessary love and support to make their children feel safe and secure, caregivers react anxiously, angrily, or indifferently. In response, the children feel pressure to be "perfect" by complying with (rather than establishing autonomy from) their parents' expectations and demands (Bruch, 1978/2001). Eating or not eating becomes a way for such children to comfort themselves and feel a sense of control in response to having been mistreated (Zerbe, 2010). As Bruch memorably described it, "though considered the perfect child, the patient herself lives in continuous fear of not being loved and acknowledged" (Bruch, 1978/2001, p. 53). Eating disorders express the child's unfulfilled desire for "independence, autonomy, and age-appropriate dependence on other people" (Zerbe, 2010, p. 342).

Psychodynamic therapies provide a corrective emotional experience (see Chapter 2) in which eating disordered patients learn that relationships can be supportive, caring, safe, and secure. To provide such an experience, therapists must help patients work through their projective identifications (see Chapter 2)—the unwanted and split-off feelings they have about themselves that they project onto their therapists. Through these projective identifications, patients reenact with their therapists the troublesome emotional and behavioral patterns they engage in outside of therapy; this creates countertransference feelings in therapists, whereby they come to experience the same negative feelings their patients project onto them (Winston, 2012). Object relations therapists make projective identifications explicit by openly discussing them with patients. The therapeutic relationship becomes a means by which eating disordered patients (a) gain insight into past relationship patterns, and (b) learn how to foster new, healthier ways of interacting with others. As new relationship patterns are learned, eating disorder symptoms disappear because they are no longer needed to cope. There aren't many randomized controlled trials on the effectiveness of psychodynamic therapies for eating problems, but existing research suggests psychodynamic approaches can be helpful (S. Murphy, Russell, & Waller, 2005; Zerbe, 2010; Zipfel et al., 2014).

Marta

Let's imagine Marta sought psychodynamic therapy for her anorexia. During the course of therapy Marta would likely begin projecting her conflicted feeling about being controlled and criticized by others onto her therapist. She might even come to feel controlled and criticized by her therapist—even if he wasn't treating her in a controlling or critical manner. As the therapist came to understand Marta's projective identification, he would openly discuss it with her. Marta would, in turn, gain insight into her relationship patterns. She would start seeing how she feels obliged to go along with what she assumes those around her want—such as pursuing ballet throughout her childhood because her mother wanted her to be a dancer. She would have what psychodynamic therapists call a "corrective emotional experience" with her therapist, realizing that just because her mother is controlling and critical doesn't mean all relationships must be like that. As Marta came to learn new and healthier ways of relating to her therapist, her anorexic symptoms—which served as a way for her to assert control in a situation where she felt she didn't have any—would dissipate. She would also begin generalizing her new relational patterns to others besides her therapist.

CASE EXAMPLES

CHAPTER 9

Interpersonal Therapy (IPT)

Interpersonal therapy (IPT) is a brief therapy influenced by interpersonal theorists like Harry Stack Sullivan. As you probably recall from Chapter 5, IPT was originally developed to alleviate depression (Klerman, Weissman, Rounsaville, & Chevron, 1984). Like the psychodynamic perspectives discussed above, IPT helps patients address interpersonal deficits. However, it is briefer and somewhat narrower in focus. As with depression, IPT for eating problems specifically emphasizes *role transitions*, *interpersonal conflicts*, and *grief* as they relate to symptoms (Apple, 1999; McIntosh et al., 2000; R. Murphy, Straebler, Basden, Cooper, & Fairburn, 2012; Tanofsky-Kraff & Wilfley, 2010). In IPT, eating disorder symptoms are viewed as ways to avoid dealing with pressing interpersonal issues. For instance, "a female patient who avoids intimacy with her husband may attribute her avoidance to body dissatisfaction related to her obesity. She may wish to discuss her body concerns at great length to circumvent actual difficulties in communication with her husband" (Tanofsky-Kraff & Wilfley, 2010, p. 282). To avoid this sort of pitfall, IPT therapists resist spending too much time talking with patients about their eating independent of its connection to dysfunctional relational patterns. Instead, IPT highlights how patients' eating symptoms serve a purpose in interpersonal relationships—for instance, helping them to avoid grief or emotional and physical intimacy. IPT aims to help clients become aware of links between their interpersonal difficulties and their anorexic symptoms (McIntosh et al., 2000).

The small number of randomized controlled trials on IPT for bulimia and binge eating have generally found it to be effective (Apple, 1999; R. Murphy et al., 2012; Tanofsky-Kraff & Wilfley, 2010). Some consider it the best alternative to CBT (discussed below) for bulimia and binge eating, although it takes longer than CBT to improve symptoms (Fairburn, Cooper, & Shafran, 2003; R. Murphy et al., 2012). When it comes to anorexia, however, the research on IPT is less encouraging. As a result, some clinicians are hesitant to recommend it (R. Murphy et al., 2012).

COGNITIVE-BEHAVIORAL PERSPECTIVES

Behavioral Interventions

Anorexia, Bulimia, and Binge Eating

Exposure therapies (introduced in Chapter 2; revisited in Chapters 6–7) expose clients to feared objects and situations to condition new emotional responses. *In vivo* **food exposure** is a type of *in vivo* exposure used to change the eating habits of people diagnosed with anorexia, bulimia, and binge-eating (Koskina, Campbell, & Schmidt, 2013); it is *in vivo* because it is exposure done in real life. One type of *in vivo* exposure technique that can be used with patients who binge and purge is exposure plus response prevention. In **exposure plus response prevention of purging**, patients are prevented from purging after bingeing (Koskina et al., 2013). The intention is to decrease patients' conditioned fear about overeating by showing them that nothing terrible happens if they don't purge. In **exposure plus response prevention of bingeing**, patients are exposed to foods they usually binge on, but are then prevented from doing so. The goal is to recondition patient behavior by no longer having these foods serve as conditioned stimuli for bingeing (Koskina et al., 2013). Finally, in **food exposure for anorexia**, patients are gradually exposed to food as a way to reduce fear of food and food avoidance (Koskina et al., 2013; J. E. Steinglass et al., 2011). There is some evidence that exposure can improve bulimia and binge eating symptoms, though these therapies can be logistically difficult to implement with patients and may be less effective than full-blown CBT or IPT (Fairburn et al., 2003; Koskina et al., 2013). There isn't a lot of research on exposure therapies for anorexia and they are rarely used to treat it (Koskina et al., 2013; J. E. Steinglass et al., 2011).

Avoidant-Restrictive Food Intake

Avoidant-restrictive food intake has only just been added to the *DSM-5* as a disorder, so research on it remains sparse. One study examined whether a behavioral parent-training intervention could help reduce symptoms of avoidant-restrictive food intake (J. Murphy & Zlomke, 2016). The approach involved psychoeducation to teach parents behavioral techniques that they could use with their children. Appropriate parenting behaviors were modeled and parents were taught how to differentially reinforce desirable eating behaviors. Preliminary evidence suggests these techniques were helpful in reducing avoidant-restrictive eating (J. Murphy & Zlomke, 2016). Of course, behavioral parent training and psychoeducation aren't limited to avoidant-restrictive food intake; they can be used with other eating problems, too.

Wendy

Were Wendy's parents to pursue behavioral parent training to help address her avoidant-restrictive eating, they would learn techniques for reinforcing desired eating behaviors. For instance, Wendy's parents would be taught to smile and respond positively when Wendy tried new foods and ate appropriately, but to ignore her whining and complaining when she didn't like a food. They would also be taught how to work with Wendy to develop a hierarchy of feared foods, from least to most frightening, for Wendy to try. For each food Wendy ate a bite of, she would receive an agreed-upon reward. For instance, if she ate a piece of carrot, she might receive a half-hour of access to her mother's iPad. Over time, Wendy would be reinforced for better eating behaviors and hopefully her overall eating habits would become less restrictive.

CASE EXAMPLES

Pica

A range of behavioral interventions can be used to effectively reduce pica (Mishori & McHale, 2014). Common techniques include (a) **aversion therapy** in which patients are punished for eating things they shouldn't (e.g., by squirting them in the face with water or squirting them in the mouth with lemon juice); (b) differentially reinforcing desired behaviors that are incompatible with pica; (c) enriching the person's environment with toys and other engaging stimuli that reinforce them for behaviors that don't involve eating non-nutritive items; and (d) **overcorrection**, in which an undesired behavior is punished by requiring the person to repeatedly engage in an opposite kind of behavior (e.g., brushing teeth and using mouthwash after eating something inappropriate such as feces) (McAdam, Sherman, Sheldon, & Napolitano, 2004). Research is needed to test whether these behavioral techniques are effective (McAdam et al., 2004). Importantly, some clinicians find aversive techniques ethically dubious, viewing them as inflicting pain or humiliation on clients; in many places, their use remains controversial (Fredericks et al., 1998).

Alastair

How could aversion therapy be used to reduce Alastair's pica? Every time he attempted to eat something inappropriate, he might be sprayed in the face with water. This would punish him for eating non-nutritive substances. In addition to aversion, Alastair might also be provided with interesting toys. The enjoyment he received from playing with these toys would serve as reinforcement for non-pica behaviors.

CASE EXAMPLES

Rumination

Behavioral conceptualizations of rumination have focused on how regurgitating, re-chewing, and re-swallowing food is reinforced because it provides oral satisfaction (Lang et al., 2011). Aversion therapy can be used (e.g., giving ruminators electric shocks or putting something bad tasting in their mouths), but often aren't for ethical reasons (Fredericks et al., 1998). *Non-aversive behavioral interventions* try to replace rumination with other satisfying oral activities, such as gum chewing (Fredericks et al., 1998; Lang et al., 2011). Finally, because rumination is one way of decreasing hunger, **satiation techniques** (in which patients' regular meals are supplemented with additional food) are used to make rumination less rewarding (Fredericks et al., 1998; Lang et al., 2011; Sharp, Phillips, & Mudford, 2012). There isn't a great deal of research on behavioral interventions for rumination, though existing research shows they sometimes help (Lang et al., 2011; Sharp et al., 2012).

Simone

If Simone underwent behavioral therapy for her rumination, she might be taught to chew gum instead of regurgitating and re-chewing her food. She also might be given snacks between meals. This would decrease reinforcement for rumination, which often serves to satisfy hunger.

CASE EXAMPLES

Enhanced Cognitive-Behavioral Therapy (CBT-E)

CHAPTER 9

Oxford University psychiatrist Christopher Fairburn and colleagues have developed an **enhanced cognitive-behavioral therapy (CBT-E)** model of eating disorders (also called the *transdiagnostic model*). This model maintains that there is a "core psychopathology" behind all eating disorders—one in which people base their self-worth not on their achievements, but on their ability to control body weight and shape (Dudek, Paweł, & Stanisław, 2014; Fairburn et al., 2003; Fairburn, Shafran, & Cooper, 1999). The transdiagnostic model challenges the long-standing tendency to divide eating problems into anorexia, bulimia, and binge eating diagnoses because it contends that people don't neatly fit into these categories. This model holds that everyone diagnosed with one of these disorders experiences the same core psychopathology in which there is a common tendency to cognitively evaluate self-worth in terms of weight and body shape.

CBT-E doesn't use traditional cognitive techniques such as the Daily Record of Dysfunctional Thoughts (DRDT) and challenging core beliefs because these techniques don't seem to work (Dalle Grave, Calugi, Doll, & Fairburn, 2013). Instead, psychoeducation is the primary technique employed (Dalle Grave et al., 2013). Patients are taught how to monitor their eating patterns and identify cognitive distortions that maintain these patterns—especially all-or-nothing thinking and selective attention (Dalle Grave et al., 2013). Research on CBT-E has found it to be effective in reducing eating disorder symptoms and improving quality of life (Dalle Grave et al., 2013; Dalle Grave, Calugi, Ghoch, Conti, & Fairburn, 2014; Fairburn et al., 2013; Fairburn et al., 2009; Watson, Allen, Fursland, Byrne, & Nathan, 2012). However, not everyone benefits. One study found that about half (51%) of patients who underwent CBT-E for bulimia and binge eating maintained improvement sixty weeks later (Fairburn et al., 2009). Studies of CBT-E for anorexia (which is notoriously difficult to treat) have yielded more varied and inconsistent results, especially when it comes to long-term maintenance of improved symptoms (Dudek et al., 2014; Fairburn et al., 2013)—although a study by Fairburn himself found CBT-E provided longer-lasting gains than those found in previous studies (Fairburn et al., 2013). Despite some people diagnosed with eating disorders not benefitting as much as we'd like from CBT-E, it is still one of the most effective treatments for eating issues. Aspects of CBT-E (as well as other therapeutic approaches) have even been incorporated into smartphone apps! See the "Try It Yourself" box for information on how you can download and explore these apps.

TRY IT YOURSELF

Can My Smartphone Help Me Overcome an Eating Disorder?

If you can download an app onto your smartphone to help you keep track of your bank account, manage your exercise regimen, and keep tabs on the weather, why not an app to help you manage an eating disorder? One journal article provided a scholarly review of various smartphone apps designed for just that purpose, with special praise for those incorporating therapeutic features backed by research (Juarascio, Manasse, Goldstein, Forman, & Butryn, 2015). Below, two of the apps are described. Because they are free, you are encouraged to download one or both of them to your smartphone and check them out for yourself.

Smartphone apps have been developed to help people diagnosed with eating disorders.
Source: Getty Images/Image Source \ Image Source

» *Recovery Record* "allows users to set clinical goals, many of which are based on cognitive-behavioral strategies" (Juarascio et al., 2015, p. 6). This app contains various features consistent with empirically supported aspects of CBT-E and ACT, including providing users with information about in-the-moment and acceptance-based coping strategies. Users can also set goals for themselves, keep track of their food intake, and record their thoughts and emotions. This app is available in both Apple iOS and Google Android formats (Healthline, n.d.).

» *Rise Up + Recover* allows users to log what they eat, their corresponding feelings, and "target" behaviors such as bingeing and purging (R. Goldman, 2018). The app incorporates CBT-E coping skills (such as contacting friends during times of distress). It also contains "modules that include topics such as cultivating positive body image, building strong relationships with others, journaling, and mindfulness practice" (Juarascio et al., 2015, p. 6). This app is only available for Apple iOS (R. Goldman, 2018).

Daemyn

Should case example client Daemyn seek CBT-E for his binge-eating, the therapist would zero in on the "core psychopathology" common in all eating issues, namely Daemyn's tendency to base his sense of self on his weight and body shape. The therapist would help Daemyn become aware of how he selectively attends to negative events (e.g., eating too much), but overlooks times when he eats properly. Therapy would also focus on making Daemyn more aware of his other accomplishments—such as his successful career as a computer programmer—and shifting his thinking so that his weight wasn't the main means by which Daemyn evaluated his self-worth.

CASE EXAMPLES

Acceptance and Commitment Therapy (ACT)

Acceptance and commitment therapy (ACT) was mentioned in Chapters 6 and 7 as it relates to anxiety and posttraumatic stress. However, ACT is used with a variety of presenting problems, including eating issues. The main premise of ACT is that people's thoughts about events—especially their desire to avoid these thoughts—are often at the root of emotional distress (Dudek et al., 2014; Hayes, 2004; Hayes & Pankey, 2002; Heffner, Sperry, Eifert, & Detweiler, 2002; K. G. Wilson & Roberts, 2002). Too often, people experience **cognitive fusion** with their thoughts (Dudek et al., 2014). That is, they mistake their private thoughts for absolute truths, fusing with these thoughts in ways that cause emotional pain and interfere with their ability to interpret things in alternative ways. Then, they try to avoid these upsetting thoughts. Those with eating disorders dodge upsetting thoughts by focusing on controlling their eating and weight.

ACT tries to alleviate eating problems not by directly challenging negative thoughts or asking clients to change them, but by having clients pay attention to and be aware of these thoughts and the fact that they are just thoughts, not absolutes (Dudek et al., 2014; Hayes & Pankey, 2002; Heffner et al., 2002; K. G. Wilson & Roberts, 2002). As discussed in Chapter 6, the idea is that moment-to-moment awareness of thoughts allows people to be less influenced by these thoughts and instead live in a way that is more consistent with their values. Many different creative techniques are used in ACT to help clients observe in a detached manner the thoughts that they typically avoid. One example of a creative ACT technique is the **thought parade exercise** in which clients are asked to calmly imagine a parade in which people carry signs reproducing their negative thoughts (Heffner et al., 2002). A few RCTs have been conducted on ACT for eating issues, but none with participants formally diagnosed with eating disorders (Dudek et al., 2014). These RCTs did find ACT to be effective, however.

CASE EXAMPLES

Zayna

If Zayna—our case example client experiencing bulimia—sought acceptance and commitment therapy, she might be asked to engage in a "thought parade" exercise. In this exercise, Zayna would visualize herself watching a parade in which people held up signs repeating her negative thoughts (e.g., "I look like a pear!" "If I can't control my eating, I'm worthless."). She also might be asked to keep track of her weight-related thoughts and behaviors, we well as how much she was able to accept these thoughts and behaviors. The idea would be to show Zayna how the more she is able to accept her thoughts, the less likely she will be to engage in bingeing and purging.

HUMANISTIC PERSPECTIVES

Emotion-Focused Therapy (EFT)

Humanistic perspectives see eating problems as meaningful solutions to psychological distress. Emotion-focused therapy (EFT) for eating issues helps clients get in touch with negative emotions such as anger, shame, disgust, fear and sadness (Dolhanty, 2006; Dolhanty & Greenberg, 2009; Ivanova & Watson, 2014). From an EFT perspective, people who restrict food intake tend to suppress negative emotions (especially anger and sadness), while those who binge and purge do so as a way to dissociate from upsetting emotions (Ivanova & Watson, 2014). The EFT perspective (discussed previously in Chapters 5 and 6) holds that people who experience anorexia, bulimia, and binge eating have been raised in environments where emotions were "dismissed, avoided, or ... expressed in unpredictable and uncontrollable ways," leading them to suffer "from an impaired capacity to access, identify, and be guided by adaptive emotions" (Ivanova & Watson, 2014, p. 283).

Emotion-focused therapists help clients diagnosed with eating disorders to better identify and feel comfortable with their emotions (Dolhanty, 2006; Dolhanty & Greenberg, 2009). By trying to empathically understand clients' feelings (a typical humanistic therapy goal) and educating clients about how these feelings can serve a useful purpose (e.g., emotions provide important information about their needs), EFT practitioners help clients to deal with feelings more effectively and stop using problematic eating habits as a way to avoid such feelings (Ivanova & Watson, 2014). EFT for eating problems can be conducted with individuals, but it has also been adapted to group and family formats (Brennan, Emmerling, & Whelton, 2015; A. L. Robinson, Dolhanty, & Greenberg, 2015). While studies have examined EFT's effectiveness for depression and interpersonal issues, the utility of EFT for eating disorders needs to be researched (Dolhanty, 2006).

CASE EXAMPLES

Marta

If EFT was used to help Marta address her anorexia, emphasis would be placed on helping her to identify and experience (rather than avoid) her emotions—especially ones she finds frightening, such as anger and sadness. The therapist would empathically reflect Marta's experiences back to her in an effort to make sure he understood what Marta was going through. As Marta became better at expressing her feelings and both she and her therapist came to have a better grasp of these feelings, the therapist would educate Marta about the importance of acknowledging and listening to these feelings. Rather than ignoring her anger at her mother for pressuring her to take dance lessons, Marta might come to identify the anger as a sign that she probably doesn't want to dance and perhaps should tell this to her mother. EFT would be successful if Marta became better able to identify and act on her emotions. This would make her anorexic behaviors—the avoidant ways she has dealt with these feelings—less necessary.

Narrative Therapy

Narrative therapy (introduced in Chapter 2 and revisited in Chapter 4) focuses on the *problem-saturated stories* that people tell themselves. One of the main techniques in narrative therapy is externalizing the problem, in which the problem is talked about as something outside the person that gets the best of him or her (Maisel, Epston, & Borden, 2004; N. Scott, Hanstock, & Patterson-Kane, 2013). This directly contradicts the medical model in which things like anorexia and bulimia are spoken of as disorders that reside inside individuals. By recasting anorexia, bulimia, or binge eating as entities outside people that get the best of them, narrative therapists help clients change the stories they tell about themselves and pinpoint *exceptions*—times when they were able to resist the pernicious influence of their eating problems (Maisel et al., 2004; Scott et al., 2013). This allows clients to identify solutions for overcoming the influence of eating issues. Narrative therapists have been slow to conduct traditional empirical research on their approach (Chang & Nylund, 2013), but one small study of narrative therapy in a group setting suggested it may be effective with eating problems (M. Weber, Davis, & McPhie, 2006). While attractive to many clinicians, a lot more research on narrative therapy, EFT, and other humanistic approaches to eating issues is necessary if they hope to catch up to CBT-E and IPT in the empirical-evidence department.

CHAPTER 9

Zayna

Imagine narrative therapy with Zayna. Instead of treating bulimia as a disease that Zayna "has," her therapist would externalize it. She might ask Zayna "How and when does bulimia get the best of you?" Zayna might reply that bulimia tells her she is worthless and ugly; she might also note that bulimia is most influential when she encounters stressful challenges in her life—such as exams in school. The therapist would then look for exceptions: "Can you think of times when bulimia had less of an influence over you? What did you do differently during those times?" Zayna might share how when she makes sure she gets proper rest, confides in close friends about her worries, and doesn't keep junk food at home she is better able to resist the influence of bulimia. The therapist would then help Zayna recognize how these are strategies she can use going forward to counteract bulimia's insidious influence.

EVALUATING PSYCHOLOGICAL PERSPECTIVES

When comparing different psychotherapies, CBT is considered by many to have the largest and most compelling evidence base, especially for bulimia (Hay, 2013). Even so, as with drug treatments, CBT clients don't always do well over the long haul—remission rates are fairly high (J. E. Mitchell et al., 2007). Like CBT, IPT is considered effective for eating problems and may be particularly beneficial to clients with interpersonal issues (J. E. Mitchell et al., 2007). In direct comparisons, CBT seems to help people more quickly, but IPT and psychodynamic therapies often "catch up," showing equivalent or better effectiveness across time (Hay, 2013; Zipfel et al., 2014). While acknowledging that IPT holds its own against CBT, not all researchers are as enthusiastic about psychodynamic therapies. Some contend that psychodynamic therapies—while effective— have a weaker evidence base and don't fare as well when directly compared to CBT (J. E. Mitchell et al., 2007; Poulsen et al., 2014). Nonetheless, it seems fair to conclude that there is evidence in favor of CBT, IPT, and even psychodynamic therapies for eating issues. By comparison, there has been minimal research on emotion-focused and narrative therapies to date.

Interestingly, the specific type of psychotherapy offered may be less important than non-specific factors common to all therapies. For anorexic patients, better client–therapist relationships are associated with better therapy outcomes (Antoniou & Cooper, 2013). Even more provocatively, some studies have found that **specialist supportive clinical management (SSCM)**—a non-theoretical approach to managing eating disorder symptoms that was originally devised to serve as a control comparison in research studies on CBT and IPT—may often be just as effective as more theoretically driven interventions (McIntosh, Jordan, & Bulik, 2010; McIntosh et al., 2006; U. Schmidt et al., 2012). In SSCM, clinicians work with patients to help them target problematic eating behaviors. They also provide nutritional advice while teaching clients how to establish a proper diet, monitor their weight, and establish a realistic weight goal. Finally, SSCM provides patients with basic guidance and suggestions on life problems that may be impacting their eating. Although SSCM compares favorably to CBT and IPT, its effects appear to dissipate over time (Hay, 2013). This makes sense if SSCM is merely a pragmatic way to "manage" clinical symptoms rather than a full-blown and theoretically developed therapy intended to "cure" eating disorders. Still, the effectiveness of SSCM suggests there may be common factors that cut across different therapies and explain why they help.

9.6 SOCIOCULTURAL PERSPECTIVES

CROSS-CULTURAL AND SOCIAL JUSTICE PERSPECTIVES

The Western Ideal of Thinness

As previously noted, eating disorders like anorexia and bulimia are generally thought to be much more common in Western industrialized countries (Makino et al., 2004; Qian et al., 2013; Swami, 2015). However, this may be changing, especially as other cultures come into closer contact with the **Western ideal of thinness** in which female bodies with small waists and minimal body fat are venerated (Sepúlveda & Calado, 2012). As non-Western countries industrialize, rates of eating disorders often increase; one example of this is South Korea, where the prevalence of eating disorder diagnoses is comparable to that found in the U.K., U.S., and Canada (M. P. Levine & Smolak, 2010). Does this mean we can consider eating disorders to be culture-bound syndromes unique to Western and Western-influenced industrialized cultures that value thinness? Perhaps, though this is debated, with many clinicians arguing that even if eating disorders are impacted by cultural influences associated with Westernization and industrialization, they can't be explained entirely in these terms; not everyone within these cultures develops an eating disorder, so there must be more to it than only culture (J. D. Brown & Witherspoon, 2002; Keel & Klump, 2003; M. P. Levine & Smolak, 2010; Pike, Dunne, & Addai, 2013). Further, is it Westernization or industrialization that is the primary culprit in the increase in eating disorders? Disentangling their relative influence is quite difficult (Swami, 2015). As a final caveat, when we sharply differentiate Western from non-Western cultures we may risk sliding into *cultural essentialism*, the idea that all members of a culture engage in certain practices; when this happens, not only do we potentially overlook differences within cultures, but we also downplay similarities across cultures (Narayan, 1998). Thus, while it is important to be aware of Western and non-Western cultural disparities in understanding eating issues, we should remain vigilant about not oversimplifying the issue.

Cultural and Ethnic Differences

Even if you don't think eating disorders are completely culture-bound, they do seem to be heavily influenced by cultural norms about eating and weight. This becomes clear when noting how even within Western industrialized countries, eating problems vary by ethnic group. In the U.S., for instance, middle- and upper middle-class white females are extremely vulnerable to anorexia and bulimia (Makino et al., 2004; Striegel-Moore, Silberstein, & Rodin, 1986). They rate very high on indices measuring body dissatisfaction, commitment to exercise, and desire for a smaller body (Yates, Edman, & Aruguete, 2004). By comparison, African American females—compared to white, Hispanic, American Indian, or Asian American females—are less likely to engage in dieting and problematic eating behaviors intended to control weight (M. P. Levine & Smolak, 2010), but are more likely to be obese (C. L. Ogden, Carroll, Fryar, & Flegal, 2015).

Unfortunately, viewing the desire for thinness as primarily an issue among middle- and upper-class white females can lead to overlooking its occurrence (even if it is less) among non-white females, those from lower socioeconomic backgrounds, males, and people in non-white majority countries (M. Brown, Cachelin, & Dohm, 2009; M. P. Levine & Smolak, 2010; Pike et al., 2013; Ricciardelli, McCabe, Williams, & Thompson, 2007). Anorexic and bulimic behaviors are increasing in many non-Western and non-white countries, including Chile, China, Japan, and Malaysia (Chisuwa & O'Dea, 2010; Mellor, McCabe, Ricciardelli, & Merino, 2008; Mellor et al., 2009; X. Xu et al., 2010). They are also increasing among minorities within majority white societies. Along these lines, dislocation studies, which look at rates of eating disorders in people who temporarily move from cultures where eating disorders are less common (e.g., Kenya, Nigeria, south Asia, Pakistan, and Greece) to ones where they are more common (e.g., the U.K., U.S., and Canada), find increased rates of eating disorders (M. P. Levine & Smolak, 2010). Immigrants who internalize Western beliefs appear to be at greater risk than native-born citizens for eating disorders such as anorexia and bulimia (M. P. Levine & Smolak, 2010).

Why might disordered eating behavior spread cross culturally? When a culture, or subcultures within it, comes to celebrate thinness as an ideal everyone should strive for, then it is only logical that more problematic eating behaviors also occur. However, given that not everyone in a given culture develops eating problems, it may be difficult to explain things like anorexia, bulimia, and binge eating exclusively in sociocultural terms (M. P. Levine & Smolak, 2010).

Gender and the Media

Gender and the media are two of the most important sociocultural factors talked about when discussing eating disorders. Women are at much higher risk than men for anorexia, bulimia, and BED. Is the media to blame? Those who answer in the affirmative point to extensive research showing that exposure to media images of thin-ideal models increases body dissatisfaction in females (J. D. Brown & Witherspoon, 2002; Derenne & Beresin, 2006; Groesz, Levine, & Murnen, 2002; Spettigue & Henderson, 2004). Television, films, magazines, the Internet, and social media are examples of media influences that have been tied to increased eating disorder risk. Investigations into the impact of social media on eating issues are relatively new; see the "In Depth" box for more on this budding area of research.

IN DEPTH

Social Media and Eating Disorders

Although there is a lot of research showing how idealization of thinness in "traditional" media such as television, films, and magazines is associated with higher rates of eating disorders (J. D. Brown & Witherspoon, 2002; Groesz et al., 2002), the impact of online environments such as social media are only beginning to be studied (G. Holland & Tiggemann, 2016). As with traditional media, researchers have consistently found that Internet and social media use are related to problematic eating and weight-related behaviors (Fardouly, Diedrichs, Vartanian, & Halliwell, 2015; Fardouly & Vartanian, 2015; Ferguson, Muñoz, Garza, & Galindo, 2014; G. Holland & Tiggemann, 2016; Latzer, Spivak-Lavi, & Katz, 2015; Mabe, Forney, & Keel, 2014; Perloff, 2014). Notably, some (but not all) studies suggest that time spent on social media sites like Facebook is "associated with increased body surveillance, greater endorsement of the thin ideal, more frequent appearance comparisons, and decreased weight satisfaction among younger girls and adolescent women" (G. Holland & Tiggemann, 2016, p. 102). This has led some people to hypothesize that exposure to negative messages about body shape and weight on social media sites like Facebook and Instagram might contribute to the development of eating disorders.

Given that not all studies have found a positive correlation between social media use and problematic eating, some researchers suspect that it may not be the amount of time people spend on social media that is the problem, but how people use social media that leads to difficulties. Posting more pictures of oneself, as well as "liking" and making a lot of comments on other people's posts, correlates with body-image dissatisfaction and a striving for thinness (G. Holland & Tiggemann, 2016). Why? It's not entirely clear, but perhaps people who engage in these activities are more likely to evaluate themselves based on their appearance, making them also more likely to engage in disordered eating as they strive to achieve their idealized body shape.

Most of the existing research on social media, body image, and eating habits has been correlational, but some experimental studies intended to root out cause-and-effect relationships have also been conducted. One such experiment found that spending as little as 20 minutes on Facebook can increase body dissatisfaction (G. Holland & Tiggemann, 2016; Mabe et al., 2014)! However, another experiment produced a rather different result; it found that spending 10 minutes on Facebook did not affect body satisfaction or result in a desire to be thinner (Fardouly et al., 2015; G. Holland & Tiggemann, 2016).

What should we conclude from all this? It's possible that social media users are at an increased risk of negatively comparing themselves to others based on appearance. This negative comparing, which Facebook and Instagram use may inadvertently encourage but which isn't something all users necessarily engage in, may lead to body image issues and problematic eating behaviors (Fardouly & Vartanian, 2015; G. Holland & Tiggemann, 2016). Some speculate that Instagram, which is primarily image-based, may be even more dangerous than Facebook when it comes to women's body image concerns (Fardouly & Vartanian, 2015). However, much more research must be done for us to better understand the precise relationship between social media and eating problems (G. Holland & Tiggemann, 2016).

CRITICAL THINKING QUESTIONS

1. Do you think social media use contributes to negative body images that increase people's vulnerability to eating disorders? What kind of evidence is required to empirically support your view?

2. Could social media be used to help decrease the prevalence of eating problems? If so, how?

3. Given that social media may place people at greater risk for developing disordered eating, should children, teens, and other vulnerable groups have their social media use limited? Why or why not?

Objectification Theory

One theoretical model used to understand the connection between media portrayals and eating problems in women is **objectification theory**. According to this theory, media images (on television, in films, in magazines, and online) present women as sexual objects to be judged based on their looks. This results in **objectification**, in which the female body is "looked at and evaluated, primarily on the basis of appearance" (Tiggemann, 2013, p. 36). According to objectification theory, **self-objectification** occurs when girls and women internalize media messages that judge them based on their appearance and then begin to appraise their own worth based on these messages (Tiggemann, 2013). The theory predicts that problematic eating and weight-related behaviors often ensue in response to self-objectification. There is a strong base of research to support objectification theory's contention that media images are associated with more negative self-assessments in females (Calogero, Davis, & Thompson, 2005; T. A. Myers & Crowther, 2007; Tiggemann, 2013). A limitation of this research, however, is that most of it has been done with "normal" samples rather than samples diagnosed with eating disorders (Tiggemann, 2013).

Zayna

When Zayna was a teenager, she began comparing her own developing body to those she saw on television and in fashion magazines. They were so much skinnier than she was. No matter how much dieting and exercising she did, Zayna just couldn't get her body to look like the actresses and models she admired. She came to believe that being thin was equal to being happy and successful. When she looked in the mirror, Zayna judged herself a failure because she could never achieve the body shape she desired.

CASE EXAMPLES

Muscle Dysmorphia

Women aren't alone in being influenced by media images that may lead to disordered eating. There is also evidence that men are increasingly affected by media portrayals that demand they have a "bulked up" and muscular body (J. D. Brown & Witherspoon, 2002; Sepúlveda & Calado, 2012). **Muscle dysmorphia** (alluded to in Chapter 6), a subtype of body dysmorphic disorder (BDD) in which (mostly) males obsessively worry that they aren't muscular enough, may be influenced by such media portrayals. This is in keeping with research suggesting that people perceive anorexia as a "female" problem and muscle dysmorphia as a "male" problem (Griffiths, Mond, Murray, & Touyz, 2014). In light of this finding, it makes sense that men who display symptoms of anorexia are perceived as having more feminine characteristics (Griffiths et al., 2014).

Social Justice Efforts to Change Media Messages

Let's close this discussion with a provocative quote about the media's impact on eating disorders, one which indicts the media for not only emphasizing the thin ideal, but for spreading problematic values that may indeed be important in understanding the origin of eating disorders:

> *Western media do not merely propagate a thin ideal, which is internalized by individuals in non-Western sites. Rather, Western media present a concoction of values that go beyond the idealization of thinness and that includes consumerism, the idealization of youthfulness, the veneration of beauty in and for itself, the notion that physical selves are malleable, and that work on the body is both healthy and required. (Swami, 2015, p. 47)*

Clinicians and researchers operating from social justice perspectives work to change these kinds of societal values, which they see as destructively encouraging disordered eating habits. Those who agree with them probably share their view that social action challenging problematic social values is essential in addressing eating problems. That is, they believe that "if certain harmful aspects of lifestyle that contribute to negative body images and eating behaviours are to be altered, it is necessary to carry out social interventions to change personal motivations that can lead to disorders" (Sepúlveda & Calado, 2012, p. 61). But what kind of social interventions are needed? Some have suggested that we place warnings on objectionable media that are thought to place people at risk for eating disorders. The "Controversial Question" feature delves deeper into this issue.

CONTROVERSIAL QUESTION

Should There Be Warning Labels on Unrealistic Images in Fashion Magazines?

Fashion magazines are filled with unrealistic photos of models. These snapshots are digitally altered, airbrushed, and tweaked to present an idealized (and often unattainable) image of the perfect body. Because exposure to media images that celebrate unrealistically thin bodies is positively correlated with body dissatisfaction and eating disorders, some countries—including Australia, France, Israel, and the U.K.—have considered the use of warning labels to educate the public about the potentially damaging impact of such images (Tiggemann, Slater, Bury, Hawkins, & Firth, 2013). The logic behind doing so is intuitive. If people are influenced by unrealistic advertising images of beauty and body size, perhaps placing disclaimers on these images (to let people know that they have been altered) might reduce their negative influence.

But can warning labels prevent or reduce body dissatisfaction? Researchers have been investigating that question and the results are a bit surprising. Of the numerous studies that have been done to date, only one found that warning labels reduced body dissatisfaction (Slater, Tiggemann, Firth, & Hawkins, 2012). Several others found little to no effect for warning labels (Ata, Thompson, & Small, 2013; Bury, Tiggemann, & Slater, 2016; Frederick, Sandhu, Scott, & Akbari, 2016; Tiggemann et al., 2013). A couple of studies even found that warning labels might increase body dissatisfaction in some instances for certain people (Bury et al., 2016; Selimbegović & Chatard, 2015; Tiggemann et al., 2013). These findings have led several investigators to conclude that warning labels, while well intentioned, may do more harm than good: "The results of these studies provide some reason for pessimism regarding the effectiveness of disclaimers" (Frederick et al., 2016, p. 173).

Why don't warning labels seem to work? It may be that different people respond to them differently (Bury et al., 2016). Women with a tendency to compare themselves to others based on appearance may be negatively impacted by warning labels, while those less likely to compare their appearance to others' may respond more positively to such labels (especially when they contain specific information about how the image has been changed) (Bury et al., 2016; Tiggemann et al., 2013). In other words, if you are inclined to compare your body to others' bodies, then highlighting differences between your body and the bodies of people in advertisements (even digitally altered advertisements!) might lead you to make more comparisons and feel more dissatisfied with your own body. But if you aren't someone who makes such comparisons, then a warning label about the ways an image has been altered might simply make you more aware of unrealistic ideals promoted in the advertisement.

CHAPTER 9

Studies on warning labels provide a nice example of how research can help us examine commonsense ideas and potentially find that they don't hold up to scrutiny. Warning labels on altered media sound like they should work, but they don't appear to. For better or worse, most researchers have reluctantly concluded that "disclaimers of digital alteration do not reduce body dissatisfaction following exposure to thin ideal fashion magazine advertisements" (Bury et al., 2016, p. 141).

CRITICAL THINKING QUESTIONS

1. Are you surprised by the results of research on warning labels? Why or why not?
2. What kinds of research studies should be done to further tease apart the influence of different kinds of warning labels and individual differences on body dissatisfaction in response to digitally altered ads?
3. Irrespective of the effectiveness of warning labels, is it ethical for advertisers to digitally alter ads? Why or why not?
4. In light of evidence that digitally altering ads may enhance body dissatisfaction and foster eating problems, should governments impose limitations on the practice? Explain your thinking.

Socioeconomic Status and Education Level

Some research finds a **negative correlation between income and obesity**, at least in industrialized countries where sufficient food is available (Achat & Stubbs, 2014; Boisvert & Harrell, 2014; O'Dea & Dibley, 2014). That is, people of lower socioeconomic status (SES) are usually more likely to be overweight. Why this is remains uncertain. However, it seems reasonable to hypothesize that lower SES people may not have access to resources that allow them to eat in a healthy manner; fast food and junk food are less expensive than healthier food choices. It also may be that people of lower SES are less educated about healthy eating. Social justice therapists advocate for programs designed to address educational and economic inequalities that perpetuate obesity among poorer people.

Teasing out the exact influences of SES and education is difficult because these factors probably influence one another while also being influenced by additional factors, such as ethnicity (Achat & Stubbs, 2014; Boisvert & Harrell, 2014). For example, one study found that non-white, high-income women reported fewer symptoms of disordered eating than non-white, low-income women (Boisvert & Harrell, 2014). In this study, both SES and ethnicity were relevant factors. However, less education and lower SES are generally correlated with binge-eating issues while more education and higher SES are usually correlated with issues tied to a drive for thinness (Boisvert & Harrell, 2014). Given that being a minority—black or Hispanic in the U.S., for instance—is associated with lower SES and less education, it is easy to see why it can be hard to discern exactly what the relative influence of education, SES, and ethnicity are when it comes to eating issues.

Cultural Pica

Pica is often rooted in cultural practices and is not always considered disordered. In rural India, pregnant women often eat "mud, clay, ash, lime, charcoal, and brick in response to cravings," while in East Africa pica plays a role in fertility rituals in which pregnant women "eat soil before, during, and after pregnancy because they believe in the soil's magical potential to ensure future offspring" (Stiegler, 2005, p. 27). As another example, tribes in Peru and Bolivia eat clay to ward off any toxins in their primary food, potatoes (Stiegler, 2005). When eating non-food substances is part of a group's usual cultural practices and "believed to be of spiritual, medicinal, or other social value," the *DSM-5* indicates that pica shouldn't be diagnosed (American Psychiatric Association, 2013b, p. 331).

CONSUMER AND SERVICE-USER PERSPECTIVES

Studies consistently find that being diagnosed with an eating disorder carries substantial stigma (Griffiths et al., 2014; Maier et al., 2014; Makowski, Mnich, Angermeyer, Löwe, & von dem Knesebeck, 2015; S. A. McLean et al., 2014; Murakami, Essayli, & Latner, 2016; Roehrig & McLean, 2010; Vartanian & Porter, 2016). To illustrate this, one study found that people rate someone with eating disorder symptoms significantly more negatively than someone with symptoms of depression (Roehrig & McLean, 2010). Interestingly, males appear to hold more negative attitudes and stigmatizing beliefs about people with anorexia and bulimia than do women (Griffiths et al., 2014; S. A. McLean et al., 2014).

Although having an eating disorder carries extensive stigma, so does being overweight. Research suggests that a lot of problematic eating behavior—such as skipping meals and bingeing—are correlated with weight stigma; people who have encountered prejudice for being overweight are more likely to engage in these behaviors (Vartanian & Porter, 2016). That said, although being obese carries substantial stigma, it appears to carry less than having an anorexia, bulimia, or binge-eating diagnosis (Murakami et al., 2016). Though the reasons for this remain speculative, it might be because people think of anorexia, bulimia, and binge-eating disorder as genetically inherited biological disorders. A qualitative study of women diagnosed with eating disorders found that even though many believed genetic explanations of eating disorders could make them less likely to be blamed for their problematic eating, others worried that such explanations might create destructive self-fulfilling prophecies in which people inappropriately blame their eating issues (and their failure to overcome them) on genetics (Easter, 2012).

SYSTEMS PERSPECTIVES

Psychosomatic Families

In Chapter 2, we discussed Salvador Minuchin's (1974) structural family therapy, which focused on how unspoken rules influence patterns of family interaction. Minuchin and colleagues proposed an early family therapy model of anorexia. They argued that anorexic children come from psychosomatic families, characterized by *enmeshment, overprotectiveness, rigidity, conflict avoidance*, and *difficulty resolving conflict* (Minuchin, Rosman, & Baker, 1978). In such families, boundaries between members are blurred. The family acts in lockstep while being overprotective and downplaying disagreement among members. Minuchin described the impact of psychosomatic families on the anorexic child's development, explaining how such families are

> *typically child-oriented. The child grows up carefully protected by parents who focus on her well-being. Parental concern is expressed in hypervigilance of the child's movements and intense observation of her psychological needs. Since the child experiences family members as focusing on her actions and commenting on them, she develops vigilance over her own actions. Since the evaluation of what she does is another's domain, the child develops an obsessive concern for perfection. (Minuchin et al., 1978, p. 59)*

Although today the notion of psychosomatic families is occasionally criticized for blaming families for causing anorexia, it was revolutionary from a family systems perspective because its main focus wasn't on the individual psychology of the anorexic patient, but on the broader family dynamics believed to foster anorexic behaviors. Not only did Minuchin move away from seeing the anorexic child as a "'sick' and helpless victim," but he also reframed anorexia as an "interpersonal problem in which all family members were involved" (Dodge, 2016, p. 221). The goal of therapy wasn't simply a changed individual, but a more functional family system (Minuchin et al., 1978). Through a variety of family therapy techniques—including the family meal, during which the therapist observed the anorexic family having a meal together in order to directly observe dysfunctional family patterns—structural family therapists came to understand (and counter) family dynamics that perpetuated anorexia (Dodge, 2016; Minuchin et al., 1978).

Despite being highly influential, research has provided little support for the notion of psychosomatic families. Numerous studies and several literature reviews have concluded that there really isn't a clear pattern that characterizes the families of those diagnosed with anorexia and other eating disorders (Dodge, 2016; Eisler, 2005; Holtom-Viesel & Allan, 2014; Kog & Vandereycken, 1985; Lyke & Matsen, 2013). In fact, there is a great deal of variability across these families. The psychosomatic family approach is no longer the first-line family therapy for eating disorders, but has influenced the family-based treatment that now is.

Family-Based Treatment (FBT) for Anorexia and Bulimia

Family-based treatment (FBT) is a manualized approach to anorexia and bulimia in teens that typically consists of 20 family therapy sessions spread over a year (Fitzpatrick, 2011). It is also called the *Maudsley approach*, after the hospital in London where it was developed. FBT differs from Minuchin's approach in that it doesn't assume eating disorders are caused by family dynamics. Instead, it tends to see anorexia and bulimia as diseases in which family patterns serve to influence and maintain symptoms. Thus, it doesn't blame parents for their children's anorexia and bulimia (Eisler, Lock, & le Grange, 2010; Fitzpatrick, 2011; Le Grange, 2005, 2010; Le Grange & Lock, 2010).

In *Phase I (renourishment)* of FBT, weekly sessions focus on weight restoration and/or the establishment of healthy eating (Eisler et al., 2010; Fitzpatrick, 2011; Le Grange & Lock, 2010). Minuchin's family meal

CHAPTER 9

technique is used early in Phase I to identify problematic family patterns around eating and coach the family on how to remedy them. Because anorexic patients, compared to bulimic patients, tend to be younger and at greater risk for serious health issues due to their self-starvation, their parents are given a great deal of authority over weight restoration. With bulimic patients, a more collaborative approach is used to negotiate appropriate rules for eating. Importantly, Phase I absolves parents of responsibility for their child's eating disorder (in comparison to Minuchin's model, which blamed parents). This is done to empower them as they work to improve their children's eating habits.

Phase II (autonomy over eating) begins when patients have reached a healthy body weight and are no longer struggling to eat normally (Eisler et al., 2010; Fitzpatrick, 2011; Le Grange & Lock, 2010). Session frequency decreases to every other week and patients are given greater autonomy over their eating and exercise habits. That is, "parents are encouraged to 'test the water'" of their child's readiness to eat in an age-appropriate way without so much parental monitoring (Eisler et al., 2010, p. 165).

Phase III (normal adolescence) occurs when the teen's eating and weight have returned to normal (Eisler et al., 2010; Fitzpatrick, 2011; Le Grange & Lock, 2010). Sessions occur only once per month and focus mainly on supporting the teen with normal developmental issues (school work, dating, peer pressure, and ordinary worries about body height, size, and shape). Any concerns that the parents or teen have about the possibility of relapse are also addressed.

Marta

If Marta underwent FBT for her anorexia, weekly sessions with her and her family would initially focus on helping her regain weight. The therapist might observe a family meal and realize that Marta's parents often contradict one another, with mom telling Marta she needn't eat everything on her plate and dad insisting the plate must be emptied. Subsequent therapy sessions would encourage Marta's parents to work together and support one another in setting appropriate expectations for Marta's eating. As they did so and Marta's eating (and weight) improved, she would be given greater autonomy and less supervision over her eating.

CASE EXAMPLES

Research suggests that FBT is effective at reducing symptoms of anorexia and bulimia, especially in first-time non-chronic cases (Le Grange, 2005; Le Grange, Lock, Agras, Bryson, & Jo, 2015; Lock, 2011). FBT doesn't help everyone—especially given that 15%–30% of families can't or won't participate in family therapy (Fitzpatrick, 2011)—but those who do engage in it appear to improve. In a critical review, Downs and Blow (2013) pointed to several weaknesses in the FBT research literature. First, many of the existing studies have small sample sizes, in part because doing family therapy studies can be quite time consuming and expensive. Second, some of the studies have significant dropout rates—making it hard to compare the outcomes of those who dropped out to those who remained. Third, studies often differ in their use of *DSM* diagnostic criteria in recruiting participants; this means that participants' symptoms may not be similar across studies. Fourth, many studies don't control for other treatments that participants receive at the same time as FBT; this makes it hard to know how much FBT versus the other simultaneous treatments contribute to patient improvement. Despite these limitations, the overall body of research does suggest that FBT effectively reduces symptoms of anorexia and bulimia (Eisler et al., 2010; Fitzpatrick, 2011; Le Grange, 2010; Le Grange & Lock, 2010; Le Grange et al., 2015).

EVALUATING SOCIOCULTURAL PERSPECTIVES

Sociocultural factors are seen as playing a central role in fostering and maintaining eating problems. In cultures where thinness is worshipped and women in particular are judged based on their looks, it makes sense that eating issues are common. Research clearly shows that media can influence body image and that people who spend more time taking in such media run a higher risk for engaging in problematic eating. Turning to family perspectives, family-based treatment (FBT) appears to be an effective therapy for anorexia and bulimia. It does well in studies comparing it to CBT and IPT. In fact, for anorexia some consider it the treatment of choice (A. E. Kass, Kolko, & Wilfley, 2013). Overall, there is less evidence for FBT's effectiveness for bulimia (Hay, 2013; Le Grange, 2010), but one recent randomized controlled trial of FBT for bulimia did find it superior to CBT (Le Grange et al., 2015). Some researchers are encouraging the combination of FBT and CBT-E in treating bulimia (Hurst, Read, & Holtham, 2015).

9.7 CLOSING THOUGHTS: ARE FEEDING AND EATING PROBLEMS UNIVERSAL OR UNIQUE TO OUR TIME?

Eating habits are intimately intertwined with not only our biology and psychology, but also with social norms and practices. What we eat, when we eat, with whom we eat, and how we eat are inevitably shaped by cultural customs that we usually take for granted. At the same time, eating is an activity with clear biological and psychological bases. Thus, when discussing feeding and eating disorders a formidable question arises. Are the various feeding and eating disorders culture-bound syndromes uniquely tied to our current historical era? Or, are they universal disorders, rooted in underlying biological and psychological dysfunctions, that are merely influenced by sociocultural factors?

Although it may be a bit of both, most of us lean one way or the other on this issue. Theorists who lean toward a view of eating disorders as culture-bound syndromes come from a perspective of **cultural relativism** in which abnormality is always relative to social norms (Isaac, 2013); eating is only "disordered" within a social context that defines it as such. In

Are eating disorders culture-bound syndromes?
Source: GOODSHOOT

contrast, theorists who lean toward a view of eating disorders as maladies that aren't dependent on culture and context come from a perspective of **cultural universalism**; how people display eating disorders in terms of specific behaviors may vary from one culture or historical period to another, but the disorders themselves cut across time and place (Isaac, 2013). Feeding and eating problems aren't unique in reminding us of continuing disagreement over whether mental disorders are universal or relative. The universalist–relativist debate can be applied to just about every presenting problem discussed in this book. However, because eating behavior is so clearly rooted in biological, psychological, and social processes, our uncertainty over the universality of feeding and eating disorders is especially noticeable.

KEY TERMS

Adapted to flee famine hypothesis
Amenorrhea
Anorexia nervosa
Anterior insula
Atypical anorexia nervosa
Atypical bulimia nervosa
Aversion therapy
Avoidant/restrictive food intake
   disorder (ARFID)
Binge eating
Binge-eating disorder (BED)
Body mass index (BMI)
Bulimia nervosa
Cognitive fusion
Compensatory behavior
Cultural relativism
Cultural universalism
Dislocation studies
Eating problems
Enhanced cognitive-behavioral therapy
   (CBT-E)

Exposure plus response prevention of
   bingeing
Exposure plus response prevention of
   purging
Family meal
Family-based treatment (FBT)
Feeding disorder of infancy and early
   childhood
Feeding problems
Food exposure for anorexia
Geophagia
In vivo food exposure
Lateral hypothalamus
Mercyism
Mesolimbic pathway
Muscle dysmorphia
Night eating syndrome
Norepinephrine-dopamine reuptake
   inhibitors (NDRIs)
Obesity
objectification
Objectification theory

Oral impregnation
Orthorexia nervosa
Other specified feeding or eating
   disorder
Overcorrection
Pica
Psychosomatic families
Purging
Purging disorder
Reproductive suppression hypothesis
Rumination disorder
Satiation techniques
Self-objectification
Sexual competition hypothesis
Specialist supportive clinical
   management (SSCM)
Thought parade exercise
Tryptophan
Ventromedial hypothalamus
Weight set point
Western ideal of thinness

Full definitions of the terms listed above can be found in the end-of-book glossary on p. 533.

CHAPTER **9**

 Go to the companion website, www.macmillanihe.com/raskin-abnormal-psych, to access a study guide, multiple choice and flashcard quizzes for this chapter, and other useful learning aids.

CHAPTER 10
SEXUAL PROBLEMS AND GENDER ISSUES

10.1 OVERVIEW

 LEARNING OBJECTIVES

After reading this chapter, you should be able to:

1. Define basic sex and gender terms and discuss the role of values in discussing sex and gender.
2. Outline *DSM-5*, *ICD-10*, and *ICD-11* diagnoses pertaining to sexual dysfunctions, paraphilias, and gender dysphoria, as well as explain controversies concerning these diagnoses.
3. Describe historical trends in the history of understanding sex and gender issues and identify significant figures from this history.
4. Explain biological perspectives on sexuality and gender issues, including those emphasizing brain chemistry, brain structure, genes, evolution, and the immune system.
5. Distinguish psychodynamic, cognitive-behavioral, and humanistic conceptualizations and interventions for sexual problems and gender issues.
6. Overview cross-cultural, social justice, and community-based program approaches to assessing and addressing sexuality and gender issues.

Photo source: © Royalty-Free/Corbis

GETTING STARTED: WHAT IS "NORMAL" SEXUAL BEHAVIOR?

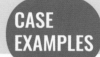
CASE EXAMPLES

Elena
Elena is a 30-year-old married woman who seeks therapy because she has lost all interest in sex. "No matter how hard my husband Hector tries to arouse me, I just can't seem to get turned on," she complains.

Ahmed
Ahmed is a 65-year-old widower who is back on the dating scene. He has a new girlfriend, Miri. Ahmed complains that even though he finds Miri very attractive, he is unable to get an erection and this is interfering with their sex life and their relationship.

Bolin
Bolin, a 22-year-old male, seeks therapy because he is not getting along with his girlfriend, May. He reluctantly admits that sex with May isn't very good because "I cum too fast." Bolin is deeply embarrassed by this, but hopes therapy might help.

Linnea
Linnea is a 48-year-old married woman who seeks medical attention because she experiences vaginal pain whenever she has sex with her husband Phillip. "I get very anxious anytime he wants to have sex because I know it's going to hurt," she says.

Lou
Lou is a 35-year-old married man who comes to therapy with his wife, Ruth. They have been arguing over Lou's insistence on wearing Ruth's undergarments when they have sex. In fact, Lou has difficulty getting aroused unless he wears women's clothes. Because Ruth finds this to be a big turnoff, she has increasingly avoided sex with Lou.

William

William is a 42-year-old man who has just been arrested for having child pornography on his computer. He admits to being turned on by pictures of naked children, but swears that he has never actually touched a real child in a sexual manner. He goes on trial in the near future and is likely to be labeled as a sex offender.

Julio

Julio is a 30-year-old man who believes he was born in the wrong body. "Inside, I feel like a woman," he says. He has felt this way as long as he can remember. "I never liked boy stuff," he recalls. "My father really wanted me to play football, but I preferred playing with dolls and dressing up in my mom's clothes." Julio seeks therapy because—even though he has been dressing and living as a man—he wants to undergo sex reassignment surgery and transition to life as a woman. "I want my outside to match what I know I am inside," he exclaims.

Sex, Gender, and Values

When it comes to sex and gender, what is normal? This is a difficult question to which different people—even different mental health professionals—give different responses. People answer this question differently because their ideas about what is normal when it comes to sex and gender are inevitably informed by their personal and cultural values. Of course, this has been true of other topics we have discussed. However, what constitutes "normal" sex and gender tends to evoke particularly opinionated responses from professionals and non-professionals alike—perhaps due to the intimate nature of the topic. Thus, don't be surprised if you find yourself having strong reactions to how various perspectives conceptualize sex and gender issues, especially if you recognize yourself in some of the issues discussed. With that in mind, it may help to remember that "ideas about what is considered to be normal sexual behavior vary considerably over time" and "atypical sexual activity is not a *de facto* indicator of mental illness" (Kamens, 2011, p. 40).

Sex and Gender: Basic Terms

One of the challenges in discussing sex and gender is sorting out what people mean when they use different terms. This task is made more difficult because terms that some people find appropriate, others object to—which may explain why accepted terms change over time. Further, how terms are defined varies, making it hard to always know exactly what is meant when they are used. Despite these challenges, let's do our best to define some basic terms.

Sex

According to the American Psychological Association (2012), sex refers to one's biological status as male, female, or intersex. A person's biological sex is indicated by physical factors such as "sex chromosomes, gonads, internal reproductive organs, and external genitalia" (American Psychological Association, 2012, p. 11). Intersex people have atypical physical features that make classifying them as male or female difficult.

Gender

Gender has to do with "the attitudes, feelings, and behaviors that a given culture associates with a person's biological sex" (American Psychological Association, 2012, p. 11). Gender conformity is when a person's behavior fits with cultural expectations about gender, whereas gender nonconformity is when a person violates such expectations (American Psychological Association, 2012). For example, a girl who wears a dress is gender conforming. A boy who does so isn't. The extent to which a person's gender conforms is often intertwined with gender identity, "one's persistent inner sense of belonging to either the male and female gender category" (Moleiro & Pinto, 2015, p. 2). Gender identity usually matches gender expression, which refers to how people behave and dress in order to convey their gender (American Psychological Association, 2012; Drescher, 2014). People's clothes, haircuts, ways of speaking, and body

Which toilet would you choose? How you answer may reflect your feelings about gender conformity.
Source: Getty Images/iStockphoto \ tomap 49, Sedat SEVEN

language (among other indicators) communicate their gender identities to others. Understandably, people whose gender identities are inconsistent with their biological sex may have difficulty expressing their gender identities and instead conform to cultural gender expectations despite the psychological stress this causes them.

Julio

For example, our case example client Julio is experiencing dissonance concerning his gender identity, gender expression, and biological sex.

CASE EXAMPLES

Sexual Orientation

To further complicate matters, gender identity may or may not be a straightforward indicator of **sexual orientation**, which refers to the "sex of those to whom one is sexually and romantically attracted" (American Psychological Association, 2012, p. 11). **Heterosexuals** are attracted to the other sex, whereas **homosexuals** are attracted to the same sex; **bisexuals** are attracted to both sexes (American Psychological Association, 2012; Drescher, 2014; Grollman, 2010). The term **gay** describes male or female homosexuals, but some women prefer the term **lesbian**, which refers to female homosexuals (Drescher, 2014). Of course, declaring one's sexual orientation isn't always easy due to **heterosexism** and **homophobia**, both of which have to do with hostility toward and prejudice against gay people (Herek, 1996). Heterosexism is the more current term, referring to any "ideological system that denies, denigrates, and stigmatizes any nonheterosexual form of behavior, identity, relationship, or community" (Herek, 1990, p. 316). The older term, homophobia, is no longer preferred by many because it implies that antigay prejudice results from an individual problem—a clinical affliction that causes people to fear and reject homosexuality—rather than from cultural ideologies that lead to discrimination and mistreatment of homosexual persons. Thus, when the term homophobia is used today, it usually refers to **internalized homophobia**, "the hostility of gay men and lesbians toward their own homosexuality" that they learn from the wider culture (Herek, 1996, p. 102).

Coming out is the process by which people come to accept and declare their sexual orientation or gender identity to others (American Psychological Association, 2012; Drescher, 2014). Due to heterosexism, coming out can be a difficult process for gay men, lesbians, and people with nonconforming gender identities. Such individuals often face discrimination and stigma for doing so—with heterosexual and gender-conforming individuals (who don't have to come out because their sexual orientation and gender identity are usually presumed) often unaware of how difficult coming out can be. Although some don't care for the term, those who have yet to come out are often referred to as **closeted**, or "in the closet" (Drescher, 2014; Grollman, 2010). Importantly, sexual orientation may not be as either/or as the categorical terms we use to describe it suggest. Although sexual orientation is often viewed as relatively consistent, there is evidence that it can be fluid across time (M. W. Ross, Daneback, & Månsson, 2012).

Transsexual and Transgender

People whose gender identity is inconsistent with their biological sex are often described as "transsexual" or "transgender." **Transsexual** is an older (and often no longer favored) term traditionally applied to people who have sought or undergone medical procedures to reduce the discrepancy between their biological sex and their gender identity; they have transitioned from one sex to the other (Markman, 2011; Moleiro & Pinto, 2015; Scutti, 2014). However, some people have moved away from this strictly medical definition and instead use the term more inclusively to refer to

> anyone who has a gender identity that is incongruent with the sex assigned at birth and therefore is currently, or is working toward, living as a member of the sex other than the one they were assigned at birth, regardless of what medical procedures they may have undergone or may desire in the future. (Moleiro & Pinto, 2015, p. 2)

Transgender is a more recent term that, in many respects, is broader and more inclusive than transsexual (Moleiro & Pinto, 2015; Scutti, 2014). The U.S.'s National Center for Transgender Equality (2015, para. 2) defines transgender as "a term for people whose gender identity, expression or behavior is different from those typically associated with their assigned sex at birth." Transgender is considered an "umbrella term to describe those people who defy societal expectations and assumptions regarding gender" (Moleiro & Pinto, 2015, p. 2). It includes not only transsexual and intersex individuals, but people whose identities fall outside the traditional male/female binary and who may express their gender in ways that defy social norms and expectations (Moleiro & Pinto, 2015). The term "transgender" is sometimes confused with the term **transvestite**. People identified as transvestites engage in **transvestism**, or cross-dressing. While some transgender people cross-dress, most cross-dressers aren't transgender because they don't experience incongruence about their gender identity. It's also worth noting that gender identity is independent of sexual orientation because "one's gender identity does not automatically reveal one's sexual attractions" (Drescher, 2014, p. 1318). What it means, then, to be transgender can vary greatly:

> *One example of a transgendered person might be a man who is attracted to women but also identifies as a cross-dresser. Other examples include people who consider themselves gender nonconforming, multigendered, androgynous, third gender, and two-spirit people. All of these definitions are inexact and vary from person to person, yet each of them includes a sense of blending or alternating the binary concepts of masculinity and femininity. Some people using these terms simply see the traditional concepts as restrictive. (Scutti, 2014, para. 4)*

Many transgender people challenge the assumption that gender identities must conform to the traditional male/female binary.
Source: iStock.com/LemonTreeImages

Transgender is increasingly being contrasted with **cisgender**, a term for people whose gender identity and birth sex do match (Drescher, 2014). Awareness of the cisgender label is relevant in thinking about abnormality because the term offers "a way of distinguishing people who do not identify themselves as transgender" without implying that the opposite of transgender is "normal" (Markman, 2011, p. 315). Terminology in the transgender community changes across time, so please see Table 10.1 for a quick guide to current transgender terminology. As you will see throughout the rest of this chapter, there is fierce debate about whether transgender identities are unfairly pathologized in the *DSM* and *ICD*, which are discussed next.

Table 10.1 Transgender Terminology

Terminology within the transgender community varies and has changed over time so we recognize the need to be sensitive to usage within particular communities.

Transgender	A term for people whose gender identity, expression or behavior is different from those typically associated with their assigned sex at birth. Transgender is a broad term and is good for nontransgender people to use. "Trans" is shorthand for "transgender." (Note: Transgender is correctly used as an adjective, not a noun, thus "transgender people" is appropriate but "transgenders" is often viewed as disrespectful.)
Transgender Man	A term for a transgender individual who currently identifies as a man (see also "FTM").
Transgender Woman	A term for a transgender individual who currently identifies as a woman (see also "MTF").
Gender Identity	An individual's internal sense of being male, female, or something else. Since gender identity is internal, one's gender identity is not necessarily visible to others.
Gender Expression	How a person represents or expresses one's gender identity to others, often through behavior, clothing, hairstyles, voice or body characteristics.
Transsexual	An older term for people whose gender identity is different from their assigned sex at birth who seeks to transition from male to female or female to male. Many do not prefer this term because it is thought to sound overly clinical.
Cross-dresser	A term for people who dress in clothing traditionally or stereotypically worn by the other sex, but who generally have no intent to live full-time as the other gender. The older term "transvestite" is considered derogatory by many in the United States.
Queer	A term used to refer to lesbian, gay, bisexual and, often also transgender, people. Some use queer as an alternative to "gay" in an effort to be more inclusive. Depending on the user, the term has either a derogatory or an affirming connotation, as many have sought to reclaim the term that was once widely used in a negative way.
Genderqueer	A term used by some individuals who identify as neither entirely male nor entirely female.
Gender Nonconforming	A term for individuals whose gender expression is different from societal expectations related to gender.

CHAPTER 10

Bi-gendered	One who has a significant gender identity that encompasses both genders, male and female. Some may feel that one side or the other is stronger, but both sides are there.
Two-spirit	A contemporary term that refers to the historical and current First Nations people [of the U.S.] whose individual spirits were a blend of male and female spirits. This term has been reclaimed by some in Native American LGBT communities in order to honor their heritage and provide an alternative to the Western labels of gay, lesbian, bisexual, or transgender.
FTM	A person who transitions from "female-to-male," meaning a person who was assigned female at birth, but identifies and lives as a male. Also known as a "transgender man."
MTF	A person who transitions from "male-to-female," meaning a person who was assigned male at birth, but identifies and lives as a female. Also known as a "transgender woman."
Sex Reassignment Surgery	Surgical procedures that change one's body to better reflect a person's gender identity. This may include different procedures, including those sometimes also referred to as "top surgery" (breast augmentation or removal) or "bottom surgery" (altering genitals). Contrary to popular belief, there is not one surgery; in fact, there are many different surgeries. These surgeries are medically necessary for some people, however not all people want, need, or can have surgery as part of their transition. "Sex change surgery" is considered a derogatory term by many.
Sexual Orientation	A term describing a person's attraction to members of the same sex and/or a different sex, usually defined as lesbian, gay, bisexual, heterosexual, or asexual.
Transition	The time when a person begins to live as the gender with which they identify rather than the gender they were assigned at birth, which often includes changing one's first name and dressing and grooming differently. Transitioning may or may not also include medical and legal aspects, including taking hormones, having surgery, or changing identity documents (e.g. driver's license, Social Security record) to reflect one's gender identity. Medical and legal steps are often difficult for people to afford.
Intersex	A term used for people who are born with a reproductive or sexual anatomy and/or chromosome pattern that does not seem to fit typical definitions of male or female. Intersex conditions are also known as differences of sex development (DSD).
Drag Queen	Used to refer to male performers who dress as women for the purpose of entertaining others at bars, clubs, or other events. It is also sometimes used in a derogatory manner to refer to transgender women.
Drag King	Used to refer to female performers who dress as men for the purposes of entertaining others at bars, clubs, or other events.

Source: Reproduced with permission from the National Center for Transgender Equality (www.transequality.org/issues/resources/transgender-terminology)

10.2 *DSM* AND *ICD* PERSPECTIVES

In a tremendously significant break with the *DSM-5* and *ICD-10*, the *ICD-11* no longer classifies sex and gender issues as mental disorders. Instead, it now includes them in a distinct chapter called "conditions related to sexual health." This chapter contains subsections for "sexual dysfunctions," "sexual pain disorders," "paraphilic disorders," and "gender incongruence." Removing sex and gender disorders from the mental disorders section of *ICD-11* could potentially decrease the stigma associated with these problems by reframing them in less psychological and more medical terms. Some have even argued that moving sex and gender concerns out of the mental disorders section of *ICD* marks an effort to move past the mind/body separation that has often ensnared understandings of these issues (G. M. Reed et al., 2016). Whatever the reasons or outcome, it's a big change.

Because the *DSM-5* (unlike the *ICD*s) restricts itself solely to mental disorders, it must consider sex and gender issues as mental disorders; if it didn't, it would need to delete these diagnoses from the manual entirely. The *DSM-5* hasn't given any indication it plans to do so. Thus, the *DSM-5* maintains separate chapters on "sexual dysfunctions," "paraphilic disorders," and "gender dysphoria"—a change from the *DSM-IV-TR*, which grouped these problems together (Downing, 2015; C. A. Ross, 2015). The *ICD-10*, like the *DSM-5*, also categorizes sex and gender issues as mental disorders. Its sexual dysfunctions are contained in its "behavioural syndromes associated with physiological disturbances and physical factors" section, while "gender identity disorders" and "disorders of sexual preference" (which include paraphilias) are grouped under the broader heading of "disorders of adult personality and behaviour."

SEXUAL DYSFUNCTIONS

The *DSM-5* defines **sexual dysfunctions** as disturbances "in a person's ability to respond sexually or to experience sexual pleasure" (American Psychiatric Association, 2013b, p. 423). The various sexual dysfunction diagnoses aren't mutually exclusive; a person can have more than one. While a good deal of clinical judgment is involved in diagnosing sexual dysfunctions, these disorders all require that the person being diagnosed feels distressed by the symptoms. Sexual dysfunctions can be further divided into *disorders of desire and arousal*, *orgasmic disorders*, and *sexual pain disorders*—all discussed below.

Disorders of Desire and Arousal

DSM-5

Disorders of desire and arousal (see Diagnostic Box 10.1) generally have to do with lack of sexual interest and/or difficulty becoming sexually aroused. The *DSM-5* lists three such disorders, one for women and two for men. **Female sexual interest/arousal disorder** is diagnosed in women who show little or no interest in or arousal from sexual activity. These women rarely or never initiate sex and don't experience pleasure from it when they do engage in it.

Elena
Elena, our case example client who is unresponsive to her husband's sexual advances, might be diagnosed with female sexual interest/arousal disorder.

Similarly, **male hypoactive sexual desire disorder** describes men who show minimal interest in sex. Such men have few sexual fantasies and don't easily become aroused. Finally, **erectile disorder** is diagnosed in men who repeatedly have trouble obtaining or maintaining erections during sexual activity.

Ahmed
Erectile disorder might be diagnosed in case example client Ahmed, who is unable to obtain an erection when engaging in sexual activity with his girlfriend, Miri.

The *DSM-5* points out that the prevalence of female sexual interest/arousal disorder isn't known, but it hypothesizes that age, culture, duration of symptoms, and degree of distress over symptoms all impact prevalence rates. The manual estimates that sexual desire complaints in men increase with age—with roughly 6% of men ages 18–24 and 41% of men ages 66–74 reporting low sexual desire. However, *DSM-5* says that only a small percentage of these men meet criteria for male hypoactive sexual desire disorder because most of them don't experience symptoms for six months or longer. Finally, *DSM-5* reports that the lifetime prevalence of erectile disorder isn't known, but that roughly 13%–21% of men between ages 40 and 80 occasionally experience difficulty obtaining or maintaining erections. The issue often becomes more significant with age.

ICD-10

The *ICD-10* classifies sexual desire and arousal disorders somewhat differently than the *DSM-5*. **Lack or loss of sexual desire** is diagnosed in men and women who have little interest in and rarely initiate sexual activity. However, if sexual activity is undertaken, arousal is usually possible. When arousal is impaired, **failure of genital response** is diagnosed. This diagnosis applies both to cases of erectile dysfunction in men (there is no separate erectile disorder diagnosis in *ICD-10*, though there is an *impotence of organic origin* code) and dryness or an inability to become lubricated in women. **Sexual aversion and lack of sexual enjoyment** is reserved for cases where the idea of sex with a partner is highly unpleasant—yielding fear, anxiety, and avoidance. To some people's dismay, *DSM-5* and *ICD-11* no longer include a sexual aversion diagnosis, both having removed it (Borg, de Jong, & Elgersma, 2014; G. M. Reed et al., 2016).

ICD-11

The *ICD-11* renamed *ICD-10*'s lack or loss of sexual desire diagnosis, calling it **hypoactive sexual desire dysfunction**. Like lack or loss of sexual desire, hypoactive sexual desire dysfunction (a) involves reduced interest in sexual activities, and (b) can be diagnosed in males or females. However, the *ICD-11* diagnosis of **female sexual arousal dysfunction** is exclusive to women. Note that *ICD-11*'s hypoactive sexual desire dysfunction and female sexual arousal dysfunction both fall under one diagnosis in the *DSM-5*: female sexual interest/arousal disorder. By dividing arousal and desire dysfunctions into separate disorders, the *ICD-11*

CHAPTER 10

allows the low desire disorder to also be diagnosed in males (the arousal disorder remains restricted to females). The division also allows the *ICD-11* to distinguish arousal from desire issues, something the *DSM-5* combines. One place where the *ICD-11* is in sync with the *DSM-5* is erectile disorder, a diagnosis that is basically the same in *ICD-11* and *DSM-5*, except that in *ICD-11* it goes by the name *male erectile dysfunction*. Consult Diagnostic Box 10.1 for details on distinguishing *DSM-5*, *ICD-10*, and *ICD-11* sexual dysfunction diagnoses.

Diagnostic Box 10.1 Disorders of Desire and Arousal

Female Sexual Interest/Arousal Disorder
- **DSM-5**: For at least six months, absence or decrease in at least three of these: (1) sexual activity; (2) sexual thoughts/fantasies; (3) initiation of sex or responsiveness to partner initiating sex; (4) sexual responsiveness (in 75%–100% of sexual encounters); (5) responsiveness to sexual cues/signals; (6) arousal (in 75%–100% of sexual encounters).

Based on American Psychiatric Association, 2013b, p. 433
- **ICD-10**: Depending on specific symptoms, diagnose as "lack or loss of sexual desire," "failure of genital response," or "sexual aversion and lack of sexual enjoyment."

Based on World Health Organization, 1992, pp. 150–151
- **ICD-11**: Depending on specific symptoms, diagnose one of these:
  o *Female sexual arousal dysfunction*: Diagnosable only in females and characterized by absent or minimal sexual arousal, even during masturbation.
  o *Hypoactive sexual desire dysfunction*: Diagnosable in males or females and characterized by absent or decreased sexual thoughts, fantasies, or desire for several months or more; the symptoms cause the person distress.

Based on http://apps.who.int/classifications/icd11/browse/l-m/en

Male Hypoactive Sexual Desire Disorder
- **DSM-5**: Absent or decreased sexual thoughts, fantasies, or desire for six months or more; symptoms accompanied by distress.

Based on American Psychiatric Association, 2013b, pp. 440–441
- **ICD-10**: Depending on specific symptoms, diagnose as "lack or loss of sexual desire" or "sexual aversion and lack of sexual enjoyment."

Based on World Health Organization, 1992, pp. 150–151
- **ICD-11**: Called "hypoactive sexual desire dysfunction" and characterized by absent or decreased sexual thoughts, fantasies, or desire for several months or more, in either males or females; the symptoms cause the person distress.

Based on http://apps.who.int/classifications/icd11/browse/l-m/en

Erectile Disorder
- **DSM-5**: At least one of these 75%–100% of the time during sexual activity: (1) getting an erection; (2) keeping an erection; (3) maintaining erectile rigidity.

Based on American Psychiatric Association, 2013b, pp. 426–427
- **ICD-10**: Diagnosed as either "failure of genital response" or "impotence of organic origin."
- **ICD-11**: Called "male erectile disorder" and characterized by inability to obtain or keep an erection long enough for sexual activity despite desire and sufficient stimulation.

Excessive Sexual Drive
- **ICD-10**: Includes "nymphomania" (excessive sexual drive or desire in females) and "satyriasis" (excessive sexual drive or desire in males).

Based on World Health Organization, 1992, p. 152
- No comparable diagnosis in *ICD-11* or *DSM-5* ("hypersexual disorder" was proposed for *DSM-5*, but not included).

Disorders of Orgasm

Female Orgasmic Disorder (DSM-5)

Female orgasmic disorder is a *DSM-5* diagnosis for women who rarely or never experience orgasms. Even when these women do have orgasms, they are often of reduced intensity. *DSM-5* reports that difficulties experiencing orgasm affect anywhere between 10% and 42% of women. They even estimate that 10% of women never experience an orgasm. However, these statistics don't tease out how many women experience distress over the issue, which is required for a diagnosis.

Anorgasmia (ICD-11)/Orgasmic Dysfunction (ICD-10)

The *ICD-11* equivalent of female orgasmic disorder is called **anorgasmia** (sometimes called **orgasmic dysfunction**, its *ICD-10* name). However, a significant difference between *ICD-11*'s anorgasmia and *DSM-5*'s female orgasmic disorder is that anorgasmia can be diagnosed in males, with the *ICD-11* distinguishing between a man's physical ability to ejaculate and his subjective experience of orgasm (G. M. Reed et al., 2016). Although it can be diagnosed in both men and women, anorgasmia is generally thought to be more common in women. See Diagnostic Box 10.2 for further details about female orgasmic disorder and anorgasmia.

Diagnostic Box 10.2 Disorders of Orgasm

Female Orgasmic Disorder
- **DSM-5**: For at least six months, one or more of these symptoms 75%–100% of the time during sexual activity: (1) delayed, infrequent, or no orgasm; (2) reduced intensity of orgasm; a diagnosis exclusive to women.
Based on American Psychiatric Association, 2013b, pp. 429–430
- **ICD-10**: Diagnose as "orgasmic dysfunction"; a diagnosis more common in, but not exclusive to, women.
Based on World Health Organization, 1992, p. 151
- **ICD-11**: Called "anorgasmia" and characterized by orgasms that are absent, infrequent, or of diminished intensity; a diagnosis more common in, but not exclusive to, women.
Based on http://apps.who.int/classifications/icd11/browse/l-m/en

Premature (Early) Ejaculation
- **DSM-5**: For at least six months, 75%–100% of the time male ejaculation occurs within one minute of vaginal penetration and earlier than the person wants.
Based on American Psychiatric Association, 2013b, pp. 443–444
- **ICD-10**: Called "premature ejaculation" and defined as inability to control ejaculation enough for both partners to enjoy sex.
Based on World Health Organization, 1992, p. 151
- **ICD-11**: Called "male early ejaculation" and characterized by ejaculation that occurs within one to three minutes of vaginal penetration.
Based on http://apps.who.int/classifications/icd11/browse/l-m/en

Delayed Ejaculation
- **DSM-5**: Delayed, infrequent, or absent ejaculation at least 75%–100% of the time during sex with a partner.
Based on American Psychiatric Association, 2013b, p. 424)
- **ICD-10**: Not included in ICD-10, but it could be diagnosed as a form of "orgasmic dysfunction."
- **ICD-11**: Called "male delayed ejaculation" and characterized by inability to ejaculate or excessive delay in ejaculation despite sufficient sexual stimulation.
Based on http://apps.who.int/classifications/icd11/browse/l-m/en

Premature (Early) Ejaculation and Delayed Ejaculation in DSM and ICD

There are two male orgasmic disorders (again, see Diagnostic Box 10.2). In the *DSM-5*, **premature (early) ejaculation** is diagnosed in men who ejaculate within one minute of vaginal penetration, while **delayed ejaculation** is diagnosed in men who show a delay in (or inability to) ejaculate despite being adequately stimulated and wanting to ejaculate more quickly. Despite minor name differences ("male early ejaculation" and "male delayed ejaculation"), these two diagnoses are basically similar in the *ICD-11*. The *ICD-10* only includes premature ejaculation; delayed ejaculation would be diagnosed in *ICD-10* using the orgasmic dysfunction diagnosis discussed above. Although the *DSM-5* notes that 20% to 30% of men between ages 18 and 70 express worry about early ejaculation, the "within one minute" criterion means that only 1%–3% of men probably qualify for a premature ejaculation diagnosis. Delayed ejaculation is thought to be much rarer, though differences in how to best define it make its prevalence unclear (American Psychiatric Association, 2013b).

Bolin
Our case example client Bolin might receive a premature (early) ejaculation diagnosis.

CASE EXAMPLES

CHAPTER 10

Disorders Involving Pain During Intercourse

Some people (usually women) experience pain during sex, a problem for which the *ICD-10* includes two diagnoses: vaginismus and dyspareunia. Let's discuss how the *ICD-10* defines these two disorders, then draw comparisons to changes made in the *DSM-5* and *ICD-11*.

ICD-10

Vaginismus is diagnosed exclusively in women in the *ICD-10*. It is characterized by pain in response to spasms in the muscles around the vagina during intercourse. **Dyspareunia**, diagnosed in both men and women in the *ICD-10*, also involves pain during intercourse—sometimes with no identifiable physical basis and other times with evidence of psychological factors (such as past sexual abuse).

DSM-5

How did *DSM-5* change the vaginismus and dyspareunia diagnoses? In light of research suggesting that clinicians can't reliably distinguish vaginismus from dyspareunia (Binik, 2010; IsHak & Tobia, 2013; Lamont, 2011; Sungur & Gündüz, 2014), the *DSM-5* combines them into a single category reserved for women only—**genito-pelvic pain/penetration disorder**—which replaces the separate diagnoses of vaginismus and dyspareunia. Because genito-pelvic pain/penetration disorder is diagnosed exclusively in women, *DSM-5* no longer includes a sexual pain disorder for men (IsHak & Tobia, 2013).

ICD-11

Like the *DSM-5*, the *ICD-11* eliminated vaginismus as a diagnosis. Instead, it includes a new diagnosis called **sexual pain-penetration disorder**. This diagnosis is roughly similar to the *DSM-5*'s genito-pelvic pain/penetration disorder, with one major exception: it excludes dyspareunia, which remains an *ICD-11* diagnosis (unlike in the *DSM-5*, which eliminated it). Although *ICD-11* has retained dyspareunia, the diagnosis is now clearly specified as having physical determinants. Further, it can now only be diagnosed in women—whereas in *ICD-10* it could be diagnosed, at least theoretically, in women or men. This makes the *ICD-11* similar to the *DSM-5* in no longer containing a male sexual pain disorder.

How Common are Sexual Pain Disorders?

Given recent changes in diagnostic terminology, the prevalence of sexual pain disorders remains unclear. The *DSM-5* says it doesn't know the prevalence of genito-pelvic pain/penetration disorder, but estimates that as many as 15% of women experience recurrent pain during sexual intercourse. Diagnostic Box 10.3 contains criteria and guidelines for the various pain disorders in *DSM-5*, *ICD-10*, and *ICD-11*.

Diagnostic Box 10.3 Pain During Intercourse

DSM-5: Genito-Pelvic Pain/Penetration Disorder
- *DSM-5* combined vaginismus and dyspareunia into one diagnosis made exclusively in females.
- Difficulty with: (1) vaginal penetration; (2) pain during vaginal intercourse or penetration; (3) fear of pain before, during, or as a consequence of penetration; or (4) pelvic floor muscles tightening during penetration.
Based on American Psychiatric Association, 2013b, p. 437

ICD-10: Nonorganic Vaginismus and Nonorganic Dyspareunia
- *ICD-10* contains two pain disorder diagnoses; one exclusive to females, the other diagnosable in both males and females.
- *Nonorganic vaginismus*: Muscle spasms around the vagina that lead to blockage of the vaginal opening; prevents penetration during intercourse, or makes it painful.
Based on World Health Organization, 1992, p. 151
- *Nonorganic dyspareunia*: In males or females, pain during sexual intercourse; sometimes caused by a known medical condition, but other times there is no known cause and emotional conflicts may be implicated.
Based on World Health Organization, 1992, pp. 151–152

ICD-11: Sexual Pain-Penetration Disorder and Dyspareunia
- *ICD-11* contains two pain disorder diagnoses, both exclusive to females.
- *Sexual pain-penetration disorder*: Difficulties with (1) vaginal penetration, in some cases due to tightening of pelvic floor muscles, (2) pain during penetration, or (3) fear of pain before, during, or as a consequence of penetration.
Based on http://apps.who.int/classifications/icd11/browse/l-m/en
- *Dyspareunia*: Genital pain before, during, or after vaginal intercourse that is caused by physical determinants other than lack of lubrication.
Based on http://apps.who.int/classifications/icd11/browse/l-m/en

Linnea

Depending on whether there is an identifiable physical cause for her pain during intercourse or not, our case study client Linnea would be diagnosed with either vaginismus or dyspareunia if using ICD-10. *Similarly, she'd be diagnosed with either sexual pain-penetration disorder or dyspareunia if using* ICD-11. *However, no diagnostic distinction would need to be made if using* DSM-5; *Linnea would simply receive the one-and-only sexual pain diagnosis in the* DSM-5, *genito-pelvic pain/penetration disorder.*

CASE EXAMPLES

PARAPHILIAS AND PARAPHILIC DISORDERS

According to the *DSM-5*, a **paraphilia** involves sexual impulses, fantasies, and behaviors directed toward unusual (and sometimes socially taboo) objects and situations. The *DSM-5* defines **paraphilic disorders** as paraphilias that cause either "significant distress and impairment to the individual" or "personal harm, or risk of harm, to others" (American Psychiatric Association, 2013b, pp. 685–686). This means that the *DSM-5* doesn't consider all paraphilias to be mental disorders. Only paraphilias that cause distress to the person experiencing them or harm to others qualify in *DSM-5* as paraphilic disorders (American Psychiatric Association, 2013b; Downing, 2015). This *DSM-5* distinction between paraphilias and paraphilic disorders, also adopted by the *ICD-11*, is new. It isn't part of *ICD-10*. Diagnostic Box 10.4 outlines the numerous paraphilias/paraphilic disorders and maps their varying names and diagnoses across the *DSM-5*, *ICD-10*, and *ICD-11*. As for prevalence, the *DSM-5* says that the prevalence rates it cites for the various paraphilic disorders are merely estimates and that actual prevalence rates aren't known. However, it is believed that the overwhelming majority of people with paraphilias are men (J. V. Becker, Johnson, & Perkins, 2014).

Lou and William

CASE EXAMPLES

The Lou and William case examples can be conceptualized as instances of paraphilias. The difference between them, of course, is that Lou's transvestism doesn't involve criminal behavior, whereas William's pedophilia does. Using DSM-5 and ICD-11 criteria, William definitely has a paraphilic disorder because his use of child pornography harms others (the children exploited to obtain the photos). Whether or not Lou has a paraphilic disorder is less clear. His behavior doesn't hurt anyone; DSM-5 and ICD-11 only consider it a disorder if Lou is distressed by it.

Diagnostic Box 10.4 Paraphilias/Paraphilic Disorders

ICD-10 does not distinguish paraphilias from paraphilic disorders, but *DSM-5* and *ICD-11* do. Additionally, the three manuals don't all include the same paraphilic diagnostic categories. This table clarifies diagnostic equivalents across the three manuals.

Disorder	Definition	DSM-5 Diagnosis	ICD-10 Diagnosis	ICD-11 Diagnosis
Exhibitionism/ exhibitionistic disorder	Sexual fantasies, urges, or behaviors related to exposing one's genitals to unsuspecting people	Exhibitionistic disorder	Exhibitionism	Exhibitionistic disorder
Fetishism/ fetishistic disorder	Sexual fantasies, urges, or behaviors related to nonliving objects or nongenital body parts	Fetishistic disorder	Fetishism	Paraphilic disorder involving solitary behavior or consenting individuals
Fetishistic transvestism/ transvestic disorder	Sexual fantasies, urges, or behaviors related to cross-dressing	Transvestic disorder	Fetishistic transvestism	Paraphilic disorder involving solitary behavior or consenting individuals
Frotteurism/ frotteuristic disorder	Sexual fantasies, urges, or behaviors related to touching or rubbing against a non-consenting person	Frotteuristic disorder	Other disorders of sexual preference	Frotteuristic disorder
Pedophilia/ pedophilic disorder	Sexual fantasies, urges, or behaviors related to sexual involvement with preteen children	Pedophilic disorder	Pedophilia	Pedophilic disorder
Sadomasochism/ sexual sadism disorder or sexual masochism disorder	Sexual fantasies, urges, or behaviors related to the physical or emotional suffering of another person (sexual sadism) or being humiliated or made to suffer (masochism)	Two diagnoses: Sexual sadism disorder Sexual masochism disorder	Sadomasochism	Two diagnoses: Coercive sexual sadism disorder Paraphilic disorder involving solitary behavior or consenting individuals
Voyeurism/ voyeuristic disorder	Sexual fantasies, urges, or behaviors related to observing an unsuspecting person naked	Voyeuristic disorder	Voyeurism	Voyeuristic disorder

- Other paraphilias—including fantasies, urges, or behaviors related to sexual activity involving dead bodies (*necrophilia*), animals (*zoophilia*), feces (*coprophilia*), urine (*urophilia*), enemas (*klismaphilia*), or making obscene phone calls (*scatalogia*)—are diagnosed as "other specified paraphilia" in *DSM-5*, "other disorder of sexual preference" in *ICD-10*, and "paraphilic disorder involving solitary behavior or consenting individuals" in *ICD-11*.
- For paraphilias that may involve criminal behavior (exhibitionism, frotteurism, pedophilia, sexual masochism, and voyeurism), *DSM-5* requires the sexual urges to last six months and must either be acted upon or cause the person distress.
- For all other paraphilias, *DSM-5* requires the sexual urges to last six months and cause the person distress in social, occupational, or other functioning (regardless of whether acted upon).
- *ICD-10* and *-11* contain no duration requirements, but *ICD-11* requires distress for paraphilic disorder diagnoses.

CHAPTER 10

Importantly, many people enjoy paraphilic or other atypical sexual interests and don't necessarily view them as abnormal. The "Try It Yourself" exercise offers you a chance to guess what people said when they were asked if they are turned on by or have ever dabbled in various paraphilias.

TRY IT YOURSELF

How Common Are Paraphilias?

A survey investigated how interested people were in various paraphilias and if they had ever tried them (Joyal & Carpentier, 2017). What percentage of people do you think reported a desire to experience the following paraphilias? What percentage do you think said they had actually tried these paraphilias at least once? Answer key is on page 346.

Paraphilia	% of People with a Desire to Experience It			% of People Who Have Tried It At Least Once		
	% of all People	% of Men	% of Women	% of all People	% of Men	% of Women
Exhibitionism: traditional definition (exposing self to unsuspecting people)						
Exhibitionism: nontraditional definition (sex with a partner in front of others or with risk of being seen)						
Fetishism: arousal from nonsexual object (other than a vibrator)						
Frotteurism: arousal from rubbing against others						
Masochism: desire to suffer, be dominated, or be humiliated						
Pedophilia: arousal by children 13 or younger while an adult						
Sadism: desire to impose suffering or humiliation on others						
Transvestism: arousal from wearing clothes of opposite sex						
Voyeurism: arousal from watching an unsuspecting stranger undress, be nude, or have sex						

GENDER DYSPHORIA/INCONGRUENCE AND RELATED DIAGNOSES

Gender Dysphoria *(DSM-5)*

DSM-5 includes **gender dysphoria** as a diagnosis for people who show incongruence between their experienced or expressed gender and their natal gender (the gender to which they were assigned to at birth) (American Psychiatric Association, 2013b). The *DSM-5* contains one all-inclusive gender dysphoria diagnostic category that has different diagnostic criteria and codes for *gender dysphoria in children* and *gender dysphoria in adolescents and adults*. Importantly, gender dysphoria is not a synonym for transgender (Moleiro & Pinto, 2015). Only those transgender people who experience conflict about their gender should be diagnosed with gender dysphoria.

Although not everyone who experiences gender dysphoria comes to clinical attention, the *DSM-5* nonetheless estimates it to be quite rare. Few natal males (0.005% to 0.014%) and even fewer natal females (0.002% to 0.003%) qualify for a diagnosis. Diagnostic Boxes 10.5 and 10.6 include *DSM-5* criteria.

Gender Incongruence *(ICD-11)*

The *ICD-11* equivalent of gender dysphoria is **gender incongruence**. Like the *DSM-5*, the *ICD-11* includes one version of its gender incongruence diagnosis for children and another for adolescents and adults. *ICD-11* guidelines for these disorders are similar to *DSM-5* criteria. One noteworthy difference is that the *DSM-5* only requires that incongruent gender feelings last for six months before a childhood gender dysphoria diagnosis can be made, while the *ICD-11* requires such feelings to last for two years. The *ICD-11* also specifies that gender incongruence shouldn't be diagnosed in children under five years old. See Diagnostic Boxes 10.5 and 10.6 for *ICD-11* gender incongruence guidelines.

Transsexualism and Gender Identity Disorder of Childhood *(ICD-10)*

The *ICD-10*, having been published in the 1990s, employs older names for gender dysphoria/incongruence (ones also found in previous *DSMs*). *ICD-10* uses the terms **gender identity disorder of childhood** (for children) and **transsexualism** (for adults) instead of gender dysphoria or incongruence. These older terms were discarded by *DSM-5* and *ICD-11*, mainly in an effort to be less pathologizing (Gosselin, 2016a). "Gender dysphoria" and "gender incongruence" are considered less pejorative diagnostic labels than "gender identity disorder" because they don't use the word "disorder." These new diagnostic terms are also preferred to "transsexualism," which emphasizes sex rather than gender. In addition, neither of the *ICD-10* terms (gender identity disorder or transsexualism) highlight gender incongruence as the primary source of emotional distress (Kamens, 2011). *ICD-10* guidelines are included in Diagnostic Boxes 10.5 and 10.6.

Diagnostic Box 10.5 Gender Dysphoria/Incongruence in Adolescents and Adults

DSM-5: Gender Dysphoria in Adolescents and Adults
- Two or more of the following for at least six months: (1) incongruence between experienced gender and assigned sex; (2) wish to eliminate sex characteristics of incongruent gender; (3) wish for the sex characteristics of the other gender; (4) wish to change genders; (5) wish to be treated as the other gender; (6) conviction that one's feelings/responses are consistent with the other gender.
- Causes distress or impaired functioning.
Based on American Psychiatric Association, 2013b, pp. 452–453

ICD-10: Transsexualism
- Wish to live and be accepted as a member of the other sex.
- Usually involves distress about one's physical sex and a wish to use hormonal therapies and surgery to make one's body as similar as possible to the other sex.
Based on World Health Organization, 1992, p. 168

ICD-11: Gender Incongruence of Adolescence or Adulthood
- Incongruence between experienced gender and assigned sex.
- Desire to "transition" to, live as, and be accepted as the other sex.
- Usually involves distress about one's physical sex and a wish to use hormonal therapies, surgery, and other medical services to make one's body as similar as possible to the other sex.
Based on http://apps.who.int/classifications/icd11/browse/l-m/en

Diagnostic Box 10.6 Gender Dysphoria in Children

DSM-5: Gender Dysphoria in Children
- For at least six months, incongruence between experienced gender and assigned sex.
- One or more of the following: (1) wish to be the other gender or assertion that one is the other gender (or some alternative gender); (2) a strong preference for wearing the clothes and/or simulating the appearance of the other gender; (3) takes on cross-gender roles during play; (4) prefers toys, games, and activities stereotypical of the other gender; (5) prefers other-gender playmates; (6) rejects activities traditionally associated with one's birth sex; (7) shows distaste for one's sexual anatomy; (8) wishes for the physical sex characteristics of one's experienced gender.
Based on American Psychiatric Association, 2013b, p. 452

ICD-10: Gender Identity Disorder of Childhood
- Wish to be (or insistence that one is) the opposite sex.
- The behavior, characteristics, and/or style of dress of the assigned sex are rejected.
- Develops prior to adolescence.
Based on World Health Organization, 1992, pp. 168–170

ICD-11: Gender Incongruence
- After age 5 and for at least two years, incongruence between experienced gender and assigned sex.
- Includes wish to be another gender; distaste for one's sexual anatomy or a wish to change sexual anatomy; preference for toys, games, and activities stereotypical of the other gender.
Based on http://apps.who.int/classifications/icd11/browse/l-m/en

CHAPTER 10

Using Diagnosis to Aid in Transitioning

The desire to depathologize gender dysphoria reflects a very important clinical fact. In mainstream practice, clinicians generally don't try to align adult transgender people's experienced gender with their natal gender. Rather, gender dysphoria diagnoses in adults are usually made to help those receiving them obtain coverage for hormone treatments, gender reassignment surgery, and other health-related services that bring their physical bodies into sync with their experienced or expressed gender. That is, these diagnoses are used to aid in the gender transitioning process. By contrast, using gender dysphoria/incongruence diagnoses to help with transitioning isn't as clear when working with minors. Because they lack maturity and legal authority, children and adolescents who qualify for a gender dysphoria diagnosis aren't typically permitted to physically alter their bodies (at least until advanced puberty). Still, a gender dysphoria diagnosis can help alert others to a child or adolescent's gender identity and assist in providing support services.

EVALUATING *DSM* AND *ICD* PERSPECTIVES

Pathologizing Normal Variations in Sexual Behavior?

One of the main criticisms lodged against the *DSM* and *ICD* sexual dysfunction, paraphilia, and gender dysphoria diagnoses is that they pathologize normal variations in human sexual interest, identity, and behavior. *DSM* and *ICD* detractors contend that "that there is little justification for granting a psychiatric manual the authority to define normal sexual function" (Kamens, 2011, p. 41). When it comes to sexual dysfunctions specifically, they note that "conditions such as delayed ejaculation, vaginismus or erectile dysfunction (ED) … may be variations of ordinary sexual responses which represent transient alterations in normal sexual activities" (Sungur & Gunduz, 2013, p. 114). Deciding what constitutes "normal sexual activities" is difficult and not everyone agrees with current diagnostic definitions. How long should it be before a man ejaculates during intercourse? How often should a woman experience orgasm? How interested in sex should men and women be? The ways that *DSM* and *ICD* answer these questions strike some people as arbitrary. Given the lack of clear scientific data, some conclude that diagnostic categories for sexual dysfunctions, paraphilias, and gender dysphoria simply reflect social norms (Goldhill, 2015; C. A. Ross, 2015; Sungur & Gunduz, 2013). In other words, "given the malleability of human sexuality and the creativity of human beings in pursuing and amplifying sexual pleasure, it remains a debated question as to what justifies the classification of a source of sexual pleasure or a type of sexual activity as a mental disorder" (J. C. Wakefield, 2011, p. 195).

Controversies Surrounding Excessive Sexual Drive and Hypersexual Disorder

Excessive sexual drive is a sexual disorder in *ICD-10* that has been removed from *DSM-5*. It is about too much, rather than too little, interest in sex. *ICD-10*'s excessive sexual drive diagnosis includes *nymphomania* (excessive sexual drive in women) and *satyriasis* (excessive sexual drive in men), two terms that really aren't used much anymore. Critics have complained that the excessive sexual drive diagnosis shamed people and used now-dated and disparaging terms such as nymphomania (R. Weiss, 2016). While there is no exact *DSM-5* or *ICD-11* equivalent of excessive sexual drive, there was an effort to add something called **hypersexual disorder** to *DSM-5*. Hypersexual disorder applies to people who show excessive interest in sexual activities. It is akin to "sex addiction," a problem that has increasingly received attention from the media and public in recent years. While there was a formal proposal (defining it as a preoccupation with and excessive engagement in sexual activities, often as a coping mechanism) and some evidence of diagnostic reliability (Kafka, 2013; Reid et al., 2012), hypersexual disorder wasn't added to *DSM-5*. This proposed disorder's exclusion was attributed to concerns about it including too many normal sexual variations, requiring more research, and being too controversial (Halpern, 2011; Kafka, 2014; Sungur & Gündüz, 2014). Some clinicians have strongly advocated that it be added to future diagnostic manuals (Kafka, 2013), but others remain opposed (Halpern, 2011; Reay, Attwood, & Gooder, 2013). The *ICD-11* has sided with those advocating a hypersexual diagnosis by including **compulsive sexual behavior disorder** as an impulse control disorder diagnosable in people who seem unable to control their sexual appetites (World Health Organization, 2018b). Compulsive sexual behavior is mentioned again in Chapter 11 when discussing behavioral addictions.

Should Gender Dysphoria Even Be a Mental Disorder?

As transgender people have become more accepted in many countries, gender dysphoria diagnoses have become increasingly controversial. Some critics assert that gender dysphoria should no longer be considered a mental disorder (Davy, 2015; Drescher, 2015b; Drescher, Cohen-Kettenis, & Winter, 2012; Markman, 2011;

Sennott, 2011). They maintain that gender incongruent feelings among transgender people aren't disordered; they are normal responses to the widespread social disapproval transgender people face by not adopting traditional gender roles. Violating taken-for-granted assumptions about what it means to be male or female—and facing the emotional stress that accompanies doing so—shouldn't be seen as a disorder, say the critics (Daley & Mulé, 2014; Markman, 2011). In their view, diagnoses such as gender dysphoria reflect questionable but commonly held beliefs that sex, gender, and sexuality are fixed biological givens rather than fluid cultural constructs (Daley & Mulé, 2014; Markman, 2011). Further, many people who identify as transgender don't wish to fit into the male–female gender binary that they believe most people (including the authors of *DSM* and *ICD*) take for granted (Wilchens, 1997). Based on these arguments, *DSM* and *ICD* critics argue that gender dysphoria diagnoses should be removed from these manuals.

Importantly, not all transgender activists agree with this view. Some support the inclusion of gender dysphoria in the *DSM* and *ICD*, even if they don't view it as a disorder (Vance et al., 2010). Why? Because—as previously mentioned—in order to obtain coverage for expensive medical interventions such as hormone treatments and sex-reassignment surgery, transgender people (at least in the U.S.) need a corresponding diagnosis (Drescher, 2015b). For this reason alone, many transgender advocates—including the World Professional Association for Transgender Health—support gender dysphoria's inclusion in *DSM* and *ICD* (Daley & Mulé, 2014; Davy, 2015; De Cuypere, Knudson, & Bockting, 2011; Drescher, 2015b; Drescher et al., 2012). Some supporters suggest that, beyond the name change in *DSM-5*, gender dysphoria will be further destigmatized by being reclassified—along with all sexual concerns—as a purely medical (not mental) disorder in *ICD-11* (Drescher et al., 2012; Drescher, Cohen-Kettenis, & Reed, 2016). However, this may not satisfy those who think gender dysphoria shouldn't be considered either a mental or physical disorder. The continued inclusion of gender dysphoria in *DSM* and *ICD* remains controversial.

10.3 HISTORICAL PERSPECTIVES
THE MEDICALIZATION OF SEXUAL DEVIANCE

The Bible's Old Testament not only prohibited homosexuality, but also condemned anal sex, cross-dressing, and masturbation (De Block & Adriaens, 2013; Gordon, 2008). Such religious attitudes clearly influenced how medical doctors later came to define sexual deviance. However, over the last two centuries there has been a shift from religious to medical perspectives. Recall from Chapter 1 how the 18th-century Swiss physician S. A. D. Tissot (1728–1797) declared masturbation (which he called onanism) to be a mental disorder (Bullough, 2002). Tissot wasn't alone in this assessment. Many 18th-century Enlightenment thinkers saw masturbation and other nonreproductive sex acts as posing dangers to mind and body (Bullough, 2002; De Block & Adriaens, 2013). Tissot's identification of masturbation as a disease is an early example of the medicalization of sexual deviance.

The Sexual Instinct

The consensus among many historians is that the medicalization of sexual deviance occurred most fully between the mid-19th and mid-20th centuries (De Block & Adriaens, 2013). It was during this time that doctors began hypothesizing about a **sexual instinct**, "thought of as a reproductive instinct, or an instinct for the propagation of the species" (De Block & Adriaens, 2013, p. 278). Sexual deviations were attributed to degeneration of the sexual instinct. According to 19th-century French physician Paul Moreau de Tours (1844–1908), the sexual instinct could be too weak, too strong, or absent entirely—which potentially explained differences in sexual interest and activity (De Block & Adriaens, 2013). However, the sexual instinct could also be misdirected—as in paraphilias and other "sexual perversions" where the instinct was believed to deviate "from its natural aim" (i.e., reproduction) (De Block & Adriaens, 2013, p. 279).

Krafft-Ebing's *Psychopathia Sexualis*

Medical explanations encouraged a shift away from seeing deviant sexual behavior as sinful or criminal and toward viewing it as having biological and psychological origins. This culminated in the publication of Austrian-German psychiatrist Richard von Krafft-Ebing's (1840–1902) influential book *Psychopathia Sexualis*. In this book, which went through multiple editions, Krafft-Ebing (1892) used vivid case studies to illustrate what he defined as sexual pathology. Krafft-Ebing identified four basic kinds of sexual deviance: *anaesthesia* (lack of sexual desire), *hyperaesthesia* (excessive sexual desire), *paradoxia* (sexual excitement during an inappropriate time of life, such as childhood or old age), and *paraesthesia* (desire directed at nonreproductive sexual ends)

CHAPTER 10

(De Block & Adriaens, 2013; Krafft-Ebing, 1892; "Richard Freiherr von Krafft-Ebing," 2008). He introduced terms such as *sadism* and *masochism* (revisit Diagnostic Box 10.4), which are still used in *DSM* and *ICD* (De Block & Adriaens, 2013; Krafft-Ebing, 1892; Oosterhuis, 2012). He was also among the first to study transsexualism (De Block & Adriaens, 2013; Krafft-Ebing, 1892; Oosterhuis, 2012).

Krafft-Ebing's work greatly influenced how doctors thought about sexual deviance. His presentation of homosexuality and masturbation as biological and psychological dysfunctions, rather than sins (Oosterhuis, 2012), shifted understandings of sexual deviance in a medical direction (De Block & Adriaens, 2013)—albeit one that continued the religious tradition of viewing such acts negatively. This is evidenced in the works of physicians such as Havelock Ellis (1859–1939) and Magnus Hirschfeld (1868–1935), who wrote extensively about sexual deviance in Britain and Germany, respectively, during the early 20th century. Like Krafft-Ebing, Ellis and Hirschfeld argued that homosexuality and masturbation are best viewed as medical entities, not sinful vices (H. Ellis, 1901; M. Hirschfeld, 1948). Despite Krafft-Ebing's medical orientation, by the end of his career he softened his stance on the abnormality of homosexuality, acknowledging "that his earlier views on the immoral and pathological nature of homosexuality had been one-sided and that there was truth in the point of view of many of his homosexual correspondents who asked for sympathy and compassion" (Oosterhuis, 2012, p. 137). Still, it would be another 70 years before homosexuality was officially declassified as a mental disorder. See the "In Depth" feature for a detailed account of homosexuality's controversial removal from the *DSM*.

IN DEPTH

Voting Homosexuality Out of the *DSM*

Homosexuality was listed as a mental disorder in *DSM-I* (1952) and *DSM-II* (1968). During this time, it was common for clinicians to engage in **conversion therapy** (also known as *reparative therapy*), which involved trying to turn homosexuals into heterosexuals (Socarides, 1978/1989). However, as social attitudes about homosexuality became more tolerant during the 1960s and 1970s, many people began questioning whether homosexuality should be considered a disorder. During the revision process for *DSM-III* in the early 1970s, those who wanted homosexuality declassified as a mental disorder began protesting at American Psychiatric Association (APA) conventions (Drescher, 2015a; Kirk & Kutchins, 1992). This produced one of the most controversial events in *DSM* history: the supposed "voting out" of homosexuality from the *DSM*.

What exactly happened? Many members of the *DSM-III* revision task force—including its leader, psychiatrist Robert Spitzer, concluded that if homosexuality didn't cause a person subjective distress, it made no sense to consider it a mental disorder. Various APA committees concurred with Spitzer's determination and in December 1973 the APA's Board of Trustees voted to remove homosexuality from the *DSM* (Drescher, 2015a; Kirk & Kutchins, 1992). Psychiatrists opposing this decision petitioned to have the entire membership of the APA vote on whether or not they agreed with the Board of Trustees. Half of the APA's 20,000 members voted, with 58% of them supporting the Board (Drescher, 2015a). Thus, homosexuality was officially removed from the *DSM*.

Critics often point to this vote as evidence that deciding what is a mental disorder is based on politics, not science (Kirk & Kutchins, 1992). After all, would we ever consider voting illnesses like diabetes or cancer out of existence? If a disorder is real, these critics claim, then voting cannot change that fact. However, others counter that this is an unfair assessment (Drescher, 2015a; Zachar & Kendler, 2012). They note that in all scientific endeavors, human decisions about how to define and classify certain things must be made. For instance, as astronomers' definition of what constitutes a planet changed, they ultimately resorted to voting on Pluto's status as a planet (and, to some people's dismay, decided it isn't one) (Zachar & Kendler, 2012). Defenders of the *DSM* say the vote on homosexuality was no different from the vote on Pluto; science often involves social consensus—and the evolving consensus among mental health professions was that homosexuals not distressed about their sexuality shouldn't be deemed ill.

But the issue didn't end there. The *DSM-III* (1980) removed homosexuality, but included a new diagnosis called **ego-dystonic homosexuality** for people who were gay and psychologically upset about it (Drescher, 2015a). Critics saw this as backsliding and a way to pacify those who wished to continue diagnosing and treating homosexuality. Why, argued these critics, was there an ego-dystonic homosexuality category but not an ego-dystonic heterosexuality diagnosis? Couldn't one be straight and conflicted about it, too? Based on these criticisms, ego-dystonic homosexuality wasn't included in *DSM-III-R* (1987), *DSM-IV* (1994), or *DSM-IV-TR* (2000). However, these manuals did note that distress over sexual orientation could continue to be diagnosed using the sexual disorder not otherwise specified (SDNOS) category (Drescher, 2015a). Critics continued to object. They argued that persistent distress about being gay or lesbian is better attributed to social disapproval than mental disorder. At last, with the publication of *DSM-5* in 2013, homosexuality was—for the first time—wholly removed from the manual (Drescher, 2015a).

Most of the controversy about homosexuality as a mental disorder has focused on the *DSM*. Yet it's worth noting that the *ICD* has generally followed in the *DSM*'s footsteps. Homosexuality was listed as a mental disorder from *ICD-6* (1948) through *ICD-9* (1975) (Drescher, 2015a). *ICD-10* echoed the *DSM-III*'s ego-dystonic homosexuality by including a category called *ego-dystonic sexual orientation*, but the *ICD-11*—like the *DSM-5*—excludes homosexuality entirely (Drescher, 2015a). Reflecting the *DSM* and *ICD* shifts away from classifying homosexuality as a disorder, professional organizations in many countries today consider conversion therapy ineffective and unethical (American Psychiatric Association, 2000; Anton, 2010; British Psychological Society, 2014, 2017; Canadian Psychological Association, n.d.; "Memorandum of understanding on conversion therapy in the UK," 2015; Veltman & Chaimowitz, 2014). Some countries—notably Malta and Taiwan—have even moved to ban it entirely (Lambert, 2017; L. Stack, 2016). However, the repudiation of homosexuality as mental disorder is not universal. In 2016, the Indonesian Psychiatrists Association (PDSKJI), despite objections from other professional organizations inside and outside of Indonesia (Lamb, 2017; S. Levin, 2016), identified homosexuality as a mental disorder and indicated that it can be cured with proper treatment (Yosephine, 2016). Thus, in certain parts of the world homosexuality remains pathologized.

CRITICAL THINKING QUESTIONS

1. What do you think of the argument that removing homosexuality from the *DSM* was influenced more by politics than science? Explain your answer.

2. When it comes to deciding whether something is a disorder, what is the exact relationship between science and politics? Can political considerations ever be taken out of the equation?

3. Most mental health professional organizations prohibit the use of conversion therapy. What would you, as a psychotherapist, say to a client who came to see you seeking conversion therapy?

4. What do you make of the fact that while many countries have been moving away from seeing homosexuality as a disorder and conversion therapy as an ethical treatment, Indonesia recently declared homosexuality a treatable mental disorder?

CHANGING ATTITUDES
Asking People About Their Sex Lives

The Kinsey Reports

The American biologist Alfred Kinsey (1894–1956) is often identified as the first **sexologist** (a scientist who studies human sexual behavior). Kinsey did a great deal to shed light on human sexual activity and to normalize sexual acts that earlier researchers had deemed atypical and/or pathological. How? By asking people about their sex lives, something no scientist before him had done to any great extent. Kinsey and his colleagues famously interviewed Americans about their sex lives and reported their results in two volumes that became known as the Kinsey Reports (Kinsey, Pomeroy, & Martin, 1948; Kinsey, Pomeroy, Martin, & Gebhard, 1953).

One of the reasons why the Kinsey Reports garnered such attention is that their findings contradicted many long-held assumptions. For instance, it was common in Kinsey's day to believe women weren't interested in and didn't enjoy sex—but Kinsey's research found this to be incorrect (Kinsey et al., 1953). His research also found that masturbation, which had usually been considered a sign of pathology up to that time (Bullough, 2002), was extremely common—as was oral sex. Finally, Kinsey's research led him to challenge the predominant view of homosexuality and heterosexuality as mutually exclusive categories (Kinsey, 1941; Kinsey et al., 1948). On the contrary, he found that many people's diverse sexual experiences made it difficult to group them solely as homosexuals or heterosexuals. Consequently, Kinsey discouraged either/or identifications of sexual orientation and instead advocated rating people using a 6-point homosexuality–heterosexuality scale (Kinsey et al., 1948; Kinsey et al., 1953). His argument against rigidly relying on homosexual and heterosexual categories calls to mind current debates between those advocating dimensional versus categorical approaches to diagnosis. Kinsey memorably (and forcefully) made his point:

> It is a fundamental taxonomy that nature rarely deals with discrete categories. Only the human mind invents categories and tries to force facts into separated pigeon-holes. The living world is a continuum in each and every one of its aspects. The sooner we learn this concerning human sexual behavior the sooner we shall reach a sound understanding of the realities of sex. (Kinsey et al., 1948, p. 639)

Kinsey's work was criticized for not using samples that adequately represented the population, which called into question the generalizability of his results (Clausen, 1954; W. G. Cochran, Mosteller, & Tukey, 1953;

CHAPTER 10

Drucker, 2012). Nonetheless, the Kinsey Reports are viewed as historically important not only because they used research to identify common sexual behaviors, but also because they showed that human sexual behavior was much more diverse and expansive than people had previously believed. In light of his research, Kinsey grew skeptical of the idea that some forms of sex were disordered or unnatural, allegedly once remarking that "the only unnatural sex act is that which one cannot perform" (H. L. Call, 1963, p. 12). The Kinsey Reports became bestsellers and greatly influenced changing social and medical attitudes about sex and sexuality (Drucker, 2012).

The Hite and Janus Reports

Later researchers followed in Kinsey's footsteps. In the 1970s and early 1980s, Shere Hite (b. 1942) published reports on the sexual behavior of American women and men (Hite, 1976, 1981). Surveying more than 1,800 women, Hite found that a majority of them didn't typically experience orgasm during vaginal intercourse, even though 95% of them did when masturbating. She therefore questioned whether lack of female orgasm during sex was a purely physical sexual dysfunction. In the 1990s, psychologist Samuel Janus (1930–2011) and gynecologist Cynthia Janus published the Janus Report, which used survey data to report on the sex lives of more than 2,600 Americans (Janus & Janus, 1993). Among the Janus Report's findings: people over age 65 were highly interested in sex, 17% of women and 22% of men reported a homosexual experience, and 23% of women and 11% of men indicated being sexually abused as children. As with Kinsey, both the Hite and Janus Reports were criticized for their non-representative samples, not using inferential statistics, and making sweeping generalizations (C. Davis, 1993; Irvine, 2005). Despite these limitations, these reports were—like Kinsey's before them—bestsellers.

Cynthia and Samuel Janus, authors of the Janus Report.
Source: Yvonne Hemsey/Getty Images

The Sexual Response Cycle

In 1966, gynecologist William H. Masters (1915–2001) and sexologist Virginia E. Johnson (1925–2013) published their famous work, *Human Sexual Response*. In it, they outlined a four-phase sexual response cycle for both men and women. This model has been highly influential in defining, conceptualizing, and treating the sexual dysfunctions found in *DSM* and *ICD*. Masters and Johnson's (1966) original four phases of the sexual response cycle are as follows:

1. *Excitement/arousal*: During this phase, sensual stimuli such as kissing, touching, and erotic imagery trigger arousal and excitement; *vasocongestion* (swelling of body tissue due to vascular blood flow) often occurs.

2. *Plateau*: Sexual pleasure peaks during this stage; heart rate and respiration increase.

3. *Orgasm*: In this phase, pelvic muscles around the sexual organs involuntarily contract; in men, ejaculation usually occurs, while in women the vagina's outer walls contract.

4. *Resolution*: After orgasm, blood pressure drops and the body relaxes; men often experience a *refractory period* during which they are incapable of having another orgasm.

Despite its historical importance and continuing influence, Masters and Johnson's sexual response cycle has faced its fair share of criticism. Some have argued that the plateau phase is misleading because the peak of sexual pleasure occurs during the orgasm phase, not the plateau phase. To address this, Helen Singer Kaplan (1929–1995) revised the sexual response cycle. She absorbed the plateau phase into the excitement phase and added a *desire* phase that could account for psychological factors such as sexual interests, fantasies, thoughts, and feelings (or the lack thereof). Thus, Kaplan's (1995) revised sexual response cycle consists of *desire*, *arousal/excitement*, *orgasm*, and *resolution* phases.

Some have complained that Masters and Johnson focused too much on the physical components of sex while overlooking psychological aspects (R. J. Levin, 2008). Others contend that many people don't experience the phases in such linear order and have proposed more circular models (Basson, 2001; ter Kuile, Both, & van Lankveld, 2010). Finally, it's been argued that the sexual response cycle unwisely assumes that sexual response is the same for everyone, regardless of gender, social class, and individual differences (Tiefer, 1991). Critiques and revisions notwithstanding, the sexual response cycle continues to influence modern conceptions of sexual dysfunction.

10.4 BIOLOGICAL PERSPECTIVES
BRAIN CHEMISTRY (AND HORMONAL) PERSPECTIVES
Sexual Dysfunctions

Hormones vs. Neurotransmitters

When discussing sexual problems, brain chemistry perspectives must be supplemented by hormonal perspectives because both hormones and neurotransmitters have been implicated in sexual dysfunctions. Recall from Chapter 5 that hormones are chemical messengers of the endocrine system, a collection of glands that are important in regulating things like sexual functioning, sleep, mood, and metabolism. Hormones are produced by endocrine glands and secreted directly into the bloodstream. This contrasts with neurotransmitters, which are part of the nervous system. As first described in Chapter 2, neurotransmitters are chemical messengers produced by neurons in the brain that are critical to neural communication. Many hormones are chemically distinct from neurotransmitters, although the neurotransmitters norepinephrine and dopamine also function as endocrine system hormones; norepinephrine in the endocrine system is usually called **noradrenaline**.

Hormones and Sexual Dysfunction

Testosterone and **estrogen**, the primary male and female sex hormones, are often implicated in sexual dysfunction (Meana, 2012; Rowland, 2012). Men and women have both these sex hormones, with men higher in testosterone and women higher in estrogen. Testosterone is an **androgen**, a type of hormone responsible for the development of male characteristics. For men, low levels of testosterone are correlated with low sexual interest and difficulty with erections (Corona, Isidori, Aversa, Burnett, & Maggi, 2016). Testosterone's role in female sexual dysfunction is less clear (C. A. Graham, 2010). Testosterone is sometimes administered to men and women experiencing low sexual interest or sexual performance difficulties (Corona et al., 2016; Rowland, 2012).

Estrogen is also implicated in sexual dysfunction. Research suggests that low estrogen levels are related to reduced sexual desire in women—especially after **menopause**, the time in life when a woman's menstrual cycle ends (usually in her 40s or 50s) and estrogen levels decrease (Wylie & Malik, 2009). Estrogen, androgens, and **progestin** (a synthetic hormone that has effects similar to **progesterone**, an endogenous sex hormone important in menstruation and pregnancy) are all sometimes prescribed to women experiencing low sexual desire (Hertlein & Weeks, 2009). These drugs are used with both pre- and postmenopausal women. With the latter they are known as **hormone replacement therapy (HRT)** because the drugs replace depleted estrogen levels suspected of decreasing sexual interest and performance (Wylie & Malik, 2009). HRT was quite popular for a while, but research showing it can increase the risks of breast cancer, stroke, and heart disease has changed many people's attitudes about it (H. D. Nelson, Humphrey, Nygren, Teutsch, & Allan, 2002).

CHAPTER 10

Linnea
The pain during intercourse that our 48-year old case study client Linnea experiences may be due to low estrogen levels that cause poor lubrication during sex. Linnea has recently gone through menopause, and her lubrication issue may be tied to lower levels of female sex hormones such as estrogen. If we can address her lubrication problem with hormone replacement therapy, Linnea's sexual interest may return. However, Linnea should be warned about the risks of HRT so she can make an informed choice about it.

CASE EXAMPLES

Neurotransmitter and Non-Neurotransmitter-Focused Drug Treatments

Dopamine, norepinephrine, and serotonin all play a role in sexual functioning (Clayton, Alkis, Parikh, & Votta, 2016; Pfaus, 2009). Dopamine—the "pleasure" neurotransmitter—is the most strongly associated with sexual behavior. However, norepinephrine is important too, especially in sexual arousal (Pfaus, 2009). The norepinephrine-dopamine reuptake inhibitor (NDRI) *bupropion* (which, as noted in Chapter 9, is an antidepressant that makes more norepinephrine and dopamine available in the brain) is sometimes used to increase sexual desire (Clayton et al., 2016; Wylie & Malik, 2009).

Unlike dopamine and norepinephrine, serotonin typically reduces sexual interest, arousal, and orgasm (Clayton et al., 2016; La Torre, Giupponi, Duffy, & Conca, 2013; Uphouse, 2014). This may explain why SSRIs, which make more serotonin available, often interfere with sexual desire and performance. The drug **flibanserin** (marketed under the trade name Addyi) aims to increase female sexual desire by reducing serotonin while enhancing dopamine and norepinephrine (Armitage, 2015; Stahl, Sommer, & Allers, 2011). It was approved for use in the U.S. in 2015 (Joffe et al., 2016). Despite its approval, some researchers have questioned the drug's effectiveness, arguing that existing studies show only small improvements in sexual satisfaction and performance while being accompanied by side effects like dizziness, sleepiness, nausea, and fatigue (Jaspers et al., 2016; Woloshin & Schwartz, 2016). Concerns about efficacy and side effects may be why flibanserin has yet to be approved in the U.K., the rest of Europe, and Australia (L. Clark, 2015).

Elena

If she was seeking treatment in the U.S., our case study client Elena, who experiences low sexual desire and difficulty becoming aroused, could be prescribed flibanserin.

Even though it is often called the "female Viagra" (Armitage, 2015), flibanserin is quite different from **sildenafil** (the chemical name of the erectile dysfunction drug marketed as Viagra) (Hertlein & Weeks, 2009). Whereas flibanserin alters brain neurochemistry to enhance a woman's psychological experience of sexual desire, sildenafil works directly on sex organs. Sildenafil and other similar drugs are **phosphodiesterase type-5 inhibitors.** They reduce levels of a chemical enzyme called *phosphodiesterase type-5 (PDE5)*. PDE5 breaks down *cyclic guanosine monophosphate (cGMP)*, a chemical that increases blood flow to the sex organs. Thus, inhibiting phosphodiesterase type-5 means more cGMP and a greater chance of sexual arousal. With men (to whom they are mainly given), PDE5 inhibitors increase blood flow to the penis and physically cause erections (Ghofrani, Osterloh, & Grimminger, 2006).

Ahmed

Our male case study patient Ahmed who—like Elena—suffers from difficulty becoming aroused, might be given sildenafil.

Note that Elena's flibanserin doesn't stimulate her sex organs. Rather, it increases arousal more circuitously by altering neurotransmitter levels. By contrast, Ahmed's sildenafil doesn't target brain neurochemistry. Instead, it directly causes erections by increasing blood flow to the penis. Does this mean female sexual arousal is more rooted in mood and brain neurochemistry, while male arousal is a purely mechanical issue having to do with sex organ malfunction? This is a controversial question to which we don't have a clear answer.

Drug-Induced Sexual Dysfunctions

Sexual dysfunction is often a side effect of medications prescribed for other presenting problems. Antidepressants, antipsychotics, mood stabilizers, and anxiolytics are all suspected of inducing sexual dysfunction (Clayton et al., 2016; La Torre, Conca, et al., 2013; La Torre, Giupponi, et al., 2013; La Torre et al., 2014). There is also modest research evidence that anxiolytics and mood stabilizers produce sexual dysfunction, but the research on this is limited and has been criticized as methodologically unsound (La Torre et al., 2014). The evidence for antipsychotics and antidepressants is stronger (Bella & Shamloul, 2013). Antidepressants (SSRIs, SNRIs, tricyclics, and MAOIs) are suspected of causing sexual dysfunction by increasing serotonin, while antipsychotics are believed to induce sexual dysfunction by reducing dopamine (Bella & Shamloul, 2013; Bijlsma et al., 2014; Clayton et al., 2016; Keks, Hope, & Culhane, 2014; La Torre, Conca, et al., 2013; La Torre, Giupponi, et al., 2013; Segraves & Balon, 2014). Unfortunately, due to methodological limitations of the existing research, the exact mechanisms behind antipsychotic and antidepressant-induced sexual dysfunction remain unclear (Bella & Shamloul, 2013; La Torre, Conca, et al., 2013; La Torre, Giupponi, et al., 2013).

Drugs to treat seizures (anticonvulsants) and high blood pressure (antihypertensives) can also induce sexual dysfunction (La Torre et al., 2014; Meana, 2012). For instance, beta blockers (high blood pressure drugs discussed in Chapter 6 because they are also prescribed for people experiencing anxiety) are suspected of causing erectile dysfunction (Manolis & Doumas, 2012). Older blood pressure medications are generally viewed as the worst culprits, with newer ones viewed as neutral or even as improving sexual performance (La Torre, Giupponi, Duffy, Conca, & Catanzariti, 2015; Manolis & Doumas, 2012). Nonetheless, the overall consensus seems to be that beta blockers are often associated with sexual dysfunction (La Torre et al., 2015; Manolis & Doumas, 2012).

Paraphilias

Paraphilias are notoriously difficult to eliminate and are therefore often considered to be lifetime disorders (Assumpção, Garcia, Garcia, Bradford, & Thibaut, 2014). To manage paraphilias, different types of drugs are prescribed, usually in combination with psychotherapy. Two of the more commonly used drugs are SSRIs and antiandrogens (Assumpção et al., 2014; J. V. Becker et al., 2014; J. M. Bradford & Fedoroff, 2009; Gosselin, 2016b). These drug treatments, discussed next, are mainly used with those who have committed sex offenses against others, regardless of whether they have been diagnosed with a paraphilic disorder.

SSRIs

SSRIs are hypothesized to decrease sexual interest in paraphilic activity by raising levels of serotonin (Assumpção et al., 2014; Guay, 2009). While SSRIs haven't shown consistent effectiveness (Gosselin, 2016b), there is some evidence that they work with paraphilias that are considered to be less severe—such as exhibitionism, compulsive masturbation, and pedophilia without acting out (Assumpção et al., 2014; Thibaut, 2012). Research on SSRIs for paraphilias hasn't progressed much in recent years, has numerous methodological flaws, and has produced few double-blind controlled studies (in which both patients and doctors in the study are unaware of whether patients are receiving SSRIs or placebos) (Assumpção et al., 2014; J. V. Becker et al., 2014; Thibaut, 2012). Therefore, its conclusions should be taken cautiously.

Antiandrogens

Antiandrogens are drugs that reduce levels of male sex hormones such as testosterone, thereby decreasing sexual interest (Thibaut, 2012). Different antiandrogens work in chemically different ways, but all reduce androgen levels. Prescribing antiandrogens to sex offenders is controversially referred to as **chemical castration** because it brings testosterone to levels as low as those found in people who have been surgically castrated (J. V. Becker et al., 2014; K. Jordan, Fromberger, Stolpmann, & Müller, 2011). Chemical castration is a less severe alternative to **surgical castration**, which involves removing a man's testicles (*orchiectomy*) or a woman's ovaries (*oophorectomy*) (K. Harrison, 2007). Chemical castration is used around the world, but the legality and ethics of chemically castrating sex offenders against their will is extremely contentious and fiercely debated (J. V. Becker et al., 2014; Berlin 1997; Grubin & Beech, 2010; K. Harrison, 2007; Stinneford, 2006). Moreover, the effectiveness of antiandrogens in reducing paraphilias remains uncertain because "few placebo-controlled double-blind studies have been performed with inconsistent results concerning treatment effects" (K. Jordan et al., 2011, p. 3020).

Gender Dysphoria/Incongruence

Prenatal Sex Hormones

Some researchers hypothesize that gender dysphoria originates in exposure to atypical levels of prenatal sex hormones such as testosterone (Gosselin, 2016a). Androgen in the womb positively correlates with finger length, especially comparative finger length between the index and ring fingers (the second and fourth digits) (Gosselin, 2016a). Consequently, measuring index to ring finger ratios offers an easy (if somewhat crude and imprecise) way to infer androgen levels. Interestingly, several (but not all) studies have found that male-to-female transsexuals' index to ring finger ratios are more similar to natal females' than non-transsexual males' (Gosselin, 2016a; Kraemer et al., 2009; H. J. Schneider, Pickel, & Stalla, 2006; Veale, Clarke, & Lomax, 2010). There is some (but less) evidence for a reverse pattern in female-to-male transsexuals (Wallien, Zucker, Steensma, & Cohen-Kettenis, 2008). While you may be tempted to start measuring the length of your fingers, remember that this evidence is correlational. Judgments about masculinity, femininity, and gender identity based on finger length ratios should be made with extreme caution.

Cross-Sex Hormonal Treatment and Sex Reassignment Surgery

Although gender dysphoria treatments (as well as attitudes toward them) vary by country, transgender individuals who are transitioning from male to female or female to male often seek **cross-sex hormonal treatment** (i.e., *hormone therapy*) that alters their physical bodies to better match their gender identities. Androgens, estrogens, and antiandrogens are prescribed (A. D. Fisher et al., 2014; Gosselin, 2016a; Manieri et al., 2014). Hormone therapy can be done with or without **sex reassignment surgery** (also called *gender reassignment surgery* and *gender affirmation surgery*), in which a person's physical body is surgically altered (often through multiple operations) to match gender identity. For men, this means removing the penis and crafting a vagina, breasts, clitoris and labia (Selvaggi & Bellringer, 2011). For women, the womb and breasts are removed and a penis and scrotum are crafted (usually using material from the clitoris and labia to do so) (Selvaggi & Bellringer, 2011). After sex reassignment surgery, patients continue to take hormones.

BRAIN STRUCTURE AND FUNCTION (AND ANATOMICAL) PERSPECTIVES
Sexual Dysfunctions

Brain scan research has been used to identify various brain regions associated with sexual desire, arousal, and performance. Among the brain structures implicated are the orbitofrontal cortex (believed to play a role in assessing the sexual relevance of faces), parietal cortex (significant in the cognitive elements of sexual desire),

CHAPTER 10

amygdala (tied to arousal and pleasurable emotions), hippocampus (important in memory, including memory of past sexual experiences), thalamus (important in erections), and hypothalamus (associated with sexual arousal) (Baird, Wilson, Bladin, Saling, & Reutens, 2007; Fonteille & Stoléru, 2011; Georgiadis, 2011; Georgiadis & Kringelbach, 2012; Pfaus, 2009; Stoléru, Fonteille, Cornélis, Joyal, & Moulier, 2012; Stoléru & Mouras, 2007). Brain scan research on sexual function is in its infancy and poses several difficulties, including: (a) it is hard to obtain ethics approval for studies in which participants engage in sexual activity; (b) measuring blood flow in people's brains during sexual activity is challenging; (c) most of the research has used young and healthy male participants, making generalizability to females and older individuals problematic; and (d) the research is correlational, leading one investigator to warn that "changes in a brain region should not be interpreted such that this or that region is solely responsible for a certain behavior or phase of the sexual pleasure cycle" (Georgiadis & Kringelbach, 2012, p. 54).

Anatomically, erectile dysfunction is sometimes conceptualized as a problem with tumescence—increased blood flow leading to swelling of the sexual organs. When penile tumescence is poor, men have difficulty getting erections. This is why they are often prescribed sildenafil (discussed earlier). When sildenafil doesn't work, doctors sometimes treat erection problems with intracavernous injection therapy, which involves injecting chemicals that increase blood flow into the penis (Atwood, 2015). Obviously, men generally find getting injections in their penises unpleasant. Further, some critics worry that medical doctors sometimes prescribe these injections even when erectile problems appear to be strictly psychological (Atwood, 2015).

Paraphilias

The neurobiology behind paraphilias is relatively unknown. Research has found that lesions in the temporal and frontal lobes can lead to disinhibited sexual behavior (Bradford & Fedoroff, 2009; Bradford, 2001; Gosselin, 2016b). This is an intriguing finding given that people with paraphilias have irresistible sexual urges. Unfortunately, frontal and temporal lobe damage correlates with disinhibition generally and therefore isn't specific to sexual disinhibition (Bradford & Fedoroff, 2009; Gosselin, 2016b).

Gender Dysphoria/Incongruence

There isn't much research on brain structures and gender dysphoria. There is evidence that the white matter microstructure of male-to-female transsexuals attracted to men may be more similar to that of natal females. Likewise, the white matter microstructure of female to male transsexuals attracted to women may be more similar to that of natal males (Kreukels & Guillamon, 2016). Research has also explored differences in gray matter and cortical thickness between transsexuals and cissexuals (E. S. Smith, Junger, Derntl, & Habel, 2015). In evaluating such research, one review noted that "many of the results are inconsistent or still need to be replicated and the sample sizes are often extremely small" (E. S. Smith et al., 2015, p. 262). Further, the findings only identify brain differences—and just because something is different doesn't make it pathological.

GENETIC AND EVOLUTIONARY PERSPECTIVES
Sexual Dysfunction

Genes

Female sexual dysfunctions appear to be influenced by genes. Various candidate genes—including genes related to dopamine, serotonin, estrogen, and testosterone—have been identified as potentially relevant to sexual dysfunction (Burri, Cherkas, & Spector, 2009). When it comes to inheritance of sexual dysfunctions, one study estimated heritability at 44% (Burri, Rahman, & Spector, 2011). This implies that genes are important, but aren't the whole story. If heritability is 44%, then more than half the variability in female sexual complaints is due to the environment (Burri, 2013; Burri et al., 2009; Burri, Rahman, et al., 2011; Burri, Spector, & Rahman, 2013). In fact, once genes are controlled for, environmental factors—particularly relationship satisfaction—are the best predictors of female problems with arousal, desire, and lubrication (Burri et al., 2013).

Evolution

Evolutionary psychologists hypothesize that premature ejaculation and erectile dysfunction in men are due to evolution not keeping up with societal changes (Apostolou, 2015). They argue that in ancestral times, premature ejaculation wasn't a big deal because the women with whom men were having sex were often in arranged marriages or slaves and had little say in choosing their sex partners; thus, even if a woman was dissatisfied with her partner's premature ejaculation, this wouldn't have impaired his ability to impregnate her and pass on his genes (Apostolou, 2015). As for erectile dysfunction, evolutionary psychologists hypothesize that women in modern societies have a lot more choice in picking their mates than preindustrial women did. This gives men less say in selecting female partners, which theoretically predisposes them to greater sexual performance anxiety—something evolution hasn't had time to weed out (Apostolou, 2015). These explanations are interesting, but (as with most evolutionary accounts) are purely speculative.

Paraphilias

There isn't much research on the genetics of paraphilias. One study found that men who have an extra male (Y) chromosome (*XYY syndrome*) are at higher risk for unconventional sexual behaviors and fantasies compared to both men who have an extra female (X) chromosome (*Klinefelter syndrome*) and men with no extra sex chromosomes (Schiavi, Theilgaard, Owen, & White, 1988). More broadly, people with extra sex chromosomes appear to be at higher risk for cognitive and behavioral difficulties in general—although the evidence base for this conclusion remains small (Leggett, Jacobs, Nation, Scerif, & Bishop, 2010).

Pedophilia has received more genetic research attention than other paraphilias. Family studies suggest that pedophilia and sex offending run in families (Gaffney, Lurie, & Berlin, 1984; Labelle, Bourget, Bradford, Alda, & Tessier, 2012; Långström, Babchishin, Fazel, Lichtenstein, & Frisell, 2015). However, teasing apart genetic from environmental influences in family studies can be difficult. There has been only one twin study of pedophilia and it yielded a very low heritability estimate of just 14.6% for pedophilic interest (Alanko, Salo, Mokros, & Santtila, 2013; Tenbergen et al., 2015). This implies that even if genes and environment interact in producing pedophilia, environment may be the greater influence. Nonetheless, a recent candidate gene study on genes linked to androgen, estrogen, and other sex-related hormones found that variations on these genes correlated with pedophilic sexual interest (Alanko, Gunst, Mokros, & Santtila, 2016).

Gender Dysphoria/Incongruence

Research on gender-related traits has yielded varied heritability estimates, anywhere from 0.11 to 0.77, with most estimates somewhere in the middle of this range (Burri, Cherkas, Spector, & Rahman, 2011; Coolidge, Thede, & Young, 2002; Klink & Den Heijer, 2014; Knafo, Iervolino, & Plomin, 2005; van Beijsterveldt, Hudziak, & Boomsma, 2006). Unfortunately, this research only gives us a sense of the heritability of gender-related traits, not gender dysphoria. However, one recent twin study reported a concordance rate of 39.1% for female identical twins diagnosed with gender identity disorder, in contrast to a 0% concordance for non-identical twins (Heylens et al., 2012). While this is a single study with a small sample size, it does suggest that gender dysphoria is influenced by genes.

When it comes to candidate genes and gender dysphoria, there are currently few studies. Those conducted, while identifying several potential candidate genes, haven't produced consistent results (Fernández et al., 2015; Fernández et al., 2014; Klink & Den Heijer, 2014). One review concluded as much, observing that "no strong candidate has emerged for the development of gender dysphoria" (Klink & Den Heijer, 2014, p. 37). Future research will no doubt continue to explore specific genes.

IMMUNE SYSTEM PERSPECTIVES

Many illnesses can negatively impact sexual interest and performance. As one example, people with autoimmune diseases are highly susceptible to sexual dysfunction—including those with *rheumatoid arthritis* (in which inflammation progressively destroys joints) and *Addison's Disease* (in which the immune system attacks the endocrine system's adrenal glands) (Granata et al., 2013; J. Hill, Bird, & Thorpe, 2003; Tristano, 2009, 2014). When it comes to rheumatoid diseases, sexual impairment can result from many factors including "pain, fatigue, stiffness, functional impairment, depression, anxiety, negative body image, reduced libido, hormonal imbalance, and drug treatment" (Tristano, 2009, p. 853). Perhaps because talking about sex is uncomfortable to many people, doctors often don't ask their rheumatoid patients about their sexual functioning (J. Hill et al., 2003; Tristano, 2014). Doing so would help bring sexual issues to light so they can be addressed (J. Hill et al., 2003; Tristano, 2014).

EVALUATING BIOLOGICAL PERSPECTIVES

Research support for treatment of sexual dysfunctions is meager, though this problem isn't limited to biological interventions: "'Lack of scientific evidence' is a recurrent theme, concerning pharmacological as well as psychological treatment methods" (Almås, 2016, p. 60). Beyond debates over effectiveness, critics who

Have we pathologized female sexuality by overemphasizing the importance of genital arousal and orgasm?
Source: Getty Images/iStockphoto Thinkstock Images\Timur Nisametdinov

favor psychosocial approaches complain that biological perspectives unnecessarily medicalize sex and gender issues. Psychologist Leonore Tiefer has been especially critical of medicalizing female sexual complaints. She has argued that medicalization yields too narrow a definition of sexual "normalcy," one that unfairly pathologizes sexual experiences that don't stress the importance of genital arousal and orgasm (Tiefer, 2002). From such a perspective, by over-medicalizing sexual complaints we become fixated on trying to "cure" them through reliance on pharmaceuticals (e.g., "Female Viagra") instead of dealing with them in more relational ways through couples counseling, sex therapy, and sex education (Tiefer, 2002). Obviously, those coming from a biological perspective might counter that while some sexual complaints do have psychological origins, medicalization is justified when there is a clear biological basis for it. The shift over the past 40 years to viewing erectile dysfunction as more often due to decreased blood flow to the penis (rather than psychological conflicts) exemplifies an instance where medicalization may be justified (Ghofrani et al., 2006). Unfortunately, on many occasions the biological basis of sexual complaints isn't easily pinpointed.

Medicalization is also a concern when it comes to paraphilias and gender dysphoria. Past efforts to medicalize rape as a paraphilia, for instance, created enormous controversy; see the "Controversial Question" feature for details. Further, although people who identify as transgender or meet criteria for gender dysphoria may ultimately turn out to have verifiable biological differences from others, critics caution against equating biological difference with disorder because difference doesn't always mean disorder (Epting, Raskin, & Burke, 1994; L. Hoffman & Lincoln, 2011). For example, biological dissimilarities between homosexuals and heterosexuals have been identified (LeVay, 1991, 2011). Yet even though most mental health professionals acknowledge such variations, almost none of them see homosexuality as a disorder anymore.

CONTROVERSIAL QUESTION

Are Rapists Mentally Ill?

Is the urge to rape a paraphilic disorder worthy of inclusion in the *DSM*? Some mental health professionals say yes indeed, while others resolutely disagree. This has resulted in an ongoing fight over whether to add something called **paraphilic coercive disorder (PCD)** (previously called *paraphilic rapism*) to the *DSM* (Dodd, 2015; Marecek & Gavey, 2013). The battle has been raging for years. PCD proposals have been put forward and rejected from *DSM-III* to *DSM-5*, and the debate is so hot that PCD isn't even listed in *DSM-5* under criteria sets for further study (Agalaryan & Rouleau, 2014; First, 2014).

So, what exactly is PCD? A variety of diagnostic criteria have been proposed over the years (Thornton, 2010). All have focused on the idea of rape as a paraphilia. The criteria proposed for *DSM-5* were as follows: (a) "recurrent, intense sexually arousing fantasies or sexual urges focused on sexual coercion" that last six months; (b) distress over these urges, or actually having acted on them at least three separate times; and (c) not having a sexual sadism diagnosis (P. Stern, 2010, p. 1444). If eventually added to the *DSM* or *ICD*, the disorder would be diagnosed almost entirely in men—those who repeatedly rape or are disturbed and upset about their ongoing impulse to do so.

Arguments about PCD have more or less focused on two not altogether distinct issues: science and politics. Regarding science, debate has concentrated on whether PCD can be reliably differentiated from other disorders. Research on this issue has often relied on the *penile plethysmograph (PPG)*, a device that gauges sexual arousal by measuring blood flow to the penis. If PPG studies can distinguish men who are aroused by rape-related imagery from those who aren't, then we potentially have an objective basis for diagnosing PCD—a development that would please those (such as RDoC researchers; see Chapter 3) who wish to see mental disorders assessed using quantifiable biomarkers. Unfortunately, although there is some evidence that rapists do experience arousal in response to coercive imagery and fantasies, PPG studies haven't yielded definitive results—or at least they haven't provided results about which those on either side of this contentious debate can agree (R. A. Knight, 2010; Thornton, 2010).

What about the politics of the PCD debate? Those who think rape should be considered a mental illness argue that officially recognizing it as a paraphilic disorder will allow us to reduce recidivism rates by medically treating paraphilic rapists who, because of their disorder, commit terrible crimes (P. Stern, 2010). This, they argue, will help both paraphilic rapists and the public at large. Those opposed to classifying rape as mental disorder take a thoroughly different stance. Some maintain that seeing rape as

Photo source: © Getty Images/iStockphoto Thinkstock Images\bahri altay a disorder excuses rapists from responsibility for their crimes—a shift that could lead to the PCD diagnosis being used in court to help rapists evade legal accountability (Dodd, 2015). Others worry that the PCD diagnosis would be used to unfairly label too many people as sexual predators, potentially justifying lengthy or indefinite institutionalizations (J. C. Wakefield, 2012). Finally, some PCD opponents insist that identifying rape as mental disorder inappropriately transforms a social problem into a medical one (Dodd, 2015; Scully & Marolla, 1985). From this standpoint, rape isn't an illness. Rather, it's an all-too-common act performed by perfectly "normal" men who live in a society that condones violence against women. By regarding rape as a disorder, we avoid examining broader societal values that perpetuate it.

The latest skirmish in the "Is rape a mental disorder?" fight may be the *ICD-11*'s addition of a new paraphilia called **coercive sexual sadism disorder**. This diagnosis is characterized "by a sustained, focused and intense pattern of sexual arousal that involves the infliction of physical or psychological suffering on a non-consenting person" (Reed et al., 2016, p. 213). Seen as a disorder highly prevalent in sex offenders (R. B. Krueger et al., 2017; Reed et al., 2016)—including serial rapists—the coercive sexual sadism diagnosis opens a new front in the ongoing battle over whether rape and other sexual offenses are not just crimes, but also—in at least some cases—expressions of mental disorder.

CRITICAL THINKING QUESTIONS

1. In what ways do those wanting to add PCD to the *DSM* espouse a medical model?
2. In what ways do those opposing the addition of PCD to the *DSM* espouse a social justice model?
3. Should PCD be added to future revisions of *DSM* and *ICD*? Why or why not?

10.5 PSYCHOLOGICAL PERSPECTIVES

PSYCHODYNAMIC PERSPECTIVES

Classic Freud

From a psychoanalytic perspective, sexual dysfunctions and paraphilias are outward expressions of unconscious conflicts. Freud (1905/1962) believed that sexual "perversions" (which today we call paraphilias) occur when people become fixated at one or more of the psychosexual stages. For instance, a fetish might originate in castration anxiety at the phallic stage, while vaginismus might be a way of coping with unresolved penis envy (Atwood, 2015; Gabbard, 2014). As a result of such fixations, the sexual instinct becomes misdirected away from the normal aim of sexual intercourse (i.e., reproduction) and towards the paraphilic activity. While Freud's stance may sound regressive by modern standards, some argue that Freud was actually challenging the idea that "perversions" only occurred in seriously disturbed individuals (H. Wood, 2003). People often point to this provocative Freud quote, which suggests "perversion" is something few of us escape entirely: "No healthy person, it appears, can fail to make some addition that might be called perverse to the normal sexual aim; and the universality of this finding is in itself enough to show how inappropriate it is to use the word perversion as a term of reproach" (S. Freud, 1905/1962, p. 51). This shows that Freud didn't firmly distinguish normal from abnormal sexuality, arguing that nearly all of us are at least somewhat "perverted" when it comes to our sexual interests. However, when sexual "perversions" interfere with our lives or cause harm to others, psychoanalysis can be undertaken to uncover the unconscious conflicts behind them.

Paraphilias as Hostile Fantasies

Even though "paraphilia" had replaced "perversion" as the accepted term by the time he was writing in the 1970s and 1980s, psychoanalyst Robert Stoller (1985, 1975/1986) actively preferred the word "perversion" because he considered it more precise and powerful. "I want to retain the word *perversion* just *because* of its nasty connotations," he provocatively explained. "*Perversion* is a sturdy word, throbbing with assumptions, while *paraphilia* is a wet noodle" (Stoller, 1985, p. 6). Stoller argued that "perverts" are people who unconsciously feel guilt over their sexual urges and behaviors because these urges and behaviors are motivated not by a desire for sexual intimacy, but by hostility. To Stoller, perversions (which he noted occur

From Robert Stoller's psychoanalytic perspective, case study client Lou's transvestism is only pathological if it stems from profound humiliation in childhood and constitutes an act of revenge.

Source: iStock.com/FatCamera

CHAPTER 10

almost exclusively in men) are traceable to instances of profound humiliation during childhood—including but not limited to being repeatedly demeaned, bullied, and abused (usually with the implication of not being masculine enough). Perversions, as responses to this mistreatment, are therefore acts of revenge. They fulfill a need to degrade others as a way to relive past traumas, but in the role of victor rather than victim. In this respect, perversions involve the defense mechanism of identification (see Chapter 2)—specifically **identification with the aggressor**, in which people identity with those who have mistreated them and adopt their characteristics. In Stoller's (1985, 1975/1986) view, perversions (or paraphilias, if you prefer today's term) prevent people from establishing genuine intimacy with their partners because rather than engaging with their partners as whole persons, they instead use their partners to extract vengeance for past humiliations.

Lou

Imagine psychodynamic therapy with Lou for his transvestism. During the course of therapy, Lou might recall how his mother verbally and physically humiliated him when he misbehaved as a young child—once even making him wear his sister's clothes. His masculinity was deeply threatened. Therapy might help Lou gain insight into how his current sexual interest in wearing women's clothes during sex is tied to these past humiliations and is a way for him to not only relive them, but to exact revenge for them by forcing his wife Ruth to be overpowered in bed by a strong man able to overcome being forced to wear women's clothes. As Lou comes to understand and work through his past issues, he ideally would find himself no longer requiring women's clothes to get sexually turned on. Even if he sometimes chose to wear women's clothes during sex, he would no longer require them for arousal. This would allow sex with Ruth to become about emotional intimacy instead of about Lou trying to work through past humiliations.

CASE EXAMPLES

Importantly, according to Stoller it is the psychodynamics behind a sex act—rather than the sex act itself—that makes it "perverted" or not: "To label someone 'perverse' says something about his or her psychodynamics, especially about a *fantasy* of harming" (Stoller, 1985, p. 41). Psychodynamic therapy helps the patient gain insight into how past humiliations restrict genuine sexual intimacy. However, when acted upon in ways that violate the rights of others (e.g., in pedophilia, exhibitionism, frotteurism, voyeurism, and some cases of sadomasochism), Stoller (1985, 1975/1986) notes that paraphilias may require legal as well as psychological intervention. The main criticism of psychodynamic perspectives like Stoller's is that—unlike the cognitive-behavioral approach discussed shortly—there is little empirical research to support them.

Interpersonal Therapy (IPT) for Transgender Clients

It has been proposed that interpersonal therapy (IPT) (see Chapters 5 and 9) can be adapted for use with transgender clients (Budge, 2013). Recall that IPT is a brief and structured therapy in which client and therapist address one or more of these areas: *interpersonal role transitions, interpersonal role disputes, grief,* or *interpersonal sensitivity*. IPT can assist clients with the inevitable role transitions that occur during the process of gender transitioning. This often involves helping clients to grieve the loss of the old gender role, express emotion related to the changing role, facilitate new social skills that let them be more genuine with people (now that they no longer must hide their true gender identities), and develop social support systems that are accepting of their transitioned gender identities (Budge, 2013). Research has found IPT effective for depression and eating issues (de Mello, de Jesus Mari, Bacaltchuk, Verdeli, & Neugebauer, 2005; Hollon & Ponniah, 2010; R. Murphy, Straebler, Basden, Cooper, & Fairburn, 2012). However, it has only recently been adapted for use with transgender clients. Thus, research on its effectiveness in addressing transgender issues is currently lacking.

COGNITIVE-BEHAVIORAL PERSPECTIVES

Behavioral Perspectives on Sexual Dysfunctions and Paraphilias

Habituation and Conditioning

From a strictly behavioral standpoint, sexual disorders and paraphilias are explicable in terms of **habituation**, classical conditioning, and operant conditioning (Plaud & Holm, 1998). Habituation is when responsiveness to a stimulus decreases after repeated exposure to it (Plaud & Holm, 1998).

Elena

For instance, our case study client Elena, who reports having lost all interest in sex with her husband Hector, may have become habituated to the conditions under which she and Hector have sex. If sex is pretty much the same every time (e.g., always at night, always in the missionary position, always in bed), then it's possible Elena's responsiveness has decreased simply due to the repetitious nature of their sexual interactions. Consequently, what previously aroused Elena no longer does. Behavior therapy might encourage Elena and Hector to experiment with different sexual times, positions, and locations whose novelty might excite her.

CASE EXAMPLES

In classical conditioning (see Chapter 2) of sexual problems, neutral stimuli become conditioned stimuli after repeatedly being paired with inherently arousing stimuli (Bolling, Terry, & Kohlneberg, 2006).

Lou

Thus, the sexual interests of Lou (our case study client who gets turned on by wearing women's clothes) may be the result of classical conditioning. For example, if contact with women's clothing (initially a neutral stimulus) occurred in conjunction with the sensual touch of a woman (an unconditioned sexually arousing stimulus), then Lou may have formed an association between women's clothes and sexual arousal. As a result, women's clothes have become a conditioned stimulus that evokes sexual excitement.

CASE EXAMPLES

Finally, operant conditioning (again, see Chapter 2) involves the strengthening or weakening of behavior based on its consequences (Bolling et al., 2006). An operant conditioning explanation might look for ways in which sexual arousal has been reinforced as a result of Lou's wearing women's clothes. Once the conditioning contingencies surrounding clients' undesirable sexual behaviors are understood (via functional analysis, discussed in Chapter 3), then behavioral interventions can be implemented to try to change them. As noted in earlier chapters, behavioral techniques for sexual issues can be done *in vivo* (real life) or imaginally.

Sexual Dysfunctions

Many behavioral interventions try to improve sexual performance. Although not exclusively tied to behavior theory, **sensate focus**—originally developed by Masters and Johnson (1970)—is perhaps the most well-known *in vivo* technique used to help those having trouble becoming sexually aroused or having orgasms. The rationale of sensate focus is to eliminate sexual performance pressure (Gosselin, 2016b; L. Weiner & Avery-Clark, 2014). Clients are instructed to engage in sensual touching with their partners, but without it leading to intercourse. Ideally, this reduces **spectatoring**—the tendency to observe and negatively evaluate one's sexual performance as if one was a third person watching it (Masters & Johnson, 1970; L. Weiner & Avery-Clark, 2014). Because sensate focus removes the pressure to perform and discourages spectatoring, clients ironically often "fail" the assignment by becoming aroused, engaging in intercourse, and even having orgasms.

Elena and Ahmed

Elena (who isn't interested in sex with husband Hector) and Ahmed (who is unable to get an erection despite finding his girlfriend Miri very attractive) might benefit from sensate focus exercises.

CASE EXAMPLES

For premature ejaculation, Masters and Johnson (1970) developed the **squeeze technique** in which the ridge at the top of the penis is repeatedly squeezed during sexual activity in order to delay ejaculation (Gosselin, 2016b). An alternative to the squeeze technique is the **stop-start technique**, where men learn to stop intercourse prior to ejaculating and to begin again only after arousal decreases (H. S. Kaplan, 1974). Both the squeeze technique and the stop-start method condition men to not ejaculate so quickly.

Bolin

Bolin, our case study client who experiences premature ejaculation, might be asked to practice the squeeze technique or the stop-start technique when having intercourse with his girlfriend, May.

CASE EXAMPLES

Pelvic floor rehabilitation is another common behavior-based technique to improve sexual interest. It tries to address suspected weaknesses of the pelvic floor muscles associated with issues such as dyspareunia and vaginismus. Patients might be assigned **Kegel exercises**, which involve tightening and relaxing pelvic floor muscles to strengthen them (ter Kuile et al., 2010; van Lankveld et al., 2006). In conjunction with Kegel exercises, biofeedback (described in Chapter 8) is sometimes employed. In biofeedback training, a device that measures pelvic floor muscle contractions positively reinforces pelvic floor muscle strengthening through rehabilitation exercises. Research has found biofeedback to be effective for this purpose (Bergeron, Morin, & Lord, 2010; Glazer, Rodke, Swencionis, Hertz, & Young, 1995). Finally, systematic desensitization (outlined in Chapter 6) can be employed to help people who are anxious about sex or have experienced past sexual traumas. By gradually exposing these individuals to sexual activities while they practice relaxation, sex becomes associated with pleasure instead of anxiety or trauma (Gosselin, 2016b).

Paraphilias

Besides improving sexual performance, behavioral techniques are also used to curtail paraphilias. Aversion therapies attempt to reduce undesirable sexual interests and behaviors by associating them with aversive (unpleasant) events (Gaither, Rosenkranz, & J., 1998). For instance, **covert sensitization** is an aversion therapy in which an unpleasant image is presented (*in vivo* or imaginally) while the client focuses on the paraphilic interest. The goal is to associate the paraphilia with the unpleasant image in order to lessen the behavior. For example, in one case of exhibitionism, a client was asked to imagine two aversive things: being scolded by the woman he exposed himself to and having

CHAPTER 10

his wife divorce him because of his exhibitionism (Gaither et al., 1998). In other words, covert sensitization aims to eliminate paraphilias by conditioning them to be associated with something negative. Two other types of aversion therapy used with paraphilias are olfactory aversion and electrical aversive therapy (Gaither et al., 1998). In olfactory aversion, the client self-administers an aversive odor during the undesired sexual activity; in electrical aversive therapy, the client is administered an electric shock instead. Both are intended to punish the paraphilia as a way to eliminate it. Finally, masturbatory satiation is also used to reduce paraphilias. The client is asked to masturbate "for a much longer time than is pleasurable" while "engaging in deviant fantasies" related to the undesirable sexual interest (Gaither et al., 1998, p. 158). The goal—supported by a variety of studies—is to have the paraphilic stimulus lose its erotic value by associating it with boredom (Gaither et al., 1998).

William

Covert sensitization and masturbatory satiation might be employed with William, our case example client who is aroused by child pornography. In covert satiation, William might be asked to focus on sexually arousing thoughts about children while his therapist talks to him about the potential consequences of being caught with child pornography: social embarrassment, ridicule, and possibly prison. This will hopefully condition William to associate child porn with negative consequences. William also might be asked to masturbate at home for two hours continuously while engaged in erotic pedophilic fantasies. Because two hours is a long time, William should eventually become bored and—if all goes well—his fantasies about children will become associated with this boredom and lose their allure.

CASE EXAMPLES

Cognitive Perspectives on Sexual Dysfunctions and Paraphilias

CBT for Sexual Dysfunctions

Cognitive-behavioral therapy (CBT) for sexual dysfunctions supplements the behavioral techniques already discussed by also considering problematic thinking that negatively impacts sexual performance. As discussed in Chapter 2, cognitive change is often accomplished through cognitive restructuring, in which the therapist uses reason and argument to change (i.e., restructure) people's thinking, replacing dysfunctional beliefs with rational ones. CBT therapists recommend cognitive restructuring for sexual dysfunctions because research has found that dysfunctional beliefs contribute to such issues (Carvalho & Nobre, 2010; Carvalho, Veríssimo, & Nobre, 2013; Géonet, De Sutter, & Zech, 2013; Nobre & Pinto-Gouveia, 2006). Among women, examples of such beliefs are: women should always be able to have orgasms during intercourse, sexual desire is sinful, morally upstanding women (especially older ones) shouldn't be sexual, women lose sexual interest with age, and postmenopausal women don't like sex (Carvalho et al., 2013; Gosselin, 2016b; Nobre & Pinto-Gouveia, 2006). Comparable problematic beliefs common to men include: "real men" have sex often, difficulty getting an erection is a personal failure, impotent men aren't masculine, and a woman's sexual satisfaction is determined by the quality of a man's erection (Gosselin, 2016b; Nobre & Pinto-Gouveia, 2006). The cognitive component of CBT involves challenging and replacing dysfunctional beliefs and cognitive distortions that interfere with sexual satisfaction. However, CBT also includes psychoeducation about sex—including bibliotherapy (see Chapter 1) in which people learn and change through reading assignments. The goal of CBT interventions is to help people more realistically assess their own sexual performance (M. P. Carey, 1998; Meana, 2012).

Bolin

With Bolin, our 22-year-old who worries about ejaculating too quickly with his girlfriend May, cognitive therapy might challenge (and help him change) his core belief that his worth as a man and his attractiveness as a boyfriend are tied exclusively to how long he lasts in bed.

CASE EXAMPLES

CBT for Paraphilias

Cognitive restructuring is also used to treat paraphilias. However, it is most relevant when a paraphilia endangers others. With paraphilias where nobody else is at risk, some practitioners question the wisdom of using cognitive restructuring. For example, in lieu of cognitive therapy, transvestic clients (such as our case study client Lou) might be encouraged to "seek alternative options to treatment, such as joining a transvestite club where they can crossdress free from social disapproval" (W. L. Marshall & Fernandez, 1998, p. 285).

For paraphilias that do violate others' rights (voyeurism, pedophilia, frotteurism, and exhibitionism), cognitive restructuring challenges cognitive distortions that rationalize sex offenses—for instance, objectionable attitudes like "Having sex with a child is a good way for an adult to teach the child about sex" (M. S. Kaplan & Krueger, 2012, p. 293). In other words, cognitive restructuring targets problematic thinking that makes sexual transgressions more likely—beliefs such as: children are sexual beings; sex isn't harmful to kids; sex is a right one is entitled to; social rules about sex are optional; and women are deceitful, manipulative, and bad (Schaffer, Jeglic, Moster, & Wnuk, 2010). Cognitive restructuring with sex offenders confronts how they justify, rationalize, excuse, minimize, and deny the negative effects of their actions. CBT therapy also aims to enhance empathy (because offenders often have a hard time understanding the impact of their behavior on others) and improve interpersonal skills (because offenders also tend to have trouble establishing intimate relationships and building support networks) (W. L. Marshall & Fernandez, 1998; Schaffer et al., 2010).

CBT is generally considered the most effective psychotherapy for sex offenders, though the evidence is mixed (Fedoroff & Marshall, 2010). For instance, some argue that research shows CBT significantly reduces recidivism rates (i.e., how often offenders commit additional sex crimes) among child molesters (J. V. Becker et al., 2014; B. Kim, Benekos, & Merlo, 2016; Lösel & Schmucker, 2005; Schaffer et al., 2010). Others disagree, arguing that existing research is meager and inconsistent in its results (J. V. Becker et al., 2014; Walton & Chou, 2015). Discussion about the effectiveness of CBT is part of a larger debate (revisited when discussing sociocultural perspectives) about the utility of intervention programs for sex offenders.

Transgender-Affirmative CBT

Transgender-affirmative CBT (TA-CBT) is a form of CBT intended to assist transgender clients as they cope with anxiety and depression caused by transphobia (social prejudice directed at transgender people) (A. Austin & Craig, 2015). TA-CBT works to help transgender clients understand how transphobia can negatively impact how they think and feel about themselves. By encouraging examination and revision of negative internalized beliefs influenced by prejudiced societal views about being transgender, TA-CBT assists transgender clients in clarifying their own thoughts and feelings about being transgender while also developing identity-affirming relationships and support systems. TA-CBT is relatively new and still being developed, so research on its effectiveness remains in its early stages (A. Austin & Craig, 2015).

Julio
TA-CBT with Julio would help him explore ways that he has internalized negative ideas about being transgender. For instance, TA-CBT might help Julio identify dysfunctional beliefs influenced by negative societal attitudes toward transgender people (e.g., "Nobody will love or accept me for who I truly am"). Over time, he would replace these beliefs with more functional ones (e.g., "Even if some people don't accept me, there are those who will love me for who I am"). Shifts like this in his thinking should not only improve Julio's emotional outlook, but also make it easier to build relationships with people who support and accept him for who he is.

CASE EXAMPLES

HUMANISTIC PERSPECTIVES
Critique of Medicalization of Sexuality

Humanistic psychotherapists often criticize what they see as the excessive medicalization of sexuality (Szasz, 1991b; Tiefer, 2006). To them, what we commonly identify as sexually disordered is rarely disordered at all, but usually just atypical and/or socially unacceptable. Consistent with their view of people as adjustment and growth-oriented, humanistic clinicians are reluctant to label unusual sexual acts or interests as disordered because, from their perspective, this unfairly pathologizes personally meaningful variations in sexual activity (L. L. Armstrong, 2006; Gunst, 2012; Kleinplatz, 1996, 2014; Tiefer, 2006). To the humanistic sensibility, sexual acts, interests, and complaints aren't merely symptoms of disorder to be eradicated. On the contrary, they reflect meaningful efforts at personal growth to be respected and understood:

> *Whether it is the rape victim's flashbacks and nightmares, the intense anxiety of the man reporting erectile dysfunction, the pain of the woman with vaginismus, or the paraphiliac's fantasies ... distressing symptoms are never to be eliminated without attention to their value, meaning, purpose and clinical usefulness. (Kleinplatz, 2014, p. 205)*

Experiential Sex Therapy

To counter the humanistic lament that sex therapy is too often "used within a medical model of symptom removal rather than as part of a focus on sexual growth and fulfilment" (Tiefer, 2006, p. 363), humanistic sex therapist Peggy Kleinplatz (1996, 2007, 2014) developed experiential sex therapy, an outgrowth of Alvin Mahrer's (1996) experiential psychotherapy. Kleinplatz's approach focuses on the experiential meaning of sex rather than on "fixing" broken parts or eliminating dysfunctional interests and activities. That is,

> *the goal of Experiential Psychotherapy is to allow the individual to fulfill—rather than contain—his or her sexual, and other, potentials. Although there is no attempt to target behaviors—sexual or otherwise, deviant or normophilic—when fundamental personality change is effected, the results are manifest in sexual and other desires, wishes, fantasies and behavior, intimate relationships and bodily phenomena. (Kleinplatz, 2014, p. 204)*

CHAPTER 10

In clinical practice, experiential sex therapy encourages clients to identify and explore strong feelings (which may not be directly related to sex). When explored, these feelings provide access to important inner experiences that suggest new possibilities for living and being. By allowing these newly discovered inner experiences to inform how they go about life, clients experience personal growth that helps them live in more self-consistent ways. Such growth transforms all aspects of their lives, including their sex lives.

Elena

If Elena and her husband Hector sought therapy for Elena's low sexual interest, an experiential sex therapist would seek an issue about which Elena feels strong emotion—perhaps her powerful desire to say "to hell with everyone else." Therapy might trace this feeling to past hurts Elena experienced over being told she was "too aggressive" and "not feminine enough" and how she compensated for this by becoming increasingly passive and compliant both interpersonally and sexually with the various men she dated (including Hector). Working to experience the world from Elena's perspective, her therapist might ask her to focus on what it would look like if she did indeed say "to hell with everyone else." In response, Elena might express a desire to be more assertive at work and with Hector—including in bed. To her surprise, Elena might find that Hector actually welcomes such changes. Experiential sex therapy would encourage Elena to be the more assertive person she feels she is down deep. Operating more assertively, Elena would likely experience changes in many areas of her life. She might find that her interpersonal relationships at home and work improve. She also might find herself aroused by the prospect of being more sexually assertive with Hector.

CASE EXAMPLES

Experiential sex therapy can be used for any of the sexual issues discussed in this chapter, including erectile dysfunction, premature ejaculation, difficulties with orgasm, and paraphilias (Gunst, 2012; Kleinplatz, 1998, 2004, 2007, 2010, 2014). However, because experiential sex therapists resist viewing sexuality as disordered, their approach isn't easily amenable to traditional outcome research to test its effectiveness with specific diagnoses (Kleinplatz, 2014). Experiential sex therapists therefore face a challenge. To have their approach accepted more broadly (as CBT and drug therapies are), they need to show via research that their therapy is effective—even if they find this hard to do in a field that emphasizes outcomes for specific problems over more comprehensive (but harder to measure) personality transformation.

EVALUATING PSYCHOLOGICAL PERSPECTIVES

Sexual Dysfunctions

For most of the psychological therapies for sexual dysfunctions, research is extremely scarce (Almås, 2016; Basson, Wierman, van Lankveld, & Brotto, 2010; de Jong, van Lankveld, & Elgersma, 2010). Not surprisingly, CBT has the most extensive evidence base and for many sexual dysfunctions it is generally considered to be effective, although not incredibly so (Faubion & Rullo, 2015; Meston & Bradford, 2007). That is, when it comes to sexual dysfunction even CBT's evidence base isn't especially large or compelling. One review—admittedly written by medical doctors who may prefer biological to psychological interventions—concluded that estrogen therapy, bupropion, and sildenafil were all preferable to CBT for treating sexual dysfunctions in women (Faubion & Rullo, 2015). Others have lamented that even though studies have found CBT helpful for issues like vaginismus, many patients' symptoms return (de Jong et al., 2010). Though both biological and psychological treatments of sexual dysfunctions require additional research support (Almås, 2016), the former are often touted as more effective than the latter. However, not everyone concurs with this assessment. A review sympathetic to psychological interventions drew a more optimistic conclusion—noting that although more research is needed, psychotherapy (especially CBT) is effective for problems such as low sexual desire and has the added advantage (compared to medication) of no side effects (Basson et al., 2010). Whether you find yourself rooting for the biological or psychological perspective in this debate probably tells you something about your own theoretical commitments.

Paraphilic Disorders and Sex Offenders

When it comes to paraphilic disorders, one of the challenges in assessing therapy research is that paraphilic therapy clients aren't an especially representative sample. After all, many people with paraphilias don't seek therapy because they don't see their behavior as problematic, are embarrassed by it, or are hiding it because it's illegal (Gosselin, 2016b). Consequently, the samples in paraphilia therapy research tend to be unrepresentative, consisting of people who have been arrested and mandated to seek therapy. Unfortunately, "these individuals are usually highly motivated to report that the treatment has worked, but may not necessarily be motivated to change" (Gosselin, 2016b, p. 251). This makes assessing the existing therapy research difficult. Further, a lot of the research focuses on the effectiveness of therapy for sex offenders—a group that overlaps with, but isn't identical to, people diagnosed with paraphilias.

The main controversy over psychotherapy for sex offenders and people with paraphilias is, quite simply, whether or not it works. Research on the effectiveness of the various psychological therapies has yielded uneven results. Some investigators interpret the research optimistically, rating CBT as the best supported psychological intervention (Fedoroff & Marshall, 2010; Lösel & Schmucker, 2005). Others take a much grimmer view, arguing that psychological therapies (including CBT) aren't especially helpful and that recidivism rates are high (Fedoroff & Marshall, 2010; Marques, Wiederanders, Day, Nelson, & van Ommeren, 2005; Walton & Chou, 2015). As with sexual dysfunctions, biological interventions with sex offenders—however controversial they may be—often seem to fare better in controlled research trials than psychological therapies, but this may be due to methodological issues rather than genuine differences in effectiveness (Lösel & Schmucker, 2005).

10.6 SOCIOCULTURAL PERSPECTIVES
CROSS-CULTURAL AND SOCIAL JUSTICE PERSPECTIVES

Prevalence rates for sexual dysfunctions, paraphilias, and gender dysphoria differ across cultures. For instance, *DSM-5* notes that the prevalence of low sexual desire varies widely based on background, ranging from 12.5% among Northern European men all the way up to 28% among Southeast Asian men. This makes sense from a cross-cultural perspective, which says that what counts as sexually deviant differs by culture, so we must be careful before assuming that the disorders listed in *DSM* and *ICD* are universal. Social justice-oriented therapists and researchers challenge the idea that sexual disorders are culture-free categories and instead argue that when it comes to sexual difficulties, we must be especially sensitive to ways in which gender, ethnicity, economic status, and other social issues shape our understanding.

The New View Critique and Reconceptualization of Sexual Dysfunctions

The **New View**, a feminist and humanistic social justice perspective, combines scholarship and social activism in challenging what its supporters see as a problematic tendency to treat women's sexual dysfunctions as strictly medical (rather than interpersonal and social) problems (McHugh, 2006; Tiefer, 2001, 2002, 2010). According to the New View, the traditional medical approach to sexual difficulties incorrectly assumes that men and women are physiologically equivalent when it comes to sexual functioning (Working Group for A New View of Women's Sexual Problems, 2001). This overlooks important gender differences, such as the fact that women often don't distinguish between desire and arousal. The medical view also problematically encourages us to see desire and arousal complaints in women as signs of sickness, rather than as responses to relationship dissatisfaction and gender discrimination. After all, it's hard to maintain interest in sex if you feel abused by your partner and discriminated against in the wider world. Finally, the medical view minimizes individual and situational differences, assuming that certain levels of desire, interest, and activity are "normal" for all women—regardless of factors such as personality, economic status, and relationship satisfaction (World Association of Sexual Health, 2014). One target of the New View's ire is the *DSM*, which New View supporters feel personifies their concerns about the medical model:

> The American Psychiatric Association's DSM *approach bypasses relational aspects of women's sexuality, which often lie at the root of sexual satisfactions and problems—e.g., desires for intimacy, wishes to please a partner, or, in some cases, wishes to avoid offending, losing, or angering a partner. The* DSM *takes an exclusively individual approach to sex, and assumes that if the sexual parts work, there is no problem; and if the parts don't work, there is a problem. But many women do not define their sexual difficulties this way. The* DSM's *reduction of "normal sexual function" to physiology implies, incorrectly, that one can measure and treat genital and physical difficulties without regard to the relationship in which sex occurs. (Working Group for A New View of Women's Sexual Problems, 2001, p. 3)*

New View therapists have developed their own classification system as an alternative to the *DSM*. The New View classification divides sexual problems into four types: (1) *sexual problems due to sociocultural, political or economic factors*; (2) *sexual problems relating to partner and relationship*; (3) *sexual problems due to psychological factors*; and (4) *sexual problems due to medical factors* (Working Group for A New View of Women's Sexual Problems, 2001). Importantly, the New View approach sees most sexual complaints as traceable to social, political, psychological, and relational factors, even while leaving room for some sexual issues to be medically based. Also note how the New View identifies sexual *problems* rather than sexual *disorders*—a clear attempt to move away from a strictly medical model, a move that excites many New View-sympathetic clinicians (Iasenza, 2001; Kleinplatz, 2012; McHugh, 2006; G. Ogden, 2001; Tiefer, 2001; S. P. Williams, 2001).

Elena
Rather than simply diagnosing Elena with female sexual interest/arousal disorder and treating it as a strictly medical problem involving faulty body parts, a New View therapist working with Elena would consider additional factors that might explain her lack of sexual interest. Exploring socioeconomic, political, and economic factors, Elena's therapist might learn that Elena is being sexually harassed by her boss at work and

 CASE EXAMPLES

CHAPTER 10

paid less than men with comparable education and experience. Her emotional stress over these goings-on could be negatively affecting her sexual interest. When it comes to relational factors, a New View therapist would be interested in the quality of Elena's relationship with her husband Hector. If the relationship is going poorly, she may not be interested in sex with him. Finally, psychological factors would be considered. If Elena is a survivor of past abuse, her ability to emotionally trust Hector and let her guard down might turn sex into a traumatic chore rather than an intimate emotional experience. Therapy would focus on these issues to help Elena address them.

There hasn't been much research on the New View classification, but one qualitative study found that it effectively accounted for 98% of women's sexual complaints—with 65% of these complaints identified as relational, 20% as sociocultural/political/economic, 8% as psychological, and 7% as medical (Nicholls, 2008). The study concluded that the New View is a valid alternative to the *DSM* (Nicholls, 2008). However, more studies demonstrating the New View classification's reliability, validity, and overall utility are needed. On a practical level, the New View (like most *DSM* and *ICD* alternatives) doesn't provide anything comparable to diagnostic codes, which help clinicians collect insurance payments and statistically track the prevalence and incidence of various problems. Without such codes, many clinicians—even those who prefer the New View perspective to the medical model—may be unwilling to adopt it.

Transgender Affirmative Therapists: Gatekeepers or Advocates?

Should transgender people who want hormone therapy or gender reassignment surgeries have to get permission from mental health professionals first? The World Professional Association of Gender Health (WPATH) says yes. WPATH recommends that before undergoing any gender-altering procedures, patients should have to get one or more referral letters from qualified professionals attesting that they (a) have been diagnosed with gender dysphoria, (b) are able to make informed decisions about treatment, (c) are of legal age, and (d) have any significant medical or mental health issues under control (Coleman et al., 2012). WPATH standards require one letter for hormone therapy or breast augmentation/reduction surgeries and two letters for genital surgeries (Coleman et al., 2012).

The WPATH standards are an example of **gatekeeping**—an approval process conducted by medical and mental health professionals intended to keep those deemed psychologically unfit from making irreversible gender-altering decisions (W. P. Bouman et al., 2014). The idea of gatekeeping is to protect people, and one case study did find that gatekeeping psychotherapy was helpful in the transition process (Budge, 2015b). Nonetheless, some people worry that gatekeeping is a paternalistic and—in some instances—oppressive process that can delay or interfere with the ability of transgender people to receive the medical interventions they desire (W. P. Bouman et al., 2014; A. A. Singh & Burnes, 2010; A. A. Singh & dickey, 2016). Consequently, there has been a subtle shift—even within WPATH—from seeing psychotherapists as gatekeepers to viewing them more as *advocates* who assist clients in overcoming obstacles in the gender transition process (Burnes et al., 2010; Singh & Burnes, 2010; Singh & dickey, 2016). Coming from a social justice orientation, transgender affirmative therapists acknowledge the ways in which discrimination, societal disapproval, and cisgender bias (even from many well-intentioned therapists) place transgender individuals at greater risk for emotional difficulties and even suicide (Blumer, Ansara, & Watson, 2013; R. T. Liu & Mustanski, 2012; McCann & Sharek, 2016). Social

The rainbow flag is often used as a symbol of LGBTQ pride.
Source: ImageSource

justice-oriented therapists encourage mental health practitioners to be more sensitive to the difficulties transgender people face and to shift their emphasis in therapy from gatekeeping to advocacy. To them, such a shift

demonstrates a call to the counseling field to acknowledge that transgender people may enter the counseling relationship having experienced multiple levels of oppression that influence their expectations of what the counseling process entails and their access to components of a potentially desired medical and social transition. (Singh & Burnes, 2010, p. 242)

CONSUMER AND SERVICE-USER PERSPECTIVES

Because doing so is both intimate and potentially stigmatizing, many people hesitate in seeking out professional help for sex and gender concerns. To rectify this, consumer and advocacy groups assist people while educating the public and working to reduce stigma over help-seeking. For example, when it comes to transgender issues specifically, there are many transgender support and advocacy groups. Some of these groups focus exclusively on transgender issues. Others are broader, offering services for anyone identifying as *LGBTQ* (an abbreviation that stands for *lesbian, gay, bisexual, transgender, and queer or questioning*) (www.thewelcomingproject.org). Table 10.2 lists some of the more prominent consumer groups that provide education, online support, referrals for counseling, and political advocacy for transgender people and others identifying under the broader LGBTQ umbrella. The website of one of these groups—The Gender Center of Australia—includes first-hand accounts of what it's like to be trans. See "The Lived Experience" for one of these autobiographical stories.

Table 10.2 Transgender and Other LGBTQ Support and Advocacy Groups

United States and Canada	
• **Trans Lifeline** (www.translifeline.org)	Non-profit organization in U.S. and Canada focused on the well-being of transgender people; runs a hotline for transgender people staffed by transgender people.
• **The Trevor Project** (www.thetrevorproject.org)	Offers crisis intervention and suicide prevention services to LGBTQ people ages 13–24.
• **PFLAG** (www.pflag.org)	Provides support, education, and advocacy for the LGBTQ community; over 400 chapters in the U.S.; has international affiliates around the world.
• **It Gets Better Project** (www.itgetsbetter.org)	Online video project to bring hope to LGBT youth around the world; started in U.S., but has an international affiliate program.
United Kingdom and Europe	
• **Beaumont Society** (www.beaumontsociety.org.uk)	Self-help body run by and for the transgender community.
• **Gender Trust** (http://gendertrust.org.uk)	Registered charity that helps transgender people and those affected by gender identity issues.
• **Mermaids** (www.mermaidsuk.org.uk)	Supports children and young people (up to age 19) facing gender identity issues; also assists their families and the professionals who care for them.
• **Transgender Europe (TGEU)** (http://tgeu.org)	Transgender support and advocacy group with 103 member organizations in 42 countries.
• **LGBT Foundation** (http://lgbt.foundation)	Offers support groups, counseling, a hotline, email support, a befriending scheme, a sexual health program, anti-homophobia projects in schools, a substance-misuse project, and other support services; also conducts research and engages in political advocacy.
• **Consortium** (www.lgbtconsortium.org.uk)	Helps develop and support LGBTQ groups, organizations and projects across the U.K.
Australia	
• **The Gender Center** (https://gendercentre.org.au)	Provides support services to people with gender issues, their partners, family members and friends in New South Wales.

CHAPTER 10

• **Transgender Victoria** (www.transgendervictoria.com)	Educates organizations and workplaces on how to provide better services for transgender people and helps provide direct services to the transgender community.
• **Transcend** (www.transcendsupport.com.au)	Parent-led peer support network and information hub for transgender children and their families.
• **QLife** (https://qlife.org.au)	Offers phone and web-based support and services service for lesbian, gay, bisexual, trans, and/or intersex individuals.
South Africa	
• **Gender DynamiX** (http://genderdynamix.org.za)	Defends and promotes rights of transgender and gender nonconforming people in South Africa, Africa, and the world; engages in public education, media outreach, research, and training.
• **PFLAG South Africa** (http://pflagsouthafrica.org)	Provides support meetings and resources to the LGBTQ community, their families, and their friends.

THE LIVED EXPERIENCE

Call Me Stephanie

My story is not unique. It's not even unusual. I am not a celebrity. I am unlikely to be feted by the media, but neither will I be pursued and abused by paparazzi. Because of these facts you may find we have more in common than if I were on every magazine cover on every news stand and negotiating for my own reality show.

Although my wish to be female probably goes back much earlier, the first times I can remember doing anything about my transgender obsession were during my time in high school in the 1970s. I would dress up after school, borrowing female gear wherever I could. Only my mother knew about my cross-dressing and her attitude was ambivalent.

On the one hand, she didn't try and stop me from "dressing up," but on the other hand she tried to control what I wore, and would criticise me for wearing "unsuitable" clothing. There was one skirt I loved but my mother said it was too short for a person my age. But it was my favourite so I kept wearing it until it literally fell apart from overuse.

When I started work I could not have been more masculine in my choice of careers. I understand this is a fairly common trait among transgenders, who often go into high risk, hyper-masculine employment to demonstrate to themselves (and the world at large) that they are not sissies and can hold their own in a masculine dominated world.

I was in the army for some time, then became an ironworker in a shipyard. From there I moved into concrete finishing work for the Council and by the time I was in my twenties I was on the gully-truck, clearing waste and keeping the Council drains and waterways clear and also clean.

Throughout this time I was still cross-dressing, but limiting myself to dressing up at home.

I had an industrial accident that injured my back early in 1994 and I was placed on light duties … and by 1996 I was invalided out of my Council employment. I started to cross-dress more after this time and by 1997 I was in touch with the Gender Centre, where I met Elizabeth Riley, the Manager. Elizabeth treated me well and I learned a lot from her. For the first time, I had a path laid out for me and I could clearly see my future as a woman in society.

[A counsellor] counselled me in 2000 and 2001 and about that time I changed doctors and started hormone therapy after consulting Professor Alfred Steinbeck on the best hormones. I prefer now to use patches rather than pills, as the hormones are absorbed through the skin, which is much kinder to the liver. I have been using hormone patches (two a week) since 2003.

I have come out to my family, including my brother and his children. I have never married so that I have not had the problems of reconciling my new personality with sons or daughters.

I am happy living in my preferred gender role, and I dress conservatively these days (even my mother would approve). I hope that all those with whom I share my experience will find their life journeys as rewarding and fulfilling as I am finding mine.

By Stephanie Annette. Reprinted with permission.
Originally published in the Australian magazine Polare *in October 2015.*
Article available at:
https://gendercentre.org.au/resources/support-resources/male-to-female/personal-stories?download=428:call-me-stephanie&start=15

SYSTEMS PERSPECTIVES
Programs for Sexual Offenders

Relapse Prevention (RP)

There are a variety of programs used by corrections agencies and prison services to rehabilitate criminal offenders, sexual offenders included. **Relapse prevention (RP)** programs are rooted in a cognitive-behavioral perspective. The RP model assumes that deviant sexual fantasies usually can't be eliminated, but they can be successfully managed to minimize the chance of relapse (Pithers, Kashima, Cumming, Beal, & Buell, 1988). RP programs contend that the best way to keep people from reoffending is to help them maintain a sense of control over their own behavior. Unfortunately, when offenders find themselves in high-risk situations with cues that arouse deviant fantasies, their sense of control is threatened. In response, they may begin to think in problematic

Relapse prevention programs view dealing with deviant sexual fantasies as something to be managed, not eliminated.
Source: iStock.com/-Antonio.

ways (e.g., "It's no use, I can't handle it") that increase the likelihood of repeat offenses (Pithers et al., 1988, p. 247). Additionally, high-risk situations lead offenders to focus on the instant gratification the sex act will provide while losing sight of its consequences. For instance, "a rapist might focus on the immediate effects of performing a sexual assault, such as a feeling of power and release of hostile emotions, rather than keeping in mind the full ramifications of the act" (Pithers et al., 1988, p. 247).

RP programs use a variety of CBT techniques. *Self-monitoring* is a behavioral technique in which people monitor their thoughts, feelings, and behaviors to identify connections among them. When relapse prevention programs use self-monitoring, the offender tracks moods, fantasies, thoughts, situations, and behaviors as a way to identify triggers associated with reoffending. *Situational competency tests* ask offenders how they would respond to various high-risk scenarios, while *self-efficacy ratings* involve having offenders rate how confident they are of being able to successfully handle those scenarios. RP programs teach offenders more effective responses to situations they don't feel equipped to handle. They also teach offenders different techniques for *avoiding lapses* (not falling back into the problematic behavior pattern)—things such as relaxation training, planning ways to avoid or escape from high-risk situations, coping strategies for dealing with deviant sexual urges, and cognitive therapy to alter beliefs that make reoffending more likely. Research findings on RP programs for sexual offenders are mixed, with some studies finding such programs helpful and others suggesting they have little or no effect (Gosselin, 2016b; Marques et al., 2005).

Risk-Need-Responsivity Model

The **risk-need-responsivity (RNR) model** is another cognitive-behavioral program for sex offenders, one consisting of three components (D. A. Andrews & Bonta, 2010; Bonta & Andrews, 2007). The first component involves assessing the *risk* of further offenses. Some risk factors may change over time (e.g., personality characteristics, substance use, educational deficiencies, social support, attitudes and beliefs about offending, whether one engages in productive or destructive recreational activities), while others are static (e.g., age, gender, criminal history) (D. A. Andrews & Bonta, 2010; Bonta & Andrews, 2007). Glenn, an antisocial substance abuser and gambler who believes that women often "ask" to be raped by dressing provocatively, poses much greater risk of offending again than Ronald, a member of his church choir who gets along well with others, doesn't use drugs or alcohol, and holds respectful attitudes toward women. Risk predictions are used to determine the second component, *need* (D. A. Andrews & Bonta, 2010; Bonta & Andrews, 2007). Low-risk offenders like Ronald need little or no intervention, while high-risk offenders like Glenn require substantial intervention. The third component, *responsivity*, specifically addresses the risk–need connection. The responsivity principle says that the best way to prevent recidivism is to correctly match risk with need in order to provide appropriate interventions to each offender (D. A. Andrews & Bonta, 2010; Bonta & Andrews, 2007).

CHAPTER 10

RNR targets changeable risk factors, mainly using CBT-based strategies (D. A. Andrews & Bonta, 2010; Stams, 2015). Because risk factors for each offender vary, the techniques used to help also vary and are tailored to the specific offender's needs. Cognitive interventions are employed to change beliefs that make new offenses more likely. Glenn, for instance, might undergo cognitive therapy to change his problematic beliefs about women. Behaviorally speaking, offenders might also be encouraged to anticipate the rewards and costs of their conduct. It may help Ronald to remember that any momentary feelings of excitement and arousal he experiences from flashing people on the subway are undoubtedly going to be eclipsed by his subsequently being arrested and jailed. Again, what is especially unique about RNR is how it personalizes interventions to the precise needs of each offender.

The RNR model has been extremely influential and is widely used around the world (Barnao & Ward, 2015). A review of research examining RNR programs for high-risk offenders in Canada, the U.S., and Australia concluded that there is reason to be optimistic about such programs even though the current evidence for their effectiveness is unclear (Olver & Wong, 2013). The mixed results aren't too shocking given that high-risk offenders are, by definition, at high risk for recidivism (which is why they are difficult to rehabilitate). Unfortunately, high-risk offenders often drop out of their RNR programs. Further, a substantial number of them are diagnosed with antisocial personality disorder (see Chapter 12), a risk factor that predicts poor outcomes. Beyond these issues, research on RNR is hard to interpret because the programs tested don't always implement RNR principles in the same ways (Polaschek, 2012). Additional research may help refine RNR program strategies. To sum up RNR's current status, one researcher noted that it remains the most established and well-respected sex offender rehabilitation model, but it isn't the "last word" on the subject (Polaschek, 2012, p. 13).

Good Lives Model

The **good lives model (GLM)** challenges what its supporters see as the overly CBT nature of the RNR model. GLM adds a humanistic component to sex offender rehabilitation, arguing that it isn't enough to simply focus on reducing risk and avoiding problematic thoughts and behaviors. GLM advocates argue that rehabilitation counselors must also remember that people—even sex offenders—have a basic need for personal growth and fulfillment (T. Ward & Brown, 2004; T. Ward, Mann, & Gannon, 2007; T, Ward & Marshall, 2004; T. Ward & Stewart, 2003). That is, GLM assumes that "human beings are naturally inclined to seek a number of basic goods that are valued states of affairs, actions, and characteristics" (T. Ward & Marshall, 2004, p. 255). GLM programs therefore help offenders identify and pursue *primary goods* (intrinsically beneficial goals such as being independent, excelling at the work they choose, and fostering intimate relationships with others). While GLM relies on many of the CBT techniques used in relapse prevention and RNR approaches, in keeping with its humanistic orientation it places additional emphasis on "offenders' overarching values, talents and preferences" (T. Ward et al., 2007, p. 98). RNR's developers have, not surprisingly, objected to the GLM's critique of their approach as insufficiently attentive to human meanings and motivations (D. A. Andrews, Bonta, & Wormith, 2011). Further, there hasn't been much in terms of controlled research on the good lives model. One case study using it with a violent (non-sex) offender found it beneficial (Whitehead, Ward, & Collie, 2007). A qualitative study with (again, non-sex) offenders didn't test the GLM specifically, but did find that in general offenders valued person-centered interventions (Barnao, Ward, & Casey, 2015). More research is sorely needed to inform future discussions about the utility of GLM, RNR, and RP programs. There is some evidence that they reduce recidivism, but how much depends on the sexual offense. For instance, outcomes for rapists and pedophiles who molest boys are particularly disappointing (Gosselin, 2016b).

From a family systems perspective, case study client Elena's lack of sexual interest in her husband Hector is not due to her having a sexual disorder; it is a product of marital conflict.
Source: Getty Images/Wavebreakmedia Ltd

Family Systems Perspectives

Family systems perspectives view sexual problems not as individual maladies, but as issues reflecting broader couple and family dynamics. That is, a systems view "stresses that sexual disorders do not exist in a vacuum but are often related to problems in the couple's emotional relationship, such as poor communication, hostility and competitiveness, and sex role problems" (Atwood, 2015, p. 452). Systems therapies aim to disrupt the usual family and relationship dynamics that perpetuate sexual problems. That doesn't mean all sexual complaints originate relationally, but "even in cases in which the sexual disorder is not related to relationship problems, the couple's emotional relationship is often damaged by the sexual problem and feelings of guilt, inadequacy, and frustration that usually accompany the sexual disorder" (Atwood, 2015, p. 452).

Elena

From a systems vantage point, our case example client Elena's lack of sexual interest may be best understood as reflecting not an individual disorder, but relational problems in her marriage. Perhaps Elena and her husband Hector are both from conflict-avoidant families and have continued this pattern in their marriage—with each quietly nursing unaddressed grievances about the other. If this problematic and unproductive marital pattern is addressed in systems-oriented couple therapy so that Elena and Hector learn to communicate more effectively, then Elena's sexual interest may return.

CASE EXAMPLES

Although systems perspectives appear to be a natural fit for working with many sexual problems (sex, after all, is a key element of most couple relationships), that hasn't necessarily been the case: "A major problem in the field is that sex therapy for the most part has not been grounded or related to systems theory, meaning that sex continues to be treated as a special area both theoretically and clinically within the couple therapy field" (Atwood, 2015, p. 452). While there have been some interesting couple and family approaches to sex therapy put forward (K. E. Jones, Meneses da Silva, & Soloski, 2011; Weeks & Gambescia, 2015), additional clinical and research work in this area would be welcome.

EVALUATING SOCIOCULTURAL PERSPECTIVES

One of the strengths of sociocultural perspectives is that they remind us that our judgments about sexual behavior are influenced by culture and context. The New View exemplifies this in challenging the medical model, which in its pure form sees sexual disorders as culturally universal diseases rather than—as New View therapists prefer—socially and relationally defined problems. Likewise, sociocultural perspectives emphasize ways in which social values lead us to discriminate against transgender people; they view advocacy and support groups as an important form of social support necessary to overcome such discrimination. In a similar social vein directed at a different problem, rehabilitation programs for sex offenders incorporate CBT and humanistic principles into concrete programs intended to reduce recidivism and reintegrate offenders back into society. Although many clinicians view them positively, the degree to which sex offender rehabilitation programs work continues to be debated. Finally, systemic therapies remain consistent with the sociocultural perspective's emphasis on seeing sexual complaints as products of problematic relational and family patterns; in sociocultural terms, sexual issues are issues between people, rather than inside them.

The main weakness of the sociocultural stance in the minds of many is that in some instances at least, sexual problems may indeed be better attributed to biological and psychological (rather than social) causes.

Ahmed

For instance, the sexual problems of Ahmed—our 65-year-old case example client who experiences difficulty with erections—may indeed be due to biological (age-related) factors effectively addressed via drugs. However, sociocultural advocates might counter that even in cases like Ahmed's, the problem isn't free of social influences. After all, Ahmed may find himself more distressed over his biologically based erectile dysfunction simply because he lives in a culture that equates erections with manhood. In a different cultural context, his erectile issues might not bother him as much.

CASE EXAMPLES

CHAPTER 10

10.7 CLOSING THOUGHTS: SEXUALITY AS SOCIALLY CONSTRUCTED?

Attitudes about what constitutes normal sexual activity change over time. Some critics argue that conceptions of sexuality—including our ideas about love, sexual desire, sexual orientation, sexual identity, sexual response, sexual dysfunction, gender, and so on—are socially constructed (DeLamater & Hude, 1998; Foucault, 1978; Halperin, 1989; Nussbaum, 1997; Tiefer, 1991). As noted in Chapter 2, a social construction is any communal way of defining, talking about, and understanding something that brings into being certain shared social realities, which in turn influence how people come to apprehend themselves (Burr, 2015; Gergen, 2015). From the social constructionist viewpoint, social constructions about sexuality shape how people understand themselves sexually (Billings & Urban, 1982; De Block & Adriaens, 2013; Fausto-Sterling, 2000; Fishman

& Mamo, 2001; D. F. Greenberg, 1988; Lavie-Ajayi, 2005; Tiefer, 2003). For instance, without the socially constructed distinction between homosexuality and heterosexuality, people could not come to experience themselves as gay or straight (Burr, 2015; D. F. Greenberg, 1988). Likewise, they could not see themselves as having sexual dysfunctions without having internalized socially agreed-upon ideas about how much interest they should have in sex, how often they should engage in it, and what constitutes "proper" performance at it (Lavie-Ajayi, 2005; Tiefer, 2003).

As you consider the perspectives on sexual dysfunctions, paraphilias, and gender dysphoria discussed in this chapter, keep in mind that social constructionists see past and current understandings of abnormal sexuality and gender as shaped by taken-for-granted social and cultural assumptions. If such understandings are indeed social constructions, then how might people one hundred years from now view what we currently accept as scientific knowledge about sex and gender disorders? How similar will these future views be to our present understandings? Are there universal truths about sex and gender that transcend time, place, and culture? Or will a comparable chapter on these issues a century from now look utterly different? These questions could apply to just about any presenting problem reviewed in this book, but seem especially pertinent when thinking about sex and gender because our ideas about them have changed so rapidly and significantly over the past century.

TRY IT YOURSELF

Try It Yourself (Answer Key): How Common Are Paraphilias?

Paraphilia	% of People with a Desire to Experience It			% of People Who Have Tried It At Least Once		
	% of all People	% of Men	% of Women	% of all People	% of Men	% of Women
Exhibitionism: traditional definition (exposing self to unsuspecting people)	4.5	5.9	3.4	5.0	7.8	**2.7**
Exhibitionism: nontraditional definition (sex with a partner in front of others or with risk of being seen)	**30.6**	35.0	26.9	**30.9**	32.6	29.4
Fetishism: arousal from nonsexual object (other than a vibrator)	**44.5**	40.4	47.9	**26.3**	30.1	23.2
Frotteurism: arousal from rubbing against others	**26.7**	34.2	20.7	**26.1**	32.4	20.5
Masochism: desire to suffer, be dominated, or be humiliated	**23.8**	19.2	27.8	**19.2**	13.9	23.7
Pedophilia: arousal by children 13 or younger while an adult	0.6	1.1	0.2	0.4	0.6	0.2
Sadism: desire to impose suffering or humiliation on others	7.1	9.5	5.1	5.5	7.4	3.9
Transvestism: arousal from wearing clothes of opposite sex	6.3	7.2	5.5	4.9	6.5	3.5
Voyeurism: arousal from watching an unsuspecting stranger undress, be nude, or have sex	**46.3**	60.0	34.7	**34.5**	50.3	21.2

Bold = higher than statistical criteria (normal curve) for unusual occurrence
Italics = significant difference between men and women

Source: Compiled using data from Table 1a and Table 1b from Joyal, C. C., & Carpentier, J. (2017). The prevalence of paraphilic interests and behaviors in the general population: A provincial survey. The Journal of Sex Research, 54(2), 161–171. doi:10.1080/00224499.2016.1139034

CRITICAL THINKING QUESTIONS

1. How generalizable are these results? Would you expect similar results in urban and rural areas, or in different cultures (this survey was done in the predominantly urban province of Quebec, Canada)? Why or why not?
2. Paraphilic interests and behaviors are more common than many of us assume. Does this influence how "normal" you think such interests and behaviors are? In what way?
3. Should the level of criminality of a paraphilic interest or behavior influence whether we consider it abnormal to be interested in it or to engage in it? Explain your thinking.

KEY TERMS

Androgen
Anorgasmia
Antiandrogens
Bisexuals
Chemical castration
Cisgender
Closeted
Coercive sexual sadism
Coming out
Compulsive sexual behavior disorder
Conversion therapy
Covert sensitization
Cross-sex hormonal treatment
Delayed ejaculation
Dyspareunia
Ego-dystonic homosexuality
Electrical aversive therapy
Erectile disorder
Estrogen
Excessive sexual drive
Experiential sex therapy
Failure of genital response
Female orgasmic disorder
Female sexual arousal dysfunction
Female sexual interest/arousal disorder
Flibanserin
Gay
Gatekeeping
Gender
Gender conformity
Gender dysphoria
Gender expression
Gender identity
Gender identity disorder of childhood

Gender incongruence
Gender nonconformity
Genito-pelvic pain/penetration disorder
Good lives model (GLM)
Habituation
Heterosexism
Heterosexuals
Homophobia
Homosexuals
Hormone replacement therapy (HRT)
Hypersexual disorder
Hypoactive sexual desire dysfunction
Identification with the aggressor
Internalized homophobia
Intersex
Intracavernous injection therapy
Kegel exercises
Lack or loss of sexual desire
Lesbian
Male hypoactive sexual desire disorder
Masturbatory satiation
Menopause
Natal gender
New View
Noradrenaline
Olfactory aversion
Orgasmic dysfunction
Paraphilia
Paraphilic coercive disorder (PCD)
Paraphilic disorders
Pelvic floor rehabilitation
Perversions
Phosphodiesterase type-5 inhibitor
Premature (early) ejaculation

Progesterone
Progestin
Recidivism rates
Relapse prevention (RP)
Risk-need-responsivity model (RNR)
   model
Sensate focus
Sex
Sex reassignment surgery
Sexologist
Sexual aversion and lack of sexual
   enjoyment
Sexual dysfunctions
Sexual instinct
Sexual orientation
Sexual pain-penetration disorder
Sexual response cycle
Sildenafil
Spectatoring
Squeeze technique
Stop-start technique
Surgical castration
Testosterone
Transgender
Transgender-affirmative CBT (TA-CBT)
Transphobia
Transsexual
Transsexualism
Transvestism
Transvestite
Tumescence
Vaginismus

Full definitions of the terms listed above can be found in the end-of-book glossary on p. 533.

Go to the companion website, www.macmillanihe.com/raskin-abnormal-psych, to access a study guide, multiple choice and flashcard quizzes for this chapter, and other useful learning aids.

CHAPTER 10

CHAPTER 11
SUBSTANCE USE AND ADDICTION

11.1 OVERVIEW

 LEARNING OBJECTIVES

After reading this chapter, you should be able to:

1. Define basic terms such as addiction, abuse, and dependence.
2. Identify different classes of drugs and describe their physiological and psychological effects.
3. Summarize *DSM* and *ICD* diagnoses related to substance use and behavioral addictions, as well as explain differences among and controversies over these diagnoses.
4. Discuss how ideas about addiction have changed across history.
5. Describe biological perspectives on substance use and behavioral addictions, including those pertaining to brain chemistry, brain structure, genes, evolution, and the immune system.
6. Summarize psychodynamic, cognitive-behavioral, and humanistic perspectives on substance use and addictions.
7. Outline sociocultural perspectives on substance use and behavioral addictions, especially the importance of socioeconomic factors.
8. Describe self-help, community treatment, and family approaches to substance use and behavioral addictions.

GETTING STARTED: SUBSTANCE USE AND OTHER BEHAVIORS AS ADDICTIVE?

Walter

Walter is a 35-year-old businessman who seeks therapy at the insistence of his wife Margaret. Since his university days, he has always considered himself the "life of the party." However, in recent years Margaret has become increasingly frustrated with Walter's drinking. "He's drunk all the time," she complains. "He drinks all day, every day. He's more interested in his next beer than in me and the kids." Walter admits he enjoys alcohol and drinks it often but denies that he's an alcoholic. "I don't drink as much as Margaret says I do. Besides, I could stop anytime I want," he insists. When it's pointed out that the reason Margaret demanded he seek therapy was because Walter was recently arrested for drunk driving, he dismisses it as "Bad luck that could happen to anyone."

CASE EXAMPLES

Ayesha

Ayesha is a 22-year-old woman who is arrested while wandering the streets in a daze late one night. She tells the police that until recently, she was a graduate student in anthropology at the local university. However, she was kicked out of school for not paying her tuition. She says she's been down on her luck economically, ever since her parents threw her out of the house. When asked why they demanded she move out, she shrugs and says she isn't sure. Further inquiry reveals that Ayesha has been shooting heroin regularly for the past year. Her parents initially tried to help her, but they grew increasingly alarmed by Ayesha's behavior and her refusal to seek help. They were upset with her when she used the tuition money they gave her to buy heroin instead, but the final straw was when she stole one of their credit cards and used it to withdraw large sums of money from their bank account. As Ayesha sits in her jail cell waiting to be arraigned, she begins to tremble, sweat, and feel sick to her stomach.

Pedro

Pedro is a 28-year-old bartender who seeks counseling after his father urges him to get help for his chronic gambling. Pedro regularly bets on sporting events online. He also spends many weekends at a nearby casino or attending high stakes poker tournaments. Pedro began gambling in high school, when he and his friends wagered small amounts of money on card games. By college, he was playing poker regularly, but only if money was involved. "Without something at stake, where's the fun in it?" Pedro asks. In recent years, his father has stepped in to pay off Pedro's debts, in one case saving him from the wrath of an angry bookmaker. Pedro indicates that when he gambles, he doesn't know when to stop. "If I lose, I just keep going back for more," he says. "I just always think the next bet is going to make up for the one before."

Liam

Liam is a 15-year-old high school student whose parents take him to therapy because they are worried about him spending too much time in his room playing video games. "It's like he cares more about the characters and stories in these games than he does about his real life!" his mother exclaims. Liam says his parents are overreacting. "Sure, I like video games and play them a lot. First of all, they're interactive, not passive—like when they sit on the couch watching television. Second of all, what's the harm in it if I enjoy it?" Liam's grades in school have dropped lately, but he says that has nothing to do with gaming too much. His parents wish he'd socialize with friends in the neighborhood. Liam says that he much prefers the people he games with online, even though he's never met any of them in person.

Deanna

Deanna is a 55-year-old woman whose partner, Lesley, brings her to psychotherapy because—in Lesley's words—she's a "shopaholic." When asked about this, Lesley says Deanna regularly runs up huge credit card bills at the mall and while shopping online. She is unable to pay these bills and is currently carrying a large credit card balance, in one case even exceeding her credit limit. "I enjoy the things I buy. Is that so wrong?" Deanna replies. Lesley says she may end their relationship if Deanna doesn't get her shopping under control.

Basic Terms: Addiction, Abuse, and Dependence

Addiction

The term **addiction** is difficult to pin down (M. Clark, 2011; Tieu, 2010). It's "a loaded term" that has "different meanings to different people" (Petry, 2016c, p. 1). It used to be reserved exclusively for situations involving drug use. Thus, older definitions refer to being unable to stop using a substance and continuing use despite negative consequences (A. Goodman, 1990). However, addiction's scope has been broadened to include problematic behaviors such as excessive shopping, internet use, and sexual activity (Black, 2007a; M. Clark, 2011; Derbyshire & Grant, 2015; Fong, Reid, & Parhami, 2012; Petry, 2016a).

Addiction is often conceptualized as a disease. The American Society of Addiction Medicine (ASAM) says "addiction is a primary, chronic disease of brain reward, motivation, memory and related circuitry" (www.asam.org/quality-practice/definition-of-addiction). Although influential, not all clinicians and researchers agree with this definition's full-throated endorsement of the medical model. To them, viewing addiction exclusively as a disease glosses over ongoing disagreements about whether people with drug problems are actually capable of controlling their behavior. Quarrels over how best to conceptualize addiction may explain why the word—although used regularly—is barely mentioned in the *ICD-10* and *ICD-11* and didn't appear in the *DSM* until *DSM-5* in 2013. Even then, the *DSM-5* authors disagreed over whether the term should be included in the manual at all (Hasin et al., 2013). It appears only minimally, mainly in the title of the "Substance Use Disorders and Addictive Disorders" chapter as a way to highlight the chapter's inclusion of not just substance problems, but also chronic gambling. Even though we rely on the term addiction, keep in mind that professional consensus over its proper meaning and usage remains elusive.

Substance Abuse and Substance Dependence

When it comes to drug use, the concept of addiction clearly includes behaviors on both sides of the not-always accepted (but nonetheless important!) distinction between substance abuse and substance dependence. **Substance abuse** is about the ongoing misuse of a substance (W. L. White, 2007). It can involve many different kinds of problematic behaviors due to drug use. Substance abusers often fail to meet school, work, and family obligations. Their substance use interferes with relationships, results in them doing hazardous things (such as driving under the influence), and gets them in trouble with the law (for things like disorderly conduct). Substance abusers misuse substances, but they aren't necessarily physically or psychologically dependent on them.

Substance abuse involves misusing a substance, but—unlike substance dependence—it does not include tolerance and withdrawal. There is controversy over whether the abuse–dependence distinction is valid and should be maintained.
Source: ImageSource

CHAPTER 11

Substance dependence has traditionally been distinguished from substance abuse by two things: tolerance and withdrawal (W. L. White, 2007). **Tolerance** refers to needing more of a drug to produce the same effects. For instance, over time someone who drinks regularly needs increasingly more alcohol to get equally inebriated. **Withdrawal** describes the unpleasant psychological and physical symptoms that result when one stops taking a drug. A common example is when a smoker runs out of cigarettes. The resulting nausea, grogginess, headache, and depressed mood are due to nicotine withdrawal.

As an example of abuse versus dependence, many university students abuse alcohol while at university. They drink too much, do foolish things, and perhaps even get in trouble. That's substance abuse. However, once these students graduate and move into the workforce, most of them stop drinking and start behaving more responsibly. Only those who continue drinking and can't seem to stop are considered dependent. As the website of a well-known addiction treatment center succinctly summed it up, "abuse is too much" and "dependence is the inability to quit" (Hazelden Betty Ford Foundation, 2016, para. 2). As you will see, the abuse–dependence distinction remains part of the *ICD* but has been done away with in the *DSM*. Nonetheless, because many people still make it, it's a distinction to remain aware of as we turn to common substances and behaviors deemed addictive.

Depressants

Depressants are drugs that slow the central nervous system (CNS). They decrease brain function, reduce breathing rate, and lower blood pressure. Dizziness, slurred speech, drowsiness, and sedation also occur. Depressants are usually ingested orally.

Alcohol

Alcohol (also called *ethanol* or *ethyl alcohol*) is the most widely used depressant, contained in many of our most popular beverages (Sussman & Ames, 2008). People have been drinking alcohol for many millennia, with wine being part of human culture for over 6,000 years (Barceloux, 2012; Oei & Hashing, 2013). Alcohol content varies by drink. Beer contains roughly 5% alcohol, wine 10%–18%, and liquors anywhere from 21% to 50% (Sussman & Ames, 2008). Alcohol is absorbed through the gastrointestinal tract, entering the bloodstream and slowing the central nervous system. It affects various neurotransmitter systems discussed in earlier chapters, such as GABA, dopamine, serotonin, and glutamate (Barceloux, 2012; Oei & Hashing, 2013). Alcohol enhances GABA activity while diminishing the effects of glutamate. Because GABA is inhibitory and glutamate excitatory, the result is relaxation. Alcohol also increases dopamine levels in the brain's reward center (Barceloux, 2012; Oei & Hashing, 2013).

Alcohol's status as a depressant can seem counterintuitive because in small amounts alcohol has a stimulant effect. As most of us know, having a drink or two can produce an enjoyable "buzz." The person loosens up (i.e., experiences *disinhibition*) and feels good. However, when the person drinks too much and becomes drunk, alcohol's depressant effects become more obvious: slurred speech, decreased physical coordination, slowed reaction time, impaired judgment, and in some instances emotional outbursts. Extreme drunkenness produces the most intense depressant effects—things like not feeling pain, vomiting, and unconsciousness (Foundation for a Drug Free World, n.d.-b). Alcohol can be deadly, usually when a person's **blood alcohol content** (the percentage of alcohol in the blood stream) reaches 0.35% or higher (Sussman & Ames, 2008). For most people, it takes about an hour for their bodies to process a single drink (Sussman & Ames, 2008), although the exact processing time is affected by a person's weight and sex (because women usually have less body water than men, their blood alcohol levels tend to increase more quickly [National Institute on Alcohol Abuse and Alcoholism, 1999]). Of course, drinks vary in their alcohol content. Further, how much alcohol counts as a single (i.e., standard) drink varies by country; there is no agreed-upon international standard. Table 11.1 lists standard drink sizes in various countries, while Figure 11.1 compares several alcoholic beverages using U.S. standards. As Figure 11.1 shows, not all drinks are created equal. Thus, when imbibing it is important to pay attention to serving sizes of different types of drinks.

Table 11.1 One Standard Drink by Country, Grams and Milliliters of Alcohol

Australia	10 g	13 mL
Canada	13.6 g	17 mL
Ireland	10 g	13 mL
New Zealand	10 g	13 mL
UK	8 g	10 mL
USA	14 g	18 mL

Alcohol is ubiquitous in most modern societies (Barceloux, 2012). Among Americans aged 12 or older, 58.6 million are believed to engage in **binge drinking** at least once a month, which involves having five or more drinks on one occasion (Kosten, Newton, De La Garza, & Haile, 2014). Americans aren't alone in this. In 2006, roughly 80 million people in the European Union aged 15 or older (over one-fifth of the adult population) reported binge drinking at least once per week (Farke & Anderson, 2007). Although drinking is often considered less

A Standard Drink in the US = 18 mL or 14 g of alcohol

Beer	**Wine**	**Liqueur**	**Spirit**
(5% ABV)	(12% ABV)	(24% ABV)	(40% ABV; 80 proof)
12 oz (355 mL)	5 oz (~150 mL)	2.5 oz (~75 mL)	1.5 oz (~45 mL)

Figure 11.1 One Standard Drink in the U.S.

serious than using other drugs, alcohol's social costs are actually enormous, "with alcohol-related injuries accounting for one-third of the global burden of disease" (Oei & Hashing, 2013, p. 648). In the U.S. alone each year, it is estimated that over 620,000 hospital emergency room visits and 40,000 automobile accident deaths are related to alcohol use (Barceloux, 2012). In New Zealand, alcohol-related hospital admissions increased by 18.4% between 2006 and 2011, for a total of 19,180 patients (R. Stewart et al., 2014). Alcohol is also a factor in many suicides, homicides, physical assaults, and rapes (Beynon, McVeigh, McVeigh, Leavey, & Bellis, 2008; Cafferky, Mendez, Anderson, & Stith, 2016; Darke, 2010; de Bruijn & de Graaf, 2016; Kuhns, Exum, Clodfelter, & Bottia, 2014; Lorenz & Ullman, 2016; M. F. Tomlinson, Brown, & Hoaken, 2016; Yuodelis-Flores & Ries, 2015). This may be because being under the influence makes people more likely to act on impulse.

Alcohol abuse takes a huge toll on families. Children raised by parents who drink excessively often have the emotional and physical scars to prove it (Christozov & Toteva, 1989; S. Park & Schepp, 2015; Rossow, Felix, Keating, & McCambridge, 2016). Unborn children of pregnant women who drink are at risk too. They can be born with **fetal alcohol syndrome (FAS)** (Khoury, Milligan, & Girard, 2015; J. J. Smith & Graden, 1998). Children with FAS are usually identified by three characteristics: (a) retarded growth, falling under the 10th percentile of normal height and weight for their age; (b) developmental delays and impaired cognitive performance; and (c) atypical facial features: small heads (*microencephaly*), small eyes (*microphthalmia*), thin upper lips with lack of vertical indentation in the middle, and flat upper jaw bones (Khoury et al., 2015; J. J. Smith & Graden, 1998).

The term **alcoholic** describes people who have difficulty managing their alcohol use. It isn't a diagnostic term included in the *DSM* or *ICD*, so—like addiction—its exact definition is somewhat imprecise. Definitional issues notwithstanding, alcoholics typically experience both tolerance and withdrawal. In roughly 5% of cases, alcohol withdrawal is highly dramatic, inducing an intense syndrome known as **delirium tremens (DTs)** during which the person becomes delirious, experiences intense body tremors, and has terrifying hallucinations (Erwin, Williams, & Speir, 1998). Chronic excessive alcohol use can produce irreversible scarring of the liver, known as **cirrhosis** (H. Popper, 1977; Rehm et al., 2010). Long-time drinkers also are at risk for **Korsakoff syndrome**, characterized by serious deterioration in short- and long-term memory, as well as an inability to recall new information (Kopelman, Thomson, Guerrini, & Marshall, 2009). To compensate for their memory problems, many Korsakoff patients engage in **confabulation**, wherein they invent explanations (which they themselves believe) to account for their gaps in recall (Kopelman et al., 2009). How does chronic alcohol use produce Korsakoff syndrome? By creating a **thiamine** (vitamin B-1) deficiency. Thiamine is a chemical compound that helps the brain convert sugar into energy, but chronic drinking decreases thiamine levels and—over time—leads to Korsakoff symptoms (Kopelman et al., 2009).

Sedative-Hypnotics

Sedative-hypnotics (sometimes just called *sedatives*) are another class of depressants. Barbiturates are one of the most well-known sedative-hypnotics (Barceloux, 2012). They go by slightly different names in the U.S. versus the rest of the world—ending in "al" or "one," respectively (Barceloux, 2012). Thus, *barbital* in the U.S. is *barbitone* elsewhere; likewise, *secobarbital* is *secorbarbitone* and *pentobarbital* is *pentobarbitone*. To further confuse things, these three drugs are often also referred to by their respective trade names: Veronal, Seconal, and Nembutal (Barceloux, 2012; Sussman & Ames, 2008). First introduced as prescription drugs in the early 20th century, barbiturates were used for a variety of medical purposes. They served as sedatives, anticonvulsants, anesthetics, headache remedies, and anxiolytics (anti-anxiety drugs). However, it was quickly realized that

CHAPTER 11

barbiturates had strong addictive qualities. Consequently, they are rarely prescribed today. Barbiturates produce effects similar to alcohol: slurred speech, decreased physical coordination, cognitive impairment and judgment issues, disinhibition, and mental confusion (Barceloux, 2012). Like alcohol, barbiturates enhance the effects of the inhibitory neurotransmitter GABA (Barceloux, 2012). They are cardiorespiratory depressants, meaning that they slow respiration and movement of the diaphragm. Thus, at high doses barbiturates can cause extreme drowsiness, coma, breathing failure, and death (Barceloux, 2012).

Benzodiazepines (previously discussed in Chapters 5, 6, 7, and 9) are the class of drug that largely replaced barbiturates. Also known as minor tranquilizers, benzodiazepines are commonly prescribed as anti-anxiety drugs, sedatives, and sleep aids. While still habit-forming, they are considered significantly less addictive than

At low doses, benzodiazepines are used as anti-anxiety drugs, but at high doses they produce effects similar to alcohol and barbiturates. Benzodiazepines can produce tolerance and withdrawal.
Source: Getty Images/iStockphoto Thinkstock Images\Evgeny Sergeev

barbiturates (Horwitz, 2013). There are many kinds of benzodiazepines. Among the best known are *diazepam* (Valium), *chlordiazepoxide* (Librium), *chlorazepate* (Tranxene), *alprazolam* (Xanax), and *lorazepram* (Ativan) (Sussman & Ames, 2008). Like alcohol and barbiturates, benzodiazepines enhance responsiveness to GABA. In low doses, they seem to help with anxiety and sleep issues. However, at high doses they produce many of the same effects as alcohol and barbiturates, including the risk of becoming addictive. People build up tolerance to benzodiazepines and undergo withdrawal symptoms when they stop taking them. Compared to barbiturates, however, benzodiazepines don't produce as much drowsiness and are less likely to kill those who overdose due to their more modest impact on respiration. While prescribed regularly and considered safe in most instances, doctors understandably try to keep patients on benzodiazepines for only limited periods due to the risks of abuse and dependence.

Let's briefly mention major tranquilizers—antipsychotic drugs such as *olanzapine* (Zyprexa), *quetiapine* (Seroquel), and *haloperidol* (Haldol). Like minor tranquilizers, major tranquilizers are depressants with sedative-like effects (Foundation for a Drug Free World, n.d.-a). They play a huge role in managing psychosis by decreasing dopamine transmission (see Chapter 4). Unlike benzodiazepines, antipsychotics aren't generally considered addictive. Nonetheless, they do produce withdrawal symptoms when a person stops taking them (Haddad & Sharma, 2007).

Stimulants

Whereas depressants slow down the central nervous system, stimulants—which can be taken orally, sniffed, smoked, or injected—speed it up (Sussman & Ames, 2008). Stimulants cause people to feel euphoric, alert, energetic, confident, and hypersensitive to their surroundings (Eaddy, 2013). Restlessness, loss of appetite, increased heart rate and blood pressure, irritability, and paranoia are additional effects (Sussman & Ames, 2008).

Cocaine

Cocaine, made from the leaves of the South American coca plant, is one of the most powerful stimulants, producing euphoria, excessive confidence, and tremendously high energy levels. It does this by stimulating the release of dopamine, while also enhancing serotonin and norepinephrine levels (Barceloux, 2012; Sussman & Ames, 2008). In powder form, cocaine can be "snorted" through the nose or dissolved in water and injected. It can also be turned into a crystal form (known as crack) via a process known as *freebasing*. In freebasing, the pure cocaine is chemically separated out from sugars and other impurities, making crack a more powerful and faster acting drug (Samokhvalov & Rehm, 2013). Crack cocaine is inhaled into the lungs using a pipe (National Institute on Drug Abuse, 2016). While many abusers begin their habit by snorting cocaine, they often later switch to smoking crack (Barceloux, 2012).

According to the World Health Organization (WHO), the lifetime prevalence of cocaine use is 1%–3%, with greater prevalence in the U.S. and countries that produce cocaine (World Health Organization, n.d.). Cocaine use peaked in the mid-1980s, when over 7 million people were estimated to be at least occasional users;

this decreased to just 2.4 million users by 1994 (Barceloux, 2012). While the global manufacture and trafficking of cocaine has dropped by approximately 24%–27% since 2007, there is some evidence that cocaine production may be creeping upward once again—especially in the Middle East and East- and South-East Asia (United Nations Office on Drugs and Crime, 2016). Cocaine dependence therefore still poses an enormous public health problem, "resulting in a significant number of medical, psychological and social problems, including the spread of infectious diseases (e.g. AIDS, hepatitis and tuberculosis), crime, violence and neonatal drug exposure" (World Health Organization, n.d., para. 4).

Cocaine, produced from the leaves of South American coca plants, is one of the most powerful stimulants.
Source: PhotoDisc/Getty Images

Amphetamines

Amphetamines, such as *amphetamine* (trade name *Benzedrine*) and *dextroamphetamine* (trade name *Dexedrine*), are laboratory-manufactured stimulants. Producing many of the same effects as cocaine, amphetamines—which remain in the blood longer—provide an "amped up" energetic feeling by (like cocaine) enhancing dopamine, serotonin, and norepinephrine levels (Sussman & Ames, 2008). As with all stimulants, amphetamines increase heart rate and respiration while reducing the need for sleep (Sussman & Ames, 2008). They are used to enhance alertness and improve performance on mental and athletic tasks. Amphetamines are commonly ingested as pills, but can also be injected or turned into crystal form and smoked. Other notable amphetamines include *methamphetamine* (trade name *Methedrine*, but also called *speed*, *crystal meth*, *ice*, and *crank*) and *3,4-methylenedioxymethamphetamine* (*MDMA*, also known as or *Ecstasy* or *Molly*) (McKetin, Kaye, Clemens, & Hermens, 2013; Ramo, Grov, & Parsons, 2013; Sussman & Ames, 2008). Despite their dangers, amphetamine or amphetamine-derived drugs are used for various medical purposes. As discussed in Chapter 13, certain kinds are prescribed to people diagnosed with attention-deficit hyperactivity disorder (ADHD).

Because they increase dopamine activity, all amphetamines can induce altered reality perception at high doses (i.e., amphetamine psychosis, discussed in Chapter 4). However, MDMA—which actually affects serotonin more than dopamine (Ramo et al., 2013)—has especially strong hallucinogenic properties (hallucinogens are discussed below) (Martins et al., 2013). People on Ecstasy mostly show stimulant effects: increased heart rate, decreased appetite, enhanced mood and energy, feelings of well-being along with lessened anxiety, and a sense of intimacy with others (Ramo et al., 2013). However, they also may experience perceptual changes, such as sensitivity to light and touch. This is what sometimes gets MDMA classified as a hallucinogen. Long popular as a "club drug" for providing partygoers with energy and a sense of connectedness, chronic MDMA use can cause permanent damage to the brain's serotonin neurons (Barceloux, 2012; Ramo et al., 2013; Sussman & Ames, 2008).

Nicotine

Some stimulants are common, easily obtained, and widely used—such as **nicotine**, found in tobacco leaves. Nicotine is most often consumed by smoking it in cigarettes or pipes. However, chewing tobacco, tobacco-based chewing gum, and snuff (a dried tobacco product inhaled by nose) are other delivery methods (Sussman & Ames, 2008). In recent times, it's become popular to ingest nicotine in vapor form via *electronic cigarettes* (or *e-cigarettes*) (Sussman & Ames, 2008). Nicotine functions as both a stimulant and a relaxant, making its users feel both alert and calm. Its effects are caused by it enhancing the neurotransmission of dopamine, glutamate, and **acetylcholine** (important in muscle movement, arousal, memory, and learning) (Sussman & Ames, 2008). Unfortunately, in addition to being habit-forming (tolerance and withdrawal are issues), nicotine is associated with many health problems. Although nicotine hasn't been directly linked to cancer, smoking tobacco (which contains nicotine) definitely has (Barceloux, 2012). Further, tobacco users who are dependent on nicotine have an overall lower quality of life, both mentally and physically. They are at increased risk for respiratory and cardiovascular disease, diabetes, and psychological problems (Attwood et al., 2013; R. A. Schnoll, Goren, Annunziata, & Suaya, 2013).

CHAPTER 11

Caffeine

Caffeine is undoubtedly the most widely used stimulant in the world—a drug taken regularly "by up to 80% of the general population" (Barceloux, 2012, p. 789). It is found in more than sixty different kinds of plants, including those used to make coffee, tea, chocolate, and soft drinks (G. N. Scott, 2013; A. P. Smith, 2013). Caffeine is a mild stimulant that isn't generally considered dangerous or excessively harmful (Sussman & Ames, 2008). It increases norepinephrine and serotonin activity, but has no discernible effect on dopamine (Sussman & Ames, 2008). In most people caffeine increases alertness and energy while also providing a sense of well-being (Barceloux, 2012). Still, people do build up tolerance to it, requiring ever more caffeine for the same pleasant effects. Withdrawal can also be an

Did you need coffee to make it to class today? If so, you're not alone. Caffeine is the most widely used stimulant, consumed by roughly 80% of the population.
Source: Getty Images\Guido Mieth

issue, with headaches and drowsiness the most common symptoms (A. P. Smith, 2013). If you haven't had your usual cup of tea, coffee, or hot cocoa this morning and are feeling lousy, you know what I mean.

Opioids

Opioids (also known as *opiates* or *narcotics*) are powerful painkillers, with mostly depressant, but also some stimulant, effects. They can be *natural* (found in nature), *semisynthetic* (derived from natural opiates), or *synthetic* (made entirely in the laboratory). In functioning as painkillers, opioid drugs mimic the **endogenous opioids** (also known as *endorphins*) created naturally by our bodies. We all have endogenous opioids in our central nervous system. They serve as chemical messengers, reducing pain and calming us down. Opioid drugs have much the same effect as endogenous opioids. Euphoria and drowsiness accompanied by impaired memory, attention, and social functioning are common symptoms of opioid intoxication (Eaddy, 2013).

Some opioid drugs are of natural origin, derived directly from **opium**—a psychoactive substance found in the sap of opium poppy plants. As far back as 3000 BCE, opium was used to relieve pain (Barceloux, 2012). Opium's downside is that it is quite addictive. Advances in chemistry have allowed us to break opium into its component alkaloids—*morphine*, *codeine*, and *thebaine* (Barceloux, 2012; Sussman & Ames, 2008). **Morphine** is an even more powerful painkiller than opium, but—like opium—has addictive qualities. **Codeine** is a milder opioid than morphine, used as a minor pain reliever and cough medicine. Both morphine and codeine—along with **thebaine**, another opium alkaloid with more stimulant than depressant effects (WHO Advisory Group, 1980)—can be used to create semisynthetic opioid drugs.

Other opioids are semisynthetic (i.e., humanly-made using natural opiates). **Heroin** is perhaps the most (in)famous of the semisynthetic opioid drugs because it is so highly addictive. Across Australia, the U.K., and the rest of Europe, it is estimated that between 3 and 8 out of every 1,000 people have a heroin problem (Barceloux, 2012). Dependence occurs quickly, with research suggesting that "signs of physical dependence in human subjects develop after the infusion of heroin 4 times daily for 2–3 days" (Barceloux, 2012, p. 555). Heroin tolerance and withdrawal are especially severe. Withdrawal symptoms include restlessness, insomnia, irritability, high blood pressure, tachycardia (heart rate over 100 beats per minute), teary eyes, runny nose, sweating, dilated pupils, goose bumps on the skin, abdominal cramps, vomiting, diarrhea, and fever (Barceloux, 2012; Samokhvalov & Rehm, 2013). Chronic users eventually reach a point where they must keep taking heroin in ever increasing doses simply to avoid withdrawal. Given the severity of heroin addiction, heroin is illegal or tightly controlled in most countries.

Ayesha
The trembling, sweating, and nausea that our case study client Ayesha experiences while sitting in her jail cell are symptoms of heroin withdrawal.

CASE EXAMPLES

Oxycodone is another semisynthetic opioid. It is less habit-forming than heroin and typically a controlled rather than illegal substance. Used as a pain reliever, it's the main ingredient in drugs marketed under names like Percocet and OxyContin.

Finally, some opioids are completely synthetic, meaning they aren't derived from opium at all. Instead, they are made entirely in the laboratory. *Meperidine* (trade name *Demerol*), *fentanyl*, and *pentazocine* are synthetic opioids used as painkillers and anesthetics. As with benzodiazepines, doctors prescribing opioids must monitor patients for signs of abuse and dependence.

Hallucinogens

Hallucinogens (also known as *psychedelics*) are drugs that induce *hallucinations*, altered thinking and perceptions, out-of-body experiences, and sometimes paranoia (Martins et al., 2013; Sussman & Ames, 2008). They can also lead to **drug-induced synesthesia**, a mixing of sensory experiences in which stimulation of one sensory mode spawns perceptual responses from another sensory mode (Sinke et al., 2012). For instance, listening to music might trigger not only auditory stimulation (i.e., hearing the notes), but also visual imagery (i.e., seeing random colors and images). There are more than 100 different hallucinogenic drugs and their mechanisms of action vary (Sussman & Ames, 2008). Let's review three types.

Indoleamine Hallucinogens

Indoleamine hallucinogens work by activating serotonin receptors in the brain's medial prefrontal cortex and anterior cingulate cortex (Halberstadt, 2015; Sussman & Ames, 2008). By enhancing sensitivity to serotonin, these drugs induce hallucinations and heighten emotional sensitivity. *LSD* (lysergic acid diethylamide), *DMT* (N,N-dimethyltryptamine), and *psilocybin* (4-phosphoryloxy-N,N-dimethyltryptamine; a.k.a., "magic mushrooms") are indoleamine hallucinogens—with LSD probably the best known of the three (Sussman & Ames, 2008). LSD was originally synthesized in 1938 (Barceloux, 2012). During the 1950s and 1960s, once its psychedelic properties were known, investigators researched LSD's effects. They explored its use as a treatment for problems such as psychosis, alcoholism, sexual problems, and autism (Barceloux, 2012). However, LSD's medical uses were limited because many people had negative reactions to it. During the 1960s, a time of social transformation and rebellion, LSD was widely used by those seeking to expand their minds.

Within an hour or two of taking it, people on an LSD "trip" experience an enhanced sense of perception. They often become highly attuned to physical and psychological changes in their bodies. Their heightened responsiveness may also lead them to become preoccupied with minute aspects of their surroundings, such as stripes on their neck tie or individual hairs on their arms. Physical and psychological responses to LSD and other hallucinogens vary widely. Some users report a sense of peaceful bliss and enlightenment, but others experience terror and intense horror—a "bad trip." Because people build tolerance to LSD, each time they take it they must increase their dose to produce the same effects. Unfortunately, as doses and frequency of use increase, so do the risks of frightening **drug flashbacks** in which, at a later date, users unexpectedly re-experience aspects of past drug trips (Barceloux, 2012).

Phenylalkylamine Hallucinogens

Phenylalkylamine hallucinogens produce both hallucinogenic and stimulant effects by affecting norepinephrine, dopamine, and serotonin receptors. *Mescaline* (peyote and trimethoxy-phenethlamine) and *DOM* (2,5-dimethoxy- 4-methylamphetamine STP) are phenylalkyalimine hallucinogens. Mescaline is derived from the peyote cactus found in the southwestern United States. According to research using radioactive carbon dating, Native Americans were using peyote for medicinal and religious purposes as far back as 5,700 years ago (El-Seedi, De Smet, Beck, Possnert, & Bruhn, 2005). Because of its addictive qualities, drugs like mescaline are illegal or tightly regulated in many countries.

Phencyclidine (PCP)

Phencyclidine (PCP) (also called *Sernyl* or *Angel Dust*) is another type of hallucinogen. It works by reducing the influence of glutamate while enhancing the effects of dopamine (Barceloux, 2012). PCP is usually classified as a hallucinogen, but also has a significant number of depressant and even some stimulant properties (Barceloux, 2012). Therefore, it is sometimes considered a depressant. This makes sense given that it was first developed in the 1950s as a surgical anesthetic and was later used as an animal tranquilizer (Sussman & Ames, 2008). However, in addition to its depressant anesthetic effects, PCP also can produce delirium, disorientation, agitation, and hallucinations (Barceloux, 2012). The *DSM-5* therefore groups it with the hallucinogens. Due to its addictive and hallucination-inducing properties, PCP is not currently considered a useful drug for any medical purpose (Barceloux, 2012).

Interestingly, the anesthetic drug ketamine (discussed in Chapter 5 as an experimental antidepressant) is a derivative of PCP (Barceloux, 2012). Ketamine is generally viewed as safer than PCP, but—like PCP—ketamine is also considered addictive. A common "club drug" taken in capsule, powder, crystal, tablet, or solution forms, ketamine goes by street names such as *K*, *Jet*, *Super Acid*, *Vitamin K*, and *Special K* (Ramo et al., 2013). Chronic use can damage the gastrointestinal system and urinary tract (Bokor & Anderson, 2014; Kamaya & Krishna, 1987; S. Ross, 2008; Y. C. Wang, Chen, & Lin, 2010; Winstock, Mitcheson, Gillatt, & Cottrell, 2012). Ketamine's addictive properties are among the reasons why its potential as an antidepressant has so far been limited.

Cannabis

The term cannabis refers to drugs made from the flowers, dried leaves, and extracts of assorted varieties of the *hemp plant* (*cannabis sativa*) (Barceloux, 2012; Grover, Zvolensky, Bonn-Miller, Kosiba, & Hogan, 2013). Tetrahydrocannabinol (THC), the active ingredient in cannabis, is responsible for its stimulant, depressant, and psychedelic effects. The more THC, the greater the potency. While hemp leaves and buds both contain THC, the highest concentration is found in the plant's flower tops. Types of cannabis include *marijuana* (consisting of hemp leaves, flowers, and buds), *ganja* (derived from small cannabis leaves), *bhang* (a drink made from cannabis leaf extract), and *hashish* (a highly potent form of cannabis made from hemp plant flowers) (Barceloux, 2012). Notably, the percentage of THC in cannabis has been increasing over the years (Grover et al., 2013). In the U.S., the average is now 11%, but in states where cannabis has been legalized, the average is notably higher—17%, with certain samples registering levels as great as 30% (United Nations Office on Drugs and Crime, 2016).

Cannabis is usually smoked, but it can be taken orally too (Sussman & Ames, 2008). How does it produce its effects? By reducing GABA and glutamate, while increasing dopamine (Barceloux, 2012; Borowicz, Kaczmarska, & Barbara, 2014). Physically, cannabis usually induces a mild and brief period of intoxication that involves increased pulse, blood pressure, and appetite along with bloodshot eyes, dizziness, and in some instances sleepiness; cognitive and motor performance on complex tasks is impaired (Grover et al., 2013). Psychologically, people's responses to cannabis depend on many factors, including the setting in which they take it, their mood at the time, and their overall personality (Barceloux, 2012). At low doses, many people report feeling relaxed and content. They lose track of time and experience perceptual distortions and heightened awareness (Grover et al., 2013). Others, however, become irritable and paranoid (Grover et al., 2013). At high doses, more intense paranoia is common; hallucinations, depersonalization, and even manic psychosis are also possible (Barceloux, 2012; Sussman & Ames, 2008).

Students often ask whether or not marijuana is truly addictive. This question provokes intense debate. There is evidence that the brain contains cannabinoid receptors (which are sensitive to cannabis) and that regular marijuana users experience withdrawal symptoms when they cease taking it (Budney & Hughes, 2006). The most common symptoms of cannabis withdrawal are irritability, anxiety, trouble sleeping, loss of appetite/weight, and depressed mood (Bonnet & Preuss, 2017; Gorelick et al., 2012). These symptoms are generally considered relatively mild and are usually managed via outpatient interventions, but in more severe cases inpatient treatment may be needed. Despite inducing dependence and withdrawal symptoms, cannabis is usually viewed as minimally harmful and addictive. In some countries, there has even been a move to legalize it. See the Controversial Question feature for an examination of arguments about legalizing marijuana.

CONTROVERSIAL QUESTION

Should Marijuana Be Legal?

There is ongoing disagreement over the dangerousness of cannabis and the extent to which it should be legally restricted (D. E. Smith, 2016). Some people argue that cannabis has many medical uses. They worry that overly strict regulation interferes with using it for legitimate health purposes. After all, there is research suggesting that cannabis may be effective in treating chronic pain, cancer, AIDS, glaucoma, and inflammatory bowel disease (Borowicz et al., 2014; Lamarine, 2012). However, others point out that when cannabis is made more accessible, overall usage rates—for both medical and recreational purposes—tend to increase (Cerdá, Wall, Keyes, Galea, & Hasin, 2012). Cannabis supporters see no problem with this, arguing that cannabis is no more (and possibly less) dangerous than alcohol or tobacco. Therefore, they believe it should be legal for both medical and leisure use. Such a view has gained traction in the past few years. For example, Uruguay and several parts of the U.S. (Alaska, California, Colorado, Maine, Massachusetts, Nevada, Oregon, Washington, and the District of Columbia) have legalized marijuana for recreational purposes (D. E. Smith, 2016; Struyk, 2018; United Nations Office on Drugs and Crime, 2016)—with numerous other U.S. states also on the verge of doing so at the time of writing (L. Sanders, 2018).

However, not everyone is pleased with such developments. Critics argue that cannabis poses serious health risks. Though not always considered addictive, roughly half of cannabis users develop

Recreational marijuana use remains illegal in most places, although Uruguay and parts of the U.S. have decriminalized it in recent years despite controversy over doing so.
Source: iStock.com/JamesBrey

tolerance and withdrawal symptoms (Lamarine, 2012). Some researchers also contend that long-term cannabis use may contribute to heart problems, cancer, anxiety, and even psychosis—though investigators disagree on the strength of the evidence (Lamarine, 2012). Other researchers opposed to legalization worry about the impact of increased access to cannabis on adolescents. High levels of teen use are associated with greater risk for mood and anxiety issues, as well as psychosis, later in life (M. J. Wright Jr, 2015). There is also concern that marijuana is a "gateway" drug that precedes and encourages more serious drug use, although most people who use marijuana don't move on to using harder drugs (National Institute on Drug Abuse, 2017). So, what to make of all the arguments about the health impact of cannabis, pro and con? Confusion may be justified. One review concluded that there is currently insufficient evidence for the strong claims on either side in this ongoing debate (Lamarine, 2012).

Though disagreement about the direct health effects of cannabis continues, there is preliminary evidence that legalizing cannabis does have indirect health costs. In 2014, the year after Colorado legalized recreational marijuana, the number of cannabis-related emergency room visits and hospitalizations increased by 29% and 38%, respectively (United Nations Office on Drugs and Crime, 2016). After legalization, the number of children in Colorado and Washington, D.C. who accidentally ingested cannabis also rose sharply. These statistics are correlational, but they hint that legalizing marijuana may place people at greater risk of injury. Further research is warranted. Of course, its outcomes can't dictate whether restricting cannabis access is the right thing to do because decisions about allowing or denying access to drugs—even when the risks and benefits are informed by science—are inevitably moral and political judgments.

CRITICAL THINKING QUESTIONS

1. Given the research on cannabis' benefits and harms, do you think it should be legal?
2. In deciding whether cannabis should be legal, how much credence do you give to evidence that easier access is associated with increased health and injury risks?
3. If there are legal restrictions on cannabis, should there also be legal restrictions on alcohol—which, as noted in this chapter, also has enormous health and financial costs? What (if any) legal restrictions would you support and why?

Using More Than One Drug (Polydrug Use)

Polydrug Use

Drug users often take more than one substance. This is known as **polydrug use** (Ives & Ghelani, 2006). Polydrug use is a broad term that applies to many different situations. It refers to taking more than one drug at the same time, but it also describes people who transition over time from one drug to another (Ives & Ghelani, 2006). Further, the term is appropriate for both mild and severe cases of drug use. The occasional drinker who every once in a while smokes cigarettes is technically a polydrug user, but so is someone who uses alcohol, cocaine, opioids, benzodiazepines, and heroin on a daily basis (United Nations Office on Drugs and Crime, 2016). Polydrug use is common, but data on it is scarce. However, it does appear that polydrug use of amphetamines and psychoactive substances is on the rise in various parts of the world (United Nations Office on Drugs and Crime, 2016).

Polydrug use can lead to cross-tolerance and potentially dangerous—even life threatening—synergistic effects.
Source: MACMILLAN SOUTH AFRICA

Cross-Tolerance

Polydrug use can lead to **cross-tolerance**. In cross-tolerance, tolerance for one drug transfers to other drugs with similar chemical effects on the brain (United Nations Office on Drugs and Crime, 2016). Thus, regular users of a drug may find themselves highly tolerant of not just that drug, but also of other drugs—even ones they haven't previously used. This allows users to replace a drug to which they have built up tolerance with another drug as a way to avoid withdrawal. Examples of cross-tolerant drug use "include the use of alcohol with benzodiazepines, cannabis or cocaine; concurrent use of heroin, benzodiazepines and antihistamines; the use of alcohol or other opioids (methadone, fentanyl etc.); and the use of cocaine and other stimulants" (United Nations Office on Drugs and Crime, 2016, p. 2). As an example, the chronic drinker who runs out of alcohol may resort to smoking marijuana or taking a friend's benzodiazepines. In so doing, this person staves off going into alcohol withdrawal.

Synergistic Effects

Drugs taken together can also produce a **synergistic effect** in which combining them affects their impact (United Nations Office on Drugs and Crime, 2016). Some drug combinations have a cumulative synergistic effect; taken at the same time, their impact multiplies, provoking a much more intense drug response. For instance, combining alcohol and barbiturates—both depressants—enhances the effects of both. It also greatly increases the risk of overdose.

Rather than enhancing one another, other synergistic drugs elicit opposite effects. When used together they cancel each other out. For instance, taking stimulants like cocaine or amphetamines with opioids—a process known as **speedballing**—can provide the highs of both drugs while reducing their negative effects (United Nations Office on Drugs and Crime, 2016). However, it's also quite dangerous. For instance, heroin and cocaine can produce intense synergistic effects (Duvauchelle, Sapoznik, & Kornetsky, 1998; Gerasimov & Dewey, 1999; Leri, Bruneau, & Stewart, 2003). When administered separately they increase dopamine by 70% and 350%, respectively; however, combining them can elevate dopamine by a whopping 1,000% (Gerasimov & Dewey, 1999; Leri et al., 2003)! The key message? Anytime multiple drugs are combined, the chances of a potentially lethal overdose are greatly increased. To illustrate this, check out the online list of famous people whose deaths were drug-related that is available at https://en.wikipedia.org/wiki/List_of_drug-related_deaths. Note how many of these deaths were attributed to polydrug use.

Beyond Substances: Behavioral Addictions?

Beginning in 1990, the concept of addiction began to expand beyond substance use to include **behavioral addictions** (Marks, 1990). As with substance addictions, behavioral addictions—involving activities like excessive gambling, sex, and shopping—can be difficult to define. Some argue a behavior must meet the following criteria to be considered an addiction:

> *(1) disrupts personal, family, social, or vocational pursuits; (2) causes significant personal distress to self or others; (3) has risk or potential for significant physical or emotional harm to self or others; (4) is uncontrollable or resistant to change (e.g., patient feels out of control or unable to reduce or change the behavior), and (5) is not better accounted for by an alternate psychiatric diagnosis. (Fong et al., 2012, p. 280)*

Failure to resist engaging in the behavior is an especially important criterion (J. E. Grant, Potenza, Weinstein, & Gorelick, 2010; Petry, 2016c)—although knowing whether someone can control his or her behavior isn't always easy to determine. Problem gambling is perhaps the most commonly accepted behavioral addiction. However, other behaviors are increasingly being proposed as addictions too—things like excessive shopping, working, eating, exercising, sexual activity, video game playing, internet use, cell phone use, and social networking (Adams, 2013; Andreassen, 2013; Carbonell, Oherst, & Beranuy, 2013; Echeburúa, 2013; Fong et al., 2012; Q. Jiang & Huang, 2013; Q. Jiang, Huang, & Tao, 2013; D. L. King, Delfabbro, & Griffiths, 2013; Lejoyeux & Weinstein, 2013; Petry, 2016a; Toneatto, 2013). But where do we draw the line? Are these problems really addictions? Maybe they are more appropriately classified as obsessive-compulsive or impulse control disorders (Fong et al., 2012)? Or perhaps they aren't disorders at all? Our uncertainty reflects concern about whether we are pathologizing too many normal variations in behavior. In this vein, some clinicians and researchers worry that, if we aren't careful, the notion of behavioral addictions could become too broad and all-inclusive (Billieux, Schimmenti, Khazaal, Maurage, & Heeren, 2015; Fong et al., 2012). A behavioral addictions expert put it this way:

> *Surely not everyone should have a psychiatric condition, and if many excessive behavioral patterns are deemed psychiatric disorders most everyone would be diagnosed with a mental illness. This concern is particularly relevant to the construct of behavioral addictions. Excessive chocolate eating, even if it is causing weight gain and some distress, does not constitute a psychiatric disorder. (Petry, 2016c, pp. 2–3)*

Table 11.3 Types of *ICD-10* and *ICD-11* Substance Disorders

ICD-10

Allows for the diagnosis of *intoxication*, *harmful use*, *dependence*, and *withdrawal* related to the following substances:

- Alcohol
- Opioids
- Cannabinoids
- Sedatives or hypnotics
- Cocaine
- Other stimulants, including caffeine
- Hallucinogens
- Tobacco
- Volatile solvents
- Multiple drug use and use of other psychoactive substances

ICD-11

Allows for the diagnosis of *intoxication*, *harmful use*, *dependence*, and *withdrawal* related to the following substances:

- Alcohol
- Cannabis
- Synthetic cannabinoids
- Opioids
- Sedatives, hypnotics, anxiolytics
- Cocaine
- Stimulants, including amphetamines, methamphetamine, and methcathinone
- Synthetic cathinone
- Caffeine (no dependence diagnosis)
- Hallucinogens
- Nicotine
- Volatile inhalants
- MDMA or related drugs, including MDA*
- Dissociative drugs, including ketamine and phencyclidine (PCP)
- Other specified or multiple specified psychoactive substances
- Unknown or unspecified psychoactive substances
- Nonpsychoactive substances

*MDA is 3,4-Methylenedioxyamphetamine (MDA), a drug closely related to MDMA; it goes by the street names "Sally," "Sass," or "Sassafras")

As already noted, *DSM-5* codes for severity (mild, moderate, or severe). However, coding can be affected by whether the individual is also being diagnosed with **intoxication** (being under the influence of the substance at the time of assessment) or withdrawal (Kosten et al., 2014). Being in **remission** (no longer displaying signs of difficulty with the substance) can also affect coding; people in remission often describe themselves as *in recovery*. As for prevalence rates, they can be difficult to determine. They vary by country and by drug, with the *DSM-5* providing U.S. rates, some of which are listed in Table 11.4. To nobody's surprise, substance use disorders often go hand in hand with other presenting problems. They are comorbid with mood disorders, anxiety disorders, posttraumatic stress disorder, personality disorders, and attention-deficit hyperactivity disorder (Hildebrand, Behrendt, & Hoyer, 2015; Hunt, Malhi, Cleary, Lai, & Sitharthan, 2016a, 2016b; Ivanov, Pearson, Kaplan, & Newcorn, 2010; Kanbur & Harrison, 2016; Korsgaard, Torgersen, Wentzel-Larsen, & Ulberg, 2016; Lai, Cleary, Sitharthan, & Hunt, 2015; McAweeney, Rogers, Huddleston, Moore, & Gentile, 2010; Souza & Spates, 2008).

Table 11.4 Twelve-Month Prevalence Rates for *DSM-5* Substance Use Disorders

Disorder Type	Ages 12–17	Ages 18+	Men	Women
Alcohol Use Disorder	4.6%	8.5%	12.4%	4.9%
Cannabis Use Disorder	3.4%	1.5%	2.2%	0.8%
Phencyclidine Use Disorder	Unknown	Unknown	Unknown	Unknown
Other Hallucinogen-Use Disorder	0.5%	0.1%	0.2%	0.1%
Inhalant Use Disorder	0.4%	0.02%	0.02%	Close to 0%
Opioid Use Disorder	1.0%	0.37%	0.49%	0.26%
Sedative, Hypnotic, or Anxiolytic Use Disorder	0.3%	0.2%	0.3% (ages 18+); 0.2% (ages 12-17)	Slightly less than 0.3% (ages 18+); 0.4% (ages 12-17).

Stimulant Use Disorder: Amphetamines	0.2%	0.2%	0.2% (ages 18+); (0.1% ages 12-17)	0.2% (ages 18+); 0.3% (ages 12-17)
Stimulant Use Disorder: Cocaine	0.2%	0.3%	0.4%	0.2%
Tobacco Use Disorder	Not reported	13%	14%	12%

Note: *DSM-5* actually reports 12-month prevalence rates for *DSM-IV* nicotine dependence criteria and estimates that because nicotine use is narrower than tobacco use, actual tobacco use disorder prevalence rates (which weren't available when *DSM-5* was published) are probably higher.
Source = *DSM-5* (American Psychiatric Association, 2013b)

GAMBLING DISORDER AND GAMING DISORDER

For the first time, the *DSM-5* and *ICD-11* group gambling and substance use issues together. This is a major change, one the *DSM-5* made partly in response to research suggesting that underlying physiological aspects of these problems are similar (Hasin et al., 2013). Using biological research to inform organization of the manual reflects the *DSM-5*'s medical model orientation.

DSM-5 classifies **gambling disorder** as a behavioral addiction characterized by recurrent problem gambling that leads to impairment and distress. This disorder is listed in the *ICD-10* as **pathological gambling**, but as a habit and impulse disorder—just as it was in the *DSM-IV*. However, the *ICD-11* is following the *DSM-5*'s

The DSM-5 *and* ICD-11 *have renamed "pathological gambling" as "gambling disorder" and now group it with substance use disorders rather than habit and impulse control disorders.*
Source: PHOTOALTO

lead by grouping problem gambling with substance use problems and adopting the *DSM-5* name "gambling disorder." For more, see Diagnostic Box 11.3.

Data across various countries—the U.S., the U.K., Canada, Australia, New Zealand, China, Singapore, Norway, Italy, Sweden, and Switzerland—indicate that gambling disorder is diagnosable in roughly 0.1% to 2% of the population (Petry, 2016b). Consistent with this, the *DSM-5* estimates lifetime prevalence for gambling disorder at 0.4%–1.0%. *DSM-5* also says that men are at greater risk (0.6%) than women (0.2%), a finding supported by earlier research concluding that 72% of problem gamblers are male (Petry, 2016b). Gambling disorder is comorbid with a number of other diagnoses, including substance use disorders, mood disorders, and anxiety disorders (Petry, 2016b). Besides gambling disorder, no other behavioral addictions (e.g., internet addiction, compulsive shopping, sex addiction, etc.) are included in *DSM-5* or *ICD-10*. However, the *ICD-11* includes **gaming disorder** (World Health Organization, 2018b), a diagnosis for people who addictively play video games (see Diagnostic Box 11.4). The *DSM-5* lists a similar diagnosis, *internet gaming disorder*, in its Section III as a potential future diagnosis requiring further study.

Diagnostic Box 11.3 Gambling Disorder/Pathological Gambling

DSM-5: Gambling Disorder
- Persistent and repeated gambling.
- Over 12 months, at least four of these: (1) must gamble larger sums for same excitement; (2) when tries to stop or reduce gambling, becomes impatient and short-tempered; (3) unsuccessfully tries to reduce or stop gambling; (4) absorbed in and focused on gambling much of the time; (5) gambles when upset; (6) tries to recoup losses by gambling more; (7) dishonest about degree of gambling; (8) risks or loses jobs, relationships, or other life prospects due to gambling; (9) relies on others to relieve financial problems caused by gambling.
- Specify severity: *mild* (4–5 symptoms), *moderate* (6–7 symptoms), or *severe* (8–9 symptoms).
Based on American Psychiatric Association, 2013b, pp. 585–586

ICD-10: Pathological Gambling
- Persistent repeated gambling.
- Despite negative consequences (e.g., poverty, strained personal relationships), keeps gambling or gambles even more often.
Based on World Health Organization, 1992, pp. 165–166

ICD-11: Gambling Disorder
- Persistent repeated gambling.
- Difficulty controlling gambling; gambling given priority over other activities and interests; keeps gambling despite negative consequences.
- Symptoms must last at least 12 months, though a diagnosis can be made when symptoms are present for less time but severe.

Based on https://icd.who.int/browse11/l-m/en

Diagnostic Box 11.4 Gaming Disorder in ICD-11
- Persistent repeated video game playing.
- Difficulty controlling gaming; gaming given priority over other activities and interests; keeps gaming despite negative consequences.
- Symptoms must last at least 12 months, though a diagnosis can be made when symptoms are present for less time but severe.

Based on https://icd.who.int/browse11/l-m/en

EVALUATING *DSM* AND *ICD* PERSPECTIVES

Should the Abuse–Dependence Distinction Be Maintained?

Much disagreement surrounded the *DSM-5* decision to combine substance abuse and substance dependence into a single substance use disorder. Defenders of this change argued that the abuse–dependence distinction made sense conceptually, but it was difficult to distinguish in practice. While substance dependence in *DSM-IV* had pretty strong diagnostic reliability, the reliability of the abuse diagnosis was more problematic (K. D. Jones, Gill, & Ray, 2012). Thus, defenders of combining abuse and dependence pointed to research showing that merging these diagnoses into one substance use disorder category enhanced diagnostic reliability (Denis, Gelernter, Hart, & Kranzler, 2015; Hasin et al., 2013; Regier et al., 2013). However, opponents remained unconvinced that the change was for the better. They marshalled evidence showing that the combined substance use disorder category increased prevalence rates by capturing more people than the old abuse/dependence criteria did (T. Chung, Martin, Maisto, Cornelius, & Clark, 2012; K. D. Jones et al., 2012; Kelly et al., 2014). The implied result: improperly classifying more people as having substance use disorders, especially those who only meet milder diagnostic criteria (K. D. Jones et al., 2012).

Because the *DSM-IV* substance abuse category had long been problematic in terms of both reliability and validity, critics expressed further dismay that many of its criteria were incorporated into *DSM-5*'s substance use disorder (J. C. Wakefield, 2015). Part of the problem with the abuse criteria is that they focus too much on the consequences of substance use—things like getting in trouble with the law or having one's family relationships negatively affected by drug use (C. S. Martin, Langenbucher, Chung, & Sher, 2014). Unfortunately, consequences aren't especially helpful for determining whether someone actually has an addiction (C. S. Martin et al., 2014). Debate over whether it was wise to combine abuse and dependence into a single disorder is likely to continue because the *ICD-11* has—in direct contrast to *DSM-5*—opted to retain harmful use and dependence as separate diagnoses (Lago, Bruno, & Degenhardt, 2016; Poznyak, 2014). Until this issue is resolved, whether abuse and dependence are distinct disorders or two aspects of the same disorder will be contingent on which diagnostic manual a clinician uses.

Should *DSM* and *ICD* Include More Behavioral Addictions?

The notion of behavioral addictions has not been without controversy. Some worry that unless we are conceptually careful in how we define them, too many behaviors can easily (and inappropriately) be classified as behavioral addictions (Billieux et al., 2015). This perhaps explains why the *DSM-5* erred on the side of caution by only including one behavioral addiction, gambling disorder. No other behavioral addictions were included. Not everyone appreciated this conservatism, arguing instead that excessive sexual behavior (see Chapter 10), compulsive buying, and internet gaming are legitimate disorders that warrant inclusion in the *DSM* and *ICD* (Black, 2007a, 2007b; Granero, Fernández-Aranda, Mestre-Bach, et al., 2016; Granero, Fernández-Aranda, Steward, et al., 2016; Kafka, 2010, 2013; Petry & O'Brien, 2013; Petry, Rehbein, Gentile, Lemmens, Rumpf, Mößle, Bischof, Tao, Fung, Borges, Auriacombe, GonzálezIbáñez, et al., 2014; Petry, Rehbein, Gentile, Lemmens, Rumpf, Mößle, Bischof, Tao, Fung, Borges, Auriacombe, Ibáñez, et al., 2014; Rehbein, Kühn, Rumpf, & Petry, 2016).

More behavioral addictions will likely be included in *DSM* and *ICD* in the future. The prospects for gaming disorder look bright given its scheduled appearance in *ICD-11* and its inclusion in *DSM-5* as a proposed disorder warranting further study. Prospects for hypersexual disorder and compulsive buying disorder are less clear.

CHAPTER 11

Criteria have been proposed, but neither *DSM* nor *ICD* have indicated that they plan to add these diagnoses. However, supporters of these diagnoses continue to advocate for their inclusion in future *DSM* and *ICD* revisions.

11.3 HISTORICAL PERSPECTIVES

DRUG USE THROUGHOUT HUMAN HISTORY

Drug use has always been a part of human history. Not only is there evidence of alcohol being traded as far back as late prehistorical times, but anthropological evidence also hints that nearly all preliterate societies used psychoactive substances (Westermeyer, 2005). North and South American tribal societies used coca leaf, tobacco leaf, coffee bean, and peyote; African and Middle Eastern ethnic groups produced stimulants like qat, as well as cannabis; and across Asia, opium was prevalent (Westermeyer, 2005). Interestingly, before Columbus traveled to North America, Old World people didn't know about smoking drugs and generally ingested them by mouth (Westermeyer, 2005). Within particular cultures, different economic and social sects didn't always use the same substances: "For example, one group in India consumed alcohol but not cannabis, whereas an adjacent group consumed cannabis but not alcohol" (Westermeyer, 2005, p. 18). Across religions, drugs were used differently, as well. Wine has traditionally been part of Jewish, Catholic, and other Christian rituals, but alcohol use is forbidden by many Muslim, Hindu, Buddhist, and fundamentalist Christian groups (Westermeyer, 2005).

Drugs and our attitudes toward them are greatly influenced by culture and context. Many religious groups incorporate alcohol into their rituals, while others forbid it.
Source: PhotoDisc/Getty Images

MORAL VS. ILLNESS MODELS OF ADDICTION

Substance abuse has caused problems throughout history. The term "addiction" (which we previously noted is hard to define) first appeared in the 16th century. It derives from the Latin word *addictionem*: "a devoting" (Westermeyer, 2013). Prior to that time, what we now call addiction was mainly understood using the moral model (M. Clark, 2011; Westermeyer, 2013). The **moral model of drug addiction** sees excessive drug-taking as a vice; those who overindulge are considered morally weak. Thus, problematic drug use is best viewed not as a sickness, but as a crime. By implication, people who freely choose such crimes ought to be held responsible for them. The criminalization of drug use can be found as far back as the Aztec tribes of North America (Westermeyer, 2005). The moral model remains influential to this day, as evidenced by both widespread drug laws and societal disapproval of many forms of drug use.

As the notion of addiction developed after the 16th century, the **illness model of drug addiction** (also called the *medical model of drug addiction*) increasingly grew in influence. The illness model—first developed in Asia, Europe, and North America—views addiction as a disease, not a vice (M. Clark, 2011; Westermeyer, 2013). One of the earliest historical examples of the illness model is found in the work of renowned physician and signatory of the U.S. Declaration of Independence, Benjamin Rush (1746–1813). Today considered the "Father of American Psychiatry," Rush developed his ideas about drinking in the late 18th and early 19th centuries, at a time when alcohol use in the U.S. was pervasive and widespread. As evidence of this point, in 1830 the annual consumption of distilled liquor in the U.S. was greater than 5 gallons per person; by comparison, in 2009 it was only 0.73 gallons (Freed, 2012). So, to put it mildly, back then "Americans drank all day, and when they drank they got drunk" (Freed, 2012, p. 28). As he studied the problem of drunkenness, Rush began seeing extreme drinking not as a moral defect, but as a sickness. Rush developed his illness model most fully in his famous book, *An Inquiry into the Effects of Ardent Spirits on the Human Body and Mind*. In the book, first published in 1784, Rush argued that alcoholism is a disease, for which the only cure is total abstinence (Freed, 2012; B. Rush, 1784/1823). Rush realized there would be resistance to his illness view, observing that "I am aware that the efforts of science and humanity, in applying their resources to the care of a disease induced by a vice, will meet with a cold reception from many people" (B. Rush, 1784/1823, p. 29). He urged compassion rather than condemnation for those he believed were sick: "Let us not, then, pass by the prostrate sufferer from strong drink, but administer the same relief, we would afford to a fellow creature, in a similar state, from an accidental and innocent cause" (B. Rush, 1784/1823, p. 29).

The illness model greatly impacted the way people thought about drug use. It influenced the 19th-century U.S. and European temperance movements, which saw eliminating alcohol from society as the best means for "curing" drunkenness (Freed, 2012; H. G. Levine, 1978; van der Stel, 2015). It also influenced early interventions for substance abuse, which increasingly adopted a medical stance. For instance, during the second half of the 19th century, chronic drunkards and excessive cocaine and opium users in the U.S. were diagnosed with *inebriety* and often committed to asylums for treatment (Freed, 2012). The illness model became increasingly influential during the 20th century. E. M. Jellinek (1890–1963), a biometrician who began studying alcohol's effects on people, and public relations specialist Marty Mann (1904–1980), one of the first female members of Alcoholics Anonymous (discussed below), worked together to advance the illness model (Freed, 2012; G. Glaser, 2015; Levine, 1978; Straussner & Attia, 2002). Mann, in particular, worked hard to "publicize the medical 'facts' about alcohol addiction" and open "information centers nationwide to advertise alcoholism as an illness" (Freed, 2012, p. 35). Even though not everyone shared their belief in alcoholism as disease, Jellinek and Mann's psychoeducation efforts largely succeeded (Freed, 2012). Professionals and the public increasingly came to see addiction as first and foremost an illness—a view that remains predominant.

THE FOUNDING OF ALCOHOLICS ANONYMOUS

Another important 20th-century development was the establishment of **12-step programs** to assist people in overcoming their addictions. The original and most famous of these groups is **Alcoholics Anonymous (AA)**, which was cofounded by William Griffith Wilson (1895–1971). Wilson (more famously known by the name he used at AA meetings, "Bill W.") was a chronic drinker who—in keeping with the illness model of addiction—came to view alcoholism as a disease, not a moral weakness. However, he believed the best "cure" for alcoholism wasn't intervention by medical professionals, but encouragement and fellowship provided by other alcoholics. AA continues to be influential to this day. At weekly AA meetings, attendees acknowledge their powerlessness over alcohol and provide one another mutual support in abstaining from drink (Freed, 2012). Perhaps because it operated outside of the medical field, the initial response to AA from doctors was quite negative. In 1939, "the *Journal of the American Medical Association* criticized Alcoholics Anonymous as 'a curious combination of organizing propaganda and religious exhortation ... [with] no scientific merit or interest'" (Freed, 2012, p. 33). Similar tensions between 12-step programs and medical professionals periodically flare to this day (L. Dodes & Dodes, 2015; Peele, 1989). AA and other 12-step programs are discussed further under "Sociocultural Perspectives."

11.4 BIOLOGICAL PERSPECTIVES

BRAIN CHEMISTRY PERSPECTIVES

Dopamine Hypothesis of Addiction

The neurotransmitter dopamine is central to many biological perspectives on addiction. This is because dopamine plays a crucial role in the mesolimbic dopamine pathway (the brain's major reward pathway, introduced in Chapter 4 and discussed again in this chapter when examining brain structure perspectives). Thus, neurochemically speaking, there are different versions of the **dopamine hypothesis of addiction**. All of them maintain that addictive drugs increase dopamine levels in the brain. **Reward deficiency syndrome theory (RDS)** hypothesizes that addicted people take drugs to compensate for having too little dopamine (Blum et al., 2014; Blum et al., 2015). RDS theory sees dopamine as producing pleasure. People with reward deficiency syndrome are suspected of being insufficiently responsive to everyday activities that other people find satisfying. Agreeable and rewarding events don't increase their dopamine levels enough to bring them pleasure. In other words, whereas most people's dopamine levels increase naturally in response to pleasant events, the levels of people suffering from a reward deficiency do not. This places them at much higher risk for addiction because when they take drugs, their dopamine levels are artificially raised—something they can't otherwise achieve.

A weakness of RDS theory is that some research suggests that dopamine isn't directly associated with pleasure ("liking"). Instead, it's increasingly viewed as a neurotransmitter of motivation and attention ("wanting") (Berridge, 2007; Berridge & Kringelbach, 2008; Littrell, 2010, 2015). Thus, an alternative dopamine hypothesis called **incentive-sensitization theory** proposes that drugs cause people to seek them out by increasing sensitivity to dopamine (the "wanting" neurotransmitter) in the brain's reward system (Berridge, 2007; Berridge & Kringelbach, 2008; T. E. Robinson & Berridge, 1993). Increased dopamine sensitivity results in people being more alert and on the lookout for drugs. In this model of addiction, drugs hijack the dopamine system by literally changing the brain (Littrell, 2010, 2015; Nestler & Malenka, 2004). The enduring nature of these brain changes may explain why relapse can occur long after drug use stops. The addicted person's brain

CHAPTER 11

remains altered. It therefore continues to be vulnerable to drug-related cues that trigger dopamine activity (Kalivas & Volkow, 2005; Littrell, 2010, 2015).

While dopamine theories of addiction have been enormously influential over the past two decades, a lot remains unanswered. First, the relationship between dopamine and reward may be a lot more complicated than initially believed (Pariyadath, Paulus, & Stein, 2013). Second, most dopamine studies have used stimulants (which directly increase dopamine), but not all drugs affect dopamine the same way that stimulants do (opiates and alcohol are good examples of this) (Badiani, Belin, Epstein, Calu, & Shaham, 2011; Nutt, Lingford-Hughes, Erritzoe, & Stokes, 2015). Third, some drugs that increase dopamine turn out not to be addictive (D. J. Nutt et al., 2015). Fourth, dopamine theories haven't led to any new addiction treatments (D. J. Nutt et al., 2015).

Other Neurotransmitters

While discussed less than dopamine, other neurotransmitters such as glutamate and serotonin have garnered increasing attention when it comes to understanding substance addiction. Glutamate, as you recall, is an excitatory neurotransmitter found in more than half the brain's synapses (Pariyadath et al., 2013). It's been hypothesized that glutamate interacts with dopamine. Animal studies suggest that stimuli associated with drug use can trigger glutamate release in addicted people (Kalivas & Volkow, 2005; Littrell, 2015). If so, this might serve to further prime and motivate addicts to obtain drugs.

In addition to glutamate, serotonin is implicated in addiction, possibly in counteracting the effects of dopamine (Cools, Nakamura, & Daw, 2011; Pariyadath et al., 2013). Because serotonin is associated with impulsivity, it may be important in understanding cravings and relapse (Ciccocioppo, 1999; Kirby, Zeeb, & Winstanley, 2011). Finally, norepinephrine and GABA are also being researched as neurotransmitters involved in rewards, motivation, and addiction (Erdozain & Callado, 2014; España, Schmeichel, & Berridge, 2016; Filip et al., 2015; Gorsane et al., 2012; Sofuoglu & Sewell, 2009; Weinshenker & Schroeder, 2007). When it comes to substance addiction, neurotransmitter research is developing rapidly, with different neurotransmitters appearing to interact in complex ways. Our grasp of these interactions is increasing, but there is much we still don't know.

Comparable Neurochemistry in Behavioral vs. Substance Addictions?

One of the reasons that the *DSM-5* placed gambling disorder in the same chapter as substance use disorders is that many brain researchers increasingly suspect that the biochemical processes behind all addictions (behavioral or substance-related) are essentially alike. Along these lines, a growing body of research suggests that the underlying neurochemistry of gambling and other behavioral addictions is remarkably similar to what occurs in substance addictions. For instance, reward deficiency syndrome is being applied to understand the role of dopamine and related neurotransmitters in gambling and other behavioral addictions (Blum et al., 2014; Fauth-Bühler, Mann, & Potenza, 2016; Y. Meng et al., 2014; Piquet-Pessôa, Ferreira, Melca, & Fontenelle, 2014). This kind of research fits within the Research Domain Criteria (RDoC) perspective first introduced in Chapter 3. RDoC's idea is that disorders should be identified by shared brain abnormalities, not differences in behavior. Thus, if it turns out that substance users, compulsive shoppers, obsessive tan-seekers, and binge-eaters all show the same reliably identifiable neurotransmitter patterns in their brain reward centers, then we should conclude that they all have the same disease. Many investigators are optimistic that future research will show this to be the case, but the fact that the *DSM-5* left out all behavioral addictions besides gambling tells us that others doubt whether sufficient evidence is available yet (Piquet-Pessôa et al., 2014).

Drug Interventions for Addiction

Detoxification is the physical process of weaning addicted individuals from the drugs they are addicted to (J. R. McKay, Kranzler, Kampman, Ashare, & Schnoll, 2015). When removed from drugs all at once (going "cold turkey"), patients can experience intense physical and psychological withdrawal symptoms. However, if drug doses are decreased gradually, detoxification can be done with far less discomfort (J. R. McKay et al., 2015). Detoxification usually occurs in clinics or hospitals, although in some cases it can be accomplished in an outpatient setting. It is "often confused with treatment, but in reality detoxification is, at best, the first step in treatment" (J. R. McKay et al., 2015, p. 764). In other words, detoxification generally needs to occur prior to other interventions.

Drugs to Treat Addiction and Prevent Relapse

Following detoxification, a variety of drugs are often prescribed to prevent relapse in substance users. We review some of them here. **Disulfiram** (trade name *Antabuse*) is given to alcoholics as a way to discourage their drinking (Franck & Jayaram-Lindström, 2013). It works by making them sick when they drink. Disulfiram inhibits an enzyme that breaks down **acetaldehyde**, a chemical metabolite left over after the liver breaks down alcohol (Franck &

Jayaram-Lindström, 2013). When a person gets drunk, the liver is unable to remove acetaldehyde from the body quickly enough; this results in a hangover. Disulfiram amplifies this effect by leaving even more acetaldehyde in the body. Thus, the alcoholic gets extremely sick immediately upon drinking. The main drawback of disulfiram is that to avoid becoming ill when they drink, many alcoholics don't take it (Fuller et al., 1986)—although compliance can be enhanced among patients in the legal system by court-mandating it (B. Martin et al., 2003).

Acamprosate (trade name *Campral*) and **n-acetylcysteine** are drugs used to diminish cravings (Franck & Jayaram-Lindström, 2013; Littrell, 2010, 2011; J. R. McKay et al., 2015). They do so by targeting glutamate (Kalivas, Peters, & Knackstedt, 2006). N-acetylcysteine's main advantage is that it has few side effects, but research on its effectiveness has yielded mixed results (Littrell, 2015). *Naltrexone* (trade name *Vivitrol*), *naloxone* (trade name *Narcan*), and *nalmefene* (trade name *Selincro*) are other drugs used to ward off cravings (Franck & Jayaram-Lindström, 2013; J. R. McKay et al., 2015). They are **opioid blockers** that inhibit the body's pleasurable response to alcohol (Littrell, 2015).

Topiramate, an anticonvulsant drug, is sometimes used to treat alcohol and cocaine problems. By decreasing GABA and enhancing glutamate, topiramate can help reduce drug cravings (J. R. McKay et al., 2015). SSRIs are also occasionally prescribed—especially to alcohol users, who are believed to have low serotonin levels; the evidence for their effectiveness is mixed (J. R. McKay et al., 2015). SSRIs and other antidepressants are also used for nicotine dependence. The atypical antidepressant *bupropion* (marketed for smoking cessation as *Zyban*) has been found to improve smoking cessation rates, as has the tricyclic antidepressant *nortriptyline* (K. Cahill, Stevens, Perera, & Lancaster, 2013; J. R. McKay et al., 2015).

Varenicline (trade name *Chantix*) is a newer drug to help smokers quit. It works by partially blocking nicotine receptors, making cigarettes less enjoyable and decreasing withdrawal symptoms (J. R. McKay et al., 2015). Varenicline is considered the most effective drug for smoking cessation (K. Cahill et al., 2013). **Cytisine** is a drug similar to varenicline that is sold in Eastern Europe under the trade names *Tabex* and *Desmoxan*; it too is considered effective (K. Cahill et al., 2013). There has been some controversy over a suspected link between varenicline and suicide. Since 2009, varenicline (and bupropion) packages in the U.S. have warned about suicide risk (Gunnell, Irvine, Wise, Davies, & Martin, 2009). However, research hasn't shown a consistent relationship between varenicline and suicide; those who favor its continued use contend that if it does increase suicide risk, the increase is small (Gunnell et al., 2009; J. R. Hughes, 2016).

Drug Replacement Treatments

One treatment that doesn't necessarily require detoxification is **drug replacement therapy**, which involves either changing the delivery method by which people take a drug or exchanging one addictive drug for another. Sometimes the goal is to wean people off drugs; other times it is to sustain them on similar but less dangerous drugs. Nicotine replacement therapy is an example of the former, while methadone maintenance therapy represents the latter.

In **nicotine replacement therapy**, the method of nicotine delivery is changed in an effort to make weaning off nicotine easier. *Nicotine gum* (chewing gum with nicotine in it), *nicotine patches* (adhesives affixed to the arm that provide the body with nicotine), *nicotine lozenges* (medicinal tablets that dissolve in the mouth), and *e-cigarettes* (battery-powered electronic devices that administer nicotine in vapor form) are examples of the alternative delivery methods used to help people stop smoking. Ideally, use of gum, patches, lozenges, or e-cigarettes is decreased over time until the person is nicotine-free. Research on the effectiveness of NRT has yielded inconsistent results, but many investigators conclude it works (J. R. Hughes, Peters, & Naud, 2011; Moore et al., 2009). Even if beneficial, NRT in combination with in-person counseling may be more advantageous than NRT alone (J. R. Hughes et al., 2011; Moore et al., 2009; Thurgood, McNeill, Clark-Carter, & Brose, 2016). As for the newer methods like e-cigarettes, the evidence is pretty shaky (Khoudigian et al., 2016). Further, the health risks of e-cigarettes remain unclear (Shahab, Brose, & West, 2013).

In **methadone maintenance therapy (MMT)**, a synthetic opioid (usually *methadone* or *buprenorphine*) is substituted for heroin in an effort to maintain patients on what most people consider a less problematic drug (Mattick, Breen, Kimber, & Davoli, 2009, 2014). Like

Nicotine replacement therapies change the method of nicotine delivery to make weaning off nicotine easier; e-cigarettes are one example of an alternate delivery method.
Source: iStock.com/prostooleh

CHAPTER 11

heroin, methadone and buprenorphine are addictive opioids. However, they provide less extreme highs, last longer (requiring one administration every day or two versus multiple daily administrations when taking heroin), and can be safely and effectively given in either inpatient or outpatient medical settings (Day & Strang, 2011). Thus, MMT works by replacing a more problematic opioid (heroin) with a less problematic but chemically similar one (methadone or buprenorphine). Importantly, the goal isn't necessarily to get patients to stop using addictive opioids because—given the power of heroin addiction, especially its intense withdrawal symptoms—that may not be feasible. Instead, MMT assumes that long-term medically supervised maintenance on methadone or buprenorphine is preferable to taking heroin out on the streets because it is associated with less criminal behavior, higher social functioning, and (although the evidence isn't clear) reduced chance of death (Fischer, Rehm, Kim, & Kirst, 2005; Mattick et al., 2009). In addition to maintenance drugs, MMT also usually involves prescribing naltrexone or naloxone to reduce cravings. Sometimes buprenorphine and naloxone are combined into a single drug (marketed as *Buprenex*, *Suboxone*, and *Subutex*).

Methadone maintenance seems effective, although more randomized clinical trials are recommended (Mattick et al., 2009, 2014). Its main drawback is very high dropout rates. In a Canadian study looking at methadone maintenance program data from 1996 to 2006, retention rates were between 52% and 59% at 6 months, 39% and 46% at 12 months, and 20% and 24% at 36 months (Nosyk, Marsh, Sun, Schechter, & Anis, 2010). A study in China found similarly low rates, with first-year retention ranging between 30% and 70% (K. Zhou & Zhuang, 2014). These high dropout rates may not simply reflect limitations of methadone maintenance as a treatment. Social stigma associated with going to a methadone clinic, as well as conflict with clinic staff, may also play roles (Anstice, Strike, & Brands, 2009; Earnshaw, Smith, & Copenhaver, 2013; Gryczynski et al., 2014; J. J. Sanders, Roose, Lubrano, & Lucan, 2013; C. B. R. Smith, 2010).

Critics contend that claims of MMT's effectiveness are overstated (Ausubel, 1983; Fischer et al., 2005). They argue that replacing one drug with another is a questionable solution to heroin addiction (Ausubel, 1983). At the very least, the possibility of permanently coming off methadone maintenance and being opioid-free is worth discussing with patients (J. J. Sanders et al., 2013; Winstock, Lintzeris, & Lea, 2011). Ironically, some evidence indicates that methadone withdrawal may actually be more severe than heroin withdrawal (Gossop & Strang, 1991). Methadone may therefore be counterproductive when the ultimate objective isn't maintenance but getting people off opioids all together.

Ayesha

Substituting methadone for heroin would be one way to help our case example client Ayesha with her heroin problem. Methadone would be administered under a doctor's supervision. This would keep Ayesha off the streets and out of dangerous situations where she might use dirty needles that carry the HIV virus and other illnesses. Further, Ayesha would only need to take methadone every other day, compared to every few hours with heroin. Because attrition rates for methadone treatment are high, psychotherapy to help Ayesha address issues that might lead her to drop out would also be important.

BRAIN STRUCTURE PERSPECTIVES

Previously discussed neurochemical explanations of addiction often focus on neurotransmitter levels in the brain's reward system. This reward system involves interactions among numerous brain areas, including the *medial prefrontal cortex, amygdala, ventral striatum, ventral tegmental area,* and *hippocampus* (A. Beck, Grace, & Heinz, 2011). One part of the brain's reward system that has gained a lot of attention in addiction research is the mesolimbic dopamine pathway (see Chapter 4 and Figure 11.2). This pathway connects the **ventral tegmental area (VTA)** (located in the midbrain and important in rewards and motivation) to the nucleus accumbens (part of the *ventral striatum,* which plays a role in reward processing). It makes sense that the mesolimbic dopamine pathway is considered important in addiction because communication along this pathway is dopamine-based (R. A. Wise & Rompré, 1989)—and dopamine theories of addiction say that addictive drugs increase dopamine levels, especially in the nucleus accumbens (A. Beck et al., 2011; Volkow, Wang, Fowler, & Tomasi, 2012). Many

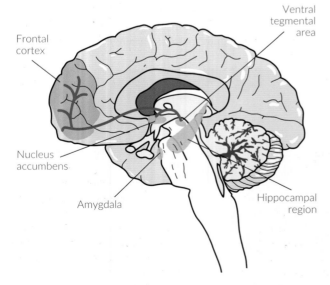

Figure 11.2 The Mesolimbic Dopamine (Reward) Pathway

Source: Figure 1 from: Kalsi, G., Prescott, C. A., Kendler, K. S., & Riley, B. P. (2009). Unraveling the molecular mechanisms of alcohol dependence. *Trends in Genetics*, 25(1), 49–55. doi:10.1016/j.tig.2008.10.005

researchers argue that all drugs of abuse directly or indirectly activate the mesolimbic dopamine pathway and that addiction is a disease of the brain's reward system (Pariyadath et al., 2013).

GENETIC AND EVOLUTIONARY PERSPECTIVES
Genetic Perspectives

Heritability of Addiction

Researchers who have conducted family, twin, and adoption studies point to a strong genetic component in addiction (Leeman & Potenza, 2013). Heritability estimates for substance disorders usually hover around 50%, but can range widely—39% to 72% by one account (D. Goldman, 2013; D. Goldman, Oroszi, & Ducci, 2005) and 40% to 60% by another (C.-Y. Li, Mao, & Wei, 2008; Oei & Hashing, 2013). When it comes to specific substances, heritability estimates for alcoholism are also roughly 50% (Epps & Wright, 2012; Verhulst, Neale, & Kendler, 2015). If correct, this means that about half the variance in alcoholism is attributable to genes and the other half to environment. The heritability for cocaine and opioid addiction is generally thought to be a bit lower than for alcoholism (Epps & Wright, 2012). However, a Swedish twin study examining cannabis, stimulant, and sedative abuse estimated the combined heritability for abusing any of these substances to be higher than 50%, ranging between 64% and 70% (Kendler et al., 2015). And what about behavioral addictions? Heritability estimates for pathological gambling are comparable to substance disorders: 50% to 60% (Grant, Odlaug, & Chamberlain, 2016; Leeman & Potenza, 2013). Based on this data, genes and environment both contribute significantly to substance and behavioral addictions, with genes playing a slightly bigger role (Ducci & Goldman, 2012; Gelernter & Kranzler, 2015; Goldman, 2013; Kendler, Ohlsson, Sundquist, & Sundquist, 2016).

Candidate Genes

Candidate gene studies and genome-wide association studies (GWAs), both described in earlier chapters, try to tease apart precisely which genes contribute to addictions. An enormous amount of research is being done to track down addiction-related candidate genes. Literally thousands of genes have been implicated—1,500 by one estimate (C.-Y. Li et al., 2008)! Given the suspected importance of dopamine in both substance and behavioral addictions, candidate genes related to both dopamine and rewards have received a lot of attention (e.g., DRD2, DRD3, DRD4, DAT1, COMT, MOA-A, SLC6A4, Mu, and GABAB) (Comings & Blum, 2000; Gold, Badgaiyan, & Blum, 2015; Grant et al., 2016; Kenny, Voren, & Johnson, 2013; Le Foll, Gallo, Le Strat, Lu, & Gorwood, 2009; Leeman & Potenza, 2013; Patriquin, Bauer, Soares, Graham, & Nielsen, 2015).

One of the central questions in candidate gene and genome-wide association studies is whether the relevant genes that predict addiction vary by substance. If they do, then a person might be genetically susceptible to alcohol addiction, for instance, but not opioid addiction. If they don't, then certain genes should be associated with all types of substance addiction—and maybe even with behavioral addictions too. While some research implies that more of the genetic vulnerability to addiction is attributable to a general (rather than substance-specific) predisposition (Kendler et al., 2015; Kendler, Ohlsson, Sundquist, & Sundquist, 2014b), specific genes have sometimes been associated with particular kinds of substance addiction. For example, various candidate genes (including GABRA2, CHRM2, and ADH4) have been tied to alcohol dependence (Epps & Wright, 2012; Yan et al., 2014).

Critique of Genetics Research on Addiction

Critic David Moore (2014) points to several weaknesses in genetic research on addiction. First, it assumes addiction is a known entity independent of the many imprecise terms used to describe it ("dependence," "abuse," "addiction," "alcoholism," etc.). Yet these terms construct as much as they reflect what is meant by "addiction." Second, genetic research doesn't always clearly operationalize addiction. How much drinking, for instance, will get one into a study on the genetics of alcoholism? Third, just as what counts as "addiction" is often taken for granted, so is what constitutes an "environmental factor." "Bad parenting," "poor family relations," and "personality traits such as 'impulsivity'" are culturally relative judgments and ways of understanding people (Moore, 2014, p. 579). If how we use these terms changes, genetic research results may shift, as well. Fourth, conclusions drawn from genetic research are often conceptually confused. Do genes and environment "cause" addiction? Or do they merely "contribute" to it? Researchers typically don't clarify whether these are similar or different things. So while genetic research on addiction is fascinating and holds much promise in many people's eyes, critics feel it is less definitive than often believed and doesn't allow us to predict addiction any better than if we simply take a family history (W. Hall, Carter, & Forlini, 2015).

CHAPTER 11

Evolutionary Perspectives

Let's examine three evolutionary hypotheses of addiction. The **mismatch hypothesis** theorizes that drug addiction is an accidental by-product of how our brains evolved (E. M. Hill, 2013). According to this hypothesis, addictive drugs interfere with evolved brain pathways, such as the mesolimbic dopamine pathway (Nesse, 1994; Nesse & Berridge, 1997). This poses difficulties because, given our technical prowess, today's drugs are much more potent than those our ancestors encountered. Therefore, addiction arises because our brains haven't evolved to handle these substances in such powerful forms (E. M. Hill, 2013).

The **mutualism hypothesis** offers a somewhat different take, arguing that our response to addictive drugs isn't a fluky anomaly. Rather, our use of drugs across many millennia has resulted in us evolving a taste for them (E. M. Hill, 2013). As one example, our ancestors were hunter-gatherers who ate a lot of fruit. Often this fruit had fermented, meaning some of its sugar had been converted to alcohol. This stopped bacteria from growing in it. Eating fermented fruit was adaptive because it kept early humans from eating bacteria-riddled fruit. Thus, over time we may have evolved a liking for alcohol, which makes us susceptible to developing a problem with it (Dudley, 2002; E. M. Hill, 2013).

Finally, the **life-history hypothesis** examines ways in which psychosocial and environmental pressures might have influenced how certain groups evolved a vulnerability to addiction (E. M. Hill, 2013; E. M. Hill & Chow, 2002). Research with different groups of people from East Asia has found a correlation between having a gene variation that makes metabolizing alcohol easier and being descended from people who fermented rice at an earlier historic date. This suggests tolerance to alcohol may have evolved in conjunction with alcohol use (E. M. Hill, 2013). The life-history hypothesis also tries to explain differences in alcohol use between men and women, holding that men are more evolutionarily prone to alcohol abuse because it lubricates social interactions and encourages risk-taking, which makes finding mates easier. Women, on the other hand, are more invested in caring for their young; therefore they evolved less vulnerability to alcohol abuse because it simply doesn't serve the demands of child rearing (E. M. Hill, 2013).

Evolutionary theories are hypothetical. They "cannot be tested experimentally ... because the argument is about past events" (E. M. Hill, 2013, p. 41). Still, they pose some fascinating hypotheses that, in conjunction with our increasing interest in identifying genes associated with addiction, make them increasingly popular (E. M. Hill, 2013; Oei & Hashing, 2013; Saah, 2005).

IMMUNE SYSTEM PERSPECTIVES

People with substance use problems are much more vulnerable to illnesses that tax their immune systems (Sarkar, Jung, & Wang, 2015). Of course, disentangling the complex interactions among substance use, stress, and the immune system can be challenging (Crews, 2012). As with many other presenting problems (see previous chapters), addiction is associated with immune system inflammation. Alcoholics, for instance, show decreased immune function and increased blood levels of pro-inflammatory cytokines (immune system cells helpful in healing that can cause swelling in large amounts; again, see previous chapters) (Crews et al., 2015; Szabo & Saha, 2015; R. J. Ward, Lallemand, & de Witte, 2014). Immunity-related inflammation has also been found among heroin users (Y. Y. Chan et al., 2015). Might immune system impairment affect behavioral addictions, too? One study found that excessive internet users reported decreased immune response, although inflammation itself wasn't measured (P. Reed, Vile, Osborne, Romano, & Truzoli, 2015).

Researchers increasingly suspect that genes related to immune functioning may predispose people to substance addiction (Crews, 2012; Crews et al., 2015). In other words, certain people may be genetically susceptible to addiction because their immune systems are especially responsive to drug use. As evidence of this, changes have been observed in the **microglia** of alcoholics (Crews et al., 2015). Microglia are *glial cells* (i.e., support cells) in the brain that are important in immune response. The microglia of alcoholics look noticeably different than those of healthy people. These differences have been linked to various genes that are increasingly suspected of enhancing vulnerability to substance use problems (Crews, 2012; Crews et al., 2015). The role of the immune system in addiction is an emerging area of research that warrants continued study.

EVALUATING BIOLOGICAL PERSPECTIVES

The main objection to biological perspectives is that they insist addiction is a "chronic, relapsing brain disease" (N. D. Campbell, 2010, p. 90), but not everyone agrees with this (W. Hall et al., 2015). The "addiction as brain disease" assumption is so prevalent that many students are surprised to learn that anyone questions it. However, some critics contend that addictive behavior is a choice, not a disease (Kerr, 1996; Schaler,

2000, 2002). They question researchers who say addicts have no control over their behavior. For example, psychologist Jeffrey Schaler (2002) rejects the idea that addicts lack choice: "Chemical rewards have no power to compel—although this notion of compulsion may be a cherished part of clinicians' folklore. I am rewarded every time I eat chocolate cake, but I often eschew this reward." This argument may remind you of the illness–moral model debate. If you like this argument, maybe you sympathize with the moral model. If not, perhaps you prefer the illness model.

Other critics complain that neuroscientists overstate the case for addiction as brain disease, pointing out that—like all *DSM* and *ICD* mental disorders—addictions are still diagnosed using behavioral (rather than biological) criteria (Hammer et al., 2013). Further, critics argue that the disease view hasn't yielded much in terms of new treatment interventions (W. Hall et al., 2015). Defenders of pharmaceutical interventions disagree, arguing that naloxone, acamprosate, and varenicline exemplify the benefits of disease model-derived drug treatments for addiction (Volkow & Koob, 2015).

Finally, some critics assert that neuroscience research emphasizes biological explanations at the expense of social influences. They see the "addiction as disease" view as a social invention whose main advantage (one not always achieved) is to destigmatize those labeled as addicts (Hammer et al., 2013). In this critique, addictive behavior—even with all its compelling biological correlates—always takes place in a social context. When we forget this, we improperly treat addiction as exclusively medical and overlook the social. A few examples: a person can't be an "alcoholic" without socially shared ideas about how much drinking is too much; "compulsive buying" makes little sense outside of capitalist environments that celebrate (yet also worry about excessive) consumer consumption; and "internet addiction" wasn't a "thing" until we invented the internet and began worrying about how much time online is okay. For one last vivid example, consider the difference between people who regularly use prescribed narcotics for pain versus those who regularly use narcotics illegally: "Among the former, neuroadaptation (dependence) is considered a normal 'side effect' of medication, and drug-seeking behavior understandable; for the latter, their neuroadaptation is regarded as pathological, their behavior criminal, and their compunction 'hijacked'" (Hammer et al., 2013, p. 30). Social context matters a lot in what "counts" as addiction.

11.5 PSYCHOLOGICAL PERSPECTIVES

PSYCHODYNAMIC PERSPECTIVES

Attachment Theory and the Self-Medication Hypothesis

Psychodynamic perspectives see compulsive drug use as a symptom of unconscious conflicts traceable to childhood. As such, they place early attachment issues front and center (L. M. Dodes & Khantzian, 2005; Fletcher, Nutton, & Brend, 2015). They believe that inadequate (sometimes downright abusive) parenting at the hands of primary caregivers during childhood leads to insecure relational attachments in adulthood. Consistent with this, many psychodynamic therapists adhere to the **self-medication hypothesis**, which holds that insecurely attached people who have difficulty recognizing and regulating their emotions are most susceptible to drug addiction (Khantzian, 1985, 1997, 2003, 2013). Substance abuse becomes a defensive strategy to avoid overwhelming and unbearable negative feelings about self and relationships (Fletcher et al., 2015; Gottdiener & Suh, 2015). In this respect, substance abusers are similar to people who somaticize in that they often exhibit alexithymia (see Chapter 8)—they have difficulty naming and describing their feelings (L. M. Dodes & Khantzian, 2005). The self-medication hypothesis goes so far as to predict that people use substances to deal with emotional problems (e.g., alcohol to manage constricted or repressed emotions; opiates to deal with anger; and cocaine to relieve boredom and fatigue or fulfill the need for sensation-seeking) (Suh, Ruffins, Robins, Albanese, & Khantzian, 2008).

In psychodynamic therapy, patients gain insight into how their substance use is an ineffective way to avoid painful emotions associated with insecure attachments. The patient–therapist relationship offers an opportunity for patients to learn how to accept, experience, and express

The self-medication hypothesis says that many people drink or use substances to cope with unpleasant emotions and defend against negative feelings about themselves.
Source: ImageSource

CHAPTER 11

their emotions (Khantzian, 2012). Transference (see Chapter 2) must be worked through, in which patients project their feelings about self and relationships onto their therapists. Substance abusers commonly idealize their therapists, but also feel guarded and worry about being controlled by them (L. M. Dodes & Khantzian, 2005). Psychodynamic therapists use therapy as a place to process patients' avoidant relational patterns and help them begin experiencing and sharing their emotions more productively, initially with their therapists and then increasingly with other people in their lives (L. M. Dodes & Khantzian, 2005; Khantzian, 2012). As patients become more emotionally expressive and self-aware (i.e., less alexithymic), they no longer need drugs to escape their feelings. There isn't much research on psychodynamic therapy for substance use, but what little there is has found it effective with alcohol and opiate addiction (Drisko & Simmons, 2012; Gottdiener & Suh, 2015; Leichsenring, Leweke, Klein, & Steinert, 2015).

As with substance addictions, psychodynamic perspectives also view behavioral addictions as expressions of unconscious conflicts. Many different hypotheses about these conflicts have been advanced. Problem gambling has been attributed to early losses and deprivation, an unconscious need to lose, the desire for approval, and unconscious feelings of not being good enough (López Viets & Miller, 1997; Rosenthal & Rugle, 1994). Compulsive shopping has been explained as an unconscious need for nurturing, an effort to deny death, and as a repressed need for sexual adventure (Black, 2016). Excessive internet use has been viewed as a way to avoid intimacy and engagement with the wider world (Allison, von Wahlde, Shockley, & Gabbard, 2006). As with substance addictions, psychodynamic therapies for behavioral addictions aim to help clients gain insight into their underlying conflicts so that they can cope better with negative feelings and improve relational patterns. Research on psychodynamic approaches to behavioral addictions is minimal and mostly consists of case studies (Black, 2016; López Viets & Miller, 1997).

Pedro

If Pedro underwent psychodynamic therapy for his gambling problem, the therapist would help him explore unconscious conflicts. Pedro would discuss his early attachment relationships with his parents: "I always wanted my dad to recognize me and pay attention to me, but he was always busy at work. He never had time for me." Over time, Pedro might gain insight into his unconscious desire for his father's approval and how he never felt good enough. He also might come to understand how the only time his father ever paid attention to him was when he got in trouble for gambling. As he becomes consciously aware of his need for recognition and approval, therapy would focus on Pedro obtaining these things in his relationship with his therapist without having to be a "screw up." As Pedro works through his past emotional injuries and develops new ways of relating and being attached to others that don't require him to be a "screw up" just to get attention, Pedro's gambling would be expected to decrease.

CASE EXAMPLES

The Addictive Personality

Early psychoanalytic theorists speculated about an **addictive personality** that originated in psychic conflicts at the oral stage (B. Johnson, 2003). The notion of an addictive personality (a set of traits that predispose people to developing an addiction) remains popular, especially in self-help books (Naken, 2009). However, among researchers it remains highly disputed. Addictive personality supporters contend that antisocial traits—reflected in behaviors like societal rule breaking, impulsivity, aggression, and lack of empathy for others—are positively correlated with addiction (Eysenck, 1997; Gerstley, Alterman, McLellan, & Woody, 1990; Nathan, 1988; Szalavitz, 2015). They even argue that the genes associated with antisocial personality may also be associated with substance addiction (Szalavitz, 2015). However, addictive personality critics aren't convinced, noting that just because drug users behave antisocially doesn't mean their behavior is attributable to an underlying personality disorder; it might simply reflect impaired judgment from being intoxicated (Amodeo, 2015; Szalavitz, 2015). Those opposed to addictive personality argue that existing evidence simply doesn't support the concept; no clear constellation of personality traits consistently predicts addiction (Amodeo, 2015; Berglund et al., 2011; Kerr, 1996; Nathan, 1988). In light of the paltry evidence, it's been argued that it's time to retire the idea of addictive personality because retaining it reinforces a stigmatizing and pessimistic view of substance abusers as having fundamentally broken personalities that make recovery unlikely (Amodeo, 2015).

COGNITIVE-BEHAVIORAL PERSPECTIVES

From a behavioral perspective, drugs serve as reinforcers—initially as positive reinforcers because taking them makes people feel good; and later as negative reinforcers when taking them relieves the unpleasant effects of withdrawal (Lejuez, Schaal, & O'Donnell, 1998). Behaviorally speaking, then, prescribing disulfiram to addicts serves as a form of aversive conditioning by trying to turn drugs from reinforcers to punishers (Lejuez et al., 1998). The nausea disulfiram induces punishes drug-taking, but—as we saw earlier—many patients simply stop taking it to avoid this. The idea of substance addiction as conditioned behavior also generalizes to behavioral addictions, which behavior therapists see as maintained by classical and operant conditioning contingencies (I. Marks, 1990; Oei & Hashing, 2013).

From a cognitive perspective, substance use problems and behavioral addictions are about dysfunctional thinking and poor problem solving (J. S. Beck, Liese, & Najavits, 2005; J. E. Grant et al., 2010). If we can get people to change their thinking, behavior change will follow. There are many different cognitive-behavioral therapies (CBT) for substance use and addictions. In fact, there are too many to cover them all. Several representative examples are discussed below. Some of these approaches are more cognitive and others more behavioral, but all fall under the broader CBT banner.

Contingency Management

Contingency management (CM) is a behavioral technique designed to reward abstinence and other desired behaviors among drug users. Rooted in the principles of operant conditioning, the goal is to positively reinforce sobriety (Higgins & Petry, 1999; M. Stitzer & Petry, 2006). How does it work? Participants in a CM program take regular drug tests. Those who pass are given rewards such as food, clothes, shelter, employment, and prizes. In some cases, instead of providing tangible rewards, participants are given vouchers that can then be exchanged for rewards. In addition to abstinence, contingency management can be used to reward medication adherence and regular attendance at treatment meetings (M. W. Lewis, 2008). CM has been used to reduce the use of many substances—including alcohol, tobacco, opioids, cocaine, and methamphetamines (Dougherty et al., 2015; Higgins & Petry, 1999; Ledgerwood, Arfken, Petry, & Alessi, 2014; Meredith & Dallery, 2013; Roll, 2007; Secades-Villa, García-Rodríguez, López-Núñez, Alonso-Pérez, & Fernández-Hermida, 2014). It has also been employed to reward people for continuing methadone maintenance treatment (M. W. Lewis, 2008; M. L. Stitzer, Iguchi, Kidorf, & Bigelow, 1993). Research evidence shows that CM works, but is mainly effective while participants remain in the program (Blonigen, Finney, Wilbourne, & Moos, 2015). Once the program is finished and regular reinforcement ends, many people revert back to earlier substance use. Because of this, CM is often used in conjunction with other interventions (such as drug treatments, AA, and cognitive therapy) in an effort to promote more enduring change (Blonigen et al., 2015).

Social Skills Training

Drug abuse is often a means of compensating for poor social skills (J. J. Platt & Husband, 1993). In social skills training, substance abusers are taught how to start social interactions, convey thoughts and feelings, handle criticism, and manage challenging interpersonal situations (Blonigen et al., 2015; Monti, Gulliver, & Myers, 1994; Monti & O'Leary, 1999; J. J. Platt & Husband, 1993). Although social skills training has cognitive and problem-solving components, its main emphasis is teaching concrete behavioral strategies that people can use when interacting with others (e.g., how to start and carry on a conversation, how to politely disagree with others, how to share feelings in a socially appropriate manner). Social skills training typically ranks as one of the most effective CBT interventions for substance use problems (Blonigen et al., 2015).

Relapse Prevention

Relapse prevention (RP), a CBT technique introduced in Chapter 10 as an intervention for sex offenders, is also used with substance abusers. RP is a bit more cognitive than social skills training. It focuses on preventing relapse by teaching those in recovery how to handle high-risk situations that tempt them to begin using again (D. Donovan & Witkiewitz, 2012; G. A. Marlatt & Witkiewitz, 2005; Witkiewitz & Marlatt, 2004). High-risk situations involve people, places, and events that are associated with past drug use (Witkiewitz & Marlatt, 2004). They are often encountered unintentionally, usually by making insignificant everyday decisions.

Ayesha
For instance, imagine that our case example client Ayesha is in recovery from her heroin addiction. She decides to go to the beach one day, where she accidentally runs into her old drug dealer. This is a high-risk situation because it exposes Ayesha to cues (in this case her drug dealer) that may tempt her to return to using drugs.

Here's another example:

> A man who is trying to abstain from drinking takes a shortcut that entails walking past his favorite bar. Although he had no intention of drinking or stopping at his favorite bar, the decision to take that particular route could present a risky situation. (Witkiewitz & Marlatt, 2004)

Relapse prevention teaches recovering substance abusers how to identify and cope with high-risk situations (D. Donovan & Witkiewitz, 2012; G. A. Marlatt & Witkiewitz, 2005; Witkiewitz & Marlatt, 2004). Clients are taught concrete behaviors such as walking away from the situation or declining invitations to use the substance. They are also encouraged to develop a social support system because people who have others around to provide support fare better in avoiding relapse. Finally, cognitive expectancies are evaluated, with the goal of helping recovering substance users feel more optimistic about their ability to navigate high-risk scenarios. The idea is that negative expectations about one's ability to handle a situation make failure a lot more likely. In other words, self-efficacy matters. Recall from Chapter 3 that self-efficacy is an estimate of one's ability to do something successfully, in this case resisting cues that encourage relapse. People who are confident that they are capable of handling risky drug-related situations are more likely to succeed in doing so. Relapse prevention has been found to be effective for alcohol, tobacco, cocaine, and polysubstance use (D. Donovan & Witkiewitz, 2012; Witkiewitz & Marlatt, 2004). However, social skills training is generally seen as somewhat more effective (W. R. Miller & Wilbourne, 2002).

Cognitive Therapy

Cognitive therapy, rooted in the work of Aaron Beck, conceptualizes substance addiction as learned behavior that—like all learned behaviors—can be changed by altering how people think and act (J. S. Beck et al., 2005). As it does for every presenting problem, cognitive therapy focuses on how people's belief systems impact problematic behavior, in this case drug use. Clients' automatic thoughts, intermediate beliefs, core beliefs, and schemas (all discussed in Chapter 2) influence how substance users respond to situations and explain why they resort to relying on drugs as a coping strategy. Cognitive therapy for substance abuse aims to have clients identify and alter dysfunctional thoughts and behavior patterns that lead to drug use. It is typically considered effective, although cognitive interventions generally don't fare quite as well as those with a behavioral or skills focus (W. R. Miller & Wilbourne, 2002). Thus, cognitive therapy often incorporates other CBT techniques, such as skills training and relapse prevention (D. Donovan & Witkiewitz, 2012; Ritvo et al., 2003).

Walter

For Walter (our alcoholic case example), dysfunctional thoughts play a central role in his drinking. In many situations, he has automatic thoughts about not being likable or interesting enough (e.g., "Nobody will like me if I'm not the life of the party" and "Unless I drink, everyone will see how boring I really am"). These are tied to one of his core beliefs: "I'm not lovable." Were Walter to see a cognitive therapist, the goal would be to examine and understand Walter's belief system in an effort to help him revise how he thinks about himself and interprets situations. He also might be taught social skills that allow him to interact more effectively with others. Finally, Walter would learn to identify high-risk situations—such as hanging out with his beer-drinking buddies or going to work-related cocktail parties—that might tempt him to fall off the wagon.

CASE EXAMPLES

HUMANISTIC PERSPECTIVES

Motivational interviewing (MI) is a technique that helps people recognize and do something about pressing problems (W. R. Miller & Rollnick, 2002; W. R. Miller & Wilbourne, 2002). Rooted in the humanistic principles of Carl Roger's person-centered therapy, it is often used as an intervention for substance abuse (Fleck & Fleck, 2013). MI is more goal-directed and focused than classic person-centered therapy (W. R. Miller & Rollnick, 1991). It is also briefer, usually lasting just 1–4 sessions (Smedslund et al., 2011). Motivational interviewers aim to do five things with substance abusing clients: (1) *express empathy* (by actively listening to, accepting, and reflecting back client concerns); (2) *develop discrepancy* (by helping clients see inconsistencies between their current behavior and broader goals); (3) *avoid argumentation* (by not labeling clients as "alcoholics" or "addicts" or placing demands on them); (4) *roll with resistance* (by accepting that clients may not share their perspective or be ready to change); and (5) *support self-efficacy* (by believing clients can change if they choose to, but are the ones ultimately responsible for such changes) (W. R. Miller & Rollnick, 1991, 2002).

MI has often been combined with the **transtheoretical model of change**, which identifies five stages that clients go through on their way to changing (DiClemente & Velasquez, 2002; Prochaska, DiClemente, & Norcross, 1992). The five stages of

Motivational interviewing might help case study client Liam reduce his video game playing by encouraging him to identify goals and become aware of discrepancies between these goals and his gaming behavior.
Source: BANANASTOCK

this model are: *precontemplation* (no awareness of a problem and no intention of changing), *contemplation* (awareness of a problem, but not committed to change), *preparation* (intends to change and makes small changes), *action* (makes decisive changes), and *maintenance* (works to prevent relapse) (DiClemente & Velasquez, 2002). Keeping these five stages in mind can be quite useful in meeting clients where they are (rolling with resistance), while also encouraging and collaboratively supporting them as they progress through the change process.

MI's humanistic framework extends to its therapy strategies, best remembered by the acronym **OARS** (use *open questions*, *affirm*, *reflect*, and *summarize*). MI is more structured than person-centered therapy. It even incorporates the CBT concept of self-efficacy. Yet in maintaining that genuine empathy and acceptance can be used to help substance users identify discrepancies between current behavior and larger life goals, MI remains firmly grounded in the humanistic tradition. It tries to tap into substance users' internal motivations to change. What's more humanistic than that?

Unlike some humanistic interventions, there is a lot of research on MI. Much of it finds MI to be effective in addressing substance use problems (Duffett & Ward, 2015; Hodgins, Currie, Currie, & Fick, 2009; Lundahl & Burke, 2009; W. R. Miller & Wilbourne, 2002; D. D. Walker et al., 2016). One comprehensive review concurred with this conclusion, but also noted that effect sizes for MI are small, other interventions are also effective, and more methodologically strong studies are needed (Smedslund et al., 2011). Another review—this one examining MI as an intervention for substance-abusing teens—didn't find it to be helpful (L. Li, Zhu, Tse, Tse, & Wong, 2016). Thus, while there is evidence supporting MI, research outcomes haven't been uniformly positive. Interestingly, MI research isn't limited to substance use; studies suggest MI may also work for problem gambling (Diskin & Hodgins, 2009; Hodgins et al., 2009; Petry, Weinstock, Morasco, & Ledgerwood, 2009; Yakovenko, Quigley, Hemmelgarn, Hodgins, & Ronksley, 2015).

Liam

Imagine Liam, our 15-year-old case example whose parents think he has a video gaming addiction, undergoes motivational interviewing. He meets four times with a therapist, who empathizes with Liam when he insists "It's my parents who have a problem, not me!" The therapist avoids arguing with Liam and trying to convince him he's addicted to video games. However, she also helps Liam identify discrepancies between his goals and his behavior. Liam reluctantly admits that having most of his social needs met by people he games with online is lonely and unsatisfying; he confesses he'd like to socialize more and develop deeper friendships with kids at school. His therapist empathically reflects this discrepancy: "You want to get out more and have more friends, but you're spending most of your time alone in your room playing games." By the end of the four sessions, Liam has come to better understand what he wants. He decides to cut back on gaming and reallocate that time to afterschool activities where he can start to make more friends.

CASE EXAMPLES

EVALUATING PSYCHOLOGICAL PERSPECTIVES

Psychological approaches to substance addiction are difficult to evaluate because the research literature on them is relatively small and differences between various treatments aren't always found (Blonigen et al., 2015; Klimas et al., 2014). One prominent review concluded that cocaine and cannabis users show the biggest gains from psychological interventions, though treatment dropout rates for cocaine users are pretty high (Dutra et al., 2008). This review also determined that polysubstance users typically improve the least, perhaps because they are often hampered by other psychological and medical problems (Dutra et al., 2008). Although psychological therapies are usually considered helpful, a comprehensive review of alcohol and illicit-drug therapies noted that studies are few and their quality is often weak, making it difficult to compare therapies or draw firm conclusions (Klimas et al., 2014). Nonetheless, contingency management, CBT, relapse prevention, and motivational interviewing are among the psychological interventions usually highlighted as most effective (Blonigen et al., 2015; B. L. Burke, Arkowitz, & Dunn, 2002; Dutra et al., 2008; W. R. Miller et al., 1995). When it comes to problem gambling, no particular therapy stands out as more effective than the rest, but CBT is used most often (Rash & Petry, 2014). There isn't a lot of research on therapies for other behavioral addictions, though there is preliminary support for CBT as a therapy for compulsive shopping (Leite, Pereira, Nardi, & Silva, 2014).

How do psychological interventions compare to pharmacological interventions? They tend to be as good or better, though there is some evidence that acamprosate and the opioid antagonists naltrexone and nalmefene perform comparably to the best psychological therapies (W. R. Miller & Wilbourne, 2002). A significant challenge in comparing psychological to pharmacological interventions is that in many studies patients are simultaneously being treated with both. This makes teasing apart their relative contributions difficult.

Of course, when evaluating therapies for addiction, an important but often overlooked question is "what counts as success?" Typically, total abstinence has been the goal, but some researchers and therapists increasingly believe that helping people reduce or moderate their drug use can also be a good outcome. For more on this provocative issue, check out the "In Depth" feature.

CHAPTER 11

IN DEPTH

Controlled Drinking vs. Total Abstinence

Must people with alcohol problems totally abstain from drinking or can they learn to control their alcohol use? While most approaches preach abstinence, controlled drinking and harm reduction perspectives argue otherwise. **Controlled drinking** treatments aim to help people reduce their drinking to acceptable levels and moderate alcohol's role in their lives, but without demanding abstinence (H. Rosenberg & Melville, 2005; Sobell & Sobell, 1995). Moderation can be achieved using both professional and self-help interventions (Witkiewitz & Marlatt, 2006). **Moderation Management (MM)** is a controlled drinking self-help group whose members generally don't identify as alcoholics. In contrast to Alcoholics Anonymous, Moderation Management sees drinking as a learned behavior, not a disease. Thus, MM promotes controlled drinking over abstinence as an appropriate goal for many problem drinkers (Klaw & Humphreys, 2000; Lembke & Humphreys, 2012).

The objective in most controlled drinking approaches is **harm reduction**—reducing individual and societal harm caused by drug and alcohol use (Heather, 2006; G. A. Marlatt, 1996; Witkiewitz & Marlatt, 2006). Harm reduction focuses less on stopping people from using substances and more on ways to minimize risk when they do. Examples of harm reduction strategies include needle exchange programs (to ensure that drug users avoid HIV by having clean needles), adding thiamine to beer (to prevent Korsakoff syndrome), and providing late-night public transportation (to decrease incidents of drunk driving) (Heather, 2006). Supporters of harm reduction argue that because many people will inevitably drink or take drugs, we should make sure they do so in a safe environment. Opponents, on the other hand, worry that such strategies encourage substance use (O'Loughlin, 2007).

Controlled drinking and harm reduction perspectives challenge both the moral and illness models of addiction (G. A. Marlatt, 1996). They deemphasize the moral model's insistence on criminalizing and punishing substance users and instead focus on health and safety issues. They also question the illness model, which in their view leans too heavily on the assumption that drinking is a disease and abstinence the only viable cure.

Does controlled drinking work? It depends on the severity of someone's alcohol problem. Some studies suggest that for less serious alcohol dependence, controlled drinking treatments are just as effective as those promoting abstinence (Ambrogne, 2002; Heather, 2006; Sobell & Sobell, 1995). However, more severely dependent people usually find moderating their drinking difficult; for them, abstinence may be preferable (Ambrogne, 2002; Heather, 2006; Sobell & Sobell, 1995). Abstinence remains the most common goal in drug treatment, especially in the U.S. (Ambrogne, 2002; Klingemann & Rosenberg, 2009; H. Rosenberg & Davis, 2014). Still, controlled drinking approaches encourage us to question the often-taken-for-granted assumption that abstinence is always the best or only option.

CRITICAL THINKING QUESTIONS

1. Do you think controlled drinking is a realistic goal for problem alcohol and drug use? Explain your reasoning.

2. Does harm reduction implicitly promote drug use? Why or why not?

3. Some controlled drinking advocates believe that the illness model sets people up for repeated relapses by seeing them as having a lifelong disease. What do you think?

Photo source: © PhotoDisc/Getty Images

11.6 SOCIOCULTURAL PERSPECTIVES

CROSS-CULTURAL AND SOCIAL JUSTICE PERSPECTIVES

Socioeconomic Status and Substance Use

From a sociocultural perspective, sociocultural factors greatly influence when, why, and how often people use drugs. This may explain why different drugs are popular in different parts of the world (see Figure 11.3). Within any given culture, important social differences may affect patterns of drug use. Let's examine one factor that is regularly tied to substance abuse: socioeconomic status (SES). Unfortunately, its precise role isn't clear. Some studies have found that adolescents and adults in low-SES neighborhoods are at higher risk for substance use and abuse (Gardner, Barajas, & Brooks-Gunn, 2010; Johansson, San Sebastian, Hammarström, & Gustafsson, 2015; Karriker-Jaffe, 2013; Kendler, Ohlsson, Sundquist, & Sundquist, 2014a). However, not all studies bear this out (Jackson, Denny, & Ameratunga, 2014; Karriker-Jaffe, 2011; Mulia & Karriker-Jaffe, 2012). Sometimes it depends on the drug being studied. While low SES consistently predicts tobacco use among adults, it doesn't as readily predict alcohol and illicit drug use (Gardner et al., 2010). Interestingly, in some cases it is high SES, not

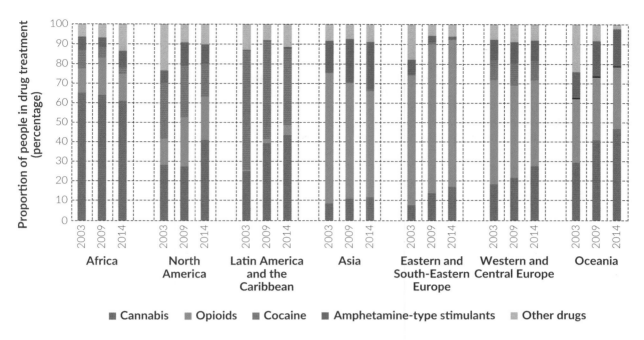

Figure 11.3 Primary Drug Used among People in Drug Treatment, by Region, 2003, 2009, and 2014

Source: Figure 10 from United Nations Office on Drugs and Crime (2016, p. 9)
Note: Based on responses to the annual report questionnaire. Data used for each point in time are based on reporting from countries in each region for the year cited or the latest year for which data are available.

low SES, that is predictive. For example, a number of studies have found that people in higher SES neighborhoods are more likely to regularly use alcohol and other drugs (Gardner et al., 2010; Kuhl, Chavez, Swisher, & Wilczak, 2016; Legleye, Beck, Khlat, Peretti-Watel, & Chau, 2012; W. Pedersen & Bakken, 2016). What neighborhood factors predict risk? In low-SES neighborhoods, relevant factors might be poor schools, economic stress, family conflict, neighborhood problems, and a lack of social support. In high-SES neighborhoods, risk factors might be job-related stress, lax parenting, and low social support (Gardner et al., 2010).

Social Support-Based Intervention Programs

Clinicians operating from a social justice perspective contend that addressing inequality and rectifying social problems are necessary in dealing with addiction. For example, justice-oriented researchers have looked at racial disparities in completing addiction treatment (Mennis & Stahler, 2016). By identifying and understanding these disparities, changes can be made to reduce and eliminate them. Social justice intervention programs for substance abuse try to identify and fix oppressive social systems while helping disadvantaged individuals gain access to services.

Prevention and Early Intervention Programs

Along these lines, **prevention and early intervention programs** aim to thwart the development of substance abuse or, if it develops, to intervene early enough to keep it from snowballing into a larger problem. There are many different kinds of prevention programs, including ones based on CBT and motivational interviewing (Botvin, Baker, Renick, Filazzola, & Botvin, 1984; Dusenbury, Botvin, & James-Ortiz, 1989; Foxcroft, Coombes, Wood, Allen, & Almeida Santimano, 2016; Sussman & Ames, 2008). The **Reclaiming Futures** program in the U.S. provides a nice example of a prevention/early intervention program rooted in a social justice perspective (Nissen, 2007, 2014; Nissen & Pearce, 2011). It was designed for juveniles arrested on drug-related charges (many of them minority group members of low SES). The program assists these adolescents by providing them with easy access to treatment, along with mentorship programs and other community-based social supports. Social inequalities are acknowledged and addressed to not only make access to services easier, but also to fit those services to the needs of those receiving them. Through nurturing and supportive means, the program tries to help kids who have had drug-related run-ins with the law turn their lives around before the problem becomes a lifelong pattern. Preliminary investigations are promising, though research on the program's effectiveness remains in the early stages (Nissen & Merrigan, 2011).

CHAPTER 11

Therapeutic Communities

Therapeutic communities (TCs) are another type of social support intervention for substance abusers. There are many kinds of therapeutic communities. Some are residential (short- or long-term), while others are day treatment programs. The goal is to treat the whole person by providing an array of services, including "medical, mental health, vocational, educational, family counseling, fiscal, administrative, and legal" (De Leon, 2015b, p. 511). Patient drug abuse is viewed as a byproduct of social deficits, such as having trouble delaying gratification, resistance to authority, difficulty managing feelings, poor communication skills, and irresponsibility in meeting social obligations (De Leon, 2015b). Treatment communities aim to re-socialize residents, providing the support and services necessary for them to develop new life skills that eventually allow them to return to society and live more effectively. Patients not only receive treatment, but—reminiscent of the community-care models for alleviating psychosis discussed in Chapter 4—are also expected to participate in the daily operation of the community (things like cooking, cleaning, and minor repair work) (De Leon, 2015b). Some research has found evidence that therapeutic communities are effective in reducing substance use (De Leon, 2010; Magor-Blatch, Bhullar, Thomson, & Thorsteinsson, 2014), but other research has questioned whether these improvements are long-lasting (Malivert, Fatséas, Denis, Langlois, & Auriacombe, 2011). Interestingly, supporters have questioned whether randomized controlled trials (RCTs) are a fair way to assess therapeutic communities, given that such communities involve complex and varied interventions over an extended period that cannot easily be tested using traditional experimental designs (De Leon, 2015a).

Ayesha

After heroin detoxification, Ayesha enters a residential therapeutic community. She has her own room and is assigned household responsibilities. She initially resists the house rules and is angry about being expected to assist in household tasks and attend regular individual and group therapy sessions. Nonetheless, Ayesha reluctantly attends these sessions and, over time, slowly begins to acknowledge her issues. In therapy, she learns how to handle overwhelming negative feelings, which she had previously avoided by getting high. Besides individual and group therapy, Ayesha also attends family therapy with her parents, in which they repair their relationship and work through dysfunctional family patterns. Through these various forms of therapy and having to navigate relationships with other residents of the community, Ayesha learns how to talk about her feelings and communicate them to others. In addition to psychotherapy, Ayesha is given financial and legal advice; the former allows her to develop the skills necessary to function economically once she gets out of treatment and the latter helps her resolve lingering legal issues stemming from her heroin arrest. As Ayesha improves, she becomes more cooperative, responsible, and respectful of house rules. She performs ever-more effectively in completing her chores and she moves up the hierarchy in the residence. Ayesha is eventually put in charge of the kitchen and—with her newfound interpersonal communication skills—takes it upon herself to mentor several new residents entering the residence, just as other members of the community had previously mentored her. After six months, Ayesha leaves the residence and begins her life anew.

CASE EXAMPLES

CONSUMER AND SERVICE-USER PERSPECTIVES

Stigma

Addiction is often accompanied by stigma and rejection (Luoma et al., 2007; L. A. Phillips, 2013). This is especially so for substance use. In one study, more social distance was desired from people described as substance users than people described as smokers or as obese (L. A. Phillips & Shaw, 2013). A large component of stigma involves blaming addicts for their substance use. Although this doesn't fit with the illness model advanced by many in the addictions field, it is common for people to condemn substance users and see them as responsible for their behavior (C. Lloyd, 2013). In this regard, people adhere more to the moral, rather than illness, model of addiction. However, the notion that the illness model always lessens stigma isn't universally accepted; some argue that it encourages us to overlook psychosocial, cultural, political, and historical factors that, if understood, might also be stigma-reducing (Acker, 1993; van Boekel, Brouwers, van Weeghel, & Garretsen, 2015).

Sadly, substance abusers often internalize stigmatized ideas about themselves. This is problematic because internalized stigma is associated with higher rates of continued drug use, longer stays in residential treatment, and poorer social functioning (Can & Tanrıverdi, 2015; Kulesza, Ramsey, Brown, & Larimer, 2014; Luoma, Kulesza, Hayes, Kohlenberg, & Larimer, 2014). Given this finding, public relations campaigns to stigmatize drug use as a way to prevent it may be risky. Even when such efforts prevent new users from starting to take drugs, they also increase self-stigmatization among existing users—something associated with worse treatment outcomes (Palamar, Halkitis, & Kiang, 2013).

Behavioral addictions also carry stigma. Compared to substance use problems, people are more likely to blame behavioral addictions on character flaws (Konkolÿ Thege et al., 2015). A qualitative study of compulsive shoppers concluded that many shopaholics work hard to conceal their addiction due to shame and a desire to avoid stigma (Demerling, 2011). To prevent this sort of stigma, some argue that we must educate people about behavioral addictions, making sure they understand that they are real disorders (Black, 2007a; Yau & Potenza, 2015). Others argue quite the opposite, expressing worry that proposed behavioral addictions such as hypersexual disorder and compulsive shopping run the risk of inadvertently stigmatizing people, many of whom are simply engaging in extreme forms of behavior (sex, shopping, work, etc.) that society encourages (S. Lee & Mysyk, 2004; Woody, 2011).

Deanna
For a long time, Deanna concealed her compulsive shopping as much as she could. She didn't tell her partner, Lesley, when she would go on an online shopping binge. Lesley would only find out when the credit card bill arrived. Nor did Deanna confide in anyone else about her problem. In therapy, when pressed to discuss her compulsive shopping, Deanna admits to feeling ashamed. She worries that others will see her as a "bad person" with "low morals" who "selfishly indulges herself when she can't afford it." Her therapist, who believes that compulsive shopping is no less of an addiction than substance use disorders, works to shift Deanna's thinking. "You have a disease," he tells her, "It's no more your fault than if you had cancer or diabetes." Still, Deanna's partner Lesley remains skeptical. "Deanna just needs to stop it. She isn't 'required' to shop!"

CASE EXAMPLES

Alcoholics Anonymous and Other 12-Step Programs

Basic Philosophy

Alcoholics Anonymous (AA) and other 12-step programs such as Narcotics Anonymous (NA), Cocaine Anonymous (CA), Gamblers Anonymous (GA), and Shopaholics Anonymous (SA) are self-help groups in which people struggling with drug and behavioral addictions meet regularly to support one another in their recovery. These groups are founded locally by addicts themselves. As such, they are organized and run entirely by non-professionals. For example, "no therapists, psychologists or physicians can attend AA meetings unless they, too, have drinking problems" (Lilienfeld & Arkowitz, 2011, para. 3).

What is the 12-step philosophy? In a nutshell, it "emphasizes the importance of accepting addiction as a disease that can be arrested but never eliminated, enhancing individual maturity and spiritual growth, minimizing self-centeredness, and providing help to other individuals who are addicted" (D. M. Donovan, Ingalsbe, Benbow, & Daley, 2013, p. 315). These goals are accomplished by following the 12 steps listed in Table 11.5. Among other things, these steps require addicts to admit their powerlessness over their addiction, accept the influence of God or a higher power in their recovery, and make amends for past wrongs (D. M. Donovan et al., 2013). The goal is total abstinence, achieved through regular attendance at meetings where members receive support and guidance from other recovering addicts (D. M. Donovan et al., 2013).

Table 11.5 The 12 Steps of Alcoholics Anonymous

1. We admitted we were powerless over alcohol—that our lives had become unmanageable.
2. Came to believe that a Power greater than ourselves could restore us to sanity.
3. Made a decision to turn our will and our lives over to the care of God *as we understood Him*.
4. Made a searching and fearless moral inventory of ourselves.
5. Admitted to God, to ourselves, and to another human being the exact nature of our wrongs.
6. Were entirely ready to have God remove all these defects of character.
7. Humbly asked Him to remove our shortcomings.
8. Made a list of all persons we had harmed, and became willing to make amends to them all.
9. Made direct amends to such people wherever possible, except when to do so would injure them or others.
10. Continued to take personal inventory and when we were wrong promptly admitted it.
11. Sought through prayer and meditation to improve our conscious contact with God *as we understood Him*, praying only for knowledge of His will for us and the power to carry that out.
12. Having had a spiritual awakening as the result of these steps, we tried to carry this message to alcoholics, and to practice these principles in all our affairs.

Source: Copyright 1952, 1953, 1981 by Alcoholics Anonymous Publishing (now known as Alcoholics Anonymous World Services, Inc.) The Twelve Steps are reprinted with permission of Alcoholics Anonymous World Services, Inc. ("A.A.W.S.") Permission to reprint the Twelve Steps does not mean that A.A.W.S. has reviewed or approved the contents of this publication, or that A.A. necessarily agrees with the views expressed herein. A.A. is a program of recovery from alcoholism only—use of the Twelve Steps in connection with programs and activities which are patterned after A.A., but which address other problems, or in any other non-A.A., does not imply otherwise. Available from www.aa.org/assets/en_US/smf-121_en.pdf

CHAPTER 11

Prevalence of 12-Step Programs

A World Health Organization (2010) survey assessed the number of 12-step programs around the globe. It found Alcoholics Anonymous in 71% of member nations, Narcotics Anonymous in 56.7%, and Cocaine Anonymous in 11.5%. The original and largest 12-step program, Alcoholics Anonymous, estimates it has roughly 114,000 groups in 170 different countries (Alcoholics Anonymous, 2013). Although it doesn't keep membership lists (Alcoholics Anonymous [Great Britain], 2017), AA estimates that it has 2.1 million members worldwide, with 1.3 million in the U.S., 100,000 in Canada, and 700,000 in other countries (Steinmetz, 2010). A 2014 demographic survey of 6,000 U.S. and Canadian AA members found that 62% were male and 89% were white; average member age was 50 and average length of sobriety was ten years (Alcoholics Anonymous, 2014).

Do 12-Step Programs Work?

Whether or not 12-step programs work has long been controversial. Researching the effectiveness of such groups is difficult because members are anonymous and not readily tracked. Further, 12-step programs don't systematically study their own outcomes—not surprising given that these groups are run by recovering addicts, not medical doctors committed to scientific inquiry. Therefore, existing 12-step program research is often methodologically weak, with few randomized controlled trials and a lack of agreement on what to make of existing studies. Some believe that, despite mixed findings, there is sufficient evidence that AA and other 12-step programs work (N. P. Johnson & Phelps, 1991; Kaskutas, 2009; Krentzman, 2007; Lilienfeld & Arkowitz, 2011; Pagano, Friend, Tonigan, & Stout, 2004). One reviewer encouragingly concluded that overall "the evidence for AA effectiveness is strong" (Kaskutas, 2009, p. 155). However, others are less enthusiastic, believing the evidence for 12-step programs to be lacking (P. E. Bebbington, 1976; L. Dodes & Dodes, 2015; Ferri, Amato, & Davoli, 2006; G. Glaser, 2015). These detractors note that no randomized clinical trial "to date has been able to prove that AA is effective at all" and that AA's success rate is, by objective measures, only 5% to 8% (L. Dodes & Dodes, 2015, p. 56). In addition to scientific objections, many 12-step critics are uncomfortable with the programs' emphasis on religion and spirituality (Ferentzy, Skinner, & Antze, 2010; Sharma & Branscum, 2010). That is, they are "put off by the faith-based approach of the 12 steps, five of which mention God" (Glaser, 2015, para. 5). The debate over 12-step programs is likely to continue. However, one thing nobody doubts is that for some people, these programs are profoundly life-altering. See "The Lived Experience" box for an example.

THE LIVED EXPERIENCE

Stu W's Story of Recovery

I'm not certain that many people can recall their first drink, but aside from a few ceremonial sips of wine around the dinner table on Fridays and Jewish Holidays, the memory of my first cocktail is well ingrained in my consciousness. It was at my friend's Bar Mitzvah during the cocktail hour. A gray-haired woman walked away from the bar and left half of a whiskey sour. Curiously and almost instinctively, I grabbed the glass, turned it so the lipstick smudges wouldn't touch my lips, and downed the fruity beverage. What happened next would be a sensation that I would seek in almost all of the high school teen dances, college fraternity parties, twenty-something-social mixers, romantic dates, and business-related functions I attended years later. I enjoyed alcohol like everyone else did. I loved the feelings it produced in me. It made me more relaxed and sociable. It made me laugh and helped me come out of my shell of shyness. It made me feel confident and "comfortable in my skin," which I never did. What I didn't realize is that, while I was drinking "normally" as others did, the internal reaction I had was different.

So, in the aftermath of my failed marriage, career challenges, lopsided custody situation and accompanying resentment and depression, I sought out situations and people where I blended in and drank to numb painful feelings. Alcohol seemed to have a different effect on me, but I didn't notice or care about it back then. After a night of enjoying too many cocktails to count, when others called a cab, I always insisted on driving. I drove as fast as my car would go. A lot. Thankfully and luckily, I never crashed or hurt anyone. Somehow, I never got caught. I engaged in many high-risk activities, spent money as if it were Monopoly currency, and ended up in places and with people that I *never ever* would have chosen to be with if I had been sober—and I did this repeatedly. When I had time with my son, I was sober and present, but the rest of the time, I sought out parties and booze to numb out.

So, on October 28, 2006, with all of this "wreckage," a feeling of hollowness in my gut, an aching heart, and an anxious mind, I took the longest walk of my life into my first 12-step recovery meeting. It was a Sunday morning in Newport Beach, California. I saw a large gathering of about 100 people on the beach about half way between the boardwalk and the ocean. I stepped onto the sand and started the walk. What was really just a few hundred feet seemed like it was a quarter mile. When I got to the circle, I sat on the periphery. About 10 minutes into the meeting, I started to sob. I did not plan to break down in front of so many complete strangers. It caught me totally by surprise, but something moved in me and I couldn't hold it back. The man sitting next to me reached over, put his arm around me, and whispered in my ear: "It's going to be okay. I'm glad you are here. Let's talk after the meeting." That man's name is Paul and every year for the last ten years, I have driven to Newport Beach to that meeting to thank him. Each year, he tells me the same thing: "Just pay it forward."

Paul sent me home with the suggestion to go to a meeting in San Diego that night, which I did. Half way through the meeting, it happened again. I started sobbing. I was just so broken inside. The people at that meeting huddled around me and hugged me and gave me books and pamphlets and meeting schedules and phone numbers. They told me to "keep coming back" and to "call anytime day or night." I was so scared and numb with bewilderment. I didn't know anyone. I didn't know how I ended up in those meetings with those people. I had never even heard of those meetings, but there they were; right smack in the middle of the town where I worked and spent so many happy hours. In that teeny church's kindergarten classroom, a whole society of recovering people gathered on a regular basis. At the time, I had no idea that those meetings were everywhere across Southern California, with hundreds offered weekly.

Consumed with anxiety, I attended another meeting the next day. With my head down, still in shock, and once again on the verge of tears, this time the leader of the meeting called on me to share. In between sobs, I choked out some words of despair. The room was dead silent. When I was done, people clapped. Slips of paper started to get passed to me from all directions. On them were the phone numbers of men offering their support and help. To this day, almost eleven years later, I still carry a card in my wallet that has the names and numbers of ten of those men on it.

Despite the things I did when drinking, I was initially confused about whether I belonged at these meetings. I didn't drink like the other attendees had. I never sat at a bar for hours and then fell off of my bar stool. I never got kicked off of an airplane for being intoxicated, never went to jail, never had a DUI, and never went to a "detox" facility, let alone rehab. I certainly didn't see myself trading late night parties, with bikini-clad women-in-heels and copious amounts of booze and drugs, for 12-step meetings. I was never going to become one of those people drinking endless cups of bad coffee, and chain smoking cigarettes. But my view shifted as I started to hear stories that sounded like mine. I began to see that I did fit in ... and I still do.

Virtually friendless, alone, nearly broke and scared, I went to two and even three meetings every day. When I stopped consuming the mind-altering elixir that soothed my nerves (and masked my pain) the underlying feelings of being irritable, depressed, ashamed, resentful and afraid set in ... and they didn't go away. I didn't know why I was feeling that way and I didn't know how to make it stop, but those people said they knew how—and they were laughing and happy. Anyway, when I shared my pain, something changed. All I know is that for the last 10 years and 10 months, I have been on a journey of recovery, which continues to this day. Whereas once, full of guilt and shame from the double-life I was living, I couldn't look my 4-year-old son in the eyes when he came to see me on Father's Day, I now have an amazingly close, emotionally open relationship with him. Back then, I was consumed with profound sadness and grief at the loss of my marriage, as well as intense resentment toward my now-former-wife. Now, I have an amicable relationship with her and her new husband.

Recovery, and the resulting Divine Power I discovered in the process, keep me sober today. I have replaced all-night parties with bottomless Jack and Cokes to a daily routine of spiritual practices and ongoing service work for others in need. But the wreckage from my partying years has left its toll. I lost two of my closest friends. I lost huge amounts of money. I lost my direction. I lost a piece of my soul. With the exception of the lost friendships, my recovery has helped me to establish balance in my life. I now have a more simplistic yet satisfying lifestyle. I am comfortable in my skin and can go anywhere and not be tempted to drink. That's the miracle of recovery.

So, with the intervention of a Power Greater than Myself, a program of recovery, and many supportive recovering friends around me, I am sober today. As I live my life, clean and sober, I now have the great responsibility and humble honor of being that man who can put his arm around another scared, suffering soul when he takes that long walk out on the sand and sits on the periphery of that circle. I am now qualified to say to him, "It's going to be okay. I'm glad you're here. Let's talk after the meeting."

By Stuart Weintraub. Reprinted with permission.

CHAPTER 11

SYSTEMS PERSPECTIVES

Family systems perspectives emphasize how family functioning plays a central role in fostering and sustaining substance abuse (C. L. Rowe, 2012). Family systems therapies address drug abuse by changing what they see as the problematic family dynamics behind it. Many different family systems therapies for substance abuse have been developed (C. L. Rowe, 2012). We review just one here: **multidimensional family therapy (MDFT)**.

MDFT is specifically designed to treat adolescents' substance issues. When using MDFT to treat teen addiction, assessment and intervention focus on individual, family, and environmental factors that contribute to ongoing substance use (Liddle, 2010; C. Rowe, Liddle, McClintic, & Quille, 2002). Interventions are done with the adolescent drug users themselves, as well as with their parents, other family members, and social systems external to the family (such as schools and the court system) (Liddle, 2010; C. Rowe et al., 2002). Many kinds of interventions are used, which is what makes it "multidimensional." The therapist conducts individual and family psychotherapy sessions directly with adolescents and their families, during which personal and relational issues are addressed (e.g., adolescent feelings of alienation and isolation, parental disengagement, and patterns of ongoing family conflict). However, MDFT also involves a therapist assistant who functions a lot like a case manager, communicating with external systems and overseeing aspects of treatment that occur outside of individual and family therapy sessions (e.g., psychosocial interventions such as tutoring, afterschool programs, and court appointments) (C. Rowe et al., 2002).

MDFT has amassed a strong base of research support. Randomized controlled trials have concluded that MDFT is equally or more effective than other interventions, including individual CBT and residential treatment (Liddle, 2010). One randomized controlled trial conducted in Belgium, France, Germany, Switzerland, and the Netherlands found an MDFT-based program highly effective in treating cannabis-using adolescents (Rigter et al., 2013; Rigter et al., 2010; Schaub et al., 2014).

EVALUATING SOCIOCULTURAL PERSPECTIVES

Sociocultural perspectives are helpful in thinking about substance use and behavioral addictions because these problems always occur within social and cultural contexts. Hence, social interventions targeting factors other than the individual can be beneficial because they draw our attention to how substance dependence and behavioral addictions don't occur in a vacuum. Social, relational, economic, political, and cultural influences all play roles not only in the development of addiction, but also in our shared social understandings of it. Socioeconomic deprivation, cultural values, problems within families, and other social stressors affect how, when, and why people drink too much, shop too much, work too much, seek out porn on the internet, get lost in video games, snort cocaine, and so on. Along these lines, any given individual's substance use may vary based on circumstances. That is, substance-specific environmental influences—different triggers at work and home, for instance—can affect drug use (Badiani, 2013). That said, not everyone facing the same social circumstances develops an addiction problem. To many, this means that sociocultural perspectives don't tell the whole story. Biological and psychological processes specific to individuals remain important in fully understanding and addressing addiction, even when taking sociocultural factors into account.

11.7 CLOSING THOUGHTS: HOW DO I KNOW IF I'M ADDICTED?

Almost all of us know someone with an addiction problem: a family member, friend, partner, boss, or colleague. Some of us may even wonder about whether we, ourselves, have a problem. To assess this, many self-administered inventories have been developed. One example is the **Alcohol Use Disorders Identification Test (AUDIT)**. Originally produced by the World Health Organization, the AUDIT is a 10-item self-report inventory to assess problem drinking and alcohol dependence (Babor, Higgins-Biddle, Saunders, & Monteiro, 2001). Because many people don't like completing surveys, numerous shortened versions of the AUDIT have been devised (K. Bush, Kivlahan, McDonell, Fihn, & Bradley, 1998; Gual, Segura, Contel, Heather, & Colom, 2002; J. W. Kim et al., 2013; Levola & Aalto, 2015). The AUDIT-C, for example, cuts the assessment down to just three items, making it easy to quickly complete and score. We conclude by sharing the AUDIT-C in our "Try It Yourself" feature, as a way to encourage students to think about how material in this chapter applies to their own lives. If you are concerned about the level of your responses, consult with your instructor, a doctor, or a mental health practitioner.

TRY IT YOURSELF

Are You Drinking Too Much?

The AUDIT was developed to quickly assess hazardous drinking behavior. Below are the first three items of the World Health Organization's original 10-item AUDIT (Alcohol Use Disorders Identification Test) measure. People completing the AUDIT enter 0–4 in the box to the right then total their score. Higher scores generally indicate more dangerous drinking behavior.

Questions	0	1	2	3	4	
1. How often do you have a drink containing alcohol?	Never	Monthly or less	2-4 times a month	2-3 times a week	4 or more times a week	
2. How many drinks containing alcohol do you have on a typical day when you are drinking?	1 or 2	3 or 4	5 or 6	7 to 9	10 or more	
3. How often do you have six or more drinks on one occasion?	Never	Less than monthly	Monthly	Weekly	Daily or almost	
					Total ⟹	

Source: The Alcohol Use Disorders Identification Test: Self-Report Version, 3 first questions and answer choices. p. 31, Appendix B. Published in: Babor, T. F., Higgins-Biddle, J. C., Saunders, J. B., & Monteiro, M. G. (2001). AUDIT: The Alcohol Use Disorders Identification Test, Guidelines for Use in Primary Care, 2nd ed. Used with permission from World Health Organization.

KEY TERMS

12-step programs
Acamprosate
Acetaldehyde
Acetylcholine
Addiction
Addictive personality
Alcohol
Alcohol Use Disorders Identification Test (AUDIT)
Alcoholic
Alcoholics Anonymous (AA)
Amphetamines
Behavioral addictions
Binge drinking
Blood alcohol content
Caffeine
Cannabis
Cirrhosis
Cocaine
Codeine
Confabulation
Contingency management (CM)
Controlled drinking
Crack
Cross-tolerance
Cytisine
Delirium tremens (DTs)
Dependence
Depressants
Detoxification
Disulfiram
Dopamine hypothesis of addiction

Drug flashbacks
Drug replacement therapy
Drug-induced synesthesia
Endogenous opioids
Fetal alcohol syndrome (FAS)
Gambling disorder
Gaming disorder
Hallucinogens
Harm reduction
Harmful use
Heroin
Illness model of drug addiction
Incentive-sensitization theory
Indolamine hallucinogens
Intoxication
Korsakoff syndrome
Life-history hypothesis
Methadone maintenance therapy (MMT)
Microglia
Mismatch hypothesis
Moderation Management (MM)
Moral model of drug addiction
Morphine
Motivational interviewing (MI)
Multidimensional family therapy (MDFT)
Mutualism hypothesis
n-acetylcysteine
Nicotine
Nicotine replacement therapy
OARS

Opioid blockers
Opioids
Opium
Oxycodone
Pathological gambling
Phencyclidine (PCP)
Phenylalkylamine hallucinogens
Polydrug use
Prevention and early intervention programs
Reclaiming Futures
Remission
Reward deficiency syndrome theory (RDS)
Sedative-hypnotics
Self-medication hypothesis
Speedballing
Stimulants
Substance abuse
Substance dependence
Substance use disorder
Synergistic effects
Tetrahydrocannabinol (THC)
Thebaine
Therapeutic communities (TCs)
Thiamine
Tolerance
Transtheoretical model of change
Varenicline
Ventral tegmental area (VTA)
Withdrawal

CHAPTER 11

Full definitions of the terms listed above can be found in the end-of-book glossary on p. 533.

 Go to the companion website, www.macmillanihe.com/raskin-abnormal-psych, to access a study guide, multiple choice and flashcard quizzes for this chapter, and other useful learning aids.

CHAPTER 12
PERSONALITY ISSUES

12.1 OVERVIEW

LEARNING OBJECTIVES

After reading this chapter, you should be able to:

1. Define basic terms such as personality, traits, temperament, character, and personality disorder.
2. Describe what the five-factor model (FFM) of personality is and how it is relevant to thinking about personality disorder.
3. Outline the difference between categorical and dimensional models of personality disorder, summarize the *DSM* and *ICD* models, and explain the debates about the strengths and weaknesses of these models.
4. Discuss historical ideas about personality and personality issues.
5. Explain how mental health professionals using brain chemistry, brain structure, genetic, evolutionary, and immune system perspectives conceptualize and treat personality issues.
6. Summarize psychodynamic, cognitive-behavioral, and humanistic approaches to thinking about and addressing personality issues.
7. Explain how sociocultural perspectives see gender bias, trauma, socioeconomic disadvantage, and racism as critical to understanding personality issues.
8. Describe systems approaches to personality issues.

Photo source: © Royalty-Free/Corbis

GETTING STARTED: WHAT IS PERSONALITY?

Harvey

Harvey is a 23-year-old African American male currently in prison for attempted murder. He has a long history of being in trouble with the law, starting at age 15 when he was arrested for dealing drugs in the inner-city neighborhood where he grew up. Based on police records, by the time Harvey was 18 he was overseeing a small drug ring. His associates found him intimidating. He often lied to them or outright threatened them with physical harm so he could get his way. Sometimes he acted on his threats, impulsively lashing out at them violently and without provocation—occasionally even injuring them. On such occasions, Harvey rarely (if ever) seemed to feel any remorse. While in prison, Harvey regularly gets into fights. The severe punishments he is subjected to for these fights (including several times in solitary confinement) do little to deter him or change his unruly and troublesome behavior. When asked about his recurrent bad behavior, Harvey scowls and says "It ain't my fault. Everyone's against me."

CASE EXAMPLES

Magdalena

Magdalena is a 25-year-old female who is referred to therapy after attempting suicide by overdosing on antidepressants her psychiatrist had prescribed. She has a history of impulsive behavior. In the past, she has gone on outrageous shopping sprees, abruptly quit various jobs, and keyed the car of an ex-boyfriend. She reports feeling depressed and "empty" much of the time. In session, Magdalena vacillates between various intense emotions: she might be clingy one minute, angry the next, and then despondent after that. At the end of one therapy session, she ingratiatingly tells her therapist how kind and compassionate he is, then wonders aloud if he would extend future sessions by 15 minutes. When the therapist politely declines this request, Magdalena's mood abruptly shifts. She expresses rage at his insensitivity and says she knew he was pretending to care about her all along. She also remarks that if she doesn't get more time in sessions, she can't promise what might happen to her. When the therapist asks Magdalena if this is a veiled suicide threat, she just shrugs and looks away. Magdalena's therapist finds her difficult to work with and often feels highly stressed by their sessions. "You never know from moment to moment what she's going to be like," he thinks to himself.

Defining and Measuring Personality

Basic Terms

Before we can discuss personality issues, we need to define "personality." Defining it isn't as straightforward as it seems. According to the American Psychological Association, personality (a term previously defined in Chapter 3) "refers to individual differences in characteristic patterns of thinking, feeling and behaving" (www.apa.org/topics/personality/). It is customarily seen as consisting of enduring **traits**—distinguishing qualities people "have," such as a tendency toward happiness, anxiousness, or aggression. Perspectives emphasizing traits are known as **trait theories**. Trait theories tend to view traits as originating in biology. That is, traits are regularly tied to (if not always clearly distinguished from) the idea of an inborn **temperament**: the automatic ways of responding to emotional stimuli that produce consistent habits and moods (Cloninger, 1994).

While personality is often treated as synonymous with traits and temperament, it can also be viewed more broadly as emerging from how traits and temperament are molded by environmental experiences (Angleitner & Ostendorf, 1994). Further muddying these already confusing conceptual waters is the concept of **character**, described as unique patterns of adaptive behavior that are relatively constant and enduring (Hertz & Hertz, 2016). Character is sometimes used as a synonym for personality, but is also defined independently of it. Compared to temperament, character is often seen as being influenced more by psychological and developmental factors than heredity (Caligor, Kernberg, & Clarkin, 2007)—as less rooted in nature than nurture (Cloninger, 1994). As you can tell, there isn't always agreement on how best to differentiate personality, character, temperament, and traits, but we do our best despite the fuzzy boundaries surrounding these terms.

Stable Traits and Personality Disorder

Trait theories typically view personality as relatively stable across settings (Markon & Jonas, 2015). For example, people high in the trait of "angry hostility" can be expected to be confrontational and antagonistic regardless of the situation. They will behave in similarly hostile ways whether at home, work, or out bowling with friends. Therefore, in the traditional view of personality, people display enduring and universal traits that they have in greater or lesser amounts. Any given person's constellation of traits constitutes his or her personality. In other words, "to satisfactorily characterize someone's personality functioning within a trait model, it is necessary to characterize his or her standing on all the traits within the model" (Markon & Jonas, 2015, p. 64). A person is often diagnosed with a **personality disorder** when his or her constellation of personality traits, or character, consistently leads to interpersonal conflict and difficulty in daily functioning (Hertz & Hertz, 2016). As you read this chapter, pay attention to the way that many (but not all) perspectives on personality disorders take for granted the trait view of personality. How much you accept or question the trait view may inform which perspectives on personality problems appeal to you.

The Five-Factor Model of Personality

Most trait theories see personality as consisting of one to five central **trait factors**, which are traits that, in research studies, have been found to be distinct from one another. The term "factor" is used because trait factor research often relies on a statistical technique called **factor analysis**, which involves identifying patterns in how people respond to different questions (i.e., items) on one or more self-report personality inventories (objective tests using standardized items with limited response choices; see Chapter 3). When responses to items are highly correlated, it can be inferred that they are measuring the same thing—and therefore constitute a single "factor." When we look at the correlated items, we might decide they all involve how much one likes to socialize with others. Thus, we might name the factor we have identified "extraversion." The goal of factor analytic personality research is to statistically identify the core factors (or traits) that account for individual differences.

According to the five-factor model, everybody's personality can be mapped along five dimensions.
Source: Getty Images/Hero Images

CHAPTER 12

Factor analytic techniques have yielded a variety of trait factor theories. However, over the past several decades, the **five-factor model (FFM)** has reigned supreme. This model, which has generated an enormous body of research, proposes that every human being's personality can be mapped along five trait dimensions: *extraversion*, *agreeableness*, *conscientiousness*, *neuroticism*, and *openness* (Digman, 1990; Goldberg, 1993; McCrae & John,

1992). These dimensions are sometimes referred to as the Big Five (mentioned in Chapter 3). For a more thorough overview of the Big Five, as well as a test you can take to assess yourself on these factors, see the "Try It Yourself" box. As we shall see, the five-factor model has greatly influenced *DSM* and *ICD* perspectives on personality disorder (Suzuki, Griffin, & Samuel, 2016; Trull, 2012; Widiger & Costa, 2012; Widiger & Presnall, 2013; Widiger, Samuel, Mullins-Sweatt, Gore, & Crego, 2012). However, it has also been subject to intense criticism by humanistic and sociocultural theorists (Kroger & Wood, 1993; McCrae & John, 1992; Nilsson, 2014).

TRY IT YOURSELF

The Big Five Project Personality Test

Want to assess yourself on the Big Five personality factors? You can do so for free at www.outofservice.com/bigfive. The factors this online test assesses are as follows:

FACTOR	IF HIGH ON THIS FACTOR:	IF LOW ON THIS FACTOR:
Extraversion	Sociable, easily excited, talkative, emotionally expressive	Reserved, quiet, less need for social engagement
Agreeableness	Kind, trusting, altruistic, affectionate, cooperative	Competitive, suspicious, manipulative, skeptical, uncooperative
Conscientiousness	Self-disciplined, dutiful, regulated, organized, detail-oriented, planned rather than spontaneous	Undisciplined, unreliable, disorganized, messy, impulsive, spontaneous rather than planned
Neuroticism	Lots of negative emotions (anger, anxiety, sadness) and emotional instability (i.e., mood swings)	Emotionally stable and resilient
Openness	Open to new experiences, creative, adventurous	Wary of new experiences, unaware of own emotions, traditional rather than creative

Photo source: © PhotoDisc/Getty Images

12.2 *DSM* AND *ICD* PERSPECTIVES

The *DSM* and *ICD* view personality issues as originating in disorders that people have. Consistent with trait theories, *DSM* and *ICD* perspectives see personality disorders as involving rigid and unbending patterns of relating to others that create interpersonal difficulties and result in emotional distress. These patterns are stable and originate early in life. In keeping with this view, the *DSM-5* defines a personality disorder as "an enduring pattern of inner experience and behavior that deviates markedly from the expectations of the individual's culture, is pervasive and inflexible, has an onset in adolescence or early adulthood, is stable over time, and leads to distress or impairment" (American Psychiatric Association, 2013b, p. 645). This is quite similar to the *ICD-10* definition: "a severe disturbance in the characterological constitution and behavioural tendencies of the individual, usually involving several areas of the personality" that begins in late childhood or early adolescence and is "nearly always associated with considerable personal and social disruption" (World Health Organization, 1992, p. 157); and also comparable to the *ICD-11* definition: "problems in functioning of aspects of the self … and/or interpersonal dysfunction … that have persisted over an extended period of time;" these problems are "manifest in patterns of cognition, emotional experience, emotional expression, and behaviour that are maladaptive" and occur "across a range of personal and social situations" (https://icd.who.int/browse11/l-m/en#/http%3a%2f%2fid.who.int%2ficd%2fentity%2f941859884). Compared to other mental disorders that emphasize more focused behavioral symptoms (e.g., being afraid of specific items or situations, having body image and eating problems, feeling depressed, or confusion about sexual orientation), personality disorders are broader and more all-encompassing in that they involve fundamental problems in the overall structure of an individual's personality and style of relating to others.

FROM CATEGORIES TO DIMENSIONS

Traditionally, the *DSM* and *ICD* have included distinct categories of personality disorder, each with its own diagnostic criteria. However, this is increasingly viewed as problematic because personality disorder categories are highly comorbid; they often overlap with each other (and with other mental disorders), resulting in many patients meeting criteria for multiple diagnoses (Aragona, 2009; B. F. Grant, Stinson, Dawson, Chou, & Ruan, 2005; Lenzenweger, Lane, Loranger, & Kessler, 2007; Paris, 2014; Tyrer, 2012). Therefore, many researchers now question the wisdom of a strictly categorical approach (B. F. Grant et al., 2005; Tyrer, 2012; Widiger, 2013, 2015).

Instead, they wish to see personality disorders move toward a *dimensional* diagnostic approach that charts degrees of severity for different personality traits instead of a *categorical* approach that divides personality issues into mutually exclusive categories (see Chapter 3). Advocates of dimensional diagnosis prefer to assess people along key personality dimensions reflecting traits consistently found in Big Five and related research (DeYoung, Carey, Krueger, & Ross, 2016; Widiger, 2015; Widiger & Costa, 2012; Widiger & Presnall, 2013).

This shift toward a dimensional emphasis means that significant changes are likely on the horizon for *DSM* and *ICD* conceptions of personality disorders. The *DSM-5* came very close to revamping its personality disorders chapter (Tyrer, Reed, & Crawford, 2015; Zachar, Krueger, & Kendler, 2016). Had it done so, it would have replaced its categorical diagnoses with a new hybrid system, combining some categories with some trait dimension assessments. However, ultimately the *DSM-5* retained the *DSM-IV-TR* personality disorders exactly as they were and designated its hybrid system as a proposal warranting further study. The *ICD-11* has gone further than the *DSM-5* in overhauling its section on personality disorders (Tyrer et al., 2015). Unlike the *DSM-5*, which kept its more dimensional model as a proposal, the *ICD-11* decided to make a clear break with the past. It has jettisoned the categorical approach to personality disorders entirely and replaced it with a new dimensional system. Below, we outline the traditional categorical personality disorder diagnoses found in *DSM-5* and *ICD-10*. Then we discuss both the *DSM-5*'s dimensional/categorical hybrid proposal and the *ICD-11*'s fully dimensional reconceptualization of personality disorders.

TRADITIONAL CATEGORIES

The *DSM-5* and *ICD-10* both break personality disorders into discrete diagnostic categories. However, the number of categories differs: *DSM-5* contains ten personality disorders, but *ICD-10* only has eight. *DSM-5* divides personality disorders into three types: *odd or eccentric* (**Cluster A**), *dramatic, emotional, or erratic* (**Cluster B**), and *anxious or fearful* (**Cluster C**). *ICD-10* doesn't emphasize clusters, listing personality disorders under "Disorders of Adult Personality and Behaviour." The categories described below are organized by *DSM-5* clusters.

Cluster A: Odd or Eccentric Personality Disorders

Paranoid Personality Disorder

People diagnosed with **paranoid personality disorder** tend to be unjustifiably suspicious of others. They have difficulty trusting people and worry that others are trying to exploit, harm, or deceive them. These individuals tend to be critical, humorless, and argumentative. They hold grudges and see conspiracies everywhere. Because of their combative and suspicious manner, they don't work and play well with others—which further confirms their sense that people are out to get them. Criteria and guidelines for paranoid personality disorder (and other Cluster A personality disorders) are recapped in Diagnostic Box 12.1. According to the *DSM-5*, between 2.3% and 4.4% of people qualify for a paranoid personality disorder diagnosis. Importantly, the *DSM-5* warns clinicians to be

Do you think we can distinguish when paranoia is justified versus indicative of a personality disorder? Are there times when people really are out to get you?
Source: Getty Images\ONOKY – Eric Herchaft

careful before diagnosing it in socially marginalized people (e.g., minority group members), whose justified anger and frustration can be misinterpreted as paranoia.

Diagnostic Box 12.1 DSM-5 and ICD-10 Cluster A (Odd or Eccentric) Personality Disorders

- **Paranoid Personality Disorder**: Ongoing pattern of suspiciousness and lack of trust; unjustifiably suspects others are conspiring against him/her, or are out to cause harm; tends not to confide in others due to doubts about their trustworthiness.

Based on American Psychiatric Association, 2013b, p. 649) and World Health Organization, 1992, p. 158

- **Schizoid Personality Disorder**: Ongoing pattern of disengagement from others and limited ability to express a range of emotions; does not like or desire close relationships and displays poor social skills; has few interests and prefers solitary activities.

Based on American Psychiatric Association, 2013b, pp. 652–653 and World Health Organization, 1992, pp. 158–159

CHAPTER 12

Schizoid Personality Disorder

Schizoid personality disorder (see Diagnostic Box 12.1) is characterized by utter disinterest in relationships and people. Individuals with this diagnosis simply have no desire to engage with others, instead preferring to be alone. Characteristically, they have no close friends and don't care what others think about them. They show little emotion, have very few interests, and have minimal to no desire for sexual experiences with others. People view them as emotionally cold and they consistently appear aloof and disconnected from their surroundings. *DSM-5* reports prevalence rates in the 3.1% to 4.9% range, with it being slightly more common in men than women.

Schizotypal Personality Disorder

The key features of **schizotypal personality disorder (STPD)** (alluded to in Chapter 4 when discussing psychosis) are eccentric thoughts, perceptions, and behaviors accompanied by difficulty forming close relationships. People who receive this diagnosis strike others as strange. Not only do they appear suspicious and paranoid, but their thinking seems bizarre or magical. For instance, they might believe they have telepathic powers or the clairvoyant ability to predict the future. Their emotional reactions often seem constricted or inappropriate, as well. Put bluntly, these individuals seem odd and peculiar and thus tend to lack close friends. In their social difficulties, people with schizotypal diagnoses are similar to those with schizoid diagnoses. People who receive either of these diagnoses lack social connections with others, but for somewhat different reasons. The social deficits found in schizotypal personality disorder are mainly a consequence of odd and eccentric behavior resulting from cognitive-perceptual distortions, whereas those found in schizoid personality disorder are simply due to not enjoying or desiring social interaction with others (Chemerinski, Triebwasser, Roussos, & Siever, 2013).

As discussed in Chapter 4, schizotypal personality disorder is a personality disorder in the *DSM-5*, but it is grouped with psychotic disorders in the *ICD-10* and *ICD-11*, where it is simply called *schizotypal disorder*. *DSM-5* reports varied prevalence rates, citing a Norwegian study that found 0.6% prevalence versus a U.S. study that found 4.6% prevalence. Slightly more men than women qualify for this diagnosis. Refer to Diagnostic Box 12.1 for diagnostic details.

Cluster B: Dramatic, Emotional, or Erratic Personality Disorders

Antisocial Personality Disorder

Antisocial personality disorder (APD) describes people who consistently violate the rights of others. Such people are deceitful, disregard social norms, and often break the law. They are impulsive, reckless, irresponsible, and (in some cases) violent. They regularly manipulate and exploit others. People diagnosed with APD show little remorse for their actions and lack empathy for those they hurt. *DSM-5* estimates APD prevalence is between 0.2% and 3.3%. Men are diagnosed far more often than women, with rates three to five times as high by some counts (Alegria et al., 2013; Compton, Conway, Stinson, Colliver, & Grant, 2005; Oltmanns & Powers, 2012; Trull, Jahng, Tomko, Wood, & Sher, 2010). The *DSM-5* estimates that upwards of 70% of men in substance abuse clinics, prisons, and other forensic settings meet APD diagnostic criteria, which are presented in condensed form in Diagnostic Box 12.2 (which contains all four Cluster B personality disorders). Note that the *ICD-10* equivalent of APD goes by a different name, **dissocial personality disorder**.

Diagnostic Box 12.2 DSM-5 and ICD-10 Cluster B (Dramatic, Emotional, or Erratic) Personality Disorders

- **Borderline Personality Disorder**: Ongoing pattern of rapidly shifting and unstable relationships, sense of self, and emotions, along with impulsive behavior; typically tries to desperately avoid abandonment (whether real or imagined), alternates between idealizing and devaluing others, has a rapidly shifting self-image, feels empty inside, has difficulty controlling anger, and behaves impulsively (often including threats of self-harm). NOTE: *ICD-10* contains a slightly broader "emotionally unstable personality disorder" diagnosis, with two subtypes: "impulsive" (involving mainly emotional instability, impulsivity, and angry outbursts in response to criticism) and "borderline" (involving emotional instability, feelings of emptiness, efforts to avoid abandonment, intense relationships, and sometimes threats of self-harm)

Based on American Psychiatric Association, 2013b, p. 663 and World Health Organization, 1992, pp. 159–160

- **Histrionic Personality Disorder**: Ongoing pattern of extreme emotionality and behavior intended to garner attention; often feels upset when not the center of attention, displays shallow and rapidly changing feelings, describes things in an impressionistic way, is dramatic or theatrical, overly focused on physical appearance, is inappropriately flirtatious, and believes relationships with others are deeper than they are.

Based on American Psychiatric Association, 2013b, p. 667 and World Health Organization, 1992, p. 160

- **Narcissistic Personality Disorder**: Ongoing pattern of grandiosity, a need to be admired, and a lack of empathy for others; tends to demand recognition, be overly focused on own importance (as powerful, beautiful, intelligent, successful, etc.), believe he/she is special or of high status, feel entitled, be jealous of others, and exploit others for own gain. NOTE: Narcissistic personality disorder is not in the *ICD-10*.

Based on American Psychiatric Association, 2013b, pp. 669–670

Harvey
Our case example client, Harvey, who is in prison for attempted murder and has a long history of violent behavior without remorse, might receive an antisocial diagnosis.

CASE EXAMPLES

APD is closely related (but not identical) to psychopathy and sociopathy, which is why people diagnosed with APD are often described as psychopaths or sociopaths. See the "In Depth" feature for more on psychopathy and sociopathy.

IN DEPTH

Psychopathy and Sociopathy

The *DSM-5*'s antisocial personality disorder (APD) and the *ICD-10*'s dissocial personality disorder are often treated as modern diagnostic equivalents of the older terms "psychopathy" and "sociopathy" (MacKenzie, 2014). However, some researchers and clinicians object to this (Hare, 1996; MacKenzie, 2014; Pemment, 2013). It's been argued that APD, with its emphasis on observable diagnostic criteria, doesn't capture some of the psychological nuances of psychopathy (Hare, 1996). Further, some symptoms of psychopathy and sociopathy, such as impulsivity, are also found in the impulsive and borderline subtypes of *ICD-10*'s emotionally unstable personality disorder (MacKenzie, 2014). Besides how to distinguish them from their *DSM* and *ICD* counterparts, abnormal psychology students often want to know: How are psychopathy and sociopathy different from one another?

Psychopathy is generally seen as originating in biology (Viding, McCrory, & Seara-Cardoso, 2014). Psychopaths exhibit *emotional/interpersonal symptoms* (Hare, 2006; Hare, Neumann, & Widiger, 2012; D. F. Thompson et al., 2014). They are glib, superficial, egocentric, and grandiose. Further, they are deceitful, manipulative, and display shallow emotions. When they wrong others, psychopaths lack remorse, guilt, and empathy. In addition to their emotional/interpersonal issues, psychopaths are also *socially deviant* (Hare, 2006; Hare et al., 2012; D. F. Thompson et al., 2014). They are impulsive and irresponsible, while having a constant need for excitement and stimulation. All these symptoms start early in life and continue into adulthood (Hare, 2006; Hare et al., 2012; D. F. Thompson et al., 2014).

Sociopathy is usually distinguished from psychopathy in that it is attributed mainly to social causes, not biology (MacKenzie, 2014). In other words, "psychopaths are born as psychopaths whereas sociopaths are the product of one's developmental environment" (MacKenzie, 2014). Sociopaths are also considered to be different from psychopaths in that although they violate the rights of others, they do sometimes feel empathy; they have a conscience, but their conscience is inconsistent with accepted cultural norms and practices (Pemment, 2013). Considering the subtle differences between them, some say psychopathy and sociopathy should be included in the *DSM-5* as subtypes of antisocial personality disorder (MacKenzie, 2014).

Although psychopathy is viewed as physiologically based, in some cases the environment is cast in a supporting role. **Primary psychopathy** is defined as psychopathy rooted entirely in biology, whereas **secondary psychopathy** is viewed as psychopathy that results when a biologically innate predisposition

CHAPTER 12

is brought out by environmental factors (MacKenzie, 2014). An additional distinction is made between **successful psychopaths** and **unsuccessful psychopaths**, with the former effectively navigating the world and avoiding punishment and the latter being criminals who are likely to be incarcerated (D. F. Thompson et al., 2014). Ruthless but influential politicians and businesspeople might be successful psychopaths, whereas serial killers in prison are unsuccessful psychopaths.

Proposed distinctions notwithstanding, it's not always clear whether psychopathy is truly distinct from sociopathy, or whether the terms reflect some clinicians' desire to attribute antisocial behavior to biology and other clinicians' desire to attribute such behavior to the environment. Although we don't dive into the importance of these distinctions later in the chapter when discussing biological brain correlates of APD, it's been suggested that psychopathy and sociopathy may be distinguishable based on brain chemistry and brain structure differences (Pemment, 2013; D. F. Thompson et al., 2014). However, others continue to downplay the psychopathy–sociopathy distinction by either using the terms interchangeably or discarding them both in favor of the less theoretically loaded antisocial personality disorder.

CRITICAL THINKING QUESTIONS

1. Do you believe there is a meaningful distinction to be made between psychopathy and sociopathy?
2. Can people be "born bad," as the concept of psychopathy implies?
3. In clinical settings, do you think psychopathy can be distinguished from sociopathy? If yes, how? If no, why not?

Borderline Personality Disorder

Borderline personality disorder (BPD) (see Diagnostic Box 12.2) describes people who show instability in their relationships, sense of self, and emotions. They have a difficult time regulating their own emotions, especially negative ones like anger and sadness. BPD clients' feelings about self and others shift rapidly depending on the circumstances. One minute they might idealize others, then the next minute disparage them. Such rapid shifts (the "unstable" aspect of being "borderline") stem from intense (and often unrealistic) fears of being abandoned by others.

Case study client Magdalena is diagnosed with borderline personality disorder; her feelings about herself and others rapidly and abruptly shift, making it difficult for her to get along with people.
Source: Getty Images/iStockphoto\Juanmonino

Magdalena

CASE EXAMPLES

Consider our case example client Magdalena, who meets the criteria for BPD. One minute Magdalena thanks her therapist profusely for being supportive and caring, then the next minute becomes furious, angry, and insulting toward the therapist when he declines her request to extend sessions by 15 minutes. Magdalena's abrupt shift is a desperate and manipulative attempt to deal with feeling abandoned.

Such sudden emotional shifts make borderline clients difficult for people (therapists included) to deal with. Other challenging characteristics of BPD are impulsive behavior (substance abuse and behavioral addictions are common), chronic feelings of emptiness, and **parasuicidal behavior**—self-harm inflicted less because one wants to die and more to manipulate others, communicate distress, or regulate emotions (Kreitman, 1977; Linehan, 1993a). Unfortunately, the behaviors BPD clients engage in get them the very outcome they most fear: many people don't like them and actively avoid them. The *DSM-5* estimates the median prevalence to be 1.6%, but possibly as high as 5.9%. It also notes that 75% of those diagnosed are women.

The *ICD-10* lists borderline as one of two types of a broader personality disorder that it calls **emotionally unstable personality disorder**. In the *ICD-10* conception, emotionally unstable personality disorder is characterized by both acting impulsively (without considering the consequences) and emotional unpredictability. People diagnosed with the *borderline type* mainly display emotional unpredictability, while those assigned to the *impulsive type* tend to act out (often in threatening or violent ways) without considering the consequences.

Histrionic Personality Disorder

Histrionic personality disorder is diagnosed in those who are excessively dramatic and emotional. Such people crave being the center of attention. They strike others as shallow and overly-theatrical, shifting rapidly from one exaggerated emotional display to another. Their style of speech is often vague and impressionistic. They can also be inappropriately flirtatious and seductive. People with this diagnosis are often disparagingly dismissed as "drama queens." Scarlett O'Hara in the classic movie *Gone with the Wind* exhibits many symptoms of histrionic personality disorder: "Her flair for the overly dramatic, the constant demand for attention, the quick foolish decisions, and emphasis on provocative clothing even during her impoverished years is typical histrionic" (Hammond, 2016, para. 4). The *DSM-5* estimates prevalence at 1.84% and cautions that even though the diagnosis is made more frequently in women, actual prevalence among males and females may be comparable. See Diagnostic Box 12.2 for diagnostic details.

"Enough about you. Let's talk about me." People deemed narcissistic desperately seek attention, have a deep-seated need to be admired, and believe they are entitled to special treatment.
Source: iStock.com/LUNAMARINA

Narcissistic Personality Disorder

People meeting criteria for **narcissistic personality disorder (NPD)** exhibit grandiosity (see Chapter 5) in that they think of themselves as extremely important. This disorder is characterized not only by an inflated sense of self, but also by a desperate need for admiration. Individuals diagnosed with NPD have an exaggerated sense of **entitlement**, the unreasonable expectation that they deserve special treatment or attention. In their minds, the usual rules don't apply to them. Thus, a narcissistic individual might expect his professor to give him an extension on a late paper even though a strict "no extensions" policy is in place and no other students were granted one. NPD clients tend to be arrogant and are often preoccupied with fantasies of unlimited power. The *DSM-5* cites prevalence rates between 0% and 6.2% in community samples while noting that 50% to 75% of those diagnosed are men. The *ICD-10* doesn't include narcissistic personality disorder. Narcissistic personality disorder is listed in Diagnostic Box 12.2.

Cluster C: Anxious or Fearful Personality Disorders

Avoidant Personality Disorder

Avoidant personality disorder is grouped with the Cluster C personality disorders found in Diagnostic Box 12.3. People with an avoidant diagnosis actively avoid social interactions because they are excessively worried about being criticized or rejected. These individuals want guaranteed acceptance from others. Without it, they are too frightened of disapproval to socially engage. Therefore, they steer clear of people to avoid being hurt. The *DSM-5* cites prevalence rates of 2.4% and indicates that the disorder affects males and females equally.

People diagnosed with avoidant personality disorder genuinely want relationships, but steer clear of social interactions because the prospect of being rejected feels emotionally unbearable to them.
Source: Getty Images/iStockphoto Thinkstock Images \ mandygodbehear

Avoidant personality disorder sometimes gets confused with schizoid personality disorder because in both cases, those diagnosed avoid dealing with people. However, their reasons for doing so differ. People identified as schizoid don't care what others think of them and dodge social contact because they have no interest in relationships. By contrast, people who are avoidant desperately want relationships and care too much about what others think of them; they are so terribly afraid of being criticized or rejected that they refuse to take the risks necessary to establish and maintain connections with others. Avoidant personality disorder is also sometimes confused with antisocial personality disorder—mainly because in everyday language the word "antisocial" is commonly used as a synonym for avoidant. However, in *DSM-5* antisocial is about violating others' rights, whereas avoidant is about not socializing with others due to fear of rejection. In the *ICD-10*, avoidant personality disorder goes by the more awkward (but potentially clearer) name **anxious (avoidant) personality disorder**.

CHAPTER **12**

Diagnostic Box 12.3 DSM-5 and ICD-10 Cluster C (Anxious or Fearful) Personality Disorders

- **Avoidant Personality Disorder**: Ongoing pattern of feeling socially inhibited, inadequate, and overly fearful of criticism or rejection by others; tends to avoid interactions with others due to fear of being judged or not receiving unconditional approval and to be socially inhibited because feels inadequate.
  NOTE: Called "anxious [avoidant] personality disorder" in *ICD-10*.

Based on American Psychiatric Association, 2013b, pp. 672–673 and World Health Organization, 1992, p. 161

- **Dependent Personality Disorder**: Ongoing pattern of submissiveness, clinginess, fear of being alone, and a wish to be cared for; tends to be deferent, to have difficulty making decisions, to need excessive reassurance, to desperately seek relationships to avoid being alone, and to bend over backwards to receive support (even agreeing to do unpleasant things).

Based on American Psychiatric Association, 2013b, p. 675 and World Health Organization, 1992, p. 161

- **Obsessive-Compulsive Personality Disorder**: Ongoing pattern of being overly focused on control, orderliness, and perfectionism; tends to excessively focus on details (rules, lists, schedules, organization, etc.), be perfectionistic to the point being unable to finish tasks, be overly conscientious and rigid, be inflexible and self-righteous, and value productivity over relationships.
  NOTE: Called "anankastic personality disorder" in *ICD-10*.

Based on American Psychiatric Association, 2013b, pp. 678–679 and World Health Organization, 1992, pp. 160–161

Dependent Personality Disorder

Dependent personality disorder (see Diagnostic Box 12.3) describes those who desperately want to be cared for. Lacking confidence in their own abilities, they regularly seek advice and reassurance from those around them. They are deferent, submissive, and emotionally needy. This results in them allowing others to make major life decisions for them. People with this diagnosis lack self-confidence and don't feel capable of taking care of themselves. Hence, they desperately cling to others because they are terrified of being left to their own devices. This diagnosis isn't common, with *DSM-5* citing low prevalence rates of 0.49% to 0.60%. The *DSM-5* reports that although dependent personality disorder is diagnosed more often in women than men, actual prevalence among men and women may be similar.

Obsessive-Compulsive Personality Disorder

People diagnosed with **obsessive-compulsive personality disorder (OCPD)** (also in Diagnostic Box 12.3) are disproportionately focused on orderliness, rules, and control. They are excessively perfectionistic and rigid, to the point that it interferes with their functioning. Struggling to see the forest through the trees, these individuals often don't complete projects because they get lost in details and nothing is ever good enough.

Although they sometimes occur together, it's important to distinguish obsessive-compulsive personality disorder from obsessive-compulsive disorder (OCD), discussed in Chapter 6. Unlike OCD, OCPD involves neither obsessions (intrusive thoughts) or compulsions (acts one feels compelled to do). Rather, OCPD is about control, orderliness, rigidity, and perfectionism. In this respect, its use of the phrase "obsessive-compulsive" is misleading. To avoid confusion, think of OCD as involving obsessions and compulsions and OCPD as describing an exceptionally controlling, rigid, and perfectionistic personality. The *ICD-10* avoids confusing OCD and OCPD by calling OCPD by a different name entirely, **anankastic personality disorder**; "anankastic" derives from the Greek word *anankastikos*, which means "compulsion." The *DSM-5* states that OCPD affects between 2.1% and 7.9% of the population and is diagnosed in males twice as often as females.

DIMENSIONAL ALTERNATIVES

DSM-5's Proposed Hybrid Trait Model

The proposed (but unofficial) ***DSM-5* alternative model for personality disorders** (sometimes called the *hybrid model*, or *hybrid trait model*) combines both dimensional and categorical assessment in diagnosing personality disorders (R. F. Krueger & Markon, 2014; J. S. Porter & Risler, 2014; Widiger, 2013). The diagnostic process is quite different (and more complicated) than the usual categorical procedure of comparing a patient's behaviors to a list of criteria to see if a diagnosis is warranted. It involves the following steps (American Psychiatric Association, 2013b; Skodol, Morey, Bender, & Oldham, 2015):

1. **Assess the patient's *level of personality functioning*.** The diagnostic process begins with the **Level of Personality Functioning Scale (LPFS)** (see Diagnostic Box 12.4). The LPFS is a 5-point scale ranging

from "0" (little or no impairment) to "4" (extreme impairment). It assesses overall personality functioning in four areas. The first two of these areas (*identity* and *self-direction*) concern *self-functioning*, while the second two of these areas (*empathy* and *intimacy*) concern *identity functioning*. A moderate level of impairment in functioning ("2" on the 5-point scale) in at least two of these areas is required to diagnose a personality disorder.

Diagnostic Box 12.4 DSM-5 Alternative Model of Personality Disorders: Levels of Personality Functioning

SELF (2 areas)

1. **Identity**: Experience of self as unique, with clear boundaries between self and others; stability of self-esteem and accuracy of self-appraisal; capacity for, and ability to regulate, a range of emotional experiences.
2. **Self-direction**: Pursuit of coherent and meaningful short-term and life goals; utilization of constructive and prosocial internal standards of behavior; ability to self-reflect productively.

INTERPERSONAL (2 areas)

1. **Empathy**: Comprehension and appreciation of others' experiences and motivations; tolerance of differing perspectives; understanding the effects of one's own behavior on others.
2. **Intimacy**: Depth and duration of connection with others; desire and capacity for closeness; mutuality of regard reflected in interpersonal behavior.

   NOTE: Each area is assessed on a 0–4 scale; a patient must be moderately impaired ("2" or higher) in at least two these areas to qualify for a personality disorder.

   Source: Reprinted with permission from the *Diagnostic and Statistical Manual of Mental Disorders*, Fifth Edition, (Copyright ©2013). American Psychiatric Association. All Rights Reserved.

2. **Assess *pathological trait domains***. If the patient's level of personality functioning is moderately impaired, the next step is to assess *pathological trait domains*. The *DSM-5* lists five domains (see Diagnostic Box 12.5), which roughly correspond to the Big Five personality factors (Crego & Widiger, 2016). Each trait domain is subdivided into *trait facets*, of which there are 25 in total (again, see Diagnostic Box 12.5). To assess these facets, a self-report inventory called the **Personality Inventory for the *DSM-5* (PID-5)** has been developed. There are currently 220-item, 100-item, and 25-item versions of this inventory available (Bach, Maples-Keller, Bo, & Simonsen, 2016; Krueger, Derringer, Markon, Watson, & Skodol, 2012; Maples et al., 2015). Because it wasn't included in the *DSM-5*, the American Psychiatric Association made the 220-item and 25-item versions available online for clinicians to use with patients (www.psychiatry.org/psychiatrists/practice/dsm/educational-resources/assessment-measures).

Diagnostic Box 12.5 DSM-5 Alternative Model of Personality Disorders: Five Trait Domains

TRAIT DOMAIN	DOMAIN DESCRIPTION	FACETS
Negative affectivity (vs. Emotional Stability)	Frequent experience of a wide range of negative emotions	1. Emotional lability (instability of mood) 2. Anxiousness 3. Separation insecurity 4. Submissiveness 5. Hostility 6. Perseveration (continuing behavior that has proven ineffective)
Detachment (vs. Extraversion)	Withdrawal from interpersonal interactions and restricted emotionality	7. Withdrawal 8. Intimacy avoidance 9. Anhedonia (lack of enjoyment from life) 10. Depressivity 11. Restricted emotionality 12. Suspiciousness
Antagonism (vs. Agreeableness)	Behaviors that place one at odds with other people	13. Manipulativeness 14. Deceitfulness 15. Grandiosity 16. Attention-seeking 17. Callousness

CHAPTER 12

| **Disinhibition**
(vs. Conscientiousness) | Orientation toward immediate gratification, leading to impulsiveness | 18. Irresponsibility
19. Impulsivity
20. Distractibility
21. Risk-taking
22. (Lack of) rigid perfectionism |
| **Psychoticism**
(vs. Lucidity) | Displaying a wide range of odd, eccentric, or unusual behaviors and cognitions | 23. Unusual beliefs and experiences
24. Eccentricity
25. Cognitive and perceptual dysregulation (including dissociation) |

Based on Table 3, American Psychiatric Association, 2013b, pp. 779–781

3. **Make categorical diagnoses (using level of personality functioning and trait facet criteria)**. This step has two parts:

   a. **Use trait facets to diagnose from among six personality disorder categories**. The *DSM-5* hybrid model retains six of the ten traditional personality disorder categories: *antisocial*, *avoidant*, *borderline*, *narcissistic*, *obsessive-compulsive*, and *schizotypal*. However, the criteria for these categories have been revamped so that they are diagnosed based on level of personality functioning and trait domain facets (see Diagnostic Box 12.6).

   b. **Use the *personality disorder-trait specified* diagnosis for patients who don't qualify for any of the six personality disorder categories**. Patients who don't meet the criteria for any of the six personality disorders are assigned a new diagnosis, personality disorder-trait specified. Level of personality functioning is described and trait facets the patient meets are listed.

4. **Apply the inclusion and exclusion criteria**. The personality pattern must include two things: It must be (a) pervasive, occurring in many personal and social contexts; and (b) stable over time. The personality pattern also must exclude three things: It can't be (a) better explained by another mental disorder diagnosis; (b) due to substance use; and (c) due to developmental or sociocultural factors. After completing all four steps, a final diagnosis is made, listing diagnostic category, level of personality functioning assessment, and trait relevant domains and facets.

Diagnostic Box 12.6 DSM-5 Alternative Model of Personality Disorders: Diagnostic Criteria

DISORDER	CRITERION A: LEVEL OF PERSONALITY FUNCTIONING Moderate impairment ("2" on 5-point scale) in two of the four areas listed below for each disorder.	CRITERION B: TRAIT DOMAINS/FACETS Assess using the PID-5.
Antisocial Personality Disorder	• **Identity:** egocentrism; self-esteem from personal gain, power, pleasure • **Self-direction:** goal-setting based on personal gratification; absence of prosocial internal standards • **Empathy:** lack of concern for others; lack of remorse after mistreating others • **Intimacy:** exploitation as main way of relating to others; use of deceit, coercion, dominance, and intimidation to control others	6 of these 7 trait facets: • **Antagonism** (4 facets: manipulativeness, callousness, deceitfulness, hostility) • **Deceitfulness** (3 facets: risk-taking, impulsivity, irresponsibility)
Avoidant Personality Disorder	• **Identity:** low self-esteem related to self-appraisal as socially inept, personally unappealing, or inferior; excessive feelings of shame • **Self-direction:** reluctance to pursue goals, take personal risks, or engage in activities involving interpersonal contact • **Empathy:** sensitivity to criticism or rejection, associated with distorted inference of being negatively evaluate • **Intimacy:** exploitation as main way of relating to others; use of deceit, coercion, dominance, and intimidation to control others	3 of these 4 trait facets: • **Negative Affectivity** (1 facet: anxiousness) • **Detachment** (3 facets: withdrawal, anhedonia, intimacy avoidance)

Borderline Personality Disorder	• **Identity:** impoverished self-image associated with excessive self-criticism; chronic feelings of emptiness; dissociation under stress • **Self-direction:** instability in goals, aspirations, values, career plans • **Empathy:** difficulty recognizing others' feelings due to interpersonal hypersensitivity and biased focus on others' negative attributes • **Intimacy:** intense, unstable, conflicted relationships; idealization and devaluation of others	4 of these 7 facets (at least one must be *): • **Negative Affectivity** (4 facets: emotional lability, anxiousness, separation insecurity, depressivity) • **Disinhibition** (2 facets: impulsivity*, risk-taking*) • **Antagonism** (1 facet: hostility*)
Narcissistic Personality Disorder	• **Identity:** reliance on others for self-definition/esteem; exaggerated self-appraisal (inflated, deflated, or vacillating); emotional regulation mirrors self-esteem fluctuations • **Self-direction:** goal-setting based on wanting others' approval; unreasonably high personal standards to see self as exceptional, or too low based on sense of entitlement; often unaware of own motivations • **Empathy:** impaired ability to recognize/identify with others' feelings/needs; excessively attuned to others' reactions (if self-relevant); over/underestimates effect on others • **Intimacy:** superficial relationships to serve self-esteem regulation; little genuine interest in others' experiences and predominance of a need for personal gain	Both these facets: • **Antagonism** (2 facets: grandiosity, attention-seeking)
Obsessive-Compulsive Personality Disorder	• **Identity:** sense of self derived mainly from work/productivity; constricted experience and expression of strong emotions • **Self-direction:** difficulty completing tasks due to rigid and unrealistic standards; overly conscientious and moralistic attitudes • **Empathy:** difficulty understanding others' ideas, feelings, or behaviors • **Intimacy:** relationships seen as secondary to work/productivity; rigidity and stubbornness affect relationships	3 of these 4 trait facets (one must be *): • **Conscientiousness** [*opposite of disinhibition*] (1 facet: rigid perfectionism*) • **Negative Affectivity** (1 facet: perseveration) • **Detachment** (2 facets: intimacy avoidance, restricted affectivity)
Schizotypal Personality Disorder	• **Identity:** confused self/other boundaries; distorted self-concept; emotional expression not consistent with context or internal experience • **Self-direction:** unrealistic/incoherent goals; no clear set of internal standards • **Empathy:** difficulty understanding impact of one's behavior on others; frequent misinterpretations of others' motivations/behaviors • **Intimacy:** impairment in developing close relationships tied to mistrust/anxiety	4 of these 6 trait facets: • **Psychoticism** (3 facets: cognitive/perceptual dysregulation, unusual beliefs/experiences; eccentricity) • **Detachment** (3 facets: restricted affectivity, withdrawal, suspiciousness)
Personality Disorder-Trait Specified	• Describe level of functioning problems in the 4 areas: **Identity, Self-direction, Empathy,** and **Intimacy**	1 or more of the 5 trait domains listed in Diagnostic Box 12.5, as indicated by any of the 25 specific trait facets within these domains.

Based on American Psychiatric Association, 2013b, pp. 763–771

ICD-11's Complete Overhaul: A Fully Dimensional Approach

The ***ICD-11* model of personality disorders** goes further than the *DSM-5* alternative model in two ways. First, its dimensional reconceptualization of personality disorders isn't a proposal for further study; it replaces the old categorical approach. Second, in supplanting the categorical approach, the *ICD-11* discards traditional personality disorder categories once and for all—something the *DSM-5* has been criticized for not doing with its hybrid model (J. S. Porter & Risler, 2014; Tyrer, 2012; Widiger, 2011). In *ICD-11*, personality disorders are diagnosed completely dimensionally. That is, the *ICD-11* "abolishes all type-specific categories of personality disorder apart from the main one, the presence of personality disorder itself" (Tyrer et al., 2015, p. 721).

One Category Only: "Personality Disorder"

Thus, the *ICD-11* limits itself to one broad category, *personality disorder*, which—as noted earlier—is defined similarly to how *DSM-5* and *ICD-10* define it, as "a pervasive disturbance in how an individual experiences and thinks about the self, others, and the world, manifested in maladaptive patterns of cognition, emotional experience, emotional expression, and behaviour" (Tyrer et al., 2015, p. 718). Personality disorders still involve inflexible and long-term patterns of dealing with people that create interpersonal problems across a range of personal and social situations. However, rather than diagnosing specific types (e.g., antisocial, histrionic, borderline, etc.), personality disorders in *ICD-11* are diagnosed by *severity* and *trait domains* (World Health Organization, 2017).

Three Levels of Severity

When it comes to severity, the lone personality disorder category has three levels (*mild*, *moderate*, and *severe*), each with its own diagnostic code (Tyrer et al., 2015; World Health Organization, 2018a). A **mild personality disorder** reflects notable problems in interpersonal relationships, but social and occupational functioning involve only minimal harm to self and others. A **moderate personality disorder** is more severe; social and occupational functioning are somewhat compromised with past and future harm to self and others expected, though not severely damaging. Finally, a **severe personality disorder** involves extreme impairment in interpersonal relationships, such that work and social functioning are profoundly disrupted and serious harm to self and others is anticipated.

Five Trait Domains

Similar to the *DSM-5* alternative model, the *ICD-11* model uses five trait domains to identify a person's most prominent trait facets (Tyrer et al., 2015). Advocates of the trait domain model are quick to point out that trait facets "are not categories, but rather represent a set of dimensions that correspond to the underlying structure of personality dysfunction" (Tyrer et al., 2015, p. 723). The *ICD-11* trait domains, presented in Diagnostic Box 12.7, are similar but not identical to those in the *DSM-5* alternative model. They differ mainly in that the *ICD-11* contains an *anankastia* domain rather than a *psychoticism* domain; right before its release, the *ICD-11* added a "borderline pattern" in addition to the five trait domains. The *ICD-11* model is also different from the *DSM-5* alternative model in that it doesn't assess level of personality functioning or require clinicians to list specific trait facets. Part of the reason for this is to keep the diagnosis of personality disorders as simple as possible (in contrast to the more complicated *DSM-5* hybrid model). This should allow general practitioners to quickly diagnose personality disorders with the expectation that specialists (psychiatrists, psychologists, and other mental health professionals) will follow up with more in-depth assessment identifying relevant trait domains and facets necessary to fully understand the patient's pathology (Tyrer et al., 2015).

Diagnostic Box 12.7 ICD-11 Model of Personality Disorders: Five Trait Domains

TRAIT DOMAIN	DOMAIN DESCRIPTION
Negative Affectivity	Tendency to manifest a broad range of distressing emotions including anxiety, anger, self-loathing, irritability, vulnerability, depression, and other negative emotional states, often in response to even relatively minor actual or perceived stressors.
Detachment	Emotional and interpersonal distance, manifested in marked social withdrawal and/or indifference to people, isolation with very few or no attachment figures, including avoidance of not only intimate relationships but also close friendships. Traits include aloofness or coldness, reserve, passivity and lack of assertiveness, and reduced experience and expression of emotion, especially positive emotions, to the point of a diminished capacity to experience pleasure.
Dissociality	Disregard for social obligations and conventions and the rights and feelings of others. Traits include callousness, lack of empathy, hostility and aggression, ruthlessness, and inability or unwillingness to maintain prosocial behavior, often manifested in an overly positive view of the self, entitlement, and a tendency to be manipulative and exploitative of others.

| Disinhibition | Tendency to act impulsively in response to immediate internal or environmental stimuli without consideration of longer-term consequences. Traits include irresponsibility, impulsivity without regard for risks or consequences, distractibility, and recklessness. |
| Anankastia | A narrow focus on the control and regulation of one's own and others' behavior to ensure that things conform to the individual's particularistic ideal. Traits include perfectionism, perseveration, emotional and behavioral constraint, stubbornness, deliberativeness, orderliness, and concern with following rules and meeting obligations. |

Source: Adapted from Tyrer et al. (2015, p. 723)

EVALUATING *DSM* AND *ICD* PERSPECTIVES
Should Personality Disorder Diagnosis Shift from Categories to Dimensions?

Scientific Objections to Categories

Although both the *ICD-10* and *DSM-5* still officially classify personality disorders categorically, the categorical approach appears to be on its way out. As noted, those who want to see it done away with point to research that consistently finds that personality disorder categories overlap or co-occur (i.e., they are comorbid), making them difficult for clinicians to differentiate (Aragona, 2009; Fowler, O'Donohue, & Lilienfeld, 2007; B. F. Grant et al., 2005; Lenzenweger et al., 2007; Samuel & Griffin, 2015; Trull, Scheiderer, & Tomko, 2012). This comorbidity calls into question the validity of personality disorder categories—that is, do they really exist as distinct entities (Fowler et al., 2007)? Considering comorbidity problems, it isn't surprising that traditional personality disorder categories also have problems with interrater reliability (a concept introduced in Chapter 3) (Fowler et al., 2007; Zimmerman, 1994). This means that different clinicians diagnosing a personality disorder in the same client often arrive at different diagnoses (e.g., one clinician might diagnose antisocial, another narcissistic, and still another histrionic). In other words, therapists often have trouble distinguishing personality disorders. This failure to consistently agree on which personality disorder someone has is a significant problem in clinical practice and an ongoing concern for *DSM* and *ICD* developers, who pride themselves on making sure that these manuals have good reliability.

Is Dimensional Diagnosis Better?

Because traditional categories have had so many problems, there has been a steady shift toward conceptualizing personality disorders dimensionally. Compared to categorical models, are these dimensional systems on stronger scientific ground? Are they more reliable? Do they help clinicians map personality disorder better? When it comes to the *DSM-5* hybrid model versus the *ICD-11* purely dimensional model, is one better than the other? These are the questions researchers are currently exploring.

Let's look at the *DSM-5* hybrid model first. A growing body of research suggests that this model performs at least as well as (and sometimes better than) the categorical approach to diagnosing personality disorders (J. Anderson, Snider, Sellbom, Krueger, & Hopwood, 2014; Chmielewski, Ruggero, Kotov, Liu, & Krueger, 2016; Samuel, 2015). For instance, studies on both borderline personality disorder and antisocial personality disorder have found the *DSM-5* hybrid system an improvement over the old categorical system (J. L. Anderson, Sellbom, Sansone, & Songer, 2016; Bach & Sellbom, 2016; Few, Lynam, Maples, MacKillop, & Miller, 2015). Nonetheless, the need for additional refinements remains. Just as categories often overlap, trait facets sometimes do too (J. Anderson et al., 2014). Thus, the proposed *DSM-5* facets may not be as structurally simple and distinct as originally assumed (R. F. Krueger & Markon, 2014). This makes reliable diagnosis more difficult. Further, there is limited evidence for the level of impairment assessment; it may need to be revised or discarded (J. L. Anderson & Sellbom, 2016). Finally, the *DSM-5* alternative model has been criticized for being an awkward mix of categories and dimensions (Widiger, 2011)—perhaps making it too cumbersome for actual use in clinical practice.

Now let's turn to the *ICD-11*'s dimensional model. Its advocates contend that it's not just convenient and practical, but also scientifically promising. The model's five trait domains have been partly validated in initial research (Y. R. Kim et al., 2015; Mulder, Horwood, Tyrer, Carter, & Joyce, 2016). There is also emerging evidence that dividing personality disorder into mild, moderate, and severe types may be diagnostically valid (Y. R. Kim, Blashfield, Tyrer, Hwang, & Lee, 2014). Some have even suggested that the *ICD-11* system is more clinically sensitive, identifying more people who have personality disorders (Tyrer et al., 2014). This contention is based on the unexpected finding that the *ICD-11* dimensions, compared to the *ICD-10* categories, result in

CHAPTER 12

more people receiving personality disorder diagnoses (Tyrer et al., 2014). Dimensional diagnosis supporters contend that this is because the *ICD-11* system more accurately uncovers those with personality disturbances, but it's also possible that the *ICD-11* system is too inclusive. Nonetheless, dimensional researchers are excited about the *ICD-11* system's potential, as evidenced by a flurry of ongoing research into its scientific standing and clinical utility.

Practitioner Support of Categories

In breaking with historical tradition by reducing or eliminating long-familiar categories, do the *DSM-5* hybrid and *ICD-11* dimensional models go too far? Are they, as some critics believe, too radical (Pull, 2013; Verheul, 2012)? Although past research pointed to professional doubts about traditional personality disorder categories (Samuel & Griffin, 2015), a survey done during the development of the *DSM-5* found that practicing clinicians from around the world overwhelmingly like the traditional categories and aren't keen to give them up (Mullins-Sweatt, Bernstein, & Widiger, 2012). Not only do high percentages of them report frequently using personality disorder diagnoses, but they also rate these diagnoses as important in clinical decision-making (Mullins-Sweatt et al., 2012). So even though many researchers are eager to discard what they see as scientifically suspect personality disorder categories, many practicing clinicians feel quite the opposite. Conflict between scientists and practitioners over the relative importance of scientific data versus clinical experience is common in the mental health field (T. B. Baker, McFall, & Shoham, 2008; Garb, Lilienfeld, & Fowler, 2016), but is especially sharp when it comes to personality disorders. While many clinicians and everyday people continue to wholeheartedly accept traditional personality disorder categories (as evidenced by the large number of self-help books about personality disorders), researchers are pushing ahead with new dimensional models because they see the old categories as having serious scientific limitations.

As dimensional trait models of personality disorder are phased in over the next few years, it will be interesting to see whether clinicians and the public warm to them. At least one study suggests they might. In this study, clinicians were asked to use both the *DSM-5* categorical and hybrid models and rate them. While they generally agreed that the categorical model was better for easy communication with other professionals, they also rated the hybrid system positively, seeing it as extremely comprehensive (L. C. Morey, Skodol, & Oldham, 2014). Increased familiarity with new dimensional models may eventually foster their acceptance.

12.3 HISTORICAL PERSPECTIVES
PERSONALITY AND BODILY HUMORS

The idea of personality as stable and enduring is found throughout history. For instance, Ancient Chinese medicine attributed differences in temperament to a person's "blood and vital essence," which starts out fluid during early life, hardens into a stable personality during adulthood, and loosens again in old age (Crocq, 2013, p. 148). History is also replete with systems for distinguishing personality types. In ancient Greece, the philosopher Theophrastus (c. 371–c. 287 BCE) identified twelve character types, including the *thankless character* (who sees the negative in everything and is unable to enjoy life) and the *suspicious character* (who, like today's paranoid personality, doesn't trust others) (Crocq, 2013). More famously, the Greek physician Galen used the four bodily humors (see Chapter 1) proposed by Hippocrates (460–367 BCE) to articulate an early classification of personality types and personality disturbance (Merenda, 1987; Tyrer et al., 2015). See Table 12.1 for details.

Table 12.1 Bodily Humor Personality Types

HUMOR	PERSONALITY TYPE	PERSONALITY CHARACTERISTICS
Blood	*Sanguine*	Optimistic, hopeful, impulsive, pleasure-seeking
Black bile	*Melancholic*	Introverted, thoughtful, sad, and depressed
Yellow bile	*Choleric*	Ambitious, persevering, easily angered and irritable
Phlegm	*Phlegmatic*	Relaxed, quiet, apathetic

MORAL INSANITY

The French physician Philippe Pinel (1745–1826), who famously unchained the inmates at Bicêtre Hospital (again, see Chapter 1), was one of the first to identify patterns of behavior that today would likely be diagnosed as personality disorders. He spoke of *manie sans délire* (**mania without delusion**), a term he used to describe patients who showed no overt symptoms of madness. They weren't hallucinatory, delusional, or incoherent. Instead, they were prone to emotional outbursts such as fits of temper or impulsive violence (Crocq, 2013). In many cases, Pinel attributed their personality problems to an improper upbringing, such as having a weak and undisciplined mother (Crocq, 2013). Pinel's work likely influenced James Cowles Prichard (1786–1848), who introduced the concept of **moral insanity**, a precursor to the *DSM*'s antisocial personality disorder. Moral insanity was characterized by impulsive, violent, and depraved behavior, but without more florid symptoms of madness (Coolidge & Segal, 1998). Prichard (1835, p. 6) vividly described it as a madness "consisting in a morbid perversion of the natural feelings, affections, inclinations, temper, habits, moral dispositions, and natural impulses, without any remarkable disorder or defect of the intellect or knowing and reasoning faculties, and particularly without any insane illusion or hallucination."

PSYCHOPATHIC PERSONALITIES

Prichard's work clearly impacted that of Emil Kraepelin (1856–1926), who (as discussed in Chapter 3) developed one of the first psychiatric classification systems. In that system he included **psychopathic personalities**, which he believed were lifelong pathologies caused by inborn "defects" (Crocq, 2013). Kraepelin's notion of "psychopathic personalities" was broader than our current use of the term "psychopathy." He identified four specific psychopathic personalities: *born criminals*, *the weak-willed*, *pathological liars/swindlers*, and *the paranoid* (Crocq, 2013). Kraepelin's ideas about psychopathic personalities were in turn further expanded by Kurt Schneider (1887–1967). Schneider "defined 'psychopathic' personalities as those individuals who suffer, or cause society to suffer, because of their personality traits" (Crocq, 2013, p. 151). Like Kraepelin, he felt psychopathic personalities were mostly innate, but influenced by environmental factors (Crocq, 2013). Schneider identified ten types of psychopathic personality: *depressive*, *insecure*, *fanatical*, *recognition-seeking*, *explosive*, *emotionally-blunted*, *weak-willed*, *asthenic* (those lacking in energy), *hyperthymic* (those with exceptionally positive moods), and *labile* (those with rapidly changing moods) (Crocq, 2013). Schneider's ten "psychopathic personalities" profoundly influenced later *DSM* and *ICD* personality disorder categories (see Table 12.2). Interestingly, Schneider was an early advocate of dimensional assessment because he felt personality couldn't be broken into discrete categories (Crocq, 2013). Thus, his work continues to influence modern conceptions of personality disorder.

Table 12.2 Links Between the Classifications of Galen with Schneider's and the *DSM* and *ICD* Classifications

	Schneider	*DSM*-IV-TR	ICD-6	*ICD*-10
Choleric	Emotionally unstable	Borderline	Emotional instability	Emotionally unstable, including borderline and impulsive
Choleric	Explosive	Antisocial	Antisocial	Antisocial
Choleric	Self-seeking	Narcissistic	—	—
Choleric	—	Histrionic	Immature	Histrionic
Melancholic	Depressive	Depressive*	Cyclothymic†	—
Melancholic	Asthenic	Avoidant	Passive dependency	Anxious (avoidant)
Melancholic	Weak-willed	Dependent	Inadequate	Dependent
Phlegmatic	Affectless	Schizoid	Schizoid	Schizoid
Phlegmatic	—	Schizotypal	Asocial	—
Not classified elsewhere	Insecure sensitive	Paranoid	Paranoid	Paranoid

CHAPTER 12

Not classified elsewhere	Insecure anankastic	Obsessive-compulsive	Anankastic	Anankastic
Not classified elsewhere	Fanatical	—	—	—
Sanguine	Hyperthymic	—	—	—

*A diagnosis listed in earlier versions of *DSM* and recommended for further study in *DSM-IV*.
†This category appeared in later revisions of *ICD* and *DSM* but was subsequently recoded under affective (mood) disorders.

Source: Adapted from p. 719 of: Tyrer, P., Reed, G. M., & Crawford, M. J. (2015). Classification, assessment, prevalence, and effect of personality disorder. *The Lancet*, 385(9969), 717–726. doi:10.1016/S0140-6736(14)61995-4

12.4 BIOLOGICAL PERSPECTIVES

Biological perspectives on personality disorder are frequently overshadowed by psychoanalytic and behavioral approaches (Perez-Rodriguez, New, & Siever, 2013). Nonetheless, personality disorders are often viewed as originating in inborn (genetic) traits and are commonly treated with medication. Most of the research on the biology of personality disorders has focused on three specific diagnoses: antisocial (APD), borderline (BPD), and schizotypal (STPD) (Perez-Rodriguez et al., 2013). We focus mostly on these diagnoses below.

BRAIN CHEMISTRY PERSPECTIVES

Neurotransmitters and Personality Disorders

Serotonin in APD and BPD

Both antisocial and borderline personality disorders have been tied to low serotonin activity (Amad, Ramoz, Thomas, Jardri, & Gorwood, 2014; Calati, Gressier, Balestri, & Serretti, 2013; Coccaro, Sripada, Yanowitch, & Phan, 2011; Fanning, Berman, Guillot, Marsic, & McCloskey, 2014; Maurex, Zaboli, Öhman, Åsberg, & Leopardi, 2010; Moul, Dobson-Stone, Brennan, Hawes, & Dadds, 2013; Ni et al., 2006; Soloff, Chiappetta, Mason, Becker, & Price, 2014; D. F. Thompson, Ramos, & Willett, 2014; Yildirim & Derksen, 2013). While some published studies on BPD haven't confirmed this link (Baca-Garcia et al., 2004; Pascual et al., 2008), the consensus seems to be that low serotonin predicts both antisocial and borderline symptoms. This makes intuitive sense given that reduced serotonin is associated with impulsive and aggressive behavior, both of which are common among those diagnosed with APD and BPD. However, the research is mainly correlational and low serotonin isn't unique to antisocial and borderline patients; it is correlated with many presenting problems.

Dopamine in STPD

Because schizotypal personality disorder is often viewed as a milder but related form of psychosis, interest in the role of dopamine is understandable. As you recall from Chapter 4, the dopamine hypothesis of schizophrenia holds that schizophrenia and other forms of psychosis are due to too much dopamine. Excessive dopamine is suspected of being important in STPD too. Research studies have provided support for this, especially for positive symptoms (additions to the personality such as hallucinations and delusions; see Chapter 4) (Abi-Dargham et al., 2004; Siever & Davis, 2004; Siever & Weinstein, 2009). It's been hypothesized that the milder symptoms of STPD compared to schizophrenia are attributable to better "buffering" ability in the brains of STPD patients; their brains are suspected of being better able to compensate for dopamine dysregulation problems, therefore making symptoms less severe (Perez-Rodriguez et al., 2013; Siever & Davis, 2004).

Polypharmacy and Non-Specificity of Drug Treatments

Many different types of drugs are used to treat personality disorders—including antidepressants, mood stabilizers, anticonvulsants, and antipsychotics (Paris, 2011; Ripoll, Triebwasser, & Siever, 2011; Stoffers et al., 2010). Often patients are prescribed multiple drugs at the same time—an approach known as **polypharmacy** (Lieb, Völlm, Rücker, Timmer, & Stoffers, 2010; Paris, 2011). For example, an antidepressant might be used to help ease sadness, a mood stabilizer or anticonvulsant given to reduce aggression and impulsivity, and an antipsychotic prescribed to address paranoia and odd thoughts and perceptions (Duggan, Huband, Smailagic, Ferriter, & Adams, 2008; M. Goodman, Vail, West, New, & Siever, 2006; Lieb et al., 2010; Silk & Feurino, 2012).

Harvey and Magdalena

Thus, our case example clients Harvey and Magdalena might both find themselves taking a variety of medications.

In thinking about polypharmacy, note that drug treatments aren't targeting underlying neurochemical imbalances specific to each personality disorder, mainly because we don't presently have the knowledge to do this. As prominent psychiatrist Joel Paris bluntly, yet optimistically, explains:

> We do not know whether personality disordered patients have a "chemical imbalance", as so many seem to believe, without much supporting evidence. It is possible that any drug with strong sedating properties can reduce anger and impulsivity. Non-specific effects of this kind can still be useful, but we need to develop more specific agents. ... Thus drugs for personality disorder are non-specific "stop-gaps" that will eventually be replaced by better and more precise alternatives. (Paris, 2011, p. 305)

Medication for Personality Disorders: Debate over Effectiveness and Use

Given that drug treatments for personality disorders are non-specific, it makes sense that research on their effectiveness has often yielded discouraging conclusions. Currently, there aren't that many empirical studies on psychopharmacology for personality disorders (Silk & Feurino, 2012). Reviews of existing studies generally conclude that medications aren't especially helpful as first-line treatments (Bateman, Gunderson, & Mulder, 2015; Duggan et al., 2008; Stoffers et al., 2010). Yes, there is some evidence that certain classes of drugs may reduce specific emotional symptoms such as impulsivity, anger, aggression, and unstable mood (Lieb et al., 2010; Paris, 2011; Ripoll et al., 2011; Stoffers et al., 2010). However, some warn against the polypharmacy approach this can lead to, arguing there is no evidence that prescribing multiple drugs works better than sticking with a single medication (Silk & Feurino, 2012).

Despite such reservations about their effectiveness, large numbers of people diagnosed with personality disorders are prescribed one or more medications (Silk & Feurino, 2012). In a U.S. sample, as many as 81% of those with borderline, schizotypal, avoidant, or obsessive-compulsive personality disorder diagnoses had a history of taking psychotropic drugs (Bender et al., 2001). A more recent European study found something similar, with roughly 90% of inpatients with a borderline diagnosis receiving medication (Bridler et al., 2015). Such high medication rates are astonishing considering that research casts doubt on these drugs' effectiveness. The high European rates are also surprising given that European professional guidelines don't recommend medication for borderline personality disorder (Bridler et al., 2015). While U.S. guidelines are less discouraging about using medication (Tyrer & Silk, 2011), it appears that in actual practice both American and European doctors overwhelmingly prescribe drugs to treat people diagnosed with borderline and other personality disorders. Although most clinicians probably don't see drugs as a panacea, they may feel compelled to use them to manage the persistent and challenging emotions and behaviors that people with personality disorders display—even when there is little evidence for doing so (Paris, 2011).

BRAIN STRUCTURE PERSPECTIVES

Antisocial Personality Disorder/Psychopathy

A good deal of brain research refers to "psychopathy" rather than "APD," treating these terms as more or less equivalent despite the former not being in the *DSM* or *ICD*. We therefore use "APD" and "psychopathy" somewhat interchangeably below when discussing biological perspectives. Although this may seem confusing, it is a confusion in the field, one that reflects the lack of widespread agreement about terminology. If you refer back to the "In Depth" feature on p. 389, it isn't surprising that biological researchers often use the term psychopathy because psychopathy has typically been viewed as originating in biology.

In individuals diagnosed with APD and/or psychopathy, overall brain volumes are often, though not always, decreased (Perez-Rodriguez et al., 2013; Skodol, Bender, Gunderson, & Oldham, 2014). Two specific brain areas that tend to show volume reduction are the prefrontal cortex and temporal cortex. Besides being smaller, the prefrontal cortexes of patients with APD are also thought to be less active and to have structural and functional deficits—in particular, in the orbitofrontal, dorsolateral frontal, and anterior cingulate regions (D. F. Thompson et al., 2014; Y. Yang & Raine, 2009). Why might changes in prefrontal and temporal areas play a part in psychopathy? Because these areas are important in decision-making, planning, and regulating social

CHAPTER 12

behavior—all problem areas for APD patients. Temporal and prefrontal cortex dysfunctions are both associated with violent outbursts, which are common in APD/psychopathy (Coccaro et al., 2011; Potegal, 2012).

Another brain area receiving attention in psychopathy research is the amygdala, which is important in primitive emotions such as fear and anger. Some studies find the amygdala is larger among those with APD, while other studies suggest it's smaller (Boccardi et al., 2011; D. F. Thompson et al., 2014). Uncertainty over changes in its size notwithstanding, exactly how might the amygdala be malfunctioning in APD? One theory says it is underactive, as evidenced by the fact that those who score high on measures of psychopathy often have deficient responses to alarming and stressful circumstances. This makes them less effective in reading situations and avoiding trouble (Blair, 2008). An alternative hypothesis is that the amygdala is overactive, not underactive. Its hyperactivity, combined with an underactive prefrontal cortex, is suspected of producing impulsive and violent behaviors characteristic of APD (Buchheim, Roth, Schiepek, Pogarell, & Karch, 2013).

Harvey
From a biological perspective, then, our case example client Harvey's violent and antisocial behavior might be attributable to biological brain factors.

Borderline Personality Disorder

Like people with antisocial tendencies, those diagnosed as borderline tend to show decreased overall brain volume. Specifically, they show reduced volume and/or activity in various prefrontal regions related to emotional control, such as the anterior cingulate gyrus and orbitofrontal cortex (Lis, Greenfield, Henry, Guilé, & Dougherty, 2007; Perez-Rodriguez et al., 2013). Certain studies have also found decreased volume in the amygdala and hippocampus (important in memory) (Buchheim et al., 2013). When it comes to the amygdala, some studies have indicated that it becomes overactive when exposed to emotional stimuli, while others have found it shuts down in response to painful stimuli (Perez-Rodriguez et al., 2013). Both results may have some truth to them because people diagnosed as borderline become easily overwhelmed by strong emotions (overactive amygdala?), but also tend to dissociate when faced with upsetting situations (underactive amygdala?). The challenge is that the various brain regions linked to BPD (and there are many more than the few highlighted here) are the same ones implicated in other disorders—including PTSD, depression, and bipolar disorder (Lis et al., 2007; Perez-Rodriguez et al., 2013). Thus, changes in these brain regions aren't specific to people displaying borderline symptoms.

Magdalena
Might the emotional responses of Magdalena, our borderline case example client, be attributable to dysfunctions in her hippocampus and amygdala?

Schizotypal Personality Disorder

One of the major brain structure anomalies found in schizophrenia—enlarged brain ventricles—is also found in schizotypal personality disorder, albeit to a lesser degree (Perez-Rodriguez et al., 2013). This isn't surprising given that both diagnoses involve psychotic symptoms, even though schizotypal symptoms are milder. What is the significance of enlarged ventricles? The larger the ventricles, the less brain matter—implying brain volume deterioration (see Chapter 4).

STDP is like schizophrenia in other ways, too. For example, people with both diagnoses (as well as other diagnoses linked to trauma, such as depression and PTSD) show decreased hippocampal volumes (Fervaha & Remington, 2013). However, one way that STPD differs from schizophrenia is that patients sometimes show increased volume in the prefrontal cortex; exactly why isn't known, but some have speculated it's the brain's way of warding off full-blown psychosis—something the brains of those who develop schizophrenia may be unable to do (Fervaha & Remington, 2013).

GENETIC AND EVOLUTIONARY PERSPECTIVES
Genetic Perspectives

Twin, Family, and Adoption Studies

Most genetic research has looked at genetic and environmental influences on normal personality, not personality disorders (South, 2015). Heritability estimates (see Chapter 2) aim to tell us what percentage of a person's phenotypic variability (differences in displayed traits) is due to genes versus environment. Twin and family studies have yielded heritability estimates between 40% and 50% for the Big Five personality traits (South, 2015). This suggests that genes and environment contribute nearly equally to personality. When it comes to personality disorders, the consensus is that they are moderately to strongly heritable (with the possible exceptions of schizoid, paranoid, and avoidant), although research results have sometimes been inconsistent in confirming this (Fontaine & Viding, 2008; Reichborn-Kjennerud, 2010).

There haven't been many personality disorder twin studies, partly because it's hard to locate affected twins (Roussos & Siever, 2012). In the studies that have been done, heritability estimates for personality disorders have varied. One well-cited study reported a median heritability of 61% with a range between 28% and 79% (Roussos & Siever, 2012; Torgersen et al., 2000). Two Norwegian studies found lower heritability: 21% to 28% for Cluster A ("odd") disorders and 27% to 35% for Cluster C ("anxious or fearful") disorders (Kendler et al., 2006; Reichborn-Kjennerud et al., 2007; Roussos & Siever, 2012).

Genetics research may help us understand the high rates of comorbidity among personality disorder diagnoses, especially if different personality disorder categories can be linked to shared genetic and environmental factors. Some studies point to common genetic and environmental influences in the Cluster A personality disorders and two of the three Cluster C personality disorders (avoidant and dependent, but not obsessive-compulsive) (Kendler et al., 2006; Reichborn-Kjennerud et al., 2007). However, other studies suggest that Clusters A, B, and C may not be the best way to carve up personality disorders; there may simply be a general genetic predisposition to personality disorders, along with specific genetic vulnerabilities to those personality disorders involving high impulsivity/low agreeableness and those involving introversion (Kendler et al., 2008; Reichborn-Kjennerud, 2010). There is continuing disagreement over how much genetics research results can effectively be used to inform *DSM* and *ICD* classifications of personality disorders (Hopwood, 2013; Iacono, 2013; Skodol & Krueger, 2013; South & DeYoung, 2013a, 2013b). Some critics warn researchers not to overemphasize genes, reminding us that adjusted and maladjusted personality patterns inevitably arise from gene–environment interactions (Fontaine & Viding, 2008; Hayden, 2013).

Candidate Genes

To date, research on candidate genes has provided many leads but few definitive answers. Genes related to dopamine and glutamate are garnering interest when it comes to Cluster A personality disorders, especially for schizotypal personality disorder (South, 2015). For Cluster C personality disorders, links have been found with various genes, including the 5-HTTLPR serotonin gene and the DRD3 and DRD4 dopamine genes; the DRD3 gene has been associated with both avoidant and obsessive-compulsive personality disorders, while the DRD4 gene with only obsessive-compulsive personality disorder (Joyce et al., 2003; Light et al., 2006; South, 2015).

Cluster B ("dramatic and emotional") personality disorder research has mostly focused on antisocial and borderline personalities. It has highlighted the importance of TPH1, TPH2 and 5-HTLLPR genes (all significant in the serotonin system) and the MAOA gene (important in the functioning of monoamine oxidase, the enzyme discussed in Chapter 5 that breaks down serotonin, norepinephrine, and dopamine) (Maurex et al., 2010; Ni, Chan, Chan, McMain, & Kennedy, 2009; Ni et al., 2006; South, 2015; Wagner, Baskaya, Lieb, Dahmen, & Tadić, 2009; S. T. Wilson et al., 2009). Because impulsivity and aggression are typical antisocial and borderline symptoms, a lot of Cluster B research has focused on genetic influences on antisocial and violent behavior. Many different genes have been identified as potentially relevant (D. Li et al., 2012; Maurex et al., 2010; Moul, Dobson-Stone, Brennan, Hawes, & Dadds, 2015; Ni et al., 2009; Ni et al., 2006; Paaver, Kurrikoff, Nordquist, Oreland, & Harro, 2008; Tadić et al., 2008; M. Yang, Kavi, Wang, Wu, & Hao, 2012; M. Yang et al., 2014). However, the MAOA and 5-HTTLPR genes are most often mentioned as important (Ficks & Waldman, 2014; Fontaine & Viding, 2008; T. D. Gunter, Vaughn, & Philibert, 2010; Hayden, 2013; Roussos & Siever, 2012; South, 2015).

Despite some tantalizing findings, not everyone is persuaded by research on the genetics of violence and criminality. Critics argue that (a) it is difficult to precisely define what counts as criminal behavior, (b) environmental and genetic influences can't be readily separated, and (c) many different genes, not just a few, probably contribute to violent behavior (Hayden, 2013). More broadly, critics feel that genetics research minimizes social influences on impulsive and violent behavior while overemphasizing genes and biology (J. Joseph, 2004; Wachbroit, 2001).

Evolutionary Perspectives

Evolutionary hypotheses try to explain how personality traits and patterns, many of which are commonly identified as disordered, are indeed adaptive and advantageous (Durisko, Mulsant, McKenzie, & Andrews, 2016; Nesse, 2005b; Nettle, 2006). Let's discuss two examples. The **frequency-dependent selection hypothesis**

CHAPTER **12**

holds that psychopathy is an evolutionarily adaptive strategy so long as its frequency in the population is low (K. N. Barr & Quinsey, 2004; Hertler, 2014b; Lalumière, Mishra, & Harris, 2008; Mealey, 1995). It maintains that personality characteristics that foster exploiting the natural human tendency to trust and cooperate are effective, but only if very few individuals engage in this sort of behavior. When too many of us prey on others, people stop trusting and become more cautious—taking away psychopathy's reproductive advantage. The **obsessive trait complex hypothesis** holds that obsessive-compulsive personality disorder traits are innate, not learned (Hertler, 2014a). It hypothesizes that the inherited traits common to OCPD (e.g., anxiety, compulsive conscientiousness, miserliness, and an ever-present sense of urgency) are what allowed early humans who migrated to colder and more inhospitable climates to survive (Hertler, 2014b, 2015a, 2015b).

Traditional medical model adherents are skeptical of evolutionary perspectives. They aren't convinced that problematic personality traits (like those found in psychopathy) are evolved adaptations functioning normally. Instead, they prefer explanations that attribute personality disorders to brain malfunctions (D. J. Stein, 1997). Critics also contend that evolutionary hypotheses are hard to test empirically and that other theories might just as readily explain personality issues (Crusio, 2004).

IMMUNE SYSTEM PERSPECTIVES

As you recall from previous chapters, stress and trauma are often associated with inflammation in the immune system. People who have experienced abuse, neglect, and deprivation early in life are more likely to behave aggressively—and behavioral aggression is a consistent predictor of immune system inflammation (Coccaro, Lee, & Coussons-Read, 2015a; Fanning, Lee, Gozal, Coussons-Read, & Coccaro, 2015). Because both early life trauma and aggressive behavior are common in personality disorders, researchers have begun looking at whether people with personality disorder diagnoses show immune system inflammation. Although correlational, evidence shows just such a link. Levels of cytokines (the small proteins produced by immune system cells that cause swelling in large amounts) and other inflammatory markers tend to be higher in people with personality disorder diagnoses (Coccaro, Lee, & Coussons-Read, 2015a; Coccaro et al., 2015b; Díaz-Marsá et al., 2012; Fanning et al., 2015).

Of course, almost all presenting problems are associated with past stress of some kind. Thus, inflammation is common to most psychiatric diagnoses and not specific to personality disorders. Nonetheless, this link between trauma and personality issues (particularly aggressive tendencies) suggests a complex interaction between environmental conditions and immunological processes that warrants further examination.

EVALUATING BIOLOGICAL PERSPECTIVES

Biological perspectives haven't yielded much in terms of treatment for personality issues; despite widespread use, medications remain minimally effective. Scientifically speaking, genetic explanations of personality disorder are usually considered the strongest of the biological approaches, built on a compelling and extensive (if occasionally contested) body of research (Cloninger, 2012; Roussos & Siever, 2012; South, 2015). Nonetheless, biological perspectives on personality difficulties are criticized for (a) minimizing social and contextual factors, and (b) relying on circular reasoning about traits. When it comes to social and contextual factors, prominent personality and social psychologist Walter Mischel has long argued that human behavior is influenced not just by innate biological traits, but also by situations and how people make sense of them (Mischel, 1973, 2009; Mischel & Shoda, 1995).

Harvey
Maybe our case example client Harvey behaves angrily not simply because he has an innately "angry personality," but also because he finds himself in many situations that he interprets as hostile.

CASE EXAMPLES

As for circular reasoning, critics contend that attributing behavior to inborn personality traits or disorders amounts to a non-explanation, one relying on a concept (traits) that can't be empirically verified (Boag, 2011).

Harvey
For example, how do we know that Harvey has innate antisocial personality traits? Because he behaves aggressively. And why does Harvey behave aggressively? Because of his innate antisocial personality traits, of course!

CASE EXAMPLES

Such circular reasoning is clearly problematic. It treats personality traits (an abstract concept) as physically real and then circularly uses them to explain behavior, even though the very behaviors that personality traits explain are simultaneously offered as "proof" that these traits exist in the first place (Boag, 2011). Many of the psychological and sociocultural perspectives discussed next try to avoid this sort of circular reasoning, though not always successfully.

12.5 PSYCHOLOGICAL PERSPECTIVES

PSYCHODYNAMIC PERSPECTIVES

Psychodynamic perspectives stress how personality is shaped by early relationships with caregivers. A dominant theme in psychodynamic psychotherapy "is the fundamental role that mental presentations, derived from early relational experiences have in shaping personality organization. These are seen to underlie the development of capacities for emotional regulation, metacognition, and interpersonal interactions" (Town & Driessen, 2013, p. 502). Thus, psychodynamic theories hold that when people experience neglect or abuse in early relationships, personality issues develop.

As examples, consider narcissistic, borderline, and obsessive-compulsive personality problems. Many psychodynamic therapists consider narcissism to be a self-protective response to defend against feelings of shame tied to parental rejection and mistreatment; narcissistic individuals compensate for these negative feelings by convincing themselves they are wonderful and seeking admiration and approval from others (O. F. Kernberg, 2001; Ronningstam, 2011). Borderline personality, on the other hand, is viewed as involving the dissociation (or splitting into "good" and "bad" parts; see Chapter 2) of incompatible ego states (Clarkin, Yeomans, & Kernberg, 2006; O. F. Kernberg, Selzer, Koenigsberg, Carr, & Appelbaum, 1989). This allows the person to keep contradictory emotions separate. Splitting feelings of hurt and rejection from those of idealization and love is how borderline clients cope with perceived slights, which they experience as intensely as the original abuse and mistreatment they received from loved ones during childhood and which fostered using splitting as a defense in the first place (Clarkin et al., 2006; Kernberg et al., 1989). Finally, psychodynamic conceptions often see obsessive-compulsive personality disorder as related to anal stage conflicts tied to toilet training; other, even more interpersonally oriented psychodynamic perspectives, view it as either an attempt to establish autonomy in response to dominating parents or as a means of overcoming anxiety, insecurity, and helplessness by controlling one's surroundings (Mallinger, 2009; Pollak, 1987; M. C. Wells, Glickauf-Hughes, & Buzzell, 1990). While specific psychodynamic explanations vary, they all focus on how child-rearing contributes to rigid personality styles. Below, after discussing the *Psychodynamic Diagnostic Manual*, we examine psychodynamic perspectives on personality disorder that are influenced by attachment and object relations theories.

Psychodynamic Diagnostic Manual (PDM)

As discussed in Chapter 3, the *Psychodynamic Diagnostic Manual* (*PDM*)—currently in its second edition (*PDM-2*)—is an alternative to the *DSM* and *ICD* (Lingiardi & McWilliams, 2017). The *PDM* system diverges from the strictly medical model of *DSM* and *ICD*, instead advancing an explicitly psychodynamic diagnostic approach (Meehan & Levy, 2015). The *PDM* is important when discussing personality issues because assessing personality is a core component of *PDM* diagnosis. Given the centrality of personality in psychodynamic theories, this makes sense. To wit, the *PDM-2* assesses all clients' personalities using one of its three central diagnostic axes, the P-Axis. This axis consists of 12 *personality syndromes* and is summarized in Table 12.3 (for more, also see Table 3.7). Notice that many of the personality syndromes listed in Table 12.3 closely correspond to the personality disorders we have been discussing. In fact, the P-Axis includes categories that are roughly comparable to all *DSM-5* personality disorders except schizotypal (Lingiardi & McWilliams, 2017; Meehan & Levy, 2015; Sperry, 2016). The *PDM* excludes schizotypal due its presumed overlap with schizoid personality disorder and the belief (shared by the *ICD*) that schizotypal is better grouped with schizophrenia and other psychoses (Meehan & Levy, 2015). Besides excluding schizotypal, the *PDM-2* also includes three personality syndromes not in the *DSM-5*: depressive, somatizing, and sadistic (Lingiardi & McWilliams, 2017).

CHAPTER 12

Table 12.3 P-Axis Personality Syndromes and their Closest *DSM-5* Equivalents

Syndrome	Tension/Preoccupation	Nearest *DSM-5* Personality Disorder Equivalent	Other Relevant *DSM-5* Disorders
Depressive	Self-critical, self-punishing, overly concerned with relatedness and/or loss	—	Mood disorders
Dependent	Maintaining relationships	Dependent personality disorder	
Anxious-avoidant and phobic	Staying safe vs. avoiding danger	Avoidant personality disorder	Anxiety disorders

Obsessive-compulsive	Submitting to vs. rebelling against the control or authority of others.	Obsessive-compulsive personality disorder	
Schizoid	Fearing intimacy vs. wanting intimacy	Schizoid personality disorder	
Somatizing	Integrity vs. fragmentation of the physical body	—	Somatic symptom and related disorders
Hysteric-histrionic	Unconscious devaluing of own gender while being envious and fearful of opposite gender	Histrionic personality disorder	
Narcissistic	Inflating vs. deflating self-esteem	Narcissistic personality disorder	
Paranoid	Attacking vs. being attacked by others	Paranoid personality disorder	
Psychopathic	Manipulating others vs. being manipulated by them	Antisocial personality disorder	
Sadistic	Suffering humiliation vs. imposing humiliation	—	Sexual sadism disorder
Borderline	Coherent vs. fragmented sense of self; enmeshed attachment vs. despair at abandonment	Borderline personality disorder	

NOTE: *DSM-5*'s schizotypal personality disorder has no direct equivalent *PDM-2* personality syndrome, but psychotic-like symptoms can be assessed in *PDM-2* using the P-Axis levels of personality organization (see Table 12.4).

Source: Lingiardi, V., & McWilliams, N. (Eds.). *Psychodynamic diagnostic manual* (2nd ed.). New York, NY: Guilford Press (2017). Adapted with permission of Guilford Press.

The importance of personality functioning in the *PDM* diagnostic system cannot be overstated. In assessing all clients on the P-Axis, the *PDM* ensures that personality issues aren't artificially separated from other types of psychological maladjustment. Rather, it evaluates personality functioning regardless of whether other (non-personality) disorders are diagnosed. The *PDM-2* does this because of its strong psychodynamic conviction that "all people have personality styles" and that personality issues naturally co-occur with other presenting problems, including "anxiety, depression, eating disorders, somatic symptoms, addictions, phobias, self-harm, trauma, and relationship problems" (Lingiardi & McWilliams, 2017, p. 17). Further, even among clients who don't formally qualify for *DSM* or *ICD* personality disorder diagnoses, the *PDM-2* contends that assessing overall personality functioning along the P-Axis provides crucial clinical information. From a *PDM*-perspective, "there is no hard and fast distinction between a personality *type* or *style* and a personality *disorder*" except that people identified as having personality disorders (or those who must interact with them) experience significantly higher levels of distress (Lingiardi & McWilliams, 2017, p. 17).

To better differentiate higher from lower functioning personality styles, the *PDM-2* distinguishes four **levels of personality organization** (see Table 12.4). The highest functioning level of organization is the *healthy level of personality organization*. People functioning at the healthy level may sometimes display elements of the personality syndromes in Table 12.3, but in a flexible and adaptive manner that allows them to function well in daily life. The next highest level of functioning is called the *neurotic level of personality organization*. Individuals at this level have many psychological strengths and function well much of the time, but tend to become rigid and restricted in their coping strategies when under distress; they may display depressive, phobic, or obsessive-compulsive styles when faced with adversity. Those at the *borderline level of functioning* experience trouble regulating emotion, thus they often experience intense worry, sadness, or anger when faced with challenging circumstances; the personality styles they rely on tend to be rigid and result in extreme disruption in relationships with others. They tend to engage in a lot of splitting (compartmentalizing of experiences) and projective identification (attributing undesired aspects of one's own experience to others); see Chapter 2 for a refresher on both these terms. Note that the borderline level of personality functioning is distinct from the borderline personality syndrome, even though they both use the term "borderline." Finally, the *psychotic level of personality organization* is the most extreme and pathological. It involves extremely poor reality testing and a diffuse sense of self. Someone "who stalks his love object in the conviction that this person 'really' loves him, despite all of the person's protestations to the contrary," would score at the psychotic level of personality organization (Lingiardi & McWilliams, 2017, p. 23).

Table 12.4 *PDM-2* Levels of Personality Organization

The Psychodiagnostic Chart below can be used to rate levels of personality organization on a 1–10 scale, with 1 most pathological and 10 least pathological.

Psychotic level	(1–2)	Break with reality; poor sense of identity; highly defensive; difficulty distinguishing fantasy and reality.
Borderline level	(3–5)	Have difficulty with emotional regulation; often overwhelmed by intense depression, anxiety, and rage.
Neurotic level	(6–8)	Respond to certain stressors with rigidity, despite having many functional capacities overall.
Healthy level	(9–10)	Have preferred coping style, but it is flexible enough to accommodate challenges of everyday life.

Source: adapted from Gordon, R. M., & Bornstein, R. F. (2018). Construct validity of the Psychodiagnostic Chart: A transdiagnostic measure of personality organization, personality syndromes, mental functioning, and symptomatology. *Psychoanalytic Psychology*, 35(2), 280–288. doi:10.1037/pap0000142

Among clinicians, the *PDM* has generated excitement about being able to diagnose personality functioning psychodynamically. However, its reliability and validity require further study (Fonagy & Luyten, 2012). Time will tell whether the *PDM-2* generates research and is incorporated into clinical practice by a sizable number of clinicians.

Attachment and Object Relations Approaches

Attachment theory (discussed in several previous chapters) holds that early experiences with caregivers lead to secure or insecure attachments (Bowlby, 1980, 1988). As you may recall, securely attached babies have reliable parents who soothe and console them when they encounter stress (Ainsworth, Blehar, Waters, & Wall, 1978). Such babies grow up to be emotionally resilient, feeling good about themselves and safe with and connected to others. Insecurely attached babies, on the other hand, struggle to modulate feelings of frustration, fear, and rage (Ainsworth et al., 1978). In response to their parents' inconsistent warmth and attention, they learn that others are unreliable. As adults, they worry about being abandoned and have difficulty handling negative emotions that arise during stressful situations. Through a psychodynamically oriented attachment theory lens, then, personality disorders are viewed as problematic patterns of

Attachment theory hypothesizes that personality disorders are traceable to negative early parent–child interactions that result in insecure attachment patterns in adulthood.
Source: PhotoDisc/Getty Images

relating tied to difficulties with early attachment. Object relations therapy (see Chapter 2) is like attachment theory in emphasizing the importance of early caregiving. Both approaches maintain that people who experience abusive, inconsistent, or indifferent parenting develop rigid and problematic patterns of relating to others—in other words, disordered personality functioning (Blatt & Levy, 2003; Caligor & Clarkin, 2010; De Bei & Dazzi, 2014; Fonagy & Luyten, 2012; Jeremy Holmes, 2015a; O. F. Kernberg et al., 1989; K. N. Levy & Blatt, 1999; Meehan & Levy, 2015). These dysfunctional personality patterns may have worked as ways to cope with difficult caregivers during childhood, but they have serious limitations when relied on as templates for adult relationships.

Object relations therapies assume that patients require a corrective emotional experience in which they learn new patterns of relating to others (Alexander & French, 1946). As such, transference and countertransference take center stage. Transference occurs when patients project feelings about past relationships onto their therapists and then defend against these feelings by engaging in their usual problematic patterns of relating. Countertransference, on the other hand, can take two forms: a useful kind and a not-so-useful kind. The not-so-useful kind is when therapists project their own issues onto patients (Cashdan, 1988; Clarkin et al., 2006; O. F. Kernberg et al., 1989). This clouds therapists' ability to clearly understand patients. The useful kind is when therapists are induced to act and feel in certain ways in response to patient behavior (Cashdan,

CHAPTER 12

1988; Clarkin et al., 2006; O. F. Kernberg et al., 1989). For example, a patient who projects dependency and neediness might evoke feelings of omnipotence in her therapist, while also leading the therapist to feel pressure to tell her what to do to solve her problems. By contrast, a narcissistic patient might elicit feelings of boredom and frustration from his therapist, who ends up feeling like little more than an audience expected to tell the patient how terrific he is. Corrective emotional experiences occur when therapists share their countertransference feelings, encouraging patients to relate to them without relying on their usual rigid and defensive patterns. By using the therapist–patient relationship to help patients gain insight into long-standing personality patterns, patients start to develop more effective and flexible ways of interacting—initially with their therapists, and eventually with others (A. Abbass, 2016; A. A. Abbass & Town, 2013; Caligor et al., 2007; Cashdan, 1988; Clarkin, Fonagy, & Gabbard, 2010; Clarkin et al., 2006; Davanloo, 1999; Eizirik & Fonagy, 2009; O. F. Kernberg et al., 1989; Levenson, 2017; Yeomans, Clarkin, & Kernberg, 2015; Yeomans & Diamond, 2010).

Magdalena

Imagine Magdalena seeks psychodynamic therapy. When she insists that the therapist doesn't care for her because he won't extend session times, the therapist would use this as an opportunity to carefully and thoroughly explore his relationship with Magdalena. He would examine with her how she was feeling during their interactions and link her frantic efforts to avoid his rejection back to previous rejecting experiences she had growing up. By patiently providing a safe and secure relationship, one in which emotionally charged topics could be openly discussed (such as Magdalena feeling abandoned), the therapy would offer an emotionally corrective experience. It might take Magdalena time to feel safe enough to not rely on her "borderline" manipulations with the therapist, but over time she would hopefully begin feeling like she didn't need to resort to such measures because she had developed faith and trust that the therapist cared for her and wouldn't abandon her. Ultimately, the goal would be to help Magdalena start developing similar secure relationships outside of therapy in which she no longer felt borderline-style behaviors were necessary.

CASE EXAMPLES

Research on Structured Psychodynamic Therapies

Various structured psychodynamic therapies have been developed for use with personality disorders, including *transference-focused psychotherapy* (*TFP*) (O. F. Kernberg, 2016; Yeomans et al., 2015; Yeomans & Diamond, 2010), *mentalization-based treatment* (*MBT*) (Bateman & Fonagy, 2010; Bateman & Fonagy, 2012; Fonagy & Luyten, 2009), and *intensive short-term dynamic psychotherapy* (*ISTDP*) (A. Abbass, 2016; A. Abbass, Sheldon, Gyra, & Kalpin, 2008; Davanloo, 1999). These therapies usually last a year or two, making them brief by psychodynamic standards. Their conceptualizations of personality problems vary somewhat, but all emphasize using the relationship between client and therapist to help rectify rigid and ineffective patterns of interaction that were learned in early childhood. Advocates of these more structured psychodynamic interventions contend that the evidence base for them is reasonably strong. Still, some psychoanalytic traditionalists remain skeptical, arguing that many of the more structured relational therapies don't sufficiently attend to sexual drives and unconscious conflicts (Fonagy & Campbell, 2015). Ironically, despite this reticence on the part of some psychodynamic therapists, it is due to this promising empirical research on more structured approaches that psychodynamic interventions are recommended for personality disorders (A. Abbass, 2016; A. Abbass, Town, & Driessen, 2012; Bateman & Fonagy, 2009; Bateman, O'Connell, Lorenzini, Gardner, & Fonagy, 2016; Biskin & Paris, 2012; Haskayne, Hirschfeld, & Larkin, 2014; Leichsenring, Abbass, Luyten, Hilsenroth, & Rabung, 2013; Leichsenring & Klein, 2014; Leichsenring, Leweke, Klein, & Steinert, 2015; Messer & Abbass, 2010; Town, Abbass, & Bernier, 2013; Town & Driessen, 2013; Verheul & Herbrink, 2007; Yeomans & Diamond, 2010). Nonetheless, a comprehensive review concluded that even though psychodynamic therapies appear effective for personality issues, more evidence is needed to draw definite conclusions (Stoffers et al., 2012).

Psychodynamic perspectives on personality disturbances have been criticized for being vague and overemphasizing the importance of upbringing. One critic argued that psychodynamic approaches are in denial about the heritability of personality issues (Hertler, 2014a). Citing a heritability of 0.78 for OCPD (Torgersen et al., 2000), this critic pushed psychodynamic clinicians to give up their long-held idea that personality problems are forged during child-rearing, remarking that "after so demonstrating the heritability of obsessive character, the principle [sic] predicate of psychoanalytic etiologies becomes patently implausible" (Hertler, 2014a, p. 172). Of course, this returns us to earlier debates about how much personality is inherited versus shaped by environment—an issue we grapple with throughout the rest of this chapter. Suffice to say, even when they acknowledge genetic influences, psychodynamic clinicians remain committed to the idea that early life attachments are central to personality problems.

COGNITIVE-BEHAVIORAL PERSPECTIVES

Cognitive-behavioral therapies (CBT) attribute personality issues to learning and thinking (A. T. Beck, Davis, & Freeman, 2015; Leahy & McGinn, 2012; Linehan, 1993a; Lobbestael & Arntz, 2012; Nysæter & Nordahl, 2008). As in psychodynamic perspectives, CBT approaches maintain that what happens to you in early childhood is important in conceptualizing personality difficulties. However, a CBT view emphasizes behavioral conditioning and the development of unhelpful but fixed beliefs about self, others, and relationships. Cognitively speaking, each personality disorder is associated with certain main beliefs developed early in life (see Table 12.5). When people stubbornly cling to such beliefs, their interpersonal relationships are disrupted and they tend to get diagnosed with personality disorders. Cognitive therapy works to loosen and change inflexible beliefs to provide people with greater latitude in how they think, feel, and behave. Below two well-established CBT approaches to personality disorders are presented: *schema therapy* and *dialectical behavior therapy*.

Table 12.5 Main Beliefs Associated with Specific Personality Disorders

Personality Disorder	Main Belief
Paranoid	I cannot trust people
Schizotypal	It's better to be isolated from others
Schizoid	Relationships are messy, undesirable
Histrionic	People are there to serve or admire me
Narcissistic	Since I am special, I deserve special rules
Borderline	I deserve to be punished
Antisocial	I am entitled to break rules
Avoidant	If people know the "real" me, they will reject me
Dependent	I need people to survive, be happy
Obsessive-compulsive	People should do better, try harder

Note: The main beliefs listed here are just some examples; this table should not be considered a complete list of main beliefs associated with the specific personality disorders.
Source: Adapted from Table 3.1: PBQ Beliefs Most Strongly Associated with Specific Personality Disorders in Beck, A., Davis, D., & Freeman, A. (2015). *Cognitive therapy of personality disorders*. New York, NY: Guilford Press, p. 61

Schema Therapy

Jeffrey E. Young's **schema therapy** (also known as *schema-focused therapy*) places the cognitive concept of schemas front and center (Arntz, van Genderen, Drost, Sendt, & Baumgarten-Kustner, 2009; Farrell, Reiss, Shaw, & Finkelmeier, 2014; Nysæter & Nordahl, 2008; J. E. Young, 1999; J. E. Young, Klosko, & Weishaar, 2003). Recall from Chapter 2 that schemas are mental structures or scripts that we use to organize information and guide our behavior. Schema therapy maintains that people diagnosed with personality disorders develop extremely rigid and deeply-rooted relationship schemas early in life as the result of abuse or neglect. These inflexible schemas originating in childhood are known as **early maladaptive schemas (EMSs)** and they reflect stable and dysfunctional life themes (Nysæter & Nordahl, 2008; J. E. Young et al., 2003). EMSs are what make people vulnerable to problematic interpersonal patterns. Young identified 18 distinct EMSs that can contribute to problematic personality functioning (Nysæter & Nordahl, 2008; J. E. Young et al., 2003). Examples include *abandonment* (the belief others will leave you in the lurch), *defectiveness* (the view that you are fundamentally broken), *insufficient control* (the assumption that others are trying to dominate you), *entitlement* (the belief that others owe you special treatment), and *mistrust/abuse* (the belief that others will mistreat you).

The "punitive parent mode" is an example of an early maladaptive schema (EMS) that may be carried into adulthood.
Source: PhotoDisc\Fuse

CHAPTER 12

When EMSs are activated, people enter cognitive, emotional, and behavioral states known as **dysfunctional schema modes** (Arntz et al., 2009; Farrell et al., 2014; Nysæter & Nordahl, 2008; J. E. Young et al., 2003). Examples of dysfunctional schema modes are the *vulnerable child mode* (you feel helpless, weak, and unable to get your needs met), *angry/impulsive child mode* (you feel angry and impulsively lash out), *avoidant protector mode* (you disconnect from yourself and others to protect yourself from painful feelings), *compliant surrender mode* (you go along with others' demands to keep others from getting angry), and *punitive parent mode* (you punish yourself for expressing needs, making mistakes, or disappointing people) (Arntz et al., 2009; Farrell et al., 2014; Nysæter & Nordahl, 2008; J. E. Young et al., 2003). Dysfunctional schema modes contrast with **healthy and functional schema modes**, consisting of adaptive states of thinking, feeling, and behaving. The *healthy adult mode* (productive thoughts and feelings lead you to feel skilled and capable) and *healthy child mode* (you feel playful and can engage others in enjoyable activities) constitute the two healthy and functional schema modes (Arntz et al., 2009; Farrell et al., 2014; Nysæter & Nordahl, 2008; J. E. Young et al., 2003).

The goal of schema therapy is to replace dysfunctional schema modes with healthy and functional ones. In schema therapy the concepts of EMSs and schema modes are explained to clients and they are encouraged to pay attention to how these operate in their daily lives. If all goes as planned, over time clients become ever-more aware of how emotionally loaded situations trigger their EMSs and dysfunctional schema modes. This allows them to get better at identifying and resisting dysfunctional schemas and to develop more healthy and functional alternative schemas.

Most of the research on schema therapy for personality disorders has focused on borderline personality disorder. Unfortunately, there aren't that many studies on schema therapy. A comprehensive review identified four—a single case study, a case series study, and two randomized controlled trials (Sempértegui, Karreman, Arntz, & Bekker, 2013). All four found evidence supporting the use of schema therapy for BPD. The case series study used an ABAB design (see Chapter 1) to map progress in six different clients (Nordahl & Nysæter, 2005). It found all six improved, but none were symptom-free after treatment. One of the randomized controlled trials (RCTs) compared schema therapy to transference-focused therapy and found that both helped, but schema therapy was more effective and had fewer patients drop out (Giesen-Bloo et al., 2006). In this trial, 45.5% of those who received schema therapy recovered, compared to only 23.8% of those who received transference-focused therapy (Giesen-Bloo et al., 2006; Sempértegui et al., 2013). While having only 45% of patients recover may seem unimpressive, for personality issues—which are enduring and hard to treat—this is considered promising.

Dialectical Behavior Therapy (DBT)

Marsha Linehan's **dialectical behavior therapy (DBT)** is a CBT-influenced approach that incorporates Zen Buddhist mindfulness; DBT was originally developed for borderline personality disorder, but is also used with other presenting problems (Heard & Linehan, 1994; Linehan, 1993a, 2003, 2015; Swales, Heard, & Williams, 2000). Usually lasting a year, DBT helps borderline clients address poor self-related boundaries, impulsive behavior, difficulty regulating emotions, and interpersonal anxiety and conflict (Linehan, 1993a, 2015). DBT combines skills training (involving CBT interventions such as reinforcement, exposure, problem-solving, behavioral rehearsal, contingency management, and cognitive restructuring) with an emphasis on **dialectics**, the rational process of reconciling opposites. As people with borderline personalities often struggle to integrate conflicting thoughts and feelings, learning to think dialectically can be beneficial.

Outpatient DBT is typically divided into three treatment modes administered simultaneously: (1) weekly individual DBT sessions; (2) weekly skills training group sessions; and (3) between-session telephone consultations with the individual DBT therapist, as needed (Heard & Linehan, 1994; Linehan, 2003, 2015). DBT group skills training is explicitly cognitive-behavioral: "There are three types of skills training procedures: (1) skill acquisition (e.g., instructions, modeling); (2) skill strengthening (e.g., behavioral rehearsal, feedback); and (3) skill generalization (e.g., homework assignments, discussion of similarities and differences in situations)" (Linehan, 1993b, p. 31). Skills training is broken into distinct modules that focus on *core mindfulness skills* (observing and accepting, rather than avoiding, negative emotions) *interpersonal effectiveness skills* (productively interacting with others), *emotion regulation skills* (managing and regulating upsetting feelings), and *distress tolerance skills* (enduring distress without being overwhelmed by it) (Linehan, 1993b, 2015). Individual sessions are more relationally focused than group sessions, emphasizing client insight into behavior patterns that impair their functioning in and out of therapy. Individual therapy tries to help clients think in more integrated ways, incorporate the coping skills they are learning in group sessions into their everyday lives, and accept themselves and their emotions (Heard & Linehan, 1994; Linehan, 2003, 2015).

Magdalena

Imagine Magdalena undergoes DBT for her borderline personality issues. In individual DBT sessions, the therapist would target specific problem behaviors—such as suicidal threats, drug use, and explosive emotional outbursts that alienate people at home and work. To target these behaviors, Magdalena might be asked to fill out a weekly diary card (a card on which clients log their thoughts, feelings, drug use, and other problematic behaviors to help identify links between them). Doing so might reveal that Magdalena relies a lot on alcohol to deal with feelings of misery. She and her therapist could then target alcohol use and feelings of misery by thinking of specific skills Magdalena is learning that she could use between sessions to cope more efficiently. Magdalena might be able to apply core mindfulness skills (which she is learning in group sessions) to the emotions causing her misery. Behaving mindfully, she might simply try to remain aware of misery-inducing feelings. Rather than avoiding, resisting, or impulsively reacting to these feelings, Magdalena would try to simply identify, label, and remain aware of them. The expectation would be that as Magdalena becomes more mindful of painful feelings (such as rage and fear), she would become better able to accept them without being ruled by them. That is, her ability to regulate feelings and tolerate emotional distress would improve. By accepting difficult feelings, they would come to cause her less misery and she would be less inclined to get drunk to guard against them.

Linehan and others have done extensive research on DBT, making it the most studied psychotherapy for borderline personality disorder (Stoffers et al., 2012). DBT researchers have found DBT to be effective in reducing suicidal behavior, self-harm, therapy dropouts, hospital admission rates, reliance on prescription drugs, anger, anxiety, and depression (Andreasson et al., 2016; Barnicot, Savill, Bhatti, & Priebe, 2014; Binks et al., 2006; Kliem, Kröger, & Kosfelder, 2010; Linehan, Armstrong, Suarez, Allmon, & Heard, 1991; Linehan et al., 2006; O'Connell & Dowling, 2014; Panos, Jackson, Hasan, & Panos, 2014; Priebe et al., 2012; Stoffers et al., 2012; van den Bosch, Koeter, Stijnen, Verheul, & van den Brink, 2005). More broadly, research studies have found DBT beneficial in both inpatient and outpatient settings, even with clients not diagnosed as borderline (Bohus et al., 2004; Panepinto, Uschold, Olandese, & Linn, 2015). A comprehensive review noted that DBT has the most robust evidence base of therapies for borderline personality disorder; even so, it concluded that more studies are needed and that those already done often suffer from small sample sizes and other methodological limitations (Stoffers et al., 2012).

HUMANISTIC PERSPECTIVES

Humanistic perspectives on personality disorders usually receive less attention than psychodynamic and CBT perspectives (A. Quinn, 2011). Some of this may be because humanistic clinicians often reject medical model diagnosis. Consequently, they generally dislike labels like "personality disorder," which they see as pejorative, demeaning, and mistaken in equating human distress with brain disease (Gunn & Potter, 2015; Szasz, 1987, 1970/1991a). The "Controversial Question" box builds on this humanistic concern by asking whether some or all personality disorders are moral evaluations masquerading as medical diagnoses. Given their skepticism about diagnostic labels, many humanistic therapists would answer "yes." What do you think?

CONTROVERSIAL QUESTION

Are Personality Disorders Merely Moral Judgements?

Philosopher and bioethicist Louis Charland (2006, 2010) has argued that the Cluster B personality disorders (antisocial, borderline, histrionic, and narcissistic—the "dramatic, emotional, and erratic" disorders) aren't disorders at all. Instead, they reflect moral judgments about people who behave in socially unacceptable ways. Those with Cluster B diagnoses lie, cheat, manipulate, and emotionally carry-on in ways others find morally reprehensible. However, just because behavior is immoral doesn't necessarily make it disordered. Charland's ideas may remind you of psychiatric gadfly Thomas Szasz, previously discussed in Chapter 1. Szasz (1987, 1970/1991a) felt that *DSM* and *ICD* too often turn moral problems into medical ones. When this happens, the medicalization of personality conflicts occurs and people whose behavior ethically offends or annoys us get labeled as ill. Rule-breakers become "psychopaths," those we find emotionally manipulative become "borderlines," and those we feel demand too much attention for themselves (and don't give enough to others) become "narcissists." But what we have here, thinkers like Charland and Szasz maintain, aren't "personality disorders" within the offending parties, but ethical conflicts between the offending parties and those who take offense. While Charland's critique of moral conflicts masquerading as mental disorders is limited to Cluster B personality disorders, Szasz's view is far broader, extending to all mental disorder diagnoses. Those who reject Szasz and Charland's ideas counter that while personality disorders do have a moral component, morally objectionable behavior may sometimes be caused by illness (Zachar, 2011; Zachar & Potter, 2010a, 2010b). Still, critiques of personality disorders as moral judgments remain compelling to those skeptical of *DSM* and *ICD* diagnosis.

Recasting "Personality Disorders" as Fragile Process

In keeping with the humanistic perspective's non-pathologizing, anti-diagnostic view, psychotherapist Margaret Warner (2013, 2014) reframes "personality disorders" as examples of **difficult process**. She explains difficult process by supplementing Carl Rogers' person-centered therapy (PCT; see Chapter 2) with Bowlby's attachment theory. For Warner, difficult process emerges in people who don't receive Rogers' core conditions (empathy, genuineness, and unconditional positive regard) during infancy. This leads to insecure attachments with caregivers. Consequently, such people have trouble establishing the kinds of supportive relationships necessary for emotional growth and self-actualization, the humanistic motivation to fulfill one's potential.

In Warner's view, clients diagnosed as "narcissistic" and "borderline" don't have mental disorders. Rather, due to their insecure attachments and failure to receive core conditions needed for positive self-development, they experience a specific type of difficult process that Warner calls **fragile process**. Fragile process clients have a hard time regulating their emotions, struggle to see others' viewpoints, and often feel emotionally overwhelmed and negated by others. What fragile process clients need, Warner argues, is non-directive person-centered therapy that provides them with a caring and empathic relationship. From a PCT viewpoint, more active therapies for fragile process are risky because "attempts to direct or explain or to teach different ways of being with these experiences often backfire" (Warner, 2013, p. 355). Thus, PCT assumes that genuinely empathizing with and unconditionally accepting fragile process clients is what they require: "When therapists can stay with client experiences, clients become more and more able to stay connected to these experiences themselves. This allows experiences to process and resolve themselves" (Warner, 2013, p. 355).

Research Evidence for Person-Centered Therapy

There isn't much research on person-centered therapy for personality issues; one review identified only three studies (Quinn, 2011). One study found PCT helpful across all personality disorders, regardless of whether medication was also used; in fact, when it came to alleviating depression, PCT alone was more effective than PCT plus medication for all personality disorders except socially dependent Cluster C diagnoses (Teusch, Böhme, Finke, & Gastpar, 2001). In the two other studies, person-centered therapy wasn't the main therapy being researched. It was merely being used as a control group. Even so, both imply PCT can help clients diagnosed with personality disorders. In one, PCT fared equally to cognitive therapy in reducing self-harm, suicidality, depression, anxiety, and—over the long haul—hopelessness (Cottraux et al., 2009). In the other, PCT was found effective, but less effective overall than dialectical behavior therapy; it did as well as DBT in addressing impulsivity, anger, and depression, but not as well at decreasing suicidal and other self-harm behaviors (Turner, 2000). In evaluating research on PCT for personality disorders, the fact that there are so few studies makes it difficult to draw firm conclusions. Further, the fact that DBT seemed to work better than PCT for reducing suicidality and self-harm calls into question Warner's assertion that more directive interventions (such as DBT skills training) often backfire. Person-centered approaches may indeed help people experiencing difficult process, but supplementing them with more directive techniques may provide additional benefits (E. Steffen, 2013).

EVALUATING PSYCHOLOGICAL PERSPECTIVES

Psychotherapy is usually recommended for personality issues. Both inpatient and outpatient psychotherapy appear to be helpful (Antonsen et al., 2014; Horn et al., 2015). When it comes to psychotherapy effectiveness, most research has focused on Cluster B disorders ("dramatic, emotional, and erratic")—especially borderline personality disorder (Dixon-Gordon, Turner, & Chapman, 2011). Compared to Cluster B, the evidence base for Cluster C disorders ("anxious and fearful") is much more meager and there is barely any research at all on therapy for Cluster A disorders ("odd and eccentric") (Dixon-Gordon et al., 2011). That said, all the therapies discussed above have some evidence supporting their use, but many investigators nonetheless contend that more research is needed due to sample size issues, concerns about the reliability and validity of the personality disorder categories, and other methodological weaknesses (Bateman et al., 2015; Budge, 2015a; Budge et al., 2013; Stoffers et al., 2012). When it comes to comparing psychotherapies, brief psychodynamic and CBT therapies are both recommended, with the former usually (but not always) holding their own against the latter (Duggan, Huband, Smailagic, Ferriter, & Adams, 2007; Emmelkamp et al., 2006). Across all types of therapy, DBT has the most extensive research support (Stoffers et al., 2012).

12.6 SOCIOCULTURAL PERSPECTIVES
CROSS-CULTURAL AND SOCIAL JUSTICE PERSPECTIVES
Personality Disorders: Culturally Universal or Culturally Relative?

When assessing personality, how much is attributable to individual differences and how much to culture? Big Five research does find personality differences across cultures. For example, Americans and Europeans are more extraverted and open to experience (but less agreeable) than their Asian and African counterparts (Allik, 2012). What this sort of finding means is hard to say because it raises once again the issue of cultural relativism versus cultural universalism first discussed in Chapter 9 (Calliess, Sieberer, Machleidt, & Ziegenbein, 2008). Are the Big Five (not to mention the very notion of personality itself) cultural universals or culture-bound social constructions (see Chapter 2)? Can *acculturation* (acquiring the characteristics of a culture one moves to) change personality traits (Allik, 2005)? If so, does this make "personality" more a product of culture than genes? And if personality is strongly affected by culture, then are "personality disorders" truly individual afflictions in the same way that culturally universal diseases like diabetes and cancer seem to be? Or are they reified social constructions that tell us more about our cultural values than they tell us about who is ill (Epstein, 2006b)? As another example, people in Western countries score higher on measures of narcissism than those from Eastern countries; in fact, narcissism appears to be on the rise in Western countries (Twenge, 2011). Is this due to individual or cultural differences? Does it mean that Westerners suffer more from something called narcissistic personality disorder? Or does it mean that cultural values influence how self-focused people are? Is that friend of yours whom you describe as "narcissistic" mentally ill or the victim of cultural indoctrination that celebrates a "Me First" mentality?

In response to such questions, cultural theorists are quite interested in how specific personality disorders are conceptualized in different societies. For instance, people diagnosed with borderline personality disorder vary by country. American and British patients identified as borderline, for example, appear to differ in terms of drug use, drug-related psychoses, aversion to dependency, and derealization/depersonalization symptoms (Jani, Johnson, Banu, & Shah, 2016). Do such differences reflect cultural variations in the expression of a universal disorder? Or is the term "borderline personality disorder" being used to describe somewhat different things in different cultures? Cultural theorists leaning toward the latter view point to more explicit ways that personality disorder diagnoses vary across nations. For example, the Chinese Society of Psychiatry has rejected borderline as a diagnosis and instead speaks only of *impulsive personality disorder*. Why? Because two of BPD's central symptoms (fear of abandonment and feelings of emptiness) are alien to Chinese culture, which is much more communally focused than Western societies (Jani et al., 2016). So, is China's impulsive personality disorder different from what other countries call borderline personality disorder? And if personality disorders vary in prevalence and symptoms by culture, how confident should we be in viewing them as universal disorders? The cultural relativism/universalism question is a tricky one that all students of abnormal psychology should be aware of, even if they don't have a definite answer to it.

Psychiatrists in China don't recognize borderline personality disorder (BPD), perhaps because in China's culture—certainly compared to the West—"fear of abandonment" is less of an issue. Does this mean that BPD is a culture-bound syndrome?
Source: Getty Images\Pavliha

Gender Bias, Trauma, Socioeconomic Disadvantage, and Racism

Feminist and other therapists adopting a social justice perspective view personality issues not as disorders, but as expectable responses to sexism, abuse, and economic disadvantage. Recall from Chapter 2 that feminist theory views the personal as political; it sees individual problems as originating in sociopolitical circumstances (L. S. Brown, 1994; Hanisch, 1969; M. P. P. Root, 1992). Thus, from a social justice perspective, those diagnosed with personality disorders aren't ill; they are struggling as best they can to deal with oppressive conditions such as gender bias, trauma, socioeconomic disadvantage, and racism (Epstein, 2006b; Moane, 2014)—each briefly discussed below.

Before discussing the potential impact of these oppressive social conditions, let's briefly review **relational-cultural theory**, which nicely exemplifies the feminist/social justice critique of personality disorders. Relational-cultural theory "challenges many of the traditional psychological theories of personality in terms of their emphasis on the growth of a separate self, their exclusive focus on intrapsychic phenomenon, and their espousal of enduring internal traits" (J. V. Jordan, 2004, p. 120). According to relational-cultural theorists, the *DSM*, *ICD*, *PDM* and other individualistic assessments of personality disorder err by improperly attributing psychological distress to internal psychopathology rather than to societal influences such as chronic social disconnection (J. V. Jordan, 2004; Nabar, 2009). By failing to consider "the importance of context beyond the traditional nuclear family and often beyond the influence of the early mother-infant relationship," those espousing the notion of "personality disorders" mistakenly locate the source of emotional suffering "in the individual" (J. V. Jordan, 2004, p. 125). The unfortunate result is that "social conditions and the relational failures emanating from these social conditions are rarely examined as the source of the problem" (J. V. Jordan, 2004, p. 125).

Magdalena

With case example client Magdalena, a relational-cultural therapist might reject the idea that Magdalena "has" borderline personality disorder and instead look for ways in which Magdalena's emotional distress is tied to social factors such as past instances of social isolation, gender bias, and traumatic abuse. A relational-cultural approach to therapy would help Magdalena address the ways such events have contributed to her difficulties, while also assisting her to develop a social support system to aid her in overcoming and resisting oppressive social influences.

CASE EXAMPLES

Gender Bias

From a feminist viewpoint, personality disorder categories are gender biased, mistaking socialized gender roles for psychopathology (L. S. Brown, 1992; Epstein, 2006b; M. Kaplan, 1983; Wirth-Cauchon, 2000). For instance, it's been argued that histrionic and borderline personality disorders are diagnosed more often in females because both involve "excessive" emotionality—thus unfairly targeting women, who are socialized to express feelings more readily than men (M. Kaplan, 1983). Equating emotional expression with being histrionic (or "hysterical") goes all the way back to Ancient Greek medicine, which—as noted in Chapter 1—attributed such symptoms to a wandering womb (Ng, 1999; Novais, Araújo, & Godinho, 2015; Palis, Rossopoulos, & Triarhou, 1985; Tasca, Rapetti, Carta, & Fadda, 2012).

By pathologizing "excessive emotionality," are histrionic and borderline personality disorder diagnoses sexist?
Source: PhotoDisc/Getty Images

Histrionic and borderline aren't the only personality disorders deemed sexist. Some see dependent personality disorder as pathologizing women by treating their learned tendencies toward deference and support-seeking as signs of disorder. However, from a feminist perspective "dependent personalities" are better explained in social terms. In cultures where women lack socioeconomic equality, many are—quite literally—dependent on men! The result? When their helplessness leads to emotional distress, they are improperly labeled as mentally ill (L. S. Brown, 1992; M. Kaplan, 1983). Instead of attributing their distress to feeling boxed in by socially oppressive gender norms, mental health professionals mistakenly diagnose dependent personality disorder.

Over thirty years ago, psychologist Marcie Kaplan (1983) famously proposed two fictitious personality disorders to illustrate her belief that the personality disorders are sexist. She proposed *independent personality disorder* and *restricted personality disorder*. The former is characterized by putting work above relationships and not considering others when making decisions; "e.g., expects spouse and children to re-locate to another city because of individual's career plans" (M. Kaplan, 1983, p. 790). The latter involves excessive emotional restraint and avoidance; "e.g., absence of crying at sad moments" and "engages others (especially spouse) to perform emotional behaviors such as writing the individual's thank-you notes or telephoning to express the individual's concern" (M. Kaplan, 1983, p. 790). Kaplan's point was that these behaviors, because they are traditionally masculine, aren't identified as disorders, but that comparable female behaviors are:

> In other words, whereas behaving in a feminine stereotyped manner alone will earn a ... diagnosis (e.g., Dependent or Histrionic Personality Disorder), behaving in a masculine stereotyped manner alone will not. A masculine stereotyped individual, to be diagnosed, cannot just be remarkably masculine. Masculinity alone is not clinically suspect; femininity alone is. (M. Kaplan, 1983, p. 791)

Does research support the notion that personality disorders are gender biased? Maybe. Some studies have indeed found evidence of gender bias in the diagnosis of personality disorders (Golomb, Fava, Abraham, & Rosenbaum, 1995; Hartung & Widiger, 1998; Jane, Oltmanns, South, & Turkheimer, 2007; Loring & Powell, 1988). However, others haven't (Boggs et al., 2005; Funtowicz & Widiger, 1999; L. C. Morey, Warner, & Boggs, 2002; Oltmanns & Powers, 2012). In the studies that have found gender bias, the personality disorders typically diagnosed more often in men are paranoid, schizoid, schizotypal, antisocial, narcissistic, and obsessive-compulsive; among women, the more common personality disorders tend to be dependent, histrionic, and borderline (Hartung & Widiger, 1998). If there are gender differences in personality disorder prevalence rates, are they because these diagnoses are scientifically invalid and rooted in sexist ideas about male and female gender roles? Or are personality disorders legitimate categories, but ones where bias in diagnosing them needs to be eliminated? The debate rages on.

Trauma

It's commonly believed that people diagnosed with personality disorders are more likely to have experienced past violence, neglect, or abuse (physical or sexual) (L. S. Brown, 1992, 1994; M. Epstein, 2006b; Herman, 2015; Nicki, 2016). Along these lines, research has linked childhood trauma to many personality disorders, including schizotypal, antisocial, avoidant, histrionic, obsessive-compulsive, and borderline (Cotter, Kaess, & Yung, 2015; Frías, Palma, Farriols, & González, 2016; Hageman, Francis, Field, & Carr, 2015; J. P. Klein, Roniger, Schweiger, Späth, & Brodbeck, 2015; MacIntosh, Godbout, & Dubash, 2015; Rubio, Krieger, Finney, & Coker, 2014; Schimmenti, Di Carlo, Passanisi, & Caretti, 2015; Stepp, Lazarus, & Byrd, 2016; Velikonja, Fisher, Mason, & Johnson, 2015). The Collaborative Longitudinal Personality Disorders Study found that 73% of people diagnosed with personality disorders reported abuse and 82% reported neglect (Battle et al., 2004). Personality disorders (as well as Chapter 8's controversial dissociative identity disorder) are so regularly associated with childhood trauma that trauma researcher Judith Herman (2015) proposed replacing them with a new diagnosis called complex PTSD (since added to *ICD-11*; see Chapter 7). The complex PTSD diagnosis "frames the root problem of personal difficulties as victimization instead of personality deficiency" (Nicki, 2016, p. 219). Instead of blaming those who have been abused by concluding they have defective personalities, a feminist social justice model "depathologizes normal responses to horrible experiences" by maintaining that "many of the behaviors we see after trauma are manifestations of specialized coping behaviors for survival" (M. P. P. Root, 1992, p. 237).

Socioeconomic Disadvantage and Racism

Like trauma, socioeconomic disadvantage often predicts personality issues. Socioeconomic status (SES), as measured by residing in a low-SES neighborhood, has been associated with lower overall functioning and higher rates of symptoms among those with personality disorder diagnoses (Z. Walsh et al., 2013). When it comes to specific personality disorders, a recent review found that children and teens of lower SES backgrounds displayed more antisocial personality disorder behaviors than those of higher SES backgrounds (Piotrowska, Stride, Croft, & Rowe, 2015). Similar results have been found for borderline and schizotypal personality disorders (P. Cohen et al., 2008). As for paranoid personality disorder, low SES is implicated there, as well (Harper, 2011).

SES isn't the only factor tied to paranoid and antisocial behavior. There is also a link to race. In the U.S., some evidence suggests that African American patients are more likely to be diagnosed as paranoid than white patients

To what extent do you believe that case study client Harvey's antisocial behavior is attributable to economic oppression and racism?
Source: PhotoDisc/Getty Images

CHAPTER 12

(Harper, 2011; Loring & Powell, 1988; Whaley, 2004). One study found that low SES and past trauma were both associated with paranoid personality symptoms among African Americans, especially those of low SES (Iacovino, Jackson, & Oltmanns, 2014).

Harvey

From a social justice perspective, our case example client Harvey's antisocial behavior is a direct result of economic oppression and racism. Raised in an environment that provided poor African-American youth with few options, Harvey grew up feeling angry and acted out in the only ways he felt he could. His idea that everyone's out to get him isn't a clinical instance of paranoia. It's a legitimate response to a social system in which Harvey faces discrimination and economic restrictions at every turn, and these severely limit his opportunities. From a social justice viewpoint, social change is the key to helping Harvey. Medicating him or offering him therapy to adjust him to his conditions does little more than propagate an oppressive social system.

CASE EXAMPLES

Although the research on SES and race is mostly correlational, it provides support for the assertion that oppressive social conditions are a major culprit in the development of personality issues. It intuitively makes sense that someone from a discriminated-against ethnic group who grows up in poverty and runs a higher risk of facing traumatic circumstances would be more likely to act out or be suspicious of others. Again, the great debate surrounds whether gender, race, and socioeconomic factors influence personality disorders, or whether personality disorders are a way of blaming people (rather than social ills) for their problems.

CONSUMER AND SERVICE-USER PERSPECTIVES

Stigma

With the occasional exception (Catthoor, Schrijvers, Hutsebaut, Feenstra, & Sabbe, 2015), research has consistently found that mental health professionals display a great deal of stigma toward people diagnosed with personality disorders (Newton-Howes, Weaver, & Tyrer, 2008; Paris, 2007; Servais & Saunders, 2007). Clinicians who work with patients carrying personality disorder diagnoses tend to hold very negative attitudes toward these patients. To be blunt, mental health professionals generally dislike people diagnosed with personality disorders. A personality disorder diagnosis is a red flag that screams "difficult" patient. Studies have found negative attitudes toward people with personality disorders among psychiatrists (G. Lewis & Appleby, 1988), psychiatric nurses (James & Cowman, 2007; C. A. Ross & Goldner, 2009; Woollaston & Hixenbaugh, 2008), prison officers (Bowers et al., 2006), and community mental health staff (Newton-Howes et al., 2008). Stigma appears to be a problem for all personality disorders, but especially borderline personality disorder—with mental health professionals regularly viewing patients with BPD diagnoses as manipulative, attention-seeking, angry, and difficult (Aviram, Brodsky, & Stanley, 2006; Kling, 2014; Nehls, 1998; K. Wright, Haigh, & McKeown, 2007). In describing psychiatric nurses' attitudes toward BPD patients, one study used the memorable (if unflattering) term "destructive whirlwind" (Woollaston & Hixenbaugh, 2008). When a mental health professional calls a patient "borderline," it may tell us as much about the clinician's feelings towards the patient as it does the patient's clinical condition!

The stigma of personality disorders is so great that in some cases, clinicians are reluctant to tell patients their diagnosis. For instance, some mental health professionals don't inform patients that they have been diagnosed with borderline personality disorder due to "worries that such a diagnosis would have deleterious effects on the patient's health and morale" (Lequesne & Hersh, 2004, p. 172). Even when they do tell patients, they often delay doing so or do it in a manner that can be alienating. One patient described the surreal experience this way:

> I actually hadn't been told until that day that I had the diagnosis of borderline. And she sat there, the psychologist, and she just talked to the advocate, she didn't talk to me. And she goes "oh this is typical behaviour for someone with borderline personality disorder." And I'm going what? And when I left I went straight to the library to find out what on earth she was meaning. (Veysey, 2014, p. 26)

While it may be ethically dubious not to tell patients their diagnoses, concerns over stigmatization may be justified because personality disorder labels can affect patients. That is, in response to the stigma and discrimination they face, people with personality disorders may engage in **self-stigmatization**. This means they internalize the negative attitudes espoused by their doctors, as well as by the media (M. L. Bowen, 2016). Consequently, they come to see themselves as others do, in a distinctly unfavorable light (Dinos, Stevens, Serfaty, Weich, & King, 2004; Grambal et al., 2016). A recent study suggests that patients diagnosed with personality disorders often feel powerless, perhaps because the culture has imposed a pathologizing diagnosis on them without understanding their point of view (Bonnington & Rose, 2014). They also feel dismissed, with many reporting that they have been subtly routed away from receiving care because their doctors view them as difficult (Sulzer, 2015). Thus, people with personality issues are often both stigmatized and denied much-needed help.

Service-User/Survivor Perspectives

Perhaps because of the stigmatizing impact of diagnostic labels and the often less-than-humane treatment that some patients report, members of the service-user/survivor movement (see Chapter 2) reject conventional mental health approaches to personality disorders (Capes, 2010; M. Epstein, 2006a, 2006b). Themselves former patients, they argue that the mental health system does great harm when it assigns personality disorder labels to people. They also contend that scientifically suspect and stigmatizing personality disorder diagnoses are unhelpful and that much of the "treatment" those who get them receive is more damaging than beneficial. "The Lived Experience" feature provides some memorable quotes from patients about being labeled as borderline. Service-user/survivor movement advocates would see these quotes as supporting their perspective. After reading the feature box, think about whether you agree with them or not and why.

THE LIVED EXPERIENCE

Photo source: © PHOTOALTO

Being Labeled as "Borderline"

What is it like to be labeled as "borderline?" These powerful quotes on the experience from a recent qualitative study suggest it can be quite difficult.

» On feeling pathologized:

It [being diagnosed] was such a shock, such a fucking slap in the face. It really was an insult actually. [The psychiatrist] invested no time in me whatsoever, and it was just like I was a naughty, dirty person ... it was like I should be ashamed of myself ... it was like being marked out differently. I'd struggled for so long not knowing who I was and then suddenly "here's a label." Well, what does that tell me then? Am I not part of humanity? ... it's made me very insecure about my worth as a person, who I am, because I used to be so capable and now I'm a nothing, a nobody. It's taken everything away from me. (Bonnington & Rose, 2014, p. 11)

» On feeling powerless:

If you say "you've got this, therefore we can help you with X, Y and Z," that's not as bad as saying "you've got this [i.e. BPD], we can no longer help you" which was basically what I was being told. "There is no treatment, we're not offering you any therapy, we're not offering you any medication and there's no point of you going into hospital" ... the use of it [i.e. the diagnosis] to the doctors was that it meant they no longer had to bother to make an effort because "she's one of those we can't help." (Bonnington & Rose, 2014, p. 13)

» On feeling stigmatized at the doctor's office when speaking with the general practitioner (GP):

When it came up on the [GP's computer] that I had BPD he spoke to me differently [compared] to what he did originally ... he was asking me to describe how I was feeling, physically, and then he asked about medication, but he was fiddling around with his PC and when it came up it was like he put it all down to that [the BPD]—"well that's why you feel like that." (Bonnington & Rose, 2014, p. 13)

» On feeling demeaned, disrespected, and violated by healthcare staff:

I had to do whatever they [nurses] were doing. I didn't even have any privacy to put a tampon in. I was followed to the toilet with someone holding the door open all the time watching. (Bonnington & Rose, 2014, p. 14)

As these quotes make clear, getting diagnosed as "borderline" doesn't make things easy. Many of the interactions that people who are labeled as borderline experience in the mental health system are, unfortunately, quite invalidating. Thus, before calling someone borderline, might it be worth considering the potential impact of doing so on the person being diagnosed? The quotes above, combined with the research on how personality disorder diagnoses are both stigmatizing and scientifically controversial, suggest that caution may indeed be called for.

CHAPTER 12

SYSTEMS PERSPECTIVES

Family Systems and Personality Issues

From a systems perspective, personality issues arise within the context of relationships—with the family system most often the focus of attention. As already noted, many (if not most) people diagnosed with borderline or other personality disorders have experienced early life trauma—and this trauma has often occurred within the family (Sansone & Sansone, 2009). Thus, thinking systemically, people with difficult personalities developed them within family systems characterized by mistreatment or neglect. For example, many of the violent behaviors found in people with antisocial personality disorder diagnoses may be attributable to family dynamics (e.g., lack of parental warmth, harsh discipline, and witnessing parental violence) (K. H. Rosen, 1998).

Harvey

Harvey, our case example client in prison for attempted murder, was raised in a family where he regularly witnessed his father's explosive temper. Harvey's father rarely expressed affection, but he displayed much anger and hostility. Physical violence in the family was common. Harvey's father often hit Harvey, his siblings, and Harvey's mother. Once, during an especially intense family argument, Harvey saw his father threaten his mother with a knife. When Harvey was 15, his father was sentenced to prison for assault during an armed robbery. Sadly, his father's prison time anticipated the similar fate that later befell Harvey.

CASE EXAMPLES

Substantial attention has been paid to the families of borderline clients. It's been argued that **borderline families** are characterized by interpersonal chaos in which family members don't know how to nurture or support one another (Sperry, 2011). This may be because many of the family members qualify for other diagnoses themselves, such as substance use disorder, conduct disorder, bipolar disorder, and schizoaffective disorder (Sansone & Sansone, 2009; Sperry, 2011). Three kinds of borderline families have been identified (E. G. Goldstein, 1990; P. E. Marcus, 1993). *Enmeshed or overinvolved families* have poor boundaries between members, are intense, and display lots of hostile conflict that the client who is later diagnosed as borderline gets caught in; one parent tends to be overprotective of the client while the other is dismissive and devaluing. *Alienated or rejecting families* see the client as different, unwelcome, bad, or the enemy; in these families, the parents are closely aligned with one another and exclude the client, who is blamed for family problems. Finally, in *idealizing or denying families* the family members see each other as perfect and downplay both the client's difficulties and other family conflicts.

Couples and Family DBT for Borderline Personality

Dialectical behavior therapy (DBT), described previously, has been adapted for use with families and couples in which borderline personality patterns are an issue (Fruzzetti & Payne, 2015). The therapy aims to help partners and other family members eliminate problematic ways of engaging one another that are typical of borderline personality (things like avoidance, withdrawal, and expressing destructive anger). Instead, the goal is to foster family skills of constructive communication, in which feelings are conveyed in a non-threatening way and each person openly receives feedback. Couple and family interactions are often video-recorded so that family members and therapists can gain insight into problematic interpersonal patterns. Diary cards (discussed earlier) are also adapted to help couples and families track their dealings with one another and reinforce appropriate interpersonal skills. There is evidence that DBT can reduce problematic family behaviors (Ekdahl, Idvall, & Perseius, 2014), though as with our earlier discussion of DBT's effectiveness, more studies are needed (Stoffers et al., 2012).

EVALUATING SOCIOCULTURAL PERSPECTIVES

Sociocultural perspectives are criticized for overlooking biological and psychological components of personality issues. In such critiques, contextual factors such as gender, race, and SES are important but don't replace other influences—especially genetic predispositions to certain personality traits (Hertler, 2014a). Critics of sociocultural perspectives wonder whether doing away with the personality disorders and instead diagnosing people with less pathologizing and more reliable disorders (such as depression and complex PTSD) can ever truly eliminate stigma (Paris, 2007). They contend that the stigma of personality disorders isn't carried solely by diagnostic labeling, but also reflects the disturbing and difficult ways that clients so labeled behave when dealing with others. For example, when it comes to clients diagnosed as borderline, "stigma cannot be removed by reclassification" because "patients who are chronically suicidal and who do not form strong treatment alliances will continue to be just as difficult, even under a different diagnostic label" (Paris, 2007, p. 36). When it comes to the stigma of personality disorders, a key question is whether diagnostic labels are causes or effects of negative attitudes. Nonetheless, sociocultural perspectives contextualize personality issues and keep us attuned to factors outside of individuals that influence their challenging interpersonal behavior.

12.7 CLOSING THOUGHTS: CAN YOUR PERSONALITY BE DISORDERED?

Is "personality disorder" a legitimate concept? Your answer to this question may depend on how you feel about the notion of personality, a concept that—despite its ubiquity in Western culture—remains fuzzy. As alluded to earlier, psychologist Walter Mischel has long challenged the idea that human behavior is best explained by attributing it to a stable and enduring personality (Mischel, 1973, 2009; Mischel & Shoda, 1995). His critique is based on the observation that people often behave very differently across situations. For example, how you act with your friends might be quite different from how you act with your family. To Mischel, what we call "personality" is often a function of situational factors and how people make sense of things, rather than an innate set of immutable traits. Extending this view, some critics contend that personality is a social construction. That is, it's "a concept that we use in our everyday lives in order to try to make sense of the things that other people and ourselves do … a theory for explaining human behaviour" (Burr, 2015, p. 40). But how good a theory is it? As noted previously, some critics complain that attributing something to personality (or, by implication, a personality disorder) is circular and not much of an explanation at all:

> Imagine that someone observes Jane acting in a consistently outgoing and friendly fashion and asks, "Why does Jane behave this way?" If the answer is that she has an "extraverted personality" by observing that she is generally outgoing and friendly, this is a tautological, pseudo-explanation. (Fowler et al., 2007, p. 6)

Do you agree with this critique or do you think it unfair? Regardless of whether we approve of the concept of personality disorders, most of us would concur that many people do rely on recurrent ways of relationally engaging people that consistently create difficulties for them and others. Exactly why this is so remains an open question. Hopefully, this chapter has offered you a variety of perspectives for you to consider in coming to your own conclusions.

KEY TERMS

Anankastic personality disorder
Antisocial personality disorder (APD)
Anxious (avoidant) personality disorder
Avoidant personality disorder
Borderline families
Borderline personality disorder (BPD)
Character
Cluster A
Cluster B
Cluster C
Dependent personality disorder
Dialectical behavior therapy (DBT)
Dialectics
Difficult process
Dissocial personality disorder
DSM-5 alternative model for personality disorders
Dysfunctional schema modes
Early maladaptive schemas (EMSs)
Emotionally unstable personality disorder
Entitlement
Factor analysis

Five-factor model (FFM)
Fragile process
Frequency-dependent selection hypothesis
Healthy and functional schema modes
Histrionic personality disorder
ICD-11 model of personality disorders
Level of Personality Functioning Scale (LPFS)
Levels of personality organization
Mania without delusion
Mild personality disorder
Moderate personality disorder
Moral insanity
Narcissistic personality disorder (NPD)
Obsessive trait complex hypothesis
Obsessive-compulsive personality disorder (OCPD)
Paranoid personality disorder
Parasuicidal behavior
Personality disorder
Personality disorder-trait specified

Personality Inventory for the DSM-5 (PID-5)
Polypharmacy
Primary psychopathy
Psychopathic personalities
Psychopathy
Relational-cultural theory
Schema therapy
Schizoid personality disorder
Schizotypal personality disorder (STPD)
Secondary psychopathy
Self-stigmatization
Severe personality disorder
Sociopathy
Successful psychopaths
Temperament
Trait factors
Trait theories
Traits
Unsuccessful psychopaths

Full definitions of the terms listed above can be found in the end-of-book glossary on p. 533.

 Go to the companion website, www.macmillanihe.com/raskin-abnormal-psych, to access a study guide, multiple choice and flashcard quizzes for this chapter, and other useful learning aids.

CHAPTER 13
DEVELOPMENTAL ISSUES INVOLVING DISRUPTIVE BEHAVIOR AND ATTACHMENT

13.1 OVERVIEW

LEARNING OBJECTIVES

After reading this chapter, you should be able to:

1. Distinguish externalizing from internalizing behaviors.
2. Outline *DSM* and *ICD* disruptive behavior diagnoses and social connection/attachment diagnoses, as well as discuss critiques of these diagnoses.
3. Describe historical perspectives on attention-deficit hyperactivity disorder (ADHD) and autism.
4. Summarize brain chemistry, brain structure, genetic, evolutionary, and immune system perspectives on disruptive behavior and autism.
5. Explain psychodynamic, cognitive-behavioral, and humanistic psychological perspectives on disruptive behavior and autism.
6. Outline sociocultural and systems perspectives on developmental issues, including how gender, race, socioeconomic status, and stigma influence such issues.

GETTING STARTED: HOW DO DEVELOPMENTAL ISSUES IMPACT BEHAVIOR?

Source: © Royalty-Free/Corbis

Mark

Mark is a 9-year-old boy whose school has referred him for a psychological assessment because of his disruptive behavior in class. Mark has trouble staying in his seat and regularly interrupts his teacher. He bothers the other children, finds it difficult to pay attention to his work for more than a few minutes at a time, and often forgets to do his homework. Mark's parents aren't sure they see what the big deal is, although Mark seems to have some of the same problems at home—he forgets to complete his chores and is often loud and unruly. "Boys will be boys!" says his father. The school, however, is demanding that something be done.

Sumiko

Sumiko is a 15-year-old girl whose parents take her to therapy. "She's insufferable!" exclaims her mother. "Anything we say, she says the opposite!" Sumiko regularly talks back, refuses to complete chores, and neglects her homework because it is "boring." Like her parents, Sumiko's teachers are also flummoxed by her behavior. "She's got a quick temper and often gets in arguments with me and the other kids in the class," says one of her teachers. While Sumiko is perceived as obnoxious, she doesn't skip school, doesn't do drugs, and she has never had a run-in with the law. When the therapist presses her about her challenging behavior, Sumiko admits that she feels sad and lonely much of the time and has a hard time sleeping.

Michael

Michael is a 15-year-old teen living in a poor part of town. He is repeatedly in trouble. Last month, he was suspended from school for assaulting another student. This month, he was arrested for stealing a car. Despite surveillance video showing him breaking into the car, Michael insists that it wasn't him. Since he was 9 years old, Michael has had little in the way of regular parental supervision. Michael's father is in prison for attempted murder and his mother works two jobs to support Michael and his three younger siblings.

Hernando

Hernando is a 3-year-old boy whose parents take him for a medical evaluation because they are concerned about his development. He rarely makes eye contact, gets extremely agitated if you touch him, and hasn't learned to speak. Hernando's only interest seems to be his collection of toy cars, which he spends hours meticulously arranging and rearranging in neat little rows. Anything that disrupts Hernando's daily routine disproportionately upsets him. His parents aren't sure what to do and worry that he won't be ready to enter pre-school in the fall.

Externalizing and Internalizing Behaviors

In thinking about developmental issues in children and adolescents, a distinction is often made between externalizing and internalizing behaviors. **Externalizing behaviors** are characterized by poor impulse-control, rule-breaking, and physical or verbal aggression (Bauminger, Solomon, & Rogers, 2010; Samek & Hicks, 2014).

Mark, Sumiko, and Hernando

Mark disrupting class, Sumiko refusing to obey her parents, and Hernando having a tantrum when his routine is changed are all examples of externalizing behaviors. They involve taking internal thoughts and feelings and directing them externally at the environment by acting out (D. D. Smith, 2007).

CASE EXAMPLES

By contrast, **internalizing behaviors** are things like social withdrawal, loneliness, depression, anxiety, and difficulty concentrating (Bauminger et al., 2010; D. D. Smith, 2007).

Mark, Sumiko, and Hernando

Mark's inability to pay attention to school work, Sumiko's feelings of loneliness and sadness, and Hernando's withdrawal from others are examples of internalizing behaviors.

CASE EXAMPLES

The problems covered in this chapter—disruptive behavior and difficulties with social connections and attachment—involve, to varying degrees, both externalizing and internalizing behaviors.

13.2 *DSM* AND *ICD* PERSPECTIVES

DISRUPTIVE BEHAVIOR

In the *DSM-5*, most disruptive behavior issues (oppositional defiant disorder, conduct disorder, intermittent explosive disorder, pyromania, and kleptomania) are included in the "Disruptive, Impulse-Control, and Conduct Disorders" chapter. However, the most well-known diagnosis involving disruptive behavior, attention-deficit/hyperactivity disorder (ADHD), is listed in the *DSM-5*'s "Neurodevelopmental Disorders" chapter because it is conceptualized as developing in childhood and being neurologically based. In the *ICD-10*, externalizing problems are all grouped together as "behavioural and emotional disorders with onset usually occurring in childhood and adolescence." The *ICD-11* places ADHD in its "neurodevelopmental disorders" section, oppositional defiant disorder and conduct disorder in its "disruptive behavior and dissocial disorders" section, and pyromania and kleptomania in its "impulse control disorders" section. In addition to the disorders described below, recall (from Chapter 5) disruptive mood dysregulation disorder (DMDD), the *DSM-5* mood disorder diagnosed in children who regularly display bursts of temper. Obviously, externalizing problems involving disruptive behavior are dispersed across the *DSM* and *ICD*'s many sections.

CHAPTER 13

Oppositional Defiant Disorder and Conduct Disorder

Oppositional defiant disorder (ODD) is diagnosed in children and adolescents who are angry, argumentative, defiant, and vindictive. People with an ODD diagnosis consistently argue with authority figures and disobey rules. They are touchy, quick to anger, and blame others for their own mistakes. Some students astutely point out that ODD seems like it would be highly comorbid with DMDD, the new *DSM-5* mood disorder just mentioned above. Well, the *ICD-11*, which doesn't include a stand-alone DMDD diagnosis, appears aware of the overlap. Consequently, it includes an ODD subtype characterized by chronic irritability and anger—and indicates that this subtype should be used in lieu of disruptive mood dysregulation disorder.

What is the relationship between oppositional defiant disorder and conduct disorder? **Conduct disorder (CD)** (called *conduct-dissocial disorder* in *ICD-11*) is more severe than ODD because, unlike ODD, it also includes serious violations of other people's rights. While people considered ODD are merely disobedient and angry, those diagnosed with conduct disorder engage in much more worrisome and frightening behaviors, preying on others in often violent ways. They are physically aggressive, destroy property, lie, steal, and engage in significant rule violations.

Sumiko

Our case example client Sumiko might get diagnosed with ODD because she is argumentative and disobeys authority figures, but she wouldn't receive a conduct disorder diagnosis because she isn't physically aggressive and doesn't engage in destructive or criminal behavior. However, the conduct disorder diagnosis would apply to one of our other case example clients, Michael, who repeatedly breaks rules and engages in violent and antisocial behaviors that violate others' rights.

CASE EXAMPLES

Although there is ongoing debate about whether they are qualitatively or quantitatively distinct (Norberg, 2010), ODD and conduct disorder are linked because many children diagnosed with ODD display increasingly troublesome behavior over time, eventually meeting the criteria for conduct disorder (Husby & Wichstrøm, 2016). Put another way, ODD often (though not always) progresses into conduct disorder. This is borne out by research suggesting that age of onset for ODD behaviors is a bit earlier than for CD behaviors—between ages 7 and 15 for ODD and ages 9 and 14 for CD (Kessler et al., 2007). The tendency for ODD to develop into conduct disorder may explain why the *ICD-10* considers oppositional-defiant disorder a specific type of conduct disorder—although in *DSM-5* and *ICD-11* they are distinct diagnoses. The progression from ODD to conduct disorder can also continue into adulthood. When conduct disordered behaviors continue past age 18, they can result in an adult diagnosis of antisocial personality disorder (see Chapter 12). Diagnostic Boxes 13.1 and 13.2 contain criteria and guidelines for ODD and conduct disorder.

Diagnostic Box 13.1 Oppositional Defiant Disorder (ODD)

DSM-5
- Anger, irritability, and defiance for six months or more, as exemplified by things like losing temper, becoming annoyed easily, being angry and resentful, resisting authority, blaming others, and behaving spitefully or vindictively.
- Symptoms occur daily if under age 5 and at least weekly if over age 5.
- Symptoms can be *mild* (occur in one setting); *moderate* (occur in two settings), or *severe* (occur in three settings or more)

Based on American Psychiatric Association, 2013b, pp. 462–463

ICD-10
- Behavior that is negative, hostile, defiant, provocative, or disruptive without violating the rights of others.
- Involves defying adults, annoying others, being angry and resentful, getting annoyed easily, difficulty handling frustration, being temperamental, resisting authority, and being uncooperative or confrontational.
- Considered a subtype of conduct disorder in the *ICD-10*.

Based on World Health Organization, 1992, p. 212

ICD-11
- Uncooperative, defiant, and disobedient behavior that lasts six months or more, as exemplified by things like arguing with adults/authority figures or refusing to obey rules, requests, or instructions.
- May also be irritable, angry, blame others, act vindictively, express resentment, purposely annoy people, behave rudely, or have trouble getting along with others.
- Two subtypes: *without chronic irritability-anger* and *with chronic irritability-anger* (can use the latter as equivalent to *DSM-5's* "disruptive mood dysregulation disorder").

Based on https://gcp.network/en/private/icd-11-guidelines/grouping

Diagnostic Box 13.2 Conduct Disorder (CD)

DSM-5
- For at least 12 months, regularly violates others' rights or breaks age-related social norms, as exemplified by aggression toward people or animals (e.g., frequent fights, cruelty to others, or use of weapons), destroying property (e.g., vandalism or fire-setting), lying and/or stealing (e.g., breaking and entering), and regular rule breaking (e.g., running away or cutting school).
- Don't diagnose in people over age 18 who qualify for antisocial personality disorder.
- Specify *mild, moderate,* or *severe.*
- Specify *with limited prosocial emotions* if lacking remorse, empathy, or concern about school or work performance.

Based on American Psychiatric Association, 2013b, pp. 469–471

ICD-10
- Class of disorders (rather than just a single disorder) in which behavior that is consistently dissocial, aggressive, or defiant in ways that are more extreme than typical childhood mischief or teen rebelliousness and exemplified by things like fighting or bullying, cruelty to people or animals, destroying property, setting fires, stealing, lying, cutting school, running away, throwing tantrums, being defiant, and being disobedient.
- Specific types of conduct disorder in *ICD-10* include: *unsocialized* (has disturbed relationships), *socialized* (has adequate and lasting friendships with peers), *oppositional-defiant disorder* (see Diagnostic Box 13.1), *depressive conduct disorder* (accompanied by depressed mood), and *confined to family context.*

Based on World Health Organization, 1992, pp. 209–213

ICD-11
- Over an extended period (e.g., 12 months) regularly violates others' rights or breaks age-related social norms, as exemplified by aggression toward people or animals (e.g., frequent fights, cruelty to others, or use of weapons), destroying property (e.g., vandalism or fire-setting), lying and/or stealing (e.g., breaking and entering), and regular rule-breaking (e.g., running away or cutting school).
- Called "conduct-dissocial disorder" in *ICD-11.*

Based on https://gcp.network/en/private/icd-11-guidelines/grouping

Prevalence estimates for ODD cited in the *DSM-5* range widely, from 1% to 11% with an average of 3.3%. This means somewhere between 1% and 11% of children and adolescents qualify for a diagnosis. Before adolescence, boys are diagnosed 1.4 times more than girls, but after adolescence the prevalence rates for boys and girls are roughly equal (American Psychiatric Association, 2013b). The *DSM-5*'s one-year prevalence estimates for conduct disorder are comparable to those for ODD, ranging from 2% to over 10% with a median of 4%. As with antisocial personality disorder (the diagnosis to which ongoing conduct problems lead in adulthood), conduct disorder is much more common in boys than girls (American Psychiatric Association, 2013b).

Intermittent Explosive Disorder, Pyromania, and Kleptomania

Intermittent explosive disorder is characterized by recurrent aggressive outbursts—verbal, physical, or both. People who get this diagnosis seem unable to control themselves when they get upset. Thus, they exhibit explosive anger. The *DSM-5* estimates U.S. prevalence around 2.7% and notes the problem is more common in people under 35–40-years-old compared to those over age 50. Onset has been estimated to typically occur between ages 13 and 21, with half of all cases thought to begin during childhood or adolescence (Kessler et al., 2007).

Pyromania and **kleptomania** are two other impulse-control diagnoses in the *DSM-5, ICD-10,* and *ICD-11.* The former involves purposeful fire-setting, while the latter involves impulsive stealing. In both disorders, those diagnosed engage in fire-setting or theft because they experience a thrill from doing so. These activities aren't undertaken for monetary gain, vengeance, or to make a political statement. They are performed because they provide a sense of gratification. The *DSM-5* notes that pyromania is very rare. Kleptomania occurs in anywhere from 4% to 24% of people arrested for shoplifting, but its overall prevalence is—like pyromania—also rare (0.3%–0.6%). The *DSM-5* notes that pyromania and kleptomania often emerge during adolescence (sometimes co-occurring with conduct issues), though they can develop and be diagnosed for the first time well into adulthood. The *DSM-5* reports kleptomania being three times more common in women than men. Diagnostic Box 13.3 displays criteria and guidelines.

Diagnostic Box 13.3 Intermittent Explosive Disorder, Pyromania, and Kleptomania

Intermittent Explosive Disorder
- *DSM-5*: Trouble controlling disproportionate and unjustified aggressive impulses, as exemplified by verbal or physical aggression (at least twice a week for three months or, when directed at people or animals, at least three times in 12 months); usually must be at least age 6 for a diagnosis.

Based on American Psychiatric Association, 2013b, p. 466

CHAPTER **13**

- **ICD-10**: Mentioned under "other habit and impulse disorders," but no guidelines provided.
Based on World Health Organization, 1992, p. 168
- **ICD-11**: Difficulty controlling aggressive impulses that lead to verbal or physical aggression.
Based on https://icd.who.int/dev11/l-m/en

Pyromania
- **DSM-5**: Multiple instances of intentionally setting fires accompanied by emotional arousal before doing so, preoccupation with fire, enjoyment or relief from fire-setting, no financial or other gain from setting fires, and no psychotic symptoms or judgment issues that lead to setting fires.
Based on American Psychiatric Association, 2013b, p. 476
- **ICD-10**: Setting fires repeatedly without being motivated by financial gain, revenge, or political reasons; shows fascination with watching fires burn and experiences tension before fire-setting and arousal after it; called "pathological fire-setting" in *ICD-10*.
Based on World Health Organization, 1992, pp. 166–167
- **ICD-11**: Intentionally and repeatedly sets or tries to set fires without a clear motive such as financial gain, revenge, or political goals; preoccupation with fire and strong urges to set fires that are hard to resist or control, along with arousal before lighting fires and relief after doing so.
Based on https://icd.who.int/dev11/l-m/en

Kleptomania
- **DSM-5**: Impulsively steals objects one has no need for, with tension right beforehand and enjoyment/relief afterwards; not motivated by anger, revenge, hallucinations, or delusions; must eliminate conduct disorder, mania, or antisocial personality disorder as causes for the stealing.
Based on American Psychiatric Association, 2013b, p. 478
- **ICD-10**: Recurrent difficulty resisting the impulse to steal things not needed for personal use or financial gain; tension beforehand and enjoyment/relief afterwards; don't always thoroughly conceal one's stealing; anxiety and guilt afterwards, but still steals again.
Based on World Health Organization, 1992, p. 167
- **ICD-11**: Intentionally and repeatedly steals objects not wanted for personal use or financial gain; strong urges to steal, along with arousal before doing so and pleasure or relief after doing so.
Based on https://icd.who.int/dev11/l-m/en

Attention-Deficit/Hyperactivity Disorder (ADHD)

The hallmark features of **attention-deficit/hyperactivity disorder (ADHD)** are difficulty sustaining attention, being revved-up and full of excessive energy, and impulsive behavior. People with this diagnosis are divided into three types: those whose issue is mainly inattention, those whose issue is mainly hyperactivity and impulsivity, and those who struggle with both inattention and hyperactivity-impulsivity. To meet the *DSM-5* criteria for ADHD, symptoms must be present before age 12 and must occur in at least two settings. That is, if a child only displays inattention and hyperactivity at school or if the symptoms didn't appear until adolescence or adulthood, then ADHD shouldn't be diagnosed. This is important given concerns about overdiagnosis, discussed more below. The *DSM-5* reports that in most cultures ADHD occurs in about 5% of children and 2.5% of adults. It's been estimated that 80% of lifetime ADHD cases develop between ages 4 and 11 (Kessler et al., 2007), though the research estimating this used older and (as discussed below, debatably) narrower *DSM-IV* criteria.

The *ICD-10* doesn't contain a stand-alone ADHD category and actually expresses skepticism about the diagnosis, sharply remarking that "in recent years the use of the diagnostic term 'attention deficit disorder' ... has been promoted. It has not been used here because it implies a knowledge of psychological processes that is not yet available" (World Health Organization, 1992, p. 206). Instead, the *ICD-10* lists two diagnoses under the heading of "hyperkinetic conduct disorders" that roughly correspond to *DSM-5*'s ADHD: **disturbance of activity and attention** and **hyperkinetic conduct disorder**. The former is explicitly mentioned in the *ICD-10* as including ADHD. The latter is diagnosed in people whose attention-deficit issues are compounded by conduct problems. The *ICD-11* doesn't share the *ICD-10*'s wariness about ADHD as a diagnosis; it is included in the *ICD-11* as a neurodevelopmental disorder with guidelines similar to *DSM-5* criteria (see Diagnostic Box 13.4).

Diagnostic Box 13.4 Attention-Deficit/Hyperactivity Disorder (ADHD)

DSM-5
- Inattention and/or hyperactivity-impulsivity in more than one setting that develops before age 12 and lasts for six months or more.
- *Inattention* involves six of these (five if age 17 or older): (1) inattention to details or careless mistakes; (2) difficulty paying attention; (3) difficulty listening; (4) trouble following instructions or completing work; (5)

disorganized; (6) avoids/doesn't like work requiring prolonged mental effort; (7) loses things needed to complete work; (8) easily distracted; (9) forgets to complete chores and errands.
- *Hyperactivity/impulsivity* involves six of these (five if age 17 or older): (1) fidgets or squirms; (2) has trouble staying seated; (3) runs or climbs inappropriately; (4) cannot play quietly; (5) always in motion (6) talks excessively; (7) answers before questions are finished; (8) cannot await turn; (9) interrupts or intrudes on conversations or activities.

Based on American Psychiatric Association, 2013b, pp. 59–61

ICD-10
- Called "hyperkinetic disorders" in *ICD-10*.
- Both impaired attention and overactivity occur in more than one setting: *impaired attention* involves leaving tasks unfinished and being easily diverted; *overactivity* involves restlessness, excessive running/jumping, inability to remain in seat, excessive talkativeness/noisiness, and fidgeting.
- Can also involve disinhibition, recklessness in dangerous situations, impulsively disobeying rules by interrupting or intruding, answering questions prematurely, and difficulty waiting for one's turn.
- Two different diagnoses: *disturbance of activity and attention* (diagnosed when no conduct issues involved) and *hyperkinetic conduct disorder* (diagnosed when both hyperkinetic and conduct disorder criteria met).

Based on World Health Organization, 1992, pp. 206–209

ICD-11
- Inattention and/or hyperactivity-impulsivity in more than one setting that develops in early to mid-childhood and lasts for six months or more.
- *Inattention* involves difficulty paying attention to tasks that provide minimal stimulation or rewards; it also involves being disorganized and easily distracted.
- *Hyperactivity* involves trouble staying still, typically in situations that require it.
- *Impulsivity* involves tendency to react immediately to stimuli without thinking or considering the consequences.

Based on https://icd.who.int/dev11/l-m/en

Mark
Look back at the description of our 9-year-old case example client, Mark. Do you think he qualifies for an ADHD diagnosis? Why or why not?

CASE EXAMPLES

SOCIAL CONNECTION AND ATTACHMENT ISSUES

Some children struggle to establish social connections with others. This can be due to difficulties understanding and engaging in social interactions, problems communicating with people, and/or an inability to form healthy relational attachments. The *DSM* and *ICD* include various diagnoses having to do with social connection and attachment issues. Several pertain to **autism**, a general term for people who—to greater or lesser degrees—struggle with social interactions, have difficulties with verbal and nonverbal communication, and engage in repetitive and ritualistic behaviors (Autism Speaks, n.d.). The diagnostic categories related to autism have changed drastically in recent years. Below we unpack how.

Autism-Related Diagnoses in the *DSM* and *ICD*

From Autistic and Asperger's Disorders to Autism Spectrum Disorder

The *DSM-IV* divided autism into two primary disorders, **autistic disorder** and **Asperger's disorder** (also called *Asperger's syndrome*). It grouped them together as **pervasive developmental disorders**, which were characterized by the usual things associated with autism: impaired social skills, poor communication skills, and repetitive and ritualized behaviors, interests, and activities. *DSM-IV*'s autistic disorder was a severe, often profound, form of autism involving not only social and communication problems, but also serious impairment in the learning and use of language. Additionally, many cases were accompanied by cognitive and intellectual deficits. Asperger's, in contrast, was milder. It didn't include problems with language acquisition and, compared to autistic disorder, social and cognitive functioning were typically at a much higher level. For patients who didn't fit neatly into either of these categories, another diagnosis was used—**pervasive developmental disorder-not otherwise specified (PDD-NOS)**. Some people found reliance on the PDD-NOS diagnosis worrisome because it suggested the autistic and Asperger's disorder categories weren't adequate for classifying people with autism (Carrascosa-Romero & De Cabo-De La Vega, 2015).

Although it was a new addition to the *DSM-IV*, Asperger's disorder quickly became a tremendously popular diagnosis. Prevalence rates rose rapidly, with one representative study finding rates ranging from 1.6 to 2.9 of every 1,000 people (Mattila et al., 2007). Because Asperger's wasn't in the *DSM* prior to the *DSM-IV*, the explosion

CHAPTER **13**

Both DSM-5 and ICD-11 have combined the older diagnoses of autistic disorder and Asperger's disorder into a single autism spectrum disorder diagnosis.
Source: Getty Images/iStockphoto\mactrunk

in diagnostic rates seemed even more striking (Frances, 2010b; Gernsbacher, Dawson, & Hill Goldsmith, 2005). A lot of people—including psychiatrist Allen Frances, who oversaw the *DSM-IV*'s development—came to believe that the *DSM-IV* had defined autism and Asperger's too loosely, resulting in many false diagnoses (Frances, 2010a, 2010b; P. Steinberg, 2012). To address such concerns, the *DSM-5* made significant changes.

What kinds of changes? First, the *DSM-5* discarded the term "pervasive developmental disorder" and moved autism to the neurodevelopmental disorders chapter of the manual. Second, it merged all forms of autism (autistic disorder, Asperger's, and PDD-NOS) into a single diagnosis, **autism spectrum disorder (ASD)**. This new category is an example of the *DSM-5*'s move toward dimensional diagnosis (see Chapter 3 for a definition and Chapter 12 for how dimensional diagnosis applies to personality disorders). Autism spectrum disorder is dimensional to the extent that people diagnosed with it are distinguished based on the seriousness of their symptoms. The diagnosis specifies three levels of severity in social communication and restricted/repetitive behaviors. A person previously diagnosed with Asperger's who shows mild symptoms would likely fall at Level 1 (requiring the least assistance), whereas someone with profound autism in which communication, behavior, and cognition are extremely disrupted would probably fall at Level 3 (requiring extensive assistance).

The *ICD-11*, like the *DSM-5*, has also moved to a single diagnosis. It combined multiple *ICD-10* autism categories (**childhood autism**, **atypical autism**, and Asperger's syndrome) into a single autism spectrum disorder. *DSM-5* criteria and *ICD-10* and *ICD-11* guidelines are listed in Diagnostic Box 13.5. The *DSM-5* estimates a 1% worldwide prevalence for autism spectrum disorder, but notes that prevalence rates remain highly debated. This issue is revisited below when evaluating *DSM* and *ICD* perspectives. Regarding gender, the *DSM-5* indicates that boys are diagnosed with autism spectrum disorder four times more often than girls, but girls—when diagnosed—are more likely to also show intellectual disabilities (discussed in Chapter 14).

Source: © Royalty-Free/Corbis

Hernando

Hernando, our 3-year-old case example client who doesn't speak, withdraws from social contact, and repetitively lines up his toy cars for hours at a time, would likely be diagnosed with autism spectrum disorder.

CASE EXAMPLES

For those interested in learning about online self-assessments for autism, see the "Try It Yourself" feature.

Diagnostic Box 13.5 Autism

DSM-5: Autism Spectrum Disorder
- Deficits in communication, social interaction, and comprehending relationships that develop in early childhood.
- Characterized by at least two of these: repetitive/exaggerated behaviors or language use, a demand for sameness or routines, narrow and rigid interests, and being under- or oversensitive to sensory information.
- Severity levels: Level 1 (*requiring support*); Level 2 (*requiring substantial support*); Level 3 (*requiring very substantial support*)
- This diagnosis should be given to patients previously diagnosed with *DSM-IV*'s autistic disorder, Asperger's disorder, or pervasive developmental disorder-not otherwise specified (PDD-NOS).

Based on American Psychiatric Association, 2013b, pp. 50–51

ICD-10: Childhood Autism, Atypical Autism, and Asperger's Syndrome
- **Childhood autism**: Present by age 3 with abnormality in three areas: social interaction, communication, and restricted/repetitive behavior.

Based on World Health Organization, 1992, pp. 198–200
- **Atypical autism**: Differs from childhood autism in age of onset or in failure to show abnormality in all three areas (social interaction, communication, and restricted/repetitive behavior).

Based on World Health Organization, 1992, p. 200
- **Asperger's syndrome**: Social interaction difficulties and repetitive/restrictive behaviors like in autism, but language and cognitive development not impaired; normal intelligence in most cases, but clumsiness is common.

Based on World Health Organization, 1992, p. 203

ICD-11: Autism Spectrum Disorder
- Ongoing deficits in social interaction and communication, as well as repetitive, restricted, and inflexible behaviors and interests.
- Typically develops in early childhood, though symptoms may not become fully apparent until later.
- Those diagnosed vary widely in their intellectual functioning and language skills.

Based on https://icd.who.int/dev11/l-m/en

TRY IT YOURSELF

Am I on the Spectrum?

A variety of online sites offer self-assessments that people can take to get a sense of whether they are "on the spectrum." Here are two of the more prominent and well-regarded ones:

» PsychCentral's Short Autism Screening: https://psychcentral.com/quizzes/autism-quiz.htm
» "Autism Spectrum Quotient" screening: https://psychology-tools.com/autism-spectrum-quotient/

While you are encouraged to check these out, please remember that an online test is not sufficient for making a diagnosis. While an advantage of such self-assessments is that they can educate people about problems they may have, they also have a big disadvantage in that they can unnecessarily alarm people by telling them they have a problem that they don't. Self-assessments like these can be fun and informative, but they shouldn't be taken too literally.

A New DSM-5 Diagnosis: Social (Pragmatic) Communication Disorder (SPCD)

In addition to autism spectrum disorder, the *DSM-5* also added an entirely new disorder called **social (pragmatic) communication disorder (SPCD)**. This diagnosis is given to individuals who, early in life, develop difficulties communicating with others. They struggle with basic verbal interactions, such as greeting people and sharing information in a socially appropriate manner. They also find it difficult to calibrate their communication style to the situation; they might speak too loudly in class or be unable to adjust their language when speaking to kids instead of adults. Following the rules of storytelling, making inferences based on what people say, and understanding subtleties of conversation such as humor, metaphors, and multiple meanings are difficult for them. Basically, SPCD is a diagnosis for people who show social communication problems, but not the restricted and repetitive behavior required to meet the criteria for autism spectrum disorder (Norbury, 2014). SPCD, while listed as a neurodevelopmental disorder, is considered a communication disorder, not a form of autism. The *DSM-5* doesn't provide prevalence estimates for SPCD.

There is no comparable SPCD diagnosis in the *ICD-10*. However, the *ICD-11* does include a category analogous to SPCD, **developmental language disorder with impairment of mainly pragmatic language**. This *ICD-11* equivalent is perhaps a bit narrower than SPCD. Unlike SPCD, its guidelines specify that it can only be diagnosed if autism spectrum disorder is ruled out (Norbury, 2014). However, this difference notwithstanding, the two diagnoses cover many of the same patients. See Diagnostic Box 13.6 for further details.

CHAPTER 13

Diagnostic Box 13.6 Disorders of Social (Pragmatic) Communication

DSM-5: Social (Pragmatic) Communication Disorder
- Verbal and nonverbal communication difficulties that begin in early childhood.
- Has hard time with social communication, matching communication to the situation, telling stories, following conversational rules, and inferring what isn't explicitly said.

Based on American Psychiatric Association, 2013b, pp. 47–48

ICD-11: Developmental Language Disorder with Impairment of Mainly Pragmatic Language
- Ongoing language impairment characterized by things like difficulty making inferences, comprehending humor, or understanding verbal ambiguity.
- Typically develops during childhood.
- Must rule out a diagnosis of autism spectrum disorder.

Based on https://icd.who.int/dev11/l-m/en

Reactive Attachment Disorder

Reactive attachment disorder is diagnosed in children who have been inadequately cared for. These kids have experienced severe environmental neglect, often with regular changes in who is taking care of them. Consequently, they don't develop an ability to form attachments. Children with this diagnosis are emotionally withdrawn and inhibited around caregivers. They don't seek comfort when distressed and, when comfort is provided, they aren't especially responsive to it. Episodes of sadness, irritability, and fear are also common. In the *ICD-10* reactive attachment disorder is grouped with "emotional disorders with onset specific to childhood," but the *DSM-5* and *ICD-11* consider it a trauma and stress-related disorder. However, given its developmental and attachment elements, reactive attachment disorder is mentioned here rather than in the chapter on trauma, stress, and loss (Chapter 7). Although the *DSM-5* indicates that the prevalence of reactive attachment disorder isn't known, it also reports it to be very rare, occurring in less than 10% of severely neglected children. Criteria and guidelines appear in Diagnostic Box 13.7.

Diagnostic Box 13.7 Reactive Attachment Disorder

DSM-5
- Inhibited and withdrawn around adult caregivers when upset; unresponsive when caregivers offer comfort during times of distress.
- The child has been neglected, repeatedly been passed from one caregiver to another, or been raised in an environment that offers little chance for attachment.
- Some symptoms evident before age 5.

Based on American Psychiatric Association, 2013b, pp. 265–266

ICD-10
- Called "reactive attachment disorder of childhood."
- Dysfunctional relationship with caregivers that started before age 5 leading to ambivalence when separating or reuniting with them.
- Includes behaviors like averting gaze from caregiver, feeling ambivalent toward caregiver when comforted, emotional unresponsiveness to caregivers, withdrawal, aggression, fear that cannot be comforted, and sometimes failure to grow or thrive.

Based on World Health Organization, 1992, pp. 219–220

ICD-11
- Child doesn't seek comfort, help, or nurturance from caregivers or other adults.
- There is a history of neglect or maltreatment from primary caregiver(s).
- Can only be diagnosed in children and features develop during first five years of life, but cannot be diagnosed before age 1 (or those with a developmental age less than 9 months).

Based on https://icd.who.int/dev11/l-m/en

EVALUATING *DSM* AND *ICD* PERSPECTIVES

Pathologizing Rebelliousness and Social Resistance?

Some critics argue that diagnoses like ODD, CD and ADHD improperly turn normal adolescent rebellion and anti-authoritarianism into mental disorders (Edwards, 2008; B. E. Levine, 2005, 2008, 2012; Worley, 2014). Had the *DSM* and *ICD* been around in the past, such critics contend, many important historical figures who resisted authority or didn't pay attention to ideas they found limiting—people like Albert Einstein, Thomas Paine, and Malcom X—might have been wrongly diagnosed with disruptive behavior disorders (B. E. Levine, 2012). For these critics, when social rebellion is treated as an indicator of mental disorder, adaptive and appropriate resistance to oppression is mistakenly pathologized and social change is potentially stifled (Edwards, 2008; B. E. Levine, 2005, 2008, 2012). Their challenge to the *DSM* and *ICD* is nicely encapsulated by this question: "Do we really want to diagnose and medicate everyone with 'deficits in rule-governed behavior'" (B. E. Levine, 2012, para. 9)? Whether you think this is a fair question or not tells you something about your take on this issue.

Critiques of ADHD

Lowered Diagnostic Threshold?

Critics worry that the criteria for ADHD have been loosened in the *DSM-5*, making more people eligible for a diagnosis (Batstra & Frances, 2012; Frances, 2015; Paris, Bhat, & Thombs, 2015). How so? Well, in the *DSM-IV-TR*, symptoms had to develop before age 7. However, in the *DSM-5* they can develop as late as age 12. This potentially inflates the number of people meeting criteria for ADHD. Whereas before people who first showed symptoms after age 7 but before age 12 were excluded from a diagnosis, now they aren't. In addition to relaxing the age threshold, adult rates are also likely to increase because the *DSM-5* reduced the number of criteria people over age 17 must meet from six to five (Whitely, 2015).

Though the *DSM-5* is still relatively new, initial research suggests that its revised criteria do indeed increase prevalence (Ghanizadeh, 2013; Matte et al., 2015; Rigler et al., 2016; Vitola et al., 2017). One study revealed an 11% jump in diagnoses among children and adolescents (Ghanizadeh, 2013), another uncovered a 27% increase among young adults (Matte et al., 2015), a third found diagnostic rates shot up by 65% in a college student sample (Rigler et al., 2016), and a fourth estimated nearly a threefold increase in prevalence compared to *DSM-IV* (Vitola et al., 2017). While the more inclusive criteria may help reduce **false negatives** (true cases that go undiagnosed), it could also increase the number of **false positives** (cases that get diagnosed even though they shouldn't) (Matte et al., 2015; Sibley, Waxmonsky, Robb, & Pelham, 2013). Those who approve of the new criteria point out that, when it comes to severity of symptoms, there aren't notable differences between those whose age of onset was before age 7 versus before age 12 (Vande Voort, He, Jameson, & Merikangas, 2014). To them, therefore, changing the age criterion was justified and the increased prevalence isn't a problem. Still, many experts remain concerned about inflated diagnostic rates (Batstra & Frances, 2012; Frances, 2015; Matte et al., 2015; Paris et al., 2015; Whitely, 2015).

Is ADHD a Valid Disorder?

Supporters of ADHD as a diagnosis cite evidence for its reliability and validity. The *DSM-5* field trials rated the interrater reliability of ADHD as "good" or "very good" (Regier et al., 2013). Further, in 2002 a group of prominent practitioners and researchers signed an international consensus statement attesting to the validity of ADHD as a diagnosis (Barkley, 2002). Nonetheless, some critics object to the very idea of ADHD, seeing it as lacking diagnostic validity. In other words, they question whether ADHD is a legitimate disorder (T. Armstrong, 1995; Quinn & Lynch, 2016; Timimi, 2004, 2015; Timimi & Leo, 2009; J. Visser & Jehan, 2009; Whitely, 2015). Instead, they view ADHD as a scientifically suspect diagnosis unfairly used to justify drugging children who irritate their teachers and parents (Timimi, 2004, 2015; J. Visser & Jehan, 2009; Whitely, 2015). As one critic explained it, "ADHD is perhaps nothing more than an example of the 'medicalisation' of behaviours in children which are the most annoying and problematic for adults to control" (Quinn & Lynch, 2016, p. 62). Another critic put it even more strongly, arguing that

> the rapid expansion in the use of culturally constructed diagnoses like ADHD, together with giving children powerful stimulant medications to control their behaviour, is a damning indictment of the position of children in neo-liberal cultures, rather than an indication of scientific progress. (Timimi, 2015, p. 575)

Not all critics are quite so adamant. *DSM-IV* chair turned *DSM-5* critic, Allen Frances, agrees with those who say ADHD is too loosely defined in the *DSM*-5. Consequently, he worries that the revised *DSM-5* criteria will trigger a fad in which many adults are unjustifiably diagnosed with ADHD (Frances, 2010a, 2012a). At the same time, Frances opposes those who reject ADHD entirely: "We need to tame the epidemic of ADHD, not eliminate the ADHD diagnosis" (Frances, 2015, p. 577). This sentiment is echoed by those who argue that the real problem is that too many doctors fail to conduct a full and thorough assessment before diagnosing ADHD, resulting in the diagnosis too often being carelessly and incorrectly assigned (Hinshaw & Scheffler, 2014; Sparrow & Erhardt, 2014). Debate is both long-standing and ongoing between those who question ADHD's diagnostic validity and those who say ADHD is valid but overdiagnosed. We revisit this issue when discussing sociocultural perspectives. In the meantime, see the "In Depth" feature for another validity-related issue that applies not just to ADHD, but to most of the developmental diagnoses we discuss in this chapter—namely, the problem of comorbidity.

CHAPTER 13

IN DEPTH

If You Have One Developmental Diagnosis, You Just Might Qualify for Another

Developmental issues consistently co-occur. In other words, they have high degrees of comorbidity. For instance, it's been reported that patients diagnosed with ADHD are diagnosed with at least one other mental disorder 50% of the time and that this rate increases as they age (Yüce, Uçar, & Nur Say,

2015). The most common comorbid ADHD diagnoses are ODD and conduct disorder. In one previous study, ODD co-occurred in 46% of children and 33% of teens with ADHD, while conduct disorder co-occurred in 25% of children and 42% of teens with ADHD (Biederman et al., 1998; Yüce et al., 2015). Other diagnoses comorbid with ADHD include learning disorders, intellectual disabilities, depression, bipolar disorder, anxiety disorders, disruptive mood dysregulation disorder, tic disorders, and enuresis and encopresis (bed wetting and soiling; see Chapter 14) (Yüce et al., 2015).

Besides these disorders, ADHD is also comorbid with autism spectrum disorder. One study found that roughly 30% of preschoolers with ADHD also met criteria for autism; for the old *DSM-IV* category of PDD-NOS, comorbidity was even higher (45%) (Carrascosa-Romero & De Cabo-De La Vega, 2015). Many researchers have also long suspected a link between autism and schizophrenia, with comorbidity estimates ranging widely from 0% to 34.8% (Chisholm et al., 2015). Comorbidity is similarly high between childhood schizophrenia and the now defunct *DSM-IV* PDD-NOS diagnosis (Chisholm et al., 2015).

What to make of these high comorbidity rates? From the Research Domain Criteria (RDoC) perspective (see Chapter 3), the problem may be that existing developmental diagnostic categories rely on behavior (rather than biological and other rigorously measurable criteria) for making diagnoses and that many of these behavioral criteria overlap—resulting in high comorbidity rates (Cuthbert & Kozak, 2013; Insel et al., 2010; Morris & Cuthbert, 2012). Thus, familiar diagnostic categories such as autism, ODD, and ADHD may not reflect the actual disorders that brain research may ultimately discover. Discussing autism, one RDoC researcher sums it up this way: "Under the RDoC framework, the current definition of ASD is a somewhat arbitrary and ill-defined clustering of symptoms that are not necessarily closely related in terms of biology" (Damiano, Mazefsky, White, & Dichter, 2014). RDoC hopes to remedy this problem with research on basic brain processes, from which we might eventually arrive at more valid diagnostic categories that can be defined and assessed using reliable physiological and cognitive assessment measures rather than relying so heavily on observed behaviors, as *DSM* and *ICD* currently do (Baroni & Castellanos, 2015; Damiano et al., 2014; F. Levy, 2014).

CRITICAL THINKING QUESTIONS

1. Do you think ADHD, disruptive behavior disorders, and autistic spectrum disorder are discrete, despite how often they co-occur? Why or why not?

2. Are current developmental disorders comorbid so often because existing diagnostic categories are unreliable and/or inadequate? Explain your reasoning.

3. Do you believe the RDoC initiative will eventually produce physiological indicators (i.e., biomarkers) that we will use to make developmental diagnoses? If yes, why? If no, why not?

Objections to Eliminating Asperger's

One of the more controversial changes in the *DSM-5* (also implemented in the *ICD-11*) was the elimination of Asperger's disorder. Many people worried that those with Asperger's diagnoses would no longer meet the criteria for an autism-related diagnosis (Autism Speaks, 2012). The practical consequences of this could be significant because having a diagnosis is what often makes people eligible for clinical services (Halfon & Kuo, 2013; W. D. Lohr & Tanguay, 2013; McPartland, Reichow, & Volkmar, 2012). Of course, part of the reason for combining autistic disorder and Asperger's into the new autism spectrum disorder was to address a perceived problem of inflated diagnostic rates. If too many people were being diagnosed with Asperger's disorder (i.e., there were too many false positives), then perhaps the new autism spectrum diagnosis would result in lower (more accurate?) prevalence rates. However, when people diagnosed with Asperger's expressed alarm at losing their diagnoses, the *DSM-5* authors assured them that anyone with an existing diagnosis would be able to retain it (Autism Speaks, 2012). To guarantee this, the *DSM-5* included an exemption (or, "grandfather clause") to protect people with well-established *DSM-IV-TR* autism diagnoses (I. C. Smith, Reichow, & Volkmar, 2015). In other words, people previously diagnosed with *DSM-IV-TR* pervasive developmental disorders wouldn't have to worry because their preexisting diagnoses would not be taken away. However, overall prevalence rates could still be expected to drop going forward because *DSM-5* made it harder for first-time patients to meet the more stringent criteria for the new autism spectrum disorder. There is some evidence that this has been the case. After plateauing in 2015, autism diagnoses appear to be down under the *DSM-5* (Bent, Barbaro, & Dissanayake, 2017).

How much has the shift to autism spectrum disorder (ASD) lowered prevalence rates? The *DSM-5*'s publisher, the American Psychiatric Association (2013a), contends not very much. They point to a study that found 91% of children with *DSM-IV-TR* pervasive developmental disorder diagnoses also met criteria for the new autism spectrum disorder (Huerta, Bishop, Duncan, Hus, & Lord, 2012). However, other studies suggest more substantial decreases in the number of people who qualify for an ASD diagnosis under new *DSM-5* criteria (Maenner et al., 2014; Mattila et al., 2011; Mayes et al., 2014; R. L. Young & Rodi, 2014). One systematic review concluded that only 50%–75% of people with a *DSM-IV-TR* autism-related diagnosis would receive a *DSM-5* ASD diagnosis (I. C. Smith et al., 2015). Thus, it's unclear whether the *DSM-5* changes have decreased prevalence a little or a lot. The situation is only made more uncertain because we have very little prevalence data for the new social (pragmatic) communication disorder—and what little data we do have has yielded inconsistent prevalence rates (Brukner-Wertman, Laor, & Golan, 2016; Y. S. Kim et al., 2014; Norbury, 2014; C. E. Wilson et al., 2013). This is relevant because SPCD was intended to capture some of the people who used to receive autism or Asperger's diagnoses in *DSM-IV*, but don't meet ASD criteria in *DSM-5*.

So, can people still be diagnosed with Asperger's? If you go by the *DSM-5* and *ICD-11*, it seems like the answer is "no" because someone who used to get an Asperger's diagnosis is now likely to be diagnosed with mild ASD. However, the answer isn't a definitive "no" because in many countries, the *ICD-10* remains the official diagnostic manual. The U.S., for instance, only switched to it in 2015. This is relevant because the *ICD-10* contains a code for Asperger's! Thus, people living in countries where *ICD-10* continues to be used could technically still receive an Asperger's diagnosis. That said, countries increasingly will be switching to the *ICD-11* and—even in countries where *ICD-10* remains in force—clinicians often defer to the *DSM-5*, which has removed Asperger's. Thus, the Asperger's diagnosis is all but defunct as a medical diagnosis; however, this hasn't prevented people who feel attached to the term from continuing to use it to describe themselves (L. J. Rudy, 2017).

Before moving on, let's briefly revisit the *DSM-5* exemption protecting people with well-established *DSM-IV-TR* autism diagnoses from losing their diagnoses. Critics note that this exemption has resulted in the simultaneous use of two different sets of diagnostic criteria. Some people's diagnoses were derived using *DSM-IV-TR* and other's using *DSM-5* (I. C. Smith et al., 2015). Practically speaking, this has some odd implications. It means that

> individuals diagnosed prior to the publication of the DSM-5 should maintain a diagnosis of ASD and continue to receive the same level of services they have been receiving, but individuals who present for first diagnosis moving forward with similar symptoms and needs may not. (I. C. Smith et al., 2015, p. 2548)

Whether this is scientifically sound, not to mention fair, remains a contentious question. Imagine a new discovery changed our understanding of cancer. Would we make an exception (or "grandfather in") people who already had cancer and only apply our fresh knowledge to diagnosing new cases? Unlikely. Is this a fair analogy? You'll have to decide for yourself.

13.3 HISTORICAL PERSPECTIVES

In thinking about developmental issues, it's important to historically locate the concept of childhood. The French historian Philippe Ariès (1962) controversially but compellingly argued that a distinct period of life called childhood—characterized by innocence and a need for nurturing—is a relatively new notion, one created by and taken for granted in modern societies. In earlier historic periods, Ariès maintained, children were thought of (and treated) as little adults. Regardless of whether you concur with Ariès' analysis (and not everyone does!), the idea that our understanding of developmental issues is rooted in historical-cultural views of both childhood and abnormality seems important (see Chapter 1 for a discussion of historical-cultural views). With that in mind, let's discuss past ideas about what today we call ADHD and autism.

ADHD

18th Century: Identifying "Lack of Attention" as a Medical Condition

The German physician Melchior Adam Weikard (1742–1803) is credited with one of the earliest references to a disorder anticipating today's ADHD (Schwarz, 2016). In 1775, Weikard identified a condition he called "lack of attention" (*attentio volubilis* in Latin) and described those who suffer from it as "unwary, careless, flighty and bacchanal" (Barkley & Peters, 2012, p. 627). Some of the treatments Weikard prescribed for lack of attention seem silly by today's standards: cold baths, sour milk, steel powder, and horseback riding; however, he also recommended exercise, something doctors still encourage (Barkley & Peters, 2012). Two decades later, in 1798, the Scottish physician Sir Alexander Crichton (1763–1856) published a more extensive description of attention difficulties (Schwarz, 2016). Crichton (1798) posited that people can either be born with or develop diseases of attention. He felt that most children outgrow their attention issues as they reach adulthood, an idea that remained popular until the 1990s (Lange, Reichl, Lange, Tucha, & Tucha, 2010).

CHAPTER 13

19th Century: Hoffmann's "Fidgety Philip"

Numerous historians believe that the German physician and obstetrician Heinrich Hoffmann (1809–1894) was writing about ADHD in his famous 1845 children's book, *Struwwelpeter* (Lange et al., 2010; Schwarz, 2016; Sparrow & Erhardt, 2014). Two of the stories, "Fidgety Philip" and "Johnny Look-in-the-Air," portray restless and inattentive boys. However, historians remain divided over whether Hoffmann was using the stories to describe attention-deficit problems or whether he was just telling amusing children's parables (Lange et al., 2010). As one skeptical historian remarked, "textbook histories of hyperactivity show how history can be exploited by interested parties to shape the understanding of a disorder" (M. Smith, 2012, p. 28). That is, we often interpret the past through our current prism, imposing our present conceptions of abnormality on past events. Some historians view "The Story of Fidgety Philip," published in 1845 by German physician Heinrich Hoffmann (1844), as an early representation of ADHD. See the excerpt below and Figure 13.1 for more on Fidgety Philip's unfortunate mealtime predicament.

"Let me see if Philip can
Be a little gentleman;
Let me see if he is able
To sit still for once at table."
Thus spoke, in earnest tone,
The father to his son;
And the mother looked very grave
To see Philip so misbehave.
But Philip he did not mind
His father who was so kind.
He wriggled
And giggled,
And then, I declare,
Swung backward and forward
And tilted his chair,
Just like any rocking horse;-

"Philip! I am getting cross!"

See the naughty, restless child,
Growing still more rude and wild,
Till his chair falls over quite.
Philip screams with all his might,
Catches at the cloth, but then
That makes matters worse again.
Down upon the ground they fall,
Glasses, bread, knives, forks and all.
How Mamma did fret and frown,
When she saw them tumbling down!
And Papa made such a face!
Philip is in sad disgrace.

Source: INTERFOTO / Alamy Stock Photo

Figure 13.1 Fidgety Philip: ADHD in 1845? An original illustration from "The Story of Fidgety Philip" in Heinrich Hoffmann's 1845 children's book, Struwwelpeter.

Early 20th Century: Attention Disorders, Lack of Moral Control, and Hyperkinetic Disease

At the turn of the 20th century, the Scottish physician Thomas Clouston (1840–1915) wrote about what he identified as attention disorders (M. Smith, 2012). Unlike later conceptions of ADHD as a lifelong disorder, Clouston believed attention disorders generally lasted only a few months. However, anticipating later medical conceptions of ADHD, he believed these disorders were caused by dysfunctions in the cerebral cortex and he treated them with *bromides* (chemical compounds used as sedatives during that era) (M. Smith, 2012).

Sir George F. Still (1868–1941), a British physician, is perhaps the most well-known figure in the history of ADHD. Like Clouston, he also wrote about attention disorders at the turn of the 20th century. His renowned

1902 lectures on the subject are viewed as the scientific starting point for modern understandings of ADHD (Lange et al., 2010). Still described children whom he believed suffered from "defects of moral control" (Lange et al., 2010; Rafalovich, 2004; M. Smith, 2012; Still, 2006). Admittedly, Still's notion of defective moral control is broader and more inclusive than modern ADHD; today, many of Still's case study children would be diagnosed with ODD or conduct disorder, not ADHD (Lange et al., 2010). Nonetheless, Still's work helped firmly establish the idea that disruptive behavior might be caused by an underlying medical condition.

In 1932, the German physicians Franz Kramer (1878–1967) and Hans Pollnow (1902–1943) described what they called a "hyperkinetic disease" in infants and children that was characterized by extreme physical restlessness (Lange et al., 2010). These children seemed to be unable to sit still for any extended time. Kramer and Pollnow's work anticipated the use of the term "hyperkinetic disorder" in past *DSM* and *ICD* manuals. It also clearly influenced current *DSM* descriptions of ADHD, especially the behavioral criterion of acting as if "driven by a motor" (Lange et al., 2010; M. Smith, 2012; Still, 2006).

Discovery of Stimulant Medication to Treat Attention Problems

In 1937, the American physician Charles Bradley (1902–1979) gave stimulant medications to neurologically impaired children to help them with headaches. The drugs didn't decrease the headaches, but—to Bradley's great surprise—they did improve the children's behavior in school (Lange et al., 2010; M. Smith, 2012). After investigating this further, Bradley concluded that children who had the shortest attention spans benefitted most from taking stimulant medications. In 1954, the stimulant **methylphenidate** was first marketed under the name **Ritalin**; to this day, it remains the most widely used drug for treating ADHD (Lange et al., 2010; Wenthur, 2016). More is said about treating ADHD with stimulants when we examine biological perspectives.

Latter 20th Century: From Hyperkinetic Reaction to Attention Deficit Disorder

By the 1960s and 1970s, researchers were hard at work studying the hyperkinetic—or hyperactive—behavior of children. Many researchers posited that hyperactivity was attributable to minimal brain dysfunction that didn't affect overall intelligence, but did impact the ability to regulate attention and activity (although this hypothesis was later criticized for being too broad and lacking evidence) (Lange et al., 2010; M. Smith, 2012). Interest in attention and hyperactivity difficulties in children continued and by 1968, the *DSM-II* included a disorder called *hyperkinetic reaction of childhood*. This became *attention deficit disorder* (*ADD*) in the *DSM-III*, which could be diagnosed "with or without hyperactivity" (Lange et al., 2010). The *DSM-5* and *ICD-11* diagnostic term, attention-deficit/hyperactivity disorder, was introduced in 1987's *DSM-III-R*. Finally, during the 1990s the long-held assumption that people outgrew attention problems fell by the wayside. Doctors began diagnosing the disorder not just in children, but also in adults (Lange et al., 2010; M. Smith, 2012). Thus, the recognition of adult ADHD is a relatively recent historical development.

AUTISM

Leo Kanner and Autism

The Austrian-American psychiatrist Leo Kanner (1894–1981) is typically credited with first identifying autism (J. P. Baker, 2013; Olmsted & Blaxill, 2016; Verhoeff, 2013; Volkmar & McPartland, 2014; S. Wolff, 2004). Prior to Kanner, there were few descriptions of anything resembling autism, although some have argued that historical accounts of allegedly feral children may actually have been describing children with autism (Volkmar & McPartland, 2014; Waltz, 2013; S. Wolff, 2004). Still, it's unclear whether the subjects of these and other past accounts fit Kanner's criteria (S. Wolff, 2004).

Kanner first wrote about what he called "infantile autism" in 1943. He described 11 cases of children whose ability to socially engage was deeply impaired (L. Kanner, 1943). These children were socially unresponsive and cut off from others. In addition to their social isolation, Kanner observed that autistic children reacted negatively to changes in their environment and insisted on maintaining sameness. Some of the children also had difficulty with language and communication. Kanner felt that autistic children were often misdiagnosed with schizophrenia. He may have accidentally furthered this confusion by using the term autism, which originally referred to symptoms of schizophrenia that involved disordered thinking and a retreat from reality (J. P. Baker, 2013; Volkmar & McPartland, 2014). Confusion with schizophrenia notwithstanding, many historians have argued that Kanner's description of autism was remarkably astute and it continues to influence

CHAPTER 13

current conceptions, even if the exact contours of the disorder have evolved over time (Verhoeff, 2013; Volkmar & McPartland, 2014).

Hans Asperger and Asperger's Syndrome

The Austrian pediatrician Hans Asperger (1906–1980) wrote a doctoral dissertation on "autistic psychopathy" in children. It was published in 1944, shortly after Kanner's seminal 1943 paper (Lyons & Fitzgerald, 2007). The children Asperger described were often quite capable in math and science, but they had difficulty with social relationships. They were extremely sensitive, had trouble empathizing with others, engaged in repetitive and ritualistic behaviors, and were clumsy; they didn't have problems learning language, but sometimes spoke in odd or idiosyncratic ways (Asperger, 1991; S. Wolff, 2004). Asperger believed these symptoms were innate and lifelong. The children Asperger spoke of appeared to be higher functioning than those Kanner described and Asperger himself thought that he and Kanner had identified different disorders (Barahona-Corrêa & Filipe, 2016). This anticipated the later distinction between autism and Asperger's syndrome.

Although Kanner and Asperger published around the same time, neither seemed to have been (at least initially) aware of the other's work (Barahona-Corrêa & Filipe, 2016), although some have wondered if Kanner might have been familiar with Asperger's ideas (Lyons & Fitzgerald, 2007). Historians find the coincidences of their work intriguing—both men were born in Austria and published on autism within a year of each other, even though they never met (Barahona-Corrêa & Filipe, 2016; Lyons & Fitzgerald, 2007). Historically, Kanner gets most of the credit for first discovering autism, perhaps because he wrote in English and took a more systematic approach in his descriptions (Barahona-Corrêa & Filipe, 2016; S. Wolff, 2004). Asperger's ideas didn't gain widespread attention until they were popularized by the English psychiatrist Lorna Wing (1928–2014), who introduced the term "Asperger's syndrome" in 1981. Although Wing (1981) saw autism and Asperger's as part of a common autism spectrum, others increasingly saw them as distinct—resulting in the *ICD-10* and *DSM-IV* including Asperger's as its own disorder within a decade and a half of Wing's 1981 paper. It's worth noting that the reign of Asperger's as a separate disorder has been brief; it's been less than 40 years since Wing (1981) first coined the term. This only makes the explosion in diagnoses throughout the 1990s and early 2000s, followed by the *DSM-5* and *ICD-11* decisions to eliminate Asperger's, that much more fascinating from a historical vantage point.

The Refrigerator Mother Theory of Autism

In the mid-20th century the **refrigerator mother theory of autism** was quite popular. Most famously advanced by the psychoanalyst Bruno Bettelheim (1903–1990), this theory attributed autism to cold and aloof parenting (Bettelheim, 1967). Although he was one of the most definitive in pushing the refrigerator mother theory, other prominent figures also advanced the idea that autism was caused by the withholding of maternal warmth and affection (Waltz, 2015). Leo Kanner, for instance, vacillated between the refrigerator mother theory (L. Kanner, 1949; L. Kanner & Eisenberg, 1957; Waltz, 2013, 2015) and the theory he originally advanced, namely that autistic children were born that way (J. P. Baker, 2013; L. Kanner, 1943; S. Wolff, 2004). He did, however, eventually reject the refrigerator mother theory and endorse the view of psychologist Bernard Rimlind (1928–2006), who in 1964 advanced a neurological perspective on autism (Rimlind, 1964). The refrigerator hypothesis is almost universally rejected and in disrepute today, as is the reputation of Bruno Bettelheim who, it was revealed after his death, had faked his educational credentials, plagiarized some of his work, and physically abused children at the group home for emotionally troubled children he ran at The University of Chicago (Pollack, 1997). Even though Bettelheim and his work have been discredited, there are some psychotherapists—especially in France—who still adhere to the refrigerator mother theory; we discuss this further under psychodynamic perspectives.

The refrigerator mother theory of autism is almost universally rejected today, but was extremely popular in the mid-20th century.
Source: Getty Images/Hemera/Thinkstock\Cathy Yeulet

13.4 BIOLOGICAL PERSPECTIVES
BRAIN CHEMISTRY PERSPECTIVES
Disruptive Behavior

The Dopamine Hypothesis of ADHD

Since the early 1970s, investigators have been researching the **dopamine hypothesis of ADHD**, which holds that ADHD is caused by deficits in the transmission of the neurotransmitter dopamine, which (as you recall from earlier chapters) is associated with pleasure, motivation, and attention (F. Levy, 1991; F. Levy & Swanson, 2001; Tripp & Wickens, 2008; Volkow et al., 2009). Researchers favoring the dopamine hypothesis of ADHD note that stimulant medications used to treat ADHD boost dopamine levels (Daughton & Kratochvil, 2009). So even though it seems counterintuitive, stimulants are the drug of choice for hyperactivity.

Dopamine has received the greatest attention and is often treated as the most important ADHD neurotransmitter (del Campo, Chamberlain, Sahakian, & Robbins, 2011; J. Wu, Xiao, Sun, Zou, & Zhu, 2012). However, dopamine isn't the only catecholamine neurotransmitter linked to ADHD; so is norepinephrine (Arnsten, 2006; del Campo et al., 2011; K. E. Knight, 2013). Stimulants prescribed for ADHD increase both dopamine and norepinephrine (Daughton & Kratochvil, 2009; del Campo et al., 2011; F. Levy, 2009). Thus, sometimes the dopamine hypothesis of ADHD is framed more broadly as the **catecholamine hypothesis of ADHD** (del Campo et al., 2011; Quist & Kennedy, 2001).

Critics of the dopamine hypothesis of ADHD note that stimulants don't only increase attention in people with ADHD; anyone who takes them shows improved attention and vigilance (Gonon, 2009). This may explain why so many non-ADHD-diagnosed college students "borrow" their friends' prescribed ADHD stimulants in attempts to improve their own academic performances (Wilens et al., 2008). The point? While stimulants enhance dopamine levels and improve attention in everyone, this doesn't necessarily mean those with poor attention spans (who, like everyone else, benefit from the stimulants) necessarily have a dopamine transmission issue in the first place (Gonon, 2009). Despite criticisms like this and the fact that research on dopamine's role in ADHD has produced inconsistent results, dopamine remains central in ongoing efforts to understand the neurochemistry of ADHD (del Campo et al., 2011).

Drugs Prescribed for ADHD

As already noted, stimulants are the most commonly used medications for ADHD. However, sometimes other drugs are used, as well. Most drugs for ADHD can be administered in short-acting (4–6 hour) or long-acting (6–12 hour) forms, which tend to be equally effective (Daughton & Kratochvil, 2009; Punja et al., 2016). Table 13.1 lists some of the more popular stimulants and their trade names. It also lists non-stimulant drugs prescribed for ADHD, often in addition to stimulants (or in place of them when stimulants don't work or aren't tolerated).

Mark
Our ADHD-diagnosed case example client, 9-year-old Mark, is likely to be prescribed Ritalin or another stimulant drug.   CASE EXAMPLES

Table 13.1 Drugs Commonly Prescribed for ADHD

DRUG(S)	DRUG TYPE	COMMON TRADE NAME(S)
Methylphenidate	Stimulant	Ritalin, Methylin, Concerta, Metadate
Dextroamphetamine (dexamfetamine)	Stimulant	Dexedrine, Adderall*
Lisdexamfetamine	Stimulant	Vyvanse, Elvanse
Atomoxetine	Norepinephrine reuptake inhibitor	Strattera
Guanfacine	Alpha agonist	Tenex, Intuiv
Clonadine	Alpha agonist	Catapres

CHAPTER 13

Bupropion†	Norepinephrine-dopamine reuptake inhibitor antidepressant	Wellbutrin
Desipramine†	Tricyclic antidepressant	Norpramin
Imipramine†	Tricyclic antidepressant	Tofranil
Nortriptyline†	Tricyclic antidepressant	Aventyl, Pamelor

* Adderall contains *both* dextroamphetamine and amphetamine.
† Not an approved medication for ADHD, but often prescribed "off label."

Do ADHD drugs work? Comprehensive reviews have found that all stimulants prescribed for ADHD improve symptoms (at least in the short term) (Pringsheim, Hirsch, Gardner, & Gorman, 2015a; Punja et al., 2016). However, there is little research on their long-term effectiveness (L. Seligman & Reichenberg, 2007) and a comprehensive review of research on methylphenidate in children determined that the quality of most studies was poor (Storebø et al., 2015). Further, stimulant drugs have unpleasant side effects that lead many people to drop out of treatment—such as difficulty sleeping, loss of appetite, and stomach pain (Castells, Ramos-Quiroga, Bosch, Nogueira, & Casas, 2011; Punja et al., 2016; Storebø et al., 2015). In the long term, the benefits of stimulants aren't clear, mainly because few randomized controlled trials (RCTs) have been conducted to test their effectiveness over extended periods (Castells et al., 2011; Punja et al., 2016; Storebø et al., 2015). Further, there has been a lot of controversy over whether stimulants are overprescribed, especially in the United States where—compared to other countries—ADHD is diagnosed at a much higher rate (Hinshaw & Scheffler, 2014; G. Russell, Rodgers, Ukoumunne, & Ford, 2014; Schwarz & Cohen, 2013). One major concern about stimulant drugs, even at the doses used for ADHD, is that they are habit-forming (Daughton & Kratochvil, 2009). Revisit Chapter 11 for more on the addictive properties of stimulants.

Non-stimulant drugs aren't considered as effective for attention issues as stimulant drugs (Daughton & Kratochvil, 2009; Pringsheim et al., 2015a). Of the non-stimulants, the tricyclic antidepressants have the largest evidence base (Budur, Mathews, Adetunji, Mathews, & Mahmud, 2005; Otasowie, Castells, Ehimare, & Smith, 2014). However, they have bad side effects such as increased blood pressure and loss of appetite (Otasowie et al., 2014). Further, there were reports in the 1980s and 1990s of children who died unexpectedly while taking them. While a clear link between tricylics and unexplained death hasn't been established, many clinicians remain hesitant about prescribing tricyclics to children (Budur et al., 2005; Varley, 2001).

Conduct Problems

Recall from Chapter 12 that being diagnosed with antisocial personality disorder is correlated with having low levels of serotonin. The same is true for conduct disorder, a childhood diagnosis that anticipates adult antisocial personality disorder. In research studies of juvenile behavior problems, low serotonin levels are often, though not always, tied to aggression (Cappadocia, Desrocher, Pepler, & Schroeder, 2009; Golubchik, Mozes, Vered, & Weizman, 2009; Lahey, Hart, Pliszka, Applegate, & McBurnett, 1993; Unis et al., 1997; J. Zhou et al., 2006). Thus, people with diagnoses like intermittent explosive disorder and conduct disorder might be good candidates for selective-serotonin reuptake inhibitors (SSRIs), especially when their symptoms are accompanied only by anxiety and depression (Cremers, Lee, Keedy, Phan, & Coccaro, 2016; Nevels, Dehon, Alexander, & Gontkovsky, 2010). However, SSRIs pose complications when conduct problems are comorbid with ADHD because SSRIs aren't that helpful for ADHD, especially attention issues (Buoli, Serati, & Cahn, 2016; C. W. Popper, 1997).

Other than SSRIs, many drugs used for ADHD are commonly given to children and teens with conduct problems. Stimulants and the norepinephrine-dopamine reuptake inhibitor (NDRI) *bupropion* (see Chapter 9) are frequently prescribed; mood stabilizers, anticonvulsants, and atypical antipsychotics are used too (Sarteschi, 2014; Searight, Rottnek, & Abby, 2001). However, as you may remember from the "In Depth" feature in Chapter 5, administering mood stabilizers and atypical antipsychotics to children is often considered ethically dubious due to these drugs' potency and side effects (Nevels et al., 2010; Sparks & Duncan, 2012; Whitaker, 2012). Additionally, reviewers have concluded that the evidence of their effectiveness for conduct issues is not very strong, with the one possible exception being the atypical antipsychotic *risperidone* (Gorman et al., 2015; Hambly, Khan, McDermott, Bor, & Haywood, 2016; Loy, Merry, Hetrick, & Stasiak, 2012; Pringsheim, Hirsch, Gardner, & Gorman, 2015b; Sarteschi, 2014). Yet it's been argued that even risperidone should only be used in the most severe cases (Pringsheim et al., 2015b).

Michael
Do you think that Michael, our 15-year-old case example client with a diagnosis of conduct disorder due to his history of aggressive and violent behavior, should be prescribed risperidone? Why or why not?

Autism

Suppressed GABA Inhibition?

Some researchers suspect that autism is linked to disequilibrium involving GABA and glutamate, the brain's respective inhibitory and excitatory neurotransmitters (see Chapter 2). The **suppressed GABA inhibition hypothesis** holds that GABA activity is reduced in those with autism, perhaps due to a communication breakdown in the brain's GABA transmission pathway (Hussman, 2001). The presumed result? Diminished GABA activity, which reduces GABA's inhibitory effects and leads to increased neural excitability and excessive glutamate activity (Brondino et al., 2016; El-Ansary & Al-Ayadhi, 2014; Hussman, 2001). If correct, this hypothesis might explain why people with autism feel overwhelmed by sensory information. Without sufficient inhibitory GABA signaling, their brains are unable to modulate responsiveness to environmental stimulation. Researchers increasingly have been testing this hypothesis (Banerjee et al., 2013; Coghlan et al., 2012; El-Ansary & Al-Ayadhi, 2014; Gaetz et al., 2014; Oblak, Gibbs, & Blatt, 2010, 2011). A 2016 study was the first ever to directly link inhibited GABA transmission to autism in humans (C. E. Robertson, Ratai, & Kanwisher, 2016). The results are correlational and other neural pathways may also be involved, but they support the proposition that impaired GABA may be important in autism.

Drugs Prescribed for Autism

Many patients with autism exhibit highly irritable and disruptive behavior such as temper tantrums, aggression, and self-injury. The atypical antipsychotic risperidone (mentioned previously) and *aripiprazole* are the most commonly used and best researched drugs for reducing these behaviors (Accordino, Kidd, Politte, Henry, & McDougle, 2016; Fung et al., 2016; Ghanizadeh, Tordjman, & Jaafari, 2015; Hirsch & Pringsheim, 2016; I. Jordan, Robertson, Catani, Craig, & Murphy, 2012; Lemmon, Gregas, & Jeste, 2011; McPheeters et al., 2011). Sometimes anticonvulsants and mood stabilizers are used instead, although the evidence for them is weaker (Accordino et al., 2016). As already noted, many worry about prescribing powerful drugs like risperidone and aripiprazole to children, pointing to side effects such as weight gain, sedation, drooling, and tremors (Fung et al., 2016; Hirsch & Pringsheim, 2016; McPheeters et al., 2011; Sparks & Duncan, 2012; Whitaker, 2012). Thus, the U.K.'s National Institute for Health and Care Excellence (NICE) recommends that antipsychotics only be prescribed to children with autism "when psychosocial or other interventions are insufficient or could not be delivered because of the severity of the behaviour" (National Institute for Health and Care Excellence, 2013, Recommendation 1.4.10). Despite being approved in the U.S. and U.K. for autism, use of atypical antipsychotics in children remains controversial.

Hernando
Would you prescribe atypical antipsychotics to 3-year-old Hernando, our case example client diagnosed with autism spectrum disorder?

Drugs are prescribed for other symptoms of autism besides disruptive behavior. Antidepressants and similar drugs (usually SSRIs, but also tricyclics, bupropion, and atomoxetine) are given to reduce repetitive behaviors and/or hyperactivity (Accordino et al., 2016). SSRIs reduce these symptoms in adults, but for children the evidence is mixed (Accordino et al., 2016).

When it comes to social withdrawal in autism, investigators have been exploring the role of **oxytocin**, an amino acid produced by the hypothalamus that functions as both a neurotransmitter and a hormone. In addition to playing a role in sex and reproduction (by stimulating labor and breastfeeding), oxytocin has been linked to social behavior (Neumann, 2008). It's been hypothesized that raising oxytocin levels might help to minimize social deficits in those with autism, although it's not clear whether people with autism necessarily have lower oxytocin levels (Parker et al., 2014). Oxytocin nasal sprays have been developed to reduce social withdrawal in autism. There is mixed evidence for their effectiveness (Alvares, Quintana, & Whitehouse, 2016; Guastella & Hickie, 2016; Preti et al., 2014; Yatawara, Einfeld, Hickie, Davenport, & Guastella, 2016). Further, some worry that their prolonged use might decrease the brain's natural production of oxytocin (Huang et al., 2014).

CHAPTER 13

BRAIN STRUCTURE PERSPECTIVES

Disruptive Behavior

Attention Issues

The precise neuroanatomy of ADHD isn't known (Kimonis & Frick, 2016; Thapar & Cooper, 2016). However, several findings are worth noting. When it comes to brain volume, people with ADHD seem to have smaller volumes, especially in the prefrontal cortex, cerebellum, corpus callosum, and basal ganglia (S. V. Faraone & Biederman, 2013; Kimonis & Frick, 2016; Tarver, Daley, & Sayal, 2014). As for specific brain regions, many have been identified as potentially relevant. Among them are the prefrontal cortex (important in attention, planning, decision-making, and goal-directed behavior); the **dorsal anterior midcingulate cortex** (which plays a role in motivational aspects of attention, cognitive processing, and response inhibition); the parietal cortex (involved in attention and spatial processing); and the striatum (a part of the brain's reward system) (G. Bush, 2011; Kimonis & Frick, 2016). These brain regions work together to help with executive functioning (defined in Chapter 3)— cognitive processes involving attention, planning, decision-making, and goal-directed behavior (Castellanos, Sonuga-Barke, Milham, & Tannock, 2006). Underactivity of these brain regions is thought to disrupt executive functioning and is suspected of being responsible for symptoms of ADHD (Cortese et al., 2012).

Promising leads notwithstanding, it's important to note that researchers haven't yet identified exact brain mechanisms in ADHD, perhaps because ADHD consists of at least two impairments: inattention and hyperactivity-impulsivity (Kimonis & Frick, 2016). Taking this further, the RDoC perspective holds that what we call ADHD should be broken into specific symptom domains and research conducted on the neural basis for each of these domains (Baroni & Castellanos, 2015). This might better help us identify and diagnose attention and impulsivity issues using biological measures. However, while brain researchers have many leads they consider promising, there are currently no known biological markers for ADHD (Thapar & Cooper, 2016).

Conduct Problems

People diagnosed with conduct disorder are suspected of having biological issues in various areas related to stress and fear-based learning. They are notably less reactive to fearful stimuli. How is this reflected in their physiology? For one thing, their autonomic nervous systems (which control heart rate, blood pressure, and emotional arousal; see Chapter 7) are underresponsive to fear conditioning, suggesting they aren't afraid of punishment and don't learn from it (Matthys, Vanderschuren, & Schutter, 2013). They also tend to have reduced levels of the stress hormone cortisol, implying they don't find aversive situations stressful (Cappadocia et al., 2009; Matthys et al., 2013). Finally, two brain regions important in emotion and stress—the amygdala and the hypothalamic-pituitary-adrenal (HPA) axis—often show decreased functioning (Cappadocia et al., 2009; Matthys et al., 2013).

Autism

It's suspected that as we learn more about neuroanatomy, autism will turn out to be multiple disorders (H. R. Park et al., 2016); at the very least, autism appears to have various biological correlates. One of the more robust findings is that brain volume is increased in young children with autism, but normal or decreased in teens and adults (Kolevzon, Wang, Grodberg, & Buxbaum, 2013). This implies accelerated brain growth early in life, followed by arrested brain growth or brain deterioration later (Kolevzon et al., 2013).

Numerous brain structures have been implicated in autism. The cerebellum (a brain area implicated in movement, attention, and language; see Chapter 2) appears to develop abnormally in children with autism, which might contribute to attention and communication difficulties (Fatemi, Aldinger et al., 2012; Kolevzon et al., 2013). Another important brain structure in autism is the amygdala, which is thought to play a role in social engagement. Researchers believe amygdala dysfunction affects two types of social withdrawal seen in autism: inability to maintain eye contact and difficulty processing faces (Kolevzon et al., 2013; Neuhaus, Beauchaine, & Bernier, 2010; H. R. Park et al., 2016). The caudate nucleus (important in goal-directed activity; see Chapter 4) is also worth mentioning. It is enlarged in many autistic patients and this may contribute to repetitive behaviors (Kolevzon et al., 2013). When it comes to executive functioning deficits that impair the thinking, emotion, communication, and social behavior of people with autism, the prefrontal cortex has been implicated (Neuhaus et al., 2010; Opris & Casanova, 2014; H. R. Park et al., 2016). Finally, the nucleus accumbens is important in reward-processing, which is significant because people with autism show decreased responsiveness to social rewards (H. R. Park et al., 2016).

GENETIC AND EVOLUTIONARY PERSPECTIVES

Genetic Perspectives

Disruptive Behavior

Those who believe ADHD originates primarily in genetics point to evidence from family, twin, and adoption studies. Family studies find that the parents and siblings of children with ADHD are two to eight times more likely to also qualify for a diagnosis (S. V. Faraone & Biederman, 2013). Consistent with this, twin studies have yielded very high heritability estimates for ADHD in children—somewhere between 0.76 and 0.80, which would place ADHD among the most highly heritable mental disorders (Brikell, Kuja-Halkola, & Larsson, 2015; S. V. Faraone & Biederman, 2013; S. V. Faraone et al., 2005; Thapar & Cooper, 2016; Thapar, Cooper, Eyre, & Langley, 2013). Interestingly, heritability estimates for adults are much lower (in the 0.30 to 0.40 range), although some attribute this to difficulties in diagnosing adult ADHD (Brikell et al., 2015; S. V. Faraone & Biederman, 2013; Franke et al., 2012). Finally, adoption studies also imply a genetic basis for ADHD. Adoptive relatives of children with ADHD diagnoses show lower rates of ADHD than biological relatives (S. V. Faraone & Biederman, 2013). As a quick comparison, the heritability of conduct disorder is somewhat lower than ADHD, around 0.50—which is still considered highly heritable (Salvatore & Dick, 2016).

What about specific genes associated with disruptive behavior? Although nearly 180 different genes have been identified that might be relevant to ADHD (Carrascosa-Romero & De Cabo-De La Vega, 2015), genome-wide association (GWA) studies have yet to yield any significant results (S. V. Faraone & Biederman, 2013; Middeldorp et al., 2016; Thapar et al., 2013). More broadly, various dopamine-related genes are being studied as potentially contributing to externalizing, conduct-related problems (Chhangur et al., 2015; Janssens et al., 2015). However, a lot more research is needed.

Autism

Concordance rates for autism in twin studies have varied, but generally have been high. Overall concordance has ranged from 36% to 95% for identical twins and 0% to 23% for fraternal twins (Ronald & Hoekstra, 2014; R. E. Rosenberg et al., 2009). Variation in these rates may depend on whether autism is defined narrowly or more broadly (to include less severe cases) (Ronald & Hoekstra, 2014). What about heritability? Its estimates also vary. A Japanese study estimated heritability at 0.73 for males and 0.87 for females (Ronald & Hoekstra, 2014; Taniai, Nishiyama, Miyachi, Imaeda, & Sumi, 2008). By comparison, a California study generated lower heritability estimates: 0.58 for male and 0.60 for female identical twins, compared to 0.21 for male and 0.27 for female fraternal twins (Hallmayer et al., 2011). This study's identical twin rates are comparable to those from a twin study in China that yielded a 0.61 heritability for social impairment (Deng et al., 2015). However, a Swedish study found lower autism heritability rates of 0.39 for identical twins and 0.15 for fraternal twins (Lichtenstein, Carlström, Råstam, Gillberg, & Anckarsäter, 2010). While one skeptical critic has argued that heritability estimates for autism are inflated and should only be estimated at 37% (J. Joseph, 2012), another review concluded that "most estimates of heritability in ASD are placed at 80% or higher" (Kolevzon et al., 2013, p. 77). Regardless of heritability estimate differences, most genetics researchers believe autism has a strong genetic component (Kolevzon et al., 2013; Ronald & Hoekstra, 2014; R. E. Rosenberg et al., 2009). In this vein, many genes have been identified as potentially important in autistic symptoms, though—as with many other disorders—genome-wide association results have been difficult to replicate (X. Liu & Takumi, 2014; H. R. Park et al., 2016; Persico & Napolioni, 2013).

Evolutionary Perspectives

Attention-Deficits and Hyperactivity

Several evolutionary theories of ADHD have been advanced. The **hunter-farmer theory** hypothesizes that ADHD traits evolved because they were adaptive for hunters and farmers, who needed to be vigilant (to protect crops) and able to quickly shift gears (to chase prey) (T. Hartmann, 1997; Thagaard, Faraone, Sonuga-Barke, & Østergaard, 2016). Similarly, the **response readiness theory** proposes that short attention spans and hyperactivity-impulsivity were necessary in ancestral environments where threats to safety were extreme and food was scarce (Jensen et al., 1997; Thagaard et al., 2016). There is also the **wader theory**, which says that over time humans evolved to have less body hair so they could better wade into water in search of food; this lack of hair made clinging to mothers for protection less adaptive, but those children able to get their mothers' attention through hyperactive behaviors were more likely to be breastfed

CHAPTER 13

(Shelley-Tremblay & Rosén, 1996; Thagaard et al., 2016). Finally, the **fighter theory** holds that hyperactivity and aggression evolved to help early Homo sapiens in their battles with Neanderthals (Shelley-Tremblay & Rosén, 1996; Thagaard et al., 2016). While these theories are interesting because they reframe hyperactivity and impulsivity as adaptive rather than disordered, a recent review concluded that they currently have little research support (Thagaard et al., 2016).

Autism

Let's discuss two evolutionary theories of autism. The **low-fitness extreme theory** proposes that children with the innate ability to charm their parents are more likely to receive attention and care; thus, being high on "charm" is a sign of fitness (Ploeger & Galis, 2011; Shaner, Miller, & Mintz, 2008). The low-fitness extreme theory posits that people with autism are on the extreme low end of the "charm" trait, so they don't elicit as much nurturance from caregivers (Ploeger & Galis, 2011; Shaner et al., 2008). There isn't a lot of research on this theory. Its supporters point to evidence that the charm trait emerges when babies wean from breastfeeding and that autistic children are often weaned early (Ploeger & Galis, 2011).

Psychologist Simon Baron-Cohen (1995) has proposed that people with autism experience **mindblindness** in that they don't appear to have the evolved capacity for theory of mind, the ability to view the world through others' eyes in order to attribute thoughts and feelings to them (see Chapter 4). Baron-Cohen's more recent work extends this idea by proposing **extreme male brain (EMB) theory**, which posits that people with autism are better at *systematizing* than *empathizing* (Baron-Cohen, 2002, 2009). People who systematize feel compelled to analyze and construct systems for organizing, predicting, and understanding; those who empathize monitor others' behavior and try to respond in an emotionally appropriate way (Baron-Cohen, 2009). EMB theory holds that men evolved a tendency toward systematizing (to aid in hunting and developing weapons) over empathizing (which would detract from their ability to kill enemies); women, by contrast, evolved strong empathizing skills to help them navigate family relationships and child-rearing (Baron-Cohen, 2002, 2009). While EMB theory doesn't claim that all men have "male" brains and all women "female" brains, it does claim that autism is about having a more "male" brain—which potentially explains why males are more likely to be autistic than females (Baron-Cohen, 2002, 2009; Ploeger & Galis, 2011). The evidence for EMB theory is mixed and it remains fiercely debated (Grossi & Fine, 2012; Hauth, de Bruijn, Staal, Buitelaar, & Rommelse, 2014; T. M. Krahn & Fenton, 2012; Kung et al., 2016; Voyer, 2014; Whitehouse, 2016). Critics contend that EMB theory endorses sexist gender stereotypes while overlooking evidence that male-female brain differences are minimal (Grossi & Fine, 2012; T. M. Krahn & Fenton, 2012; Voyer, 2014). Supporters of EMB theory disagree and have continued to write about and research this controversial theory (Baron-Cohen et al., 2014; Hauth et al., 2014; Whitehouse, 2016).

IMMUNE SYSTEM PERSPECTIVES

Inflammatory Hypothesis

As you recall from earlier chapters, the inflammatory hypothesis holds that many psychiatric disorders—ADHD and autism included—are tied to immune system inflammation (R. H. B. Mitchell & Goldstein, 2014). A comprehensive review identified three studies linking inflammation with ADHD in children and adolescents (R. H. B. Mitchell & Goldstein, 2014). However, by far the largest number of immune system inflammation studies (at least 39) have been on children classified along the autism spectrum (R. H. B. Mitchell & Goldstein, 2014). Inflammation studies often measure levels of pro-inflammatory cytokines, the proteins produced by immune system cells (Masi et al., 2015; V. M. Miller, Racine, & Zalcman, 2014; R. H. B. Mitchell & Goldstein, 2014). High pro-inflammatory cytokine levels cause swelling and reflect ongoing immune system activity. Research suggests a positive correlation between autism and numerous types of cytokines; as these cytokine counts rise, so do rates of autism (Gottfried, Bambini-Junior, Francis, Riesgo, & Savino, 2015; Masi et al., 2015; V. M. Miller et al., 2014; R. H. B. Mitchell & Goldstein, 2014). Of course, because this is correlational data, we can't pinpoint the exact relationship between autism and inflammation. However, research in this area is expanding rapidly (Rossignol & Frye, 2012).

Viral Infection and Autoimmune Disease Theories

The inflammatory hypothesis is deeply entwined with other immune system research examining the **viral theory of autism**. The viral theory (first mentioned in Chapter 2) holds that children with autism are more likely to have had mothers who had a viral or bacterial infection during pregnancy, especially (and maybe only) in cases warranting hospitalization (Atladóttir et al., 2010; H. Jiang et al., 2016; Lee et al., 2015; H. R. Park et al., 2016; Zerbo et al., 2015). This hypothesis is reminiscent of the viral theory of schizophrenia (see Chapter 4), which linked schizophrenia to maternal viral infections. The fact that investigators are studying similar viral theories for both autism and schizophrenia is interesting given that some symptoms of autism and schizophrenia overlap (Chisholm, Lin, Abu-Akel, & Wood, 2015; Volkmar & Cohen, 1991).

The viral theory hypothesizes that a compromised maternal immune system during pregnancy may be a risk factor for autism. A related and compatible hypothesis is the **autoimmune disease hypothesis**, which proposes that there is a connection between a family history of autoimmune disease and autism. Correlations have been found between maternal autoimmune disorders and autism in offspring (Gottfried et al., 2015; Lyall, Ashwood, Water, & Hertz-Picciotto, 2014). Similarly, an analysis of existing studies found that the chances of autism were increased by 28% in families with a history of autoimmune disorders; specific autoimmune disorders that increased risk the most were juvenile diabetes (49%), rheumatoid arthritis (51%), and psoriasis (59%) (S. Wu et al., 2015). These numbers seem alarming, but another researcher cautions that the increased risk of autism remains modest (Lyall et al., 2014).

We'd be remiss to conclude our discussion of immune system issues without addressing the purported relationship between the measles-mumps-rubella (MMR) vaccine and autism. Does getting the MMR vaccine increase the chances of autism? See the "Controversial Question" feature for more on this extremely polarizing issue.

Do Vaccines Cause Autism?

CONTROVERSIAL QUESTION

A 1998 study in the leading medical journal *The Lancet* found a link between receiving the measles-mumps-rubella (MMR) vaccine (typically administered between 12 and 15 months of age) and the development of autism symptoms (A. J. Wakefield et al., 1998). The study led to the widespread belief that the MMR vaccine can cause autism. However, most researchers and practicing doctors believe the study has been thoroughly debunked. How so? First, it's been refuted on scientific grounds, with study after study consistently finding no evidence that the MMR vaccine leads to autism (Ahearn, 2010; Demicheli, Rivetti, Debalini, & Di Pietrantonj, 2012; DeStefano, 2002; A. Jain et al., 2016; A. Jain et al., 2015; L. E. Taylor, Swerdfeger, & Eslick, 2014; Uchiyama, Kurosawa, & Inaba, 2007). Second, the study was retracted by *The Lancet* following allegations that the lead author of the paper, Dr. Andrew Wakefield, and several of his co-authors manipulated their data (T. S. S. Rao & Andrade, 2011; "Retraction—Ileal-lymphoid-nodular hyperplasia, non-specific colitis, and pervasive developmental disorder in children," 2010). It was also alleged that Wakefield had a financial conflict of interest because he received funding from a legal group seeking evidence that it could use to sue vaccine manufacturers (Deer, 2004; Godlee, Smith, & Marcovitch, 2011). In the aftermath of the controversy and his study's retraction, Wakefield's medical license was revoked by the U.K.'s General Medical Council (2010).

Despite the scandal and the consensus among most researchers that the MMR vaccine doesn't pose an autism risk, many parents continue to worry (Fischbach, Harris, Ballan, Fischbach, & Link, 2016). Because this can influence whether they have their children vaccinated, most health professionals warn that providing effective education about the safety of vaccines is critical—especially considering evidence that when vaccination rates go down, health and financial costs go up (K. F. Brown et al., 2012; Centers for Disease Control and Prevention, 2014; Demicheli et al., 2012; Godlee et al., 2011; C. King & Leask, 2017). The U.S. Centers for Disease Control and Prevention (2014) notes that before the measles vaccine, hundreds of children died every year from measles and that a 1964–65 outbreak of rubella (German measles) resulted in 12.5 million infections, 11,000 miscarriages, and the deaths of 2,000 babies.

Nonetheless, many people—including prominent celebrities such as Robert De Niro and Jenny McCarthy—continue to assert that the MMR vaccine contributes to autism and that further research on the topic is necessary (*Frontline*, 2015; H. Parry, 2016). Many research scientists have strongly pushed back, arguing that those who keep advocating the vaccine–autism link

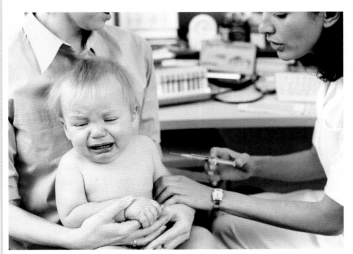

Despite a large body of research evidence suggesting otherwise, many people still believe that vaccines can cause autism.
Source: BANANASTOCK

Photo source: © Getty Images/iStockphoto Thinkstock Images\bahri altay

CHAPTER 13

aren't just wrong, but are doing serious harm (Ahearn, 2010; Godlee et al., 2011; J. F. A. Murphy, 2011). In the words of one such critic, "the damage to public health continues, fueled by unbalanced media reporting and an ineffective response from government, researchers, journals, and the medical profession" (Godlee et al., 2011, p. 65). Clearly, we haven't heard the last of this contentious debate, despite the one-sided nature of the research evidence.

CRITICAL THINKING QUESTIONS

1. Why, despite so much evidence against the vaccine–autism connection and the debunking of the original study showing such a link, do you think that some people continue to believe the MMR vaccine can cause autism?
2. Has the media perpetuated the vaccine–autism link, as some researchers believe?
3. Should more research on the vaccine–autism hypothesis be conducted or is the existing evidence that shows no link sufficient? Explain your position.

EVALUATING BIOLOGICAL PERSPECTIVES

Biological perspectives provide intriguing ways of thinking about developmental issues, but they aren't without critics. One challenge for biological perspectives is that biomarkers that can be used to make diagnoses haven't yet been discovered. Referring to ADHD, for example, one biological perspective detractor observed that "no child labeled as ADHD has met a medical standard that confirms the existence of a specific pathology connoting the disease. It can't be done because no such standard exists" (Olsen, 2012, p. 53). In other words, despite much tantalizing brain research, we currently can't diagnose ADHD and other disruptive behavior issues biologically. Perhaps because of this, some biological perspective critics worry that we too often inappropriately attribute such problems to biology rather than learning (Worley, 2014).

Similarly, while developmental problems are suspected of being highly heritable, some believe the evidence is frequently overstated. For example, certain critics argue that researchers conducting ADHD twin studies improperly make the equal environments assumption (see Chapter 4), erroneously assuming monozygotic and dizygotic twins experience identical environments even though identical twins (who look the same) are more likely to be treated similarly than fraternal twins (who don't) (J. Joseph, 2000). In ignoring this, the critics argue, twin studies minimize environmental factors and overestimate genetic ones (J. Joseph, 2000).

Finally, a lot of biological perspective research is correlational. We haven't yet identified precise causal connections between physiological factors and developmental problems. Thus, critics assert that when it comes to problems like ADHD, biological viewpoints tend to overstate the belief that it is primarily biological (Gonon, Bezard, & Boraud, 2011). Criticisms notwithstanding, biological hypotheses are highly compelling and will undoubtedly continue to influence how we conceptualize and treat developmental issues.

13.5 PSYCHOLOGICAL PERSPECTIVES

PSYCHODYNAMIC PERSPECTIVES

Disruptive Behavior

From a purely psychodynamic perspective, disruptive behavior reflects unconscious conflicts and/or attachment difficulties. Research has linked oppositional defiance, conduct issues, and other disruptive behavior problems to poor early childhood attachment relationships (Abell & Dauphin, 2009; J. P. Allen, Hauser, & Borman-Spurrell, 1996; Guttmann-Steinmetz & Crowell, 2006; Madigan, Moran, Schuengel, Pederson, & Otten, 2007; M. Nowak, Gawęda, Jelonek, & Janas-Kozik, 2013; Waters, Posada, Crowell, & Keng-ling, 1993). The implications are quite intuitive when you think about them. Children lacking secure attachments to caregivers are more likely to develop disruptive behavior problems.

Regarding ADHD specifically, some psychodynamic conceptions are consistent with attachment perspectives. For instance, object relations therapy views ADHD as tied to disturbed early parent–child interactions and attachment trauma (Conway, 2012, 2014, 2015; Salomonsson, 2004, 2011; Sugarman, 2006; Widener, 1998). In a slightly different vein, other psychodynamic approaches to ADHD emphasize ego functioning. Recall that in psychoanalytic theory, the ego is governed by the reality principle; the ego tries to fulfill id impulses based on what's practical and possible. From an ego psychology perspective, ADHD is attributable to a dysfunctional ego—which is why executive functioning is impaired (Conway, 2012; Gilmore, 2000, 2002). In both object relations and ego-oriented therapies, therapists work with transference and countertransference issues in session (Conway, 2014, 2015; Salomonsson, 2004).

A psychodynamic case study provides a vivid example of interpreting transference (Conway, 2014). Jason, a 10-year-old boy diagnosed with ADHD, is bored during a session and begins climbing on the furniture. When he nearly falls, the therapist asks him to stop climbing and Jason responds that she is no fun. The therapist replies, "Being expected to follow the rules when you are feeling the need to do something about your 'boredom' may seem to benefit me more than you." When Jason agrees, the therapist responds by saying "I believe I now understand how difficult it has been for you" (Conway, 2014, p. 108), then adds "Can you describe other times that you have experienced being bored and how you handled it?" This is a nice example of the therapist using the unfolding dynamic between herself and Jason to explore how Jason feels and behaves in other relationships. In other words, the therapist explores transference issues to help Jason share his own feelings, which in turn reduces his need to express those feelings through disruptive behavior. Most research on psychodynamic conceptions of disruptive behavior are case studies like this one, but experimental studies are increasingly being done and, according to a report by the American Academy of Child and Adolescent Psychiatry, show some promise (P. F. Kernberg, Ritvo, & Keable, 2012).

Autism

Given their past tendency to blame "refrigerator mothers," psychodynamic perspectives on autism remain controversial. Not surprisingly then, psychoanalysis for autism is rare. One place where it remains influential is France. However, there has been a strong backlash against this—with parents, autism advocacy groups, and behavior therapists lambasting the continued use of psychoanalysis with autistic patients (C. Harris, 2016; Schofield, 2012). French psychoanalysts counter that viewing autism strictly as brain dysfunction to be managed through medication and behavioral conditioning overlooks the central underlying conflicts behind the disturbance. However, critics insist that psychoanalysis for autism doesn't work and that French psychoanalysts stubbornly cling to an outdated view autism as a form of psychosis rooted in early family dynamics (C. Harris, 2016; Schofield, 2012).

Some psychoanalysts do take a more moderate stance, accepting autism as a neurodevelopmental brain disorder (Emanuel, 2015; Sherkow, Harrison, & Singletary, 2014). They employ psychoanalysis to help people with autism be more relationally attuned, thus improving perspective-taking and social skills. Rather than blaming parents, this sort of psychoanalytic approach sees analysts as "sensitive translators" who decode and convey to parents what children with autism are thinking and feeling (Emanuel, 2015; D. Mann, 2008; Sherkow et al., 2014). There is little research on psychoanalysis for autism, mostly case studies. Thus, psychodynamic perspectives remain controversial and on the fringes of autism treatment.

COGNITIVE-BEHAVIORAL PERSPECTIVES

Disruptive Behavior

Behavior Therapy for ADHD

Behavior therapies are probably the most well-regarded interventions for ADHD. Behavior modification techniques such as contingency management (see Chapter 11) are often used, which involve analyzing and then altering the environment to reinforce desired behaviors and ignore or discourage undesired ones (Waschbusch & Waxmonsky, 2015). In school settings, this might involve "developing specific and concrete rules for the child to follow, developing a system for tracking rule adherence and rule violations, and developing positive and negative consequences that are contingent on the child's performance during school" (Waschbusch & Waxmonsky, 2015, p. 399). Behavior therapies for ADHD have fared extremely well in studies examining their effectiveness, resulting in them being consistently recommended as empirically supported interventions (Fabiano et al., 2009; Hodgson, Hutchinson, & Denson, 2014; Vallerand, Kalenchuk, & McLennan, 2014; Waschbusch & Waxmonsky, 2015). While beneficial, the effects of behavior therapies aren't permanent; when such therapies end, problematic behaviors often return (something also true of medication) (Waschbusch & Waxmonsky, 2015). Further, not all children respond to behavior therapies, though this might be because the therapies are often poorly implemented (Waschbusch & Waxmonsky, 2015). Limitations notwithstanding, behavior therapies are considered highly effective for ADHD, perhaps equally or more effective than medication (S. Baldwin, 1999; Pelham et al., 2014; Pelham et al., 2016).

CHAPTER 13

CBT for ADHD

Cognitive-behavioral therapy (CBT) for ADHD combines cognitive and behavioral techniques. Common interventions include social skills training (teaching clients to read social cues and respond accordingly), **problem-solving skills training** (teaching planning, organization, and management skills), psychoeducation (teaching clients about how ADHD influences them so they can better implement cognitive strategies for overcoming it), and cognitive restructuring (helping clients better identify and reduce automatic, negative thoughts and cognitive distortions) (He & Antshel, 2016; Knouse & Fleming, 2016; J. T. Mitchell, Benson, Knouse, Kimbrel, & Anastopoulos, 2013; Puente & Mitchell, 2016; J. R. Ramsay, 2010, 2017; Sprich, Knouse, Cooper-Vince, Burbridge, & Safren, 2010; Storebø et al., 2011). When it comes to effectiveness, the evidence base for CBT is mixed. Some studies imply that CBT for ADHD is reasonably effective (Emilsson et al., 2011; Toplak, Connors, Shuster, Knezevic, & Parks, 2008; Virta et al., 2010). Others suggest that the more cognitive-oriented interventions—while intuitively appealing and promising—may not consistently work (Antshel & Olszewski, 2014; Barry & Haraway, 2005; Hodgson et al., 2014; L. Seligman & Reichenberg, 2007; Waschbusch & Waxmonsky, 2015). Of course, ADHD involves both attention and hyperactivity-impulsivity; some believe CBT works better for the former than the latter (He & Antshel, 2016). Unfortunately, one of the difficulties in evaluating CBT studies is that CBT is a broad term and the interventions tested aren't always comparable, making it hard to generalize (He & Antshel, 2016). The overall takeaway message is that when it comes to CBT for ADHD, cognitive techniques are usually viewed as less effective than behavioral ones (Antshel & Olszewski, 2014; Waschbusch & Waxmonsky, 2015).

CBT and Other Disruptive Behaviors

There isn't much research on treatment for impulse-control diagnoses such as kleptomania, pyromania, and intermittent explosive disorder. Nonetheless, behavioral interventions are commonly used (e.g., relaxation training, systematic desensitization, aversive conditioning, and assertiveness training) (L. Seligman & Reichenberg, 2007). One review found CBT especially helpful in reducing oppositional-defiance (Battagliese et al., 2015). However, another study found that when comorbid with ADHD, oppositional-defiant children were viewed by their parents as responding less well to CBT than children experiencing depression and anxiety (Antshel, Faraone, & Gordon, 2014). More research is clearly needed.

Autism

Applied Behavior Analysis (ABA)

Behavioral perspectives for autism are among the most researched and utilized (Seligman & Reichenberg, 2007). They are often rooted in **applied behavior analysis (ABA)**, which employs behavioral principles to understand how, on a case-by-case basis, environmental stimuli condition behavior in patients with developmental disabilities (Vismara & Rogers, 2010). The goal of ABA, which is often implemented in school or residential settings, is to use the resulting knowledge to change the environment and therefore condition alternative behaviors. A type of ABA used for autism is **discrete trial training (DTT)**. DTT is a highly structured approach that teaches concrete skills in a step-by-step manner using reinforcement and other behavioral techniques (Kodak & Grow, 2011; T. Smith, 2001; Vismara & Rogers, 2010). When DTT is used with patients under age 5, it is called **early and intensive behavioral intervention (EIBI)** (Vismara & Rogers, 2010). As its name implies, EIBI aims to intervene early in the child's life (before age 5) and intensively (20–40 hours per week) (Vismara & Rogers, 2010).

Discrete trial training (DTT) is a type of applied behavior analysis (ABA) often used to treat autism; when conducted with children under age 5, it is called early and intensive behavioral intervention (EIBI).
Source: iStock.com/SerrNovik

DTT and EIBI involve taking complex skills that people with autism often struggle with and dividing them into concrete subskills, which are then intensively taught to patients using behavioral learning strategies. For example, social skills training might be employed in which social interactions are broken into specific skills, such as making eye contact, listening to what the other person says, and speaking in turn. Children are reinforced for mastering these subskills and combining them into more complex behaviors. For children with more limited language skills, the **Picture Exchange Communication System (PECS)** can be used, in which the child learns to communicate using picture cards. In PECS, behavioral techniques help autistic children use the cards to build complete sentences, ask and answer questions, and convey increasingly intricate ideas (Bondy & Frost, 2002; Vismara & Rogers, 2010). Although the number of controlled studies isn't that large and some have methodological shortcomings, research does find that DTT, EIBI, PECS, social skills training, and other ABA interventions are helpful in treating autism (Axelrod, McElrath, & Wine, 2012; Bishop-Fitzpatrick, Minshew, & Eack, 2013; Palmen, Didden, & Lang, 2012; T. Smith & Iadarola, 2015; Vismara & Rogers, 2010). Many professionals and parents see behavioral approaches as the best supported psychotherapeutic interventions for autism, but investigators nonetheless point out that additional research is needed to refine behavioral strategies (Kodak & Grow, 2011; Vismara & Rogers, 2010).

Hernando

Hernando, our 3-year-old autistic case example client, undergoes EIBI until he turns 5, when he enrolls in a special school for autistic children. At that time, he begins DTT. During his DTT sessions, appropriate forms of communication and social interaction are positively reinforced, while problematic behaviors are ignored. For instance, when Hernando averts his gaze from his DTT instructor, the instructor asks him to look at her. When he does, the therapist positively reinforces this by praising him and giving him a Cheerio to eat. Over the course of many DTT sessions, Hernando's social interaction skills improve.

CASE EXAMPLES

Cognitive-Behavioral Therapy (CBT)

CBT is often employed to reduce accompanying anxiety and depression in people with autism. When using CBT with autistic populations, some adjustments must be made to accommodate and help patients overcome communication difficulties, problems with tolerating change and uncertainty, and alexithymia (difficulty identifying and expressing emotions; see Chapter 8) (Spain, Sin, Chalder, Murphy, & Happé, 2015). CBT perspectives must also account for the **weak central coherence theory**, which holds that people with autism prefer focusing on parts, not wholes (Happé & Frith, 2006). This cognitive emphasis on details over the more global picture helps explain why people with autism often struggle to see the forest through the trees (Happé & Frith, 2006). Thus, to reduce depression and anxiety, CBT cognitively teaches autistic patients to be aware of the cognitive distortions they make, while also working with them behaviorally on concrete skill development. More studies are needed, but existing evidence suggests CBT interventions do indeed reduce anxiety and depression in children with autism, though there is less agreement on whether the reductions are as great as those that occur in children without autism (Sukhodolsky, Bloch, Panza, & Reichow, 2013; Ung, Selles, Small, & Storch, 2015; van Steensel & Bögels, 2015; J. J. Wood et al., 2015).

HUMANISTIC PERSPECTIVES

Person-Centered Perspectives

Child-Centered Play Therapy for Externalizing and Internalizing Problems

Child-centered play therapy (also called *person-centered play therapy*) is used for both externalizing and internalizing childhood problems, including disruptive behavior issues and autism (J. L. Cochran, Cochran, Cholette, & Nordling, 2011; J. L. Cochran, Cochran, Nordling, McAdam, & Miller, 2010; Paone & Douma, 2009; Ray, Sullivan, & Carlson, 2012; VanFleet, Sywulak, & Sniscak, 2010). Pioneered by psychologist Virginia Axline (1947a, 1947b, 1950, 1964), it adapts Carl Rogers' (1951, 1959) non-directive person-centered therapy (PCT) for use with children (see Chapter 2 for a refresher on PCT). Child-centered play therapists rely on carefully selected toys, games, sandboxes, arts and crafts, and other play activities as the means for children to express feelings and work through issues (Ray et al., 2013). Consistent with the person-centered tradition, the child-centered play therapist provides core conditions for change by being genuine, empathic, and unconditionally accepting of the child

Child-centered play therapy uses toys to help children express their feelings and work through issues; the therapist provides core conditions for change—empathy, genuineness, and unconditional positive regard.
Source: BRAND X

CHAPTER 13

(Behr, Nuding, & McGinnis, 2013; Bratton, Ray, Edwards, & Landreth, 2009; Ray & Jayne, 2016; VanFleet et al., 2010). Person-centered therapists believe such a nurturing relationship promotes the child's innate tendency toward growth and self-actualization (Behr et al., 2013; Ray & Jayne, 2016). The following quote from a client-centered play therapist working with of a 6-year-old autistic boy named Andrew captures how different this approach is compared to behavioral interventions:

> *Andrew's increased desire to be in relationship with the play therapist was not the result of being rewarded for staying on task or demonstrating particular play behaviors but because he was open to receiving the acceptance and unconditional positive regard offered by the play therapist, demonstrating his intrinsic motivation. (Ray et al., 2012, p. 172)*

Consistent with their emphasis on unconditional positive regard, humanistic therapists are skeptical of diagnostic labels like ADHD, oppositional defiant disorder, conduct disorder, intermittent explosive disorder, and even autism—which they see as judgmental and often scientifically unsupported diagnoses reflecting the medicalization of human conflicts and differences (Breggin, 2001; Dowling, 2006; Edwards, 2008; B. E. Levine, 2005; Quinn & Lynch, 2016; Rutten, 2014; Worley, 2014). Instead, child-centered play therapy relies on a nonjudgmental relationship that accepts children for who they are and assumes that providing core conditions will naturally foster change (Axline, 1947b; Behr et al., 2013; Ray & Jayne, 2016). Research on child-centered play therapy in educational and clinical settings points to its effectiveness, both for disruptive behavior problems and autism (Bratton et al., 2013; Bratton et al., 2009; Ray, Armstrong, Balkin, & Jayne, 2015; Ray, Blanco, Sullivan, & Holliman, 2009; Ray & Jayne, 2016; Ray, Schottelkorb, & Tsai, 2007; Salter, Beamish, & Davies, 2016; VanFleet et al., 2010). However, as with other humanistic therapy research, the methodological rigor of child-centered play therapy studies has been questioned (R. D. Phillips, 2010).

Hernando

Child-centered play therapy with our autistic client, Hernando, at age 5 would involve the therapist trying to enter and understand Hernando's world. Although Hernando might not initially engage much with the therapist, the therapist would use reflective listening to empathize with him. If Hernando was to neatly line up his toy cars in a row, the therapist could say, "Now they're just how you want them." When, after several sessions, if Hernando engages the therapist by handing her several of his toy cars, she might respond, "You want me to play, too." The idea would be to help Hernando tap into his innate need for connection and personal growth by accepting him as he is.

CASE EXAMPLES

From "Autism" to "Autistic Process"

Humanistic therapists caution against seeing autism as something unacceptable that must be changed (Ray et al., 2012; Rutten, 2014). Many prefer to speak of **autistic process**, not autistic disorder (Rutten, 2014). In this line of thinking, people with autistic process experience the world differently than **neurotypicals** (people without autism or other neurodevelopmental diagnoses), but they aren't broken or ill.

Person-centered therapy doesn't see autistic process as disordered, so it doesn't try to cure it. Rather, person-centered therapy for autistic process provides core conditions to help clients understand and accept themselves (Rutten, 2014). When more severe communication difficulties are present, pre-therapy (a variant of person-centered therapy used for psychosis; see Chapter 4) can be used (Rutten, 2014). Thus, all person-centered therapies assume that even though "clients with autism may have a qualitatively different process, there is nothing 'wrong' with that and it does not need 'fixing'" (Rutten, 2014, p. 84). Unfortunately, research on person-centered approaches to autistic process remains underdeveloped (Rutten, 2014). "The Lived Experience" box offers a powerful firsthand account of what it's like to experience autistic process from someone who wasn't diagnosed until adulthood but always knew he was different.

THE LIVED EXPERIENCE

Growing Up Undiagnosed

Early Signs of Autism

My parents knew something was wrong from the time I was two weeks old. I screamed for no apparent reason throughout the day and night for many months. My early life was complicated by the onset of severe eczema and a number of allergies, including intolerance to dairy products.

I didn't demand attention, wouldn't smile or wave goodbye and also responded poorly to speech. I barely babbled and did not engage in proto conversations. I showed very little interest in the environment and was very sensitive to smells, less so to noise.

Misreading the Characteristics

I didn't like to be cuddled and showed no desire to be picked up and at first my parents suspected that this may have been caused by the eczema.

Growing up, I did not respond to physical affection or seek comfort when I was distressed. I lacked empathy and tended to stare a lot at people. My parents and I made a number of visits to both doctors and psychologists, hoping to get an answer for my odd behaviours but they only focused on my skin and epilepsy.

Coping with Mainstream School and Making Friends

I coped relatively well in mainstream schools and I think over the years I have learnt to modify my behaviour and learnt a lot mainly thanks to the help from the communications class at my last ever school, where I first heard about Asperger syndrome. It was from there that I slowly but surely started to like myself, rather than wondering why I was indifferent.

I'm lucky compared to others as I always had a small group of friends, who were always there for me regardless of my need. We are still in touch with each other, which is a good sign as they have seen it all through my highs and lows. I tried so hard to fit in with others outside my circle of real friends back at high school, probably too hard.

I just wanted to let them know that I always liked them, I just couldn't put my thoughts into words back then and sometimes couldn't control what I said, I just came out with things without thinking. I still occasionally fall back into that habit but very rarely these days, I guess it is part of autism. Today, I have a fantastic social life and a number of great friends—they know who they are and I will always thank them and regard it a pleasure to be part of their lives.

Trying to Find a Job

The only downside that remains ever since I left college upbeat and really happy, has been the lack of job opportunities. Over the past five years my jobs have been very limited. I've only been lucky enough to have had seasonal and voluntary positions in gardening and working for a local charity but never had a full or even a part-time job, which made me feel pretty down and depressed in the past.

Those who denied me an opportunity should think again; I've remained cheerful and positive considering the outcome and believed in my own ability, regardless.

I'm 26 years old and just lately things are starting to take shape. I've been taking driving lessons and was given the all clear by my medical centre back in the summer of 2009, the same time I finally got diagnosed with high functioning autism.

The way I see it, I have already beaten the odds and should I pass my driving test I will see it as a bonus more than anything else, as it will almost certainly improve my independence and could open many doors for me—but I won't stop there.

Getting Qualifications

I'm also about to start a sports coaching course at a residential college. I know I've managed to cope in mainstream schools and colleges over the years and believe I've got to the age where I'm more mature and see this by no means as a backwards step but as a forwards step.

This will be the first time I will be going into special education. I will make up for the mistakes I made in my past and know that I can get the right support there if I ask, something I didn't really have as such in the past when I needed it the most.

I am more keen to learn than ever before and I believe the only way from here is up. I hope to reward my whole family and friends for their support and understanding. All my past, present and future success is for you lot.

Thank you so much for your time and efforts, it means a lot to me—I wouldn't be who I am today without you and I'm no way ashamed of my autism; it makes me who I am today and now I have the social skills, am proud and most importantly see the strengths it brings.

By Andy Kirtland.
Reproduced with permission from The National Autistic Society—www.autism.org.uk

Narrative Therapy

Narrative therapy (see Chapter 2) emphasizes externalizing the problem, in which clients reframe their problems as separate entities outside themselves that sometimes get the best of them (White & Epston, 1990). In so doing, clients distinguish times they resisted the problem, which highlights solutions for coping with it. Externalizing also reduces self-stigmatization (defined in Chapter 12) because clients come to view the problem as distinct from them rather than at the core of who they are (White & Epston, 1990).

Narrative therapy can be used to address aggression and other disruptive behaviors in children diagnosed with things like ADHD, oppositional-defiant disorder, conduct-disorder, and autism (Cashin, 2008; Cashin, Browne, Bradbury, & Mulder, 2013; Ingamells & Epston, 2014; J. Johnson, 2012; Nylund & Corsiglia, 1996). For example, a case study on Justin, an Asperger's client with an explosive temper, described how he externalized his anger as "the bang" (Cashin, 2008). Justin was asked to keep a diary in which he mapped times when "the bang" snuck up on him. He and his therapist also wrote a letter to the school asking them to assist Justin in keeping "the bang" in check. As Justin and his school cooperated in finding exceptions (times they outsmarted "the bang" and kept it from influencing Justin), Justin's anger outbursts decreased. Research on narrative therapy for disruptive behavior is almost non-existent, but one exploratory study did find it improved the school behavior of 9- to 11-year-old girls diagnosed with ADHD (Yoosefi Looyeh, Kamali, & Shafieian, 2012).

EVALUATING PSYCHOLOGICAL PERSPECTIVES
Behavior Therapy vs. Drugs for ADHD

Among psychological interventions for ADHD, behavior therapies stand out as having the most extensive and compelling research support (Fabiano, Schatz, Aloe, Chacko, & Chronis-Tuscano, 2015; Waschbusch & Waxmonsky, 2015). Given their strong research base, many consider them a viable alternative to medication—especially those concerned about giving stimulant medications to children. Those favoring behavior therapies for ADHD point to evidence that such therapies are equally, if not more, effective than drugs (S. Baldwin, 1999; Pelham et al., 2014). Consistent with this, one study found that providing behavioral treatment before medication produced better outcomes than providing medication before behavioral treatment (Pelham et al., 2016). Another study found supplementing CBT with medication was no more effective than using CBT alone to treat ADHD (M. Weiss et al., 2012). Of course, not all research supports these findings; other ADHD research has found stimulant drugs more effective than psychological interventions (E. Chan, Fogler, & Hammerness, 2016; Sonuga-Barke et al., 2013).

Those who believe behavior therapies are equally as effective as medication sometimes wonder why behavior therapies are often overlooked in favor of drug treatments. Medications have the advantage of being quick and easy to provide; behavior therapies are more time-consuming and complicated to administer. Still, for those who disapprove of prescribing stimulants to children, behavior interventions are preferable. You'll need to resolve the therapy versus drugs debate for yourself. Whatever you conclude, it's worth remembering that neither behavior therapies nor medication are cure-alls. Both are only effective while being used; once withdrawn, symptoms tend to return (Waschbusch & Waxmonsky, 2015). Thus, behavior therapies and medication manage, but don't eliminate, ADHD symptoms.

Psychological Therapies for Autism

Most research on psychological interventions for autism focus on ABA and CBT approaches. While existing research suggests these interventions can be beneficial, the number of studies remains small (Bishop-Fitzpatrick et al., 2013; Kodak & Grow, 2011). Further research, especially on long-term effectiveness, is needed (Vismara & Rogers, 2010).

13.6 SOCIOCULTURAL PERSPECTIVES
CROSS-CULTURAL AND SOCIAL JUSTICE PERSPECTIVES
Cultural and Social Influences

Culture Bias, Gender Bias, and Inequality

Sociocultural theorists are interested in how factors like gender, race, culture, and economic inequality influence or lead to the developmental issues many children face. They ask a variety of provocative questions, thereby challenging conventional understandings of childhood difficulties that don't pay much attention to social influences. As a few examples of such questions, consider the following:

» Why are boys diagnosed with ADHD, conduct problems, and autism more than girls? Is this due to differences in the prevalence of these problems or, alternatively, is there gender bias in how we interpret boy versus girl behavior (Abell & Dauphin, 2009; Rollins, 2007)?

» Why are levels of autism often higher among those from socially deprived or immigrant backgrounds (Delobel-Ayoub et al., 2015)?

» Why are racial and ethnic minorities less likely to have their autism correctly identified (Burkett, Morris, Manning-Courtney, Anthony, & Shambley-Ebron, 2015; Mandell, Wiggins, & Carpenter, 2009)?

» Why are rates of ADHD much higher in the U.S. (G. Russell et al., 2014)? Are U.S. children intrinsically more hyperactive or might there be something about American culture that increases rates of ADHD diagnosis?

Those coming from a sociocultural perspective warn us not to overlook these sorts of questions. They argue that more individualized perspectives (both biological and psychological) regularly downplay the extent to which childhood developmental issues are impacted by or reflect social customs and cultural values. Yet teasing out sociocultural influences on developmental problems that are typically considered to be biological brain disorders isn't easy.

Importantly, many sociocultural theorists see their perspective as supplementing, not replacing, biological and psychological viewpoints. They accept traditional developmental diagnoses such as ADHD, ODD, conduct disorder, reactive attachment disorder, and autism spectrum disorder, but believe that important social variables are ignored. As noted, critics complain that rates of ADHD diagnosis are grossly inflated, especially in the United States (Hinshaw & Scheffler, 2014; G. Russell et al., 2014; Schwarz, 2016; Schwarz & Cohen, 2013). They attribute this to various social factors. One suspected social factor is a short-attention-span culture that discourages patience and prolonged attention by operating at an increasingly frenetic pace while simultaneously demanding enhanced performance, attention, and productivity (T. Armstrong, 1995; Schwarz, 2016). Other suspected social factors include problematic parenting dynamics, boring classrooms, a breakdown in social hierarchies such that children no longer respect and obey authority figures, and normal gender differences between boys and girls (in which boys, due to a combination of nature and nurture, struggle to sit still and pay attention) (T. Armstrong, 1995). To a sociocultural sensibility, addressing these sorts of relational and social issues would lead to fewer people being misdiagnosed with ADHD and other disruptive behavior problems.

Reframing Developmental Disorders as Social Constructions

Unlike those who accept biological and psychological conceptions but want social factors to be weighted more heavily, other sociocultural theorists push in a more thoroughly social direction. Some of these theorists see developmental disorders not as biological or psychological givens, but as social constructions—socially shared ways of defining, talking about, and understanding things that establish how people experience them (see Chapter 2). In the social constructionist view, medicalized childhood diagnoses such as ADHD, ODD, conduct disorder, and autism spectrum disorder are contestable culturally rooted social inventions, not universal disorders (Abell & Dauphin, 2009; Danforth & Navarro, 2001; Rafalovich, 2004; M. Smith, 2012; Timimi & Taylor, 2003). When children behave in ways that are deemed to be "disruptive," we rely on taken-for-granted Western social constructions that attribute problematic behaviors to something biologically or psychologically broken inside people. The result? Socially constructed diagnostic categories are treated as universally true things, rather than culturally derived understandings that reflect the social and political commitments of those who invented them. For example, many Western societies are committed to the Protestant work ethic, in which people are expected to direct focused time and energy toward reaching high levels of achievement. Such societies "might well be expected to define deviance in terms of distractibility, impulsiveness, and lack of motivation," making the socially constructed notion of ADHD "a means through which our society attempts to preserve its underlying value system" (T. Armstrong, 1995, p. 27).

Some critics argue that this boy's disruptive behavior might be better understood as a response to social conditions (e.g., underfunded schools, overworked parents, and a culture that encourages instant gratification) rather than a mental disorder.
Source: Brand X Pictures\Rubberball/Nicole Hill

In other words, "a medicalized approach often fails to acknowledge that researchers who 'discover' childhood disorders and professionals making diagnoses of those disorders operate within a constructive and contested discursive field of political and normative meanings about the lives of children" (Danforth & Navarro, 2001, p. 167). From a social justice point of view, when social constructions are mistaken for universal truths, oppression often results. Disruptive behavior problems are conceptualized as illnesses, rather than interpersonal or political conflicts (Rafalovich, 2004). Consequently, the individual unfairly becomes the target of intervention instead of previously mentioned social problems such as poor parenting, bad schools, and a short-attention-span culture. Oppression is perpetuated because current social inequities are maintained. As one stern critic of medical models of ADHD and other disruptive behavior problems explained it, "what better way to maintain the status quo than to view inattention,

CHAPTER 13

anger, anxiety, and depression as biochemical problems of those who are mentally ill rather than normal reactions to an increasingly authoritarian society" (B. E. Levine, 2012, para. 18)?

Sumiko and Michael

CASE EXAMPLES

A social justice perspective might conceptualize case example client Sumiko's "ODD" as a socially constructed label that reflects cultural biases against girls who are assertive rather than compliant. Sumiko's refusal to do as she is told might be the only way she knows how to resist social norms that demand she behave in more deferent ways. Similarly, a social justice perspective might deconstruct 15-year-old Michael's "conduct disorder" diagnosis, viewing it as a convenient way to lay the blame on Michael rather than on broader social forces such as racism and economic inequality that have prevented Michael from getting the support he needs to develop in more prosocial ways. Social justice-oriented therapy with Sumiko and Michael might help them better understand—and resist—oppressive social norms and restrictions while challenging the idea that their problems are purely due to individual deficits.

Environmental Factors

Environmental Toxins

Environmental toxin hypotheses posit that developmental difficulties in children are associated with exposure to pollution and other environmental toxins (Dietrich, 2010). ADHD has been linked to a variety of such toxins—especially lead and tobacco, but also pesticides, mercury, PCBs (chemicals used as coolants), PBDEs (chemicals used as flame retardant building materials), PFCs (chemicals used to make products grease and stain resistant), Bisphenol A (a synthetic compound in some plastics), and airborne pollutants (Braun, Kahn, Froehlich, Auinger, & Lanphear, 2006; Lanphear, 2015; Polańska, Jurewicz, & Hanke, 2012). Conduct disorder and other externalizing behavior problems have also been tied to environmental toxins, most notably lead exposure and maternal smoking during pregnancy (Braun et al., 2008; Desrosiers et al., 2013; Gaysina et al., 2013; Lanphear, 2015; Slotkin, 2013). Finally, autism has been linked to toxins, as well. Prenatal exposure to lead, alcohol, mercury, folate (a type of Vitamin B), and insecticides have all been correlated with increased autism risk in offspring (A. S. Brown et al., 2018; Landrigan, 2010; Lanphear, 2015; Raghavan et al., 2016).

The major weaknesses of environmental toxin research are that (a) its results haven't always been replicated (Braun et al., 2014; van Wijngaarden et al., 2017); and (b) it is correlational and cannot be used to infer cause (though it often is, perhaps unnecessarily alarming people) (Hamblin, 2016). Still, if environmental pollutants do contribute to developmental issues, then we face a social justice issue—one in which taking political action to prevent toxin exposure becomes an important preventative measure to reduce the prevalence of internalizing and externalizing problems (Koger, Schettler, & Weiss, 2005). From a social justice perspective, decreasing toxin exposure also demands addressing economic inequality. Why? Because research has found environmental toxin exposure is greatest among people of low socioeconomic status (SES) (Tyrrell, Melzer, Henley, Galloway, & Osborne, 2013).

Diet

A variety of dietary hypotheses about ADHD have been proposed. Over forty years ago, pediatric allergist Benjamin Feingold advanced a **food additives hypothesis**, which holds that additives in food (such as synthetic food coloring) lead to ADHD (M. Smith, 2011). He developed and recommended the **Feingold Diet**, which eliminates food additives from the diets of ADHD-diagnosed children (Schnoll, Burshteyn, & Cea-Aravena, 2003; M. Smith, 2011). In a similar vein, the **excessive sugar-intake hypothesis** holds that ADHD symptoms are caused or made worse by too much intake of refined sugars (R. Schnoll et al., 2003). Diets based on this hypothesis recommend restricting sugar consumption to lessen ADHD symptoms. Finally, the **polyunsaturated fatty acids (PUFA) hypothesis** proposes that ADHD is caused or exacerbated by PUFA deficiencies (Gillies, Sinn, Lad, Leach, & Ross, 2012; Hawkey & Nigg, 2014). Thus, the dietary solution is to increase PUFA intake.

The evidence base for these diets is mixed. Recent research suggests that while food additives probably don't cause ADHD, eliminating them from a child's diet may sometimes reduce ADHD symptoms (how much remains debated and because such diets can be difficult to implement, they can be disruptive in certain families) (Arnold, Lofthouse, & Hurt, 2012; K. Eagle, 2014; Millichap & Yee, 2012; Nigg, Lewis, Edinger, & Falk, 2012;

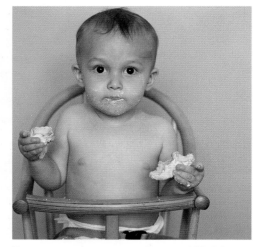

Does too much sugar contribute to ADHD?
Source: © Royalty-Free/Corbis

Sonuga-Barke et al., 2013; Stevenson et al., 2014). Likewise, some studies have linked sugar consumption to childhood and adolescent ADHD and conduct problems (Lien, Lien, Heyerdahl, Thoresen, & Bjertness, 2006; Yu et al., 2016); others haven't (Ghanizadeh & Haddad, 2015). Finally, some investigators have found PUFA diets produce small decreases in ADHD symptoms (Hawkey & Nigg, 2014; Sonuga-Barke et al., 2013; Stevenson et al., 2014), but other investigators have concluded there is no effect (Gillies et al., 2012). While the overall quality of existing dietary studies has been questioned, the last few years have seen renewed enthusiasm about and research into dietary interventions for ADHD (Nigg, 2013; Nigg et al., 2012; Tarver et al., 2014).

Mark
Should case example client Mark's parents have concerns about stimulant medication, one alternative would be for them to explore whether dietary changes might help reduce his ADHD symptoms.

ADHD and conduct problems aren't the only developmental issues where dietary factors are considered important. The **gluten/casein-free diet hypothesis** maintains that a diet low in *gluten* (proteins in wheat) and *casein* (a protein in milk) can reduce symptoms of autism (J. H. Elder, 2008). This hypothesis posits that when the gut fails to fully breakdown foods high in gluten and casein, high levels of opioid peptides result. These peptides enter the blood stream, cross the blood–brain barrier, and negatively affect neural transmission, leading to autism symptoms (J. H. Elder, 2008). While a few researchers contend that a gluten/casein-free diet can improve autism symptoms (Whiteley, 2015; Whiteley et al., 2010), a larger number argue that there is little or no scientific support for such a claim (Ahearn, 2010; Hurwitz, 2013; S. L. Hyman et al., 2016; Lange, Hauser, & Reissmann, 2015; Marí-Bauset, Zazpe, Mari-Sanchis, Llopis-González, & Morales-Suárez-Varela, 2014; Mulloy et al., 2010, 2011). As an alternative, the PUFA diet used for ADHD is also sometimes used for autism, but—as with ADHD—there isn't much evidence for its effectiveness (Ahearn, 2010; Gillies et al., 2012). Despite their weak evidence base, many parents of children diagnosed with autism nonetheless swear by these diets.

CONSUMER AND SERVICE-USER PERSPECTIVES

Stigma

Children and adolescents diagnosed with developmental issues often experience stigma (Linton, 2014; O'Driscoll, Heary, Hennessy, & McKeague, 2012; Ohan, Visser, Moss, & Allen, 2013; Rogalin & Nencini, 2015; J. S. Walker, Coleman, Lee, Squire, & Friesen, 2008). Of special concern is self-stigmatization. When people self-stigmatize, they internalize negative beliefs about themselves. There is some evidence that children and teens with developmental diagnoses self-stigmatize (Ali, Hassiotis, Strydom, & King, 2012; McKeague, Hennessy, O'Driscoll, & Heary, 2015; Wiener et al., 2012). Interestingly, age of diagnosis may impact degree of stigma, especially in autism; in one study, people diagnosed earlier in life tended to have higher levels of self-esteem and reported less workplace discrimination when disclosing their diagnosis (T. D. Johnson & Joshi, 2016). Thus, an autism diagnosis may not have purely negative consequences. Such a diagnosis—while stigmatizing—can also provoke self-discovery by providing a framework for understanding one's experiences (Linton, 2014).

Thinking beyond patients themselves, children with disorders like ADHD and autism aren't alone in their experience of stigma. Their parents and families often feel stigmatized, too (Broady, Stoyles, & Morse, 2017). This is called **courtesy stigma** (or *associative stigma*) and it involves being stigmatized simply by being associated with a family member with a developmental issue or other stigmatized problem (Ali et al., 2012; dosReis, Barksdale, Sherman, Maloney, & Charach, 2010; Koro-Ljungberg & Bussing, 2009; Thibodeau & Finley, 2016). A recent qualitative study captured the lived experience of courtesy stigma. It found parents of autistic children tended to feel judged, rejected, and unsupported (Broady et al., 2017). As one parent put it, "we lost a lot of friends because no one wants to hang out with people with a baby that's screaming and yelling and bashing against the wall" (Broady et al., 2017, p. 229). When it comes to developmental issues, stigma is often a family affair.

Identity and Asperger's

When the *DSM-5* announced the removal of Asperger's, many self-declared "Aspies" were upset (Annear, 2013; Rosin, 2014). The diagnosis had provided them with a strong sense of identity and many "felt like something … was being ripped away from them" (Annear, 2013, para. 10). This sentiment was confirmed in a qualitative study examining identity concerns of people previously diagnosed with the now-defunct Asperger's diagnosis. A lot of patients worried about what this meant for their sense of identity, especially given that many people who identify as "Aspies" reject the idea that they have a disorder to be cured. Thus, they worry about being pathologized by the new autism spectrum disorder diagnosis. As the study's authors put it, "by taking away the term Asperger's, the [*DSM*-5] workgroup has eliminated (in the eyes of participants in this study) an entire culture—a culture separate from those with low-functioning autism" (Spillers, Sensui,

& Linton, 2014, p. 257). The fascinating question here is to what extent should a strong sense of communal identity about a diagnosis influence its scientific status? Is defining autism or Asperger's something that should be restricted to psychiatric researchers or should the attitudes and opinions of those who receive the diagnoses count, too?

SYSTEMS PERSPECTIVES

Systems perspectives attribute disruptive behavior less to individual mental disorders and more to the social systems in which children and adolescents are embedded. Numerous systems-based approaches for addressing externalizing behaviors have been developed. Let's discuss one representative example: **multisystemic therapy (MST)**. MST was originally developed for juvenile offenders and is used for oppositional, conduct, and other externalizing behavior problems (Zajac, Randall, & Swenson, 2015). It is rooted in a systems perspective because it sees disruptive behaviors as being collectively determined by the multiple social systems in which children and adolescents function: home, school, peer groups, and neighborhoods (Henggeler & Borduin, 1990; Swenson, Henggeler, Taylor, & Addison, 2005; Zajac et al., 2015). MST starts by identifying factors in these social systems that contribute to (i.e., are "drivers" of) disruptive behaviors. Once these drivers are identified, clients and families are encouraged to come up with ways of altering each system so that disruptive behaviors are reduced (Henggeler & Borduin, 1990; Swenson et al., 2005; Zajac et al., 2015).

Because different systems might require different solutions, MST employs a variety of eclectic interventions. It uses CBT techniques to target problematic family member behaviors and intensive family therapy to remedy troublesome family dynamics. MST involves frequent visits to clients' homes, making it easier for them to receive services. However, MST isn't limited to individual and family interventions. In a broader systemic way, it also incorporates **neighborhood-based projects** to address community issues that contribute to disruptive behavior. Neighborhood-based projects involve working with not only the families of individual clients, but also with local politicians, community and business-leaders, the police, and community members to collaboratively identify and address neighborhood issues that contribute to disruptive behavior (Swenson et al., 2005). The idea is to intervene on individual, family, and community levels to make the systems in which clients live less likely to produce disruptive behaviors. A review conducted by its developer concluded that MST reduces behavior problems, improves family relations, and offers considerable cost savings to communities where it's implemented (Carr, 2016; Henggeler, 2011). However, other researchers have drawn somewhat less optimistic conclusions about the quality of evidence for MST's clinical and cost effectiveness (Goorden et al., 2016; van der Stouwe, Asscher, Stams, Deković, & van der Laan, 2014). They conclude that it has modest benefits and appears to work best for teens under age 15 who display the most severe behavior issues (van der Stouwe et al., 2014).

Source: Getty Images/iStockphoto\bowdenimages

Michael

MST for Michael, our 15-year-old client with a conduct disorder diagnosis, would involve his entire family. An MST therapist would make regular visits to Michael's house and would work with him, his mother, and his siblings. His mother might be taught parenting skills to help her more effectively parent Michael. Family therapy might help Michael and his family examine and alter long-standing problematic family dynamics that have contributed to Michael's conduct problems. More broadly, the MST therapy team might initiate a neighborhood-based project that brings all the major stakeholders together to address issues in the schools and larger community that contribute to conduct problems like Michael's. In this case, the neighborhood-based project might identify ways to improve community–police relations, while also developing an after-school program for at-risk youth that gives children and adolescents somewhere to go after school when their parents are still at work.

CASE EXAMPLES

EVALUATING SOCIOCULTURAL PERSPECTIVES

Sociocultural perspectives help us contextualize developmental issues. Understanding the roles of culture, gender, socioeconomic conditions, and family dynamics seems important, as does paying attention to the influence of stigma. Still, critics argue that sociocultural perspectives underestimate the role of individual factors such as genetics. Sure, social factors influence how we understand problems like ADHD and autism, but heritability estimates for both these diagnoses are consistently high, implying a strong genetic component (Brikell et al., 2015; S. V. Faraone & Biederman, 2013; S. V. Faraone et al., 2005; Kolevzon et al., 2013; Ronald & Hoekstra, 2014; R. E. Rosenberg et al., 2009; Thapar & Cooper, 2016; Thapar et al., 2013). To critics of purely social explanations, this establishes ADHD and autism as more than just social constructions.

Further, when it comes to treatment effectiveness, few health care professionals believe that addressing dietary, environmental, and family influences alone is sufficient for alleviating developmental issues. From a biological perspective, both psychological and social interventions (e.g., social advocacy, stigma-reduction, individual therapy, and family therapy) can merely help manage what ultimately are neurological disorders. In this critique, psychosocial approaches play second fiddle to biological ones; they can offer beneficial support services, but ultimate explanations must be brain-based. Nonetheless, those coming from a sociocultural viewpoint continue to argue that developmental issues inevitably emerge from a social context and that paying attention to social factors remains critically important.

13.7 CLOSING THOUGHTS: NEURODIVERSITY

How do we know what constitutes "normal" development? When do worrisome childhood behaviors—such as resisting authority, breaking rules, being socially uncommunicative, struggling to pay attention, or feeling overwhelmed by environmental stimulation—reflect underlying disorders rather than socially unacceptable behavior (i.e., deviance)? Even when deviant childhood behaviors can be tied to neurological factors, how do we know what is neurologically normal? In recent years, some people have started advancing a **neurodiversity** argument—the contention that those carrying diagnoses like autism and ADHD are neurologically different, not disordered. Neurodiversity advocates stress appreciating (rather than trying to change) those whose brains function differently. To them, conditions like autism and ADHD are better thought of as gifts, not disorders (Honos-Webb, 2010; S. Silberman, 2015). They argue that "instead of viewing this gift as an error of nature ... society should regard it as a valuable part of humanity's genetic legacy" (S. Silberman, 2015, p. 470). Champions of neurodiversity agree that we should try to ameliorate aspects of autism, ADHD, and other neurological differences that are disabling, but without pathologizing them. Such an approach challenges a central assumption in abnormal psychology, namely that developmental issues (or any presenting problem, for that matter) can be cleanly divided into normal and abnormal varieties. Even if you aren't fully convinced by the neurodiversity argument, it's worth remembering because (at the very least) it keeps us humble as we struggle to identify, conceptualize, and treat developmental issues.

KEY TERMS

Applied behavior analysis (ABA)
Asperger's Disorder
Attention-deficit/hyperactivity disorder (ADHD)
Atypical autism
Autism
Autism spectrum disorder (ASD)
Autistic disorder
Autistic process
Autoimmune disease hypothesis
Catecholamine hypothesis of ADHD
Child-centered play therapy
Childhood autism
Conduct disorder (CD)
Courtesy stigma
Developmental language disorder with impairment of mainly pragmatic language
Discrete trial training (DTT)
Disturbance of activity and attention
Dopamine hypothesis of ADHD
Dorsal anterior midcingulate cortex

Early and intensive behavioral intervention (EIBI)
Environmental toxin hypotheses
Excessive sugar-intake hypothesis
Externalizing behaviors
Extreme male brain (EMB) theory
False negatives
False positives
Feingold diet
Fighter theory
Food additives hypothesis
Gluten/casein-free diet hypothesis
Hunter-farmer theory
Hyperkinetic conduct disorder
Intermittent explosive disorder
Internalizing behaviors
Kleptomania
Low-fitness extreme theory
Methylphenidate
Mindblindness
Multisystemic therapy (MST)
Neighborhood-based projects
Neurodiversity

Neurotypicals
Oppositional defiant disorder (ODD)
Oxytocin
Pervasive developmental disorder-not otherwise specified (PDD-NOS)
Pervasive developmental disorders
Picture Exchange Communication System (PECS)
Polyunsaturated fatty acids (PUFA) hypothesis
Problem-solving skills training
Pyromania
Reactive attachment disorder
Refrigerator mother theory of autism
Response readiness theory
Ritalin
Social (pragmatic) communication disorder (SPCD)
Suppressed GABA inhibition hypothesis
Viral theory of autism
Wader theory
Weak central coherence theory

CHAPTER 13

Full definitions of the terms listed above can be found in the end-of-book glossary on p. 533.

Go to the companion website, www.macmillanihe.com/raskin-abnormal-psych, to access a study guide, multiple choice and flashcard quizzes for this chapter, and other useful learning aids.

CHAPTER 14
OTHER PRESENTING PROBLEMS

14.1 OVERVIEW

LEARNING OBJECTIVES

After reading this chapter, you should be able to:

1. Describe *DSM* and *ICD* sleep-wake disorder diagnoses and the history of sleep issues.

2. Summarize the sleep cycle, biological theories of and interventions for sleep difficulties, the psychodynamic theory of nightmares, cognitive-behavioral therapy for insomnia (CBT-I), and the organizational injustice perspective on sleep issues.

3. Describe *DSM* and *ICD* elimination disorder diagnoses, as well as the history of elimination issues.

4. For elimination issues, outline biological theories and interventions, psychological therapies (behavioral, cognitive-behavioral, psychodynamic, and humanistic), and sociocultural approaches (including family systems and alternative therapies).

5. Distinguish *DSM* and *ICD* definitions of intellectual and learning disabilities, as well as the history of intellectual disabilities.

6. Summarize biological, psychological, and sociocultural perspectives on intellectual and learning disabilities.

7. Identify *DSM* and *ICD* motor disorder diagnoses and discuss the history of Tourette's syndrome.

8. Describe these perspectives on Tourette's syndrome: biological (genetics, immune system dysfunction, and treatments), psychological (behavior and cognitive therapies), and sociocultural (the impact of stigma).

9. Describe *DSM* and *ICD* communication disorder diagnoses.

10. Explain these perspectives on stuttering: biological (the roles of genes, dopamine, and drug interventions), psychological (cognitive-behavioral and constructivist therapies), and sociocultural (the impact of stigma).

11. Summarize *DSM* and *ICD* perspectives on delirium and dementia, as well as the history of Alzheimer's disease.

12. For Alzheimer's dementia, outline biological perspectives (the amyloid hypothesis, genetic influences, and drugs used), psychological perspectives (cognitive and behavioral therapies), and sociocultural perspectives (day care and long-term care plus cultural factors).

Photo source: © Royalty-Free/Corbis

GETTING STARTED: A BIT OF THIS AND THAT

One of the big challenges in teaching abnormal psychology is that there is simply so much material to cover. This chapter touches on a variety of topics not covered in earlier chapters, but which seem important to review. Because these topics aren't all tightly related, the chapter is organized somewhat differently than earlier presenting problem chapters, with a variety of problems introduced separately and only some perspectives for each examined.

14.2 SLEEP DISTURBANCES

Cassandra

Cassandra is a 46-year-old business executive for a large corporation who is married with three young children. For the past six months, Cassandra has had difficulty sleeping. Although tired when she gets in bed at night, she finds herself lying there unable to sleep. When she does finally fall asleep, she doesn't sleep well, often waking up in the middle of the night or very early the next morning. "Although I desperately want to sleep, I instead find myself thinking about other things: work, the kids, our upcoming family vacation. I'm exhausted during the day, but still can't get to sleep at night."

CASE EXAMPLES

Hubert

Hubert is a 30-year-old man who has begun experiencing sudden periods of extreme sleepiness for no apparent reason. "Out of the blue, I'll just fall asleep." When this happens, his muscles often go limp and he collapses. "Besides being embarrassing, I'm worried that if I don't get help for this, I'm going to get hurt when I fall down during one of these episodes."

DSM AND *ICD* PERSPECTIVES

The *DSM-5* lists sleep-related issues in its "sleep-wake disorders" chapter, while the *ICD-10* groups them as "nonorganic sleep disorders." Notably, some *ICD-10* sleep disorders are coded as disorders of the nervous system rather than as mental disorders. The *ICD-11* takes things even further. It doesn't classify sleep disorders as mental disorders at all. Instead, they have been relocated to a new "sleep-wake disorders" section of the manual. Still, sleep disorders are often viewed as problems that commonly accompany mental disorders, ones about which mental health professionals should be knowledgeable (Fawcett, 2015).

Insomnia, Hypersomnia, and Narcolepsy

People diagnosed with **insomnia** (*insomnia disorder* in the *DSM-5*, *nonorganic insomnia* in the *ICD-10*, and *chronic insomnia* in the *ICD-11*) have difficulty falling asleep or staying asleep. They also often wake up early and can't go back to sleep. Basically, insomniacs can't seem to get sufficient sleep.

Cassandra

Our case example client Cassandra could be diagnosed with insomnia.

CASE EXAMPLES

Even if you don't qualify for an insomnia diagnosis, it's quite possible you don't get enough sleep. The "Try It Yourself" feature provides a quick assessment tool that can be used to measure your subjective sense of sleepiness.

Most of us can recall times when couldn't fall asleep at night, but for people diagnosed with insomnia it is a recurrent and debilitating problem.
Source: Getty Images/PhotoAlto\PhotoAlto/Frederic Cirou

TRY IT YOURSELF

What's Your Sleep Like?

Sleep Quiz

Instructions: Please answer the questions below about your sleep habits over **the past 4 weeks**. This quiz takes most people about 5 minutes to complete. Take your time and answer truthfully for the most accurate results.

1. Do you have trouble falling asleep?
   - ☐ Not at all
   - ☐ Just a little
   - ☐ Somewhat
   - ☐ A good bit of the time
   - ☐ Most of the time
   - ☐ All the time

2. Do you have trouble staying awake during the day?
   - ☐ Not at all
   - ☐ Just a little
   - ☐ Somewhat
   - ☐ A good bit of the time
   - ☐ Most of the time
   - ☐ All the time

3. Do you get enough sleep to feel rested when you first wake in the morning?
   - ☐ Not at all
   - ☐ Just a little
   - ☐ Somewhat
   - ☐ A good bit of the time
   - ☐ Most of the time
   - ☐ All the time

CHAPTER 14

4. Do you get the amount of sleep you needed?
   ☐ Not at all
   ☐ Just a little
   ☐ Somewhat
   ☐ A good bit of the time
   ☐ Most of the time
   ☐ All the time

5. Do you snore when you sleep?
   ☐ Not at all
   ☐ Just a little
   ☐ Somewhat
   ☐ A good bit of the time
   ☐ Most of the time
   ☐ All the time

6. Do you feel drowsy or sleepy during the day?
   ☐ Not at all
   ☐ Just a little
   ☐ Somewhat
   ☐ A good bit of the time
   ☐ Most of the time
   ☐ All the time

7. Do you take naps that are 5 minutes or longer during the day?
   ☐ Not at all
   ☐ Just a little
   ☐ Somewhat
   ☐ A good bit of the time
   ☐ Most of the time
   ☐ All the time

8. Do you feel that your sleep was not quiet (e.g. feeling tense, moving restlessly, can't get comfortable)?
   ☐ Not at all
   ☐ Just a little
   ☐ Somewhat
   ☐ A good bit of the time
   ☐ Most of the time
   ☐ All the time

9. Do you awaken short of breath or with a headache in the morning?
   ☐ Not at all
   ☐ Just a little
   ☐ Somewhat
   ☐ A good bit of the time
   ☐ Most of the time
   ☐ All the time

10. Do you awaken in the middle of the night and have trouble falling asleep again?
    ☐ Not at all
    ☐ Just a little
    ☐ Somewhat
    ☐ A good bit of the time
    ☐ Most of the time
    ☐ All the time

11. How long did it usually take you to fall asleep during the past 4 weeks?
    ☐ 0-15 minutes
    ☐ 16-30 minutes
    ☐ 31-45 minutes
    ☐ 46-60 minutes
    ☐ More than 60 minutes

12. On average, how many hours did you sleep each night during the past 4 weeks?
    ☐ 0-4 hours
    ☐ 5-6 hours
    ☐ 7-8 hours
    ☐ 9-10 hours
    ☐ 11-24 hours

Take this quiz online to have it scored: https://psychcentral.com/quizzes/sleep-quiz/

Source: Adapted from Hays, R. D., & Stewart, A. L. (1992). Sleep measures. In A. L. Stewart & J. E. Ware (eds.), Measuring functioning and well-being: The Medical Outcomes Study approach (pp. 235–259). Durham, NC: Duke University Press. Printed with permission from RAND Corporation.

By contrast, people with **hypersomnia** get enough sleep, but nevertheless are perpetually tired and sometimes find themselves falling asleep during the day. This disorder is technically called *hypersomnolence disorder* in *DSM-5*, *nonorganic hypersomnia* in *ICD-10*, and *behaviorally induced hypersomnia* in *ICD-11*. It is easily confused with another disorder, **narcolepsy**. Narcolepsy is characterized by periods of unexpected and uncontrollable sleepiness, often resulting in abrupt lapses into sleep. In many instances, narcolepsy involves something called **cataplexy**, a sudden but temporary loss of muscle tone. Narcolepsy is typically attributed to purely biological causes—which is why it is included in *ICD-10* and *ICD-11*, but not coded as a mental disorder.

Hubert
Case example client Hubert meets narcolepsy criteria.

See Diagnostic Boxes 14.1, 14.2, and 14.3 for more on diagnosing insomnia, hypersomnia, and narcolepsy.

When it comes to prevalence, insomnia is extremely common. The *DSM-5* reports that one-third of adults show some symptoms and 6%–10% qualify for an insomnia disorder diagnosis. Insomnia's prevalence goes up in middle-aged and older people; further, women are more likely to experience it than men. Hypersomnia is far less common than insomnia, with *DSM-5* reporting that 1% of Americans and Europeans meet diagnostic criteria. Not surprisingly, the prevalence of narcolepsy is even lower, with the *DSM-5* estimating its occurrence in just 0.02%–0.04% of the population.

Diagnostic Box 14.1 Insomnia

DSM-5: Insomnia Disorder
- Trouble falling asleep, staying asleep, or waking up early and being unable to go back to sleep.
- Occurs at least 3 nights per week for 3 months or longer and isn't caused by drugs, lack of opportunity for sleep, or another sleep-wake disorder.
Based on American Psychiatric Association, 2013b, pp. 362–363

ICD-10: Nonorganic Insomnia
- Trouble falling asleep, staying asleep, or having poor quality sleep.
- Occurs at least 3 times per week for 1 month or longer and the person is preoccupied or excessively worried about the lack of sleep.
Based on World Health Organization, 1992, pp. 144–145

ICD-11: Chronic Insomnia
- Trouble falling asleep, staying asleep, or having poor quality sleep.
- Persists for an extended period of time.
Based on https://icd.who.int/browse11/l-m/en

Diagnostic Box 14.2 Hypersomnia

DSM-5: Hypersomnolence Disorder
- Excessive sleepiness despite at least 7 hours of sleep, with either lapsing into sleep during the day or sleeping more than 9 hours per day and not feeling rested.
- Occurs at least 3 nights per week for 3 months or longer and isn't caused by drugs or another sleep-wake disorder.
Based on American Psychiatric Association, 2013b, pp. 368–369

ICD-10: Nonorganic Hypersomnia
- Extreme sleepiness/sleep during the day or difficulty waking up not caused by inadequate sleep.
- Occurs daily for at least 1 month and not caused by other sleep problems or medical conditions.
Based on World Health Organization, 1992, pp. 144–145

ICD-11: Behaviorally Induced Hypersomnia
- Extreme sleepiness/sleep during the day or difficulty waking up not caused by inadequate sleep.
- When there is no physical explanation for the hypersomnia, it is usually associated with mental disorders.
Based on https://icd.who.int/browse11/l-m/en

CHAPTER 14

Diagnostic Box 14.3 Narcolepsy

DSM-5
- Uncontrollable need to sleep or lapsing into sleep during the day.
- Occurs at least three nights per week for three months or longer and isn't caused by drugs or another sleep-wake disorder; there are also low levels of the neurotransmitter hypocretin-1 and decreased rapid-eye movement (REM) sleep.
- May involve *cataplexy* (muscle weakness).

Based on American Psychiatric Association, 2013b, pp. 372–373

ICD-10
- Narcolepsy is not grouped with the mental and behavioral disorders.

ICD-11
- Narcolepsy is not grouped with the mental and behavioral disorders.
- Two types:
  o *Type 1*: Uncontrollable need to sleep or lapsing into sleep during the day, accompanied by cataplexy.
  o *Type 2*: Uncontrollable need to sleep or lapsing into sleep during the day, accompanied by *muscle paralysis, hypnagogic hallucinations* (sensory experiences during the transition from wakefulness to sleep), or *automatic behaviors* (continue with behavior one was engaging in before narcoleptic episode, but without conscious awareness).

Based on https://icd.who.int/browse11/l-m/en

Parasomnias

Parasomnias are sleep disturbances involving undesired events or experiences during sleep (see Diagnostic Box 14.4). In **non-rapid eye movement (NREM) sleep arousal disorder**, deep sleep is disrupted by either sleepwalking or sleep terrors. **Sleepwalking** (also called *somnambulism*) involves getting out of bed and walking around while still asleep; the sleepwalker has a blank expression, is unresponsive to others, and is difficult to awaken. Sleepwalking is much more common in children than adults (Zadra, Desautels, Petit, & Montplaisir, 2013). The *DSM-5* estimates that 10%–30% of children have engaged in sleepwalking at least once, but only 1%–5% of people who sleepwalk meet criteria for a NREM sleep arousal disorder diagnosis.

Sleep terrors (also called *night terrors*) are episodes of intense terror that jerk the person abruptly from deep sleep, often with a panicked scream and a scramble to escape the room. The individual isn't fully awakened, rarely leaves the room, and usually has little memory of the incident later. The *DSM-5* says the prevalence of sleep terrors is unknown, but—like sleepwalking—it's more common in children than adults. Younger children tend to experience sleep terrors the most. The *DSM-5* notes that 36.9% of 18-month-olds have experienced a sleep terror episode (not the full-blown disorder), compared to only 19.7% of 30-month-olds and just 2.2% of adults. In contrast to the *DSM-5*, the *ICD-10* and *ICD-11* list sleepwalking and sleep terrors as separate diagnoses rather than as subtypes of a single non-REM sleep arousal disorder.

The *DSM-5* and *ICD-11* (but not the *ICD-10*) also include **rapid eye movement (REM) sleep behavior disorder**. It is characterized by acting out the dreams one experiences during REM sleep. The patient might speak, shout, kick, punch, or even leap out of bed (National Sleep Foundation, n.d.-b). Finally, all three manuals—*DSM-5*, *ICD-10*, and *ICD-11*—contain another parasomnia known as **nightmare disorder** (simply *nightmares* in the *ICD-10*), which is diagnosed in people who regularly have vivid and upsetting dreams in which their safety, security, or very survival is at risk. For good measure, although we don't discuss them further in this book, Diagnostic Box 14.5 provides definitions for other sleep-wake disorders: the **breathing-related sleep disorders** (which are diagnosed using *polysomnography*, a procedure that measures breathing, brain waves, eye movement, leg movement, and blood oxygen levels during sleep), the **circadian rhythm sleep-wake disorders**, and **restless legs syndrome**.

Diagnostic Box 14.4 Parasomnias

Non-Rapid Eye Movement (NREM) Sleep Arousal Disorder
- **DSM-5**: Partial awakening, usually during first third of sleep, that involves either:
  o *Sleepwalking* (getting out of bed and walking around, usually with a blank face and lack of responsiveness to others), or
  o *Sleep terrors* (abrupt arousal from sleep, typically accompanied by a panicked scream, rapid breathing, excessive heart rate, and perspiration)

Based on American Psychiatric Association, 2013b, p. 399
- **ICD-10**: Divided into two disorders: "sleepwalking" (or "somnambulism") and "sleep terrors" (or "night terrors").

Based on World Health Organization, 1992, pp. 146–148
- **ICD-11**: Divided into two disorders: "sleepwalking disorder" and "sleep terrors."

Based on World Health Organization, https://icd.who.int/browse11/l-m/en

Rapid Eye Movement (REM) Sleep Behavior Disorder (DSM-5 *and* ICD-11)
- Arousal during REM sleep characterized by talking or physical movement.

Based on American Psychiatric Association (2013b, pp. 407–408 and World Health Organization, https://icd.who.int/browse11/l-m/en

Nightmare Disorder (DSM-5 *and* ICD-11)/*Nightmares* (ICD-10)
- Repeated vivid and upsetting dreams of a frightening nature that usually involve threats to safety, security, or survival that usually occur during second half of sleep and result in abruptly waking up.

Based on American Psychiatric Association, 2013b, p. 404; World Health Organization, 1992, p. 149; and World Health Organization, https://icd.who.int/browse11/l-m/en.

Diagnostic Box 14.5 Other Sleep Disorders

The following sleep issues are in the *DSM-5, ICD-10,* and *ICD-11,* but—as with all sleep disorders—are grouped as sleep disorders, not mental disorders, in *ICD-10* or *ICD-11.*

Breathing-Related Sleep Disorders
- **Central Sleep Apnea:** Five or more incidences of apnea (temporary cessation of breathing) per hour during sleep, as measured by polysomnography.
- **Obstructive Sleep Apnea Hypopnea:** Obstructive breathing disturbances that occur at least five times per hour during sleep (snoring, snorting/gasping, breathing interruptions); these must be measured by polysomnography.
- **Sleep-Related Hypoventilation:** Slowed respiration related to increased carbon dioxide levels.

Circadian Rhythm Sleep-Wake Disorders
These are disorders of the *circadian rhythm* (see Chapter 5) that interfere with sleep. Subtypes:
- *Delayed sleep phase type*: Delays in falling asleep and waking up, so that the person goes to sleep and wakes up later than desired.
- *Advanced sleep-phase type*: Prematurely falling asleep and waking up, so that the person goes to sleep and wakes up earlier than desired.
- *Irregular sleep-wake cycle*: Disorganized sleep in which there is no regular pattern of going to sleep and waking up.
- *Non-24-hour sleep-wake cycle*: Sleep cycle that doesn't adhere to the 24-hour-day clock; the person's sleep cycle consistently shifts, usually to ever-later times.
- *Shift-work type*: Insomnia during waking hours and excessive sleepiness during nighttime hours, induced by unconventional work hours.

Restless Legs Syndrome
- Irresistible desire to move one's legs that gets worse when resting or trying to sleep.
- Symptoms improve when walking.

Based on American Psychiatric Association, 2013b; World Health Organization, 1992; and https://icd.who.int/browse11/l-m/en.

Evaluating *DSM* and *ICD* Sleep Disorders

Primary vs. Secondary Insomnia

One of the more notable changes in *DSM-5, ICD-11,* and 2014's revision of the *International Classification of Sleep Disorders* (*ICSD-3*) was the elimination of the long-time distinction between **primary insomnia** and **secondary insomnia** (Gupta et al., 2014). In *DSM-IV,* primary insomnia was diagnosed when insomnia occurred in the absence of another medical or psychiatric disorder; secondary insomnia was diagnosed when another medical or psychiatric disorder occurred along with the insomnia (Gupta et al., 2014). However, in practice it was difficult to make this diagnostic distinction, so it was eliminated (Gupta et al., 2014).

The Comorbidity of Sleep Disorders

Because sleep disorders frequently co-occur with one another and with other mental and physical disorders, we again face the thorny issue of comorbidity. Consider insomnia. It is comorbid with other sleep-wake disorders such as **central sleep apnea**, circadian rhythm sleep-wake disorders, and restless legs syndrome (all defined in Diagnostic Box 14.5). More broadly, insomnia is also quite common in people diagnosed with other mental disorders—especially anxiety disorders, posttraumatic stress, depression, alcohol dependence, and schizophrenia (Mackie & Winkelman, 2015; Spiegelhalder, Regen, Nanovska, Baglioni, & Riemann, 2013;

CHAPTER **14**

Winokur, 2015). Many non-mental disorders are also highly comorbid with insomnia, including respiratory, gastrointestinal, neurological, and immune system disorders, as well as chronic pain and diabetes (Dikeos & Georgantopoulos, 2011). Of course, it's quite intuitive that these sorts of problems might disrupt sleep. Think of how your own sleep was affected the last time you felt anxious, sad, sick, or were having difficulties breathing properly. So, is insomnia a disorder in and of itself or a sign of some other problem? The *DSM-5*, with its elimination of the primary–secondary insomnia distinction, says insomnia is a mental disorder all its own. However, can it be a single disorder if there are so many potentially different causes for it? While this question may not get a final answer, mental health professionals should be familiar with sleep problems because many clients will present with them.

HISTORICAL PERSPECTIVES

Sleep habits have changed throughout history, which means our ideas about what constitutes normal sleep have changed, too. Early hunter-gatherers (circa 8000 BCE) likely slept in the fetal position in shallow pits next to cave walls (Bulger, 2016). By the time of the ancient Egyptians, sleep was regarded as a revered near-death state; however, the later Romans didn't focus much on sleep—possibly seeing it as a distraction from building roads, aqueducts, and the Coliseum (Bulger, 2016). In Europe during the Middle Ages, times were tough for most people, who huddled together to stay warm while they slept; thus, sleep wasn't an especially comfortable or private experience (Bulger, 2016). It was during the Renaissance that Europeans began focusing on comfort during sleep. Mattresses were made more comfortable by placing them on ropes weaved back and forth across bed frames; some historians even attribute the phrase "sleep tight" to the fact that these ropes needed to be tightened each evening before bed (Fisher, 2011). Perhaps most notably, before nighttime lighting was developed, people usually went to sleep for several hours after sunset, then woke in the middle of the night to pray, talk, or have sex; after that, they went back to sleep for several hours before rising at dawn (Ekirch, 2005). Thus, the notion of an uninterrupted night's sleep is a modern conception that inevitably influences current ideas about normal sleep habits.

BIOLOGICAL PERSPECTIVES
The Sleep Cycle

How can we understand what is going on in the brain during sleep? Using a machine called an *electroencephalogram (EEG)*, brain researchers can record the brain's electrical activity during sleep and wakefulness. Different patterns of electrical activity (referred to as *brain waves*) occur while awake versus while asleep. Once asleep, electrical activity goes through four distinct stages known as the **sleep cycle**. The first three stages are **non-rapid eye movement (NREM) sleep**, in which there is little or no eye movement and dreaming is extremely rare (Chieh, 2015; L. Martin, 2013; National Sleep Foundation, n.d.-c). The final stage is **rapid eye movement (REM) sleep**, characterized by rapid eye movement, muscle paralysis, and dreaming (Chieh, 2015; L. Martin, 2013; National Sleep Foundation, n.d.-c; Nordqvist, 2015). During an eight-hour night of sleep, a person goes through the sleep cycle five times (see Figures 14.1 and 14.2). The stages of the sleep cycle are as follows:

» *NREM Stage 1*: This stage is somewhere between wakefulness and falling asleep. It usually lasts about five minutes and is often described as light sleep. The brain's electrical activity shifts from *beta waves* (those characteristic of everyday wakefulness) into slower *alpha waves* (associated with feelings of peacefulness and relaxation), but there are also some *theta waves* more typical of Stage 2 sleep.

» *NREM Stage 2*: In this stage, brain waves slow down further into theta waves, but there are periodic bursts of electrical activity known as *sleep spindles*, which may reflect the brain's efforts to decrease responsiveness to environmental stimulation that would otherwise wake the person. People spend the most time in Stage 2 while sleeping. Stage 2 sleep usually lasts about 20 minutes.

» *NREM Stage 3*: Stage 3 marks the beginning of deep sleep. Brain waves slow even further into a pattern known as *delta waves*, although early in this stage there is still some faster activity. There is no eye movement or muscle activity during this stage. Stage 3 used to be divided into two stages (with the latter being the deepest stage of sleep), but the American Academy of Sleep Medicine (AASM) combined these stages into a single stage in 2007 (http://healthysleep.med.harvard.edu/glossary/n-p). Stage 3 sleep lasts about 30 minutes, although as the night goes on the duration of Stage 3 sleep decreases and toward the end of the night disappears entirely (see Figure 14.1).

» *REM Stage 4*: REM sleep occurs in Stage 4. Theta, alpha, and sometimes beta waves occur, but the person remains sound asleep. During REM sleep, the body undergoes *atonia* (muscle paralysis) and the person experiences dreams. People don't necessarily remember their dreams (and when they do, those recalled are usually from the last REM stage before waking). Importantly, during REM sleep, the frontal lobes of the brain responsible for rational thinking shut down, but the amygdala, hippocampus, and limbic system (brain regions responsible for emotional processing and recall) are active. Thus, although the muscles shut off during REM sleep, the brain remains highly active. The duration of REM sleep is about 10 minutes initially, but typically increases as the night goes on (again, see Figure 14.1).

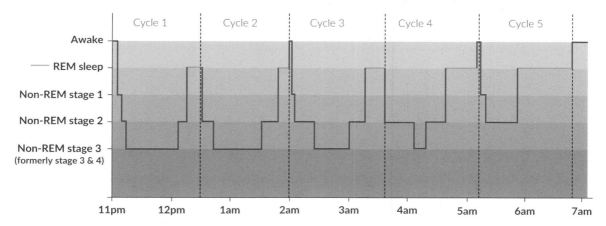

Figure 14.1 Hypnogram Showing the Sleep Cycle During an Eight-Hour Night of Sleep
Source: Reprinted with permission from Luke Mastin. Available from: www.howsleepworks.com/types_cycles.html

The sleep cycle described applies to children and adults. Babies sleep a lot more. Newborns typically sleep 16–20 hours a day (usually in 30–50 minute spurts), waking up regularly to feed ("Changes in sleep with age," 2007; Raising Children Network, 2016). By 3–4 months of age, babies start sleeping for longer periods, eventually remaining asleep throughout the night (but still taking naps during the day, usually until age 6 or 7) ("Changes in sleep with age," 2007). It is older children and adults who settle into the sleep cycle outlined above. However, sleep difficulties often arise with age ("Changes in sleep with age," 2007). Older adults generally sleep less, take longer to fall asleep, report less satisfying sleep, and experience decreased REM sleep; some of these problems may be a result of normal aging, but in many cases are attributable to physical illnesses or psychological disturbances, along with the drugs used to treat them (National Sleep Foundation, n.d.-a).

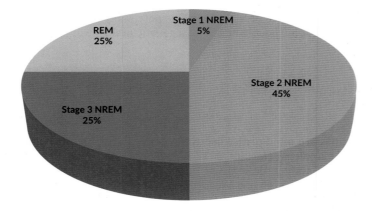

Figure 14.2 Percentage of Sleep Spent in Each of the Sleep Stages
Source: Reprinted with permission from Luke Mastin. Available from: www.howsleepworks.com/types_cycles.html

Biological Explanations of Sleep Disturbances

Biological researchers see underlying physiological malfunctions as the primary culprits in sleep difficulties. They often assume that susceptibility to sleep disorders is genetic (or heritable) and they point to a growing body of evidence to support this claim (Gehrman, Keenan, Byrne, & Pack, 2015; Kripke et al., 2015). Below we briefly touch on a few biological explanations of sleep-wake disorders.

CHAPTER 14

Hyperarousal and Insomnia

The **hyperarousal theory of insomnia** is a well-known example of a sleep disorder theory that includes the belief that sleep problems are heritable. This theory combines biological and cognitive-behavioral ways of thinking in proposing that insomnia is a disorder of chronic *hyperarousal* (Riemann et al., 2010). It hypothesizes that people with chronic insomnia are genetically vulnerable to it. Consequently, they are more likely to biologically experience arousal, which—through classical conditioning—becomes associated with various cognitive and behavioral events like worrying or lying in bed at night (Riemann et al., 2010). Thus, those with insomnia remain in a hyper-aroused physiological state much of the time, making sleep difficult.

Cassandra

According to hyperarousal theory, our case example client Cassandra may be genetically predisposed to hyperarousal—so much so that even stimuli that should evoke rest, such as her bed, have become associated with an aroused physiological state.

CASE EXAMPLES

Orexin, Neurodevelopmental Degeneration, and Narcolepsy

Narcolepsy is associated with too little **orexin** (also called *hypocretin*), a neurotransmitter secreted by the lateral hypothalamus (Howell, 2012). Orexin—which comes in two varieties, orexin-A and orexin-B (Dubey, Handu, & Mediratta, 2015)—regulates wakefulness and appetite. It has been implicated in cataplexy, the loss of muscle tone that often occurs in narcolepsy. Orexin appears important not just in narcolepsy, but also in REM sleep behavior disorder (Howell, 2012). However, REM sleep behavior disorder has other biological correlates, as well. It has been linked to diseases involving neurological degeneration, including Parkinson's disease, Alzheimer's disease, and dementia with Lewy bodies (all implicated in dementia, discussed later), as well as amyotrophic lateral sclerosis (ALS) (Howell, 2012).

NREM Sleep Disruption and Parasomnias

Finally, NREM parasomnias such as sleepwalking and sleep terrors are believed to result when there is an inadequate shift from NREM sleep to wakefulness (Howell, 2012; Howell, Khawaja, & Schenck, 2015). People with NREM sleep disorders such as sleepwalking seem to experience disrupted sleep cycles, especially during delta wave periods of sleep (Zadra et al., 2013). They appear sensitive to sleep distractions (e.g., noise), sleep deprivation, and medications—all of which have been linked to sleepwalking (Howell et al., 2015; Pilon, Montplaisir, & Zadra, 2008; Zadra et al., 2013). Regarding medication specifically, there have been reports that antipsychotics may increase the chances of sleepwalking—although a lot more research is needed to support this suspicion (M. V. Seeman, 2011b). Dysfunctional relationships between brain regions associated with cognitively demanding tasks (the motor and cingulate cortices) and those active during rest states (the medial prefrontal and lateral parietal cortices) have been identified as potentially important in sleepwalking (Zadra et al., 2013). It's also suspected that some people may have a genetic predisposition to NREM sleep problems (Modi, Camacho, & Valerio, 2014).

Drug Treatments for Sleep Problems

Too Much Sleep

Stimulants such as amphetamines are often prescribed to people who have difficulty staying awake due to problems like hypersomnia and narcolepsy (Mignot, 2012; M. S. Wise, Arand, Auger, Brooks, & Watson, 2007). By stimulating the central nervous system, these drugs inhibit sleep. However, the obvious disadvantage is that stimulants can be addictive. People often use a less problematic stimulant—caffeine—to help them stay awake, although it is not considered efficient as a treatment for hypersomnia and at high doses it can cause cardiovascular issues (Mignot, 2012). A non-stimulant prescription alternative to amphetamines and caffeine is a drug called **modafinil** (sold around the world under many different trade names, including *Provogil* in the U.S.). It's a wake-promoting drug that doesn't appear to be habit-forming (M. S. Wise et al., 2007). Although it reduces sleepiness, its precise mechanism of action remains unclear (Gerrard & Malcolm, 2007; M. S. Wise et al., 2007).

Sodium oxybate is a central nervous system depressant that is sometimes prescribed for cataplexy (L. E. Krahn, 2003; Mayer, 2012; M. S. Wise et al., 2007). It is believed to reduce cataplexy by improving nighttime sleep. In high doses, it's also used to treat excessive daytime sleepiness, often in conjunction with other drugs such as modafinil (Mayer, 2012). Unfortunately, sodium oxybate is—like stimulant drugs—potentially addictive (Mayer,

2012). The drug is controversial not only due to its habit-forming qualities, but because of its well-publicized misuse. Also known as *gamma-hydroxybutyrate* (*GHB*), it has been slipped into the drinks of unsuspecting people to sedate them against their wishes, resulting in media references to it as the "date-rape drug" (L. E. Krahn, 2003). Besides these drugs, antidepressants (SSRIs, SNRIs, and tricyclics) are sometimes prescribed for narcolepsy because they suppress REM sleep and can reduce cataplexy.

Hubert

To treat his narcolepsy, Hubert could be prescribed amphetamines. However, given concerns about the addictive potential of long-term amphetamine use, he might instead be prescribed modafinil. While the modafinil is likely to help keep Hubert awake during the day, his cataplexy might be more responsive to sodium oxybate. Of course, his doctor will need to monitor Hubert closely to make sure the sodium oxybate doesn't become habit-forming.

CASE EXAMPLES

Lack of Sleep

Drugs are commonly prescribed to people who experience insomnia and other lack of sleep problems. For example, sedative-hypnotics are often used to treat insomnia. Many patients are prescribed benzodiazepines (a class of anxiolytic sedative-hypnotic drugs, first discussed in Chapter 6). As you may recall, benzodiazepines enhance the activity of gamma-aminobutyric acid (GABA), an inhibitory neurotransmitter that reduces anxiety. Benzodiazepines are prescribed for numerous sleep issues, including insomnia (M. D. Reed & Findling, 2002). Unfortunately, they have a variety of worrisome side effects. Besides being habit-forming, they can cause cognitive impairments such as confusion and forgetfulness in elderly patients (Dubey et al., 2015; Proctor & Bianchi, 2012). Thus, newer **non-benzodiazepine sleep aids** are commonly prescribed for insomnia. Like benzodiazepines, these drugs enhance GABA activity, but their chemical structure and mechanism of action are somewhat different (Sanger, 2004). *Zolpidem* (trade names *Ambien*, *Edluar*, *Zolpimist*, *Intermezzo*), eszopiclone (trade name *Lunesta*), and *zaleplon* (trade name *Sonata*) are among the more commonly prescribed non-benzodiazepine sleep aids (L. Anderson, 2016). These drugs—sometimes referred to as "Z drugs"—seem to be less habit-forming than benzodiazepines. Research suggests that they are somewhat effective in reducing insomnia, especially in younger female patients and in higher doses; however, some of the research may be biased and overlook potential placebo effects (Huedo-Medina, Kirsch, Middlemass, Klonizakis, & Siriwardena, 2012).

"Z drugs" are non-benzodiazepine sleep aids that many studies find reduce insomnia, although some of the effect may be placebo.
Source: Getty Images\Peter Dazeley

Besides benzodiazepine and non-benzodiazepine sedative-hypnotics, other drugs are sometimes prescribed to combat sleep difficulties. Let's discuss several of them, beginning with older antidepressants—specifically, the tricyclics. Tricyclics are occasionally used as sleep aids because, unlike newer SSRIs and SNRIs, they can cause sleepiness (Proctor & Bianchi, 2012). *Amitriptyline* and *nortriptyline* are the tricyclics most commonly prescribed for insomnia (Proctor & Bianchi, 2012). Though often taken to relieve seasonal allergies, **antihistamines** are also used to treat insomnia. They work by inhibiting **histamine**, another wake-promoting neurotransmitter (Barbier & Bradbury, 2007; Proctor & Bianchi, 2012). The main drawback of antihistamines is that they can take a long time to wear off (leaving a "hangover" effect) and they can alter cognition (Proctor & Bianchi, 2012). Many antihistamines (such as *diphenhydramine*, sold as *Benadryl* and *Unisom Sleep Gels*) can be purchased over the counter. Melatonin, a hormone important in regulating sleep-wake cycles, is another popular over-the-counter sleep aid. However, there hasn't been much research on taking melatonin for insomnia (Proctor & Bianchi, 2012).

The newest prescription drugs for insomnia are **orexin-receptor antagonists**. These drugs block the activity of orexin, the neurotransmitter implicated in arousal and wakefulness (Bennett, Bray, & Neville, 2014; Dubey et al., 2015). By blocking the action of orexin, arousal is decreased, making sleep more likely. The first orexin-receptor antagonist approved for use in the U.S. is *suvoxerant* (trade name *Belsomra*) (Bennett et al., 2014; Dubey et al., 2015). Because it's a new drug, there isn't much data comparing suvoxerant to other drug treatments for insomnia (Bennett et al., 2014; Dubey et al., 2015; Kishi, Matsunaga, & Iwata, 2015). However, initial evidence suggests that suvoxerant reduces insomnia, but without the negative side effects of benzodiazepines (Bennett et al., 2014; Dubey et al., 2015; Kishi et al., 2015).

CHAPTER 14

Cassandra

Cassandra, our case example client with insomnia, could be prescribed benzodiazepines to help her sleep. However, because of these drugs' potential for addiction, it might be better to try a non-benzodiazepine sleep aid such as zolpidem. Another possibility would be to prescribe her the newest sleep aid drug, suvoxerant. Regardless of which drug she used, it's likely to help only so long as she continues to take it.

In evaluating drug interventions for insomnia, it's important to realize that while they can improve sleep, they aren't a panacea. Many people on these drugs continue to struggle with sleep issues. Further, once the drugs are stopped, symptoms may return. As one researcher summed it up in discussing non-benzodiazepine sleep aids, "current evidence suggests that reliance on hypnotic drugs as the only treatment option for insomnia is misguided. It is important to consider other effective treatments ... to optimise outcomes for patients with insomnia" (Cunnington, 2012, p. 1). It is to some of those treatments that we turn next.

PSYCHOLOGICAL PERSPECTIVES

Psychodynamic Theory and Nightmares

From a psychodynamic perspective, people's psychological symptoms—including those related to sleep—always reflect underlying unconscious conflicts. There isn't much psychodynamic scholarship on sleep disorders, specifically. However, psychodynamic therapists have written a great deal about dreams. Recall from Chapter 2 that in classic psychoanalysis, every dream is a wish fulfillment—that is, dreams express unconscious (and sometimes unacceptable and, therefore, disguised) wishes (S. Freud, 1900/1965). The *DSM* and *ICD* sleep disorders most tied to dreaming are nightmares and night terrors. Psychodynamic therapists offer various explanations of the nightmares that people with these diagnoses experience (Lansky & Bley, 1995; Novellino, 2012). What these explanations share is an emphasis on the underlying meaning and function of nightmares. From a psychodynamic perspective, the key is to access the unconscious meaning of a nightmare and then to work through the underlying emotional conflict (Lansky & Bley, 1995; Novellino, 2012). There is minimal research on psychodynamic perspectives on nightmares and night terrors, but many people remain convinced that nightmares (and dreams in general) are best conceptualized as unconscious communications that must be analyzed and understood in order to resolve them.

Cognitive-Behavioral Therapy for Insomnia (CBT-I)

Cognitive-behavioral perspectives see sleep problems as emerging from dysfunctional thought processes and behavioral conditioning. Thus, **cognitive-behavioral therapy for insomnia (CBT-I)** employs a variety of CBT interventions developed specifically to target difficulty sleeping. It generally relies on the following CBT techniques (Baron et al., 2017; Edinger & Means, 2005; Rybarczyk, Lund, Garroway, & Mack, 2013):

» *Stimulus control therapy*: **Stimulus control therapy** assumes that bedtime and the bedroom have been classically conditioned to be associated with wakefulness and failed efforts to sleep. The goal is to recondition them to be associated with sleep. This is accomplished by having clients only go to bed when tired, get out of bed when they can't sleep (so bed isn't associated with being awake), and only use the bedroom for sleeping (so it isn't associated with other activities, such as reading or watching TV).

» *Sleep restriction therapy*: In **sleep restriction therapy**, the total amount of time allowed in bed is restricted so that it eventually matches the amount of time needed for sleep. The client keeps a sleep log, from which the therapist determines how many hours per night the client sleeps. The therapist then sets a time limit for staying in bed that is typically the number of hours of sleep needed plus thirty minutes. The idea is to train the person to remain in bed only as long as necessary to sleep.

» *Sleep hygiene education*: During **sleep hygiene education**, the client is taught habits that are conducive to getting a good night's sleep, including the importance of regular exercise; avoiding caffeine, alcohol, and nicotine; having a small snack before bed; and keeping the bedroom dark, noise-free, and comfortable.

» *Cognitive therapy*: Cognitive interventions aim to alter illogical beliefs and irrational fears about sleeping.

» *Relaxation training*: The client is taught to relax via methods such as progressive relaxation, biofeedback, hypnosis, and meditation.

CBT-I has been extensively researched and its advocates contend that it is highly effective and preferable to medication because, even though it doesn't work as well in the short term, its long-term effects are superior to medication (M. D. Mitchell, Gehrman, Perlis, & Umscheid, 2012; Rybarczyk et al., 2013). CBT-I has been found effective with children, older patients, and those with comorbid psychiatric diagnoses (M. D. Mitchell et al.,

2012; Owens, Palermo, & Rosen, 2002; D. J. Taylor & Pruiksma, 2014; M. Y. Wang, Wang, & Tsai, 2005). The main challenge is getting clients (and their families, when the clients happen to be children) to adhere to CBT-I. It is labor intensive and can sometimes decrease sleep while clients are first implementing it. Thus, not all clients stick with CBT-I and some who do implement it less than optimally (E. E. Matthews, Arnett, McCarthy, Cuddihy, & Aloia, 2013; Owens et al., 2002). However, for those who implement it properly and persevere in following through with it, CBT-I can be quite beneficial.

Cassandra

Were Cassandra to pursue CBT-I for her insomnia, she would likely be asked to keep a sleep log so that her therapist could better understand when, where, and how often she sleeps. If the sleep log indicates that Cassandra typically sleeps six hours per night, he might restrict her to no more than 6½ hours in bed per night. He also might have her avoid non-sleeping activities in bed—including reading, eating, thinking, watching TV, or even having sex with her husband ("Find another room in the house for that!"). The goal would be to recondition the bedroom as a place associated solely with sleep and rest. Any irrational thoughts Cassandra might have, such as "I must get eight hours of sleep every night or I won't be able to function" and "I am incapable of sleeping through the night" would be challenged using cognitive therapy. Finally, the therapist would educate Cassandra about proper sleeping habits so that she engages in sleep-promoting behaviors like keeping her bedroom dark at night while avoiding sleep-impairing actions like drinking caffeinated drinks that stimulate wakefulness.

CASE EXAMPLES

SOCIOCULTURAL PERSPECTIVES

Think of that terrible job you once had. Did you lose sleep over it? Was your distress because you were being mistreated? In other words, can sleep disturbances be due to social injustice? From a social justice perspective, indeed they can be. For instance, sleep problems might be tied to *organizational injustice*, in which workplace conditions are so unfair or oppressive that they cause stress that interferes with employees' sleep. Along these lines, research has found that that reduced pay, workplace inequality, and workplace stress all predict inadequate sleep (Elovainio et al., 2009; J. Greenberg, 2006).

How else might social inequality interfere with sleep? A demographic study of American's sleep habits found that people who got too little sleep were more likely to work two jobs, work long hours, and spend a lot of time commuting to work (Basner, Spaeth, & Dinges, 2014). The study also found that too much or too little sleep was associated with lower levels of education and with belonging to a minority group. In other words, lower social status was linked to poor sleep (Basner et al., 2014). Why does this matter? Because too much or too little sleep is correlated with higher mortality rates and other health-related problems (L. Hale, 2014).

Thus, from a social justice perspective, sleep loss is often not a sign of mental disorder, but of inequality. The question that therapists seeking social justice ask is this: If we addressed socioeconomic inequalities, discrimination, and other social issues that predict inadequate sleep, might we be able to improve people's sleep and thus improve their health? As the data linking sleep problems to social unfairness are correlational rather than causal, we can't know for sure (L. Hale, 2014). However, justice advocates believe that social change is at least as important as individual change in addressing sleep difficulties. These advocates worry that casting sleep issues exclusively as individual disorders may result in us failing to look at broader societal inequalities requiring attention and reform.

14.3 ELIMINATION ISSUES

Maribel

Maribel is an 8-year-old girl who began regularly wetting her bed six months ago. Her parents are upset and confused. "Before this began," her mother lamented, "she hadn't had any accidents since she was three." Maribel feels embarrassed by her bedwetting and hopes her friends from school don't find out. However, when asked about it she shrugs and says that it's "no big deal."

CASE EXAMPLES

Arjun

Arjun, a 6-year-old boy, has been defecating in his pants for the past three months. Even worse, sometimes Arjun "plays" with his stool, smearing it on the wall on several occasions. His parents are extremely worried. They acknowledge that Arjun has experienced problems with constipation in the past and that he often avoids going to the toilet because defecating when constipated is painful and anxiety-provoking.

CHAPTER 14

DSM AND *ICD* PERSPECTIVES

Enuresis and Encopresis

The *DSM-5* and *ICD-11* both contain chapters entitled "Elimination Disorders," which include two diagnoses: enuresis and encopresis. **Enuresis** is diagnosed in people five years or older who wet their beds or clothes, whereas **encopresis** is diagnosed in people four years or older who repeatedly have bowel movements in inappropriate places, such as in their pants or on the floor. In the *ICD-10*, enuresis and encopresis are not separated into an "Elimination Disorders" chapter but are instead grouped with "behavioural and emotional disorders with onset usually occurring in childhood and adolescence."

The *DSM-5* estimates that enuresis occurs in 5%–10% of 5-year-olds, 3%–5% of 10-year-olds, and 1% of people 15-years-old or older. Encopresis is far less common, according to the *DSM-5*, occurring in only 1% of 5-year-olds. Both enuresis and encopresis are more common in boys than girls. See Diagnostic Box 14.6 for details on diagnosing these two disorders. There is a lot more research on enuresis than encopresis, which is why enuresis receives greater attention below.

Maribel and Arjun

In thinking about our two case example clients, Maribel qualifies for an enuresis diagnosis while Arjun meets criteria for encopresis.

CASE EXAMPLES

Diagnostic Box 14.6 Elimination Disorders

Enuresis
- **DSM-5: Enuresis**
  - Unintentionally or intentionally urinates into bed or clothes at least twice weekly for three months.
  - Must be at least 5 years old or at equivalent developmental level.
  - The problem can't be caused by drugs or another medical condition

Based on American Psychiatric Association, 2013b, p. 355
- **ICD-10: Nonorganic Enuresis**
  - Unintentional urination during the day or night several times per week.
  - Diagnosed in people aged 5 years or older or with a mental age of at least 4 years.
  - Specify *primary* if the person has wet the bed since birth and *secondary* if the person developed bladder control and then lost it (typically between ages 5 and 7).

Based on World Health Organization, 1992, pp. 223–224
- **ICD-11: Enuresis**
  - Unintentional urination during the day or night several times per week.
  - Diagnosed in people aged 5 years or older or with a mental age of at least 4 years.
  - Specify *primary* if the person has wet the bed since birth and *secondary* if the person developed bladder control and then lost it (typically between ages 5 and 7).

Based on https://icd.who.int/browse11/l-m/en

Encopresis
- **DSM-5: Encopresis**
  - Unintentionally or intentionally placing bowel movements in inappropriate places (e.g., in pants or on floor) at least once a month for three months.
  - Must be at least 4 years old or at equivalent developmental level.
  - Must attend to whether the problem is accompanied by constipation.
  - The problem can't be caused by drugs or another medical condition besides constipation.

Based on American Psychiatric Association, 2013b, pp. 357–358
- **ICD-10: Nonorganic Encopresis**
  - Unintentional passing of feces in inappropriate locations.
  - Must attend to whether the problem is accompanied by constipation.

Based on World Health Organization, 1992, pp. 224–225
- **ICD-11: Encopresis**
  - Unintentionally or intentionally placing bowel movements in inappropriate places (e.g., in pants or on floor) at least once a month for several months.
  - Must be at least 4 years old or at equivalent developmental level.
  - Must attend to whether the problem is accompanied by constipation.
  - The problem can't be caused by drugs or another medical condition besides constipation.

Based on https://icd.who.int/browse11/l-m/en

Criticisms of *DSM* and *ICD* Perspectives

Evaluating DSM-5 Changes

The *DSM-5* criteria for enuresis (adopted almost verbatim by *ICD-11*) have been criticized for being inconsistent with current research standards and for defining the disorder too broadly (von Gontard, 2013). Critics note that there is a difference between nighttime bedwetting (which is always involuntary) and daytime urinating in one's pants (which can be intentional or unintentional), a difference they feel the *DSM-5* doesn't sufficiently accentuate (von Gontard, 2013). The *DSM-5* criteria for encopresis have evoked fewer complaints, but this may be because they remain essentially unchanged from the *DSM-IV-TR* (von Gontard, 2013).

Comorbidity Issues

There is substantial comorbidity between enuresis and other presenting problems. It's quite common for children with enuresis to also be diagnosed with attention-deficit/hyperactivity disorder (ADHD) or oppositional defiant disorder (ODD), as well with mood disorders (Ghanizadeh, 2010; Gontkovsky, 2011; Tsai et al., 2017; von Gontard & Equit, 2015). Physical and intellectual disabilities are often common in children with enuresis (Gontkovsky, 2011). Further, enuresis sometimes occurs in children identified as having posttraumatic stress disorder (PTSD) (Eidlitz-Markus, Shuper, & Amir, 2000). The high comorbidity rates raise the question of whether elimination issues are independent problems in their own right or, as some believe, merely symptoms of other problems.

HISTORICAL PERSPECTIVES

The first known reference to nocturnal enuresis occurred around 1550 BCE when it was mentioned in the Ebers Papyrus, a document containing ancient Egyptian medical knowledge (Glicklich, 1951; McDonald & Trepper, 1977; M. A. Salmon, 1975). During Roman times, the philosopher and naturalist Pliny the Elder (23–79 CE) proposed various interventions to prevent incontinence, including feeding children boiled mice (M. A. Salmon, 1975). The Persian physician Abū Bakr Muhammad ibn Zakariyyā al-Rāzī (known as Rhazes; c. 865–925 CE) wrote about enuresis and put forward some ideas that seem quite consistent with modern views. He speculated that enuresis could have many causes, including deep sleep, drinking too much before bed, small bladder capacity, and delayed development (Changizi Ashtiyani, Shamsi, Cyrus, & Tabatabayei, 2013). Later European views strike us today as more befuddling. In 1545, the English pediatrician Thomas Phaire recommended that enuresis be treated by burning the windpipe of a cock or the testicles of a hedgehog into powder and ingesting it two or three times a day (M. A. Salmon, 1975).

By the 17th and 18th centuries, enuresis treatments became increasingly medicalized. Fluid restriction, enemas, alarm clocks, and cold or warm baths were all prescribed (Hurl, 2011; M. A. Salmon, 1975). More invasively, there are 19th-century accounts of the urethra being sealed to prevent urination; in other cases, devices of various kinds were attached to the penis—including some that delivered electric shocks when urine was detected (Hurl, 2011; M. A. Salmon, 1975). By the 20th century, many of the current explanations of enuresis discussed below began to develop. Importantly, throughout history there have been many explanations for enuresis, yet "no method or treatment has ever fully contained this elusive condition" and "no analysis has sufficiently defined its causes" (Hurl, 2011, p. 49). Some believe that there is a lack of clarity in explaining and treating enuresis because medical and psychological perspectives have developed independently of one another (M. L. Brown, Pope, & Brown, 2011). However, this may simply reflect how much disagreement there is about whether enuresis is best conceptualized in medical or psychosocial terms.

BIOLOGICAL PERSPECTIVES

Genetics and Enuresis

Enuresis and encopresis are often approached from a biological perspective. Some researchers believe that enuresis occurs in children with weak bladders (in some instances due to developmental delays), though other researchers aren't so sure about this (R. J. Butler, 2004; Scharf, Pravda, Jennings, Kauffman, & Ringel, 1987; Wille, 1994). Enuresis does appear to run in families and twin studies have found higher concordance rates among identical twins than fraternal twins, although this finding applies more to boys than girls (R. J. Butler, 2004; Scharf et al., 1987; von Gontard, Heron, & Joinson, 2011). Further, several potential genetic markers for enuresis have been identified (R. J. Butler, 2004; Eiberg, Berendt, & Mohr, 1995; von Gontard et al., 1997;

CHAPTER 14

von Gontard, Schaumburg, Hollmann, Eiberg, & Rittig, 2001). However, the genetics research is still relatively modest and more studies are needed.

Maribel

Like Maribel, Maribel's mother was also a bedwetter growing up. So were several of Maribel's cousins on her mother's side. "We have a long history of weak bladders in our family," Maribel's mother awkwardly jokes. Whether this is due to genetics or shared family environment isn't clear.

CASE EXAMPLES

Drug Treatments for Enuresis

In many cases of childhood enuresis, it's suspected that there are insufficient levels of **vasopressin**, a hormone that reduces urine production (Nevéus et al., 2000). Thus, the most common drug treatment for enuresis is to prescribe a synthetic (i.e., humanly made) version of vasopressin called **desmopressin** (marketed under the trade name *DDAVP*). The goal is to decrease urine production to reduce or eliminate nighttime bedwetting (Arda, Cakiroglu, & Thomas, 2016; Kiddoo, 2011; National Clinical Guideline Centre, 2010; Thurber, 2016). There is a solid body of research that shows desmopressin is effective for managing nocturnal enuresis, but taking desmopressin doesn't provide a permanent cure. When the medication is stopped, bedwetting problems often recur (Glazener & Evans, 2002; Glazener, Evans, & Peto, 2004). Further, desmopressin can cause side effects such as headaches and stomachaches (National Clinical Guideline Centre, 2010). Most seriously, desmopressin can lead to *water intoxication* in which the child taking it gets extremely thirsty and drinks too much fluid. As a result, the child can experience side effects ranging from dizziness and fatigue to seizures and even death (Thurber, 2016). These side effects can be avoided if fluid intake is carefully monitored (National Clinical Guideline Centre, 2010), but this risk makes some parents hesitant to have their children take the drug.

Besides desmopressin, the tricyclics *imipramine* and *desipramine* are sometimes prescribed (Kiddoo, 2011; Nevéus et al., 2000). Tricyclic antidepressants effectively reduce nocturnal bedwetting while being used, but—like desmopressin—when patients stop taking them, bedwetting returns (Arda et al., 2016; Kiddoo, 2011). Precisely why antidepressants work isn't known, but they may cause people to sleep less heavily, making them more likely to wake up when they need to urinate (M. L. Brown et al., 2011). Because tricyclics are older drugs with potentially serious side effects, they aren't recommended as often as desmopressin (Arda et al., 2016; Kiddoo, 2011).

Anticholinergic medications such as *oxybutynin* and *tolterodine* constitute the final class of drugs prescribed for enuresis (Arda et al., 2016; Kiddoo, 2011). These drugs block the activity of the neurotransmitter acetylcholine, which is important in both activating muscles and in regulating cognitive processes such as attention and memory (Nikolas, Markon, & Tranel, 2016). The evidence for using anticholinergic drugs to treat enuresis is mixed. Some researchers conclude they clearly work and others say the evidence is uncertain (Arda et al., 2016; Kiddoo, 2011). Thus, desmopressin remains the drug most recommended and used for nocturnal bedwetting (Nevéus, 2011).

Maribel

Maribel's pediatrician prescribes desmopressin for her nocturnal bedwetting. Maribel takes the medication for six months and her enuresis all-but disappears. However, because the desmopressin gives Maribel stomach aches, her parents agree to let her stop taking it. Unfortunately, once Maribel goes off the desmopressin, her bedwetting returns.

CASE EXAMPLES

PSYCHOLOGICAL PERSPECTIVES

Behavior Therapy for Enuresis

When it comes to psychological interventions for enuresis, behavior therapy is by far the most utilized approach. The **enuresis alarm** (originally—and sometimes still—called the *bell and pad method*) is a well-established behavioral intervention for nocturnal bedwetting in children (Michaels, 1939; Mowrer & Mowrer, 1938; Shapira & Dahlen, 2010; Thurber, 2016). During the nighttime hours, a battery-operated alarm is attached to the child's underwear or to a pad placed on the bed. The alarm is programmed to go off when urine is detected. This wakes up the child, who can then get out of bed and go to the toilet. Research consistently finds that the enuresis alarm is an effective intervention for nocturnal bedwetting (Kiddoo, 2011, 2015; Thurber, 2016). It is frequently used in combination with desmopressin, but when compared to desmopressin it is often considered more effective because it tends to produce longer-lasting changes while desmopressin tends to work only so long as one takes it (Kiddoo, 2015; Perrin, Sayer, & While, 2015; Thurber, 2016).

Behavioral theorists believe that the enuresis alarm works due to both classical and operant conditioning. In classical conditioning terms, the alarm is an unconditioned stimulus. It automatically awakens the child without any learning necessary. When the alarm is repeatedly paired with having a full bladder, having a full bladder goes from being a neutral stimulus to a conditioned stimulus. That is, a full bladder gets associated with the alarm and eventually wakes up the child on its own, even when no alarm sounds (M. L. Brown et al., 2011; Thurber, 2016). This classically conditioned response of waking up to a full bladder is then further strengthened by operant conditioning (M. L. Brown et al., 2011; Keeley, Graziano, & Geffken, 2009). Waking up and going to the toilet is negatively reinforced because it allows the child to avoid something unpleasant (wetting the bed). As a result, the child is more likely to get up and go to the toilet the next time he or she has a full bladder at night (Keeley et al., 2009).

Sometimes the enuresis alarm is combined with **dry-bed training**, a behavioral intervention that involves having parents wake up children during the night, praise them when they don't wet the bed, and punish them when they do (often by making them wash their bedding) (Azrin & Foxx, 1974; Thurber, 2016). Due to the punitive nature of making children wash their bedding, dry-bed training has fallen into disrepute. For instance, the U.K.'s National Institute for Health Care and Clinical Excellence (NICE) maintains that because it relies on potentially humiliating punishments, dry-bed training is not an appropriate and ethical intervention (National Clinical Guideline Centre, 2010). Despite ethical concerns about its use of punishment, research on dry-bed training finds that adding it to treatment with an enuresis alarm may increase the number of nights without bedwetting (M. L. Brown et al., 2011; Kiddoo, 2015). Whether combining dry-bed training with an enuresis alarm is more effective than using an enuresis alarm alone remains a matter of disagreement (Kiddoo, 2015; Thurber, 2016)—one that ethical objections to dry-bed training only amplify.

Despite research support for them, behavioral techniques for enuresis do have one very notable downside, namely that they are highly demanding of the children and parents implementing them (Keeley et al., 2009; Kiddoo, 2015). Many parents and their children ignore the alarms or don't get up during the night to follow through on the procedure. Such families often prefer desmopressin and other drug interventions because they are far less labor intensive.

Maribel

After taking her off desmopressin, Maribel's parents try an enuresis alarm. Every night when Maribel goes to sleep, her parents attach the alarm to a pad placed on her bed. The alarm wakes Maribel whenever it detects urine on the pad. Because Maribel's parents both must get up early for work, they initially struggle to implement the enuresis alarm, either sleeping through it or forgetting to turn it on before Maribel goes to sleep. However, when they become more diligent about turning on the alarm and arising to assist Maribel when it sounds, they notice a definite decrease in her bedwetting.

CASE EXAMPLES

Cognitive-Behavioral Therapy (CBT) for Encopresis

Cognitive-behavioral therapy (CBT) is used for encopresis with constipation. In such cases, laxatives and enemas are given to empty the patient's bowels; patients are also placed on high fiber and high fluid diets that are low in constipating dairy products (L. T. Hardy, 2009). The explicitly CBT part of the intervention is a 12-session structured therapy (van Dijk, Benninga, Grootenhuis, Nieuwenhuizen, & Last, 2007). This therapy provides psychoeducation to the parents of the constipated and incontinent child. The psychoeducation teaches parents how to effectively reinforce desired toilet behaviors while ignoring undesired toilet behaviors. The therapy also aims to improve parent–child interactions and reduce anxiety about the child's encopresis problem. Reinforcement is used to encourage proper toilet behavior—stickers and other rewards are provided (L. T. Hardy, 2009; van Dijk et al., 2007). Skills training is also employed, in which the constipated child learns techniques for properly expelling a stool. There isn't much research on this CBT program for encopresis, which fits with the broader observation that encopresis simply hasn't received as much clinical or research attention as enuresis.

Arjun

Arjun's family undergoes CBT for his encopresis. His parents are taught techniques for reinforcing Arjun when he goes to the toilet. Whenever Arjun defecates on the toilet, he gets a sticker and praise from his parents. Arjun is taught techniques for defecating that reduce pain. Negative cognitions that he and his parents hold are also examined, with the idea of getting them to see Arjun's problem as a learned habit that can be changed rather than a sign that they and Arjun are "seriously disturbed."

CASE EXAMPLES

CHAPTER 14

Psychodynamic and Humanistic Alternatives

Psychodynamic and humanistic therapists believe it is important to distinguish *organic* cases of enuresis and encopresis (which have medical/genetic causes) from *functional* cases (which are attributable to psychological conflicts). Given their theoretical commitments, they often focus on the latter, viewing enuresis and encopresis as expressions of underlying psychological distress. Psychodynamic and humanistic therapists believe that addressing this distress in therapy, rather than simply focusing on changing bathroom behavior, is critical to eliminating enuresis and encopresis.

Psychodynamic Perspectives

Psychodynamic perspectives view elimination issues as representations of unconscious conflicts (G. Goodman, 2013; Mishne, 1993; Protinsky & Dillard, 1983). Many psychodynamic explanations have been offered over the years, including ones that attribute enuresis to "distortion of body image, castration fantasies, and conflicts related to sexual identification" (Mishne, 1993, p. 474). Some psychodynamic therapists see cases of **primary enuresis** (when the child has never attained bladder control) as an expression of separation/individuation issues; the child is fearful of separating from the parent (Mishne, 1993). Other psychodynamic theorists view **secondary enuresis** (when the child starts bedwetting after having previously attained bladder control) as caused by a stressful event that results in the child relying on the psychological defense mechanism of regression to return to an earlier (and emotionally less anxiety-provoking) developmental level (Mishne, 1993). Finally, encopresis has been conceptualized in psychodynamic terms as due to unresolved attachment issues; in this analysis, encopresis distracts the child from painful emotions related to insecure attachment by having the child focus on "the pleasure derived from one's own bodily products" (G. Goodman, 2013, p. 441). Although intriguing, there is little research to support these psychodynamic views.

Child-Centered Play Therapy

Child-centered play therapy (introduced in Chapter 13), which grows out of Carl Rogers' person-centered therapy, uses the medium of play to help children work through their issues. Therapists provide core conditions for change and, in providing a safe and accepting environment, children move from a state of psychological incongruence (being self-inconsistent) to a state of congruence (being self-consistent, or true to who they really are). Child-centered play therapy makes sense as an intervention for enuresis and encopresis, but there is almost no humanistic research in this area. The only known published article is a case study of an 8-year-old boy named Tom who displayed self-soiling behaviors (Cuddy-Casey, 1997). The therapist used non-directive child-centered play therapy to help Tom work through his emotional conflicts. The therapy was thought to work by allowing Tom to explore his feelings without being judged or ridiculed. This allowed him to become more self-consistent, which made self-soiling behaviors unnecessary (Cuddy-Casey, 1997). Unfortunately, a single case study—however vivid—provides almost no basis for drawing broader conclusions about the effectiveness of child-centered play therapy for enuresis and encopresis.

Narrative Therapy

Narrative therapy, initially developed by Michael White and David Epston (1990), helps people overcome problems by encouraging them to tell a different story about them. This is often done through externalizing the problem (discussed in several previous chapters). Recall that when clients externalize, they shift their narratives from ones in which the problem is a part of them (a disorder they "have") to ones in which the problem is external to them (something independent of them that gets the best of them). One of White and Epston's (1990) most famous examples of externalizing the problem involved a case of encopresis, in which a little boy named Nick kept smearing his poo on the walls, creating much dissension in his family. White and Epston helped Nick and his parents, Ron and Sue, to externalize "Sneaky Poo." They each came to understand the "requirements" of the problem; that is, how Sneaky Poo affected them. Ron avoided others out of shame, Sue became depressed, and Nick played with his excrement. Once each family member understood how Sneaky Poo influenced him or her, exceptions could be identified by recalling instances when they didn't abide by Sneaky Poo's demands. Nick recognized times when Sneaky Poo didn't convince him to play with his feces, Sue identified moments when she listened to music rather than letting Sneaky Poo depress her, and Ron learned when he was able to socially engage despite Sneaky Poo's protestations to the contrary. Understanding exceptions (times they didn't go along with Sneaky Poo) gave them each insight into effective strategies for sidestepping the problem, which they were able to implement over the course of therapy.

SOCIOCULTURAL PERSPECTIVES

Culture, Stigma, and Socioeconomic Impact

Is enuresis' status as a disorder a reflection of Western values? Some think so, noting that bedwetting hasn't always been regarded as a major problem in other cultures. For example, Native Americans weren't especially concerned about bedwetting and West Africans considered it a "cute" and curable childhood problem (McDonald & Trepper, 1977). Perhaps because Western cultures regard bedwetting so negatively, it carries a lot of stigma (Cendron, 2002). Children who wet the bed or soil themselves are believed to experience a great deal of shame and embarrassment; they often become socially avoidant because they feel isolated from and ostracized by others (R. J. Butler, 2004). Shame and low self-esteem aren't the only negative impacts of enuresis. The financial, as well as emotional, costs to parents of constantly having to launder soiled clothes and sheets and eliminate bad odors in the home are often underestimated (Schulpen, 1997). More broadly, coming from deprived social environments, including being of lower socioeconomic status (SES), has sometimes (but not always) been linked to enuresis (R. J. Butler, 2004; Dolgun, Savaser, Balci, & Yazici, 2012; Scharf et al., 1987; Van Hoecke, Baeyens, Walle, Hoebeke, & Roeyers, 2003). Considering these findings, it's been argued that attending to how social factors influence elimination issues is vitally important.

Arjun
Arjun's parents live on a limited income and most months they barely make ends meet. Arjun's constant soiling of his clothes and bedding has forced his mother to go to the laundromat daily. The cost of this is putting additional stress on Arjun's family.

CASE EXAMPLES

Family Systems Approaches

Various family factors predict nocturnal enuresis, including family instability, parental divorce, and having a mother who smokes or is under age 20 (R. J. Butler, 2004). Thus, from a family systems approach, family context matters. One family systems perspective, structural family therapy, conceptualizes the child with enuresis as the identified patient (the member of the family whose outward symptoms represent the problem) (Protinsky & Dillard, 1983). However, the problem isn't seen as specific to the child, but as a problem in the relational dynamics of the family (T. B. Fletcher, 2000; Protinsky & Dillard, 1983). There might be enmeshed boundaries between the child and one parent, with the other parent becoming increasingly disengaged. This dynamic often reflects unresolved conflicts between the parents, which the child's bedwetting distracts everyone from. Family systems therapy aims to address enuresis (and the family conflicts it masks) by shifting the usual patterns of family interaction. There isn't a lot of research on systems approaches to elimination issues, but many people nonetheless find them compelling.

Maribel's
From a family systems perspective, Maribel's bedwetting distracts from unspoken and unaddressed marital tension between her parents. Maribel is enmeshed with her mother, but this alignment between Maribel and her mother pushes her father to increasingly disengage. Family therapy would disrupt the usual dynamics, perhaps by placing Maribel's father in charge of her enuresis. This would force all members of the family to approach Maribel's bedwetting in a new way, changing ingrained patterns. As Maribel's bedwetting decreased, attention might turn to marital conflict between her parents. Better family communication patterns would be worked on and, as they developed, both Maribel's bedwetting and her parent's marriage would improve.

CASE EXAMPLES

Alternative Therapies: Hypnosis and Acupuncture

Hypnosis is occasionally used as a less traditional, alternative therapy for enuresis. So is **acupuncture**, an ancient Chinese technique in which designated points on the body are stimulated by needles (although in modern acupuncture, lasers are often used instead) (Pearl & Schrollinger, 1999). In hypnosis for enuresis, the patient is often placed into a trance state and offered suggestions that emphasize increased bladder capacity, confidence in the ability to not have accidents, and all-around tension reduction (S. D. Edwards & Van der Spuy, 1985). The patient might be asked to drink several glasses of sweet tea before the hypnotherapy session and then, during the session, be given suggestions to wake up from the trance when feeling the urge to urinate (Tomic, 2011). There isn't a particularly strong evidence base for hypnotherapy for enuresis and it can be time-consuming, but it has worked in some instances and may be appealing to families seeking non-traditional approaches (Iglesias & Iglesias, 2008; Kiddoo, 2015; Seabrook, Gorodzinsky, & Freedman, 2005). The evidence may be a little better for using acupuncture for enuresis, suggesting that adding it to desmopressin or behavior therapy can improve outcomes (Alsharnoubi, Sabbour, Shoukry, & Abdelazeem, 2017; Moursy, Kamel, & Kaseem, 2014). However, two literature reviews concluded that methodological limitations in existing studies make it difficult to draw firm conclusions (Kiddoo, 2015; Lv et al., 2015).

CHAPTER 14

14.4 INTELLECTUAL AND LEARNING DIFFICULTIES

Yolanda

Yolanda is a 22-year-old female born with Down syndrome. As a result, her intellectual functioning is much lower than most other people her age. She has an IQ of 48, according to a recent standardized intelligence assessment; this is significantly below the average, which is roughly 100. Currently, Yolanda lives with her parents, but as they get older they worry about what will become of her when they are no longer physically or financially able to care for her.

Alfred

Alfred is a 10-year-old boy who struggles in school. He dislikes reading and isn't good at it. Standardized assessments find that his reading proficiency is well below where it should be for a boy his age. The other children in school often tease him for being "stupid" and his teachers worry about his increasingly angry and disruptive behavior in the classroom. Despite his poor reading skills, Alfred's IQ is in the average range and he functions well outside of school, as evidenced by the fact that he was recently chosen to be captain of his travel football team.

DSM AND *ICD* PERSPECTIVES

Intellectual Disability

The *DSM-5* and *ICD-11* distinguish intellectual disability from learning disorder, although both are classified as neurodevelopmental disorders. These manuals define **intellectual disability** (also called *intellectual developmental disorder*) as involving deficits in intellectual and adaptive functioning that emerge early in a child's development. Intellectual disability is diagnosed by assessing (a) intelligence (using intelligence tests; see Chapter 3), and (b) impairment in everyday functioning. Typically, children qualify for an intellectual disability if their intelligence quotient (IQ) is below 70, which is substantially lower than the average IQ of 100 (two standard deviations lower, for those of you with knowledge of statistics). See Chapter 3 for more on IQ score ranges. Intellectual disabilities are divided into four types: *mild* (IQ 50–69), *moderate* (IQ 35–49), *severe* (IQ 20–34), and *profound* (IQ less than 20) (Bhaumik et al., 2016). Both IQ score and level of adaptive functioning are used to determine severity.

Yolanda

Case example client Yolanda qualifies for an intellectual disability diagnosis of moderate severity, due to her IQ of 48.

Importantly, the *DSM-5* cautions that clinical judgment is necessary and that IQ scores alone shouldn't determine whether someone receives an intellectual disability diagnosis. People with mild and moderate intellectual disabilities are usually able to live on their own and hold down skilled or semiskilled jobs; those with severe intellectual disabilities require daily supervision and assistance; and those with profound intellectual disabilities often need help with even the most basic tasks, such as feeding themselves, walking, talking, and getting dressed. The *ICD-10* divides intellectual disabilities into the same mild, moderate, severe, and profound categories as the *DSM-5* and *ICD-11*, but because it was published in the 1990s, it still uses the now out-of-fashion (due to it being perceived as derogatory) term **mental retardation** (Martínez, Nellis, White, Jochim, & Peterson, 2016). See Diagnostic Box 14.7 for criteria and guidelines. The *DSM-5* estimates that intellectual disabilities affect 1% of the population.

Diagnostic Box 14.7 Intellectual Disability

DSM-5: Intellectual Disability (Intellectual Developmental Disorder)
- Intellectual deficits.
- Adaptive functioning deficits (doesn't meet developmental and social standards for independent functioning).
- Onset in early development.
- Specify: *mild, moderate, severe,* or *profound.*

Based on American Psychiatric Association, 2013b, p. 33

ICD-10: Mental Retardation
- Reduced intellectual functioning.
- Diminished adaptability to everyday demands.
- Onset during early development.
- Specify: *mild, moderate, severe,* or *profound.*

Based on World Health Organization, 1992, pp. 176–180

ICD-11: Disorder of Intellectual Development
- Reduced intellectual functioning.
- Diminished adaptability to everyday demands.
- Functioning two or more standard deviations below average.
- Specify: *mild, moderate, severe,* or *profound.*

Based on https://icd.who.int/browse11/l-m/en

Learning Disorders

Intellectual disabilities must be distinguished from *learning disorders* (also called *learning disabilities*). **Specific learning disorder** (see Diagnostic Box 14.8) is the *DSM-5* disorder that is diagnosed when a child exhibits difficulty learning and performing in school. There is an equivalent category in the *ICD-11* called *developmental learning disorder*. Children who qualify for a specific learning disorder diagnosis have trouble with things like reading, writing, spelling, and math. Their academic performance is substantially below expectations for their age, but—and this is an important distinction—it isn't caused by an intellectual disability. That is, academic performance is poor even though there aren't deficits in intellectual and adaptive functioning.

Diagnostic Box 14.8 Learning Disorders

DSM-5: Specific Learning Disorder
- Difficulties with learning or academic skills, as evidenced by academic skills that are significantly below what is expected for one's age and that interfere with performance at work, school, or in everyday life.
- One or more: (1) incorrect or slow reading requiring extensive effort; (2) trouble with reading comprehension; (3) poor spelling; (4) poor writing; (5) trouble with understanding or calculating numbers; (6) difficulty solving math problems.
- The problem develops during school years but may not become apparent until academic demands exceed skills.
- Cannot be due to an intellectual disability, uncorrected vision or hearing problem, other mental/neurological disorders, socioeconomic adversity, lack of proficiency with language used in school, or poor-quality schooling.
- Specify: *with impairment in reading, with impairment in written expression,* or *with impairment in mathematics.*

Based on American Psychiatric Association, 2013b, pp. 66–68

ICD-10: Specific Developmental Disorders of Scholastic Skills
Four separate diagnoses:
- **Specific reading disorder**: Impaired reading skills, not attributable to mental retardation, vision problems, or poor schooling.
- **Specific spelling disorder**: Impaired spelling, not attributable to mental retardation, vision problems, or poor schooling; no history of specific reading disorder.
- **Specific disorder of arithmetical skills**: Impaired math skills, not attributable to mental retardation or extremely poor schooling.
- **Mixed disorder of scholastic skills**: Unclearly defined residual category for anyone with reading, spelling, or math problems that don't fit the other three categories, and which are not attributable to mental retardation or poor schooling.

Based on World Health Organization, 1992, pp. 188–195

ICD-11: Developmental Learning Disorder
- Difficulties with learning or academic skills, as evidenced by academic skills that are significantly below what is expected for one's age and that interfere with performance at work, school, or in everyday life.
- Cannot be due to an intellectual disability, uncorrected vision or hearing problem, other mental/neurological disorders, socioeconomic adversity, lack of proficiency with language used in school, or poor-quality schooling.
- Separate diagnoses for: *with impairment in reading, with impairment in written expression, with impairment in mathematics,* or *with other specified impairment in learning.*

Based on https://icd.who.int/browse11/l-m/en

The *DSM-5* lists three types of specific learning disorder: *with impairment in reading, with impairment in writing,* and *with impairment in mathematics.* Sometimes the impairment in reading type is referred to as **dyslexia**, which involves difficulty decoding information when reading; it is characterized by trouble recognizing, deciphering, or spelling words (Shaywitz & Shaywitz, 2005; Snowling & Hulme, 2012). Likewise, the type involving impairment with mathematics (e.g., processing and calculating numbers) is often identified as **dyscalculia**. Notably, for the impaired reading type, reading comprehension problems are occasionally distinguished from dyslexia, but are still coded as specific learning disorders with impairment in reading (Snowling & Hulme, 2012). The *ICD-11* lists the same three types as *DSM-5,* but it includes a fourth type (*with other specified impairment in learning*) for children whose learning problems don't have to do with reading,

Children performing well below their expected age-level in math may receive the DSM-5 *diagnosis of specific learning disorder with impairment in mathematics, which is also called dyscalculia.*
Source: www.imagesource.com

written expression, or math. Similarly, the *ICD-10* lists four distinct "developmental disorders of scholastic skills" (disorders of reading, spelling, math, and mixed skills).

Alfred

Using DSM-5 criteria, Alfred (our 9-year-old case example client who struggles with reading) may qualify for a diagnosis of specific learning disorder (with impairment in reading); further assessment might identify Alfred's reading problem as dyslexia.

CASE EXAMPLES

When do academic struggles constitute a learning disorder and how can we best assess this? These issues continue to be debated in the field.
Source: Getty Images/Onoky\Eric Audras

The *DSM-5* says learning disorders affect 5%–15% of school-age children and 4% of adults. Dyslexia is usually considered the most common specific learning disorder. As evidence of this, a study of second to sixth graders in Brazil found greater prevalence of reading impairment (7.5%) compared to writing (5.4%) or math (6.0%) (Fortes et al., 2016). However, reading, writing, and math impairments show a great deal of comorbidity (Landerl & Moll, 2010; Moll, Kunze, Neuhoff, Bruder, & Schulte-Körne, 2014). Thus, someone with difficulties in one of these academic areas may also struggle with one or both of the others. In recent years, there has been much controversy over how best to assess whether a child has a learning disorder. The "Controversial Question" feature examines this issue.

CONTROVERSIAL QUESTION

How Should We Diagnose Learning Disabilities?

Diagnosing learning disabilities has long been controversial. Starting in the late 1970s in the United States, it became common practice to make diagnoses using the **IQ-achievement discrepancy model**. In this model, discrepancies between IQ scores and achievement scores are used to diagnose learning disabilities (Cakiroglu, 2015). When children's IQ scores (which ostensibly assess natural ability) are significantly higher than their performance on achievement tests (which ostensibly test mastery of material), learning disabilities are diagnosed. The assumption is that a learning disability, rather than an intellectual deficit, is the cause of these children's poor academic performances.

While IQ-achievement discrepancy was the predominant way of diagnosing learning disabilities for quite some time, it has received a great deal of criticism. Many have questioned the validity of the discrepancy model, arguing that research finds it doesn't distinguish children with learning disabilities from those without them (Fuchs, Mock, Morgan, & Young, 2003; Humphries & Bone, 1993; Stuebing et al., 2002). Further, it is considered to be a "wait-to-fail" model because children can't be diagnosed with a learning disability until after they have been in school a while and accrued a record of poor performance relative to their IQ scores (Cakiroglu, 2015; Fuchs et al., 2003; Kavale, Holdnack, & Mostert, 2006; Martinez et al., 2016). Thus, critics have argued that the IQ-achievement discrepancy model leads to learning disorder labels being "arbitrarily assigned" and "unfairly withheld from children who are as needy and deserving as those to whom the label is given" (Fuchs et al., 2003, p. 158).

Since the mid-2000s, the **response-to-intervention model (RTI)** has provided an alternative to the discrepancy model. RTI's main idea is "to identify the academic difficulties of students as early as possible to provide the necessary supplemental educational services" (Cakiroglu, 2015, p. 171). RTI aims to provide students with high quality instruction that meets their academic needs, using research data as a guide to what kind of instruction does so (Grosche & Volpe, 2013). Each child's performance in school the previous year is evaluated. There are various ways in which RTI programs have been structured, but one of the most common ways is using a three-tier approach (Cakiroglu, 2015; Fuchs et al., 2003; McKenzie, 2009). Children who are meeting grade-level standards are considered *Tier 1*; this is most children in regular classroom settings. Those whose performances don't meet these standards are placed in *Tier 2* and provided academic assistance in small groups (2–4 students) that meet 3–4 times per week for 9–12 weeks. Tier 2 children who respond to this intervention are returned to the normal classroom (Tier 1). Those who don't are moved to Tier 3, where they are given much more intensive academic assistance, provided by special education teachers, over a longer period in groups up to three students. Tier 3 also includes individualized assessment to rule out intellectual disabilities, autism, vision and hearing impairments, and other issues besides a learning disorder that could be the reason for poor academic performance (Grosche & Volpe, 2013). Children who respond to Tier 3 interventions are reintegrated into Tiers 2 and 1, but those who don't are placed into special education programs (Cakiroglu, 2015; Fuchs et al., 2003).

Like the discrepancy model, RTI also has come in for criticism. Those skeptical of RTI complain that it has worse, not better, validity than the discrepancy model. Why? Because RTI blurs the line between learning and intellectual disabilities by no longer using IQ discrepancy to identify learning disorders (Kavale & Spaulding, 2008; McKenzie, 2009). Thus, any student who does poorly in school, regardless of IQ score, potentially qualifies for a learning disability. Detractors therefore contend that "when analyzed critically, RTI does not appear to be a complete identification procedure" (Kavale & Spaulding, 2008, p. 174). Some have suggested that RTI be used as a form of prevention, rather than as a means of diagnosing learning disabilities; only once a child fails to respond at Tier 3 should efforts to diagnose a learning disorder begin, using both IQ-achievement discrepancy and other relevant data (Kavale & Spaulding, 2008). Using discrepancy versus RTI models for assessing learning disabilities remains an ongoing controversy in the field of special education and one about which students planning to pursue careers in education should be aware.

CRITICAL THINKING QUESTIONS

1. Do you prefer the IQ-achievement discrepancy model or the response-to-intervention model? Why?

2. Can you think of ways to move beyond the discrepancy-RTI debate and more adequately conceptualize learning disabilities?

3. To what extent do you think that ways of assessing learning disabilities are intertwined with the priorities and values of the educational system?

HISTORICAL PERSPECTIVES

Attitudes toward people with intellectual disabilities have changed a lot over the last century or so. During the early 20th century, the **eugenics movement** took hold in many countries (Diekema, 2003). Eugenicists believed that intelligence and other traits were primarily inherited. Based on this belief, they felt that humanity could be improved by encouraging selective breeding between people with "desirable" traits while preventing it among those with "undesirable" traits. At various points throughout the 20th century, many countries—including the U.S., Canada, Australia, Germany, Japan, Denmark, and Iceland—allowed the legal sterilization of intellectually disabled and other "mentally defective" people against their will (Diekema, 2003; A. Roy, Roy, & Roy, 2012; Stefánsdóttir, 2014). Sometimes this was done surgically; other times via chemical castration in men (see Chapter 10) or birth control pills in women. There are still some instances of involuntary sterilization today, but the practice has generally fallen out of favor as attitudes toward people with intellectual disabilities have become less negative. Still, this history reminds us that helping professionals always have the potential to do harm.

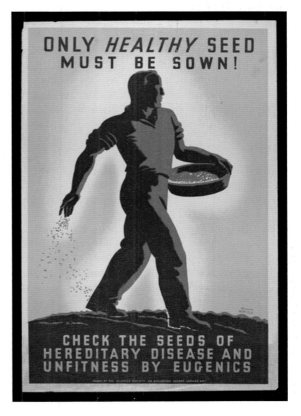

A 1930 British Eugenics poster.
Source: © Galton Institute London

BIOLOGICAL PERSPECTIVES

Intellectual Disabilities

Some intellectual disabilities are attributed to genetically inherited recessive-gene diseases. For instance, **phenylketonuria (PKU)** is a rare inherited disease. Babies born with it are deficient in the liver enzyme, *phenylalanine hydroxylase*. This results in their bodies being unable to break down phenylalanine and

CHAPTER 14

phenylpyruvic acid, which leads to brain damage and intellectual impairment (R. A. Williams, Mamotte, & Burnett, 2008).

Other intellectual disabilities are caused by abnormalities with chromosomes (which, as discussed in Chapter 2, are the 23 thread-like structures made up of DNA that carry genetic information). Two examples of disorders attributed to chromosomal abnormalities are Down syndrome and fragile X syndrome. People with **Down syndrome** have an extra copy of the chromosome *trisomy 21* (Nikolas et al., 2016). In addition to intellectual disability, Down syndrome is associated with certain physical signs, including eyes that slant upwards; short, stocky bodies; flat faces and noses; small heads, ears, and mouths; and poor muscle tone (National Institute of Health, n.d.-a).

Yolanda

Yolanda, our case example client with an intellectual disability, has Down Syndrome.

CASE EXAMPLES

Fragile X syndrome is linked to a mutation in the *fMRI1* gene on the *X chromosome* (Maenner et al., 2013; I. Newman, Leader, Chen, & Mannion, 2015). During adolescence, children with fragile X syndrome develop thin faces, long ears, large heads, prominent foreheads, flat feet, and extremely flexible joints (National Institute of Health, n.d.-b; Newman et al., 2015). Demographically, Fragile X is more common in boys than girls, but women are more likely to carry the recessive gene that causes it than men (Maenner et al., 2013; National Institute of Health, n.d.-b). Further, Fragile X syndrome is comorbid with aggression, disruptive behavior, and attention-deficit hyperactivity disorder (ADHD) (Newman et al., 2015; Wheeler, Raspa, Bishop, & Bailey, 2016). Patients diagnosed with it often show autism spectrum disorder symptoms: sensitivity to noise and bright lights, speech and language difficulties, and intense anxiety in unfamiliar situations (National Institute of Health, n.d.-b). Might this mean that fragile X shares underlying genetic links to disorders with which it commonly co-occurs?

Besides genetics, intellectual disabilities are attributed to other biological factors. Intellectual disabilities can originate in *problems during pregnancy*—such as maternal drug use, infections, and malnutrition (Bhaumik et al., 2016). *Complications during childbirth*, such as the baby's brain being denied oxygen, can also produce intellectual disabilities (Bhaumik et al., 2016). Other sources of intellectual disabilities are *illnesses* such as whooping cough, meningitis, or the measles. Finally, *brain injuries*—due to head injuries (e.g., in car accidents) or exposure to environmental toxins (e.g., lead, mercury, or environmental pollutants)—are common causes of intellectual disabilities (Bhaumik et al., 2016).

Learning Disorders

Biological investigators have been searching for genetic correlates of learning disorders, too. Dyslexia has received the most attention in this regard. Researchers point to studies showing dyslexia to be heritable, as well as to research that has identified numerous candidate genes associated with it (Carrion-Castillo, Franke, & Fisher, 2013; Kong et al., 2016; B. Mueller et al., 2014). There is less research on the genetics of dyscalculia, but what evidence there is has been interpreted as suggesting that dyscalculia has a genetic/familial component while also being genetically distinct from dyslexia (Kuhn, 2015; Shalev et al., 2001). As for brain structures, posterior regions of the brain (specifically the left *temporoparietal area* and *occipitotemporal area*) have been identified as less active in people with dyslexia; the assumption is that underactivity in these areas impairs *phonological awareness* (awareness of the structure and sounds of words) (Shaywitz & Shaywitz, 2005).

When it comes to medication, in some cases (especially when other behavior problems are present) stimulants and other ADHD drugs are prescribed to children diagnosed with reading disabilities (C. Gray & Climie, 2016). More broadly, it's estimated that drugs are prescribed to 20%–45% of people diagnosed with learning disorders (Deb, 2007). The types of drugs prescribed include not only stimulants, but also antipsychotics, antidepressants, benzodiazepines, *antiepileptics*, *buspirone*, beta blockers, mood stabilizers, and opioid antagonists (Deb, 2007). Most of these drugs have not been extensively researched for use in patients diagnosed with learning disorders, but nonetheless are used to manage comorbid behavior and mood problems (Deb, 2007).

Alfred

Should Alfred's behavior in school continue to be disruptive, his doctors might prescribe him one of these drugs. If you were Alfred's parents, would you support or oppose this? Why?

CASE EXAMPLES

PSYCHOLOGICAL PERSPECTIVES

Intellectual Disabilities

Cognitive-behavioral interventions are often used to help people with intellectual disabilities. Early interventions rooted in the principles of applied behavior analysis (ABA) (see Chapter 13) are commonly employed, along with CBT techniques that teach people with intellectual disabilities how to complete everyday tasks by breaking them down into manageable steps (Luiselli, 2016). There is evidence that such interventions can have positive effects (Hassiotis et al., 2011; Haymes, Storey, Maldonado, Post, & Montgomery, 2013; Luiselli, 2016).

Yolanda

When Yolanda's intellectual disability was first identified during her childhood, she might have undergone ABA. Using reinforcement, she would have been taught how to complete basic tasks such as bathing, getting dressed, and making her bed. As she got older, more complex tasks—such as taking the bus, ordering in a restaurant, and paying bills online could have been taught to her in a step-by-step way using reinforcement of desired responses.

Learning Disorders

When it comes to learning disorders, psychological interventions that focus on teaching both *reading skills* and *phonological awareness* can significantly improve reading performance in children diagnosed with dyslexia (Snowling & Hulme, 2012). There is also support for using *oral language interventions* that teach speaking and listening skills, narrative skills, and vocabulary. However, although oral language interventions do appear to improve vocabulary, they don't necessarily improve reading skills (Snowling & Hulme, 2012). Finally, **music education** is sometimes used to treat dyslexia. Rooted in the idea that phonological awareness is correlated with musical abilities, the goal is to help people with dyslexia to develop the skills necessary for reading more effectively by improving their musical skills. The evidence that music education improves reading skills is slim because, although some studies support it, few of them are randomized controlled trials (RCTs) (Cogo-Moreira et al., 2012; Rolka & Silverman, 2015).

Music education is sometimes used to treat dyslexia. It's thought to help because phonological awareness and musical abilities are positively correlated.
Source: COMSTOCK IMAGES

SOCIOCULTURAL PERSPECTIVES

Intellectual Disabilities

Socioeconomic Inequality

Although intellectual disabilities are commonly thought to originate in impaired brain functioning, social factors are extremely important. Social justice advocates point to an alarming finding, namely that intellectual disabilities are correlated with poverty. Those living in poverty are at higher risk for developing intellectual disabilities (Emerson, 2007). Why might this be? One reason is that poor people have less access to resources that foster intellectual development; another reason is that they are more likely to be exposed to toxins and other environmental dangers that cause intellectual disabilities (Emerson, 2007). In addition to poverty placing people at higher risk for intellectual disabilities, it's also the case that intellectual disabilities foster poverty (Emerson & Hatton, 2007; Emerson, Shahtahmasebi, Lancaster, & Berridge, 2010). How come? Because having an intellectual disability is economically draining. People with such disabilities lack earning potential. They are also expensive to care for, thus families with a member who is intellectually disabled often slide down the socioeconomic ladder.

CHAPTER 14

Yolanda

For instance, our case example client Yolanda's parents have found it extremely difficult to make ends meet given the costs Yolanda's intellectual disability incurs (medication, schooling, therapies, etc.).

Social justice advocates argue that remediating social inequality is a critical, but neglected, way in which we can both prevent intellectual disabilities and assist those who do have them (Emerson & Parish, 2010).

Group Homes

People with intellectual disabilities most often live in community settings, typically with the assistance of family members and various social support services (Lakin & Stancliffe, 2007). When circumstances don't permit patients to live on their own or with family members, residential treatment in **group homes** is a common alternative. Group homes typically house a small number of residents, providing them with medical care and live-in aides who assist them in their daily routines. The main advantage of group homes is that, compared to hospitals and nursing homes, they allow residents to live in the community rather than a more institutional setting.

Yolanda
One possibility for Yolanda is to eventually move into a group home. Should she find a group home she likes, she will be able to live independently in the community while also receiving necessary social support. The challenge is finding high-quality group homes that are adequately funded and staffed.

Learning Disorders

How should people learn? What things should they be good at learning? How do we know when they aren't learning properly? Sociocultural critics of learning disorders like to ask such questions. Some even argue that "learning disorders" aren't objectively true things we discovered. Instead, they are concepts that people in Western, individualized cultures invented and now take for granted. In other words, to many sociocultural critics, "learning disorders" are social constructions. Why? Because they reflect a socially shared way of defining, talking about, and understanding poor academic performance—one overly rooted in a "deficit" orientation (Dudley-Marling, 2004; Katchergin, 2016).

A social constructionist perspective encourages us to consider alternative ways of collectively talking about and defining learning problems. It holds that current definitions of learning disorder (and strategies for "fixing" it) are products of a Western worldview that assumes learning problems originate in individual defects (Dudley-Marling, 2004; Katchergin, 2016). Further, socially invented categories of "learning disability" serve powerful social interests by sorting children in ways that advantage the privileged in society. According to one social constructionist analysis, "students are rank-ordered and classified for instruction such that those from advantaged social groups tend to be prepared for the better jobs, while those from disadvantaged backgrounds tend to be channeled into low pay, low status work" (Sleeter, 1986, p. 48).

The social constructionist view encourages us to question the idea that learning disabilities are context-free disorders that occur within individuals and instead reframe learning problems in more social and relational terms. For instance, we might ask why learning disorder diagnoses are more commonly assigned to children from certain racial and ethnic minority groups, as well as in boys and those who are *language minorities* (their first language isn't the one being taught in school) (Shifrer, Muller, & Callahan, 2011). To a social constructionist way of thinking, such differences may reflect the minimization of sociocultural factors and the overemphasis of individual factors in thinking about children who experience trouble with learning. As such, learning problems become as much a social justice issue as a medical one.

14.5 MOTOR PROBLEMS

Greta
Greta is a 6-year-old girl who recently developed multiple vocal and motor tics. These tics involve recurrently blinking, grunting, and making odd clicking noises with her tongue. Previously an outgoing child and good student, Greta's performance in school has deteriorated since she began exhibiting these tics.

DSM AND *ICD* PERSPECTIVES

Besides some of the other problems discussed in this chapter and Chapter 13, the *DSM-5*'s "Neurodevelopmental Disorders" chapter also includes a section on "motor disorders." The three major diagnostic categories in this section are developmental coordination disorder, stereotypic movement disorder, and tic disorders.

Developmental coordination disorder is diagnosed in children who show motor coordination skills that are well below what would be expected given their age. They are excessively clumsy and bad at activities requiring physical coordination—things like catching a ball, using scissors, riding a bike, writing with a pen, or playing sports. **Stereotypic movement disorder** involves repetitive and purposeless movements that begin early in development and which the child seems driven to perform; according to the *DSM-5*, examples include waving one's hands, rocking back and forth, banging one's head, and biting or hitting oneself. The last of the three motor disorder categories contain the **tic disorders**, which are characterized by abrupt and repetitive motor or vocal movements (i.e., **tics**). There are four different kinds of tics (Shaw & Coffey, 2014):

Developmental coordination disorder is diagnosed in children who struggle with activities like catching a ball, cutting with scissors, riding a bike, or writing with a pen.
Source: Flickr Open\EujarimPhotography

» *Simple motor tics* are the most common; they involve simple repetitive movements like eye-blinking, shoulder shrugging, or head jerking.

» *Complex motor tics* are comprised of more coordinated and purposeful movements, such as hopping, skipping, tapping, stepping in certain patterns, and touching specific objects.

» *Simple vocal tics* involve brief utterances or sounds; repetitive throat clearing, coughing, sniffling, grunting, gurgling, and spitting are all examples.

» *Complex vocal tics* are characterized by repeating words, sounds, and phrases; examples are repeating one's own words (**palilalia**), repeating other's words (echolalia; see Chapter 4), and involuntary cursing (**copralalia**).

The most well-known tic disorder is **Tourette's disorder** (or *Tourette's syndrome*), which involves both motor and vocal tics that have persisted for over a year. However, the *DSM-5* also includes two less severe tic disorder diagnoses: **persistent (chronic) motor or vocal tic disorder** (in which the patient displays either motor or vocal tics—but not both—for over a year) and **provisional tic disorder** (in which the patient displays motor and/or verbal tics, but for less than one year). To qualify for any of these tic disorders, symptoms must begin before age 18. However, tics most often develop between ages 4 and 6, reaching their peak severity between ages 10 and 12 (Shaw & Coffey, 2014).

Greta

Our case example client, Greta, probably would be diagnosed with provisional tic disorder until her tics persist for more than a year; once they do, her diagnosis would change to Tourette's disorder because she exhibits both motor and vocal tics.

CASE EXAMPLES

The *ICD-10* and *ICD-11* include movement disorder diagnoses that are roughly equivalent to the three *DSM-5* categories just described. However, the *ICD-11* lists tic disorders as movement disorders of the nervous system, rather than as mental disorders. See Diagnostic Box 14.9 for details. Herein, we focus mainly on tic disorders, especially Tourette's disorder.

Diagnostic Box 14.9 Motor Disorders

DSM-5

- **Developmental coordination disorder**: Coordination and motor skills that are lower than what is expected for one's age and are not due to an intellectual disability, vision problem, or another neurological disorder; begins early in development and results in clumsiness (e.g., bumping into things) or poor motor skills (e.g., difficulty catching a ball, using scissors, riding a bike, writing with a pen, or playing sports).
Based on American Psychiatric Association, 2013b, p. 74
- **Stereotypic movement disorder**: Repetitive and purposeless motor behavior that one seems driven to perform that begins early in development. Specify *with injurious behavior* or *without injurious behavior*.
Based on American Psychiatric Association, 2013b, pp. 77–78

CHAPTER 14

- **Tic disorders**: Characterized by abrupt and repetitive motor or vocal movements (i.e., tics). Three types
  - **Provisional tic disorder**: One or more tics (motor and/or vocal) that have persisted for less than 12 months and began before age 18.
  - **Persistent (chronic) motor or vocal tic disorder**: Either motor or vocal tics (but not both) that have persisted for more than 12 months and began before age 18.
  - **Tourette's disorder**: Multiple motor tics and at least one vocal tic (though not necessarily at the same time) that have persisted for more than 12 months and began before age 18.

Based on American Psychiatric Association, 2013b, p. 81

ICD-10

- **Specific developmental disorder of motor function**: Seriously impaired motor coordination not due to mental retardation or another neurological disorder; results in clumsiness (e.g., dropping things, bumping into things, poor handwriting, and being bad at puzzles, building models, drawing, or comprehending maps).
- **Stereotyped movement disorders**: Involve intentional, repeated, stereotyped, and purposeless movements that are often rhythmic but are not part of any recognized mental or neurological disorder.
- **Tic disorders**: Characterized by abrupt and repetitive motor or vocal movements (i.e., tics). Three types:
  - **Transient tic disorder**: Recurrent tics that have not persisted for more than 12 months; usually develop by age 4 or 5.
  - **Chronic motor or vocal tic disorder**: Either motor or vocal tics (but not both) that have persisted for more than 12 months.
  - **Combined motor or vocal tic disorder (Tourette's syndrome)**: Multiple motor tics and at least one vocal tic (though not necessarily at the same time); the motor tics often develop first; typically develops in childhood or adolescence.

Based on World Health Organization, 1992, pp. 196–197 (specific developmental disorder of motor function), pp. 226–227 (stereotyped movement disorders), and pp. 221–223 (tic disorders)

ICD-11

- **Developmental coordination disorder**: Motor skills that are well below what is expected given the person's age and intellectual level; delayed acquisition of motor skills that results in clumsy and slow motor behavior.
- **Stereotyped movement disorder**: Involve intentional, repeated, stereotyped, and purposeless movements that are often rhythmic but are not part of any recognized mental or neurological disorder.
- **Tic disorders**: Characterized by abrupt and repetitive motor or vocal movements (i.e., tics). Three types:
  - **Transient motor tic disorder**: Motor tics that have persisted for less than 12 months.
  - **Chronic motor tic disorder**: Motor tics that have persisted for at least 12 months.
  - **Transient vocal tic disorder**: Vocal tics that have persisted for less than 12 months.
  - **Chronic phonic tic disorder**: Vocal tics that have persisted for at least 12 months.
  - **Tourette's syndrome:** Both chronic motor and vocal tics that develop in childhood or adolescence; the motor and vocal tics must have persisted for at least 12 months but may not occur simultaneously or persistently during that time.

Based on https://icd.who.int/browse11/l-m/en

Regarding prevalence, the *DSM-5* estimates that 5%–6% of children meet criteria for developmental coordination disorder, with boys two to seven times more likely than girls to receive this diagnosis. As for stereotypic movement disorder, it is especially prevalent among children in residential facilities who are diagnosed with intellectual disabilities; 10%–15% of such children may qualify for a diagnosis, according to the *DSM-5*. When it comes to tic disorders, Tourette's disorder is estimated to occur in 1% of the world's population (Shaw & Coffey, 2014). More generally, the *DSM-5* indicates that tic disorders occur in three to five out of every 1,000 children and are two to four times more common in males than females. The prevalence of tic disorders is higher in people diagnosed with numerous other mental disorders. For instance, tic disorders are comorbid with obsessive-compulsive disorder, ADHD, disruptive behavior disorders, autism spectrum disorder, major depressive disorder, bipolar disorder, personality disorders, and sleep disorders (Eapen, Cavanna, & Robertson, 2016; Ferreira, Pio-Abreu, & Januário, 2014; Kalyva, Kyriazi, Vargiami, & Zafeiriou, 2016; M. M. Robertson, Cavanna, & Eapen, 2015). Tic disorders also commonly co-occur with epilepsy (L. C. Wong et al., 2016).

HISTORICAL PERSPECTIVES

Tourette's syndrome is named after Georges Albert Édouard Brutus Gilles de la Tourette (1857–1904), who was a French physician and student of the famous neurologist Jean-Martin Charcot (1825–1893). In 1885, Gilles de la Tourette published a two-part article describing nine patients who had vocal and motor tics (Kushner, 1999, 2000; McNaught, 2010). One of the cases that Gilles de la Tourette wrote about was previously described by the French physician Jean Marc Gaspard Itard (1775–1838). The case was that of the Marquise de Dampierre, a French noblewoman who, despite being highly educated and sophisticated, was infamous for publically shouting out curse words in the middle of conversations. Gilles de la Tourette named the syndrome he described *maladie des tics*, but Charcot later renamed it Tourette's syndrome in honor of the man who described it (McNaught, 2010).

Importantly, Charcot and Gilles de la Tourette viewed Tourette's syndrome as an incurable brain disease; as Gilles de la Tourette himself put it, "once a ticcer, always a ticcer" (Kushner, 2000, p. 76). However, throughout much of the 20th century, psychodynamic theories of Tourette's were quite influential. For example, the prominent psychoanalyst Margaret Mahler (1897–1985) believed that Tourette's only developed in biologically susceptible children with severely repressed psychological conflicts tied to family dynamics (Kushner, 1999; Mahler & Rangell, 1943). Although not very effective, psychodynamic interventions for Tourette's were far less invasive than the psychosurgery technique of lobotomy (see Chapter 1), which—despite its damage to overall mental functioning—was sometimes used in severe cases (Hashemiyoon, Kuhn, & Visser-Vandewalle, 2017). The influence of psychodynamic therapy for treating tics didn't wane until the antipsychotic drug *haloperidol* showed more promise and began to be used instead during the 1960s. This led to the reemergence of genetic and other biological theories of tic disorders, which we discuss next.

BIOLOGICAL PERSPECTIVES

Genetics and Tourette's

The causes of tic disorders remain largely unknown (Shaw & Coffey, 2014). Compared to other disorders suspected of having a strong genetic component, existing research on the genetics of tic disorders is relatively modest (Pauls, Fernandez, Mathews, State, & Scharf, 2014). Still, based on this research, the consensus is that tic disorders are highly heritable (Motlagh, Fernandez, & Leckman, 2012; Pauls et al., 2014; Shaw & Coffey, 2014). Although only two twin studies have been published, these studies estimate concordance rates for Tourette's to be 50%–77% for monozygotic (identical) twins, but only 10%–23% for dizygotic (fraternal) twins (O'Rourke, Scharf, Yu, & Pauls, 2009; Pauls et al., 2014; Shaw & Coffey, 2014). Further, tic disorders run in families (O'Rourke et al., 2009; Pauls et al., 2014). If you have a first degree relative with a tic disorder, your chances of having one increase by 5 to 15 times (Shaw & Coffey, 2014).

Numerous candidate genes have been linked to Tourette's. Genes related to dopamine and serotonin are being studied, with the **dopamine hypothesis of Tourette's disorder** holding that too much dopamine activity may play a role in the disorder (with some researchers adding that too little serotonin may be important too) (Motlagh et al., 2012; Paschou, 2013; Shaw & Coffey, 2014). Chromosomal abnormalities on the *SLITRK1 gene* (important in *neurite outgrowth*, which involves the growth of neuron dendrites and axons) have also received a lot of attention (Motlagh et al., 2012; O'Rourke et al., 2009; Pauls et al., 2014; Shaw & Coffey, 2014). Another candidate gene worthy of mention is the *HDC gene*, which is important in the activity of histamine, a neurotransmitter involved in immune system response and mentioned earlier when discussing sleep (A. Hartmann, Martino, & Murphy, 2016; Paschou, 2013).

Tics Due to Immune System Dysfunction?

Some research has found a relationship between tics and autoimmune functioning. Children who have had viral infections such as strep throat appear to be at higher risk of developing tics. This has led to the **PANDAS hypothesis** (i.e., the *Pediatric Autoimmune Neuropsychiatric Disorders Associated with Streptococcal Infection hypothesis*), which holds that tics develop in genetically susceptible individuals who contract strep or other viruses (Elamin, Edwards, & Martino, 2013; Hoekstra, Dietrich, Edwards, Elamin, & Martino, 2013; Hoekstra, Kallenberg, Korf, & Minderaa, 2002; Hornig & Lipkin, 2013; Kushner, 2000). The PANDAS hypothesis continues to be researched and debated, but not everyone accepts it or thinks it applies to all tic disorder cases (Hoekstra et al., 2013).

Biological Interventions

Drugs Prescribed

When it comes to drug treatments for Tourette's disorder, antipsychotics are commonly prescribed because extreme dopamine sensitivity (possibly due to having too many dopamine receptors) in the **basal ganglia** (a part of the brain important in controlling movement) is suspected of playing a role in causing Tourette's (A. Hartmann et al., 2016; Kushner, 1999; Roessner et al., 2011). There are different dopamine pathways and many antipsychotics affect the D2 dopamine pathways; however, recent research suggests that targeting the D1 pathway with drugs like *ecopipam* (which doesn't affect D2 dopamine receptors or serotonin) may hold promise in Tourette's treatment (A. Hartmann et al., 2016). Overall, research on the effectiveness of antipsychotics for Tourette's has produced mixed results at best, although there is some hope that newer

CHAPTER 14

atypical antipsychotics like *aripiprazole* and *risperidone* may be more effective (and have fewer negative side effects) than older first-generation antipsychotics like *haloperidol* (Roessner et al., 2011; Roessner et al., 2013; C. Yang et al., 2016; Zheng et al., 2016). Unfortunately, the evidence base for atypical antispychotic use for Tourette's is currently small; a lot more research is needed (Roessner et al., 2011; Roessner et al., 2013; Zheng et al., 2016). Though antipsychotics are used most often, drugs affecting histamine, acetylcholine, GABA, and glutamate are all receiving attention as treatments for tic disorders, as are antiepileptic drugs and cannabis (A. Hartmann et al., 2016; Roessner et al., 2011; Roessner et al., 2013; C. Yang et al., 2016). This reflects how neurochemical explanations of Tourette's remain muddy, leading to speculation that many neurotransmitters may interact in causing tics (Roessner et al., 2011; Roessner et al., 2013).

Deep Brain Stimulation (DBS)

When other interventions fail to produce results, deep brain stimulation (DBS) is sometimes used to treat Tourette's. As you may remember from Chapter 5, DBS involves permanently implanting electrodes in the brain and then delivering low levels of electrical current using a transmitter the person wears. DBS is generally seen as preferable to more invasive brain surgeries sometimes undertaken in extreme cases to reduce or eliminate tics (Müller-Vahl et al., 2011). However, it remains an intervention of last resort because it is more invasive than drugs or cognitive-behavioral interventions and there isn't that much research yet on its effectiveness (Müller-Vahl et al., 2011).

PSYCHOLOGICAL PERSPECTIVES

Behavior Therapies

Behavior therapies are the most researched and used psychological interventions for Tourette's and other tic disorders. Consequently, they are often tried before (or in combination with) prescribing medication. Of the behavioral techniques, perhaps the most popular and effective is **habit reversal training (HRT)**. In HRT, the patient is trained to recognize sensory experiences that indicate the onset of a tic. Patients are then taught to engage in a behavioral response (breathing or movement) that is incompatible with the tic (Flessner, 2011; Hartmann et al., 2016; Verdellen, van de Griendt, Hartmann, & Murphy, 2011).

Greta

For example, our case example client Greta might learn to identify when her need to blink repeatedly is about to begin, perhaps by paying attention to sensations that typically precede the tic. She would then be encouraged to engage in a competing response, such as keeping her eyes wide open until the urge to blink passes.

CASE EXAMPLES

HRT has a strong body of research support and appears to reduce both vocal and motor tics (Frank & Cavanna, 2013; A. Hartmann et al., 2016; Verdellen et al., 2011). It is also sometimes used to treat trichotillomania (hair-pulling disorder), discussed in Chapter 6 (Flessner, 2011).

In addition to HRT, exposure plus response prevention is also commonly used to treat tics (A. Hartmann et al., 2016; Verdellen et al., 2011). As in HRT, patients are taught to identify sensations that predict when a tic is about to begin. Once they can do this, patients are asked to resist engaging in the tic; that is, they attempt to prevent the tic response. In so doing, they become habituated to the sensations that precede the tic, eventually causing these sensations to no longer function as conditioned stimuli that trigger the tic. The research evidence for exposure plus response prevention isn't as extensive as that for HRT, but it is widely viewed as an effective therapy for reducing tics (Frank & Cavanna, 2013; A. Hartmann et al., 2016; Verdellen et al., 2011).

Greta

If Greta's tics were treated using exposure plus response prevention, she would be taught to identify sensations preceding her tics, then actively resist doing them for as long as possible. With practice, she would hopefully begin to habituate to the sensations that came before the tics and no longer feel such a strong urge to engage in them.

CASE EXAMPLES

Cognitive Therapies

Cognitive therapies are sometimes used to complement behavioral interventions. Cognitive restructuring, acceptance and commitment therapy (ACT) and mindfulness-based cognitive therapy (MBCT) are increasingly being added to more strictly behavioral techniques (A. Hartmann et al., 2016). The goal is to help patients with tics to accept their experience and not judge themselves too harshly when they have tics. Negative beliefs surrounding tics are examined and in-the-moment acceptance and awareness of unpleasant feelings and experiences is encouraged. The evidence for supplementing traditional behavioral therapies for tics with these more cognitive approaches is minimal, but interest in developing and improving them for use with tic disorders continues (A. Hartmann et al., 2016).

SOCIOCULTURAL PERSPECTIVES

People with tics, as well as their parents and families, experience a great deal of social stigma (J. L. Davis & Manago, 2016; Malli, Forrester-Jones, & Murphy, 2016; H. Smith, Fox, & Trayner, 2015). Those who experience frequent tics often feel as if others don't understand their condition or blame them for tics that are difficult to control. As a result, they report encountering negative reactions from others at work and at home. One tic sufferer described his experience in school: "I feel like I somehow get left out of all the games, and I feel like I'm a dork and that stuff, and I don't really have much friends … and mostly I get picked on at school" (H. Smith et al., 2015, p. 625). Another indicated feeling highly self-conscious: "In class I felt embarrassed, I couldn't pay attention because I heard a laugh and I thought my colleagues were laughing at me and I always kept an eye on what my colleagues thought, said, or did and I had a bad time" (H. Smith et al., 2015, p. 623). A third tic sufferer, a 55-year-old man, summed up the challenge of wanting to have positive and supportive relationships with others despite having tics: "I can't control my tics but I want to be taken as I am for myself" (H. Smith et al., 2015, p. 625). As you can see, people with Tourette's and other tic disorders experience a lot of social stigma and struggle to cope with others responding negatively to them. For an extended and powerful firsthand account of what it's like to have Tourette's, see "The Lived Experience" box.

THE LIVED EXPERIENCE

Overcoming the Bully: My Life with Tourette Syndrome

"Happy Easter Eve!" I yelled, jumping into bed for what seemed like the thousandth time, but was probably only the seventeenth. It was April 15, 1995 and I couldn't sleep, not because I was excited about what the Easter bunny might bring, but because I was stuck in a maddening routine: wash hands, turn bathroom lights on and off, jump into bed, yell this odd salutation, repeat. I'd been having a tough time of it as of late, but I think this was the night that we all knew something was really wrong.

I have Tourette Syndrome. Popular culture would have you believe that this means I involuntarily shout four letter words and other obscenities at the least socially acceptable times possible. While this may make for good slapstick, it's never been true of me, nor is it the case for the vast majority of Tourette's sufferers. Tourette Syndrome is characterized by chronic motor and vocal tics that can vary from essentially unnoticeable to nearly debilitating. Because the range of severity is so vast, it's hard to say exactly what percent of people suffer from Tourette's, but the current estimate is between 3–6 children out of 1,000 are affected by the disorder.

Incidence is measured in children because many with Tourette's show significant improvement in their late teens and early twenties, but try telling that to an 8-year-old who feels she has completely lost control of her body and mind. At that age, I thought the chance I'd ever be "normal" was just slightly lower than the chance I'd walk on the moon.

Let's go back to 1995. What had started with minor facial and vocal tics had quickly escalated. In hindsight, I'd shown signs much earlier—a bout of obsessive hand washing as a toddler and "games" I played that involved not stepping on certain tiles on our kitchen floor. But it wasn't long after the Easter Eve incident that I was diagnosed. In some ways, the diagnosis came as a relief because at least we knew what we were dealing with. We knew that other people were affected by this disorder, and that many of them are able to control it quite successfully with medication.

People have often asked me what my tics feel like. The best way I can describe it is to compare them to a really bad itch that needs to be scratched. Can you avoid scratching it? Sure, but you can't think of anything else until you do. That isn't to say that it's impossible to suppress tics at important moments. Take internationally renowned soccer star Tim Howard, who has been outspoken about his struggle with Tourette Syndrome. He has said that the stress of a big game causes his tics to flare, but when an opposing striker approaches the goal, all of a sudden he is in control of them. I've read stories of surgeons and pilots who can control their tics while in the operating room or in flight, and I believe it. At the peak of my struggle with Tourette's, I was especially self-conscious about my tics and struggled constantly to hide them. I remember in elementary school, I would go all day suppressing my tics as much as possible. I had always been teased, and I was terrified my peers might notice and use them as new ammunition. I would come home both physically and mentally exhausted, and with all of my power to resist depleted I could barely do anything but tic.

As if tics aren't enough, 86 percent of kids with Tourette's are diagnosed with at least one additional mental, behavioral or developmental disorder. Common co-disorders include Attention Deficit Disorder (ADD), Obsessive Compulsive Disorder (OCD), anxiety, depression and learning difficulties. I was blessed with both OCD and ADD, although I don't know that I demonstrated the latter more than any other kid growing up in the '90s. The OCD, however, played a compounding roll in my struggle with Tourette's. Whereas someone with only Tourette's has the "itch," the OCD causes me to imagine serious negative repercussions if I don't scratch it. Not every tic is this conscious, but the longer I try to put off a certain tic or routine, the more vividly I imagine whatever my biggest fear is at the time occurring as a result. One time I burnt myself on our wood stove because that was better than what would have happened if I hadn't touched my belly button to it. I still have the scar.

My Tourette's was the most severe between the ages of eight and eleven. During those years, there were times that it felt nearly debilitating. Nighttime was the hardest. I developed a bedtime ritual that seemed to get longer each night. At one point, this ritual included going outside to touch a specific tree in our yard, coming inside and jump-spinning three times before running and launching myself into my bed just the right way and yelling "good night!" If I didn't do it correctly the first time, I would have to do it all over again, sometimes half a dozen times. This could go on for hours, and sometimes I wouldn't get to sleep until well after 2:00 a.m. I distinctly remember nights I ran barefoot in the snowy New England winters to touch that tree ... or trees, actually; my parents had recently divorced, and I had a tree at each house.

I began to struggle in school. Behavioral problems and lack of self-control are common in kids with Tourette's. My parents had many discussions with the small private school I was attending at the time about my disorder, but my teacher didn't know how to handle me and by fourth grade I was spending a good part of the school day sitting in the office. She tried at the start, but I think she came to resent the fact the tools that she had in her toolbox weren't working with me. Eventually, she began to be a bully, doing and saying things that she knew would rile me up. I remember one incident in particular when I was still trying desperately to keep everything a secret from my classmates. One of my tics at the time was spitting. While it's actually a fairly common tic in Tourette's patients, it was the one that absolutely mortified me. Little girls aren't supposed to spit. We were on the annual class trip to climb Mount Monadnock, a day I looked forward to all year. I was making my way up the mountain with a group of friends when my teacher came up behind us and said so the whole group could hear, "Johanna, I can tell exactly where you've been. There's a path of trail mix and spit!" Everyone laughed except me. Eventually, I had to leave that school.

My parents have always fought for me in every way imaginable, but there were times that even they didn't know how to handle me. I think they struggled with how much leeway to give me on account of my Tourette's. "What can she control, and what can't she?" was always the question on their minds. At times I resented the special treatment from my parents and teachers, as it was just further proof that I wasn't normal.

Academically, I always excelled. The only assignment I remember really struggling with was a simple diary. The Journal. Each night, I would sit for hours writing each and every detail of my day; what I ate, said and thought at each moment. Leaving anything out was not an option. By the end of each entry, my hands ached and my handwriting had noticeably declined. Even today, I think it would be painful to look back at that journal.

After my diagnosis, my parents took me to a slew of specialists. Eventually we did find a cocktail of drugs that allowed me to get my tics under control, but I came to resent those visits. I think one of the reasons I refuse to go to the doctor's office now is because I spent so much time there as a child. The one visit I never resented was my weekly session with my counselor Marti. Marti loved me, and she did it with the tough love I desperately needed at that time. She taught me to think of the voice in my head that was telling me what to do as "the Bully." In my mind, he looked like the Genie from Aladdin, except he was a bad guy. Villainizing that voice helped me talk back to it and say I wasn't going to take it. I credit Marti greatly with making some of those toughest years manageable.

Luckily, through some combination of age and medication, things improved drastically by high school. My detentions subsided and I made friends. Eventually I graduated and got into a good college. It was my Junior year of college that I decided I didn't want to rely on medication any more. I remember how scary it was to stop taking it. What if all the progress I made was lost and suddenly I became that out of control kid again? Luckily, that didn't happen. In fact, the first full semester after going cold turkey I got a 4.0 GPA for the first time in my life. This was such a proud moment for me, as it was finally an achievement I could take full credit for without the "crutch" of meds or special treatment.

Most of my friends have no idea I have Tourette's, and when it does come up it's always met with surprise. This isn't because my tics have gone away completely. In fact, as I sit writing this, they're flaring up. I've stood up and sat back down three times and writing about throat clearing and eye-blinking is causing me to do it. Sometimes I still touch my belly button or get up and leave the room before I eat or go to sleep. But I am in control to the point that people rarely notice. These days I no longer see my Tourette's as a bully, but as something that has made me stronger. I've always believed that everybody has their challenges to face, this just happened to be mine.

Today I'm happily married, have a good job and a loving network of friends. My life is as normal as I would ever want life to be. But my biggest fear at age 10 wasn't the dark, or monsters under my bed. My biggest fear was that I would never live a normal life. I wish someone could have told that scared little girl that not only would she grow up to be functional, she would grow up to be successful. I wish someone could have told her that she would meet a man who didn't just love her in spite of her tics, but who actually found them cute and charming. I wish someone could have told her that she would make friends, lots of them, and that they would love her because of her quirks. But the thing is, I don't think she would have believed it. If my story can help just one little girl or boy believe that all these things will be true for them too, it was a story worth telling.

By Johanna Elsemore. Reproduced with permission. Original article available at:
www.huffingtonpost.com/johanna-elsemore/my-life-with-tourette-syndrome_b_5914626.html

14.6 COMMUNICATION PROBLEMS

Bobby
Bobby is an 18-year-old male who has stuttered since age 3. His parents were not always very supportive, especially his father—who used to get angry with Bobby for his lack of speech fluency. At school, Bobby was often teased about his speech difficulty and this led him to become highly anxious about speaking to people he doesn't know. Now, as he proceeds to university, his fear of speaking in front of others poses an ongoing challenge.

CASE EXAMPLES

DSM AND *ICD* PERSPECTIVES
Communication Disorders in *DSM-5*

The *DSM-5*'s "Neurodevelopmental Disorders" chapter includes a "communication disorders" section. Besides social (pragmatic) communication disorder (which we discussed in Chapter 13 alongside autism), this communication disorders section lists three other diagnoses: language disorder, speech-sound disorder, and childhood-onset fluency disorder. People with **speech-sound disorder** comprehend and can generate speech, but their speech is extremely hard to understand due to difficulty making speech sounds. By contrast, **language disorder** is diagnosed in children who have trouble acquiring and using language. They struggle with speaking and writing because they have difficulty understanding language and forming spoken sentences. For many with this diagnosis, conducting conversations is extremely difficult. Finally, **childhood-onset fluency disorder (stuttering)** is characterized by repeating sounds or prolonging consonants or vowels. People who stutter sometimes substitute different words to avoid words that are hard to say. They also tend to repeat one-syllable words. Stuttering not only interferes with speech fluency, but also results in much anxiety about speaking.

Bobby
Our case example client Bobby meets criteria for a stuttering diagnosis.

CASE EXAMPLES

Communication Disorders in *ICD-10* and *ICD-11*

The *ICD-10* classifies language difficulties using different diagnoses than the *DSM-5*, though these diagnoses cover much of the same ground. In the *ICD-10*'s **specific speech articulation disorder**, a child's speech development is below the expected level. Because the child has difficulty articulating words, comprehending what the child says can be challenging. **Expressive language disorder** involves limited ability to use expressive language. Children with this diagnosis have very limited vocabularies for their age. **Receptive language disorder** is diagnosed in children whose ability to understand language is below their developmental level. Finally, like the *DSM-5*, the *ICD-10* includes stuttering (also known as *stammering*).

The *ICD-11* includes a *developmental speech sound disorder* which is comparable to speech sound disorder in *DSM-5* and specific speech articulation disorder in *ICD-10*. Like *DSM-5* and *ICD-10*, it also contains a stuttering diagnosis, *developmental speech fluency disorder*. However, rather than a single language disorder diagnosis (as in *DSM-5*), *ICD-11* follows in the footsteps of *ICD-10* and includes two *developmental language disorders*—one for those with expressive language issues (**developmental language disorder with impairment of mainly expressive language**) and another for those with both receptive and expressive language issues

CHAPTER 14

(**developmental language disorder with impairment of receptive and expressive language**). Diagnostic Box 14.10 provides a diagnostic overview of the somewhat varied ways that the *DSM-5*, *ICD-10*, and *ICD-11* classify communication disorders. Below we limit our discussion to stuttering.

Diagnostic Box 14.10 Communication Disorders

DSM-5: Communication Disorders
- **Speech-sound disorder**: Difficulty producing speech sounds that makes one's speech hard to understand.
Based on American Psychiatric Association, 2013b, p. 44
- **Language disorder**: Trouble acquiring and using language in written, spoken, and other forms due to difficulty comprehending and producing it; limited vocabulary and impaired ability to form sentences and conduct conversations.
Based on American Psychiatric Association, 2013b, p. 42
- **Childhood-onset fluency disorder (stuttering)**: Characterized by things like repeating sounds or syllables, extending consonants or vowels, substituting different words to avoid words that are hard to say, and repeating one-syllable words; arises in childhood.
Based on American Psychiatric Association, 2013b, pp. 45–46
- **Social (pragmatic) communication disorder**: See Chapter 13.

ICD-10: Specific Developmental Disorders of Speech and Language
- **Specific speech articulation disorder**: Speech difficulty in which the child's development of speech is below expected level; problems with articulation and word use make comprehending the child difficult.
Based on World Health Organization, 1992, pp. 184–185
- **Expressive language disorder**: Limited ability to use expressive language; vocabulary is restricted for what is expected at the child's age.
Based on World Health Organization, 1992, pp. 185–186
- **Receptive language disorder**: The child's ability to understand language is below what is expected at the child's age.
Based on World Health Organization, 1992, pp. 186–187
- **Stuttering (stammering)**: Characterized by things like repeating or prolonging sounds, syllables, or words and frequent hesitations that disrupt speech flow; arises in childhood (not classified as a "specific developmental disorder of speech and language," but with "other behavioral and emotional disorders with onset usually occurring in childhood and adolescence").
Based on World Health Organization, 1992, p. 227

ICD-11: Developmental Speech or Language Disorders
- **Developmental speech sound disorder**: Difficulty learning, producing, and understanding speech; arises during development and results in pronunciation and speech errors that make understanding the person's speech difficult.
- **Developmental language disorder with impairment of mainly expressive language**: Limited ability to use expressive language; vocabulary is restricted for what is expected at the child's age.
- **Developmental language disorder with impairment of receptive and expressive language**: The child's ability to understand language is below what is expected at the child's age and this is accompanied by difficulty with producing spoken or sign language.
- **Developmental speech fluency disorder**: Characterized by things like repeating sounds or syllables, extending consonants or vowels, substituting different words to avoid words that are hard to say, and repeating one-syllable words; arises in childhood.
- **Developmental language disorder with impairment of mainly pragmatic language**: See Chapter 13.
Based on https://icd.who.int/browse11/l-m/en

BIOLOGICAL PERSPECTIVES

Genetics and Stuttering

Stuttering, like motor problems, has long been known to run in families (Kraft & Yairi, 2012; Yairi, Ambrose, & Cox, 1996). Twin studies have also found evidence that stuttering has a genetic component, with concordance in past studies ranging anywhere from 20% to 83% for identical twins, but only 5.4% to 31% for fraternal twins (Kraft & Yairi, 2012).

Bobby
Case example client Bobby has several relatives—including his maternal grandfather—who also stuttered.

CASE EXAMPLES

What about specific genes and stuttering? Because stuttering often co-occurs with ADHD, research has examined whether dopamine-related genes linked to ADHD are also associated with stuttering. However, currently the evidence base for this is meager (Kraft & Yairi, 2012). Additionally, the GNPTAB gene has been studied for its potential connection to stuttering, with a highly publicized 2010 study finding a link (C. Kang et al., 2010). As with dopamine-related genes, the evidence base for the GNPTAB gene's role in stuttering is small and a lot more research is needed (Casa Futura Technologies, 2013; Kraft & Yairi, 2012). Genetic linkage research on stuttering faces the same daunting problem that all genetic research faces, namely the challenge of replicating results (Kraft & Yairi, 2012).

Dopamine and Drug Treatments

The **dopamine hypothesis of stuttering**, like the dopamine hypothesis of Tourette's, proposes that stuttering is related to excessive dopamine transmission in the basal ganglia (Alm, 2004). Thus, it makes sense that haloperidol and other antipsychotics used to treat Tourette's have sometimes been prescribed for stuttering (Alm, 2004; Bothe, Davidow, Bramlett, Franic, & Ingham, 2006; Boyd, Dworzynski, & Howell, 2011). These drugs decrease dopamine. Paradoxically, stimulant drugs that increase dopamine also reduce stuttering in some instances (even though they cause it in others); this has led to speculation that there might be two types of people who stutter—those responsive to drugs that increase dopamine and those responsive to drugs that decrease dopamine (Alm, 2004). Some of the contradictory findings may be due to diagnostic issues; it can be difficult to agree on what counts as stuttering, so not everyone diagnosed necessarily has the same suspected (but still debated) neurochemical problem (Alm, 2004). This may be why so many drugs besides antipsychotics and stimulants have been tried as treatments for stuttering—including antidepressants, anticonvulsants, and beta blockers. Yet it isn't clear that any of these drugs work. Comprehensive reviews have concluded that there isn't much high-quality research on drug treatments for stuttering; further, what little exists hasn't found drugs to be especially helpful (Bothe et al., 2006; Boyd et al., 2011).

Bobby
When Bobby was 9 years old, he was briefly placed on an antipsychotic medication. It wasn't clear how much it reduced his stuttering. Bobby's parents took him off the drug after a few months due to its highly unpleasant side effects.

CASE EXAMPLES

PSYCHOLOGICAL PERSPECTIVES
Cognitive-Behavioral Therapy

The Lidcombe Program

Behavior therapies are often used to address stuttering in children. The most well-known and researched behavioral intervention is the **Lidcombe Program**, which is named after the Sydney, Australia suburb where it was developed (Blomgren, 2013). Aimed at children aged 5 and younger who stutter, this program consists of the following two stages:

» In *Stage 1*, the child and his or her parents have regular appointments at the speech clinic. The child's stuttering is analyzed to assess both its severity and the specific speech errors being made. Parents are trained to rate the child's stuttering on a 1 to 10 scale, with 1 being least severe and 10 being most severe. Then, the parents are taught contingency management (CM) skills (see Chapters 11 and 13), in which *verbal contingencies* are used to encourage fluent speech. Verbal contingencies are the verbal responses parents give when their child stutters or speaks fluently. They involve positive reinforcement of stutter-free speech by providing *praise* (e.g., "Fantastic smooth talking!"), *acknowledgement* (e.g., "That was smooth"), and *requests for self-evaluation* (e.g., "Did you say that smoothly?") (Packman et al., 2014, p. 6). The verbal contingencies for stuttering are a bit different; they involve *acknowledgment* (e.g., "That was a stuck word"), but also *requests for self-correction* (e.g., "Can you try that again?") (Packman et al., 2014, p. 6). All responses are rooted in the principles of operant conditioning, with the verbal contingencies intended to reinforce fluent speech (Blomgren, 2013; Packman et al., 2014).

» In *Stage 2*, visits to the speech clinic become less frequent while the parents continue to implement the contingency management program at home. The goal is to prevent relapse, a common problem in stuttering treatment (Blomgren, 2013; Packman et al., 2014; B. P. Ryan, 2004).

The Lidcombe program is the most researched behavioral intervention for stuttering. Studies consistently find it to be effective (Arnott et al., 2014; Femrell, Åvall, & Lindström, 2012; M. Jones et al., 2005; Nye et al., 2013; O'Brian et al., 2013; B. P. Ryan, 2004). The biggest risk with the Lidcombe program, as with any stuttering intervention, is the likelihood of relapse (B. P. Ryan, 2004). That is, in a significant number of cases, stuttering returns.

CHAPTER 14

CBT

Many adults who stutter develop intense feelings of anxiety about speaking to others (A. Craig & Tran, 2014). To address this, behavior therapy to reduce stuttering is often supplemented by cognitive-behavioral therapy (CBT) to manage stuttering-related anxiety. Much of the emphasis is on changing the cognitions of those who stutter by "challenging unhelpful beliefs about possible negative evaluations by others" (Blomgren, 2013, p. 14). Negative thought patterns are identified and examined and behavioral techniques for managing and reducing anxiety—including interventions like systematic desensitization (see Chapters 2, 6, and 10)—are employed to condition people to associate talking to others with relaxation rather than stress (Blomgren, 2013). There isn't a lot of research on using CBT and other techniques to manage anxiety associated with stuttering; what's more, even when anxiety about conversing is reduced, the frequency of stuttering doesn't necessarily decrease along with it (Blomgren, 2013).

Bobby

Imagine Bobby seeks CBT to help him address the anxiety that accompanies his stuttering. Cognitive restructuring might be used. Bobby's negative beliefs—such as "Everyone thinks I'm stupid because of how I talk" and "Nobody will ever like me if I can't speak properly"—would be challenged and replaced with more rational beliefs, such as "Some people can see past difficulties with speaking" and "Those who truly care about you love you no matter how you talk." As Bobby's beliefs about people's reactions to him change, he should experience less anxiety about talking to people, making it easier for him to speak more fluently.

CASE EXAMPLES

Constructivist Therapy and Stuttering Relapse

In Chapter 2, we introduced constructivist therapy, which focuses on how people meaningfully create unique understandings of self and world, which they then use to make sense of themselves and the events they encounter. One type of constructivist therapy, *personal construct psychology*, has been used to address the problem of relapse in stuttering treatment. From a personal construct psychology perspective, relapse often occurs when people who stutter continue to construe lack of fluency as central to their sense of self (DiLollo & Neimeyer, 2008; DiLollo, Neimeyer, & Manning, 2002; Fransella, 1987). As one person who stutters put it, "I often feel that when I'm fluent and people like me, I feel like it's a façade … like they're gonna find out I'm not what they thought I was. I'm an imposter" (DiLollo & Neimeyer, 2008, p. 167). For individuals like this, stuttering is part of their core role, or identity. It is therefore difficult for them to not relapse because they haven't integrated being a fluent speaker into their sense of who they are. In other words,

> *for the person who stutters, despite experiencing fluent speech (for example, following successful behavioral therapy), it is likely that the experience will not be meaningful, and, thus, behavior will likely revert back to that which is compatible with the dominant construct system based on stuttering. (DiLollo, Manning, & Neimeyer, 2003, p. 180)*

Constructivist therapy for stuttering therefore focuses not simply on correcting speech, but also on having clients incorporate being fluent into their core constructions of self. One way of accomplishing this is through narrative therapy, which uses the technique of externalizing the problem (introduced in Chapter 2 and revisited in several other chapters) (DiLollo & Neimeyer, 2008; DiLollo, Neimeyer, & Constantino, 2014; DiLollo et al., 2002; F. Ryan, O'Dwyer, & Leahy, 2015). Externalizing the problem involves encouraging clients to talk about the problem (in this case stuttering) as something outside themselves that sometimes gets the best of them. This allows clients to identify exceptions—times when stuttering didn't triumph, and fluent speech occurred instead. Personal construct research has found that people who construe stuttering as part of their core role are more likely to continue struggling to achieve fluency (DiLollo et al., 2003; DiLollo, Manning, & Neimeyer, 2005; DiLollo & Neimeyer, 2008; DiLollo et al., 2014; DiLollo et al., 2002; Fransella, 1987). However, there aren't any published outcome studies yet on using narrative therapy as a stuttering intervention (F. Ryan et al., 2015).

SOCIOCULTURAL PERSPECTIVES

Stuttering carries a lot of stigma. Research consistently finds that people who stutter are viewed negatively by others (Erickson & Block, 2013; Ip, St. Louis, Myers, & Xue, 2012; Przepiorka, Blachnio, St. Louis, & Wozniak, 2013; St. Louis et al., 2016). This can detrimentally impact quality of life, with those who moderately or severely stutter more likely to report physical pain and anxiety/depression (Koedoot, Bouwmans, Franken, & Stolk, 2011). The stigma of stuttering can also affect work life. Along these lines, one study found that 70% of people who stutter believe stuttering makes them less likely to be hired or promoted at work (J. F. Klein & Hood, 2004). How best to reduce the stigma of stuttering? As with many types of stigma, contact and education decrease people's negative attitudes toward those who stutter (M. P. Boyle, Dioguardi, & Pate,

2016). As people learn about stuttering and have face-to-face interactions with people who stutter, they become less likely to view stuttering in negative and stigmatizing ways (M. P. Boyle et al., 2016).

14.7 DELIRIUM AND DEMENTIA

Sanjay

Sanjay is a 74-year-old man who began experiencing memory difficulties several years ago. Initially, these problems were mild—forgetting words, losing track of where he left things, or becoming disoriented for a few moments. Sanjay dismissed these occurrences as normal forgetfulness. "My senior moments," he laughingly called them. However, over time Sanjay's memory problems steadily worsened. Sometimes he wouldn't remember how to drive home from the store. Other times, he'd be temporarily unable to recall the names of friends and family members. Increasingly, he found himself struggling with basic household tasks; he'd forget how to operate the vacuum cleaner, washer-dryer, and other home appliances. It was the day when Sanjay didn't recognize his grandchildren that his wife, Marsha, demanded he go see a doctor.

CASE EXAMPLES

DSM AND *ICD* PERSPECTIVES

Delirium

The *DSM-5*'s "Neurocognitive Disorders" chapter lists three main disorders: delirium, mild neurocognitive disorder, and major neurocognitive disorder. **Delirium**, which is also included in *ICD-10* and *ICD-11*, involves diminished attention to and awareness of one's surroundings. The hallmarks of delirium are memory problems, impaired perceptual functioning, and an overall state of confusion and disorientation. Delirium usually develops quickly (over a few hours or days) and fluctuates in severity. Importantly, there must be evidence of a biological reason for delirium, such as a medical condition, drug intoxication, or drug withdrawal. Depending on its cause, in some cases delirium lifts all together, while in other cases it comes and goes. The *DSM-5* notes that while overall prevalence of delirium is only 1%, it rises as high as 14% among people over age 85. Diagnostic details are in Diagnostic Box 14.11.

Diagnostic Box 14.11 Delirium

DSM-5
- Disturbed attention to and awareness of the environment that develops over a short period (hours or days) and changes throughout the day.
- Involves disrupted cognition (memory problems, confusion, communication and perception difficulties) that isn't due to mild or major neurocognitive disorder but is biologically attributable to another medical condition or drug use/withdrawal.
- Must determine whether delirium is *substance-induced, medication-induced, due to another medical condition,* or *due to multiple etiologies.*
Based on American Psychiatric Association, 2013b, pp. 596–598

ICD-10
- Impaired attention or awareness.
- Distorted cognition (perceptual impairment, trouble with abstract thinking, incoherence, memory problems, disorientation).
- Disrupted sleep and emotional disturbances (e.g., depression, anxiety, irritability, euphoria).
- Must determine whether delirium is *not induced by alcohol or other psychoactive substances, not superimposed on dementia,* or *superimposed on dementia.*
Based on World Health Organization, 1992, pp. 56–57

ICD-11
- Disturbed attention to and awareness of the environment that develops over a short period (hours or days) and changes throughout the day.
- Involves disrupted cognition (memory problems, confusion, communication and perception difficulties) and disturbed sleep-wake cycle may also occur; is biologically attributable to another medical condition or drug use/withdrawal.
- Must determine whether delirium is *substance or medication-induced, due to causes other than substances including medications, due to multiple etiologies,* or *due to unknown etiologies.*
Based on https://icd.who.int/browse11/l-m/en

CHAPTER 14

Dementia

Delirium can be difficult to distinguish from **dementia**, which is diagnosed when there is a permanent and usually progressive cognitive decline in functioning as the result of a specific brain disease or injury (see Diagnostic Box 14.12). Alzheimer's disease, Parkinson's disease, vascular disease, traumatic brain injury, Huntington's disease, and numerous other brain diseases listed in Table 14.1 can cause dementia. Consequently, the diagnostic codes used when diagnosing dementia depend on the brain disease suspected of causing it. Interestingly, the *DSM-5* no longer uses the term dementia. Instead, what it previously called dementia it now divides into two diagnoses: **major neurocognitive disorder** (for cases of severe cognitive decline) and **mild neurocognitive disorder** (for cases of mild cognitive decline). The *ICD-11* has partly imitated the *DSM-5* in this regard. Like the *DSM-5*, it now calls less severe cases of dementia mild neurocognitive disorder. However, unlike the *DSM-5*, it still refers to more serious cases as dementia, not major neurocognitive disorder.

Diagnostic Box 14.12 Dementia

DSM-5: Major and Mild Neurocognitive Disorders
- Cognitive deterioration (not due to delirium) in one or more of these areas: attention, language, perception, social cognition, executive function, or learning and memory.
- Evidence of cognitive deterioration is based on: (a) reports of the patient, the clinician, or someone who knows the patient well, and (b) impaired mental functioning documented by observation and assessment.
- The person's ability to function independently is impaired.
- **Major neurocognitive disorder**: The decline is significant.
- **Mild neurocognitive disorder**: The decline is modest.

Based on American Psychiatric Association, 2013b, pp. 596–598

ICD-10: Dementia
- Chronic impairment and decline in areas such as memory, thinking, learning, communication, and decision-making that is caused by a brain disease and impairs functioning.
- Can follow or co-occur with delirium.

Based on World Health Organization, 1992, pp. 45–49

ICD-11: Mild Neurocognitive Disorder and Dementia
- **Mild neurocognitive disorder**: Subjectively experienced decline in cognitive functioning beyond what is expected for age and intellectual level that does not significantly affect daily living and is not explainable as due to normal aging; may be due to underlying disease, trauma, infection, chronic drug/medication use, or unknown cause.
- **Dementia**: Decline in cognitive functioning with impairment in at least two cognitive areas (e.g., memory, executive functioning, attention, speech, social understanding, motor speed, visual/spatial perception or skills) that significantly affects daily living and is not explainable as due to normal aging; may be due to underlying disease, trauma, infection, chronic drug/medication use, or unknown cause. Three levels of severity: *mild dementia syndrome, moderate dementia syndrome,* and *severe dementia syndrome.*

Based on https://icd.who.int/browse11/l-m/en

Table 14.1 Common Dementia-Inducing Brain Diseases

- Alzheimer's disease
- Frontotemporal degeneration (Pick's disease)
- Human immunodeficiency virus (HIV)
- Huntington's disease
- Lewy body disease
- Parkinson's disease
- Prion disease (includes Creutzfeldt-Jakob disease)
- Traumatic brain injury
- Substance/medication use
- Vascular disease

The prevalence of neurocognitive disorder (NCD) varies based on the prevalence of the underlying brain disease causing it, but the *DSM-5* states that the likelihood of dementia (now neurocognitive disorder) increases with age, with it affecting 1%–2% of 65-year-olds and as many as 30% of 85-year-olds. When it comes to mild NCD, some critics worry that its addition to the *DSM-5* runs the risk of pathologizing normal and expected cognitive declines that occur as people age; critics also complain that the scientific support for the mild NCD diagnosis remains limited (Kamens, Elkins, & Robbins, 2017; Stokin, Krell-Roesch, Petersen, & Geda, 2015). Below, we limit our discussion of dementia mostly to dementia due to Alzheimer's disease, the likely diagnosis for our case example patient, Sanjay.

HISTORICAL PERSPECTIVES

The term "dementia" derives from Latin words for "off" ("de") and "mind" ("mens") (G. Cipriani, Dolciotti, Picchi, & Bonuccelli, 2011). Dementia has been identified and discussed throughout history. As far back as 2000 BCE, the ancient Egyptians were aware that old age often involved memory loss (Boller & Forbes, 1998). In the early Roman Empire (during the 1st and 2nd centuries CE), Greek physicians like Galen and Aretheus of Cappadocia distinguished cognitive declines that were temporary (delirium) from those that were permanent (dementia) (Boller & Forbes, 1998). Many centuries later, Philippe Pinel (1745–1826)—famous for unchaining the inmates at Bicêtre Hospital in France (revisit Chapter 1)—provided extensive descriptions of patients experiencing dementia; his student and colleague, Jean-Étienne-Dominique Esquirol (1772–1840), also wrote about dementia and speculated about its causes (Boller & Forbes, 1998; G. Cipriani et al., 2011).

The early 20th-century discovery of **Alzheimer's disease** is attributed to the German physician Alois Alzheimer (1864–1915) (G. Cipriani et al., 2011; Dahm, 2006; Ramirez-Bermudez, 2012; N. S. Ryan, Rossor, & Fox, 2015; Toodayan, 2016). Dr. Alzheimer worked with a 51-year-old female patient named Auguste Deter (written about as "Auguste D."), who exhibited severe and progressive cognitive decline; she was confused, disoriented, and had extensive memory problems. After Deter died, Alzheimer examined her brain and identified **senile plaques** (the sticky buildup of *beta-amyloid protein* in the area surrounding neurons) and **neurofibrillary tangles** (the twisting of *tau protein fibers*, which help neurons keep their shape and allow them to transmit nutrients). Plaques and tangles are still considered primary biomarkers of Alzheimer's disease (Bird, 1998; M. W. Weiner et al., 2015). Dr. Alzheimer's discovery greatly influenced later biological brain research on Alzheimer's disease, which we briefly summarize next. But first, see the "In Depth" feature for more on Auguste Deter's experience of Alzheimer's dementia.

IN DEPTH

The First Documented Case of Alzheimer's Disease

The Case of "Auguste D." was the first fully documented case of what became known as Alzheimer's Disease. The patient, Auguste Deter, came under the care of Dr. Alois Alzheimer in 1901 in Frankfurt, Germany. She displayed mental confusion and had difficulty communicating. Her condition steadily worsened and she eventually died. Here are two excerpts from Alzheimer's medical notes on Deter's case, recorded on November 26, 1901. Dr. Alzheimer's questions are in regular font, while Deter's responses are in italics. These exchanges provide a harrowing glimpse into the experience of Alzheimer's disease.

Exchange 1

What year is it? *Eighteen hundred.* Are you ill? *Second month.* What are the names of the patients? She answers quickly and correctly. What month is it now? *The 11th.* What is the name of the 11th month? *The last one, if not the last one.* Which one? *I don't know.* What colour is snow? *White.* Soot? *Black.* The sky? *Blue.* Meadows? *Green.* How many fingers do you have? *5.* Eyes? *2.* Legs? *2.* (Maurer, Volk, & Gerbaldo, p. 1547)

Exchange 2

If you buy 6 eggs, at 7 dimes each, how much is it? *Differently.* On what street do you live? *I can tell you, I must wait a bit.* What did I ask you? *Well, this is Frankfurt am Main.* On what street do you live? *Waldemarstreet, not, no. ...* When did you marry? *I don't know at present. The woman lives on the same floor.* Which woman? *The woman where we are living.* The patient calls *Mrs G, Mrs G, here a step deeper, she lives. ...* I show her a key, a pencil and a book and she names them correctly. What did I show you? *I don't know, I don't know.* It's difficult isn't it? *So anxious, so anxious.* I show her 3 fingers; how many fingers? *3.* Are you still anxious *Yes.* How many fingers did I show you? *Well this is Frankfurt am Main.* (Maurer et al., p. 1547)

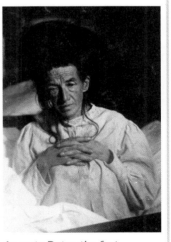

Auguste Deter, the first documented case of Alzheimer's disease.
Source: Maurer et al. (1997, p. 1547)

CHAPTER **14**

CRITICAL THINKING QUESTIONS

1. Alzheimer's disease is terrifying today, when it's long been identified as a disorder. What do you think it must have been like for people suffering from this disease—as well as their friends and families—before Dr. Alzheimer identified it as a disease?

2. Dr. Alzheimer identified Alzheimer's as a disease after Auguste D. died and he could examine her brain. Researchers are working to develop methods for diagnosing it while patients are alive, but Alzheimer's has traditionally been diagnosed postmortem. What challenges has this posed for doctors with patients who appeared to have this deadly and debilitating disorder?

BIOLOGICAL PERSPECTIVES

The Amyloid Hypothesis of Alzheimer's Disease

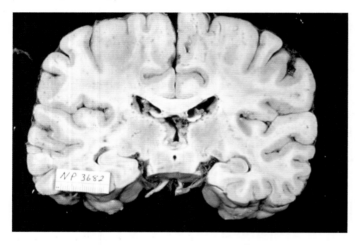

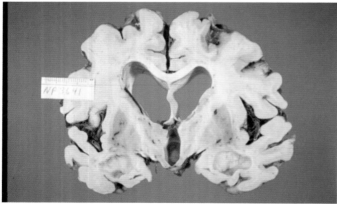

Figure 14.3 The Atrophying Brain in Alzheimer's Disease

Top: A normal adult brain. *Bottom*: The brain of an adult with Alzheimer's disease, reflecting the brain shrinkage commonly associated with the disorder.

Source: Figure 1 from: Bird, T. D. (2008). Genetic aspects of Alzheimer disease. *Genetics In Medicine: Official Journal Of The American College Of Medical Genetics*, 10(4), 231–239. doi:10.1097/GIM.0b013e31816b64dc

Consistent with the pioneering work of Alois Alzheimer, senile plaques and neurofibrillary tangles are found in various brain regions in Alzheimer's patients, including the hippocampus (important in memory and, as noted in Chapter 2, often decreased in volume in Alzheimer's patients) (Hill et al., 2014; Wolz et al., 2014; L. N. Zhao, Lu, Chew, & Mu, 2014). The **amyloid hypothesis** holds that—more than anything else—it is the senile plaques that are critical (J. Hardy & Selkoe, 2002; Yoshiyama, Lee, & Trojanowski, 2013). According to this hypothesis, the senile plaques (also called *amyloid plaques* because they consist of beta-amyloid proteins) trigger tau protein malfunctioning. This, in turn, produces neurofibrillary tangles. As the plaques and tangles impair brain functioning, many neurons die, and the brain literally shrinks. At the same time, the patient's cognitive functioning progressively gets worse. Despite the amyloid hypothesis, why plaques and tangles produce Alzheimer's isn't entirely understood; other brain mechanisms likely also play a role. Although most researchers agree that senile plaques and tau protein problems are critical, the former may not lead to the latter—that is, tau protein problems may develop for other reasons (Ballatore, Lee, & Trojanowski, 2007; Karch, Jeng, & Goate, 2013; Yoshiyama et al., 2013). Even though senile plaques and neurofibrillary tangles are biomarkers for Alzheimer's disease, until recently they could only be identified by examining the brain after death, which posed challenges to diagnosing Alzheimer's in living patients. However, promising new research is identifying ways to diagnose Alzheimer's and related forms of dementia using PET scan brain imaging technology (K. A. Johnson et al., 2013; Siderowf et al., 2014; Tateno et al., 2015).

Genetics of Alzheimer's

Why do some people develop senile plaques and neurofibrillary tangles? Most researchers suspect that genes play a central role. In 25% of cases, Alzheimer's disease seems to run in the family (Bird, 2008). However, this number goes up substantially in early-onset cases (those that develop before age 65), with 60% of such cases believed to run in families and 13% estimated to be *autosomal dominant* (meaning if the gene is passed to you by one of your parents, you will develop the disorder) (Bird, 2008). Given these statistics, it's understandable why early-onset cases are often referred to as *early-onset familial Alzheimer's* (Duara et al., 1993). However, early-onset familial Alzheimer's only makes up about 1%–6% of total cases (Bird, 2008). Most of the remaining cases are *late-onset sporadic Alzheimer's* that develop after age 65 and are less likely to run in families (hence the term "sporadic") (Duara et al., 1993). In late-onset sporadic cases, genetic vulnerability remains important, but environmental factors are thought to also play a significant role (Bird, 2008; Fiske et al., 2016; J. Williamson, Goldman, & Marder, 2009; L. N. Zhao et al., 2014). For instance, people who have had more years of education are at less of a risk for Alzheimer's, as are those with higher IQ scores (Contador et al., 2017; X. Meng & D'Arcy, 2012; W. Xu et al., 2016). According to the cognitive reserve hypothesis, education and intelligence may provide a buffer against Alzheimer's and other forms of dementia by affording people "the ability to tolerate the age-related changes and disease related pathology in the brain without developing clinical symptoms or signs of disease" (X. Meng & D'Arcy, 2012, p. 2).

What genes specifically are suspected in Alzheimer's disease? Three genes are believed to contribute to early-onset cases: *amyloid precursor protein (APP)*, *presenilin 1 (PSEN1)*, and *presenilin 2 (PSEN2)*; these genes are important in the brain's production of the beta-amyloid protein, as well as another protein called *presenilin* (Bird, 2008; J. Williamson et al., 2009). Late-onset cases have most often been linked to a gene known as *apolipoprotein E (APOE)*, though various other genes are also attracting attention (Bird, 1998; El Haj et al., 2016; Fiske et al., 2016; X. Meng & D'Arcy, 2012; J. Williamson et al., 2009; L. N. Zhao et al., 2014). An analogue study using mice found that deactivating the BASE1 gene reversed the development of amyloid plaques and improved performance on cognitive tasks; this could one day lead to the development of effective Alzheimer's treatments, though we aren't near achieving such treatments yet (X. Hu, Das, Hou, He, & Yan, 2018). As with all genetics research, study results aren't always replicated and currently no specific gene mutations have been identified that directly lead to Alzheimer's (J. Williamson et al., 2009). Nonetheless, research on the genetics of Alzheimer's disease continues in the hope of eventually understanding how genetic and environmental factors contribute to it.

Drugs Prescribed for Alzheimer's

There are presently no biological treatments that can reverse the steady progression of Alzheimer's disease. However, drugs are prescribed to slow down or temporarily relieve symptoms. Many of these drugs—such as *donezepil* (trade name *Aricept*), *galantamine* (trade names *Razadyne*, *Nivalin*, *Reminyl*, and *Lycoremine*), and *rivastigmine* (trade name *Exelon*)—enhance the activity of the neurotransmitter acetylcholine (Atri, 2011; Bishara, Sauer, & Taylor, 2015; Eleti, 2016). Use of these drugs is based on the cholinergic hypothesis of Alzheimer's, which maintains that because acetylcholine is important in memory, making more of it available reduces memory problems (Bishara et al., 2015). Unfortunately, unpleasant side effects of these drugs include nausea, vomiting, and diarrhea; exhaustion, sleeplessness, headaches, and tremors also sometimes occur (Mossello & Ballini, 2012).

Not all anti-Alzheimer's drugs target acetylcholine. For people who don't respond to or can't tolerate acetylcholine-focused drugs, the glutamate-enhancing drug *memantine* (trade names *Namenda*, *Auxura*, *Ebixa*, and *Memary*) is used instead (Atri, 2011; Bishara et al., 2015; Eleti, 2016). It's not clear why it helps, though it might influence amyloid and tau proteins (Eleti, 2016).

Sometimes people with Alzheimer's disease behave in agitated and aggressive ways; in some instances, they become paranoid, or even develop signs of psychosis. In such cases, antidepressants and/or antipsychotic drugs are sometimes prescribed. Prescribing antipsychotics for Alzheimer's is controversial—not only because of these drugs' serious side effects (see Chapter 4), but also because mortality rates in elderly people who take them are 1.5 to 1.7 times higher compared to patients not given such drugs (Antai-Otong, 2008; M. Steinberg & Lyketsos, 2012). Thus, in the U.S. there is a black box warning on antipsychotics for use in older patients (Antai-Otong, 2008; M. Steinberg & Lyketsos, 2012). Nonetheless, these drugs are still sometimes prescribed to Alzheimer's patients whose aggressive behavior is difficult to manage (Antai-Otong, 2008; T. Casey, 2014; C. S. Liu et al., 2016). It has been argued that when such drugs are used, doctors have an obligation to educate patients and their families about the risks and benefits (M. Steinberg & Lyketsos, 2012). Some clinicians encourage the use of alternative drugs (such as cannabis, lithium, nonsteroidal anti-inflammatory drugs, analgesics, antiepileptic drugs, and narcotics) to manage aggression in patients with dementia, but the research base for these is presently slim (C. S. Liu et al., 2016). Others believe that Vitamin E can further help slow mental decline in Alzheimer's, though a comprehensive review found little evidence for this (Farina, Llewellyn, Isaac, & Tabet, 2017).

CHAPTER 14

The drugs described so far are all prescribed after a person is diagnosed with Alzheimer's disease. However, several drugs are suspected of preventing Alzheimer's dementia from developing in the first place. Some believe that taking the female sex hormone estrogen or nonsteroidal anti-inflammatory drugs (NSAIDs) such as *aspirin*, *ibuprofen* (trade names *Advil*, *Motrin*, and *Nuprin*), and *naproxen* (trade names *Aleve* and *Naprosyn*) can decrease the chances of developing Alzheimer's disease, but current research support for this is minimal (Jaturapatporn, Isaac, McCleery, & Tabet, 2012; Tabet & Feldman, 2003).

Sanjay

Sanjay is diagnosed with Alzheimer's dementia and prescribed donezepil, a drug that increases acetylcholine levels to improve memory functioning. The donezepil slows down Sanjay's mental deterioration but can't stop it. Over time, Sanjay loses the ability to communicate effectively and experiences a shift in temperament. While Sanjay had always been a pleasant and gentle man, as his Alzheimer's advances, he becomes increasingly angry and sometimes even physically violent. His doctor recommends placing Sanjay on an antipsychotic to help manage these outbursts. Sanjay's wife, Marsha, reluctantly agrees despite the health risks such drugs pose to older patients. "I don't know how else to manage him," she laments.

CASE EXAMPLES

PSYCHOLOGICAL PERSPECTIVES

Cognitive and Behavioral Interventions for Alzheimer's Disease

Cognitive enhancement therapies assume that the progression of Alzheimer's and other forms of dementia can be slowed down by boosting patients' cognitive engagement with their surroundings (Choi & Twamley, 2013; Clare, 2003). The idea—borne out in some research studies—is that cognitive engagement fosters brain changes that counteract or delay the course of dementia (Choi & Twamley, 2013; L. Hall, Orrell, Stott, & Spector, 2013). There are three well-known types of cognitive enhancement therapy: *cognitive stimulation*, *cognitive training*, and *cognitive rehabilitation* (Choi & Twamley, 2013; Clare, 2003; Clare & Woods, 2004). Each is a bit different in the exact strategies it uses, but all three engage patients in exercises intended to improve cognitive functioning. Patients might be asked to recall names, faces, or events; play word games; practice situation-specific tasks; or organize everyday tasks (such as paying bills or going grocery shopping) so that it is easier to remember and complete them (Choi & Twamley, 2013). Clearly, the severity of a patient's dementia may influence which cognitive exercises can be used. There is evidence that cognitive enhancement therapies are effective, though—like drugs—they slow, rather than stop, the impact of dementia (Aguirre et al., 2013; Bamidis et al., 2014; Woods, Aguirre, Spector, & Orrell, 2012).

Cognitive enhancement therapies engage patients in cognitive activities (e.g., games, exercises, and everyday tasks); research suggests such activities can stave off the progression of Alzheimer's and other forms of dementia.
Source: Getty Images/Westend61\Westend61

Sanjay

Early in the progression of Sanjay's Alzheimer's disease, he undergoes cognitive interventions intended to counteract his memory deterioration. He is shown pictures of famous people and family members and asked to name them. He also is encouraged to play "Words with Friends" on his iPhone and to practice everyday tasks such as heating up food in the microwave. For a while, Sanjay can perform these tasks and his functioning improves a bit. Over time, however, his functioning worsens and eventually he is unable to engage in cognitive therapy tasks any longer.

CASE EXAMPLES

Other Psychological Interventions: Physical Activity and Pre-Therapy

Behaviorally, physical activity is encouraged as an intervention to counter the advance of dementia. Older people who engage in such activity (e.g., walking, biking, household chores, games, sports, and exercise) are less likely to show cognitive and physical decline (Bamidis et al., 2014). Further, humanistic therapists have employed pre-therapy with patients experiencing dementia (Dodds, Bruce-Hay, & Stapleton, 2014). As discussed in Chapter 4, pre-therapy is a more structured version of person-centered therapy that tries to make emotional contact with patients who are difficult to reach—such as those isolated by the experiences of psychosis, autistic process, or dementia. The idea isn't that pre-therapy can reverse dementia, but that it provides patients with necessary, but often overlooked, emotional and relational support. As one group of humanistic therapists put it, when working in long-term care settings, "there is a danger that the person with dementia may become remote and we need emotion-oriented work to help staff sustain a sense of continuing to see the person alongside the dementia" (Dodds et al., 2014, p. 115).

Like cognitive activity, physical activity is often encouraged as a way to slow the progress of dementia.
Source: BANANASTOCK

SOCIOCULTURAL PERSPECTIVES
Social Factors and Dementia

Education and Intelligence

A variety of social factors have been linked to dementia. As already noted, education and intelligence are both correlated with lower Alzheimer's risk (Chen, Lin, & Chen, 2009; Yeo, Arden, & Jung, 2011). People who score higher on measures of intelligence, as well as those who engage in intellectual-cultural activities during early and middle adulthood are less likely to develop Alzheimer's or other forms of dementia (Yeo et al., 2011). The extent to which such findings reflect the relative influence of genes versus sociocultural factors remains unclear. The cognitive reserve hypothesis, mentioned earlier, suggests that gene–environment interactions (in which intellectual ability and socialized habits both play roles) may combine to protect people from dementia.

Gender

Gender is also correlated with dementia. Women appear to be at significantly higher risk for dementia than men (Alzheimer's Disease International, 2015, 2016; Azad, Al Bugami, & Loy-English, 2007; Bamford & Walker, 2012; Chen et al., 2009; Erol, Booker, & Peel, 2015). For instance, it's been estimated that roughly two-thirds of dementia cases in Canada, Mexico, and the U.S. occur in women; the percentage is even higher (75%) in South Africa (Alzheimer's Disease International, 2016; Erol et al., 2015). The exact reasons for this are unknown, but one explanation offered is that women tend to live longer than men. Given that dementia is more likely the older one gets, women's greater longevity may place them at increased risk for dementia (Bamford & Walker, 2012). However, not only are women more likely than men to be afflicted by dementia. They are also more likely to become caregivers for family members who develop it (Erol et al., 2015). Thus, even when women don't directly suffer from dementia, they are more vulnerable to the physical and psychological burdens associated with caring for someone who does. Social justice advocates encourage policymakers to consider such findings in developing public policies to support both those with dementia and those to whom their care typically falls (Erol et al., 2015).

Stress and Socioeconomic Status

Two other social factors associated with dementia are socioeconomic status and stress. People who experience chronic or posttraumatic stress are at enhanced risk for dementia (Alzheimer's Society, 2017; M. S. Greenberg, Tanev, Marin, & Pitman). So are people who come from lower socioeconomic classes (Russ et al., 2013; Yaffe et al., 2013). Of course, stress and socioeconomic status may be related; those from poorer backgrounds may experience more stress in daily life as they struggle to get by. Some researchers suspect that prolonged stress could directly contribute to dementia—with high levels of the immune system stress hormone cortisol possibly leading to dysfunctions in the hypothalamic-pituitary-adrenal (HPA) axis and hippocampus (Alzheimer's Society, 2017; M. S. Greenberg et al.). However, few studies have been done so far, thus hypotheses about the effects of stress and socioeconomic status on dementia remain tentative (M. S. Greenberg et al.). Continued examination of these important social factors' relationship to dementia is called for.

CHAPTER 14

Day Care and Long-Term Care

Day care programs are outpatient programs for people with dementia and other cognitive difficulties; patients attend these programs during the day and then go home at night. Ideally, such programs provide helpful interventions for patients, improving their moods and reducing their risk of additional psychiatric problems (J. S. M. Curran, 1995). Day care centers also provide a respite for family caretakers, lifting some of their burden (Tretteteig, Vatne, & Rokstad, 2016). Unfortunately, in many cases day care programs are inadequately staffed and funded, making them less effective than they could be (J. S. M. Curran, 1995). **Long-term care** in a hospital, nursing home, or assisted-living facility is also an option. Long-term care is expensive and, especially in more institutional settings, it is sometimes associated with poor health outcomes for patients with dementia (Tam-Tham, Cepoiu-Martin, Ronksley, Maxwell, & Hemmelgarn, 2013).

Sanjay

For a while, Sanjay participates in a day care program. The program includes a variety of activities—exercise and cognitive therapy, for example—intended to mentally stimulate Sanjay. The day care program provides a break for Sanjay's wife Marsha, his primary caretaker. As Sanjay's functioning deteriorates and it becomes too difficult for Marsha to care for him at home, Sanjay enters a nursing home where he receives long-term care.

CASE EXAMPLES

Culture, Context, and Dementia

Sociocultural perspectives look at how culture and context shape our understanding of presenting problems. When it comes to dementia, some sociocultural theorists believe that industrialized Western countries tend to overly medicalize and stigmatize cognitive decline in old age, but not all cultures do (G. Cipriani & Borin, 2015). As one example, Native American culture often views psychosis and other cognitively atypical experiences common to dementia not as pathological, but as ways of connecting with the afterlife as "part of an elder's transition to the next world" (G. Cipriani & Borin, 2015, p. 200). As another example, in less individualistic cultures where family is more valued (such as Hispanic/Latino culture), dementia is regarded less negatively. Instead of treating it as a dreaded disease, these cultures see it as an expected component of aging. Thus, they are less likely to institutionalize family members with dementia and more likely to care for them at home (G. Cipriani & Borin, 2015).

14.8 CLOSING THOUGHTS: INFINITE VARIETY IN PRESENTING PROBLEMS

From Chapter 4 on, we have covered a wide variety of presenting problems that mental health care professionals typically encounter in everyday practice. As you are hopefully now quite aware, one of the recurring challenges that professionals run into is the regular co-occurrence of more than one presenting problem at a time—what we have repeatedly identified as the issue of comorbidity. One of the reasons why problems are often comorbid is because, despite our best efforts to organize presenting problems into discrete categories, people don't always come in neat little packages. Their life concerns don't necessarily fit precisely into one presenting problem category that is mutually exclusive from all others. Nonetheless, the need to distinguish certain things as problems worthy of attention is necessary to make our conversations about what is or isn't abnormal (and what to do about it) manageable. Of course, as may be clear by now, the distinctions we make (and how to help people once we make them) are often contested and aren't the only ones possible. Further, these distinctions greatly influence the conduct of clinical practice and are influential in shaping wider social policies pertaining to those identified as abnormal. Much of our final chapter is devoted to examining such policies as we turn our attention to legal and ethical perspectives.

KEY TERMS

Acupuncture
Alzheimer's disease
Amyloid hypothesis
Antihistamines
Basal ganglia
Breathing-related sleep disorders
Cataplexy
Central sleep apnea
Childhood-onset fluency disorder (stuttering)
Cholinergic hypothesis of Alzheimer's
Circadian rhythm sleep-wake disorders
Cognitive enhancement therapies
Cognitive reserve hypothesis

Cognitive-behavioral therapy for insomnia (CBT-I)
Constructivist therapy for stuttering
Copralalia
Day care programs
Delirium
Dementia
Desmopressin
Developmental coordination disorder
Developmental language disorder with impairment of mainly expressive language

Developmental language disorder with impairment of receptive and expressive language
Dopamine hypothesis of stuttering
Dopamine hypothesis of Tourette's disorder
Down syndrome
Dry-bed training
Dyscalculia
Dyslexia
Encopresis
Enuresis
Enuresis alarm
Eugenics movement

Expressive language disorder
Fragile X syndrome
Group homes
Habit reversal training (HRT)
Histamine
Hyperarousal theory of insomnia
Hypersomnia
Insomnia
Intellectual disability
IQ-achievement discrepancy model
Language disorder
Lidcombe Program
Long-term care
Major neurocognitive disorder
Mental retardation
Mild neurocognitive disorder
Modafinil
Music education
Narcolepsy
Neurofibrillary tangles
Nightmare disorder

Non-benzodiazepine sleep aids
Non-rapid eye movement
  (NREM) sleep
Non-rapid eye movement (NREM)
  sleep arousal disorder
Orexin
Orexin-receptor antagonists
Palilalia
PANDAS hypothesis
Parasomnias
Persistent (chronic) motor or vocal tic
  disorder
Phenylketonuria (PKU)
Primary enuresis
Primary insomnia
Provisional tic disorder
Rapid eye movement (REM) sleep
Rapid eye movement (REM) sleep
  behavior disorder
Receptive language disorder
Response-to-intervention model (RTI)

Restless legs syndrome
Secondary enuresis
Secondary insomnia
Senile plaques
Sleep cycle
Sleep hygiene education
Sleep restriction therapy
Sleep terrors
Sleepwalking
Sodium oxybate
Specific learning disorder
Specific speech articulation disorder
Speech-sound disorder
Stereotypic movement disorder
Stimulus control therapy
Tic disorders
Tics
Tourette's disorder
Vasopressin

Full definitions of the terms listed above can be found in the end-of-book glossary on p. 533.

 Go to the companion website, www.macmillanihe.com/raskin-abnormal-psych, to access a study guide, multiple choice and flashcard quizzes for this chapter, and other useful learning aids.

CHAPTER 14

CHAPTER 15
SUICIDE, ETHICS, AND LAW

15.1 OVERVIEW

LEARNING OBJECTIVES

After reading this chapter, you should be able to:

1. Define suicide, subintentional death, and Shneidman's specific types of suicide and subintentional death.
2. Describe the proposed suicidal behavior disorder and nonsuicidal self-injury disorder (NSSI), as well as the debate over these proposed diagnoses.
3. Discuss biological perspectives on suicide, including the search for biomarkers, the suspected role of serotonin, and the use of medication.
4. Distinguish psychodynamic, cognitive-behavioral, and humanistic perspectives on suicide.
5. Explain sociocultural perspectives on suicide, including Durkheim's four types of suicide, as well as issues related to gender, socioeconomic status, age, and social contagion.
6. Describe forms of suicide prevention.
7. Discuss ethical issues pertaining to informed consent, confidentiality, privilege, competence conflicts of interest, and access to care.
8. Define insanity and the insanity defense, as well as outline various legal tests of insanity and arguments for and against the insanity defense.
9. Distinguish fitness to plead from competency to stand trial, outline criteria used to legally determine whether someone is fit or competent, and summarize ethical and other challenges involved in declaring defendants unfit or incompetent.
10. Differentiate types of civil commitment and outline arguments for and against civil commitment.
11. Define the right to refuse treatment, the right to treatment, and the duty to warn and protect, while also identifying controversies surrounding these three issues.

GETTING STARTED: ABNORMALITY IN MORAL AND LEGAL CONTEXTS

Dahlia (Suicide Prevention)
Dahlia is a 24-year-old woman who calls a suicide prevention hotline feeling extremely depressed. She was recently laid off at work and is now struggling to pay her bills. "I think about dying most of the time and have tried to kill myself several times before—most recently about six months ago by swallowing the entire bottle of antidepressants my doctor prescribed me," she reluctantly admits. Dahlia also reports that she has little family support because her mother died when she was 9 years old and the rest of her family stopped speaking to her when she came out to them as a lesbian several years ago. "Life just seems too pointless and painful," she laments, "and when it comes to getting my family to talk to me again, I'd rather be dead than violate who I am." When asked if she has the means to kill herself, Dahlia responds elusively and declines to answer directly.

CASE EXAMPLES

Dr. S (Duty to Warn)
Dr. S, a local psychologist, consults a colleague for advice after his first session with a new patient. The patient, Norman, is a 35-year-old man who came for therapy because of "scary thoughts" he is having about his 22-year-old neighbor, Tammy. Norman reports fantasies in which he rapes and murders Tammy. Norman has a history of impulse-control issues and did once spend a night in jail after getting into a fist fight with a man in a bar. When asked directly by Dr. S if he plans to follow through on his fantasies about Tammy, Norman looks away and mutters, "Not if I can help it."

Niki (Competency to Stand Trial)
Niki was recently arrested for possession of opioids. Mr. B, the attorney assigned to defend Niki in court, finds her difficult to communicate with when they meet to discuss her case. When Mr. B asks Niki if she wants to plead innocent or guilty to

possession of an illegal substance, Niki stares at the ceiling and repeatedly says she wants to go home. Unsure about whether Niki comprehends what he is telling her or the circumstances she faces, Mr. B ponders whether to ask the court to bring in a psychologist to assess her fitness to stand trial. However, he is hesitant and conflicted about doing so.

Marta (Civil Commitment)

Marta, a 21-year-old woman studying at the local university, has begun seeing and hearing things that alarm her psychotherapist, Dr. Y. During sessions, she keeps talking about how the university president monitors her via the thermostat in the classroom where her psychology class is held. Marta's appearance has deteriorated in recent weeks. She has lost weight and looks gaunt and tired, as if she has been getting little sleep. Marta's lack of grooming also concerns Dr. Y. Her hair is unkempt and tangled and it appears as if she hasn't been bathing regularly. Dr. Y begins to wonder if Marta is currently able to take proper care of herself.

Dr T. (Testifying in Court)

Dr. T receives a subpoena from the courts to release information about his client, Juanita, a government employee who is on trial for sharing sensitive government data with an underground organization that has previously engaged in terrorist activity. The courts want Dr. T to share both a written summary of his work with Juanita and to testify about Juanita's mental status in open court. Juanita has not signed a release form giving Dr. T permission to communicate with the court and her attorney recently contacted Dr. T to tell him that Juanita does not want him to disclose personal information she shared in their therapy sessions. Dr. T knows that Juanita never discussed any illegal activities in sessions with him, although she did confide her distrust and anger at the government office that employed her due to what she perceived to be gender discrimination that kept her from getting a promotion.

Self-Harm and Other Ethical and Legal Dilemmas

The presenting problems that we have reviewed throughout this text do not occur in a vacuum. When people's behavior is labeled as abnormal, such judgments always arise within a social context—one governed by ethical and legal principles. In the second half of this chapter, we explore ethical perspectives that helping professionals bring to their work, as well as legal perspectives that society applies in deciding permissible patient behaviors and clinician practices in various situations. However, before turning to ethical and legal perspectives, we examine suicide, which—in addition to accompanying almost every presenting problem we have reviewed—has many ethical and legal implications. Suicide is an action that poses extremely difficult and complex dilemmas for clients, their families, and mental health professionals. At the same time, suicide is increasingly being viewed not just as an ethically challenging act that accompanies other presenting problems, but as a presenting problem all its own. Thus, rather than considering suicide as a side issue emerging from other presenting problems (such as depression, the topic under which many abnormal texts subsume it), we explore suicide in its own right. Due to its many ethical and legal implications, suicide segues nicely into an examination of ethical and legal dilemmas—hence the inclusion of these topics side by side in our final chapter. Before diving into these challenging matters, check out the "Try It Yourself" feature for an opportunity to think through how you might handle the tricky ethical and legal scenarios described in the case examples.

TRY IT YOURSELF

How Would You Resolve These Ethical and Legal Dilemmas?

Answer the following questions about the case examples that open the chapter. Then, read the rest of the chapter and return to this feature. Reread the case examples and revisit your answers, this time employing what you have learned. How, if at all, did your responses change? Even when you are aware of ethical and legal guidelines, determining the best course of action in specific situations can be difficult, especially when ethical and legal standards conflict!

Dilemma #1: Suicide Prevention?
1. Do you think Dahlia is likely to hurt herself? Why or why not?
2. Should Dahlia be involuntarily hospitalized to prevent her from self-harm? What rationale are you relying on to make this determination?
3. If Dahlia is involuntarily hospitalized to prevent her from attempting suicide, what positive and negative consequences might result?

Dilemma #2: Duty to Warn?

1. How would you feel if you were in Dr. S's position?
2. What ethical and legal principles are at play in this scenario?
3. Should Dr. S warn Tammy about Norman? Why or why not?

Dilemma #3: Competent to Stand Trial?

1. Should Mr. B raise the issue of competency to stand trial with the court?
2. Why might Mr. B be unsure whether to raise the issue of Niki's competency?
3. What would you do if you were Mr. B?

Dilemma #4: Civil Commitment?

1. Should Dr. Y pursue emergency civil commitment of Marta?
2. If Dr. Y does pursue civil commitment, what ethical and legal issues should he consider?
3. Let's imagine Dr. Y does have Marta civilly committed. Her condition improves after a brief stint on antipsychotic drugs. However, after she is released from the hospital, she refuses to see Dr. Y (or any other therapist, for that matter) because she feels Dr. Y broke her trust by having her hospitalized. How would you feel if you were Dr. Y? Would you regret your decision or feel you did the right thing?

Dilemma #5: Testify in Court?

1. What ethical principles are important in this case?
2. How should Dr. T handle this situation?
3. What would you do if you were in Dr. T's position?

For those of you who wish to grapple with additional dilemmas, a rich assortment is available at www.ethicalpsychology.com/p/vignette-warehouse.html

15.2 PERSPECTIVES ON SUICIDE

DEFINING SUICIDE

Suicide involves intentionally ending one's own life; it is "the human act of self-inflicted, self-intentioned cessation" (Shneidman, 1981b, p. 198). Thus, when clients present with suicidal thoughts and feelings, a myriad of ethical and legal issues arise. Understandably, the notion of people killing themselves provokes strong feelings in most of us, making suicide one of the more controversial topics we discuss. Below we examine perspectives on suicide and related forms of self-harm.

HOW MANY PEOPLE DIE BY SUICIDE?

The World Health Organization (WHO) (2014), author of the *ICD*, estimates that in 2012 suicide was the fifteenth leading cause of death, accounting for 1.4% of deaths worldwide. They report that more than 800,000 people die every year from suicide and that suicide is the second leading cause of death among 15–29 year olds (road accidents are first). WHO (2014) concludes that for every successful suicide there are 20 unsuccessful attempts—although it is difficult to know with certainty because people don't always report suicide attempts and, as we shall see, not every effort to hurt oneself is necessarily an attempt to end one's life. Seventy-five percent of suicides occur in low and middle-income countries and the most common methods of suicide are ingesting pesticides, hanging, and firearms (World Health Organization, 2014).

WHO (2014) notes that in wealthy countries suicide rates generally are the highest among middle-aged men, while in low- and middle-income countries young adults and elderly women are more likely to kill themselves. Overall, men kill themselves more than women, regardless of country—however this varies by nation. In affluent countries, men kill themselves three times more often than women, but in less prosperous countries men only kill themselves one-and-a-half times more often than women. Even though men have a higher suicide rate, women attempt suicide more often (Schrijvers, Bollen, & Sabbe, 2012). This paradox has been explained by noting how women choose less deadly means than men, resulting in lower death rates (Schrijvers et al., 2012). However, an interesting study conducted in Germany found that regardless of means chosen, men succeed in killing themselves at a higher frequency than women; why this is remains something of a mystery (Cibis et al., 2012).

TYPES OF SUICIDE

Suicide

The clinical psychologist Edwin S. Shneidman is perhaps the most well-known psychological theorist of suicide, having spent most of his career studying suicide and how to prevent it. Shneidman (1993, 1998) believed suicide was traceable to intense psychological hurt, pain, and anguish—which he called **psychache**. Importantly, he argued that not all suicides are alike (Shneidman, 1981a, 1985). Thus, he divided those who kill themselves into the following four types, which many researchers and clinicians have found extremely useful:

» **Death seekers** are people who attempt suicide because they actively seek their own deaths. They want to die much of the time, although this desire tends to wax and wane. Death seekers often make multiple suicide attempts, with many of them ultimately succeeding in killing themselves.

Dahlia
Because our case example client Dahlia thinks about dying most of the time and has tried to kill herself several times before, she may best be classified as a death seeker.

CASE EXAMPLES

» **Death initiators** want to die because they believe that the process of dying is already underway. Many, but not all of them, suffer from fatal illnesses. They kill themselves to accelerate what they see as the inevitability of imminent death. A person in the last stages of terminal cancer who takes her own life to just "get this over with already" is a death initiator.

» **Death ignorers** view death as a beginning, rather than an ending. They think their deaths mark the start of something new. Some believe in an afterlife, seeing death as an escape to a better and more peaceful place. Others think of death as temporary or reversible; young children who lack a grasp of the finality of death may think this way when they end their lives.

» **Death darers** are unsure about wanting to die. Their ambivalence leads them to take risks that could result in death. For example, they might play "Russian roulette" or purposely overdose on drugs, but then call for help. Although death darers tempt fate, their behavior doesn't ensure death. In many instances, death darers engage in parasuicidal behavior (see Chapter 12), in which they inflict self-harm to manipulate others, express distress, or regulate feelings (rather than because they truly wish to die).

Subintentional Death

Shneidman (1981a, 1985) also spoke of **subintentional death** (or *indirect suicide*), which is a death caused by an unconscious wish to die that leads to reckless or negligent actions. Subintentional deaths aren't overt suicide attempts because there isn't an active effort to kill oneself, but at some level, there is an unrecognized desire to die. Shneidman (1981a) identified four types of subintentional deaths:

» **Death chancers** take unnecessary risks just to see what will happen. They might cross the street without looking or rock climb without safety gear. They take chances but are consciously unaware of any desire to die.

» **Death hasteners** engage in unhealthy lifestyles that hasten their own deaths. They mistreat their bodies by doing things like taking drugs, eating poorly, or not getting enough sleep. Again, no overtly suicidal feelings or behaviors occur.

» **Death capitulators** give in to death. Their anxiety and depression lead them to psychologically capitulate, making death more likely. A person who psychologically gives up after having a stroke meets the definition of a death capitulator.

Death chancers might rock climb without safety gear.
Source: ImageState

» **Death experimenters** don't actively try to end their lives, but instead experiment with living in a continuously altered and foggy state. Substance users who regularly take drugs to remain chronically altered can be considered death experimenters.

Notice how in all four types of subintentional death, the actions engaged in reflect an unacknowledged desire to die. However, there is no active suicide attempt. Because they are less overt than suicides, subintentional deaths can be hard to identify. This makes it difficult to estimate how many deaths are subintentional. It's quite possible that a lot more people die subintentional deaths than we realize.

HISTORICAL PERSPECTIVES

Views about suicide have changed over the course of history. In Ancient Greece, "suicide was viewed as a moral response to disgrace and an appropriate method of making a political statement" (Pridmore, 2011, p. 78). However, by the 4th century, the early Christian philosopher St. Augustine (354–430 AD) strongly rejected suicide as a sinful act; by 693 AD, the Roman Catholic Church decided that suicide attempts should be punished by excommunication (Shneidman, 1981b). Consistent with this position, more than 500 years later St. Thomas Aquinas (1225–1274) argued that "suicide was a mortal sin in that it usurped God's power over man's life and death" (Shneidman, 1981b, p. 202). Eventually, however, as Renaissance Humanism took hold in Europe, thinkers like Jean Jacques Rousseau (1712–1778) and David Hume (1711–1776) began challenging the "sin" model of suicide (Hume, 1783; J. J. Rousseau, 1810; Shneidman, 1981b; Szasz, 2011). Rousseau blamed suicide not on individuals, but on an oppressive society that prevents people from meeting their needs; whereas Hume argued that "suicide is not a transgression of our duties to God, to our fellow citizens, or to ourselves" (Shneidman, 1981b, p. 202). The famous 19th-century French psychiatrist Jean-Étienne Esquirol (1772–1840)—previously mentioned in Chapters 1, 6, and 14—shifted further away from the sin model by conceptualizing suicide in medical terms. He was one of the first to gather epidemiological data on suicide, cataloging common methods people used to kill themselves and comparing suicide rates in different countries (https://ethicsofsuicide. lib.utah.edu/selections/esquirol/). Since Esquirol, it has been common to treat suicide as a medical problem (Pridmore, 2011). The most common medical conceptions of suicide are in the *DSM* and *ICD*.

DSM AND *ICD* PERSPECTIVES

Suicidal Behavior Disorder

As you may remember from Chapter 3, the *DSM-5*'s Section III contains proposed disorders that aren't officially recognized because they are contested and/or require additional research. The *DSM-5* includes a new disorder in Section III called **suicidal behavior disorder**, which, if eventually approved, would be diagnosed in anyone who has attempted suicide in the last two years. Suicide attempts due to delirium or mental confusion, or done for political or religious reasons, would be excluded. However, all other suicide attempts would qualify a person for this disorder. Further, if the individual's attempted suicide occurred one to two years before the evaluation, then the disorder would be considered "in remission." See Diagnostic Box 15.1 for criteria.

Diagnostic Box 15.1 Suicidal Behavior Disorder

Proposed *DSM-5* Disorder
- A suicide attempt within the last two years.
- Must rule out nonsuicidal self-injury and suicidal ideation (thoughts and preparation for the suicide attempt).
- The attempt isn't due to delirium or mental confusion.
- The attempt isn't a political or religious act.
- Specify if *current* (no more than one year since last attempt) or *in early remission* (1–2 years since last attempt).

Dahlia
Although not an officially approved DSM-5 disorder, our case example client Dahlia meets the criteria for suicidal behavior disorder because she has tried to kill herself within the last two years.

CASE EXAMPLES

Proponents of suicidal behavior disorder argue that adding it to the *DSM* will make clinicians more likely to assess for suicidal risk, thereby better integrating attention to suicide into everyday practice (Oquendo & Baca-Garcia, 2014). They also argue that suicidal behavior disorder is a reliable and valid diagnostic category (Oquendo & Baca-Garcia, 2014). However, critics disagree, arguing instead that suicidal overtures are symptomatic of other disorders or a response to life stressors (Oquendo & Baca-Garcia, 2014). These critics point to the high comorbidity between **suicidal ideation** (a technical term for suicidal thoughts and feelings) and having a mental disorder diagnosis (Nock, Hwang, Sampson, & Kessler, 2010). Along these lines, suicidal ideation tends to be quite comorbid with depression and anxiety—although, interestingly, conduct issues, impulse-control problems, interpersonal conflict, antisocial behavior, and substance abuse are better predictors of actual suicide attempts (Turecki & Brent, 2016). Still, the objection is that if suicidal ideation and behavior consistently co-occur with other presenting problems, then it may be unwise to view suicidal behavior as a discrete disorder.

Other critics go even further, bristling at what they see as the medicalization of suicide (Pridmore, 2011; Szasz, 2010). To them, the risk is that we will improperly turn a meaningful (if, in most people's view, usually misguided) response to emotional difficulties and life stressors into a medicalized diagnostic category. To these critics, suicide is a moral act, not a medical one (Szasz, 1999, 2010). Further, some of these critics see a slippery slope. Once suicide is conceived of in medical terms, they ask, how long before homicide is transformed from a crime into a disorder and people are excused for it (Oquendo & Baca-Garcia, 2014)? You will need to decide for yourself whether you feel concerns about overly medicalizing self-harm are warranted.

Nonsuicidal Self-Injury Disorder

In addition to suicidal behavior disorder, the *DSM-5* also includes a Section III proposal for a disorder called **nonsuicidal self-injury (NSSI)**. NSSI has attracted a lot of attention in recent years and, in addition to being in the *DSM-5* as a disorder for further study, it is also in the *ICD-11* (World Health Organization, 2018a). NSSI involves deliberately injuring oneself, but without suicidal intent (American Psychiatric Association, 2013b; Wilkinson & Goodyer, 2011). Rather than having the intention of ending one's life, NSSI is undertaken to escape negative thoughts and feelings (such as anxiety or depression), cope with interpersonal conflicts, or provide comfort and positive feelings (American Psychiatric Association, 2013b). The most common type of NSSI behavior is *self-cutting* (in which people repeatedly cut themselves with a sharp object). However, other NSSI forms of self-injury include scratching, burning, hitting, punching, excessive rubbing, carving words or symbols on the skin, or picking at wounds to keep them from healing (Mayo Clinic Staff, 2017; Wilkinson, 2013; Wilkinson & Goodyer, 2011). NSSI occurs most often in adolescents (Brady, 2014; B. Hall & Place, 2010; A. L. Miller & Smith, 2008; Wilkinson, 2013). Proposed *DSM-5* criteria are contained in Diagnostic Box 15.2.

Diagnostic Box 15.2 Nonsuicidal Self Injury (NSSI)

Proposed *DSM-5* Disorder
- Intentional self-inflicted damage to the surface of one's body during at least five days over the past year (e.g., cutting, burning, stabbing, hitting, excessive rubbing) without any intent of suicide.
- The self-injury is intended to accomplish at least one of these: (a) reduce negative thoughts and feelings; (b) address interpersonal conflict; (c) produce a state of positive feeling.
- The self-injury is related to at least one of these: (a) interpersonal conflicts or negative thoughts and feelings (e.g., depression, anxiety, tension, anger, self-criticism, or emotional upset) that occur immediately prior to the self-injury; (b) being preoccupied with the self-injurious behavior before doing it; (c) recurrent thoughts about the self-injury, whether acted on or not.
- The self-injury isn't socially approved (e.g., a tattoo, body piercing, or religious ritual) and is more serious than just picking a scab or biting one's nails.
- The behavior isn't due to delirium, psychosis, substance use, or substance withdrawal; it also isn't better explained by another disorder (e.g., autism spectrum disorder, stereotypic movement disorder, or hair-pulling disorder).

Based on American Psychiatric Association, 2013b, p. 803

ICD-11
- Intentional self-injury (e.g., cutting, scraping, burning, biting, or hitting).
- The self-injuring person expects no significant harm from the self-injury.

Based on https://icd.who.int/browse11/l-m/en

NSSI is comorbid with many other problems. People—especially girls—who have faced adversity (for instance, a greater number of life stressors, interpersonal conflict, or sexual abuse) are more prone to NSSI (Bedi, Muller, & Classen, 2014; J. D. Ford & Gómez, 2015; R. T. Liu et al., 2014). Consistent with this, NSSI co-occurs among people diagnosed with posttraumatic stress disorder (PTSD), panic disorder, borderline personality disorder, mood disorders, and most anxiety disorders (Bentley, Cassiello-Robbins, Vittorio, Sauer-Zavala, & Barlow, 2015; Ford & Gómez, 2015). Further, NSSI is also comorbid with suicidal behavior (Hamza, Stewart, & Willoughby, 2012). That is, even though people who engage in NSSI aren't typically viewed as wanting to die, there is evidence that NSSI and suicidal behavior are related (Cheung et al., 2013). Indeed, research

Nonsuicidal self-injury (NSSI)—proposed in DSM-5 but included in ICD-11—is a diagnosis for people who injure themselves without wanting to end their lives; self-cutting is the most common NSSI behavior.
Source: iStock.com/grummanaa5

has found a link between NSSI behavior and a history of suicide attempts, with one study finding that 86.8% of people diagnosed with NSSI engaged in suicide attempts compared to only 43.8% of those without an NSSI diagnosis (Andover & Gibb, 2010). Importantly, the NSSI–suicide attempt relationship appears stronger than the established link between NSSI and other problems such as depression, hopelessness, and borderline personality disorder (Andover & Gibb, 2010). The implications of this are a bit confusing given that NSSI is usually conceptualized as distinct from suicidality. Does the NSSI–suicide attempt correlation point to a relationship between two distinct problems? Or does it suggest that NSSI isn't clearly distinguishable from suicidality and from other mental disorder diagnoses? This issue remains unresolved and investigators have called for additional research to determine if NSSI is a discrete and reliable diagnostic category (Selby, Kranzler, Fehling, & Panza, 2015; Zetterqvist, 2015).

BIOLOGICAL PERSPECTIVES
The Search for Suicide Biomarkers

Consistent with the Research Domain Criteria (RDoC) initiative, brain researchers hope to eventually predict who will die by suicide using biomarkers (biological measures that tell us whether someone has a given disorder; see Chapter 3). No such biomarkers have been established yet, but biological researchers remain optimistic about several leads. Twin and family studies have often found that suicide appears to be heritable and run in families (N. L. Pedersen & Fiske, 2010; Petersen, Sørensen, Andersen, Mortensen, & Hawton, 2014; Tomassini, Juel, Holm, Skytthe, & Christensen, 2003). However, how much this is due to genes versus environmental influences isn't always clear. Still, genetics research has identified a long list of genes potentially related to suicidal behavior (Oquendo et al., 2014). Many of these genes play a role in serotonin transmission (discussed more below). Further, certain areas of the prefrontal cortex—most notably the orbitofrontal cortex and dorsolateral prefrontal cortex (both important in decision-making)—have been implicated in suicidal behavior (Desmyter, van Heeringen, & Audenaert, 2011; van Heeringen, Bijttebier, & Godfrin, 2011). Could the decision to kill oneself be due to these brain areas malfunctioning? That's what some investigators suspect, though more research is needed.

The hypothalamic-pituitary-adrenal (HPA) axis (see numerous previous chapters) plays an important role in stress-related responding; overactive HPA response is believed by many to be related to suicidal behavior (J. J. Mann & Currier, 2012). Consistent with this, suicidal individuals—like those who are depressed—experience immune system inflammation, a sign of prolonged stress (Brundin, Erhardt, Bryleva, Achtyes, & Postolache, 2015; J.-W. Kim, Szigethy, Melhem, Saghafi, & Brent, 2014). This fits with research indicating that suicidal people often fail the *dexamethasone suppression test* (*DST*), which measures levels of the stress hormone cortisol in the bloodstream (Blasco-Fontecilla & Oquendo, 2016; Oquendo et al., 2014). Failing this test suggests that suicidal people are unable to suppress their stress response, which may explain their high cortisol levels even after taking dexamethasone, a synthetic steroid that decreases cortisol. Brain researchers consider DST results to be one of the more promising potential biomarkers for suicidal behavior (Blasco-Fontecilla & Oquendo, 2016).

As mentioned previously, low levels of serotonin have been repeatedly linked to suicidal behavior (Blasco-Fontecilla & Oquendo, 2016; J. J. Mann & Currier, 2012; Oquendo et al., 2014). This makes sense given that serotonin deficiencies, as we saw in Chapters 12 and 13, are often associated with impulsivity, aggression, and violence (Cappadocia, Desrocher, Pepler, & Schroeder, 2009; Coccaro, Sripada, Yanowitch, & Phan, 2011; Fanning, Berman, Guillot, Marsic, & McCloskey, 2014; Golubchik, Mozes, Vered, & Weizman, 2009; Moul, Dobson-Stone, Brennan, Hawes, & Dadds, 2013; Moul, Dobson-Stone, Brennan, Hawes, & Dadds, 2015; J. Zhou et al., 2006). Low serotonin is also implicated in depression (see Chapter 5), a presenting problem that is often tied to suicide (Di Benedetto, Rupprecht, & Rammes, 2010; Hillhouse & Porter, 2015).

The question is whether we will eventually be able to biologically differentiate depression, suicidality, impulsivity, and aggression from one another. So far, we cannot because of their similar biological correlates. However, researchers continue to investigate. The other challenge is that, as with most biomarker research, we are dealing with correlational data. This makes it hard to know whether (a) suicidal feelings lead to neurochemical and inflammatory changes, (b) neurochemical and inflammatory changes lead to suicidal feelings, or (c) some other factor explains the suspected relationship.

Medication for Suicide Prevention

Considering evidence that suicidal individuals suffer from low serotonin levels, antidepressants that make more serotonin available (SSRIs, SNRIs, and tricyclics) are often prescribed (Hawton et al., 2015; J. J. Mann & Currier, 2012). Mood stabilizers (such as lithium) and antipsychotics are also sometimes used. Why? Because mood stabilizers increase serotonin in some brain regions, while antipsychotics bind with 5-HT-2A serotonin receptors (counterintuitively, this blocks serotonin but sometimes reduces depression) (J. J. Mann & Currier, 2012). Comprehensive reviews usually conclude that the research support for using medication to reduce suicides is weak; there is little evidence that these drugs are consistently effective in preventing suicidal behavior (Hawton et al., 2015; J. J. Mann & Currier, 2012).

Dahlia
After her first suicide attempt, our case example client Dahlia's doctor prescribed her an SSRI antidepressant. However, it had little effect on her suicidal ideation. CASE EXAMPLES

PSYCHOLOGICAL PERSPECTIVES

Psychodynamic Perspectives

Sigmund Freud and the early psychoanalysts conceptualized suicide as a response to anger toward others that is internalized and then redirected at oneself (Lester, 1994). As Freud himself put it, "no neurotic harbours thoughts of suicide which he has not turned back upon himself from murderous impulses against others" (S. Freud, 1917/1953, p. 252). Later in his career, Freud theorized that people have a built-in **death instinct** (or *Thanatos*), which he contrasted with the **life instinct** (or *Eros*). Freud used the death instinct to explain why people are driven to behave in self-destructive ways. Though usually directed outwardly toward the world, sometimes the death instinct is turned against the self, which results in suicidal thoughts and actions.

Instead of stressing a death instinct, many modern psychodynamic theories attribute suicidal ideation to early life losses, such as parental death or divorce (Kaslow et al., 1998). From this perspective, "behind every suicidal gesture, even the most superficial one, there is always a tragedy" (Mikhailova, 2005, p. 42).

Dahlia
Our case example client Dahlia, for example, lost her mother when she was 9 years old. CASE EXAMPLES

Psychodynamic therapy for suicidal clients emphasizes the importance of making unconscious conflicts conscious and using the therapeutic relationship to help patients identify and work through problematic attachment and relationship patterns (Lester, 1994). As a historical footnote, at the end of his life when he was in severe pain and dying from cancer of the mouth, Freud had his doctor assist him in committing suicide by injecting him with large doses of morphine (L. Cohen, 2014). Might Freud's actions to hasten his own death as he reached the late stages of his incurable and painful cancer qualify him as a death initiator, one of Shneidman's four types of suicidal people?

Cognitive-Behavioral (CBT) Perspectives

From the perspective of cognitive-behavioral therapy (CBT), it is distorted thinking that leads to suicidal ideation (Lester, 1994; B. Stanley et al., 2009; Wenzel & Beck, 2008). Cognitively, suicidal people display rigid thought patterns that keep them from finding workable solutions to their problems. Consequently, they "have polarized and

Many modern psychodynamic therapists see suicidal ideation as tied to early childhood losses, such as the death of a parent.
Source: iStock.com/patat

CHAPTER 15

extreme views of themselves, life, and death and have closed themselves off to examining alternative solutions to suicide" (Lester, 1994, p. 367). Behaviorally, suicide is more likely when people's environments haven't adequately reinforced their initiatives. For instance, people who learn that their behavior has no effect on their environments experience learned helplessness (see Chapter 5); such people may see suicide as their only option for escaping situations they believe they cannot change (Lester, 1994).

Dahlia
Dahlia may be experiencing learned helplessness; no matter what she does, her life doesn't seem to get better.

Many CBT perspectives adopt a **diathesis-stress model of suicide** (B. Stanley et al., 2009). Like the diathesis-stress model of psychosomatic illness (see Chapter 8), the diathesis-stress model of suicide says that people try to kill themselves when a preexisting vulnerability (*diathesis*) is exacerbated by environmental *stress*. Thus, suicide is most likely when a predisposing dispositional vulnerability (e.g., a temperament that leads to impulsivity, irrational thinking, or difficulty solving problems) is brought to the breaking point by seemingly unmanageable life stressors (e.g., interpersonal conflicts, financial difficulties, or work issues) (B. Stanley et al., 2009; Wenzel & Beck, 2008).

Dahlia
Our case example client, Dahlia, has a number of predisposing vulnerabilities: She may not have developed sufficient problem-solving skills given the minimal family support she received while growing up; it's also possible she is prone to irrational thinking that leads her to see suicide as her only alternative. Further, Dahlia faces several extremely challenging life stressors—including being unemployed, interpersonal conflicts with her family over her sexual orientation, and unresolved emotional issues regarding her mother dying when Dahlia was just 9 years old.

CBT interventions emphasize changing people's cognitive distortions (see Chapter 2), particularly those that lead to feelings of hopelessness (B. Stanley et al., 2009; Wenzel & Beck, 2008). CBT therapists have developed a 12-session **cognitive-behavioral therapy for suicide prevention (CBT-SP)**, though research on it is just beginning (B. Stanley et al., 2009). Rooted in the diathesis-stress model of suicide, CBT-SP uses several structured strategies to prevent further suicide attempts, including the following:

» *Chain analysis* involves identifying activating events that previously pushed the client toward suicide. Beliefs about these activating events and how these beliefs led to past suicide attempts are examined.

» *Safety plan development* allows the client to generate concrete coping strategies to prevent further suicide attempts. The client develops a list of concrete actions to counter suicidal urges. Some of these actions can be taken without help from others (such as listening to music, watching a comforting television program, or going to the gym), while others require the client to seek assistance (calling a friend, not being alone, or driving to the emergency room).

» *Skill building* occurs when the client is taught problem-solving strategies for addressing life's challenges. This often involves cognitive restructuring, in which the client's irrational beliefs and cognitive distortions are challenged and substituted with more effective beliefs. Instead of cognitively concluding that suicide is the only option, the client instead becomes able to resolve problems by breaking them into manageable steps.

Dahlia
In CBT-SP, Dahlia's belief that things will never get better might be questioned and replaced with a new belief acknowledging her difficulties but seeing them as potentially surmountable.

While there is some encouraging evidence that CBT helps reduce suicidal behavior, the evidence base remains somewhat small and there have been calls for further research (Hawton et al., 2016). You may recall that dialectical behavior therapy (DBT), a type of CBT developed for people diagnosed with personality disorders (see Chapter 12), is also used to reduce suicidal behavior. While DBT researchers have found their approach to be effective for reducing self-harm, a recent comprehensive review concluded that DBT may be better at reducing, rather than eliminating, such behaviors (Hawton et al., 2016).

Humanistic Perspectives

In a more humanistic/existential vein, suicide is a personal and meaningful reaction to humiliation, anger, hurt, or loss (G. A. Kelly, 1961; R. A. Neimeyer, 1983; J. R. Rogers, Bromley, McNally, & Lester, 2007; J. R. Rogers & Soyka, 2004). Humanistically speaking, suicide isn't an irrational act; it's a purposeful act in response to ongoing psychological upset. It can be a means of remaining self-consistent ("I'd rather be dead than violate who I am," according to our case example client, Dahlia). It can also be a way to exert control when one feels humiliated, angry, hurt, or dominated by others (J. R. Rogers et al., 2007). Rather than focusing primarily on getting clients to agree not to hurt themselves (which calms therapists' nerves, but may alienate and demean some clients), humanistic therapists instead stress empathically understanding the psychological meaning behind suicidal thoughts and acts (J. R. Rogers & Soyka, 2004). In doing so, they treat suicide not as a disorder or brain disease, but as a personally meaningful response to psychological conflict and pain. The idea of simply listening to suicidal clients is consistent with the client-centered focus of Carl Rogers' person-centered therapy, but because psychotherapists tend to become anxious about suicidal clients and feel that they need to actively intervene to stop them from hurting themselves, a purely person-centered model of suicide prevention isn't commonly utilized in everyday practice (Lester, 1994).

SOCIOCULTURAL PERSPECTIVES

Durkheim and the Sociology of Suicide

In 1897, Emile Durkheim published a seminal book on the sociology of suicide. Rather than explaining suicide as mainly due to individual influences (as biological and psychological perspectives do), he instead stressed the importance of social and cultural factors (Durkheim, 1897/1951). Durkheim argued that two social factors are most important in explaining suicide: *social integration* and *social regulation*. Social integration is a person's sense of being socially included and accepted, while social regulation concerns itself with communal rules used to monitor, influence, and control people's behavior. Using the concepts of integration and regulation, Durkheim (1897/1951) proposed four different types of suicide:

» **Egoistic suicide** occurs when people experience *low social integration*. Because they feel like they don't belong, they become alienated and unhappy. People who feel isolated and alone are more likely to kill themselves. As just one example, research finds that gay, lesbian, and transgender people—who often face social rejection and discrimination—are at higher risk for both suicide and nonsuicidal self-injury (Haas et al., 2011; E. Marshall, Claes, Bouman, Witcomb, & Arcelus, 2016). Societies in which many people feel excluded or ostracized might be expected to have higher egoistic suicide rates.

Low social integration can lead to egoistic suicide, according to the classic sociological theorizing of Emile Durkheim.
Source: Image Source/Christopher Robbins

» **Altruistic suicide** occurs when people experience *high social integration*. In fact, they are so well integrated into society that they willingly sacrifice themselves for the greater good. A soldier who jumps on a grenade, a parent who takes a bullet for her child, or a protestor willing to die for a cause are examples of altruistic suicides. Altruistic suicides should be most common in cultures that are highly integrated, where honor and serving the collective good are valued.

» **Anomic suicide** occurs when people experience *low social regulation*. In such cases, suicide results because society doesn't provide dependable social structures for its members. Lack of adequate community support—from one's family, church, schools, workplace, or government—lead to people feeling isolated and let down. For instance, war veterans who return home but don't receive necessary assistance run a higher risk of suicide (Bruce, 2010).

» **Fatalistic suicide** occurs when people experience *high social regulation*. Rules, expectations, and social demands are so great that death feels like the only way out. Slaves and prisoners who kill themselves to escape their fate would be examples of fatalistic suicide. Other examples might be people committing suicide because they feel trapped by the demands of work, school, or home.

As you can see, what makes Durkheim's view so different from biological and psychological perspectives is that it portrays suicide as emerging from social, not individual, factors. From a strictly sociological perspective suicide is a social problem, not a medical one. Below we highlight several areas where social factors are worth considering when it comes to understanding suicide.

CHAPTER 15

Gender and Socioeconomic Status (SES)

As already mentioned, women are more likely to attempt suicide, but men succeed at it more. How might we explain this in social terms? Perhaps women are more socially integrated. That is, compared to men, they may be socialized to maintain closer social connections to family and friends, making egoistic suicide less likely (Wray, Colen, & Pescosolido, 2010). Divorced men, widowed men, and single men who live by themselves run a higher risk for suicide—all instances in which men may be less socially integrated (Wray et al., 2010). Interestingly, when socioeconomic status is controlled for, the risk is limited to divorced men (Wray et al., 2010). This fits with the broader finding that people of lower socioeconomic status (SES) die by suicide more often than those of higher SES (J. C. Franklin et al., 2017). From a social justice perspective, then, suicide may be more of a social and economic issue than a medical one. Figure 15.1 shows the percentage of violent deaths that were suicides in different regions of the world in 2012 by gender. As the figure indicates, a greater percentage of violent deaths in high-income countries, compared to low- and middle-income countries, were attributed to suicide in many (but not all) parts of the world. What hypotheses can you generate to explain this?

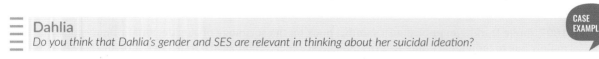

Dahlia

Do you think that Dahlia's gender and SES are relevant in thinking about her suicidal ideation?

CASE EXAMPLES

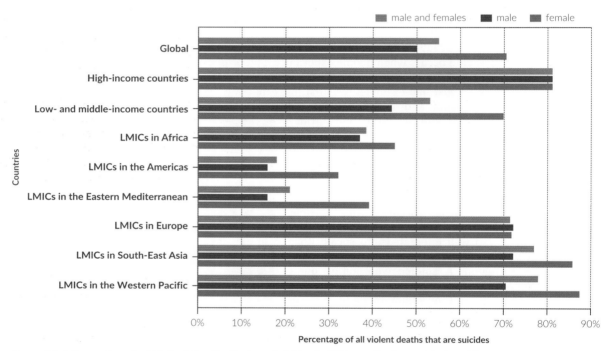

Figure 15.1 Proportion of all Violent Deaths that are Suicides in Different Regions of the World, 2012
Source: World Health Organization (2014, p. 23, Figure 4).

Age

Suicide rates vary by age. People under age 15 are least likely to kill themselves, while those over age 70 are most likely to kill themselves—and this pattern holds in most locations around the globe (World Health Organization, 2014). In some countries, suicide rates steadily increase with age; however, in other countries suicides peak among young adults, then drop off among middle-aged people before increasing again in old age (World Health Organization, 2014). Young adults and elderly women are at greater risk of suicide in low- and middle-income countries than they are in high-income countries, but middle-aged-men's risk is significantly greater in high-income countries. (World Health Organization, 2014).

In many countries, there has been a recent spike in adolescent suicides (L. Holmes, 2017; Illmer, 2017; Rachel Lewis, 2017). There have been sharp increases in suicides among both teenage boys and girls, but particularly in girls. A 2015 study by the U.S. Centers for Disease Control found that the suicide rate for girls aged 15–19 had doubled since 2007, hitting its highest rate in 40 years (Rachel Lewis, 2017). The suicide rate increased significantly for teen boys, too—30% since 2007 (L. Holmes, 2017). Still, in keeping with adult suicide rates, more U.S. teenage boys (1,537) than girls (524) killed themselves in 2015 (L. Holmes, 2017). While adolescent suicide rates are higher in the U.S. than other countries (such as the U.K.), the highest teen suicide rates in the developed world are in New Zealand, where teen suicide is twice as likely as in the U.S. and five times as likely as in the U.K. (Illmer, 2017). Some have speculated that New Zealand's high child poverty rates, high incidence of bullying in schools, and discrimination against Maori and Pacific Islanders may all be contributing to such high suicide rates, but the answer remains unclear (Illmer, 2017).

Across all developed countries, some have attributed the spike in adolescent suicides to the rise of cell phones, which critics complain has resulted in teens spending less time socializing and dating and more time at home alone with their phones and other cherished electronic devices (Twenge, 2017). This has purportedly left many adolescents isolated and depressed, interfering with their ability to develop the necessary emotional resilience to handle adversity and keep suicidal ideation at bay. While the cell phone argument is compelling and provocative, there is little research on whether it explains the alarming increase in teen suicides.

Social Contagion

Is suicide socially "contagious"—meaning when someone takes his own life, can it influence others to do the same? Some argue yes, pointing to research evidence for the **Werther effect**, which is the tendency for suicide rates to go up following a highly publicized suicide (Phillips, 1974). The Werther effect is named after the lead character who kills himself in Johann Wolfgang von Goethe's popular 1774 novel, *The Sorrows of Young Werther*. Following the book's publication, people noticed (although never definitely confirmed) an uptick in suicide rates. However, social science research over the past several decades has provided compelling evidence for the Werther effect, finding that the more publicity a suicide receives, the more suicide rates tend to increase (D. P. Phillips, 1974; M. Schäfer & Quiring, 2015).

Many have theorized that the Werther effect results from social modeling. Basically, people learn about a suicide from the media, then imitate it. But only some people are inspired to kill themselves after a highly publicized suicide, so who is most vulnerable? Recent research suggests, unsurprisingly, that experiencing depressed mood is what makes people susceptible to contagion effects (Ma-Kellams, Baek, & Or, 2016). In other words, "depressed affect stands as a critical determinant of whether contagion occurs" (Ma-Kellams et al., 2016, p. 5). This provides a nice example of how social and individual characteristics may combine in contributing to suicidal behavior.

SUICIDE PREVENTION
Suicide Prevention Counseling

Suicide prevention counseling is a form of crisis counseling in which a professional or trained volunteer talks with the suicidal person to prevent a suicide. It can occur in a variety of formats—face-to-face interviews, telephone hotlines, online chats, social media interventions, or crisis texting via mobile phones (D. C. Clark, 1998; Hvidt, Ploug, & Holm, 2016; Perry, Werner-Seidler, Calear, & Christensen, 2016; J. Robinson et al., 2016). The goal is to provide suicidal people with an outlet to express their feelings and concerns to a supportive listener.

Dahlia
Returning once again to our case client Dahlia, by using person-centered listening skills to empathize with her experience, a crisis counselor would provide Dahlia the opportunity to process her feelings about wanting to kill herself.

At the same time, suicide prevention counseling often moves beyond simply lending an empathic ear, especially with clients who seem like they might follow through with hurting themselves. Most suicide prevention counseling involves assessing suicidal risk. That is, how likely does it seem that the client will eventually self-harm? To make such determinations, the counselor must ask directly about suicidal ideation with questions such as: "Have you had thoughts of killing yourself?" "If yes, have you thought about how you'd kill yourself?" "Do you have a specific plan for killing yourself?" "Have you in any way acted to advance the plan?" The goal is to estimate the suicide risk.

Dahlia
The suicide counselor that Dahlia speaks to might ask her these sorts of questions to assess how likely she is to hurt herself again.

CHAPTER **15**

When it comes to telephone hotlines, some point to evidence that they can help to reduce suicide risk in the short term, but there isn't much research on long-term outcomes (Hvidt et al., 2016). Overall, we simply don't know how effective suicide prevention programs are because existing research results are mixed (Lester, 2011). Further, a lot of suicidal people don't reach out for help.

No-Suicide Contracts

When dealing with suicidal clients, many professionals like to use **no-suicide contracts**. No-suicide contracting involves asking suicidal clients to explicitly state that they will not hurt themselves for an agreed-upon amount of time, ranging from a few hours or days or until the next therapy or crisis-intervention session (Drye, Goulding, & Goulding, 1973; S. Edwards & Harries, 2007; Range, Campbell, Kovac, Marion-Jones, & Aldridge, 2002). A specific list of contingencies is developed—actions to be taken should a client feel unable to abide by the contract (Drye et al., 1973; S. Edwards & Harries, 2007; Range et al., 2002). Figure 15.2 contains an example of a no-suicide contract that a suicidal client might be asked to sign.

I, _____ agree that I will not do anything that would cause harm to myself or anyone else, for the following length of time: _____.

I realize that I am responsible for my own actions, and that if I feel my life is becoming too difficult, I agree to do one or more of the following actions so that there is no harm to myself or others.

  1. Call _____ at _____, or

  2. _____ at _____, or

  3. _____ at _____, or

I will go to the emergency room.

Client Signature _____   Date _____

Witness/Counselor Signature: _____   Date _____

Figure 15.2 Example of a No-Suicide Contract

Source: Reproduced from: Range, L. M., Campbell, C., Kovac, S. H., Marion-Jones, M., & Aldridge, H. (2002). No-suicide contracts: An overview and recommendations. *Death Studies*, 26(1), 51–74. doi:10.1080/07481180210147

No-suicide contracts are controversial, with some professionals arguing strongly in favor of them and others firmly against them. Table 15.1 summarizes some of the main arguments for and against no-suicide contracts. Research-wise, there isn't much evidence for no-suicide contracts (McMyler & Pryjmachuk, 2008; Rudd, Mandrusiak, & Joiner, 2006). As an alternative to no-suicide contracts, some professionals use a **commitment to treatment statement (CTS)**, in which suicidal clients commit to (a) life and the therapy process, (b) being honest about their suicidal thoughts and actions, and (c) seeking emergency services should they experience a crisis between sessions (Rudd et al., 2006). The CTS differs from a no-suicide contract in that it doesn't ask clients to contractually agree not to harm themselves. However, there is little in the way of published research on the effectiveness of commitment to treatment statements. Debate about no-suicide contracts continues.

Table 15.1 Some Arguments For and Against No-Suicide Contracts

ARGUMENTS FOR	ARGUMENTS AGAINST
No-suicide contracts foster a cooperative working relationship between client and counselor with a shared goal (namely, preventing the client's suicide).	No-suicide contracts unfairly coerce clients.
No-suicide contracts allow therapists to learn which clients are resistant to suicide prevention efforts.	No-suicide contracts are improperly viewed by therapists as a protection against legal liability should one of their clients attempt suicide.
No-suicide contracts permit clinicians to express genuine concern for clients' welfare.	No-suicide contracts are not merely ineffective, but potentially harmful—especially when clients believe that acknowledging suicidal overtures might violate the contract to which they agreed.

Source: These arguments draw on the works of S. J. Edwards and Sachmann (2010); J. B. Lee and Bartlett (2005); A. Weiss (2001).

Public Education

Public education programs try to prevent suicides by providing psychoeducational information, often via mass media campaigns that "deliver messages across multiple media platforms, including print media, television, billboards, and posters" (Torok, Calear, Shand, & Christensen, 2016, p. 2). These anti-suicide public service announcements convey a variety of messages—such as the importance of people openly discussing suicide, the value of the suicidal person's life, the suffering that suicidal people experience, and the incredible anguish experienced by those left behind after a successful suicide (Ftanou et al., 2017). While widely used, evidence for the effectiveness of public service announcements is currently limited (Ftanou et al., 2017). Table 15.2 provides information common to many suicide prevention public service announcements. The idea in disseminating such information is not only to educate people about the problem of suicide, but to overcome social taboos against discussing it openly.

Table 15.2 Myths about Suicide

Myth #1	Once suicidal, always suicidal	Suicidal feelings are often temporary and specific to the situation. Someone feeling suicidal is unlikely to always feel that way and can usually go on to live a long life.
Myth #2	People who talk about suicide won't try to kill themselves	People who discuss killing themselves are often trying to reach out for help. Take them seriously. They may indeed follow through on their threats.
Myth #3	People who talk about suicide always have mental disorders	Feeling suicidal doesn't mean you have a mental disorder. Lots of people who are suicidal don't meet the criteria for a mental disorder. Others who are diagnosed with a mental disorder don't ever feel suicidal.
Myth #4	Talking to a suicidal person is bad because it encourages suicide	Talking about it actually gives the suicidal person a chance to discuss difficult feelings and consider alternatives to suicide.
Myth #5	Suicides usually happen suddenly with no warning	While some suicides do occur without warning, most have clear warning signs. Suicidal people often say or do things that suggest suicide is on their minds.
Myth #6	Suicidal people want to die	Suicidal people are often ambivalent about dying. They may do something rash that ends their lives, but this doesn't mean they necessarily were determined to die. Many suicide attempts are cries for help in which the person is communicating a genuine sense of intense unhappiness.

Source: Inspired by ideas expressed in World Health Organization (2014).

Method Restriction

Another approach to suicide prevention is **method restriction**, in which access to common ways that people kill themselves is limited or made more difficult (Sarchiapone, Mandelli, Iosue, Andrisano, & Roy, 2011). Gun control, regulating the availability of pesticides, detoxifying gasoline used in motor vehicles, and curbing access to alcohol and other drugs are all examples of method restriction. Other examples of method restriction include altering the physical environment to make suicides more difficult (e.g., placing barriers at sites where people might hang themselves or jump to their deaths), prescribing fewer barbiturates and tricyclic antidepressants (which suicidal people often use to overdose), and using "safe rooms" in prisons and hospitals (built to make it much harder for people to harm themselves).

Dahlia
At one point Dahlia considered jumping off the roof of her 10-story apartment building, but she couldn't because the roofline had recently been edged with a tall fence.

CASE EXAMPLES

Some but not all evidence suggests that method restriction may lower suicide rates, although there is always the risk that highly determined people will simply seek alternative means for ending their lives (Anestis, Anestis, & Butterworth, 2017; Barber & Miller, 2014; Beautrais et al., 2007; Habenstein, Steffen, Bartsch,

CHAPTER 15

Michaud, & Reisch, 2013; McPhedran & Baker, 2012; Sarchiapone et al., 2011). Of course, some might argue that denying everyone access to items like guns and pesticides because certain people misuse them is unfair. However, others disagree, arguing that society has a right to impose commonsense restrictions on individual liberty for the greater good.

Hospitalization

Suicidal people who are judged to be an imminent threat to themselves can be hospitalized using civil commitment procedures (discussed later). Typically, such individuals are temporarily committed for a brief hospital stay. For a more extended commitment, those wanting the person hospitalized must go to court. The **"thank you" theory of involuntary commitment** in such cases holds that people who threaten or attempt suicide will thank us later if we have them hospitalized and that their future appreciativeness, rather than a mental health professional's limited ability to judge how dangerous they are, is the best legal justification for committing them (J. C. Beck & Golowka, 1988; A. A. Stone, 1975). Although the "thank you" theory predominates in clinical practice, some civil libertarians take a very different view. They argue that not only is involuntary hospitalization of suicidal people a violation of their rights, but also that people have a legal right to suicide—even when we morally disagree with their choice to end their lives (Szasz, 1986, 1999, 2011). What are your thoughts on this contentious question? Do we do more harm than good by coercively stopping people from harming themselves? Or do we do our clients an invaluable service by preventing them from taking an action that they may later regret?

Can We Predict Who Will Die By Suicide?

Although several factors—such as past suicide attempts, a family history of suicide, prior treatment for a serious presenting problem, and general maladjustment—provide some information about who might attempt suicide, these factors aren't consistently strong predictors of suicide (although the more of them that are present, the better the predictions) (J. C. Franklin et al., 2017). Perhaps because these risk factors aren't always dependable predictors, counselors aren't especially good at figuring out who will or won't self-harm (J. C. Franklin et al., 2017). This difficulty may be further compounded because clients don't always tell the truth about whether they're planning suicide. But even if we account for client deception, it is still very difficult for people—even trained counselors—to predict future behavior.

Interestingly, some new research is experimenting with using computer technology to sort through data and make suicide predictions. One promising study yielded 80%–90% accuracy in predicting suicide using machine learning algorithms (C. G. Walsh, Riberio, & Franklin, 2017). Given these results, some speculate that suicide-predicting algorithms could be integrated into social media sites like Facebook to identify people at risk for suicide. This could be used to intervene to prevent suicides, though some might view social media sites sorting through their posts to determine their suicidality as an invasion of privacy. As with so many topics we have discussed throughout the text, the issue of suicide and its prevention remains one where there are many competing perspectives. Further, when people attempt suicide, it raises numerous ethical and legal issues. When is it acceptable to involuntarily treat suicidal and other clients deemed dangerous? What rights do such clients have? How do we balance protecting client rights to self-determination while also safeguarding both clients and those around them? These sorts of ethical and legal concerns—with suicidal and other challenging clients—are examined next.

15.3 ETHICAL PERSPECTIVES
PROFESSIONAL ETHICS CODES

Psychologists, psychiatrists, counselors, couples and family therapists, social workers, and psychiatric nurses all have ethics codes designed to protect the service-users with whom they work. The American Psychological Association's (2002) ethics code is representative of such codes. It contains five general principles to guide professional research and practice (see Table 15.3), as well as specific ethical standards psychologists are expected to uphold. More generally, Table 15.4 provides online links to the ethics codes of selected associations of psychologists and psychiatrists from around the globe. Familiarity with such codes is crucial for mental health professionals working in clinical and research capacities as they grapple daily with ethical issues. We examine several of these issues below.

Table 15.3 General Principles of the Ethics Code of the American Psychological Association

Principle A: Beneficence and Nonmaleficence	Psychologists strive to benefit those with whom they work and take care to do no harm.
Principle B: Fidelity and Responsibility	Psychologists establish relationships of trust with those with whom they work. They are aware of their professional and scientific responsibilities to society and to the specific communities in which they work.
Principle C: Integrity	Psychologists seek to promote accuracy, honesty, and truthfulness in the science, teaching, and practice of psychology.
Principle D: Justice	Psychologists recognize that fairness and justice entitle all persons to access and benefit from the contributions of psychology and to equal quality in the processes, procedures, and services being conducted by psychologists.
Principle E: Respect for People's Rights and Dignity	Psychologists respect the dignity and worth of all people, and the rights of individuals to privacy, confidentiality, and self-determination.

Source: Adapted from the American Psychological Association (2002, pp. 1062–1063).

Table 15.4 Ethics Codes and Committees in Psychology and Psychiatry

PSYCHOLOGY	
• American Psychological Association (APA)	www.apa.org/ethics/code/
• Australian Psychological Society (APS)	www.bps.org.uk/news-and-policy/bps-code-ethics-and-conduct
• British Psychological Society (BPS)	www.bps.org.uk/news-and-policy/bps-code-ethics-and-conduct
• Canadian Psychological Society (CPS)	www.cpa.ca/aboutcpa/committees/ethics/codeofethics/
• European Federation of Psychologists' Associations (EFPA)	http://efpa.eu/ethics/meta-code-of-ethics-
• New Zealand Psychological Society (NZPsS)	www.psychology.org.nz/wp-content/uploads/2014/04/code-of-ethics.pdf
• Psychological Society of South Africa (PsySSA)	www.psyssa.com/other-sage-journals-2/
PSYCHIATRY	
• American Psychiatric Association (APA)	www.psychiatry.org/psychiatrists/practice/ethics
• Canadian Psychiatric Association (CPA)	www.cpa-apc.org/news-policy-advocacy/advocacy-policy/position-papers-statements/#tab-3-3
• European Psychiatric Association (EPA)	www.europsy.net/committees/committee-on-ethical-issues/
• Royal Australian and New Zealand College of Psychiatrists (RANZCP)	www.ranzcp.org/Files/Resources/College_Statements/Practice_Guidelines/code_ethics_2010-pdf.aspx
• Royal College of Psychiatrists (U.K.)	www.rcpsych.ac.uk/usefulresources/publications/collegereports/cr/cr186.aspx
• World Psychiatric Association	www.wpanet.org/detail.php?section_id=5&category_id=9&content_id=31

CHAPTER 15

INFORMED CONSENT

Throughout this book, we have regularly cited research studies, many of them using participants who were vulnerable because they were experiencing a debilitating presenting problem. While it is important to study such people, it is also important to remember that professional ethics demands that people never be required to participate in a study or be misled about a study in order to secure their participation. In other words, study participants must always consent to participate based on a full understanding of what they are getting themselves into. The process of providing prospective research participants with sufficient information about a study—including why it is being conducted and what the risks and benefits of participating are—is called **informed consent**.

Although the importance of informed consent in protecting research participants may seem obvious, the history of medical and psychological research is marred by gross violations in which informed consent was never obtained. Nazi doctors during the Second World War conducted horrible experiments on nonconsenting subjects. After the war, Nazi researchers accused of war crimes were tried by an international tribunal representing the U.S., U.K., France, and the Soviet Union in what is now known as the Nuremberg trials. Most of the researchers tried were "physicians accused of murder and torture in the conduct of medical experiments on concentration-camp inmates" (Shuster 1997, p. 1437). To help better protect human subjects, the tribunal issued what came to be known as the **Nuremburg Code**, "a sophisticated set of 10 research principles centered not on the physician but on the research subject" (Shuster 1997, p. 1439). Informed consent was the first principle outlined in this code. Informed consent was further codified in 1964 when the World Medical Association (WMA) approved the **Declaration of Helsinki**, a set of ethical principles designed to govern medical research, but which are more broadly applied to any research involving human subjects. The Declaration has undergone seven revisions, most recently in 2013 (World Medical Association, 2013).

Unfortunately, Nazi doctors aren't the only researchers to violate participants' rights before or after the Nuremburg Code and the Declaration of Helsinki. The infamous *Tuskegee experiment*, which continued for 40 years (1932–1972), was undertaken by the United States Public Health Service to study the natural course of syphilis (Chadwick, 1997; Heintzelman, 2003). Without obtaining any kind of informed consent, roughly 400 African American men were infected with (and then not treated for) syphilis—even though safe antibiotic treatments became available in the 1940s. Similarly, between the 1940s and 1970s, the U.S. government conducted experiments in which they exposed people to harmful radiation in order to see its effects, with no clear medical knowledge to be gleaned (by the 1950s and 1960s, the effects of radiation were already known) and often without informed consent (Chadwick, 1997; N. E. Kass & Sugarman, 1996; Subcommittee on Energy Conservation and Power, 1986). According to a report by the U.S. House of Representatives, "in some cases, the human subjects were captive audiences or populations that experimenters might frighteningly have considered 'expendable': the elderly, prisoners, hospital patients suffering from terminal diseases or who might not have retained their full faculties for informed consent" (Subcommittee on Energy Conservation and Power, 1986, p. 1).

Informed consent is imperative when conducting research of any kind. However, when working with vulnerable clinical populations, extra special care is needed—particularly when there is doubt about participants' ability to comprehend the study well enough to understand the risks and appropriately consent. Researchers studying psychosis, for instance, have developed strategies for evaluating whether prospective participants diagnosed with schizophrenia can give informed consent and—when it is determined that they can—how to best explain studies to them so that they can make genuinely informed decisions to participate (or not!) (K. K. Anderson & Mukherjee, 2007; Beebe & Smith, 2010; W. T. Carpenter et al., 2000; S. Y. H. Kim et al., 2007; B. W. Palmer, 2006). Students of abnormal psychology who are interested in conducting research must fully comprehend ethical issues involving the use of human subjects, including informed consent.

CONFIDENTIALITY AND PRIVILEGE

Confidentiality

Have you ever shared something personal with a friend, assuming what you confided would be kept private, only to have that person tell others what you said? Did this encourage you to confide in that person again? Probably not. Treating personal information with reverence and care is key for psychotherapists and other professionals working with clients, especially because most clients are experiencing emotionally painful and difficult presenting problems that they may wish to keep private. Thus, professional ethics codes demand that practicing clinicians maintain client **confidentiality**—the requirement that they not disclose what clients tell them unless their clients give them permission to do so (Guraya, London, & Guraya, 2014; Konrad & Bath, 2014; Smith-Bell & Winslade, 1994; Younggren & Harris, 2008). In other words, confidentiality is a professional obligation or duty of mental health professionals, one that demands they protect clients by avoiding the unauthorized release of information about them. It "is the key to most models of effective psychotherapy. Without this privacy, clients cannot be expected to reveal embarrassing, sometimes personally damaging, information in treatment" (Younggren & Harris, 2008, p. 589).

By keeping what clients say confidential, practicing clinicians make it more likely their clients feel willing to share sensitive personal information with them.
Source: Digital Vision/Getty Images

Should you seek psychotherapy or other professional services for a presenting problem, it is important to understand that your clinician is ethically required to keep what you disclose confidential. When sessions are covered by your health insurance, you usually must give written consent to have your therapist release information to the insurer; of course, specific consent requirements vary by country (Yarmohammadian, Raeisi, Tavakoli, & Nansa, 2010). Often, what is shared is merely a diagnostic code, but sometimes the release of additional information is required. When clients give consent to have confidential information released, it's important that clinicians make clear to them precisely what's being shared. It should also be explained that, once released, clinicians no longer control what those who receive the information do with it.

While confidentiality is a core ethical commitment of all mental health professions, there are several important situations in which clinicians can choose to or are required to violate confidentiality. Clinicians accused of malpractice, for instance, are permitted to disclose information to defend themselves in court. Also, when people are considered dangerous to self or others, therapists are legally obligated to break confidentiality as part of their duty to protect the public (an issue discussed later in the chapter). Importantly, even though circumstances requiring clinicians to break confidentiality are relatively uncommon, such situations place clinicians in a difficult quandary because the decision to break confidentiality is never easy (Winters, 2013). The violation of trust that breaking confidentiality entails can have negative consequences for clients even when the decision is deemed justified (Winters, 2013).

Confidentiality applies not just to clinical practice, but also to research. Although the goal of research is to disseminate new knowledge, in doing so researchers are ethically obliged to keep participant data protected so that participants' identities and responses can't be identified. Additionally, researchers have an ethical duty to protect research participants by storing their data safely and securely. When data is shared with other researchers, all identifying information must be removed to protect participants' confidentiality.

Privilege

Privilege is distinct from, but related to, confidentiality. It is a legal rule that makes it easier for clinicians to safeguard client confidentiality. Privilege holds that certain relationships are protected, meaning that those in them are exempt from being legally compelled to share what was confided in the context of that relationship. Traditionally, communications between married people, clergy and their parishioners, lawyers and their clients, and doctors and their patients (including psychotherapists and their clients) are privileged (Guraya et al., 2014; Konrad & Bath, 2014; Smith-Bell & Winslade, 1994). By designating confidential client communications as privileged, the legal system permits mental health professionals to withhold confidential information that they would otherwise be legally bound to share if asked (Guraya et al., 2014; Konrad & Bath, 2014; Smith-Bell & Winslade, 1994).

For example, imagine that you go to see a psychotherapist. Later, you get arrested for shoplifting and, while on trial, the attorneys prosecuting you subpoena your therapist to release details of what you shared with her in therapy—perhaps by requesting that she hand over her therapy notes. The therapist asserts that, based on her ethical obligation to protect your confidentiality, she cannot share notes detailing your discussions. That is, she asserts that this information is privileged and—unlike other witnesses being subpoenaed—she is legally protected from having to share what she knows. Luckily for you, the judge concurs and indicates that because the notes are privileged under the therapist–client relationship, your therapist is not required to hand them over. This excellent example notwithstanding, a lot of people struggle to see the difference between confidentiality and privilege. A handy way to keep the distinction clear is to remember that "confidentiality is a professional duty to refrain from speaking about certain matters, while privilege is a relief from the duty to speak in a court proceeding about certain matters" (Smith-Bell & Winslade, 1994, p. 184). Depending on particular laws in specific jurisdictions, the courts may rule that certain communications between clients and their therapists aren't covered by privilege. When this happens, therapists must make a difficult choice between obeying the court and upholding their professional commitment to protect client confidentiality.

COMPETENCE

The ethical standard of **competence** holds that clinicians only conduct therapies, assessments, and research when they are properly trained and competent to do so (American Psychological Association, 2002). Knowing the limits of one's expertise is critical for ethical practice. For example, psychologists, counselors, couple and family therapists, and social workers shouldn't be giving medication advice to their clients because these professionals typically do not have the medical training or authority to do so—just as those psychiatrists who lack training and experience in psychotherapy should refer patients requesting such services. As another example, therapists trained only in cognitive-behavioral therapy (CBT) shouldn't begin conducting psychodynamic therapy without appropriate training and supervision to ensure that they can do so competently. Similarly, if conducting assessments (see Chapter 3), a clinician should stick to assessment instruments that he or she has been trained to use. For instance, it's unethical to administer, score, and interpret the Minnesota Multiphasic Personality Inventory (MMPI) without appropriate training. As one additional example, when clients present with problems outside a clinician's area of expertise, the clinician has a duty to either refer the client to someone trained to work with that problem or to obtain the necessary training and supervision necessary to competently provide clinical services.

CONFLICTS OF INTEREST

Most ethics codes warn professionals to avoid **conflicts of interest**. The American Psychological Association's ethics code, for instance, states the following:

> *Psychologists refrain from taking on a professional role when personal, scientific, professional, legal, financial, or other interests or relationships could reasonably be expected to (1) impair their objectivity, competence, or effectiveness in performing their functions as psychologists or (2) expose the person or organization with whom the professional relationship exists to harm or exploitation. (American Psychological Association, 2002, p. 1065)*

There are many potential conflicts of interest that clinicians and researchers must attend to. Having a dual role with a client could pose a conflict of interest. If I am your psychology professor and have grading power over you, I probably shouldn't also see you as a therapy client—especially if your student evaluations of me could influence whether my teaching contract is renewed! Similarly, I shouldn't see friends, family members, or people with whom I have a business relationship in therapy because I may have a vested interest in the decisions they make and this could negatively affect my clinical judgment. Financial conflicts are something ethical clinicians must especially pay heed to. The "In Depth" feature examines the debate over alleged conflicts of interest in a particularly contentious area, namely whether psychiatrists' financial ties to pharmaceutical companies have compromised the development of the *DSM-5*.

IN DEPTH

Financial Conflicts of Interest and the *DSM-5*

Did *DSM-5* task force committee members with financial ties to pharmaceutical companies have a conflict of interest? Psychologist Lisa Cosgrove and colleagues contend that very well might have been the case (Cosgrove, Bursztajn, Erlich, Wheeler, & Shaughnessy, 2013; Cosgrove, Krimsky, Vijayaraghavan, & Schneider, 2006; Cosgrove et al., 2014). Their research found that 56% of *DSM-5* committee members had at least one financial association with a drug company (Cosgrove et al., 2006). That means more than half the psychiatrists who worked on the *DSM-5* were financially connected to a pharmaceutical company. However, this percentage jumped to 100% for those serving on the mood disorder and schizophrenia panels (Cosgrove et al., 2006). In a more recent study, Cosgrove found that in 13 research trials overseen by *DSM-5* committee members to test psychiatric drugs for new *DSM-5* disorders, financial conflicts of interest with a drug company were reported in all but one (Cosgrove et al., 2014). Examples of financial conflicts of interest are "research grants, consultation, honoraria, speakers bureau participation, and/or stock" (Cosgrove et al., 2014, p. 110). Critics of medicalization in psychiatry have interpreted Cosgrove's findings as proof that psychiatrists have a financial conflict of interest that makes it impossible for them to objectively evaluate *DSM-5* disorders and the psychiatric drugs used to treat those disorders (J. Davies, 2017; Whitaker, 2017; Whitaker & Cosgrove, 2015). To these critics, *DSM-5* committee members' judgment is compromised due to conflicts of interest.

However, defenders of the *DSM-5* and psychiatric research counter that Cosgrove's research indicates no such thing. First, they point to the fact that the American Psychiatric Association placed clear (and what they considered reasonable) limits on how much money a *DSM-5* committee member could take from a drug company—no more than US $10,000 a year from industry sources while holding a maximum of US $50,000 in stocks or shares and no more than US $10,000 in dividends from these stocks and shares (A. Kaplan, 2009). Second, they argue that the fact that 100% of the mood disorder and schizophrenia panel members had ties to pharmaceutical companies tells us nothing more than that these disorders are biologically based and commonly treated with medications (Kupfer & Regier, 2009). Thus, it makes perfect sense that panel members would often be connected to drug companies working on treatments for these disorders. In the words of David Kupfer and Darrel Regier (2009, para. 5), who oversaw the development of *DSM-5*, Cosgrove and her coauthors "seem not to appreciate or understand how the collaborative relationships among government, academia, and industry are vital to the current and future development of pharmacological treatments for mental disorders." Thus, to the *DSM-5* defenders, there is nothing sinister going on and no conflict of interest significant enough to influence scientific and clinical judgements.

Yet those skeptical of the *DSM-5* remain unconvinced, noting that $50,000 in stock and $10,000 in annual dividends is still a lot of money—surely enough to influence decision-making. To Cosgrove, "the APA's efforts at creating a conflict of interest (COI) policy have failed to ensure that the process for revising diagnostic and therapeutic guidelines is one that the public can trust" (Cosgrove & Bursztajn, 2009, para. 1). Debate over the potential conflict of interest related to psychiatrists' financial ties to the pharmaceutical industry is unlikely to abate anytime soon. You will need to draw your own conclusions about this thorny ethical issue.

CRITICAL THINKING QUESTIONS

1. Does Cosgrove's research convince you that *DSM-5* committee members had a financial conflict of interest? Explain your reasoning.

2. Even if there was a conflict of interest, do you see evidence that *DSM-5* decisions were influenced by these conflicts?

3. Do you think the limits that the American Psychiatric Association established for how much money a *DSM-5* committee member can receive from pharmaceutical companies are reasonable? Explain.

4. Cosgrove's critics counter that ties between government, academia, and industry are necessary to advance psychiatric knowledge and that suggesting these ties imply conflicts of interest is unfair. Do you agree with this statement and why?

ACCESS TO CARE

Developing effective interventions for presenting problems is important, but these interventions can only benefit people if they have access to them. Thus, the issue of **access to care** is critical to ethical practice. What is access to care? The Institute of Medicine defines it as "the timely use of personal health services to achieve the best possible health outcomes" (Institute of Medicine, 1993, p. 4). People can be said to have access when they are able to obtain medical, psychological, and social services and are helped by doing so.

Barriers to Care

Unfortunately, not everyone has equal access to care. Access isn't equitable when there are "systematic differences in use and outcomes among groups" and when financial barriers or other barriers prevent certain people from receiving effective services (Institute of Medicine, 1993, p. 4). Thus, many argue that clinicians must attend to issues of access to make sure that services are available to all who need them. Barriers that prevent access to care include the following:

1. *Financial barriers.* Many people simply can't afford to seek help for their problems (Rowan, McAlpine, & Blewett, 2013; Social Solutions, 2016). This may be especially true in the United States, where there is no nationalized health insurance, which means that a sizable number of people lack coverage entirely or have health plans that provide limited coverage of mental health services (Rowan et al., 2013). In such

cases, psychiatric and psychological services are often prohibitively expensive, reducing people's access to them (Rowan et al., 2013).

2. *Insufficient services available.* Sometimes people lack access due to a scarcity of services. For example, people in rural areas with fewer trained professionals are often unable to obtain care (Jain, 2014). In the U.S., it's estimated that 89.3 million people live in geographic regions with shortages of mental health professionals (Social Solutions, 2016). Similarly, in the U.K., cuts to mental health coverage by the National Health Service between 2008 and 2014 resulted in a dearth of available services; the shortage became so severe that up to 75% of people diagnosed with mental illnesses were estimated to go without any treatment at all (Docherty & Thornicroft, 2015). Canada has a shortage of clinicians, as well. One study found that only six out of 230 Vancouver psychiatrists were available to provide services in a timely manner, while another reported that only 13% of people in British Columbia diagnosed with depression received minimally adequate counseling and psychotherapy (Gratzer & Goldbloom, 2017). When services aren't offered due to lack of funding or lack of providers, people can't benefit from them.

3. *Racial and cultural barriers.* Being from a racial or ethnic minority group or being an immigrant often predicts poorer access to care (Derr, 2016; National Collaborating Centre for Mental Health, 2011). Some evidence implies that members of certain racial and ethnic minority groups find services less acceptable than members of other groups (National Collaborating Centre for Mental Health, 2011). It's possible that these perceptions are due to stigmatized attitudes within these racial and cultural groups toward those who pursue professional help for psychological problems. However, it's also possible that social discrimination against these groups leads their members to distrust mental health professionals and avoid seeking services.

4. *Language barriers.* Language barriers overlap with racial and cultural barriers. Research consistently finds that people who lack proficiency in the language native to where they live underutilize psychiatric services (National Collaborating Centre for Mental Health, 2011; Ohtani, Suzuki, Takeuchi, & Uchida, 2015). Finding ways to overcome language barriers— such as increasing the number of bilingual practitioners—could improve access to care (National Collaborating Centre for Mental Health, 2011).

5. *Age-related barriers.* Age can be a barrier to seeking services. Many older people who experience depression don't see it as a problem worthy of clinical attention and therefore are less likely to pursue professional help (National Collaborating Centre for Mental Health, 2011). Further, older people feeling depressed or anxious often present with physical symptoms rather than psychological complaints, making them less likely to be offered psychological services (National Collaborating Centre for Mental Health, 2011).

6. *Stigma.* Most of the presenting problems reviewed in this text carry a great deal of stigma (National Collaborating Centre for Mental Health, 2011; Social Solutions, 2016). One unfortunate consequence of this is that people may be less willing to seek services because of the stigma that accompanies doing so. Efforts to reduce stigma might result in more people being willing to request professional help for their problems.

Age is often a barrier to mental health care. For instance, many older people who experience depression do not seek psychological services.
Source: Getty Images Thinkstock Images\Stockbyte

Enhancing Access in the Digital Age via e-Mental Health

One intriguing and increasingly common way of enhancing access to care is through technology. Many practitioners find themselves relying on email, text messaging, videoconferencing, and other forms of modern technology when communicating with their clients. The burgeoning area of **e-mental health**, in which telecommunication and information technologies are used to provide mental health services at a distance, grants access to care to those who might otherwise be unable to obtain it (Mucic & Hilty, 2016). The oldest and perhaps the most widely used form of e-mental health is **telepsychiatry** (or *telepsychology*, as psychologists often call it). Telepsychiatry employs real-time videoconferencing, allowing services such as medication management and short-term psychotherapy to be provided remotely by video (Lauckner & Whitten, 2016; Saeed, Johnson, Bagga, & Glass, 2016). It has been used extensively when providing services to veterans, children, and students (Lauckner & Whitten, 2016). Because telepsychiatry appointments occur in real time, they are a *synchronous* form of e-mental health services.

However, many newer e-mental health interventions are *asynchronous*—meaning that they don't involve live interactions in the immediate moment, but rather utilize alternating interactions that occur at times convenient to the participants (Myers & Vander Stoep, 2017). Email, social media, online discussion boards, and smartphone apps (such as those discussed in Chapter 9's "Try It Yourself" feature) are all examples of asynchronous technologies used in e-mental health (Mucic & Hilty, 2016; Myers & Vander Stoep, 2017). Some e-mental health smartphone apps offer professional services via phone conversations and instant messaging; others help clients by encouraging them to participate in psychological exercises (such as visualization or attending to their thoughts and feelings), or to monitor or maintain their progress (using symptom self-assessments or medication reminders) (Bardram et al., 2013; S. Chan, Torous, Hinton, & Yellowlees, 2016). E-mental health interventions are still in their infancy and, when using them, clinicians must be careful to safeguard client privacy and confidentiality (Mucic & Hilty, 2016). Special attention must also be paid to the limits of assessing and diagnosing people via the internet—where important clinical information available in face-to-face interactions may not be available (Andersson & Titov, 2014). That said, initial research suggests that e-mental health techniques hold much promise and that they will be steadily integrated into everyday practice (Andersson & Titov, 2014; Lal & Adair, 2014). Given the ubiquity of smartphones, using e-mental health apps is viewed by many as an excellent way to increase access to care (Myers & Vander Stoep, 2017). To those who see e-mental health as the wave of the future, "technology is providing tools to help rectify the disparities in access to quality mental health care that we all see, but from which we have often turned away" (Myers & Vander Stoep, 2017, p. 6).

15.4 LEGAL PERSPECTIVES

Sometimes the presenting problems people experience pose not just ethical, but also legal, challenges. How does the legal system handle such issues? Below we examine four issues where abnormality and the legal system come into contact: the insanity defense, determining fitness or competency to stand trial, civil commitment, and the duties to warn and protect. As you will see, legal and mental health perspectives don't always conceptualize abnormality similarly, which can pose difficulties.

THE INSANITY DEFENSE

Insanity and the Insanity Defense as Legal Terms

Insanity isn't a psychiatric concept. It's a legal one. The term is used in legal proceedings and defined by legislators, not mental health professionals. In other words, the term insanity is "informed by mental health professionals, but the term today is primarily legal, not psychological. There's no 'insane' diagnosis listed in the DSM" (R. Howes, 2009, para. 4). Legally speaking, insanity is typically defined as "mental illness of such a severe nature that a person cannot distinguish fantasy from reality, cannot conduct her/his affairs due to psychosis, or is subject to uncontrollable impulsive behavior" ("Insanity," n.d., para. 1). This definition is used in the legal system to make judgements about guilt and innocence (R. Howes, 2009). Hence, the **insanity defense** is a legal plea that challenges criminal responsibility by arguing that defendants aren't responsible for a crime if, under certain circumstances, they were suffering from a mental disorder when the crime was committed ("Insanity," n.d.). Defendants who wish to invoke the insanity defense plead **not guilty by reason of insanity (NGBRI)**. If the plea is successful, they are committed to mental hospitals for treatment (rather than sentenced to prison) and only released when judged to have recovered. Although used in only a very small number of legal cases (and rarely successful even when invoked, as we discuss further) (Justice Center, 2009; Perlin, 2017b), the insanity defense remains a hot topic both in abnormal psychology classes and the wider culture. Below we examine the history, use, and arguments for and against the insanity defense.

Historical Origins

The insanity defense as a legal tactic has mainly developed over the past two-and-a-half centuries, but the notion existed in some form before that. The ancient Greek philosopher Plato, for instance, argued that mentally disturbed individuals shouldn't be held responsible or punished for their crimes (R. J. Simon & Ahn-Redding, 2006). Further, precursors to the insanity defense can be found in both ancient Jewish and Islamic law (R. J. Simon & Ahn-Redding, 2006). Modern versions of the insanity defense grew out of British common law (law based mainly on precedents from judicial rulings rather than from codified statutes). For instance, in 1265, the British jurist Lord Bracton proposed the **wild beast test**, which "likened the defendant to a wild beast due to his complete lack of understanding" (R. J. Simon & Ahn-Redding, 2006, p. 6). Thus, even before modern legal tests of insanity developed, the idea of not holding people responsible for crimes due to their mental state was percolating.

CHAPTER 15

Legal Tests of Insanity

M'Naghten Test

The first widely established (and still used, in many places) test of insanity is the **M'Naghten test** (or *M'Naghten rule*) ("M'Naghten's case," n.d.; D. N. Robinson, 1996; Rolf, 2006; R. J. Simon & Ahn-Redding, 2006). This test was developed in the aftermath of a landmark 1843 British murder case. In this famous case, a jury acquitted Scotsman Daniel M'Naghten by reason of insanity in the murder of Edwin Drummond, the secretary to British Prime Minister Robert Peel. M'Naghten had shot and killed Drummond, whom he'd mistaken for Peel. After being arrested, M'Naghten told the police that he had set out to kill the prime minister because "the tories in my city follow and persecute me wherever I go, and have destroyed my peace of mind. They do everything in their power to harass and persecute me; in fact they wish to murder me" ("M'Naghten's case," n.d.). At trial, several witnesses testified that M'Naghten was delusional at the time of the murder. Nonetheless, the acquittal provoked a great deal of public uproar, leading the House of Lords to clarify the criteria for reaching an insanity defense verdict, which became known as the M'Naghten test:

> It must be clearly proven that at the time of the act, the accused was under such a defect of reason from disease of the mind that he did not know the nature and quality of the act he was committing; or if he did know, he did not know what he was doing was wrong. ("M'Naghten's case," n.d.)

The key question in making insanity determinations under the M'Naghten test is this: At the time of the crime, did the defendant have a mental disorder that made him or her unable to understand the actions taken or that these actions were wrong? The M'Naghten test remains widely used today. For instance, it is still employed in the U.K., as well as in many U.S. states; Brazil, Israel, and parts of Australia also use tests derived from or influenced by M'Naghten (R. J. Simon & Ahn-Redding, 2006).

Irresistible Impulse Test

Although the U.K. and most of the U.S. had adopted the M'Naghten test within 10 years of the M'Naghten case, the test was criticized for focusing too much on defendants' ability to understand their actions while overlooking another important issue—namely, whether they could control those actions (Rolf, 2006; R. J. Simon & Ahn-Redding, 2006). In response to such criticism, an alternative to the M'Naghten test was adopted in parts of United States. Known as the **irresistible impulse test**, it held that defendants could be acquitted by reason of insanity when their crimes were attributable to impulses they couldn't resist. Under the irresistible impulse test, people could be acquitted when a mental disease caused them to lose their free will, making it unreasonable to hold them responsible for what they'd done ("The irresistible impulse test," n.d.; D. N. Robinson, 1996; Rolf, 2006; R. J. Simon & Ahn-Redding, 2006).

When first developed, the irresistible impulse test was sometimes used in addition to the M'Naghten test, but at other times it was used instead of it ("The irresistible impulse test," n.d.). Either way, it came in for extensive criticism ("The irresistible impulse test," n.d.; D. N. Robinson, 1996; Rolf, 2006; R. J. Simon & Ahn-Redding, 2006). The biggest objection was that the irresistible impulse test offered no clear way for deciding which defendants could or couldn't control their behavior. What was to stop defendants from faking insanity by claiming they weren't responsible for their actions? That is, they could say their crimes had been the result of uncontrollable impulses caused by mental disorders—and how could anyone prove otherwise, especially with both sides in a trial bringing in dueling experts to plead their case? Consequently, the irresistible impulse test was often deemed too broad and too vague. Although some U.S. states still use a version of it today, they typically do so in conjunction with the stricter M'Naghten test (R. J. Simon & Ahn-Redding, 2006).

Durham Test

The **Durham test** (or *Durham rule*) originated in New Hampshire and was briefly used at the federal level in the U.S. between 1954 and 1972 ("The 'Durham Rule'," n.d.). The test was named after Monte Durham, a troubled 26-year-old resident of Washington, DC who was arrested for breaking and entering. Durham had a long history of emotional difficulties, including at least two suicide attempts (R. J.Simon & Ahn-Redding, 2006). He was acquitted on grounds that his illegal behavior was caused by a mental disorder. This established the Durham test, which held that "a criminal defendant cannot be convicted of a crime if the act was the result of a mental disease or defect at the time of the incident" ("The 'Durham Rule'," n.d., para. 3).

The Durham test only requires that criminal behavior be caused by a mental disease or defect. This makes it even more inclusive than the irresistible impulse test, which demands that defendants be unable to control their behavior. In fact, the Durham test has been rejected for being overly inclusive. Under it, anyone who claims a mental defect—even those who understood their actions and could control them—may plead insanity ("The 'Durham Rule'," n.d.; D. N. Robinson, 1996; Rolf, 2006; R. J. Simon & Ahn-Redding, 2006). The Durham test has also been criticized for being exceedingly dependent on mental health professionals to determine whether a defendant has a mental disorder. Thus, U.S. courts overwhelmingly rejected the Durham test. New Hampshire is the only state that still uses it ("The 'Durham Rule'," n.d.).

Model Penal Code Test

In the U.S., the **model penal code test** combines aspects of the M'Naghten and irresistible impulse

The insanity defense is controversial and there are different legal requirements for it depending on the state or country.
Source: Getty Images/Caiaimage\Paul Bradbury

rules. Also known as the *American Law Institute test*, or *ALI test* (because it was proposed in 1955 by the American Law Institute), it holds that defendants can be acquitted by reason of insanity if at the time of their crimes they had a mental disorder that prevented them from either (a) having substantial capacity to appreciate the wrongfulness of their actions, or (b) controlling their behavior ("The 'Model Penal Code' test for legal insanity," n.d.; D. N. Robinson, 1996; Rolf, 2006; R. J. Simon & Ahn-Redding, 2006). This test is still used in some U.S. states, but it came under fire following John Hinckley, Jr.'s attempted assassination of President Ronald Reagan in 1981 (D. N. Robinson, 1996; Rolf, 2006; R. J. Simon & Ahn-Redding, 2006). What was Hinckley's motivation for shooting Reagan? He was trying to impress the actress Jodie Foster, whom he had been stalking. Under the model penal code test, Hinckley—who pleaded insanity after being diagnosed with schizophrenia—was acquitted. Afterwards, the public was outraged and efforts were made to abolish or curtail use of the insanity defense in the United States (Rolf, 2006; R. J. Simon & Ahn-Redding, 2006).

Insanity Defense Reform Act

In the aftermath of the Hinckley verdict, the U.S. Congress passed the **Insanity Defense Reform Act (IDRA)**, which implemented strict federal standards in insanity defense cases (D. N. Robinson, 1996; Rolf, 2006; R. J. Simon & Ahn-Redding, 2006). Under this act, the insanity defense is limited to instances where the mental defect or disorder is "severe." Psychosis is still included, but milder diagnoses typically no longer qualify. In addition, the irresistible impulse component of the ALI rule was eliminated entirely, while the M'Naghten component was narrowed (instead of merely lacking "substantial capacity to appreciate" wrongfulness, defendants now must be "unable to appreciate" it). Finally, the burden of proof was shifted from the prosecution to the defense; rather than prosecutors having to prove defendants sane, defense lawyers now have to prove their clients insane. For better or worse (something you must judge for yourself), IDRA reforms make it more difficult for defendants to successfully plead insanity.

The Insanity Defense Around the World

As noted, many countries still rely on the M'Naghten test or something similar in making judgments of insanity. In Germany, for instance, people aren't criminally responsible when their actions are attributable to psychosis or a comparable mental disorder that prevented them from understanding that what they did was wrong (R. J. Simon & Ahn-Redding, 2006); a clear echo of the M'Naghten test. France's insanity defense, on the other hand, incorporates elements of the irresistible impulse test; people can avoid criminal responsibility if able to show their behavior resulted from a mental disorder that destroyed judgement or the ability to control actions (R. J. Simon & Ahn-Redding, 2006). South Africa's insanity defense requires that defendants not understand the wrongfulness of their actions or be unable to behave in accordance with their understanding, which calls to mind the ALI test (R. J. Simon & Ahn-Redding, 2006). Similarly, parts of Australia have grappled with expanding M'Naghten to include the inability to control behavior (R. J. Simon & Ahn-Redding, 2006), which is reminiscent of the ALI test. Interestingly, both the Australian and Canadian legal systems have stopped using the term "insanity" because it is considered stigmatizing ("The insanity defense," n.d.). Australia now refers to a *mental illness defence* (Nedim, 2015), while in Canada the NGBRI verdict has been replaced with a new verdict called **not criminally responsible on account of mental**

CHAPTER 15

disorder (NCRMD) (CBC News, 2011; R. J. Simon & Ahn-Redding, 2006). Canadian law says offenders can be held not criminally responsible when they are unable to either (a) appreciate the nature or quality of the act, or (b) know it was wrong. Like the M'Naghten test, the Canadian Criminal Code focuses on grasping the meaning of one's actions, but because "appreciating" is considered broader than "knowing," the Canadian insanity defense is regarded as more inclusive than M'Naghten (R. J. Simon & Ahn-Redding, 2006).

Not all countries have an insanity defense. Sweden abolished the insanity defense in 1965, although convicted offenders who are judged mentally ill can be sent to psychiatric hospitals (R. J. Simon & Ahn-Redding, 2006). Denmark, Norway, and The Netherlands also don't have an insanity defense; instead, offenders who the courts deem to be mentally ill are convicted, but not punished (although they are often required to receive treatment, which—as we discuss below—can be experienced as punishment) (Sreevatsa, 2012). In a similar vein, many U.S. states have a **guilty but mentally ill (GBMI)** plea as an alternative to the insanity defense. If convicted under GBMI, the offender is supposed to receive treatment concurrent with a prison sentence. The GBMI plea was developed to hold people responsible for their crimes and reduce insanity defense pleas, but critics say the plea tends to confuse jurors and that those convicted under GBMI don't consistently receive the treatment they are supposed to (Melville & Naimark, 2002; C. A. Palmer & Hazelrigg, 2000; Plaut, 1983).

Evaluating the Insanity Defense

Letting People Get Away with Crimes?

The insanity defense has always been controversial—and it continues to be. Many people complain that the insanity defense lets people get away with crimes. But does it? First, the insanity defense isn't nearly as common as people think. In the U.S., for instance, it's been estimated that fewer than 1% of defendants plead insanity and, when they do, only a fraction of them are acquitted (Justice Center, 2009). Second, when acquitted, defendants aren't typically freed, despite many people assuming otherwise. Instead, they are usually confined to mental hospitals until judged well enough to be released back into society. Some critics object to the insanity defense for this very reason. They don't like the possibility that insanity acquittal leads to an indefinite stay in a mental hospital (Coleman, 1984; Szasz, 1963). In fact, people acquitted by reason of insanity are often incarcerated for longer than they would have been if actually convicted of their crimes—on average, almost twice as long as those sent to prison for similar offenses (Perlin, 2017b). While incarceration in a hospital is arguably preferable to prison in most instances, the assumption that people acquitted by reason of insanity walk off unpunished strikes many people as incorrect; most of us, they argue, would find being involuntarily detained—even in a hospital—quite punishing (Coleman, 1984; Szasz, 1963).

Can Experts Truly Determine Who Is Insane?

The insanity defense is also criticized because many people question if it is possible to validly distinguish the sane from the insane (Coleman, 1984; Szasz, 1963). Most legal definitions of insanity don't specify what counts as a "disease of the mind." Therefore, expert testimony from mental health professionals is often required. Some critics have complained that this leads to "battles of the experts" in which each side in a trial lines up professionals to say whatever they are paid to say (Bergman, 2009). Others have argued that this "battle of the experts" idea is a myth and point to data that 80%–90% of the time, the prosecution and defense reach consensus on whether a case warrants an insanity plea (Perlin, 2017b). Even if insanity defense trials aren't dominated by dueling experts, some insanity defense detractors contend that we shouldn't place so much stock in experts. After all, these critics maintain, mental health professionals cannot determine in any sort of definite way whether someone's actions are due to a "mental defect" (Coleman, 1984; Szasz, 1963). Thus, to many of these critics the insanity defense should be abolished.

Free Will vs. Determinism

Perhaps the insanity defense is so controversial because the very notion of insanity challenges a core assumption of the legal system, namely that people have free will—that is, they autonomously choose their actions. Free will is the basis for holding people responsible for their behavior. By this logic, those who make bad choices and harm others deserve punishment. In contrast, many perspectives on abnormality reject free will and instead adopt a more deterministic stance, attributing erratic behavior to biological, psychological, or sociocultural causes. Does it make sense to hold people responsible for actions caused by their brains, by psychological processes, or by social determinants? Once we shift to a deterministic stance, the wisdom of holding people accountable for their actions becomes less clear. Ultimately, whether one supports or opposes the insanity defense often depends on one's stance on the thorny issue of free will versus determinism.

FITNESS TO PLEAD/COMPETENCY TO STAND TRIAL

Defining Fitness and Competency

Sometimes people charged with crimes are considered incapable of properly mounting a defense due to their mental state. Historically, courts grappling with defendants who seem unable or unwilling to participate in their own defense is nothing new; it's been going on for centuries. As far back as 1583 in England, "juries were appointed by courts to determine whether someone was mute by malice or by visitation of God" (Mudathikundan, Chao, & Forrester, 2014, p. 135). However, rather than suspending trials in such cases (as is typically done in many countries today), defendants were pressured to participate. To coerce them, food was withheld or they were "pressed"—i.e., placed under a gradually increasing weight—until they either entered a plea or died (from starvation or being crushed to death) (Mudathikundan et al., 2014; A. Shah, 2012). Such practices continued until the 18th century (Mudathikundan et al., 2014).

In England and Wales today, the legal standard for determining whether someone is capable of participation in legal proceedings is called **fitness to plead** (Exworthy, 2006; Mudathikundan et al., 2014). Fitness to plead is traceable to the 1836 case of *R v. Pritchard*, in which a man who was deaf and mute was charged with bestiality (having sex with an animal) (Mudathikundan et al., 2014; T. P. Rogers, Blackwood, Farnham, Pickup, & Watts, 2008). It was determined that he was unfit to stand trial. The *Pritchard* case, along with later cases, led to the current fitness to plead standard. This standard holds that for a trial to proceed, those charged must be able to (a) enter a plea, (b) understand the court proceedings, (c) instruct their lawyers, (d) contest a juror, and (e) comprehend the evidence offered (Exworthy, 2006; Mossman et al., 2007; Mudathikundan et al., 2014; T. P. Rogers et al., 2008). The legal term "fitness to plead" isn't just used in England and Wales. It is also used in other places (such as Canada, Australia, New Zealand, and Scotland), although its precise interpretation and application can vary (O'Shaughnessy, 2007; Shah, 2012).

The U.S. equivalent of fitness to plead is called **competency to stand trial** (Mossman et al., 2007; Palermo, 2015; Perlin, 2017a; Schug & Fradella, 2015; Stork, 2013). The requirement that defendants be mentally competent was established by the Supreme Court in the case of *United States v. Dusky* (1961). The defendant, Milton Dusky, was charged with kidnapping a girl and assisting two teens who raped her (Stork, 2013). When his attorney raised the issue of whether Dusky was mentally competent, a psychiatric evaluation was ordered. Dusky was diagnosed with schizophrenia and judged incompetent to stand trial. The Dusky ruling established that "to be competent, a defendant must have the present sufficient ability to rationally consult with counsel and rationally and factually understand the proceedings against him" (Stork, 2013, p. 931). That is, the person must be able to (a) comprehend the proceedings, (b) participate in his or her own defense, and (c) consult with legal counsel (Mossman et al., 2007; T. P. Rogers et al., 2008; Stork, 2013). Someone incapable of these three things can be declared mentally incompetent. Interestingly, the *Dusky* case only required that defendants lack an ability to understand and participate. However, roughly a quarter-century later, the U.S. passed a law requiring that defendants also have a diagnosable mental disorder or defect (Palermo, 2015; Perlin, 2017a; Stork, 2013). Likewise, the 2005 *Mental Capacity Act (MCA)* in England and Wales holds that a person lacks legal capacity if unable to make decisions due to a temporary or permanent disturbance in the mind or brain; however, the MCA doesn't apply to fitness to plead in criminal trials, a fact lamented by those who wish to see fitness to plead rules reformed (T. P. Rogers et al., 2008; Shah, 2012).

Although their respective fitness and competency criteria share much in common, courts in England and Wales rarely find people unfit to plead compared to U.S. courts. By one estimate, the U.S. conducts 60,000 competency hearings per year and finds 20% of the defendants to be incompetent (Mossman et al., 2007; van den Anker, Dalhuisen, & Stokkel, 2011). Some have speculated that U.S. courts find people incompetent more often because U.S. competency hearings stress the importance of decisional competency, while English (as well as Canadian) fitness-to-plead criteria place greater emphasis on the ability to communicate with one's attorney (Mackay, 2007; O'Shaughnessy, 2007).

Determining Competency

How is competency determined? To begin with, someone raises the issue of competency. This could be the defendant's attorney, but prosecutors and judges are free to bring it up, too (Exworthy, 2006). Next, the defendant must be sent for psychological assessment to determine whether he or she has a diagnosable mental disorder, as well as an inability to understand and participate in the legal proceeding (Schug & Fradella, 2015). In the U.K., defendants who are deemed by a judge to be unfit to plead can be released (especially if it has been established they did not commit the acts they are accused of) or sent to a hospital for treatment (Mental Health Cop, 2013). In the U.S., if the defendant is declared incompetent to stand trial, then the trial is suspended and the defendant sent to a mental hospital for treatment (Palermo, 2015). The length of stay in the hospital varies, with the expectation that after treatment the person will have sufficiently recovered to be legally competent, at which point the trial resumes. In cases where recovery isn't adequate, there are limits to how long defendants can be kept in the hospital. When defendants aren't restored to competency within a certain period (up to five years, in some U.S. states), they must either be released without facing trial or civilly committed (a process discussed later in the chapter) (Schug & Fradella, 2015).

The Difficulty and Ethics of Declaring Defendants Incompetent

Fitness to plead and incompetency to stand trial are controversial legal concepts. The process of determining fitness or competency has been criticized for being inconsistent, leading to widely different rulings from case to case (T. P. Rogers et al., 2008). The U.S. Supreme Court has acknowledged that there aren't fixed signs for deciding when competency is an issue (Shah, 2012). In discussing fitness to plead and competency standards, many critics feel "the current process does not incorporate any systematic way of detecting defendants who may be potentially unfit to plead" (Shah, 2012, p. 191).

Equally significant to many critics, being declared incompetent has adverse consequences for defendants (Stork, 2013). Most are sent to mental hospitals and forced to take medication against their will so they can be restored to competency and tried (Bullock, 2002). After what might turn out to be a lengthy hospital stay (often with no clear discharge date), they could wind up incarcerated again if later convicted and sentenced to prison (Schug & Fradella, 2015; Stork, 2013). While defense attorneys may feel ethically obligated to raise the issue of competency when they truly believe their clients are unable to meaningfully grasp and participate in a trial, they may be reluctant to do so because of the potentially negative results this can yield:

> A defense attorney who has a potentially incompetent client faces a difficult situation. If the client has been charged with a misdemeanor, a finding of incompetency could easily keep him in a criminal psychiatric hospital for longer than he would have been in prison if he had been convicted (which could be zero days in jail since many misdemeanors only result in a fine). (Stork, 2013, p. 966)

Debate over fitness to plead and competency to stand trial is intense. In 2006, the United Nations General Assembly adopted a resolution on the rights of persons with disabilities. In this resolution, the U.N. asserted that "the existence of a disability shall in no case justify a deprivation of liberty" (United Nations General Assembly, 2006, Article 14b). Incarcerating people in mental hospitals after they are declared incompetent may violate this principle because it results in involuntarily committing mentally disabled people for potentially long periods without a conviction of any kind. Some critics even argue that mental health professionals sometimes use fitness to plead and competency procedures paternalistically to treat people against their will by having them declared incompetent. In the words of one legal analyst, the fitness process is sometimes "being used for purposes other than assessing fitness ... specifically to assess and treat individuals with psychotic illnesses" who resist or avoid treatment (O'Shaughnessy, 2007, p. 507). Consequently, "it could be argued that ... mental health professionals ... work around some of the logistical difficulties in providing treatment to mentally ill persons, arguably at the expense of the integrity of the legal process" (O'Shaughnessy, 2007, p. 507). However, those in favor of such practices dismiss this critique and counter that pushing forward with a trial (rather than hospitalizing and medicating those deemed incompetent) is the unethical act, as it potentially violates defendants' rights to due process and sends people with mental disabilities to prisons instead of providing them with needed treatment (Perlin, 2017a). Which view on this difficult issue do you favor and why?

CIVIL COMMITMENT

So far, we have been talking about **criminal commitment**, which involves placing people in mental hospitals because of crimes they committed. Both the insanity defense and being declared incompetent to stand trial result in criminal commitment. However, another equally controversial form of commitment is **civil commitment** (also known as *involuntary commitment*; or, in the U.K., *sectioning* or *detaining*). In civil commitment, people considered harmful to themselves or others are treated against their will, either in hospital or outpatient settings (Menninger, 2001; Schug & Fradella, 2015; Testa & West, 2010). Involuntarily committed individuals haven't broken the law, but their behavior frightens and appears dangerous to others. They act in ways that place themselves or others at risk, or they appear to desperately need treatment but refuse it.

Temporary Commitment

The basis for civil commitment stems from two forms of government power: **police power** (the state's authority to confine people who pose a danger to society) and *parens patriae* (a legal concept that says the state can restrict the freedom of children and people deemed mentally incompetent; it is Latin for "state as parent") (Menninger, 2001; Schug & Fradella, 2015). Using these two forms of power, how does civil commitment occur? In most jurisdictions, family members, the police, and medical/mental health professionals can initiate short-term psychiatric hospitalizations of those they believe pose a danger to self or others. This is known as **temporary commitment** (or *emergency commitment*) and it happens in crisis situations (Menninger, 2001). For example, highly suicidal individuals or those in the throes of extreme psychosis might be placed in the hospital by the police or by doctors, usually with little or no legal approval required. This allows leeway to quickly intervene in emergencies. However, because so little approval is necessary, temporary commitment is typically limited to just a few days.

Extended Commitment

Until the not-so-distant past (the mid-20th century, in many countries), there was no distinction between temporary and longer-term commitment. People hospitalized for psychiatric reasons had very little recourse and often spent years (sometimes their whole lives) involuntarily committed in mental hospitals (Schug & Fradella, 2015). In the U.S., sweeping reforms in the 1950s and 1960s—as well as the development of antipsychotics that could be used to quell erratic behavior, making it easier to justify letting people out of hospitals—led to the widespread deinstitutionalization of many long-term mental patients (see Chapter 1) and the establishment of more extensive due process rights for those wishing to challenge efforts to hospitalize them (Schug & Fradella, 2015). Thus, civilly committing people for longer periods is now known as **extended commitment** and requires a formal legal proceeding to convince a court that hospitalization is the least restrictive treatment available (Menninger, 2001; Schug & Fradella, 2015).

Still, those facing civil commitment procedures typically don't have as many due process rights as those facing criminal proceedings, even though the outcome in both cases could be involuntary incarceration (Schug & Fradella, 2015). This is because the burden of proof in civil commitment cases is usually lower than in criminal cases. For example, in U.S. criminal cases, the *beyond a reasonable doubt* standard is employed, which requires that jurors be all-but-certain of a defendant's guilt (the 90% certain rule). By contrast, civil cases have a much lower standard of proof because they don't result in anyone being incarcerated; thus, they only require *preponderance of the evidence*, in which the decision merely needs to more likely correct than incorrect (the 50% rule). When it comes to civil commitment, an intermediate standard called *clear and convincing proof* (the 75% rule) is used. Why? Because, according to the courts, psychiatry is an inexact science when it comes to predicting risk and thus "beyond a reasonable doubt" is too burdensome and would prevent proper care of those who clearly require hospitalization (Testa & West, 2010). Given that involuntary commitment results in loss of freedom, use of clear and convincing proof (rather than beyond a reasonable doubt) remains controversial (Testa & West, 2010; Tsesis, 2011).

The stated goals of extended civil commitment are to (a) rehabilitate people diagnosed with mental illnesses, and (b) protect the public from such people (Schug & Fradella, 2015). Extended commitment typically requires that the person be diagnosed with a mental illness and be judged dangerous, gravely disabled, or in need of treatment (Menninger, 2001). In determining *dangerousness*, the courts typically look at the type of danger (harm to self, others, or property?), its immediacy (when is it expected to occur?), and its likelihood (what are the chances of it occurring?) (Schug & Fradella, 2015). Of course, in some instances the danger isn't because of what people do, but because of what they don't do. In such cases, individuals can be committed for being *gravely disabled*, which means they are deemed unable to take care of their basic needs (for food, clothes, shelter, health, and safety) (Menninger, 2001; Schug & Fradella, 2015). Dangerousness and being gravely disabled have increasingly taken precedence over *need for treatment* (which can be harder to agree on) in making extended commitment decisions (Menninger, 2001).

Involuntary Outpatient Commitment (IOC)

Not all civil commitment involves inpatient hospitalization. **Involuntary outpatient commitment (IOC)** (also called *outpatient civil commitment*, *compulsory community treatment*, *assisted outpatient treatment*, or *community treatment orders*) occurs when a person is legally mandated to receive treatment in a community, rather than hospital, setting (O'Brien, McKenna, & Kydd, 2009; Saks, 2003; Testa & West, 2010). IOC is a more recent and less restrictive form of civil commitment in the sense that it mandates treatment against someone's will, but doesn't confine the person to a hospital (Testa & West, 2010). It first originated in the U.S. in the 1960s, during the early deinstitutionalization movement (see Chapter 1). IOC began being implemented more widely during the 1980s and 1990s (O'Brien et al., 2009). Today, 46 U.S. states plus the District of Columbia utilize some form of it (Center for Public Health Law Research, 2016). Other countries have also adopted versions of IOC, including Australia (during the 1980s and 1990s), New Zealand (in 1992), much of Canada (in 1994), Scotland (in 2005), and England (in 2008) (J. E. Gray & O'Reilly, 2005; O'Brien et al., 2009). IOC can be used with people who the legal system determines need ongoing treatment, but for whom hospitalization seems unnecessary. IOC might be used as an alternative to hospitalization, as a condition of being released from a hospital following more intensive treatment, or as a preventative measure to avert the need for hospitalization (O'Brien et al., 2009; Saks, 2003).

> *In contrast to inpatient civil commitment, which involves separation of a mentally ill person from society through placement behind a locked door, outpatient civil commitment allows people suffering from mental disorders to remain in their communities. It is an alternative means of mandating the treatment of individuals who could potentially become dangerous to themselves or others without forcing them to be hospitalized. (Testa & West, 2010, p. 37)*

Debate over Civil Commitment

Civil commitment has long been controversial. Those in favor of it argue that it protects people with mental illnesses who are dangerous, gravely disabled, or in need of treatment. Thus, by forcing people into treatment, it helps those who cannot help themselves. Patient advocacy groups like the National Alliance on Mental Illness (NAMI, see Chapter 1) and prominent psychiatrists such as E. Fuller Torrey are long-time advocates of civil commitment. As Torrey put it:

> *Most people will agree on the necessity of treating people who are a danger to themselves or others. Many disagree on treating people who are "in need of treatment." I personally am inclined to give people who are not aware of their illness a shot at treatment and would hospitalize them at least briefly and involuntarily to give them an attempt at medication to see if it does improve things. (D. Miller & Hanson, 2016, p. 23)*

Opponents of civil commitment vigorously disagree with such sentiments. Psychiatric survivor groups such as MindFreedom International (see Chapter 2) and antipsychiatry groups like the Citizens Commission on Human Rights (CCHR; cofounded by the psychiatrist Thomas Szasz and the Church of Scientology) wish to see civil commitment abolished. They argue that civil commitment not only incarcerates people who haven't committed crimes, but adds insult to injury by forcing them to take psychiatric drugs (D. Miller & Hanson, 2016). Civil commitment, its most vocal critics argue, is a form of unjust punishment rather than a humane treatment. Thomas Szasz, who throughout his long career vociferously and controversially argued against civil commitment, contended that "whether we admit it or not, we have a choice between caring for others coercively and caring for them only with their consent" (Szasz, 1994, p. 205). He continued:

> *It is dishonest to pretend that caring coercively for the mentally ill invariably helps him, and that abstaining from such coercion is tantamount to "withholding treatment" from him. Every social policy entails benefits as well as harms. Although our ideas about benefits and harms vary from time to time, all history teaches us to beware of benefactors who deprive their beneficiaries of liberty. (Szasz, 1994, p. 205)*

Civil libertarians like Szasz note that in some countries such as China and the former Soviet Union, civil commitment has been used as a form of social control or to punish political dissidents (S. Faraone, 1982; X. Zhao & Dawson, 2014). They worry that even in countries with greater civil liberties, declaring people mentally ill can be used to justify taking away their rights.

Other critics argue that even if we don't wish to abolish civil commitment, its effectiveness is brought into question by the difficulty of predicting dangerousness, meaning mental health professionals cannot definitively distinguish who poses a threat to self or others (Monahan & Shah, 1989). Further, some fear that the threat of involuntary treatment discourages people from seeking mental health services and—as in the case of psychiatric survivors represented by groups like MindFreedom—does psychological damage to people by forcing them to take psychiatric drugs against their will (D. Miller & Hanson, 2016; O'Reilly, 2004). As with many other topics in this chapter, you will need to reach your own conclusions about civil commitment. Table 15.5 provides a succinct summary of the major arguments for and against it, while "The Lived Experience" feature presents a prominent psychiatrist's critical reflections on civil commitment.

Table 15.5 Some Arguments For and Against Civil Commitment

ARGUMENTS FOR	ARGUMENTS AGAINST
Society has an obligation to care for those who can't care for themselves and must commit those in desperate need of help.	Society has an obligation to protect individual rights and should never force people into treatment.
Civil commitment protects people from themselves.	Civil commitment violates people's civil rights.
Mentally ill people often don't know they are mentally ill, requiring that we overlook their opposition to civil commitment and involuntary treatment.	People who resist being committed are justified in not wanting to be incarcerated against their will and forced to take psychiatric drugs with serious side effects.
Many of those civilly committed might otherwise end up in jail or homeless, which are worse fates.	Civil commitment isn't fundamentally different than jail because, like jail, it involves restriction of freedom.
Civil commitment is the most effective way to intervene in situations where people are dangerous to self or others.	Voluntary community services, which are currently underfunded and difficult to access, are preferable to civil commitment.
People who are civilly committed will thank us when they are recovered and can better understand why we had to intervene and treat them.	Coercion, however well intentioned, inevitably causes people to fear and avoid the mental health system.

THE LIVED EXPERIENCE

Involuntary Hospitalization

Dr. Sederer, Chief Medical Officer of the New York State Office of Mental Health, describes his experience involuntarily hospitalizing patients.

When I have personally committed a patient of mine for what I believed to be a life threatening mental illness the result was that short-term safety was achieved—but at an unwelcome price.

... An intervention may be necessary but it may not be helpful—for more than the moment. People who are subject to loss of liberty, to the deeply unsettling experience of having the police intervene, of being transported in restraints, and of being put behind a locked hospital door never forget the experience. Some come to terms with it and a few even come to understand (even if they don't forgive). But this is a traumatic experience and a normal response to it is to not want to put yourself back into an environment, like a mental health clinic or hospital, where that could happen again.

Would I do what I did again should circumstances reach crisis and life-threatening proportions? I don't know what other responsible thing there would be to do. Thus, good answers seem to lie with solutions that avoid the use of coercion and loss of liberty, whenever possible. These are solutions, I believe, that require that mental health interventions be made more humane while we also work to reengineer services to intervene earlier and more effectively in the course of a person's illness.

We owe people with mental illness what has been called "patient centered" care—not as a slogan but as a standard of practice. What this would look like would include open access to an appointment where, instead of waiting for days or weeks, people in crisis could come to a clinic the same day they want to be seen. There would be the ability for clinicians to meet with patients (and families) outside the four walls of a clinic, in settings more natural and less stigmatizing (this is particularly necessary for younger people). Special attention needs to be paid to what is needed to keep youth in school and adults in work, or on a path to work. Shared decision-making where patients are made partners in their care is an important way to engage and retain people in treatment. The use of medications needs to be highly judicious and attentive to managing the side effects that frequently discourage patients from taking them. We need to enlist the help of families who can serve as an early warning system for problems in their loved ones. Most often (though not always) families are the most important and enduring source of support for a person with a medical illness, including mental disorders. ... What I describe here is not new but it calls for changes that will take leadership and relentless persistence since change is hard, even when clearly needed.

We also owe people with mental illness and our communities an alternative to the demoralizing experience of a condition advancing to a severe, persistent and even dangerous state that makes involuntary commitment almost inescapable. This requires giving people with mental illness, their families and communities, and our mental health system the means to identify problems early, typically in adolescence, and new methods of engaging people with illness in effective treatments that also

CHAPTER **15**

support their families. ... This is the kind of overhaul the mental health system needs. This is the kind of overhaul that could provide more effective care with dignity and probably save lives and money.

Humane, patient-centered services and early intervention are paths out of coercion. Imagine their impact on people with mental illness, their families and communities, and doctors who may not need to find themselves in situations such as I have described. Achieving these goals would be something to be proud of.

By Lloyd I. Sederer, MD. Reprinted with permission.

RIGHT TO REFUSE TREATMENT

Why Might a Patient Refuse Treatment?

Sometimes civilly committed patients refuse treatment, which usually consists of psychiatric drugs. There are many reasons why they might do so. Sometimes they refuse due to problems in the doctor–patient relationship. Their doctors may have done a bad job explaining the benefits of treatment or have had difficulty establishing doctor–patient rapport, leading patients to reject treatment recommendations (Wettstein, 1999). Patients also refuse treatment in many instances because of its unpleasant side effects—as is the case with many psychiatric drugs and electroconvulsive therapy (ECT) (Wettstein, 1999). Further complicating matters, some patients may decide against treatment to resist or accommodate the wishes of family and friends, who may have their own agendas regarding whether treatment is administered (Wettstein, 1999). Additional reasons why patients refuse treatment include religious objections, the stigma that accompanies a psychiatric diagnosis, or legal motivations (such as wanting to appear sicker in court to help win a case) (Wettstein, 1999).

What Happens When a Patient Refuses Treatment?

If treatment is voluntary, then the patient has the right to decline (Appelbaum, 1988; Sederer, 2013). Someone who checks into a hospital voluntarily is legally entitled to reject whatever interventions are offered—or to leave the hospital entirely. However, in cases where treatment is involuntary (as in civil or criminal commitment), things get a lot more complicated. Until the 1970s, it was commonly assumed that involuntarily committed patients didn't have a right to decline treatment (Appelbaum, 1988). However, this view has shifted since then (Appelbaum, 1988; Barrett, Taylor, Pullo, & Dunlap, 1998; Kapp, 1994; Wettstein, 1999). For example, U.S. courts have often ruled that patients do indeed have a **right to refuse treatment** (Kapp, 1994; Rebecca Lewis, 2014)—especially given that civil commitment laws have increasingly emphasized dangerousness over the need for treatment as a rationale for committing people involuntarily: "If commitment was now for the purpose of preventing dangerous behavior ... there was some logic in asking where the state derived the additional interest in imposing treatment on unwilling patients" (Appelbaum, 1988, p. 414). Thus, the patient's right to refuse treatment is recognized in many psychiatric situations (Rebecca Lewis, 2014). Ironically, this can lead to patients being involuntarily hospitalized for being dangerous, but then receiving no treatment because treatment is refused (Sederer, 2013). In many countries, treatment can be administered involuntarily despite a refusal if the patient is declared legally incompetent (Barrett et al., 1998; Center for Addiction and Mental Health, n.d.; "Consent to treatment," n.d.; L. Davidson, 2016; Mental Health Coordinating Council, 2015).

Debate Surrounding Right to Refuse Treatment

Critics of the right to refuse treatment maintain that a central issue remains unresolved, namely that mentally ill people often don't understand their situations well enough to make informed choices about declining interventions intended to restore them to health. These critics contend that when non-mentally ill patients refuse treatment for, let's say, cancer or diabetes, they have a legal right to do so because they are rational and cogent agents capable of freely making informed decisions. By contrast, patients diagnosed as seriously mentally ill are often deemed incapable of making rational decisions for themselves—which, right-to-refuse-treatment critics argue, calls into question whether they should legally be allowed to reject treatment. That is, "deprivation of the liberty of the mentally ill rests on the prospects that their disorders will be treated—benefitting both society and the patients themselves—and that treatment will allow them to be restored to freedom" (Appelbaum, 1988, p. 417). Further, critics insist that involuntarily treated patients will be appreciative once recovered. According to the "thank you" test introduced when discussing suicide, clients will "thank the clinician afterward for treating them against their objections, thereby proving that the ostensible refusals were based on mental pathology rather than on principle or rational analysis" (Kapp, 1994, p. 228).

However, those skeptical of involuntary treatment strongly defend the right to refuse treatment and argue that all-too-often mental health professionals become paternalistic and fail to respect patient rights: "Although the underlying sentiments are honorable and sincere, in many cases beneficence or concern for patient well-being has been overextended into the sort of parentalistic 'doctor knows best' attitude that helped to inspire external oversight in the first place" (Kapp, 1994, p. 228). Right-to-refuse-treatment defenders insist that regardless of the psychological issues involved, patients should always have a say in accepting or declining treatments that impact their lives, especially when those treatments have serious and sometimes debilitating side effects. But critics of the right to refuse treatment remain unconvinced. As with many of the topics reviewed in this chapter, the right to refuse treatment remains a contentious and ethically difficult topic in legal and practice circles.

RIGHT TO TREATMENT

Involuntarily committed patients not only have a right to refuse treatment in some instances, but they also have a **right to treatment** because, according to some court decisions, failing to provide it renders hospitals indistinguishable from jails (Schwitzgebel, 1974). Using the U.S. as a representative example, legal rulings have found that it isn't acceptable simply to keep patients in the hospital (Schwitzgebel, 1974; Subedi, 2014). For example, in the case of *Wyatt v. Stickney* (1971),

> *a federal court in Alabama held for the first time that people who are involuntarily committed to state institutions because of mental illness or developmental disabilities have a constitutional right to treatment that will afford them a realistic opportunity to return to society. (Disability Justice, n.d.)*

This means that people who are involuntarily hospitalized are entitled to treatment, as opposed to simply being warehoused. The *Wyatt v. Stickney* ruling held that civilly committed patients are legally entitled to minimal care, including "(1) a humane psychological and physical environment; (2) qualified staff in numbers sufficient to administer adequate treatment; and (3) individualized treatment plans" (Subedi, 2014, p. 52). See "The Controversial Question" feature for discussion of an interesting debate over whether a patient's right to treatment includes a right to empirically supported treatment.

CONTROVERSIAL QUESTION

Does the Right to Treatment Require Empirically Supported Treatments (ESTs)?

Way back in Chapter 1, we introduced the concept of empirically supported treatments (ESTs), which are treatments that have been found to be effective for specific presenting problems in randomized controlled trials (RCTs). If patients have a right to treatment, does this include a right to empirically supported treatment? American psychiatry grappled with this issue in the aftermath of the famous case of *Osheroff v. Chestnut Lodge* (1985). The case was brought by Dr. Raphael J. Osheroff, a successful 41-year-old nephrologist (a doctor specializing in kidney care) who had been experiencing anxiety and depression for two years when, in 1979, he had himself admitted to Chestnut Lodge, a prestigious private mental hospital in Maryland (Boodman, 1989; Hirschkop & Mook, 2012; Klerman, 1990; Knoll, 2013; Packer, 2013). Psychodynamic perspectives had long dominated at Chestnut Lodge; earlier in its long history, the prominent psychodynamic therapists Harry Stack Sullivan and Frieda Fromm-Reichmann had both been employed there (Boodman, 1989; Knoll, 2013; Packer, 2013). During his 7-month hospitalization, Osheroff was provided intensive psychoanalysis but no psychiatric drugs because "Chestnut Lodge offered psychoanalytic approaches only, without prescribing medication" (Packer, 2013, para. 3). Unfortunately, Osheroff's condition deteriorated during his stay at Chestnut Lodge. He began pacing the halls uncontrollably, to the point that his feet blistered and he lost 40 pounds (Boodman, 1989; Klerman, 1990; Packer, 2013). Nonetheless, Chestnut Lodge declined requests by Osheroff for psychiatric drugs. Osheroff's elderly parents became so alarmed at their son's worsening condition that they had him transferred to Silver Hill, a private hospital in Connecticut (Boodman, 1989). At Silver Hill, Osheroff was prescribed antidepressants and antipsychotics and his condition improved (Klerman, 1990). He stopped pacing at three weeks and was discharged at nine weeks (Boodman, 1989; Knoll, 2013). Three years later, Osheroff sued Chestnut Lodge for negligence (Boodman, 1989; Klerman, 1990). Although the case was settled out of court (Klerman, 1990), it provoked debate in the psychiatric community over whether mental health professionals have an ethical and legal duty to use empirically supported treatments.

The debate that ensued pitted psychodynamic perspectives against biological perspectives. However, it also highlighted a more comprehensive and ongoing disagreement among mental health professionals over whether treatment decisions are best rooted in *scientific research* or *clinical experience* (Garb, Lilienfeld, & Fowler, 2016; Norcross, Beutler, & Levant, 2006). Those who sided with Osheroff tended to favor scientific research. The psychiatrist Gerald Klerman (1990) best expressed this point of view in arguing

CHAPTER 15

that Chestnut Lodge erred by treating Osheroff with scientifically unsupported psychodynamic therapy rather than empirically supported medications. Klerman (1990, p. 417) contended that "the psychiatrist has a responsibility to use effective treatment" and that failure to do so places the psychiatrist in legal jeopardy. Quite simply, patients have a right to empirically supported treatments.

Not everyone agreed it was that simple, however. Some stressed clinical experience and patient preferences. Psychiatrist Alan A. Stone (1990) objected to Klerman's argument, not because he opposed science or medication (he agreed that Chestnut Lodge should have been less rigid in refusing to prescribe), but because he questioned whether the scientific evidence is so definitive that only certain treatments are permissible. Along these lines, Stone could point to evidence (found throughout this text) that existing research often leaves it less-than-clear which interventions are best. To Stone, patients and clinicians deserve freedom of choice, even if this means they sometimes select interventions with uncertain empirical support. To do otherwise forecloses too many options and runs the risk of becoming dictatorial. As Stone (1990, p. 426) put it, "in his quest for efficacious standards, Klerman endorses an authoritarian control over psychiatric practice." The precise balance between scientific data and clinical judgement in professional practice remains hotly debated.

CRITICAL THINKING QUESTIONS

1. Should Raphael Osheroff have been prescribed psychiatric drugs by Chestnut Lodge? Justify your answer.
2. How did the *Osheroff* case highlight theoretical tensions between psychoanalysis and biological psychiatry?
3. How much should clinical practice be based on scientific research versus clinical experience?
4. Do you find yourself agreeing more with Klerman or Stone? Explain why.

DUTIES TO WARN AND PROTECT

Should clinicians be required to violate confidentiality when their clients make threats against others? Such a legal duty isn't consistently recognized in the U.K. (Thomas, 2009). However, in the U.S. it is known as the **duty to warn** (E. Henderson, 2015; R. W. Lee & Gillam, 2000). The duty to warn requires therapists to break confidentiality and make sure people are informed of threats made against them by clients. It originates in the famous case of *Tarasoff v. Regents of the University of California* (1974). This case concerned a student from India named Prosenjit Poddar who was studying at the University of California at Berkeley in 1969. He began spending time with a female student named Tatiana (Tanya) Tarasoff. After a New Year's Eve kiss, Poddar expected a romantic relationship to develop. However, Tarasoff said she was seeing other men and wasn't interested in a relationship with Poddar. Despondent, Poddar's schoolwork suffered and his behavior became erratic. He sought therapy on an outpatient basis at the university hospital and, during a session, he told his therapist that he planned to kill Tanya Tarasoff. The therapist informed his supervisors of the threat. The university police were also notified. The police interviewed Poddar but didn't detain him. Shortly thereafter, Poddar stabbed Tanya Tarasoff to death. Tarasoff's family sued, claiming that the therapist had a duty not just to inform the police about Poddar's threat, but also to warn Tanya Tarasoff herself. The California Supreme Court agreed and a legal duty to warn was established. This duty requires mental health professionals to take reasonable steps to warn people they believe might be harmed by a potentially violent client. Most other U.S. states followed suit and established comparable duty to warn rules (E. Henderson, 2015; Yufik, 2005). Under these rules, it isn't sufficient for therapists to just tell the police about someone's threats; they must ensure that threatened individuals themselves are duly informed.

Since the original Tarasoff case, the duty to warn has become ever broader. U.S. courts have ruled that clinicians have such a duty not only when they learn of threats directly from clients, but also when this information is shared with them by clients' families, friends, or associates (Simone & Fulero, 2005; Thomas, 2009; Yufik, 2005). The courts have also determined that therapists have a duty to warn not just potential victims of their clients' direct threats, but also those close to them—such as their children or significant others—because these people might also be in danger (Simone & Fulero, 2005; Thomas, 2009; Yufik, 2005). As one last example of far-reaching duty to warn expectations, in a highly controversial legal decision, a clinician was held responsible when her client followed through on a threat made in therapy to burn down his father's barn. The court held that the therapist's duty to warn extended beyond protecting people's physical safety to also safeguarding their property (Simone & Fulero, 2005; Thomas, 2009; Yufik, 2005).

Building on the *Tarasoff* ruling, the duty to warn has become part of a more general **duty to protect**. The duty to protect applies anytime a therapist suspects a client is dangerous and could do harm to others, even when no direct threats are made. Under such circumstances, more general steps to protect the public must be taken—such as contacting the police or having someone civilly committed. Although most people acknowledge that having mental health professionals break confidentiality can protect the public, critics contend that clinicians can't predict dangerousness very accurately, thus imposing a duty to protect on them is unfairly burdensome (Thomas, 2009). Additionally, some argue that duties to warn and protect turn therapists from confidants into informants, making clients potentially reluctant to honestly share their thoughts in session lest their therapists break confidentiality (Bollas & Sundelson, 1995). Others complain that imposing these duties on therapists causes them to become preoccupied with being sued (E. Henderson, 2015). Consequently, they operate defensively to protect themselves rather than in the best interests of their clients. Still, those in favor of the duties to warn and protect counter that clinicians have an ethical, as well as legal, obligation to safeguard the public and that the duties to warn and protect are an important part of that. What do you think?

15.5 CLOSING THOUGHTS: SUICIDE AS ONE EXAMPLE OF A PROBLEM THAT POSES ETHICAL AND LEGAL DILEMMAS

Let's conclude our discussion of suicide, ethics, and law by highlighting how suicide provides one vivid example (among others we've touched on in this chapter) of how clinical practice poses many ethical and legal dilemmas. Harking back to the general ethical principles of the American Psychological Association (revisit Table 15.3), you can see that psychologists face quite a predicament with suicidal clients. Invoking the principle of beneficence and nonmaleficence, it could be argued that there is a professional ethical duty to involuntarily commit suicidal clients for their own protection. At the same time, appealing to the principle of respecting people's rights and dignity, an alternative argument could be made that hospitalization should be a last resort (or rejected entirely) out of concern for clients' rights to privacy, confidentiality, and self-determination—all three of which involuntary commitment violates. Thus, psychologists working with suicidal clients must make some very difficult ethical decisions, ones over which reasonable people often disagree.

To further confuse matters, whatever ethical determinations a clinician makes inevitably occur within the confines of the broader legal system. A clinician who, in trying to abide by the general principle of respecting people's rights and dignity, decides a no-suicide contract is ethically preferable to involuntary hospitalization, may nonetheless receive a different answer from the legal system. If that clinician's client later dies by suicide, the courts may determine that the therapist acted improperly by not hospitalizing the client, even if the therapist explains the ethical rationale for her actions. Thus, in suicide cases—or more broadly, all cases that wind up in the legal system—ethical and legal perspectives may not always be in agreement.

Finally, to add one more layer of complication, the ethical codes of mental health professionals and the laws of society may not only conflict with each other; they also may conflict with the ethical beliefs of clients. Even when therapists and judges agree in a given instance on a particular remedy (e.g., a potentially self-harming client warrants involuntary commitment or a possibly dangerous client necessitates a duty to warn), this doesn't mean that the clients (or others) impacted by such decisions necessarily agree. For instance, a client might strongly assert his right to end his own life, but professional ethics codes and legal statutes might be interpreted otherwise. Whenever clinical practice, the legal system, and the infinite variety of client ethical beliefs come into contact, things will often get messy. This is not to suggest you shouldn't form your own ideas in each of these realms. However, as with all the topics we have covered in this book, you will inevitably face alternative (and often conflicting) perspectives, each with its own internal rationale pointing toward a preferred course of action.

15.6 EPILOGUE

We have, at last, reached the end of our journey together. In reflecting on abnormal psychology, most students find it to be a fascinating, yet contentious, field of study. In good measure, this is because there are so many ways of classifying, conceptualizing, and rectifying problems identified as abnormal. Diagnostic, biological, psychological, and sociocultural perspectives each have their own ways of thinking about what constitute problems, what causes them, and how best to remedy them. No doubt, this book has exposed you to many perspectives that take very different stances in defining, theorizing about, researching, and addressing a multitude of presenting problems.

Certainly, when it comes to different perspectives, "contrasting" does not necessarily mean "incompatible." There are countless efforts to integrate various perspectives. Along these lines, many clinicians and researchers consider themselves advocates of a biopsychosocial model of abnormality (Engel, 1977). This model, previously mentioned in Chapter 4, holds that presenting problems inevitably are an interaction among biological, psychological, and social factors and that trying to reduce "abnormality" to one of these factors is simplistic and counterproductive.

CHAPTER 15

In other words, a helping professional's skills "must span the social, psychological, and biological" (Engel, 1977, p. 133). Thus, the biopsychosocial model became popular in the 1980s and 1990s, with even the *DSM* espousing it as an integrative way of thinking about its proposed disorders. The biopsychosocial model appeals to those who seek a respite from long-standing conflicts among seemingly irreconcilable perspectives.

Integration at last, you say? Not so fast. If you've learned anything from reading this text, it's that there's always a contrasting point of view—even on integrative efforts like the biopsychosocial model. Critics of the model complain that it leads to what they consider a mindless eclecticism (Ghaemi, 2009, 2010; Henriques, 2015). Eclecticism is an approach to practice in which clinicians draw from multiple theories depending on what is useful in the moment. To critics, eclecticism leads to an unreflective (and therefore dangerous) pluralism in which one is free to pick whatever intervention one likes without thoroughly thinking things through (Ghaemi, 2009, 2010; Henriques, 2015). Eclecticism, its critics contend,

> borders on anarchy: one can emphasise the 'bio' if one wishes, or the 'psycho' (which is usually psychoanalytical among many biopsychosocial advocates), or the 'social'. But there is no rationale why one heads in one direction or the other in deciding what interventions to use. (Ghaemi, 2009, p. 3)

Of course, not everyone has given up on the biopsychosocial approach. Some argue that it needs to be revived and then more thoroughly developed so that it incorporates both medical and humanistic threads (Frances, 2014; McKay, McDonald, Lie, & McGowan, 2012). Whether this can or will occur remains to be seen. Surely, we aren't going to resolve debate over the biopsychosocial model here. But such debate serves as one final reminder that, even with ongoing efforts at integration, the field of abnormal psychology will continue to be one where contrasting perspectives reign and where there are many ways to think about and deal with presenting problems. Hopefully, reading this book has whet your appetite to further explore the perspectives presented in these pages, even if your journey doesn't lead to simple and singular answers.

In closing, 20th-century American psychologist George Kelly (1955/1991a, 1955/1991b), whose personal construct psychology was mentioned in several previous chapters, once remarked that the questions we ask are often more important than the answers we give them. There are a lot of questions in abnormal psychology and, depending on the perspective of the person responding, many different answers in response to those questions. Learning to live with ambiguity and uncertainty is par for the abnormal psychology course. Sometimes the more you know, the less you know for sure. Hopefully, your knowledge of abnormal psychology has expanded sufficiently to make you keenly aware of how many questions remain to be asked.

KEY TERMS

Access to care	Diathesis-stress model of suicide	Nonsuicidal self-injury (NSSI)
Altruistic suicide	Durham test	Not criminally responsible on account of mental disorder (NCRMD)
Anomic suicide	Duty to protect	Not guilty by reason of insanity (NGBRI)
Civil commitment	Duty to warn	Nuremburg Code
Cognitive-behavioral therapy for suicide prevention (CBT-SP)	e-mental health	*Parens patriae*
Commitment to treatment statement (CTS)	Eclecticism	Police power
Competence	Egoistic suicide	Privilege
Competency to stand trial	Extended commitment	Psychache
Confidentiality	Fatalistic suicide	Public education programs
Conflicts of interest	Fitness to plead	Right to refuse treatment
Criminal commitment	Guilty but mentally ill (GBMI)	Right to treatment
Death capitulators	Informed consent	Subintentional death
Death chancers	Insanity	Suicidal behavior disorder
Death darers	Insanity defense	Suicidal ideation
Death experimenters	Insanity Defense Reform Act (IDRA)	Suicide
Death hasteners	Involuntary outpatient commitment (IOC)	Suicide prevention counseling
Death ignorers	Irresistible impulse test	Telepsychiatry
Death initiators	Life instinct	Temporary commitment
Death instinct	M'Naghten test	Thank you" theory of involuntary commitment
Death seekers	Method restriction	Werther effect
Declaration of Helsinki	Model penal code test	Wild beast test
	No-suicide contracts	

Full definitions of the terms listed above can be found in the end-of-book glossary on p. 533.

 Go to the companion website, www.macmillanihe.com/raskin-abnormal-psych, to access a study guide, multiple choice and flashcard quizzes for this chapter, and other useful learning aids.

NOTE: Numbers in parentheses refer to the chapter where the term is first introduced or most fully defined; use the index to track additional references to terms.

4P model of case formulation: Model of formulation in which clinicians gather information about four areas: (1) preconditions; (2) precipitating factors; (3) perpetuating factors; and (4) protective factors. (3)

12-step programs: Self-help groups such as Alcoholics Anonymous that see addiction as disease; by following the 12 steps (see Table 11.5), group members recover from their addictions. (11)

ABAB design: Type of single-subject experiment that alternates between presenting and removing the independent variable manipulation to see its effect on the single participant; also called a *reversal design*. (1)

ABC recording: Behavioral assessment technique that involves directly observing and recording client behaviors ("B"), while also writing down their antecedents (what comes before them, or "A") and their consequences (what comes after them, or "C"); the goal is to assess how antecedents and consequences maintain a behavior. (3)

ABCDE model: REBT model of how psychological problems originate and how to fix them; A = activating event; B = beliefs; C = emotional consequences of beliefs; D = disputing beliefs; and E = more effective beliefs that replace those that were disputed. (2)

Aberrant salience hypothesis: Ascribes psychosis to overactivity of the mesolimbic dopamine pathway; this results in excess dopamine, which leads to over-attributing meaning (i.e., salience) to extraneous and irrelevant events. (4)

Abnormal motor behavior: A symptom of psychosis in which the person seems physically agitated/restless or catatonic (unresponsive to surroundings). (4)

Acamprosate: Drug to treat addiction that reduces cravings by targeting glutamate; trade name *Campral*. (11)

Acceptance and commitment therapy (ACT): CBT intervention designed to help people stay focused and in touch with the present moment; acceptance of negative emotions encouraged as a method to defuse them. (6)

Access to care: Extent to which people can obtain medical, psychological, and social services and are helped by doing so. (15)

Accommodation: Process by which patients' relatives or significant others collude with them to help them avoid anxiety-provoking situations or repeatedly reassure them that everything is okay; associated with poorer patient outcomes. (6)

Acedia: Term used during the early Christian era to describe low mood, boredom, and longing; involved despair arising from pressure to avoid temptation; became incorporated into Western conceptions of melancholia. (5)

Acetaldehyde: A chemical metabolite left over after the liver breaks down alcohol; when people drink a lot, their bodies can't break down acetalaldehyde quickly enough, resulting in hangover symptoms. (11)

Acetylcholine: Neurotransmitter that plays a role in muscle movement, arousal, memory, and learning. (11)

Achievement: Successful performance following learning. (3)

Action potential: Triggers the sending of an electrical impulse along a neuron's axis; occurs when sufficient neurotransmitters bond with receptors on a neuron's dendrites, causing the electrical charge within the neuron to shift from negative to positive; central process in neural communication. (2)

Actualizing tendency: In humanistic theories, the innate motivation to fulfill one's full potential. (2)

Acupuncture: An ancient Chinese technique in which designated points on the body are stimulated by needles; in modern acupuncture, lasers are often used instead. (14)

Acute and transient psychotic disorder (ATPD): *ICD-10* and *ICD-11* equivalent diagnosis to the *DSM-5*'s brief psychotic disorder. (4)

Acute stress disorder (ASD): *DSM-5* disorder in which a person experiences PTSD-like symptoms for between three days and one month after the traumatic event. (7)

Acute stress reaction: *ICD-10* disorder in which a person experiences PTSD-like symptoms lasting between a few minutes and three days following a traumatic event; included in *ICD-11* but not considered a disorder. (7)

Adaptationist models: Models of depression that claim depression may serve an adaptive purpose—such as helping people avoid social risks, minimize losses, ruminate about problems they need to address, fight infection and recover from sickness, conserve energy, give in when socially defeated, and solicit resources by encouraging others to help them. (5)

Adapted to flee famine hypothesis: Evolutionary theory that claims anorexia evolved to assist those facing famine; anorexic symptoms of feeling energetic and restless while remaining in denial about weight loss encourages migration to new locations in search for food. (9)

Addiction: A non-diagnostic term that has often referred to being unable to stop using a substance and continuing use despite negative consequences; in recent times, also refers to problematic behaviors such as excessive shopping, internet use, and sexual activity. (11)

Addictive personality: Supposed set of personality traits that predisposes people to addiction—most commonly antisocial traits such as societal rule breaking, impulsivity, aggression, and lack of empathy. (11)

Adjustment disorders: *DSM-5*, *ICD-10*, and *ICD-11* diagnoses used to identify emotional reactions to ongoing stressors; milder than most other disorders and often used as catch-all categories for people facing continuing life stress who don't qualify for another mental disorder. (7)

Adoption studies: Look at rates of schizophrenia among siblings adopted early in life and reared in separate environments. (4)

Affect: Clinical term for "emotion." (3)

Agoraphobia: *DSM-5*, *ICD-10*, and *ICD-11* disorder diagnosed in people who fear being in situations where they may have an intense and embarrassing fear reaction (such as a panic attack) and won't be able to escape. (6)

Alcohol: A depressant drug found in many popular beverages (also called *ethanol* or *ethyl alcohol*). (11)

Alcohol Use Disorders Identification Test (AUDIT): A 10-item World Health Organization inventory to assess problem drinking and alcohol dependence; shortened versions such as the 3-item AUDIT-C have also been developed for even quicker assessment. (11)

Alcoholic: Non-diagnostic term for people who have difficulty managing their alcohol use. (11)

Alcoholics Anonymous (AA): The largest and most well-known 12-step group for recovering alcoholics. (11)

Alexithymia: Difficulty naming, describing, or expressing emotions verbally. (8)

Algoia: Negative symptom of psychosis that involves a reduction in speech; the person doesn't say much. (4)

Algorithmic model: Diagnostic approach in which clinicians observe countable criteria; used in *DSM*. (3)

Alienists: Early term for psychiatrists, used during the 18th and 19th centuries. (1)

Allele: Name for each of the two different versions of every gene; *dominant alleles* take priority in influencing how particular characteristics genetically unfold, while *recessive alleles* only influence development when a person inherits two of them (one from each parent). (2)

Alter: Any of the personalities present in dissociative identity disorder; each one is referred to as an "alter." (8)

Altruistic suicide: According to Durkheim, occurs when people experience *high social integration*; they are so well integrated into society that they willingly sacrifice themselves for the greater good. (15)

Alzheimer's disease: Form of dementia characterized by senile plaques and neurofibrillary tangles in the brain; *early-onset familial Alzheimer's* occurs before age 65 and is thought to run in families, while *late-onset sporadic Alzheimer's* occurs after age 65 and is thought to be influenced by a combination of genetic and environmental factors. (14)

Amenorrhea: Loss of menstruation in females; often occurs in cases of anorexia as a result of malnutrition. (9)

Amino acids: Chemical compounds consisting of carbon, hydrogen, nitrogen, and oxygen; GABA and glutamate are amino acid-based neurotransmitters. (2)

Amnesia: Memory gaps; sometimes occur in dissociation. (7)

Amphetamine psychosis: Psychosis induced by taking large doses of amphetamines. (4)

Amphetamines: Laboratory-manufactured stimulants; includes *amphetamine* (trade name *Benzedrine*), *dextroamphetamine* (trade name *Dexedrine*), and *methamphetamine* (trade name *Methedrine*). (11)

Amygdala: Almond-sized area deep in the limbic system area of the brain that has been implicated in regulation of emotions such as fear and anger. (2)

Amyloid hypothesis: Holds that senile plaques are critical to Alzheimer's disease. (14)

Anaclitic depression: Historically used to describe depression in young children, but now refers to attachment-related depression in adults who are clingy, helpless, dependent, and fear abandonment. (5)

Anal-expulsive: Fixated anal stage personality style characterized by resisting the need for ego regulation; anal-expulsive individuals are messy, reckless, disobedient, and disorganized. (2)

Anal-retentive: Fixated anal stage personality style characterized by strict ego regulation; anal-retentive individuals are rigid, neat, stingy, stubborn, and highly organized. (2)

Anal stage: Second stage of psychosexual development, from ages 1½ to 3, during which toilet training serves as the basis for ego development; fixation here results in becoming anal-retentive or anal-expulsive. (2)

Analogue behavioral observation: Type of behavioral assessment used to arrive at a functional analysis in which a person is naturally observed in an environment established by the clinician/researcher. (3)

Analogue experiment: An experiment in which the researchers create laboratory scenarios that are similar (*analogous*) to those they want to study and use them to draw inferences about the situation they are interested in but can't practically study; animal studies are one common form of analogue study. (1)

Anankastic personality disorder: *ICD-10* equivalent of *DSM-5*'s obsessive-compulsive personality disorder; "anankastic" derives from the Greek word *anankastikos*, which means "compulsion." (12)

Androgen: A type of hormone responsible for the development of male characteristics; testosterone is the most well-known androgen. (10)

Anhedonia: Negative symptom of psychosis in which the person gets little pleasure from previously enjoyed activities. (4)

Animal studies: One of the best-known examples of analogue studies; the animals serve as analogues for human beings; often used to study new drug treatments that can't ethically be tested on humans. (1)

Anomic suicide: According to Durkheim, occurs when people experience *low social regulation*; suicide results because society doesn't provide dependable social structures for its members, leading to people feeling isolated and let down. (15)

Anorexia nervosa: *DSM-5*, *ICD-10*, and *ICD-11* disorder involving seriously low body weight due to restricted food intake. (9)

Anorgasmia: *ICD-11* diagnosis for men and women who experience absent, infrequent, or diminished orgasms; also called *orgasmic dysfunction*, its name in *ICD-10*. (10)

Anterior cingulate cortex: Front area of cingulate cortex that is important in decision-making, anticipating rewards, emotion, and impulse control. (6)

Anterior insula: Brain region that links a variety of brain areas important in regulating autonomic activities such as hunger; activity in the anterior insular has been correlated with feelings of disgust in anorexics. (9)

Antiandrogens: Drugs that reduce levels of male sex hormones such as testosterone, thereby decreasing sexual interest. (10)

Anticonvulsants: Drugs initially developed to treat seizures, but also used as mood stabilizers to treat bipolar disorder; they enhance GABA activity. (5)

Antidepressants: Drugs used to alleviate depression and many other presenting problems; they work by affecting monoamine neurotransmitters in the brain. (5)

Antihistamines: Drugs that inhibit histamine; used to relieve allergies, as well as insomnia. (14)

Antipsychotics: Drugs used to alleviate psychotic symptoms; they work by affecting neurotransmitters in the brain—typically dopamine; also called *neuroleptics* and *major tranquilizers*. (4)

Antisocial personality disorder (APD): *DSM-5* diagnosis describing people who consistently violate the rights of others; in addition to being deceitful, disregarding social norms, and often breaking the law, people with APD are reckless, irresponsible, and (in some cases) violent as they manipulate and exploit others. (12)

Anxiety: An emotion characterized by feelings of tension, worried thoughts, and physical changes like increased blood pressure; involves cognitive appraisals related to more basic fear responses. (6)

Anxiolytics: Drugs used to relieve anxiety; usually refers to benzodiazepines. (6)

Anxious (avoidant) personality disorder: *ICD-10* equivalent of *DSM-5*'s avoidant personality disorder. (12)

Applied behavior analysis (ABA): Uses behavioral principles to understand how, on a case-by-case basis, environmental stimuli condition behavior; the resulting knowledge is used to change the environment and therefore condition alternative behaviors. (13)

Asociality: Negative symptom of psychosis in which a person lacks interest in social contact. (4)

Asperger's Disorder: *DSM-IV* and *ICD-10* diagnosis that was removed from *DSM-5* and *ICD-11*; like autism, characterized by impairments in social skills, communication skills, and restricted interests that develop in early childhood, but milder and without significant deficits in language acquisition or cognitive functioning (called *Asperger's disorder* in *DSM-IV*, but *Asperger's syndrome* in *ICD-10*). (13)

Assertive community treatment (ACT): A way to organize services for those diagnosed with schizophrenia and other severe psychological disorders in which team members from a variety of professions work together to coordinate services for outpatients with schizophrenia and other chronic mental disorder diagnoses. (4)

Assessment: Gathering information to understand or diagnose a person's difficulties. (3)

Assimilative integration: Process by which therapists operating from one theoretical perspective, when incorporating a technique from another theoretical perspective, carefully consider how the theory they are using and the theory from which they are co-opting a technique are both changed. (2)

Asylums: Institutional housing for abnormal people that spread throughout Europe during the Renaissance. (1)

Attachment-based family therapy: Integrates attachment theory into family therapy to help strengthen parent–child attachment relationships in depressed and suicidal adolescents. (5)

Attachment theory: Emphasizes how early childhood relational attachments affect later psychological functioning. (2)

Attention-deficit/hyperactivity disorder (ADHD): *DSM-5* and *ICD-11* disorder involving difficulty sustaining attention, being revved-up and full of excessive energy, and impulsive behavior. (13)

Attenuated psychosis syndrome (APS): A proposed but unofficial *DSM* diagnosis for people whose behavior is odd or eccentric and might eventually develop into full-blown psychosis—but doesn't yet technically qualify. (4)

Atypical anorexia nervosa: Diagnosed in cases where significant weight loss doesn't occur but the person meets all other criteria for anorexia; diagnosed in *DSM-5* using the other specified feeding or eating disorder category. (9)

Atypical antipsychotics: Antipsychotic drugs that are often thought to have fewer side effects than first-generation antipsychotics; also called *second-generation antipsychotics* (see separate entry). (4)

Atypical autism: *ICD-10* diagnosis involving abnormalities in three domains: social interaction, communication, and restricted/repetitive behavior; differs from childhood autism in terms of age of onset and not necessarily showing abnormality in all three domains. (13)

Atypical bulimia nervosa: Diagnosed in cases when bingeing and compensatory behaviors don't occur often enough for a bulimia nervosa diagnosis (they occur less than once a week and for fewer than 3 months); diagnosed in *DSM-5* using the other specified feeding or eating disorder category. (9)

Augmenting agents: Secondary drugs used to improve the impact of primary drugs; for example, benzodiazepines are sometimes used to augment the effect of SSRIs for OCD. (6)

Authenticity: In existential theory, when one is aware of one's responsibility for creating meaning and living by it. (2)

Autism: A general term for people who—to greater or lesser degrees—struggle with social interactions, have difficulties with verbal and nonverbal communication, and engage in repetitive and ritualistic behaviors. (13)

Autism spectrum disorder (ASD): *DSM-5* diagnosis that combines the *DSM-IV*'s autistic and Asperger's disorder categories; characterized by deficits in communication, social interaction, and comprehending relationships that develop in early childhood. (13)

Autistic disorder: *DSM-IV* diagnosis that was removed from the *DSM-5*; characterized by impairments in social skills, communication, and comprehending relationships that develop in early childhood. (13)

Autistic process: Term used by those who see autism as a way of processing and responding to the world, but not a disorder. (13)

Autoimmune disease hypothesis: Proposes that there is a connection between a family history of autoimmune disease and autism. (13)

Automatic thoughts: Spontaneous thoughts that occur to us throughout daily life. (2)

Autonomic nervous system (ANS): Responsible for regulating automatic biological functions affected by prolonged stress—such as heart rate, blood pressure, and emotional arousal. (7)

Aversion therapy: Behavior therapy in which undesired behaviors are associated with something unpleasant to decrease these behaviors. (9)

Avoidance model of worry: Cognitive explanation of anxiety that maintains people are often anxious about negative events potentially befalling them in the future; worry about events that haven't happened yet is negatively reinforced because thinking about anxiety-provoking possibilities is less stressful than experiencing more intense physiological symptoms of anxiety. (6)

Avoidant personality disorder: *DSM-5* diagnosis for those who actively avoid social interactions because they are excessively worried about being criticized or rejected; these individuals want guaranteed acceptance from others. (12)

Avoidant/restrictive food intake disorder (ARFID): *DSM-5* and *ICD-11* disorder characterized by extremely picky eating and a failure to eat enough to meet basic nutritional needs. (9)

Avolition: Negative symptom of psychosis characterized by decreased motivation. (4)

Awfulizing: REBT term for the irrational tendency to interpret things as more awful than they truly are. (2)

B cells: Lymphocytes that produce *antibodies*, which attack invading viruses and bacteria to stop them from entering cells. (8)

Barbiturates: Highly addictive sedative-hypnotic drugs such as *secobarbital* and *pentobarbital*; previously used as anti-anxiety drugs, but have generally been replaced by benzodiazepines. (6)

Basal ganglia: Area at the base of the forebrain important in numerous functions, including voluntary motor movement. (14)

Beck Depression Inventory (BDI): 21-item self-administered inventory for measuring depression. (3)

Behavior that disturbs others: A criterion for abnormality that identifies as abnormal those whose behavior upsets others; is influenced a great deal by social norms and values. (1)

Behavior therapy: Applies the principles of classical and operant conditioning, as well as social learning, to alter behavior deemed abnormal. (2)

Behavioral activation: Behavioral technique in which client schedules activities that bring positive reinforcement; intended to alleviate depression. (5)

Behavioral addictions: Addictions involving behaviors rather than substances; includes activities such as excessive gambling, sex, eating, and shopping. (11)

Behavioral assessment: Identifies conditions in the environment that sustain undesirable behaviors. (3)

Behavioral experiments: CBT technique used for psychosis in which patients test the reality of their delusional beliefs. (4)

Behavioral perspectives: Define abnormality in terms of behavior, and see abnormal behavior as caused by environmental conditioning and social learning. (2)

Behavioral rehearsal: Behavioral technique in which the client role-plays how to act in specific social situations. (4)

Bender Visual Motor Gestalt Test: Neuropsychological test consisting of nine cards with geometrical designs; test-takers are asked to examine the designs and then draw them from memory; difficulty doing so is often interpreted as an indicator of brain damage. (3)

Benzodiazepines: Anxiolytic drugs that enhance the functioning of GABA (the brain's primary inhibitory neurotransmitter) to reduce anxiety; sometimes also used as mood stabilizers. (5)

Bereavement: The situation of having recently lost a significant person through death. (7)

Bereavement exclusion: *DSM-IV* criterion for major depressive disorder that discouraged clinicians from diagnosing major depression in people grieving the loss of a loved one; removed from *DSM-5*. (5)

Beta blockers: Blood pressure reducing drugs that block norepinephrine receptors; used to relieve anxiety. (6)

Bibliotherapy: Therapy in which people learn and change through completing reading assignments. (1)

Big Five: The five traits measured by the Five-Factor Model (FFM) of personality: *extraversion, agreeableness, conscientiousness, neuroticism,* and *openness*. (3)

Bilateral stimulation: Component of EMDR that involves rhythmically exposing people to alternating stimulation on their left and right sides. (7)

Binge drinking: Having five or more drinks on one occasion. (11)

Binge eating: Form of overeating in which a person eats a huge amount of food in a single sitting—much more than most people would eat during a comparable period of time. (9)

Binge-eating disorder (BED): *DSM-5* and *ICD-11* disorder characterized by recurrent binge eating. (9)

Bioenergetics exercises: Breathing and other exercises intended to enhance bodily awareness. (8)

Biofeedback: Technique in which patients are hooked up to a machine that measures one or more biological functions (e.g., heart rate, breathing rate, muscle tension, or temperature); patients are reinforced for desired changes to these biological functions; used to help reinforce patients with psychosomatic illnesses for altering biological functions they typically assume they have little control over. (8)

Biological perspectives: View abnormality as caused by medical illnesses; they see mental illnesses as diseases that afflict people. (1)

Biomarkers: Biological measures used to make diagnoses; *DSM* and *ICD* disorders cannot yet be diagnosed using them, but they are widely sought in psychiatric research. (3)

Biopsychosocial model: Holds that presenting problems inevitably are an interaction among biological, psychological, and social factors, and that trying to reduce "abnormality" to one of these factors is simplistic and counterproductive. (4)

Bipolar affective disorder: *ICD-10* disorder diagnosed in those who experience some combination of manic, hypomanic, and depressive episodes; various subtypes identify the specific combination of episodes present in a patient. (5)

Bipolar I disorder: *DSM-5* and *ICD-11* disorder diagnosed in those who experience one or more manic episodes. (5)

Bipolar II disorder: *DSM-5* and *ICD-11* disorder diagnosed in those who have experienced hypomanic and depressive episodes, but have never had a manic episode. (5)

Bisexuals: People who are attracted to both sexes. (10)

Bizarre delusions: Delusions that are unrealistic and odd, such as believing that the government is monitoring you via radar implanted in the fillings of your teeth. (4)

Black box warning: A government warning that informs people that a drug may have hazardous consequences; antidepressants in the U.S. carry one that says they may increase suicidal tendencies in teens; antipsychotics also carry one indicating that they may increase mortality rates among the elderly. (5)

Blood alcohol content: Amount of alcohol in the blood stream. (11)

Bodily Distress Disorder: *ICD-11* characterized by physical symptoms that the person finds distressing and pays excessive attention to; even when the symptoms have a physical explanation, worry about them is excessive and the person cannot be reassured, even by doctors; roughly equivalent to the *DSM-5*'s *somatic symptom disorder*. (8)

Bodily humors: Four biological substances identified by the ancient Greeks and long considered important in understanding abnormal behavior; the four humors were *black bile, yellow bile, phlegm,* and *blood.* (1)

Body dysmorphic disorder (BDD): *DSM-5* and *ICD-11* disorder in which people display obsessional preoccupation with one or more perceived physical flaws in their appearance; listed as a variant of hypochondriasis in the *ICD-10*. (6)

Body mass index (BMI): A weight by height index used to measure whether people are underweight, normal, or overweight. (9)

Body-oriented psychotherapies: Incorporate dance, meditation, martial arts, yoga, and awareness through movement techniques into the therapeutic encounter. (8)

Borderline families: Families characterized by interpersonal chaos in which family members don't know how to nurture or support one another; three kinds of borderline families: *enmeshed or overinvolved, alienated or rejecting,* and *idealizing or denying.* (12)

Borderline personality disorder (BPD): *DSM-5* diagnosis describing people who show instability in their relationships, sense of self, and emotions; BPD clients have a difficult time regulating their own emotions and their feelings about self and others often shift rapidly. (12)

Boundaries: In family therapy, the ability to distinguish between different family members' thoughts and feelings; can be too rigid or too loose. (2)

Bracketing: Phenomenological research method in which the researcher tries to lay aside (or "bracket") taken-for-granted beliefs about what is being studied. (1)

Brain chemistry perspectives: Biological approaches to abnormality that focus on neurotransmitters (chemicals in the brain) and how they influence cognition, emotion, and behavior. (2)

Brain stem: Connects the brain to the spinal cord; plays a role in many involuntary activities, such as breathing, heart rate, digestion, blood pressure, body temperature, perspiration, and sleeping. (2)

Brain structure and function perspectives: Biological approaches to abnormality emphasizing how the functioning (or malfunctioning) of different areas in the brain influences abnormal behavior. (2)

Brain waves: The electrical activity of neurons firings. (3)

Breathing-related sleep disorders: Sleep disorders that involve *sleep apnea* (temporary cessation of breathing during sleep) or *hypoventilation* (slowed respiration during sleep related to carbon dioxide levels). (14)

Brief psychotic disorder: *DSM-5* disorder in which psychotic symptoms only last a short time (one day to one month); also see *acute and transient psychotic disorder.* (4)

Bulimia nervosa: *DSM-5, ICD-10,* and *ICD-11* disorder characterized by binge-eating followed by compensatory behavior. (9)

Buspirone: An anxiolytic drug that decreases serotonin levels, but not by blocking serotonin reuptake; thus, it is not classified as an SSRI. (6)

Caffeine: A mild and commonly used stimulant found in many plants, including those used to make coffee, tea, chocolate, and soft drinks; increases alertness and energy while providing a sense of well-being. (11)

Candidate gene studies: Studies in which allele frequencies on genes of interest are statistically analyzed to see if some allele variations are present more often among case subjects compared to controls. (5)

Cannabis: Drugs made from the flowers, dried leaves, and extracts or assorted varieties of the hemp plant; cannabis high includes feeling relaxed and content, losing track of time, perceptual distortions, and heightened awareness; *marijuana, ganja, bhang,* and *hashish* are types of cannabis. (11)

Case study: Type of qualitative design in which a specific instance of something is examined in depth, often using a theoretical perspective to organize the data and to generalize to other instances; its focus can be on a person, a small group, an organization, a partnership, a community, a relationship, a decision, or a project. (1)

Cataplexy: A sudden but temporary loss of muscle tone; often occurs in *narcolepsy*. (14)

Catastrophic misinterpretation model of panic disorder: Holds that people prone to recurrent, unexpected panic attacks catastrophically misinterpret certain bodily sensations; the more they interpret sensations in an anxious way, the stronger the sensations become—eventually resulting in a full-blown panic attack. (6)

Catatonia: Form of abnormal motor behavior that sometimes occurs in psychosis; characterized by decreased responsiveness to one's surroundings as evidenced by reduced movement, holding oneself in a rigid posture, or a *catatonic stupor* (ceasing to respond verbally or physically). (4)

Catecholamine hypothesis of ADHD: Slightly broader than the dopamine hypothesis of ADHD, it holds that ADHD is caused by deficits in both dopamine and norepinephrine. (13)

Catecholamines: A type of monoamine neurotransmitter; dopamine and norepinephrine are catecholamines. (2)

Categorical diagnosis: Approach to diagnosis where similar patterns of symptoms and signs are grouped into categories and distinguished as distinct disorders; disorders are divided into discrete and mutually exclusive categories. (3)

Categorizing: Grounded theory data analysis method in which the researcher examines codes and looks for links among them, eventually sorting them into categories that seem to best fit. (1)

Catharsis: Strong emotional release of pent-up feelings. (2)

Caudate nucleus: Basal ganglia brain region important in goal-directed activity. (4)

Central sleep apnea: Sleep-related disorder in which there is temporary cessation of breathing five or more times per hour during sleep. (14)

Cerebellum: A lower area of the brain behind the brain stem that is implicated in voluntary movement, balance, attention, and language. (2)

Cerebrum: Larger upper area of the brain that consists of two hemispheres which are connected by and communicate via the corpus callosum; consists of four lobes (occipital, frontal, parietal, and temporal lobes) that are important in many psychological functions—including speech, vision, hearing, movement, sensation, and intelligence. (2)

Character armor: Reich's idea that the physical postures people adopt—including how they walk, talk, breathe, and carry themselves—tell us a great deal about their psychological functioning; also called *body armor*. (8)

Character: Unique patterns of adaptive behavior that are relatively constant and enduring; sometimes used as a synonym for personality, but also defined independently of it. (12)

Chemical castration: Use of antiandrogens to bring testosterone levels as low as those found in people who have been surgically castrated. (10)

Child-centered play therapy: Child therapy approach that believes that person-centered therapy's core conditions for change (genuineness, empathy, and unconditional positive regard) are necessary and sufficient to address developmental issues; also called *person-centered play therapy*. (13)

Childhood autism: *ICD-10* diagnosis roughly comparable to the *DSM-IV*'s autistic disorder; involves abnormalities in social interaction, communication, and restricted/repetitive behavior that must be present by age 3. (13)

Childhood-onset fluency disorder (stuttering): *DSM-5* diagnosis characterized by repeating sounds or prolonging consonants or vowels; called both *stuttering* and *stammering* in the *ICD-10* and called *developmental speech fluency disorder* in the *ICD-11*. (14)

Cholinergic hypothesis of Alzheimer's: Maintains that because acetylcholine is important in memory, making more of it available reduces memory problems and can stave off the progression of Alzheimer's dementia. (14)

Chromosomes: Each person has 23 sets of them; they are made of DNA; genes are contained at random intervals along them. (2)

Circadian rhythms: Mental and behavioral changes in alertness and energy that are tied to levels of light and dark in the environment; circadian rhythm disruptions have been implicated in symptoms associated with bipolar disorder. (5)

Circadian rhythm sleep-wake disorders: Sleep-related difficulties due to disruptions in one's circadian rhythm (patterns of alertness and energy tied to levels of light and dark in the environment). (14)

Cirrhosis: Irreversible scarring of the liver due to chronic excessive alcohol use. (11)

Cisgender: Term for people whose gender identity and birth sex match. (10)

Civil commitment: When people deemed dangerous to self or others or in serious need of treatment are treated against their will, either in hospital or outpatient settings; also known as *involuntary commitment*; or, in the U.K., *sectioning* or *detaining*. (15)

Classical conditioning: An unconditioned stimulus is paired with a neutral stimulus, which turns the neutral stimulus into a conditioned stimulus that evokes the same response as the unconditioned stimulus, even when the unconditioned stimulus isn't present. (2)

Cliff-edge fitness theory: Proposes that schizophrenia occurs when people's theory of mind abilities (their ability to sensitively read others) crosses a line from being exceedingly sensitive to over-interpreting others' behaviors; this subtle shift explains the difference between highly attuned and psychotic. (4)

Clinical interview: Assessment procedure in which clinician talks to client to gather information about the presenting problem. (3)

Clinical psychologists: Applied psychologists trained in the assessment, diagnosis, and treatment of abnormality; compared to counseling psychologists, they often work with clients experiencing more severe presenting problems. (1)

Closeted: Nonheterosexual people who have yet to come out. (10)

Cluster A: Odd or eccentric personality disorders (paranoid, schizoid, and schizotypal). (12)

Cluster B: Dramatic, emotional, or erratic personality disorders (antisocial, borderline, histrionic, and narcissistic). (12)

Cluster C: Anxious or fearful personality disorders (avoidant, dependent, and obsessive-compulsive). (12)

Coalitions: In family therapy, when some family members align with one another against other family members; can lead to dysfunctional interactions. (2)

Cocaine: Stimulant made from the leaves of the South American coca plant; one of the most powerful stimulants, producing euphoria, excessive confidence, and tremendously high energy levels. (11)

Codeine: A natural opioid derived from opium that is used mainly as a pain reliever and cough medicine. (11)

Coding: Grounded theory data analysis method in which the researcher goes through the data line by line, jotting down relevant phrases and codes; the goal is to distill key ideas. (1)

Coercive sexual sadism: *ICD-11* paraphilic disorder characterized by fantasies, urges and behaviors involving physically or psychologically imposing harm on nonconsenting others. (10)

Cognitive distortions: Errors in thinking that lead to emotional distress. (2)

Cognitive enhancement therapies: Assume that the progression of Alzheimer's and other forms of dementia can be slowed by boosting patients' cognitive engagement with their surroundings. (14)

Cognitive fusion: Concept from acceptance and commitment therapy (ACT) in which people mistake their private thoughts for absolute truths, fusing with these thoughts in ways that cause emotional pain and interfere with their ability to interpret things in alternative ways. (9)

Cognitive perspectives: Emphasize thoughts and beliefs as the root causes of abnormal behavior. (2)

Cognitive processing therapy (CPT): Specific cognitive therapy for PTSD that combines exposure therapy with a more primary focus on having clients examine and revise their cognitions about the traumatic event. (7)

Cognitive reserve hypothesis: Hypothesis that education and intelligence provide a buffer against Alzheimer's and other forms of dementia. (14)

Cognitive restructuring: Cognitive therapy techniques designed to help people think more rationally. (2)

Cognitive specificity hypothesis: Holds that each disorder has a unique way in which its sufferers cognitively interpret events. (2)

Cognitive therapy: Aaron Beck's therapy approach, which focuses on correcting the client's dysfunctional thoughts. (2)

Cognitive triad: Negative beliefs about self, experience, and future that cognitive therapists believe result in depression. (5)

Cognitive-behavioral therapy (CBT): Therapy that combines elements of two distinct perspectives that are often blended together: *cognitive therapy* and *behavior therapy*. (2)

Cognitive-behavioral conjoint therapy (CBCT): 15-session manualized PTSD treatment for couples and families in which cognitive therapy techniques are used to teach conflict management. (7)

Cognitive-behavioral therapy for insomnia (CBT-I): Uses CBT to reduce insomnia; techniques include stimulus control therapy, sleep restriction, sleep hygiene education, cognitive therapy, and relaxation training. (14)

Cognitive-behavioral therapy for psychosis (CBTp): Emphasizes how thought processes and behavioral conditioning influence psychotic behavior; uses cognitive and behavioral techniques to challenge the psychotic patient's abnormal perceptions and behavior. (4)

Cognitive-behavioral therapy for suicide prevention (CBT-SP): Uses several structured strategies to prevent further suicide attempts, including *chain analysis* (identifying activating events that push one toward suicide), *safety plan development* (concrete coping strategies to prevent further suicide attempts, and *skill building* (teaching problem-solving strategies to better handle life's challenges). (15)

Coming out: Process by which people come to accept and declare their sexual orientation or gender identity to others. (10)

Commitment to treatment statement (CTS): Suicide prevention technique in which suicidal clients commit to (a) life and the therapy process, (b) being honest about their suicidal thoughts and actions, and (c) seeking emergency services should they experience a crisis between sessions; an alternative to no-suicide contracts. (15)

Common factors: Factors believed to be present in all effective psychotherapies. (2)

Community care: Care that integrates people with chronic mental health issues into the social environment, often by housing them in group homes or other shared living situations; emphasizes continuity of care, encouraging independence, and advocacy that insures patients receive necessary services and are treated properly. (4)

Community mental health care: provides an integrated array of outpatient services (medication management, therapy, family support, job training, etc.) to mental health service users, often via government-funded programs. (1)

Comorbidity: When multiple disorders co-occur, or are diagnosed at the same time. (3)

Compensatory behavior: Behavior a person engages in to counteract having binged; includes purging, fasting, and excessive exercise. (9)

Competence: Ethical standard that clinicians only conduct therapies, assessments, and research when they are properly trained and competent to do so. (15)

Competency to stand trial: Legal standard used in the U.S. that says those charged with a crime must be able to (a) comprehend the proceedings, (b) participate in his or her own defense, and (c) consult with legal counsel. (15)

Complex PTSD: *ICD-11* diagnosis for PTSD patients who have (a) difficulties managing emotions; (b) negative beliefs about themselves as worthless; and (c) trouble maintaining relationships. (7)

Compulsions: Behaviors or mental acts that a person feels driven to perform. (6)

Compulsive sexual behavior disorder: An *ICD-11* impulse control disorder diagnosable in people who seem unable to control their sexual appetites. (10)

Conceptualize: To think about client problems using the terms of a given theory; an important part of formulation. (3)

Concordance rates: Percentage of time that both twins in a pair are diagnosed with schizophrenia. (4)

Conditional positive regard: In person-centered therapy, when others only accept a person if certain conditions are met; leads to incongruence. (2)

Conditioned response (CR): A response to a conditioned stimulus (e.g., salivation in response to a bell that has been paired with dog food). (2)

Conditioned stimulus (CS): A stimulus that has been paired with an unconditioned stimulus so that it now evokes the same response as the unconditioned stimulus (e.g., bell evokes salivation after being paired with dog food). (2)

Conduct disorder (CD): *DSM-5*, *ICD-10*, and *ICD-11* diagnosis made in children and adolescents who engage in serious violations of other people's rights, such as physical aggression, destroying property, lying, stealing, and engaging in serious rule violations; called *conduct-dissocial disorder* in *ICD-11*. (13)

Confabulation: Inventing explanations to account for gaps in memory recall; occurs in Korsakoff syndrome patients. (11)

Confidentiality: The ethical requirement that practicing clinicians not disclose what clients tell them unless their clients give them permission to do so. (15)

Conflicts of interest: Situations in which a clinician or researcher has a professional, legal, financial, or other interest that might impair his or her objectivity, competence, or effectiveness or that could lead to exploitation or harm. (15)

Confounding variable: Any variable in an experiment that interferes with the independent variable manipulation. (1)

Congruence: Rogers' term for when a person is self-consistent, behaving in accordance with the actualizing tendency. (2)

Conscious: Psychodynamic term for the rational and adult part of the mind; all that we are currently focused on and aware of is conscious. (2)

Consciousness-raising: Educating clients about racism, sexism, and other economic and social inequalities that they have unwittingly accepted and which lead to emotional distress. (2)

Constant comparison: Grounded theory data analysis method that involves comparing instances highlighted in various codes, categories, and memos to assist in the process of developing a grounded theory. (1)

Constructivist perspectives: Emphasize how people create meaningful ways of understanding themselves, their world, and their relationships, which they then use to guide their lives; difficulties occur when people mistake their constructed meanings for reality itself and get locked into meanings that are no longer helpful. (2)

Constructivist therapy for stuttering: Focuses not simply on correcting speech, but also on having clients incorporate being fluent into their core constructions of self. (14)

Consumer and service-user perspectives: Focus on the experience and concerns of people receiving psychiatric services. (2)

Consumer movement: Movement of consumers of psychiatric services that accepts psychiatric views of mental disorder and often finds traditional treatments helpful; largely directed toward reducing stigma, reforming policies and practices that interfere with access to services, and generating more mental health treatment choices. (2)

Contingency management (CM): Operant conditioning behavioral technique in which abstinence and other desired behaviors are positively reinforced to strengthen them. (11)

Control group: A group of experimental participants who do not receive the treatment; gives us something to compare the treatment group to. (1)

Controlled drinking: Treatments that help people reduce their drinking to acceptable levels and moderate alcohol's role in their lives, but without demanding abstinence. (11)

Conversion disorder: *DSM-5* somatic symptom diagnosis that involves physical loss or alteration for which there is no known neurological or medical explanation; also called *functional neurological symptom disorder*. (8)

Conversion therapy: Therapy to turn homosexuals into heterosexuals; popular in the past, but almost universally rejected today as unethical. (10)

Convulsion therapy: Early 20th-century treatment for schizophrenia in which epileptic-like convulsions were induced by inducing insulin shock or administering electroconvulsive therapy. (1)

Copralalia: Speech problem involving involuntary cursing. (14)

Core beliefs: Basic philosophies or mindsets we hold about ourselves that influence intermediate beliefs and automatic thoughts. (2)

Core conditions for change: Rogers' three necessary and sufficient conditions; in person-centered therapy, these are provided to help clients reconnect with their actualizing tendency; consist of empathy, genuineness, and unconditional positive regard. (2)

Corpus callosum: Bundle of nerves that connects the two hemispheres of the cerebrum. (2)

Corrective emotional experience: A new kind of relationship in which the patient learns to assess others more realistically and no longer rely on projective identification during interpersonal relationships. (2)

Correlation: When two variables are related; changes in one are systematically associated with changes in the other; correlations can be *positive* or *negative*. (1)

Correlation coefficient: A statistically calculated number between −1.0 and +1.0; a positive correlation coefficient is closer to +1.0; a negative correlation coefficient is closer to −1.0; no correlation hovers around 0. (1)

Correlational research: Looks at the relationship between two variables to see whether changes in one are systematically tied to changes in the other. (1)

Corticostriatal pathophysiological models: Models that hold that OCD is explicable in terms of the complex circuitry by which various areas of the brain communicate. (6)

Cortisol: The primary stress hormone; high levels are correlated with problems like depression and mania, while low levels may occur in response to posttraumatic stress. (5)

Counseling psychologists: Applied psychologists trained to emphasize the emotional strengths and positive aspects of client functioning; compared to clinical psychologists, they often work with clients experiencing less severe presenting problems. (1)

Countertransference: In classic psychoanalysis, occurs when therapists generalize (i.e., transfer) their feelings about important people in their lives onto their patients; in object relations and time limited dynamic therapies, also refers to times when therapists feel certain ways because of how their patients interpersonally interact with them. (2)

Courtesy stigma: Stigma simply by being associated with a family member with a developmental issue or other stigmatized problem; also called *associative stigma*. (13)

Covert sensitization: Aversion therapy in which an unpleasant image is presented (*in vivo* or imaginally) while the client focuses on the paraphilic interest; the goal is to associate the paraphilic interest with the unpleasant image in order to lessen the behavior. (10)

Crack: Purer, more powerful crystal form of cocaine; inhaled via a pipe. (11)

Criminal commitment: Placing people in mental hospitals because of crimes they committed. (15)

Critical incident stress debriefing (CISD): An extended single-session post-trauma intervention during which trauma victims are asked to recall the event in vivid detail shortly after it occurs; controversial because some research suggests CISD can be harmful. (7)

Cross-sex hormonal treatment: Prescription of sex hormones (androgens, estrogens, and antiandrogens) to alter people's physical appearance as they transition from one sex to the other; also called *hormone therapy*. (10)

Cross-tolerance: When tolerance for one drug transfers to other drugs with similar chemical effects on the brain. (11)

Cultural adaptations: Modifying empirically supported treatments to account for cultural differences. (7)

Cultural formulation interview (CFI): Structured clinical interview included in the *DSM-5* in which clinicians inquire about cultural factors potentially impacting the presenting problem. The CFI assesses four domains: cultural definition of the problem; cultural perceptions of cause, context, and support; cultural factors affecting self-coping and past help seeking; and cultural factors affecting current help seeking. (3)

Cultural relativism: Perspective that says abnormality is always relative to social norms. (9)

Cultural universalism: Perspective on abnormality that says mental disorders are universal, cutting across time, culture, and context—even when cultural factors influence how people display symptoms. (9)

Culture: The values, beliefs, and practices of any ethnic or cultural group. (2)

Culture bias: Occurs when diagnostic, formulation, or assessment approaches reflect the cultural assumptions of those devising them. (3)

Culture-bound syndromes: Diagnoses that reflect the cultural values of a specific historical time and place rather than universally true disorders. (2)

Cyclical maladaptive pattern: The problematic interpersonal pattern produced in relationship after relationship. (2)

Cyclothymic disorder: Diagnosis reserved for those who have hypomanic and depressive symptoms that don't rise to the level of hypomanic and depressive episodes. (5)

Cytisine: Smoking-cessation drug that blocks nicotine receptors, making cigarettes less enjoyable and decreasing withdrawal symptoms (trade names *Tabex* and *Desmoxan*); sold primarily in Eastern Europe. (11)

Cytokines: Small proteins produced by immune system cells that are helpful in healing, but which cause swelling in large amounts; levels are elevated in people with presenting problems such as depression, suggesting highly active immune systems. (4)

Daily Record of Dysfunctional Thoughts (DRDT): A form used by cognitive therapists to help clients track events, their emotional reactions, their automatic thoughts, their behavioral response, and their errors in logic. (2)

Dancing mania: A form of "mass madness" that sometimes occurred during the Middle Ages in which people felt an unstoppable urge to dance. (1)

Dark therapy: Treatment sometimes combined with light therapy for those diagnosed with bipolar disorder; patient kept in the dark for several hours to correct circadian rhythm disruptions suspected of causing mania. (5)

Day care programs: Outpatient programs for people with dementia and other cognitive difficulties; patients attend these programs during the day and then go home at night. (14)

Death capitulators: According to Shneidman, people who give in to death; their anxiety and depression lead them to psychologically capitulate, making subintentional death more likely. (15)

Death chancers: According to Shneidman, people who take unnecessary risks just to see what will happen; can lead to subintentional death. (15)

Death darers: According to Shneidman, suicide attempters who are unsure about wanting to die, leading them to take risks that could result in death—such as playing Russian Roulette or purposely overdosing on drugs but then calling for help. (15)

Death experimenters: According to Shneidman, people who don't actively try to end their lives, but instead experiment with living in a continuously altered and foggy state; can lead to subintentional death. (15)

Death hasteners: According to Shneidman, people who engage in unhealthy lifestyles that hasten their own subintentional deaths. (15)

Death ignorers: According to Shneidman, suicide attempters who view death as a beginning, rather than an ending; they think their deaths mark the start of something new and may see death as an escape to a better and more peaceful place, or as temporary or reversible. (15)

Death initiators: According to Shneidman, suicide attempters who want to die because they believe that the process of dying is already underway; many, but not all of them, suffer from terminal illnesses. (15)

Death instinct: Unconscious instinct proposed by Freud that drives people to behave in self-destructive ways, including self-harm and suicide; also called *Thanatos*. (15)

Death seekers: According to Shneidman, suicide attempters who attempt suicide because they actively seek their own deaths; they want to die, although this desire tends to wax and wane. (15)

Decathexis: Psychoanalytic term that describing the process by which psychic energy is divested from an object. (7)

Declaration of Helsinki: A set of ethical principles designed to govern medical research, but which are more broadly applied to any research involving human subjects; revised in 2013. (15)

Deep brain stimulation (DBS): Treatment in which electrodes are permanently implanted in the brain and then low levels of electrical current are sent to these electrodes using a transmitter the person wears; used to treat movement disorders such as Parkinson's disease and Tourette's disorder, as well as chronic depression that doesn't respond to antidepressants. (5)

Defense mechanisms: In psychodynamic theories, partly unconscious mental processes used to ward off or reduce anxiety and cope with emotionally upsetting experiences. (2)

Deinstitutionalization: Wide-scale releasing of patients from mental hospitals; widespread in the latter 20th century at mental institutions across North America and Europe. (1)

Delay of gratification: The ego's ability to postpone expressing id impulses. (2)

Delayed ejaculation: *DSM-5* diagnosis for men who show a delay in (or inability to) ejaculate despite being stimulated and wanting to ejaculate more quickly. (10)

Delirium: *ICD-10* and *ICD-11* diagnosis describing a cognitive disturbance that fluctuates in severity and involves diminished attention to and awareness of one's surroundings; there must be a biological reason for the delirium, such as a medical condition, drug intoxication, or drug withdrawal—and, depending on the reason, it lifts all together or comes and goes. (14)

Delirium tremens (DTs): Syndrome in extreme cases of alcohol withdrawal in which the person becomes delirious, experiences intense body tremors, and has terrifying hallucinations. (11)

Delusional disorder: *DSM-5*, *ICD-10*, and *ICD-11* disorder characterized by delusional thinking. (4)

Delusions: False beliefs that a person won't give up, despite overwhelming evidence against them; for specific types of delusions, see *bizarre delusions*, *erotomanic delusions*, *grandiose delusions*, *jealous delusions*, *non-bizarre delusions*, *persecutory delusions*, and *somatic delusions*. (4)

Dementia: *ICD-10* and *ICD-11* disorder diagnosed when there is a permanent and usually progressive cognitive decline in functioning because of a specific brain disease or injury. (14)

Dementia praecox: Early term used to describe what is today called schizophrenia; it means "premature dementia." (4)

Demonological perspective: Views abnormal behavior as due to possession by evil spirits; also called the *supernatural perspective*. (1)

Dependence: *ICD-10* and *ICD-11* diagnosis in which use of a substance takes on a higher priority than it once had; involves things like feeling compelled to take a substance, difficulty controlling use, tolerance, and withdrawal. (11)

Dependent personality disorder: *DSM-5* and *ICD-10* disorder describing those who desperately want to be cared for; lacking confidence in their own abilities, they regularly seek advice and reassurance from those around them. (12)

Dependent variable: The variable that depends on the manipulation of the independent variable; the observed result in an experiment. (1)

Depersonalization: Form of dissociation characterized by disconnecting from one's self and one's emotions; the self seems unreal or changed. (7)

Depersonalization/derealization disorder: *DSM-5* and *ICD-11* dissociative disorder diagnosed in those who experience depersonalization, derealization, or both; called *depersonalization/derealization syndrome* in *ICD-10*. (8)

Depressants: Drugs that slow the central nervous system (CNS). (11)

Depression: Feelings of intense and often debilitating sadness and melancholy, along with a generally pessimistic worldview and loss of interest in previously enjoyed activities. (5)

Depressive episode: At least two weeks of intense sadness and depressed mood or loss of interest in daily activities; other symptoms include change in appetite, sleep disturbance, tiredness, indecisiveness, feelings of worthlessness, lethargy or restlessness, and suicidal feelings. (5)

Derealization: Form of dissociation characterized by disconnecting from one's surroundings; the world seems remote, altered, or unreal. (7)

Description: Phenomenological research method in which the researcher obtains descriptions of what is being studied from participants. (1)

Descriptive psychopathology: Diagnostic approach that relies on descriptions of how people think, feel, and behave for making diagnoses. (3)

Desmopressin: Synthetic form of the hormone vasopressin prescribed to decrease urine production to reduce or eliminate nighttime bedwetting. (14)

Detoxification: The physical process of weaning addicted individuals from the drugs they are addicted to. (11)

Developmental coordination disorder: *DSM-5* disorder diagnosed in children who show motor coordination skills well below what is expected given their age; called *developmental motor coordination disorder* in *ICD-11*. (14)

Developmental language disorder with impairment of mainly expressive language: *ICD-11* disorder for those with a limited ability to use expressive language; somewhat similar to *ICD-10* diagnosis, *expressive language disorder*. (14)

Developmental language disorder with impairment of mainly pragmatic language: *ICD-11* disorder that is similar to the *DSM-5*'s social (pragmatic) communication disorder (SPCD); involves development of communication difficulties early in life. (13)

Developmental language disorder with impairment of receptive and expressive language: *ICD-11* disorder for those with a limited ability to understand language, as well as difficulty producing spoken or sign language; somewhat similar to *ICD-10* diagnosis, *receptive language disorder*. (14)

Deviance: Behavior that violates social norms and values. Deviant people behave in socially unacceptable ways, but may or may not be viewed as suffering from mental disorders. (1, 13)

Diagnosis: In medical terms, a procedure for determining the nature and circumstances of a diseased condition; in psychological and social terms, seeking the cause or nature of a problem or situation. (3)

Diagnostic and Statistical Manual of Mental Disorders (DSM): Diagnostic manual of the American Psychiatric Association. (1)

Diagnostic code: An alphanumeric key assigned to disorder categories. (3)

Diagnostic criteria: Lists of symptoms in *DSM-5* that are used to make diagnoses; they specify the required number of symptoms and their duration; use an algorithmic model to enhance diagnostic reliability. (3)

Diagnostic guidelines: *ICD-10* and *ICD-11* descriptors used to gauge whether a patient qualifies for a diagnosis; written broadly using a prototype model to allow for diagnostic flexibility. (3)

Dialectical behavior therapy (DBT): CBT-influenced approach developed for borderline personality disorder that combines CBT skill-training with an emphasis on dialectics. (12)

Dialectics: The rational process of reconciling opposites; important in dialectical behavior therapy for borderline personality disorder, in which patients often struggle to integrate conflicting thoughts and feelings. (12)

Diathesis-stress model of psychosomatic illness: Maintains that psychosomatic illness emerges from a combination of *diathesis* (a predisposing biological vulnerability) and *stress*. (8)

Diathesis-stress model of suicide: Holds that people try to kill themselves when a preexisting vulnerability (*diathesis*) is exacerbated by environmental *stress*. (15)

Differentiation: In family therapy, when family members come to distinguish their own thoughts and feelings from others in the family so they can resist and eliminate problematic family patterns. (2)

Difficult process: Humanistic term that reframes psychological abnormality in a non-pathologizing and anti-diagnostic way; psychological problems are not attributed to mental disorder, but to a failure to receive the necessary and sufficient core conditions for self-actualization due to problems in early attachment relationships. (12)

Dimensional diagnosis: Approach to diagnosis that charts degrees of severity for different symptoms rather than dividing disorders into discrete categories. (3)

Diminished emotional expression: Negative symptom of psychosis in which a person's emotional expression seems decreased or flattened. (4)

Discontinuation syndrome: Syndrome that occurs when people discontinue antidepressants; can include flu-like symptoms, dizziness, insomnia, nausea, diarrhea, irritability, nightmares, and depressive symptoms due to stopping the drug. (5)

Discrete trial training (DTT): Applied behavior analysis (ABA) technique for working with developmental issues; teaches concrete skills in a step-by-step manner using reinforcement and other behavioral techniques. (13)

Dislocation studies: Studies that look at rates of eating disorders in people who temporarily move from cultures where eating disorders are less common to ones where they are more common. (9)

Disorganized thinking: Thinking pattern in psychosis characterized by disturbances in the form of thought; loose associations (leaping from topic to topic during conversation) and tangential responding (responding to something other than what was asked) are common, as is incoherent or disrupted language use; also called *formal thought disorder*. (4)

Disruptive mood dysregulation disorder (DMDD): *DSM-5* disorder diagnosed in children and adolescents who show depressive symptoms combined with temper outbursts. (5)

Dissocial personality disorder: *ICD-10* equivalent of antisocial personality disorder. (12)

Dissociation: Detaching from experience. (7)

Dissociative amnesia: *DSM-5*, *ICD-10*, and *ICD-11* dissociative disorder that involves difficulty recalling important autobiographical information; diagnosed with or without fugue in *DSM-5* and *ICD-11*. (8)

Dissociative disorders of movement and sensation: *ICD-10* term for conversion disorder; see also *dissociative neurological symptom disorder*, its *ICD-11* equivalent. (8)

Dissociative fugue: *ICD-10* dissociative disorder in which a person experiences dissociative amnesia, leaves home, travels to a new location, and establishes a new identity; considered a subtype of dissociative amnesia in *DSM-5* and *ICD-11*. (8)

Dissociative identity disorder (DID): *DSM-5* and *ICD-11* dissociative disorder describing people who have two or more distinct "personalities," with only one being present at any given time; called *multiple personality disorder* in *ICD-10*. (8)

Dissociative neurological symptom disorder: *ICD-11* disorder in which there is lost or altered sensory, motor, or cognitive functioning inconsistent with any known disease or health condition; see also *conversion disorder* (the *DSM-5* equivalent) and *dissociative disorders of movement and sensation* (the *ICD-10* equivalent). (8)

Disturbance of activity and attention: One of two *ICD-10* diagnoses that roughly correspond to ADHD in *DSM-5* and *ICD-11*; diagnosed when there are attention and hyperactivity-impulsivity symptoms, but no conduct problems. (13)

Disulfiram: Drug given to alcoholics that makes them sick when they drink by inhibiting an enzyme that prevents the breakdown of acetaldehyde, a metabolite left over when the liver breaks down alcohol. (11)

Dizygotic twins: Fraternal twins who come from separate fertilized eggs; they are siblings who share half their genes despite being in utero at the same time. (4)

DNA (deoxyribonucleic acid): Chromosomes are made of this; it consists of four chemical compounds (adenine, cytosine, guanine, and thymine). (2)

Dopamine: An inhibitory neurotransmitter implicated in memory, motivation, and reward/pleasure; too much is associated with psychosis; can also function as a hormone. (2)

Dopamine hypothesis of addiction: Theory that all addictive drugs increase dopamine in the brain, even though this is often by different biological mechanisms. (11)

Dopamine hypothesis of ADHD: Hypothesis that ADHD is caused by deficits in the transmission of dopamine. (13)

Dopamine hypothesis of schizophrenia: Most influential brain chemistry theory of schizophrenia, which hypothesizes that schizophrenia results from too much of the brain neurotransmitter dopamine. (4)

Dopamine hypothesis of stuttering: Proposes that stuttering is related to excessive dopamine transmission in the basal ganglia. (14)

Dopamine hypothesis of Tourette's disorder: Holds that too much dopamine activity in the basal ganglia plays a role in Tourette's disorder. (14)

Dorsal anterior midcingulate cortex: Brain region that plays a role in motivational aspects of attention, cognitive processing, and response inhibition. (13)

Dorsolateral prefrontal cortex: Brain region important in decision-making, working memory, and planning; has been associated with conversion symptoms. (8)

Double bind: Occurs when someone is placed in a situation where there are two contradictory demands, neither of which can be satisfied or avoided; Gregory Bateson theorized that children who grow up in families where double binds are the norm are at higher risk for developing schizophrenia. (4)

Double-blind studies: Experiments in which neither the participants nor researchers testing them know which treatment group participants belong to. (1)

Down syndrome: Caused by having an extra copy of the chromosome trisomy 21; physical signs include stocky body, short stature, flat faces and noses, small heads, small ears, small mouths, and poor muscle tone; also associated with intellectual disabilities. (14)

Drapetomania: Diagnostic term coined in the 1850s to describe American slaves who ran away to escape captivity. (1)

Dream analysis: Psychoanalytic technique in which patients report their dreams and the analyst seeks to interpret wish fulfillments. (2)

Drug flashbacks: Unexpected re-experiencing of past drug trips. (11)

Drug replacement therapy: Substance dependence treatment that involves either changing the delivery method of a drug or exchanging one drug for a chemically similar one; goal is either to wean people off drugs or sustain them on a similar but less dangerous drug. (11)

Drug-induced synesthesia: A mixing of sensory experiences in which stimulation of one sensory mode spawns perceptual responses from another; often caused by hallucinogens. (11)

Dry-bed training: Behavior therapy intervention for enuresis that involves having parents wake up children during the night, praise them when they don't wet the bed, and punish them when they do (often by making them wash their bedding); opposed by many due to its punitive nature. (14)

DSM: See *Diagnostic and Statistical Manual of Mental Disorders* (*DSM*).

***DSM-5* alternative model for personality disorders**: Currently unofficial alternative to the *DSM-5* categorical model of personality disorders that combines dimensional and categorical assessment in diagnosing personality disorders; also known as the *hybrid model* or *hybrid trait model*. (12)

***DSM-5* definition of mental disorder**: "A syndrome characterized by clinically significant disturbance in an individual's cognition, emotion regulation, or behavior that reflects a dysfunction in the psychological, biological, or developmental processes underlying mental functioning." (3)

Dual representation theory (DRT): Holds that people cognitively encode trauma memories in two ways: through *verbally accessible memories (VAMs)*, which can be actively remembered and expressed in words; and *situationally accessible memories (SAMs)*, which aren't consciously available and are only elicited by stimuli that remind the person of the trauma. (7)

Durham test: Legal test of insanity that says defendants can be acquitted when their illegal behavior was caused by a mental disorder; also called the *Durham rule*. (15)

Duty to protect: Legal duty that applies anytime a therapist suspects a client is dangerous and could do harm to others, even when no direct threats are made. Under such circumstances, steps to protect the public must be taken—such as contacting the police or having someone civilly committed. (15)

Duty to warn: Legal duty that requires therapists to break confidentiality and inform people of threats made against them by clients. (15)

Dynamic interpersonal therapy (DIT): Short-term psychodynamic therapy that emphasizes uncovering and remedying one major unconscious interpersonal pattern that contributes to the client's depression. (5)

Dyscalculia: Learning disorder that involves impairment with mathematics; difficulty processing and calculating numbers. (14)

Dysfunctional schema modes: Schema therapy term for cognitive, emotional, and behavioral states that people enter when their early maladaptive schemas (EMSs) are activated). (12)

Dyslexia: Learning disorder that involves difficulty decoding information when reading; characterized by trouble recognizing, deciphering, or spelling words. (14)

Dyspareunia: *ICD-10* diagnosis for women and men who experience pain during intercourse—sometimes with no physical basis and other times with evidence of psychological factors (such as past sexual abuse); also in *ICD-11*, where it must have physical determinants. (10)

Dysregulation models: Hold that the adaptive mechanism behind normal sadness is broken and runs amok in severe and recurrent cases of depression. (5)

Dysthymia: *ICD-10* disorder describing ongoing depression that is milder than major depression; closest equivalent is *dysthymic disorder* in *ICD-11* and *persistent depressive disorder* in the *DSM-5*. (5)

E-mental health: Mental health services provided at a distance via telecommunication and information technologies. (15)

Early and intensive behavioral intervention (EIBI): Version of discrete trial training (DTT) used with patients under age 5. (13)

Early maladaptive schemas (EMSs): Schema therapy concept for dysfunctional schemas developed in early childhood due to abuse or neglect. (12)

Eating problems: Characterized by disturbed body image; involve concerns about being overweight or experiencing one's body negatively or in ways that appear distorted. (9)

Echolalia: Psychotic symptom in which the person repeats back what is said word for word. (4)

Eclecticism: An approach to practice in which clinicians draw from multiple theories depending on what is useful in the moment. (15)

Ego: Partly conscious/partly unconscious psychoanalytic personality structure that tries to satisfy id impulses while considering superego demands and constraints in the external environment; motivated by the reality principle. (2)

Ego-dystonic homosexuality: *DSM-III* diagnosis for people who were gay and psychologically upset about it; removed from subsequent editions of *DSM* and not in *ICD-11*, but a comparable diagnosis (*ego-dystonic sexual orientation*) is in *ICD-10*. (10)

Egoistic suicide: According to Durkheim, occurs when people experience *low social integration*; because they feel like they don't belong, they become alienated, unhappy, and are more likely to kill themselves. (15)

Electra complex: Occurs at phallic stage in girls; the little girl experiences *castration anxiety* until she realizes she has no penis; then she experiences *penis envy*; ends when little girl identifies with mom and represses the experience; results in superego, but a weak superego because castration anxiety is never fully resolved. (2)

Electrical aversive therapy: Aversive therapy in which an electric shock is administered in order to associate it with an undesired sexual activity. (10)

Electroconvulsive therapy (ECT): Treatment in which an electrical current is delivered to the brain to produce a seizure; used mainly for treatment-resistant depression, but sometimes also used for bipolar disorder and psychosis. (1)

Electroencephalogram (EEG): Device that records the electrical activity of neuronal firing, or brain waves. (3)

Emotion-focused couple therapy (EFCT) for trauma: 10–20 session approach that—like other emotion-focused interventions—stresses processing emotions to help the couple identify and eliminate negative relational interaction patterns. (7)

Emotion-focused therapy (EFT): Brief humanistic psychotherapy that combines person-centered, Gestalt, and constructivist ideas. (5)

Emotional cutoff: When family members place emotional or physical distance between one another to avoid dealing with conflicts. (2)

Emotional dysregulation model: Cognitive explanation of anxiety that contends anxious people have difficulty regulating their emotions and therefore find strong emotions highly aversive. (6)

Emotional processing theory: A cognitive theory that attributes posttraumatic stress (as well as other fear and anxiety responses) to dysfunctional *fear structures* (closely associated thoughts, feelings, beliefs, and behaviors that are simultaneously elicited when faced with a threatening event); contends that for exposure therapy to be most effective, fear structures must be activated during exposure. (7)

Emotional suffering: Defines abnormality in terms of emotional suffering and upset that goes beyond what is typical or reasonable; coming to agreement on what is typical or reasonable can be difficult. (1)

Emotionally unstable personality disorder: *ICD-10* diagnosis characterized by acting impulsively and emotional unpredictability; divided into two types: *borderline type* (characterized by emotional instability) and *impulsive type* (characterized by acting out, often in threatening or violent ways, without considering the consequences). (12)

Empathy: Understanding another's point of view; involves actively listening to them and reflecting what is heard; one of Rogers' core conditions for change. (2)

Empirically supported treatments (ESTs): Treatments that have been found to be effective for specific presenting problems in randomized controlled trials. (1)

Encopresis: *DSM-5*, *ICD-10*, and *ICD-11* diagnosis given to children who repeatedly have bowel movements in inappropriate places, such as in their pants or on the floor. (14)

Endocrine system: Collection of glands important in regulating things like sexual functioning, sleep, mood, and metabolism. (5)

Endogenous depression: Depression believed to originate inside the person via faulty physiological processes. (5)

Endogenous opioids: Chemicals produced by our bodies that reduce pain and calm us down; also called *endorphins*. (11)

Enhanced cognitive behavioral therapy (CBT-E): Form of CBT used with eating disorders that maintains there is a "core psychopathology" associated with all eating disorders—one in which people base their self-worth not on their achievements, but on their ability to control body weight and shape; uses psychoeducation to help people monitor their eating patterns and identify cognitive distortions that maintain these patterns; also called the *transdiagnostic model*. (9)

Enmeshed families: Families in which the boundaries between members are loose or blurred, making it difficult for members to distinguish their own beliefs and feelings from other family members' beliefs and feelings; can lead to intense relationships and, in some cases, hostile conflict. (2)

Entitlement: The unreasonable expectation that one deserves special attention or treatment. (12)

Entorhinal cortex: Limbic system area of brain associated with memory. (2)

Enuresis: *DSM-5*, *ICD-10*, and *ICD-11* diagnosis given to children who wet their beds or clothes; also known as *bedwetting*. (14)

Enuresis alarm: Battery-operated alarm used in behavior therapy for enuresis; it is attached to the child's underwear or to a pad placed on the bed and it goes off when urine is detected, waking up the child; also called the *bell and pad method*. (14)

Environmental toxin hypotheses: Posit that developmental difficulties in children are associated with exposure to pollution and other environmental toxins. (13)

Epidemiological research: Form of correlational research used to study the prevalence and incidence of *DSM* and *ICD* mental disorders. (1)

Equal environments assumption: Assumption made in twin studies that the environments of monozygotic twins and dizygotic twins are identical. (4)

Erectile disorder: *DSM-5* disorder diagnosed in men who repeatedly have trouble obtaining or maintaining erections during sexual activity; called *male erectile dysfunction* in the *ICD-11* and diagnosed as either *failure of genital response* or *impotence of organic origin* in the *ICD-10*. (10)

Erotomanic delusions: Delusions in which you falsely believe a person is in love with you. (4)

Estrogen: Primary female sex hormone. (10)

Etiology: Medical term for "cause." (3)

Eugenics movement: 20th-century movement that believed intelligence and other traits were primarily inherited and felt humanity could be improved by encouraging breeding between those with "desirable" traits while preventing it among those with "undesirable" traits; in numerous countries, led to forced sterilization of those deemed "mentally defective." (14)

Evidential analysis: CBT technique for psychosis in which client and therapist list evidence for and against the client's psychotic beliefs. (4)

Evolutionary perspectives: Use Darwin's evolutionary theory to understand how presenting problems evolved, seeing them as both genetically inherited and often having been adaptive at some point in early human history. (2)

Excessive sexual drive: *ICD-10* diagnosis for people who show too much (i.e., excessive) interest in sex. (10)

Excessive sugar-intake hypothesis: Holds that ADHD symptoms are caused or made worse by too much intake of refined sugars. (13)

Excoriation (skin-picking disorder): *DSM-5* and *ICD-11* disorder that involves compulsive picking of the skin; listed as "neurotic excoriation" in the *ICD-10*. (6)

Executive functioning: Cognitive processes involving attention, planning, decision-making, and goal-directed behavior. (3)

Exhibitionism/exhibitionistic disorder: Paraphilic disorder involving sexual fantasies, urges, or behaviors related to exposing one's genitals to unsuspecting people. (10)

Existential anxiety: Normal and expected anxiety that motivates people to construct meaningful lives for themselves; emerges from the four basic existential givens. (6)

Existential givens: death, freedom, isolation, and meaninglessness. (6)

Existential psychotherapies: Therapies that focus on people creating their own meanings to live by and accepting responsibility for these meanings and the choices they make in life. (2)

Exogenous depression: Depression seen as originating outside the person—in external circumstances such as poverty, racism, and sexism; or in situational factors such as job or marital dissatisfaction. (5)

Experiential sex therapy: Humanistic approach to sex therapy that views sexual problems as having an underlying and personal meaning to those suffering from them; helps clients identify important feelings that can guide them in how they wish to live their lives; the resulting personal growth transforms and improves their lives and this indirectly leads to the resolution of sexual issues. (10)

Experiments: Research studies in which controlled variables are manipulated in order to identify causal relationships among variables. (1)

Exposure plus response prevention: Exposure technique in which client is thrust into contact with the conditioned stimulus and prevented from leaving the situation; client learns that nothing bad happens when in contact with the stimulus; also called *flooding and response prevention*. (2)

Exposure plus response prevention of bingeing: Form of exposure plus response prevention in which patients are exposed to foods they usually binge on but are then prevented from bingeing; goal is to recondition patient behavior by no longer having these foods serve as conditioned stimuli for bingeing. (9)

Exposure plus response prevention of purging: Form of exposure plus response prevention in which patients are prevented from purging after bingeing; goal is to decrease conditioned fear of overeating by showing them nothing terrible happens if they don't purge. (9)

Exposure therapies: Therapy techniques in which the client is placed in the presence of the conditioned stimulus to extinguish the old response and condition a new one. (2)

Expressed emotion: The degree to which family members respond to a patient in a hostile, critical, or emotionally overinvolved way; associated with poorer outcomes for the patient. (4)

Expressive language disorder: *ICD-10* disorder that involves limited ability to use expressive language; children with this diagnosis have very limited vocabularies for their age; somewhat similar to *ICD-11* diagnosis, *developmental language disorder with impairment of mainly expressive language*. (14)

Extended commitment: Civilly committing people for longer periods; usually requires a formal legal proceeding to convince a court that hospitalization is the least restrictive treatment available; *dangerousness, grave disability*, and *need for treatment* are the criteria used to make extended commitment decisions. (15)

External validity: The extent to which experimental results can be generalized to everyday life. (1)

Externalizing behaviors: Behaviors that involve taking internal thoughts and feelings and directing them externally at the environment by acting out; characterized by poor impulse-control, rule-breaking, and physical or verbal aggression. (13)

Externalizing the problem: Narrative therapy technique in which clients are asked to talk about their problems as something separate from them that sometimes gets the best of them (as opposed to disorders they "have"). (2)

Extinction: When a conditioned stimulus is no longer paired with an unconditioned stimulus, the conditioned stimulus stops eliciting a conditioned response. (2)

Extrapyramidal side effects: Side effects of antipsychotic drugs that include muscle tremors, a shuffling gait, and drooling. (4)

Extreme male brain (EMB) theory: Evolutionary theory of autism that posits that people with autism are better at systematizing (a trait more evolved in males) than empathizing (a trait more evolved in females); potentially explains why autism occurs more in males than females. (13)

Eye movement desensitization and reprocessing (EMDR): Technique used for a variety of anxiety-related problems in which people imagine anxiety-provoking or traumatic events while engaging in bilateral stimulation. (7)

Factitious disorder: *DSM-5, ICD-10*, and *ICD-11* diagnosis for people who physically tamper with themselves or otherwise exaggerate or simulate symptoms in order to produce signs of illness and convince others they are sick; the goal is to get medical attention. (8)

Factor analysis: A statistical procedure that involves identifying patterns in how people respond to different items on one or more psychological inventories; items on which responses correlate with one another are grouped together as measuring the same thing (i.e., a common factor). (12)

Failure of genital response: *ICD-10* diagnosis for men with erectile dysfunction and women who have difficulty becoming lubricated. (10)

False consciousness: When oppressed people fail to realize they are oppressed and internalize the values of their oppressors. (2)

False negatives: Cases that incorrectly don't get diagnosed with a disorder even though they should. (13)

False positives: Cases that incorrectly get diagnosed with a disorder even though they shouldn't. (13)

Family-based treatment (FBT): Manualized therapy for anorexia and bulimia that focuses on weight restoration and/or the establishment of healthy eating while not blaming parents; the family is encouraged to work together to help address the family member's eating disorder; also called the *Maudsley approach*. (9)

Family focused grief therapy: 10-session therapy that teaches families to communicate and share emotions more effectively to help with the mourning process; differentiates more functional families that are supportive or conflict-resolving from more dysfunctional families that are hostile, sullen, or intermediate. (7)

Family-focused therapy (FFT): Family therapy approach emphasizing psychoeducation, improving communication skills, and problem solving. (5)

Family meal: Technique originated in structural family therapy—and used also in family-based treatment (FBT)—in which the therapist observes a family meal to directly observe dysfunctional family patterns. (9)

Family rules: In Minuchin's structural family therapy, unspoken rules that influence family members' behaviors. (2)

Family studies: Studies looking at how often the relatives of those with schizophrenia are also diagnosed with schizophrenia. (4)

Family systems therapy: Looks at couple and family dynamics in trying to understand and remediate psychological issues. (2)

Family systems therapy for PTSD: Family systems perspective is used to address dysfunctional family patterns that exacerbate the PTSD patient's symptoms. (7)

Fatalistic suicide: According to Durkheim, occurs when people experience *high social regulation*; rules, expectations, and social demands are so great that death feels like the only way out. (15)

Fear: A basic emotion in response to something specific that is perceived as dangerous with distinct physiological symptoms that are universal, automatic, and brief. (6)

Feeding disorder of infancy and early childhood: *ICD-10* disorder that involves fussy or faddish eating or refusal of food; can also involve rumination. (9)

Feeding problems: Characterized by concern over food preferences; involve fussy or faddish eating habits in which certain foods are avoided or refused because of taste, texture, or a basic dislike for them. (9)

Feingold diet: Eliminates food additives from the diets of ADHD-diagnosed children. (13)

Female orgasmic disorder: *DSM-5* diagnosis for women who rarely or never experience orgasms. (10)

Female sexual arousal dysfunction: *ICD-11* diagnosis for women who show little or no arousal from sexual activity. (10)

Female sexual interest/arousal disorder: *DSM-5* diagnosis for women who show little or no interest in or arousal from sexual activity. (10)

Feminist therapy: Therapy which holds that patriarchy (the structuring of society so that men are in charge) is the root cause of many problems commonly labeled as mental disorders; reconceptualizes therapy as a collaborative relationship between therapist and client, one in which both work for social reform. (2)

Fetal alcohol syndrome (FAS): Characterized by retarded growth, developmental delays, and atypical facial features such as *microencephaly* (small heads), *microphthalmia* (small eyes), thin upper lips with no ventromedial indentation in the middle, and flat upper jaw bones; occurs in children of mothers who drank excessively during pregnancy. (11)

Fetishism/fetishistic disorder: Paraphilic disorder involving sexual fantasies, urges, or behaviors related to nonliving objects or nongenital body parts. (10)

Fetishistic transvestism/transvestic disorder: Paraphilic disorder involving sexual fantasies, urges, or behaviors related to cross-dressing. (10)

Fight or flight response: Controlled by the sympathetic nervous system; process by which organism decides whether to flee from danger, engage it, or freeze. (7)

Fighter theory: Evolutionary theory of ADHD that holds that hyperactivity and impulsivity evolved to help early Homo sapiens in their battles with Neanderthals. (13)

First-generation antipsychotics: Original antipsychotic drugs used to treat schizophrenia and other forms of psychosis; also referred to by the name *phenothiazines*. (4)

Fitness: Evolutionary theory term used to describe organisms that are adapted to their environments; adaptation occurs when organisms are successful in reproducing and passing on their genes. (2)

Fitness to plead: Legal standard used in England and Wales that says those charged with a crime must be able to (a) enter a plea, (b) understand the court proceedings, (c) instruct their lawyers, (d) contest a juror, and (e) comprehend the evidence offered; versions of this rule are also used in Canada, Australia, New Zealand, and Scotland. (15)

Five-factor model (FFM): A model that proposes that every human being's personality can be mapped along five trait dimensions: *extraversion, agreeableness, conscientiousness, neuroticism,* and *openness*. (12)

Five-stage theory of grief: Kübler-Ross's theory of grief in which a mourner progresses through discrete stages of *denial, anger, bargaining, depression,* and *acceptance*. (7)

Fixation: When a child gets stuck at one of psychoanalytic theory's psychosexual stages of development. (2)

Flashbacks: PTSD symptom in which a person feels and acts as if the traumatic event is happening again. (7)

Flattened affect: Negative symptom of psychosis tied to diminished emotional expression; the person speaks in an unemotional voice with few inflections and little expressive body language. (4)

Flibanserin: Drug that aims to increase female sexual desire by reducing serotonin and increasing norepinephrine; marketed as Addyi. (10)

Food additives hypothesis: Holds that additives in food (such as synthetic food coloring) lead to ADHD. (13)

Food exposure for anorexia: Behavioral technique in which patients are gradually exposed to food as a way to reduce fear of food and food avoidance. (9)

Formulation: A hypothesis about a person's difficulties, which draws from psychological theory. (3)

Four P model of case formulation: See *4P model of case formulation*.

Fragile process: In humanistic theory, a type of *difficult process* characteristic of those usually diagnosed as "narcissistic" or "borderline." (12)

Fragile X syndrome: Mutation on the X chromosome that leads to the development during adolescence of thin faces, long ears, large heads, prominent foreheads, flat feet, and extremely flexible joints; more common in boys than girls and associated with intellectual disabilities. (14)

Free association: Psychoanalytic technique in which patient is instructed to say whatever comes to mind. (2)

Frequency-dependent selection hypothesis: Hypothesis that psychopathy is an evolutionarily adaptive strategy so long as its frequency in the population is low. (12)

Frontal lobe: Brain region important in executing behavior; often appears to have decreased volume in many cases of depression and mania. (5)

Frotteurism/frotteuristic disorder: Paraphilic disorder involving sexual fantasies, urges, or behaviors related to touching or rubbing against a nonconsenting person. (10)

Functional analysis: Behavioral assessment in which judgments are made about the relationships between environmental conditions and client behavior, along with estimates of how these relationships might be modified. (3)

Functional analysis interview (FAI): A structured behavioral assessment method in which an interviewer gathers information from the client about the behavior of interest, its antecedents, its consequences, and circumstances and strategies that seem to increase or decrease the behavior. (3)

Functional relaxation: A body-oriented relaxation technique to increase body awareness; used to reduce psychosomatic symptoms associated with asthma, tension headaches, and irritable bowel syndrome. (8)

Gambling disorder: *DSM-5* and *ICD-11* behavioral addiction characterized by recurrent problem gambling that leads to impairment and distress; called *pathological gambling* and considered a habit and impulse disorder in *ICD-10*. (11)

Gaming disorder: *ICD-11* beta-draft disorder for those who compulsively play video games; a similar proposed *DSM-5* disorder is called *internet gaming disorder*. (11)

Gamma-aminobutyric acid (GABA): The brain's primary inhibitory neurotransmitter. (2)

Gatekeeping: Approval process conducted by medical and mental health professionals intended to keep people with gender dysphoria who are deemed psychologically unfit from making irreversible gender-altering decisions. (10)

Gay: Term to describe male or female homosexuals. (10)

Gender: Attitudes, feelings, and behaviors a culture associates with a person's biological sex. (10)

Gender conformity: When a person's behavior fits with cultural expectations about gender. (10)

Gender dysphoria: *DSM-5* diagnosis for children, adolescents, and adults who display incongruence between their birth sex (natal gender) and experienced/expressed gender; see also *gender incongruence* (*ICD-11*), *transsexualism* (*ICD-10*), and *gender identity disorder of childhood* (*ICD-10*). (10)

Gender expression: How people behave and dress to convey their gender. (10)

Gender identity: One's persistent sense of belonging to the male or female gender category. (10)

Gender identity disorder of childhood: *ICD-10* diagnosis for children who display incongruence between birth sex and experienced/expressed gender; see also *gender dysphoria* (*DSM-5*), *gender incongruence* (*ICD-11*), and *transsexualism* (*ICD-10*). (10)

Gender incongruence: *ICD-11* diagnosis for children, adolescents, and adults who display incongruence between their birth sex (natal gender) and experienced/expressed gender; see also *gender dysphoria* (*DSM-5*), *transsexualism* (*ICD-10*), and *gender identity disorder of childhood* (*ICD-10*). (10)

Gender nonconformity: When a person's behavior violates cultural expectations about gender. (10)

General adaptation syndrome: Hans Selye's theory that defined stress in terms of three stages: alarm, resistance, and exhaustion. (7)

General paresis: Psychological syndrome characterized by progressive decline in mental functioning; progressive symptoms include mania, psychosis, delusions, physical deterioration, and death; caused by the syphilis virus. (2)

Generalized anxiety disorder (GAD): *DSM-5*, *ICD-10*, and *ICD-11* diagnosis characterized by excessive and consistent worry that is global rather than specific. (6)

Genes: Parts of a chromosome's DNA molecules; contain biological instructions for building a person; humans have roughly 30,000 of them. (2)

Genetic marker studies: Look for specific gene indicators associated with schizophrenia. (4, 8, 9)

Genetic perspectives: Focus on the role of genes in explaining the origins of presenting problems. (2)

Genital stage: Fifth stage of psychosexual development, from adolescence onward; conflicts from fixations at first three stages emerge. (2)

Genito-pelvic pain/penetration disorder: *DSM-5* diagnosis for women only that combines what used to be divided into vaginismus and dyspareunia into a single diagnostic category; characterized by pain during penetration and/or intercourse. (10)

Genome: The complete set of genetic information for each human. (2)

Genome-wide association (GWA) study: A study that examines all the genes of the genome to identify associations between specific genes and specific traits or disorders; contrasts with candidate gene studies, which look specifically at a smaller number of genes suspected of being involved in a trait or disorder. (6)

Genotype: A person's entire genetic makeup; includes all alleles, even non-dominant ones that aren't reflected in the person's physical and psychological makeup. (2)

Genuineness: Self-consistency; behaving in a manner that is congruent with one's actualizing tendency; one of Rogers' core conditions. (2)

Geophagia: Form of pica in which a person intentionally eats dirt, soil, or clay. (9)

Glutamate: The brain's main excitatory neurotransmitter. (2)

Glutamate hypothesis of depression: Proposes that depression is associated with high levels of glutamate, the brain's main excitatory neurotransmitter. (5)

Glutamate hypothesis of OCD: Contends that obsessive-compulsive disorder (OCD) may be the result of excess glutamate. (6)

Glutamate hypothesis of schizophrenia: Hypothesizes that lack of the neurotransmitter glutamate is behind many symptoms of schizophrenia. (4)

Gluten/casein-free diet hypothesis: Maintains that a diet low in gluten (proteins in wheat) and casein (a protein in milk) can reduce symptoms of autism. (13)

Good lives model (GLM): Humanistic program for sex offenders that emphasizes their basic need for personal growth and fulfillment; helps offenders identify *primary goods* (intrinsically beneficial goals such as being independent, excelling at work, and fostering intimate relationships) that can guide their rehabilitation. (10)

Grandiose delusions: Delusions in which you view yourself as important or special in some way. (4)

Grandiosity: Belief that one is very important. (5)

Grief: Primary emotional response to bereavement, consisting of emotional and physical reactions. (7)

Grounded theory methods: Qualitative methods that attempt to help researchers develop *grounded theories*—conceptual theoretical models of the topics they study. (1)

Group homes: Typically house a small number of adult residents with special needs, providing them with medical care and live-in aides who assist them in their daily routines. (14)

Group selection: Hypothesized process by which different members of a species or social group evolve specialized functions that benefit the larger community. (6)

Group selection theory of OCD: Proposes that OCD behaviors developed via group selection; having some group members partake in time-consuming behaviors such as checking, cleaning, and hoarding benefits the entire group without everyone needing to expend energy on such behaviors. (6)

Guilty but mentally ill (GBMI): Legal plea used as an alternative to the insanity defense in some U.S. states; designed to hold people responsible for their crimes and reduce insanity pleas; if convicted under GBMI, the offender is supposed to receive treatment concurrent with a prison sentence. (15)

Gut-brain axis: The system of biochemical connections between the *gut* (or *gastrointestinal tract*) and brain; the gut contains *bacteria* (also known as *gut microbiome*) and imbalances in these bacteria are suspected of playing roles in anxiety, OCD, depression, autism, psychosis, and perhaps other presenting problems. (6)

Habit reversal training (HRT): Behavior therapy technique used to treat tic disorders; patients taught to recognize sensory experiences that indicate the onset of a tic and then engage in a behavioral response (breathing or movement) that is incompatible with the tic. (14)

Habituation: Behavioral term for when responsiveness to a stimulus decreases after repeated exposure to it. (10)

Hair-pulling disorder: See *Trichotillomania*.

Hallucinations: Sensory experiences in the absence of sensory stimulation; can be auditory (hearing things), visual (seeing things), olfactory (smelling things), gustatory (tasting things), or tactile (feeling things touching you). (4)

Hallucinogens: Drugs that induce hallucinations, altered thinking and perceptions, out-of-body experiences, and sometimes paranoia; also known as *psychedelics*. (11)

Halstead-Reitan Neuropsychological Test Battery (HRB): Neuropsychological battery consisting of eight tests that assess visual, auditory, and tactile functioning; verbal communication; spatial and sequential perception; ability to analyze information; motor ability; and attention, concentration, and memory. (3)

Harm reduction: Intervention strategies for reducing individual and societal harm caused by drug and alcohol use; examples include needle exchange programs, adding thiamine to beer, and providing late-night public transportation. (11)

Harmful internal dysfunction: Jerome Wakefield's definition of mental disorder that has two components: (a) a mental mechanism that fails to operate according to its naturally designed function (i.e., an internal dysfunction), and (b) behavior that society deems harmful which is caused by the internal dysfunction. (1)

Harmful use: *ICD-10* and *ICD-11* diagnosis that involves ongoing misuse of a substance leading to physical or mental health problems, adverse social consequences, and criticism from others; also called *substance abuse*. (11)

Harmfulness to self or others: Criterion that identifies those whose behavior is harmful to self or others as abnormal. Judgments often differ about how much harm is acceptable and what counts as a harmful behavior. (1)

Healthy and functional schema modes: In schema therapy, adaptive states of thinking, feeling, and behaving; the two healthy modes are the *healthy adult mode* (productive thoughts and feelings lead you to feel skilled and capable) and *healthy child mode* (you feel playful and can engage others in enjoyable activities). (12)

Heritability: The percentage of phenotypic variation that can be attributed to genes, as opposed to environment. (2)

Heritability estimate: A score from 0.0 to 1.0 that estimates the degree to which a trait is genetic; for instance, a 0.60 heritability score would mean the trait at hand was 60% attributable to genetics and 40% attributable to the environment. (2)

Heroin: A highly addictive semisynthetic opioid to which dependence develops quickly; heroin tolerance and withdrawal are especially severe. (11)

Heterosexism: Hostility and prejudice against homosexuals (and other people with nonconforming sexual identities) that originates in ideologies that deny, denigrate, and stigmatize nonheterosexual behavior, identities, relationships, and communities. (10)

Heterosexuals: People who are attracted to the opposite sex. (10)

Hierarchical Taxonomy of Psychopathology (HiTOP): An emerging approach to diagnosis that offers a dimensional (rather than categorical) approach; see also *HiTOP spectra*. (3)

Highway hypnosis: Form of dissociation in which people drive long distances without paying conscious attention to what they are doing. (8)

Hippocampus: Limbic system brain structure that plays a role in memory. (2)

Histamine: A wake-promoting neurotransmitter; in the immune system, helps remove allergens from the body. (14)

Historical-cultural views: Views that see abnormality as historically situated; what is considered abnormal in one historical period may not be in another. (1)

Histrionic personality disorder: *DSM-5* and *ICD-10* diagnosis for those who are excessively dramatic and emotional; these individuals crave being the center of attention and strike others as shallow and overly theatrical, shifting from one exaggerated emotional display to another. (12)

HiTOP spectra: In the Hierarchical Taxonomy of Psychopathology (HiTOP) system, the six basic dimensions of psychopathology (detachment, antagonistic externalizing, disinhibited externalizing, thought disorder, internalizing, and somatoform). (3)

Hoarding disorder: *DSM-5* and *ICD-11* diagnosis given to people who have a hard time giving up possessions, even when they have too many or the possessions are no longer useful or valuable; not included in the *ICD-10*. (6)

Homeostasis: Biological process of maintaining the status quo for things like body temperature, body weight, fluid balances, and heart rate; regulated by the hypothalamus. (7)

Homophobia: Hostility and prejudice against homosexuals; some consider it an outdated term due to its implication that antigay prejudice originates from a dysfunction inside the individual rather than from cultural ideologies and practices. (10)

Homosexuals: People who are attracted to the same sex. (10)

Hopelessness theory: Predicts that people who make stable, global, and internal attributions will experience depression. (5)

Hormone replacement therapy (HRT): Therapy in which postmenopausal women are given female sex hormones to replace depleted hormone levels. (10)

Hormones: Chemical messengers of the endocrine systems. (5)

Humanistic perspectives: Perspectives that maintain people are proactive meaning-makers who strive to develop their full potential; includes humanistic, existential, and constructivist perspectives. (2)

Hunter-farmer theory: Hypothesizes that ADHD traits evolved because they were adaptive for hunters and farmers, who needed to be vigilant (to protect crops) and able to quickly shift gears (to chase prey). (13)

Hydrotherapy: Historical treatment for schizophrenia in which the patient was voluntarily or involuntarily wrapped in wet sheets of varied temperatures for several hours at a time. (4)

Hyperarousal theory of insomnia: Combines biological and cognitive-behavioral theories in proposing that some people are genetically predisposed to experience arousal and that such people become classically conditioned to associate hyperarousal state with sleep-related stimuli, making it difficult for them to fall or stay sleep. (14)

Hyperkinetic conduct disorder: One of two *ICD-10* diagnoses that roughly correspond to *DSM-5*'s ADHD; diagnosed when attention and hyperactivity-impulsivity symptoms are compounded by conduct problems. (13)

Hypersexual disorder: Proposed *DSM-5* disorder that is roughly equivalent to *ICD-10*'s excessive sexual drive; akin to "sexual addiction," a term used by the media and public but which is not an official diagnosis in *DSM* or *ICD*; proposed criteria define it as a preoccupation with and excessive engagement in sexual activities, often as a coping mechanism. (10)

Hypersomnia: Sleep problem in which one feels perpetually tired and sometimes even falls asleep despite getting sufficient sleep; called *hypersomnolence disorder* in the *DSM-5*, *idiopathic hypersomnolence disorder* in the *ICD-11*, and *nonorganic hypersomnia* in the *ICD-10*. (14)

Hypnosis: Combines deep relaxation (a *trance* state) with suggestion (requests that hypnotic subjects can follow if they wish to). (8)

Hypoactive sexual desire dysfunction: *ICD-11* diagnosis for men and women who have absent or reduced sexual thoughts, fantasies, or desires. (10)

Hypochondriasis: *ICD-11* diagnosis describing excessive worry about being physically ill, traditionally with the assumption that there is little or no basis for such concern; called *hypochondriacal disorder* in the *ICD-10*. (8)

Hypomanic episode: Shorter version of a manic episode, lasting just a few days. (5)

Hypothalamic-pituitary-adrenal (HPA) axis: Interconnected brain structures that play a role in managing stress and releasing cortisol (the primary stress hormone); appears to be overactive in many cases of depression and perhaps mania. (5)

Hypothalamus: A limbic system brain region that regulates homeostasis (the process of maintaining the status quo for things like body temperature, body weight, fluid balances, and heart rate). (7)

Hypothesis: A prediction we make about how variables will affect one another. (1)

Hysteria: A malady involving numerous psychological and physical symptoms that the ancient Greeks diagnosed exclusively in women. (1)

Iatrogenic condition: A condition or disorder induced when mental health professionals subtly encourage their patients that they have it; sociocognitive theorists claim that dissociative identity disorder is an iatrogenic condition. (8)

ICD: See *International Classification of Diseases (ICD)*

ICD definition of mental disorder: An underlying dysfunction in psychological, biological, or developmental processes that affects cognition, emotional regulation, and behavior. (3)

ICD-11 model of personality disorders: Model of personality disorders in which there is one diagnostic category (*personality disorder*) that is identified as *mild*, *moderate*, or *severe* depending on how someone scores along five personality trait domains (*negative affect*, *detachment*, *dissocial features*, *disinhibition*, and *anankastic features*). (12)

Id: Unconscious psychoanalytic personality structure consisting of the infant's aggressive, selfish, and sexual desires; motivated by the pleasure principle. (2)

Identification with the aggressor: Psychodynamic defense mechanism in which people identify with those who mistreat them and adopt their characteristics. (10)

Identified patient: In family therapy, the family member displaying symptoms who bears the burden of "carrying" the family's pathology. (2)

Identity alteration: Form of dissociation that sometimes accompanies identity confusion, in which a person establishes a new identity in lieu of the old one. (8)

Identity confusion: Form of dissociation in which a person is confused about and/or has a hard time recalling his or her identity. (8)

Illness anxiety disorder: *DSM-5* somatic symptom diagnosis for people who worry about having one or more physical illnesses; differs from the *ICD* diagnosis of *hypochondriasis* by not requiring that those diagnosed with it aren't actually sick. (8)

Illness model of drug addiction: Sees addiction as a disease, not a vice; also called the *medical model of drug addiction*). (11)

Imaginal exposure: Exposure technique in which client is simply asked to imagine the feared scenario to condition a new, non-anxious response to them. (6, 7)

Immune system perspectives: Emphasize the importance of the immune system (the system of cells and biological processes used to fight off pathogens) in understanding psychopathology. (2)

In vivo exposure: Exposure technique in which client is exposed to the actual anxiety-provoking objects or situations in order to condition a new, non-anxious response to them. (6)

In vivo food exposure: Behavioral technique in which *in vivo* exposure is used to change the eating habits of people diagnosed with eating disorders. (9)

Inauthenticity: In existential theory, when one denies responsibility for one's choices. (2)

Incentive-sensitization theory: Theory that drugs cause people to seek them out by increasing sensitivity to dopamine (the "wanting" neurotransmitter), which results in people being more alert and on the lookout for drugs. (11)

Incidence: The number of new cases of a mental disorder that are diagnosed within a specified period. (1)

Incongruence: Rogers' term for when people behave in self-inconsistent ways to maintain conditional positive regard. (2)

Independent variable: The variable the researcher controls; its manipulation should cause a result in the dependent variable. (1)

Indolamine hallucinogens: Drugs that induce hallucinations and heighten emotional sensitivity by activating serotonin receptors in the prefrontal cortex and anterior cingulate cortex; *LSD, DMT,* and *psilocybin* are indolamine hallucinogens. (11)

Indolamines: A type of monoamine neurotransmitter; serotonin is an indolamine. (2)

Inflammatory hypothesis: Postulates that many psychiatric disorders (psychosis, anxiety, mood problems, etc.) may be tied to immune system inflammation. (4)

Informed consent: The process of providing prospective research participants with sufficient information about a study, including why it is being conducted and the risks and benefits of participating. (15)

Inhibitory learning: Classical conditioning term for what occurs during extinction, when new conditioning teaches an organism that a previously conditional stimulus (CS) no longer predicts an unconditioned stimulus (US). (6)

Insanity: Legal term for a mental illness that is so severe that it prevents someone from distinguishing fantasy from reality, conducting daily affairs due to psychosis, or exerting control over behavior. (15)

Insanity defense: A legal plea that challenges criminal responsibility by arguing that a defendant isn't responsible for a crime if suffering from a mental disorder when the crime was committed. (15)

Insanity Defense Reform Act (IDRA): U.S. law that implemented strict federal standards in insanity defense cases, limiting it to cases where the mental defect or disorder was "severe." (15)

Insomnia: Sleep problem involving difficulty falling or staying asleep; called *insomnia disorder* in the *DSM-5, chronic insomnia* in the *ICD-11,* and *nonorganic insomnia* in the *ICD-10.* (14)

Insula: A small area deep within the cerebral cortex that appears to play a role in basic emotions, sense of self, awareness of desires, and awareness of bodily states; excessive insula activity is associated with anxiety. (6)

Insulin coma therapy: Historical treatment for schizophrenia in which insulin injections were used to bring patients in and out of comas daily over several weeks. (1)

Integrated sociodevelopmental-cognitive model of schizophrenia: Asserts that schizophrenia emerges from a circular and mutually influencing interaction among biological, cognitive, and sociocultural factors; genetic vulnerability and social disadvantage/adversity lead to dopamine dysregulation, which produces cognitive misattributions of salience, which yields psychosocial stress, which in turn further impacts dopamine transmission, and so on in an ongoing cycle. (4)

Integrative behavioral couples therapy: A behavioral couples therapy approach to PTSD that teaches emotional acceptance while also using exposure techniques to eliminate interpersonal avoidance. (7)

Integrative evidence-based case formulation: Four step model of formulation in which the steps are (1) create a problem list; (2) make a diagnosis; (3) develop an explanatory hypothesis; and (4) plan treatment. (3)

Intellectual disability: *DSM-5* and *ICD-11* diagnosis made in those who show deficits in intellectual and adaptive functioning that emerge early in development; also called *intellectual developmental disorder* by the *DSM-5* and *ICD-11,* but in the *ICD-10* goes by the now out-of-fashion name *mental retardation.* (14)

Intelligence: Cognitive capacities to acquire knowledge or engage successfully in sensory, perceptual, associative, and relational processes; seen as generally stable over time. (3, 14)

Intelligence quotient (IQ): Mental age (a score reflecting level of performance on an intelligence test) divided by chronological age (how old one is) multiplied by 100. (3)

Intelligence tests: Assessment measures used to evaluate intelligence. (3)

Intentionality: Phenomenological idea that mental events always refer to or "intend" something in the world. (1)

Intermediate beliefs: General rules and beliefs that influence automatic thoughts. (2)

Intermittent explosive disorder: *DSM-5, ICD-10,* and *ICD-11* diagnosis characterized by recurrent aggressive outbursts that are verbal, physical, or both. (13)

Internal family systems therapy (IFS): Systemic approach to thinking about the internal psychological functioning of individuals facing various presenting problems; conceptualizes human personality as a series of "parts" that relate to one another. (8)

Internal validity: The degree to which experimental results are caused by the manipulation of the independent variable. (1)

Internalized homophobia: Hostility of gay men and lesbians toward themselves that they learn from the wider culture. (10)

Internalizing behaviors: Behaviors that do not involve acting out against the environment; social withdrawal, loneliness, depression, anxiety, and difficulty concentrating are examples. (13)

***International Classification of Diseases* (*ICD*)**: Diagnostic manual of the World Health Organization. (3)

Interpersonal and social rhythm therapy (IPSRT): Short-term therapy for bipolar symptoms that uses interpersonal therapy (IPT) techniques to help clients regulate their sleep habits and overcome suspected circadian rhythm disruptions. (5)

Interpersonal PTSD groups/PTSD process groups: emphasize helping group members gain awareness of their feelings and patterns of relating to others; the group setting provides an excellent forum for members to give one another interpersonal feedback. (7)

Interpersonal therapy (IPT): Short-term therapy that focuses on improving relationships to alleviate depression and other presenting problems. (5)

Interrater reliability: Type of diagnostic reliability in which different raters using the same diagnostic system reach the same diagnosis much of the time. (3)

Intersex: People who have atypical physical features that make classifying them as male or female difficult. (10)

Intolerance of uncertainty model: Cognitive explanation of anxiety that sees ongoing anxiety as occurring in those who have difficulty with uncertainty; holds that anxious individuals tend to have a negative problem orientation, see challenges as threatening, and believe that worry is necessary to motivate problem-solving. (6)

Intoxication: Being under the influence of a substance; *DSM-5*, *ICD-10*, and *ICD-11* contain distinct intoxication criteria/ guidelines for each substance they describe. (11)

Intracavernous injection therapy: Injecting drugs into the sex organs to increase blood flow; often done with men who have erectile problems and don't respond to drug treatments. (10)

Involuntary outpatient commitment (IOC): When a person is legally mandated to receive treatment in a community, rather than hospital, setting; also called *outpatient civil commitment*, *compulsory community treatment*, *assisted outpatient treatment*, or *community treatment orders*. (15)

IQ-achievement discrepancy model: Model that uses discrepancies between IQ scores and achievement scores to diagnose learning disabilities. (14)

Irresistible impulse test: Legal test of insanity that says defendants can be acquitted when their crimes are attributable to impulses that they couldn't resist. (15)

Jealous delusions: Delusions in which you are preoccupied with the idea that your partner is cheating on you despite there being no evidence of this. (4)

Kegel exercises: Pelvic floor muscle rehabilitation exercise in which women learn to tighten and relax pelvic floor muscles as a way to strengthen them; used to treat sexual pain disorders such as dyspareunia and vaginismus. (10)

Ketamine: An anesthetic drug that inhibits glutamate and has antidepressant and anti-anxiety effects. (5)

Kleptomania: *DSM-5*, *ICD-10*, and *ICD-11* impulse control disorder that involves impulsive stealing that provides a thrill and isn't done for personal gain; called *pathological stealing* in *ICD-10*. (13)

Korsakoff syndrome: Syndrome resulting from chronic excessive alcohol use involving serious deterioration in short- and long-term memory, as well as inability to recall new information. (11)

La belle indifférence: Term used by Charcot to describe the tendency of patients diagnosed with hysteria to be indifferent to their physical symptoms; suggests these symptoms may serve a psychological purpose. (8)

Lack or loss of sexual desire: *ICD-10* diagnosis for men and women who have little interest in and rarely initiate sex. (10)

Language disorder: *DSM-5* diagnosis made in children who have trouble acquiring and using language. (14)

Latency stage: Fourth stage of psychosexual development, from age 6 to pre-adolescence; a period of relative calm and quiet. (2)

Lateral hypothalamus: Part of the hypothalamus responsible for making people feel hungry and maintaining a state of arousal. (9)

Learned helplessness: Conditioned response in which an organism learns its behavior has no effect on its environment so it stops engaging in that behavior and endures unpleasant situations—even when they can be avoided. (5)

Lesbian: Term referring specifically to female homosexuals. (10)

Level of Personality Functioning Scale (LPFS): A 5-point scale used in the *DSM-5* alternative model for personality disorders; it assesses self-functioning and identity functioning using a scale of "0" (no impairment) to "4" (extreme impairment) that assesses personality. (12)

Levels of personality organization: Component of the S-Axis in *PMD-2* diagnosis; patients are rated on a 10-point scale assessing their level of personality functioning, with "10" being most healthy and "1" being least healthy: *healthy level* (9–10), *neurotic level* (6–8), *borderline level* (3–5), and *psychotic level* (1–2). (12).

Libido: Freudian term for sexual instincts; the drive to seek pleasure and avoid pain. (2)

Lidcombe Program: Behavioral program for stuttering that uses contingency management, in which fluency is praised or acknowledged and stuttering acknowledged or corrected; used with children whose stuttering begins before age 5 and involves training their parents to implement contingency management techniques at home. (14)

Life instinct: Unconscious instinct proposed by Freud that drives people to survive and seek pleasure; also called *Eros*. (15)

Life-history hypothesis: Evolutionary hypothesis that examines how psychosocial and environmental pressures might have influenced how certain groups of people evolved a vulnerability to addiction. (11)

Light therapy: Therapy for those diagnosed with seasonal affective disorder in which patient sits next to a box that projects bright light. (5)

Limbic system: Area of the brain that developed early in human evolution and which contains several structures associated with the regulation of emotion. (2)

Lithium: Metallic mineral salt used as a mood stabilizer to treat bipolar disorders. (5)

Little Albert: The 18-month-old boy who John Watson classically conditioned to fear white rats and other similar objects. (1)

Little Hans: Freud's famous case study of a 5-year-old boy who developed an intense fear of horses; Freud interpreted Hans' phobia as due to unresolved *castration anxiety*. (6)

Lobotomy: Historical treatment for schizophrenia in which the prefrontal cortex was surgically disconnected from the rest of the brain; also called a *leucotomy*. (1)

Logotherapy: Existential treatment method developed by Victor Frankl that emphasizes helping clients find meaning in life. (6)

Long-term care: Ongoing care in a hospital, nursing home, or assisted-living facility. (14)

Loose associations: Form of disorganized psychotic thinking in which a person regularly shifts from topic to topic during everyday conversations; responses to questions are often *tangential* in that they are unrelated to what was asked. (4)

Low-fitness extreme theory: Evolutionary theory of autism that proposes that the ability to "charm" reflects high levels of fitness and that children innately able to charm their parents are more likely to receive attention and care; children with autism are on the low end of the charm trait. (13)

Lowering of diagnostic thresholds: Changes in *DSM* diagnostic criteria resulting in more people qualifying for a diagnosis; its benefits and disadvantages are hotly debated. (3)

Luria-Nebraska Neuropsychological Battery (LNNB): 269-item neuropsychological inventory consisting of 11 clinical scales assessing areas such as reading, writing, math, memory, language, and motor function. (3)

Lycanthropy: The belief that one is possessed by or has been transformed into a wolf; widely reported during the Middle Ages, but occasionally still seen today. (1)

Lymphocytes: White blood cells important in fighting off illness. (8)

M-Axis (Profile of Mental Functioning): *PDM* axis used to evaluate and describe nine categories of mental functioning. (3)

M'Naghten test: Legal test of insanity that says defendants can be acquitted if, at the time their crimes, they were suffering from a disease of the mind that prevented them from understanding the nature of their acts or that these acts were wrong. (15)

Magnetic resonance imaging (MRI): Neuroimaging technique that creates an x-ray-like picture of the brain using the magnetic activity of hydrogen atoms; one kind, the fMRI (functional MRI), tracks oxygen levels in the brain's hemoglobin, allowing assessment of blood flow in various brain areas while the person is thinking, feeling, or completing a task. (3)

Major depressive disorder (MDD): *DSM-5* disorder diagnosed in those who experience one or more major depressive episodes. (5)

Major neurocognitive disorder: *DSM-5* term for cases of severe cognitive decline; this term and minor neurocognitive disorder are now used by the *DSM-5* instead of dementia. (14)

Major tranquilizers: An alternative name for antipsychotic drugs; this name contrasts with minor tranquilizers, which are used to reduce anxiety. (4)

Malarial therapy: 20th-century treatment in which patients were injected with malaria to induce a high fever, which was thought to relieve symptoms of schizophrenia. (1)

Male hypoactive sexual desire disorder: *DSM-5* diagnosis for men who show minimal interest in sex. (10)

Malingering: Term used to describe people who are "just faking" symptoms, typically to gain something, such as disability benefits or being relieved of responsibilities at work. (8)

Malleus Maleficarum: A book written by monks Heinrich Kramer and James Sprenger during the Middle Ages that examined witchcraft and demonic possession; reflected the demonological perspective on abnormality. (1)

Mania: Characterized by euphoric mood, boundless energy, and a sometimes-distorted sense of one's capabilities. (5)

Mania without delusion: Phillipe Pinel's term for patients who showed no overt symptoms of madness (they weren't hallucinatory, delusional, or incoherent), but who were prone to emotional outbursts such as fits of temper or impulsive violence; *manie sans délire* in the original French. (12)

Manic episode: One week or more of persistently elevated mood accompanied by high energy and intense goal-directed activity; often involves inflated self-esteem, grandiosity, decreased need for sleep, extreme talkativeness, racing thoughts, distractibility, and impulsive/risky behavior. (5)

MAO inhibitors (MAOIs): Type of antidepressant that works by inhibiting monoamine oxidase (MAO), a brain enzyme that breaks down excess monoamine neurotransmitters; this leaves more monoamine neurotransmitters available. (5)

Masturbatory satiation: Behavioral technique in which the client is asked to masturbate to paraphilic imagery for a much longer time than is pleasurable as a way to associate the paraphilia with boredom. (10)

Matched control groups: A control group whose participants are selected to make sure the control group is comparable to the experimental group participants along various confounding variables (such as age, socioeconomic status, ethnicity, etc.); often used in quasi-experiments to compensate for the fact that random assignment isn't possible. (1)

Medial prefrontal cortex: Brain region important in memory and decision-making; may be underresponsive in patients diagnosed with PTSD. (7)

Medical 203: Diagnostic nomenclature developed by the U.S. Army and Surgeon General during World War II; direct predecessor of the *DSM*. (3)

Medical model: Model of abnormality holding that presenting problems are caused by physiological malfunctions; the medical model organizes presenting problems into categories that are thought to reflect underlying biological illnesses. (1)

Medicalization: Inappropriately classifying non-medical problems as medical. (1)

Melancholia: Term traceable to Ancient Greece that described those experiencing seemingly baseless sadness and fear, but sometimes other symptoms such as hallucinations. (1)

Memo writing: Grounded theory method in which the researcher writes down analytical reactions to the data to help shape the emerging understanding of the topic. (1)

Menopause: The time in life when a woman's menstrual cycle ends (usually in her 40s or 50s) and estrogen levels decrease. (10)

Mental disorder: Defined by the American Psychiatric Association as a syndrome characterized by clinically significant disturbance in a person's cognition, emotional regulation, or behavior reflecting a dysfunction in psychological, biological, or developmental processes. (1)

Mental illness: Defined by the American Psychiatric Association as an illness affecting or located in a person's brain that affects how a person thinks, behaves, and interacts with other people. (1)

Mental retardation: *ICD-10* term for intellectual disability; this term is now out-of-fashion in most settings, but because the *ICD-10* was published more than two decades ago, it still includes this term. (14)

Mental status exam: Type of structured clinical interview used to assess a person's current mental status; data is gathered about the person's appearance, attitude, and activity; mood and affect; speech and language; thought processes, thought content, and perception; cognition; and insight and judgment. (3)

Mercyism: Another name for rumination in humans; used in past historic eras. (9)

Mesolimbic dopamine pathway: Part of the brain's reward system that connects the ventral tegmental area (VTA) to the nucleus accumbens; implicated in addiction and psychosis. (4)

Mesolimbic pathway: Brain pathway important in responding to rewards. (9)

Metacognition: The ability to think about one's thinking. (4)

Metacognitive model: Cognitive explanation of anxiety that focuses on how people think about worrying; hypothesizes that people hold both positive and negative beliefs about worry. (6)

Methadone maintenance therapy: Drug replacement therapy in which synthetic opioids (usually *methadone* or *buprenorphine*) are substituted for heroin in order to maintain heroin addicts on what most people consider a less problematic drug. (11)

Method restriction: Suicide prevention strategy in which access to common ways that people kill themselves is limited or made more difficult. (15)

Methylphenidate: Stimulant drug prescribed for attention-deficit/hyperactivity disorder; marketed as Ritalin. (13)

Microglia: Support cells in the brain important in immune response; those of alcoholics look noticeably different than those of healthy people, suggesting a genetic vulnerability to substance use problems. (11)

Mild personality disorder: Diagnosis in the *ICD-11*'s dimensional model of personality disorders; for those who show notable problems in interpersonal relationships, but social and occupational functioning involve minimal harm to self and others. (12)

Mindblindness: Baron-Cohen's idea that people with autism don't have the evolved capacity for theory of mind (the ability to view the world through others' eyes in order to attribute thoughts and feelings to them). (13)

Mindfulness-based cognitive therapy (MBCT): Combines mindfulness training (in which client is taught to simply observe and be aware of thoughts) with cognitive therapy in treating depression. (5)

Mindfulness-based stress reduction (MBSR): A variation of mindfulness-based cognitive therapy that facilitates awareness of one's thoughts without trying to influence or stop them; used to reduce stress associated with psychosomatic illness. (8)

Mindfulness training: Zen Buddhist-influenced technique in which people are taught to simply observe and be aware of their thoughts (as opposed to trying to stop or change them). (5, 6)

Minnesota Multiphasic Personality Inventory (MMPI): 567-item objective self-report personality inventory used to assess the total personality; contains ten clinical scales plus validity scales to determine if test-taker is faking good or bad. (3)

Minor neurocognitive disorder: *DSM-5* term for cases of mild cognitive decline; this term and major neurocognitive disorder are now used by the *DSM-5* instead of dementia. (14)

Minor tranquilizers: An alternative name for benzodiazepines; this name is in contrast to major tranquilizers, another name for antipsychotic drugs. (6)

Mismatch hypothesis: Evolutionary hypothesis that drug addiction is an accidental by-product of how our brains evolved; today's more potent drugs happen to interfere with evolved brain pathways, something our brains haven't evolved to handle. (11)

Misperception of reality: Criterion that defines abnormality in terms of a person's inability to perceive things realistically; questions about whose perceptions best reflect reality pose the biggest challenge for using this criterion. (1)

Mixed anxiety and depressive disorder: Proposed *DSM-5* and official *ICD-11* diagnosis for people who display symptoms of both depression and anxiety for two weeks or more, but whose symptoms don't qualify them for other mood or anxiety disorders. (6)

Mixed episode: *ICD*-only mood episode in which manic and depressive symptoms rapidly alternate or co-occur for at least two weeks; replaced with "with mixed features" specifier in *DSM-5*. (5)

Mixed methods: Approach to research in which qualitative and quantitative research methods are combined in studying a specific issue. (1)

Modafinil: A non-stimulant wake-promoting drug used to reduce sleepiness. (14)

Model penal code test: Legal test of insanity that combines aspects of the M'Naghten and irresistible impulse tests; says defendants can be acquitted if, at the time of their crimes, they had a mental disorder that prevented them from either (a) having substantial capacity to appreciate the wrongfulness of their actions, or (b) controlling their behavior; also called the *American Law Institute test* or *ALI test*. (15)

Modeling: Indirect form of exposure in which the therapist models the aversive behavior for the client, demonstrating that the fear is unjustified. (4)

Moderate personality disorder: Diagnosis in the *ICD-11*'s dimensional model of personality disorders; for those whose social and occupational functioning are somewhat compromised with past and future harm to self and others expected, but not severely damaging. (12)

Moderation Management (MM): Controlled drinking self-help group in which members generally don't identify as alcoholics; drinking is viewed as a learned behavior (not a disease) and controlled drinking is deemed an appropriate goal. (11)

Monoamine hypothesis: Hypothesis that depression is due to a shortage of the monoamine neurotransmitters serotonin, norepinephrine, and dopamine. (5)

Monoamine oxidase (MAO): Brain enzyme that breaks down excess monoamine neurotransmitters in the synapses between neurons. (5)

Monoamine oxidase (MAO) inhibitors: See *MAO inhibitors*.

Monoamines: Chemical compounds derived from ammonia; norepinephrine, serotonin, and dopamine are monoamine neurotransmitters. (2)

Monozygotic twins: Identical twins that come from a single fertilized egg that split in two; they share the same genes. (4)

Mood stabilizers: Various types of drugs used to treat manic symptoms of bipolar disorder. (5)

Moral insanity: James Cowles Prichard's 18th-century precursor to *DSM-5*'s antisocial personality disorder, characterized by impulsive, violent, and depraved behavior, but without more florid symptoms of madness. (12)

Moral model of drug addiction: Sees excessive drug-taking as a vice of the morally weak. (11)

Moral therapy: An early treatment for abnormality in which the provision of a warm and nurturing environment was used to help people overcome madness (also called *moral treatment*). (1)

Morphine: A natural opioid derived from opium with more powerful painkilling qualities than opium. (11)

Motivational interviewing (MI): Humanistic technique rooted in person-centered theory that helps people recognize and do something about pressing problems. (11)

MRI: See *magnetic resonance imaging (MRI)*.

Multicultural perspectives: Hold that what is considered abnormal often is a function of culture and that clinicians must be aware of how cultural differences impact their work with clients. (2)

Multidimensional family therapy: Family therapy intervention for adolescents with substance issues; addresses individual, family, and social circumstances that contribute to substance abuse. (11)

Multifamily group psychoeducation: Various families are brought together in a group format to share stories and provide one another with support. (7)

Multigenerational family therapy: Bowen's approach to family therapy, which stresses how families pass dysfunctional patterns down across generations. (2)

Multigenerational transmission process: The process by which families pass their dysfunctional patterns down from generation to generation. (2)

Multiple personality disorder: *ICD-10* name for dissociative identity disorder; this name used to be used by *DSM* too but was replaced with DID in both *DSM-5* and *ICD-11*. (8)

Multisystemic therapy (MST): Systems treatment for externalizing behavior problems that sees disruptive behaviors as collectively determined by the multiple social systems in which children and adolescents function (home, school, peer groups, and neighborhoods). (13)

Munchausen syndrome: Another name for factitious disorder. (8)

Muscle dysmorphia: A type of body dysmorphia in which (mostly) males obsessively worry that they aren't muscular enough. (9)

Music education: Treatment for dyslexia that tries to reduce reading problems by improving musical skills; based on the idea that phonological awareness is correlated with musical abilities. (14)

Musterbating: REBT term for the irrational belief that certain things must be a certain way or life can't go on. (2)

Mutualism hypothesis: Evolutionary hypothesis that people evolved a taste for drugs as they used them over many millennia. (11)

N-acetylcysteine: Drug to treat addiction that reduces cravings by targeting glutamate; has fewer side effects than acamprosate, but mixed effectiveness. (11)

Naltrexone: Opioid antagonist that may reduce dissociation. (8)

Narcissistic personality disorder (NPD): *DSM-5* diagnosis for people who exhibit grandiosity in that they think of themselves as extremely important; characterized by an inflated sense of self and a desperate need for admiration. (12)

Narcolepsy: Sleep problem characterized by periods of unexpected and uncontrollable sleepiness, often resulting in abrupt lapses into sleep; often accompanied by *cataplexy*. (14)

Narrative therapy: Constructivist therapy in which clients are asked to examine and revise the stories they tell about their lives. (2)

Natal gender: One's birth sex. (10)

Natural killer (NK) cells: Lymphocytes important in fighting off viral infections and tumors. (8)

Negative appraisals theory: Hypothesizes that people develop symptoms of posttraumatic stress when they process past traumatic events in a manner that produces an ongoing sense of threat; they interpret the external world as dangerous and come to see themselves as damaged and no longer able to function effectively. (7)

Negative correlation: As one variable increases, the other decreases. (1)

Negative emotionality (NEM): The tendency toward negative moods such as anger, anxiety, and depression. (7)

Negative punishment: Something desirable is removed after a behavior, making that behavior less likely in the future. (2)

Negative reinforcement: Something undesirable is removed after a behavior, making that behavior more likely in the future. (2)

Negative symptoms: Things detracted from the personality in psychosis; symptoms such as diminished emotional expression, flattened affect, avolition, algoia, anhedonia, and asociality. (4)

Neighborhood-based projects: Projects undertaken by mental health professionals that involve working with local politicians, community and business-leaders, the police, and community members to collaboratively identify and address neighborhood issues that contribute to disruptive behavior problems in clients. (13)

Neurasthenia: Diagnosis popular during the late 19th and early 20th centuries that was given to sad and anxious people whose nervous systems were thought to be exhausted. (5)

Neurodiversity: Emphasizes that those carrying diagnoses like autism and ADHD are neurologically different, not disordered. (13)

Neurofibrillary tangles: Twisting of tau protein fibers that help neurons keep their shape and allow them to transmit nutrients; these tangles are common in patients with Alzheimer's disease. (14)

Neuroimaging techniques: Neurological measures that photograph brain activity, such as *positron-emission topography (PET scan)* and *magnetic resonance imaging (MRI)*. (3)

Neurological tests: Physiological tests that measure brain functioning directly. (3)

Neurons: Brain cells that communicate with one another both electrically and chemically. (2)

Neuropsychological tests: Psychological tests used to evaluate perceptual, cognitive, and motor skills; often used to infer underlying brain dysfunction. (3)

Neurosis: In psychoanalytic theory, occurs when the ego is overwhelmed in its efforts to balance id impulses, superego demands, and external reality constraints. (2)

Neurotic anxiety: Pathological anxiety that occurs in people who refuse to acknowledge existential givens that demand they invest their lives with meaning. (6)

Neurotransmitters: Brain chemicals involved in neural communication. (2)

Neurotypicals: People without autism or other neurodevelopmental diagnoses. (13)

New View: Feminist and humanistic social justice perspective on female sexual problems that critiques medical model approach and instead divides female sexual problems into four types: (1) *sexual problems due to sociocultural, political or economic factors*; (2) *sexual problems relating to partner and relationship*; (3) *sexual problems due to psychological factors*; and (4) *sexual problems due to medical factors*. (10)

Nicotine replacement therapy: Drug replacement therapy used in smoking cessation in which the delivery method is changed in an effort to make weaning off nicotine easier; gum, patches, lozenges, and e-cigarettes are examples of alternative delivery methods. (11)

Nicotine: A stimulant found in tobacco leaves that is most commonly consumed by smoking it in cigarettes or pipes. (11)

Night eating syndrome: Characterized by waking up during the night and eating excessively; diagnosed in *DSM-5* using the other specified feeding or eating disorder category. (9)

Nightmare disorder: A *DSM-5* and *ICD-11* parasomnia diagnosed in those who regularly have vivid and upsetting dreams in which their safety, security, or survival is at risk; called *nightmares* in the *ICD-10*. (14)

No correlation: There is no relationship between the variables in a correlational study. (1)

No-suicide contracts: Suicide prevention technique in which suicidal clients are asked to explicitly state that they will not hurt themselves for an agreed-upon amount of time, ranging from a few hours or days or until the next therapy or crisis-intervention session. (15)

Nomenclature: Any system of names used in a field of study; in abnormal psychology, refers to diagnostic nomenclatures. (3)

Non-benzodiazepine sleep aids: Drugs that enhance GABA activity and promote sleep; sometimes referred to as the *Z drugs*, they include drugs marketed under names like Ambien and Sonata. (14)

Non-bizarre delusions: Delusions that don't seem outlandish, such as believing others are spying on you. (4)

Non-rapid eye movement (NREM) sleep: Sleep in which there is little or no eye movement and dreaming is extremely rare. (14)

Non-rapid eye movement (NREM) sleep arousal disorder: A *DSM-5* parasomnia in which sleep is disrupted by sleepwalking or sleep terrors. (14)

Nonsteroidal anti-inflammatory drugs (NSAIDs): Drugs being researched for use in reducing depression based on the inflammatory hypothesis. (5)

Nonsuicidal self-injury disorder (NSSI): Proposed *DSM-5* disorder that involves deliberately injuring oneself, but without suicidal intent; in *ICD-11*, it is coded not as a disorder, but as a mental or behavioral symptom or sign and called *non-suicidal self-injury*. (15)

Noradrenaline: Name of norepinephrine when it is secreted as a hormone in the endocrine system. (10)

Norepinephrine: An excitatory neurotransmitter associated with anxiety and depression. (2)

Norepinephrine-dopamine reuptake inhibitors (NDRIs): Drugs that block reuptake of norepinephrine and dopamine, leaving more available; *bupropion* is an NDRI. (9)

Normalization: CBT technique used for psychosis in which the therapist explains that what the client is experiencing is more common than the client thinks. (4)

Not criminally responsible on account of mental disorder (NCRMD): Legal verdict in Canada that replaces not guilty by reason of insanity (NGBRI); says offenders can be held not criminally responsible when they are unable to either (a) appreciate the nature or quality of the act, or (b) know it was wrong. (15)

Not guilty by reason of insanity (NGBRI): Legal plea used in insanity defense cases. (15)

Nucleotides: Chemical compounds (*adenine, cytosine, guanine*, and *thymine*) that together constitute DNA. (2)

Nucleus accumbens: Brain area implicated in reward processing and addictive behavior. (2)

Nuremburg Code: A set of 10 research principles intended to protect the rights of research participants; *informed consent* is the first principle. (15)

OARS: Acronym for the humanistic therapy strategies used in motivational interviewing: *use open questions, affirm, reflect,* and *summarize*; these strategies are used to help elicit change talk in clients. (11)

Obesity: According to the World Health Organization, extremely high body mass index (greater than 30). (9)

Object: In object relations theory, any person or thing for which someone develops an internal mental representation, known as an *introjection*. (2)

Object relations therapy: Refers to a loose cluster of psychodynamic therapies that emphasize how early attachment relationships with caregivers lead to psychologically internalized expectations, which result in recurring patterns of interacting with others later in life; these patterns are worked through and changed using the patient–therapist relationship. (2)

Objectification: When the female body is looked at and evaluated primarily based on its appearance; key term in objectification theory. (9)

Objectification theory: Theory that holds that media images present women as sexual objects to be judged based on their looks; this leads women to objectify their bodies and makes them more vulnerable to body image and eating issues. (9)

Objective test: Test that uses standardized items with limited response choices (e.g., multiple choice, "true/false," or "yes/no"); self-report personality inventories are objective tests. (3)

Objective/universal/legal views: Views that see certain psychological experiences as abnormal across history, regardless of how they might have been explained at the time; certain states are pathological no matter the historical context. (1)

Observational learning: Process by which people learn behavioral and emotional reactions by watching other people model responses to situations. (6)

Obsessions: Persistent thoughts, images, or urges that are hard to dismiss or stop thinking about. (6)

Obsessive trait complex hypothesis: Holds that obsessive-compulsive personality disorder traits are innate and that these traits (e.g., anxiety, compulsive conscientiousness, miserliness, and an ever-present sense of urgency) are what allowed early humans who migrated to colder and more inhospitable climates to survive. (12)

Obsessive-compulsive disorder (OCD): *DSM-5, ICD-10*, and *ICD-11* disorder marked by the presence of obsessions and compulsions. (6)

Obsessive-compulsive personality disorder (OCPD): *DSM-5* diagnosis for people disproportionately focused on orderliness, rules, and control; these people are excessively perfectionistic and rigid, to the point that it interferes with their functioning. (12)

Oedipus complex: Occurs at phallic stage in boys; the little boy wants mom for himself; *castration anxiety* occurs when the boy fears father finding out; ends when little boy identifies with dad and represses the experience; results in superego. (2)

Olfactory aversion: Aversion therapy in which an unpleasant odor is self-administered in order to associate it with an undesired sexual activity. (10)

Onanism: Diagnostic term describing non-procreative sexual activities such as masturbation, which were often associated with psychopathology in the 18th century. Illustrates how social norms and values can change over time when it comes to defining abnormality. (1)

Open Dialogue: A community-care approach rooted in narrative and dialogical theories that aims to create a support network that can intervene and assist the person experiencing psychosis. (4)

Operant conditioning: Behavioral approach focused on how the consequences of behavior (reinforcement of punishment) influence whether it is likely to be repeated in the future. (2)

Opioid antagonists: Drugs traditionally used to treat substance addiction; they bond to opioid receptors, preventing other opioid substances (such as heroin) from doing the same. (8)

Opioid blockers: Prescription drugs that ward off cravings by inhibiting the body's pleasurable response to addictive substances; commonly used in alcohol dependence and methadone maintenance therapy; *Naloxone, naltrexone,* and *nalmefene* are opioid blockers (trade names *Narcan, Vivitrol,* and *Selincro*). (11)

Opioids: Natural, synthetic, or semisynthetic drugs that depress the central nervous system and serve as powerful painkillers; highly addictive, they mimic the endogenous opioids created naturally by our bodies (also called *opiates* and *narcotics*). (11)

Opium: A natural opioid found in the sap of opium poppy plants. (11)

Oppositional defiant disorder (ODD): *DSM-5*, *ICD-10*, and *ICD-11* diagnosis given to children who are angry, argumentative, defiant, and vindictive. (13)

Oral impregnation: Psychodynamic conceptualization of eating disorders in which patients have an unconscious Oedipal wish to become pregnant by oral means. (9)

Oral stage: First stage of psychosexual development, from birth to age 1½, when id impulses are best satisfied through activities involving the mouth; fixation at this stage results in issues with autonomy and dependence. (2)

Orbitofrontal cortex: Brain area that plays a role in decision-making. (2)

Orexin: A neurotransmitter that plays a role in regulating wakefulness and appetite. (14)

Orexin-receptor antagonists: Drugs that block the activity of the wake-promoting neurotransmitter orexin, thereby promoting sleep; *suvoxerant* was the first orexin-receptor antagonist approved for use in the United States. (14)

Organismic valuing process: Rogers' term for the innate ability to seek experiences that enhance them and avoid those that don't. (2)

Orgasmic dysfunction: *ICD-10* diagnosis for men and women who experience absent, infrequent, or diminished orgasms; called *anorgasmia* in *ICD-11*. (10)

Orthorexia nervosa: Proposed mental disorder characterized by preoccupation with healthy eating. (9)

Other specified feeding or eating disorder: *DSM-5* category for those who don't meet full criteria for any other feeding or eating disorder diagnosis, but who show symptoms warranting a diagnosis. (9)

Overcorrection: Behavioral technique in which an undesired behavior is punished by requiring the person to repeatedly engage in an opposite kind of behavior. (9)

Oxycodone: A semisynthetic opioid that is less habit-forming than heroin and is typically a controlled rather than illegal substance; used as a pain reliever, it is the main ingredient in drugs marketed under names like *Percocet* and *OxyContin*. (11)

Oxytocin: An amino acid produced by the hypothalamus that functions as both a neurotransmitter and a hormone; plays a role in sex and reproduction (by stimulating labor and breastfeeding) and is also linked to social behavior. (13)

P-Axis (Personality Syndromes): *PDM* axis used to map healthy and disordered personality functioning; includes four levels of personality organization and 12 personality syndromes. (3)

Palilalia: Speech problem involving repeating other's words. (14)

PANDAS hypothesis: Holds that tics develop in genetically susceptible individuals who contract strep throat or other viruses; full name of this hypothesis is the *Pediatric Autoimmune Neuropsychiatric Disorders Associated with Streptococcal Infection hypothesis*. (14)

Panic attack: An intense anxiety reaction that comes on abruptly; symptoms include pounding heart, trembling, shortness of breath, chest pain, nausea, dizziness, feeling chilled or hot, tingling sensations, and detachment from self or world. (6)

Panic disorder: *DSM-5*, *ICD-10*, and *ICD-11* disorder characterized by recurrent and unexpected panic attacks. (6)

Paranoid personality disorder: *DSM-5* and *ICD-10* diagnosis for people who tend to be unjustifiably superstitious of others; they have difficulty trusting others and worry that others are trying to exploit, harm, or deceive them. (12)

Paraphilia: Sexual impulses, fantasies, and behaviors directed toward unusual (and sometimes socially taboo) objects and situations. (10)

Paraphilic coercive disorder: Controversial proposed *DSM* disorder in which ongoing fantasies of and repeated acts of rape are considered a paraphilia. (10)

Paraphilic disorders: In *DSM-5* and *ICD-11*, term for pathological paraphilias that are considered disordered because they either impair or distress the person engaging in them or they cause (or run the risk of causing) harm. (10)

Parasomnias: Sleep disturbances involving undesired events or experiences during sleep; parasomnias include sleepwalking, sleep terrors, nightmares, or acting out dreams. (14)

Parasuicidal behavior: Self-harm inflicted less because one wants to die and more to manipulate others, communicate distress, or regulate emotions. (12)

Parasympathetic nervous system (PNS): Branch of the autonomic nervous system that counters the sympathetic nervous system, slowing down breathing and heart rates, normalizing pupils, reestablishing hunger, and lowering blood pressure. (7)

Parens patriae: Legal concept that says the state can restrict the freedom of children and people deemed mentally incompetent; it is Latin for "state as parent." (15)

Parent management training: Teaches PTSD patients and their partners effective parenting techniques. (7)

Parietal cortex: Brain region involved in movement, attention, and spatial processing. (8)

Participant modeling: Type of modeling wherein the client is invited to partake in the anxiety-provoking activity with the therapist. (6)

Participants: The people who partake in an experiment; also called *subjects*. (1)

Pathogens: Foreign bodies that cause disease (e.g., viruses, bacteria, parasites, and cancer cells); pathogens can compromise the immune system. (2)

Pathological gambling: *ICD-10* habit and impulse disorder for those with chronic gambling issues; comparable to *gambling disorder* in *DSM-5* and *ICD-11*, but—unlike in those manuals—it is not identified as a behavioral addiction in *ICD-10*. (11)

Pedophilia/pedophilic disorder: Paraphilic disorder involving sexual fantasies, urges, or behaviors related to sexual involvement with preteen children. (10)

Pelvic floor rehabilitation: Behavior-based technique to improve sexual interest in which the patient is assigned physical exercises (such as Kegel exercises) to strengthen weak pelvic floor muscles associated with issues such as dyspareunia and vaginismus. (10)

Persecutory delusions: Delusions in which you believe you are being unfairly treated or pursued by others; also known as *paranoid delusions*. (4)

Persistent (chronic) motor or vocal tic disorder: *DSM* disorder in which a person displays either motor or vocal tics—but not both—for over a year; *ICD-10* and *ICD-11* contain equivalent diagnoses. (14)

Persistent complex bereavement disorder: Proposed for people who have a difficult time getting over the loss of a loved one; characterized by intense grief for an extended period of time and difficulty moving on with life; also called *persistent grief*, *complicated grief*, *pathological grief*, or (in *ICD-11*, where it is a recognized disorder) *prolonged grief*. (7)

Persistent depressive disorder (PDD): *DSM-5* disorder diagnosed in those who experience chronic depression and may or may not also meet criteria for a depressive episode; related to, but different in some respects from, the *ICD-10* and *ICD-11* diagnoses of *dysthymia* and *dysthymic disorder*. (5)

Person-centered play therapy: See *child-centered play therapy*.

Person-centered therapy: Rogers' humanistic and non-directive therapy in which therapists provide core conditions for change (empathy, genuineness, and unconditional positive regard) and in so doing help clients get back on a path toward self-actualization. (2)

Personality: Stable and characteristic patterns of thinking, feeling, behaving, and interacting with others. (3)

Personality disorder: When one's constellation of personality traits, or character, consistently leads to interpersonal conflict and difficulty in daily functioning. (12)

Personality disorder-trait specified: Proposed diagnosis in the *DSM-5* alternative model for personality disorders; used for people who don't meet the trait-based criteria for any of the other six personality disorder categories in the alternative model system. (12)

Personality Inventory for the *DSM-5* (PID-5): A self-report inventory used to assess pathological trait domains in the *DSM-5* alternative model for personality disorders; 220-item, 100-item, and 25-item versions currently available. (12)

Personality test: Any test that measures emotions, interpersonal relationship patterns, levels of motivation and interest, and attitudes; includes self-report inventories and projective tests. (3)

Pervasive developmental disorders: *DSM-IV* and *ICD-10* term for disorders that develop early in life and that are characterized by impaired social skills, communication problems, and repetitive/ritualized behavior; autism and its variations were considered pervasive developmental disorders. (13)

Pervasive developmental disorder-NOS (PDD-NOS): *DSM-IV* diagnosis for patients with autism-like symptoms who didn't fit neatly into the autism or Asperger's disorder categories. (13)

Perversions: Old-fashioned term for paraphilias preferred by psychodynamic therapist Robert Stoller, who saw them as acts of revenge intended to compensate for profound humiliation during childhood. (10)

PET scan: See *positron-emission topography (PET scan)*.

Phallic stage: Third stage of psychosexual development, from ages 3 to 5; Oedipus/Electra complex occurs, leading to formation of the superego; fixation at this stage results in narcissistic, proud, competitive, and vain personality traits. (2)

Phencyclidine: A hallucinogen with hallucinogenic, depressant, and even some stimulant properties; reduces influence of glutamate while enhancing effects of dopamine. (11)

Phenomenological methods: Qualitative research approaches rooted in the phenomenological research tradition; the idea is to describe the essence of something by setting aside one's biases and preconceptions and studying conscious experience. (1)

Phenomenological reduction: Consists of two parts: (a) bracketing preconceptions, and (b) allowing objects in the world to "present" themselves to us so we can interpretively describe and make sense of them. (1)

Phenotype: A person's actual properties and psychological traits; the physical and psychological traits a person has developed because of genetic and environmental influences. (2)

Phenylalkylamine hallucinogens: Produce both hallucinogenic and stimulant effects by affecting norepinephrine, dopamine, and serotonin receptors; *mescaline* and *DOM* are phenylalkylamine hallucinogens. (11)

Phenylketonuria (PKU): Rare inherited disease in which babies are born deficient in the liver enzyme, phenylalanine hydroxylase, resulting in the inability to break down phenylalanine and phenylpyruvic acid; this leads to brain damage and intellectual impairment. (14)

Phosphodiesterase type-5 inhibitor: Drug that inhibits the chemical enzyme *phosphodiesterase type-5 (PED5)*; PDE5 breaks down *cyclic guanosine monophosphate (cGMP)*, which increases blood flow to the sex organs; by reducing PDE5, therefore, blood flow to sex organs is increased. (10)

Pica: *DSM-5*, *ICD-10*, and *ICD-11* disorder involving the eating of nonfood substances. (9)

Picture Exchange Communication System (PECS): Applied behavior analysis (ABA) technique for children with communication difficulties in which the children learn to communicate using picture cards. (13)

Placebo control group: A control group that gets an activity that is comparable to the treatment, but not the treatment. (1)

Placebo effect: Occurs when placebo control group activity induces results like those expected from the treatment group; in drug studies, it is when participants who receive an inert pill (often a sugar pill) show improvement despite not receiving the active ingredient being tested. (1)

Pleasure principle: Guiding principle that rules the id; consists of the desire to experience pleasure and avoid pain. (2)

Police power: The state's legal authority to confine people who pose a danger to society. (15)

Polydrug use: When drug users take more than one substance. (11)

Polygenic: When multiple genes are implicated in the expression of a trait; in abnormal psychology, most of the psychological problems discussed are polygenic, meaning there are numerous genes that contribute to them. (2)

Polypharmacy: The practice of prescribing multiple drugs at the same time. (12)

Polyunsaturated fatty acids (PUFA) hypothesis: Proposes that ADHD is caused or exacerbated by polyunsaturated fat deficiencies. (13)

Population: All people of a given class; for instance, all people suffering from depression. (1)

Positive correlation: As one variable increases, so does the other. (1)

Positive punishment: Something undesirable is added after a behavior, making that behavior less likely in the future. (2)

Positive reinforcement: Something desirable is added after a behavior, making that behavior more likely in the future. (2)

Positive symptoms: Additions to the personality that occur in psychosis; hallucinations and delusions are examples; also called *Type I symptoms*. (4)

Positron-emission topography (PET scan): Neuroimaging technique in which radioactive isotopes are placed in the bloodstream and gamma rays are used to generate images reflecting changes in cerebral blood flow; allows assessment of which brain areas are active during a given task. (3)

Post-hypnotic suggestion: A suggestion made during hypnosis that is obeyed when no longer hypnotized. (8)

Postpartum depression: Diagnosis describing depression that develops in women who are pregnant or have given birth within the last four weeks. (5)

Posttraumatic Growth (PTG): Positive changes following crises, traumas, losses, and other stressful events. (7)

Posttraumatic model: Holds that somatic and dissociative symptoms are usually tied to stressful or traumatizing life events; also called the *traumagenic position*. (8)

Posttraumatic stress disorder (PTSD): *DSM-5*, *ICD-10*, and *ICD-11* disorder diagnosed in people who, following a traumatic event, experience significant psychological difficulty for an extended period. (7)

Power hierarchies: In family therapy, when some coalitions dominate others in detrimental ways. (2)

Power Threat Meaning (PTM) Framework: Psychosocial alternative to traditional diagnosis, which attributes distress to economic and social injustice, not individual disorders; maps three elements that contribute to distress: *power* (what happened to a person; how the person had power used against them), *threat* (a person's response to what happened), and *meaning* (how a person makes sense of what happened). (3)

Pre-therapy: Version of client-centered therapy specifically for use with psychotic individuals; goal is to make *psychological contact* with the psychotic client as a necessary pre-condition for effective therapy. (4)

Preconscious: Unrepressed memories currently out of awareness; can easily be made conscious if focused on. (2)

Prefrontal cortex: Brain area important in decision-making, emotional regulation, goal-oriented behavior, and speech. (4)

Premature (early) ejaculation: *DSM-5*, *ICD-10*, and *ICD-11* diagnosis for men who ejaculate too soon. (10)

Premenstrual dysphoric disorder (PMDD): *DSM-5* and *ICD-11* disorder diagnosed in women who show depressive symptoms during the week before their menstrual periods. (5)

Prepared conditioning: Conditioning that is easier to accomplish because the organism is evolutionarily predisposed to it. (6)

Presenting problems: The problems for which clients request help when consulting with mental health professionals. Presenting problems may or may not ultimately be the primary focus of treatment. (1)

Prevalence: Percentage of people in the population believed to currently suffer from a specific mental disorder. (1)

Prevention and early intervention programs: Programs designed to prevent or intervene in the early stages of substance use. (11)

Primary enuresis: Enuresis in which the child has never attained bladder control. (14)

Primary gain: The reason for a symptom; the central (or *primary*) conflict the symptom is intended to address. (8)

Primary insomnia: Prior to *DSM-5*, a diagnosis given when insomnia occurred in the absence of another medical or psychiatric disorder. (14)

Primary psychopathy: Psychopathy attributed entirely to biology. (12)

Privilege: Legal rule that holds certain relationships are protected, meaning that those in them are exempt from being legally compelled to share what was confided in the context of that relationship. (15)

Problem Behavior Questionnaire (PBQ): A 15-item behavioral assessment scale that asks questions about the target behavior; people completing it rate the percentage of the time the behavior occurs (never, 10%, 25%, 50%, 75%, 90%, or always). (3)

Problem-solving skills training: Type of behavioral skills training that teaches planning, organization, and management skills. (13)

Problem-solving therapy: Cognitive-behavioral therapy (CBT) approach in which therapist helps client define specific problems and then generate solutions that can be implemented. (5)

Problems in living: Thomas Szasz's term for the problems that people encounter in daily life that are often incorrectly, in his view, identified as mental illnesses. (1)

Progesterone: Female sex hormone important in menstruation and pregnancy. (10)

Progestin: A synthetic hormone that has effects similar to the female sex hormone progesterone; sometimes prescribed to address low sexual desire in women. (10)

Progressive relaxation: Technique often used in systematic desensitization wherein the client is taught to alternately relax and tense each muscle in the body. (6)

Projective identification: Object relations theory term referring to the tendency of people to project unwanted and split-off feelings about themselves onto others, including their therapists. (2)

Projective test: Test in which responses to some form of artistic representation are used to infer aspects of psychological functioning. (3)

Prolonged grief disorder: *ICD-11* diagnosis for people who have a difficult time getting over the loss of a loved one; characterized by intense grief for an extended period of time and difficulty moving on with life; also called *persistent grief*, *complicated grief*, *pathological grief*, or (in *DSM-5*) *persistent complex bereavement*. (7)

Prototype model: Diagnostic approach that provides general guidelines describing a syndrome, which clinicians use impressionistically to make a diagnosis; used in *ICD*. (3)

Provisional tic disorder: *DSM-5* diagnosis in which a person displays motor and/or verbal tics, but for less than one year; called *transient tic disorder* in the *ICD-10* and divided into *transient phonic tic disorder* and *transient motor tic disorder* in *ICD-11*. (14)

Pseudopatient study: Rosenhan's classic study in which eight people faking auditory hallucinations (pseudopatients) sought admission at 12 hospitals; all were admitted and none were discovered as impostors; controversial to this day, but raises issues about the validity of psychiatric diagnosis. (3)

Psychache: Schneidman's term for the intense psychological hurt, pain, and anguish that is often behind suicide. (15)

Psychiatric diagnosis: medical model diagnostic approach of psychiatry in which clusters of symptoms and signs grouped into discrete categories. (3)

Psychiatrists: Physicians who have completed specialized training in psychiatry, a medical specialty concerned with mental disorders and their treatment. (1)

Psychic determinism: The psychoanalytic idea that every mental event is caused. (2)

Psychic energy: In psychoanalytic theory, the hypothesized substance that gets distributed across id, ego, and superego; the way psychic energy is distributed in one's system determines one's personality. (2)

Psychoanalysis: Approach to therapy grounded in Freud's original psychoanalytic theory; patient lies on couch facing away from analyst; uses techniques of free association, dream analysis, and examination of transference. (2)

***Psychodynamic Diagnostic Manual* (PDM)**: Diagnostic manual of the American Psychoanalytic Association. (3)

Psychodynamic PTSD groups: Aim to make members' traumatic memories conscious so feelings about them can be worked through in the group setting. (7)

Psychodynamic perspectives: Include all theories that trace their origins back to Freud's work; early life attachments and unconscious processes emphasized. (2)

Psychoeducation: Technique in which clients are taught about the problem they are diagnosed with to help them better cope with it. (4)

Psychogenic movement disorder: Another term for conversion cases in which there is medically unexplained difficulty moving a limb or body part. (8)

Psychological and behavioral factors associated with disorders or diseases classified elsewhere: *ICD-10* and *ICD-11* equivalents to the *DSM-5* diagnosis of *psychological factors affecting other medical conditions*. (8)

Psychological factors affecting other medical conditions: *DSM-5* somatic symptom diagnosis for people who have a known medical symptom that is brought on or made worse by ongoing psychological stress. Called *psychological and behavioral factors associated with disorders or diseases classified elsewhere* in *ICD-10*. (8)

Psychological first aid (PFA): A less invasive intervention than CISD that builds on research showing most people are resilient in the face of trauma; offers help to victims in the aftermath of a traumatic event in a non-intrusive way. (7)

Psychological perspectives: Conceptualize abnormality in psychological terms as involving problematic thoughts, feelings, and behaviors; abnormality is attributed to psychological conflicts. (1)

Psychologists: People who have a graduate degree (usually a doctorate) in psychology, a discipline that studies mental processes and behavior; unlike psychiatrists, psychologists are not medical doctors. (1)

Psychoneuroimmunology (PNI): Field that studies how psychological stress influences the central nervous system, endocrine system, and immune system. (8)

Psychopathic personalities: Emil Kraepelin's psychiatric term for people with one of four pathological personality types: *born criminals, the weak-willed, pathological liars/swindlers,* and *the paranoid*; Kurt Schneider later identified ten types of psychopathic personalities, which influenced the categories found in the *DSM*. (12)

Psychopathology: Focuses on abnormality as caused by an internal dysfunction or sickness inside the individual. (1)

Psychopathy: Attributed to mainly biological origins; characterized by *emotional/interpersonal symptoms* (being glib and superficial, egocentric and grandiose, lacking remorse or guilt, lacking empathy, being deceitful and manipulative, and displaying shallow emotions) and *social deviance* (impulsivity, poor control over behavior, a need for excitement, irresponsibility, behavior problems early in life, and antisocial behavior in adulthood). (12)

Psychosis: A broad term used to describe people whose thoughts, behaviors, and perceptions are so strange that they appear to have lost contact with reality. (4)

Psychosomatic: Term for when prolonged psychological stress results in or exacerbates a real medical condition; sometimes also referred to as *psychophysiological*. (8)

Psychosomatic families: Name used by early structural and family therapists to describe the dynamics of families with an anorexic child; such families are characterized by enmeshment, overprotectiveness, rigidity, conflict avoidance, and difficulty resolving conflict. (9)

Psychosomatogenic families: Families in which there is a great deal of enmeshment, rigidity, overprotectiveness, and difficulty with conflict resolution; in such families, somatic symptoms are believed to be more likely. (8)

Psychosurgery: Twentieth-century treatment of severe psychological abnormality in which surgery was used to sever connections between prefrontal lobes and other parts of the brain. (1)

Psychotherapy: Psychological intervention for presenting problems that involves conversation between a professional helper (the therapist) and the person being helped (the client or patient, depending on the preferred term); also called *talk therapy*. (1)

Psychotherapy integration: Process by which links among different theories are identified and used together to develop effective therapy interventions. (2)

PTSD: See *Posttraumatic stress disorder (PTSD)*.

Public education programs: Programs that try to prevent suicides by providing psychoeducational information about it, often via mass media campaigns. (15)

Punishers: Consequences that decrease the likelihood of the behavior they follow. (2)

Purging: Removal of food from one's body through self-induced vomiting or misuse of laxatives, diuretics, or other drugs. (9)

Purging disorder: Characterized by recurrent purging; diagnosed in *DSM-5* using the other specified feeding or eating disorder category. (9)

Purposive sampling: Sampling technique in which participants are recruited to participate in a study because they have characteristics that allow the research question to be examined in depth; used in a variety of research methods, including grounded theory approaches. (1)

Pyromania: *DSM-5*, *ICD-10*, and *ICD-11* impulse control disorder that involves purposeful fire-setting that provides a thrill and isn't done for personal gain; called *pathological fire-setting* in *ICD-10*. (13)

Q-sort: Person-centered assessment in which 100 cards with descriptors written on them are sorted into piles to describe client personality using everyday language. (3)

Qualitative methods: Research methods in which the researcher gathers data about subjective experiences or sociocultural phenomena, usually with the goal of comprehending the specific worldviews reflected in what is being studied. (1)

Quantitative methods: Research methods in which the researcher uses mathematical statistics to test hypotheses. (1)

Quasi-experiment: Variation on an experiment in which the researchers are unable to randomly assign participants to groups. (1)

Questions About Behavioral Function (QABF): A 25-item behavioral assessment inventory that assesses the extent to which behaviors are reinforced by providing social attention, escape from undesirable situations, tangible rewards, a way of coping with physical discomfort, or a way to entertain or pacify themselves in nonsocial situations. (3)

Random assignment: The practice of assigning an experiment's participants to different independent variable conditions at random. (1)

Random sample: A sample that is chosen arbitrarily from the population; choosing participants randomly gives us the best chance that the sample will be representative of the larger population. (1)

Randomized controlled trial (RCT): A kind of experiment designed to compare different therapies' effectiveness in treating specific presenting problems. (1)

Rape trauma syndrome: A term used to describe the reaction to being sexually assaulted; characterized by symptoms similar to PTSD. (7)

Rapid eye movement (REM) sleep: Sleep characterized by rapid eye movement, muscle paralysis, and dreaming. (14)

Rapid eye movement (REM) sleep behavior disorder: A *DSM-5* parasomnia characterized by acting out the dreams one experiences during REM sleep. (14)

Rat Man: Freud's case study of a man in his late 20s with obsessions about rats boring into his father's and fiancée's anuses; Freud reported curing the Rat Man using psychoanalysis. (6)

Rational emotive behavior therapy (REBT): Albert Ellis' cognitive therapy, which focuses on disputing clients' irrational beliefs. (2)

RDoC: See *Research Domain Criteria (RDoC)*.

RDoC's five domains: Negative valence systems, positive valence systems, cognitive systems, systems for social processes, and regulatory systems. (3)

Reaching Out About Depression (ROAD): Community outreach program to assist low-income women experiencing depression; combined a psychoeducational workshop series and an advocacy program in which participants worked one-on-one with law or counseling graduate students who helped them obtain necessary social services. (5)

Reactive attachment disorder: *DSM-5*, *ICD-10*, and *ICD-11* diagnosis given to children who have experienced severe environmental neglect and don't develop the ability to form attachments; they are withdrawn and inhibited around caregivers; called *reactive attachment disorder of childhood* in the *ICD-10*. (13)

Reality principle: Guiding principle of the ego; the need to consider the requirements of the external world in expressing id impulses. (2)

Receptive language disorder: *ICD-10* diagnosis in which a child's ability to understand language is below developmental level; somewhat similar to the *ICD-10* diagnosis, *developmental language disorder with impairment of receptive and expressive language*. (14)

Recidivism rates: How often sex offenders commit additional sex crimes. (10)

Reclaiming Futures: Social justice-based early intervention program for juveniles arrested on drug-related charges; provides easy access to treatment, mentorship, and community-based social support to counter social inequality that puts some adolescents at risk. (11)

Recurrent depressive disorder: *ICD-10* and *ICD-11* disorder for those who experience multiple depressive episodes. (5)

Reductionism: The idea that we can break complex human experience into its components such as thoughts, behaviors, and drives or genes, neurochemicals, or brain parts; rejected by adherents of the humanistic perspective. (2)

Refrigerator mother theory of autism: Theory that attributed autism to cold and aloof parenting. (13)

Reification: Tendency to treat one's invented categories as if they are real. (3)

Reinforcers: Consequences that increase the likelihood of the behavior they follow. (2)

Relapse prevention (RP): CBT technique that focuses on preventing relapse by teaching those in recovery how to handle high-risk situations that tempt them to engage in the problematic activity again; typically used with substance users, people experiencing behavioral addictions, and sexual offenders. (10)

Relational-cultural theory: Holds that many approaches to personality psychology err by improperly attributing psychological distress to internal psychopathology rather than to societal influences such as chronic social disconnection. (12)

Relaxation training: Various techniques in which clients are taught how to calm themselves; examples include *progressive relaxation* and *functional relaxation*. (6)

Reliability: Regarding diagnosis, the degree to which a diagnostic system yields similar results each time it is used. (3)

Remission: no longer displaying signs of difficulty with a substance; people in remission often describe themselves as *in recovery*. (11)

Repression: Occurs when the conscious mind pushes unacceptable ideas and impulses into the unconscious mind. (2)

Reproductive suppression hypothesis: Evolutionary theory that holds anorexia is a female strategy for maximizing long-term productive success by shutting down reproductive capacity through self-starvation during times when current conditions aren't optimal for having babies. (9)

Research Domain Criteria (RDoC): U.S. National Institute of Mental Health (NIMH) initiative to devise a diagnostic system that uses biological measures (i.e., biomarkers) to diagnose mental disorders; currently a research initiative rather than a diagnostic system. (3)

Resistance: When patients reject their psychoanalysts' interpretations. (2)

Response readiness theory: Evolutionary theory of ADHD that proposes that short attention spans and hyperactivity-impulsivity were necessary in ancestral environments where threats to safety were extreme and food was scarce. (13)

Response-to-intervention model (RTI): Model for assessing learning disorders that uses a preventative approach; using three tiers, RTI identifies children who don't meet grade-level standards and then provides services tailored to their needs; if responsive, the children are reintegrated into the normal classroom, but if not, they are assigned to a special education classroom. (14)

Restless legs syndrome: Sleep-related disorder diagnosed in people who have an irresistible desire to move their legs, which gets worse when resting or trying to sleep. (14)

Reward deficiency syndrome theory (RDS): Hypothesis that addicted people take drugs to compensate for having too little dopamine. (11)

Rhodiola rosea: Herbal remedy for depression and other presenting problems; active ingredients are *rosavin*, *rosin* and *rosarian*. (5)

Right anterior prefrontal cortex: Suspected of helping people perform tasks related to one goal while simultaneously keeping information about a different goal in working memory; has been associated with factitious symptoms and malingering. (8)

Right to refuse treatment: Legal right to decline treatment unless judged incompetent to make such a decision. (15)

Right to treatment: Legal right of individuals to receive appropriate treatment while involuntarily committed. (15)

Risk-need-responsivity model (RNR): CBT-based program for sexual offenders that tailors interventions to each offender by assessing offender *risk* and *need* in order to determine *responsivity* (the appropriate kind and level of intervention needed to prevent repeat offenses). (10)

Ritalin: Name under which the stimulant methylphenidate is marketed as a treatment for attention-deficit/hyperactivity disorder. (13)

RNA (ribonucleic acid): Consists of three of the same four nucleotides as DNA (*adenine*, *cytosine*, and *guanine*), along with a fourth nucleotide (*uracil*); RNA carries out DNA's instructions. (2)

Role construct repertory test: Personality test in which a client's *personal constructs* (bipolar dimensions of meaning created by the client) are elicited and their relationships mapped; allows for an assessment using the client's personal meanings rather than the clinician's diagnostic categories. (3)

Rorschach Inkblot Method (RIM): Projective assessment technique in which test-taker responds to 10 inkblots; various scoring systems available, but Rorschach Comprehensive System (CS) is currently the most widely used. (3)

Rumination disorder: *DSM-5* term describing those who regularly re-chew, re-swallow, or spit out food after intentionally regurgitating it; included as a specific form of "feeding disorder of infancy and early childhood" in the *ICD-10* and called *rumination-regurgitation disorder* in *ICD-11*. (9)

S-Axis (Subjective Experience): *PDM* axis that describes *DSM* categories in psychoanalytic experience, with the goal of conveying what it is like to have each disorder. (3)

Sadomasochism/sexual sadism disorder or **sexual masochism disorder**: Paraphilic disorder involving sexual fantasies, urges, or behaviors related to the physical or emotional suffering of another person (sexual sadism) or being humiliated or made to suffer (masochism). (10)

Sample: Members of a population chosen to participate in a study. (1)

Satiation techniques: Behavioral technique in which patients' regular meals are supplemented with additional food; because rumination often occurs when hungry, it is used to discourage rumination by making the patient less hungry. (9)

Scatterplot: Behavioral assessment method in which the client's behavior in a specific environment is continuously observed over time to identify temporal patterns. (3)

Schema therapy: Maintains that people diagnosed with personality disorders develop extremely rigid and deeply rooted schemas early in life due to abuse and neglect; encourages clients to become aware of how situations trigger dysfunctional schemas so they can develop more healthy and functional alternative responses. (12)

Schemas: Mental structures used to organize information; generalized scripts about how the world works that we use to anticipate what will happen in each situation. (2)

Schizoaffective disorder: *DSM-5*, *ICD-10*, and *ICD-11* disorder in which the person displays aspects of psychosis and depression. (4)

Schizoid personality disorder: *DSM-5* and *ICD-10* diagnosis characterized by utter disinterest in relationships and people; these people have no desire to engage with others, preferring to be alone. (12)

Schizophrenia: The best known and perhaps most severe psychotic disorder in the *DSM-5*, *ICD-10*, and *ICD-11*; characterized by hallucinations, delusions, and disorganized speech. (4)

Schizophreniform disorder: *DSM-5* disorder that shows same basic symptoms as schizophrenia, but they don't last as long. Not included in *ICD-10* or *ICD-11*, but included in *ICD-10-CM* (the U.S. modification of the *ICD*). (4)

Schizophrenogenic mothers: Cold, demanding, and domineering mothers whose parenting style Fromm-Reichman, in her psychodynamic theory, hypothesized contributed to their children's schizophrenia. (4)

Schizotypal disorder: *ICD-10* and *ICD-11* diagnosis that is equivalent to the *DSM-5* diagnosis of schizotypal personality disorder; the *ICD* groups this disorder with psychotic disorders, whereas the *DSM-5* groups it with personality disorders. (4)

Schizotypal personality disorder (STPD): *DSM-5* diagnosis for people with eccentric thoughts, perceptions, and behaviors accompanied by difficulty forming close relationships; people with this diagnosis strike others as strange; see also *schizotypal disorder*. (12)

Scientific method: Systematic collection of data through various means of observation and measurement. (1)

Search for essences: Phenomenological research method in which the researcher breaks participants' descriptions down into meaningful units, looking for commonalities across participants.; the result constitutes the essence of the experience. (1)

Seasonal affective disorder (SAD): Diagnosis describing depression that occurs during the winter months when there are fewer hours of daylight. (5)

Second-generation antipsychotics: Antipsychotic drugs that are often thought to have fewer side effects than first-generation antipsychotics; also called *atypical antipsychotics* (see separate entry). (4)

Secondary enuresis: Enuresis in which the child starts bedwetting after having previously attained bladder control. (14)

Secondary gain: Any other advantages a symptom provides beyond the original unconscious conflict that it expresses. (8)

Secondary insomnia: Prior to *DSM-5*, a diagnosis given when insomnia was diagnosed alongside another medical or psychiatric condition. (14)

Secondary psychopathy: Psychopathy seen as resulting when a biologically innate predisposition is brought out by environmental factors. (12)

Sedative-hypnotics: A class of depressants sometimes simply called *sedatives*; barbiturates and benzodiazepines are types of sedative-hypnotic drugs. (11)

Selective mutism: *DSM-5*, *ICD-10*, and *ICD-11* disorder diagnosed mainly in children who fail to speak in social situations where doing so is expected; term "elective mutism" also used in *ICD-10*. (6)

Selective serotonin reuptake inhibitors (SSRIs): Class of antidepressant drugs that work by preventing the reuptake or reabsorption of serotonin by the neurons that released it; this leaves more serotonin available. (5)

Self-actualization: Process by which people draw on their actualizing tendency and move towards enhancement and personal growth, fulfilling their full potential. (2)

Self-efficacy: An estimate of one's ability to do something successfully. (3)

Self-hypnosis: The ability to enter a hypnotic trance on one's own without guidance from others; people with a tendency to dissociate—especially those with dissociative identity disorder—are thought to be good at self-hypnosis. (8)

Self-medication hypothesis: Psychodynamic hypothesis that insecurely attached people who have difficulty recognizing and regulating their emotions are most susceptible to drug addiction. (11)

Self-objectification: When girls and women internalize media messages that judge them based on their appearance and begin to appraise their own based on these messages. (9)

Self-report personality inventory: Objective test using standardized items with limited response choices; easy to administer and score because it has clear answer choices and scoring systems. (3)

Self-stigmatization: The process of internalizing negative attitudes about oneself espoused by others. (12)

Senile plaques: Sticky buildup of beta-amyloid protein in the areas surrounding neurons that is implicated in Alzheimer's disease; also called *amyloid plaques*. (14)

Sensate focus: Masters and Johnson technique to help those having trouble with arousal and orgasm; clients are instructed to engage in sensual touching with their partners, but without it leading to intercourse; removes pressure to perform and clients often "fail" by becoming aroused. (10)

Separation anxiety disorder: *DSM-5*, *ICD-10*, and *ICD-11* disorder in which one shows excessive anxiety about being separated from significant attachment figures; not specific to children in *DSM-5*, but specific to children and called "separation anxiety disorder of childhood" in *ICD-10*. (6)

Serotonin: An inhibitory neurotransmitter associated with depression and anxiety. (2)

Serotonin and norepinephrine reuptake inhibitors (SNRIs): Antidepressants that work by blocking the reuptake of both serotonin and norepinephrine, leaving more of both available. (5)

Service-user/survivor movement: Rejects mainstream psychiatric perspectives, contending that many interventions—especially prescription drugs and involuntary treatments—are often inhumane, abusive, and fail to take into consideration the desires of the people forced to endure them; sometimes also called the *psychiatric survivor movement*. (2)

Severe personality disorder: Diagnosis in the *ICD-11*'s dimensional model of personality disorders; for those who show extreme impairment in interpersonal relationships and whose social and occupational functioning are profoundly disrupted and serious harm to self and others is anticipated. (12)

Sex reassignment surgery: Surgery in which a person's physical body is altered (often through multiple operations) to match gender identity; also called *gender reassignment surgery* and *gender affirmation surgery*). (10)

Sex: One's biological status as male, female, or intersex. (10)

Sexologist: A scientist who studies human sexual behavior. (10)

Sexual aversion and lack of sexual enjoyment: *ICD-10* diagnosis reserved for cases where the idea of sex with a partner is highly unpleasant—yielding fear, anxiety, and avoidance. (10)

Sexual competition hypothesis: Evolutionary theory that says eating problems emerge because women must compete with one another to attract men by maintaining a "nubile" hour-glass shape; in industrial societies where there is less familial help in securing a mate, even greater emphasis on maintaining a thin shape emerges. (9)

Sexual dysfunctions: Defined by *DSM-5* as disturbances in a person's ability to respond sexually or experience sexual pleasure. (10)

Sexual instinct: A reproductive instinct for the propagation of the species; proposed by early doctors as part of the process of medicalizing sexual deviance. (10)

Sexual masochism disorder: See *Sadomasochism/sexual sadism disorder or sexual masochism disorder*.

Sexual orientation: The sex of those to whom one is sexually and romantically attracted. (10)

Sexual pain-penetration disorder: *ICD-11* diagnosis for people who experience difficulties with vaginal penetration (often due to tightening of pelvic floor muscles); pain during penetration; or fear of painful penetration; similar to the *DSM-5*'s genito-pelvic pain/penetration disorder, except it excludes dyspareunia. (10)

Sexual response cycle: In Masters and Johnson's original formulation, involved four phases: *excitement/arousal*, *plateau*, *orgasm*, *resolution*. Revised by Kaplan to consist of *desire*, *arousal/excitement*, *orgasm*, and *resolution* phases. (10)

Sexual sadism disorder: See *Sadomasochism/sexual sadism disorder or sexual masochism disorder*.

Shell shock: First World War diagnosis used with soldiers who experienced emotional difficulties due to combat; called shell shock because it was thought to originate from repeated exposure to exploding artillery shells. (7)

Short-term dynamic therapy of stress syndromes: Psychodynamic therapy for PTSD and grief that helps patients navigate five proposed phases of dealing with trauma and grief: (a) initial outcry; (b) denial and numbness; (c) intrusive thoughts and feelings; (d) "working through;" and (e) completion. (7)

Short-term psychoanalytic supportive therapy (SPST): Brief psychodynamic therapy that helps depressed people revise problematic internalized relationship patterns. (5)

Signs: In psychiatric diagnosis, the physical changes that occur as part of a syndrome. (3)

Sildenafil: A phosphodiesterase type-5 inhibitor used to increase blood flow to sex organs; given mainly to men to help provide blood flow to penis necessary for erections; marketed as Viagra. (10)

Silencing the self (STS) theory: Proposes that depression in women is a product of deeply rooted cultural assumptions that direct women to silence or suppress certain thoughts or feelings to satisfy the demands of a male-centered world. (5)

Single episode depressive disorder: *ICD-10* and *ICD-11* depressive disorder diagnosis for people who only experience one lifetime depressive episode. (5)

Single-subject experiments: Experiments conducted on just one person. (1)

Sixteen Personality Factor (16PF) Questionnaire: 185 multiple-choice self-report personality inventory yielding scores on 16 primary personality factors (*warmth*, *reasoning*, *emotional stability*, *dominance*, *liveliness*, *rule-consciousness*, *social boldness*, *sensitivity*, *vigilance*, *abstractedness*, *privateness*, *apprehension*, *openness to change*, *self-reliance*, *perfectionism*, and *tension*), plus the "Big-Five" global personality traits (*extraversion*, *anxiety*, *tough-mindedness*, *independence*, and *self-control*). (3)

Sleep cycle: Cycle a person typically goes through five times during a normal night's sleep, consisting of four distinct stages; the first three are non-rapid eye movement (NREM) sleep and the fourth is rapid eye movement (REM) sleep. (14)

Sleep hygiene education: CBT-I treatment for insomnia in which client is taught habits conducive to getting a good night's sleep, including importance of regular exercise; avoiding caffeine, alcohol, and nicotine; having a snack before bed; and keeping the bedroom dark, noise-free, and comfortable. (14)

Sleep restriction therapy: CBT-I treatment for insomnia in which the total amount of time allowed in bed is restricted so that it eventually matches the amount of time needed for sleep; idea is to train the person to remain in bed only so long as is needed to sleep. (14)

Sleep terrors: Episodes of intense terror that jerk a person abruptly from deep sleep, often with a panicked scream and a scramble to escape the room; also called *night terrors*. (14)

Sleepwalking: Getting out of bed and walking around while still asleep; the sleepwalker has a blank expression, is unresponsive to others, and is difficult to awaken; also called *somnambulism*. (14)

Slips of the tongue: In psychoanalytic theory, occur when a person accidentally uses wrong words and in so doing expresses an unconscious conflict. (2)

Snowball sampling: Sampling technique in which additional participants are recruited by asking initial participants if they know anyone else with similar experiences; often used in grounded theory research. (1)

SNRI: See *serotonin and norepinephrine reuptake inhibitors*.

Social (pragmatic) communication disorder (SPCD): *DSM-5* disorder given to individuals who, early in life, develop difficulties communicating with others; unlike those diagnosed with autism spectrum disorder, SPCD patients don't display restricted/repetitive behavior; see also *developmental language disorder with impairment of mainly pragmatic language*. (13)

Social anxiety disorder (social phobia): *DSM-5*, *ICD-10*, and *ICD-11* disorder diagnosed in people who become anxious and fear embarrassing or humiliating themselves in social situations where they might be scrutinized. (6)

Social construction: Any socially shared way of defining, talking about, and understanding something that influences how people come to experience it. (2)

Social drift: Tendency of those diagnosed with severe mental disorders such as schizophrenia to slide (or drift) down the socioeconomic ladder. (4)

Social justice perspectives: Approaches that view abnormality as the product of social inequality; they rely on consciousness raising and social action to help clients overcome oppression and relieve emotional distress. (2)

Social learning theory: Behavioral approach that focuses on how observation and modeling contribute to learning. (2)

Social oppression: Idea that abnormality results from or is exacerbated by unjust social conditions; sees abnormality as a product of oppressive and inequitable social circumstances, rather than as a product of disorder or dysfunction inside the person. (1)

Social skills training: CBT technique in which complicated social scenarios—such as making friends, dating, ordering food in a restaurant, or going on a job interview—are broken down into discrete steps and taught to clients. (4)

Sociocognitive model: Model that maintains there is no such thing as dissociative identity disorder; media accounts and therapists who believe in DID iatrogentically induce it; also known as the *fantasy model* and the *iatrogenic position*. (8)

Sociocultural perspectives: Attribute abnormality to social causes; factors such as socioeconomic conditions, cultural influences, and social oppression are the root causes of people's emotional upset. (1)

Socioeconomic status (SES): A measure of a person's social standing based on income, education, and employment. (1)

Sociopathy: Distinguished from psychopathy in that it is mainly attributed to social causes, not biology. (12)

Socratic questioning: Cognitive-behavioral technique in which the therapist asks questions designed to help therapists and clients better understand the client's experiences. (4)

Sodium oxybate: A central nervous system depressant prescribed to reduce cataplexy by improving nighttime sleep; also known as *gamma-hydroxybutrate* (GHB). (14)

Somatic complaint: A presenting problem that involves experiencing or worrying about physical symptoms. (8)

Somatic delusions: Delusions in which you falsely believe you have a disease. (4)

Somatic symptom disorder (SSD): *DSM-5* somatic symptom diagnosis describing people who have one or more somatic symptoms that they think and worry about excessively; replaced the *DSM-IV-TR* and *ICD-10* diagnosis of somatization disorder; roughly equivalent to *bodily distress disorder* in ICD-11. (8)

Somatization: The process of expressing psychological problems in physical terms. (8)

Somatization disorder: *ICD-10* disorder characterized by multiple changing and frequent physical symptoms lacking adequate physical explanation; also called *Briquet's syndrome*; replaced by *bodily distress disorder* in *ICD-11* and *somatic symptom disorder* in *DSM-5*, both of which do away with the requirement that symptoms lack adequate physical explanation. (8)

Soteria model: A community-based approach to schizophrenia that applies humanistic-existential ideas to therapeutic communities for people diagnosed with schizophrenia. (4)

Specialist supportive clinical management (SSCM): A non-theoretical approach to managing eating disorder symptoms originally devised as a control comparison for research on other therapies but found to be effective in its own right; SSCM helps patients target problematic eating behaviors, establish a proper diet, monitor weight, establish realistic weight goals, and deal with life problems that may be affecting their eating. (9)

Specific learning disorder: *DSM-5* diagnosis given when a child exhibits learning difficulties in school, showing trouble with things like reading, writing, spelling and math; academic performance is lower than expected for the child's age, but isn't caused by an intellectual disability; commonly referred to more informally using the term *learning disorder*. (14)

Specific phobia: *DSM-5*, *ICD-10*, and *ICD-11* disorder characterized by the fear associated with a given object or situation; the fear is focused, with the phobic individual afraid of something specific. (6)

Specific speech articulation disorder: *ICD-10* diagnosis in which a child's speech development is below expected level. (14)

Spectatoring: The tendency to observe and negatively evaluate one's sexual performance as if one was a third person watching it. (10)

Speech-sound disorder: *DSM-5* diagnosis in which a person can generate speech, but the speech is extremely hard to understand due to difficulty making speech sounds. (14)

Speedballing: Taking stimulants with opioids to produce a synergistic effect in which the highs of both drugs are experienced but the negative effects are reduced; increases risk of overdose. (11)

Splitting: Object relations term for the mental process of dividing an object into "good" and "bad" parts. (2)

Squeeze technique: Masters and Johnson's technique in which the top of the penis is repeatedly squeezed during sexual activity to delay ejaculation; conditions men to not ejaculate so quickly. (10)

SSRI: See *selective serotonin reuptake inhibitors*.

St. John's wort: Herbal remedy for depression and other presenting problems that is derived from a plant found in parts of Europe and Asia; active ingredients are *hyperforin* and *hypericin*. (5)

Standardization: Establishment of clearly defined rules for administering and interpreting an assessment instrument. (3)

State-dependent learning: The idea that people's ability to recall something is affected by their psychological or emotional state. (8)

Statistical deviation: Defines abnormality as what is statistically atypical. Whether what is atypical is abnormal in the sense of being psychopathological is often debated. (1)

Stereotypic movement disorder: *DSM-5* and *ICD-11* disorder involving repetitive and purposeless movements that begin early in development and which the child seems driven to perform; examples of such movements include waving one's hands, rocking back and forth, banging one's head, and biting or hitting oneself. (14)

Stigma: Society's negative and often hostile responses to people carrying certain marks or labels; mental disorder diagnoses often carry significant stigma. (2)

Stimulants: Drugs that speed up the central nervous system (CNS). (11)

Stimulus control therapy: CBT-I treatment for insomnia that tries to recondition clients to associate bed and bedroom with sleeping; clients only go to bed when tired, get out of bed when they can't sleep, and only use the bedroom for sleeping. (14)

Stop-start technique: Alternative to squeeze technique in which men learn to stop intercourse prior to ejaculating and to begin again only after arousal decreases; conditions men to not ejaculate so quickly. (10)

Strategic approach therapy (SAT): 10-session manualized therapy in which stress inoculation and other coping skills are taught. (7)

Stress: A feeling of being overwhelmed, worried, or run-down. (7)

Stress inoculation training (SIT): Therapy that combines a variety of CBT techniques (such as education, relaxation training, breathing retraining, role playing, covert modeling, guided self-dialogue, graduated *in vivo* exposure, and thought stopping) to decrease avoidance and anxiety. (7)

Stress-induced analgesia: Pain suppression that occurs when exposed to frightening or potentially traumatizing situations. (8)

Stress-vulnerability-coping skills model: Model that says a *biological vulnerability* to psychosis is triggered by *environmental stress*; the degree to which someone has sufficient cognitive coping skills then influences whether stress triggers the biological vulnerability or, once triggered, allows the resulting psychotic symptoms to be dealt with effectively. (4)

Striatum: Brain region that is part of the brain's reward system. (6)

Structural family therapy: Minuchin's family therapy, which emphasizes how the structure of a family system—including its rules, boundaries, and power hierarchies—contribute to its dysfunction. (2)

Structural model: Later psychoanalytic model that added the psychic structures of id, ego and superego. (2)

Structured Clinical Interview for *DSM* Disorders (SCID): Semi-structured interview for making *DSM* diagnoses. (3)

Structured interview: Clinical interviewing technique in which clinician employs a clearly defined and predetermined set of questions. (3)

Stuttering: See *Childhood-onset fluency disorder*.

Subintentional death: A death caused by an unconscious wish to die that leads to reckless or negligent actions, rather than overt suicide attempts; also called *indirect suicide*. (15)

Substance abuse: Ongoing misuse of a substance; can involve many different kinds of problematic behaviors, including failing to meet school, work, and family obligations. (11)

Substance dependence: Misuse of a substance that typically involves tolerance and withdrawal. (11)

Substance use disorder: *DSM-5* diagnosis that combines symptoms of abuse and dependence; assessment based on type of drug being used and severity of use. (11)

Successful psychopaths: Psychopaths who effectively navigate the world and avoid punishment. (12)

Suicidal behavior disorder: Proposed *DSM-5* disorder that, if eventually approved, would be diagnosed in anyone who has attempted suicide in the last two years; in *ICD-11*, it is coded not as a disorder, but as a mental or behavioral symptom or sign and called *suicide attempt*. (15)

Suicidal ideation: Technical term for suicidal thoughts and feelings. (15)

Suicide: Intentionally ending one's own life. (15)

Suicide prevention counseling: Form of crisis counseling in which a professional or trained volunteer talks with the suicidal person to prevent a suicide. (15)

Superego: Partly conscious/partly unconscious psychoanalytic personality structure that houses moral beliefs. (2)

Supportive PTSD groups: Focus on having group members provide each other with emotional support and encouragement; the idea is that by fostering supportive relationships, those coping with trauma can assist one another. (7)

Suppressed GABA inhibition hypothesis: Holds that GABA activity is reduced in those with autism, perhaps due to a breakdown in the brain's GABA transmission pathway. (13)

Surgical castration: Removing a man's testicles (*orchiectomy*) or a woman's ovaries (*oophorectomy*). (10)

Survival of the fittest: Evolutionary theory concept that says only those organisms well suited to an environment are able to reproduce and keep their species alive. (2)

Sympathetic nervous system (SNS): Branch of the autonomic nervous system activated when a person is under stress, causing physiological changes such as increased breathing and heart rates, pupil dilation, inhibition of appetite, and higher blood pressure. (7)

Symptoms: In psychiatric diagnosis, the presenting complaint elements of a syndrome. (3)

Syndrome: In psychiatric diagnosis, a discrete category consisting of symptoms and signs. (3)

Synergistic effects: Effect from taking drugs together; some combinations enhance the effects of both drugs, while other combinations cancel out some of the effects of both drugs. (11)

System: In systems perspectives, an integrated and dynamic whole that consists of individual parts; couples, families, and social groups are examples. (2)

Systematic desensitization: Exposure technique that combines *relaxation training* and use of a *fear hierarchy* (ranking potential experiences with the feared object or situation and from least to most scary); the client is gradually exposed to the conditioned stimulus while in a relaxed state, with the goal of conditioning a new response. (2)

Systems perspectives: Look at how individuals are influenced by and function within "systems" of relationships. (2)

T cells: Lymphocytes that work to kill viruses and bacteria once they have entered cells. (8)

Tardive dyskinesia: Irreversible syndrome from prolonged use of antipsychotics; involves repetitive and involuntary muscle movements; symptoms such as lip smacking, tongue wagging, and repeated eye blinking are common. (4)

Technical eclecticism: Combining whatever psychotherapy techniques are shown to work, regardless of the theory from which they originate. (2)

Telepsychiatry: Uses real-time videoconferencing to provide services such as medication management and short-term psychotherapy; when done by psychologists, called *telepsychology*. (15)

Temperament: The automatic ways of responding to emotional stimuli that produce consistent habits and moods. (12)

Temporal cortex: Brain area that plays a part in language, emotion, and memory. (4)

Temporary commitment: In most jurisdictions, when family members, the police, or medical/mental health professionals initiate short-term psychiatric hospitalizations of those they believe pose a danger to self or others; also called *emergency commitment*. (15)

Test batteries: assessments consisting of various tasks intended to assess multiple aspects of an area of psychological functioning. (3)

Test-retest reliability: Degree to which an assessment measure yields similar results each time. (4)

Testosterone: Primary male sex hormone. (10)

Tetrahydrocannabinol (THC): Active ingredient in cannabis, responsible for its stimulant, depressant, and psychedelic effects. (11)

Thalamus: Small midbrain region that relays sensory information from parts of the body to other areas of the brain. (6)

"Thank you" theory of involuntary commitment: Holds that people who threaten or attempt suicide will thank us later if we have them hospitalized and that their future appreciativeness is the best legal justification for committing them. (15)

Thebaine: An opium alkaloid with more stimulant than depressant effects. (11)

Thematic Apperception Test (TAT): Projective assessment technique in which test-taker tells stories about pictures on 20 cards (determined by age and gender); scored for thematic content reflecting personality functioning. (3)

Theoretical coding: Grounded theory data analysis method in which latent links among codes, categories, and memos are sought and an integrated conception of the topic being studied starts to emerge. (1)

Theoretical sampling: Grounded theory technique that entails devising and revising strategies for recruiting participants as the research project goes along; the tactics used may change as the researcher learns more about the topic being studied and figures out what kinds of additional data are needed. (1)

Theoretical sensitivity: Grounded theory technique in which the researcher's knowledge and expertise about a topic informs the research question asked about it. (1)

Theory of mind: The evolved human ability to view the world through others' eyes and generate interpretations of why others behave as they do, as well as to infer and comprehend one's own mental states and behavior. (4)

Therapeutic communities: Social support intervention for substance abusers; residential or day treatment programs that provide an array of services; re-socializes participants by helping them develop new life skills. (11)

Thiamine: A chemical compound that helps the brain convert sugar into energy (also known as *Vitamin B-1*); chronic drinking decreases thiamine levels and can lead to Korsakoff syndrome. (11)

Thought parade exercise: Acceptance and commitment therapy (ACT) technique in which clients are asked to calmly imagine a parade in which people carry signs reproducing their negative thoughts; helps clients observe their thoughts in a detached manner, with the idea that calmly accepting these thoughts reduces their influence. (9)

Thought stopping: CBT technique in which clients are taught to stop their thoughts, often by saying or thinking "Stop!" whenever an intrusive thought occurs. (6)

Tic disorders: Movement disorders characterized by abrupt and repetitive motor or vocal movements (i.e., tics). (14)

Tics: Abrupt and repetitive motor or vocal movements; four types: *simple motor tics* (simple repetitive movements like eye-blinking, shoulder shrugging, and head jerking), *complex motor tics* (more coordinated and purposeful movements, such as hopping, skipping, tapping, stepping in certain patterns, and touching specific objects), *simple vocal tics* (brief utterances or sounds, such as repetitive throat clearing, coughing, sniffling, grunting, gurgling, and spitting), and *complex vocal tics* (repeating words, sounds, and phrases; includes palilalia, echolalia, and copralalia). (14)

Time-limited dynamic psychotherapy (TLDP): Short-term psychodynamic therapy that shares object relations therapy's emphasis on using therapy to identify and revise problematic interpersonal patterns, but does so more quickly by establishing clear therapeutic goals and addressing them in 20–25 sessions. (2)

Tolerance: Needing more of a drug to produce the same effects. (11)

Topographic model: Early psychoanalytic model that conceived of unconscious and conscious as locations in the mind where memories are stored. (2)

Tourette's disorder: *DSM-5*, *ICD-10*, and *ICD-11* disorder that involves motor and vocal tics that have persisted for over a year; also called *Tourette's syndrome*. (14)

Trait factors: Traits that are distinct from one another; trait factors are often derived from the statistical procedure of factor analysis. (12)

Trait theories: Perspectives emphasizing the importance of traits in personality; often view traits as originating in biology. (12)

Traits: Distinguishing qualities people "have," such as a tendency toward happiness, anxiousness, or aggression. (12)

Transcranial magnetic stimulation (TMS): Treatment for depression and sometimes bipolar symptoms in which magnetic energy is sent through the brain via electromagnetic coils placed on the scalp. (5)

Transference: Occurs when patients generalize (i.e., transfer) their feelings about important people in their lives onto their therapists. (2)

Transgender-affirmative CBT (TA-CBT): Form of CBT intended to assist transgender clients as they cope with anxiety and depression caused by transphobia; negative internalized beliefs about being transgender are examined and changed. (10)

Transgender: A term for people whose gender identity, expression, or behavior is different from what is typically associated with their birth sex. (10)

Transphobia: Social prejudice directed at transgender people. (10)

Transsexual: Traditionally, a medical term for people who have undergone medical procedures to reduce the discrepancy between their biological sex and their gender identity; they have transitioned from one sex to the other. (10)

Transsexualism: *ICD-10* diagnosis for adults who display incongruence between their birth sex and experienced/expressed gender; see also *gender dysphoria (DSM-5)*, *gender incongruence (ICD-11)*, and *gender identity disorder of childhood (ICD-10)*. (10)

Transtheoretical model of change: Model of therapeutic change that identifies five stages clients go through during the change process (*precontemplation*, *contemplation*, *preparation*, *action*, and *maintenance*). (11)

Transvestism: The practice of cross-dressing; when done for the purpose of sexual arousal, it is sometimes considered a paraphilia (see *fetishistic transvestism/transvestic disorder*). (10)

Transvestite: Term referring to people who engage in cross-dressing (transvestism). (10)

Trauma: Exposure to actual or threatened death, serious injury, or sexual violence. (7)

Trauma-focused cognitive-behavioral groups: More structured group approach that educates members about trauma and uses various exposure and relaxation techniques to address anxiety. (7)

Traumatic context: A set of circumstances in which there is a prolonged and intense exposure to trauma; spending a lot of time in such a context makes developing PTSD more likely. (7)

Traumatic neurosis: Historical diagnosis for emotional difficulties following trauma proposed by Herman Oppenheim in the 1880s; its causes were often originally attributed to organic factors, but in the 1900s Abram Kardiner said psychological factors were also relevant. (7)

Trepanation: Prehistoric treatment of abnormal behavior in which holes were drilled in the skull, ostensibly to free evil spirits; also called *trephination*. (1)

Triangulation: In family therapy, when two family members deal with conflict between them by involving a third family member; often exacerbates family conflict. (2)

Trichotillomania (hair-pulling disorder): *DSM-5*, *ICD-10*, and *ICD-11* disorder describing those who compulsively pull out their own hair. (6)

Tricyclics: Antidepressants that mainly affect norepinephrine and serotonin (usually with more impact on norepinephrine); they work by inhibiting reabsorption of these neurotransmitters, leaving more available. (5)

Trustworthiness: Characteristic of good qualitative research; evaluated by looking at the study's social validity, whether it acknowledges its biases, and whether it provides adequate data. (1)

Tryptophan: Amino acid obtained from food that is required to produce the neurotransmitter serotonin. (9)

Tumescence: Increased blood flow leading to swelling of sexual organs; men with poor tumescence have difficulty obtaining erections. (10)

Twelve-step programs: See *12-step programs*.

Twin studies: Studies in which identical twins, who are genetically the same, are compared to see if both develop schizophrenia. (4)

Type A personality: Driven, impatient, and competitive style with which some people aggressively engage the world. (8)

Type B personality: Opposite of Type A personality; easygoing individuals who lack drive, ambition, and urgency. (8)

Type C personality: People who appear easygoing like Type B personalities, but are anxious and insecure. (8)

Type D personality: Characterized by emotional negativity and social inhibition. (8)

Unconditional positive regard: In person-centered therapy, when others unconditionally accept a person; leads to congruence; one of Rogers' core conditions. (2)

Unconditioned response (UR): A response to an unconditioned stimulus (e.g., dog salivates in response to dog food). (2)

Unconditioned stimulus (US): A stimulus that naturally evokes a response without any learning necessary (e.g., dog food elicits salivation). (2)

Unconscious: Psychodynamic term for the childish and immature part of the mind that is out of awareness (i.e., repressed). (2)

Unified psychodynamic therapy protocol for anxiety disorders (UPP-ANXIETY): Psychodynamic protocol designed for use with all anxiety disorders; therapy is broken into concrete steps (or "modules"), each with empirical support for its effectiveness. (6)

Unstructured interview: Clinical interviewing technique in which clinician asks client open-ended questions. (3)

Unsuccessful psychopaths: Psychopaths who are criminals and likely to be incarcerated. (12)

Vaginismus: *ICD-10* diagnosis for women who experience pain in response to spasms in the muscles around the vagina during intercourse; no longer included as a stand-alone diagnosis in *DSM-5* or *ICD-11*. (10)

Validity: The degree to which a diagnostic system or assessment instrument measures what it claims to; types of validity include *descriptive validity* (does a measure accurately describe what is being observed?), *face validity* (on the face of it, does a measure seem accurate?), *predictive validity* (does a measure allow us to predict outcomes?), *construct validity* (does a measure correlate with other measures that we think are getting at the same thing?), and *concurrent validity* (are a measure's results consistent with other measures given concurrently—that is, at the same time?). (3)

Varenicline: Smoking-cessation drug that blocks nicotine receptors, making cigarettes less enjoyable and decreasing withdrawal symptoms (trade name *Chantix*). (11)

Variables: Aspects of the world that can change; measured in correlational and experimental research studies. (1)

Vasopressin: Hormone that reduces urine production. (14)

Ventral tegmental area (VTA): Structure in the midbrain that is important in rewards and motivation. (11)

Ventricles: Four empty spaces in the brain filled with cerebrospinal fluid; they tend to be larger in people diagnosed with schizophrenia, suggesting decreased brain volume. (4)

Ventromedial hypothalamus: Part of the hypothalamus responsible for inducing feelings of satiation. (9)

Violation of social norms and values: Defines abnormality in terms of the degree to which someone behaves in ways that others deem troublesome; social norms and values are used to evaluate whether a behavior is normal or not. Because social norms change over time and across cultures, the interpretation of this criterion varies widely. (1)

Viral explanation of general paresis: Found that general paresis is caused by the syphilis virus. (2)

Viral theories: Hypothesize that psychological disorders can be caused by viral infections. (2)

Viral theory of autism: Holds that children with autism are more likely to have had mothers who had a viral or bacterial infection during pregnancy, especially (and maybe only in) cases involving hospitalization. (13)

Viral theory of schizophrenia: Holds that people whose mothers had a virus while pregnant with them are at higher risk for schizophrenia. (4)

Virtual reality exposure: Exposure technique in which client is exposed to the anxiety-provoking objects or situations using computer-generated virtual reality experiences to condition a new, non-anxious response to them. (6)

Voyeurism/voyeuristic disorder: Paraphilic disorder involving sexual fantasies, urges, or behaviors related to observing an unsuspecting person naked. (10)

Vulnerability paradox: Paradoxical research finding that people from wealthier and more sheltered countries, who tend to believe that the world is safe, show higher prevalence rates of PTSD than people from poorer and more vulnerable countries who don't have similar expectations of safety. (7)

Wader theory: Evolutionary theory of ADHD that says that over time, humans evolved to have less body hair and this made clinging to mothers for protection less adaptive; however, children able to get their mothers' attention through hyperactive behaviors were more likely to be breastfed. (13)

Wandering womb theory: The ancient Greek physician Hippocrates' biological theory that attributed hysteria to a woman's uterus detaching from its natural location and wandering around her body. (1)

War neurasthenia: A term popular in the late 19th and early 20th centuries to describe the emotional responses of war veterans; their emotional difficulties were attributed to a weak nervous system. (7)

Weak central coherence theory: Holds that people with autism prefer focusing on parts, not wholes; thus, they cognitively emphasize details over the more global picture. (13)

Weight set point: The weight one's body tries to maintain. (9)

Werther effect: The tendency for suicide rates to go up following a highly publicized suicide. (15)

Western ideal of thinness: Beauty ideal advanced in many Western cultures that values thin female bodies with small waists and minimal body fat; some believe that this beauty ideal, when internalized, contributes to eating disorders. (9)

Wild beast test: Precursor to the insanity defense developed in 1265 in the U.K.; it compared defendants who did not understand their crimes to wild beasts. (15)

Wish fulfillment: Psychoanalytic idea that every dream contains a wish, often an unconscious one. (2)

Withdrawal: The unpleasant psychological and physical symptoms that result when someone stops taking a drug. (11)

Word salad: Form of psychotic behavior in which a person's speech seems like a jumble of random words; believed to reflect disorganized thinking. (4)

Working through: In psychoanalysis, the period after catharsis during which patients integrate unconscious conflicts that have been discovered into their lives. (2)

York Retreat: A Quaker retreat in York, England where William Tuke's version of moral therapy was offered; emphasized Quaker values in supporting patients as they worked to overcome madness. (1)

REFERENCES

///////////////////////

Aaltonen, J., Seikkula, J., & Lehtinen, K. (2011). The comprehensive open-dialogue approach in Western Lapland: I. The incidence of non-affective psychosis and prodromal states. *Psychosis: Psychological, Social and Integrative Approaches, 3*(3), 179–191. doi:10.1080/1752 2439.2011.601750

Abbass, A. (2016). The emergence of psychodynamic psychotherapy for treatment resistant patients: Intensive short-term dynamic psychotherapy. *Psychodynamic Psychiatry, 44*(2), 245–280. doi:10.1521/pdps.2016.44.2.245

Abbass, A. A., & Town, J. M. (2013). Key clinical processes in intensive short-term dynamic psychotherapy. *Psychotherapy, 50*(3), 433–437. doi:10.1037/a0032166

Abbass, A., Sheldon, A., Gyra, J., & Kalpin, A. (2008). Intensive short-term dynamic psychotherapy for DSM-IV personality disorders: A randomized controlled trial. *Journal of Nervous and Mental Disease, 196*(3), 211–216. doi:10.1097/NMD.0b013e3181662ff0

Abbass, A., Town, J., & Driessen, E. (2012). Intensive short-term dynamic psychotherapy: A systematic review and meta-analysis of outcome research. *Harvard Review of Psychiatry, 20*(2), 97–108. doi:10.3109/10673 229.2012.677347

Abed, R. T. (1998). The sexual competition hypothesis for eating disorders. *British Journal of Medical Psychology, 71*(4), 525–547. doi:10.1111/j.2044-8341.1998.tb01007.x

Abell, S., & Dauphin, B. (2009). The perpetuation of patriarchy: The hidden factor of gender bias in the diagnosis and treatment of children. *Clinical Child Psychology and Psychiatry, 14*(1), 117–133. doi:10.1177/1359104508096773

Abi-Dargham, A., Kegeles, L. S., Zea-Ponce, Y., Mawlawi, O., Martinez, D., Mitropoulou, V., ... Siever, L. J. (2004). Striatal amphetamine-induced dopamine release in patients with schizotypal personality disorder studied with single photon emission computed tomography and [123I]Iodobenzamide. *Biological Psychiatry, 55*(10), 1001–1006. doi:10.1016/j.biopsych.2004.01.018

Abramowitz, J. S., & Jacoby, R. J. (2014). Obsessive-compulsive disorder in the DSM-5. *Clinical Psychology: Science and Practice, 21*(3), 221–235. doi:10.1111/cpsp.12076

Abramowitz, J. S., Fabricant, L. E., Taylor, S., Deacon, B. J., McKay, D., & Storch, E. A. (2014). The relevance of analogue studies for understanding obsessions and compulsions. *Clinical Psychology Review, 34*(3), 206–217. doi:10.1016/j.cpr.2014.01.004

Abramson, L. Y., Metalsky, G. I., & Alloy, L. B. (1989). Hopelessness depression: A theory-based subtype of depression. *Psychological Review, 96*(2), 358–372. doi:10.1037/0033-295X.96.2.358

Abramson, L. Y., Seligman, M. E., & Teasdale, J. D. (1978). Learned helplessness in humans: Critique and reformulation. *Journal of Abnormal Psychology, 87*(1), 49–74. doi:10.1037/0021-843X.87.1.49

Abreu, T., & Bragança, M. (2015). The bipolarity of light and dark: A review on bipolar disorder and circadian cycles. *Journal of Affective Disorders, 185*, 219–229. doi:10.1016/j.jad.2015.07.017

Accordino, R. E., Kidd, C., Politte, L. C., Henry, C. A., & McDougle, C. J. (2016). Psychopharmacological interventions in autism spectrum disorder. *Expert Opinion on Pharmacotherapy, 17*(7), 937–952. doi:10.151 7/14656566.2016.1154536

Achat, H. M., & Stubbs, J. M. (2014). Socio-economic and ethnic differences in the prevalence of overweight and obesity among school children. *Journal of Paediatrics and Child Health, 50*(10), E77–E84. doi:10.1111/j.1440-1754.2012.02474.x

Acker, C. J. (1993). Stigma or legitimation? A historical examination of the social potentials of addiction disease models. *Journal of Psychoactive Drugs, 25*(3), 193–205. doi:10.10 80/02791072.1993.10472271

Adame, A. L. (2014). 'There needs to be a place in society for madness': The psychiatric survivor movement and new directions in mental health care. *Journal of Humanistic Psychology, 54*(4), 456–475. doi:10.1177/0022167813510207

Adams, J. (2013). Exercise dependence. In P. M. Miller, S. A. Ball, M. E. Bates, A. W. Blume, K. M. Kampman, D. J. Kavanagh, M. E. Larimer, N. M. Petry, & P. De Witte (Eds.), *Comprehensive addictive behaviors and disorders, Vol. 1: Principles of addiction* (pp. 827–835). San Diego, CA: Elsevier Academic Press.

Adityanjee, Raju, G. S., & Khandelwal, S. K. (1989). Current status of multiple personality disorder in India. *The American Journal of Psychiatry, 146*(12), 1607–1610.

Adriaens, P. R. (2008). Debunking evolutionary psychiatry's schizophrenia paradox. *Medical Hypotheses, 70*(6), 1215–1222. doi:http://dx.doi.org/10.1016/j.mehy.2007.10.014

Adriaens, P. R., & De Block, A. (2010). The evolutionary turn in psychiatry: A historical overview. *History of Psychiatry, 21*(2), 131–143. doi:10.1177/0957154X10370632

Agalaryan, A., & Rouleau, J.-L. (2014). Paraphilic coercive disorder: An unresolved issue. *Archives of Sexual Behavior, 43*(7), 1253–1256. doi:10.1007/s10508-014-0372-5

Aguirre, E., Hoare, Z., Streater, A., Spector, A., Woods, B., Hoe, J., & Orrell, M. (2013). Cognitive stimulation therapy (CST) for people with dementia—Who benefits most? *International Journal of Geriatric Psychiatry, 28*(3), 284–290. doi:10.1002/gps.3823

Aharoni, R., & Hertz, M. M. (2012). Disgust sensitivity and anorexia nervosa. *European Eating Disorders Review, 20*(2), 106–110. doi:10.1002/erv.1124

Ahearn, W. H. (2010). What every behavior analyst should know about the 'MMR causes autism' hypothesis. *Behavior Analysis in Practice, 3*(1), 46–50.

Ainsworth, M. D. S., Blehar, M. C., Waters, E., & Wall, S. (1978). *Patterns of attachment: A psychological study of the strange situation.* Oxford, UK: Lawrence Erlbaum.

Akyüz, G., Doğan, O., Şar, V., Yargiç, L. İ., & Tutkun, H. (1999). Frequency of dissociative identity disorder in the general population in Turkey. *Comprehensive Psychiatry, 40*(2), 151–159. doi:10.1016/S0010-440X(99) 90120-7

Alanen, Y. O. (2009). Can we approach patients with schizophrenic psychoses from a psychological basis? In Y. O. Alanen, M. González de Chávez, A.-L. S. Silver, & B. Martindale (Eds.), *Psychotherapeutic approaches to schizophrenic psychoses* (pp. 3–9). London, UK: Routledge.

Alanko, K., Gunst, A., Mokros, A., & Santtila, P. (2016). Genetic variants associated with male pedophilic sexual interest. *Journal of Sexual Medicine, 13*(5), 835–842. doi:10.1016/j.jsxm.2016.02.170

Alanko, K., Salo, B., Mokros, A., & Santtila, P. (2013). Evidence for heritability of adult men's sexual interest in youth under age 16 from a population-based extended twin design. *Journal of Sexual Medicine, 10*(4), 1090–1099. doi:10.1111/jsm.12067

Albert, U., Bogetto, F., Maina, G., Saracco, P., Brunatto, C., & Mataix-Cols, D. (2010). Family accommodation in obsessive-compulsive disorder: Relation to symptom dimensions, clinical and family characteristics. *Psychiatry Research, 179*(2), 204–211. doi:http://dx.doi.org/10.1016/j.psychres.2009.06.008

Albus, C. (2010). Psychological and social factors in coronary heart disease. *Annals of Medicine, 42*(5), 487–494. doi:10.3109/07853890.201 0.515605

Alcoholics Anonymous [Great Britain]. (2017). Membership. Retrieved from http://www.alcoholics-anonymous.org.uk/About-AA/Membership

Alcoholics Anonymous. (2013, April 7). AA around the globe. Retrieved from http://www.aa.org/assets/en_US/smf-165_en.pdf

Alcoholics Anonymous. (2014). 2014 membership survey. Retrieved from http://www.aa.org/assets/en_US/p-48_membershipsurvey.pdf

Aldarondo, E. (Ed.) (2007). *Advancing social justice through clinical practice.* Mahwah, NJ: Lawrence Erlbaum.

Alegria, A. A., Blanco, C., Petry, N. M., Skodol, A. E., Liu, S.-M., Grant, B., & Hasin, D. (2013). Sex differences in antisocial personality disorder: Results from the National Epidemiological Survey on Alcohol and Related Conditions. *Personality Disorders: Theory, Research, and Treatment, 4*(3), 214–222. doi:10.1037/a0031681

Alexander, F., & French, T. (1946). *Psychoanalytic therapy: Principles and applications.* New York, NY: Ronald Press.

Ali, A., Hassiotis, A., Strydom, A., & King, M. (2012). Self stigma in people with intellectual disabilities and courtesy stigma in family carers: A systematic review. *Research in Developmental Disabilities, 33*(6), 2122–2140. doi:10.1016/j.ridd.2012.06.013

Allen, J. G., & Smith, W. H. (1993). Diagnosing dissociative disorders. *Bulletin of the Menninger Clinic, 57*(3), 328–343.

Allen, J. P., Hauser, S. T., & Borman-Spurrell, E. (1996). Attachment theory as a framework for understanding sequelae of severe adolescent psychopathology: An 11-year follow-up study. *Journal of Consulting and Clinical Psychology, 64*(2), 254–263. doi:10.1037/0022-006X.64.2.254

Allen, L. A., & Woolfolk, R. L. (2010). Cognitive behavioral therapy for somatoform disorders. *Psychiatric Clinics of North America, 33*(3), 579–593. doi:10.1016/j.psc.2010.04.014

Allen, N. B., & Badcock, P. B. T. (2006). Darwinian models of depression: A review of evolutionary accounts of mood and mood disorders. *Progress in Neuro-Psychopharmacology & Biological Psychiatry, 30*(5), 815–826. doi:10.1016/j.pnpbp.2006.01.007

Allik, J. (2005). Personality dimensions across cultures. *Journal of Personality Disorders, 19*(3), 212–232. doi:10.1521/pedi.2005.19.3.212

Allik, J. (2012). National differences in personality. *Personality and Individual Differences, 53*(2), 114–117. doi:10.1016/j.paid.2011.05.011

Allison, S. E., von Wahlde, L., Shockley, T., & Gabbard, G. O. (2006). The development of the self in the era of the internet and role-playing fantasy games. *The American Journal of Psychiatry, 163*(3), 381–385.

Alm, P. A. (2004). Stuttering and the basal ganglia circuits: A critical review of possible relations. *Journal of Communication Disorders, 37*(4), 325–369. doi:10.1016/j.jcomdis.2004.03.001

Almås, E. (2016). Psychological treatment of sexual problems. Thematic analysis of guidelines and recommendations, based on a systematic literature review 2001–2010. *Sexual and Relationship Therapy, 31*(1), 54–69. doi:10.1080/14681994.2015.1086739

Almli, L. M., Fani, N., Smith, A. K., & Ressler, K. J. (2014). Genetic approaches to understanding post-traumatic stress disorder. *International Journal of Neuropsychopharmacology, 17*(2), 355–370. doi:10.1017/S1461145713001090

Alonso, J., Angermeyer, M. C., Bernert, S., Bruffaerts, R., Brugha, T. S., Bryson, H., ... Vollebergh, W. A. M. (2004). Prevalence of mental disorders in Europe: Results from the European Study of the Epidemiology of Mental Disorders (ESEMeD) project. *Acta Psychiatrica Scandinavica, 109*(Suppl420), 21–27.

Alonso, J., Buron, A., Bruffaerts, R., He, Y., Posada-Villa, J., Lepine, J. P., ... Von Korff, M. (2008). Association of perceived stigma and mood and anxiety disorders: Results from the World Mental Health Surveys. *Acta Psychiatrica Scandinavica, 118*(4), 305–314. doi:10.1111/j.1600-0447.2008.01241.x

Alsharnoubi, J., Sabbour, A. A., Shoukry, A. I., & Abdelazeem, A. M. (2017). Nocturnal enuresis in children between laser acupuncture and medical treatment: A comparative study. *Lasers in Medical Science, 32*, 95–99.

Altemus, M. (2006). Sex differences in depression and anxiety disorders: Potential biological determinants. *Hormones and Behavior, 50*(4), 534–538. doi:10.1016/j.yhbeh.2006.06.031

Altemus, M., Sarvaiya, N., & Epperson, C. N. (2014). Sex differences in anxiety and depression clinical perspectives. *Frontiers in Neuroendocrinology, 35*(3), 320–330. doi:10.1016/j.yfrne.2014.05.004

Alvares, G. A., Quintana, D. S., & Whitehouse, A. J. O. (2016). Beyond the hype and hope: Critical considerations for intranasal oxytocin research in autism spectrum disorder. *Autism Research.* doi:10.1002/aur.1692

Alzheimer's Disease International. (2015). *World Alzheimer's Report 2015.* Retrieved from https://www.alz.co.uk/research/WorldAlzheimerReport2016.pdf

Alzheimer's Disease International. (2016). *World Alzheimer Report 2016.* Retrieved from https://www.alz.co.uk/research/WorldAlzheimerReport2016.pdf

Alzheimer's Society. (2017, April 15). Is there a link between stress and dementia risk? Retrieved from https://blog.alzheimers.org.uk/research/stress-and-dementia/

Amad, A., Ramoz, N., Thomas, P., Jardri, R., & Gorwood, P. (2014). Genetics of borderline personality disorder: Systematic review and proposal of an integrative model. *Neuroscience and Biobehavioral Reviews, 40*, 6–19. doi:10.1016/j.neubiorev.2014.01.003

Ambrogne, J. A. (2002). Reduced-risk drinking as a treatment goal: What clinicians need to know. *Journal of Substance Abuse Treatment, 22*(1), 45–53. doi:http://dx.doi.org/10.1016/S0740-5472(01)00210-0

American Institute of Stress. (n.d.). What is stress? Retrieved from http://www.stress.org/what-is-stress/

American Psychiatric Association. (1952). *Diagnostic and statistical manual of mental disorders.* Washington, DC: Author.

American Psychiatric Association. (1980). *Diagnostic and statistical manual of mental disorders* (3rd ed.). Washington, DC: Author.

American Psychiatric Association. (1998). *Position statement on psychiatric treatment and sexual orientation.* Washington, DC: Author.

American Psychiatric Association. (2000). Position statement on therapies focused on attempts to change sexual orientation (reparative or conversion therapies). *The American Journal of Psychiatry, 157*(10), 1719–1721.

American Psychiatric Association. (2013a). Autism spectrum disorder. Retrieved from https://www.psychiatry.org/psychiatrists/practice/dsm/educational-resources/dsm-5-fact-sheets

American Psychiatric Association. (2013b). *Diagnostic and statistical manual of mental disorders* (5th ed.). Washington, DC: American Psychiatric Publishing.

American Psychiatric Association. (2013c). Feeding and eating disorders. Retrieved from http://www.dsm5.org/documents/eating%20disorders%20fact%20sheet.pdf

American Psychiatric Association. (2013d). Substance-related and addictive disorders. Retrieved from https://www.psychiatry.org/psychiatrists/practice/dsm/educational-resources/dsm-5-fact-sheets

American Psychiatric Association. (n.d.-a). DSM-5: Frequently asked questions. Retrieved from https://www.psychiatry.org/psychiatrists/practice/dsm/feedback-and-questions/frequently-asked-questions

American Psychiatric Association. (n.d.-b). What is psychiatry? Retrieved from http://www.psychiatry.org/about-apa--psychiatry/more-about-psychiatry

American Psychoanalytic Association. (2006). *Psychodynamic diagnostic manual.* Silver Spring, MD: Alliance of Psychoanayltic Organizations.

American Psychological Association. (2002). Ethical principles of psychologists and code of conduct. *American Psychologist, 57*(12), 1060–1073. doi:10.1037/0003-066X.57.12.1060

American Psychological Association. (2012). Guidelines for psychological practice with lesbian, gay, and bisexual clients. *American Psychologist, 67*(1), 10–42. doi:10.1037/a0024659

American Psychological Association. (2017, March 23). The Hierarchical Taxonomy of Psychopathology (HiTOP). Retrieved from http://www.apa.org/pubs/highlights/spotlight/issue-88.aspx

American Psychological Association. (n.d.-a). Anxiety. Retrieved from http://www.apa.org/topics/anxiety/

American Psychological Association. (n.d.-b). Understanding chronic stress. Retrieved from http://www.apa.org/helpcenter/understanding-chronic-stress.aspx

Amianto, F., Caroppo, P., D'Agata, F., Spalatro, A., Lavagnino, L., Caglio, M., ... Fassino, S. (2013). Brain volumetric abnormalities in patients with anorexia and bulimia nervosa: A voxel-based morphometry study. *Psychiatry Research: Neuroimaging, 213*(3), 210–216. doi:10.1016/j.pscychresns.2013.03.010

Amodeo, M. (2015). The addictive personality. *Substance Use & Misuse, 50*(8–9), 1031–1036. doi:10.3109/10826084.2015.1007646

Amos, T., Stein, D. J., & Ipser, J. C. (2014). Pharmacological interventions for preventing post-traumatic stress disorder (PTSD). *Cochrane Database of Systematic Reviews, 2014*(7), 1–64. doi:10.1002/14651858.CD006239.pub2

Anastasi, A., & Urbina, S. (1997). *Psychological testing* (7th ed.). Upper Saddle River, NJ: Prentice Hall.

Anders, S., Tanaka, M., & Kinney, D. K. (2013). Depression as an evolutionary strategy for defense against infection. *Brain, Behavior, and Immunity, 31*, 9–22. doi:http://dx.doi.org/10.1016/j.bbi.2012.12.002

Andersen, I., Thielen, K., Nygaard, E., & Diderichsen, F. (2009). Social inequality in the prevalence of depressive disorders. *Journal of Epidemiology and Community Health, 63*(7), 575–581. doi:10.1136/jech.2008.082719

Anderson, J. L., & Sellbom, M. (2016). Evaluating the DSM-5 Section III personality disorder impairment criteria. *Personality Disorders: Theory, Research, and Treatment*. doi:10.1037/per0000217

Anderson, J. L., Sellbom, M., Sansone, R. A., & Songer, D. A. (2016). Comparing external correlates of DSM-5 Section II and Section III dimensional trait operationalizations of borderline personality disorder. *Journal of Personality Disorders, 30*(2), 193–210. doi:10.1521/pedi_2015_29_189

Anderson, J., Snider, S., Sellbom, M., Krueger, R., & Hopwood, C. (2014). A comparison of the DSM-5 Section II and Section III personality disorder structures. *Psychiatry Research, 216*(3), 363–372. doi:10.1016/j.psychres.2014.01.007

Anderson, K. K., & Mukherjee, S. D. (2007). The need for additional safeguards in the informed consent process in schizophrenia research. *Journal of Medical Ethics: Journal of the Institute of Medical Ethics, 33*(11), 647–650. doi:10.1136/jme.2006.017376

Anderson, K. N., Jeon, A. B., Blenner, J. A., Wiener, R. L., & Hope, D. A. (2015). How people evaluate others with social anxiety disorder: A comparison to depression and general mental illness stigma. *American Journal of Orthopsychiatry, 85*(2), 131–138. doi:10.1037/ort0000046

Anderson, L. (2016). Insomnia treatment with non-benzodiazepines Ambien, Lunesta & Sonata. Retrieved from https://www.drugs.com/slideshow/insomnia-treatment-nonbenzodiazepines-1072

Anderson, R. J., Frye, M. A., Abulseoud, O. A., Lee, K. H., McGillivray, J. A., Berk, M., & Tye, S. J. (2012). Deep brain stimulation for treatment-resistant depression: Efficacy, safety and mechanisms of action. *Neuroscience and Biobehavioral Reviews, 36*(8), 1920–1933. doi:10.1016/j.neubiorev.2012.06.001

Andersson, G., & Ghaderi, A. (2006). Overview and analysis of the behaviourist criticism of the Diagnostic and Statistical Manual of Mental Disorders (DSM). *Clinical Psychologist, 10*(2), 67–77. doi:10.1080/13284200600690461

Andersson, G., & Titov, N. (2014). Advantages and limitations of Internet-based interventions for common mental disorders. *World Psychiatry, 13*(1), 4–11. doi:10.1002/wps.20083

Andover, M. S., & Gibb, B. E. (2010). Non-suicidal self-injury, attempted suicide, and suicidal intent among psychiatric inpatients. *Psychiatry Research, 178*(1), 101–105. doi:http://dx.doi.org/10.1016/j.psychres.2010.03.019

Andreasen, N. C. (2010). Posttraumatic stress disorder: A history and a critique. *Annals of the New York Academy of Sciences, 1208*, 67–71. doi:10.1111/j.1749-6632.2010.05699.x

Andreassen, C. S. (2013). Work addiction. In P. M. Miller, S. A. Ball, M. E. Bates, A. W. Blume, K. M. Kampman, D. J. Kavanagh, M. E. Larimer, N. M. Petry, & P. De Witte (Eds.), *Comprehensive addictive behaviors and disorders, Vol. 1: Principles of addiction* (pp. 837–845). San Diego, CA: Elsevier Academic Press.

Andreasson, K., Krogh, J., Wenneberg, C., Jessen, H. K. L., Krakauer, K., Gluud, C., ... Nordentoft, M. (2016). Effectiveness of dialectical behavior therapy versus collaborative assessment and management of suicidality treatment for reduction of self-harm in adults with borderline personality traits and disorder—A randomized observer-blinded clinical trial. *Depression and Anxiety, 33*(6), 520–530. doi:10.1002/da.22472

Andrews, D. A., & Bonta, J. (2010). Rehabilitating criminal justice policy and practice. *Psychology, Public Policy, and Law, 16*(1), 39–55. doi:10.1037/a0018362

Andrews, D. A., Bonta, J., & Wormith, J. S. (2011). The risk-need-responsivity (RNR) model: Does adding the good lives model contribute to effective crime prevention? *Criminal Justice and Behavior, 38*(7), 735–755. doi:10.1177/0093854811406356

Andrews, G., & Hobbs, M. J. (2010). The effect of the draft DSM-5 criteria for GAD on prevalence and severity. *Australian and New Zealand Journal of Psychiatry, 44*(9), 784–790.

Andrews, J. (2007). The (un)dress of the mad poor in England, c.1650–1850. Part 2. *History of Psychiatry, 18*(2), 131–156. doi:10.1177/0957154X06067246

Andrews, J. A., & Neises, K. D. (2012). Cells, biomarkers, and post-traumatic stress disorder: evidence for peripheral involvement in a central disease. *Journal of Neurochemistry, 120*(1), 26–36. doi:10.1111/j.1471-4159.2011.07545.x

Andrews, P. W., & Thomson, J. A., Jr. (2009). The bright side of being blue: Depression as an adaptation for analyzing complex problems. *Psychological Review, 116*(3), 620–654. doi:10.1037/a0016242

Anestis, M. D., Anestis, J. C., & Butterworth, S. E. (2017). Handgun legislation and changes in statewide overall suicide rates. *American Journal of Public Health, 107*(4), 579–581. doi:10.2105/AJPH.2016.303650

Angell, B., Cooke, A., & Kovac, K. (2005). First-person accounts of stigma. In P. W. Corrigan (Ed.), *On the stigma of mental illness: Practical strategies for research and social change* (pp. 69–98). Washington, DC: American Psychological Association.

Angier, N. (2003, June 22). Short men, short shrift. Are drugs the answer? *The New York Times*. Retrieved from http://www.nytimes.com

Angleitner, A., & Ostendorf, F. (1994). Temperament and the Big Five factors of personality. In C. F. Halverson, Jr., G. A. Kohnstamm, & R. P. Martin (Eds.), *The developing structure of temperament and personality from infancy to adulthood* (pp. 69–90). Hillsdale, NJ: Lawrence Erlbaum.

Anglin, D. M., Lighty, Q., Greenspoon, M., & Ellman, L. M. (2014). Racial discrimination is associated with distressing subthreshold positive psychotic symptoms among US urban ethnic minority young adults. *Social Psychiatry and Psychiatric Epidemiology, 49*(10), 1545–1555. doi:10.1007/s00127-014-0870-8

Anglin, R., Moayyedi, P., & Leontiadis, G. I. (2015). Anti-inflammatory intervention in depression: Comment. *JAMA Psychiatry, 72*(5), 512–512. doi:10.1001/jamapsychiatry.2014.3246

Annear, K. (2013, May 27). The disorder formerly known as Asperger's. Retrieved from http://www.abc.net.au/rampup/articles/2013/05/24/3766915.htm

Anstice, S., Strike, C. J., & Brands, B. (2009). Supervised methadone consumption: Client issues and stigma. *Substance Use & Misuse, 44*(6), 794–808. doi:10.1080/10826080802483936

Antai-Otong, D. (2008). Pharmacological management of psychosis in Alzheimer's disease: Clinical challenges associated with second-generation antipsychotic medications. *Perspectives In Psychiatric Care, 44*(2), 120–123. doi:10.1111/j.1744-6163.2008.00161.x

Anton, B. S. (2010). Proceedings of the American Psychological Association for the legislative year 2009: Minutes of the annual meeting of the Council of Representatives and minutes of the meetings of the Board of Directors. *American Psychologist, 65*(5), 385–475. doi:10.1037/a0019553

Antoni, M. H., Lehman, J. M., Kilbourn, K. M., Boyers, A. E., Culver, J. L., Alferi, S. M., ... Carver, C. S. (2001). Cognitive-behavioral stress management intervention decreases the prevalence of depression and enhances benefit finding among women under treatment for early-stage breast cancer. *Health Psychology, 20*(1), 20–32. doi:10.1037/0278-6133.20.1.20

Antoniou, P., & Cooper, M. (2013). Psychological treatments for eating disorders: What is the importance of the quality of the therapeutic alliance for outcomes? *Counselling Psychology Review, 28*(4), 34–46.

Antonsen, B. T., Klungsøyr, O., Kamps, A., Hummelen, B., Johansen, M. S., Pedersen, G., ... Wilberg, T. (2014). Step-down versus outpatient psychotherapeutic treatment for personality disorders: 6-year follow-up of the Ullevål personality project. *BMC Psychiatry, 14.* doi:10.1186/1471-244X-14-119

Antshel, K. M., & Olszewski, A. K. (2014). Cognitive behavioral therapy for adolescents with ADHD. *Child and Adolescent Psychiatric Clinics of North America, 23*(4), 825–842. doi:10.1016/j.chc.2014.05.001

Antshel, K. M., Faraone, S. V., & Gordon, M. (2014). Cognitive behavioral treatment outcomes in adolescent ADHD. *Journal of Attention Disorders, 18*(6), 483–495. doi:10.1177/1087054712443155

Apostolou, M. (2015). Sexual dysfunctions in men: An evolutionary perspective. *Evolutionary Psychological Science, 1*, 220–231. doi:10.1007/s40806-015-0026-4

Appelbaum, P. S. (1988). The right to refuse treatment with antipsychotic medications: Retrospect and prospect. *The American Journal of Psychiatry, 145*(4), 413–419. doi:10.1176/ajp.145.4.413

Apple, R. F. (1999). Interpersonal therapy for bulimia nervosa. *Journal of Clinical Psychology, 55*(6), 715–725. doi:10.1002/(SICI)1097-4679(199906)55:6<715::AID-JCLP5>3.0.CO;2-B

Aragona, M. (2009). The role of comorbidity in the crisis of the current psychiatric classification system. *Philosophy, Psychiatry, & Psychology, 16*(1), 1–11. doi:10.1353/ppp.0.0211

Arch, J. J., Eifert, G. H., Davies, C., Vilardaga, J. C. P., Rose, R. D., & Craske, M. G. (2012). Randomized clinical trial of cognitive behavioral therapy (CBT) versus acceptance and commitment therapy (ACT) for mixed anxiety disorders. *Journal of Consulting and Clinical Psychology, 80*(5), 750–765. doi:10.1037/a0028310

Archer, J. (2001). Grief from an evolutionary perspective. In M. S. Stroebe, R. O. Hansson, W. Stroebe, & H. Schut (Eds.), *Handbook of bereavement research: Consequences, coping, and care* (pp. 263–283). Washington, DC: American Psychological Association.

Arda, E., Cakiroglu, B., & Thomas, D. T. (2016). Primary nocturnal enuresis: A review. *Nephro-Urology Monthly, 8*(4), e35809–e35809.

Ariès, P. (1962). *Centuries of childhood: A social history of family life* (R. Baldick, Trans.). New York, NY: Random House.

Aring, C. D. (1974). The Gheel experience: Eternal spirit of the chainless mind. *JAMA: Journal of the American Medical Association, 230*(7), 998–1001. doi:10.1001/jama.230.7.998

Arizmendi, B. J., & O'Connor, M.-F. (2015). What is "normal" in grief? *Australian Critical Care, 28*(2), 58–62. doi:http://dx.doi.org/10.1016/j.aucc.2015.01.005

Arkhipov, V. I. (1999). Memory dissociation: The approach to the study of retrieval processes. *Behavioural Brain Research, 106*(1–2), 39–46. doi:10.1016/S0166-4328(99)00090-X

Armando, M., Pontillo, M., & Vicari, S. (2015). Psychosocial interventions for very early and early-onset schizophrenia: A review of treatment efficacy. *Current Opinion in Psychiatry, 28*(4), 312–323. doi:10.1097/YCO.0000000000000165

Armitage, H. (2015, August 24). How does the new 'female Viagra' work? *Science.*

Armon, G. (2014). Personality and serum lipids: Does lifestyle account for their concurrent and long-term relationships. *European Journal of Personality, 28*(6), 550–559.

Armstrong, L. L. (2006). Barriers to intimate sexuality: Concerns and meaning-based therapy approaches. *The Humanistic Psychologist, 34*(3), 281–298. doi:10.1207/s15473333thp3403_5

Armstrong, T. (1995). *The myth of the A.D.D. child: 50 ways to improve your child's attention span without drugs, labels, or coercion.* New York, NY: Plume.

Arnedo, J., Svrakic, D. M., del Val, C., Romero-Zaliz, R., Hernández-Cuervo, H., Fanous, A. H., ... Zwir, I. (2015). Uncovering the hidden risk architecture of the schizophrenias: Confirmation in three independent genome-wide association studies. *The American Journal of Psychiatry, 172*(2), 139–153. doi:10.1176/appi.ajp.2014.14040435

Arnold, L. E., Lofthouse, N., & Hurt, E. (2012). Artificial food colors and attention-deficit/hyperactivity symptoms: Conclusions to dye for. *Neurotherapeutics, 9*(3), 599–609. doi:10.1007/s13311-012-0133-x

Arnone, D., McIntosh, A. M., Ebmeier, K. P., Munafò, M. R., & Anderson, I. M. (2012). Magnetic resonance imaging studies in unipolar depression: Systematic review and meta-regression analyses. *European Neuropsychopharmacology, 22*(1), 1–16. doi:http://dx.doi.org/10.1016/j.euroneuro.2011.05.003

Arnott, S., Onslow, M., O'Brian, S., Packman, A., Jones, M., & Block, S. (2014). Group Lidcombe Program treatment for early stuttering: A randomized controlled trial. *Journal of Speech, Language, and Hearing Research, 57*(5), 1606–1618. doi:10.1044/2014_JSLHR-S-13-0090

Arnsten, A. F. T. (2006). Fundamentals of attention-deficit/hyperactivity disorder: circuits and pathways. *Journal of Clinical Psychiatry, 67 Suppl 8*, 7–12.

Arntz, A., van Genderen, H., Drost, J., Sendt, K., & Baumgarten-Kustner, S. (2009). *Schema therapy for borderline personality disorder.* Chichester, UK: Wiley-Blackwell.

Aromaa, E., Tolvanen, A., Tuulari, J., & Wahlbeck, K. (2011). Personal stigma and use of mental health services among people with depression in a general population in Finland. *BMC Psychiatry, 11.* doi:10.1186/1471-244X-11-52

Asami, T., Hyuk Lee, S., Bouix, S., Rathi, Y., Whitford, T. J., Niznikiewicz, M., ... Kubicki, M. (2014). Cerebral white matter abnormalities and their associations with negative but not positive symptoms of schizophrenia. *Psychiatry Research: Neuroimaging, 222*(1–2), 52–59. doi:http://dx.doi.org/10.1016/j.pscychresns.2014.02.007

Asmundson, G. J. G., Taylor, S., & Smits, J. A. J. (2014). Panic disorder and agoraphobia: An overview and commentary on DSM-5 changes. *Depression and Anxiety, 31*(6), 480–486. doi:10.1002/da.22277

Asperger, H. (1991). Autistic psycopathy in childhood. In U. Frith (Ed.), *Autism and Asperger syndrome.* Cambridge, UK: Cambridge University Press.

Assumpção, A. A., Garcia, F. D., Garcia, H. D., Bradford, J. M. W., & Thibaut, F. (2014). Pharmacologic treatment of paraphilias. *Psychiatric Clinics of North America, 37*(2), 173–181. doi:10.1016/j.psc.2014.03.002

Astbury, J. (2010). The social causes of women's depression: A question of rights violated? In D. C. Jack & A. Ali (Eds.), *Silencing the self across cultures: Depression and gender in the social world* (pp. 19–45). New York, NY: Oxford University Press.

Ata, R. N., Thompson, J. K., & Small, B. J. (2013). Effects of exposure to thin-ideal media images on body dissatisfaction: Testing the inclusion of a disclaimer versus warning label. *Body Image, 10*(4), 472–480. doi:http://dx.doi.org/10.1016/j.bodyim.2013.04.004

Atladóttir, H. Ó., Thorsen, P., Østergaard, L., Schendel, D. E., Lemcke, S., Abdallah, M., & Parner, E. T. (2010). Maternal infection requiring hospitalization during pregnancy and autism spectrum disorders. *Journal of Autism and Developmental Disorders, 40*(12), 1423–1430. doi:10.1007/s10803-010-1006-y

Atmaca, M., Yildirim, H., Ozdemir, H., Ozler, S., Kara, B., Ozler, Z., ... Tezcan, E. (2008). Hippocampus and amygdalar volumes in patients with refractory obsessive-compulsive disorder. *Progress in Neuro-Psychopharmacology & Biological Psychiatry, 32*(5), 1283–1286. doi:10.1016/j.pnpbp.2008.04.002

Atri, A. (2011). Effective pharmacological management of Alzheimer's disease. *The American Journal of Managed Care, 17 Suppl 13*, S346–S355.

Attia, E., & Roberto, C. A. (2009). Should amenorrhea be a diagnostic criterion for anorexia nervosa? *International Journal of Eating Disorders, 42*(7), 581–589. doi:10.1002/eat.20720

Attia, E., Becker, A. E., Bryant-Waugh, R., Hoek, H. W., Kreipe, R. E., Marcus, M. D., ... Wonderlich, S. (2013). Feeding and eating disorders in DSM-5. *The American Journal of Psychiatry, 170*(11), 1237–1239. doi:10.1176/appi.ajp.13030326

Attwood, A., Aveyard, P., Bauld, L., Britton, J., Hajek, P., Hastings, G., ... West, R. (2013). Tobacco. In P. M. Miller, S. A. Ball, M. E. Bates, A. W. Blume, K. M. Kampman, D. J. Kavanagh, M. E. Larimer, N. M. Petry, & P. De Witte (Eds.), *Comprehensive addictive behaviors and disorders, Vol. 1: Principles of addiction* (pp. 767–776). San Diego, CA: Elsevier Academic Press.

Atwood, J. D. (2015). Sexual disorders and sex therapy. In J. L. Wetchler & L. L. Hecker (Eds.), *An introduction to marriage and family therapy* (2nd ed., pp. 431–467). New York, NY: Routledge.

Aucott, C., & Soni, A. (2016). Reflections on the use of Critical Incident Stress Debriefing in schools. *Educational Psychology in Practice, 32*(1), 85–99. doi:10.1080/02667363.2015.1112257

Aupperle, R. L., Melrose, A. J., Stein, M. B., & Paulus, M. P. (2012). Executive function and PTSD: Disengaging from trauma. *Neuropharmacology, 62*(2), 686–694. doi:10.1016/j.neuropharm.2011.02.008

Austin, A., & Craig, S. L. (2015). Transgender affirmative cognitive behavioral therapy: Clinical considerations and applications. *Professional Psychology: Research and Practice, 46*(1), 21–29. doi:10.1037/a0038642

Austin, D. W., & Richards, J. C. (2001). The catastrophic misinterpretation model of panic disorder. *Behaviour Research and Therapy, 39*(11), 1277–1291. doi:http://dx.doi.org/10.1016/S0005-7967(00)00095-4

Austin, D. W., & Richards, J. C. (2006). A test of core assumptions of the catastrophic misinterpretation model of panic disorder. *Cognitive Therapy and Research, 30*(1), 53–68. doi:10.1007/s10608-006-9010-4

Ausubel, D. P. (1983). Methadone maintenance treatment: The other side of the coin. *International Journal of the Addictions, 18*(6), 851–862. doi:10.3109/10826088309033052

Autism Speaks. (2012, December 2). American Psychiatric Association approves DSM-5 revisions. Retrieved from https://www.autismspeaks.org/science/science-news/american-psychiatric-association-approves-dsm-5-revisions

Autism Speaks. (n.d.). What is autism? Retrieved from https://www.autismspeaks.org/what-autism

Aviram, R. B., Brodsky, B. S., & Stanley, B. (2006). Borderline personality disorder, stigma, and treatment implications. *Harvard Review of Psychiatry, 14*(5), 249–256. doi:10.1080/10673220600975121

Axelrod, S., McElrath, K. K., & Wine, B. (2012). Applied behavior analysis: Autism and beyond. *Behavioral Interventions, 27*(1), 1–15. doi:10.1002/bin.1335

Axline, V. M. (1947a). Nondirective therapy for poor readers. *Journal of Consulting Psychology, 11*(2), 61–69. doi:10.1037/h0063079

Axline, V. M. (1947b). *Play therapy; the inner dynamics of childhood.* Oxford, UK: Houghton Mifflin.

Axline, V. M. (1950). Play therapy experiences as described by child participants. *Journal of Consulting Psychology, 14*(1), 53–63. doi:10.1037/h0056179

Axline, V. M. (1964). *Dibs: In search of self.* New York, NY: Ballantine Books.

Azad, N. A., Al Bugami, M., & Loy-English, I. (2007). Gender differences in dementia risk factors. *Gender Medicine, 4*(2), 120–129. doi:http://dx.doi.org/10.1016/S1550-8579(07)80026-X

Azibo, D. A. (2013). Unmasking materialistic depression as a mental health problem: Its effect on depression and materialism in an African–United States undergraduate sample. *Journal of Affective Disorders, 150*(2), 623–628. doi:10.1016/j.jad.2013.03.001

Azrin, N. H., & Foxx, R. M. (1974). *Toilet training in less than a day.* New York, NY: Pocket Books.

Azzone, P. (2013). *Depression as a psychoanalytic problem.* Lanham, MD: University Press of America.

Babor, T. F., Higgins-Biddle, J. C., Saunders, J. B., & Monteiro, M. G. (2001). *The Alcohol Use Disorders Identification Test: Guidelines for use in primary care.* Retrieved from http://apps.who.int/iris/bitstream/10665/67205/1/WHO_MSD_MSB_01.6a.pdf

Baca-Garcia, E., Vaquero, C., Diaz-Sastre, C., García-Resa, E., Saiz-Ruiz, J., Fernández-Piqueras, J., & de Leon, J. (2004). Lack of association between the serotonin transporter promoter gene polymorphism and impulsivity or aggressive behavior among suicide attempters and healthy volunteers. *Psychiatry Research, 126*(2), 99–106. doi:10.1016/j.psychres.2003.10.007

Bach, B., & Sellbom, M. (2016). Continuity between DSM-5 categorical criteria and traits criteria for borderline personality disorder. *The Canadian Journal of Psychiatry/La Revue Canadienne De Psychiatrie, 61*(8), 489–494. doi:10.1177/0706743716640756

Bach, B., Maples-Keller, J. L., Bo, S., & Simonsen, E. (2016). The alternative DSM-5 personality disorder traits criterion: A comparative examination of three self-report forms in a Danish population. *Personality Disorders: Theory, Research, and Treatment, 7*(2), 124–135. doi:10.1037/per0000162

Badiani, A. (2013). Substance-specific environmental influences on drug use and drug preference in animals and humans. *Current Opinion in Neurobiology, 23*(4), 588–596. doi:10.1016/j.conb.2013.03.010

Badiani, A., Belin, D., Epstein, D., Calu, D., & Shaham, Y. (2011). Opiate versus psychostimulant addiction: The differences do matter. *Nature Reviews Neuroscience, 12*(11), 685–700. doi:10.1038/nrn3104

Baer, R. A. (2003). Mindfulness training as a clinical intervention: A conceptual and empirical review. *Clinical Psychology: Science and Practice, 10*(2), 125–143.

Bafiti, T. V. (2001). The function of the parental family system and the sense of coherence as factors related to psychosomatic health. *Psychology: The Journal of the Hellenic Psychological Society, 8*(2), 249–266.

Baheretibeb, Y., Law, S., & Pain, C. (2008). The girl who ate her house—Pica as an obsessive-compulsive disorder: A case report. *Clinical Case Studies, 7*(1), 3–11. doi:10.1177/1534650106298917

Bailey, A., Le Couteur, A., Gottesman, I., & Bolton, P. (1995). Autism as a strongly genetic disorder: Evidence from a British twin study. *Psychological Medicine, 25*(1), 63–77. doi:10.1017/S0033291700028099

Baird, A. D., Wilson, S. J., Bladin, P. F., Saling, M. M., & Reutens, D. C. (2007). Neurological control of human sexual behaviour: Insights from lesion studies. *Journal of Neurology, Neurosurgery & Psychiatry, 78*(10), 1042–1049. doi:10.1136/jnnp.2006.107193

Baker, C. (2004). *Behavioral genetics: An introduction to how genes and environments interact through development to shape differences in mood, personality, and intelligence.* Washington, DC: American Association for the Advancement of Science and The Hastings Center.

Baker, J. P. (2013). Autism at 70—Redrawing the boundaries. *The New England Journal of Medicine, 369*(12), 1089–1091. doi:10.1056/NEJMp1306380

Baker, K. G. (2015). Bowen family systems couple coaching. In A. S. Gurman, J. L. Lebow, & D. K. Snyder (Eds.), *Clinical handbook of couple therapy* (5th ed., pp. 246–267). New York, NY: Guilford Press.

Baker, R. W., & Trzepacz, P. T. (2013). Conducting a mental status examination. In G. P. Koocher, J. C. Norcross, & B. A. Greene (Eds.), *Psychologists' desk reference* (3rd ed., pp. 17–22). Oxford, UK: Oxford University Press.

Baker, T. B., McFall, R. M., & Shoham, V. (2008). Current status and future prospects of clinical psychology: Toward a scientifically principled approach to mental and behavioral health care. *Psychological Science in the Public Interest, 9*(2), 67–103. doi:10.1111/j.1539-6053.2009.01036.x

Bakker, G. M. (2009). In defence of thought stopping. *Clinical Psychologist, 13*(2), 59–68. doi:10.1080/13284200902810452

Baldessarini, R. J., Pérez, J., Salmtore, P., Trede, K., & Maggini, C. (2015). History of bipolar manic-depressive disorder. In A. Yildiz, P. Ruiz, & C. B. Nemeroff (Eds.), *The bipolar book: History, neurobiology, and treatment* (pp. 3–19). New York, NY: Oxford University Press.

Baldessarini, R. J., Vieta, E., Calabrese, J. R., Tohen, M., & Bowden, C. L. (2010). Bipolar depression: Overview and commentary. *Harvard Review of Psychiatry, 18*(3), 143–157. doi:10.3109/10673221003747955

Baldwin, D. V. (2013). Primitive mechanisms of trauma response: An evolutionary perspective on trauma-related disorders. *Neuroscience and Biobehavioral Reviews, 37*(8), 1549–1566. doi:10.1016/j.neubiorev.2013.06.004

Baldwin, M. L., & Marcus, S. C. (2007). Labor market outcomes of persons with mental disorders. *Industrial Relations: A Journal of Economy & Society, 46*(3), 481–510. doi:10.1111/j.1468-232X.2007.00478.x

Baldwin, S. (1999). Applied behavior analysis in the treatment of ADHD: A review and rapprochement. *Ethical Human Sciences & Services, 1*(1), 35–59.

Baldwin, S. A., Williams, D. C., & Houts, A. C. (2004). The creation, expansion, and embodiment of posttraumatic stress disorder: A case study in historical critical psychopathology. *The Scientific Review of Mental Health Practice, 3*(1), 33–52. Retrieved from http://www.srmhp.org/0301/hcp.html

Ballatore, C., Lee, V. M. Y., & Trojanowski, J. Q. (2007). Tau-mediated neurodegeneration in Alzheimer's disease and related disorders. *Nature Reviews. Neuroscience, 8*(9), 663–672.

Balsam, R. H. (2013). Appreciating difference: Roy Schafer on psychoanalysis and women. *The Psychoanalytic Quarterly, 82*(1), 23–38. doi:10.1002/j.2167-4086.2013.00003.x

Bamford, S.-M., & Walker, T. (2012). Women and dementia – not forgotten. *Maturitas, 73*(2), 121–126. doi:http://dx.doi.org/10.1016/j.maturitas.2012.06.013

Bamidis, P. D., Vivas, A. B., Styliadis, C., Frantzidis, C., Klados, M., Schlee, W., … Papageorgiou, S. G. (2014). A review of physical and cognitive interventions in aging. *Neuroscience and Biobehavioral Reviews, 44*, 206–220. doi:10.1016/j.neubiorev.2014.03.019

Banca, P., Voon, V., Vestergaard, M. D., Philipiak, G., Almeida, I., Pocinho, F., … Castelo-Branco, M. (2015). Imbalance in habitual versus goal directed neural systems during symptom provocation in obsessive-compulsive disorder. *Brain: A Journal of Neurology, 138*(3), 798–811. doi:10.1093/brain/awu379

Bandelow, B., Lichte, T., Rudolf, S., Wiltink, J., & Beutel, M. E. (2014). The diagnosis of and treatment recommendations for anxiety disorders. *Deutsches Ärzteblatt International, 111*(27–28), 473–480.

Bandelow, B., Lichte, T., Rudolf, S., Wiltink, J., & Beutel, M. E. (2015). The German guidelines for the treatment of anxiety disorders. *European Archives of Psychiatry and Clinical Neuroscience, 265*(5), 363–373. doi:10.1007/s00406-014-0563-z

Bandelow, B., Reitt, M., & Wedekind, D. (2012). Selective serotonin reuptake inhibitors, reversible inhibitors of monoamine oxidase-A, and buspirone. In S. G. Hofmann (Ed.), *Psychobiological approaches for anxiety disorders: Treatment combination strategies* (pp. 61–74). Chichester, UK: Wiley-Blackwell.

Bandelow, B., Reitt, M., Röver, C., Michaelis, S., Görlich, Y., & Wedekind, D. (2015). Efficacy of treatments for anxiety disorders: A meta-analysis. *International Clinical Psychopharmacology, 30*(4), 183–192. doi:10.1097/YIC.0000000000000078

Bandini, J. (2015). The medicalization of bereavement: (Ab)normal grief in the DSM-5. *Death Studies, 39*(6), 347–352. doi:10.1080/07481187.2014.951498

Bandura, A. (1965). Influence of models' reinforcement contingencies on the acquisition of imitative responses. *Journal of Personality and Social Psychology, 1*(6), 589–595. doi:10.1037/h0022070

Bandura, A., Ross, D., & Ross, S. A. (1961). Transmission of aggression through imitation of aggressive models. *The Journal of Abnormal and Social Psychology, 63*(3), 575–582. doi:10.1037/h0045925

Bandura, A., Ross, D., & Ross, S. A. (1963a). A comparative test of the status envy, social power, and secondary reinforcement theories of identificatory learning. *The Journal of Abnormal and Social Psychology, 67*(6), 527–534. doi:10.1037/h0046546

Bandura, A., Ross, D., & Ross, S. A. (1963b). Imitation of film-mediated aggressive models. *The Journal of Abnormal and Social Psychology, 66*(1), 3–11. doi:10.1037/h0048687

Bandura, A., Ross, D., & Ross, S. A. (1963c). Vicarious reinforcement and imitative learning. *The Journal of Abnormal and Social Psychology, 67*(6), 601–607. doi:10.1037/h0045550

Banerjee, A., García-Oscos, F., Roychowdhury, S., Galindo, L. C., Hall, S., Kilgard, M. P., & Atzori, M. (2013). Impairment of cortical GABAergic synaptic transmission in an environmental rat model of autism. *International Journal of Neuropsychopharmacology, 16*(6), 1309–1318. doi:10.1017/S1461145712001216

Bär, K.-J., de la Cruz, F., Berger, S., Schultz, C. C., & Wagner, G. (2015). Structural and functional differences in the cingulate cortex relate to disease severity in anorexia nervosa. *Journal of Psychiatry & Neuroscience, 40*(4), 269–278. doi:10.1503/jpn.140193

Barahona-Corrêa, J. B., & Filipe, C. N. (2016). A concise history of Asperger Syndrome: The short reign of a troublesome diagnosis. *Frontiers In Psychology, 6*, 2024–2024. doi:10.3389/fpsyg.2015.02024

Barber, C. W., & Miller, M. J. (2014). Reducing a suicidal person's access to lethal means of suicide: A research agenda. *American Journal of Preventive Medicine, 47*(3 Suppl 2), S264–S272. doi:10.1016/j.amepre.2014.05.028

Barbier, A. J., & Bradbury, M. J. (2007). Histaminergic control of sleep-wake cycles: recent therapeutic advances for sleep and wake disorders. *CNS & Neurological Disorders Drug Targets, 6*(1), 31–43.

Barceloux, D. G. (2012). *Medical toxicology of drug abuse: Synthesized chemicals and psychoactive plants.* Hoboken, NJ: John Wiley.

Bardram, J. E., Frost, M., Szántó, K., Faurholt-Jepsen, M., Vinberg, M., & Kessing, L. V. (2013). Designing mobile health technology for bipolar disorder: A field trial of the MONARCA system. *Proceedings of the SIGCHI conference on human factors in computing systems, 2013*, 2627–2636.

Bargenquast, R., & Schweitzer, R. D. (2014). Enhancing sense of recovery and self-reflectivity in people with schizophrenia: A pilot study of metacognitive narrative psychotherapy. *Psychology and Psychotherapy: Theory, Research and Practice, 87*(3), 338–356. doi:10.1111/papt.12019

Barker, R. (2015). Using pre-therapy in forensic settings. In A. Meaden & A. Fox (Eds.), *Innovations in psychosocial interventions for psychosis: Working with the hard to reach* (pp. 22–37). London, UK: Routledge.

Barkley, R. A. (2002). International consensus statement on ADHD. *Clinical Child and Family Psychology Review, 5*(2), 89–111.

Barkley, R. A., & Peters, H. (2012). The earliest reference to ADHD in the medical literature? Melchior Adam Weikard's description in 1775 of 'attention deficit' (Mangel der aufmerksamkeit, attentio volubilis). *Journal of Attention Disorders, 16*(8), 623–630. doi:10.1177/1087054711432309

Barlow, M. R., & Freyd, J. J. (2009). Adaptive dissociation: Information processing and response to betrayal. In P. F. Dell & J. A. O'Neil (Eds.), *Dissociation and the dissociative disorders: DSM-V and beyond* (pp. 93–105). New York, NY: Routledge.

Barnao, M., & Ward, T. (2015). Sailing uncharted seas without a compass: A review of interventions in forensic mental health. *Aggression and Violent Behavior, 22*, 77–86. doi:10.1016/j.avb.2015.04.009

Barnao, M., Ward, T., & Casey, S. (2015). Looking beyond the illness: Forensic service users' perceptions of rehabilitation. *Journal of Interpersonal Violence, 30*(6), 1025–1045. doi:10.1177/0886260514539764

Barnes, A. (2004). Race, schizophrenia, and admission to state psychiatric hospitals. *Administration and Policy in Mental Health, 31*(3), 241–252. doi:10.1023/B:APIH.0000018832.73673.54

Barnes, A. (2008). Race and hospital diagnoses of schizophrenia and mood disorders. *Social Work, 53*(1), 77–83. doi:10.1093/sw/53.1.77

Barnes, M. A., & Caltabiano, M. L. (2017). The interrelationship between orthorexia nervosa, perfectionism, body image and attachment style. *Eating and Weight Disorders, 22*(1), 177–184. doi:10.1007/s40519-016-0280-x

Barnett, J. H., & Smoller, J. W. (2009). The genetics of bipolar disorder. *Neuroscience, 164*(1), 331–343. doi:http://dx.doi.org/10.1016/j.neuroscience.2009.03.080

Barnicot, K., Savill, M., Bhatti, N., & Priebe, S. (2014). A pragmatic randomised controlled trial of dialectical behaviour therapy: Effects on hospitalisation and post-treatment follow-up. *Psychotherapy and Psychosomatics, 83*(3), 192–193. doi:10.1159/000357365

Baron, K. G., Perlis, M. L., Nowakowski, S., Smith, M. T., Jr., Jungquist, C. R., & Orff, H. J. (2017). Cognitive behavioral therapy for insomnia. In H. P. Attarian (Ed.), *Clinical handbook of insomnia* (pp. 75–96). Totowa, NJ: Humana Press.

Baron-Cohen, S. (1995). *Mindblindness: An essay on autism and theory of mind.* Cambridge, MA: The MIT Press.

Baron-Cohen, S. (2002). The extreme male brain theory of autism. *Trends in Cognitive Sciences, 6*(6), 248–254.

Baron-Cohen, S. (2009). Autism: The empathizing-systemizing (E-S) theory. *Annals of the New York Academy of Sciences, 1156*, 68–80. doi:10.1111/j.1749-6632.2009.04467.x

Baron-Cohen, S., Cassidy, S., Auyeung, B., Allison, C., Achoukhi, M., Robertson, S., … Lai, M.-C. (2014). Attenuation of typical sex differences in 800 adults with autism vs. 3,900 controls. *PLOS One, 9*(7), e102251–e102251. doi:10.1371/journal.pone.0102251

Baroni, A., & Castellanos, F. X. (2015). Neuroanatomic and cognitive abnormalities in attention-deficit/hyperactivity disorder in the era of 'high definition' neuroimaging. *Current Opinion in Neurobiology, 30*, 1–8. doi:10.1016/j.conb.2014.08.005

Barr, K. N., & Quinsey, V. L. (2004). Is psychopathy pathology or a life strategy? Implications for social policy. In C. Crawford & C. Salmon (Eds.), *Evolutionary psychology, public policy and personal decisions* (pp. 293–317). Mahwah, NJ: Lawrence Erlbaum.

Barr, R., & Abernethy, V. (1977). Conversion reaction: Differential diagnosis in the light of biofeedback research. *Journal of Nervous and Mental Disease, 164*(4), 287–292. doi:10.1097/00005053-197704000-00010

Barrett, K. E., Taylor, D. W., Pullo, R. E., & Dunlap, D. A. (1998). The right to refuse medication: Navigating the ambiguity. *Psychiatric Rehabilitation Journal, 21*(3), 241–249. doi:10.1037/h0095307

Barrowclough, C., Gregg, L., & Tarrier, N. (2008). Expressed emotion and causal attributions in relatives of post-traumatic stress disorder patients. *Behaviour Research and Therapy, 46*(2), 207–218. doi:10.1016/j.brat.2007.11.005

Barry, L. M., & Haraway, D. L. (2005). Self-management and ADHD: A literature review. *The Behavior Analyst Today, 6*(1), 48–64. doi:10.1037/h0100051

Bartels, J. M., & Peters, D. (2017). Coverage of Rosenhan's 'On being sane in insane places' in abnormal psychology textbooks. *Teaching of Psychology, 44*(2), 169–173. doi:10.1177/0098628317692634

Basner, M., Spaeth, A. M., & Dinges, D. F. (2014). Sociodemographic characteristics and waking activities and their role in the timing and duration of sleep. *Sleep: Journal of Sleep and Sleep Disorders Research, 37*(12), 1889–1906.

Bass, C., & Halligan, P. (2014). Factitious disorders and malingering: Challenges for clinical assessment and management. *The Lancet, 383*(9926), 1422–1432. doi:10.1016/S0140-6736(13)62186-8

Bassett, A. M., & Baker, C. (2015). Normal or abnormal? 'Normative uncertainty' in psychiatric practice. *Journal of Medical Humanities, 36*(2), 89–111. doi:10.1007/s10912-014-9324-2

Bassman, R. (2001). Whose reality is it anyway? Consumers/survivors/ex-patients can speak for themselves. *Journal of Humanistic Psychology, 41*(4), 11–35. doi:10.1177/0022167801414002

Basson, R. (2001). Human sex-response cycles. *Journal of Sex & Marital Therapy, 27*(1), 33–44. doi:10.1080/00926230152035831

Basson, R., Wierman, M. E., van Lankveld, J., & Brotto, L. (2010). Summary of the recommendations on sexual dysfunctions in women. *Journal of Sexual Medicine, 7*(1, Pt 2), 314–326. doi:10.1111/j.1743-6109.2009.01617.x

Bastian, B., Jetten, J., & Ferris, L. J. (2014). Pain as social glue: Shared pain increases cooperation. *Psychological Science, 25*(11), 2079–2085. doi:10.1177/0956797614545886

Bateman, A., & Fonagy, P. (2009). Randomized controlled trial of outpatient mentalization-based treatment versus structured clinical management for borderline personality disorder. *The American Journal of Psychiatry, 166*(12), 1355–1364. doi:10.1176/appi.ajp.2009.09040539

Bateman, A., & Fonagy, P. (2010). Mentalization based treatment for borderline personality disorder. *World Psychiatry, 9*(1), 11–15.

Bateman, A. W., & Fonagy, P. (2012). Mentalization-based treatment of borderline personality disorder. In T. A. Widiger (Ed.), *The Oxford handbook of personality disorders* (pp. 767–784). New York, NY: Oxford University Press.

Bateman, A. W., Gunderson, J., & Mulder, R. (2015). Treatment of personality disorder. *The Lancet, 385*(9969), 735–743. doi:http://dx.doi.org/10.1016/S0140-6736(14)61394-5

Bateman, A., O'Connell, J., Lorenzini, N., Gardner, T., & Fonagy, P. (2016). A randomised controlled trial of mentalization-based treatment versus structured clinical management for patients with comorbid borderline personality disorder and antisocial personality disorder. *BMC Psychiatry, 16*.

Bateson, G., Jackson, D. D., Haley, J., & Weakland, J. (1956). Toward a theory of schizophrenia. *Behavioral Science, 1*, 251–264. doi:10.1002/bs.3830010402

Batstra, L., & Frances, A. (2012). DSM-5 further inflates attention deficit hyperactivity disorder. *Journal of Nervous and Mental Disease, 200*(6), 486–488. doi:10.1097/NMD.0b013e318257c4b6

Battagliese, G., Caccetta, M., Luppino, O. I., Baglioni, C., Cardi, V., Mancini, F., & Buonanno, C. (2015). Cognitive-behavioral therapy for externalizing disorders: A meta-analysis of treatment effectiveness. *Behaviour Research and Therapy, 75*, 60–71. doi:10.1016/j.brat.2015.10.008

Batterham, P. J., Griffiths, K. M., Barney, L. J., & Parsons, A. (2013). Predictors of generalized anxiety disorder stigma. *Psychiatry Research, 206*(2–3), 282–286. doi:10.1016/j.psychres.2012.11.018

Battle, C. L., Shea, M. T., Johnson, D. M., Yen, S., Zlotnick, C., Zanarini, M. C., ... Morey, L. C. (2004). Childhood maltreatment associated with adult personality disorders: Findings from the collaborative longitudinal personality disorders study. *Journal of Personality Disorders, 18*(2), 193–211. doi:10.1521/pedi.18.2.193.32777

Bauer, M., & Dinan, T. (2015). Hypothalamic-pituitary-adrenal axis and hypothalamic-pituitary-thyroid axis and their treatment impact. In A. Yildiz, P. Ruiz, & C. B. Nemeroff (Eds.), *The bipolar book: History, neurobiology, and treatment* (pp. 137–148). New York, NY: Oxford University Press.

Bauer, M., Pfennig, A., Severus, E., Whybrow, P. C., Angst, J., & Möller, H.-J. (2013). World Federation of Societies of Biological Psychiatry (WFSBP) guidelines for biological treatment of unipolar depressive disorders, Part 1: Update 2013 on the acute and continuation treatment of unipolar depressive disorders. *The World Journal of Biological Psychiatry, 14*(5), 334–385. doi:10.3109/15622975.2013.804195

Bauer, M., Severus, E., Köhler, S., Whybrow, P. C., Angst, J., & Möller, H.-J. (2015). World Federation of Societies of Biological Psychiatry (WFSBP) guidelines for biological treatment of unipolar depressive disorders. Part 2: Maintenance treatment of major depressive disorder-update 2015. *The World Journal of Biological Psychiatry, 16*(2), 76–95. doi:10.3109/15622975.2014.1001786

Baum, M. (1970). Extinction of avoidance responding through response prevention (flooding). *Psychological Bulletin, 74*(4), 276–284. doi:10.1037/h0029789

Bauminger, N., Solomon, M., & Rogers, S. J. (2010). Externalizing and internalizing behaviors in ASD. *Autism Research, 3*(3), 101–112. doi:10.1002/aur.131

Bayliss, P., & Holttum, S. (2015). Experiences of antidepressant medication and cognitive-behavioural therapy for depression: A grounded theory study. *Psychology and Psychotherapy: Theory, Research and Practice, 88*(3), 317–334. doi:10.1111/papt.12040

Beahrs, J. O. (1994). Dissociative identity disorder: Adaptive deception of self and others. *Bulletin of the American Academy of Psychiatry & the Law, 22*(2), 223–237.

Beautrais, A., Fergusson, D., Coggan, C., Collings, C., Doughty, C., Ellis, P., ... Surgenor, L. (2007). Effective strategies for suicide prevention in New Zealand: a review of the evidence. *The New Zealand Medical Journal, 120*(1251), U2459–U2459.

Bebbington, P. (2013). The classification and epidemiology of unipolar depression. In M. Power (Ed.), *The Wiley-Blackwell handbook of mood disorders* (2nd ed., pp. 3–37). Chichester, UK: Wiley-Blackwell.

Bebbington, P. E. (1976). The efficacy of Alcoholics Anonymous: The elusiveness of hard data. *The British Journal of Psychiatry, 128*, 572–580. doi:10.1192/bjp.128.6.572

Beck, A., Grace, A. A., & Heinz, A. (2011). Reward processing. In B. Adinoff & E. A. Stein (Eds.), *Neuroimaging in addiction.* (pp. 107–129). Chichester, UK: Wiley-Blackwell.

Beck, A. T. (1979). *Cognitive therapy of depression.* New York, NY: The Guilford Press.

Beck, A. T., & Rector, N. A. (2000). Cognitive therapy of schizophrenia: a new therapy for the new millennium. *American Journal of Psychotherapy, 54*(3), 291–300.

Beck, A. T., Davis, D. D., & Freeman, A. (2015). *Cognitive therapy of personality disorders* (3rd ed.). New York, NY: Guilford Press.

Beck, A. T., Epstein, N., Brown, G., & Steer, R. A. (1988). An inventory for measuring clinical anxiety: Psychometric properties. *Journal of Consulting and Clinical Psychology, 56*(6), 893–897. doi:10.1037/0022-006X.56.6.893

Beck, A. T., Rush, A. J., Shaw, B. F., & Emery, G. (1979). *Cognitive therapy of depression.* New York, NY: Guilford Press.

Beck, J. (2016, March 11). 'Americanitis': The disease of living too fast. *The Atlantic.*

Beck, J. C., & Golowka, E. A. (1988). A study of enforced treatment in relation to Stone's 'thank you' theory. *Behavioral Sciences & the Law, 6*(4), 559–566. doi:10.1002/bsl.2370060411

Beck, J. G., & Sloan, D. M. (2014). Group treatments for PTSD: What do we know and what do we need to know? In M. J. Friedman, T. M. Keane, & P. A. Resick (Eds.), *Handbook of PTSD: Science and practice* (2nd ed., pp. 466–481). New York, NY: Guilford Press.

Beck, J. S. (2011). *Cognitive behavior therapy: Basics and beyond* (2nd ed.). New York, NY: Guilford Press.

Beck, J. S., Liese, B. S., & Najavits, L. M. (2005). Cognitive therapy. In R. J. Frances, S. I. Miller, & A. H. Mack (Eds.), *Clinical textbook of addictive disorders* (3rd ed., pp. 474–501). New York, NY: Guilford Press.

Becker, A. E., Keel, P., Anderson-Fye, E. P., & Thomas, J. J. (2004). Genes and/or jeans?: Genetic and socio-cultural contributions to risk for eating disorders. *Journal of Addictive Diseases, 23*(3), 81–103. doi:10.1300/J069v23n03_07

Becker, C. B., Zayfert, C., & Anderson, E. (2004). A survey of psychologists' attitudes towards and utilization of exposure therapy for PTSD. *Behaviour Research and Therapy, 42*(3), 277–292. doi:10.1016/S0005-7967(03)00138-4

Becker, J. V., Johnson, B. R., & Perkins, A. (2014). Paraphilic disorders. In R. E. Hales, S. C. Yudofsky, & L. W. Roberts (Eds.), *The American Psychiatric Publishing textbook of psychiatry* (6th ed., pp. 895–925). Arlington, VA: American Psychiatric Publishing.

Becker-Blease, K. A., Deater-Deckard, K., Eley, T., Freyd, J. J., Stevenson, J., & Plomin, R. (2004). A genetic analysis of individual differences in dissociative behaviors in childhood and adolescence. *Journal of Child Psychology and Psychiatry, 45*(3), 522–532. doi:10.1111/j.1469-7610.2004.00242.x

Bedi, R., Muller, R. T., & Classen, C. C. (2014). Cumulative risk for deliberate self-harm among treatment-seeking women with histories of childhood abuse. *Psychological Trauma: Theory, Research, Practice, and Policy, 6*(6), 600–609. doi:10.1037/a0033897

Beebe, L. H., & Smith, K. (2010). Informed consent to research in persons with schizophrenia spectrum disorders. *Nursing Ethics, 17*(4), 425–434. doi:10.1177/0969733010364581

Beer, M. D. (1996). Psychosis: A history of the concept. *Comprehensive Psychiatry, 37*(4), 273–291. doi:10.1016/S0010-440X(96)90007-3

Behar, E., DiMarco, I. D., Hekler, E. B., Mohlman, J., & Staples, A. M. (2009). Current theoretical models of generalized anxiety disorder (GAD): Conceptual review and treatment implications. *Journal of Anxiety Disorders, 23*(8), 1011–1023. doi:10.1016/j.janxdis.2009.07.006

Behr, M., Nuding, D., & McGinnis, S. (2013). Person-centred psychotherapy and counselling with children and young people. In M. Cooper, M. O'Hara, P. F. Schmid, & A. C. Bohart (Eds.), *The handbook of person-centred psychotherapy and counselling* (pp. 266–281). New York, NY: Palgrave Macmillan.

Bell, A. C., & D'Zurilla, T. J. (2009). Problem-solving therapy for depression: A meta-analysis. *Clinical Psychology Review, 29*(4), 348–353. doi:http://dx.doi.org/10.1016/j.cpr.2009.02.003

Bella, A. J., & Shamloul, R. (2013). Psychotropics and sexual dysfunction. *Central European Journal of Urology, 66*(4), 466–471. doi:10.5173/ceju.2013.04.art22

Bello, N. T., & Hajnal, A. (2010). Dopamine and binge eating behaviors. *Pharmacology Biochemistry and Behavior, 97*(1), 25–33. doi:http://dx.doi.org/10.1016/j.pbb.2010.04.016

Ben-Shahar, A. R. (2014). *Touching the relational edge: Body psychotherapy.* London, UK: Karnac Books.

Bender, D. S., Dolan, R. T., Skodol, A. E., Sanislow, C. A., Dyck, I. R., McGlashan, T. H., ... Gunderson, J. G. (2001). Treatment utilization by patients with personality disorders. *The American Journal of Psychiatry, 158*(2), 295–302. doi:10.1176/appi.ajp.158.2.295

Benedek, D. M., Friedman, M. J., Zatzick, D., & Ursano, R. J. (2009). *Guidelines watch (March 2009): Practice guideline for the treatment of patients with acute stress disorder and posttraumatic stress disorder.* Retrieved from http://psychiatryonline.org/pb/assets/raw/sitewide/practice_guidelines/guidelines/acutestressdisorderptsd-watch.pdf

Benish, S. G., Imel, Z. E., & Wampold, B. E. (2008). The relative efficacy of bona fide psychotherapies for treating post-traumatic stress disorder: A meta-analysis of direct comparisons. *Clinical Psychology Review, 28*(5), 746–758. doi:http://dx.doi.org/10.1016/j.cpr.2007.10.005

Benjamin, S., & Taylor, W. D. (2010). Nature and nurture: Genetic influences and gene-environment interactions in depression. *Current Psychiatry Reviews, 6*(2), 82–90. doi:10.2174/157340010791196484

Bennett, T., Bray, D., & Neville, M. W. (2014). Suvorexant, a dual orexin receptor antagonist for the management of insomnia. *Pharmacy and Therapeutics, 39*(4), 264–266.

Benros, M. E., Nielsen, P. R., Nordentoft, M., Eaton, W. W., Dalton, S. O., & Mortensen, P. B. (2011). Autoimmune diseases and severe infections as risk factors for schizophrenia: A 30-year population-based register study. *The American Journal of Psychiatry, 168*(12), 1303–1310. doi:10.1176/appi.ajp.2011.11030516

Benson, E. (2003, February). Intelligent intelligence testing: Psychologists are broadening the concept of intelligence and how to test it. *Monitor on Psychology, 34,* 48.

Bent, C. A., Barbaro, J., & Dissanayake, C. (2017). Change in autism diagnoses prior to and following the introduction of DSM-5. *Journal of Autism and Developmental Disorders, 47*(1), 163–171. doi:10.1007/s10803-016-2942-y

Bentall, R. P. (2013). Would a rose, by any other name, smell sweeter? *Psychological Medicine, 43*(7), 1560–1562. doi:10.1017/S0033291713000925

Bentall, R. P., Jackson, H. F., & Pilgrim, D. (1988). Abandoning the concept of 'schizophrenia': Some implications of validity arguments for psychological research into psychotic phenomena. *British Journal of Clinical Psychology, 27*(4), 303–324. doi:10.1111/j.2044-8260.1988.tb00795.x

Bentley, K. H., Cassiello-Robbins, C. F., Vittorio, L., Sauer-Zavala, S., & Barlow, D. H. (2015). The association between nonsuicidal self-injury and the emotional disorders: A meta-analytic review. *Clinical Psychology Review, 37,* 72–88. doi:10.1016/j.cpr.2015.02.006

Benzodiazepine Drug Information. (n.d.). Retrieved from http://www.rxlist.com/benzodiazepines/drugs-condition.htm

Berg, A. O., Melle, I., Rossberg, J. I., Romm, K. L., Larsson, S., Lagerberg, T. V., ... Hauff, E. (2011). Perceived discrimination is associated with severity of positive and depression/anxiety symptoms in immigrants with psychosis: A cross-sectional study. *BMC Psychiatry, 11.* doi:10.1186/1471-244X-11-77

Bergeron, S., Morin, M., & Lord, M.-J. (2010). Integrating pelvic floor rehabilitation and cognitive-behavioural therapy for sexual pain: What have we learned and where do we go from here? *Sexual and Relationship Therapy, 25*(3), 289–298. doi:10.1080/14681994.2010.486398

Berglund, K., Roman, E., Balldin, J., Berggren, U., Eriksson, M., Gustavsson, P., & Fahlke, C. (2011). Do men with excessive alcohol consumption and social stability have an addictive personality? *Scandinavian Journal of Psychology, 52*(3), 257–260. doi:10.1111/j.1467-9450.2010.00872.x

Bergman, S. (2009, July 13). The farce of dueling psychiatrists. *The Boston Globe.* Retrieved from http://archive.boston.com/bostonglobe/editorial_opinion/oped/articles/2009/07/13/the_farce_of_dueling_psychiatrists/

Berlim, M. T., van den Eynde, F., Tovar-Perdomo, S., & Daskalakis, Z. J. (2014). Response, remission and drop-out rates following high-frequency repetitive transcranial magnetic stimulation (rTMS) for treating major depression: a systematic review and meta-analysis of randomized, double-blind and sham-controlled trials. *Psychological Medicine, 44*(2), 225–239. doi:10.1017/S0033291713000512

Berlin , F. S. (1997). "Chemical Castration" for Sex Offenders. *The New England Journal of Medicine, 336*(14), 1030–1031. doi:doi:10.1056/NEJM199704033361420

Berridge, K. C. (2007). The debate over dopamine's role in reward: The case for incentive salience. *Psychopharmacology, 191*(3), 391–431.

Berridge, K. C., & Kringelbach, M. L. (2008). Affective neuroscience of pleasure: Reward in humans and animals. *Psychopharmacology, 199*(3), 457–480. doi:10.1007/s00213-008-1099-6

Berzoff, J. (2003). Psychodynamic theories in grief and bereavement. *Smith College Studies in Social Work, 73*(3), 273–298. doi:10.1080/00377310309517686

Bettelheim, B. (1967). *The empty fortress.* New York, NY: Free Press.

Beynon, C. M., McVeigh, C., McVeigh, J., Leavey, C., & Bellis, M. A. (2008). The involvement of drugs and alcohol in drug-facilitated sexual assault: A systematic review of the evidence. *Trauma, Violence, & Abuse, 9*(3), 178–188. doi:10.1177/1524838008320221

Bhatia, M. S., & Gupta, R. (2009). Pica responding to SSRI: An OCD spectrum disorder? *The World Journal of Biological Psychiatry, 10*(4 Pt 3), 936–938.

Bhaumik, S., Kiani, R., Michael, D. M., Gangavati, S., Khan, S., Torales, J., ... Ventriglio, A. (2016). World Psychiatric Association (WPA) report on mental health issues in people with intellectual disability: Paper 1: Intellectual disability and mental health: An overview. *International Journal of Culture and Mental Health, 9*(4), 417–429. doi:10.1080/17542863.2016.1228687

Biederman, J., Faraone, S. V., Taylor, A., Sienna, M., Williamson, S., & Fine, C. (1998). Diagnostic continuity between child and adolescent ADHD: Findings from a longitudinal clinical sample. *Journal of the American Academy of Child & Adolescent Psychiatry, 37*(3), 305–313. doi:10.1097/00004583-199803000-00016

Bijlsma, E. Y., Chan, J. S. W., Olivier, B., Veening, J. G., Millan, M. J., Waldinger, M. D., & Oosting, R. S. (2014). Sexual side effects of serotonergic antidepressants: Mediated by inhibition of serotonin on central dopamine release? *Pharmacology, Biochemistry and Behavior, 121,* 88–101. doi:10.1016/j.pbb.2013.10.004

Billieux, J., Schimmenti, A., Khazaal, Y., Maurage, P., & Heeren, A. (2015). Are we overpathologizing everyday life? A tenable blueprint for behavioral addiction research. *Journal of Behavioral Addictions, 4*(3), 119–123. doi:10.1556/2006.4.2015.009

Billings, D. B., & Urban, T. (1982). The socio-medical construction of transsexualism: An interpretation and critique. *Social Problems, 29*(3), 266–282. doi:10.1525/sp.1982.29.3.03a00050

Binik, Y. M. (2010). The DSM diagnostic criteria for dyspareunia. *Archives of Sexual Behavior, 39*(2), 292–303. doi:10.1007/s10508-009-9563-x

Binks, C., Fenton, M., McCarthy, L., Lee, T., Adams, C. E., & Duggan, C. (2006). Psychological therapies for people with borderline personality disorder (Review). *Cochrane Database of Systematic Reviews, 2006*(1), 1–77. doi: 10.1002/14651858.CD005653

Bird, T. D. (1998, updated September 24, 2015). Alzheimer disease overview. *Gene Reviews.* Retrieved from https://www.ncbi.nlm.nih.gov/books/NBK1161/

Bird, T. D. (2008). Genetic aspects of Alzheimer disease. *Genetics In Medicine: Official Journal Of The American College Of Medical Genetics, 10*(4), 231–239. doi:10.1097/GIM.0b013e31816b64dc

Bishara, D., Sauer, J., & Taylor, D. (2015). The pharmacological management of Alzheimer's disease. *Progress in Neurology and Psychiatry, 19*(4), 16–22. Retrieved from http://www.progressnp.com/article/the-pharmacological-management-of-alzheimers-disease/

Bishop-Fitzpatrick, L., Minshew, N. J., & Eack, S. M. (2013). A systematic review of psychosocial interventions for adults with autism spectrum disorders. *Journal of Autism and Developmental Disorders, 43*(3), 687–694. doi:10.1007/s10803-012-1615-8

Biskin, R. S., & Paris, J. (2012). Management of borderline personality disorder. *Canadian Medical Association Journal, 184*(17), 1897–1902. doi:10.1503/cmaj.112055

Bisson, J. I., & Sakhuja, D. (2006). Adjustment disorders. *Psychiatry, 5*(7), 240–242. doi:http://dx.doi.org/10.1053/j.mppsy.2006.04.004

Bisson, J. I., Ehlers, A., Matthews, R., Pilling, S., Richards, D., & Turner, S. (2007). Psychological treatments for chronic post-traumatic stress disorder: Systematic review and meta-analysis. *The British Journal of Psychiatry, 190*(2), 97–104. doi:10.1192/bjp.bp.106.021402

Bisson, J. I., McFarlane, A. C., Rose, S., Ruzek, J. I., & Watson, P. J. (2009). Psychological debriefing for adults. In E. B. Foa, T. M. Keane, M. J. Friedman, & J. A. Cohen (Eds.), *Effective treatments for PTSD: Practice guidelines from the International Society for Traumatic Stress Studies* (2nd ed., pp. 83–105). New York, NY: Guilford Press.

Black, D. W. (2007a). Compulsive buying disorder: A review of the evidence. *CNS Spectrums, 12*(2), 124–132. doi:10.1017/S1092852900020630

Black, D. W. (2007b). A review of compulsive buying disorder. *World Psychiatry, 6*(1), 14–18.

Black, D. W. (2016). Compulsive shopping as a behavioral addiction. In N. M. Petry (Ed.), *Behavioral addictions: DSM-5® and beyond* (pp. 125–156). New York, NY: Oxford University Press.

Blair, R. J. R. (2008). The amygdala and ventromedial prefrontal cortex: functional contributions and dysfunction in psychopathy. *Philosophical Transactions of the Royal Society B: Biological Sciences, 363*(1503), 2557–2565. doi:10.1098/rstb.2008.0027

Blais, R. K., & Renshaw, K. D. (2014). Self-stigma fully mediates the association of anticipated enacted stigma and help-seeking intentions in National Guard service members. *Military Psychology, 26*(2), 114–119. doi:10.1037/mil0000036

Blasco-Fontecilla, H., & Oquendo, M. A. (2016). Biomarkers of suicide: Predicting the predictable? In P. Courtet (Ed.), *Understanding suicide: From diagnosis to personalized treatment* (pp. 77–83). Cham, Switzerland: Springer.

Blashfield, R. K., Keeley, J. W., Flanagan, E. H., & Miles, S. R. (2014). The cycle of classification: DSM-I through DSM-5. *Annual Review of Clinical Psychology, 10*, 25–51. doi:10.1146/annurev-clinpsy-032813-153639

Blatt, S. J., & Homann, E. (1992). Parent-child interaction in the etiology of dependent and self-critical depression. *Clinical Psychology Review, 12*(1), 47–91. doi:10.1016/0272-7358(92)90091-L

Blatt, S. J., & Levy, K. N. (2003). Attachment theory, psychoanalysis, personality development, and psychopathology. *Psychoanalytic Inquiry, 23*(1), 102–150. doi:10.1080/07351692309349028

Bleichhardt, G., Timmer, B., & Rief, W. (2004). Cognitive-behavioural therapy for patients with multiple somatoform symptoms—a randomised controlled trial in tertiary care. *Journal of Psychosomatic Research, 56*(4), 449–454. doi:http://dx.doi.org/10.1016/S0022-3999(03)00630-5

Blewett, A., & Bottéro, A. (1995). L.-V. Marcé and the psychopathology of eating disorders. *History of Psychiatry, 6*(21, Pt 1), 69–85. doi:10.1177/0957154X9500602104

Block, J. (2008). *The Q-Sort in character appraisal.* Washington, DC: American Psychological Association.

Blom, J. D. (2014). When doctors cry wolf: A systematic review of the literature on clinical lycanthropy. *History of Psychiatry, 25*(1), 87–102. doi:10.1177/0957154X13512192

Blomgren, M. (2013). Behavioral treatments for children and adults who stutter: A review. *Psychology Research and Behavior Management, 6.*

Blomstedt, P., Sjöberg, R. L., Hansson, M., Bodlund, O., & Hariz, M. I. (2011). Deep brain stimulation in the treatment of depression. *Acta Psychiatrica Scandinavica, 123*(1), 4–11. doi:10.1111/j.1600-0447.2010.01625.x

Blonigen, D. M., Finney, J. W., Wilbourne, P. L., & Moos, R. H. (2015). Psychosocial treatments for substance use disorders. In P. E. Nathan & J. M. Gorman (Eds.), *A guide to treatments that work* (4th ed., pp. 731–761). New York, NY: Oxford University Press.

Blow, F. C., Zeber, J. E., McCarthy, J. F., Valenstein, M., Gillon, L., & Bingham, C. R. (2004). Ethnicity and diagnostic patterns in veterans with psychoses. *Social Psychiatry and Psychiatric Epidemiology, 39*(10), 841–851.

Bluett, E. J., Homan, K. J., Morrison, K. L., Levin, M. E., & Twohig, M. P. (2014). Acceptance and commitment therapy for anxiety and OCD spectrum disorders: An empirical review. *Journal of Anxiety Disorders, 28*(6), 612–624. doi:10.1016/j.janxdis.2014.06.008

Blum, K., Febo, M., McLaughlin, T., Cronjé, F. J., Han, D., & Gold, M. S. (2014). Hatching the behavioral addiction egg: Reward Deficiency Solution System (RDSS)™ as a function of dopaminergic neurogenetics and brain functional connectivity linking all addictions under a common rubric. *Journal of Behavioral Addictions, 3*(3), 149–156. doi:10.1556/JBA.3.2014.019

Blum, K., Hauser, M., Agan, G., Giordano, J., Fratantonio, J., Badgaiyan, R. D., & Febo, M. (2015). Understanding the importance of dopaminergic deficit in Reward Deficiency Syndrome (RDS): Redeeming joy overcoming 'darkness' in recovery. *Psychology, 6*(4), 435–439. doi:10.4236/psych.2015.64040

Blumer, M. L. C., Ansara, Y. G., & Watson, C. M. (2013). Cisgenderism in family therapy: How everyday clinical practices can delegitimize people's gender self-designations. *Journal of Family Psychotherapy, 24*(4), 267–285. doi:10.1080/08975353.2013.849551

Boag, S. (2011). Explanation in personality psychology: "Verbal magic" and the five-factor model. *Philosophical Psychology, 24*(2), 223–243. doi:10.1080/09515089.2010.548319

Boccardi, M., Frisoni, G. B., Hare, R. D., Cavedo, E., Najt, P., Pievani, M., ... Tiihonen, J. (2011). Cortex and amygdala morphology in psychopathy. *Psychiatry Research: Neuroimaging, 193*(2), 85–92. doi:http://dx.doi.org/10.1016/j.pscychresns.2010.12.013

Bockoven, J. S. (1972). *Moral treatment in community mental health.* Oxford, UK: Springer Publishing.

Bodell, L. P., & Devlin, M. J. (2010). Pharmacotherapy for binge-eating disorder. In C. M. Grilo & J. E. Mitchell (Eds.), *The treatment of eating disorders: A clinical handbook* (pp. 402–413). New York, NY: Guilford Press.

Bodell, L. P., & Keel, P. K. (2010). Current treatment for anorexia nervosa: Efficacy, safety, and adherence. *Psychology Research and Behavior Management, 3.*

Bodenmann, G., & Randall, A. (2013). Marital therapy for dealing with depression. In M. Power (Ed.), *The Wiley-Blackwell handbook of mood disorders* (2nd ed., pp. 215–227). Chichester, UK: Wiley-Blackwell.

Boeding, S. E., Paprocki, C. M., Baucom, D. H., Abramowitz, J. S., Wheaton, M. G., Fabricant, L. E., & Fischer, M. S. (2013). Let me check that for you: Symptom accommodation in romantic partners of adults with obsessive–compulsive disorder. *Behaviour Research and Therapy, 51*(6), 316–322. doi:http://dx.doi.org/10.1016/j.brat.2013.03.002

Boelen, P. A., de Keijser, J., van den Hout, M. A., & van den Bout, J. (2007). Treatment of complicated grief: A comparison between cognitive-behavioral therapy and supportive counseling. *Journal of Consulting and Clinical Psychology, 75*(2), 277–284. doi:10.1037/0022-006X.75.2.277

Boelen, P. A., van den Hout, M., & van den Bout, J. (2013). Prolonged grief disorder: Cognitive-behavioral theory and therapy. In M. Stroebe, H. Schut, & J. van den Bout (Eds.), *Complicated grief: Scientific foundations for health care professionals.* (pp. 221–234). New York, NY: Routledge.

Boeree, C. G. (2006). Victor Frankl. Retrieved from http://webspace.ship.edu/cgboer/frankl.html

Boggs, C. D., Morey, L. C., Skodol, A. E., Shea, M. T., Sanislow, C. A., Grilo, C. M., ... Gunderson, J. G. (2005). Differential impairment as an indicator of sex bias in DSM-IV criteria for four personality disorders. *Psychological Assessment, 17*(4), 492–496. doi:10.1037/1040-3590.17.4.492

Bohman, M., Cloninger, C. R., von Knorring, A.-L., & Sigvardsson, S. (1984). An adoption study of somatoform disorders: III. Cross-fostering analysis and genetic relationship to alcoholism and criminality. *Archives of General Psychiatry, 41*(9), 872–878. doi:10.1001/archpsyc.1984.01790200054007

Bohnett, C. (2013). The history of ICD-10. Retrieved from https://www.webpt.com/blog/post/history-icd-10

Bohus, M., Haaf, B., Simms, T., Limberger, M. F., Schmahl, C., Unckel, C., ... Linehan, M. M. (2004). Effectiveness of inpatient dialectical behavioral therapy for borderline personality disorder: a controlled trial. *Behaviour Research and Therapy, 42*(5), 487–499. doi:http://dx.doi.org/10.1016/S0005-7967(03)00174-8

Boisvert, J. A., & Harrell, W. A. (2014). Ethnicity, socioeconomic status, and eating disorder symptomatology in Canada: Implications for mental health care. *Ethnicity and Inequalities in Health and Social Care, 7*(4), 158–177. doi:10.1108/EIHSC-10-2013-0038

Bokor, G., & Anderson, P. D. (2014). Ketamine: An update on its abuse. *Journal of Pharmacy Practice, 27*(6), 582–586. doi:10.1177/0897190014525754

Boksa, P. (2008). Maternal infection during pregnancy and schizophrenia. *Journal of Psychiatry & Neuroscience, 33*(3), 183–185.

Bola, J. R., & Mosher, L. R. (2003). Treatment of acute psychosis without neuroleptics: Two-year outcomes from the Soteria project. *Journal of Nervous and Mental Disease, 191*(4), 219–229. doi:10.1097/00005053-200304000-00002

Bola, J. R., Lehtinen, K., Aaltonen, J., Räkköläinen, V., Syvälahti, E., & Lehtinen, V. (2006). Predicting Medication-Free Treatment Response in Acute Psychosis: Cross-Validation From the Finnish Need-Adapted Project. *Journal of Nervous and Mental Disease, 194*(10), 732–739. doi:10.1097/01.nmd.0000243080.90255.88

Bollas, C., & Sundelson, D. (1995). *The new informants: The betrayal of confidentiality in psychoanalysis and psychotherapy.* Northvale, NJ: Jason Aronson.

Boller, F., & Forbes, M. M. (1998). History of dementia and dementia in history: An overview. *Journal of the Neurological Sciences, 158*(2), 125–133.

Bolling, M. Y., Terry, C. M., & Kohlneberg, R. J. (2006). Behavioral therapies. In J. C. Thomas & D. L. Segel (Eds.), *Comprehensive handbook of personality and psychopathology: Vol. 1. Personality and everyday functioning* (pp. 142–172). Hoboken, NJ: John Wiley.

Bolton, J. W. (2014). Case formulation after Engel—The 4P model: A philosophical case conference. *Philosophy, Psychiatry, & Psychology, 21*(3), 179–189. doi:10.1353/ppp.2014.0027

Bomba, J., & Cichocki, Ł. (2009). Will neuroscience account for the psychotherapeutic outcome in schizophrenia? *Archives of Psychiatry and Psychotherapy, 11*(3), 11–16.

Bonanno, G. A., Galea, S., Bucciarelli, A., & Vlahov, D. (2007). What predicts psychological resilience after disaster? The role of demographics, resources, and life stress. *Journal of Consulting and Clinical Psychology, 75*(5), 671–682. doi:10.1037/0022-006X.75.5.671

Bonanno, G. A., Papa, A., Lalande, K., Zhang, N., & Noll, J. G. (2005). Grief processing and deliberate grief avoidance: A prospective comparison of bereaved spouses and parents in the United States and the People's Republic of China. *Journal of Consulting and Clinical Psychology, 73*(1), 86–98. doi:10.1037/0022-006X.73.1.86

Bond, K., & Anderson, I. M. (2015). Psychoeducation for relapse prevention in bipolar disorder: A systematic review of efficacy in randomized controlled trials. *Bipolar Disorders, 17*(4), 349–362. doi:10.1111/bdi.12287

Bondy, A., & Frost, L. (2002). *A picture's worth: PECS and other visual communication strategies in autism.* Bethesda, MD: Woodbine House.

Bonfils, K. A., Lysaker, P. H., Minor, K. S., & Salyers, M. P. (2016). Affective empathy in schizophrenia: A meta-analysis. *Schizophrenia Research, 175*(1–3), 109–117. doi:10.1016/j.schres.2016.03.037

Bonnet, U., & Preuss, U. W. (2017). The cannabis withdrawal syndrome: Current insights. *Substance Abuse and Rehabilitation, 8*, 9–37. doi:10.2147/SAR.S109576

Bonnington, O., & Rose, D. (2014). Exploring stigmatisation among people diagnosed with either bipolar disorder or borderline personality disorder: A critical realist analysis. *Social Science & Medicine, 123*, 7–17. doi:10.1016/j.socscimed.2014.10.048

Bonta, J., & Andrews, D. A. (2007). Risk-need-responsivity model for offender assessment and rehabilitation. *Rehabilitation, 6*, 1–22.

Boodman, S. G. (1989, October 8). A horrible place a wonderful place. *The Washington Post.* Retrieved from https://www.washingtonpost.com/archive/lifestyle/magazine/1989/10/08/a-horrible-place-a-wonderful-place/ee4d7572-7ac0-4159-baf8-e8112a983e50/?utm_term=.fd65b34ab409

Bora, E., Fornito, A., Pantelis, C., & Yücel, M. (2012). Gray matter abnormalities in Major Depressive Disorder: A meta-analysis of voxel based morphometry studies. *Journal of Affective Disorders, 138*(1–2), 9–18. doi:http://dx.doi.org/10.1016/j.jad.2011.03.049

Bora, E., Yucel, M., & Pantelis, C. (2009). Theory of mind impairment in schizophrenia: Meta-analysis. *Schizophrenia Research, 109*(1-3), 1–9. doi:10.1016/j.schres.2008.12.020

Boraska, V., Davis, O. S. P., Cherkas, L. F., Helder, S. G., Harris, J., Krug, I., ... Zeggini, E. (2012). Genome-wide association analysis of eating disorder-related symptoms, behaviors, and personality traits. *American Journal of Medical Genetics. Part B, Neuropsychiatric Genetics: The Official Publication of The International Society of Psychiatric Genetics, 159B*(7), 803–811. doi:10.1002/ajmg.b.32087

Boraska, V., Franklin, C. S., Floyd, J. A. B., Thornton, L. M., Huckins, L. M., Southam, L., ... Tortorella, A. (2014). A genome-wide association study of anorexia nervosa. *Molecular Psychiatry, 19*(10), 1085–1094. doi:10.1038/mp.2013.187

Borg, C., de Jong, P. J., & Elgersma, H. (2014). Sexual aversion and the DSM-5: An excluded disorder with unabated relevance as a trans-diagnostic symptom. *Archives of Sexual Behavior, 43*(7), 1219–1223. doi:10.1007/s10508-014-0341-z

Borgwardt, S. J., Smieskova, R., Fusar-Poli, P., Bendfeldt, K., & Riecher-Rössler, A. (2009). The effects of antipsychotics on brain structure: what have we learnt from structural imaging of schizophrenia? *Psychological Medicine, 39*(11), 1781–1782. doi:http://dx.doi.org/10.1017/S0033291709006060

Borkovec, T. D., Alcaine, O. M., & Behar, E. (2004). Avoidance theory of worry and generalized anxiety disorder. In R. G. Heimberg, C. L. Turk, & D. S. Mennin (Eds.), *Generalized anxiety disorder: Advances in research and practice* (pp. 77–108). New York, NY: Guilford Press.

Bornstein, R. F. (2011). From symptom to process: How the PDM alters goals and strategies in psychological assessment. *Journal of Personality Assessment, 93*(2), 142–150. doi:10.1080/00223891.2011.542714

Bornstein, R. F., Denckla, C. A., & Chung, W.-J. (2013). Psychodynamic models of personality. In H. Tennen & J. Suls (Eds.), *Handbook of psychology: Vol. 5. Personality and social psychology* (2nd ed., pp. 43–64). Hoboken, NJ: John Wiley.

Borowicz, K. K., Kaczmarska, P., & Barbara, S. (2014). Medical uses of marijuana. *Archives of Physiotherapy and Global Researches, 18*(4), 13–17. doi:10.15442/apgr.18.1.20

Bosker, F. J., Tanke, M. A. C., Jongsma, M. E., Cremers, T. I. F. H., Jagtman, E., Pietersen, C. Y., ... den Boer, J. A. (2010). Biochemical and behavioral effects of long-term citalopram administration and discontinuation in rats: Role of serotonin synthesis. *Neurochemistry International, 57*(8), 948–957. doi:10.1016/j.neuint.2010.10.001

Boss, J. M. (1979). The seventeenth-century transformation of the hysteric affection, and Sydenham's Baconian medicine. *Psychological Medicine, 9*(2), 221–234. doi:10.1017/S0033291700030725

Botella, C., Serrano, B., Baños, R. M., & Garcia-Palacios, A. (2015). Virtual reality exposure-based therapy for the treatment of post-traumatic stress disorder: A review of its efficacy, the adequacy of the treatment protocol, and its acceptability. *Neuropsychiatric Disease and Treatment, 11*.

Bothe, A. K., Davidow, J. H., Bramlett, R. E., Franic, D. M., & Ingham, R. J. (2006). Stuttering treatment research 1970–2005: II. Systematic review incorporating trial quality assessment of pharmacological approaches. *American Journal of Speech-Language Pathology, 15*(4), 342–352. doi:10.1044/1058-0360(2006/032)

Botvin, G. J., Baker, E., Renick, N. L., Filazzola, A. D., & Botvin, E. M. (1984). A cognitive-behavioral approach to substance abuse prevention. *Addictive Behaviors, 9*(2), 137–147. doi:10.1016/0306-4603(84)90051-0

Bouchard, T. J., & McGue, M. (1981). Familial studies of intelligence: A review. *Science, 212*(4498), 1055–1059. doi:10.1126/science.7195071

Bouman, T. K. (2014). Cognitive and behavioral models and cognitive-behavioral and related therapies for health anxiety and hypochondriasis. In V. Starcevic & R. Noyes, Jr. (Eds.), *Hypochondriasis and health anxiety: A guide for clinicians* (pp. 149–198). New York, NY: Oxford University Press.

Bouman, W. P., Richards, C., Addinall, R. M., de Montis, I. A., Arcelus, J., Duisin, D., ... Wilson, D. (2014). Yes and yes again: Are standards of care which require two referrals for genital reconstructive surgery ethical? *Sexual and Relationship Therapy, 29*(4), 377–389. doi:10.1080/14681994.2014.954993

Bowen, M. (1978). *Family therapy in clinical practice.* Lanham, MD: Jason Aronson.

Bowen, M. L. (2016). Stigma: Content analysis of the representation of people with personality disorder in the UK popular press, 2001–2012. *International Journal of Mental Health Nursing.* doi:10.1111/inm.12213

Bower, G. (1994). Temporary emotional states act like multiple personalities. In R. M. Klein & B. K. Doane (Eds.), *Psychological concepts and dissociative disorders* (pp. 207–234). Hillsdale, NJ: Lawrence Erlbaum.

Bower, G. H. (1981). Mood and memory. *American Psychologist, 36*(2), 129–148. doi:10.1037/0003-066X.36.2.129

Bowers, L., Carr-Walker, P., Allan, T., Callaghan, P., Nijman, H., & Paton, J. (2006). Attitude to personality disorder among prison officers working in a dangerous and severe personality disorder unit. *International Journal of Law and Psychiatry, 29*(5), 333–342. doi:10.1016/j.ijlp.2005.10.005

Bowl, R. (1996). Legislating for user involvement in the United Kingdom: Mental health services and the NHS and Community Care Act 1990. *International Journal of Social Psychiatry, 42*(3), 165–180.

Bowlby, J. (1980). *Attachment and loss.* New York, NY: Basic Books.

Bowlby, J. (1988). *A secure base: Parent-child attachment and healthy human development.* New York, NY: Basic Books.

Boyd, A., Dworzynski, K., & Howell, P. (2011). Pharmacological agents for developmental stuttering in children and adolescents: A systematic review. *Journal of Clinical Psychopharmacology, 31*(6), 740–744. doi:10.1097/JCP.0b013e318234ee3b

Boyer, P., Phillips, J. L., Rousseau, F. L., & Ilivitsky, S. (2007). Hippocampal abnormalities and memory deficits: New evidence of a strong pathophysiological link in schizophrenia. *Brain Research Reviews, 54*(1), 92–112. doi:10.1016/j.brainresrev.2006.12.008

Boyle, M. (2002). *Schizophrenia: A scientific delusion?* (2nd ed.). London, UK: Routledge.

Boyle, M. P., Dioguardi, L., & Pate, J. E. (2016). A comparison of three strategies for reducing the public stigma associated with stuttering. *Journal of Fluency Disorders, 50*, 44–58. doi:10.1016/j.jfludis.2016.09.004

Bozkurt, H., Mutluer, T. D., Kose, C., & Zoroglu, S. (2015). High psychiatric comorbidity in adolescents with dissociative disorders. *Psychiatry and Clinical Neurosciences, 69*(6), 369–374. doi:10.1111/pcn.12256

Bradford, J. M. W. (2001). The neurobiology, neuropharmacology, and pharmacological treatment of the paraphilias and compulsive sexual behaviour. *The Canadian Journal of Psychiatry / La Revue Canadienne De Psychiatrie, 46*(1), 26–34.

Bradford, J. M., & Fedoroff, J. P. (2009). The neurobiology of sexual behavior and the paraphilias. In F. M. Saleh, A. J. Grudzinskas, Jr., J. M. Bradford, & D. J. Brodsky (Eds.), *Sex offenders: Identification, risk assessment, treatment, and legal issues* (pp. 36–46). New York, NY: Oxford University Press.

Brady, M. T. (2014). Cutting the silence: Initial, impulsive self-cutting in adolescence. *Journal of Child Psychotherapy, 40*(3), 287–301. doi:10.1080/007541 7X.2014.965430

Braff, D. L., Ryan, J., Rissling, A. J., & Carpenter, W. T. (2013). Lack of use in the literature from the last 20 years supports dropping traditional schizophrenia subtypes from DSM-5 and ICD-11. *Schizophrenia Bulletin, 39*(4), 751–753. doi:10.1093/schbul/sbt068

Brambilla, F., Bellodi, L., Arancio, C., Ronchi, P., & Limonta, D. (2001). Central dopaminergic function in Anorexia and Bulimia Nervosa: A psychoneuroendocrine approach. *Psychoneuroendocrinology, 26*(4), 393–409. doi:http://dx.doi.org/10.1016/S0306-4530(00)00062-7

Brand, B. L. (2012). What we know and what we need to learn about the treatment of dissociative disorders. *Journal of Trauma & Dissociation, 13*(4), 387–396. doi:10.1080/152 99732.2012.672550

Brand, B. L., Classen, C. C., McNary, S. W., & Zaveri, P. (2009). A review of dissociative disorders treatment studies. *Journal of Nervous and Mental Disease, 197*(9), 646–654. doi:10.1097/NMD.0b013e3181b3afaa

Brand, B. L., Lanius, R., Vermetten, E., Loewenstein, R. J., & Spiegel, D. (2012). Where are we going? An update on assessment, treatment, and neurobiological research in dissociative disorders as we move toward the DSM-5. *Journal of Trauma & Dissociation, 13*(1), 9–31. doi:10.1080/15299 732.2011.620687

Brand, B., Loewenstein, R. J., & Spiegel, D. (2013). Disinformation about dissociation: Dr Joel Paris's notions about dissociative identity disorder. *Journal of Nervous and Mental Disease, 201*(4), 354–356. doi:10.1097/NMD.0b013e318288d2ee

Brand, B. L., Loewenstein, R. J., & Spiegel, D. (2014). Dispelling myths about dissociative identity disorder treatment: An empirically based approach. *Psychiatry: Interpersonal and Biological Processes, 77*(2), 169–189.

Brandys, M. K., de Kovel, C. G. F., Kas, M. J., van Elburg, A. A., & Adan, R. A. H. (2015). Overview of genetic research in anorexia nervosa: The past, the present and the future. *International Journal of Eating Disorders, 48*(7), 814–825. doi:10.1002/eat.22400

Bratman, S. (1997, September/October). The health food eating disorder. *Yoga Journal,* 42–50.

Bratman, S. (2014, January 23). What is orthorexia. Retrieved from http://www.orthorexia.com/what-is-orthorexia/

Bratton, S. C., Ceballos, P. L., Sheely-Moore, A. I., Meany-Walen, K., Pronchenko, Y., & Jones, L. D. (2013). Head start early mental health intervention: Effects of child-centered play therapy on disruptive behaviors. *International Journal of Play Therapy, 22*(1), 28–42. doi:10.1037/a0030318

Bratton, S. C., Ray, D. C., Edwards, N. A., & Landreth, G. (2009). Child-centered play therapy (CCPT): Theory, research, and practice. *Person-Centered and Experiential Psychotherapies, 8*(4), 266–281. doi:10.1080/1 4779757.2009.9688493

Brattström, A. (2009). Long-term effects of St. John's wort (Hypericum perforatum) treatment: A 1-year safety study in mild to moderate depression. *Phytomedicine, 16*(4), 277–283. doi:http://dx.doi.org/10.1016/j.phymed.2008.12.023

Braun, J. M., Froehlich, T. E., Daniels, J. L., Dietrich, K. N., Hornung, R., Auinger, P., & Lanphear, B. P. (2008). Association of environmental toxicants and conduct disorder in U.S. children: NHANES 2001–2004. *Environmental Health Perspectives, 116*(7), 956–962. doi:10.1289/ehp.11177

Braun, J. M., Froehlich, T., Kalkbrenner, A., Pfeiffer, C. M., Fazili, Z., Yolton, K., & Lanphear, B. P. (2014). Brief report: Are autistic-behaviors in children related to prenatal vitamin use and maternal whole blood folate concentrations? *Journal of Autism and Developmental Disorders, 44*(10), 2602–2607. doi:10.1007/s10803-014-2114-x

Braun, J. M., Kahn, R. S., Froehlich, T., Auinger, P., & Lanphear, B. P. (2006). Exposures to environmental toxicants and attention deficit hyperactivity disorder in U.S. children. *Environmental Health Perspectives, 114*(12), 1904–1909.

Breen, L. J., & O'Connor, M. (2007). The fundamental paradox in the grief literature: A critical reflection. *Omega: Journal of Death and Dying, 55*(3), 199–218. doi:10.2190/OM.55.3.c

Breggin, P. R. (2001). *Talking back to Ritalin: What doctors aren't telling you about stimulants and ADHD* (rev. ed.). Cambrdige, MA: Perseus Publishing.

Breggin, P. R. (2007). ECT damages the brain: Disturbing news for patients and shock doctors alike. *Ethical Human Psychology and Psychiatry, 9*(2), 83–86. doi:10.1891/152315007782021196

Breggin, P. R. (2009). Electroshock forced on children and involuntary adults. *Ethical Human Psychology and Psychiatry, 11*(2), 80–82. doi:10.1891/1559-4343.11.2.80

Breggin, P. R. (2010). The FDA should test the safety of ECT machines. *Ethical Human Psychology and Psychiatry, 12*(2), 139–143. doi:10.1891/1559-4343.12.2.139

Breitborde, N. J. K., López, S. R., & Nuechterlein, K. H. (2010). Expressed emotion and the course of schizophrenia: The role of human agency. *Directions in Psychiatry, 30*(1), 29–40.

Breitenfeld, T., Jurasic, M. J., & Breitenfeld, D. (2014). Hippocrates: The forefather of neurology. *Neurological Sciences, 35*(9), 1349–1352. doi:10.1007/s10072-014-1869-3

Bremner, J. D. (1999). Does stress damage the brain? *Biological Psychiatry, 45*(7), 797–805. doi:10.1016/S0006-3223(99)00009-8

Bremner, J. D. (2001). Hypotheses and controversies related to effects of stress on the hippocampus: An argument for stress-induced damage to the hippocampus in patients with posttraumatic stress disorder. *Hippocampus, 11*(2), 75–81. doi:10.1002/hipo.1023

Brennan, M. A., Emmerling, M. E., & Whelton, W. J. (2015). Emotion-focused group therapy: Addressing self-criticism in the treatment of eating disorders. *Counselling & Psychotherapy Research, 15*(1), 67–75.

Bresch, A., Rullmann, M., Luthardt, J., Arelin, K., Becker, G. A., Patt, M., ... Hesse, S. (2016). In-vivo serotonin transporter availability and somatization in healthy subjects. *Personality and Individual Differences, 94*, 354–359. doi:10.1016/j.paid.2016.01.042

Breur, J., & Freud, S. (2013). *Studies on hysteria* (J. Strachey, Trans.). London, UK: Forgotten Books. (Original work published 1893–1895)

Brewerton, T. D. (2007). Eating disorders, trauma, and comorbidity: Focus on PTSD. *Eating Disorders, 15*(4), 285–304. doi:10.1080/10640260701454311

Brewin, C. R., & Burgess, N. (2014). Contextualisation in the revised dual representation theory of PTSD: A response to Pearson and colleagues. *Journal of Behavior Therapy and Experimental Psychiatry, 45*(1), 217–219. doi:10.1016/j.jbtep.2013.07.011

Brewin, C. R., & Holmes, E. A. (2003). Psychological theories of posttraumatic stress disorder. *Clinical Psychology Review, 23*(3), 339–376. doi:10.1016/S0272-7358(03)00033-3

Brewin, C. R., Andrews, B., & Valentine, J. D. (2000). Meta-analysis of risk factors for posttraumatic stress disorder in trauma-exposed adults. *Journal of Consulting and Clinical Psychology, 68*(5), 748–766. doi:10.1037/0022-006X.68.5.748

Brewin, C. R., Gregory, J. D., Lipton, M., & Burgess, N. (2010). Intrusive images in psychological disorders: Characteristics, neural mechanisms, and treatment implications. *Psychological Review, 117*(1), 210–232. doi:10.1037/a0018113

Bridler, R., Häberle, A., Müller, S. T., Cattapan, K., Grohmann, R., Toto, S., ... Greil, W. (2015). Psychopharmacological treatment of 2195 in-patients with borderline personality disorder: A comparison with other psychiatric disorders. *European Neuropsychopharmacology, 25*(6), 763–772. doi:10.1016/j.euroneuro.2015.03.017

Brigola, A. G., Silva Manzini, C. S., Silveira Oliveira, G. B., Ottaviani, A. C., Sako, M. P., & Carvalho Vale, F. A. (2015). Subjective memory complaints associated with depression and cognitive impairment in the elderly: A systematic review. *Dementia & Neuropsychologia, 9*(1), 51–57.

Brikell, I., Kuja-Halkola, R., & Larsson, H. (2015). Heritability of attention-deficit hyperactivity disorder in adults. *American Journal of Medical Genetics Part B: Neuropsychiatric Genetics, 168*(6), 406–413. doi:10.1002/ajmg.b.32335

British Psychological Society. (2011). *Response to the American Psychiatric Association: DSM-5 development.* Retrieved from http://www.bps.org.uk/system/files/consultationpapers/responses/DSM-5%202011%20-%20BPS%20response.pdf

British Psychological Society. (2014). Conversion therapy: Consensus statement. Retrieved from http://www.bps.org.uk/system/files/Public%20files/conversion_therapy_final_version.pdf

British Psychological Society. (2017, January 16). UK organisations unite against conversion therapy. Retrieved from https://beta.bps.org.uk/news-and-policy/uk-organisations-unite-against-conversion-therapy

Broady, T. R., Stoyles, G. J., & Morse, C. (2017). Understanding carers' lived experience of stigma: The voice of families with a child on the autism spectrum. *Health & Social Care in the Community, 25*(1), 224–233. doi:10.1111/hsc.12297

Brockman, R., & Murrell, E. (2015). What are the primary goals of cognitive behavior therapy for psychosis? A theoretical and empirical review. *Journal of Cognitive Psychotherapy, 29*(1), 45–67. doi:10.1891/0889-8391.29.1.45

Broft, A., Berner, L. A., & Walsh, B. T. (2010). Pharmacotherapy for bulimia nervosa. In C. M. Grilo & J. E. Mitchell (Eds.), *The treatment of eating disorders: A clinical handbook* (pp. 388–401). New York, NY: Guilford Press.

Brondino, N., Fusar-Poli, L., Panisi, C., Damiani, S., Barale, F., & Politi, P. (2016). Pharmacological modulation of GABA function in autism spectrum disorders: A systematic review of human studies. *Journal of Autism and Developmental Disorders, 46*(3), 825–839. doi:10.1007/s10803-015-2619-y

Brown, A. S. (2011). The environment and susceptibility to schizophrenia. *Progress in Neurobiology, 93*(1), 23–58. doi:http://dx.doi.org/10.1016/j.pneurobio.2010.09.003

Brown, A. S., & Derkits, E. J. (2010). Prenatal infection and schizophrenia: A review of epidemiologic and translational studies. *The American Journal of Psychiatry, 167*(3), 261–280. doi:10.1176/appi.ajp.2009.09030361

Brown, A. S., Cheslack-Postava, K., Rantakokko, P., Kiviranta, H., Hinkka-Yli-Salomäki, S., McKeague, I. W., ... Sourander, A. (2018). Association of maternal insecticide levels with autism in offspring from a national birth cohort. *The American Journal of Psychiatry.* Advance online publication. doi:10.1176/appi.ajp.2018.17101129

Brown, J. D., & Witherspoon, E. M. (2002). The mass media and American adolescents' health. *Journal of Adolescent Health, 31*(6, Supplement), 153–170. doi:http://dx.doi.org/10.1016/S1054-139X(02)00507-4

Brown, K. F., Long, S. J., Ramsay, M., Hudson, M. J., Green, J., Vincent, C. A., ... Sevdalis, N. (2012). U.K. parents' decision-making about measles-mumps-rubella (MMR) vaccine 10 years after the MMR-autism controversy: a qualitative analysis. *Vaccine, 30*(10), 1855–1864. doi:10.1016/j.vaccine.2011.12.127

Brown, L. S. (1992). A feminist critique of the personality disorders. In L. S. Brown & M. Ballou (Eds.), *Personality and psychopathology: Feminist reappraisals.* (pp. 206–228). New York, NY: Guilford Press.

Brown, L. S. (1994). *Subversive dialogues: Theory in feminist therapy.* New York, NY: Basic Books.

Brown, L. S. (1997). The private practice of subversion: Psychology as Tikkun Olam. *American Psychologist, 52*(4), 449–462. doi:10.1037/0003-066X.52.4.449

Brown, M. L., Pope, A. W., & Brown, E. J. (2011). Treatment of primary nocturnal enuresis in children: A review. *Child: Care, Health and Development, 37*(2), 153–160. doi:10.1111/j.1365-2214.2010.01146.x

Brown, M., Cachelin, F. M., & Dohm, F.-A. (2009). Eating disorders in ethnic minority women: A review of the emerging literature. *Current Psychiatry Reviews, 5*(3), 182–193. doi:10.2174/157340009788971119

Brown, R. F., Bartrop, R., & Birmingham, C. L. (2008). Immunological disturbance and infectious disease in anorexia nervosa: A review. *Acta Neuropsychiatrica, 20*(3), 117–128. doi:10.1111/j.1601-5215.2008.00286.x

Brown, R. J. (2006). Different types of 'dissociation' have different psychological mechanisms. *Journal of Trauma & Dissociation, 7*(4), 7–28. doi:10.1300/J229v07n04_02

Brown, T. A., Holland, L. A., & Keel, P. K. (2014). Comparing operational definitions of DSM-5 anorexia nervosa for research contexts. *International Journal of Eating Disorders, 47*(1), 76–84. doi:10.1002/eat.22184

Brown, T. J. (1998). *Dorothea Dix: New England reformer.* Cambridge, MA: Harvard University Press.

Browne, H. A., Gair, S. L., Scharf, J. M., & Grice, D. E. (2014). Genetics of obsessive-compulsive disorder and related disorders. *Psychiatric Clinics of North America, 37*(3), 319–335. doi:10.1016/j.psc.2014.06.002

Browning, M., Paul Fletcher, D., & Sharpe, M. (2011). Can neuroimaging help us to understand and classify somatoform disorders? A systematic and critical review. *Psychosomatic Medicine, 73*(2), 173–184. doi:10.1097/PSY.0b013e31820824f6

Bruce, M. L. (2010). Suicide risk and prevention in veteran populations. *Annals of the New York Academy of Sciences, 1208*(1), 98–103. doi:10.1111/j.1749-6632.2010.05697.x

Bruch, H. (1962). Perceptual and conceptual disturbances in anorexia nervosa. *Psychosomatic Medicine, 24*(2), 187–194.

Bruch, H. (1963). Disturbed communication in eating disorders. *American Journal of Orthopsychiatry, 33*(1), 99–104. doi:10.1111/j.1939-0025.1963.tb00363.x

Bruch, H. (1971). Family transactions in eating disorders. *Comprehensive Psychiatry, 12*(3), 238–248. doi:10.1016/0010-440X(71)90021-6

Bruch, H. (2001). *The golden cage: The enigma of anorexia nervosa.* Cambridge, MA: Harvard University Press. (Original work published 1978)

Brühl, A. B., Delsignore, A., Komossa, K., & Weidt, S. (2014). Neuroimaging in social anxiety disorder—A meta-analytic review resulting in a new neurofunctional model. *Neuroscience and Biobehavioral Reviews, 47,* 260–280. doi:10.1016/j.neubiorev.2014.08.003

Brukner-Wertman, Y., Laor, N., & Golan, O. (2016). Social (pragmatic) communication disorder and its relation to the autism spectrum: Dilemmas arising from the DSM-5 classification. *Journal of Autism and Developmental Disorders, 46*(8), 2821–2829. doi:10.1007/s10803-016-2814-5

Brundin, L., Erhardt, S., Bryleva, E. Y., Achtyes, E. D., & Postolache, T. T. (2015). The role of inflammation in suicidal behaviour. *Acta Psychiatrica Scandinavica, 132*(3), 192–203. doi:10.1111/acps.12458

Brüne, M. (2004). Schizophrenia–an evolutionary enigma? *Neuroscience and Biobehavioral Reviews, 28*(1), 41–53. doi:10.1016/j.neubiorev.2003.10.002

Brüne, M. (2005). 'Theory of mind' in schizophrenia: A review of the literature. *Schizophrenia Bulletin, 31*(1), 21–42. doi:10.1093/schbul/sbi002

Brüne, M., & Brüne-Cohrs, U. (2006). Theory of mind—evolution, ontogeny, brain mechanisms and psychopathology. *Neuroscience and Biobehavioral Reviews, 30*(4), 437–455. doi:10.1016/j.neubiorev.2005.08.001

Bryant, R. A., Felmingham, K. L., Falconer, E. M., Pe Benito, L., Dobson-Stone, C., Pierce, K. D., & Schofield, P. R. (2010). Preliminary evidence of the short allele of the serotonin transporter gene predicting poor response to cognitive behavior therapy in posttraumatic stress disorder. *Biological Psychiatry, 67*(12), 1217–1219. doi:10.1016/j.biopsych.2010.03.016

Bryant-Waugh, R., Markham, L., Kreipe, R. E., & Walsh, B. T. (2010). Feeding and eating disorders in childhood. *International Journal of Eating Disorders, 43*(2), 98–111.

Brymer, M., Layne, C., Jacobs, A., Pynoos, R., Ruzek, J., Steinberg, A., ... Watson, P. (2006). *Psychological first aid: Field operations guide* (2nd ed.). Los Angeles, CA: National Child Traumatic Stress Network and National Center for PTSD.

Brytek-Matera, A. (2012). Orthorexia nervosa—An eating disorder, obsessive-compulsive disorder or disturbed eating habit? *Archives of Psychiatry and Psychotherapy, 14*(1), 55–60.

Buchanan, R. W., Freedman, R., Javitt, D. C., Abi-Dargham, A., & Lieberman, J. A. (2007). Recent advances in the development of novel pharmacological agents for the treatment of cognitive impairments in schizophrenia. *Schizophrenia Bulletin, 33*(5), 1120–1130. doi:10.1093/schbul/sbm083

Buchheim, A., Roth, G., Schiepek, G., Pogarell, O., & Karch, S. (2013). Neurobiology of borderline personality disorder (BPD) and antisocial personality disorder (APD). *Schweizer Archiv für Neurologie und Psychiatrie, 164*(4), 115–122.

Budge, S. L. (2013). Interpersonal psychotherapy with transgender clients. *Psychotherapy, 50*(3), 356–359. doi:10.1037/a0032194

Budge, S. L. (2015a). The effectiveness of psychotherapeutic treatments for personality disorders: A review and critique of current research practices. *Canadian Psychology/Psychologie Canadienne, 56*(2), 191–196. doi:10.1037/a0038534

Budge, S. L. (2015b). Psychotherapists as gatekeepers: An evidence-based case study highlighting the role and process of letter writing for transgender clients. *Psychotherapy, 52*(3), 287–297. doi:10.1037/pst0000034

Budge, S. L., Moore, J. T., Del Re, A. C., Wampold, B. E., Baardseth, T. P., & Nienhuis, J. B. (2013). The effectiveness of evidence-based treatments for personality disorders when comparing treatment-as-usual and bona fide treatments. *Clinical Psychology Review, 33*(8), 1057–1066. doi:10.1016/j.cpr.2013.08.003

Budney, A. J., & Hughes, J. R. (2006). The cannabis withdrawal syndrome. *Current Opinion in Psychiatry, 19*(3), 233–238.

Budur, K., Mathews, M., Adetunji, B., Mathews, M., & Mahmud, J. (2005). Non-stimulant treatment for attention deficit hyperactivity disorder. *Psychiatry, 2*(7), 44–48.

Bugental, J. F. T. (1987). *The art of the psychotherapist*. New York, NY: Norton.

Bühren, K., Schwarte, R., Fluck, F., Timmesfeld, N., Krei, M., Egberts, K., ... Herpertz-Dahlmann, B. (2014). Comorbid psychiatric disorders in female adolescents with first-onset anorexia nervosa. *European Eating Disorders Review, 22*(1), 39–44. doi:10.1002/erv.2254

Bui, E., Nadal-Vicens, M., & Simon, N. M. (2012). Pharmacological approaches to the treatment of complicated grief: rationale and a brief review of the literature. *Dialogues in Clinical Neuroscience, 14*(2), 149–157.

Bulger, A. (2016, November 11). A brief history of how we slept, from 8,000 BCE to today. *Van Winkle's*.

Bulik, C. M., Sullivan, P. F., Tozzi, F., Furberg, H., Lichtenstein, P., & Pedersen, N. L. (2006). Prevalence, heritability, and prospective risk factors for anorexia nervosa. *Archives of General Psychiatry, 63*(3), 305–312. doi:10.1001/archpsyc.63.3.305

Bulik, C. M., Sullivan, P. F., Wade, T. D., & Kendler, K. S. (2000). Twin studies of eating disorders: a review. *International Journal of Eating Disorders, 27*(1), 1–20.

Bullock, J. L. (2002). Involuntary treatment of defendants found incompetent to stand trial. *Journal of Forensic Psychology Practice, 2*(4), 1–33. doi:10.1300/J158v02n04_01

Bullough, V. L. (2002). Masturbation: A historical overview. *Journal of Psychology and Human Sexuality, 14*(2/3), 17–33.

Buoli, M., Serati, M., & Cahn, W. (2016). Alternative pharmacological strategies for adult ADHD treatment: A systematic review. *Expert Review of Neurotherapeutics, 16*(2), 131–144. doi:10.1586/14737175.2016.1135735

Burgess, A. W. (1983). Rape trauma syndrome. *Behavioral Sciences & the Law, 1*(3), 97–113. doi:10.1002/bsl.2370010310

Burgess, A. W., & Holmstrom, L. L. (1974). Rape trauma syndrome. *The American Journal of Psychiatry, 131*(9), 981–986.

Burke, B. L., Arkowitz, H., & Dunn, C. (2002). The efficacy of motivational interviewing and its adaptations: What we know so far. In W. R. Miller & S. Rollnick (Eds.), *Motivational interviewing: Preparing people for change* (2nd ed., pp. 217–250). New York, NY: Guilford Press.

Burke, H. M., Davis, M. C., Otte, C., & Mohr, D. C. (2005). Depression and cortisol responses to psychological stress: A meta-analysis. *Psychoneuroendocrinology, 30*(9), 846–856. doi:10.1016/j.psyneuen.2005.02.010

Burke, R. J. (1985). Beliefs and fears underlying Type A behavior: Correlates of time urgency and hostility. *The Journal of General Psychology, 112*(2), 133–145.

Burkett, K., Morris, E., Manning-Courtney, P., Anthony, J., & Shambley-Ebron, D. (2015). African American families on autism diagnosis and treatment: The influence of culture. *Journal of Autism and Developmental Disorders, 45*(10), 3244–3254. doi:10.1007/s10803-015-2482-x

Burnes, T. R., Singh, A. A., Harper, A. J., Harper, B., Maxon-Kann, W., Pickering, D. L., ... Hosea, J. (2010). American Counseling Association: Competencies for counseling with transgender clients. *Journal of LGBT Issues in Counseling, 4*(3–4), 135–159.

Burns, J. K. (2006). Psychosis: A costly by-product of social brain evolution in Homo sapiens. *Progress in Neuro-Psychopharmacology & Biological Psychiatry, 30*(5), 797–814. doi:10.1016/j.pnpbp.2006.01.006

Burokas, A., Arboleya, S., Moloney, R. D., Peterson, V. L., Murphy, K., Clarke, G., ... Cryan, J. F. (2017). Targeting the microbiota-gut-brain axis: Prebiotics have anxiolytic and antidepressant-like effects and reverse the impact of chronic stress in mice. *Biological Psychiatry*. doi:10.1016/j.biopsych.2016.12.031

Burr, V. (2015). *Social constructionism* (3rd ed.). New York, NY: Routledge.

Burri, A. (2013). Bringing sex research into the 21st century: Genetic and epigenetic approaches on female sexual function. *Journal of Sex Research, 50*(3–4), 318–328. doi:10.1080/00224499.2012.753027

Burri, A. V., Cherkas, L. M., & Spector, T. D. (2009). The genetics and epidemiology of female sexual dysfunction: A review. *Journal of Sexual Medicine, 6*(3), 646–657. doi:10.1111/j.1743-6109.2008.01144.x

Burri, A., Cherkas, L., Spector, T., & Rahman, Q. (2011). Genetic and environmental influences on female sexual orientation, childhood gender typicality and adult gender identity. *PLOS One, 6*(7), e21982–e21982. doi:10.1371/journal.pone.0021982

Burri, A., Rahman, Q., & Spector, T. (2011). Genetic and environmental risk factors for sexual distress and its association with female sexual dysfunction. *Psychological Medicine, 41*(11), 2435–2445. doi:10.1017/S0033291711000493

Burri, A., Spector, T., & Rahman, Q. (2013). A discordant monozygotic twin approach to testing environmental influences on sexual dysfunction in women. *Archives of Sexual Behavior, 42*(6), 961–972. doi:10.1007/s10508-013-0089-x

Burrows, V. (2015). The medicalization of stress: Hans Selye and the transformation of the postwar medical marketplace. *CUNY Academic Works*. Retrieved from http://academicworks.cuny.edu/gc_etds/877

Burstow, B. (2005). A critique of posttraumatic stress disorder and the DSM. *Journal of Humanistic Psychology, 45*(4), 429–445. doi:10.1177/0022167805280265

Bury, B., Tiggemann, M., & Slater, A. (2016). The effect of digital alteration disclaimer labels on social comparison and body image: Instructions and individual differences. *Body Image, 17*, 136–142. doi:10.1016/j.bodyim.2016.03.005

Busch, F. N., & Milrod, B. L. (2015). Generalized anxiety disorder and other anxiety disorders. In P. Luyten, L. C. Mayes, P. Fonagy, M. Target, & S. J. Blatt (Eds.), *Handbook of psychodynamic approaches to psychopathology* (pp. 152–164). New York, NY: Guilford Press.

Busch, F. N., Milrod, B. L., & Shear, K. (2010). Psychodynamic concepts of anxiety. In D. J. Stein, E. Hollander, & B. O. Rothbaum (Eds.), *Textbook of anxiety disorders* (2nd ed., pp. 117–128). Arlington, VA: American Psychiatric Publishing.

Bush, G. (2011). Cingulate, frontal and parietal cortical dysfunction in attention-deficit/hyperactivity disorder. *Biological Psychiatry, 69*(12), 1160–1167. doi:10.1016/j.biopsych.2011.01.022

Bush, K., Kivlahan, D. R., McDonell, M. B., Fihn, S. D., & Bradley, K. A. (1998). The AUDIT alcohol consumption questions (AUDIT-C): An effective brief screening test for problem drinking. *Archives of Internal Medicine, 158*(16), 1789–1795.

Butcher, J. N., Atlas, M. M., & Hahn, J. (2004). The Minnesota Multiphasic Personality Inventory-2. In M. J. Hilsenroth & D. L. Segal (Eds.), *Comprehensive handbook of psychological assessment: Vol. 2. Personality assessment* (pp. 30–38). Hoboken, NJ: John Wiley.

Butler, A. C., Chapman, J. E., Forman, E. M., & Beck, A. T. (2006). The empirical status of cognitive-behavioral therapy: A review of meta-analyses. *Clinical Psychology Review, 26*(1), 17–31. doi:10.1016/j.cpr.2005.07.003

Butler, L. D. (2004). The dissociations of everyday life. *Journal of Trauma & Dissociation, 5*(2), 1–11. doi:10.1300/J229v05n02_01

Butler, R. J. (2004). Childhood nocturnal enuresis: Developing a conceptual framework. *Clinical Psychology Review, 24*(8), 909–931. doi:10.1016/j.cpr.2004.07.001

Butterworth, P., Olesen, S. C., & Leach, L. S. (2012). The role of hardship in the association between socio-economic position and depression. *Australian and New Zealand Journal of Psychiatry, 46*(4), 364–373. doi:10.1177/0004867411433215

Butts, H. F. (2002). The black mask of humanity: Racial/ethnic discrimination and post-traumatic stress disorder. *Journal of the American Academy of Psychiatry and the Law, 30*(3), 336–339.

Buwalda, F. M., Bouman, T. K., & van Duijn, M. A. J. (2007). Psychoeducation for hypochondriasis: A comparison of a cognitive-behavioural approach and a problem-solving approach. *Behaviour Research and Therapy, 45*(5), 887–899. doi:http://dx.doi.org/10.1016/j.brat.2006.08.004

Caddy, C., Amit, B. H., McCloud, T. L., Rendell, J. M., Furukawa, T. A., McShane, R., ... Cipriani, A. (2015). Ketamine and other glutamate receptor modulators for depression in adults. *Cochrane Database of Systematic Reviews*(9), CD011612. doi:10.1002/14651858.CD011612.pub2

Cafferky, B. M., Mendez, M., Anderson, J. R., & Stith, S. M. (2016). Substance use and intimate partner violence: A meta-analytic review. *Psychology of Violence*. doi:10.1037/vio0000074

Cahill, K., Stevens, S., Perera, R., & Lancaster, T. (2013). Pharmacological interventions for smoking cessation: an overview and network meta-analysis. *Cochrane Database of Systematic Reviews, 2013*(5), 1–50. doi:10.1002/14651858.CD009329.pub2

Cahill, S. P., Rothbaum, B. O., Resick, P. A., & Follette, V. M. (2009). Cognitive-behavioral therapy for adults. In E. B. Foa, T. M. Keane, M. J. Friedman, & J. A. Cohen (Eds.), *Effective treatments for PTSD: Practice guidelines from the International Society for Traumatic Stress Studies* (2nd ed., pp. 139–222). New York, NY: Guilford Press.

Cahn, W., Rais, M., Stigter, F. P., van Haren, N. E. M., Caspers, E., Pol, H. E. H., ... Kahn, R. S. (2009). Psychosis and brain volume changes during the first five years of schizophrenia. *European Neuropsychopharmacology, 19*(2), 147–151. doi:10.1016/j.euroneuro.2008.10.006

Cain, D. J. (2010). *Person-centered psychotherapies.* Washington, DC: American Psychological Association.

Cakiroglu, O. (2015). Response to intervention: Early identification of students with learning disabilities. *International Journal of Early Childhood Special Education, 7*(1), 170–182.

Calati, R., Gressier, F., Balestri, M., & Serretti, A. (2013). Genetic modulation of borderline personality disorder: Systematic review and meta-analysis. *Journal of Psychiatric Research, 47*(10), 1275–1287. doi:http://dx.doi.org/10.1016/j.jpsychires.2013.06.002

Calhoun, L. G., & Tedeschi, R. G. (2006). The foundations of posttraumatic growth: An expanded framework. In L. G. Calhoun & R. G. Tedeschi (Eds.), *Handbook of posttraumatic growth: Research and practice* (pp. 3–23). Mahwah, NJ: Lawrence Erlbaum.

Caligor, E., & Clarkin, J. F. (2010). An object relations model of personality and personality pathology. In J. F. Clarkin, P. Fonagy, & G. O. Gabbard (Eds.), *Psychodynamic psychotherapy for personality disorders: A clinical handbook* (pp. 3–35). Arlington, VA: American Psychiatric Publishing.

Caligor, E., Kernberg, O. F., & Clarkin, J. F. (2007). *Handbook of dynamic psychotherapy for higher level personality pathology.* Arlington, VA: American Psychiatric Publishing.

Call, C., Walsh, B. T., & Attia, E. (2013). From DSM-IV to DSM-5: Changes to eating disorder diagnoses. *Current Opinion in Psychiatry, 26*(6), 532–536.

Call, H. L. (1963). The hypocrisy of sexual morality. *Mattachine Review, 9*(8), 4–16. Retrieved from http://outhistory.org/items/show/4290

Calliess, I. T., Sieberer, M., Machleidt, W., & Ziegenbein, M. (2008). Personality disorders in a cross-cultural perspective: Impact of culture and migration on diagnosis and etiological aspects. *Current Psychiatry Reviews, 4*(1), 39–47. doi:10.2174/157340008783743776

Calogero, R. M., Davis, W. N., & Thompson, J. K. (2005). The role of self-objectification in the experience of women with eating disorders. *Sex Roles, 52*(1–2), 43–50. doi:10.1007/s11199-005-1192-9

Calton, T., Ferriter, M., Huband, N., & Spandler, H. (2008). A systematic review of the Soteria paradigm for the treatment of people diagnosed with schizophrenia. *Schizophrenia Bulletin, 34*(1), 181–192. doi:10.1093/schbul/sbm047

Campanini, R. F. B., Schoedl, A. F., Pupo, M. C., Costa, A. C. H., Krupnick, J. L., & Mello, M. F. (2010). Efficacy of interpersonal therapy-group format adapted to post-traumatic stress disorder: An open-label add-on trial. *Depression and Anxiety, 27*(1), 72–77. doi:10.1002/da.20610

Campbell, D. T., & Stanley, J. C. (1963). *Experimental and quasi-experimental designs for research.* Boston, MA: Houghton Mifflin Company.

Campbell, N. D. (2010). Toward a critical neuroscience of 'addiction'. *BioSocieties, 5*(1), 89–104.

Campbell, P. (2013). Service users and survivors. In J. Cromby, D. Harper, & P. Reavey (Eds.), *Psychology, mental health and distress* (pp. 139-157). New York, NY: Palgrave Macmillan.

Can, G., & Tanrıverdi, D. (2015). Social functioning and internalized stigma in individuals diagnosed with substance use disorder. *Archives of Psychiatric Nursing.* doi:10.1016/j.apnu.2015.07.008

Canadian Psychological Association. (n.d.). CPA policy statement on conversion/reparative therapy for sexual orientation. Retrieved from http://www.cpa.ca/docs/File/Position/SOGII%20Policy%20Statement%20-%20LGB%20Conversion%20Therapy%20FINALAPPROVED2015.pdf

Caparrotta, L., & Ghaffari, K. (2006). A historical overview of the psychodynamic contributions to the understanding of eating disorders. *Psychoanalytic Psychotherapy, 20*(3), 175–196. doi:10.1080/02668730600868807

Capes, A. (2010). Borderline Personality Disorder—a feminist critique. Retrieved from https://www.thefword.org.uk/2010/06/borderline_pers/

Caplan, P. J. (1995). *They say you're crazy: How the world's most powerful psychiatrists decide who's normal.* Reading, MA: Addison-Wesley.

Cappadocia, M. C., Desrocher, M., Pepler, D., & Schroeder, J. H. (2009). Contextualizing the neurobiology of conduct disorder in an emotion dysregulation framework. *Clinical Psychology Review, 29*(6), 506–518. doi:10.1016/j.cpr.2009.06.001

Carbonell, X., Oherst, U., & Beranuy, M. (2013). The cell phone in the twenty-first century: A risk for addiction or a necessary tool? In P. M. Miller, S. A. Ball, M. E. Bates, A. W. Blume, K. M. Kampman, D. J. Kavanagh, M. E. Larimer, N. M. Petry, & P. De Witte (Eds.), *Comprehensive addictive behaviors and disorders: Vol. 1. Principles of addiction* (pp. 901–909). San Diego, CA: Elsevier Academic Press.

Carey, B. (2015a, October 11). The chains of mental illness in West Africa. *The New York Times.* Retrieved from http://www.nytimes.com/2015/10/12/health/the-chains-of-mental-illness-in-west-africa.html

Carey, B. (2015b, October 20). New approach advised to treat schizophrenia. *The New York Times.* Retrieved from http://www.nytimes.com/2015/10/20/health/talk-therapy-found-to-ease-schizophrenia.html?_r=0

Carey, M. P. (1998). Cognitive-behavioral treatment of sexual dysfunctions. In V. E. Caballo (Ed.), *International handbook of cognitive and behavioural treatments for psychological disorders* (pp. 251–280). Oxford, UK: Pergamon/Elsevier Science.

Carey, T. A., & Stiles, W. B. (2015). Some problems with randomized controlled trials and some viable alternatives. *Clinical Psychology & Psychotherapy.* doi:10.1002/cpp.1942

Carlson, G. A., & Glovinsky, I. (2009). The concept of bipolar disorder in children: A history of the bipolar controversy. *Child and Adolescent Psychiatric Clinics of North America, 18*(2), 257–271. doi:10.1016/j.chc.2008.11.003

Carpenter, W. T. (2013). RDoC and DSM-5: What's the fuss? *Schizophrenia Bulletin, 39*(5), 945–946. doi:10.1093/schbul/sbt101

Carpenter, W. T., & Tandon, R. (2013). Psychotic disorders in DSM-5: Summary of changes. *Asian Journal of Psychiatry, 6*(3), 266–268. doi:10.1016/j.ajp.2013.04.001

Carpenter, W. T., & van Os, J. (2011). Should attenuated psychosis syndrome be a DSM-5 diagnosis? *The American Journal of Psychiatry, 168*(5), 460–463. doi:10.1176/appi.ajp.2011.10121816

Carpenter, W. T., Regier, D., & Tandon, R. (2014). Misunderstandings about Attenuated Psychosis Syndrome in the DSM-5. *Schizophrenia Research, 152*(1), 303–303.

Carpenter, W. T., Jr., & Buchanan, R. W. (2002). Commentary on the Soteria project: Misguided therapeutics. *Schizophrenia Bulletin, 28*(4), 577–581.

Carpenter, W. T., Jr., & Davis, J. M. (2012). Another view of the history of antipsychotic drug discovery and development. *Molecular Psychiatry, 17*(12), 1168–1173. doi:10.1038/mp.2012.121

Carpenter, W. T., Jr., Gold, J. M., Lahti, A. C., Queern, C. A., Conley, R. R., Bartko, J. J., ... Appelbaum, P. S. (2000). Decisional capacity for informed consent in schizophrenia research. *Archives of General Psychiatry, 57*(6), 533–538. doi:10.1001/archpsyc.57.6.533

Carr, A. (2014). The evidence base for couple therapy, family therapy and systemic interventions for adult-focused problems. *Journal of Family Therapy, 36*(2), 158–194. doi:10.1111/1467-6427.12033

Carr, A. (2016). Family therapy for adolescents: A research-informed perspective. *Australian and New Zealand Journal of Family Therapy, 37*(4), 467–479. doi:10.1002/anzf.1184

Carrascosa-Romero, M. C., & De Cabo-De La Vega, C. (2015). The comorbidity of ADHD and autism spectrum disorders (ASDs) in community preschoolers. In J. M. Norvilitis (Ed.), *ADHD—New directions in diagnosis and treatment* (pp. 109–164). Rijeka, Croatia: InTech.

Carrion-Castillo, A., Franke, B., & Fisher, S. E. (2013). Molecular genetics of dyslexia: An overview. *Dyslexia: An International Journal of Research and Practice, 19*(4), 214–240. doi:10.1002/dys.1464

Carroll, B. J. (2013). Biomarkers in DSM-5: Lost in translation. *Australian and New Zealand Journal of Psychiatry, 47*(7), 676–678. doi:10.1177/0004867413491162

Carta, M. G., Balestrieri, M., Murru, A., & Hardoy, M. C. (2009). Adjustment disorder: Epidemiology, diagnosis and treatment. *Clinical Practice and Epidemiology in Mental Health, 5.* doi:10.1186/1745-0179-5-15

Carter, R. T. (2007). Racism and psychological and emotional injury: Recognizing and assessing race-based traumatic stress. *The Counseling Psychologist, 35*(1), 13–105. doi:10.1177/0011000006292033

Cartwright, S. A. (1851). Diseases and peculiarities of the Negro race. *DeBow's Review, 11.* Retrieved from Africans in America (PBS) website: http://www.pbs.org/wgbh/aia/part4/4h3106t.html

Carvalho, J., & Nobre, P. (2010). Sexual desire in women: An integrative approach regarding psychological, medical, and relationship dimensions. *Journal of Sexual Medicine, 7*(5), 1807–1815. doi:10.1111/j.1743-6109.2010.01716.x

Carvalho, J., Veríssimo, A., & Nobre, P. J. (2013). Cognitive and emotional determinants characterizing women with persistent genital arousal disorder. *Journal of Sexual Medicine, 10*(6), 1549–1558. doi:10.1111/jsm.12122

Casa Futura Technologies. (2013, June 19). The controversial genetics of stuttering. Retrieved from http://www.casafuturatech.com/stuttering-genetics/

Casey, P. (2001). Multiple personality disorder. *Primary Care Psychiatry, 7*(1), 7–11. doi:10.1185/135525701750167447

Casey, P., & Bailey, S. (2011). Adjustment disorders: the state of the art. *World Psychiatry, 10*(1), 11–18.

Casey, T. (2014, November 19). Despite FDA warning, antipsychotic medications are still used in older patients with dementia.

Cashdan, S. (1988). *Object relations therapy: Using the relationship.* New York, NY: Norton.

Cashin, A. (2008). Narrative therapy: A psychotherapeutic approach in the treatment of adolescents with Asperger's disorder. *Journal of Child and Adolescent Psychiatric Nursing, 21*(1), 48–56. doi:10.1111/j.1744-6171.2008.00128.x

Cashin, A., Browne, G., Bradbury, J., & Mulder, A. (2013). The effectiveness of narrative therapy with young people with autism. *Journal of Child and Adolescent Psychiatric Nursing, 26*(1), 32–41. doi:10.1111/jcap.12020

Caspi, A., Sugden, K., Moffitt, T. E., Taylor, A., Craig, I. W., Harrington, H., … Poulton, R. (2003). Influence of life stress on depression: Moderation by a polymorphism in the 5-HTT gene. *Science, 301*(5631), 386–389. doi:10.1126/science.1083968

Castellanos, F. X., Sonuga-Barke, E. J. S., Milham, M. P., & Tannock, R. (2006). Characterizing cognition in ADHD: Beyond executive dysfunction. *Trends in Cognitive Sciences, 10*(3), 117–123. doi:10.1016/j.tics.2006.01.011

Castells, X., Ramos-Quiroga, J. A., Bosch, R., Nogueira, M., & Casas, M. (2011). Amphetamines for attention deficit hyperactivity disorder (ADHD) in adults. *Cochrane Database of Systematic Reviews, 2011*(6), CD007813. doi:10.1002/14651858.CD007813.pub2

Cattell, H. E. P. (2004). The Sixteen Personality Factor (16PF) Questionnaire. In M. J. Hilsenroth & D. L. Segal (Eds.), *Comprehensive handbook of psychological assessment: Vol. 2. Personality assessment* (pp. 39–49). Hoboken, NJ: John Wiley.

Catthoor, K., Schrijvers, D., Hutsebaut, J., Feenstra, D., & Sabbe, B. (2015). Psychiatric stigma in treatment-seeking adults with personality problems: Evidence from a sample of 214 patients. *Frontiers in Psychiatry, 6.*

Causadias, J. M. (2013). A roadmap for the integration of culture into developmental psychopathology. *Development and Psychopathology, 25*(4, Pt 2), 1375–1398. doi:10.1017/S0954579413000679

CBC News. (2011, July 6). What does 'not criminally responsible' really mean? *CBC News.* Retrieved from http://www.cbc.ca/news/canada/what-does-not-criminally-responsible-really-mean-1.1012505

Cechnicki, A., Bielańska, A., Hanuszkiewicz, I., & Daren, A. (2013). The predictive validity of expressed emotions (EE) in schizophrenia. A 20-year prospective study. *Journal of Psychiatric Research, 47*(2), 208–214. doi:10.1016/j.jpsychires.2012.10.004

Cendron, M. (2002). Removing the stigma: Helping reduce the psychosocial impact of bedwetting. *Urologic Nursing, 22*(4), 286–287.

Center for Public Health Law Research. (2016, March 9). Involuntary outpatient commitment in the US. Retrieved from http://blogs.harvard.edu/billofhealth/2016/03/09/involuntary-outpatient-commitment-in-the-us/

Centers for Disease Control and Prevention. (2014). What would happen if we stopped vaccinations? Retrieved from https://www.cdc.gov/vaccines/vac-gen/whatifstop.htm

Centers for Disease Control and Prevention. (2017, February 2). International Classification of Diseases, Tenth Revision, Clinical Modification (ICD-10-CM). Retrieved from https://www.cdc.gov/nchs/icd/icd10cm.htm

Centre for Addiction and Mental Health. (n.d.). Understanding your rights. Retrieved from http://www.camh.ca/en/hospital/visiting_camh/rights_and_policies/Pages/Understanding-your-rights.aspx

Centre for Studies on Human Stress. (n.d.). What is stress? History of stress. Retrieved from http://humanstress.ca/stress/what-is-stress/history-of-stress/

Cerdá, M., Wall, M., Keyes, K. M., Galea, S., & Hasin, D. (2012). Medical marijuana laws in 50 states: Investigating the relationship between state legalization of medical marijuana and marijuana use, abuse and dependence. *Drug and Alcohol Dependence, 120*(1–3), 22–27. doi:http://dx.doi.org/10.1016/j.drugalcdep.2011.06.011

Cerezuela, G. P., Tejero, P., Chóliz, M., Chisvert, M., & Monteagudo, M. J. (2004). Wertheim's hypothesis on 'highway hypnosis': Empirical evidence from a study on motorway and conventional road driving. *Accident Analysis and Prevention, 36*(6), 1045–1054. doi:10.1016/j.aap.2004.02.002

Chadwick, G. L. (1997). Historical perspective: Nuremberg, Tuskegee, and the radiation experiments. *Journal of the International Association of Physicians in AIDS Care, 3*(1), 27–28.

Chahine, G., Diekhof, E. K., Tinnermann, A., & Gruber, O. (2015). On the role of the anterior prefrontal cortex in cognitive 'branching': An fMRI study. *Neuropsychologia, 77,* 421–429.

Chalavi, S., Vissia, E. M., Giesen, M. E., Nijenhuis, E. R. S., Draijer, N., Cole, J. H., … Reinders, A. A. T. S. (2015). Abnormal hippocampal morphology in dissociative identity disorder and post-traumatic stress disorder correlates with childhood trauma and dissociative symptoms. *Human Brain Mapping, 36*(5), 1692–1704. doi:10.1002/hbm.22730

Chalder, M., Wiles, N. J., Campbell, J., Hollinghurst, S. P., Haase, A. M., Taylor, A. H., … Lewis, G. (2012). Facilitated physical activity as a treatment for depressed adults: Randomised controlled trial. *BMJ : British Medical Journal, 344.* doi:10.1136/bmj.e2758

Chamberlain, S. R., Odlaug, B. L., Boulougouris, V., Fineberg, N. A., & Grant, J. E. (2009). Trichotillomania: Neurobiology and treatment. *Neuroscience and Biobehavioral Reviews, 33*(6), 831–842. doi:10.1016/j.neubiorev.2009.02.002

Chambless, D. L. (2012). Adjunctive couple and family intervention for patients with anxiety disorders. *Journal of Clinical Psychology, 68*(5), 536–547. doi:10.1002/jclp.21851

Chambless, D. L., Bryan, A. D., Aiken, L. S., Steketee, G., & Hooley, J. M. (2001). Predicting expressed emotion: A study with families of obsessive–compulsive and agoraphobic outpatients. *Journal of Family Psychology, 15*(2), 225–240. doi:10.1037/0893-3200.15.2.225

Chambless, D. L., Floyd, F. J., Rodebaugh, T. L., & Steketee, G. S. (2007). Expressed emotion and familial interaction: A study with agoraphobic and obsessive-compulsive patients and their relatives. *Journal of Abnormal Psychology, 116*(4), 754–761. doi:10.1037/0021-843X.116.4.754

Chan, E., Fogler, J. M., & Hammerness, P. G. (2016). Treatment of attention-deficit/hyperactivity disorder in adolescents: A systematic review. *JAMA: Journal of the American Medical Association, 315*(18), 1997–2008. doi:10.1001/jama.2016.5453

Chan, S., Torous, J. B., Hinton, L., & Yellowlees, P. M. (2016). Psychiatric apps: Patient self-assessment, communication, and potential treatment interventions. In D. Mucic & D. M. Hilty (Eds.), *e-Mental health* (pp. 217–229). Cham, Switzerland: Springer International Publishing.

Chan, Y.-Y., Yang, S.-N., Lin, J.-C., Chang, J.-L., Lin, J.-G., & Lo, W.-Y. (2015). Inflammatory response in heroin addicts undergoing methadone maintenance treatment. *Psychiatry Research, 226*(1), 230–234. doi:10.1016/j.psychres.2014.12.053

Chan, Z. C. Y., Fung, Y., & Chien, W. (2013). Bracketing in phenomenology: Only undertaken in the data collection and analysis process? *The Qualitative Report, 18,* 1–9. Retrieved from http://www.nova.edu/ssss/QR/QR18/chan59.pdf

Chang, J., & Nylund, D. (2013). Narrative and solution-focused therapies: A twenty-year retrospective. *Journal of Systemic Therapies, 32*(2), 72–88.

Changes in sleep with age. (2007, December 18). Retrieved from http://healthysleep.med.harvard.edu/healthy/science/variations/changes-in-sleep-with-age

Changizi Ashtiyani, S., Shamsi, M., Cyrus, A., & Tabatabayei, S. M. (2013). Rhazes, a genius physician in the diagnosis and treatment of nocturnal enuresis in medical history. *Iranian Red Crescent Medical Journal, 15*(8), 633–638. doi:10.5812/ircmj.5017

Chard, K. M., Ricksecker, E. G., Healy, E. T., Karlin, B. E., & Resick, P. A. (2012). Dissemination and experience with cognitive processing therapy. *Journal of Rehabilitation Research and Development, 49*(5), 667–678.

Charland, L. C. (2006). Moral nature of the DSM-IV Cluster B personality disorders. *Journal of Personality Disorders, 20*(2), 116-125. doi:10.1521/pedi.2006.20.2.116

Charland, L. C. (2007). Benevolent theory: Moral treatment at the York Retreat. *History of Psychiatry, 18*(1), 61–80. doi:10.1177/0957154X07070320

Charland, L. C. (2010). Medical or moral kinds? Moving beyond a false dichotomy. *Philosophy, Psychiatry, & Psychology, 17*(2), 119–125. doi:10.1353/ppp.0.0292

Charmaz, K. (2014). *Constructing grounded theory* (2nd ed.). Thousand Oaks, CA: SAGE Publications.

Chauvet-Gélinier, J. C., Trojak, B., Lemogne, C., Aho-Glélé, L. S., Brindisi, M. C., Bouillet, B., ... Vergès, B. (2016). Potential influence of Type A personality on plasma C-reactive protein levels in people with diabetes. *Diabetes & Metabolism, 42*(2), 88–95. doi:10.1016/j.diabet.2015.08.001

Chaves, C., Zuardi, A. W., & Hallak, J. E. C. (2015). The role of inflammation in schizophrenia: An overview. *Trends in Psychiatry and Psychotherapy, 37*(2), 104–105. doi:10.1590/2237-6089-2015-0007

Chemerinski, E., Triebwasser, J., Roussos, P., & Siever, L. J. (2013). Schizotypal personality disorder. *Journal of Personality Disorders, 27*(5), 652–679. doi:10.1521/pedi_2012_26_053

Chen, J.-H., Lin, K.-P., & Chen, Y.-C. (2009). Risk factors for dementia. *Journal of the Formosan Medical Association, 108*(10), 754–764. doi:http://dx.doi.org/10.1016/S0929-6646(09)60402-2

Cheng, F., & Jones, P. B. (2013). Drug treatments for schizophrenia: Pragmatism in trial design shows lack of progress in drug design. *Epidemiology and Psychiatric Sciences, 22*(3), 223–233. doi:10.1017/S204579601200073X

Cherian, A. V., Pandian, D., Math, S. B., Kandavel, T., & Janardhan Reddy, Y. C. (2014). Family accommodation of obsessional symptoms and naturalistic outcome of obsessive–compulsive disorder. *Psychiatry Research, 215*(2), 372–378. doi:10.1016/j.psychres.2013.11.017

Cheung, Y. T. D., Wong, P. W. C., Lee, A. M., Lam, T. H., Fan, Y. S. S., & Yip, P. S. F. (2013). Non-suicidal self-injury and suicidal behavior: Prevalence, co-occurrence, and correlates of suicide among adolescents in Hong Kong. *Social Psychiatry and Psychiatric Epidemiology, 48*(7), 1133–1144. doi:10.1007/s00127-012-0640-4

Chhangur, R. R., Overbeek, G., Verhagen, M., Weeland, J., Matthys, W., & Engels, R. C. M. E. (2015). DRD4 and DRD2 genes, parenting, and adolescent delinquency: Longitudinal evidence for a gene by environment interaction. *Journal of Abnormal Psychology, 124*(4), 791–802. doi:10.1037/abn0000091

Chiari, G., & Nuzzo, M. L. (2010). *Constructivist psychotherapy: A narrative hermeneutic approach.* London, UK: Routledge.

Chieh, A. (2015, March 17). The 4 different stages of sleep. Retrieved from https://blog.health.nokia.com/blog/2015/03/17/the-4-different-stages-of-sleep/

Chiesa, A., Castagner, V., Andrisano, C., Serretti, A., Mandelli, L., Porcelli, S., & Giommi, F. (2015). Mindfulness-based cognitive therapy vs. psycho-education for patients with major depression who did not achieve remission following antidepressant treatment. *Psychiatry Research, 226*(2-3), 474–483. doi:10.1016/j.psychres.2015.02.003

Chiesa, A., Mandelli, L., & Serretti, A. (2012). Mindfulness-based cognitive therapy versus psycho-education for patients with major depression who did not achieve remission following antidepressant treatment: A preliminary analysis. *The Journal of Alternative and Complementary Medicine, 18*(8), 756–760. doi:10.1089/acm.2011.0407

Childress, J. E., McDowell, E. J., Dalai, V. V. K., Bogale, S. R., Ramamurthy, C., Jawaid, A., ... Schulz, P. E. (2013). Hippocampal volumes in patients with chronic combat-related posttraumatic stress disorder: A systematic review. *The Journal of Neuropsychiatry and Clinical Neurosciences, 25*(1), 12–25. doi:10.1176/appi.neuropsych.12010003

Chiodo, G. T., Tolle, S. W., & Bevan, L. (2000). Placebo-controlled trials: good science or medical neglect? *Western Journal of Medicine, 172*(4), 271–273.

Chisholm, K., Lin, A., Abu-Akel, A., & Wood, S. J. (2015). The association between autism and schizophrenia spectrum disorders: A review of eight alternate models of co-occurrence. *Neuroscience and Biobehavioral Reviews, 55*, 173–183. doi:10.1016/j.neubiorev.2015.04.012

Chisuwa, N., & O'Dea, J. A. (2010). Body image and eating disorders amongst Japanese adolescents. A review of the literature. *Appetite, 54*(1), 5-15. doi:10.1016/j.appet.2009.11.008

Chmielewski, M., Ruggero, C. J., Kotov, R., Liu, K., & Krueger, R. F. (2016). Comparing the dependability and associations with functioning of the DSM-5 Section III trait model of personality pathology and the DSM-5 Section II personality disorder model. *Personality Disorders: Theory, Research, and Treatment.* doi:10.1037/per0000213

Choi, J., & Twamley, E. W. (2013). Cognitive rehabilitation therapies for Alzheimer's disease: A review of methods to improve treatment engagement and self-efficacy. *Neuropsychology Review, 23*(1), 48–62. doi:10.1007/s11065-013-9227-4

Chrisler, J. C., & Erchull, M. J. (2011). The treatment of evolutionary psychology in social psychology textbooks. *Sex Roles, 64*(9-10), 754–757. doi:10.1007/s11199-010-9783-5

Christopher, M. (2004). A broader view of trauma: A biopsychosocial-evolutionary view of the role of the traumatic stress response in the emergence of pathology and/or growth. *Clinical Psychology Review, 24*(1), 75–98. doi:http://dx.doi.org/10.1016/j.cpr.2003.12.003

Christozov, C., & Toteva, S. (1989). Abuse and neglect of children brought up in families with an alcoholic father in Bulgaria. *Child Abuse & Neglect, 13*(1), 153–155. doi:10.1016/0145-2134(89)90039-2

Chung, R. C.-Y., & Bemak, F. P. (2012). *Social justice counseling: The next steps beyond multiculturalism.* Los Angeles, CA: SAGE Publications.

Chung, T., Martin, C. S., Maisto, S. A., Cornelius, J. R., & Clark, D. B. (2012). Greater prevalence of proposed DSM-5 nicotine use disorder compared to DSM-IV nicotine dependence in treated adolescents and young adults. *Addiction, 107*(4), 810–818. doi:10.1111/j.1360-0443.2011.03722.x

Cibis, A., Mergl, R., Bramesfeld, A., Althaus, D., Niklewski, G., Schmidtke, A., & Hegerl, U. (2012). Preference of lethal methods is not the only cause for higher suicide rates in males. *Journal of Affective Disorders, 136*(1–2), 9–16. doi:http://dx.doi.org/10.1016/j.jad.2011.08.032

Ciccocioppo, R. (1999). The role of serotonin in craving: From basic research to human studies. *Alcohol and Alcoholism, 34*(2), 244–253. doi:10.1093/alcalc/34.2.244

Cipriani, A., Furukawa, T. A., Salanti, G., Chaimani, A., Atkinson, L. Z., Ogawa, Y., ... Geddes, J. R. (2018). Comparative efficacy and acceptability of 21 antidepressant drugs for the acute treatment of adults with major depressive disorder: A systematic review and network meta-analysis. *The Lancet. 391*, 1357–1366. doi:10.1016/S0140-6736(17)32802-7

Cipriani, G., & Borin, G. (2015). Understanding dementia in the sociocultural context: A review. *International Journal of Social Psychiatry, 61*(2), 198–204. doi:10.1177/0020764014560357

Cipriani, G., Dolciotti, C., Picchi, L., & Bonuccelli, U. (2011). Alzheimer and his disease: A brief history. *Neurological Sciences, 32*(2), 275-279. doi:10.1007/s10072-010-0454-7

Claes, L., Bijttebier, P., Van Den Eynde, F., Mitchell, J. E., Faber, R., de Zwaan, M., & Mueller, A. (2010). Emotional reactivity and self-regulation in relation to compulsive buying. *Personality and Individual Differences, 49*(5), 526–530. doi:10.1016/j.paid.2010.05.020

Clare, L. (2003). Cognitive training and cognitive rehabilitation for people with early-stage dementia. *Reviews in Clinical Gerontology, 13*(1), 75–83. doi:10.1017/S0959259803013170

Clare, L., & Woods, R. T. (2004). Cognitive training and cognitive rehabilitation for people with early-stage Alzheimer's disease: A review. *Neuropsychological Rehabilitation, 14*(4), 385-401. doi:10.1080/09602010443000074

Clark, D. C. (1998). The evaluation and management of the suicidal patient. In P. M. Kleespies (Ed.), *Emergencies in mental health practice: Evaluation and management.* (pp. 75–94). New York, NY: Guilford Press.

Clark, D. M. (1986). A cognitive approach to panic. *Behaviour Research and Therapy, 24*(4), 461–470. doi:10.1016/0005-7967(86)90011-2

Clark, D. M., & Ehlers, A. (1993). An overview of the cognitive theory and treatment of panic disorder. *Applied & Preventive Psychology, 2*(3), 131–139. doi:10.1016/S0962-1849(05)80119-2

Clark, L. (2015, August 19). Why 'female viagra' approved in the US isn't coming to the UK. *Wired*.

Clark, M. (2011). Conceptualising addiction: How useful is the construct? *International Journal of Humanities and Social Science, 1*(13), 55–64.

Clarke, D. E., Narrow, W. E., Regier, D. A., Kuramoto, S. J., Kupfer, D. J., Kuhl, E. A., ... Kraemer, H. C. (2013). DSM-5 field trials in the United States and Canada, part I: Study design, sampling strategy, implementation, and analytic approaches. *The American Journal of Psychiatry, 170*(1), 43–58. doi:10.1176/appi.ajp.2012.12070998

Clarkin, J. F., Fonagy, P., & Gabbard, G. O. (Eds.). (2010). *Psychodynamic psychotherapy for personality disorders: A clinical handbook*. Arlington, VA: American Psychiatric Publishing.

Clarkin, J. F., Yeomans, F. E., & Kernberg, O. F. (2006). *Psychotherapy for borderline personality: Focusing on object relations*. Arlington, VA: American Psychiatric Publishing.

Classen, C. C., Palesh, O. G., Cavanaugh, C. E., Koopman, C., Kaupp, J. W., Kraemer, H. C., ... Spiegel, D. (2011). A comparison of trauma-focused and present-focused group therapy for survivors of childhood sexual abuse: A randomized controlled trial. *Psychological Trauma: Theory, Research, Practice, and Policy, 3*(1), 84–93. doi:10.1037/a0020096

Clausen, J. A. (1954). Biological bias and methodological limitations in the Kinsey studies. *Social Problems, 1*(4), 126–133. doi:10.2307/799383

Clayton, A. H., Alkis, A. R., Parikh, N. B., & Votta, J. G. (2016). Sexual dysfunction due to psychotropic medications. *Psychiatric Clinics of North America*. doi:10.1016/j.psc.2016.04.006

Cleare, A. J., & Rane, L. J. (2013). Biological models of unipolar depression. In M. Power (Ed.), *The Wiley-Blackwell handbook of mood disorders* (pp. 39–67). Chichester, UK: Wiley-Blackwell.

Clem, R. L., & Huganir, R. L. (2010). Calcium-permeable AMPA receptor dynamics mediate fear memory erasure. *Science, 330*(6007), 1108–1112. doi:10.1126/science.1195298

Cloninger, C. R. (1994). Temperament and personality. *Current Opinion in Neurobiology, 4*, 266–273.

Cloninger, C. R. (2012). Genetics of personality disorders. In J. I. Nurnberger, Jr. & W. H. Berrettini (Eds.), *Principles of psychiatric genetics* (pp. 316–323). New York, NY: Cambridge University Press.

Coccaro, E. F., Lee, R., & Coussons-Read, M. (2015a). Cerebrospinal fluid and plasma C-reactive protein and aggression in personality-disordered subjects: A pilot study. *Journal of Neural Transmission, 122*(2), 321–326. doi:10.1007/s00702-014-1263-6

Coccaro, E. F., Lee, R., & Coussons-Read, M. (2015b). Cerebrospinal fluid inflammatory cytokines and aggression in personality disordered subjects. *International Journal of Neuropsychopharmacology, 18*(7), 1–7. doi:10.1093/ijnp/pyv001

Coccaro, E. F., Sripada, C. S., Yanowitch, R. N., & Phan, K. L. (2011). Corticolimbic function in impulsive aggressive behavior. *Biological Psychiatry, 69*(12), 1153–1159. doi:http://dx.doi.org/10.1016/j.biopsych.2011.02.032

Cochran, J. L., Cochran, N. H., Cholette, A., & Nordling, W. J. (2011). Limits and relationship in child-centered play therapy: Two case studies. *International Journal of Play Therapy, 20*(4), 236–251. doi:10.1037/a0025425

Cochran, J. L., Cochran, N. H., Nordling, W. J., McAdam, A., & Miller, D. T. (2010). Two case studies of child-centered play therapy for children referred with highly disruptive behavior. *International Journal of Play Therapy, 19*(3), 130–143. doi:10.1037/a0019119

Cochran, W. G., Mosteller, F., & Tukey, J. W. (1953). Statistical problems of the Kinsey report. *Journal of the American Statistical Association, 48*, 673–716. doi:10.2307/2281066

Coe, C. L., & Laudenslager, M. L. (2007). Psychosocial influences on immunity, including effects on immune maturation and senescence. *Brain, Behavior, and Immunity, 21*(8), 1000–1008. doi:10.1016/j.bbi.2007.06.015

Coghlan, S., Horder, J., Inkster, B., Mendez, M. A., Murphy, D. G., & Nutt, D. J. (2012). GABA system dysfunction in autism and related disorders: From synapse to symptoms. *Neuroscience & Biobehavioral Reviews, 36*(9), 2044–2055. doi:http://dx.doi.org/10.1016/j.neubiorev.2012.07.005

Cogo-Moreira, H., Andriolo, R. B., Yazigi, L., Ploubidis, G. B., Brandão de Ávila, C. R., & Mari, J. J. (2012). Music education for improving reading skills in children and adolescents with dyslexia. *Cochrane Database of Systematic Reviews*(8). doi:10.1002/14651858.CD009133.pub2

Cohen, L. (2014). How Sigmund Freud wanted to die. *The Atlantic*.

Cohen, M., Granger, S., & Fuller-Thomson, E. (2015). The association between bereavement and biomarkers of inflammation. *Behavioral Medicine, 41*(2), 49–59. doi:10.1080/08964289.2013.866539

Cohen, P., Chen, H., Gordon, K., Johnson, J., Brook, J., & Kasen, S. (2008). Socioeconomic background and the developmental course of schizotypal and borderline personality disorder symptoms. *Development and Psychopathology, 20*(2), 633–650. doi:10.1017/S095457940800031X

Cohen, P., Rogol, A. D., Deal, C. L., Saenger, P., Reiter, E. O., Ross, J. L., ... Wit, J. M. (2008). Consensus statement on the diagnosis and treatment of children with idiopathic short stature: A summary of the Growth Hormone Research Society, the Lawson Wilkins Pediatric Endocrine Society, and the European Society for Paediatric Endocrinology Workshop. *Journal of Clinical Endocrinology & Metabolism, 93*(11), 4210–4217. doi:10.1210/jc.2008-0509

Cohen, S., Frank, E., Doyle, W. J., Skoner, D. P., Rabin, B. S., & Gwaltney, J. M., Jr. (1998). Types of stressors that increase susceptibility to the common cold in healthy adults. *Health Psychology, 17*(3), 214–223. doi:10.1037/0278-6133.17.3.214

Cohen, S., Kamarck, T., & Mermelstein, R. (1983). A global measure of perceived stress. *Journal of Health and Social Behavior, 24*(4), 385–396. doi:10.2307/2136404

Colameco, S., Becker, L. A., & Simpson, M. (1983). Sex bias in the assessment of patient complaints. *The Journal of Family Practice, 16*(6), 1117–1121.

Coleman, D. (2004). Theoretical Evaluation Self-Test (TEST): A preliminary validation study. *Social Work Research, 28*(2), 117–127. doi:10.1093/swr/28.2.117

Coleman, E., Bockting, W., Botzer, M., Cohen-Kettenis, P., DeCuypere, G., Feldman, J., ... Zucker, K. (2012). Standards of care for the health of transsexual, transgender, and gender-nonconforming people, version 7. *International Journal of Transgenderism, 13*(4), 165–232. doi:10.1080/15532739.2011.700873

Coleman, L. (1984). *The reign of error: Psychiatry, authority, and law*. Boston, MA: Beacon Press.

Collin, G., Derks, E. M., van Haren, N. E. M., Schnack, H. G., Hulshoff Pol, H. E., Kahn, R. S., & Cahn, W. (2012). Symptom dimensions are associated with progressive brain volume changes in schizophrenia. *Schizophrenia Research, 138*(2–3), 171–176. doi:10.1016/j.schres.2012.03.036

Columbia University Medical Center. (2017). Select memories can be erased, leaving others intact [Press release]. Retrieved from http://newsroom.cumc.columbia.edu/blog/2017/06/22/select-memories-can-erased-leaving-others-intact/

Comings, D. E., & Blum, K. (2000). Reward deficiency syndrome: genetic aspects of behavioral disorders. *Progress in Brain Research, 126*, 325–341.

Compton, W. M., Conway, K. P., Stinson, F. S., Colliver, J. D., & Grant, B. F. (2005). Prevalence, correlates, and comorbidity of DSM-IV antisocial personality syndromes and alcohol and specific drug use disorders in the United States: Results from the National Epidemiologic Survey on Alcohol and Related Conditions. *Journal of Clinical Psychiatry, 66*(6), 677–685. doi:10.4088/JCP.v66n0602

Condén, E., Ekselius, L., & Åslund, C. (2013). Type D personality is associated with sleep problems in adolescents. Results from a population-based cohort study of Swedish adolescents. *Journal of Psychosomatic Research, 74*(4), 290–295. doi:10.1016/j.jpsychores.2012.11.011

Condit, V. K. (1990). Anorexia nervosa: Levels of causation. *Human Nature, 1*(4), 391–413. doi:10.1007/BF02734052

Connan, F., Lightman, S. L., Landau, S., Wheeler, M., Treasure, J., & Campbell, I. C. (2007). An investigation of hypothalamic-pituitary-adrenal axis hyperactivity in anorexia nervosa: The role of CRH and AVP. *Journal of Psychiatric Research, 41*(1–2), 131–143. doi:10.1016/j.jpsychires.2005.12.005

Consent to treatment. (n.d.). Retrieved from http://www.mind.org.uk/information-support/legal-rights/consent-to-treatment/#.WPudrVKZOt8

Contador, I., del Ser, T., Llamas, S., Villarejo, A., Benito-León, J., & Bermejo-Pareja, F. (2017). Impact of literacy and years of education on the diagnosis of dementia: A population-based study. *Journal of Clinical and Experimental Neuropsychology, 39*(2), 112–119. doi:10.1080/13803395.2016.1204992

Conway, F. (2012). Psychodynamic psychotherapy of ADHD: A review of the literature. *Psychotherapy, 49*(3), 404–417. doi:10.1037/a0027344

Conway, F. (2014). The use of empathy and transference as interventions in psychotherapy with attention deficit hyperactive disorder latency-aged boys. *Psychotherapy, 51*(1), 104–109. doi:10.1037/a0032596

Conway, F. (2015). Current research and future directions in psychodynamic treatment of ADHD: Is empathy the missing link? *Journal of Infant, Child & Adolescent Psychotherapy, 14*(3), 280–287. doi:10.1080/15289168.2015.1069235

Cook, B. G., & Rumrill, P. D., Jr. (2005). Using and interpreting analogue designs. *Work: Journal of Prevention, Assessment & Rehabilitation, 24*(1), 93–97.

Cook, R. (2014). *Diagnosing the Diagnostic and Statistical Manual of Mental Disorders.* London, UK: Karnac.

Coolidge, F. L., & Segal, D. L. (1998). Evolution of personality disorder diagnosis in the Diagnostic and Statistical Manual of Mental Disorders. *Clinical Psychology Review, 18*(5), 585–599. doi:10.1016/S0272-7358(98)00002-6

Coolidge, F. L., Thede, L. L., & Young, S. E. (2002). The heritability of gender identity disorder in a child and adolescent twin sample. *Behavior Genetics, 32*(4), 251–257.

Cools, R., Nakamura, K., & Daw, N. D. (2011). Serotonin and dopamine: Unifying affective, activational, and decision functions. *Neuropsychopharmacology, 36*(1), 98–113. doi:10.1038/npp.2010.121

Cooney, G. M., Dwan, K., Greig, C. A., Lawlor, D. A., Rimer, J., Waugh, F. R., ... Mead, G. E. (2013). Exercise for depression. *Cochrane Database of Systematic Reviews, 2013*(9), 1–123. doi:10.1002/14651858.CD004366.pub6

Cooper, C., Morgan, C., Byrne, M., Dazzan, P., Morgan, K., Hutchinson, G., ... Fearon, P. (2008). Perceptions of disadvantage, ethnicity and psychosis. *The British Journal of Psychiatry, 192*(3), 185–190. doi:10.1192/bjp.bp.107.042291

Cooper, M. (2017). *Existential therapies* (2nd ed.). London, UK: Sage.

Corcos, M., Guilbaud, O., Paterniti, S., Moussa, M., Chambry, J., Chaouat, G., ... Jeammet, P. (2003). Involvement of cytokines in eating disorders: A critical review of the human literature. *Psychoneuroendocrinology, 28*(3), 229–249. doi:http://dx.doi.org/10.1016/S0306-4530(02)00021-5

Corley, C. (2015). Coping while black: A season of traumatic news takes a psychological toll. Retrieved from http://www.npr.org/sections/codeswitch/2015/07/02/419462959/coping-while-black-a-season-of-traumatic-news-takes-a-psychological-toll

Corona, G., Isidori, A. M., Aversa, A., Burnett, A. L., & Maggi, M. (2016). Endocrinologic control of men's sexual desire and arousal/erection. *Journal of Sexual Medicine, 13*(3), 317–337. doi:10.1016/j.jsxm.2016.01.007

Corradi, R. B. (2011). Schizophrenia as a human process. *Journal of the American Academy of Psychoanalysis & Dynamic Psychiatry, 39*(4), 717–736. doi:10.1521/jaap.2011.39.4.717

Corrigan, P. W. (Ed.) (2005). *On the stigma of mental illness: Practical strategies for research and social change.* Washington, DC: American Psychological Association.

Corrigan, P. W., & Kleinlein, P. (2005). The impact of mental illness stigma. In P. W. Corrigan (Ed.), *On the stigma of mental illness: Practical strategies for research and social change* (pp. 11–44). Washington, DC: American Psychological Association.

Cortese, S., Kelly, C., Chabernaud, C., Proal, E., Di Martino, A., Milham, M. P., & Castellanos, F. X. (2012). Toward systems neuroscience of ADHD: A meta-analysis of 55 fMRI studies. *The American Journal of Psychiatry, 169*(10), 1038–1055. doi:10.1176/appi.ajp.2012.11101521

Coryell, W. (2009). Maintenance treatment in bipolar disorder: A reassessment of lithium as the first choice. *Bipolar Disorders, 11*(Suppl2), 77–83. doi:10.1111/j.1399-5618.2009.00712.x

Cosgrove, L., & Bursztajn, H. J. (2009). Toward credible conflict of interest policies in clinical psychiatry. *Psychiatric Times.* Retrieved from http://www.psychiatrictimes.com/articles/toward-credible-conflict-interest-policies-clinical-psychiatry

Cosgrove, L., Bursztajn, H. J., Erlich, D. R., Wheeler, E. E., & Shaughnessy, A. F. (2013). Conflicts of interest and the quality of recommendations in clinical guidelines. *Journal of Evaluation in Clinical Practice, 19*(4), 674–681. doi:10.1111/jep.12016

Cosgrove, L., Krimsky, S., Vijayaraghavan, M., & Schneider, L. (2006). Financial ties between DSM-IV panel members and the pharmaceutical industry. *Psychotherapy and Psychosomatics, 75*(3), 154–160. doi:10.1159/000091772

Cosgrove, L., Krimsky, S., Wheeler, E. E., Kaitz, J., Greenspan, S. B., & DiPentima, N. L. (2014). Tripartite conflicts of interest and high stakes patent extensions in the DSM-5. *Psychotherapy and Psychosomatics, 83*(2), 106–113. doi:10.1159/000357499

Costa, L. d. S., Alencar, Á. P., Neto, P. J. N., Santos, M. d. S. V. d., da Silva, C. G. L., Pinheiro, S. d. F. L., ... Neto, M. L. R. (2015). Risk factors for suicide in bipolar disorder: A systematic review. *Journal of Affective Disorders, 170*, 237–254. doi:http://dx.doi.org/10.1016/j.jad.2014.09.003

Costello, S. J. (2011). An existential analysis of anxiety: Frankl, Kierkegaard, Voegelin. *International Forum for Logotherapy, 34*(2), 65–71.

Cotter, J., Kaess, M., & Yung, A. R. (2015). Childhood trauma and functional disability in psychosis, bipolar disorder and borderline personality disorder: A review of the literature. *Irish Journal of Psychological Medicine, 32*(Spec Iss1), 21–30. doi:10.1017/ipm.2014.74

Cottraux, J., Note, I. D., Boutitie, F., Milliery, M., Genouihlac, V., Yao, S. N., ... Gueyffier, F. (2009). Cognitive therapy versus Rogerian supportive therapy in borderline personality disorder: Two-year follow-up of a controlled pilot study. *Psychotherapy and Psychosomatics, 78*(5), 307–316. doi:10.1159/000229769

Coulon, S. M. (2015). *A bioecological approach to understanding the interaction of environmental stress and genetic susceptibility in influencing cortisol and blood pressure in African American adults.* (76), ProQuest Information & Learning, US. Retrieved from https://libdatabase.newpaltz.edu/login?url=http://search.ebscohost.com/login.aspx?direct=true&db=psyh&AN=2015-99140-180&site=ehost-live Available from EBSCOhost psyh database

Craig, A., & Tran, Y. (2014). Trait and social anxiety in adults with chronic stuttering: Conclusions following meta-analysis. *Journal of Fluency Disorders, 40*, 35–43. doi:10.1016/j.jfludis.2014.01.001

Craig, T. K. J., Cox, A. D., & Klein, K. (2002). Intergenerational transmission of somatization behaviour: A study of chronic somatizers and their children. *Psychological Medicine, 32*(5), 805–816. doi:10.1017/S0033291702005846

Craighead, L. W., & Smith, L. T. (2008). Eating disorders: Bulimia nervosa and binge eating. In W. E. Craighead, D. J. Miklowitz, & L. W. Craighead (Eds.), *Psychopathology: History, diagnosis, and empirical foundations* (pp. 435–466). Hoboken, NJ: John Wiley.

Cramer, P. (1999). Future directions for the Thematic Apperception Test. *Journal of Personality Assessment, 72*(1), 74–92. doi:10.1207/s15327752jpa7201_5

Craske, M. G. (2017). *Cognitive-behavioral therapy* (2nd ed.). Washington, DC: American Psychological Association.

Craske, M. G. (2012). The R-DoC initiative: Science and practice. *Depression and Anxiety, 29*(4), 253–256. doi:10.1002/da.21930

Craske, M. G., Treanor, M., Conway, C. C., Zbozinek, T., & Vervliet, B. (2014). Maximizing exposure therapy: An inhibitory learning approach. *Behaviour Research and Therapy, 58*, 10–23. doi:10.1016/j.brat.2014.04.006

Creed, F., & Gureje, O. (2012). Emerging themes in the revision of the classification of somatoform disorders. *International Review of Psychiatry, 24*(6), 556–567. doi:10.3109/09540261.2012.741063

Crego, C., & Widiger, T. A. (2016). Personality disorders. In J. E. Maddux & B. A. Winstead (Eds.), *Psychopathology: Foundations for a contemporary understanding* (4th ed., pp. 218–236). New York, NY: Routledge.

Cremers, H., Lee, R., Keedy, S., Phan, K. L., & Coccaro, E. (2016). Effects of escitalopram administration on face processing in intermittent explosive disorder: An fMRI study. *Neuropsychopharmacology, 41*(2), 590–597. doi:10.1038/npp.2015.187

Creswell, J. W. (2011). *Research design: Qualitative, quantitative, and mixed methods approaches* (4th ed.). Thousand Oaks, CA: SAGE Publications.

Crews, F. T. (2012). Immune function genes, genetics, and the neurobiology of addiction. *Alcohol Research: Current Reviews, 34*(3), 355–361.

Crews, F. T., Sarkar, D. K., Qin, L., Zou, J., Boyadjieva, N., & Vetreno, R. P. (2015). Neuroimmune function and the consequences of alcohol exposure. *Alcohol Research: Current Reviews, 37*(2), 331–351.

Crichton, A. (1798). *An inquiry into the nature and origin of mental derangement: Comprehending a concise system of the physiology and pathology of the human mind and a history of the passions and their effects* (Vol. 2). London, UK: T. Cadell, Jr., and W. Davies.

Cristancho, M. A., Helmer, A., Connolly, R., Cristancho, P., & O'Reardon, J. P. (2013). Transcranial magnetic stimulation maintenance as a substitute for maintenance electroconvulsive therapy: a case series. *The Journal of ECT, 29*(2), 106–108. doi:10.1097/YCT.0b013e31827a70ba

Criswell, E., & Serlin, I. A. (2015). Humanistic psychology, mind-body medicine, and whole-person health care. In K. J. Schneider, J. F. Pierson, & J. F. T. Bugental (Eds.), *The handbook of humanistic psychology: Theory, research, and practice* (pp. 653–666). Thousand Oaks, CA: SAGE Publications.

Crocq, M.-A. (2013). Milestones in the history of personality disorders. *Dialogues in Clinical Neuroscience, 15*(2), 147–153.

Cronin, E., Brand, B. L., & Mattanah, J. F. (2014). The impact of the therapeutic alliance on treatment outcome in patients with dissociative disorders. *European Journal of Psychotraumatology, 5.*

Crossley, N. (2004). Not being mentally ill: Social movements, system survivors and the oppositional habitus. *Anthropology & Medicine, 11*(2), 161–180. doi:10.1080/13648470410001678668

Crow, T. J. (1988). The viral theory of schizophrenia. *The British Journal of Psychiatry, 153,* 564–566.

Crow, T. J. (2000). Schizophrenia as the price that Homo sapiens pays for language: A resolution of the central paradox in the origin of the species. *Brain Research Reviews, 31*(2–3), 118–129. doi:http://dx.doi.org/10.1016/S0165-0173(99)00029-6

Crow, T. J. (2011). 'The missing genes: What happened to the heritability of psychiatric disorders?'. *Molecular Psychiatry, 16*(4), 362–364. doi:10.1038/mp.2010.92

Crumeyrolle-Arias, M., Jaglin, M., Bruneau, A., Vancassel, S., Cardona, A., Daugé, V., ... Rabot, S. (2014). Absence of the gut microbiota enhances anxiety-like behavior and neuroendocrine response to acute stress in rats. *Psychoneuroendocrinology, 42,* 207–217. doi:10.1016/j.psyneuen.2014.01.014

Crusio, W. E. (2004). The sociobiology of sociopathy: An alternative hypothesis. *Behavioral and Brain Sciences, 27*(1), 154–155. doi:10.1017/S0140525X04220040

Cuddy-Casey, M. (1997). A case study using child-centered play therapy approach to treat enuresis and encopresis. *Elementary School Guidance & Counseling, 31*(3), 220–225.

Cuijpers, P., Berking, M., Andersson, G., Quigley, L., Kleiboer, A., & Dobson, K. S. (2013). A meta-analysis of cognitive-behavioural therapy for adult depression, alone and in comparison with other treatments. *The Canadian Journal of Psychiatry / La Revue Canadienne De Psychiatrie, 58*(7), 376–385.

Cuijpers, P., Karyotaki, E., Weitz, E., Andersson, G., Hollon, S. D., & van Straten, A. (2014). The effects of psychotherapies for major depression in adults on remission, recovery and improvement: A meta-analysis. *Journal of Affective Disorders, 159,* 118–126. doi:http://dx.doi.org/10.1016/j.jad.2014.02.026

Cuijpers, P., Sijbrandij, M., Koole, S. L., Andersson, G., Beekman, A. T., & Reynolds, C. F. (2013). The efficacy of psychotherapy and pharmacotherapy in treating depressive and anxiety disorders: a meta-analysis of direct comparisons. *World Psychiatry, 12*(2), 137–148. doi:10.1002/wps.20038

Cuijpers, P., Sijbrandij, M., Koole, S., Huibers, M., Berking, M., & Andersson, G. (2014). Psychological treatment of generalized anxiety disorder: A meta-analysis. *Clinical Psychology Review, 34*(2), 130-140. doi:10.1016/j.cpr.2014.01.002

Cuijpers, P., van Straten, A., & Warmerdam, L. (2007). Problem solving therapies for depression: A meta-analysis. *European Psychiatry, 22*(1), 9–15. doi:http://dx.doi.org/10.1016/j.eurpsy.2006.11.001

Čukić, I., & Bates, T. C. (2015). The association between neuroticism and heart rate variability is not fully explained by cardiovascular disease and depression. *PLOS One, 10*(5).

Cukor, J., Spitalnick, J., Difede, J., Rizzo, A., & Rothbaum, B. O. (2009). Emerging treatments for PTSD. *Clinical Psychology Review, 29*(8), 715–726. doi:http://dx.doi.org/10.1016/j.cpr.2009.09.001

Culbert, K. M., Racine, S. E., & Klump, K. L. (2015). Research review: What we have learned about the causes of eating disorders—A synthesis of sociocultural, psychological, and biological research. *Journal of Child Psychology and Psychiatry, 56*(11), 1141–1164. doi:10.1111/jcpp.12441

Cummings, C. M., Caporino, N. E., & Kendall, P. C. (2014). Comorbidity of anxiety and depression in children and adolescents: 20 years after. *Psychological Bulletin, 140*(3), 816–845. doi:10.1037/a0034733

Cunnington, D. (2012). Non-benzodiazepine hypnotics: do they work for insomnia? *BMJ: British Medical Journal, 346* (8699), 1–2. doi:10.1136/bmj.e8699

Curran, G., & Ravindran, A. (2014). Lithium for bipolar disorder: A review of the recent literature. *Expert Review of Neurotherapeutics, 14*(9), 1079–1098. doi:10.1586/14737175.2014.947965

Curran, J. S. M. (1995). Current provision and effectiveness of day care services for people with dementia. *Reviews in Clinical Gerontology, 5*(3), 313–320. doi:10.1017/S0959259800004354

Cuthbert, B. N. (2014). The RDoC framework: Facilitating transition from ICD/DSM to dimensional approaches that integrate neuroscience and psychopathology. *World Psychiatry, 13*(1), 28–35. doi:10.1002/wps.20087

Cuthbert, B. N., & Kozak, M. J. (2013). Constructing constructs for psychopathology: The NIMH research domain criteria. *Journal of Abnormal Psychology, 122*(3), 928–937. doi:10.1037/a0034028

Czarnecki, K., Jones, D. T., Burnett, M. S., Mullan, B., & Matsumoto, J. Y. (2011). SPECT perfusion patterns distinguish psychogenic from essential tremor. *Parkinsonism & Related Disorders, 17*(5), 328–332. doi:10.1016/j.parkreldis.2011.01.012

da Mota Gomes, M., & Engelhardt, E. (2014). A neurological bias in the history of hysteria: From the womb to the nervous system and Charcot. *Arquivos de Neuro-Psiquiatria, 72*(12), 972–975. doi:10.1590/0004-282X20140149

Dahm, R. (2006). Alzheimer's discovery. *Current Biology, 16*(21), R906–R910. doi:10.1016/j.cub.2006.09.056

Dalenberg, C. J., Brand, B. L., Gleaves, D. H., Dorahy, M. J., Loewenstein, R. J., Cardeña, E., ... Spiegel, D. (2012). Evaluation of the evidence for the trauma and fantasy models of dissociation. *Psychological Bulletin, 138*(3), 550–588. doi:10.1037/a0027447

Daley, A., & Mulé, N. J. (2014). LGBTQs and the DSM-5: A critical queer response. *Journal of Homosexuality, 61*(9), 1288–1312. doi:10.1080/00918369.2014.926766

Dalle Grave, R., Calugi, S., Doll, H. A., & Fairburn, C. G. (2013). Enhanced cognitive behaviour therapy for adolescents with anorexia nervosa: An alternative to family therapy? *Behaviour Research and Therapy, 51*(1), R9-R12. doi:10.1016/j.brat.2012.09.008

Dalle Grave, R., Calugi, S., Ghoch, M. E., Conti, M., & Fairburn, C. G. (2014). Inpatient cognitive behavior therapy for adolescents with anorexia nervosa: Immediate and longer-term effects. *Frontiers in Psychiatry, 5.*

Dallos, R., & Stedmon, J. (2014). Systemic formulation: Mapping the family dance. In L. Johnstone & R. Dallos (Eds.), *Formulation in psychology and psychotherapy: Making sense of people's problems* (2nd ed., pp. 67–95). London, UK: Routledge.

Damiano, C. R., Mazefsky, C. A., White, S. W., & Dichter, G. S. (2014). Future directions for research in autism spectrum disorders. *Journal of Clinical Child and Adolescent Psychology, 43*(5), 828–843. doi:10.1080/15374416.2014.945214

Danforth, S., & Navarro, V. (2001). Hyper talk: Sampling the social construction of ADHD in everyday language. *Anthropology & Education Quarterly, 32*(2), 167–190.

Daniel, A. E., Burn, R. J., & Horarik, S. (1999). Patients' complaints about medical practice. *The Medical Journal Of Australia, 170*(12), 598–602.

Darke, S. (2010). The toxicology of homicide offenders and victims: A review. *Drug and Alcohol Review, 29*(2), 202–215. doi:10.1111/j.1465-3362.2009.00099.x

Darwin, C. (2008). *On the origin of species* (Rev. ed.). Oxford, UK: Oxford University Press. (Original work published 1839)

Daughton, J. M., & Kratochvil, C. J. (2009). Review of ADHD pharmacotherapies: Advantages, disadvantages, and clinical pearls. *Journal of the American Academy of Child & Adolescent Psychiatry, 48*(3), 240–248. doi:10.1097/CHI.0b013e3181977481

Davanloo, H. (1999). Intensive short-term dynamic psychotherapy—Central dynamic sequence: Head-on collision with resistance. *International Journal of Intensive Short-Term Dynamic Psychotherapy, 13*(4), 263–282. doi:10.1002/(SICI)1099-1182(199912)13:4<263::AID-SHO152>3.0.CO;2-E

Davidson, J. (2015). Vintage treatments for PTSD: A reconsideration of tricyclic drugs. *Journal of Psychopharmacology, 29*(3), 264–269. doi:10.1177/0269881114565143

Davidson, L. (2016). Capacity to consent to or refuse psychiatric treatment: an analysis of South African and UK law. *South African Journal on Human Rights, 32*(3), 457–489. doi:10.1080/02587203.2016.1263417

Davies, J. (2017). Political pills: Psychopharmaceuticals and neoliberalism as mutually supporting. In J. Davies (Ed.), *The sedated society: The causes and harms of our psychiatric drug epidemic* (pp. 189–225). New York, NY: Palgrave Macmillan.

Davies, L. M., Lewis, S., Jones, P. B., Barnes, T. R. E., Gaughran, F., Hayhurst, K., ... Lloyd, H. (2007). Cost-effectiveness of first- v. second-generation antipsychotic drugs: Results from a randomised controlled trial in schizophrenia responding poorly to previous therapy. *The British Journal of Psychiatry, 191*, 14–22. doi:10.1192/bjp.bp.106.028654

Davies, M. N., Verdi, S., Burri, A., Trzaskowski, M., Lee, M., Hettema, J. M., ... Spector, T. D. (2015). Generalised anxiety disorder—A twin study of genetic architecture, genome-wide association and differential gene expression. *PLOS One, 10*(8).

Davis, C. (1993). Review of the book, *A reader's guide to the Janus report*. [The Janus Report on sexual behavior]. *Journal of Sex Research, 30*(4), 336-338.

Davis, C., Levitan, R. D., Yilmaz, Z., Kaplan, A. S., Carter, J. C., & Kennedy, J. L. (2012). Binge eating disorder and the dopamine D2 receptor: Genotypes and sub-phenotypes. *Progress in Neuro-Psychopharmacology & Biological Psychiatry, 38*(2), 328–335. doi:10.1016/j.pnpbp.2012.05.002

Davis, D. A. (1976). On being detectably sane in insane places: Base rates and psychodiagnosis. *Journal of Abnormal Psychology, 85*(4), 416–422. doi:10.1037/0021-843X.85.4.416

Davis, E. B., & Strawn, B. D. (2010). The Psychodynamic Diagnostic Manual: An adjunctive tool for diagnosis, case formulation, and treatment. *Journal of Psychology and Christianity, 29*(2), 109–115.

Davis, J. L., & Manago, B. (2016). Motherhood and associative moral stigma: The moral double bind. *Stigma and Health, 1*(2), 72–86. doi:10.1037/sah0000019

Davis, L. L., Frazier, E. C., Williford, R. B., & Newell, J. M. (2006). Long-term pharmacotherapy for post-traumatic stress disorder. *CNS Drugs, 20*(6), 465–476. doi:10.2165/00023210-200620060-00003

Davis, L. W., Lysaker, P. H., Kristeller, J. L., Salyers, M. P., Kovach, A. C., & Woller, S. (2015). Effect of mindfulness on vocational rehabilitation outcomes in stable phase schizophrenia. *Psychological Services, 12*(3), 303–312. doi:10.1037/ser0000028

Davis, T. D., Sullivan, G., Vasterling, J. J., Tharp, A. L. T., Han, X., Deitch, E. A., & Constans, J. I. (2012). Racial variations in postdisaster PTSD among veteran survivors of Hurricane Katrina. *Psychological Trauma: Theory, Research, Practice, and Policy, 4*(5), 447–456. doi:10.1037/a0025501

Davy, Z. (2015). The DSM-5 and the politics of diagnosing transpeople. *Archives of Sexual Behavior, 44*(5), 1165–1176. doi:10.1007/s10508-015-0573-6

Day, E., & Strang, J. (2011). Outpatient versus inpatient opioid detoxification: A randomized controlled trial. *Journal of Substance Abuse Treatment, 40*(1), 56–66. doi:10.1016/j.jsat.2010.08.007

De Bei, F., & Dazzi, N. (2014). Attachment and relational psychoanalysis: Bowlby according to Mitchell. *Psychoanalytic Dialogues, 24*(5), 562–577. doi:10.1080/10481885.2014.949492

De Berardis, D., Campanella, D., Serroni, N., Gambi, F., Carano, A., La Rovere, R., ... Ferro, F. M. (2008). Insight and perceived expressed emotion among adult outpatients with obsessive-compulsive disorder. *Journal of Psychiatric Practice, 14*(3), 154–159. doi:10.1097/01.pra.0000320114.38434.5f

De Block, A., & Adriaens, P. R. (2013). Pathologizing sexual deviance: A history. *Journal of Sex Research, 50*(3–4), 276–298. doi:10.1080/00224499.2012.738259

de Bruijn, D. M., & de Graaf, I. M. (2016). The role of substance use in same-day intimate partner violence: A review of the literature. *Aggression and Violent Behavior.* doi:10.1016/j.avb.2016.02.010

De Cuypere, G., Knudson, G., & Bockting, W. (2011). Second response of the world professional association for transgender health to the proposed revision of the diagnosis of gender dysphoria for DSM 5. *International Journal of Transgenderism, 13*(2), 51–53. doi:10.1080/15532739.2011.624047

de Graaf, C. (2006). Effects of snacks on energy intake: An evolutionary perspective. *Appetite, 47*(1), 18–23. doi:http://dx.doi.org/10.1016/j.appet.2006.02.007

De Gucht, V., & Fischler, B. (2002). Somatization: A critical review of conceptual and methodological issues. *Psychosomatics, 43*(1), 1–9. doi:http://dx.doi.org/10.1176/appi.psy.43.1.1

de Jong, P. J., van Lankveld, J., & Elgersma, H. J. (2010). Sexual problems. In D. McKay, J. S. Abramowitz, & S. Taylor (Eds.), *Cognitive-behavioral therapy for refractory cases: Turning failure into success* (pp. 255–275). Washington, DC: American Psychological Association.

de Jonghe, F., de Maat, S., Van, R., Hendriksen, M., Kool, S., van Aalst, G., & Dekker, J. (2013). Short-term psychoanalytic supportive psychotherapy for depressed patients. *Psychoanalytic Inquiry, 33*(6), 614–625. doi:10.1080/07351690.2013.835184

de Kloet, C. S., Vermetten, E., Geuze, E., Kavelaars, A., Heijnen, C. J., & Westenberg, H. G. M. (2006). Assessment of HPA-axis function in posttraumatic stress disorder: Pharmacological and non-pharmacological challenge tests, a review. *Journal of Psychiatric Research, 40*(6), 550–567. doi:http://dx.doi.org/10.1016/j.jpsychires.2005.08.002

de Lange, F. P., Toni, I., & Roelofs, K. (2010). Altered connectivity between prefrontal and sensorimotor cortex in conversion paralysis. *Neuropsychologia, 48*(6), 1782–1788. doi:http://dx.doi.org/10.1016/j.neuropsychologia.2010.02.029

De Leon, G. (2010). Is the therapeutic community an evidence-based treatment? What the evidence says. *Therapeutic Communities, 31*(2), 104–128.

De Leon, G. (2015a). 'The gold standard' and related considerations for a maturing science of substance abuse treatment. Therapeutic communities; A case in point. *Substance Use & Misuse, 50*(8–9), 1106–1109. doi:10.3109/10826084.2015.1012846

De Leon, G. (2015b). Therapeutic communities. In M. Galanter, H. D. Kleber, & K. T. Brady (Eds.), *The American Psychiatric Publishing textbook of substance abuse treatment* (5th ed., pp. 511–530). Arlington, VA: American Psychiatric Publishing.

de Mello, M. F., de Jesus Mari, J., Bacaltchuk, J., Verdeli, H., & Neugebauer, R. (2005). A systematic review of research findings on the efficacy of interpersonal therapy for depressive disorders. *European Archives of Psychiatry and Clinical Neuroscience, 255*(2), 75–82. doi:10.1007/s00406-004-0542-x

de Ruiter, M. B., Veltman, D. J., Phaf, R. H., & van Dyck, R. (2007). Negative words enhance recognition in nonclinical high dissociators: An fMRI study. *NeuroImage, 37*(1), 323–334.

de Waal, M. W. M., Arnold, I. A., Eekhof, J. A. H., & van Hemert, A. M. (2004). Somatoform disorders in general practice: Prevalence, functional impairment and comorbidity with anxiety and depressive disorders. *The British Journal of Psychiatry, 184*(6), 470–476. doi:10.1192/bjp.184.6.470

Deacon, B. J. (2013). The biomedical model of mental disorder: A critical analysis of its validity, utility, and effects on psychotherapy research. *Clinical Psychology Review, 33*(7), 846–861.

Deacon, M. (2015). Personal experience: Being depressed is worse than having advanced cancer. *Journal of Psychiatric and Mental Health Nursing, 22*(6), 457–459. doi:10.1111/jpm.12219

Deb, S. (2007). The role of medication in the management of behaviour problems in people with learning disabilities. *Advances in Mental Health and Intellectual Disabilities, 1*(2), 26–31. doi:10.1108/1753018020070 0017

Decker, H. S. (2013). *The making of DSM-III*. Oxford, UK: Oxford University Press.

Dedovic, K., & Ngiam, J. (2015). The cortisol awakening response and major depression: Examining the evidence. *Neuropsychiatric Disease and Treatment, 11*.

Deer, B. (2004, February 22). Revealed: MMR research scandal. *The Sunday Times.* Retrieved from http://briandeer.com/mmr/lancet-deer-1.htm

Dekker, J. J. M., Hendriksen, M., Kool, S., Bakker, L., Driessen, E., De Jonghe, F., ... Van, H. L. (2014). Growing evidence for psychodynamic therapy for depression. *Contemporary Psychoanalysis, 50*(1–2), 131–155. doi:10.1080/00107530.2014.880312

del Campo, N., Chamberlain, S. R., Sahakian, B. J., & Robbins, T. W. (2011). The roles of dopamine and noradrenaline in the pathophysiology and treatment of attention-deficit/hyperactivity disorder. *Biological Psychiatry, 69*(12), e145-e157. doi:10.1016/j.biopsych.2011.02.036

Del Casale, A., Kotzalidis, G. D., Rapinesi, C., Serata, D., Ambrosi, E., Simonetti, A., ... Girardi, P. (2011). Functional neuroimaging in obsessive-compulsive disorder. *Neuropsychobiology, 64*(2), 61–85. doi:10.1159/000325223

Del Giudice, M. (2014). An evolutionary life history framework for psychopathology. *Psychological Inquiry, 25*(3–4), 261–300. doi:10.1080/1047840X.2014.884918

DeLamater, J. D., & Hude, J. S. (1998). Essentialism vs. social constructionism in the study of human sexuality. *Journal of Sex Research, 35*(1), 10–18.

Dell, P. F. (2013). The weakness of the sociocognitive model of dissociative identity disorder. *Journal of Nervous and Mental Disease, 201*(5), 483–483.

Delobel-Ayoub, M., Ehlinger, V., Klapouszczak, D., Maffre, T., Raynaud, J.-P., Delpierre, C., & Arnaud, C. (2015). Socioeconomic disparities and prevalence of autism spectrum disorders and intellectual disability. *PLOS One, 10*(11).

Deltito, J., & Beyer, D. (1998). The scientific, quasi-scientific and popular literature on the use of St. John's Wort in the treatment of depression. *Journal of Affective Disorders, 51*(3), 345–351. doi:10.1016/S0165-0327(99)00008-7

DeLuca, N. L., Moser, L. L., & Bond, G. R. (2008). Assertive community treatment. In K. T. Mueser & D. V. Jeste (Eds.), *Clinical handbook of schizophrenia* (pp. 329–338). New York, NY: Guilford Press.

Demerling, R. (2011). Resisting stigma, embracing solidarity: An ethnographic study of shopaholics anonymous. *Qualitative Studies, 2*(1), 1–15.

Demicheli, V., Rivetti, A., Debalini, M. G., & Di Pietrantonj, C. (2012). Vaccines for measles, mumps and rubella in children. *Cochrane Database of Systematic Reviews, 2012*(2), 1–166. doi:10.1002/14651858.CD004407.pub3

Deng, W., Zou, X., Deng, H., Li, J., Tang, C., Wang, X., & Guo, X. (2015). The relationship among genetic heritability, environmental effects, and autism spectrum disorders: 37 pairs of ascertained twin study. *Journal of Child Neurology, 30*(13), 1794–1799. doi:10.1177/0883073815580645

Denis, C. M., Gelernter, J., Hart, A. B., & Kranzler, H. R. (2015). Inter-observer reliability of DSM-5 substance use disorders. *Drug and Alcohol Dependence, 153*, 229–235. doi:http://dx.doi.org/10.1016/j.drugalcdep.2015.05.019

Denney, D. R., Sullivan, B. J., & Thiry, M. R. (1977). Participant modeling and self-verbalization training in the reduction of spider fears. *Journal of Behavior Therapy and Experimental Psychiatry, 8*(3), 247–253. doi:10.1016/0005-7916(77)90062-3

Derbyshire, K. L., & Grant, J. E. (2015). Compulsive sexual behavior: A review of the literature. *Journal of Behavioral Addictions, 4*(2), 37–43. doi:10.1556/2006.4.2015.003

Derenne, J. L., & Beresin, E. V. (2006). Body image, media, and eating disorders. *Academic Psychiatry, 30*(3), 257–261. doi:10.1176/appi.ap.30.3.257

DeRosse, P., Nitzburg, G. C., Kompancaril, B., & Malhotra, A. K. (2014). The relation between childhood maltreatment and psychosis in patients with schizophrenia and non-psychiatric controls. *Schizophrenia Research, 155*(1–3), 66–71. doi:http://dx.doi.org/10.1016/j.schres.2014.03.009

Derr, A. S. (2016). Mental health service use among immigrants in the United States: A systematic review. *Psychiatric Services, 67*(3), 265–274. doi:10.1176/appi.ps.201500004

DeRubeis, R. J., Siegle, G. J., & Hollon, S. D. (2008). Cognitive therapy vs. medications for depression: Treatment outcomes and neural mechanisms. *Nature Reviews. Neuroscience, 9*(10), 788–796. doi:10.1038/nrn2345

Desmyter, S., van Heeringen, C., & Audenaert, K. (2011). Structural and functional neuroimaging studies of the suicidal brain. *Progress in Neuro-Psychopharmacology and Biological Psychiatry, 35*(4), 796–808. doi:http://dx.doi.org/10.1016/j.pnpbp.2010.12.026

Desrosiers, C., Boucher, O., Forget-Dubois, N., Dewailly, É., Ayotte, P., Jacobson, S. W., … Muckle, G. (2013). Associations between prenatal cigarette smoke exposure and externalized behaviors at school age among Inuit children exposed to environmental contaminants. *Neurotoxicology and Teratology, 39*, 84–90. doi:10.1016/j.ntt.2013.07.010

DeStefano, F. (2002). MMR vaccine and autism: A review of the evidence for a causal association. *Molecular Psychiatry, 7*(Suppl 2), S51–S52. doi:10.1038/sj.mp.4001181

Devlin, M. (2014). 10 crazy facts from Bedlam, history's most notorious asylum. Retrieved from http://listverse.com/2014/04/02/10-crazy-facts-from-bedlam-historys-most-notorious-asylum/

DeVylder, J. E., Oh, H. Y., Yang, L. H., Cabassa, L. J., Chen, F., & Lukens, E. P. (2013). Acculturative stress and psychotic-like experiences among Asian and Latino immigrants to the United States. *Schizophrenia Research, 150*(1), 223–228. doi:http://dx.doi.org/10.1016/j.schres.2013.07.040

DeYoung, C. G., Carey, B. E., Krueger, R. F., & Ross, S. R. (2016). Ten aspects of the Big Five in the Personality Inventory for DSM–5. *Personality Disorders: Theory, Research, and Treatment, 7*(2), 113–123. doi:10.1037/per0000170

Dhabhar, F. S. (2014). Effects of stress on immune function: The good, the bad, and the beautiful. *Immunologic Research, 58*(2–3), 193–210. doi:10.1007/s12026-014-8517-0

Di Benedetto, B., Rupprecht, R., & Rammes, G. (2010). Beyond the monoamine hypothesis: The quest for an integrative etiology of depression and new therapeutic strategies. In J. T. Van Leeuwen (Ed.), *Antidepressants: Types, efficiency and possible side effects* (pp. 155–167). New York, NY: Nova Science Publishers.

Diamond, G. M. (2014). Attachment-based family therapy interventions. *Psychotherapy, 51*(1), 15–19. doi:10.1037/a0032689

Díaz-Marsá, M., MacDowell, K. S., Guemes, I., Rubio, V., Carrasco, J. L., & Leza, J. C. (2012). Activation of the cholinergic anti-inflammatory system in peripheral blood mononuclear cells from patients with borderline personality disorder. *Journal of Psychiatric Research, 46*(12), 1610–1617. doi:10.1016/j.jpsychires.2012.09.009

Dickerson, F. B. (2000). Cognitive behavioral psychotherapy for schizophrenia: A review of recent empirical studies. *Schizophrenia Research, 43*(2–3), 71–90. doi:10.1016/S0920-9964(99)00153-X

Dickerson, F. B. (2004). Update on Cognitive Behavioral Psychotherapy for Schizophrenia: Review of Recent Studies. *Journal of Cognitive Psychotherapy, 18*(3), 189–205. doi:10.1891/jcop.18.3.189.65654

Dickerson, F. B., & Lehman, A. F. (2011). Evidence-based psychotherapy for schizophrenia. *Journal of Nervous and Mental Disease, 199*(8), 520–526. doi:10.1097/NMD.0b013e318225ee78

DiClemente, C. C., & Velasquez, M. M. (2002). Motivational interviewing and the stages of change. In W. R. Miller & S. Rollnick (Eds.), *Motivational interviewing: Preparing people for change* (2nd ed., pp. 201–216). New York, NY: Guilford Press.

Dictionary.com. (n.d.-a). Assessment. Retrieved from http://dictionary.reference.com/browse/diagnosis

Dictionary.com. (n.d.-b). Bedlam. Retrieved from Retrieved from http://dictionary.reference.com/browse/bedlam?s=t

Dictionary.com. (n.d.-c). Diagnosis. Retrieved from http://dictionary.reference.com/browse/diagnosis

Diekema, D. S. (2003). Involuntary sterilization of persons with mental retardation: An ethical analysis. *Mental Retardation and Developmental Disabilities Research Reviews, 9*(1), 21–26.

Dietrich, K. N. (2010). Environmental toxicants. In K. O. Yeates, M. D. Ris, H. G. Taylor, & B. F. Pennington (Eds.), *Pediatric neuropsychology: Research, theory, and practice* (2nd ed., pp. 211–264). New York, NY: Guilford Press.

Digman, J. M. (1990). Personality structure: Emergence of the five-factor model. *Annual Review of Psychology, 41*, 417–440. doi:10.1146/annurev.ps.41.020190.002221

Dijkstra-Kersten, S. M. A., Biesheuvel-Leliefeld, K. E. M., van der Wouden, J. C., Penninx, B. W. J. H., & van Marwijk, H. W. J. (2015). Associations of financial strain and income with depressive and anxiety disorders. *Journal of Epidemiology and Community Health, 69*(7), 660–665. doi:10.1136/jech-2014-205088

Dikeos, D., & Georgantopoulos, G. (2011). Medical comorbidity of sleep disorders. *Current Opinion in Psychiatry, 24*(4), 346–354. doi:10.1097/YCO.0b013e3283473375

Dillen, L., Fontaine, J. R. J., & Verhofstadt-Denève, L. (2008). Are normal and complicated grief different constructs? A confirmatory factor analytic test. *Clinical Psychology & Psychotherapy, 15*(6), 386–395. doi:10.1002/cpp.590

DiLollo, A., & Neimeyer, R. A. (2008). Talking back to stuttering: Constructivist contributions to stuttering treatment. In J. D. Raskin & S. K. Bridges (Eds.), *Studies in meaning 3: Constructivist psychotherapy in the real world* (pp. 165–181). New York, NY: Pace University Press.

DiLollo, A., Manning, W. H., & Neimeyer, R. A. (2003). Cognitive anxiety as a function of speaker role for fluent speakers and persons who stutter. *Journal of Fluency Disorders, 28*(3), 167–186. doi:10.1016/S0094-730X(03)00043-3

DiLollo, A., Manning, W. H., & Neimeyer, R. A. (2005). Cognitive complexity as a function of speaker role for adult persons who stutter. *Journal of Constructivist Psychology, 18*(3), 215–236. doi:10.1080/10720530590948773

DiLollo, A., Neimeyer, R. A., & Constantino, C. D. (2014). *Counseling in speech-language pathology and audiology: Reconstructing personal narratives*. San Diego, CA: Plural Publishing.

DiLollo, A., Neimeyer, R. A., & Manning, W. H. (2002). A personal construct psychology view of relapse: Indications for a narrative therapy component to stuttering treatment. *Journal of Fluency Disorders, 27*(1), 19–42. doi:10.1016/S0094-730X(01)00109-7

DiMauro, J., Carter, S., Folk, J. B., & Kashdan, T. B. (2014). A historical review of trauma-related diagnoses to reconsider the heterogeneity of PTSD. *Journal of Anxiety Disorders, 28*(8), 774–786. doi:10.1016/j.janxdis.2014.09.002

Dimsdale, J. E., Creed, F., Escobar, J., Sharpe, M., Wulsin, L., Barsky, A., ... Levenson, J. (2013). Somatic symptom disorder: An important change in DSM. *Journal of Psychosomatic Research, 75*(3), 223–228. doi:10.1016/j.jpsychores.2013.06.033

Dinos, S., Stevens, S., Serfaty, M., Weich, S., & King, M. (2004). Stigma: The feelings and experiences of 46 people with mental illness. *Qualitative study, 184*(2), 176–181. doi:10.1192/bjp.184.2.176

Disability Justice. (n.d.). Wyatt v. Stickney. Retrieved from http://disabilityjustice.org/wyatt-v-stickney/

Diskin, K. M., & Hodgins, D. C. (2009). A randomized controlled trial of a single session motivational intervention for concerned gamblers. *Behaviour Research and Therapy, 47*(5), 382–388. doi:10.1016/j.brat.2009.01.018

Division of Clinical Psychology. (2010). Understanding bipolar disorder. Retrieved from British Psychological Society website: http://www.bps.org.uk/networks-and-communities/member-microsite/division-clinical-psychology/understanding-psychosis-and-schizophrenia

Division of Clinical Psychology. (2014). Understanding psychosis and schizophrenia. Retrieved from British Psychological Society website: http://www.bps.org.uk/networks-and-communities/member-microsite/division-clinical-psychology/understanding-psychosis-and-schizophrenia

Dix, D. (2006). 'I Tell What I Have Seen': The Reports of Asylum Reformer Dorothea Dix. *American Journal of Public Health, 96*(4), 622–625. doi:10.2105/AJPH.96.4.622 (First published 1843).

Dixon, L., Perkins, D., & Calmes, C. (2009). *Guideline watch (September, 2009): Practice guideline for the treatment of patients with schizophrenia*. Retrieved from http://psychiatryonline.org/pb/assets/raw/sitewide/practice_guidelines/guidelines/schizophrenia-watch.pdf

Dixon-Gordon, K. L., Turner, B. J., & Chapman, A. L. (2011). Psychotherapy for personality disorders. *International Review of Psychiatry, 23*(3), 282–302. doi:10.3109/09540261.2011.586992

Dmytriw, A. A. (2015). Gender and sex manifestations in hysteria across medicine and the arts. *European Neurology, 73*(1–2), 44–50. doi:10.1159/000367891

Docherty, M., & Thornicroft, G. (2015). Specialist mental health services in England in 2014: Overview of funding, access and levels of care. *International Journal of Mental Health Systems, 9*.

Dockery, L., Jeffery, D., Schauman, O., Williams, P., Farrelly, S., Bonnington, O., ... Clement, S. (2015). Stigma- and non-stigma-related treatment barriers to mental healthcare reported by service users and caregivers. *Psychiatry Research, 228*(3), 612–619. doi:10.1016/j.psychres.2015.05.044

Dodd, J. (2015). 'The name game': Feminist protests of the DSM and diagnostic labels in the 1980s. *History of Psychology, 18*(3), 312–323. doi:10.1037/a0039520

Dodds, P., Bruce-Hay, P., & Stapleton, S. (2014). Pre-therapy and dementia—the opportunity to put Person-Centred theory into everyday practice. In P. Pearce & L. Sommerbeck (Eds.), *Person-centred practice at the difficult edge* (pp. 102–118). Ross-on-Wye, UK: PCCS Books.

Dodes, L., & Dodes, Z. (2015). *The sober truth: Debunking the bad science behind 12-step programs and the rehab industry*. Boston, MA: Beacon Press.

Dodes, L. M., & Khantzian, E. J. (2005). Individual psychodynamic psychotherapy. In R. J. Frances, S. I. Miller, & A. H. Mack (Eds.), *Clinical textbook of addictive disorders* (3rd ed., pp. 457–473). New York, NY: Guilford Press.

Dodge, E. (2016). Forty years of eating disorder-focused family therapy—The legacy of 'psychosomatic families'. *Advances in Eating Disorders, 4*(2), 219–227. doi:10.1080/21662630.2015.1099452

Dodgson, G., & Gordon, S. (2009). Avoiding false negatives: Are some auditory hallucinations an evolved design flaw? *Behavioural and Cognitive Psychotherapy, 37*(3), 325–334. doi:10.1017/S1352465809005244

Dold, M., Aigner, M., Klabunde, M., Treasure, J., & Kasper, S. (2015). Second-generation antipsychotic drugs in anorexia nervosa: A meta-analysis of randomized controlled trials. *Psychotherapy and Psychosomatics, 84*(2), 110–116. doi:10.1159/000369978

Dolgun, G., Savaser, S., Balci, S., & Yazici, S. (2012). Prevalence of nocturnal enuresis and related factors in children aged 5–13 in Istanbul. *Iranian Journal of Pediatrics, 22*(2), 205–212.

Dolhanty, J. (2006). Emotion-focused therapy for eating disorders. Retrieved from http://nedic.ca/emotion-focused-therapy-eating-disorders

Dolhanty, J., & Greenberg, L. S. (2009). Emotion-focused therapy in a case of anorexia nervosa. *Clinical Psychology & Psychotherapy, 16*(4), 366–382. doi:10.1002/cpp.624

Donofry, S. D., Roecklein, K. A., Wildes, J. E., Miller, M. A., Flory, J. D., & Manuck, S. B. (2014). COMT met allele differentially predicts risk versus severity of aberrant eating in a large community sample. *Psychiatry Research, 220*(1–2), 513–518. doi:10.1016/j.psychres.2014.08.037

Donovan, D., & Witkiewitz, K. (2012). Relapse prevention: From radical idea to common practice. *Addiction Research & Theory, 20*(3), 204–217. doi:10.3109/16066359.2011.647133

Donovan, D. M., Ingalsbe, M. H., Benbow, J., & Daley, D. C. (2013). 12-step interventions and mutual support programs for substance use disorders: An overview. *Social Work in Public Health, 28*, 313–332. doi:10.1080/19371918.2013.774663

Dorahy, M. J. (2006). The dissociative processing style: A cognitive organization activated by perceived or actual threat in clinical dissociators. *Journal of Trauma & Dissociation, 7*(4), 29–53. doi:10.1300/J229v07n04_03

Dorahy, M. J., & van der Hart, O. (2006). Fable or fact? Did Janet really come to repudiate his dissociation theory? *Journal of Trauma & Dissociation, 7*(2), 29–37. doi:10.1300/J229v07n02_03

Dorahy, M. J., Brand, B. L., Sar, V., Krüger, C., Stavropoulos, P., Martínez-Taboas, A., ... Middleton, W. (2014). Dissociative identity disorder: An empirical overview. *Australian and New Zealand Journal of Psychiatry, 48*(5), 402–417. doi:10.1177/0004867414527523

Doron, G., Mikulincer, M., Kyrios, M., & Sar-Ei, D. (2015). Obsessive-compulsive disorder. In P. Luyten, L. C. Mayes, P. Fonagy, M. Target, & S. J. Blatt (Eds.), *Handbook of psychodynamic approaches to psychopathology* (pp. 199–215). New York, NY: Guilford Press.

dosReis, S., Barksdale, C. L., Sherman, A., Maloney, K., & Charach, A. (2010). Stigmatizing experiences of parents of children with a new diagnosis of ADHD. *Psychiatric Services, 61*(8), 811–816. doi:10.1176/appi.ps.61.8.811

Dougherty, D. M., Lake, S. L., Hill-Kapturczak, N., Liang, Y., Karns, T. E., Mullen, J., & Roache, J. D. (2015). Using contingency management procedures to reduce at-risk drinking in heavy drinkers. *Alcoholism: Clinical and Experimental Research, 39*(4), 743–751. doi:10.1111/acer.12687

Dowbiggin, I. R. (2009). High anxieties: The social construction of anxiety disorders. *The Canadian Journal of Psychiatry/La Revue Canadienne De Psychiatrie, 54*(7), 429–436.

Dowling, T. (2006). Who are you calling angry? *The Guardian*. Retrieved from https://www.theguardian.com/lifeandstyle/2006/jun/08/healthandwellbeing.health

Downing, L. (2015). Heteronormativity and repronormativity in sexological 'perversion theory' and the DSM-5's 'paraphilic disorder' diagnoses. *Archives of Sexual Behavior, 44*(5), 1139–1145. doi:10.1007/s10508-015-0536-y

Downs, K. J., & Blow, A. J. (2013). A substantive and methodological review of family-based treatment for eating disorders: The last 25 years of research. *Journal of Family Therapy, 35*(Suppl 1), 3–28. doi:10.1111/j.1467-6427.2011.00566.x

Dozios, D. J. A., & Covin, R. (2004). The Beck Depression Inventory (BDI-II), Beck Hopelessness Scale, and Beck Scale for Suicide Ideation. In M. J. Hilsenroth & D. L. Segal (Eds.), *Comprehensive handbook of psychological assessment: Vol. 2. Personality assessment* (pp. 50–69). Hoboken, NJ: John Wiley.

Dreher, D. E. (2013). Abnormal psychology in the Renaissance. In T. G. Plante (Ed.), *Abnormal psychology across the ages: Vol. 1. History and conceptualizations* (pp. 33–50). Santa Barbara, CA: Praeger/ABC-CLIO.

Drescher, J. (2012). The removal of homosexuality from the DSM: Its impact on today's marriage equality debate. *Journal of Gay & Lesbian Mental Health, 16*(2), 124–135. doi:10.1080/19359705.2012.653255

Drescher, J. (2014). Treatment of lesbian, gay, bisexual, and transgender patients. In R. E. Hales, S. C. Yudofsky, & L. W. Roberts (Eds.), *The American Psychiatric Publishing textbook of psychiatry* (6th ed., pp. 1293–1318). Arlington, VA: American Psychiatric Publishing.

Drescher, J. (2015a). Can sexual orientation be changed? *Journal of Gay & Lesbian Mental Health, 19*(1), 84–93. doi:10.1080/19359705.2014.944460

Drescher, J. (2015b). Queer diagnoses revisited: The past and future of homosexuality and gender diagnoses in DSM and ICD. *International Review of Psychiatry, 27*(5), 386–395. doi:10.3109/09540261.2015.1053847

Drescher, J., Cohen-Kettenis, P. T., & Reed, G. M. (2016). Gender incongruence of childhood in the ICD-11: Controversies, proposal, and rationale. *The Lancet Psychiatry, 3*(3), 297–304. doi:10.1016/S2215-0366(15)00586-6

Drescher, J., Cohen-Kettenis, P., & Winter, S. (2012). Minding the body: Situating gender identity diagnoses in the ICD-11. *International Review of Psychiatry, 24*(6), 568–577. doi:10.3109/09540261.2012.741575

Drisko, J. W., & Simmons, B. M. (2012). The evidence base for psychodynamic psychotherapy. *Smith College Studies in Social Work, 82*(4), 374–400. doi:10.1080/00377317.2012.717014

Drucker, D. J. (2012). 'A most interesting chapter in the history of science': Intellectual responses to Alfred Kinsey's Sexual Behavior in the Human Male. *History of the Human Sciences, 25*(1), 75–98. doi:10.1177/0952695111432523

Dryden, W., & Ellis, A. (2001). Rational emotive behavior therapy. In K. S. Dobson (Ed.), *Handbook of cognitive-behavioral therapies* (2nd ed., pp. 295–348). New York, NY: Guilford Press.

Drye, R. C., Goulding, R. L., & Goulding, M. E. (1973). No-suicide decisions: Patient monitoring of suicidal risk. *The American Journal of Psychiatry, 130*(2), 171–174. doi:10.1176/ajp.130.2.171

Duara, R., Lopez-Alberola, R. F., Barker, W. W., Loewenstein, D. A., Zatinsky, M., Eisdorfer, C. E., & Weinberg, G. B. (1993). A comparison of familial and sporadic Alzheimer's disease. *Neurology, 43*(7), 1377–1384.

Dubey, A. K., Handu, S. S., & Mediratta, P. K. (2015). Suvorexant: The first orexin receptor antagonist to treat insomnia. *Journal of Pharmacology & Pharmacotherapeutics, 6*(2), 118–121. doi:10.4103/0976-500X.155496

Ducci, F., & Goldman, D. (2012). The genetic basis of addictive disorders. *Psychiatric Clinics of North America, 35*(2), 495–519. doi:10.1016/j.psc.2012.03.010

Dückers, M. L. A., & Brewin, C. R. (2016). A paradox in individual versus national mental health vulnerability: Are higher resource levels associated with higher disorder prevalence? *Journal of Traumatic Stress, 29*(6), 572–576. doi:10.1002/jts.22144

Dückers, M. L. A., & Olff, M. (2017). Does the vulnerability paradox in PTSD apply to women and men? An exploratory study. *Journal of Traumatic Stress.* doi:10.1002/jts.22173

Dückers, M. L. A., Alisic, E., & Brewin, C. R. (2016). A vulnerability paradox in the cross-national prevalence of post-traumatic stress disorder. *The British Journal of Psychiatry, 209*(4), 300–305.

Dudek, J., Paweł, O., & Stanisław, M. (2014). Transdiagnostic models of eating disorders and therapeutic methods: The example of Fairburn's cognitive behavior therapy and acceptance and commitment therapy. *Rockzniki Psychologiczne / Annals of Psychology, 17*(1), 25–39.

Dudley, R. (2002). Fermenting fruit and the historical ecology of ethanol ingestion: Is alcoholism in modern humans an evolutionary hangover? *Addiction, 97*(4), 381–388. doi:10.1046/j.1360-0443.2002.00002.x

Dudley, R., Dodgson, G., Sarll, G., Halhead, R., Bolas, H., & McCarthy-Jones, S. (2014). The effect of arousal on auditory threat detection and the relationship to auditory hallucinations. *Journal of Behavior Therapy and Experimental Psychiatry, 45*(3), 311–318. doi:10.1016/j.jbtep.2014.02.002

Dudley-Marling, C. (2004). The social construction of learning disabilities. *Journal of Learning Disabilities, 37*(6), 482–489.

Duffett, L., & Ward, C. L. (2015). Can a motivational-interviewing-based outpatient substance abuse treatment achieve success? A theory-based evaluation. *African Journal of Drug and Alcohol Studies, 14*(1), 1–12.

Dugas, M. J., & Koerner, N. (2005). Cognitive-behavioral treatment for generalized anxiety disorder: Current status and future directions. *Journal of Cognitive Psychotherapy, 19*(1), 61–81. doi:10.1891/jcop.19.1.61.66326

Dugas, M. J., Freeston, M. H., & Ladouceur, R. (1997). Intolerance of uncertainty and problem orientation in worry. *Cognitive Therapy and Research, 21*(6), 593–606. doi:10.1023/A:1021890322153

Dugas, M. J., Gagnon, F., Ladouceur, R., & Freeston, M. H. (1998). Generalized anxiety disorder: A preliminary test of a conceptual model. *Behaviour Research and Therapy, 36*(2), 215–226. doi:10.1016/S0005-7967(97)00070-3

Dugas, M. J., Marchand, A., & Ladouceur, R. (2005). Further validation of a cognitive-behavioral model of generalized anxiety disorder: Diagnostic and symptom specificity. *Journal of Anxiety Disorders, 19*(3), 329–343. doi:10.1016/j.janxdis.2004.02.002

Duggan, C., Huband, N., Smailagic, N., Ferriter, M., & Adams, C. (2007). The use of psychological treatments for people with personality disorder: A systematic review of randomized controlled trials. *Personality and Mental Health, 1*(2), 95–125. doi:10.1002/pmh.22

Duggan, C., Huband, N., Smailagic, N., Ferriter, M., & Adams, C. (2008). The use of pharmacological treatments for people with personality disorder: A systematic review of randomized controlled trials. *Personality and Mental Health, 2*(3), 119–170. doi:10.1002/pmh.41

Duggins, R., & Veitch, P. (2013). Evaluating the impact of an embedded psychodynamic psychotherapist in an early intervention in psychosis service. *Journal of Psychiatric and Mental Health Nursing, 20*(9), 853–856.

Dumont, M. P., & Dumont, D. M. (2008). Deinstitutionalization in the United States and Italy: A historical survey. *International Journal of Mental Health, 37*(4), 61–70. doi:10.2753/IMH0020-7411370405

Duncan, L. E., Ratanatharathorn, A., Aiello, A. E., Almli, L. M., Amstadter, A. B., Ashley-Koch, A. E., ... Koenen, K. C. (2018). Largest GWAS of PTSD (N=20[thinsp]070) yields genetic overlap with schizophrenia and sex differences in heritability. *Molecular Psychiatry, 23*, 666–673. doi:10.1038/mp.2017.77

Dunlop, J., & Brandon, N. J. (2015). Schizophrenia drug discovery and development in an evolving era: Are new drug targets fulfilling expectations? *Journal of Psychopharmacology, 29*(2), 230–238. doi:10.1177/0269881114565806

Dunn, E. C., Brown, R. C., Dai, Y., Rosand, J., Nugent, N. R., Amstadter, A. B., & Smoller, J. W. (2015). Genetic determinants of depression: Recent findings and future directions. *Harvard Review of Psychiatry, 23*(1), 1–18. doi:10.1097/HRP.0000000000000054

Dunn, T. M., & Bratman, S. (2016). On orthorexia nervosa: A review of the literature and proposed diagnostic criteria. *Eating Behaviors, 21*, 11–17. doi:10.1016/j.eatbeh.2015.12.006

The 'Durham Rule'. (n.d.). Retrieved from http://criminal.findlaw.com/criminal-procedure/the-durham-rule.html

Durisko, Z., Mulsant, B. H., & Andrews, P. W. (2015). An adaptationist perspective on the etiology of depression. *Journal of Affective Disorders, 172*, 315–323. doi:10.1016/j.jad.2014.09.032

Durisko, Z., Mulsant, B. H., McKenzie, K., & Andrews, P. W. (2016). Using evolutionary theory to guide mental health research. *The Canadian Journal of Psychiatry/La Revue Canadienne De Psychiatrie, 61*(3), 159–165. doi:10.1177/0706743716632517

Durkheim, E. (1951). *Suicide: A study in sociology* (J. A. Spaulding & G. Simpson, Trans. G. Simpson Ed.). New York, NY: The Free Press. (Original work published 1897)

Dusenbury, L., Botvin, G. J., & James-Ortiz, S. (1989). The primary prevention of adolescent substance abuse through the promotion of personal and social competence. *Prevention in Human Services, 7*(1), 201–224. doi:10.1300/J293v07n01_10

Dutra, L., Stathopoulou, G., Basden, S. L., Leyro, T. M., Powers, M. B., & Otto, M. W. (2008). A meta-analytic review of psychosocial interventions for substance use disorders. *The American Journal of Psychiatry, 165*(2), 179–187. doi:10.1176/appi.ajp.2007.06111851

Dutta, A., McKie, S., & Deakin, J. F. W. (2015). Ketamine and other potential glutamate antidepressants. *Psychiatry Research, 225*(1–2), 1–13. doi:http://dx.doi.org/10.1016/j.psychres.2014.10.028

Duvauchelle, C. L., Sapoznik, T., & Kornetsky, C. (1998). The synergistic effects of combining cocaine and heroin ("speedball") using a progressive-ratio schedule of drug reinforcement. *Pharmacology Biochemistry and Behavior, 61*(3), 297–302. doi:http://dx.doi.org/10.1016/S0091-3057(98)00098-7

Eaddy, J. L. (2013). Prescription and over-the-counter medications. In P. M. Miller, S. A. Ball, M. E. Bates, A. W. Blume, K. M. Kampman, D. J. Kavanagh, M. E. Larimer, N. M. Petry, & P. De Witte (Eds.), *Comprehensive addictive behaviors and disorders: Vol. 1. Principles of addiction* (pp. 755–766). San Diego, CA: Elsevier Academic Press.

Eagle, K. (2014). ADHD impacted by sulfotransferase (SULT1A) inhibition from artificial food colors and plant-based foods. *Physiology & Behavior, 135*, 174–179. doi:10.1016/j.physbeh.2014.06.005

Eagle, M. N. (2011). *From classical to contemporary psychoanalysis: A critique and integration.* New York, NY: Routledge.

Eapen, V., Cavanna, A. E., & Robertson, M. M. (2016). Comorbidities, social impact, and quality of life in Tourette syndrome. *Frontiers in Psychiatry, 7.*

Earnshaw, V., Smith, L., & Copenhaver, M. (2013). Drug addiction stigma in the context of methadone maintenance therapy: An investigation into understudied sources of stigma. *International Journal of Mental Health and Addiction, 11*(1), 110–122. doi:10.1007/s11469-012-9402-5

Easter, M. M. (2012). 'Not all my fault': Genetics, stigma, and personal responsibility for women with eating disorders. *Social Science & Medicine, 75*(8), 1408–1416. doi:10.1016/j.socscimed.2012.05.042

Ebdrup, B. H., Glenthøj, B., Rasmussen, H., Aggernaes, B., Langkilde, A. R., Paulson, O. B., ... Baaré, W. (2010). Hippocampal and caudate volume reductions in antipsychotic-naive first-episode schizophrenia. *Journal of Psychiatry & Neuroscience, 35*(2), 95–104. doi:10.1503/jpn.090049

Echeburúa, E. (2013). Overuse of social networking. In P. M. Miller, S. A. Ball, M. E. Bates, A. W. Blume, K. M. Kampman, D. J. Kavanagh, M. E. Larimer, N. M. Petry, & P. De Witte (Eds.), *Comprehensive addictive behaviors and disorders: Vol. 1. Principles of addiction* (pp. 911–920). San Diego, CA: Elsevier Academic Press.

Edinger, J. D., & Means, M. K. (2005). Cognitive-behavioral therapy for primary insomnia. *Clinical Psychology Review, 25*(5), 539–558. doi:10.1016/j.cpr.2005.04.003

Edvardsen, J., Torgersen, S., Røysamb, E., Lygren, S., Skre, I., Onstad, S., & Øien, P. A. (2008). Heritability of bipolar spectrum disorders. Unity or heterogeneity? *Journal of Affective Disorders, 106*(3), 229–240. doi:10.1016/j.jad.2007.07.001

Edwards, D. A. (2008). *Opposition and defiance: A critical-theoretical approach to understanding subjugation and control through pathologizing hope.* (Doctoral dissertation), The Chicago School of Professional Psychology, Chicago, IL, US. Retrieved from https://libdatabase.newpaltz.edu/login?url=http://search.ebscohost.com/login.aspx?direct=true&db=psyh&AN=2010-99180-369&site=ehost-live Available from EBSCOhost psyh database

Edwards, S., & Harries, M. (2007). No-suicide contracts and no-suicide agreements: A controversial life. *Australasian Psychiatry, 15*(6), 484–489. doi:10.1080/10398560701435846

Edwards, S. D., & Van der Spuy, H. I. (1985). Hypnotherapy as a treatment for enuresis. *Child Psychology & Psychiatry & Allied Disciplines, 26*(1), 161–170. doi:10.1111/j.1469-7610.1985.tb01635.x

Edwards, S. J., & Sachmann, M. D. (2010). No-suicide contracts, no-suicide agreements, and no-suicide assurances: A study of their nature, utilization, perceived effectiveness, and potential to cause harm. *Crisis, 31*(6), 290–302. doi:10.1027/0227-5910/a000048

Eels, T. D. (2015). *Psychotherapy case formulation.* Washington, DC: American Psychological Association.

Efran, J., & Fauber, R. (2015). Spitting in the client's soup: Don't overthink your interventions. *Psychotherapy Networker.* Retrieved from https://www.psychotherapynetworker.org/magazine/recentissues/2015-marapr/item/2638-spitting-in-the-clients-soup

Egger, J. F., & Hebert, C. (2011). Buspirone: Anxiolytic, antidepressant, or neither? *Psychiatric Annals, 41*(3), 166–175.

Ehlers, A. (2006). Understanding and treating complicated grief: What can we learn from posttraumatic stress disorder? *Clinical Psychology: Science and Practice, 13*(2), 135–140. doi:10.1111/j.1468-2850.2006.00015.x

Ehlers, A., & Clark, D. M. (2000). A cognitive model of posttraumatic stress disorder. *Behaviour Research and Therapy, 38*(4), 319–345. doi:10.1016/S0005-7967(99)00123-0

Ehlers, A., Bisson, J., Clark, D. M., Creamer, M., Pilling, S., Richards, D., ... Yule, W. (2010). Do all psychological treatments really work the same in posttraumatic stress disorder? *Clinical Psychology Review, 30*(2), 269–276. doi:10.1016/j.cpr.2009.12.001

Ehlers, A., Clark, D. M., Hackmann, A., McManus, F., & Fennell, M. (2005). Cognitive therapy for post-traumatic stress disorder: Development and evaluation. *Behaviour Research and Therapy, 43*(4), 413–431. doi:https://doi.org/10.1016/j.brat.2004.03.006

Ehlers, A., Hackmann, A., Grey, N., Wild, J., Liness, S., Albert, I., ... Clark, D. M. (2014). A randomized controlled trial of 7-day intensive and standard weekly cognitive therapy for PTSD and emotion-focused supportive therapy. *The American Journal of Psychiatry, 171*(3), 294–304. doi:10.1176/appi.ajp.2013.13040552

Eiberg, H., Berendt, I., & Mohr, J. (1995). Assignment of dominant inherited nocturnal enuresis (ENUR1) to chromosome 13q. *Nature Genetics, 10*(3), 354–356.

Eidlitz-Markus, T., Shuper, A., & Amir, J. (2000). Secondary enuresis: Post-traumatic stress disorder in children after car accidents. *The Israel Medical Association Journal: IMAJ, 2*(2), 135–137.

Eisler, I. (2005). The empirical and theoretical base of family therapy and multiple family day therapy for adolescent anorexia nervosa. *Journal of Family Therapy, 27*(2), 104–131. doi:10.1111/j.1467-6427.2005.00303.x

Eisler, I., Lock, J., & le Grange, D. (2010). Family-based treatments for adolescents with anorexia nervosa: Single-family and multifamily approaches. In C. M. Grilo & J. E. Mitchell (Eds.), *The treatment of eating disorders: A clinical handbook* (pp. 150–174). New York, NY: Guilford Press.

Eizirik, M., & Fonagy, P. (2009). Mentalization-based treatment for patients with borderline personality disorder: An overview. *Revista Brasileira de Psiquiatria, 31*(1), 72–75. doi:10.1590/S1516-44462009000100016

Ekdahl, S., Idvall, E., & Perseius, K.-I. (2014). Family skills training in dialectical behaviour therapy: The experience of the significant others. *Archives of Psychiatric Nursing, 28*(4), 235–241. doi:10.1016/j.apnu.2014.03.002

Ekirch, A. R. (2005). *At day's close: Night in times past.* New York, NY: Norton.

El Haj, M., Antoine, P., Amouyel, P., Lambert, J.-C., Pasquier, F., & Kapogiannis, D. (2016). Apolipoprotein E (APOE) ε4 and episodic memory decline in Alzheimer's disease: A review. *Ageing Research Reviews, 27*, 15–22. doi:10.1016/j.arr.2016.02.002

El-Ansary, A., & Al-Ayadhi, L. (2014). GABAergic/glutamatergic imbalance relative to excessive neuroinflammation in autism spectrum disorders. *Journal of Neuroinflammation, 11*, 189–189. doi:10.1186/s12974-014-0189-0

El-Sayed, M., Steen, R. G., Poe, M. D., Bethea, T. C., Gerig, G., Lieberman, J., & Sikich, L. (2010). Brain volumes in psychotic youth with schizophrenia and mood disorders. *Journal of Psychiatry & Neuroscience, 35*(4), 229–236. doi:10.1503/jpn.090051

El-Seedi, H. R., De Smet, P. A. G. M., Beck, O., Possnert, G., & Bruhn, J. G. (2005). Prehistoric peyote use: Alkaloid analysis and radiocarbon dating of archaeological specimens of Lophophora from Texas. *Journal of Ethnopharmacology, 101*(1–3), 238–242.

Elamin, I., Edwards, M. J., & Martino, D. (2013). Immune dysfunction in Tourette syndrome. *Behavioural Neurology, 27*(1), 23–32. doi:10.1155/2013/329375

Elder, B. L., & Mosack, V. (2011). Genetics of depression: An overview of the current science. *Issues in Mental Health Nursing, 32*(4), 192–202. doi:10.3109/01612840.2010.541588

Elder, J. H. (2008). The gluten-free, casein-free diet in autism: An overview with clinical implications. *Nutrition in Clinical Practice, 23*(6), 583–588. doi:10.1177/0884533608326061

Eleti, S. (2016). Drugs in Alzheimer's disease dementia: An overview of current pharmacological management and future directions. *Psychiatria Danubina, 28*(Suppl-1), 136–140.

Elkins, D. N. (2016). *The human elements of psychotherapy: A nonmedical model of emotional healing.* Washington, DC: American Psychological Association.

Ellenhorn, R. (2015). Assertive community treatment: A 'living-systems' alternative to hospital and residential care. *Psychiatric Annals, 45*(3), 120–125. doi:10.3928/00485713-20150304-06

Elliott, A. (2015). *Psychoanalytic theory: An introduction* (3rd ed.). London, UK: Palgrave Macmillan.

Elliott, R. (2013). Person-centered/experiential psychotherapy for anxiety difficulties: Theory, research and practice. *Person-Centered and Experiential Psychotherapies, 12*(1), 16–32. doi: 10.1080/14779757.2013.767750

Elliott, R., Greenberg, L. S., Watson, J., Timulak, L., & Freire, E. F. (2013). Research on humanistic-experiential psychotherapies. In M. Lambert (Ed.), *Bergin and Garfield's handbook of psychotherapy and behavior change* (6th ed., pp. 495–538). Hoboken, NJ: John Wiley.

Ellis, A. (1998). *How to control your anxiety before it controls you.* New York, NY: Citadel Press.

Ellis, A., & Ellis, D. J. (2011). *Rational emotive behavior therapy.* Washington, DC: American Psychological Association.

Ellis, B. J., Jackson, J. J., & Boyce, W. T. (2006). The stress response systems: Universality and adaptive individual differences. *Developmental Review, 26*(2), 175–212. doi:http://dx.doi.org/10.1016/j.dr.2006.02.004

Ellis, H. (1901). *Studies in the psychology of sex: Sexual inversion* (2nd ed.). London, UK: F. A. Davis.

Elofsson, U. O. E., von Schèele, B., Theorell, T., & Söndergaard, H. P. (2008). Physiological correlates of eye movement desensitization and reprocessing. *Journal of Anxiety Disorders, 22*(4), 622–634. doi:10.1016/j.janxdis.2007.05.012

Elovainio, M., Ferrie, J. E., Gimeno, D., Vogli, R. D., Shipley, M., Brunner, E. J., ... Kivimäki, M. (2009). Organizational justice and sleeping problems: The Whitehall II study. *Psychosomatic Medicine, 71*(3), 334–340. doi:10.1097/PSY.0b013e3181960665

Emanuel, C. (2015). An accidental Pokemon expert: Contemporary psychoanalysis on the autism spectrum. *International Journal of Psychoanalytic Self Psychology, 10*(1), 53–68. doi:10.1080/15551024.2015.977485

Emerson, E. (2004). Deinstitutionalisation in England. *Journal of Intellectual and Developmental Disability, 29*(1), 79–84. doi:10.1080/13668250410001662838

Emerson, E. (2007). Poverty and people with intellectual disabilities. *Mental Retardation and Developmental Disabilities Research Reviews, 13*(2), 107-113. doi:10.1002/mrdd.20144

Emerson, E., & Hatton, C. (2007). Poverty, socio-economic position, social capital and the health of children and adolescents with intellectual disabilities in Britain: A replication. *Journal of Intellectual Disability Research, 51*(11), 866–874. doi:10.1111/j.1365-2788.2007.00951.x

Emerson, E., & Parish, S. (2010). Intellectual disability and poverty: Introduction to the special section. *Journal of Intellectual and Developmental Disability, 35*(4), 221–223. doi:10.3109/13668250.2010.525869

Emerson, E., Shahtahmasebi, S., Lancaster, G., & Berridge, D. (2010). Poverty transitions among families supporting a child with intellectual disability. *Journal of Intellectual and Developmental Disability, 35*(4), 224–234. doi:10.3109/13668250.2010.518562

Emilsson, B., Gudjonsson, G., Sigurdsson, J. F., Baldursson, G., Einarsson, E., Olafsdottir, H., & Young, S. (2011). Cognitive behaviour therapy in medication-treated adults with ADHD and persistent symptoms: A randomized controlled trial. *BMC Psychiatry, 11.* doi:10.1186/1471-244X-11-116

Emmelkamp, P. M. G., Benner, A., Kuipers, A., Feiertag, G. A., Koster, H. C., & van Apeldoorn, F. J. (2006). Comparison of brief dynamic and cognitive-behavioural therapies in avoidant personality disorder. *The British Journal of Psychiatry, 189*(1), 60–64. doi:10.1192/bjp.bp.105.012153

Endleman, R. (1990). *Deviance and psychopathology: The sociology and psychology of outsiders.* Malabar, FL: Krieger.

Endler, N. S. (1988). The origins of electroconvulsive therapy (ECT). *Convulsive Therapy, 4*(1), 5–23.

Engel, G. L. (1977). The need for a new medical model: a challenge for biomedicine. *Science, 196*(4286), 129–136.

Epps, C., & Wright, E. L. (2012). The genetic basis of addiction. In E. O. Bryson (Ed.), *Perioperative addiction: Clinical management of the addicted patient.* (pp. 35–50). New York, NY: Springer Science + Business Media.

Epstein, M. (2006a). *The emperor's new clothes: On being invisible and neglected within the mental health system - A gendered perspective from a "borderline pioneer."* Paper presented at the 16th Annual Conference of The Mental Health Services (theMHS), Townsville, Australia. Retrieved from http://www.takver.com/epstein/articles/emperors_new_clothes_themhs_2006.pdf

Epstein, M. (2006b). "Let's face it! She's just too f*****d"— the politics of borderline personality disorder. Retrieved from http://www.sistersinside.com.au/media/papermepstein.pdf

Epting, F. R., Raskin, J. D., & Burke, T. B. (1994). Who is a homosexual? A critique of the heterosexual-homosexual dimension. *The Humanistic Psychologist, 22,* 353–370. doi:10.1080/08873267.1994.9976959

Erdozain, A. M., & Callado, L. F. (2014). Neurobiological alterations in alcohol addiction: A review. *Adicciones, 26*(4), 360–370. doi:10.20882/adicciones.40

Erickson, S., & Block, S. (2013). The social and communication impact of stuttering on adolescents and their families. *Journal of Fluency Disorders, 38*(4), 311–324. doi:10.1016/j.jfludis.2013.09.003

Erol, R., Booker, D., & Peel, E. (2015). *Women and dementia: A global research review.* London, UK: Alzheimer's Disease International. Retrieved from https://www.alz.co.uk/sites/default/files/pdfs/Women-and-Dementia.pdf.

Erwin, W. E., Williams, D. B., & Speir, W. A. (1998). Delirium tremens. *Southern Medical Journal, 91*(5), 425–432.

Esan, O. B., Ojagbemi, A., & Gureje, O. (2012). Epidemiology of schizophrenia—An update with a focus on developing countries. *International Review of Psychiatry, 24*(5), 387–392.

España, R. A., Schmeichel, B. E., & Berridge, C. W. (2016). Norepinephrine at the nexus of arousal, motivation and relapse. *Brain Research, 1641*(Part B), 207–216. doi:10.1016/j.brainres.2016.01.002

Esterling, B. A., Kiecolt-Glaser, J. K., Bodnar, J. C., & Glaser, R. (1994). Chronic stress, social support, and persistent alterations in the natural killer cell response to cytokines in older adults. *Health Psychology, 13*(4), 291–298. doi:10.1037/0278-6133.13.4.291

Etkin, A. (2012). Neurobiology of anxiety: From neural circuits to novel solutions? *Depression and Anxiety, 29*(5), 355–358. doi:10.1002/da.21957

Etkin, A., & Wager, T. D. (2007). Functional neuroimaging of anxiety: A meta-analysis of emotional processing in PTSD, social anxiety disorder, and specific phobia. *The American Journal of Psychiatry, 164*(10), 1476–1488. doi:10.1176/appi.ajp.2007.07030504

Etzi, J. (2014). The Psychodynamic Diagnostic Manual M Axis: Toward an articulation of what it can assess. *Psychoanalytic Psychology, 31*(1), 119–133. doi:10.1037/a0031907

Ewing, E. S. K., Diamond, G., & Levy, S. (2015). Attachment-based family therapy for depressed and suicidal adolescents: Theory, clinical model and empirical support. *Attachment & Human Development, 17*(2), 136–156. doi:10.1080/14616734.2015.1006384

Exworthy, T. (2006). Commentary: UK perspective on competency to stand trial. *Journal of the American Academy of Psychiatry and the Law, 34*(4), 466–471.

Eysenck, H. J. (1997). Addiction, personality and motivation. *Human Psychopharmacology: Clinical and Experimental, 12*(Suppl 2), S79–S87. doi:10.1002/(SICI)1099-1077(199706)12:2+<S79::AID-HUP905>3.0.CO;2-T

Ezkurdia, I., Juan, D., Rodriguez, J. M., Frankish, A., Diekhans, M., Harrow, J., ... Tress, M. L. (2014). Multiple evidence strands suggest that there may be as few as 19,000 human protein-coding genes. *Human Molecular Genetics, 23*(22), 5866–5878. doi:10.1093/hmg/ddu309

Fabiano, G. A., Pelham, W. E., Jr., Coles, E. K., Gnagy, E. M., Chronis-Tuscano, A., & O'Connor, B. C. (2009). A meta-analysis of behavioral treatments for attention-deficit/hyperactivity disorder. *Clinical Psychology Review, 29*(2), 129–140. doi:10.1016/j.cpr.2008.11.001

Fabiano, G. A., Schatz, N. K., Aloe, A. M., Chacko, A., & Chronis-Tuscano, A. (2015). A systematic review of meta-analyses of psychosocial treatment for attention-deficit/hyperactivity disorder. *Clinical Child and Family Psychology Review, 18*(1), 77–97. doi:10.1007/s10567-015-0178-6

Faer, L. M., Hendriks, A., Abed, R. T., & Figueredo, A. J. (2005). The evolutionary psychology of eating disorders: Female competition for mates or for status? *Psychology and Psychotherapy: Theory, Research and Practice, 78*(3), 397–417. doi:10.1348/147608305X42929

Fairburn, C. G., Cooper, Z., & Shafran, R. (2003). Cognitive behaviour therapy for eating disorders: A "transdiagnostic" theory and treatment. *Behaviour Research and Therapy, 41*(5), 509–528. doi:http://dx.doi.org/10.1016/S0005-7967(02)00088-8

Fairburn, C. G., Cooper, Z., Doll, H. A., O'Connor, M. E., Palmer, R. L., & Grave, R. D. (2013). Enhanced cognitive behaviour therapy for adults with anorexia nervosa: A UK-Italy study. *Behaviour Research and Therapy, 51*(1), R2–R8. doi:10.1016/j.brat.2012.09.010

Fairburn, C. G., Cooper, Z., Doll, H. A., O'Connor, M. E., Bohn, K., Hawker, D. M., ... Palmer, R. L. (2009). Transdiagnostic cognitive-behavioral therapy for patients with eating disorders: A two-site trial with 60-week follow-up. *The American Journal of Psychiatry, 166*(3), 311–319. doi:10.1176/appi.ajp.2008.08040608

Fairburn, C. G., Shafran, R., & Cooper, Z. (1999). A cognitive behavioural theory of anorexia nervosa. *Behaviour Research and Therapy, 37*(1), 1–13. doi:10.1016/S0005-7967(98)00102-8

Fairweather-Schmidt, A. K., & Wade, T. D. (2015). Changes in genetic and environmental influences on disordered eating between early and late adolescence: A longitudinal twin study. *Psychological Medicine, 45*(15), 3249–3258. doi:10.1017/S0033291715001257

Faivre, E., & Hölscher, C. (2013). D-Ala²GIP facilitated synaptic plasticity and reduces plaque load in aged wild type mice and in an Alzheimer's disease mouse model. *Journal of Alzheimer's Disease, 35*(2), 267–283.

Fallon, B. A. (2004). Pharmacotherapy of somatoform disorders. *Journal of Psychosomatic Research, 56*(4), 455–460. doi:http://dx.doi.org/10.1016/S0022-3999(03)00631-7

Fang, A., Matheny, N. L., & Wilhelm, S. (2014). Body dysmorphic disorder. *Psychiatric Clinics of North America, 37*(3), 287–300. doi:10.1016/j.psc.2014.05.003

Fanning, J. R., Berman, M. E., Guillot, C. R., Marsic, A., & McCloskey, M. S. (2014). Serotonin (5-HT) augmentation reduces provoked aggression associated with primary psychopathy traits. *Journal of Personality Disorders, 28*(3), 449–461. doi:10.1521/pedi_2012_26_065

Fanning, J. R., Lee, R., Gozal, D., Coussons-Read, M., & Coccaro, E. F. (2015). Childhood trauma and parental style: Relationship with markers of inflammation, oxidative stress, and aggression in healthy and personality disordered subjects. *Biological Psychology, 112*, 56–65. doi:10.1016/j.biopsycho.2015.09.003

Fanous, A. H. (2015). Can genomics help usher schizophrenia into the age of RDoC and DSM-6? *Schizophrenia Bulletin, 41*(3), 535–541. doi:10.1093/schbul/sbv029

Faraone, S. (1982). Psychiatry and political repression in the Soviet Union. *American Psychologist, 37*(10), 1105–1112. doi:10.1037/0003-066X.37.10.1105

Faraone, S. V., & Biederman, J. (2013). Neurobiology of attention deficit/hyperactivity disorder. In D. S. Charney, J. D. Buxbaum, P. Sklar, & E. J. Nestler (Eds.), *Neurobiology of mental illness* (4th ed., pp. 1034–1047). New York, NY: Oxford University Press.

Faraone, S. V., Perlis, R. H., Doyle, A. E., Smoller, J. W., Goralnick, J. J., Holmgren, M. A., & Sklar, P. (2005). Molecular genetics of attention-deficit/hyperactivity disorder. *Biological Psychiatry, 57*(11), 1313–1323. doi:http://dx.doi.org/10.1016/j.biopsych.2004.11.024

Fardouly, J., & Vartanian, L. R. (2015). Negative comparisons about one's appearance mediate the relationship between Facebook usage and body image concerns. *Body Image, 12*, 82–88. doi:http://dx.doi.org/10.1016/j.bodyim.2014.10.004

Fardouly, J., Diedrichs, P. C., Vartanian, L. R., & Halliwell, E. (2015). Social comparisons on social media: The impact of Facebook on young women's body image concerns and mood. *Body Image, 13*, 38–45. doi:10.1016/j.bodyim.2014.12.002

Farina, N., Llewellyn, D., Isaac, M. G. E. K. N., & Tabet, N. (2017). Vitamin E for Alzheimer's dementia and mild cognitive impairment. *Cochrane Database of Systematic Reviews, 2017*(1). doi:10.1002/14651858.CD002854.pub4

Farke, W., & Anderson, P. (2007). Binge drinking in Europe. *Adicciones, 19*(4), 333–339.

Farrell, J. M., Reiss, N., Shaw, I. A., & Finkelmeier, B. (2014). *The schema therapy clinician's guide: A complete resource for building and delivering individual, group and integrated schema mode treatment programs.* Chichester, UK: Wiley-Blackwell.

Farrelly, S., Jeffery, D., Rüsch, N., Williams, P., Thornicroft, G., & Clement, S. (2015). The link between mental health-related discrimination and suicidality: Service user perspectives. *Psychological Medicine, 45*(10), 2013–2022. doi:10.1017/S0033291714003158

Farstad, S. M., McGeown, L. M., & von Ranson, K. M. (2016). Eating disorders and personality, 2004–2016: A systematic review and meta-analysis. *Clinical Psychology Review, 46*, 91–105. doi:10.1016/j.cpr.2016.04.005

Fatemi, S. H., Aldinger, K. A., Ashwood, P., Bauman, M. L., Blaha, C. D., Blatt, G. J., ... Welsh, J. P. (2012). Consensus paper: Pathological role of the cerebellum in autism. *The Cerebellum, 11*(3), 777–807. doi:10.1007/s12311-012-0355-9

Fatemi, S. H., Folsom, T. D., Rooney, R. J., Mori, S., Kornfield, T. E., Reutiman, T. J., ... Patel, D. H. (2012). The viral theory of schizophrenia revisited: Abnormal placental gene expression and structural changes with lack of evidence for H1N1 viral presence in placentae of infected mice or brains of exposed offspring. *Neuropharmacology, 62*(3), 1290–1298. doi:10.1016/j.neuropharm.2011.01.011

Faubion, S. S., & Rullo, J. E. (2015). Sexual dysfunction in women: A practical approach. *American Family Physician, 92*(4), 281–288.

Faucher, J., Koszycki, D., Bradwejn, J., Merali, Z., & Bielajew, C. (2016). Effects of CBT versus MBSR treatment on social stress reactions in social anxiety disorder. *Mindfulness, 7*(2), 514–526. doi:10.1007/s12671-015-0486-4

Fausto-Sterling, A. (2000). *Sexing the body: Gender politics and the construction of sexuality.* New York, NY: Basic Books.

Fauth-Bühler, M., Mann, K., & Potenza, M. N. (2016). Pathological gambling: A review of the neurobiological evidence relevant for its classification as an addictive disorder. *Addiction Biology.* doi:10.1111/adb.12378

Fava, G. A., Gatti, A., Belaise, C., Guidi, J., & Offidani, E. (2015). Withdrawal symptoms after selective serotonin reuptake inhibitor discontinuation: A systematic review. *Psychotherapy and Psychosomatics, 84*(2), 72–81. doi:10.1159/000370338

Fawcett, J. (2015). Sleep disorders: A major factor in psychiatry. *Psychiatric Annals, 45*(1), 4–4. doi:10.3928/00485713-20150106-01

Fawcett, J., Cameron, R. P., & Schatzberg, A. F. (2010). Mixed anxiety-depressive disorder: An undiagnosed and undertreated severity spectrum? In D. J. Stein, E. Hollander, & B. O. Rothbaum (Eds.), *Textbook of anxiety disorders* (2nd ed., pp. 241–257). Arlington, VA: American Psychiatric Publishing.

Fedoroff, J. P., & Marshall, W. L. (2010). Paraphilias. In D. McKay, J. S. Abramowitz, & S. Taylor (Eds.), *Cognitive-behavioral therapy for refractory cases: Turning failure into success* (pp. 369–384). Washington, DC: American Psychological Association.

Feigenson, K. A., Kusnecov, A. W., & Silverstein, S. M. (2014). Inflammation and the two-hit hypothesis of schizophrenia. *Neuroscience and Biobehavioral Reviews, 38*, 72–93. doi:10.1016/j.neubiorev.2013.11.006

Feiring, C., Cleland, C. M., & Simon, V. A. (2010). Abuse-specific self-schemas and self-functioning: A prospective study of sexually abused youth. *Journal of Clinical Child and Adolescent Psychology, 39*(1), 35–50. doi:10.1080/15374410903401112

Felger, J. C., & Lotrich, F. E. (2013). Inflammatory cytokines in depression: Neurobiological mechanisms and therapeutic implications. *Neuroscience, 246*, 199–229. doi:http://dx.doi.org/10.1016/j.neuroscience.2013.04.060

Femrell, L., Åvall, M., & Lindström, E. (2012). Two-year follow-up of the Lidcombe Program in ten Swedish-speaking children. *Folia Phoniatrica et Logopaedica:International Journal of Phoniatrics, Speech Therapy and Communication Pathology, 64*(5), 248–253. doi:10.1159/000342149

Fennell, D., & Boyd, M. (2014). Obsessive-compulsive disorder in the media. *Deviant Behavior, 35*(9), 669–686. doi:10.1080/01639625.2013.872526

Fennell, D., & Liberato, A. S. Q. (2007). Learning to live with OCD: Labeling, the self, the stigma. *Deviant Behavior, 28*(4), 305–331. doi:10.1080/01639620701233274

Fenton, W. S. (2000). Evolving perspectives on individual psychotherapy for schizophrenia. *Schizophrenia Bulletin, 26*(1), 47–72.

Ferentzy, P., Skinner, W., & Antze, P. (2010). The Serenity Prayer: Secularism and spirituality in Gamblers Anonymous. *Journal of Groups in Addiction & Recovery, 5*(2), 124–144. doi:10.1080/15560351003766125

Ferguson, C. J., Muñoz, M. E., Garza, A., & Galindo, M. (2014). Concurrent and prospective analyses of peer, television and social media influences on body dissatisfaction, eating disorder symptoms and life satisfaction in adolescent girls. *Journal of Youth and Adolescence, 43*(1), 1–14. doi:10.1007/s10964-012-9898-9

Fernández, R., Cortés-Cortés, J., Esteva, I., Gómez-Gil, E., Almaraz, M. C., Lema, E., ... Pásaro, E. (2015). The CYP17 MspA1 Polymorphism and the Gender Dysphoria. *Journal of Sexual Medicine, 12*(6), 1329–1333. doi:10.1111/jsm.12895

Fernández, R., Esteva, I., Gómez-Gil, E., Rumbo, T., Almaraz, M. C., Roda, E., ... Pásaro, E. (2014). The (CA)n polymorphism of ERβ gene is associated with FtM transsexualism. *Journal of Sexual Medicine, 11*(3), 720–728. doi:10.1111/jsm.12398

Fernández-Álvarez, H., Consoli, A. J., & Gómez, B. (2016). Integration in psychotherapy: Reasons and challenges. *American Psychologist, 71*(8), 820–830. doi:10.1037/amp0000100

Ferreira, B. R., Pio-Abreu, J. L., & Januário, C. (2014). Tourette's syndrome and associated disorders: A systematic review. *Trends in Psychiatry and Psychotherapy, 36*(3), 123–133. doi:10.1590/2237-6089-2014-1003

Ferri, M., Amato, L., & Davoli, M. (2006). Alcoholics Anonymous and other 12-step programmes for alcohol dependence (Review). *Cochrane Database of Systematic Reviews, 2006*(3), 1–26. doi:10.1002/14651858. CD005032.pub2

Fervaha, G., & Remington, G. (2013). Neuroimaging findings in schizotypal personality disorder: A systematic review. *Progress in Neuro-Psychopharmacology & Biological Psychiatry, 43*, 96–107. doi:10.1016/j.pnpbp.2012.11.014

Fetters, M. D., Curry, L. A., & Creswell, J. W. (2013). Achieving integration in mixed methods designs—Principles and practices. *Health Services Research, 48*(6, Pt 2), 2134–2156. doi:10.1111/1475-6773.12117

Few, L. R., Lynam, D. R., Maples, J. L., MacKillop, J., & Miller, J. D. (2015). Comparing the utility of DSM-5 Section II and III antisocial personality disorder diagnostic approaches for capturing psychopathic traits. *Personality Disorders: Theory, Research, and Treatment, 6*(1), 64–74. doi:10.1037/per0000096

Feygin, D. L., Swain, J. E., & Leckman, J. F. (2006). The normalcy of neurosis: Evolutionary origins of obsessive-compulsive disorder and related behaviors. *Progress in Neuro-Psychopharmacology & Biological Psychiatry, 30*(5), 854–864. doi:10.1016/j.pnpbp.2006.01.009

Ficks, C. A., & Waldman, I. D. (2014). Candidate genes for aggression and antisocial behavior: A meta-analysis of association studies of the 5HTTLPR and MAOA-uVNTR. *Behavior Genetics, 44*(5), 427–444. doi:10.1007/s10519-014-9661-y

Fields, A. J. (2010). Multicultural research and practice: Theoretical issues and maximizing cultural exchange. *Professional Psychology: Research and Practice, 41*(3), 196–201. doi:10.1037/a0017938

Filip, M., Frankowska, M., Sadakierska-Chudy, A., Suder, A., Szumiec, Ł., Mierzejewski, P., ... Cryan, J. F. (2015). GABAB receptors as a therapeutic strategy in substance use disorders: Focus on positive allosteric modulators. *Neuropharmacology, 88*, 36–47. doi:10.1016/j.neuropharm.2014.06.016

Fink, M. (2009). *Electroconvulsive therapy: A guide for professionals and their patients.* New York, NY: Oxford University Press.

First, M. B. (2014). DSM-5 and paraphilic disorders. *Journal of the American Academy of Psychiatry and the Law, 42*(2), 191–201.

First, M. B., & Gibbon, M. (2004). The Structured Clinical Interview for *DSM-IV* Axis 1 disorders (SCID-I) and the Structured Clinical Interview for *DSM-IV* Axis II disorders (SCID-II). In M. J. Hilsenroth & D. L. Segal (Eds.), *Comprehensive handbook of psychological assessment: Vol. 2. Personality assessment* (pp. 134–143). Hoboken, NJ: John Wiley.

First, M. B., Kendler, K. S., & Leibenluft, E. (2017). The future of the DSM: Implementing a continuous improvement model. *JAMA Psychiatry, 74*(2), 115–116. doi:10.1001/jamapsychiatry.2016.3004

First, M. B., Reed, G. M., Hyman, S. E., & Saxena, S. (2015). The development of the ICD-11 Clinical Descriptions and Diagnostic Guidelines for Mental and Behavioural Disorders. *World Psychiatry, 14*(1), 82–90. doi:10.1002/wps.20189

Fischbach, R. L., Harris, M. J., Ballan, M. S., Fischbach, G. D., & Link, B. G. (2016). Is there concordance in attitudes and beliefs between parents and scientists about autism spectrum disorder? *Autism, 20*(3), 353–363. doi:10.1177/1362361315585310

Fischer, B., Rehm, J., Kim, G., & Kirst, M. (2005). Eyes wide shut?—A conceptual and empirical critique of methadone maintenance treatment. *European Addiction Research, 11*(1), 1–9.

Fishbain, D. A. (1994). Secondary gain concept: Definition problems and its abuse in medical practice. *APS Journal, 3*(4), 264–273. doi:http://dx.doi.org/10.1016/S1058-9139(05)80274-8

Fisher, A. D., Castellini, G., Bandini, E., Casale, H., Fanni, E., Benni, L., ... Rellini, A. H. (2014). Cross-sex hormonal treatment and body uneasiness in individuals with gender dysphoria. *Journal of Sexual Medicine, 11*(3), 709–719. doi:10.1111/jsm.12413

Fisher, H. L., Jones, P. B., Fearon, P., Craig, T. K., Dazzan, P., Morgan, K., ... Morgan, C. (2010). The varying impact of type, timing and frequency of exposure to childhood adversity on its association with adult psychotic disorder. *Psychological Medicine, 40*(12), 1967–1978. doi:http://dx.doi.org/10.1017/S0033291710000231

Fisher, P. L., & Wells, A. (2011). Conceptual models of generalized anxiety disorder. *Psychiatric Annals, 41*(2), 127–132.

Fisher, T. (2011, October 16). The surprising origins of "sleep tight" and other common phrases. *Van Winkle's.*

Fishman, J. R., & Mamo, L. (2001). What's in a disorder? A cultural analysis of medical and pharmaceutical constructions of male and female sexual dysfunction. *Women & Therapy, 24*(1–2), 179–193. doi:10.1300/J015v24n01_20

Fiske, A., Lutz, J., Ciliberti, C. M., Clegg-Kraynok, M. M., Gould, C. E., Stahl, S. T., & Nazem, S. (2016). Mental health and aging. In J. E. Maddux & B. A. Winstead (Eds.), *Psychopathology: Foundations for a contemporary understanding* (4th ed., pp. 341–361). New York, NY: Routledge.

Fitzpatrick, K. K. (2011). Family-based therapy for adolescent anorexia: The nuts and bolts of empowering families to renourish their children. *Adolescent Psychiatry, 1*(4), 267–276. doi:10.2174/2210677411101040267

Flamarique, I., Baeza, I., de la Serna, E., Pons, A., Bernardo, M., & Castro-Fornieles, J. (2015). Long-term effectiveness of electroconvulsive therapy in adolescents with schizophrenia spectrum disorders. *European Child & Adolescent Psychiatry, 24*(5), 517–524. doi:10.1007/s00787-014-0602-3

Flament, M. F., Bissada, H., & Spettigue, W. (2012). Evidence-based pharmacotherapy of eating disorders. *International Journal of Neuropsychopharmacology, 15*(2), 189–207. doi:10.1017/S1461145711000381

Flament, M. F., Buchholz, A., Henderson, K., Obeid, N., Maras, D., Schubert, N., ... Goldfield, G. (2015). Comparative distribution and validity of DSM-IV and DSM-5 diagnoses of eating disorders in adolescents from the community. *European Eating Disorders Review, 23*(2), 100–110. doi:10.1002/erv.2339

Fleck, J. R., & Fleck, D. T. (2013). A person-centred approach to addiction treatment. In M. Cooper, M. O'Hara, P. F. Schmid, & A. C. Bohart (Eds.), *The handbook of person-centred psychotherapy and counselling* (2nd ed., pp. 371–390). New York, NY: Palgrave Macmillan.

Fleming, M. P., & Martin, C. R. (2011). Genes and schizophrenia: A pseudoscientific disenfranchisement of the individual. *Journal of Psychiatric and Mental Health Nursing, 18*(6), 469–478. doi:10.1111/j.1365-2850.2011.01690.x

Flessner, C. A. (2011). Cognitive-behavioral therapy for childhood repetitive behavior disorders: Tic disorders and trichotillomania. *Child and Adolescent Psychiatric Clinics of North America, 20*(2), 319–328. doi:10.1016/j.chc.2011.01.007

Fletcher, K., Nutton, J., & Brend, D. (2015). Attachment, a matter of substance: The potential of attachment theory in the treatment of addictions. *Clinical Social Work Journal, 43*(1), 109–117. doi:10.1007/s10615-014-0502-5

Fletcher, T. B. (2000). Primary nocturnal enuresis: A structural and strategic family systems approach. *Journal of Mental Health Counseling, 22*(1), 32–44.

Flint, J., & Kendler, K. S. (2014). The genetics of major depression. *Neuron, 81*(3), 484–503. doi:http://dx.doi.org/10.1016/j.neuron.2014.01.027

Flor, H., & Turk, D. C. (1989). Psychophysiology of chronic pain: Do chronic pain patients exhibit symptom-specific psychophysiological responses? *Psychological Bulletin, 105*(2), 215–259. doi:10.1037/0033-2909.105.2.215

Flor, H., Birbaumer, N., Schugens, M. M., & Lutzenberger, W. (1992). Symptom-specific psychophysiological responses in chronic pain patients. *Psychophysiology, 29*(4), 452–460. doi:10.1111/j.1469-8986.1992.tb01718.x

Flor, H., Birbaumer, N., & Turk, D. C. (1990). The psychobiology of chronic pain. *Advances in Behaviour Research & Therapy, 12*(2), 47–84. doi:10.1016/0146-6402(90)90007-D

Fluitman, S., Denys, D., Vulink, N., Schutters, S., Heijnen, C., & Westenberg, H. (2010). Lipopolysaccharide-induced cytokine production in obsessive–compulsive disorder and generalized social anxiety disorder. *Psychiatry Research, 178*(2), 313–316. doi:10.1016/j.psychres.2009.05.008

Foa, E. B., & Kozak, M. J. (1986). Emotional processing of fear: Exposure to corrective information. *Psychological Bulletin, 99*(1), 20–35. doi:10.1037/0033-2909.99.1.20

Foa, E. B., & Kozak, M. J. (1991). Emotional processing: Theory, research, and clinical implications for anxiety disorders. In J. D. Safran & L. S. Greenberg (Eds.), *Emotion, psychotherapy, and change.* (pp. 21–49). New York, NY: Guilford Press.

Foa, E. B., Hearst-Ikeda, D., & Perry, K. J. (1995). Evaluation of a brief cognitive-behavioral program for the prevention of chronic PTSD in recent assault victims. *Journal of Consulting and Clinical Psychology, 63*(6), 948–955. doi:10.1037/0022-006X.63.6.948

Foa, E. B., Huppert, J. D., & Cahill, S. P. (2006). Emotional processing theory: An update. In B. O. Rothbaum (Ed.), *Pathological anxiety: Emotional processing in etiology and treatment* (pp. 3–24). New York, NY: Guilford Press.

Follette, V. M., La Bash, H. A. J., & Sewell, M. T. (2010). Adult disclosure of a history of childhood sexual abuse: Implications for behavioral psychotherapy. *Journal of Trauma & Dissociation, 11*(2), 228–243. doi:10.1080/15299730903502953

Fonagy, P. (2001). *Attachment theory and psychoanalysis.* London, UK: Karnac.

Fonagy, P., & Campbell, C. (2015). Bad blood revisited: Attachment and psychoanalysis, 2015. *British Journal of Psychotherapy, 31*(2), 229–250. doi:10.1111/bjp.12150

Fonagy, P., & Luyten, P. (2009). A developmental, mentalization-based approach to the understanding and treatment of borderline personality disorder. *Development and Psychopathology, 21*(4), 1355–1381. doi:10.1017/S0954579409990198

Fonagy, P., & Luyten, P. (2012). Psychodynamic models of personality disorders. In T. A. Widiger (Ed.), *The Oxford handbook of personality disorders* (pp. 345–371). New York, NY: Oxford University Press.

Fone, D., White, J., Farewell, D., Kelly, M., John, G., Lloyd, K., … Dunstan, F. (2014). Effect of neighborhood deprivation and social cohesion on mental health inequality: A multilevel population-based longitudinal study. *Psychological Medicine, 44*(11), 2449–2460. doi:10.1017/S0033291713003255

Fong, T. W., Reid, R. C., & Parhami, I. (2012). Behavioral addictions: Where to draw the lines? *Psychiatric Clinics of North America, 35*(2), 279–296. doi:10.1016/j.psc.2012.03.001

Fontaine, N., & Viding, E. (2008). Genetics of personality disorders. *Psychiatry, 7*(3), 137–141. doi:http://dx.doi.org/10.1016/j.mppsy.2008.01.002

Fonteille, V., & Stoléru, S. (2011). The cerebral correlates of sexual desire: Functional neuroimaging approach. *Sexologies, 20*(3), 142–148. doi:http://dx.doi.org/10.1016/j.sexol.2010.03.011

Forbes, D., Creamer, M., Phelps, A., Bryant, R., McFarlane, A., Devilly, G. J., … Newton, S. (2007). Australian guidelines for the treatment of adults with acute stress disorder and post-traumatic stress disorder. *Australian and New Zealand Journal of Psychiatry, 41*(8), 637–648. doi:10.1080/00048670701449161

Forbes, D., Wolfgang, B., Cooper, J., Creamer, M., & Barton, D. (2009). Post-traumatic stress disorder—best practice GP guidelines. *Australian Family Physician, 38*(3), 106–111.

Forbes, J., & Sashidharan, S. P. (1997). User involvement in services—Incorporation or challenge? *British Journal of Social Work, 27*(4), 481–498. doi:10.1093/oxfordjournals.bjsw.a011237

Ford, C. V., & Folks, D. G. (1985). Conversion disorders: An overview. *Psychosomatics: Journal of Consultation and Liaison Psychiatry, 26*(5), 371–383. doi:10.1016/S0033-3182(85)72845-9

Ford, J. D., & Gómez, J. M. (2015). The relationship of psychological trauma and dissociative and posttraumatic stress disorders to nonsuicidal self-injury and suicidality: A review. *Journal of Trauma & Dissociation, 16*(3), 232–271. doi:10.1080/15299732.2015.989563

Forrest, K. A. (2001). Toward an etiology of dissociative identity disorder: A neurodevelopmental approach. *Consciousness and Cognition, 10*(3), 259–293. doi:http://dx.doi.org/10.1006/ccog.2001.0493

Fortes, I. S., Paula, C. S., Oliveira, M. C., Bordin, I. A., de Jesus Mari, J., & Rohde, L. A. (2016). A cross-sectional study to assess the prevalence of DSM-5 specific learning disorders in representative school samples from the second to sixth grade in Brazil. *European Child & Adolescent Psychiatry, 25*(2), 195–207. doi:10.1007/s00787-015-0708-2

Foster, J. A., & McVey Neufeld, K.-A. (2013). Gut–brain axis: How the microbiome influences anxiety and depression. *Trends in Neurosciences, 36*(5), 305–312. doi:https://doi.org/10.1016/j.tins.2013.01.005

Foucault, M. (1978). *The history of sexuality: Vol. 1. An introduction* (R. Hurley, Trans.). New York, NY: Pantheon Books.

Foundation for a Drug Free World. (n.d.-a). Depressants. Retrieved from http://www.drugfreeworld.org/drugfacts/prescription/depressants.html

Foundation for a Drug Free World. (n.d.-b). What is alcohol? Retrieved from http://www.drugfreeworld.org/drugfacts/alcohol.html

Fowler, K. A., O'Donohue, W., & Lilienfeld, S. O. (2007). Introduction: Personality disorders in perspective. In W. O'Donohue, K. A. Fowler, & S. O. Lilienfeld (Eds.), *Personality disorders: Toward the DSM-V* (pp. 1–19). Thousand Oaks, CA: SAGE Publications.

Foxcroft, D. R., Coombes, L., Wood, S., Allen, D., & Almeida Santimano, N. M. L. M., M. T. (2016). Motivational interviewing for the prevention of alcohol misuse in young adults (Review). *Cochrane Database of Systematic Reviews, 2016*(7), 1–221. doi:10.1002/14651858.CD008063.pub2

France, C. M., Lysaker, P. H., & Robinson, R. P. (2007). The 'chemical imbalance' explanation for depression: Origins, lay endorsement, and clinical implications. *Professional Psychology: Research and Practice, 38*(4), 411–420. doi:10.1037/0735-7028.38.4.411

Frances, A. (2010a, July 6). Normality is an endangered species: Psychiatric fads and overdiagnosis. *Psychiatric Times.* Retrieved from http://www.psychiatrictimes.com/dsm-5/normality-endangered-species-psychiatric-fads-and-overdiagnosis

Frances, A. (2010b). Will DSM5 contain or worsen the epidemic of autism? Retrieved from https://www.psychologytoday.com/blog/dsm5-in-distress/201003/will-dsm5-contain-or-worsen-the-epidemic-autism

Frances, A. (2012a). DSM-5 is a guide, not a bible: Simply ignore its 10 worst changes (December 3, 2012). Retrieved from http://www.huffingtonpost.com/allen-frances/dsm-5_b_2227626.html

Frances, A. J. (2012b). Mislabeling medical illness as mental disorder. Retrieved from https://www.psychologytoday.com/blog/dsm5-in-distress/201212/mislabeling-medical-illness-mental-disorder

Frances, A. J. (2013a). Bad news: DSM-5 refuses to correct somatic symptom disorder. Retrieved from https://www.psychologytoday.com/blog/dsm5-in-distress/201301/bad-news-dsm-5-refuses-correct-somatic-symptom-disorder

Frances, A. (2013b, November 26). Psychosis risk syndrome is back. *Psychiatric Times.* Retrieved from http://www.psychiatrictimes.com/blogs/dsm-5/psychosis-risk-syndrome-back

Frances, A. (2013c). *Saving normal: An insider's revolt against out-of-control psychiatric diagnosis, DSM-5, big pharma, and the medicalization of ordinary life.* New York, NY: Morrow.

Frances, A. (2014). Resuscitating the biopsychosocial model. *The Lancet Psychiatry, 1*(7), 496–497. doi:10.1016/S2215-0366(14)00058-3

Frances, A. (2015). Don't throw out the baby with the bath water. *Australian and New Zealand Journal of Psychiatry, 49*(6), 577. doi:10.1177/0004867415579467

Frances, A., & Chapman, S. (2013). DSM-5 somatic symptom disorder mislabels medical illness as mental disorder. *Australian and New Zealand Journal of Psychiatry, 47*(5), 483–484. doi:10.1177/0004867413484525

Frances, A. J., & Nardo, J. M. (2013). ICD-11 should not repeat the mistakes made by DSM-5. *The British Journal of Psychiatry, 203*(1), 1–2.

Frances, A. J., & Widiger, T. (2012). Psychiatric diagnosis: Lessons from the DSM-IV past and cautions for the DSM-5 future. *Annual Review of Clinical Psychology, 8*, 109–130. doi:10.1146/annurev-clinpsy-032511-143102

Franck, J., & Jayaram-Lindström, N. (2013). Pharmacotherapy for alcohol dependence: Status of current treatments. *Current Opinion in Neurobiology, 23*(4), 692–699. doi:10.1016/j.conb.2013.05.005

Franco-Paredes, K., Mancilla-Díaz, J. M., Vázquez-Arévalo, R., López-Aguilar, X., & Álvarez-Rayón, G. (2005). Perfectionism and eating disorders: A review of the literature. *European Eating Disorders Review, 13*(1), 61–70. doi:10.1002/erv.605

Frank, M., & Cavanna, A. E. (2013). Behavioural treatments for Tourette syndrome: An evidence-based review. *Behavioural Neurology, 27*(1), 105–117. doi:10.1155/2013/134863

Franke, B., Faraone, S. V., Asherson, P., Buitelaar, J., Bau, C. H. D., Ramos-Quiroga, J. A., … Reif, A. (2012). The genetics of attention deficit/hyperactivity disorder in adults, a review. *Molecular Psychiatry, 17*(10), 960–987. doi:10.1038/mp.2011.138

Frankenburg, F. R., & Baldessarini, R. J. (2008). Neurosyphilis, malaria, and the discovery of antipsychotic agents. *Harvard Review of Psychiatry, 16*(5), 299–307. doi:10.1080/10673220802432350

Frankl, V. E. (1959). *Man's search for meaning* (I. Lasch, Trans.). New York, NY: Pocket Books.

Frankl, V. E. (1968). *The doctor and the soul: From psychotherapy to logotherapy* (R. Winston & C. Winston, Trans.). New York, NY: Alfred A. Knopf.

Franklin, J. C., Ribeiro, J. D., Fox, K. R., Bentley, K. H., Kleiman, E. M., Huang, X., ... Nock, M. K. (2017). Risk factors for suicidal thoughts and behaviors: A meta-analysis of 50 years of research. *Psychological Bulletin, 143*(2), 187–232. doi:10.1037/bul0000084

Franklin, M. E., Goss, A., & March, J. S. (2012). Cognitive behavioural therapy in obsessive-compulsive disorder: State of the art. In J. Zohar (Ed.), *Obsessive compulsive disorder: Current science and clinical practice* (pp. 58–74). Chichester, UK: Wiley-Blackwell.

Fransella, F. (1987). Stuttering to fluency via reconstruing. In R. A. Neimeyer & G. J. Neimeyer (Eds.), *Personal construct therapy casebook* (pp. 290–308). New York, NY: Springer.

Frederick, D. A., Sandhu, G., Scott, T., & Akbari, Y. (2016). Reducing the negative effects of media exposure on body image: Testing the effectiveness of subvertising and disclaimer labels. *Body Image, 17,* 171–174. doi:10.1016/j.bodyim.2016.03.009

Fredericks, D. W., Carr, J. E., & Larry Williams, W. (1998). Overview of the treatment of rumination disorder for adults in a residential setting. *Journal of Behavior Therapy and Experimental Psychiatry, 29*(1), 31–40. doi:http://dx.doi.org/10.1016/S0005-7916(98)00002-0

Freed, C. R. (2012). Historical perspectives on addiction. In H. J. Shaffer, D. A. LaPlante, & S. E. Nelson (Eds.), *APA addiction syndrome handbook: Vol. 1. Foundations, influences, and expressions of addiction.* (pp. 27–47). Washington, DC: American Psychological Association.

Freedman, R., Lewis, D. A., Michels, R., Pine, D. S., Schultz, S. K., Tamminga, C. A., ... Yager, J. (2013). The initial field trials of DSM-5: New blooms and old thorns. *The American Journal of Psychiatry, 170*(1), 1–5.

Freeman, C. (2006). Psychological and drug therapies for post-traumatic stress disorder. *Psychiatry, 5*(7), 231–237. doi:http://dx.doi.org/10.1053/j.mppsy.2006.06.001

Fresco, D. M., Mennin, D. S., Heimberg, R. G., & Ritter, M. (2013). Emotion regulation therapy for generalized anxiety disorder. *Cognitive and Behavioral Practice, 20*(3), 282–300. doi:10.1016/j.cbpra.2013.02.001

Freud, A. (1966). *The ego and the mechanisms of defense* (C. Baines, Trans.). London, UK: Karnac Books. (Original work published 1937)

Freud, S. (1914). *Psychopathology of everyday life* (A. A. Brill, Trans.). New York, NY: Macmillan.

Freud, S. (1953). Mourning and melancholia (J. Strachey, Trans.). In J. Strachey, A. Freud, A. Strachey, & A. Tyson (Eds.), *The standard edition of the complete psychological works of Sigmund Freud* (Vol. 14, pp. 243–258). London, UK: Hogarth Press & The Institute of Psycho-analysis. (Original work published 1917)

Freud, S. (1955a). Analysis of a phobia in a five-year-old boy (J. Strachey, Trans.). In J. Strachey, A. Freud, A. Strachey, & A. Tyson (Eds.), *The standard edition of the complete psychological works of Sigmund Freud* (Vol. 10, pp. 3–149). London, UK: Hogarth Press & The Institute of Psycho-analysis. (Original work published 1909)

Freud, S. (1955b). Notes upon a case of obsessional neurosis (J. Strachey, Trans.). In J. Strachey, A. Freud, A. Strachey, & A. Tyson (Eds.), *The standard edition of the complete psychological works of Sigmund Freud* (Vol. 10, pp. 153–326). London, UK: Hogarth Press & The Institute of Psycho-analysis. (Original work published 1909)

Freud, S. (1959). Neurosis and psychosis (J. Riviere, Trans.) *Collected papers* (Vol. 2, pp. 250–254). New York, NY: Basic Books. (Original work published 1924)

Freud, S. (1960). *The ego and the id.* New York, NY: Norton. (Original work published 1923)

Freud, S. (1962). *Three essays on the theory of sexuality* (J. Strachey, Trans.). New York, NY: Avon Books. (Original work published 1905)

Freud, S. (1965a). *The interpretation of dreams* (J. Strachey, Trans.). New York, NY: Avon Books. (Original work published 1900)

Freud, S. (1965b). *New introductory lectures on psychoanalysis* (J. Strachey, Trans.). New York, NY: Norton. (Original work published 1933)

Frías, Á., Palma, C., Farriols, N., & González, L. (2016). Sexuality-related issues in borderline personality disorder: A comprehensive review. *Personality and Mental Health, 10*(3), 216–231. doi:10.1002/pmh.1330

Friedan, J. (2015). Don't like ICD-10? Don't worry—ICD-11 is on the horizon. Retrieved from http://www.medpagetoday.com/PracticeManagement/InformationTechnology/50256

Friederich, H. C., Walther, S., Bendszus, M., Biller, A., Thomann, P., Zeigermann, S., ... Herzog, W. (2012). Grey matter abnormalities within cortico-limbic-striatal circuits in acute and weight-restored anorexia nervosa patients. *NeuroImage, 59.* doi:10.1016/j.neuroimage.2011.09.042

Friedl, M. C., & Draijer, N. (2000). Dissociative disorders in Dutch psychiatric inpatients. *The American Journal of Psychiatry, 157*(6), 1012–1013.

Friedlander, L., & Desrocher, M. (2006). Neuroimaging studies of obsessive-compulsive disorder in adults and children. *Clinical Psychology Review, 26*(1), 32–49. doi:http://dx.doi.org/10.1016/j.cpr.2005.06.010

Friedman, M. (1977). Type A behavior pattern: some of its pathophysiological components. *Bulletin of the New York Academy of Medicine, 53*(7), 593–604.

Friedman, M. J., & Davidson, J. R. T. (2014). Pharmacotherapy for PTSD. In M. J. Friedman, T. M. Keane, & P. A. Resick (Eds.), *Handbook of PTSD: Science and practice* (2nd ed., pp. 482–501). New York, NY: Guilford Press.

Friedman, M., & Rosenman, R. H. (1959). Association of specific overt behavior pattern with blood and cardiovascular findings; blood cholesterol level, blood clotting time, incidence of arcus senilis, and clinical coronary artery disease. *Journal of the American Medical Association, 169*(12), 1286–1296.

Friedman, R. (2013). The book stops here. *The New York Times.* Retrieved from http://www.nytimes.com/2013/05/21/health/the-dsm-5-as-a-guide-not-a-bible.html?_r=0

Friedman, R. A. (2014). Antidepressants' black-box warning—10 years later. *The New England Journal of Medicine, 371*(18), 1666–1668. doi:10.1056/NEJMp1408480

Frith, C. D. (2004). Schizophrenia and theory of mind. *Psychological Medicine, 34*(3), 385–389. doi:10.1017/S0033291703001326

Frith, C. D., & Corcoran, R. (1996). Exploring 'theory of mind' in people with schizophrenia. *Psychological Medicine, 26*(3), 521–530. doi:10.1017/S0033291700035601

Fromm, M. (2004). *Introduction to the repertory grid interview.* New York, NY: Waxmann Münster. (Original work published 1995)

Fromm-Reichmann, F. (1939). Transference problems in schizophrenics. *The Psychoanalytic Quarterly, 8,* 412–426.

Fromm-Reichmann, F. (1948). Notes on the development of treatment of schizophrenics by psychoanalytic therapy. *Psychiatry: Journal for the Study of Interpersonal Processes, 11,* 263–273.

Fromm-Reichmann, F. (1954). Psychotherapy of schizophrenia. *The American Journal of Psychiatry, 111,* 410–419.

Frontline. (2015). Jenny McCarthy: "We're not an anti-vaccine movement ... We're pro-safe vaccine." Retrieved from http://www.pbs.org/wgbh/frontline/article/jenny-mccarthy-were-not-an-anti-vaccine-movement-were-pro-safe-vaccine/

Frost, N. (Ed.) (2011). *Qualitative research methods in psychology: Combining core approaches.* Maidenhead, UK: McGraw Hill/Open University Press.

Frost, R. O., Steketee, G., & Tolin, D. F. (2011). Comorbidity in hoarding disorder. *Depression and Anxiety, 28*(10), 876–884. doi:10.1002/da.20861

Fruzzetti, A. E., & Payne, L. (2015). Couple therapy and borderline personality disorder. In A. S. Gurman, J. L. Lebow, & D. K. Snyder (Eds.), *Clinical handbook of couple therapy* (5th ed., pp. 606–634). New York, NY: Guilford Press.

Fryers, T., Melzer, D., Jenkins, R., & Brugha, T. (2005). The distribution of the common mental disorders: Social inequalities in Europe. *Clinical Practice and Epidemiology in Mental Health, 1.* doi:10.1186/1745-0179-1-14

Ftanou, M., Cox, G., Nicholas, A., Spittal, M. J., Machlin, A., Robinson, J., & Pirkis, J. (2017). Suicide prevention public service announcements (PSAs): Examples from around the world. *Health Communication, 32*(4), 493–501. doi:10.1080/10410236.2016.1140269

Fuchs, D., Mock, D., Morgan, P. L., & Young, C. L. (2003). Responsiveness-to-intervention: Definitions, evidence, and implications for the learning disabilities construct. *Learning Disabilities Research & Practice, 18*(3), 157–171. doi:10.1111/1540-5826.00072

Fujii, Y., Suzuki, K., Sato, T., Murakami, Y., & Takahashi, T. (1998). Multiple personality disorder in Japan. *Psychiatry and Clinical Neurosciences, 52*(3), 299–302.

Fujisawa, T. X., Yatsuga, C., Mabe, H., Yamada, E., Masuda, M., & Tomoda, A. (2015). Anorexia nervosa during adolescence is associated with decreased gray matter volume in the inferior frontal gyrus. *PLOS One, 10*(6), e0128548. doi:10.1371/journal.pone.0128548

Fuller, R. K., Branchey, L., Brightwell, D. R., Derman, R. M., Emrick, C. D., Iber, F. L., ... et al. (1986). Disulfiram treatment of alcoholism. A Veterans Administration cooperative study. *JAMA: Journal of the American Medical Association, 256*(11), 1449–1455.

Fung, L. K., Mahajan, R., Nozzolillo, A., Bernal, P., Krasner, A., Jo, B., ... Hardan, A. Y. (2016). Pharmacologic treatment of severe irritability and problem behaviors in autism: A systematic review and meta-analysis. *Pediatrics, 137 Suppl 2*, S124–S135. doi:10.1542/peds.2015-2851K

Funtowicz, M. N., & Widiger, T. A. (1999). Sex bias in the diagnosis of personality disorders: An evaluation of DSM-IV criteria. *Journal of Abnormal Psychology, 108*(2), 195–201. doi:10.1037/0021-843X.108.2.195

Furtado, M., & Katzman, M. A. (2015). Neuroinflammatory pathways in anxiety, posttraumatic stress, and obsessive compulsive disorders. *Psychiatry Research, 229*(1–2), 37–48. doi:10.1016/j.psychres.2015.05.036

Fusar-Poli, P., & Yung, A. R. (2012). Should attenuated psychosis syndrome be included in DSM-5? *The Lancet, 379*(9816), 591–592. doi:10.1016/S0140-6736(11)61507-9

Fusar-Poli, P., Smieskova, R., Kempton, M. J., Ho, B. C., Andreasen, N. C., & Borgwardt, S. (2013). Progressive brain changes in schizophrenia related to antipsychotic treatment? A meta-analysis of longitudinal MRI studies. *Neuroscience and Biobehavioral Reviews, 37*(8), 1680–1691. doi:10.1016/j.neubiorev.2013.06.001

Gabbard, G. O. (2014). *Psychodynamic psychiatry in clinical practice* (5th ed.). Arlington, VA: American Psychiatric Publishing.

Gable, R. A., Quinn, M. M., Rutherford, R. B., Jr., Howell, K. W., & Hoffman, C. C. (1999). *Addressing student problem behavior-part II: Conducting a functional behavioral assessment.* Washington, DC: American Institutes for Research.

Gaebel, W., Zielasek, J., & Cleveland, H.-R. (2012). Classifying psychosis—Challenges and opportunities. *International Review of Psychiatry, 24*(6), 538–548. doi:10.3109/09540261.2012.737313

Gaebel, W., Zielasek, J., & Falkai, P. (2015). Psychotic disorders in ICD-11. *Die Psychiatrie: Grundlagen & Perspektiven, 12*(2), 71–76.

Gaetz, W., Bloy, L., Wang, D. J., Port, R. G., Blaskey, L., Levy, S. E., & Roberts, T. P. L. (2014). GABA estimation in the brains of children on the autism spectrum: Measurement precision and regional cortical variation. *NeuroImage, 86*, 1–9. doi:http://dx.doi.org/10.1016/j.neuroimage.2013.05.068

Gaffney, G. R., Lurie, S. F., & Berlin, F. S. (1984). Is there familial transmission of pedophilia? *Journal of Nervous and Mental Disease, 172*(9), 546–548. doi:10.1097/00005053-198409000-00006

Gahlsdorf, T., Krause, R., & Beal, M. W. (2007). Efficacy of St. John's wort for treating mild to moderate depression. *Complementary Health Practice Review, 12*(3), 184–195.

Gaither, G. A., Rosenkranz, R. R., & J., P. J. (1998). Sexual disorders. In J. J. Plaud & G. H. Eifert (Eds.), *From behavior theory to behavior therapy* (pp. 152–171). Needham Heights, MA: Allyn & Bacon.

Gambini, B. (2017). Research consortium develops evidence-based diagnostic model for mental illness [Press release]. Retrieved from http://www.buffalo.edu/news/releases/2017/03/044.html

Gambrill, E. (2014). The *Diagnostic and Statistical Manual of Mental Disorders* as a major form of dehumanization in the modern world. *Research on Social Work Practice, 24*(1), 13–36. doi:10.1177/1049731513499411

Gandal, M. J., Haney, J. R., Parikshak, N. N., Leppa, V., Ramaswami, G., Hartl, C., ... Geschwind, D. H. (2018). Shared molecular neuropathology across major psychiatric disorders parallels polygenic overlap. *Science, 359*(6376), 693–697.

Gannon, L. (2002). A critique of evolutionary psychology. *Psychology, Evolution & Gender, 4*(2), 173–218. doi:10.1080/1461666031000063665

Gao, K., Wu, R., Grunze, H., & Calabrese, J. R. (2015). Pharmacological treatment bipolar depression. In A. Yildiz, P. Ruiz, & C. B. Nemeroff (Eds.), *The bipolar book: History, neurobiology, and treatment* (pp. 281–297). New York, NY: Oxford University Press.

Garb, H. N. (1998). Recommendations for training in the use of the Thematic Apperception Test (TAT). *Professional Psychology: Research and Practice, 29*(6), 621–622. doi:10.1037/0735-7028.29.6.621.b

Garb, H. N., Lilienfeld, S. O., & Fowler, K. A. (2016). Psychological assessment and clinical judgment. In J. E. Maddux & B. A. Winstead (Eds.), *Psychopathology: Foundations for a contemporary understanding* (4th ed., pp. 111–126). New York, NY: Routledge.

García-Campayoa, J., Fayed, N., Serrano-Blanco, A., & Roca, M. (2009). Brain dysfunction behind functional symptoms: Neuroimaging and somatoform, conversive, and dissociative disorders. *Current Opinion in Psychiatry, 22*(2), 224–231. doi:10.1097/YCO.0b013e3283252d43

Gardner, M., Barajas, R. G., & Brooks-Gunn, J. (2010). Neighborhood influences on substance use etiology: Is where you live important? In L. Scheier (Ed.), *Handbook of drug use etiology: Theory, methods, and empirical findings.* (pp. 423–441). Washington, DC: American Psychological Association.

Garety, P. A., Fowler, D. G., Freeman, D., Bebbington, P., Dunn, G., & Kuipers, E. (2008). Cognitive-behavioural therapy and family intervention for relapse prevention and symptom reduction in psychosis: Randomised controlled trial. *The British Journal of Psychiatry, 192*(6), 412–423. doi:10.1192/bjp.bp.107.043570

Garfinkel, S. N., & Liberzon, I. (2009). Neurobiology of PTSD: A review of neuroimaging findings. *Psychiatric Annals, 39*(6), 370–372. doi:10.3928/00485713-20090527-01

Garrett, A., & Chang, K. (2008). The role of the amygdala in bipolar disorder development. *Development and Psychopathology, 20*(4), 1285–1296. doi:10.1017/S0954579408000618

Gaysina, D., Fergusson, D. M., Leve, L. D., Horwood, J., Reiss, D., Shaw, D. S., ... Harold, G. T. (2013). Maternal smoking during pregnancy and offspring conduct problems: Evidence from 3 independent genetically sensitive research designs. *JAMA Psychiatry, 70*(9), 956–963. doi:10.1001/jamapsychiatry.2013.127

Geddes, J. R., & Miklowitz, D. J. (2013). Treatment of bipolar disorder. *The Lancet, 381*(9878), 1672–1682. doi:http://dx.doi.org/10.1016/S0140-6736(13)60857-0

Gee, B. A., Hood, H. K., & Antony, M. M. (2013). Anxiety disorders—A historical perspective. In T. G. Plante (Ed.), *Abnormal psychology across the ages: Vol. 2. Disorders and treatments* (pp. 31–47). Santa Barbara, CA: Praeger/ABC-CLIO.

Gehrman, P. R., Keenan, B. T., Byrne, E. M., & Pack, A. I. (2015). Genetics of sleep disorders. *Psychiatric Clinics of North America, 38*(4), 667–681. doi:10.1016/j.psc.2015.07.004

Gelernter, J., & Kranzler, H. R. (2015). Genetics of addiction. In M. Galanter, H. D. Kleber, & K. T. Brady (Eds.), *The American Psychiatric Publishing textbook of substance abuse treatment* (5th ed., pp. 25–45). Arlington, VA: American Psychiatric Publishing.

Geller, R. E., & Goldberg, J. F. (2007). A review of evidence-based psychotherapies for bipolar disorder. *Primary Psychiatry, 14*(3), 59–69.

General Medical Council. (2010). *General Medical Council, Fitness to Practise Panel Hearing, 24 May 2010, Andrew Wakefield, determination of serious professional misconduct.* Retrieved from https://web.archive.org/web/20110809092833/http://www.gmc-uk.org/Wakefield_SPM_and_SANCTION.pdf_32595267.pdf

Gentile, J. P., Dillon, K. S., & Gillig, P. M. (2013). Psychotherapy and pharmacotherapy for patients with dissociative identity disorder. *Innovations in Clinical Neuroscience, 10*(2), 22–29.

Géonet, M., De Sutter, P., & Zech, E. (2013). Cognitive factors in female hypoactive sexual desire disorder. *Sexologies: European Journal of Sexology and Sexual Health / Revue européenne de sexologie et de santé sexuelle, 22*(1), e9–e15. doi:10.1016/j.sexol.2012.01.011

George, B., & Klijn, A. (2013). A modern name for schizophrenia (PSS) would diminish self-stigma. *Psychological Medicine, 43*(7), 1555–1557. doi:10.1017/S0033291713000895

Georgiadis, J. R. (2011). Exposing orgasm in the brain: A critical eye. *Sexual and Relationship Therapy, 26*(4), 342–355. doi:10.1080/14681994.2011.647904

Georgiadis, J. R., & Kringelbach, M. L. (2012). The human sexual response cycle: Brain imaging evidence linking sex to other pleasures. *Progress in Neurobiology, 98*(1), 49–81. doi:http://dx.doi.org/10.1016/j.pneurobio.2012.05.004

Gerasimov, M. R., & Dewey, S. L. (1999). Gamma-vinyl gamma-aminobutyric acid attenuates the synergistic elevations of nucleus accumbens dopamine produced by a cocaine/heroin (speedball) challenge. *European Journal of Pharmacology, 380*(1), 1–4.

Gergen, K. J. (2015). *An invitation to social construction* (3rd ed.). Thousand Oaks, CA: SAGE Publications.

Gergen, K. J., & McNamee, S. (2000). From disordering discourse to transformative dialogue. In R. A. Neimeyer & J. D. Raskin (Eds.), *Constructions of disorder: Meaning-making frameworks for psychotherapy* (pp. 333–349). Washington, DC: American Psychological Association.

Gernsbacher, M. A., Dawson, M., & Hill Goldsmith, H. (2005). Three reasons not to believe in an autism epidemic. *Current Directions in Psychological Science, 14*(2), 55–58. doi:10.1111/j.0963-7214.2005.00334.x

Gerrard, P., & Malcolm, R. (2007). Mechanisms of modafinil: A review of current research. *Neuropsychiatric Disease and Treatment, 3*(3), 349–364.

Gerstley, L. J., Alterman, A. I., McLellan, A. T., & Woody, G. E. (1990). Antisocial personality disorder in patients with substance abuse disorders: A problematic diagnosis? *The American Journal of Psychiatry, 147*(2), 173–178. doi:10.1176/ajp.147.2.173

Ghaemi, N. (2014). Psychopathology for what purpose? *Acta Psychiatrica Scandinavica, 129*(1), 78–79. doi:10.1111/acps.12198

Ghaemi, S. N. (2009). The rise and fall of the biopsychosocial model. *The British Journal of Psychiatry, 195*(1), 3–4. doi:10.1192/bjp.bp.109.063859

Ghaemi, S. N. (2010). *The rise and fall of the biopsychosocial model: Reconciling art and science in psychiatry.* Baltimore, MD: Johns Hopkins University Press.

Ghaemi, S. N., & Vöhringer, P. A. (2011). The heterogeneity of depression: An old debate renewed. *Acta Psychiatrica Scandinavica, 124*(6), 497–497. doi:10.1111/j.1600-0447.2011.01746.x

Ghaemi, S. N., Vohringer, P. A., & Whitham, E. A. (2013). Antidepressants from a public health perspective: Re-examining effectiveness, suicide, and carcinogenicity. *Acta Psychiatrica Scandinavica, 127*(2), 89–93. doi:10.1111/acps.12059

Ghanizadeh, A. (2010). Comorbidity of enuresis in children with attention-deficit/hyperactivity disorder. *Journal of Attention Disorders, 13*(5), 464–467. doi:10.1177/1087054709332411

Ghanizadeh, A. (2013). Agreement between Diagnostic and Statistical Manual of Mental Disorders, Fourth Edition, and the proposed DSM-V attention deficit hyperactivity disorder diagnostic criteria: An exploratory study. *Comprehensive Psychiatry, 54*(1), 7–10. doi:http://dx.doi.org/10.1016/j.comppsych.2012.06.001

Ghanizadeh, A., & Haddad, B. (2015). The effect of dietary education on ADHD, a randomized controlled clinical trial. *Annals of General Psychiatry, 14.* doi:10.1186/s12991-015-0050-6

Ghanizadeh, A., Tordjman, S., & Jaafari, N. (2015). Aripiprazole for treating irritability in children & adolescents with autism: A systematic review. *The Indian Journal of Medical Research, 142*(3), 269–275. doi:10.4103/0971-5916.166584

Ghofrani, H. A., Osterloh, I. H., & Grimminger, F. (2006). Sildenafil: From angina to erectile dysfunction to pulmonary hypertension and beyond. *Nature Reviews. Drug Discovery, 5*(8), 689–702.

Giacobbe, P., & Kennedy, S. H. (2006). Deep brain stimulation for treatment-resistant depression: A psychiatric perspective. *Current Psychiatry Reports, 8*(6), 437–444.

Gibney, P. (2006). The double bind theory: Still crazy-making after all these years. *Psychotherapy in Australia, 12*(3), 48–55.

Gibson, A. (2014). Insulin coma therapy. *The Psychiatric Bulletin, 38*(4), 198–198. doi:10.1192/pb.38.4.198

Gibson, S., Brand, S. L., Burt, S., Boden, Z. V. R., & Benson, O. (2013). Understanding treatment non-adherence in schizophrenia and bipolar disorder: A survey of what service users do and why. *BMC Psychiatry, 13.*

Giesen-Bloo, J., van Dyck, R., Spinhoven, P., van Tilburg, W., Dirksen, C., van Asselt, T., ... Arntz, A. (2006). Outpatient Psychotherapy for Borderline Personality Disorder: Randomized Trial of Schema-Focused Therapy vs Transference-Focused Psychotherapy. *Archives of General Psychiatry, 63*(6), 649–658. doi:10.1001/archpsyc.63.6.649

Gigante, A. D., Lafer, B., & Yatham, L. N. (2012). Long-acting injectable antipsychotics for the maintenance treatment of bipolar disorder. *CNS Drugs, 26*(5), 403–420. doi:10.2165/11631310-000000000-00000

Gilbertson, M. W., Shenton, M. E., Ciszewski, A., Kasai, K., Lasko, N. B., Orr, S. P., & Pitman, R. K. (2002). Smaller hippocampal volume predicts pathologic vulnerability to psychological trauma. *Nature Neuroscience, 5*(11), 1242–1247. doi:10.1038/nn958

Gill, J. H., DeWitt, J. R., & Nielson, H. C. (1986). Dissociation of maze performance in the original learning state following drugged-state feeding. *Physiological Psychology, 14*(3-4), 104–110.

Gill, J. M., & Szanton, S. (2011). Inflammation and traumatic stress: The society to cells resiliency model to support integrative interventions. *Journal of the American Psychiatric Nurses Association, 17*(6), 404–416. doi:10.1177/1078390311418652

Gill, J. M., Saligan, L., Woods, S., & Page, G. (2009). PTSD is associated with an excess of inflammatory immune activities. *Perspectives In Psychiatric Care, 45*(4), 262–277. doi:10.1111/j.1744-6163.2009.00229.x

Gillan, C. M., Apergis-Schoute, A. M., Morein-Zamir, S., Urcelay, G. P., Sule, A., Fineberg, N. A., ... Robbins, T. W. (2015). Functional neuroimaging of avoidance habits in obsessive-compulsive disorder. *The American Journal of Psychiatry, 172*(3), 284–293. doi:10.1176/appi.ajp.2014.14040525

Gilleland, J., Suveg, C., Jacob, M. L., & Thomassin, K. (2009). Understanding the medically unexplained: Emotional and familial influences on children's somatic functioning. *Child: Care, Health and Development, 35*(3), 383–390. doi:10.1111/j.1365-2214.2009.00950.x

Gillespie, N. A., Zhu, G., Heath, A. C., Hickie, I. B., & Martin, N. G. (2000). The genetic aetiology of somatic distress. *Psychological Medicine, 30*(5), 1051–1061. doi:10.1017/S0033291799002640

Gillies, D., Sinn, J. K., Lad, S. S., Leach, M. J., & Ross, M. J. (2012). Polyunsaturated fatty acids (PUFA) for attention deficit hyperactivity disorder (ADHD) in children and adolescents. *Cochrane Database of Systematic Reviews*(7), CD007986. doi:10.1002/14651858.CD007986.pub2

Gilmore, K. (2000). A psychoanalytic perspective on attention-deficit/hyperactivity disorder. *Journal of the American Psychoanalytic Association, 48*(4), 1259–1293. doi:10.1177/00030651000480040901

Gilmore, K. (2002). Diagnosis, dynamics, and development: Considerations in the psychoanalytic assessment of children with AD/HD. *Psychoanalytic Inquiry, 22*(3), 372–390. doi:10.1080/07351692209348993

Ginsberg, D. L. (2004). Women and anxiety disorders: Implications for diagnosis and treatment. *CNS Spectrums, 9*(9), 1–16.

Ginsberg, D. L. (2006). Bupropion SR for nicotine-craving pica in a developmentally disabled adult. *Primary Psychiatry, 13*(12), 28–28.

Giorgi, A. (1970). *Psychology as a human science: A phenomenologically based approach.* New York, NY: Harper & Row.

Giorgi, A. (1997). The theory, practice, and evaluation of the phenomenological method as a qualitative research procedure. *Journal of Phenomenological Psychology, 28*(2), 235–260. doi:10.1163/156916297X00103

Gipps, R. G. T. (2013). Cognitive behavior therapy: A philosophical appraisal. In K. W. M. Fulford, M. Davies, R. G. T. Gipps, G. Graham, J. Z. Sadler, G. Stanghellini, & T. Thornton (Eds.), *The Oxford handbook of philosophy and psychiatry* (pp. 1245–1263). New York, NY: Oxford University Press.

Glaser, G. (2015, April). The irrationality of Alcoholics Anonymous. *The Atlantic.*

Glaser, R. (2005). Stress-associated immune dysregulation and its importance for human health: A personal history of psychoneuroimmunology. *Brain, Behavior, and Immunity, 19*(1), 3–11. doi:10.1016/j.bbi.2004.06.003

Glasersfeld, Ernst von. (1995). *Radical constructivism: A way of knowing and learning.* London, UK: The Falmer Press.

Glass, D. J. (2012). Evolutionary clinical psychology, broadly construed: Perspectives on obsessive-compulsive disorder. *Journal of Social, Evolutionary, and Cultural Psychology, 6*(3), 292–308. doi:10.1037/h0099250

Glatt, S. J. (2008). Genetics. In K. T. Mueser & D. V. Jeste (Eds.), *Clinical handbook of schizophrenia* (pp. 55–64). New York, NY: Guilford Press.

Glazener, C. M. A., & Evans, J. H. C. (2002). Desmopressin for nocturnal enuresis in children. *Cochrane Database of Systematic Reviews, 2002*(3). doi:10.1002/14651858.CD002112

Glazener, C. M. A., Evans, J. H. C., & Peto, R. E. (2004). Treating nocturnal enuresis in children: review of evidence. *Journal Of Wound, Ostomy, And Continence Nursing: Official Publication Of The Wound, Ostomy And Continence Nurses Society / WOCN, 31*(4), 223–234.

Glazer, H. I., Rodke, G., Swencionis, C., Hertz, R., & Young, A. W. (1995). Treatment of vulvar vestibulitis syndrome with electromyographic biofeedback of pelvic floor musculature. *The Journal of Reproductive Medicine, 40*(4), 283–290.

Gleaves, D. H. (1996). The sociocognitive model of dissociative identity disorder: A reexamination of the evidence. *Psychological Bulletin, 120*(1), 42–59. doi:10.1037/0033-2909.120.1.42

Gleaves, D. H., May, M. C., & Cardeña, E. (2001). An examination of the diagnostic validity of dissociative identity disorder. *Clinical Psychology Review, 21*(4), 577–608. doi:http://dx.doi.org/10.1016/S0272-7358(99)00073-2

Glicklich, L. B. (1951). An historical account of enuresis. *Pediatrics, 8*(6), 859–876.

Godlee, F., Smith, J., & Marcovitch, H. (2011). Wakefield's article linking MMR vaccine and autism was fraudulent. *BMJ: British Medical Journal, 342*, c7452–c7452. doi:10.1136/bmj. c7452

Gold, M. S., Badgaiyan, R. D., & Blum, K. (2015). A shared molecular and genetic basis for food and drug addiction: Overcoming hypodopaminergic trait/state by incorporating dopamine agonistic therapy in psychiatry. *Psychiatric Clinics of North America, 38*(3), 419–462. doi:10.1016/j. psc.2015.05.011

Goldberg, L. R. (1993). The structure of phenotypic personality traits. *American Psychologist, 48*(1), 26–34. doi:10.1037/0003-066X.48.1.26

Golden, C. J. (2004). The Adult Luria-Nebraska Neuropsychological Battery. In G. Goldstein & S. R. Beers (Eds.), *Comprehensive handbook of psychological assessment: Vol. 1. Intellectual and neuropsychological assessment* (pp. 133–146). Hoboken, NJ: John Wiley.

Goldhill, S. (2015). The imperialism of historical arrogance: Where is the past in the DSM's idea of sexuality? *Archives of Sexual Behavior, 44*(5), 1099–1108. doi:10.1007/s10508-015-0556-7

Goldin, P. R., Morrison, A., Jazaieri, H., Brozovich, F., Heimberg, R., & Gross, J. J. (2016). Group CBT versus MBSR for social anxiety disorder: A randomized controlled trial. *Journal of Consulting and Clinical Psychology, 84*(5), 427–437. doi:10.1037/ccp0000092

Goldman, D. (2013). The genetic basis of addictive disorders. In D. S. Charney, J. D. Buxbaum, P. Sklar, & E. J. Nestler (Eds.), *Neurobiology of mental illness* (4th ed., pp. 696–705). New York, NY: Oxford University Press.

Goldman, D., Oroszi, G., & Ducci, F. (2005). The genetics of addictions: Uncovering the genes. *Nature Reviews. Genetics, 6*(7), 521–532.

Goldman, R. (2018, April 19). Best eating disorder recovery apps of 2018. Retrieved from https://www.healthline.com/health/top-eating-disorder-iphone-android-apps

Goldman, R. N., & Greenberg, L. S. (2015a). *Case formulation in emotion-focused psychotherapy: Co-creating clinical maps for change.* Washington, DC: American Psychological Association.

Goldman, R. N., & Greenberg, L. S. (2015b). Fundamentals of emotion-focused therapy. In R. Goldman & L. S. Greenberg (Eds.), *Case formulation in emotion-focused therapy: Co-creating clinical maps for change* (pp. 21–42). Washington, DC: American Psychological Association.

Goldsmith, L. P., Lewis, S. W., Dunn, G., & Bentall, R. P. (2015). Psychological treatments for early psychosis can be beneficial or harmful, depending on the therapeutic alliance: An instrumental variable analysis. *Psychological Medicine, 45*(11), 2365–2373. doi:10.1017/S003329171500032X

Goldstein, E. G. (1990). *Borderline disorders: Clinical models and techniques.* New York, NY: Guilford Press.

Goldstein, J. L., & Godemont, M. M. L. (2003). The legend and lessons of Geel, Belgium: A 1500-year-old legend, a 21st-century model. *Community Mental Health Journal, 39*(5), 441–458. doi:10.1023/A:1025813003347

Goldstein, M., Peters, L., Thornton, C. E., & Touyz, S. W. (2014). The treatment of perfectionism within the eating disorders: A pilot study. *European Eating Disorders Review, 22*(3), 217–221. doi:10.1002/erv.2281

Gollaher, D. (1995). *Voice for the mad: The life of Dorothea Dix.* New York, NY: The Free Press.

Golomb, M., Fava, M., Abraham, M., & Rosenbaum, J. F. (1995). Gender differences in personality disorders. *The American Journal of Psychiatry, 152*(4), 579–582. doi:10.1176/ajp.152.4.579

Golubchik, P., Mozes, T., Vered, Y., & Weizman, A. (2009). Platelet poor plasma serotonin level in delinquent adolescents diagnosed with conduct disorder. *Progress in Neuro-Psychopharmacology & Biological Psychiatry, 33*(7), 1223–1225. doi:10.1016/j.pnpbp.2009.07.003

Gonçalves, R., Pedrozo, A. L., Coutinho, E. S. F., Figueira, I., & Ventura, P. (2012). Efficacy of virtual reality exposure therapy in the treatment of PTSD: A systematic review. *PLOS One, 7*(12). doi:10.1371/journal.pone.0048469

Gonon, F. (2009). The dopaminergic hypothesis of attention-deficit/hyperactivity disorder needs re-examining. *Trends in Neurosciences, 32*(1), 2–8. doi:10.1016/j.tins.2008.09.010

Gonon, F., Bezard, E., & Boraud, T. (2011). What should be said to the lay public regarding ADHD etiology. *American Journal of Medical Genetics Part B: Neuropsychiatric Genetics, 156*(8), 989–991. doi:10.1002/ajmg.b.31236

Gontkovsky, S. T. (2011). Prevalence of enuresis in a community sample of children and adolescents referred for outpatient clinical psychological evaluation: Psychiatric comorbidities and association with intellectual functioning. *Journal of Child and Adolescent Mental Health, 23*(1), 53–58. doi:10.2989/17280583.2011.594253

Goodheart, C. D. (2014). *A primer for ICD-10-CM users: Psychological and behavioral conditions.* Washington, DC: American Psychological Association.

Goodman, A. (1990). Addiction: Definition and implications. *British Journal of Addiction, 85*(11), 1403–1408. doi:10.1111/j.1360-0443.1990.tb01620.x

Goodman, G. (2013). Encopresis happens: Theoretical and treatment considerations from an attachment perspective. *Psychoanalytic Psychology, 30*(3), 438–455. doi:10.1037/a0030894

Goodman, L. A. (n.d.). Reaching Out About Depression: A brief description. Retrieved from http://www.bc.edu/schools/lsoe/research-outreach/road.html

Goodman, L. A., Glenn, C., Bohlig, A., Banyard, V., & Borges, A. (2009). Feminist relational advocacy: Processes and outcomes from the perspective of low-income women with depression. *The Counseling Psychologist, 37*(6), 848–876. doi:10.1177/0011000008326325

Goodman, L. A., Liang, B., Helms, J. E., Latta, R. E., Sparks, E., & Weintraub, S. R. (2004). Training counseling psychologists as social justice agents: Feminist and multicultural principles in action. *The Counseling Psychologist, 32*, 793–837. doi:10.1177/0011000004268802

Goodman, L. A., Litwin, A., Bohlig, A., Weintraub, S. R., Green, A., Walker, J., ... Ryan, N. (2007). Applying feminist theory to community practice: A multilevel empowerment intervention for low-income women with depression. In E. Aldarondo (Ed.), *Advancing social justice through clinical practice* (pp. 265–290). Mahwah, NJ: Lawrence Erlbaum.

Goodman, L. A., Pugach, M., Skolnik, A., & Smith, L. (2013). Poverty and mental health practice: Within and beyond the 50-minute hour. *Journal of Clinical Psychology, 69*(2), 182–190. doi:10.1002/jclp.21957

Goodman, L. A., Smyth, K. F., & Banyard, V. (2010). Beyond the 50-minute hour: Increasing control, choice, and connections in the lives of low-income women. *American Journal of Orthopsychiatry, 80*(1), 3–11. doi:10.1111/j.1939-0025.2010.01002.x

Goodman, M., Vail, L., West, S., New, A., & Siever, L. (2006). The pharmacological and psychological treatment of personality disorders--From neurobiology to treatment strategies. *Journal of Family Psychotherapy, 17*(3–4), 53–81. doi:10.1300/J085v17n03_04

Goodman, W. K., Grice, D. E., Lapidus, K. A. B., & Coffey, B. J. (2014). Obsessive-compulsive disorder. *Psychiatric Clinics of North America, 37*(3), 257–267. doi:10.1016/j.psc.2014.06.004

Goodman, W. K., Price, L. H., Rasmussen, S. A., Delgado, P. L., Heninger, G. R., & Charney, D. S. (1989). Efficacy of fluvoxamine in obsessive-compulsive disorder: A double-blind comparison with placebo. *Archives of General Psychiatry, 46*(1), 36–44. doi:10.1001/archpsyc.1989.01810010038006

Goorden, M., Schawo, S. J., Bouwmans-Frijters, C. A. M., van der Schee, E., Hendriks, V. M., & Hakkaart-van Roijen, L. (2016). The cost-effectiveness of family/family-based therapy for treatment of externalizing disorders, substance use disorders and delinquency: A systematic review. *BMC Psychiatry, 16.*

Goracci, A., di Volo, S., Casamassima, F., Bolognesi, S., Benbow, J., & Fagiolini, A. (2015). Pharmacotherapy of binge-eating disorder: A review. *Journal of Addiction Medicine, 9*(1), 1–19. doi:10.1097/ADM.0000000000000089

Gordon, H. (2008). Editorial: The treatment of paraphilias: An historical perspective. *Criminal Behaviour and Mental Health, 18*(2), 79–87. doi:10.1002/cbm.687

Gordon, R. A. (2010). Drugs don't talk: Do medication and biological psychiatry contribute to silencing the self? In D. C. Jack & A. Ali (Eds.), *Silencing the self across cultures: Depression and gender in the social world* (pp. 47–72). New York, NY: Oxford University Press.

Gordon, R. M. (2009). Reactions to the Psychodynamic Diagnostic Manual (PDM) by psychodynamic, CBT and other non-psychodynamic psychologists. *Issues in Psychoanalytic Psychology, 31*(1), 53–59.

Gordon, R. M. & Bornstein, R. F. (2018). Construct validity of the Psychodiagnostic Chart: A transdiagnostic measure of personality organization, personality syndromes, mental functioning, and symptomatology. *Psychoanalytic Psychology. 35*(2), 280–288. doi:10.1037/pap0000142

Gorelick, D. A., Levin, K. H., Copersino, M. L., Heishman, S. J., Liu, F., Boggs, D. L., & Kelly, D. L. (2012). Diagnostic criteria for cannabis withdrawal syndrome. *Drug and Alcohol Dependence, 123*(1–3), 141–147. doi:10.1016/j.drugalcdep.2011.11.007

Gorman, D. A., Gardner, D. M., Murphy, A. L., Feldman, M., Bélanger, S. A., Steele, M. M., ... Pringsheim, T. (2015). Canadian guidelines on pharmacotherapy for disruptive and aggressive behaviour in children and adolescents with attention-deficit hyperactivity disorder, oppositional defiant disorder, or conduct disorder. *The Canadian Journal of Psychiatry/La Revue Canadienne De Psychiatrie, 60*(2), 62–76.

Gornall, J. (2013). DSM-5: A fatal diagnosis? *BMJ: British Medical Journal, 346*, 18–20. doi:10.1136/bmj.f3256

Gorsane, M.-A., Kebir, O., Hache, G., Blecha, L., Aubin, H.-J., Reynaud, M., & Benyamina, A. (2012). Is baclofen a revolutionary medication in alcohol addiction management? Review and recent updates. *Substance Abuse, 33*(4), 336–349. doi:10.1080/08897077.2012.663326

Gosselin, J. T. (2016a). Gender dysphoria. In J. E. Maddux & B. A. Winstead (Eds.), *Psychopathology: Foundations for a contemporary understanding* (4th ed., pp. 459–468). New York, NY: Routledge.

Gosselin, J. T. (2016b). Sexual dysfunctions and paraphilic disorders. In J. E. Maddux & B. A. Winstead (Eds.), *Psychopathology: Foundations for a contemporary understanding* (4th ed., pp. 237–265). New York, NY: Routledge.

Gossop, M., & Strang, J. (1991). A comparison of the withdrawal responses of heroin and methadone addicts during detoxification. *The British Journal of Psychiatry, 158*, 697–699. doi:10.1192/bjp.158.5.697

Gotlib, I. H., & LeMoult, J. (2014). The 'ins' and 'outs' of the depressive disorders section of DSM-5. *Clinical Psychology: Science and Practice, 21*(3), 193–207. doi:10.1111/cpsp.12072

Gottdiener, W. H., & Suh, J. J. (2015). Substance use disorders. In P. Luyten, L. C. Mayes, P. Fonagy, M. Target, & S. J. Blatt (Eds.), *Handbook of psychodynamic approaches to psychopathology* (pp. 216–233). New York, NY: Guilford Press.

Gottesman, I. I. (1991). *Schizophrenia genesis: The origins of madness*. New York, NY: Freeman.

Gottesman, I. I., Laursen, T. M., Bertelsen, A., & Mortensen, P. B. (2010). Severe mental disorders in offspring with 2 psychiatrically ill parents. *Archives of General Psychiatry, 67*(3), 252–257. doi:10.1001/archgenpsychiatry.2010.1

Gottfried, C., Bambini-Junior, V., Francis, F., Riesgo, R., & Savino, W. (2015). The impact of neuroimmune alterations in autism spectrum disorder. *Frontiers in Psychiatry, 6*.

Graham, C. A. (2010). The DSM diagnostic criteria for female sexual arousal disorder. *Archives of Sexual Behavior, 39*(2), 240–255. doi:10.1007/s10508-009-9535-1

Graham, J. R. (2011). *MMPI-2: Assessing personality and psychopathology*. New York, NY: Oxford.

Grambal, A., Prasko, J., Kamaradova, D., Latalova, K., Holubova, M., Marackova, M., ... Slepecky, M. (2016). Self-stigma in borderline personality disorder—Cross-sectional comparison with schizophrenia spectrum disorder, major depressive disorder, and anxiety disorders. *Neuropsychiatric Disease and Treatment, 12*.

Granata, A., Tirabassi, G., Pugni, V., Arnaldi, G., Boscaro, M., Carani, C., & Balercia, G. (2013). Sexual dysfunctions in men affected by autoimmune addison's disease before and after short-term gluco- and mineralocorticoid replacement therapy. *Journal of Sexual Medicine, 10*(8), 2036–2043. doi:10.1111/j.1743-6109.2012.02673.x

Granero, R., Fernández-Aranda, F., Mestre-Bach, G., Steward, T., Baño, M., del Pino-Gutiérrez, A., ... Jiménez-Murcia, S. (2016). Compulsive buying behavior: Clinical comparison with other behavioral addictions. *Frontiers In Psychology, 7*, 914. doi:10.3389/fpsyg.2016.00914

Granero, R., Fernández-Aranda, F., Steward, T., Mestre-Bach, G., Baño, M., del Pino-Gutiérrez, A., ... Jiménez-Murcia, S. (2016). Compulsive buying behavior: Characteristics of comorbidity with gambling disorder. *Frontiers In Psychology, 7*.

Grant, B. F., Stinson, F. S., Dawson, D. A., Chou, S. P., & Ruan, W. J. (2005). Co-occurrence of DSM-IV personality disorders in the United States: results from the National Epidemiologic Survey on Alcohol and Related Conditions. *Comprehensive Psychiatry, 46*(1), 1–5.

Grant, J. E., Odlaug, B. L., & Chamberlain, S. R. (2016). Neural and psychological underpinnings of gambling disorder: A review. *Progress in Neuro-Psychopharmacology & Biological Psychiatry, 65*, 188–193. doi:10.1016/j.pnpbp.2015.10.007

Grant, J. E., Potenza, M. N., Weinstein, A., & Gorelick, D. A. (2010). Introduction to behavioral addictions. *The American Journal of Drug and Alcohol Abuse, 36*(5), 233–241. doi:10.3109/00952990.2010.491884

Gratzer, D., & Goldbloom, D. (2017). New government, new opportunity, and an old problem with access to mental health care. *The Canadian Journal of Psychiatry/La Revue Canadienne De Psychiatrie, 62*(1), 8–10. doi:10.1177/0706743716669084

Gray, C., & Climie, E. A. (2016). Children with attention deficit/hyperactivity disorder and reading disability: A review of the efficacy of medication treatments. *Frontiers in Psychology, 7*.

Gray, J. E., & O'Reilly, R. L. (2005). Canadian compulsory treatment laws: Recent reforms. *International Journal of Law and Psychiatry, 28*(1), 13–22. doi:http://dx.doi.org/10.1016/j.ijlp.2004.12.002

Green, M. F. (2001). *Schizophrenia revealed: From neurons to social interactions*. New York, NY: Norton.

Green, M. J., & Benzeval, M. (2011). Ageing, social class and common mental disorders: Longitudinal evidence from three cohorts in the West of Scotland. *Psychological Medicine, 41*(3), 565–574. doi:10.1017/S0033291710000851

Greenberg, D. F. (1988). *The construction of homosexuality*. Chicago, IL: The University of Chicago Press.

Greenberg, G. (2013). *The book of woe: The DSM and the unmaking of psychiatry*. New York, NY: Plume.

Greenberg, J. (2006). Losing sleep over organizational injustice: Attenuating insomniac reactions to underpayment inequity with supervisory training in interactional justice. *Journal of Applied Psychology, 91*(1), 58–69. doi:10.1037/0021-9010.91.1.58

Greenberg, L. S., & Goldman, R. (2006). Case formulation in emotion-focused therapy. In T. D. Eels (Ed.), *Handbook of psychotherapy case formulation* (pp. 379–411). New York, NY: Guilford.

Greenberg, L. S., & Watson, J. C. (2006). *Emotion-focused therapy for depression*. Washington, DC: American Psychological Association.

Greenberg, M. S., Tanev, K., Marin, M.-F., & Pitman, R. K. Stress, PTSD, and dementia. *Alzheimer's & Dementia, 10*(3), S155–S165. doi:10.1016/j.jalz.2014.04.008

Greeven, A., van Balkom, A. J. L. M., van der Leeden, R., Merkelbach, J. W., van den Heuvel, O. A., & Spinhoven, P. (2009). Cognitive behavioral therapy versus paroxetine in the treatment of hypochondriasis: An 18-month naturalistic follow-up. *Journal of Behavior Therapy and Experimental Psychiatry, 40*(3), 487–496. doi:http://dx.doi.org/10.1016/j.jbtep.2009.06.005

Gressier, F., Rotenberg, S., Cazas, O., & Hardy, P. (2015). Postpartum electroconvulsive therapy: A systematic review and case report. *General Hospital Psychiatry, 37*(4), 310–314. doi:10.1016/j.genhosppsych.2015.04.009

Griebel, G., & Holmes, A. (2013). 50 years of hurdles and hope in anxiolytic drug discovery. *Nature Reviews. Drug Discovery, 12*(9), 667–687. doi:10.1038/nrd4075

Griffiths, S., Mond, J. M., Murray, S. B., & Touyz, S. (2014). Young peoples' stigmatizing attitudes and beliefs about anorexia nervosa and muscle dysmorphia. *International Journal of Eating Disorders, 47*(2), 189–195. doi:10.1002/eat.22220

Grob, G. N. (1994). *The mad among us: A history of the care of America's mentally ill*. New York, NY: The Free Press.

Groesz, L. M., Levine, M. P., & Murnen, S. K. (2002). The effect of experimental presentation of thin media images on body satisfaction: A meta-analytic review. *International Journal of Eating Disorders, 31*(1), 1–16. doi:10.1002/eat.10005

Grollman, E. A. (2010). What Is "sexual identity"? Is it the same as sexual orientation? Retrieved from http://kinseyconfidential.org/sexual-identity-sexual-orientation/

Gropalis, M., Bleichhardt, G., Hiller, W., & Witthöft, M. (2013). Specificity and modifiability of cognitive biases in hypochondriasis. *Journal of Consulting and Clinical Psychology, 81*(3), 558–565. doi:10.1037/a0028493

Grosche, M., & Volpe, R. J. (2013). Response-to-intervention (RTI) as a model to facilitate inclusion for students with learning and behaviour problems. *European Journal of Special Needs Education, 28*(3), 254–269. doi:10.1080/08856257.2013.768452

Grossi, G., & Fine, C. (2012). The role of fetal testosterone in the development of the "essential difference" between the sexes: Some essential issues. In R. Bluhm, A. J. Jacobson, & H. L. Maibom (Eds.), *Neurofeminism: Issues at the intersection of feminist theory and cognitive science* (pp. 73–104). London, UK: Palgrave Macmillan.

Grossman, P., Niemann, L., Schmidt, S., & Walach, H. (2004). Mindfulness-based stress reduction and health benefits: A meta-analysis. *Journal of Psychosomatic Research, 57*(1), 35–43. doi:http://dx.doi.org/10.1016/S0022-3999(03)00573-7

Grover, K. W., Zvolensky, M. J., Bonn-Miller, M. O., Kosiba, J., & Hogan, J. (2013). Marijuana use and abuse. In P. M. Miller, S. A. Ball, M. E. Bates, A. W. Blume, K. M. Kampman, D. J. Kavanagh, M. E. Larimer, N. M. Petry, & P. De Witte (Eds.), *Comprehensive addictive behaviors and disorders: Vol. 1. Principles of addiction* (pp. 679–687). San Diego, CA: Elsevier Academic Press.

Grubaugh, A. L. (2014). Trauma and stressor-related disorders: Posttraumatic stress disorder, acute stress disorder, and adjustment disorders. In D. C. Beidel, B. C. Frueh, & M. Hersen (Eds.), *Adult psychopathology and diagnosis* (7th ed., pp. 387–406). Hoboken, NJ: John Wiley.

Grubin, D., & Beech, A. (2010). Chemical castration for sex offenders. *BMJ: British Medical Journal, 340*, c74–c74. doi:10.1136/bmj.c74

Grünblatt, E., Hauser, T. U., & Walitza, S. (2014). Imaging genetics in obsessive-compulsive disorder: linking genetic variations to alterations in neuroimaging. *Progress in Neurobiology, 121*, 114–124. doi:10.1016/j.pneurobio.2014.07.003

Gryczynski, J., Mitchell, S. G., Jaffe, J. H., O'Grady, K. E., Olsen, Y. K., & Schwartz, R. P. (2014). Leaving buprenorphine treatment: Patients' reasons for cessation of care. *Journal of Substance Abuse Treatment, 46*(3), 356–361. doi:10.1016/j.jsat.2013.10.004

Grzywacz, J. G., Almeida, D. M., Neupert, S. D., & Ettner, S. L. (2004). Socioeconomic status and health: A micro-level analysis of exposure and vulnerability to daily stressors. *Journal of Health and Social Behavior, 45*(1), 1–16. doi:10.1177/002214650404500101

Gual, A., Segura, L., Contel, M., Heather, N., & Colom, J. (2002). AUDIT-3 and AUDIT-4: Effectiveness of two short forms of the Alcohol Use Disorders Identification Test. *Alcohol and Alcoholism, 37*(6), 591–596. doi:10.1093/alcalc/37.6.591

Guang, Y., Lei, Z., Nan, X., Hui, L., Soufu, X., & Junting, X. (2014). Analysis of quantitative genetic characteristics of schizophrenia using combined allele frequency as a genetic marker. *Psychiatry Research, 220*(1-2), 722–722. doi:10.1016/j.psychres.2014.08.038

Guastella, A. J., & Hickie, I. B. (2016). Oxytocin treatment, circuitry, and autism: A critical review of the literature placing oxytocin into the autism context. *Biological Psychiatry, 79*(3), 234–242. doi:10.1016/j.biopsych.2015.06.028

Guay, D. R. P. (2009). Drug treatment of paraphilic and nonparaphilic sexual disorders. *Clinical Therapeutics: The International Peer-Reviewed Journal of Drug Therapy, 31*(1), 1–31. doi:10.1016/j.clinthera.2009.01.009

Guillin, O., Abi-Dargham, A., & Laruelle, M. (2007). Neurobiology of dopamine in schizophrenia. *International Review of Neurobiology, 78*, 1–39.

Guisinger, S. (2003). Adapted to flee famine: Adding an evolutionary perspective on anorexia nervosa. *Psychological Review, 110*(4), 745–761. doi:10.1037/0033-295X.110.4.745

Gull, W. W. (1954). Anorexia nervosa (apepsia hysterica, anorexia hysterica). *Bulletin of the Isaac Ray Medical Library, 2*, 173–181. (Original work published 1874)

Gumber, S., & Stein, C. H. (2013). Consumer perspectives and mental health reform movements in the United States: 30 years of first-person accounts. *Psychiatric Rehabilitation Journal, 36*(3), 187–194. doi:10.1037/prj0000003

Gundogar, D., Demir, S. B., & Eren, I. (2003). Is pica in the spectrum of obsessive-compulsive disorders? *General Hospital Psychiatry, 25*(4), 293–294. doi:http://dx.doi.org/10.1016/S0163-8343(03)00039-2

Gunn, J. S., & Potter, B. (2015). *Borderline personality disorder: New perspectives on a stigmatizing and overused diagnosis.* Santa Barbara, CA: Praeger.

Gunnell, D., Irvine, D., Wise, L., Davies, C., & Martin, R. M. (2009). Varenicline and suicidal behaviour: A cohort study based on data from the General Practice Research Database. *BMJ: British Medical Journal, 339*(7729).

Gunst, E. (2012). Experiential psychotherapy with sex offenders: Experiencing as a way to change, to live more fulfilling lives, to desist from offending. *Person-Centered and Experiential Psychotherapies, 11*(4), 321–334. doi:10.1080/14779757.2012.740324

Gunter, R. W., & Bodner, G. E. (2008). How eye movements affect unpleasant memories: Support for a working-memory account. *Behaviour Research and Therapy, 46*(8), 913–931. doi:10.1016/j.brat.2008.04.006

Gunter, T. D., Vaughn, M. G., & Philibert, R. A. (2010). Behavioral genetics in antisocial spectrum disorders and psychopathy: a review of the recent literature. *Behavioral Sciences & the Law, 28*(2), 148–173. doi:10.1002/bsl.923

Gupta, R., Zalai, D., Spence, D. W., BaHammam, A. S., Ramasubramanian, C., Monti, J. M., & Pandi-Perumal, S. R. (2014). When insomnia is not just insomnia: The deeper correlates of disturbed sleep with reference to DSM-5. *Asian Journal of Psychiatry, 12*, 23–30. doi:10.1016/j.ajp.2014.09.003

Guraya, S. Y., London, N. J. M., & Guraya, S. S. (2014). Ethics in medical research. *Journal of Microscopy and Ultrastructure, 2*(3), 121–126. doi:http://doi.org/10.1016/j.jmau.2014.03.003

Gureje, O., & Reed, G. M. (2016). Bodily distress disorder in ICD-11: problems and prospects. *World Psychiatry, 15*(3), 291–292. doi:10.1002/wps.20353

Guttmann-Steinmetz, S., & Crowell, J. A. (2006). Attachment and externalizing disorders: A developmental psychopathology perspective. *Journal of the American Academy of Child & Adolescent Psychiatry, 45*(4), 440–451. doi:10.1097/01.chi.0000196422.42599.63

Guze, S. B., Cloninger, C. R., Martin, R. L., & Clayton, P. J. (1986). A follow-up and family study of Briquet's syndrome. *The British Journal of Psychiatry, 149*, 17–23. doi:10.1192/bjp.149.1.17

Guze, S. B., Woodruff, R. A., & Clayton, P. J. (1972). Sex, age, and the diagnosis of hysteria (Briquet's syndrome). *The American Journal of Psychiatry, 129*(6), 745–748.

Haack, S. A., Borghesani, P. R., Green, A. J., Neumaier, J. F., & Shyn, S. I. (2014). Electroconvulsive therapy for catatonia in an 18-year-old patient presenting with mixed features of schizophrenia and obsessive-compulsive disorder. *Journal of Child and Adolescent Psychopharmacology, 24*(7), 411–413.

Haagen, J. F. G., Smid, G. E., Knipscheer, J. W., & Kleber, R. J. (2015). The efficacy of recommended treatments for veterans with PTSD: A metaregression analysis. *Clinical Psychology Review, 40*, 184–194. doi:10.1016/j.cpr.2015.06.008

Haas, A. P., Eliason, M., Mays, V. M., Mathy, R. M., Cochran, S. D., D'Augelli, A. R., ... Clayton, P. J. (2011). Suicide and suicide risk in lesbian, gay, bisexual, and transgender populations: Review and recommendations. *Journal of Homosexuality, 58*(1), 10–51. doi:10.1080/00918369.201 1.534038

Habenstein, A., Steffen, T., Bartsch, C., Michaud, K., & Reisch, T. (2013). Chances and limits of method restriction: A detailed analysis of suicide methods in Switzerland. *Archives of Suicide Research, 17*(1), 75–87. doi:10.1080/1 3811118.2013.748418

Hadaway, S. M., & Brue, A. W. (2016). *Practitioner's guide to functional behavioral assessment: Process, purpose, planning, and prevention.* Cham, Switzerland: Springer International Publishing.

Haddad, P. M., & Sharma, S. G. (2007). Adverse effects of atypical antipsychotics: Differential risk and clinical implications. *CNS Drugs, 21*(11), 911–936.

Hadjistavropoulos, T., Craig, K. D., Duck, S., Cano, A., Goubert, L., Jackson, P. L., ... Fitzgerald, T. D. (2011). A biopsychosocial formulation of pain communication. *Psychological Bulletin, 137*(6), 910–939. doi:10.1037/a0023876

Hageman, T. K., Francis, A. J. P., Field, A. M., & Carr, S. N. (2015). Links between childhood experiences and avoidant personality disorder symptomatology. *International Journal of Psychology & Psychological Therapy, 15*(1), 101–116.

Hagman, G. (2001). Beyond decathexis: Toward a new psychoanalytic understanding and treatment of mourning. In R. A. Neimeyer (Ed.), *Meaning reconstruction and the experience of loss.* (pp. 13–31). Washington, DC: American Psychological Association.

Hagman, J., Gralla, J., Sigel, E., Ellert, S., Dodge, M., Gardner, R., ... Wamboldt, M. Z. (2011). A double-blind, placebo-controlled study of risperidone for the treatment of adolescents and young adults with anorexia nervosa: A pilot study. *Journal of the American Academy of Child & Adolescent Psychiatry, 50*(9), 915–924. doi:10.1016/j.jaac.2011.06.009

Haijma, S. V., Van Haren, N., Cahn, W., Koolschijn, P. C. M. P., Pol, H. E. H., & Kahn, R. S. (2013). Brain volumes in schizophrenia: A meta-analysis in over 18,000 subjects. *Schizophrenia Bulletin, 39*(5), 1129–1138. doi:10.1093/schbul/sbs118

Halberstadt, A. L. (2015). Recent advances in the neuropsychopharmacology of serotonergic hallucinogens. *Behavioural Brain Research, 277,* 99–120. doi:10.1016/j.bbr.2014.07.016

Hale, L. (2014). Inadequate sleep duration as a public health and social justice problem: Can we truly trade off our daily activities for more sleep? *Sleep: Journal of Sleep and Sleep Disorders Research, 37*(12), 1879–1880.

Hale, L., Strauss, C., & Taylor, B. L. (2013). The effectiveness and acceptability of mindfulness-based therapy for obsessive compulsive disorder: A review of the literature. *Mindfulness, 4*(4), 375–382. doi:10.1007/s12671-012-0137-y

Hale, T. (2015, November 11). Which countries consume the most antidepressants? Retrieved from http://www.iflscience.com/health-and-medicine/which-countries-consume-most-antidepressants

Haleem, D. J. (2012). Serotonin neurotransmission in anorexia nervosa. *Behavioural Pharmacology, 23*(5-6), 478–495. doi:10.1097/FBP.0b013e328357440d

Halfon, N., & Kuo, A. A. (2013). What DSM-5 could mean to children with autism and their families. *JAMA Pediatrics, 167*(7), 608–613. doi:10.1001/jamapediatrics.2013.2188

Hall, B., & Place, M. (2010). Cutting to cope—A modern adolescent phenomenon. *Child: Care, Health and Development, 36*(5), 623–629. doi:10.1111/j.1365-2214.2010.01095.x

Hall, L., Orrell, M., Stott, J., & Spector, A. (2013). Cognitive stimulation therapy (CST): Neuropsychological mechanisms of change. *International Psychogeriatrics, 25*(3), 479–489. doi:10.1017/S1041610212001822

Hall, W., Carter, A., & Forlini, C. (2015). The brain disease model of addiction: Is it supported by the evidence and has it delivered on its promises? *The Lancet Psychiatry, 2*(1), 105–110. doi:10.1016/S2215-0366(14)00126-6

Hallmayer, J., Cleveland, S., Torres, A., Phillips, J., Cohen, B., Torigoe, T., ... Risch, N. (2011). Genetic heritability and shared environmental factors among twin pairs with autism. *Archives of General Psychiatry, 68*(11), 1095–1102. doi:10.1001/archgenpsychiatry.2011.76

Halmi, K. A. (2013). Perplexities of treatment resistance in eating disorders. *BMC Psychiatry, 13.* doi:10.1186/1471-244X-13-292

Halperin, D. M. (1989). Is there a history of sexuality? *History and Theory, 28*(3), 257–274. doi:10.2307/2505179

Halpern, A. L. (2011). The proposed diagnosis of hypersexual disorder for inclusion in DSM-5: Unnecessary and harmful. *Archives of Sexual Behavior, 40*(3), 487–488. doi:10.1007/s10508-011-9727-3

Halstead-Reitan Battery. (n.d.). *Encyclopedia of Mental Disorders, 40*(9), 63. Retrieved from http://www.minddisorders.com/Flu-Inv/Halstead-Reitan-Battery.html

Halter, M. J., Rolin-Kenny, D., & Grund, F. (2013). DSM-5 historical perspectives. *Journal of Psychosocial Nursing and Mental Health Services, 51*(4), 22–29. doi:10.3928/02793695-20130226-03

Hamblin, J. (2016, May 12). Concerns about folate causing autism are premature. *The Atlantic.*

Hambly, J. L., Khan, S., McDermott, B., Bor, W., & Haywood, A. (2016). Pharmacotherapy of conduct disorder: Challenges, options and future directions. *Journal of Psychopharmacology, 30*(10), 967–975. doi:10.1177/0269881116658985

Hameed, U., Schwartz, T. L., Malhotra, K., West, R. L., & Bertone, F. (2005). Antidepressant treatment in the primary care office: Outcomes for adjustment disorder versus major depression. *Annals of Clinical Psychiatry, 17*(2), 77–81. doi:10.1080/10401230590932344

Hamilton, J. P. (2015). Amygdala reactivity as mental health risk endophenotype: A tale of many trajectories. *The American Journal of Psychiatry, 172*(3), 214–215. doi:10.1176/appi.ajp.2014.14121491

Hamlin, A., & Oakes, P. (2008). Reflections on deinstitutionalization in the United Kingdom. *Journal of Policy and Practice in Intellectual Disabilities, 5*(1), 47–55. doi:10.1111/j.1741-1130.2007.00139.x

Hamm, J. A., Hasson-Ohayon, I., Kukla, M., & Lysaker, P. H. (2013). Individual psychotherapy for schizophrenia: Trends and developments in the wake of the recovery movement. *Psychology Research and Behavior Management, 6.*

Hammer, R., Dingel, M., Ostergren, J., Partridge, B., McCormick, J., & Koenig, B. A. (2013). Addiction: Current criticism of the brain disease paradigm. *AJOB neuroscience,* (3), 27–32. doi:10.1080/21507740.2013.796328

Hammond, C. (2016, March 18). Understanding histrionic personality disorder. Retrieved from http://pro.psychcentral.com/exhausted-woman/2016/03/understanding-histrionic-personality-disorder/

Hamza, C. A., Stewart, S. L., & Willoughby, T. (2012). Examining the link between nonsuicidal self-injury and suicidal behavior: A review of the literature and an integrated model. *Clinical Psychology Review, 32*(6), 482–495. doi:http://dx.doi.org/10.1016/j.cpr.2012.05.003

Hanisch, C. (1969). The personal is political. Retrieved from http://www.carolhanisch.org/CHwritings/PIP.html

Hanley, A. W., Abell, N., Osborn, D. S., Roehrig, A. D., & Canto, A. I. (2016). Mind the gaps: Are conclusions about mindfulness entirely conclusive? *Journal of Counseling & Development, 94*(1), 103–113. doi:10.1002/jcad.12066

Hans-Joachim, H., & Wuld, R. (1999). Deinstitutionalization of psychiatric patients in central Europe. *European Archives of Psychiatry and Clinical Neuroscience, 249*(3), 115–122. doi:10.1007/s004060050075

Happé, F., & Frith, U. (2006). The weak coherence account: Detail-focused cognitive style in autism spectrum disorders. *Journal of Autism and Developmental Disorders, 36*(1), 5–25. doi:10.1007/s10803-005-0039-0

Hardy, J., & Selkoe, D. J. (2002). The amyloid hypothesis of Alzheimer's disease: Progress and problems on the road to therapeutics. *Science, 297*(5580), 353–356.

Hardy, L. T. (2009). Encopresis: A guide for psychiatric nurses. *Archives of Psychiatric Nursing, 23*(5), 351–358. doi:10.1016/j.apnu.2008.09.002

Hare, R. D. (1996, February 1). Psychopathy and antisocial personality disorder: A case of diagnostic confusion. *Psychiatric Times.* Retrieved from http://www.psychiatrictimes.com/antisocial-personality-disorder/psychopathy-and-antisocial-personality-disorder-case-diagnostic-confusion

Hare, R. D. (2006). The profile: Feelings and relationships. Retrieved from http://www.pbs.org/wgbh/pages/frontline/shows/execution/who/profile.html

Hare, R. D., Neumann, C. S., & Widiger, T. A. (2012). Psychopathy. In T. A. Widiger (Ed.), *The Oxford handbook of personality disorders* (pp. 478–504). New York, NY: Oxford University Press.

Harlow, H. F. (1958). The nature of love. *American Psychologist, 13*(12), 673–685. doi:10.1037/h0047884

Harlow, H. F., & Suomi, S. J. (1974). Induced depression in monkeys. *Behavioral Biology, 12*(3), 273–296. doi:10.1016/S0091-6773(74)91475-8

Harlow, J. M. (1848). Passage of an iron rod through the head. *Boston Medical and Surgical Journal, 39,* 389–393.

Harney, P. A., & Harvey, M. R. (1999). Group psychotherapy: An overview. In B. H. Young & D. D. Blake (Eds.), *Group treatments for post-traumatic stress disorder* (pp. 1–14). Philadelphia, PA: Brunner/Mazel.

Harper, D. J. (2011). Social inequality and the diagnosis of paranoia. *Health Sociology Review, 20*(4), 423–436. doi:10.5172/hesr.2011.20.4.423

Harris, B. (1979). Whatever happened to little Albert? *American Psychologist, 34*(2), 151–160. doi:10.1037/0003-066X.34.2.151

Harris, C. (2016, March 30). Autistic kids losing out in France as 'retrograde vision' leaves country lagging behind rest of Europe. *Euronews.* Retrieved from http://www.euronews.com/2016/03/30/children-losing-out-as-france-lags-rest-of-europe-on-autism-vision

Harris, J. C. (2003). A rake's progress: 'Bedlam'. *Archives of General Psychiatry, 60*(4), 338–339. doi:10.1001/archpsyc.60.4.338

Harris, M. G., Burgess, P. M., Pirkis, J., Siskind, D., Slade, T., & Whiteford, H. A. (2011). Correlates of antidepressant and anxiolytic, hypnotic or sedative medication use in an Australian community sample. *Australian and New Zealand Journal of Psychiatry, 45*(3), 249–260. doi:10.3109/00048674.2010.531459

Harrison, B. J., Soriano-Mas, C., Pujol, J., Ortiz, H., López-Solà, M., Hernández-Ribas, R., ... Cardoner, N. (2009). Altered corticostriatal functional connectivity in obsessive-compulsive disorder. *Archives of General Psychiatry, 66*(11), 1189–1200. doi:10.1001/archgenpsychiatry.2009.152

Harrison, K. (2007). The high-risk sex offender strategy in England and Wales: Is chemical castration an option? *The Howard Journal of Criminal Justice, 46*(1), 16–31. doi:10.1111/j.1468-2311.2007.00451.x

Harrison, P. J. (2015). Recent genetic findings in schizophrenia and their therapeutic relevance. *Journal of Psychopharmacology, 29*(2), 85–96. doi:10.1177/0269881114553647

Hartmann, A., Martino, D., & Murphy, T. (2016). Gilles de la Tourette syndrome—A treatable condition? *Revue Neurologique, 172*(8-9), 446–454. doi:10.1016/j.neurol.2016.07.004

Hartmann, A. S., Becker, A. E., Hampton, C., & Bryant-Waugh, R. (2012). Pica and rumination disorder in DSM-5. *Psychiatric Annals, 42*(11), 426–430. doi:10.3928/00485713-20121105-09

Hartmann, T. (1997). *Attention deficit disorder: A different perception* (2nd ed.). Grass Valley, CA: Underwood Books.

Hartung, C. M., & Widiger, T. A. (1998). Gender differences in the diagnosis of mental disorders: Conclusions and controversies of the DSM–IV. *Psychological Bulletin, 123*(3), 260–278. doi:10.1037/0033-2909.123.3.260

Hartwell, C. E. (1996). The schizophrenogenic mother concept in American psychiatry. *Psychiatry: Interpersonal and Biological Processes, 59*(3), 274–297.

Harvey, A. G., Bryant, R. A., & Tarrier, N. (2003). Cognitive behaviour therapy for posttraumatic stress disorder. *Clinical Psychology Review, 23*(3), 501–522. doi:10.1016/S0272-7358(03)00035-7

Harvey, B. H., & Slabbert, F. N. (2014). New insights on the antidepressant discontinuation syndrome. *Human Psychopharmacology: Clinical and Experimental, 29*(6), 503–516. doi:10.1002/hup.2429

Harvey, P. D. (2017). Inflammation in schizophrenia: What it means and how to treat it. *The American Journal of Geriatric Psychiatry, 25*(1), 62–63. doi:10.1016/j.jagp.2016.10.012

Hashemi, A. H., & Cochrane, R. (1999). Expressed emotion and schizophrenia: A review of studies across cultures. *International Review of Psychiatry, 11*(2–3), 219–224. doi:10.1080/09540269974401

Hashemiyoon, R., Kuhn, J., & Visser-Vandewalle, V. (2017). Putting the pieces together in Gilles de la Tourette syndrome: Exploring the link between clinical observations and the biological basis of dysfunction. *Brain Topography, 30*(1), 3–29. doi:10.1007/s10548-016-0525-z

Hashimoto, K. (2009). Emerging role of glutamate in the pathophysiology of major depressive disorder. *Brain Research Reviews, 61*(2), 105–123. doi:http://dx.doi.org/10.1016/j.brainresrev.2009.05.005

Hashimoto, K. (2011). The role of glutamate on the action of antidepressants. *Progress in Neuro-Psychopharmacology & Biological Psychiatry, 35*(7), 1558–1568. doi:10.1016/j.pnpbp.2010.06.013

Hasin, D. S., O'Brien, C. P., Auriacombe, M., Borges, G., Bucholz, K., Budney, A., ... Grant, B. F. (2013). DSM-5 criteria for substance use disorders: Recommendations and rationale. *The American Journal of Psychiatry, 170*(8), 834–851. doi:doi:10.1176/appi.ajp.2013.12060782

Haskayne, D., Hirschfeld, R., & Larkin, M. (2014). The outcome of psychodynamic psychotherapies with individuals diagnosed with personality disorders: A systematic review. *Psychoanalytic Psychotherapy, 28*(2), 115–138. doi:10.1080/02668734.2014.888675

Hassiotis, A., Canagasabey, A., Robotham, D., Marston, L., Romeo, R., & King, M. (2011). Applied behaviour analysis and standard treatment in intellectual disability: 2-year outcomes. *The British Journal of Psychiatry, 198*(6), 490–491. doi:10.1192/bjp.bp.109.076646

Hauser, J. (n.d.). Mood stabilizers for bipolar disorder. Retrieved from http://psychcentral.com/lib/mood-stabilizers-for-bipolar-disorder/59/

Hauth, I., de Bruijn, Y. G. E., Staal, W., Buitelaar, J. K., & Rommelse, N. N. (2014). Testing the extreme male brain theory of autism spectrum disorder in a familial design. *Autism Research, 7*(4), 491–500. doi:10.1002/aur.1384

Havens, L. L. (1966). Charcot and hysteria. *Journal of Nervous and Mental Disease, 141*(5), 505–516.

Hawkey, E., & Nigg, J. T. (2014). Omega–3 fatty acid and ADHD: Blood level analysis and meta-analytic extension of supplementation trials. *Clinical Psychology Review, 34*(6), 496–505. doi:10.1016/j.cpr.2014.05.005

Hawton, K., Witt, K. G., Taylor Salisbury, T. L., Arensman, E., Gunnell, D., Hazell, P., ... van Heeringen, K. (2015). Pharmacological interventions for self-harm in adults. *Cochrane Database of Systematic Reviews*(7), 1–57. doi:10.1002/14651858.CD011777

Hawton, K., Witt, K. G., Taylor Salisbury, T. L., Arensman, E., Gunnell, D., Hazell, P., ... van Heeringen, K. (2016). Psychosocial interventions for self-harm in adults. *Cochrane Database of Systematic Reviews, 2016*(5). doi:10.1002/14651858.CD012189

Hay, P. (2013). A systematic review of evidence for psychological treatments in eating disorders: 2005–2012. *International Journal of Eating Disorders, 46*(5), 462–469.

Hayden, E. C. (2013). Taboo genetics. *Nature, 502*(7469), 26–28. doi:10.1038/502026a

Hayes, S. C. (2004). Acceptance and commitment therapy, relational frame theory, and the third wave of behavioral and cognitive therapies. *Behavior Therapy, 35*(4), 639–665. doi:https://doi.org/10.1016/S0005-7894(04)80013-3

Hayes, S. C., & Pankey, J. (2002). Experiential avoidance, cognitive fusion, and an ACT approach to anorexia nervosa. *Cognitive and Behavioral Practice, 9*(3), 243–247. doi:10.1016/S1077-7229(02)80055-4

Haymes, L. K., Storey, K., Maldonado, A., Post, M., & Montgomery, J. (2013). Using applied behavior analysis and smart technology for meeting the health needs of individuals with intellectual disabilities. *Developmental Neurorehabilitation, 18*(6), 407–419. doi:10.3109/17518423.2013.850750

Haynes, S. N. (1998). The changing nature of behavioral assessment. In A. S. Bellack & M. Hersen (Eds.), *Behavioral assessment: A practical handbook* (2nd ed., pp. 1–21). Boston, MA: Allyn and Bacon.

Hazelden Betty Ford Foundation. (2016, July 24). What is the difference between alcohol abuse and dependence? Retrieved from http://www.hazeldenbettyford.org/articles/what-is-the-difference-between-alcohol-abuse-and-dependence

He, J. A., & Antshel, K. M. (2016). Cognitive behavioral therapy for attention-deficit/hyperactivity disorder in college students: A review of the literature. *Cognitive and Behavioral Practice.* doi:10.1016/j.cbpra.2016.03.010

Heard, H. L., & Linehan, M. M. (1994). Dialectical behavior therapy: An integrative approach to the treatment of borderline personality disorder. *Journal of Psychotherapy Integration, 4*(1), 55–82. doi:10.1037/h0101147

Hearon, B. A., & Otto, M. W. (2012). Benzodiazepines. In S. G. Hofmann (Ed.), *Psychobiological approaches for anxiety disorders: Treatment combination strategies* (pp. 25–39). Chichester, UK: Wiley-Blackwell.

Heather, N. (2006). Controlled drinking, harm reduction and their roles in the response to alcohol-related problems. *Addiction Research & Theory, 14*(1), 7–18. doi:10.1080/16066350500489170

Heckers, S., Barch, D. M., Bustillo, J., Gaebel, W., Gur, R., Malaspina, D., ... Carpenter, W. (2013). Structure of the psychotic disorders classification in DSM-5. *Schizophrenia Research, 150*(1), 11–14. doi:10.1016/j.schres.2013.04.039

Heffner, M., Sperry, J., Eifert, G. H., & Detweiler, M. (2002). Acceptance and commitment therapy in the treatment of an adolescent female with anorexia nervosa: A case example. *Cognitive and Behavioral Practice, 9*(3), 232–236. doi:10.1016/S1077-7229(02)80053-0

Heibach, E., Brabban, A., & Lincoln, T. M. (2014). How much priority do clinicians give to cognitive behavioral therapy in the treatment of psychosis and why? *Clinical Psychology: Science and Practice, 21*(3), 301–312. doi:10.1111/cpsp.12074

Heiby, E. M., & Haynes, S. N. (2004). Introduction to behavioral assessment. In S. N. Haynes & E. M. Heiby (Eds.), *Comprehensive handbook of psychological assessment: Vol. 3. Behavioral assessment* (pp. 3–18). Hoboken, NJ: John Wiley.

Heim, G., & Bühler, K.-E. (2006). Psychological trauma and fixed ideas in Pierre Janet's conception of dissociative disorders. *American Journal of Psychotherapy, 60*(2), 111–127.

Heintzelman, C. A. (2003). The Tuskegee syphilis study and its implications for the 21st century. *The New Social Worker, 10*(4). Retrieved from http://www.socialworker.com/feature-articles/ethics-articles/The_Tuskegee_Syphilis_Study_and_Its_Implications_for_the_21st_Century/

Helms, J. E., Nicolas, G., & Green, C. E. (2012). Racism and ethnoviolence as trauma: Enhancing professional and research training. *Traumatology, 18*(1), 65–74. doi:10.1177/1534765610396728

Helzer, J. E., Kraemer, H. C., & Krueger, R. F. (2006). The feasibility and need for dimensional psychiatric diagnoses. *Psychological Medicine, 36*(12), 1671–1680. doi:10.1017/S003329170600821X

Henderson, E. (2015). Potentially dangerous patients: a review of the duty to warn. *Journal of Emergency Nursing, 41*(3), 193–200. doi:10.1016/j.jen.2014.08.012

Henderson, S. W., & Martin, A. (2014). Case formulation and integration of information in child and adolescent mental health. In J. M. Rey (Ed.), *IACAPAP e-textbook of child and adolescent mental health* (pp. 1–20). Geneva, Switzerland: International Association for Child and Adolescent Psychiatry and Allied Professions.

Hengartner, M. P., Kawohl, W., Haker, H., Rössler, W., & Ajdacic-Gross, V. (2016). Big five personality traits may inform public health policy and preventive medicine: Evidence from a cross-sectional and a prospective longitudinal epidemiologic study in a Swiss community. *Journal of Psychosomatic Research, 84*, 44–51. doi:10.1016/j.jpsychores.2016.03.012

Henggeler, S. W. (2011). Efficacy studies to large-scale transport: The development and validation of multisystemic therapy programs. *Annual Review of Clinical Psychology, 7*, 351–381. doi:10.1146/annurev-clinpsy-032210-104615

Henggeler, S. W., & Borduin, C. M. (1990). *Family therapy and beyond: A multisystemic approach to treating behavior problems of children and adolescents.* Belmont, CA: Brooks/Cole.

Henriques, G. R. (2002). The harmful dysfunction analysis and the differentiation between mental disorder and disease. *The Scientific Review of Mental Health Practice: Objective Investigations of Controversial and Unorthodox Claims in Clinical Psychology, Psychiatry, and Social Work, 1*(2), 157–173.

Henriques, G. (2015, October 30). The biopsychosocial model and its limitations. Retrieved from https://www.psychologytoday.com/blog/theory-knowledge/201510/the-biopsychosocial-model-and-its-limitations

Herbert, J. D., Lilienfeld, S. O., Lohr, J. M., Montgomery, R. W., O'Donohue, W. T., Rosen, G. M., & Tolin, D. F. (2000). Science and pseudoscience in the development of eye movement desensitization and reprocessing: Implications for clinical psychology. *Clinical Psychology Review, 20*(8), 945–971. doi:10.1016/S0272-7358(99)00017-3

Herek, G. M. (1990). The context of anti-gay violence: Notes on cultural and psychological heterosexism. *Journal of Interpersonal Violence, 5*(3), 316–333. doi:10.1177/088626090005003006

Herek, G. M. (1996). Heterosexism and homophobia. In R. P. Cabaj & T. S. Stein (Eds.), *Textbook of homosexuality and mental health* (pp. 101–113). Arlington, VA: American Psychiatric Association.

Hergüner, S., Özyıldırım, İ., & Tanıdır, C. (2008). Is pica an eating disorder or an obsessive-compulsive spectrum disorder? *Progress in Neuro-Psychopharmacology & Biological Psychiatry, 32*(8), 2010–2011. doi:10.1016/j.pnpbp.2008.09.011

Herman, J. (2015). *Trauma and recovery: The aftermath of violence—from domestic abuse to political terror.* New York, NY: Basic Books.

Hermans, D., De Cort, K., Noortman, D., Vansteenwegen, D., Beckers, T., Spruyt, A., & Schruers, K. (2010). Priming associations between bodily sensations and catastrophic misinterpretations: Specific for panic disorder? *Behaviour Research and Therapy, 48*(9), 900–908. doi:10.1016/j.brat.2010.05.015

Hermus, I. P. M., Willems, S. J. B., Bogman, A. C. C. F., Janssen, P. K. C., Brabers, L., & Schieveld, J. N. M. (2016). Cyclic vomiting syndrome: An update illustrated by a case report. *The Primary Care Companion for CNS Disorders, 18*(3), 10.4088/PCC.4015br01912. doi:10.4088/PCC.15br01912

Hertlein, K. M., & Weeks, G. R. (2009, March–April). Sexual health. *Family Therapy Magazine,* 48–58.

Hertler, S. C. (2014a). The continuum of conscientiousness: The antagonistic interests among obsessive and antisocial personalities. *Polish Psychological Bulletin, 45*(1), 52–63. doi:10.2478/ppb-2014-0008

Hertler, S. C. (2014b). A review and critique of obsessive-compulsive personality disorder etiologies. *Europe's Journal of Psychology, 10*(1), 168–184. Retrieved from http://ejop.psychopen.eu/article/view/679

Hertler, S. C. (2015a). The evolutionary logic of the obsessive trait complex: Obsessive compulsive personality disorder as a complementary behavioral syndrome. *Psychological Thought, 8*(1), 18. doi:10.5964/psyct.v8i1.125

Hertler, S. C. (2015b). Obsessive compulsive personality disorder as an adaptive anachronism: The operation of phylogenetic inertia upon obsessive populations in Western modernity. *Psihologijske Teme, 24*(2), 207–232.

Hertz, P. (2016). The psychoses, with a special emphasis on schizophrenia spectrum disorders. In J. Berzoff, L. M. Flanagan, & P. Hertz (Eds.), *Inside out and outside in: Psychodynamic clinical theory and psychopathology in contemporary multicultural contexts* (4th ed., pp. 330–362). Lanham, MD: Rowman & Littlefield.

Hertz, P., & Hertz, M. (2016). Personality disorders, with a special emphasis on borderline and narcissistic syndromes. In J. Berzoff, L. M. Flanagan, & P. Hertz (Eds.), *Inside out and outside in: Psychodynamic clinical theory and psychopathology in contemporary multicultural contexts* (4th ed., pp. 363–411). Lanham, MD: Rowman & Littlefield.

Hervey, N. (1986). Advocacy or folly: the Alleged Lunatics' Friend Society, 1845–63. *Medical History, 30*(3), 245–275.

Heston, L. L. (1966). Psychiatric disorders in foster home reared children of schizophrenic mothers. *The British Journal of Psychiatry, 112*(489), 819–825. doi:10.1192/bjp.112.489.819

Hettema, J. M., Neale, M. C., & Kendler, K. S. (2001). A review and meta-analysis of the genetic epidemiology of anxiety disorders. *The American Journal of Psychiatry, 158*(10), 1568–1578. doi:10.1176/appi.ajp.158.10.1568

Hewson, H. (2015). A narrative approach to individuals with psychosis. In A. Meaden & A. Fox (Eds.), *Innovations in psychosocial interventions for psychosis: Working with the hard to reach* (pp. 146–163). New York, NY: Routledge.

Heylens, G., De Cuypere, G., Zucker, K. J., Schelfaut, C., Elaut, E., Vanden Bossche, H., ... T'Sjoen, G. (2012). Gender identity disorder in twins: A review of the case report literature. *Journal of Sexual Medicine, 9*(3), 751–757. doi:10.1111/j.1743-6109.2011.02567.x

Heyman, R. E., & Smith Slep, A. M. (2004). Analogue behavioral observation. In S. N. Haynes & E. M. Heiby (Eds.), *Comprehensive handbook of psychological assessment: Vol. 3. Behavioral assessment* (pp. 162–180). Hoboken, NJ: John Wiley.

Heyvaert, M., Maes, B., & Onghena, P. (2013). Mixed methods research synthesis: Definition, framework, and potential. *Quality & Quantity: International Journal of Methodology, 47*(2), 659–676. doi:10.1007/s11135-011-9538-6

Higgins, S. T., & Petry, N. M. (1999). Contingency management: Incentives for sobriety. *Alcohol Research & Health, 23*(2), 122–127.

Hildebrand, A., Behrendt, S., & Hoyer, J. (2015). Treatment outcome in substance use disorder patients with and without comorbid posttraumatic stress disorder: A systematic review. *Psychotherapy Research, 25*(5), 565–582. doi:10.1080/10503307.2014.923125

Hildebrandt, T. B., & Downey, A. (2013). The neurobiology of eating disorders. In D. S. Charney, J. D. Buxbaum, P. Sklar, & E. J. Nestler (Eds.), *Neurobiology of mental illness* (4th ed., pp. 1171–1185). New York, NY: Oxford University Press.

Hill, D. L. G., Schwarz, A. J., Isaac, M., Pani, L., Vamvakas, S., Hemmings, R., ... Stephenson, D. (2014). Coalition against major diseases/European medicines agency biomarker qualification of hippocampal volume for enrichment of clinical trials in predementia stages of Alzheimer's disease. *Alzheimer's & Dementia, 10*(4), 421–429. doi:10.1016/j.jalz.2013.07.003

Hill, E. M. (2013). An evolutionary perspective on addiction. In P. M. Miller, S. A. Ball, M. E. Bates, A. W. Blume, K. M. Kampman, D. J. Kavanagh, M. E. Larimer, N. M. Petry, & P. De Witte (Eds.), *Comprehensive addictive behaviors and disorders: Vol. 1. Principles of addiction* (pp. 41–50). San Diego, CA: Elsevier Academic Press.

Hill, E. M., & Chow, K. (2002). Life-history theory and risky drinking. *Addiction, 97*(4), 401–413. doi:10.1046/j.1360-0443.2002.00020.x

Hill, J., Bird, H., & Thorpe, R. (2003). Effects of rheumatoid arthritis on sexual activity and relationships. *Rheumatology, 42*(2), 280–286.

Hill, S. K., Bishop, J. R., Palumbo, D., & Sweeney, J. A. (2010). Effect of second-generation antipsychotics on cognition: Current issues and future challenges. *Expert Review of Neurotherapeutics, 10*(1), 43–57. doi:10.1586/ern.09.143

Hillhouse, T. M., & Porter, J. H. (2015). A brief history of the development of antidepressant drugs: From monoamines to glutamate. *Experimental and Clinical Psychopharmacology, 23*(1), 1–21. doi:10.1037/a0038550

Himei, A., & Okamura, T. (2006). Discontinuation Syndrome Associated with Paroxetine in Depressed Patients: A Retrospective Analysis of Factors Involved in the Occurrence of the Syndrome. *CNS Drugs, 20*(8), 665–672. doi:10.2165/00023210-200620080-00005

Hinney, A., & Volckmar, A.-L. (2013). Genetics of eating disorders. *Current Psychiatry Reports, 15*(12), 423–423. doi:10.1007/s11920-013-0423-y

Hinshaw, S. P., & Scheffler, R. M. (2014). *The ADHD explosion: Myths, medicine, money, and today's push for performance.* New York, NY: Oxford University Press.

Hirsch, L. E., & Pringsheim, T. (2016). Aripiprazole for autism spectrum disorders (ASD). *Cochrane Database of Systematic Reviews, 2016*(6), CD009043. doi:10.1002/14651858.CD009043.pub3

Hirschfeld, M. (1948). *Sexual anomalies: The origins, nature, and treatment of sexual disorders* (Rev. ed.). New York, NY: Emerson Books.

Hirschfeld, R. M. A. (2001). The comorbidity of major depression and anxiety disorders: Recognition and management in primary care. *Primary Care Companion to the Journal of Clinical Psychiatry, 3*(6), 244-254.

Hirschkop, P. K., & Mook, J. R. (2012). *Revisiting the lessons of Osheroff v. Chestnut Lodge.* Paper presented at the 43rd Annual Meeting of the American Academy of Psychiatry and the Law, Montreal, Canada.

Hirschowitz, J., Kolevzon, A., & Garakani, A. (2010). The pharmacological treatment of bipolar disorder: The question of modern advances. *Harvard Review of Psychiatry, 18*(5), 266–278. doi:10.3109/10673229.2010.507042

Hite, S. (1976). *The Hite report: A nationwide study on female sexuality.* Oxford, UK: Macmillan.

Hite, S. (1981). *The Hite report on male sexuality.* New York, NY: Alfred A. Knopf.

Hiyoshi, A., Fall, K., Netuveli, G., & Montgomery, S. (2015). Remarriage after divorce and depression risk. *Social Science & Medicine, 141*, 109–114. doi:10.1016/j.socscimed.2015.07.029

Hjeltnes, A., Molde, H., Schanche, E., Vøllestad, J., Svendsen, J. L., Moltu, C., & Binder, P. E. (2017). An open trial of mindfulness-based stress reduction for young adults with social anxiety disorder. *Scandinavian Journal of Psychology, 58*(1), 80–90. doi:10.1111/sjop.12342

Ho, M. S. K., & Lee, C. W. (2012). Cognitive behaviour therapy versus eye movement desensitization and reprocessing for post-traumatic disorder—Is it all in the homework then? *European Review of Applied Psychology/Revue Européenne de Psychologie Appliquée, 62*(4), 253–260. doi:10.1016/j.erap.2012.08.001

Ho, P., & Ross, D. A. (2017). More than a gut feeling: The implications of the gut microbiota in psychiatry. *Biological Psychiatry, 81*(5), e35–e37. doi:10.1016/j.biopsych.2016.12.018

Hodgins, D. C., Currie, S. R., Currie, G., & Fick, G. H. (2009). Randomized trial of brief motivational treatments for pathological gamblers: More is not necessarily better. *Journal of Consulting and Clinical Psychology, 77*(5), 950–960. doi:10.1037/a0016318

Hodgson, K., Hutchinson, A. D., & Denson, L. (2014). Nonpharmacological treatments for ADHD: A meta-analytic review. *Journal of Attention Disorders, 18*(4), 275–282. doi:10.1177/1087054712444732

Hoekstra, P. J., Dietrich, A., Edwards, M. J., Elamin, I., & Martino, D. (2013). Environmental factors in Tourette syndrome. *Neuroscience & Biobehavioral Reviews, 37*(6), 1040–1049. doi:http://dx.doi.org/10.1016/j.neubiorev.2012.10.010

Hoekstra, P. J., Kallenberg, C. G. M., Korf, J., & Minderaa, R. B. (2002). Is Tourette's syndrome an autoimmune disease? *Molecular Psychiatry, 7*, 437–445. doi:10.1038/sj.mp.4000972

Hoffman, H. (1844). *Strewwelpeter: Merry stories and funny pictures* (1848, Trans.). New York, NY: Frederick Warne.

Hoffman, I. Z. (2009). Doublethinking our way to 'scientific' legitimacy: The desiccation of human experience. *Journal of the American Psychoanalytic Association, 57*(5), 1043–1069. doi:10.1177/0003065109343925

Hoffman, L., & Lincoln, J. (2011). Science, interpretation, and identity in the sexual orientation debate: What does finger length have to do with understanding a person? *PsycCRITIQUES, 56*(15). doi:10.1037/a0023178

Hofmann, S. G., & Hinton, D. E. (2014). Cross-cultural aspects of anxiety disorders. *Current Psychiatry Reports, 16*(6), 450–450. doi:10.1007/s11920-014-0450-3

Hofmann, S. G., Asnaani, A., & Hinton, D. E. (2010). Cultural aspects in social anxiety and social anxiety disorder. *Depression and Anxiety, 27*(12), 1117–1127. doi:10.1002/da.20759

Hofmann, S. G., Asnaani, A., Vonk, I. J. J., Sawyer, A. T., & Fang, A. (2012). The efficacy of cognitive behavioral therapy: A review of meta-analyses. *Cognitive Therapy and Research, 36*(5), 427–440. doi:10.1007/s10608-012-9476-1

Hofmann, S. G., Moscovitch, D. A., & Heinrichs, N. (2002). Evolutionary mechanisms of fear and anxiety. *Journal of Cognitive Psychotherapy, 16*(3), 317–330. doi:10.1891/jcop.16.3.317.52519

Hoge, E. A., Bui, E., Goetter, E., Robinaugh, D. J., Ojserkis, R. A., Fresco, D. M., & Simon, N. M. (2015). Change in decentering mediates improvement in anxiety in mindfulness-based stress reduction for generalized anxiety disorder. *Cognitive Therapy and Research, 39*(2), 228–235. doi:10.1007/s10608-014-9646-4

Hoge, E. A., Bui, E., Palitz, S. A., Schwarz, N. R., Owens, M. E., Johnston, J. M., ... Simon, N. M. (2017). The effect of mindfulness meditation training on biological acute stress responses in generalized anxiety disorder. *Psychiatry Research.* doi:10.1016/j.psychres.2017.01.006

Holland, G., & Tiggemann, M. (2016). A systematic review of the impact of the use of social networking sites on body image and disordered eating outcomes. *Body Image, 17*, 100–110. doi:10.1016/j.bodyim.2016.02.008

Holland, J. M., Rozalski, V., Thompson, K. L., Tiongson, R. J., Schatzberg, A. F., O'Hara, R., & Gallagher-Thompson, D. (2014). The unique impact of late-life bereavement and prolonged grief on diurnal cortisol. *The Journals of Gerontology: Series B: Psychological Sciences and Social Sciences, 69B*(1), 4–11. doi:10.1093/geronb/gbt051

Holliday, K. L., Macfarlane, G. J., Nicholl, B. I., Creed, F., Thomson, W., & McBeth, J. (2010). Genetic variation in neuroendocrine genes associates with somatic symptoms in the general population: Results from the EPIFUND study. *Journal of Psychosomatic Research, 68*(5), 469–474. doi:10.1016/j.jpsychores.2010.01.024

Hölling, I. (2001). About the impossibility of a single (ex-)user and survivor of psychiatry position. *Acta Psychiatrica Scandinavica. Supplementum, 104*, 102–106. doi:10.1034/j.1600-0447.2001.1040s2102.x

Hollon, S. D. (2006). Randomized clinical trials. In J. C. Norcross, L. E. Beutler, & R. F. Levant (Eds.), *Evidenced-based practices in mental health* (pp. 96–105). Washington, DC: American Psychological Association.

Hollon, S. D., & Ponniah, K. (2010). A review of empirically supported psychological therapies for mood disorders in adults. *Depression and Anxiety, 27*(10), 891–932. doi:10.1002/da.20741

Holmes, E. A., Brown, R. J., Mansell, W., Fearon, R. P., Hunter, E. C. M., Frasquilho, F., & Oakley, D. A. (2005). Are there two qualitatively distinct forms of dissociation? A review and some clinical implications. *Clinical Psychology Review, 25*(1), 1–23. doi:http://dx.doi.org/10.1016/j.cpr.2004.08.006

Holmes, J. [Jamie] (2015, August 24). The case for teaching ignorance. *The New York Times*, p. A21. Retrieved from http://www.nytimes.com/2015/08/24/opinion/the-case-for-teaching-ignorance.html?smid=nytcore-ipad-share&smprod=nytcore-ipad&_r=0

Holmes, J. [Jeremy] (2015). Attachment theory in clinical practice: A personal account. *British Journal of Psychotherapy, 31*(2), 208–228. doi:10.1111/bjp.12151

Holmes, L. (2017, August 4). Suicide rates for teen boys and girls are climbing. *Huffington Post.* Retrieved from http://www.huffingtonpost.com/entry/suicide-rates-teen-girls_us_59848b64e4b0cb15b1be13f4

Holtom-Viesel, A., & Allan, S. (2014). A systematic review of the literature on family functioning across all eating disorder diagnoses in comparison to control families. *Clinical Psychology Review, 34*(1), 29–43. doi:10.1016/j.cpr.2013.10.005

Honos-Webb, L. (2010). *The gift of ADHD: How to transform your child's problems into strengths* (2nd ed.). Oakland, CA: New Harbinger Publications.

Hopwood, C. J. (2013). The role of behavior genetics in personality disorder classification: Comment on South and DeYoung (2013). *Personality Disorders: Theory, Research, and Treatment, 4*(3), 289–290. doi:10.1037/per0000004

Horesh, D., Lowe, S. R., Galea, S., Aiello, A. E., Uddin, M., & Koenen, K. C. (2017). An in-depth look into PTSD-depression comorbidity: A longitudinal study of chronically-exposed Detroit residents. *Journal of Affective Disorders, 208*, 653–661. doi:10.1016/j.jad.2016.08.053

Horn, E. K., Bartak, A., Meerman, A. M. M. A., Rossum, B. V., Ziegler, U. M., Thunnissen, M., ... Verheul, R. (2015). Effectiveness of psychotherapy in personality disorders not otherwise specified: A comparison of different treatment modalities. *Clinical Psychology & Psychotherapy, 22*(5), 426–442. doi:10.1002/cpp.1904

Horner, M. D., & Hamner, M. B. (2002). Neurocognitive functioning in posttraumatic stress disorder. *Neuropsychology Review, 12*(1), 15–30. doi:10.1023/A:1015439106231

Horney, K. (1924). On the genesis of the castration complex in women. *The International Journal of Psychoanalysis, 5*, 50–65.

Hornig, M., & Lipkin, W. I. (2013). Immune-mediated animal models of Tourette syndrome. *Neuroscience and Biobehavioral Reviews, 37*(6), 1120–1138. doi:10.1016/j.neubiorev.2013.01.007

Horowitz, M. J. (1973). Phase oriented treatment of stress response syndromes. *American Journal of Psychotherapy, 27*(4), 506–515.

Horowitz, M. J. (1991). Short-term dynamic therapy of stress response syndromes. In P. Crits-Christoph & J. P. Barber (Eds.), *Handbook of short-term dynamic psychotherapy* (pp. 166–198). New York, NY: Basic Books.

Horowitz, M. J. (2014). Grieving: The role of self-reorganization. *Psychodynamic Psychiatry, 42*(1), 89–97. doi:10.1521/pdps.2014.42.1.89

Horowitz, M. J., Wilner, N., Kaltreider, N., & Alvarez, W. (1980). Signs and symptoms of posttraumatic stress disorder. *Archives of General Psychiatry, 37*(1), 85–92. doi:10.1001/archpsyc.1980.01780140087010

Horowitz, M. J., Wilner, N., Marmar, C., & Krupnick, J. (1980). Pathological grief and the activity of latent self-images. *The American Journal of Psychiatry, 137*(10), 1157–1162.

Horowitz, R. (2002). Psychotherapy and schizophrenia: The mirror of countertransference. *Clinical Social Work Journal, 30*(3), 235–244. doi:10.1023/A:1016041330728

Horwitz, A. V. (2013). *Anxiety: A short history.* Baltimore, MD: The Johns Hopkins University Press.

Horwitz, A. V., & Wakefield, J. C. (2007). *The loss of sadness: How psychiatry transformed normal sadness into depressive disorder.* New York, NY: Oxford University Press.

Horwitz, B. N., Marceau, K., Narusyte, J., Ganiban, J., Spotts, E. L., Reiss, D., … Neiderhiser, J. M. (2015). Parental criticism is an environmental influence on adolescent somatic symptoms. *Journal of Family Psychology, 29*(2), 283–289. doi:10.1037/fam0000065

Hoskins, M., Pearce, J., Bethell, A., Dankova, L., Barbui, C., Tol, W. A., … Bisson, J. I. (2015). Pharmacotherapy for post-traumatic stress disorder: Systematic review and meta-analysis. *The British Journal of Psychiatry, 206*(2), 93–100. doi:10.1192/bjp.bp.114.148551

Hotopf, M., Hardy, R., & Lewis, G. (1997). Discontinuation rates of SSRIs and tricyclic antidepressants: A meta-analysis and investigation of heterogeneity. *The British Journal of Psychiatry, 170*(2), 120–127. doi:10.1192/bjp.170.2.120

Hou, R., & Baldwin, D. S. (2012). A neuroimmunological perspective on anxiety disorders. *Human Psychopharmacology: Clinical and Experimental, 27*(1), 6–14. doi:10.1002/hup.1259

Hou, R., Garner, M., Holmes, C., Osmond, C., Teeling, J., Lau, L., & Baldwin, D. S. (2017). Peripheral inflammatory cytokines and immune balance in Generalised Anxiety Disorder: Case-controlled study. *Brain, Behavior, and Immunity, 62*, 212–218. doi:10.1016/j.bbi.2017.01.021

Houts, A. C. (1996). Harmful dysfunction and the search for value neutrality in the definition of mental disorder: Response to Wakefield, part 2. *Behaviour Research and Therapy, 39*, 1099–1132. doi:10.1016/S0005-7967(01)00053-5

Howard, C. (2016). Understanding the dfference between a feeding and eating disorder in your child. Retrieved from http://www.eatingdisorderhope.com/blog/understanding-the-difference-between-a-feeding-and-eating-disorder-in-your-child

Howard, S., & Hughes, B. M. (2013). Type D personality is associated with a sensitized cardiovascular response to recurrent stress in men. *Biological Psychology, 94*(2), 450–455. doi:10.1016/j.biopsycho.2013.09.001

Howe, L., Tickle, A., & Brown, I. (2014). 'Schizophrenia is a dirty word': Service users' experiences of receiving a diagnosis of schizophrenia. *The Psychiatric Bulletin, 38*(4), 154–158. doi:10.1192/pb.bp.113.045179

Howell, M. J. (2012). Parasomnias: An updated review. *Neurotherapeutics, 9*(4), 753–775. doi:10.1007/s13311-012-0143-8

Howell, M. J., Khawaja, I. S., & Schenck, C. H. (2015). Parasomnias: An update. *Psychiatric Annals, 45*(1), 30–34. doi:10.3928/00485713-20150106-07

Howes, O. D., & Murray, R. M. (2014). Schizophrenia: An integrated sociodevelopmental-cognitive model. *The Lancet, 383*(9929), 1677–1687. doi:10.1016/S0140-6736(13)62036-X

Howes, O. D., & Nour, M. M. (2016). Dopamine and the aberrant salience hypothesis of schizophrenia. *World Psychiatry, 15*(1), 3–4. doi:10.1002/wps.20276

Howes, O. D., McCutcheon, R., & Stone, J. (2015). Glutamate and dopamine in schizophrenia: An update for the 21st century. *Journal of Psychopharmacology, 29*(2), 97–115. doi:10.1177/0269881114563634

Howes, R. (2009, July 27). The definition of insanity is…. Retrieved from https://www.psychologytoday.com/blog/in-therapy/200907/the-definition-insanity-is

Hu, J., Ferguson, L., Adler, K., Farah, C. A., Hastings, M. H., Sossin, W. S., & Schacher, S. (2017). Selective erasure of distinct forms of long-term synaptic plasticity underlying different forms of memory in the same postsynaptic neuron. *Current Biology, 27*(13), 1888–1899. doi:10.1016/j.cub.2017.05.081

Hu, T., Zhang, D., & Yang, Z. (2015). The relationship between attributional style for negative outcomes and depression: A meta-analysis. *Journal of Social and Clinical Psychology, 34*(4), 304–321. doi:10.1521/jscp.2015.34.4.304

Hu, X., Das, B., Hou, H., He, W., & Yan, R. (2018). BACE1 deletion in the adult mouse reverses preformed amyloid deposition and improves cognitive functions. *The Journal of Experimental Medicine. 215*(3), 927–940. doi:10.1084/jem.20171831

Huang, H., Michetti, C., Busnelli, M., Managò, F., Sannino, S., Scheggia, D., … Papaleo, F. (2014). Chronic and acute intranasal oxytocin produce divergent social effects in mice. *Neuropsychopharmacology, 39*(5), 1102–1114. doi:10.1038/npp.2013.310

Hudson, B. (1991). Deinstitutionalisation: What went wrong? *Disability, Handicap & Society, 6*(1), 21–36. doi:10.1080/02674649166780021

Hudson, J. I., Pope, H. G., Jonas, J. M., Yurgelun-Todd, D., & Frankenburg, F. R. (1987). A controlled family history study of bulimia. *Psychological Medicine, 17*(4), 883–890. doi:10.1017/S0033291700000684

Huedo-Medina, T. B., Kirsch, I., Middlemass, J., Klonizakis, M., & Siriwardena, A. N. (2012). Effectiveness of non-benzodiazepine hypnotics in treatment of adult insomnia: Meta-analysis of data submitted to the Food and Drug Administration. *BMJ: British Medical Journal, 345*.

Huerta, M., Bishop, S. L., Duncan, A., Hus, V., & Lord, C. (2012). Application of DSM-5 criteria for autism spectrum disorder to three samples of children with DSM-IV diagnoses of pervasive developmental disorders. *The American Journal of Psychiatry, 169*(10), 1056–1064. doi:10.1176/appi.ajp.2012.12020276

Hughes, D. (1990). Participant modeling as a classroom activity. *Teaching of Psychology, 17*(4), 238–240. doi:10.1207/s15328023top1704_6

Hughes, J. R. (2016). Editor's choice: Varenicline as a cause of suicidal outcomes. *Nicotine & Tobacco Research, 18*(1), 2–9.

Hughes, J. R., Peters, E. N., & Naud, S. (2011). Effectiveness of over-the-counter nicotine replacement therapy: A qualitative review of nonrandomized trials. *Nicotine & Tobacco Research, 13*(7), 512–522. doi:10.1093/ntr/ntr055

Hume, D. (1783). Essays on suicide and the immortality of the soul: The complete 1783 edition. Retrieved from http://www.geocities.ws/iloveselfinjury/ebooks/essaysonsuicide.pdf

Humphreys, C. L., Rubin, J. S., Knudson, R. M., & Stiles, W. B. (2005). The assimilation of anger in a case of dissociative identity disorder. *Counselling Psychology Quarterly, 18*(2), 121–132. doi:10.1080/09515070500136488

Humphries, T., & Bone, J. (1993). Validity of IQ-achievement discrepancy criteria for identifying learning disabilities. *Canadian Journal of School Psychology, 9*(2), 181–191. doi:10.1177/082957359400900206

Hunsely, J., Elliott, K., & Therrien, Z. (2013). *The efficacy and effectiveness of psychological treatments.* Retrieved from http://www.cpa.ca/docs/File/Practice/TheEfficacyAndEffectivenessOfPsychologicalTreatments_web.pdf

Hunt, G. E., Malhi, G. S., Cleary, M., Lai, H. M. X., & Sitharthan, T. (2016a). Comorbidity of bipolar and substance use disorders in national surveys of general populations, 1990–2015: Systematic review and meta-analysis. *Journal of Affective Disorders.* doi:10.1016/j.jad.2016.06.051

Hunt, G. E., Malhi, G. S., Cleary, M., Lai, H. M. X., & Sitharthan, T. (2016b). Prevalence of comorbid bipolar and substance use disorders in clinical settings, 1990–2015: Systematic review and meta-analysis. *Journal of Affective Disorders.* doi:10.1016/j.jad.2016.07.011

Hunter, E. C. M., Sierra, M., & David, A. S. (2004). The epidemiology of depersonalisation and derealisation: A systematic review. *Social Psychiatry and Psychiatric Epidemiology, 39*(1), 9–18. doi:10.1007/s00127-004-0701-4

Hunter, M. D., & Woodruff, P. W. R. (2005). History, aetiology and symptomatology of schizophrenia. *Psychiatry, 4*(10), 2–6. doi:http://dx.doi.org/10.1383/psyt.2005.4.10.2

Huprich, S. K. (2011). Reclaiming the value of assessing unconscious and subjective psychological experience. *Journal of Personality Assessment, 93*(2), 151–160. doi:10.1080/00223891.2010.542531

Hurl, C. (2011). Urine trouble: a social history of bedwetting and its regulation. *History of the Human Sciences, 24*(2), 48–64.

Hurst, K., Read, S., & Holtham, T. (2015). Bulimia nervosa in adolescents: A new therapeutic frontier. *Journal of Family Therapy.* doi:10.1111/1467-6427.12095

Hurwitz, S. (2013). The gluten-free, casein-free diet and autism: Limited return on family investment. *Journal of Early Intervention, 35*(1), 3–19. doi:10.1177/1053815113484807

Husby, S. M., & Wichstrøm, L. (2016). Interrelationships and continuities in symptoms of oppositional defiant and conduct disorders from age 4 to 10 in the community. *Journal of Abnormal Child Psychology.* doi:10.1007/s10802-016-0210-4

Hussman, J. P. (2001). Suppressed GABAergic inhibition as a common factor in suspected etiologies of autism. *Journal of Autism and Developmental Disorders, 31*(2), 247–248. doi:10.1023/A:1010715619091

Husted, J. A., Ahmed, R., Chow, E. W. C., Brzustowicz, L. M., & Bassett, A. S. (2010). Childhood trauma and genetic factors in familial schizophrenia associated with the NOS1AP gene. *Schizophrenia Research, 121*(1–3), 187–192. doi:http://dx.doi.org/10.1016/j.schres.2010.05.021

Husted, J. A., Ahmed, R., Chow, E. W. C., Brzustowicz, L. M., & Bassett, A. S. (2012). Early environmental exposures influence schizophrenia expression even in the presence of strong genetic predisposition. *Schizophrenia Research, 137*(1–3), 166–168. doi:http://dx.doi.org/10.1016/j.schres.2012.02.009

Hvidt, E. A., Ploug, T., & Holm, S. (2016). The impact of telephone crisis services on suicidal users: A systematic review of the past 45 years. *Mental Health Review Journal, 21*(2), 141–160. doi:10.1108/MHRJ-07-2015-0019

Hyman, S. (2014). Mental health: depression needs large human-genetics studies. *Nature, 515*(7526), 189–191. doi:10.1038/515189a

Hyman, S. L., Stewart, P. A., Foley, J., Cain, U., Peck, R., Morris, D. D., … Smith, T. (2016). The gluten-free/casein-free diet: A double-blind challenge trial in children with autism. *Journal of Autism and Developmental Disorders, 46*(1), 205–220. doi:10.1007/s10803-015-2564-9

Hypericum Depression Trial Study, G. (2002). Effect of hypericum perforatum (St. John's Wort) in major depressive disorder: A randomized controlled trial. *JAMA: Journal of the American Medical Association, 287*(14), 1807–1814. doi:10.1001/jama.287.14.1807

Iacono, W. G. (2013). Looking forward to the new personality disorder classification for DSM-5. *Personality Disorders: Theory, Research, and Treatment, 4*(3), 284–285. doi:10.1037/per0000002

Iacovino, J. M., Jackson, J. J., & Oltmanns, T. F. (2014). The relative impact of socioeconomic status and childhood trauma on Black-White differences in paranoid personality disorder symptoms. *Journal of Abnormal Psychology, 123*(1), 225–230. doi:10.1037/a0035258

Iasenza, S. (2001). Sex therapy with 'A New View.'. *Women & Therapy, 24*(1–2), 43–46.

ICD vs. DSM. (2009). *Monitor on Psychology, 40*(9), 63. Retrieved from http://www.apa.org/monitor/2009/10/icd-dsm.aspx

Iglesias, A., & Iglesias, A. (2008). Secondary diurnal enuresis treated with hypnosis: A time-series design. *International Journal of Clinical and Experimental Hypnosis, 56*(2), 229–240. doi:10.1080/00207140701849601

Iglewicz, A. M. D., Seay, K. B. S., Vigeant, S. B. S., Jouhal, S. K. M. D., & Zisook, S. M. D. (2013). The Bereavement Exclusion: the Truth between Pathology and Politics. *Psychiatric Annals, 43*(6), 261–266. doi:http://dx.doi.org/10.3928/00485713-20130605-05

Illmer, A. (2017, June 15). What's behind New Zealand's shocking youth suicide rate? *BBC News.* Retrieved from http://www.bbc.com/news/world-asia-40284130

Inder, M. L., Crowe, M. T., Luty, S. E., Carter, J. D., Moor, S., Frampton, C. M., & Joyce, P. R. (2015). Randomized, controlled trial of interpersonal and social rhythm therapy for young people with bipolar disorder. *Bipolar Disorders, 17*(2), 128–138. doi:10.1111/bdi.12273

Ingamells, K., & Epston, D. (2014). Love is not all you need: A revolutionary approach to parental abuse. *Australian and New Zealand Journal of Family Therapy, 35*(3), 364–382. doi:10.1002/anzf.1069

Insanity. (n.d.). *Collins Dictionary of Law.* Retrieved from http://legal-dictionary.thefreedictionary.com/insanity

The insanity defense. (n.d.). Retrieved from http://www.lectlaw.com/mjl/cl031.htm

Insel, T. (2013, April 29). Transforming diagnosis. Retrieved from http://www.nimh.nih.gov/about/director/2013/transforming-diagnosis.shtml

Insel, T. (2015). Psychiatry is reinventing itself thanks to advances in biology. *New Scientist,* (3035). Retrieved from https://www.newscientist.com/article/mg22730353-000-psychiatry-is-reinventing-itself-thanks-to-advances-in-biology/

Insel, T., Cuthbert, B., Garvey, M., Heinssen, R., Pine, D. S., Quinn, K., … Wang, P. (2010). Research domain criteria (RDoC): Toward a new classification framework for research on mental disorders. *The American Journal of Psychiatry, 167*(7), 748–751. doi:10.1176/appi.ajp.2010.09091379

Institute of Medicine. (1993). *Access to health care in America.* Washington, DC: National Academy Press.

International Society for the Study of Trauma and Dissociation. (2011). Guidelines for treating dissociative identity disorder in adults, third revision: Summary version. *Journal of Trauma & Dissociation, 12*(2), 188–212. doi:10.1080/15299732.2011.537248

Ip, M. L., St. Louis, K. O., Myers, F. L., & Xue, S. A. (2012). Stuttering attitudes in Hong Kong and adjacent Mainland China. *International Journal of Speech-Language Pathology, 14*(6), 543–556. doi:10.3109/17549507.2012.712158

Ipser, J. C., & Stein, D. J. (2012). Evidence-based pharmacotherapy of post-traumatic stress disorder (PTSD). *International Journal of Neuropsychopharmacology, 15*(6), 825–840. doi:10.1017/s1461145711001209

Ironson, G., Cruess, D., & Kumar, M. (2007). Immune and neuroendocrine alterations in post-traumatic stress disorder. In R. Ader (Ed.), *Psychoneuroimmunology* (Vol. 1, pp. 531–547). Burlington, MA: Elsevier Academic Press.

The irresistible impulse test. (n.d.). Retrieved from http://criminal.findlaw.com/criminal-procedure/the-irresistible-impulse-test.html

Irvine, J. (2005). *Disorders of desire: Sexuality and gender in modern American sexology* (revised and expanded ed.). Philadelphia, PA: Temple University Press.

Isaac, D. (2013). Culture-bound syndromes in mental health: A discussion paper. *Journal of Psychiatric and Mental Health Nursing, 20*(4), 355–361. doi:10.1111/jpm.12016

IsHak, W. W., & Tobia, G. (2013). DSM-5 changes in diagnostic criteria of sexual dysfunctions. *Reproductive System & Sexual Disorders: Current Research, 2*(2). Retrieved from http://www.omicsonline.org/dsm-5-changes-in-diagnostic-criteria-of-sexual-dysfunctions-2161-038X.1000122.php?aid=18508. doi:10.4172/2161-038X.1000122

Itoi, K., & Sugimoto, N. (2010). The brainstem noradrenergic systems in stress, anxiety and depression. *Journal of Neuroendocrinology, 22*(5), 355–361. doi:10.1111/j.1365-2826.2010.01988.x

Ivanov, I., Pearson, A., Kaplan, G., & Newcorn, J. (2010). Treatment of adolescent ADHD and comorbid substance abuse. *International Journal of Child and Adolescent Health, 3*(2), 163–177.

Ivanova, I., & Watson, J. (2014). Emotion-focused therapy for eating disorders: Enhancing emotional processing. *Person-Centered and Experiential Psychotherapies, 13*(4), 278–293. doi:10.1080/14779757.2014.910132

Ives, R., & Ghelani, P. (2006). Polydrug use (the use of drugs in combination): A brief review. *Drugs: Education, Prevention & Policy, 13*(3), 225–232. doi:10.1080/09687630600655596

Iwata, M., Ota, K. T., & Duman, R. S. (2013). The inflammasome: Pathways linking psychological stress, depression, and systemic illnesses. *Brain, Behavior, and Immunity, 31*, 105–114. doi:10.1016/j.bbi.2012.12.008

Jack, D. C. (1991). *Silencing the self: Women and depression.* New York, NY: HarperCollins.

Jack, D. C., & Ali, A. (2010a). Introduction: Culture, self-silencing, and depression: A contextual-relational perspective. In D. C. Jack & A. Ali (Eds.), *Silencing the self across cultures: Depression and gender in the social world* (pp. 3–17). New York, NY: Oxford University Press.

Jack, D. C., & Ali, A. (2010b). *Silencing the self across cultures: Depression and gender in the social world.* New York, NY: Oxford University Press.

Jackson, M. (2009). Great Britain, Part 1: The contribution of Kleinian innovations to the treatment of psychotic patients. In Y. O. Alanen, M. González de Chávez, A.-L. S. Silver, & B. Martindale (Eds.), *Psychotherapeutic approaches to schizophrenic psychoses* (pp. 78–92). London, UK: Routledge.

Jackson, M. (2014). Evaluating the role of Hans Selye in the modern history of stress. In D. Cantor & E. Ramsden (Eds.), *Stress, shock, and adaptation in the twentieth century* (pp. 21–48). Rochester, NY: University of Rochester Press.

Jackson, M. R. (2015). Resistance to qual/quant parity: Why the 'paradigm' discussion can't be avoided. *Qualitative Psychology, 2*(2), 181–198. doi:10.1037/qup0000031

Jackson, N., Denny, S., & Ameratunga, S. (2014). Social and socio-demographic neighborhood effects on adolescent alcohol use: A systematic review of multi-level studies. *Social Science & Medicine, 115*, 10–20. doi:10.1016/j.socscimed.2014.06.004

Jackson, S., & Rees, A. (2007). The appalling appeal of nature: The popular influence of evolutionary psychology as a problem for sociology. *Sociology, 41*(5), 917–930. doi:10.1177/0038038507080445

Jaeger, J. A., Echiverri, A., Zoellner, L. A., Post, L., & Feeny, N. C. (2010). Factors associated with choice of exposure therapy for PTSD. *International Journal of Behavioral Consultation and Therapy, 5*(3–4), 294–310. doi:10.1037/h0100890

Jain, A., Marshall, J., Buikema, A., Bancroft, T., Kelly, J. P., & Newschaffer, C. J. (2015). Autism occurrence by MMR vaccine status among US children with older siblings with and without autism. *JAMA: Journal of the American Medical Association, 313*(15), 1534–1540. doi:10.1001/jama.2015.3077

Jain, A., Marshall, J., Buikema, A., Bancroft, T., Kelly, J. P., & Newschaffer, C. (2016). Correction of description of MMR vaccine receipt coding and minor errors in MMR vaccine and autism study. *JAMA: Journal of the American Medical Association, 315*(2), 202–204. doi:10.1001/jama.2015.17065

Jain, S. (2014, February 6). Understanding lack of access to mental healthcare in the US: 3 lessons from the Gus Deeds story. Retrieved from http://blogs.plos.org/mindthebrain/2014/02/06/understanding-lack-access-mental-healthcare-3-lessons-gus-deeds-story/

Jakšić, N., Brajković, L., Ivezić, E., Topić, R., & Jakovljević, M. (2012). The role of personality traits in posttraumatic stress disorder (PTSD). *Psychiatria Danubina, 24*(3), 256–266.

Jakupcak, M., Wagner, A., Paulson, A., Varra, A., & McFall, M. (2010). Behavioral activation as a primary care-based treatment for PTSD and depression among returning veterans. *Journal of Traumatic Stress, 23*(4), 491–495. doi:10.1002/jts.20543

James, P. D., & Cowman, S. (2007). Psychiatric nurses' knowledge, experience and attitudes towards clients with borderline personality disorder. *Journal of Psychiatric and Mental Health Nursing, 14*(7), 670–678. doi:10.1111/j.1365-2850.2007.01157.x

Janca, A., Isaac, M., Bennett, L. A., & Tacchini, G. (1995). Somatoform disorders in different cultures: A mail questionnaire survey. *Social Psychiatry and Psychiatric Epidemiology, 30*(1), 44–48. doi:10.1007/BF00784434

Jane, J. S., Oltmanns, T. F., South, S. C., & Turkheimer, E. (2007). Gender bias in diagnostic criteria for personality disorders: An item response theory analysis. *Journal of Abnormal Psychology, 116*(1), 166–175. doi:10.1037/0021-843X.116.1.166

Janeck, A. S., Calamari, J. E., Riemann, B. C., & Heffelfinger, S. K. (2003). Too much thinking about thinking?: Metacognitive differences in obsessive-compulsive disorder. *Journal of Anxiety Disorders, 17*(2), 181–195. doi:10.1016/S0887-6185(02)00198-6

Janet, P. (1886). Unconscious acts and the doubling of personality during provoked somnambulism. *Revue Philosophique, 22*, 577–592. Retrieved from https://sites.google.com/site/psychiatryfootnotes/translations/unconscious-acts

Jang, K. L., Paris, J., Zweig-Frank, H., & Livesley, W. J. (1998). Twin study of dissociative experience. *Journal of Nervous and Mental Disease, 186*(6), 345–351. doi:10.1097/00005053-199806000-00004

Jani, S., Johnson, R. S., Banu, S., & Shah, A. (2016). Cross-cultural bias in the diagnosis of borderline personality disorder. *Bulletin of the Menninger Clinic, 80*(2), 146–165. doi:10.1521/bumc.2016.80.2.146

Janicak, P. G., & Carpenter, L. (2014). The efficacy of transcranial magnetic stimulation for major depression: A review of the evidence. *Psychiatric Annals, 44*(6), 284–292. doi:10.3928/00485713-20140609-06

Jankowski, K. (2016). PTSD and physical health. Retrieved from http://www.ptsd.va.gov/professional/co-occurring/ptsd-physical-health.asp

Jansen, J. E., Wøldike, P. M., Haahr, U. H., & Simonsen, E. (2015). Service user perspectives on the experience of illness and pathway to care in first-episode psychosis: A qualitative study within the TOP project. *Psychiatric Quarterly, 86*(1), 83–94. doi:10.1007/s11126-014-9332-4

Janssens, A., Van Den Noortgate, W., Goossens, L., Verschueren, K., Colpin, H., De Laet, S., ... Van Leeuwen, K. (2015). Externalizing problem behavior in adolescence: Dopaminergic genes in interaction with peer acceptance and rejection. *Journal of Youth and Adolescence, 44*(7), 1441–1456. doi:10.1007/s10964-015-0304-2

Janus, S. S., & Janus, C. L. (1993). *The Janus report on sexual behavior.* New York, NY: John Wiley.

Jaspers, L., Feys, F., Bramer, W. M., Franco, O. H., Leusink, P., & Laan, E. T. M. (2016). Efficacy and safety of flibanserin for the treatment of hypoactive sexual desire disorder in women: A systematic review and meta-analysis. *JAMA Internal Medicine, 176*(4), 453–462. doi:10.1001/jamainternmed.2015.8565

Jaturapatporn, D., Isaac, M. G. E. K. N., McCleery, J., & Tabet, N. (2012). Aspirin, steroidal and non-steroidal anti-inflammatory drugs for the treatment of Alzheimer's disease. *Cochrane Database of Systematic Reviews, 2012*(2). doi:10.1002/14651858.CD006378.pub2

Jauhar, S., McKenna, P. J., Radua, J., Fung, E., Salvador, R., & Laws, K. R. (2014). Cognitive-behavioural therapy for the symptoms of schizophrenia: Systematic review and meta-analysis with examination of potential bias. *The British Journal of Psychiatry, 204*(1), 20–29. doi:10.1192/bjp.bp.112.116285

Javaras, K. N., Laird, N. M., Reichborn-Kjennerud, T., Bulik, C. M., Pope, H. G., Jr., & Hudson, J. I. (2008). Familiality and heritability of binge eating disorder: Results of a case-control family study and a twin study. *International Journal of Eating Disorders, 41*(2), 174–179. doi:10.1002/eat.20484

Jeffreys, M., Capehart, B., & Friedman, M. J. (2012). Pharmacotherapy for posttraumatic stress disorder: Review with clinical applications. *Journal of Rehabilitation Research and Development, 49*(5), 703–715.

Jeffries, F. W., & Davis, P. (2013). What is the role of eye movements in eye movement desensitization and reprocessing (EMDR) for post-traumatic stress disorder (PTSD)? A review. *Behavioural and Cognitive Psychotherapy, 41*(3), 290–300. doi:10.1017/S1352465812000793

Jelovac, A., Kolshus, E., & McLoughlin, D. M. (2013). Relapse following successful electroconvulsive therapy for major depression: A meta-analysis. *Neuropsychopharmacology, 38*(12), 2467–2474. doi:10.1038/npp.2013.149

Jennings, J. H., Rizzi, G., Stamatakis, A. M., Ung, R. L., & Stuber, G. D. (2013). The inhibitory circuit architecture of the lateral hypothalamus orchestrates feeding. *Science, 341*(6153), 1517–1521. doi:10.1126/science.1241812

Jensen, P. S., Mrazek, D., Knapp, P. K., Steinberg, L., Pfeffer, C., Schowalter, J., & Shapiro, T. (1997). Evolution and revolution in child psychiatry: ADHD as a disorder of adaptation. *Journal of the American Academy of Child & Adolescent Psychiatry, 36*(12), 1672–1681. doi:10.1097/00004583-199712000-00015

Jiang, H., Xu, L., Shao, L., Xia, R., Yu, Z., Ling, Z., ... Ruan, B. (2016). Maternal infection during pregnancy and risk of autism spectrum disorders: A systematic review and meta-analysis. *Brain, Behavior, and Immunity, 58*, 165–172. doi:10.1016/j.bbi.2016.06.005

Jiang, Q., & Huang, X. (2013). Internet: Immersive virtual worlds. In P. M. Miller, S. A. Ball, M. E. Bates, A. W. Blume, K. M. Kampman, D. J. Kavanagh, M. E. Larimer, N. M. Petry, & P. De Witte (Eds.), *Comprehensive addictive behaviors and disorders: Vol. 1. Principles of addiction* (pp. 881–890). San Diego, CA: Elsevier Academic Press.

Jiang, Q., Huang, X., & Tao, R. (2013). Internet addiction: Cybersex. In P. M. Miller, S. A. Ball, M. E. Bates, A. W. Blume, K. M. Kampman, D. J. Kavanagh, M. E. Larimer, N. M. Petry, & P. De Witte (Eds.), *Comprehensive addictive behaviors and disorders: Vol. 1 Principles of addiction* (pp. 809–818). San Diego, CA: Elsevier Academic Press.

Jimerson, D. C., Wolfe, B. E., Metzger, E. D., Finkelstein, D. M., Cooper, T. B., & Levine, J. M. (1997). Decreased serotonin function in bulimia nervosa. *Archives of General Psychiatry, 54*(6), 529–534. doi:10.1001/archpsyc.1997.01830180043005

Joffe, H. V., Chang, C., Sewell, C., Easley, O., Nguyen, C., Dunn, S., ... Beitz, J. (2016). FDA approval of flibanserin—Treating hypoactive sexual desire disorder. *The New England Journal of Medicine, 374*(2), 101–104. doi:10.1056/NEJMp1513686

Johansson, K., San Sebastian, M., Hammarström, A., & Gustafsson, P. E. (2015). Neighbourhood disadvantage and individual adversities in adolescence and total alcohol consumption up to mid-life—Results from the Northern Swedish Cohort. *Health & Place, 33*, 187–194. doi:10.1016/j.healthplace.2015.03.005

John, A., Marchant, A. L., McGregor, J. I., Tan, J. O. A., Hutchings, H. A., Kovess, V., ... Lloyd, K. (2015). Recent trends in the incidence of anxiety and prescription of anxiolytics and hypnotics in children and young people: An e-cohort study. *Journal of Affective Disorders, 183*, 134–141. doi:https://doi.org/10.1016/j.jad.2015.05.002

Johns, M. W. (1991). A new method for measuring daytime sleepiness: The Epworth Sleepiness Scale. *Sleep, 14*(6), 540–545.

Johnson, B. (2003). Psychological addiction, physical addiction, addictive character, and addictive personality disorder: A nosology of addictive disorders. *Canadian Journal of Psychoanalysis/Revue Canadienne de Psychanalyse, 11*(1), 135–160.

Johnson, J. (2012). Using externalization as a means to regulate emotion in children with autism spectrum disorders. *Journal of Family Psychotherapy, 23*(2), 163–168. doi:10.1080/08975353.2012.679906

Johnson, J. (2014). *American lobotomy: A rhetorical history.* Ann Arbor, MI: University of Michigan Press.

Johnson, J. G., Cohen, P., Kasen, S., & Brook, J. S. (2006). Dissociative disorders among adults in the community, impaired functioning, and axis I and II comorbidity. *Journal of Psychiatric Research, 40*(2), 131–140. doi:10.1016/j.jpsychires.2005.03.003

Johnson, J. G., First, M. B., Block, S., Vanderwerker, L. C., Zivin, K., & Zhang, B. (2009). Stigmatization and receptivity to mental health services among recently bereaved adults. *Death Studies, 33*(8), 691–711. doi:10.1080/07481180903070392

Johnson, K. A., Sperling, R. A., Gidicsin, C. M., Carmasin, J. S., Maye, J. E., Coleman, R. E., ... Skovronsky, D. M. (2013). Florbetapir (F18-AV-45) PET to assess amyloid burden in Alzheimer's disease dementia, mild cognitive impairment, and normal aging. *Alzheimer's & Dementia, 9*(5, Suppl), S72–S83. doi:10.1016/j.jalz.2012.10.007

Johnson, N. P., & Phelps, G. L. (1991). Effectiveness in self-help groups: Alcoholics Anonymous as a prototype. *Family & Community Health: The Journal of Health Promotion & Maintenance, 14*(1), 22–27. doi:10.1097/00003727-199104000-00006

Johnson, S. (2001). Family therapy saves the planet: Messianic tendencies in the family systems literature. *Journal of Marital and Family Therapy, 27*(1), 3–11. doi:10.1111/j.1752-0606.2001.tb01132.x

Johnson, T. D., & Joshi, A. (2016). Dark clouds or silver linings? A stigma threat perspective on the implications of an autism diagnosis for workplace well-being. *Journal of Applied Psychology, 101*(3), 430–449. doi:10.1037/apl0000058

Johnstone, L. (2014a). Controversies and debates about formulation. In L. Johnstone & R. Dallos (Eds.), *Formulation in psychology and psychotherapy* (2nd ed., pp. 260–289). London, UK: Routledge.

Johnstone, L. (2014b). *A straight talking introduction to psychiatric diagnosis.* Ross-on-Wye, UK: PCCS Books.

Johnstone, L., & Dallos, R. (Eds.). (2014a). *Formulation in psychology and psychotherapy* (2nd ed.). London, UK: Routledge.

Johnstone, L., & Dallos, R. (2014b). Introduction to formulation. In L. Johnstone & R. Dallos (Eds.), *Formulation in psychology and psychotherapy* (2nd ed., pp. 1–17). London, UK: Routledge.

Johnstone, L., & Boyle, M. (with Cromby, J., Dillon, J., Harper, D., Kinderman, P., Longden, E., Pigrim, D., & Read, J.) (2018). *The Power Threat Meaning Framework: Towards the identification of patterns in emotional distress, unusual experiences and troubled or troubling behaviour, as an alternative to functional psychiatric diagnosis.* Leicester, UK: British Psychological Society. Retrieved from www.bps.org.uk/PTM-Main

Jokela, M., Pulkki-Råback, L., Elovainio, M., & Kivimäki, M. (2014). Personality traits as risk factors for stroke and coronary heart disease mortality: Pooled analysis of three cohort studies. *Journal of Behavioral Medicine, 37*(5), 881–889. doi:10.1007/s10865-013-9548-z

Jonathan, L. J., Chee, K.-T., & Ng, B.-Y. (2013). Schizoaffective disorder—An issue of diagnosis. *ASEAN Journal of Psychiatry, 14*(1), 76–81.

Jones, C., Hacker, D., Cormac, I., Meaden, A., & Irving, C. B. (2012). Cognitive behavior therapy versus other psychosocial treatments for schizophrenia. *Schizophrenia Bulletin, 38*(5), 908–910. doi:10.1093/schbul/sbs090

Jones, E., & Wessely, S. (2006). Psychological trauma: a historical perspective. *Psychiatry, 5*(7), 217–220. doi:http://dx.doi.org/10.1053/j.mppsy.2006.04.011

Jones, E., & Wessely, S. (2007). A paradigm shift in the conceptualization of psychological trauma in the 20th century. *Journal of Anxiety Disorders, 21*(2), 164–175. doi:10.1016/j.janxdis.2006.09.009

Jones, K. D. (2010). The unstructured clinical interview. *Journal of Counseling & Development, 88*(2), 220–226. doi:10.1002/j.1556-6678.2010.tb00013.x

Jones, K. D. (2012). A critique of the DSM-5 field trials. *Journal of Nervous and Mental Disease, 200*(6), 517–519.

Jones, K. D., Gill, C., & Ray, S. (2012). Review of the proposed DSM-5 substance use disorder. *Journal of Addictions & Offender Counseling, 33*(2), 115–123. doi:10.1002/j.2161-1874.2012.00009.x

Jones, K. E., Meneses da Silva, A. M., & Soloski, K. L. (2011). Sexological Systems Theory: An ecological model and assessment approach for sex therapy. *Sexual and Relationship Therapy, 26*(2), 127–144. doi:10.1080/14681994.2011.574688

Jones, M., Onslow, M., Packman, A., Williams, S., Ormond, T., Schwarz, I., & Gebski, V. (2005). Randomised controlled trial of the Lidcombe programme of early stuttering intervention. *BMJ: British Medical Journal, 331*(7518), 659–659. doi:10.1136/bmj.38520.451840.E0

Jones, S. (2004). Psychotherapy of bipolar disorder: a review. *Journal of Affective Disorders, 80*(2–3), 101–114. doi:http://dx.doi.org/10.1016/S0165-0327(03)00111-3

Jordan, A. H., & Litz, B. T. (2014). Prolonged grief disorder: Diagnostic, assessment, and treatment considerations. *Professional Psychology: Research and Practice, 45*(3), 180–187. doi:10.1037/a0036836

Jordan, I., Robertson, D., Catani, M., Craig, M., & Murphy, D. (2012). Aripiprazole in the treatment of challenging behaviour in adults with autism spectrum disorder. *Psychopharmacology, 223*(3), 357–360. doi:10.1007/s00213-012-2723-z

Jordan, J. V. (2004). Personality disorder or relational disconnection? In J. J. Magnavita (Ed.), *Handbook of personality disorders: Theory and practice* (pp. 120–134). Hoboken, NJ: John Wiley.

Jordan, K., Fromberger, P., Stolpmann, G., & Müller, J. L. (2011). The role of testosterone in sexuality and paraphilia—A neurobiological approach. Part II: Testosterone and paraphilia. *Journal of Sexual Medicine, 8*(11), 3008–3029. doi:10.1111/j.1743-6109.2011.02393.x

Jorge, R. E. (2015). Posttraumatic stress disorder. *CONTINUUM: Lifelong Learning in Neurology, 21*(3), 789–805.

Joseph, J. (2000). Not in their genes: A critical view of the genetics of attention-deficit hyperactivity disorder. *Developmental Review, 20*(4), 539–567. doi:http://dx.doi.org/10.1006/drev.2000.0511

Joseph, J. (2004). *The gene illusion: Genetic research in psychiatry and psychology under the microscope.* New York, NY: Algora Publishing.

Joseph, J. (2012). The 'missing heritability' of psychiatric disorders: Elusive genes or non-existent genes? *Applied Developmental Science, 16*(2), 65–83. doi:10.1080/10888691.2012.667343

Joseph, S., & Linley, P. A. (2006). Growth following adversity: Theoretical perspectives and implications for clinical practice. *Clinical Psychology Review, 26*(8), 1041–1053. doi:10.1016/j.cpr.2005.12.006

Joyal, C. C., & Carpentier, J. (2017). The prevalence of paraphilic interests and behaviors in the general population: A provincial survey. *The Journal of Sex Research, 54*(2), 161–171. doi:10.1080/00224499.2016.1139034

Joyce, P. R. (1980). The medical model—why psychiatry is a branch of medicine. *Australian and New Zealand Journal of Psychiatry, 14*(4), 269–278.

Joyce, P. R., Rogers, G. R., Miller, A. L., Mulder, R. T., Luty, S. E., & Kennedy, M. A. (2003). Polymorphisms of DRD4 and DRD3 and risk of avoidant and obsessive personality traits and disorders. *Psychiatry Research, 119*(1–2), 1–10. doi:10.1016/S0165-1781(03)00124-0

Juarascio, A. S., Manasse, S. M., Goldstein, S. P., Forman, E. M., & Butryn, M. L. (2015). Review of smartphone applications for the treatment of eating disorders. *European Eating Disorders Review, 23*(1), 1–11. doi:10.1002/erv.2327

Julian, L. J. (2011). Measures of Anxiety. *Arthritis care & research, 63*(S11), 10.1002/acr.20561. doi:10.1002/acr.20561

Jung, E., Wiesjahn, M., & Lincoln, T. M. (2014). Negative, not positive symptoms predict the early therapeutic alliance in cognitive behavioral therapy for psychosis. *Psychotherapy Research, 24*(2), 171–183. doi:10.1080/10503307.2013.851425

Justice Center. (2009). *The advocacy handbook: A guide to implementing recommendations of the criminal justice/mental health consensus project.* Retrieved from https://csgjusticecenter.org/cp/publications/the-advocacy-handbook-a-guide-to-implementing-recommendations-of-the-criminal-justicemental-health-consensus-project/

Juuhl-Langseth, M., Hartberg, C. B., Holmén, A., Thormodsen, R., Groote, I. R., Rimol, L. M., ... Rund, B. R. (2015). Impaired verbal learning is associated with larger caudate volumes in early onset schizophrenia spectrum disorders. *PLOS One, 10*(7).

Kaczkurkin, A. N., & Foa, E. B. (2015). Cognitive-behavioral therapy for anxiety disorders: An update on the empirical evidence. *Dialogues in Clinical Neuroscience, 17*(3), 337–346.

Kafka, M. P. (2010). Hypersexual disorder: A proposed diagnosis for DSM-V. *Archives of Sexual Behavior, 39*(2), 377–400. doi:10.1007/s10508-009-9574-7

Kafka, M. P. (2013). The development and evolution of the criteria for a newly proposed diagnosis for DSM-5: Hypersexual disorder. *Sexual Addiction & Compulsivity, 20*(1–2), 19–26.

Kafka, M. P. (2014). What happened to hypersexual disorder? *Archives of Sexual Behavior, 43*(7), 1259–1261. doi:10.1007/s10508-014-0326-y

Kalivas, P. W., & Volkow, N. D. (2005). The neural basis of addiction: A pathology of motivation and choice. *The American Journal of Psychiatry, 162*(8), 1403–1413.

Kalivas, P. W., Peters, J., & Knackstedt, L. (2006). Animal models and brain circuits in drug addiction. *Molecular Interventions, 6*(6), 339–344.

Kalsi, G., Prescott, C. A., Kendler, K. S., & Riley, B. P. (2009). Unraveling the molecular mechanisms of alcohol dependence. *Trends in Genetics, 25*(1), 49–55. doi:10.1016/j.tig.2008.10.005

Kalyva, E., Kyriazi, M., Vargiami, E., & Zafeiriou, D. I. (2016). A review of co-occurrence of autism spectrum disorder and Tourette syndrome. *Research in Autism Spectrum Disorders, 24*, 39–51. doi:10.1016/j.rasd.2016.01.007

Kamaya, H., & Krishna, P. R. (1987). Ketamine addiction. *Anesthesiology, 67*(5), 861–862.

Kamens, S. R. (2011). On the proposed sexual and gender identity diagnoses for DSM-5: History and controversies. *The Humanistic Psychologist, 39*(1), 37–59. doi:10.1080/08873267.2011.539935

Kamens, S. R. (2013). Attenuated psychosis syndrome was not actually removed from DSM-5. Retrieved from http://dxsummit.org/archives/1728

Kamens, S. R., Elkins, D. N., & Robbins, B. D. (2017). Open letter to the DSM-5. *Journal of Humanistic Psychology, 57*, 675–687. doi:10.1177/0022167817698261

Kanbur, N., & Harrison, A. (2016). Co-occurrence of substance use and eating disorders: An approach to the adolescent patient in the context of family centered care. A literature review. *Substance Use & Misuse, 51*(7), 853–860. doi:10.3109/10826084.2016.1155614

Kane, J. M., Robinson, D. G., Schooler, N. R., Mueser, K. T., Penn, D. L., Rosenheck, R. A., … Heinssen, R. K. (2016). Comprehensive versus usual community care for first-episode psychosis: 2-year outcomes from the NIMH RAISE Early Treatment Program. *The American Journal of Psychiatry, 173*(4), 362–372. Retrieved from doi:10.1176/appi.ajp.2015.15050632

Kang, C., Riazuddin, S., Mundorff, J., Krasnewich, D., Friedman, P., Mullikin, J. C., & Drayna, D. (2010). Mutations in the lysosomal enzyme-targeting pathway and persistent stuttering. *The New England Journal of Medicine, 362*(8), 677–685. doi:10.1056/NEJMoa0902630

Kang, H.-J., Kim, S.-Y., Bae, K.-Y., Kim, S.-W., Shin, I.-S., Yoon, J.-S., & Kim, J.-M. (2015). Comorbidity of depression with physical disorders: Research and clinical implications. *Chonnam Medical Journal, 51*(1), 8–18. doi:10.4068/cmj.2015.51.1.8

Kanner, A. M. (2004). Is major depression a neurologic disorder with psychiatric symptoms? *Epilepsy & Behavior, 5*(5), 636–644. doi:10.1016/j.yebeh.2004.07.008

Kanner, L. (1943). Autistic disturbance of affective contact. *Nervous Child, 2*, 217–250.

Kanner, L. (1949). Problems of nosology and psychodynamics of early infantile autism. *American Journal of Orthopsychiatry, 19*(3), 416–426. doi:10.1111/j.1939-0025.1949.tb05441.x

Kanner, L., & Eisenberg, L. (1957). Early infantile autism, 1943–1955. *Psychiatric Research Reports, 7*, 55–65.

Kantor, E. M., & Beckert, D. R. (2011). Psychological first aid. In F. J. Stoddard, Jr., A. Pandya, & C. L. Katz (Eds.), *Disaster psychiatry: Readiness, evaluation, and treatment* (pp. 203–212). Arlington, VA: American Psychiatric Publishing.

Kantrowitz, R. E., & Ballou, M. (1992). A feminist critique of cognitive-behavioral therapy. In L. S. Brown & M. Ballou (Eds.), *Personality and psychopathology: Feminist reappraisals* (pp. 70–87). New York, NY: Guilford Press.

Kaplan, A. (2009). DSM-V controversies. *Psychiatric Times*. Retrieved from http://www.psychiatrictimes.com/articles/dsm-v-controversies

Kaplan, A. S., & Howlett, A. (2010). Pharmacotherapy for anorexia nervosa. In C. M. Grilo & J. E. Mitchell (Eds.), *The treatment of eating disorders: A clinical handbook* (pp. 175–186). New York, NY: Guilford Press.

Kaplan, H. S. (1974). *The new sex therapy: Active treatment of sexual dysfunctions.* Oxford, UK: Brunner/Mazel.

Kaplan, H. S. (1995). *The sexual desire disorders: Dysfunctional regulation of sexual motivation.* Philadelphia, PA: Brunner/Mazel.

Kaplan, J. S., & Tolin, D. F. (2011). Exposure therapy for anxiety disorders. *Psychiatric Times*, (September 6). Retrieved from http://www.psychiatrictimes.com/anxiety/exposure-therapy-anxiety-disorders

Kaplan, M. (1983). A woman's view of DSM-III. *American Psychologist, 38*(7), 786–792. doi:10.1037/0003-066X.38.7.786

Kaplan, M. J. (2014). A psychodynamic perspective on treatment of patients with conversion and other somatoform disorders. *Psychodynamic Psychiatry, 42*(4), 593–615. doi:10.1521/pdps.2014.42.4.593

Kaplan, M. S., & Krueger, R. B. (2012). Cognitive-behavioral treatment of paraphilias. *Israeli Journal of Psychiatry, 49*(4), 291–296. Retrieved from http://doctorsonly.co.il/wp-content/uploads/2013/03/08_-Cognitive-behavioral-treatment.pdf

Kaplan, R. M. (2013). A history of insulin coma therapy in Australia. *Australasian Psychiatry, 21*(6), 587–591. doi:10.1177/1039856213500361

Kaplan, S. L. (2011). *Your child does not have bipolar disorder: How bad science and good public relations created the diagnosis.* Santa Barbara, CA: Praeger.

Kapp, M. B. (1994). Treatment and refusal rights in mental health: Therapeutic justice and clinical accommodation. *American Journal of Orthopsychiatry, 64*(2), 223–234. doi:10.1037/h0079524

Kapur, S. (2003). Psychosis as a state of aberrant salience: A framework linking biology, phenomenology, and pharmacology in schizophrenia. *The American Journal of Psychiatry, 160*(1), 13–23. doi:10.1176/appi.ajp.160.1.13

Kapur, S. (2004). How antipsychotics become anti-'psychotic' – from dopamine to salience to psychosis. *Trends in Pharmacological Sciences, 25*(8), 402–406. doi:https://doi.org/10.1016/j.tips.2004.06.005

Kapur, S., Mizrahi, R., & Li, M. (2005). From dopamine to salience to psychosis—linking biology, pharmacology and phenomenology of psychosis. *Schizophrenia Research, 79*(1), 59–68. doi:10.1016/j.schres.2005.01.003

Karam, E. G., Tabet, C. C., & Itani, L. A. (2013). The bereavement exclusion: Findings from a field study. *Psychiatric Annals, 43*(6), 267–271. doi:10.3928/00485713-20130605-06

Karch, C. M., Jeng, A. T., & Goate, A. M. (2013). Calcium phosphatase calcineurin influences tau metabolism. *Neurobiology of Aging, 34*(2), 374–386. doi:10.1016/j.neurobiolaging.2012.05.003

Kardiner, A., & Spiegel, H. (1947). *War stress and neurotic illness* (2nd ed.). Oxford, UK: P. B. Hoeber.

Kardum, I., Gračanin, A., & Hudek-Knežević, J. (2008). Evolutionary explanations of eating disorders. *Psihologijske Teme, 17*(2), 247–263.

Karl, A., Schaefer, M., Malta, L. S., Dörfel, D., Rohleder, N., & Werner, A. (2006). A meta-analysis of structural brain abnormalities in PTSD. *Neuroscience and Biobehavioral Reviews, 30*(7), 1004–1031. doi:10.1016/j.neubiorev.2006.03.004

Karl, T., & Arnold, J. C. (2014). Schizophrenia: A consequence of gene-environment interactions? *Frontiers in Behavioral Neuroscience, 8*.

Karon, B. P. (1992). The fear of understanding schizophrenia. *Psychoanalytic Psychology, 9*(2), 191–211. doi:10.1037/h0079355

Karon, B. P. (2000). The clinical interpretation of the Thematic Apperception Test, Rorschach, and other clinical data: A reexamination of statistical versus clinical prediction. *Professional Psychology: Research and Practice, 31*(2), 230–233. doi:10.1037/0735-7028.31.2.230

Karon, B. P. (2003). The tragedy of schizophrenia without psychotherapy. *Journal of the American Academy of Psychoanalysis, 31*(1), 89–119. doi:10.1521/jaap.31.1.89.21931

Karon, B. P. (2008a). An "incurable" schizophrenic: The case of Mr. X. *Pragmatic Case Studies in Psychotherapy, 4*(1), 1–24.

Karon, B. P. (2008b). Psychotherapy of schizophrenia works. *Pragmatic Case Studies in Psychotherapy, 4*(1), 55–61.

Karow, A., Reimer, J., König, H.-H., Heider, D., Bock, T., Huber, C., … Lambert, M. (2012). Cost-effectiveness of 12-month assertive community treatment as part of integrated care versus standard care in patients with schizophrenia treated with quetiapine immediate release (ACCESS Trial). *Journal of Clinical Psychiatry, 73*(3), e402–e408. doi:10.4088/JCP.11m06875

Karriker-Jaffe, K. J. (2011). Areas of disadvantage: A systematic review of effects of area-level socioeconomic status on substance use outcomes. *Drug and Alcohol Review, 30*(1), 84–95. doi:10.1111/j.1465-3362.2010.00191.x

Karriker-Jaffe, K. J. (2013). Neighborhood socioeconomic status and substance use by U.S. adults. *Drug and Alcohol Dependence, 133*(1), 212–221. doi:10.1016/j.drugalcdep.2013.04.033

Kaskutas, L. A. (2009). Alcoholics Anonymous effectiveness: Faith meets science. *Journal of Addictive Diseases, 28*(2), 145–157. doi:10.1080/10550880902772464

Kaslow, N. J., Reviere, S. L., Chance, S. E., Rogers, J. H., Hatcher, C. A., Wasserman, F., ... Seelig, B. (1998). An empirical study of the psychodynamics of suicide. *Journal of the American Psychoanalytic Association, 46*(3), 777–796. doi:10.1177/000306519804600 30701

Kass, A. E., Kolko, R. P., & Wilfley, D. E. (2013). Psychological treatments for eating disorders. *Current Opinion in Psychiatry, 26*(6), 549–555. doi:10.1097/YCO.0b013e328365a30e

Kass, N. E., & Sugarman, J. (1996). Are research subjects adequately protected? A review and discussion of studies conducted by the Advisory Committee on Human Radiation Experiments. *Kennedy Institute of Ethics Journal, 6*(3), 271–282.

Katchergin, O. (2016). The DSM and learning difficulties: Formulating a genealogy of the learning-disabled subject. *History of Psychiatry, 27*(2), 190–207. doi:10.1177/0957154X16633406

Kaufer, D. I. (2007). The dorsolateral and cingulate cortex. In B. L. Miller & J. L. Cummings (Eds.), *The human frontal lobes: Functions and disorders* (2nd ed., pp. 44–58). New York, NY: Guilford Press.

Kavalali, E. T., & Monteggia, L. M. (2015). How does ketamine elicit a rapid antidepressant response? *Current Opinion in Pharmacology, 20*, 35–39. doi:http://dx.doi.org/10.1016/j.coph.2014.11.005

Kavale, K. A., & Spaulding, L. S. (2008). Is response to intervention good policy for specific learning disability? *Learning Disabilities Research & Practice, 23*(4), 169–179. doi:10.1111/j.1540-5826.2008.00274.x

Kavale, K. A., Holdnack, J. A., & Mostert, M. P. (2006). Responsiveness to intervention and the identification of specific learning disability: A critique and alternative proposal. *Learning Disability Quarterly, 29*(2), 113–127. doi:10.2307/30035539

Kawa, S., & Giordano, J. (2012). A brief historicity of the Diagnostic and Statistical Manual of Mental Disorders: Issues and implications for the future of psychiatric canon and practice. *Philosophy, Ethics, and Humanities in Medicine, 7*(2). Retrieved from http://www.peh-med.com/content/7/1/2

Kaye, W. (2008). Neurobiology of anorexia and bulimia nervosa. *Physiology & Behavior, 94*(1), 121–135. doi:http://dx.doi.org/10.1016/j.physbeh.2007.11.037

Kaye, W. H., Ebert, M. H., Gwirtsman, H. E., & Weiss, S. R. (1984). Differences in brain serotonergic metabolism between nonbulimic and bulimic patients with anorexia nervosa. *The American Journal of Psychiatry, 141*(12), 1598–1601.

Kaye, W. H., Ebert, M. H., Raleigh, M., & Lake, R. (1984). Abnormalities in CNS monoamine metabolism in anorexia nervosa. *Archives of General Psychiatry, 41*(4), 350–355.

Kaye, W. H., Frank, G. K. W., & McConaha, C. (1999). Altered dopamine activity after recovery from restricting-type anorexia nervosa. *Neuropsychopharmacology, 21*(4), 503–506. doi:10.1016/S0893-133X(99)00053-6

Kaye, W. H., Frank, G. K., Bailer, U. F., Henry, S. E., Meltzer, C. C., Price, J. C., ... Wagner, A. (2005). Serotonin alterations in anorexia and bulimia nervosa: New insights from imaging studies. *Physiology & Behavior, 85*(1), 73–81. doi:10.1016/j.physbeh.2005.04.013

Kaye, W. H., Fudge, J. L., & Paulus, M. (2009). New insights into symptoms and neurocircuit function of anorexia nervosa. *Nature Reviews Neuroscience, 10*(8), 573–584. doi:10.1038/nrn2682

Kaye, W. H., Gendall, K., & Strober, M. (1998). Serotonin neuronal function and selective serotonin reuptake inhibitor treatment in anorexia and bulimia nervosa. *Biological Psychiatry, 44*(9), 825–838. doi:10.1016/S0006-3223(98)00195-4

Kaye, W. H., Gwirtsman, H. E., George, D. T., & Ebert, M. H. (1991). Altered serotonin activity in anorexia nervosa after long-term weight restoration: Does elevated cerebrospinal fluid 5-hydroxyindoleacetic acid level correlate with rigid and obsessive behavior? *Archives of General Psychiatry, 48*(6), 556–562. doi:10.1001/archpsyc.1991.01810300068010

Kaye, W. H., Wierenga, C. E., Bailer, U. F., Simmons, A. N., & Bischoff-Grethe, A. (2013). Nothing tastes as good as skinny feels: The neurobiology of anorexia nervosa. *Trends in Neurosciences, 36*(2), 110–120. doi:10.1016/j.tins.2013.01.003

Kaye, W. H., Wierenga, C. E., Bailer, U. F., Simmons, A. N., Wagner, A., & Bischoff-Grethe, A. (2013). Does a shared neurobiology for foods and drugs of abuse contribute to extremes of food ingestion in anorexia and bulimia nervosa? *Biological Psychiatry, 73*(9), 836–842. doi:http://dx.doi.org/10.1016/j.biopsych.2013.01.002

Kaysen, D., Resick, P. A., & Wise, D. (2003). Living in danger: The impact of chronic traumatization and the traumatic context on posttraumatic stress disorder. *Trauma, Violence, & Abuse, 4*(3), 247–264. doi:10.1177/1524838003004003004

Keck, P. E., Jr., McElroy, S. L., & Yildiz, A. (2015). Treatment of mania. In A. Yildiz, P. Ruiz, & C. B. Nemeroff (Eds.), *The bipolar book: History, neurobiology, and treatment* (pp. 263–279). New York, NY: Oxford University Press.

Keel, P. K., & Klump, K. L. (2003). Are eating disorders culture-bound syndromes? Implications for conceptualizing their etiology. *Psychological Bulletin, 129*(5), 747–769. doi:10.1037/0033-2909.129.5.747

Keeley, M. L., Graziano, P., & Geffken, G. R. (2009). Nocturnal enuresis and encopresis: Empirically supported approaches for refractory cases. In D. McKay & E. A. Storch (Eds.), *Cognitive-behavior therapy for children: Treating complex and refractory cases* (pp. 445–473). New York, NY: Springer.

Keesey, R. E., & Hirvonen, M. D. (1997). Body weight set-points: determination and adjustment. *The Journal of Nutrition, 127*(9), 1875S–1883S.

Keks, N. A., Hope, J., & Culhane, C. (2014). Management of antidepressant-induced sexual dysfunction. *Australasian Psychiatry, 22*(6), 525–528. doi:10.1177/1039856214556323

Kelleher, I., Jenner, J. A., & Cannon, M. (2010). Psychotic symptoms in the general population—An evolutionary perspective. *The British Journal of Psychiatry, 197*(3), 167–169. doi:10.1192/bjp.bp.109.076018

Keller, M. B., & Boland, R. J. (1998). Implications of failing to achieve successful long-term maintenance treatment of recurrent unipolar major depression. *Biological Psychiatry, 44*(5), 348–360. doi:10.1016/S0006-3223(98)00110-3

Kelley, M. E., LaRue, R. H., Roane, H. S., & Gadaire, D. M. (2011). Indirect behavioral assessments: Interviews and rating. In W. W. Fisher, C. C. Piazza, & H. S. Roane (Eds.), *Handbook of applied behavior analysis* (pp. 182–190). New York, NY: Guilford Press.

Kellner, C. H., & Fink, M. (2015). Electroconvulsive therapy versus pharmacotherapy for bipolar depression. *The American Journal of Psychiatry, 172*(3), 295–295. doi:10.1176/appi.ajp.2014.14101284

Kellner, R. (1994). Psychosomatic syndromes, somatization and somatoform disorders. *Psychotherapy and Psychosomatics, 61*(1–2), 4–24. doi:10.1159/000288868

Kelly, G. A. (1961). Suicide: The personal construct point of view. In N. L. Farberow & E. S. Shneidman (Eds.), *The cry for help.* New York, NY: McGraw-Hill.

Kelly, G. A. (1991a). *The psychology of personal constructs: Vol. 1. A theory of personality.* London, UK: Routledge. (Original work published 1955)

Kelly, G. A. (1991b). *The psychology of personal constructs: Vol. 2. Clinical diagnosis and psychotherapy.* London, UK: Routledge. (Original work published 1955)

Kelly, S. M., Gryczynski, J., Mitchell, S. G., Kirk, A., O'Grady, K. E., & Schwartz, R. P. (2014). Concordance between DSM-5 and DSM-IV nicotine, alcohol, and cannabis use disorder diagnoses among pediatric patients. *Drug and Alcohol Dependence, 140*, 213–216. doi:10.1016/j.drugalcdep.2014.03.034

Kemeny, M. E., & Schedlowski, M. (2007). Understanding the interaction between psychosocial stress and immune-related diseases: A stepwise progression. *Brain, Behavior, and Immunity, 21*(8), 1009–1018. doi:10.1016/j.bbi.2007.07.010

Kendler, K. S. (2005). Toward a Philosophical Structure for Psychiatry. *The American Journal of Psychiatry, 162*(3), 433–440.

Kendler, K. S., & Schaffner, K. F. (2011). The dopamine hypothesis of schizophrenia: An historical and philosophical analysis. *Philosophy, Psychiatry, & Psychology, 18*(1), 41–63. doi:10.1353/ppp.2011.0005

Kendler, K. S., Aggen, S. H., Czajkowski, N., Røysamb, E., Tambs, K., Torgersen, S., ... Reichborn-Kjennerud, T. (2008). The structure of genetic and environmental risk factors for DSM-IV personality disorders: A multivariate twin study. *Archives of General Psychiatry, 65*(12), 1438–1446. doi:10.1001/archpsyc.65.12.1438

Kendler, K. S., Czajkowski, N., Tambs, K., Torgersen, S., Aggen, S. H., Neale, M. C., & Reichborn-Kjennerud, T. (2006). Dimensional representations of DSM-IV Cluster A personality disorders in a population-based sample of Norwegian twins: A multivariate study. *Psychological Medicine, 36*(11), 1583–1591. doi:10.1017/S0033291706008609

Kendler, K. S., MacLean, C., Neale, M., Kessler, R. C., Heath, A., & Eaves, L. (1991). The genetic epidemiology of bulimia nervosa. *The American Journal of Psychiatry, 148*(12), 1627–1637.

Kendler, K. S., Ohlsson, H., Maes, H. H., Sundquist, K., Lichtenstein, P., & Sundquist, J. (2015). A population-based Swedish twin and sibling study of cannabis, stimulant and sedative abuse in men. *Drug and Alcohol Dependence, 149*, 49–54. doi:10.1016/j.drugalcdep.2015.01.016

Kendler, K. S., Ohlsson, H., Sundquist, K., & Sundquist, J. (2014a). Clinical features of drug abuse that reflect genetic risk. *Psychological Medicine, 44*(12), 2547–2556. doi:10.1017/S0033291713003267

Kendler, K. S., Ohlsson, H., Sundquist, K., & Sundquist, J. (2014b). The causal nature of the association between neighborhood deprivation and drug abuse: A prospective national Swedish co-relative control study. *Psychological Medicine, 44*(12), 2537–2546. doi:10.1017/S0033291713003048

Kendler, K. S., Ohlsson, H., Sundquist, K., & Sundquist, J. (2016). The rearing environment and risk for drug abuse: A Swedish national high-risk adopted and not adopted co-sibling control study. *Psychological Medicine, 46*(7), 1359–1366. doi:10.1017/S0033291715002858

Kendler, K. S., Walters, E. E., Truett, K. R., Heath, A. C., Neale, M. C., Martin, N. G., & Eaves, L. J. (1995). A twin-family study of self-report symptoms of panic-phobia and somatization. *Behavior Genetics, 25*(6), 499–515. doi:10.1007/BF02327574

Kennedy, J. J., & Bush, A. J. (1985). *An introduction to the design and analysis of experiments.* Lanham, MD: University Press of America.

Kennerley, H. (1996). Cognitive therapy of dissociative symptoms associated with trauma. *British Journal of Clinical Psychology, 35*(3), 325–340. doi:10.1111/j.2044-8260.1996.tb01188.x

Kenny, P. J., Voren, G., & Johnson, P. M. (2013). Dopamine D2 receptors and striatopallidal transmission in addiction and obesity. *Current Opinion in Neurobiology, 23*(4), 535–538. doi:10.1016/j.conb.2013.04.012

Kern, R. S., Glynn, S. M., Horan, W. P., & Marder, S. R. (2009). Psychosocial treatments to promote functional recovery in schizophrenia. *Schizophrenia Bulletin, 35*(2), 347–361. doi:10.1093/schbul/sbn177

Kernberg, O. F. (2001). Object relations, affects, and drives: Toward a new synthesis. *Psychoanalytic Inquiry, 21*(5), 604–619. doi:10.1080/07351692109348963

Kernberg, O. F. (2016). New developments in transference focused psychotherapy. *The International Journal of Psychoanalysis, 97*(2), 385–407. doi:10.1111/1745-8315.12289

Kernberg, O. F., Selzer, M. A., Koenigsberg, H. W., Carr, A. C., & Appelbaum, A. H. (1989). *Psychodynamic psychotherapy of borderline patients.* New York, NY: Basic Books.

Kernberg, P. F., Ritvo, R., & Keable, H. (2012). Practice parameter for psychodynamic psychotherapy with children. *Journal of the American Academy of Child & Adolescent Psychiatry, 51*(5), 541–557. doi:10.1016/j.jaac.2012.02.015

Kerr, J. S. (1996). Two myths of addiction: The addictive personality and the issue of free choice. *Human Psychopharmacology: Clinical and Experimental, 11*(Suppl 1), S9–S13. doi:10.1002/(SICI)1099-1077(199602)11:1+<S9::AID-HUP747>3.0.CO;2-6

Kersting, A., Kroker, K., Horstmann, J., Baune, B. T., Hohoff, C., Mortensen, L. S., ... Domschke, K. (2007). Association of MAO-A variant with complicated grief in major depression. *Neuropsychobiology, 56*(4), 191–196. doi:10.1159/000120624

Keshavan, M. S., Nasrallah, H. A., & Tandon, R. (2011). Schizophrenia, 'just the facts' 6. Moving ahead with the schizophrenia concept: From the elephant to the mouse. *Schizophrenia Research, 127*(1–3), 3–13. doi:10.1016/j.schres.2011.01.011

Keshavan, M. S., Tandon, R., Boutros, N. N., & Nasrallah, H. A. (2008). Schizophrenia, "just the facts": What we know in 2008: Part 3: Neurobiology. *Schizophrenia Research, 106*(2–3), 89–107. doi:http://dx.doi.org/10.1016/j.schres.2008.07.020

Kessler, R. C., Amminger, G. P., Aguilar-Gaxiola, S., Alonso, J., Lee, S., & Üstün, T. B. (2007). Age of onset of mental disorders: A review of recent literature. *Current Opinion in Psychiatry, 20*(4), 359–364. doi:10.1097/YCO.0b013e32816ebc8c

Kessler, R. C., Berglund, P., Demler, O., Jin, R., Koretz, D., Merikangas, K. R., ... Wang, P. S. (2003). The epidemiology of major depressive disorder: Results from the National Comorbidity Survey Replication (NCS-R). *JAMA: Journal of the American Medical Association, 289*(23), 3095–3105.

Kessler, R. C., Birnbaum, H. G., Shahly, V., Bromet, E., Hwang, I., McLaughlin, K. A., ... Stein, D. J. (2010). Age differences in the prevalence and co-morbidity of DSM-IV major depressive episodes: Results from the WHO World Mental Health Survey Initiative. *Depression and Anxiety, 27*(4), 351–364. doi:10.1002/da.20634

Kety, S. S. (1988). Schizophrenic illness in the families of schizophrenic adoptees: Findings from the Danish National Sample. *Schizophrenia Bulletin, 14*(2), 217–222.

Keuthen, N. J., Tung, E. S., Reese, H. E., Raikes, J., Lee, L., & Mansueto, C. S. (2015). Getting the word out: Cognitive-behavioral therapy for trichotillomania (hair-pulling disorder) and excoriation (skin-picking) disorder. *Annals of Clinical Psychiatry, 27*(1), 10–15.

Key, B. L., Rowa, K., Bieling, P., McCabe, R., & Pawluk, E. J. (2017). Mindfulness-based cognitive therapy as an augmentation treatment for obsessive–compulsive disorder. *Clinical Psychology & Psychotherapy.* doi:10.1002/cpp.2076

Khantzian, E. J. (1985). The self-medication hypothesis of addictive disorders: Focus on heroin and cocaine dependence. *The American Journal of Psychiatry, 142*(11), 1259–1264. doi:10.1176/ajp.142.11.1259

Khantzian, E. J. (1997). The self-medication hypothesis of substance use disorders: A reconsideration and recent applications. *Harvard Review of Psychiatry, 4*(5), 231–244. doi:10.3109/10673229709030550

Khantzian, E. J. (2003). Understanding addictive vulnerability: An evolving psychodynamic perspective. *Neuro-Psychoanalysis, 5*(1), 5–21. doi:10.1080/15294145.2003.10773403

Khantzian, E. J. (2012). Reflections on treating addictive disorders: A psychodynamic perspective. *The American Journal on Addictions, 21*(3), 274–279. doi:10.1111/j.1521-0391.2012.00234.x

Khantzian, E. J. (2013). Addiction as a self-regulation disorder and the role of self-medication. *Addiction, 108*(4), 668–669. doi:10.1111/add.12004

Khayyam-Nekouei, Z., Neshatdoost, H., Yousefy, A., Sadeghi, M., & Manshaee, G. (2013). Psychological factors and coronary heart disease. *ARYA Atherosclerosis, 9*(1), 102–111.

Khazan, I. Z. (2013). *The clinical handbook of biofeedback: A step-by-step guide for training and practice with mindfulness.* Chichester, UK: Wiley-Blackwell.

Khoudigian, S., Devji, T., Lytvyn, L., Campbell, K., Hopkins, R., & O'Reilly, D. (2016). The efficacy and short-term effects of electronic cigarettes as a method for smoking cessation: A systematic review and a meta-analysis. *International Journal of Public Health.* doi:10.1007/s00038-016-0786-z

Khoury, J. E., Milligan, K., & Girard, T. A. (2015). Executive functioning in children and adolescents prenatally exposed to alcohol: A meta-analytic review. *Neuropsychology Review, 25*(2), 149–170. doi:10.1007/s11065-015-9289-6

Khusid, M. A., & Vythilingam, M. (2016). The emerging role of mindfulness meditation as effective self-management strategy, Part 1: Clinical implications for depression, post-traumatic stress disorder, and anxiety. *Military Medicine, 181*(9), 961–968. doi:10.7205/MILMED-D-14-00677

Kiddoo, D. (2011). Nocturnal enuresis. *BMJ Clinical Evidence, 2011*, 0305.

Kiddoo, D. (2015). Nocturnal enuresis: Non-pharmacological treatments. *BMJ Clinical Evidence, 2015*, 0305.

Kiecolt-Glaser, J. K., & Glaser, R. (1992). Psychoneuroimmunology: Can psychological interventions modulate immunity? *Journal of Consulting and Clinical Psychology, 60*(4), 569–575. doi:10.1037/0022-006X.60.4.569

Kihlstrom, J. F., Glisky, M. L., & Angiulo, M. J. (1994). Dissociative tendencies and dissociative disorders. *Journal of Abnormal Psychology, 103*(1), 117–124. doi:10.1037/0021-843X.103.1.117

Kim, B., Benekos, P. J., & Merlo, A. V. (2016). Sex offender recidivism revisited: Review of recent meta-analyses on the effects of sex offender treatment. *Trauma, Violence, & Abuse, 17*(1), 105–117. doi:10.1177/1524838014566719

Kim, J. W., Lee, B. C., Lee, D. Y., Seo, C. H., Kim, S., Kang, T.-C., & Choi, I.-G. (2013). The 5-item Alcohol Use Disorders Identification Test (AUDIT-5): An effective brief screening test for problem drinking, alcohol use disorders and alcohol dependence. *Alcohol and Alcoholism, 48*(1), 68–73. doi:10.1093/alcalc/ags082

Kim, J.-W., Szigethy, E. M., Melhem, N. M., Saghafi, E. M., & Brent, D. A. (2014). Inflammatory markers and the pathogenesis of pediatric depression and suicide: A systematic review of the literature. *Journal of Clinical Psychiatry, 75*(11), 1242–1253. doi:10.4088/JCP.13r08898

Kim, S. Y. H., Appelbaum, P. S., Swan, J., Stroup, T. S., McEvoy, J. P., Goff, D. C., ... Caine, E. D. (2007). Determining when impairment constitutes incapacity for informed consent in schizophrenia research. *The British Journal of Psychiatry, 191*, 38–43. doi:10.1192/bjp.bp.106.033324

Kim, Y. R., Blashfield, R., Tyrer, P., Hwang, S. T., & Lee, H. S. (2014). Field trial of a putative research algorithm for diagnosing ICD-11 personality disorders in psychiatric patients: 1. Severity of personality disturbance. *Personality and Mental Health, 8*(1), 67–78. doi:10.1002/pmh.1248

Kim, Y. R., Tyrer, P., Lee, H. S., Kim, S. G., Hwang, S. T., Lee, G. Y., & Mulder, R. (2015). Preliminary field trial of a putative research algorithm for diagnosing ICD-11 personality disorders in psychiatric patients: 2. Proposed trait domains. *Personality and Mental Health, 9*(4), 298–307. doi:10.1002/pmh.1305

Kim, Y. S., Fombonne, E., Koh, Y.-J., Kim, S.-J., Cheon, K.-A., & Leventhal, B. L. (2014). A comparison of DSM-IV pervasive developmental disorder and DSM-5 autism spectrum disorder prevalence in an epidemiologic sample. *Journal of the American Academy of Child & Adolescent Psychiatry, 53*(5), 500–508. doi:10.1016/j.jaac.2013.12.021

Kimerling, R., Weitlauf, J. C., Iverson, K. M., Karpenko, J. A., & Jain, S. (2014). Gender issues in PTSD. In M. J. Friedman, T. M. Keane, & P. A. Resick (Eds.), *Handbook of PTSD: Science and practice* (2nd ed., pp. 313–330). New York, NY: Guilford Press.

Kimonis, E. R., & Frick, P. J. (2016). Externalizing disorders of childhood and adolescence. In J. E. Maddux & B. A. Winstead (Eds.), *Psychopathology: Foundations for a contemporary understanding* (4th ed., pp. 365–389). New York, NY: Routledge.

Kinderman, P. (2014a, August 18). Shh . . . just whisper it, but there might just be a revolution underway. Retrieved from http://www.madinamerica.com/2014/08/shh-just-whisper-might-just-revolution-underway/

Kinderman, P. (2014b). *A prescription for psychiatry: Why we need a whole new approach to mental health and wellbeing.* New York, NY: Palgrave Macmillan.

Kinderman, P. (2017). A manifesto for psychological health and wellbeing. In J. Davies (Ed.), *The sedated society: The causes and harms of our psychiatric drug epidemic* (pp. 271–301). New York, NY: Palgrave Macmillan.

Kinderman, P., & Cooke, A. (2017). Responses to the publication of the American Psychiatric Association's DSM-5. *Journal of Humanistic Psychology, 57*(6), 625–649. doi:10.1177/0022167817698262

Kinderman, P., Schwannauer, M., Pontin, E., & Tai, S. (2013). Psychological processes mediate the impact of familial risk, social circumstances and life events on mental health. *PLOS One, 8*(10). doi:10.1371/journal.pone.0076564

King, C., & Leask, J. (2017). The impact of a vaccine scare on parental views, trust and information needs: A qualitative study in Sydney, Australia. *BMC Public Health, 17*(1), 106. doi:10.1186/s12889-017-4032-2

King, D. L., Delfabbro, P. H., & Griffiths, M. D. (2013). Video game addiction. In P. M. Miller, S. A. Ball, M. E. Bates, A. W. Blume, K. M. Kampman, D. J. Kavanagh, M. E. Larimer, N. M. Petry, & P. De Witte (Eds.), *Comprehensive addictive behaviors and disorders: Vol. 1. Principles of addiction* (pp. 819–825). San Diego, CA: Elsevier Academic Press.

Kinrys, G., & Wygant, L. E. (2005). Anxiety disorders in women: Does gender matter to treatment? *Revista Brasileira de Psiquiatria, 27*, s43–s50.

Kinsey, A. C. (1941). Homosexuality; criteria for a hormonal explanation of the homosexual. *Journal of Clinical Endocrinology, 1*, 424–428. doi:10.1210/jcem-1-5-424

Kinsey, A. C., Pomeroy, W. B., & Martin, C. E. (1948). *Sexual behavior in the human male.* Oxford, UK: Saunders.

Kinsey, A. C., Pomeroy, W. B., Martin, C. E., & Gebhard, P. H. (1953). *Sexual behavior in the human female.* Oxford, UK: Saunders.

Kirby, L. G., Zeeb, F. D., & Winstanley, C. A. (2011). Contributions of serotonin in addiction vulnerability. *Neuropharmacology, 61*(3), 421–432. doi:10.1016/j.neuropharm.2011.03.022

Kirk, S. A., & Kutchins, H. (1992). *The selling of DSM: The rhetoric of science in psychiatry.* New York, NY: Aldine de Gruyter.

Kirkner, R. M. (2015). On ICD-10, the empire strikes back. Retrieved from http://www.managedcaremag.com/archives/2015/3/icd-10-empire-strikes-back

Kirsch, I. (2010). *The emperor's new drugs: Exploding the antidepressant myth.* New York, NY: Basic Books.

Kirsch, I. (2014). Antidepressants and the placebo effect. *Zeitschrift für Psychologie, 222*(3), 128–134. doi:10.1027/2151-2604/a000176

Kishi, T., Kafantaris, V., Sunday, S., Sheridan, E. M., & Correll, C. U. (2012). Are antipsychotics effective for the treatment of anorexia nervosa? Results from a systematic review and meta-analysis. *Journal of Clinical Psychiatry, 73*(6), e757–e766. doi:10.4088/JCP.12r07691

Kishi, T., Matsunaga, S., & Iwata, N. (2015). Suvorexant for primary insomnia: A systematic review and meta-analysis of randomized placebo-controlled trials. *PLOS One, 10*(8), e0136910–e0136910. doi:10.1371/journal.pone.0136910

Kissane, D. W., & Lichtenthal, W. G. (2008). Family focused grief therapy: From palliative care into bereavement. In M. S. Stroebe, R. O. Hansson, H. Schut, & W. Stroebe (Eds.), *Handbook of bereavement research and practice: Advances in theory and intervention* (pp. 485–510). Washington, DC: American Psychological Association.

Kissane, D. W., McKenzie, M., Block, S., Moskowitz, C., McKenzie, D. P., & O'Neill, I. (2006). Family focused grief therapy: A randomized, controlled trial in palliative care and bereavement. *The American Journal of Psychiatry, 163*(7), 1208–1218. doi:10.1176/appi.ajp.163.7.1208

Klaw, E., & Humphreys, K. (2000). Life stories of Moderation Management mutual help group members. *Contemporary Drug Problems: An Interdisciplinary Quarterly, 27*(4), 779–803.

Klein, J. F., & Hood, S. B. (2004). The impact of stuttering on employment opportunities and job performance. *Journal of Fluency Disorders, 29*(4), 255–273. doi:http://dx.doi.org/10.1016/j.jfludis.2004.08.001

Klein, J. P., Roniger, A., Schweiger, U., Späth, C., & Brodbeck, J. (2015). The association of childhood trauma and personality disorders with chronic depression: A cross-sectional study in depressed outpatients. *Journal of Clinical Psychiatry, 76*(6), e794–e801. doi:10.4088/JCP.14m09158

Klein, M., Heimann, P., Isaacs, S., & Riviere, J. (1952). *Developments in psychoanalysis* (J. Riviere Ed.). London, UK: Karnac.

Klein Hofmeijer-Sevink, M., Batelaan, N. M., van Megen, H. J. G. M., Penninx, B. W., Cath, D. C., van den Hout, M. A., & van Balkom, A. J. L. M. (2012). Clinical relevance of comorbidity in anxiety disorders: A report from the Netherlands Study of Depression and Anxiety (NESDA). *Journal of Affective Disorders, 137*(1-3), 106–112. doi:10.1016/j.jad.2011.12.008

Kleinman, A. M. (1977). Depression, somatization and the new cross-cultural psychiatry. *Social Science & Medicine, 11*(1), 3–10. doi:10.1016/0037-7856(77)90138-X

Kleinplatz, P. J. (1996). Transforming sex therapy: Integrating erotic potential. *The Humanistic Psychologist, 24*(2), 190–202. doi:10.1080/08873267.1996.9986850

Kleinplatz, P. J. (1998). Sex therapy for vaginismus: A review, critique, and humanistic alternative. *Journal of Humanistic Psychology, 38*(2), 41–81. doi:10.1177/00221678980382004

Kleinplatz, P. J. (2004). Beyond sexual mechanics and hydraulics: Humanizing the discourse surrounding erectile dysfunction. *Journal of Humanistic Psychology, 44*(2), 215–242. doi:10.1177/0022167804263130

Kleinplatz, P. J. (2007). Coming out of the sex therapy closet: Using experiential psychotherapy with sexual problems and concerns. *American Journal of Psychotherapy, 61*(3), 333–348.

Kleinplatz, P. J. (2010). 'Desire disorders' or opportunities for optimal erotic intimacy? In S. R. Leiblum (Ed.), *Treating sexual desire disorders: A clinical casebook* (pp. 92–113). New York, NY: Guilford Press.

Kleinplatz, P. J. (2012). Is that all there is? A new critique of the goals of sex therapy. In P. J. Kleinplatz (Ed.), *New directions in sex therapy: Innovations and alternatives* (2nd ed., pp. 101–118). New York, NY: Routledge.

Kleinplatz, P. J. (2014). The paraphilias: An experiential approach to 'dangerous' desires. In Y. M. Binik & K. S. K. Hall (Eds.), *Principles and practice of sex therapy* (5th ed., pp. 195–218). New York, NY: Guilford Press.

Klerman, G. L. (1990). The psychiatric patient's right to effective treatment: Implications of Osheroff v. Chestnut Lodge. *The American Journal of Psychiatry, 147*(4), 409–418. doi:10.1176/ajp.147.4.409

Klerman, G. L., Weissman, M. M., Rounsaville, B. J., & Chevron, E. S. (1984). *Interpersonal psychotherapy of depression: A brief, focused, specific strategy.* Lanham, MD: Jason Aronson.

Klest, B. (2012). Childhood trauma, poverty, and adult victimization. *Psychological Trauma: Theory, Research, Practice, and Policy, 4*(3), 245–251. doi:10.1037/a0024468

Klest, B., Freyd, J. J., & Foynes, M. M. (2013). Trauma exposure and posttraumatic symptoms in Hawaii: Gender, ethnicity, and social context. *Psychological Trauma: Theory, Research, Practice, and Policy, 5*(5), 409–416. doi:10.1037/a0029336

Klest, B., Freyd, J. J., Hampson, S. E., & Dubanoski, J. P. (2013). Trauma, socioeconomic resources, and self-rated health in an ethnically diverse adult cohort. *Ethnicity & Health, 18*(1), 97–113. doi:10.1080/13557858.2012.700916

Kliem, S., Kröger, C., & Kosfelder, J. (2010). Dialectical behavior therapy for borderline personality disorder: A meta-analysis using mixed-effects modeling. *Journal of Consulting and Clinical Psychology, 78*(6), 936–951. doi:10.1037/a0021015

Klimas, J., Tobin, H., Field, C., O'Gorman, C. S. M., Glynn, L. G., Keenan, E., ... Cullen, W. (2014). Psychosocial interventions to reduce alcohol consumption in concurrent problem alcohol and illicit drug users. *Cochrane Database of Systematic Reviews, 2014*(12), 1–56. doi:10.1002/14651858.CD009269. pub3

Kling, R. (2014). Borderline personality disorder, language, and stigma. *Ethical Human Psychology and Psychiatry, 16*(2), 114–119. doi:10.1891/1559-4343.16.2.114

Klingemann, H., & Rosenberg, H. (2009). Acceptance and therapeutic practice of controlled drinking as an outcome goal by Swiss alcohol treatment programmes. *European Addiction Research, 15*(3), 121–127. doi:10.1159/000210041

Klink, D., & Den Heijer, M. (2014). Genetic aspects of gender identity development and gender dysphoria. In B. P. C. Kreukels, T. D. Steensma, & A. L. C. de Vries (Eds.), *Gender dysphoria and disorders of sex development: Progress in care and knowledge* (pp. 25–51). New York, NY: Springer Science + Business Media.

Kluft, R. P. (2000). The psychoanalytic psychotherapy of dissociative identity disorder in the context of trauma therapy. *Psychoanalytic Inquiry, 20*(2), 259–286. doi:10.1080/07351692009348887

Kluge, M., Schüssler, P., Künzel, H. E., Dresler, M., Yassouridis, A., & Steiger, A. (2007). Increased nocturnal secretion of ACTH and cortisol in obsessive compulsive disorder. *Journal of Psychiatric Research, 41*(11), 928–933. doi:10.1016/j.jpsychires.2006.08.005

Klump, K. L., & Culbert, K. M. (2007). Molecular genetic studies of eating disorders: Current status and future directions. *Current Directions in Psychological Science, 16*(1), 37–41. doi:10.1111/j.1467-8721.2007.00471.x

Klump, K. L., Miller, K. B., Keel, P. K., McGue, M., & Iacono, W. G. (2001). Genetic and environmental influences on anorexia nervosa syndromes in a population-based twin sample. *Psychological Medicine, 31*(4), 737–740. doi:10.1017/S0033291701003725

Knafo, A., Iervolino, A. C., & Plomin, R. (2005). Masculine girls and feminine boys: Genetic and environmental contributions to atypical gender development in early childhood. *Journal of Personality and Social Psychology, 88*(2), 400–412. doi:10.1037/0022-3514.88.2.400

Knapp, M., Beecham, J., McDaid, D., Matosevic, T., & Smith, M. (2011). The economic consequences of deinstitutionalisation of mental health services: Lessons from a systematic review of European experience. *Health & Social Care in the Community, 19*(2), 113–125.

Kneeland, R. E., & Fatemi, S. H. (2013). Viral infection, inflammation and schizophrenia. *Progress in Neuro-Psychopharmacology & Biological Psychiatry, 42,* 35–48. doi:10.1016/j. pnpbp.2012.02.001

Knight, K. E. (2013). *Attention deficit hyperactivity disorder (ADHD) in adolescents: An investigative study of dopamine and norepinephrine systems.* (Doctoral dissertation), University of Arizona, Tucson, AZ, US. Retrieved from http://arizona.openrepository.com/arizona/bitstream/10150/247127/1/azu_etd_12403_sip1_m.pdf Available from EBSCOhost psyh database

Knight, R. A. (2010). Is a diagnostic category for paraphilic coercive disorder defensible? *Archives of Sexual Behavior, 39*(2), 419–426. doi:10.1007/s10508-009-9571-x

Knoll, J. L., IV. (2013). The humanities and psychiatry: The rebirth of mind. *Psychiatric Times.* Retrieved from http://www.psychiatrictimes.com/forensic-psychiatry/humanities-and-psychiatry-rebirth-mind

Knouse, L. E., & Fleming, A. P. (2016). Applying cognitive-behavioral therapy for ADHD to emerging adults. *Cognitive and Behavioral Practice.* doi:10.1016/j.cbpra.2016.03.008

Kocovski, N. L., Fleming, J. E., Hawley, L. L., Huta, V., & Antony, M. M. (2013). Mindfulness and acceptance-based group therapy versus traditional cognitive behavioral group therapy for social anxiety disorder: A randomized controlled trial. *Behaviour Research and Therapy, 51*(12), 889–898. doi:10.1016/j. brat.2013.10.007

Kodak, T., & Grow, L. L. (2011). Behavioral treatment of autism. In W. W. Fisher, C. C. Piazza, & H. S. Roane (Eds.), *Handbook of applied behavior analysis* (pp. 402–416). New York, NY: Guilford Press.

Koedoot, C., Bouwmans, C., Franken, M.-C., & Stolk, E. (2011). Quality of life in adults who stutter. *Journal of Communication Disorders, 44*(4), 429–443. doi:http://dx.doi. org/10.1016/j.jcomdis.2011.02.002

Koehler, B., & Silver, A.-L. S. (2009). Psychodynamic treatment of psychosis in the USA: Promoting development beyond biological reductionism. In Y. O. Alanen, M. González de Chávez, A.-L. S. Silver, & B. Martindale (Eds.), *Psychotherapeutic approaches to schizophrenic psychoses* (pp. 215–232). London, UK: Routledge.

Koehler, B., Silver, A.-L. S., & Karon, B. P. (2013). Psychodynamic approaches to understanding psychosis: Defenses against terror. In J. Read & J. Dillon (Eds.), *Models of madness: Psychological, social and biological approaches to psychosis* (pp. 238–248). London, UK: Routledge.

Koelen, J. A., Houtveen, J. H., Abbass, A., Luyten, P., Eurelings-Bontekoe, E. H. M., Van Broeckhuysen-Kloth, S. A. M., ... Geenen, R. (2014). Effectiveness of psychotherapy for severe somatoform disorder: meta analysis. *The British Journal of Psychiatry, 204*(1), 12–19. doi:10.1192/bjp.bp.112.121830

Koenders, L., Machielsen, M. W. J., van der Meer, F. J., van Gasselt, A. C. M., Meijer, C. J., van den Brink, W., ... de Haan, L. (2015). Brain volume in male patients with recent onset schizophrenia with and without cannabis use disorders. *Journal of Psychiatry & Neuroscience, 40*(3), 197–206.

Koenen, K. C., Amstadter, A. B., & Nugent, N. R. (2009). Gene–environment interaction in posttraumatic stress disorder: An update. *Journal of Traumatic Stress, 22*(5), 416–426. doi:10.1002/jts.20435

Koenigs, M., & Grafman, J. (2009). Posttraumatic stress disorder: The role of medial prefrontal cortex and amygdala. *The Neuroscientist, 15*(5), 540–548. doi:10.1177/1073858409333072

Kog, E., & Vandereycken, W. (1985). Family characteristics of anorexia nervosa and bulimia: A review of the research literature. *Clinical Psychology Review, 5*(2), 159–180. doi:10.1016/0272-7358(85)90020-0

Kog, E., Vandereycken, W., & Vertommen, H. (1985). The psychosomatic family model: A critical analysis of family interaction concepts. *Journal of Family Therapy, 7*(1), 31–44. doi:10.1046/j..1985.00663.x

Koger, S. M., Schettler, T., & Weiss, B. (2005). Environmental toxicants and developmental disabilities: A challenge for psychologists. *American Psychologist, 60*(3), 243–255. doi:10.1037/0003-066X.60.3.243

Koh, K. B., Choi, E. H., Lee, Y., & Han, M. (2011). Serotonin-related gene pathways associated with undifferentiated somatoform disorder. *Psychiatry Research, 189*(2), 246–250. doi:10.1016/j.psychres.2011.04.002

Kohler, C. G., Walker, J. B., Martin, E. A., Healey, K. M., & Moberg, P. J. (2010). Facial emotion perception in schizophrenia: A meta-analytic review. *Schizophrenia Bulletin, 36*(5), 1009–1019. doi:10.1093/schbul/sbn192

Köhler, O., Benros, M. E., Nordentoft, M., Farkouh, M. E., Iyengar, R. L., Mors, O., & Krogh, J. (2014). Effect of anti-inflammatory treatment on depression, depressive symptoms, and adverse effects: A systematic review and meta-analysis of randomized clinical trials. *JAMA Psychiatry, 71*(12), 1381–1391. doi:10.1001/jamapsychiatry.2014.1611

Köhler, S., Hoffmann, S., Unger, T., Steinacher, B., Dierstein, N., & Fydrich, T. (2013). Effectiveness of cognitive–behavioural therapy plus pharmacotherapy in inpatient treatment of depressive disorders. *Clinical Psychology & Psychotherapy, 20*(2), 97–106.

Kolevzon, A., Wang, A. T., Grodberg, D., & Buxbaum, J. D. (2013). Autism spectrum disorders. In D. S. Charney, J. D. Buxbaum, P. Sklar, & E. J. Nestler (Eds.), *Neurobiology of mental illness* (4th ed., pp. 1022–1033). New York, NY: Oxford University Press.

Kong, R., Shao, S., Wang, J., Zhang, X., Guo, S., Zou, L., ... Song, R. (2016). Genetic variant in DIP2A gene is associated with developmental dyslexia in Chinese population. *American Journal of Medical Genetics Part B: Neuropsychiatric Genetics, 171*(2), 203–208. doi:10.1002/ajmg.b.32392

Konkolÿ Thege, B., Colman, I., el-Guebaly, N., Hodgins, D. C., Patten, S. B., Schopflocher, D., ... Wild, T. C. (2015). Social judgments of behavioral versus substance-related addictions: A population-based study. *Addictive Behaviors, 42,* 24–31. doi:10.1016/j. addbeh.2014.10.025

Konrad, S. S., & Bath, E. (2014). Confidentiality and privilege. In E. Ford & M. Rotter (Eds.), *Landmark cases in forensic psychiatry* (pp. 3–9). New York, NY: Oxford University Press.

Koopmans, M. (2001). From Double Bind to N-Bind: Toward a new theory of schizophrenia and family interaction. *Nonlinear Dynamics, Psychology, and Life Sciences, 5*(4), 289–323. doi:10.1023/A:1009518729645

Kopelman, M. D., Thomson, A. D., Guerrini, I., & Marshall, E. J. (2009). The Korsakoff syndrome: Clinical aspects, psychology and treatment. *Alcohol and Alcoholism, 44*(2), 148–154. doi:10.1093/alcalc/agn118

Koro-Ljungberg, M., & Bussing, R. (2009). The management of courtesy stigma in the lives of families with teenagers with ADHD. *Journal of Family Issues, 30*(9), 1175–1200. doi:10.1177/0192513X09333707

Korsgaard, H. O., Torgersen, S., Wentzel-Larsen, T., & Ulberg, R. (2016). Substance abuse and personality disorder comorbidity in adolescent outpatients: Are girls more severely ill than boys? *Child and Adolescent Psychiatry and Mental Health, 10*. doi:10.1186/s13034-016-0096-5

Koskina, A., Campbell, I. C., & Schmidt, U. (2013). Exposure therapy in eating disorders revisited. *Neuroscience and Biobehavioral Reviews, 37*(2), 193–208. doi:10.1016/j.neubiorev.2012.11.010

Kosten, T. R., Newton, T. F., De La Garza, R., II, & Haile, C. N. (2014). Substance-related and addictive disorders. In R. E. Hales, S. C. Yudofsky, & L. W. Roberts (Eds.), *The American Psychiatric Publishing textbook of psychiatry* (6th ed., pp. 735–813). Arlington, VA: American Psychiatric Publishing.

Koszycki, D., Thake, J., Mavounza, C., Daoust, J.-P., Taljaard, M., & Bradwejn, J. (2016). Preliminary investigation of a mindfulness-based intervention for social anxiety disorder that integrates compassion meditation and mindful exposure. *The Journal of Alternative and Complementary Medicine, 22*(5), 363–374. doi:10.1089/acm.2015.0108

Kotov, R., Krueger, R. F., Watson, D., Achenbach, T. M., Althoff, R. R., Bagby, R. M., … Zimmerman, M. (2017). The Hierarchical Taxonomy of Psychopathology (HiTOP): A dimensional alternative to traditional nosologies. *Journal of Abnormal Psychology, 126*(4), 454–477. doi:10.1037/abn0000258

Kotsiubinskii, A. P. (2002). A biopsychosocial model of schizophrenia. *International Journal of Mental Health, 31*(2), 51–60.

Koven, N. S., & Abry, A. W. (2015). The clinical basis of orthorexia nervosa: Emerging perspectives. *Neuropsychiatric Disease and Treatment, 11.*

Kozlowska, K., English, M., & Savage, B. (2013). Connecting body and mind: The first interview with somatising patients and their families. *Clinical Child Psychology and Psychiatry, 18*(2), 224–245. doi:10.1177/1359104512447314

Kraemer, B., Noll, T., Delsignore, A., Milos, G., Schnyder, U., & Hepp, U. (2009). Finger length ratio (2D:4D) in adults with gender identity disorder. *Archives of Sexual Behavior, 38*(3), 359–363. doi:10.1007/s10508-007-9262-4

Kraemer, H. C., Kupfer, D. J., Clarke, D. E., Narrow, W. E., & Regier, D. A. (2012). DSM-5: How reliable is reliable enough? *The American Journal of Psychiatry, 169*(1), 13–15. doi:10.1176/appi.ajp.2011.11010050

Krafft-Ebing, R. von. (1892). *Psychopathia sexualis, with special reference to contrary sexual instinct: A medico-legal study* (C. G. Chaddock, Trans. 7th ed.). Oxford, UK: F. A. Davis.

Kraft, S. J., & Yairi, E. (2012). Genetic bases of stuttering: The state of the art, 2011. *Folia Phoniatrica et Logopaedica:International Journal of Phoniatrics, Speech Therapy and Communication Pathology, 64*(1), 34–47. doi:10.1159/000331073

Krahn, L. E. (2003). Sodium oxybate: A new way to treat narcolepsy. *Current Psychiatry, 2*(8), 65–69.

Krahn, T. M., & Fenton, A. (2012). The extreme male brain theory of autism and the potential adverse effects for boys and girls with autism. *Journal of Bioethical Inquiry, 9*(1), 93–103. doi:10.1007/s11673-011-9350-y

Kramer, H., & Sprenger, J. (n.d.). *The malleus maleficarum.* Retrieved from http://www.malleusmaleficarum.org/downloads/MalleusAcrobat.pdf

Kramer, P. (2011, July 10). In defense of antidepressants. *The New York Times.* Retrieved from http://www.nytimes.com/2011/07/10/opinion/sunday/10antidepressants.html?_r=0

Krasne, F. B. (1962). General disruption resulting from electrical stimulus of ventromedial hypothalamus. *Science, 138*(3542), 822–823.

Kreitman, N. (1977). *Parasuicide.* London, UK: John Wiley.

Kremen, W. S., Koenen, K. C., Afari, N., & Lyons, M. J. (2012). Twin studies of posttraumatic stress disorder: Differentiating vulnerability factors from sequelae. *Neuropharmacology, 62*(2), 647–653. doi:10.1016/j.neuropharm.2011.03.012

Krentzman, A. R. (2007). The evidence base for the effectiveness of Alcoholics Anonymous: Implications for social work practice. *Journal of Social Work Practice in the Addictions, 7*(4), 27–48. doi:10.1300/J160v07n04_03

Kreukels, B. P. C., & Guillamon, A. (2016). Neuroimaging studies in people with gender incongruence. *International Review of Psychiatry, 28*(1), 120–128. doi:10.3109/09540261.2015.1113163

Krieg, R. G. (2001). An interdisciplinary look at the deinstitutionalization of the mentally ill. *The Social Science Journal, 38*(3), 367–380. doi:10.1016/S0362-3319(01)00136-7

Krigbaum, G. (2013). Abnormal psychology in a multicultural context. In T. G. Plante (Ed.), *Abnormal psychology across the ages: Vol. 3. Trends and future directions* (pp. 231–241). Santa Barbara, CA: Praeger/ABC-CLIO.

Kripke, D. F., Kline, L. E., Nievergelt, C. M., Murray, S. S., Shadan, F. F., Dawson, A., … Hahn, E. K. (2015). Genetic variants associated with sleep disorders. *Sleep Medicine, 16*(2), 217–224. doi:10.1016/j.sleep.2014.11.003

Krishnamurthy, S., Garabadu, D., & Joy, K. P. (2013). Risperidone ameliorates post-traumatic stress disorder-like symptoms in modified stress re-stress model. *Neuropharmacology, 75*, 62–77. doi:10.1016/j.neuropharm.2013.07.005

Kristensen, D., Hageman, I., Bauer, J., Jørgensen, M. B., & Correll, C. U. (2013). Antipsychotic polypharmacy in a treatment-refractory schizophrenia population receiving adjunctive treatment with electroconvulsive therapy. *The Journal of ECT, 29*(4), 271–276. doi:10.1097/YCT.0b013e31828b34f6

Kroenke, K. (2003). Patients presenting with somatic complaints: epidemiology, psychiatric comorbidity and management. *International Journal of Methods in Psychiatric Research, 12*(1), 34–43.

Kroenke, K. (2007). Efficacy of treatment for somatoform disorders: A review of randomized controlled trials. *Psychosomatic Medicine, 69*(9), 881–888. doi:10.1097/PSY.0b013e31815b00c4

Kroger, R. O., & Wood, L. A. (1993). Reification, 'faking,' and the Big Five. *American Psychologist, 48*(12), 1297–1298. doi:10.1037/0003-066X.48.12.1297

Krueger, R. B., Reed, G. M., First, M. B., Marais, A., Kismodi, E., & Briken, P. (2017). Proposals for paraphilic disorders in the international classification of diseases and related health problems, eleventh revision (ICD-11). *Archives of Sexual Behavior.* doi:10.1007/s10508-017-0944-2

Krueger, R. F., & Markon, K. E. (2014). The role of the DSM-5 personality trait model in moving toward a quantitative and empirically based approach to classifying personality and psychopathology. *Annual Review of Clinical Psychology, 10*, 477–501. doi:10.1146/annurev-clinpsy-032813-153732

Krueger, R. F., Derringer, J., Markon, K. E., Watson, D., & Skodol, A. E. (2012). Initial construction of a maladaptive personality trait model and inventory for DSM-5. *Psychological Medicine, 42*(9), 1879–1890.

Krupnick, J. L. (2002). Brief psychodynamic treatment of PTSD. *Journal of Clinical Psychology, 58*(8), 919–932. doi:10.1002/jclp.10067

Krycka, K. C. (2010). Multiplicity: A first-person exploration of dissociative experiencing. *Person-Centered and Experiential Psychotherapies, 9*(2), 145–156.

Krystal, J. H., Sanacora, G., & Duman, R. S. (2013). Rapid-Acting Glutamatergic Antidepressants: The Path to Ketamine and Beyond. *Biological Psychiatry, 73*(12), 1133–1141. doi:http://dx.doi.org/10.1016/j.biopsych.2013.03.026

Kübler-Ross, E. (1970). *On death and dying.* New York, NY: Collier Books/Macmillan.

Kübler-Ross, E., Wessler, S., & Avioli, L. V. (1972). On death and dying. *JAMA: Journal of the American Medical Association, 221*(2), 174–179.

Kudler, H. S., Krupnick, J. L., Blank, A. S., Jr., Herman, J. L., & Horowitz, M. J. (2009). Psychodynamic therapy for adults. In E. B. Foa, T. M. Keane, M. J. Friedman, & J. A. Cohen (Eds.), *Effective treatments for PTSD: Practice guidelines from the International Society for Traumatic Stress Studies* (2nd ed., pp. 346–369). New York, NY: Guilford Press.

Kuhl, D. C., Chavez, J. M., Swisher, R. R., & Wilczak, A. (2016). Social class, family formation, and delinquency in early adulthood. *Sociological Perspectives, 59*(2), 345–367. doi:10.1177/0731121415586635

Kuhn, J.-T. (2015). Developmental dyscalculia: Neurobiological, cognitive, and developmental perspectives. *Zeitschrift für Psychologie, 223*(2), 69–82. doi:10.1027/2151-2604/a000205

Kuhns, J. B., Exum, M. L., Clodfelter, T. A., & Bottia, M. C. (2014). The prevalence of alcohol-involved homicide offending: A meta-analytic review. *Homicide Studies: An Interdisciplinary & International Journal, 18*(3), 251–270. doi:10.1177/1088767913493629

Kulesza, M., Ramsey, S. E., Brown, R. A., & Larimer, M. E. (2014). Stigma among individuals with substance use disorders: Does it predict substance use, and does it diminish with treatment? *Journal of Addictive Behaviors, Therapy & Rehabilitation, 3*(1), 1000115. doi:10.4172/2324-9005.1000115

Kung, K. T. F., Spencer, D., Pasterski, V., Neufeld, S., Glover, V., O'Connor, T. G., ... Hines, M. (2016). No relationship between prenatal androgen exposure and autistic traits: Convergent evidence from studies of children with congenital adrenal hyperplasia and of amniotic testosterone concentrations in typically developing children. *Journal of Child Psychology and Psychiatry, 57*(12), 1455–1462. doi:10.1111/jcpp.12602

Kupfer, D. J., & Regier, D. A. (2009). Toward credible conflict of interest policies in clinical psychiatry. *Psychiatric Times.* Retrieved from http://www.psychiatrictimes.com/articles/toward-credible-conflict-interest-policies-clinical-psychiatry/page/0/2

Kusalaruk, P., Saipanish, R., & Hiranyatheb, T. (2015). Attitudes of psychiatrists toward obsessive–compulsive disorder patients. *Neuropsychiatric Disease and Treatment, 11.*

Kushner, H. I. (1999). *A cursing brain? The histories of Tourette's syndrome.* Cambridge, MA: Harvard University Press.

Kushner, H. I. (2000). A brief history of Tourette syndrome. *Revista Brasileira de Psiquiatria, 22*, 76–79. doi:http://dx.doi.org/10.1590/S1516-44462000000200008

Kymalainen, J. A., & Weisman de Mamani, A. G. (2008). Expressed emotion, communication deviance, and culture in families of patients with schizophrenia: A review of the literature. *Cultural Diversity and Ethnic Minority Psychology, 14*(2), 85–91. doi:10.1037/1099-9809.14.2.85

La Torre, A., Conca, A., Duffy, D., Giupponi, G., Pompili, M., & Grözinger, M. (2013). Sexual dysfunction related to psychotropic drugs: A critical review. Part II: Antipsychotics. *Pharmacopsychiatry, 46*(6), 201–208. doi:10.1055/s-0033-1347177

La Torre, A., Giupponi, G., Duffy, D. M., Pompili, M., Grözinger, M., Kapfhammer, H. P., & Conca, A. (2014). Sexual dysfunction related to psychotropic drugs: A critical review. Part III: Mood stabilizers and anxiolytic drugs. *Pharmacopsychiatry, 47*(1), 1–6. doi:10.1055/s-0033-1358683

La Torre, A., Giupponi, G., Duffy, D., & Conca, A. (2013). Sexual dysfunction related to psychotropic drugs: A critical review — Part I: Antidepressants. *Pharmacopsychiatry, 46*(5), 191–199. doi:10.1055/s-0033-1345205

La Torre, A., Giupponi, G., Duffy, D., Conca, A., & Catanzariti, D. (2015). Sexual dysfunction related to drugs: A critical review. Part IV: Cardiovascular drugs. *Pharmacopsychiatry, 48*(1), 1–6. doi:10.1055/s-0034-1395515

Labelle, A., Bourget, D., Bradford, J. M. W., Alda, M., & Tessier, P. (2012). Familial paraphilia: A pilot study with the construction of genograms. *ISRN Psychiatry, 2012*, 692813–692813. doi:10.5402/2012/692813

Lacasse, J. R. (2014). After DSM-5: A critical mental health research agenda for the 21st century. *Research on Social Work Practice, 24*(1), 5–10. doi:10.1177/1049731513510048

Lago, L., Bruno, R., & Degenhardt, L. (2016). Concordance of ICD-11 and DSM-5 definitions of alcohol and cannabis use disorders: A population survey. *The Lancet Psychiatry, 3*(7), 673–684. doi:10.1016/S2215-0366(16)00088-2

Lahelma, E., Laaksonen, M., Martikainen, P., Rahkonen, O., & Sarlio-Lähteenkorva, S. (2006). Multiple measures of socioeconomic circumstances and common mental disorders. *Social Science & Medicine, 63*(5), 1383–1399. doi:http://dx.doi.org/10.1016/j.socscimed.2006.03.027

Lahera, G., Bayón, C., Bravo-Ortiz, M. F., Rodríguez-Vega, B., Barbeito, S., Sáenz, M., . . . de Dios, C. (2014). Mindfulness-based cognitive therapy versus psychoeducational intervention in bipolar outpatients with sub-threshold depressive symptoms: A randomized controlled trial. *BMC Psychiatry, 14.*

Lahey, B. B., Hart, E. L., Pliszka, S., Applegate, B., & McBurnett, K. (1993). Neurophysiological correlates of conduct disorder: A rationale and a review of research. *Journal of Clinical Child Psychology, 22*(2), 141–153. doi:10.1207/s15374424jccp2202_2

Lahmann, C., Nickel, M., Schuster, T., Sauer, N., Ronel, J., Noll-Hussong, M., ... Loew, T. (2009). Functional relaxation and guided imagery as complementary therapy in asthma: A randomized controlled clinical trial. *Psychotherapy and Psychosomatics, 78*(4), 233–239. doi:10.1159/000214445

Lahmann, C., Röhricht, F., Sauer, N., Noll-Hussong, M., Ronel, J., Henrich, G., ... Loew, T. (2010). Functional relaxation as complementary therapy in irritable bowel syndrome: A randomized, controlled clinical trial. *The Journal of Alternative and Complementary Medicine, 16*(1), 47–52. doi:10.1089/acm.2009.0084

Lai, H. M. X., Cleary, M., Sitharthan, T., & Hunt, G. E. (2015). Prevalence of comorbid substance use, anxiety and mood disorders in epidemiological surveys, 1990–2014: A systematic review and meta-analysis. *Drug and Alcohol Dependence, 154*, 1–13. doi:10.1016/j.drugalcdep.2015.05.031

Laing, R. D. (1965). *The divided self.* Baltimore, MD: Penguin.

Laing, R. D. (1967). *The politics of experience.* New York, NY: Ballantine Books.

Lakin, K. C., & Stancliffe, R. J. (2007). Residential supports for persons with intellectual and developmental disabilities. *Mental Retardation and Developmental Disabilities Research Reviews, 13*(2), 151–159. doi:10.1002/mrdd.20148

Lal, S., & Adair, C. E. (2014). E-mental health: A rapid review of the literature. *Psychiatric Services, 65*(1), 24–32. doi:10.1176/appi.ps.201300009

Lalonde, J. K., Hudson, J. I., Gigante, R. A., & Pope, H. G., Jr. (2001). Canadian and American psychiatrists' attitudes toward dissociative disorders diagnoses. *The Canadian Journal of Psychiatry/La Revue Canadienne De Psychiatrie, 46*(5), 407–412.

Lalumière, M. L., Mishra, S., & Harris, G. T. (2008). In cold blood: The evolution of psychopathy. In J. D. Duntley & T. K. Shackelford (Eds.), *Evolutionary forensic psychology: Darwinian foundations of crime and law* (pp. 176–197). New York, NY: Oxford University Press.

Lamarine, R. J. (2012). Marijuana: Modern medical Chimaera. *Journal of Drug Education, 42*(1), 1–11. doi:10.2190/DE.42.1.a

Lamb, K. (2017, February 22). Why LGBT hatred suddenly spiked in Indonesia. *The Guardian.* Retrieved from https://www.theguardian.com/global-development-professionals-network/2017/feb/22/why-lgbt-hatred-suddenly-spiked-in-indonesia

Lambe, E. K., Katzman, D. K., Mikulis, D. J., Kennedy, S. H., & Zipursky, R. B. (1997). Cerebral gray matter volume deficits after weight recovery from anorexia nervosa. *Archives of General Psychiatry, 54.* doi:10.1001/archpsyc.1997.01830180055006

Lambert, M. (2017, January 3). Taiwan publishes plan to ban conversion therapy. *Out.* Retrieved from https://www.out.com/news-opinion/2017/1/03/taiwan-publishes-plan-ban-conversion-therapy

Lamberty, G. J. (2007). *Understanding somatization in the practice of clinical neuropsychology.* Oxford, UK: Oxford University Press.

Lamers, F., Vogelzangs, N., Merikangas, K. R., de Jonge, P., Beekman, A. T. F., & Penninx, B. W. J. H. (2013). Evidence for a differential role of HPA-axis function, inflammation and metabolic syndrome in melancholic versus atypical depression. *Molecular Psychiatry, 18*(6), 692–699.

Lamont, J. A. (2011). Dyspareunia and vaginismus. Retrieved from https://www.glowm.com/section_view/heading/Dyspareunia%20and%20Vaginismus/item/429. doi:10.3843/GLOWM.10430

Landerl, K., & Moll, K. (2010). Comorbidity of learning disorders: Prevalence and familial transmission. *Journal of Child Psychology and Psychiatry, 51*(3), 287–294. doi:10.1111/j.1469-7610.2009.02164.x

Landrigan, P. J. (2010). What causes autism? Exploring the environmental contribution. *Current Opinion in Pediatrics, 22*(2), 219–225. doi:10.1097/MOP.0b013e328336eb9a

Lang, R., Mulloy, A., Giesbers, S., Pfeiffer, B., Delaune, E., Didden, R., ... O'Reilly, M. (2011). Behavioral interventions for rumination and operant vomiting in individuals with intellectual disabilities: A systematic review. *Research in Developmental Disabilities, 32*(6), 2193–2205. doi:http://dx.doi.org/10.1016/j.ridd.2011.06.011

Lange, K. W., Hauser, J., & Reissmann, A. (2015). Gluten-free and casein-free diets in the therapy of autism. *Current Opinion in Clinical Nutrition and Metabolic Care, 18*(6), 572–575. doi:10.1097/MCO.0000000000000228

Lange, K. W., Reichl, S., Lange, K. M., Tucha, L., & Tucha, O. (2010). The history of attention deficit hyperactivity disorder. *ADHD Attention Deficit and Hyperactivity Disorders, 2*(4), 241–255. doi:10.1007/s12402-010-0045-8

Langer, E. (1989). *Mindfulness.* Reading, MA: Addison-Wesley.

Långström, N., Babchishin, K. M., Fazel, S., Lichtenstein, P., & Frisell, T. (2015). Sexual offending runs in families: A 37-year nationwide study. *International Journal of Epidemiology, 44*(2), 713–720.

Lanovaz, M. J., Argumedes, M., Roy, D., Duquette, J. R., & Watkins, N. (2013). Using ABC narrative recording to identify the function of problem behavior: A pilot study. *Research in Developmental Disabilities, 34*(9), 2734–2742. doi:10.1016/j.ridd.2013.05.038

Lanphear, B. P. (2015). The impact of toxins on the developing brain. *Annual Review of Public Health, 36*, 211–230. doi:10.1146/annurev-publhealth-031912-114413

Lansky, M. R., & Bley, C. R. (1995). *Posttraumatic nightmares: Psychodynamic explorations.* Hillsdale, NJ: Analytic Press.

Larsen, T. K. (2009). Biological and psychological treatments for psychosis: An overdue alliance? In J. F. M. Gleeson, E. Killackey, & H. Krstev (Eds.), *Psychotherapies for the psychoses: Theoretical, cultural and clinical integration* (pp. 75–88). London, UK: Routledge.

Latzer, Y., Spivak-Lavi, Z., & Katz, R. (2015). Disordered eating and media exposure among adolescent girls: The role of parental involvement and sense of empowerment. *International Journal of Adolescence and Youth, 20*(3), 375–391. doi:10.1080/02673843.2015.1014925

Lauckner, C., & Whitten, P. (2016). The state and sustainability of telepsychiatry programs. *The Journal of Behavioral Health Services & Research, 43*(2), 305–318. doi:10.1007/s11414-015-9461-z

Lavie-Ajayi, M. (2005). "Because all real women do": The construction and deconstruction of "female orgasmic disorder." *Sexualities, Evolution & Gender, 7*(1), 57–72. doi:10.1080/14616660500123664

Lavretsky, H. (2008). History of schizophrenia as a psychiatric disorder. In K. T. Mueser & D. V. Jeste (Eds.), *Clinical handbook of schizophrenia* (pp. 3–13). New York, NY: Guilford Press.

Law, R. (2011). Interpersonal psychotherapy for depression. *Advances in Psychiatric Treatment, 17*(1), 23–31.

Lawlor, C. (2012). *From melancholia to Prozac: A history of depression.* Oxford, UK: Oxford University Press.

Lawson, W. B. (2008). Schizophrenia in African Americans. In K. T. Mueser & D. V. Jeste (Eds.), *Clinical handbook of schizophrenia* (pp. 616–623). New York, NY: Guilford Press.

Le Foll, B., Gallo, A., Le Strat, Y., Lu, L., & Gorwood, P. (2009). Genetics of dopamine receptors and drug addiction: A comprehensive review. *Behavioural Pharmacology, 20*(1), 1–17. doi:10.1097/FBP.0b013e3283242f05

Le Grange, D. (2005). The Maudsley family-based treatment for adolescent anorexia nervosa. *World Psychiatry, 4*(3), 142–146.

Le Grange, D. (2010). Family-based treatment for adolescents with bulimia nervosa. *Australian and New Zealand Journal of Family Therapy, 31*(2), 165–175. doi:10.1375/anft.31.2.165

Le Grange, D., & Lock, J. (2010). Family-based treatment for adolescents with bulimia nervosa. In C. M. Grilo & J. E. Mitchell (Eds.), *The treatment of eating disorders: A clinical handbook* (pp. 372–387). New York, NY: Guilford Press.

Le Grange, D., Lock, J., Agras, W. S., Bryson, S. W., & Jo, B. (2015). Randomized clinical trial of family-based treatment and cognitive-behavioral therapy for adolescent bulimia nervosa. *Journal of the American Academy of Child & Adolescent Psychiatry, 54*(11), 886–894.

Leahy, R. L., & McGinn, L. K. (2012). Cognitive therapy for personality disorders. In T. A. Widiger (Ed.), *The Oxford handbook of personality disorders* (pp. 727–750). New York, NY: Oxford University Press.

Leahy, R. L., & Rego, S. A. (2012). Cognitive restructuring. In W. T. O'Donohue & J. E. Fisher (Eds.), *Cognitive behavior therapy: Core principles for practice* (pp. 133–158). Hoboken, NJ: John Wiley.

Leark, R. A. (2004). The Luria-Nebraska Neuropsychological Battery—Children's Revision. In G. Goldstein & S. R. Beers (Eds.), *Comprehensive handbook of psychological assessment: Vol. 1. Intellectual and neuropsychological assessment* (pp. 147–156). Hoboken, NJ: John Wiley.

LeBlanc, A. (2001). The origins of the concept of dissociation: Paul Janet, his nephew Pierre, and the problem of post-hypnotic suggestion. *History of Science, 39*(1), 57–69. doi:10.1177/007327530103900103

Lebowitz, E. R., Panza, K. E., Su, J., & Bloch, M. H. (2012). Family accommodation in obsessive-compulsive disorder. *Expert Review of Neurotherapeutics, 12*(2), 229–238. doi:10.1586/ern.11.200

Leboyer, M., Oliveira, J., Tamouza, R., & Groc, L. (2016). Is it time for immunopsychiatry in psychotic disorders? *Psychopharmacology, 233*(9), 1651–1660. doi:10.1007/s00213-016-4266-1

Ledgerwood, D. M., Arfken, C. L., Petry, N. M., & Alessi, S. M. (2014). Prize contingency management for smoking cessation: A randomized trial. *Drug and Alcohol Dependence, 140*, 208–212. doi:http://dx.doi.org/10.1016/j.drugalcdep.2014.03.032

LeDoux, J. (2015). *Anxious: Using the brain to understand and treat fear and anxiety.* New York, NY: Penguin Books.

Lee, B. K., Magnusson, C., Gardner, R. M., Blomström, Å., Newschaffer, C. J., Burstyn, I., … Dalman, C. (2015). Maternal hospitalization with infection during pregnancy and risk of autism spectrum disorders. *Brain, Behavior, and Immunity, 44*, 100–105. doi:10.1016/j.bbi.2014.09.001

Lee, C. C., Liem, S. K., Leung, J., Young, V., Wu, K., Kenny, K. K. W., … Lo, W. (2015). From deinstitutionalization to recovery-oriented assertive community treatment in Hong Kong: What we have achieved. *Psychiatry Research, 228*(3), 243–250. doi:10.1016/j.psychres.2015.05.106

Lee, E. E., Hong, S., Martin, A. S., Eyler, L. T., & Jeste, D. V. (2017). Inflammation in schizophrenia: Cytokine levels and their relationships to demographic and clinical variables. *The American Journal of Geriatric Psychiatry, 25*(1), 50–61. doi:10.1016/j.jagp.2016.09.009

Lee, J. B., & Bartlett, M. L. (2005). Suicide prevention: Critical elements for managing suicidal clients and counselor liability without the use of a no-suicide contract. *Death Studies, 29*(9), 847–865. doi:10.1080/07481180500236776

Lee, R. W., & Gillam, S. L. (2000). Legal and ethical issues involving the duty to warn: Implications for supervisors. *The Clinical Supervisor, 19*(1), 123–136. doi:10.1300/J001v19n01_07

Lee, S., & Mysyk, A. (2004). The medicalization of compulsive buying. *Social Science & Medicine, 58*(9), 1709–1718. doi:http://dx.doi.org/10.1016/S0277-9536(03)00340-X

Lee, Y., & Lin, P.-Y. (2010). Association between serotonin transporter gene polymorphism and eating disorders: a meta-analytic study. *International Journal of Eating Disorders, 43*(6), 498–504. doi:10.1002/eat.20732

Leeman, R. F., & Potenza, M. N. (2013). A targeted review of the neurobiology and genetics of behavioural addictions: An emerging area of research. *The Canadian Journal of Psychiatry/La Revue Canadienne De Psychiatrie, 58*(5), 260–273.

Leggett, V., Jacobs, P., Nation, K., Scerif, G., & Bishop, D. V. M. (2010). Neurocognitive outcomes of individuals with a sex chromosome trisomy: XXX, XYY, or XXY: A systematic review. *Developmental Medicine & Child Neurology, 52*(2), 119–129. doi:10.1111/j.1469-8749.2009.03545.x

Legleye, S., Beck, F., Khlat, M., Peretti-Watel, P., & Chau, N. (2012). The influence of socioeconomic status on cannabis use among French adolescents. *Journal of Adolescent Health, 50*(4), 395–402. doi:10.1016/j.jadohealth.2011.08.004

Leichsenring, F., & Klein, S. (2014). Evidence for psychodynamic psychotherapy in specific mental disorders: A systematic review. *Psychoanalytic Psychotherapy, 28*(1), 4–32. doi:10.1080/02668734.2013.865428

Leichsenring, F., & Salzer, S. (2014). A unified protocol for the transdiagnostic psychodynamic treatment of anxiety disorders: An evidence-based approach. *Psychotherapy, 51*(2), 224–245. doi:10.1037/a0033815

Leichsenring, F., Abbass, A., Luyten, P., Hilsenroth, M., & Rabung, S. (2013). The emerging evidence for long-term psychodynamic therapy. *Psychodynamic Psychiatry, 41*(3), 361–384.

Leichsenring, F., Leweke, F., Klein, S., & Steinert, C. (2015). The empirical status of psychodynamic psychotherapy—An update: Bambi's alive and kicking. *Psychotherapy and Psychosomatics, 84*(3), 129–148. doi:10.1159/000376584

Leichsenring, F., Salzer, S., Beutel, M. E., Herpertz, S., Hiller, W., Hoyer, J., … Leibing, E. (2014). Long-term outcome of psychodynamic therapy and cognitive-behavioral therapy in social anxiety disorder. *The American Journal of Psychiatry, 171*(10), 1074–1082. doi:10.1176/appi.ajp.2014.13111514

Leichsenring, F., Salzer, S., Jaeger, U., Kächele, H., Kreische, R., Leweke, F., … Leibing, E. (2009). Short-term psychodynamic psychotherapy and cognitive-behavioral therapy in generalized anxiety disorder: A randomized, controlled trial. *The American Journal of Psychiatry, 166*(8), 875–881. doi:10.1176/appi.ajp.2009.09030441

Leichtman, M. (2004). Projective tests: The nature of the task. In M. J. Hilsenroth & D. L. Segal (Eds.), *Comprehensive handbook of psychological assessment: Vol. 2. Personality assessment* (pp. 297–314). Hoboken, NJ: John Wiley.

Leigh, H. (2015). Dissociative disorders. In H. Leigh & J. Strltzer (Eds.), *Handbook of consultation-liaison psychiatry* (2nd ed., pp. 259–264). New York, NY: Springer Science + Business Media.

Leite, P. L., Pereira, V. M., Nardi, A. E., & Silva, A. C. (2014). Psychotherapy for compulsive buying disorder: A systematic review. *Psychiatry Research, 219*(3), 411–419. doi:10.1016/j.psychres.2014.05.037

Lejoyeux, M., & Weinstein, A. (2013). Shopping addiction. In P. M. Miller, S. A. Ball, M. E. Bates, A. W. Blume, K. M. Kampman, D. J. Kavanagh, M. E. Larimer, N. M. Petry, & P. De Witte (Eds.), *Comprehensive addictive behaviors and disorders: Vol. 1. Principles of addiction* (pp. 847–853). San Diego, CA: Elsevier Academic Press.

Lejuez, C. W., Schaal, D. W., & O'Donnell, J. (1998). Behavioral pharmacology and the treatment of substance abuse. In J. J. Plaud & G. H. Eifert (Eds.), *From behavior theory to behavior therapy* (pp. 116–135). Needham Heights, MA: Allyn & Bacon.

Lembke, A., & Humphreys, K. (2012). Moderation management: A mutual-help organization for problem drinkers who are not alcohol-dependent. *Journal of Groups in Addiction & Recovery, 7*(2–4), 130–141. doi:10.1080/1556035X.2012.557657

Lemma, A., Target, M., & Fonagy, P. (2010). The development of a brief psychodynamic protocol for depression: Dynamic Interpersonal Therapy (DIT). *Psychoanalytic Psychotherapy, 24*(4), 329–346. doi:10.1080/02668734.2010.513547

Lemma, A., Target, M., & Fonagy, P. (2011). The development of a brief psychodynamic intervention (Dynamic Interpersonal Therapy) and its application to depression: A pilot study. *Psychiatry: Interpersonal and Biological Processes, 74*(1), 41–48. doi:10.1521/psyc.2011.74.1.41

Lemma, A., Target, M., & Fonagy, P. (2013). Dynamic interpersonal therapy (DIT): Developing a new psychodynamic intervention for the treatment of depression. *Psychoanalytic Inquiry, 33*(6), 552–566. doi:10.1080/07351690.2013.815092

Lemmens, L. H. J. M., Arntz, A., Peeters, F., Hollon, S. D., Roefs, A., & Huibers, M. J. H. (2015). Clinical effectiveness of cognitive therapy v. interpersonal psychotherapy for depression: Results of a randomized controlled trial. *Psychological Medicine, 45*(10), 2095–2110. doi:10.1017/S0033291715000033

Lemmon, M. E., Gregas, M., & Jeste, S. S. (2011). Risperidone use in autism spectrum disorders: A retrospective review of a clinic-referred patient population. *Journal of Child Neurology, 26*(4), 428–432. doi:10.1177/0883073810382143

Lemogne, C., Delaveau, P., Freton, M., Guionnet, S., & Fossati, P. (2012). Medial prefrontal cortex and the self in major depression. *Journal of Affective Disorders, 136*(1–2), e1–e11. doi:10.1016/j.jad.2010.11.034

Lemogne, C., Mayberg, H., Bergouignan, L., Volle, E., Delaveau, P., Lehéricy, S., ... Fossati, P. (2010). Self-referential processing and the prefrontal cortex over the course of depression: A pilot study. *Journal of Affective Disorders, 124*(1–2), 196–201. doi:10.1016/j.jad.2009.11.003

Lener, M. S., & Iosifescu, D. V. (2015). In pursuit of neuroimaging biomarkers to guide treatment selection in major depressive disorder: a review of the literature. *Annals of the New York Academy of Sciences, 1344*, 50–65. doi:10.1111/nyas.12759

Lenzenweger, M. F., Lane, M. C., Loranger, A. W., & Kessler, R. C. (2007). DSM-IV personality disorders in the national comorbidity survey replication. *Biological Psychiatry, 62*(6), 553–564. doi:10.1016/j.biopsych.2006.09.019

Leombruni, P., Lavagnino, L., & Fassino, S. (2009). Treatment of obese patients with binge eating disorder using topiramate: A review. *Neuropsychiatric Disease and Treatment, 5*.

Leon, A. C. (2007). The revised warning for antidepressants and suicidality: Unveiling the black box of statistical analyses. *The American Journal of Psychiatry, 164*(12), 1786–1789.

Leong, K., Tham, J. C. W., Scamvougeras, A., & Vila-Rodriguez, F. (2015). Electroconvulsive therapy treatment in patients with somatic symptom and related disorders. *Neuropsychiatric Disease and Treatment, 11*.

Lequesne, E. R., & Hersh, R. G. (2004). Disclosure of a diagnosis of borderline personality disorder. *Journal of Psychiatric Practice, 10*(3), 170–176. doi:10.1097/00131746-200405000-00005

Leri, F., Bruneau, J., & Stewart, J. (2003). Understanding polydrug use: Review of heroin and cocaine co-use. *Addiction, 98*(1), 7–22. doi:10.1046/j.1360-0443.2003.00236.x

Lerner, P. M. (1998). *Psychoanalytic perspectives on the Rorschach*. Hillsdale, NJ: The Analytic Press.

Lester, D. (1994). Psychotherapy for suicidal clients. *Death Studies, 18*(4), 361–374. doi:10.1080/07481189408252683

Lester, D. (2011). Evidence-based suicide prevention by lethal methods restriction. In M. Pompili & R. Tatarelli (Eds.), *Evidence-based practice in suicidology: A source book* (pp. 233–241). Cambridge, MA: Hogrefe Publishing.

LeVay, S. (1991). A difference in hypothalamic structure between heterosexual and homosexual men. *Science, 253*(5023), 1034–1037.

LeVay, S. (2011). *Gay, straight, and the reason why: The science of sexual orientation*. New York, NY: Oxford University Press.

Levenson, H. (2017). *Brief dynamic therapy* (2nd ed.). Washington, DC: American Psychological Association.

Levin, R. J. (2008). Critically revisiting aspects of the human sexual response cycle of Masters and Johnson: Correcting errors and suggesting modifications. *Sexual and Relationship Therapy, 23*(4), 393–399. doi:10.1080/14681990802488816

Levin, S. (2016, May 10). Homosexuality as a mental disorder simply not backed up by science. Retrieved from https://www.psychiatry.org/news-room/apa-blogs/apa-blog/2016/03/homosexuality-as-a-mental-disorder-simply-not-backed-up-by-science

Levine, B. E. (2005). Mental illness or rebellion? *Ethical Human Psychology and Psychiatry, 7*(2), 125–129.

Levine, B. E. (2008). How teenage rebellion has become a mental illness. Retrieved from http://www.alternet.org/story/75081/how_teenage_rebellion_has_become_a_mental_illness

Levine, B. E. (2012). Why anti-authoritarians are diagnosed as mentally ill. Retrieved from https://www.madinamerica.com/2012/02/why-anti-authoritarians-are-diagnosed-as-mentally-ill/

Levine, H. G. (1978). The discovery of addiction: Changing conceptions of habitual drunkenness in America. *Journal of Studies on Alcohol, 39*(1), 143–174. doi:10.15288/jsa.1978.39.143

Levine, M. P., & Smolak, L. (2010). Cultural influences on body image and the eating disorders. In W. S. Agras (Ed.), *The Oxford handbook of eating disorders* (pp. 223–246). New York, NY: Oxford University Press.

Levinson, D. F., & Mowry, B. J. (2000). Genetics of schizophrenia. In D. W. Pfaff, W. H. Berrettini, T. H. Joh, & S. C. Maxson (Eds.), *Genetic influences on neural and behavioral functions* (pp. 47–82). Boca Raton, FL: CRC Press.

Levinson, D., Lakoma, M. D., Petukhova, M., Schoenbaum, M., Zaslavsky, A. M., Angermeyer, M., ... Kessler, R. C. (2010). Associations of serious mental illness with earnings: Results from the WHO World Mental Health surveys. *The British Journal of Psychiatry, 197*(2), 114–121. doi:10.1192/bjp.bp.109.073635

Levitt, H. M. (2016). Qualitative methods. In J. C. Norcross, G. R. VandenBos, D. K. Freedheim, & B. O. Olatunji (Eds.), *APA handbook of clinical psychology: Vol. II. Clinical psychology: Theory and research* (pp. 335–348). Washington, DC: American Psychological Association.

Levola, J., & Aalto, M. (2015). Screening for at-risk drinking in a population reporting symptoms of depression: A validation of the AUDIT, AUDIT-C, and AUDIT-3. *Alcoholism: Clinical and Experimental Research, 39*(7), 1186–1192. doi:10.1111/acer.12763

Levy, F. (1991). The dopamine theory of attention deficit hyperactivity disorder (ADHD). *Australian and New Zealand Journal of Psychiatry, 25*(2), 277–283. doi:10.3109/00048679109077746

Levy, F. (2009). Dopamine vs noradrenaline: Inverted-U effects and ADHD theories. *Australian and New Zealand Journal of Psychiatry, 43*(2), 101–108. doi:10.1080/00048670802607238

Levy, F. (2014). DSM-5, ICD-11, RDoC and ADHD diagnosis. *Australian and New Zealand Journal of Psychiatry, 48*(12), 1163–1164. doi:10.1177/0004867414557527

Levy, F., & Swanson, J. M. (2001). Timing, space and ADHD: The dopamine theory revisited. *Australian and New Zealand Journal of Psychiatry, 35*(4), 504–511. doi:10.1046/j.1440-1614.2001.00923.x

Levy, K. N., & Blatt, S. J. (1999). Attachment theory and psychoanalysis: Further differentiation within insecure attachment patterns. *Psychoanalytic Inquiry, 19*(4), 541–575. doi:10.1080/07351699909534266

Lewin, A. B., Wu, M. S., McGuire, J. F., & Storch, E. A. (2014). Cognitive behavior therapy for obsessive-compulsive and related disorders. *Psychiatric Clinics of North America, 37*(3), 415–445. doi:10.1016/j.psc.2014.05.002

Lewis, A. J. (2009). Neuropsychological deficit and psychodynamic defence models of schizophrenia: Towards an integrated psychotherapeutic model. In J. F. M. Gleeson, E. Killackey, & H. Krstev (Eds.), *Psychotherapies for the psychoses: Theoretical, cultural and clinical integration* (pp. 52–69). London, UK: Routledge.

Lewis, D. A. (2009). Brain volume changes in schizophrenia: How do they arise? What do they mean? *Psychological Medicine, 39*(11), 1779–1780. doi:10.1017/S003329170900573X

Lewis, D. A. (2011). Antipsychotic medications and brain volume: Do we have cause for concern? *Archives of General Psychiatry, 68*(2), 126–127. doi:10.1001/archgenpsychiatry.2010.187

Lewis, G., & Appleby, L. (1988). Personality disorder: The patients psychiatrists dislike. *The British Journal of Psychiatry, 153*, 44–49. doi:10.1192/bjp.153.1.44

Lewis, G., Bebbington, P., Brugha, T., Farrell, M., Gill, B., Jenkins, R., & Meltzer, H. (2003). Socio-economic status, standard of living, and neurotic disorder. *International Review of Psychiatry, 15*(1–2), 91–96. doi:10.1080/0954026021000045994

Lewis, M. W. (2008). Application of contingency management-prize reinforcement to community practice with alcohol and drug problems: A critical examination. *Behavior and Social Issues, 17*(2), 119–138. doi:10.5210/bsi.v17i2.2038

Lewis, Rachel (2017, August 4). Suicide rate for teen girls hits 40-year high. *Time.*

Lewis, Rebecca (2014). Right to treatment. In E. Ford & M. Rotter (Eds.), Landmark cases in forensic psychiatry (pp. 54–58). New York, NY: Oxford University Press.

Lewis, S. W., & Buchanan, R. W. (2002). *Schizophrenia* (2nd ed.). Oxford, UK: Health Press.

Lewis, T. J., Scott, T., & Sugai, G. (1994). The Problem Behavior Questionnaire: A teacher-based instrument to develop functional hypotheses of problem behavior in general education classrooms. *Diagnostique, 19*(2–3), 103–115.

Lewis-Fernández, R., Hinton, D. E., Laria, A. J., Patterson, E. H., Hofmann, S. G., Craske, M. G., … Liao, B. (2010). Culture and the anxiety disorders: Recommendations for DSM-V. *Depression and Anxiety, 27*(2), 212–229. doi:10.1002/da.20647

Lewis-Fernández, R., Martínez-Taboas, A., Sar, V., Patel, S., & Boatin, A. (2007). The cross-cultural assessment of dissociation. In J. P. Wilson & C. S. Tang (Eds.), *Cross-cultural assessment of psychological trauma and PTSD* (pp. 279–317). New York, NY: Springer Science + Business Media.

Leza, J. C., García-Bueno, B., Bioque, M., Arango, C., Parellada, M., Do, K., … Bernardo, M. (2015). Inflammation in schizophrenia: A question of balance. *Neuroscience and Biobehavioral Reviews, 55*, 612–626. doi:10.1016/j.neubiorev.2015.05.014

Li, C.-Y., Mao, X., & Wei, L. (2008). Genes and (common) pathways underlying drug addiction. *PLOS Computational Biology, 4*(1), e2–e2. doi:10.1371/journal.pcbi.0040002

Li, D., Zhao, H., Kranzler, H. R., Oslin, D., Anton, R. F., Farrer, L. A., & Gelernter, J. (2012). Association of COL25A1 with Comorbid Antisocial Personality Disorder and Substance Dependence. *Biological Psychiatry, 71*(8), 733–740. doi:http://dx.doi.org/10.1016/j.biopsych.2011.12.011

Li, L., Wu, M., Liao, Y., Ouyang, L., Du, M., Lei, D., … Gong, Q. (2014). Grey matter reduction associated with posttraumatic stress disorder and traumatic stress. *Neuroscience and Biobehavioral Reviews, 43*, 163–172. doi:10.1016/j.neubiorev.2014.04.003

Li, L., Zhu, S., Tse, N., Tse, S., & Wong, P. (2016). Effectiveness of motivational interviewing to reduce illicit drug use in adolescents: A systematic review and meta-analysis. *Addiction, 111*(5), 795–805. doi:10.1111/add.13285

Liberzon, I., & Phan, K. L. (2003). Brain-Imaging Studies of Posttraumatic Stress Disorder. *CNS Spectrums, 8*(9), 641–650.

Lichtenstein, P., Carlström, E., Råstam, M., Gillberg, C., & Anckarsäter, H. (2010). The genetics of autism spectrum disorders and related neuropsychiatric disorders in childhood. *The American Journal of Psychiatry, 167*(11), 1357–1363. doi:10.1176/appi.ajp.2010.10020223

Licinio, J., Wong, M.-L., & Gold, P. W. (1996). The hypothalamic-pituitary-adrenal axis in anorexia nervosa. *Psychiatry Research, 62*(1), 75–83. doi:10.1016/0165-1781(96)02991-5

Liddle, H. A. (2010). Multidimensional family therapy: A science-based treatment system for adolescent drug abuse. *Sucht: Zeitschrift für Wissenschaft und Praxis, 56*(1), 43–50. doi:10.1024/0939-5911/a000011

Lieb, K., Völlm, B., Rücker, G., Timmer, A., & Stoffers, J. M. (2010). Pharmacotherapy for borderline personality disorder: Cochrane systematic review of randomised trials. *The British Journal of Psychiatry, 196*(1), 4–12. doi:10.1192/bjp.bp.108.062984

Lieberman, J. (2015, April 30). From fever cure to coma therapy: Psychiatric treatments through time. Retrieved from https://www.sciencefriday.com/articles/from-fever-cure-to-coma-therapy-psychiatric-treatments-through-time/

Lieblich, S. M., Castle, D. J., Pantelis, C., Hopwood, M., Young, A. H., & Everall, I. P. (2015). High heterogeneity and low reliability in the diagnosis of major depression will impair the development of new drugs. *British Journal of Psychiatry Open, 1*(2), e5–e7.

Liebman, L. S., Ahle, G. M., Briggs, M. C., & Kellner, C. H. (2015). Electroconvulsive therapy and bipolar disorder. In A. Yildiz, P. Ruiz, & C. B. Nemeroff (Eds.), *The bipolar book: History, neurobiology, and treatment* (pp. 367–375). New York, NY: Oxford University Press.

Lien, L., Lien, N., Heyerdahl, S., Thoresen, M., & Bjertness, E. (2006). Consumption of soft drinks and hyperactivity, mental distress, and conduct problems among adolescents in Oslo, Norway. *American Journal of Public Health, 96*(10), 1815–1820. doi:10.2105/AJPH.2004.059477

Light, K. J., Joyce, P. R., Luty, S. E., Mulder, R. T., Frampton, C. M. A., Joyce, L. R. M., … Kennedy, M. A. (2006). Preliminary evidence for an association between a dopamine D3 receptor gene variant and obsessive-compulsive personality disorder in patients with major depression. *American Journal of Medical Genetics Part B: Neuropsychiatric Genetics, 141B*(4), 409–413. doi:10.1002/ajmg.b.30308

Lilenfeld, L. R., Kaye, W. H., Greeno, C. G., Merikangas, K. R., Plotnicov, K., Pollice, C., … Nagy, L. (1998). A controlled family study of anorexia nervosa and bulimia nervosa: Psychiatric disorders in first-degree relatives and effects of proband comorbidity. *Archives of General Psychiatry, 55*(7), 603–610. doi:10.1001/archpsyc.55.7.603

Lilienfeld, S. O., & Arkowitz, H. (2011, March 1). Does Alcoholics Anonymous work? *The Atlantic.*

Lilienfeld, S. O., & Marino, L. (1995). Mental disorder as a Roschian concept: A critique of Wakefield's 'harmful dysfunction' analysis. *Journal of Abnormal Psychology, 104*(3), 411–420. doi:10.1037/0021-843X.104.3.411

Lilienfeld, S. O., & Marino, L. (1999). Essentialism revisited: Evolutionary theory and the concept of mental disorder. *Journal of Abnormal Psychology, 108*(3), 400–411. doi:10.1037/0021-843X.108.3.400

Lilienfeld, S. O., Kirsch, I., Sarbin, T. R., Lynn, S. J., Chaves, J. F., Ganaway, G. K., & Powell, R. A. (1999). Dissociative identity disorder and the sociocognitive model: Recalling the lessons of the past. *Psychological Bulletin, 125*(5), 507–523. doi:10.1037/0033-2909.125.5.507

Lilienfeld, S. O., Wood, J. M., & Garb, H. N. (2000). The scientific status of projective techniques. *Psychological Science in the Public Interest, 1*(2), 27–66. doi:10.1111/1529-1006.002

Lin, L. A., Rosenheck, R., Sugar, C., & Zbrozek, A. (2015). Comparing antipsychotic treatments for schizophrenia: A health state approach. *Psychiatric Quarterly, 86*(1), 107–121. doi:10.1007/s11126-014-9326-2

Lincoln, T. M., Ziegler, M., Mehl, S., Kesting, M.-L., Lüllmann, E., Westermann, S., & Rief, W. (2012). Moving from efficacy to effectiveness in cognitive behavioral therapy for psychosis: A randomized clinical practice trial. *Journal of Consulting and Clinical Psychology, 80*(4), 674–686. doi:10.1037/a0028665

Linde, K., Berner, M., Egger, M., & Mulrow, C. (2005). St John's wort for depression. *The British Journal of Psychiatry, 186*(2), 99.

Lindgren, I., Hogstedt, M. F., & Cullberg, J. (2006). Outpatient vs. comprehensive first-episode psychosis services, a 5-year follow-up of Soteria Nacka. *Nordic Journal of Psychiatry, 60*(5), 405–409. doi:10.1080/08039480600937686

Lindsay, D. S. (1998). Recovered memories and social justice. *American Psychologist, 53*(4), 486–487. doi:10.1037/0003-066X.53.4.486

Lindsley, O. R. (1956). Operant conditioning methods applied to research in chronic schizophrenia. *Psychiatric Research Reports, 5*, 118–139.

Lindsley, O. R. (1960). Characteristics of the behavior of chronic psychotics as revealed by free-operant conditioning methods. *Diseases of the Nervous System, 21*(2)Suppl, 66–78.

Linehan, M. M. (1993a). *Cognitive-behavioral treatment of borderline personality disorder.* New York, NY: Guilford Press.

Linehan, M. M. (1993b). *Skills training manual for treating borderline personality disorder.* New York, NY: Guilford Press.

Linehan, M. M. (2003). Dialectical behavior therapy (DBT) for borderline personality disorder. Retrieved from http://www.dbtselfhelp.com/html/linehan_dbt.html

Linehan, M. M. (2015). *DBT skills training manual* (2nd ed.). New York, NY: Guilford Press.

Linehan, M. M., Armstrong, H. E., Suarez, A., Allmon, D., & Heard, H. L. (1991). Cognitive-behavioral treatment of chronically parasuicidal borderline patients. *Archives of General Psychiatry, 48*(12), 1060–1064. doi:10.1001/archpsyc.1991.01810360024003

Linehan, M. M., Comtois, K. A., Murray, A. M., Brown, M. Z., Gallop, R. J., Heard, H. L., ... Lindenboim, N. (2006). Two-Year Randomized Controlled Trial and Follow-up of Dialectical Behavior Therapy vs Therapy by Experts for Suicidal Behaviors and Borderline Personality Disorder. *Archives of General Psychiatry, 63*(7), 757–766. doi:10.1001/archpsyc.63.7.757

Ling Young, S., Taylor, M., & Lawrie, S. M. (2015). 'First do no harm.' A systematic review of the prevalence and management of antipsychotic adverse effects. *Journal of Psychopharmacology, 29*(4), 353–362. doi:10.1177/0269881114562090

Lingiardi, V., & McWilliams, N. (Eds.). (2017). *Psychodynamic diagnostic manual* (2nd ed.). New York, NY: Guilford Press.

Lingiardi, V., McWilliams, N., Bornstein, R. F., Gazzillo, F., & Gordon, R. M. (2015). The Psychodynamic Diagnostic Manual Version 2 (PDM-2): Assessing patients for improved clinical practice and research. *Psychoanalytic Psychology, 32*(1), 94–115. doi:10.1037/a0038546

Linton, K. F. (2014). Clinical diagnoses exacerbate stigma and improve self-discovery according to people with autism. *Social Work in Mental Health, 12*(4), 330–342. doi:10.1080/15332985.2013.861383

Lipke, H. (1999). Comments on 'Thirty years of behavior therapy...' and the promise of the application of scientific principles. *the Behavior Therapist, 22*(1), 11–14.

Lipowski, Z. J. (1987). Somatization: The experience and communication of psychological distress as somatic symptoms. *Psychotherapy and Psychosomatics, 47*(3-4), 160–167. doi:10.1159/000288013

Lis, E., Greenfield, B., Henry, M., Guilé, J. M., & Dougherty, G. (2007). Neuroimaging and genetics of borderline personality disorder: a review. *Journal of Psychiatry & Neuroscience, 32*(3), 162–173.

Lisanby, S. H. (2007). Electroconvulsive therapy for depression. *The New England Journal of Medicine, 357*(19), 1939–1945.

Lisik, M. Z. (2014). Molecular aspects of autism spectrum disorders. *Psychiatria Polska, 48*(4), 689–700.

Littrell, J. (2010). Perspectives emerging from neuroscience on how people become addicted and what to do about it. *Journal of Social Work Practice in the Addictions, 10*(3), 229–256. doi:10.1080/1533256X.2010.498741

Littrell, J. (2011). How addiction happens, how change happens, and what social workers need to know to be effective facilitators of change. *Journal of Evidence-Based Social Work, 8*(5), 469–486. doi:10.1080/10911359.2011.547748

Littrell, J. (2015). *Neuroscience for psychologists and other mental health professionals.* New York, NY: Springer.

Litz, B. T., Gray, M. J., Bryant, R. A., & Adler, A. B. (2002). Early intervention for trauma: Current status and future directions. *Clinical Psychology: Science and Practice, 9*(2), 112–134. doi:10.1093/clipsy/9.2.112

Liu, C. S., Ruthirakuhan, M., Chau, S. A., Herrmann, N., Carvalho, A. F., & Lanctôt, K. L. (2016). Pharmacological management of agitation and aggression in Alzheimer's disease: A review of current and novel treatments. *Current Alzheimer Research, 13*(10), 1134–1144.

Liu, R. T., & Mustanski, B. (2012). Suicidal ideation and self-harm in lesbian, gay, bisexual, and transgender youth. *American Journal of Preventive Medicine, 42*(3), 221–228. doi:http://dx.doi.org/10.1016/j.amepre.2011.10.023

Liu, R. T., Frazier, E. A., Cataldo, A. M., Simon, V. A., Spirito, A., & Prinstein, M. J. (2014). Negative life events and non-suicidal self-injury in an adolescent inpatient sample. *Archives of Suicide Research, 18*(3), 251–258. doi:10.1080/13811118.2013.824835

Liu, X., & Takumi, T. (2014). Genomic and genetic aspects of autism spectrum disorder. *Biochemical and Biophysical Research Communications, 452*(2), 244–253. doi:http://dx.doi.org/10.1016/j.bbrc.2014.08.108

Lloyd, C. (2013). The stigmatization of problem drug users: A narrative literature review. *Drugs: Education, Prevention & Policy, 20*(2), 85–95. doi:10.3109/09687637.2012.743506

Lloyd, S., Schmidt, U., Khondoker, M., & Tchanturia, K. (2015). Can psychological interventions reduce perfectionism? A systematic review and meta-analysis. *Behavioural and Cognitive Psychotherapy, 43*(6), 705–731. doi:10.1017/S1352465814000162

Lo Sauro, C., Ravaldi, C., Cabras, P. L., Faravelli, C., & Ricca, V. (2008). Stress, hypothalamic-pituitary-adrenal axis and eating disorders. *Neuropsychobiology, 57*(3), 95–115. doi:10.1159/000138912

Lobbestael, J., & Arntz, A. (2012). Cognitive contributions to personality disorders. In T. A. Widiger (Ed.), *The Oxford handbook of personality disorders.* (pp. 325–344). New York, NY: Oxford University Press.

Lobel, D. S. (2013). History of psychosis. In T. G. Plante (Ed.), *Abnormal psychology across the ages: Vol. 2. Disorders and treatments* (pp. 15–29). Santa Barbara, CA: Praeger/ABC-CLIO.

Lochner, C., Seedat, S., Hemmings, S. M. J., Moolman-Smook, J. C., Kidd, M., & Stein, D. J. (2007). Investigating the possible effects of trauma experiences and 5-HTT on the dissociative experiences of patients with OCD using path analysis and multiple regression. *Neuropsychobiology, 56*(1), 6–13. doi:10.1159/000109971

Lock, J. (2011). Evaluation of family treatment models for eating disorders. *Current Opinion in Psychiatry, 24*(4), 274–279. doi:10.1097/YCO.0b013e328346f71e

Lock, J., & Kirz, N. (2008). Eating disorders: Anorexia nervosa. In W. E. Craighead, D. J. Miklowitz, & L. W. Craighead (Eds.), *Psychopathology: History, diagnosis, and empirical foundations* (pp. 467–494). Hoboken, NJ: John Wiley.

Loew, T. H., Sohn, R., Martus, P., Tritt, K., & Rechlin, T. (2000). Functional relaxation as a somatopsychotherapeutic intervention: a prospective controlled study. *Alternative Therapies in Health and Medicine, 6*(6), 70–75.

Loewenstein, R. J. (2005). Psychopharmacologic treatments for dissociative identity disorder. *Psychiatric Annals, 35*(8), 666–673.

Loewenstein, R. J., & Ross, D. R. (1992). Multiple personality and psychoanalysis: An introduction. *Psychoanalytic Inquiry, 12*(1), 3–48. doi:10.1080/07351699209533881

Loftus, E. F. (2011). Crimes of memory: False memories and societal justice. In M. A. Gernsbacher, R. W. Pew, L. M. Hough, & J. R. Pomerantz (Eds.), *Psychology and the real world: Essays illustrating fundamental contributions to society* (pp. 83–88). New York, NY: Worth Publishers.

Loftus, E. F., & Ketcham, K. (1994). *The myth of repressed memory: False memories and allegations of sexual abuse* New York, NY: St. Martin's Press.

Lohoff, F. W. (2010). Overview of the genetics of major depressive disorder. *Current Psychiatry Reports, 12*(6), 539–546. doi:10.1007/s11920-010-0150-6

Lohr, J. M., Lilienfeld, S. O., Tolin, D. F., & Herbert, J. D. (1999). Eye movement desensitization and reprocessing: An analysis of specific versus nonspecific treatment factors. *Journal of Anxiety Disorders, 13*(1–2), 185–207. doi:10.1016/S0887-6185(98)00047-4

Lohr, J. M., Tolin, D. F., & Lilienfeld, S. O. (1998). Efficacy of eye movement desensitization and reprocessing: Implications for behavior therapy. *Behavior Therapy, 29*(1), 123–156. doi:10.1016/S0005-7894(98)80035-X

Lohr, W. D., & Tanguay, P. (2013). DSM-5 and proposed changes to the diagnosis of autism. *Pediatric Annals, 42*(4), 161–166. doi:10.3928/00904481-20130326-12

Lombardo, T. W., & Turner, S. M. (1979). Thought-stopping in the control of obsessive ruminations. *Behavior Modification, 3*(2), 267–272. doi:10.1177/014544557932008

Long-Smith, C. M., Manning, S., McClean, P. L., Coakley, M. F., O'Halloran, D. J., Holscher, C., & O'Neill, C. (2013). The diabetes drug liraglutide ameliorates aberrant insulin receptor localisation and signalling in parallel with decreasing both amyloid-β plaque and glial pathology in a mouse model of Alzheimer's disease. *Neuromolecular Medicine, 15*(1), 102–114. doi:10.1007/s12017-012-8199-5

Longden, E., Madill, A., & Waterman, M. G. (2012). Dissociation, trauma, and the role of lived experience: Toward a new conceptualization of voice hearing. *Psychological Bulletin, 138*(1), 28–76. doi:10.1037/a0025995

Looper, K. J., & Kirmayer, L. J. (2004). Perceived stigma in functional somatic syndromes and comparable medical conditions. *Journal of Psychosomatic Research, 57*(4), 373–378. doi:10.1016/j.jpsychores.2004.03.005

López, S. R., & Guarnaccia, P. J. (2016). Cultural dimensions of psychopathology: The social world's impact on mental disorders. In J. E. Maddux & B. A. Winstead (Eds.), *Psychopathology: Foundations for a contemporary understanding* (4th ed., pp. 59–75). New York, NY: Routledge.

López-Muñoz, F., Álamo, C., & García-García, P. (2011). The discovery of chlordiazepoxide and the clinical introduction of benzodiazepines: Half a century of anxiolytic drugs. *Journal of Anxiety Disorders, 25*(4), 554–562. doi:10.1016/j.janxdis.2011.01.002

López Viets, V. C., & Miller, W. R. (1997). Treatment approaches for pathological gamblers. *Clinical Psychology Review, 17*(7), 689–702. doi:10.1016/S0272-7358(97)00031-7

Lorenz, K., & Ullman, S. E. (2016). Alcohol and sexual assault victimization: Research findings and future directions. *Aggression and Violent Behavior.* doi:10.1016/j.avb.2016.08.001

Lorenzetti, V., Allen, N. B., Fornito, A., & Yücel, M. (2009). Structural brain abnormalities in major depressive disorder: A selective review of recent MRI studies. *Journal of Affective Disorders, 117*(1–2), 1–17. doi:http://dx.doi.org/10.1016/j.jad.2008.11.021

Loring, M., & Powell, B. (1988). Gender, race, and DSM-III: A study of the objectivity of psychiatric diagnostic behavior. *Journal of Health and Social Behavior, 29*(1), 1–22. doi:10.2307/2137177

Lösel, F., & Schmucker, M. (2005). The effectiveness of treatment for sexual offenders: A comprehensive meta-analysis. *Journal of Experimental Criminology, 1*(1), 117–146. doi:10.1007/s11292-004-6466-7

Louch, P., Goodman, C., & Greenhalgh, T. (2005). Involving service users in the evaluation and redesign of primary care services for depression: A qualitative study. *Primary Care & Community Psychiatry, 10*(3), 109–117. doi:10.1185/135525706X56682

Lowe, G. (1983). Alcohol and state-dependent learning. *Substance & Alcohol Actions/Misuse, 4*(4), 273–282.

Lowen, A. (1971). *The language of the body.* New York, NY: Collier.

Loy, J. H., Merry, S. N., Hetrick, S. E., & Stasiak, K. (2012). Atypical antipsychotics for disruptive behaviour disorders in children and youths. *Cochrane Database of Systematic Reviews, 2012*(9), 1–62. doi:10.1002/14651858.CD008559.pub2

Lu, S. (2015, February). Erasing bad memories. *Monitor on Psychology.*

Luiselli, J. K. (2016). Intellectual disability. In C. M. Nezu & A. M. Nezu (Eds.), *The Oxford handbook of cognitive and behavioral therapies* (pp. 401–418). New York, NY: Oxford University Press.

Lund, B. C., Abrams, T. E., Bernardy, N. C., Alexander, B., & Friedman, M. J. (2013). Benzodiazepine prescribing variation and clinical uncertainty in treating posttraumatic stress disorder. *Psychiatric Services, 64*(1), 21–27.

Lundahl, B., & Burke, B. L. (2009). The effectiveness and applicability of motivational interviewing: A practice-friendly review of four meta-analyses. *Journal of Clinical Psychology, 65*(11), 1232–1245. doi:10.1002/jclp.20638

Luoma, J. B., Kulesza, M., Hayes, S. C., Kohlenberg, B., & Larimer, M. (2014). Stigma predicts residential treatment length for substance use disorder. *The American Journal of Drug and Alcohol Abuse, 40*(3), 206–212. doi:10.3109/00952990.2014.901337

Luoma, J. B., Twohig, M. P., Waltz, T., Hayes, S. C., Roget, N., Padilla, M., & Fisher, G. (2007). An investigation of stigma in individuals receiving treatment for substance abuse. *Addictive Behaviors, 32*(7), 1331–1346. doi:10.1016/j.addbeh.2006.09.008

Luria-Nebraska Neuropsychological Battery. (n.d.). *Encyclopedia of Mental Disorders, 40*(9), 63. Retrieved from http://www.minddisorders.com/Kau-Nu/Luria-Nebraska-Neuropsychological-Battery.html

Lustyk, M. K., Chawla, N., Nolan, R. S., & Marlatt, G. A. (2009). Mindfulness meditation research: issues of participant screening, safety procedures, and researcher training. *Advances in mind-body medicine, 24*(1), 20.

Luszczynska, A., Scholz, U., & Schwarzer, R. (2005). The general self-efficacy scale: Multicultural validation studies. *The Journal of Psychology: Interdisciplinary and Applied, 139*(5), 439–457. doi:10.3200/JRLP.139.5.439-457

Luty, S. E., Carter, J. D., McKenzie, J. M., Rae, A. M., Frampton, C. M. A., Mulder, R. T., & Joyce, P. R. (2007). Randomised controlled trial of interpersonal psychotherapy and cognitive-behavioural therapy for depression. *The British Journal of Psychiatry, 190*, 496–502. doi:10.1192/bjp.bp.106.024729

Lv, Z.-T., Song, W., Wu, J., Yang, J., Wang, T., Wu, C.-H., ... Li, M. (2015). Efficacy of acupuncture in children with nocturnal enuresis: A systematic review and meta-analysis of randomized controlled trials. *Evidence-Based Complementary and Alternative Medicine, 2015*, 320701–320701. doi:10.1155/2015/320701

Lyall, K., Ashwood, P., Water, J., & Hertz-Picciotto, I. (2014). Maternal immune-mediated conditions, autism spectrum disorders, and developmental delay. *Journal of Autism and Developmental Disorders, 44*(7), 1546–1555. doi:10.1007/s10803-013-2017-2

Lyke, J., & Matsen, J. (2013). Family functioning and risk factors for disordered eating. *Eating Behaviors, 14*(4), 497–499. doi:http://dx.doi.org/10.1016/j.eatbeh.2013.08.009

Lynch, D., Laws, K. R., & McKenna, P. J. (2010). Cognitive behavioural therapy for major psychiatric disorder: Does it really work? A meta-analytical review of well-controlled trials. *Psychological Medicine, 40*(1), 9–24. doi:10.1017/S003329170900590X

Lynn, S. J., Knox, J. A., Fassler, O., Lilienfeld, S. O., & Loftus, E. F. (2004). Memory, trauma, and dissociation. In G. M. Rosen (Ed.), *Posttraumatic stress disorder: Issues and controversies* (pp. 163–186). New York, NY: John Wiley.

Lynn, S. J., Lilienfeld, S. O., Merckelbach, H., Giesbrecht, T., & van der Kloet, D. (2012). Dissociation and dissociative disorders: Challenging conventional wisdom. *Current Directions in Psychological Science, 21*(1), 48–53. doi:10.1177/0963721411429457

Lynn, S. J., Lilienfeld, S. O., Merckelbach, H., Maxwell, R., Baltman, J., & Giesbrecht, T. (2016). Dissociative disorders. In J. E. Maddux & B. A. Winstead (Eds.), *Psychopathology: Foundations for a contemporary understanding* (4th ed., pp. 298–317). New York, NY: Routledge.

Lyons, V., & Fitzgerald, M. (2007). Asperger (1906–1980) and Kanner (1894–1981), the two pioneers of autism (Vol. 37, pp. 2022–2023): Springer Science & Business Media B.V.

Lysaker, P. H., & Lysaker, J. T. (2006). A typology of narrative impoverishment in schizophrenia: Implications for understanding the processes of establishing and sustaining dialogue in individual psychotherapy. *Counselling Psychology Quarterly, 19*(1), 57–68. doi:10.1080/09515070600673703

Lysaker, P. H., Buck, K. D., Fogley, R. L., Ringer, J., Harder, S., Hasson-Ohayon, I., ... Dimaggio, G. (2013). The mutual development of intersubjectivity and metacognitive capacity in the psychotherapy for persons with schizophrenia. *Journal of Contemporary Psychotherapy, 43*(2), 63–72. doi:10.1007/s10879-012-9218-4

Lysaker, P. H., Clements, C. A., Plascak-Hallberg, C. D., Knipscheer, S. J., & Wright, D. E. (2002). Insight and personal narratives of illness in schizophrenia. *Psychiatry: Interpersonal and Biological Processes, 65*(3), 197–206. doi:10.1521/psyc.65.3.197.20174

Lysaker, P. H., Glynn, S. M., Wilkniss, S. M., & Silverstein, S. M. (2010). Psychotherapy and recovery from schizophrenia: A review of potential applications and need for future study. *Psychological Services, 7*(2), 75–91. doi:10.1037/a0019115

Lysaker, P. H., Lysaker, J. T., & Lysaker, J. T. (2001). Schizophrenia and the collapse of the dialogical self: Recovery, narrative and psychotherapy. *Psychotherapy: Theory, Research, Practice, Training, 38*(3), 252–261. doi:10.1037/0033-3204.38.3.252

Lysaker, P. H., Wickett, A. M., Campbell, K., & Buck, K. D. (2003). Movement towards coherence in the psychotherapy of schizophrenia: A method for assessing narrative transformation. *Journal of Nervous and Mental Disease, 191*(8), 538–541. doi:10.1097/01.nmd.0000082182.77891.89

M'Naghten's case. (n.d.). *Bloomberg's Law.* Retrieved from http://www.casebriefs.com/blog/law/criminal-law/criminal-law-keyed-to-kadish/exculpation/mnaghtens-case/

Ma-Kellams, C., Baek, J. H., & Or, F. (2016). Suicide contagion in response to widely publicized celebrity deaths: The roles of depressed affect, death-thought accessibility, and attitudes. *Psychology of Popular Media Culture.* doi:10.1037/ppm0000115

Mabe, A. G., Forney, K. J., & Keel, P. K. (2014). Do you 'like' my photo? Facebook use maintains eating disorder risk. *International Journal of Eating Disorders, 47*(5), 516–523. doi:10.1002/eat.22254

MacGill, M. (2016, January 29). What is a randomized controlled trial in medical research? *Medical News Today.* Retrieved from http://www.medicalnewstoday.com/articles/280574.php

MacIntosh, H. B., Godbout, N., & Dubash, N. (2015). Borderline personality disorder: Disorder of trauma or personality, a review of the empirical literature. *Canadian Psychology/Psychologie Canadienne, 56*(2), 227–241. doi:10.1037/cap0000028

Mackay, R. D. (2007). AAPL practice guideline for the forensic psychiatric evaluation of competence to stand trial: An English legal perspective. *Journal of the American Academy of Psychiatry and the Law, 35*(4), 501–504.

MacKenzie, P. M. (2014). Psychopathy, antisocial personality & sociopathy: The basics. *The Forensic Examiner*. Retrieved from https://www.all-about-forensic-psychology.com/support-files/psychopathy-antisocial-personality-and-sociopathy.pdf

Mackie, S., & Winkelman, J. W. (2015). Insomnia. *Psychiatric Annals, 45*(1), 14–18. doi:10.3928/00485713-20150106-04

MacKinaw-Koons, B., & Vasey, M. W. (2000). Considering sex differences in anxiety and its disorders across the life span: A construct-validation approach. *Applied and Preventive Psychology, 9*(3), 191–209. doi:http://dx.doi.org/10.1016/S0962-1849(05)80004-6

MacLean, P. D. (1985). Evolutionary psychiatry and the triune brain. *Psychological Medicine, 15*(2), 219–221. doi:10.1017/S0033291700023485

MacLellan, L. (2017, April 30). There's no such thing as "mild depression." *Quartz*. Retrieved from https://qz.com/969943/theres-no-such-thing-as-mild-depression/

MacLeod, A. K. (2013). Suicide and attempted suicide. In M. Power (Ed.), *The Wiley-Blackwell handbook of mood disorders* (2nd ed., pp. 413–431). Chichester, UK: Wiley-Blackwell.

MacLeod, R., & Elliott, R. (2012). Emotion-focused therapy for social anxiety: A hermeneutic single case efficacy design study of a low-outcome case. *Counselling Psychology Review, 27*(2), 7–22.

MacLeod, R., Elliott, R., & Rodgers, B. (2012). Process-experiential/emotion-focused therapy for social anxiety: A hermeneutic single-case efficacy design study. *Psychotherapy Research, 22*(1), 67–81. doi:10.1080/10503307.2011.626805

MacQueen, G., Surette, M., & Moayyedi, P. (2017). The gut microbiota and psychiatric illness. *Journal of Psychiatry & Neuroscience, 42*(2), 75–77. doi:10.1503/jpn.170028

Maddux, J. E., Gosselin, J. T., & Winstead, B. A. (2016). Conceptions of psychopathology: A social constructionist perspective. In J. E. Maddux & B. A. Winstead (Eds.), *Psychopathology: Foundations for a contemporary understanding* (4th ed., pp. 3–17). New York, NY: Routledge.

Madigan, S. (2011). *Narrative therapy*. Washington, DC: American Psychological Association.

Madigan, S., Moran, G., Schuengel, C., Pederson, D. R., & Otten, R. (2007). Unresolved maternal attachment representations, disrupted maternal behavior and disorganized attachment in infancy: Links to toddler behavior problems. *Journal of Child Psychology and Psychiatry, 48*(10), 1042–1050. doi:10.1111/j.1469-7610.2007.01805.x

Maenner, M. J., Baker, M. W., Broman, K. W., Tian, J., Barnes, J. K., Atkins, A., ... Mailick, M. R. (2013). FMR1 CGG expansions: Prevalence and sex ratios. *American Journal of Medical Genetics Part B: Neuropsychiatric Genetics, 162*(5), 466–473. doi:10.1002/ajmg.b.32176

Maenner, M. J., Rice, C. E., Arneson, C. L., Cunniff, C., Schieve, L. A., Carpenter, L. A., ... Durkin, M. S. (2014). Potential impact of DSM-5 criteria on autism spectrum disorder prevalence estimates. *JAMA Psychiatry, 71*(3), 292–300. doi:10.1001/jamapsychiatry.2013.3893

Maercker, A., Brewin, C. R., Bryant, R. A., Cloitre, M., Reed, G. M., van Ommeren, M., ... Saxena, S. (2013). Proposals for mental disorders specifically associated with stress in the International Classification of Diseases-11. *The Lancet, 381*(9878), 1683–1685. doi:10.1016/S0140-6736(12)62191-6

Maercker, A., Brewin, C. R., Bryant, R. A., Cloitre, M., van Ommeren, M., Jones, L. M., ... Reed, G. M. (2013). Diagnosis and classification of disorders specifically associated with stress: proposals for ICD-11. *World Psychiatry, 12*(3), 198–206. doi:10.1002/wps.20057

Mago, R., Borra, D., & Mahajan, R. (2014). Role of adverse effects in medication nonadherence in bipolar disorder. *Harvard Review of Psychiatry, 22*(6), 363–366. doi:10.1097/HRP.0000000000000017

Magor-Blatch, L., Bhullar, N., Thomson, B., & Thorsteinsson, E. (2014). A systematic review of studies examining effectiveness of therapeutic communities. *Therapeutic Communities, 35*(4), 168–184. doi:10.1108/TC-07-2013-0024

Maher, W. B., & Maher, B. (1982). The ship of fools: Stultifera Navis or ignis fatuus? *American Psychologist, 37*(7), 756–761. doi:10.1037/0003-066X.37.7.756

Mahler, M. S., & Rangell, L. (1943). A psychosomatic study of maladie des tics (Gilles de la Tourette's disease). *Psychiatric Quarterly, 17*, 579–603. doi:10.1007/BF01561841

Mahrer, A. R. (1996). *The complete guide to experiential psychotherapy*. Oxford, UK: John Wiley.

Mai, F. M. (1983). Pierre Briquet: 19th Century savant with 20th Century ideas. *The Canadian Journal of Psychiatry/La Revue Canadienne De Psychiatrie, 28*(6), 418–421.

Mai, F. M., & Merskey, H. (1980). Briquet's treatise on hysteria: A synopsis and commentary. *Archives of General Psychiatry, 37*(12), 1401–1405. doi:10.1001/archpsyc.1980.01780250087010

Mai, F. M., & Merskey, H. (1981). Briquet's concept of hysteria: An historical perspective. *The Canadian Journal of Psychiatry /La Revue Canadienne De Psychiatrie, 26*(1), 57–63.

Maier, A., Ernst, J. P., Müller, S., Gross, D., Zepf, F. D., Herpertz-Dahlmann, B., & Hagenah, U. (2014). Self-perceived stigmatization in female patients with anorexia nervosa—Results from an explorative retrospective pilot study of adolescents. *Psychopathology, 47*(2), 127–132. doi:10.1159/000350505

Maisel, R., Epston, D., & Borden, A. (2004). *Biting the hand that starves you: Inspiring resistance to anorexia/bulimia*. New York, NY: Norton.

Maj, M. (2013). Mood disorders in ICD-11 and DSM-5: A brief overview. *Die Psychiatrie: Grundlagen & Perspektiven, 10*(1), 24–29.

Maj, M. (2015). The media campaign on the DSM-5: Recurring comments and lessons for the future of diagnosis in psychiatric practice. *Epidemiology and Psychiatric Sciences, 24*(3), 97–202. doi:10.1017/S2045796014000572

Mak, L., Streiner, D. L., & Steiner, M. (2015). Is serotonin transporter polymorphism (5-HTTLPR) allele status a predictor for obsessive-compulsive disorder? A meta-analysis. *Archives of Women's Mental Health, 18*(3), 435–445. doi:10.1007/s00737-015-0526-z

Makino, M., Tsuboi, K., & Dennerstein, L. (2004). Prevalence of eating disorders: A comparison of Western and non-Western countries. *Medscape General Medicine, 6*(3), 49.

Makowski, A. C., Mnich, E. E., Angermeyer, M. C., Löwe, B., & von dem Knesebeck, O. (2015). Sex differences in attitudes towards females with eating disorders. *Eating Behaviors, 16*, 78–83. doi:10.1016/j.eatbeh.2014.10.017

Malchow, B., Hasan, A., Schneider-Axmann, T., Jatzko, A., Gruber, O., Schmitt, A., ... Wobrock, T. (2013). Effects of cannabis and familial loading on subcortical brain volumes in first-episode schizophrenia. *European Archives of Psychiatry and Clinical Neuroscience, 263*(Suppl 2), S155–S168. doi:10.1007/s00406-013-0451-y

Maldonado, J. R., & Spiegel, D. (2014). Dissociative disorders. In R. E. Hales, S. C. Yudofsky, & L. W. Roberts (Eds.), *The American Psychiatric Publishing textbook of psychiatry* (6th ed., pp. 499–530). Arlington, VA: American Psychiatric Publishing.

Maletic, V., & Raison, C. (2014). Integrated neurobiology of bipolar disorder. *Frontiers in Psychiatry, 5*.

Malhi, G. S., Hitching, R., Berk, M., Boyce, P., Porter, R., & Fritz, K. (2013). Pharmacological management of unipolar depression. *Acta Psychiatrica Scandinavica, 127*(Suppl 443), 6–23. doi:10.1111/acps.12122

Malhi, G. S., Tanious, M., Das, P., Coulston, C. M., & Berk, M. (2013). Potential mechanisms of action of lithium in bipolar disorder: Current understanding. *CNS Drugs, 27*(2), 135–153. doi:10.1007/s40263-013-0039-0

Malivert, M., Fatséas, M., Denis, C., Langlois, E., & Auriacombe, M. (2011). Effectiveness of therapeutic communities: A systematic review. *European Addiction Research, 18*(1), 1–11. doi:10.1159/000331007

Malli, M. A., Forrester-Jones, R., & Murphy, G. (2016). Stigma in youth with Tourette's syndrome: A systematic review and synthesis. *European Child & Adolescent Psychiatry, 25*(2), 127–139. doi:10.1007/s00787-015-0761-x

Mallinger, A. (2009). The myth of perfection: Perfectionism in the obsessive personality. *American Journal of Psychotherapy, 63*(2), 103–131.

Malykhin, N. V., & Coupland, N. J. (2015). Hippocampal neuroplasticity in major depressive disorder. *Neuroscience, 309*, 200–213. doi:http://dx.doi.org/10.1016/j.neuroscience.2015.04.047

Management of Post-Traumatic Stress Working Group. (2010). *Veterans Administration/Department of Defense clinical practice guidelines for management of post-traumatic stress*. Retrieved from http://www.healthquality.va.gov/guidelines/MH/ptsd/cpg_PTSD-FULL-201011612.pdf

Mancini, A. D., Griffin, P., & Bonanno, G. A. (2012). Recent trends in the treatment of prolonged grief. *Current Opinion in Psychiatry, 25*(1), 46–51. doi:10.1097/YCO.0b013e32834de48a

Mandell, D. S., Wiggins, L. D., & Carpenter, L. A. (2009). Racial/ethnic disparities in the identification of children with autism spectrum disorders. *American Journal of Public Health, 99*(3), 493–498. doi:10.2105/AJPH.2007.131243

Manieri, C., Castellano, E., Crespi, C., Di Bisceglie, C., Dell'Aquila, C., Gualerzi, A., & Molo, M. (2014). Medical treatment of subjects with gender identity disorder: The experience in an Italian public health center. *International Journal of Transgenderism, 15*(2), 53–65. doi:10.1080/15532739.2014.899174

Mann, D. (2008, January 25). Psychoanalysis helps kids with autism. *WebMD.* Retrieved from http://www.webmd.com/brain/autism/news/20080125/psychoanalysis-helps-kids-with-autism#1

Mann, J. J., & Currier, D. (2012). Medication in suicide prevention Insights from *Neurobiology of Suicidal Behavior.* In Y. Dwivedi (Ed.), The Neurobiological Basis of Suicide. Boca Raton, FL: CRC Press/Taylor & Francis. Retrieved from https://www.ncbi.nlm.nih.gov/books/NBK107195/

Manolis, A., & Doumas, M. (2012). Antihypertensive treatment and sexual dysfunction. *Current Hypertension Reports, 14*(4), 285–292. doi:10.1007/s11906-012-0276-5

Mao, J. J., Xie, S. X., Zee, J., Soeller, I., Li, Q. S., Rockwell, K., & Amsterdam, J. D. (2015). Rhodiola rosea versus sertraline for major depressive disorder: A randomized placebo-controlled trial. *Phytomedicine: International Journal Of Phytotherapy And Phytopharmacology, 22*(3), 394–399. doi:10.1016/j.phymed.2015.01.010

Maples, J. L., Carter, N. T., Few, L. R., Crego, C., Gore, W. L., Samuel, D. B., ... Miller, J. D. (2015). Testing whether the DSM-5 personality disorder trait model can be measured with a reduced set of items: An item response theory investigation of the Personality Inventory for DSM-5. *Psychological Assessment, 27*(4), 1195–1210. doi:10.1037/pas0000120

Marazziti, D., Mucci, F., Lombardi, A., Falaschi, V., & Dell'Osso, L. (2015). The cytokine profile of OCD: Pathophysiological insights. *International Journal of Interferon, Cytokine and Mediator Research, 7*, 35–42. doi:10.2147/IJICMR.S76710

Marcos, A. (1997). The immune system in eating disorders: An overview. *Nutrition, 13*(10), 853–862.

Marcos, A. (2000). Eating disorders: A situation of malnutrition with peculiar changes in the immune system. *European Journal of Clinical Nutrition, 54 Suppl 1*, S61–S64.

Marcos, A., Nova, E., & Montero, A. (2003). Changes in the immune system are conditioned by nutrition. *European Journal of Clinical Nutrition, 57 Suppl 1*, S66–S69.

Marcus, D. K., Gurley, J. R., Marchi, M. M., & Bauer, C. (2007). Cognitive and perceptual variables in hypochondriasis and health anxiety: A systematic review. *Clinical Psychology Review, 27*(2), 127–139. doi:10.1016/j.cpr.2006.09.003

Marcus, P. E. (1993). Borderline families. In C. S. Fawcett (Ed.), *Family psychiatric nursing* (pp. 328–341). St Louis, MO: Mosby.

Marecek, J., & Gavey, N. (2013). DSM-5 and beyond: A critical feminist engagement with psychodiagnosis. *Feminism & Psychology, 23*(1), 3–9. doi:10.1177/0959353512467962

Margulies, D. M., Weintraub, S., Basile, J., Grover, P. J., & Carlson, G. A. (2012). Will disruptive mood dysregulation disorder reduce false diagnosis of bipolar disorder in children? *Bipolar Disorders, 14*(5), 488–496. doi:10.1111/j.1399-5618.2012.01029.x

Marí-Bauset, S., Zazpe, I., Mari-Sanchis, A., Llopis-González, A., & Morales-Suárez-Varela, M. (2014). Evidence of the gluten-free and casein-free diet in autism spectrum disorders: A systematic review. *Journal of Child Neurology, 29*(12), 1718–1727. doi:10.1177/0883073814531330

Markman, E. R. (2011). Gender identity disorder, the gender binary, and transgender oppression: Implications for ethical social work. *Smith College Studies in Social Work, 81*(4), 314–327. doi:10.1080/00377317.2011.616839

Markon, K. E., & Jonas, K. G. (2015). The role of traits in describing, assessing, and understanding personality pathology. In S. K. Huprich (Ed.), *Personality disorders: Toward theoretical and empirical integration in diagnosis and assessment* (pp. 63–84). Washington, DC: American Psychological Association.

Markowitz, J. C. (2013). Interpersonal psychotherapy of depression. In M. Power (Ed.), *The Wiley-Blackwell handbook of mood disorders* (2nd ed., pp. 193–214). Chichester, UK: Wiley-Blackwell.

Markowitz, J. C., Petkova, E., Neria, Y., Van Meter, P. E., Zhao, Y., Hembree, E., ... Marshall, R. D. (2015). Is exposure necessary? A randomized clinical trial of interpersonal psychotherapy for PTSD. *The American Journal of Psychiatry, 172*(5), 430–440. doi:10.1176/appi.ajp.2014.14070908

Marks, I. (1990). Behavioural (non-chemical) addictions. *British Journal of Addiction, 85*(11), 1389–1394. doi:10.1111/j.1360-0443.1990.tb01618.x

Marks, I. M., & Nesse, R. M. (1994). Fear and fitness: An evolutionary analysis of anxiety disorders. *Ethology & Sociobiology, 15*(5–6), 247–261. doi:10.1016/0162-3095(94)90002-7

Marlatt, G. A. (1996). Harm reduction: Come as you are. *Addictive Behaviors, 21*(6), 779–788. doi:http://dx.doi.org/10.1016/0306-4603(96)00042-1

Marlatt, G. A., & Witkiewitz, K. (2005). Relapse prevention for alcohol and drug problems. In G. A. Marlatt & D. M. Donovan (Eds.), *Relapse prevention: Maintenance strategies in the treatment of addictive behaviors* (2nd ed., pp. 1–44). New York, NY: Guilford Press.

Marlatt, M. W., & Lucassen, P. J. (2010). Neurogenesis and Alzheimer's disease: Biology and pathophysiology in mice and men. *Current Alzheimer Research, 7*(2), 113–125. doi:10.2174/156720510790691362

Marlock, G., & Weiss, H. (Eds.). (2015). *The handbook of body psychotherapy & somatic psychology.* Berkeley, CA: North Atlantic Books.

Marmer, S. S. (2003). Theories of the mind and psychopathology. In R. E. Hales & S. C. Yudofsky (Eds.), *The American Psychiatric Publishing textbook of clinical psychiatry* (4th ed., pp. 107–154). Arlington, VA: American Psychiatric Publishing.

Maron, E., Hettema, J. M., & Shlik, J. (2010). Advances in molecular genetics of panic disorder. *Molecular Psychiatry, 15*(7), 681–701. doi:10.1038/mp.2009.145

Marques, J. K., Wiederanders, M., Day, D. M., Nelson, C., & van Ommeren, A. (2005). Effects of a relapse prevention program on sexual recidivism: Final results from California's Sex Offender Treatment and Evaluation Project (SOTEP). *Sexual Abuse: Journal of Research and Treatment, 17*(1), 79–107. doi:10.1177/107906320501700108

Marshall, E., Claes, L., Bouman, W. P., Witcomb, G. L., & Arcelus, J. (2016). Non-suicidal self-injury and suicidality in trans people: A systematic review of the literature. *International Review of Psychiatry, 28*(1), 58–69. doi:10.3109/09540261.2015.1073143

Marshall, R. D., Spitzer, R., & Liebowitz, M. R. (1999). Review and critique of the new DSM-IV diagnosis of acute stress disorder. *The American Journal of Psychiatry, 156*(11), 1677–1685.

Marshall, W. L., & Fernandez, Y. M. (1998). Cognitive-behavioral approaches to the treatment of the paraphilias: Sexual offenders. In V. E. Caballo (Ed.), *International handbook of cognitive and behavioural treatments for psychological disorders* (pp. 281–312). Oxford, UK: Pergamon/Elsevier Science.

Martell, C. R., Dimidjian, S., & Herman-Dunn, R. (2010). *Behavioral activation for depression: A clinician's guide.* New York, NY: Guilford Press.

Martin, B., Clapp, L., Bialkowski, D., Bridgeford, D., Amponsah, A., Lyons, L., & Beresford, T. P. (2003). Compliance to supervised disulfiram therapy: A comparison of voluntary and court-ordered patients. *The American Journal on Addictions, 12*(2), 137-143. doi:10.1080/10550490390201399

Martin, C. S., Langenbucher, J. W., Chung, T., & Sher, K. J. (2014). Truth or consequences in the diagnosis of substance use disorders. *Addiction, 109*(11), 1773–1778. doi:10.1111/add.12615

Martin, L. (2013). Types and stages of sleep: Sleep cycles. Retrieved from http://www.howsleepworks.com/types_cycles.html

Martin, W. E., & Bridgmon, K. D. (2012). *Quantitative and statistical research methods: From hypothesis to results.* San Francisco, CA: Jossey-Bass.

Martínez, R. S., Nellis, L. M., White, S. E., Jochim, M. L., & Peterson, R. K. (2016). Learning disorders of childhood and adolescence. In J. E. Maddux & B. A. Winstead (Eds.), *Psychopathology: Foundations for a contemporary understanding* (4th ed., pp. 419–430). New York, NY: Routledge.

Martínez, R. S., White, S. E., Jochim, M. L., & Nellis, L. M. (2012). Language, learning, and cognitive disorders. In J. E. Maddux & B. A. Winstead (Eds.), *Psychopathology: Foundations for a contemporary understanding* (3rd ed., pp. 499–515). New York, NY: Routledge.

Martins, S. S., Lee, G. P., Sanchez, Z. M., Harrell, P., Ghandour, L. A., & Storr, C. L. (2013). Hallucinogens. In P. M. Miller, S. A. Ball, M. E. Bates, A. W. Blume, K. M. Kampman, D. J. Kavanagh, M. E. Larimer, N. M. Petry, & P. De Witte (Eds.), *Comprehensive addictive behaviors and disorders: Vol. 1. Principles of addiction* (pp. 699–709). San Diego, CA: Elsevier Academic Press.

Masi, A., Quintana, D. S., Glozier, N., Lloyd, A. R., Hickie, I. B., & Guastella, A. J. (2015). Cytokine aberrations in autism spectrum disorder: A systematic review and meta-analysis. *Molecular Psychiatry, 20*(4), 440–446. doi:10.1038/mp.2014.59

Maslow, A. H. (1968). *Toward a psychology of being* (2nd ed.). New York, NY: Van Nostrand Reinhold.

Masson, J. M. (1984). *The assault on truth: Freud's suppression of the seduction theory.* New York, NY: Farrar, Straus and Giroux.

Masters, W. H., & Johnson, V. E. (1966). *Human sexual response.* Boston, MA: Little, Brown, and Company.

Masters, W. H., & Johnson, V. E. (1970). *Human sexual inadequacy.* Boston, MA: Little, Brown, and Company.

Mataix-Cols, D. (2006). Deconstructing obsessive-compulsive disorder: A multidimensional perspective. *Current Opinion in Psychiatry, 19*(1), 84–89. doi:10.1097/01.yco.0000194809.98967.49

Matheny, K. B., Brack, G. L., McCarthy, C. J., & Penick, J. M. (1996). The effectiveness of cognitively-based approaches in treating stress-related symptoms. *Psychotherapy: Theory, Research, Practice, Training, 33*(2), 305–320. doi:10.1037/0033-3204.33.2.305

Matson, J. L., Tureck, K., & Rieske, R. (2012). The Questions About Behavioral Function (QABF): Current status as a method of functional assessment. *Research in Developmental Disabilities, 33*(2), 630–634. doi:https://doi.org/10.1016/j.ridd.2011.11.006

Mattar, S. (2011). Educating and training the next generations of traumatologists: Development of cultural competencies. *Psychological Trauma: Theory, Research, Practice, and Policy, 3*(3), 258–265. doi:10.1037/a0024477

Matte, B., Anselmi, L., Salum, G. A., Kieling, C., Gonçalves, H., Menezes, A., ... Rohde, L. A. (2015). ADHD in DSM-5: A field trial in a large, representative sample of 18- to 19- year-old adults. *Psychological Medicine, 45*(2), 361–373. doi:10.1017/S0033291714001470

Matthews, E. E., Arnedt, J. T., McCarthy, M. S., Cuddihy, L. J., & Aloia, M. S. (2013). Adherence to cognitive behavioral therapy for insomnia: A systematic review. *Sleep Medicine Reviews, 17*(6), 453–464. doi:http://dx.doi.org/10.1016/j.smrv.2013.01.001

Matthews, J. R., & Matthews, L. H. (2013). Influences of the Greeks and Romans. In T. G. Plante (Ed.), *Abnormal psychology across the ages: Vol. 1. History and conceptualizations* (pp. 1–14). Santa Barbara, CA: Praeger/ABC-CLIO.

Matthys, W., Vanderschuren, L. J. M. J., & Schutter, D. J. L. G. (2013). The neurobiology of oppositional defiant disorder and conduct disorder: Altered functioning in three mental domains. *Development and Psychopathology, 25*(1), 193–207. doi:10.1017/S0954579412000272

Mattick, R. P., Breen, C., Kimber, J., & Davoli, M. (2009). Methadone maintenance therapy versus no opioid replacement therapy for opioid dependence. *Cochrane Database of Systematic Reviews, 2009*(3), 1–32. doi:10.1002/14651858.CD002209.pub2

Mattick, R. P., Breen, C., Kimber, J., & Davoli, M. (2014). Buprenorphine maintenance versus placebo or methadone maintenance for opioid dependence. *Cochrane Database of Systematic Reviews, 2014*(2), 1–84. doi:10.1002/14651858.CD002207.pub4

Mattila, M.-L., Kielinen, M., Jussila, K., Linna, S.-L., Bloigu, R., Ebeling, H., & Moilanen, I. (2007). An epidemiological and diagnostic study of Asperger Syndrome according to four sets of diagnostic criteria. *Journal of the American Academy of Child & Adolescent Psychiatry, 46*(5), 636–646. doi:10.1097/chi.0b013e318033ff42

Mattila, M.-L., Kielinen, M., Linna, S.-L., Jussila, K., Ebeling, H., Bloigu, R., ... Moilanen, I. (2011). Autism spectrum disorders according to DSM-IV-TR and comparison with DSM-5 draft criteria: An epidemiological study. *Journal of the American Academy of Child & Adolescent Psychiatry, 50*(6), 583–592. doi:10.1016/j.jaac.2011.04.001

Maurer, K., Volk, S., & Gerbaldo, H. (1997). Auguste D and Alzheimer's disease. *The Lancet, 349*(9064), 1546–1549. doi:10.1016/S0140-6736(96)10203-8

Maurex, L., Zaboli, G., Öhman, A., Åsberg, M., & Leopardi, R. (2010). The serotonin transporter gene polymorphism (5-HTTLPR) and affective symptoms among women diagnosed with borderline personality disorder. *European Psychiatry, 25*(1), 19–25. doi:10.1016/j.eurpsy.2009.05.001

Mayberg, H. S., Lozano, A. M., Voon, V., McNeely, H. E., Seminowicz, D., Hamani, C., ... Kennedy, S. H. (2005). Deep brain stimulation for treatment-resistant depression. *Neuron, 45*(5), 651–660. doi:http://dx.doi.org/10.1016/j.neuron.2005.02.014

Mayer, G. (2012). The use of sodium oxybate to treat narcolepsy. *Expert Review of Neurotherapeutics, 12*(5), 519–529. doi:10.1586/ern.12.42

Mayes, S. D., Calhoun, S. L., Murray, M. J., Pearl, A., Black, A., & Tierney, C. D. (2014). Final DSM-5 under-identifies mild Autism Spectrum Disorder: Agreement between the DSM-5, CARS, CASD, and clinical diagnoses. *Research in Autism Spectrum Disorders, 8*(2), 68–73. doi:http://dx.doi.org/10.1016/j.rasd.2013.11.002

Mayo Clinic Staff. (2017). Self-injury/cutting. Retrieved from http://www.mayoclinic.org/diseases-conditions/self-injury/symptoms-causes/dxc-20165427

Mayo Clinic. (n.d.-a). Deep brain stimulation: Overview. Retrieved from http://www.mayoclinic.org/tests-procedures/deep-brain-stimulation/home/ovc-20156088

Mayo Clinic. (n.d.-b). Transcranial magnetic stimulation: Risks. Retrieved from http://www.mayoclinic.org/tests-procedures/transcranial-magnetic-stimulation/basics/risks/prc-20020555

Mazzeo, S. E., & Bulik, C. M. (2009). Environmental and genetic risk factors for eating disorders: What the clinician needs to know. *Child and Adolescent Psychiatric Clinics of North America, 18*(1), 67–82. doi:10.1016/j.chc.2008.07.003

Mazzucchelli, T., Kane, R., & Rees, C. (2009). Behavioral activation treatments for depression in adults: A meta-analysis and review. *Clinical Psychology: Science and Practice, 16*(4), 383–411. doi:10.1111/j.1468-2850.2009.01178.x

McAdam, D. B., Sherman, J. A., Sheldon, J. B., & Napolitano, D. A. (2004). Behavioral interventions to reduce the pica of persons with developmental disabilities. *Behavior Modification, 28*(1), 45–72. doi:10.1177/0145445503259219

McAweeney, M., Rogers, N. L., Huddleston, C., Moore, D., & Gentile, J. P. (2010). Symptom prevalence of ADHD in a community residential substance abuse treatment program. *Journal of Attention Disorders, 13*(6), 601–608. doi:10.1177/1087054708329973

McCabe, R. E., Miller, J. L., Laugesen, N., Antony, M. M., & Young, L. (2010). The relationship between anxiety disorders in adults and recalled childhood teasing. *Journal of Anxiety Disorders, 24*(2), 238–243. doi:http://dx.doi.org/10.1016/j.janxdis.2009.11.002

McCann, E., & Sharek, D. (2016). Mental health needs of people who identify as transgender: A review of the literature. *Archives of Psychiatric Nursing, 30*(2), 280–285. doi:10.1016/j.apnu.2015.07.003

McClelland, L. (2014). Reformulating the impact of social inequalities: Power and social justice. In L. Johnstone & R. Dallos (Eds.), *Formulation in psychology and psychotherapy: Making sense of people's problems* (2nd ed., pp. 121–144). London, UK: Routledge.

McClintock, S. M., Brandon, A. R., Husain, M. M., & Jarrett, R. B. (2011). A systematic review of the combined use of electroconvulsive therapy and psychotherapy for depression. *The Journal of ECT, 27*(3), 236–243. doi:10.1097/YCT.0b013e3181faaeca

McConnell, J. V. (1990). Negative reinforcement and positive punishment. *Teaching of Psychology, 17*(4), 247–249. doi:10.1207/s15328023top1704_10

McCrae, R. R., & John, O. P. (1992). An introduction to the five-factor model and its applications. *Journal of Personality, 60*(2), 175–215. doi:10.1111/j.1467-6494.1992.tb00970.x

McCullumsmith, C. B., & Ford, C. V. (2011). Simulated illness: The factitious disorders and malingering. *Psychiatric Clinics of North America, 34*(3), 621–641. doi:10.1016/j.psc.2011.05.013

McDonald, J. E., & Trepper, T. (1977). Enuresis: An historical, cultural, and contemporary account of etiology and treatment. *Psychology in the Schools, 14*(3), 308–314. doi:10.1002/1520-6807(197707)14:3<308::AID-PITS2310140310>3.0.CO;2-1

McElroy, S. L., Guerdjikova, A. I., O'Melia, A. M., Mori, N., & Keck, J. P. E. (2010). Pharmacotherapy of the eating disorders. In W. S. Agras (Ed.), *The Oxford handbook of eating disorders* (pp. 417–451). New York, NY: Oxford University Press.

McGrath, J. J. (2005). Myths and plain truths about schizophrenia epidemiology—The NAPE lecture 2004. *Acta Psychiatrica Scandinavica, 111*(1), 4–11.

McGuffin, P., & Farmer, A. (2014). Moving from DSM-5 to ICD-11: A joint problem? *Australian and New Zealand Journal of Psychiatry, 48*(2), 194–196. doi:10.1177/0004867413520254

McGuffin, P., Alsabban, S., & Uher, R. (2011). The truth about genetic variation in the serotonin transporter gene and response to stress and medication. *The British Journal of Psychiatry, 198*(6), 424–427.

McGuire, T. M., Lee, C. W., & Drummond, P. D. (2014). Potential of eye movement desensitization and reprocessing therapy in the treatment of post-traumatic stress disorder. *Psychology Research and Behavior Management, 7*.

McHenry, J., Carrier, N., Hull, E., & Kabbaj, M. (2014). Sex differences in anxiety and depression: Role of testosterone. *Frontiers in Neuroendocrinology, 35*(1), 42–57. doi:10.1016/j.yfrne.2013.09.001

McHugh, M. C. (2006). What do women want? A new view of women's sexual problems. *Sex Roles, 54*(5–6), 361–369. doi:10.1007/s11199-006-9006-2

McIntosh, V. V. W., Jordan, J., & Bulik, C. M. (2010). Specialist supportive clinical management for anorexia nervosa. In C. M. Grilo & J. E. Mitchell (Eds.), *The treatment of eating disorders: A clinical handbook* (pp. 108–129). New York, NY: Guilford Press.

McIntosh, V. V., Bulik, C. M., McKenzie, J. M., Luty, S. E., & Jordan, J. (2000). Interpersonal psychotherapy for anorexia nervosa. *International Journal of Eating Disorders, 27*(2), 125–139. doi:10.1002/(SICI)1098-108X(200003)27:2<125::AID-EAT1>3.0.CO;2-4

McIntosh, V. V. W., Jordan, J., Luty, S. E., Carter, F. A., McKenzie, J. M., Bulik, C. M., & Joyce, P. R. (2006). Specialist supportive clinical management for anorexia nervosa. *International Journal of Eating Disorders, 39*(8), 625–632.

McIntyre, R. S., & Konarski, J. Z. (2005). Tolerability profiles of atypical antipsychotics in the treatment of bipolar disorder. *Journal of Clinical Psychiatry, 66*(Suppl3), 28–36.

McKay, J. R., Kranzler, H. R., Kampman, K. M., Ashare, R. L., & Schnoll, R. A. (2015). Psychopharmacological treatments for substance use disorders. In P. E. Nathan & J. M. Gorman (Eds.), *A guide to treatments that work* (4th ed., pp. 763–800). New York, NY: Oxford University Press.

McKay, R., McDonald, R., Lie, D., & McGowan, H. (2012). Reclaiming the best of the biopsychosocial model of mental health care and 'recovery' for older people through a 'person-centred' approach. *Australasian Psychiatry: Bulletin Of Royal Australian And New Zealand College Of Psychiatrists, 20*(6), 492–495. doi:10.1177/1039856212460286

McKeague, L., Hennessy, E., O'Driscoll, C., & Heary, C. (2015). Retrospective accounts of self-stigma experienced by young people with attention-deficit/hyperactivity disorder (ADHD) or depression. *Psychiatric Rehabilitation Journal, 38*(2), 158–163. doi:10.1037/prj0000121

McKenna, P., & Kingdon, D. (2014). Has cognitive behavioural therapy for psychosis been oversold? *BMJ: British Medical Journal, 348*, g2295–g2295. doi:10.1136/bmj.g2295

McKenzie, R. G. (2009). Obscuring vital distinctions: The oversimplification of learning disabilities within RTI. *Learning Disability Quarterly, 32*(4), 203–215. doi:10.2307/27740373

McKetin, R., Kaye, S. S., Clemens, K. J., & Hermens, D. (2013). Methamphetamine addiction. In P. M. Miller, S. A. Ball, M. E. Bates, A. W. Blume, K. M. Kampman, D. J. Kavanagh, M. E. Larimer, N. M. Petry, & P. De Witte (Eds.), *Comprehensive addictive behaviors and disorders: Vol. 1. Principles of addiction* (pp. 689–698). San Diego, CA: Elsevier Academic Press.

McLaren, N. (2011). Cells, circuits, and syndromes: A critical commentary on the NIMH Research Domain Criteria project. *Ethical Human Psychology and Psychiatry, 13*(3), 229–236. doi:10.1891/1559-4343.13.3.229

McLaughlin, K. A., Breslau, J., Green, J. G., Lakoma, M. D., Sampson, N. A., Zaslavsky, A. M., & Kessler, R. C. (2011). Childhood socio-economic status and the onset, persistence, and severity of DSM-IV mental disorders in a US national sample. *Social Science & Medicine, 73*(7), 1088–1096. doi:10.1016/j.socscimed.2011.06.011

McLean, C. P., Asnaani, A., Litz, B. T., & Hofmann, S. G. (2011). Gender differences in anxiety disorders: Prevalence, course of illness, comorbidity and burden of illness. *Journal of Psychiatric Research, 45*(8), 1027–1035. doi:10.1016/j.jpsychires.2011.03.006

McLean, S. A., Paxton, S. J., Massey, R., Hay, P. J., Mond, J. M., & Rodgers, B. (2014). Stigmatizing attitudes and beliefs about bulimia nervosa: Gender, age, education and income variability in a community sample. *International Journal of Eating Disorders, 47*(4), 353–361. doi:10.1002/eat.22227

McLoughlin, G. (2002). Is depression normal in human beings? A critique of the evolutionary perspective. *International Journal of Mental Health Nursing, 11*(3), 170–173. doi:10.1046/j.1440-0979.2002.00244.x

McMyler, C., & Pryjmachuk, S. (2008). Do 'no-suicide' contracts work? *Journal of Psychiatric and Mental Health Nursing, 15*(6), 512–522. doi:10.1111/j.1365-2850.2008.01286.x

McNaught, K. S. P. (2010). 125 years of Tourette syndrome: The discovery, early history and future of the disorder. Retrieved from https://www.tourette.org/resource/125-years-tourette-syndrome-discovery-early-history-future-disorder/

McPartland, J. C., Reichow, B., & Volkmar, F. R. (2012). Sensitivity and specificity of proposed DSM-5 diagnostic criteria for autism spectrum disorder. *Journal of the American Academy of Child & Adolescent Psychiatry, 51*(4), 368–383. doi:10.1016/j.jaac.2012.01.007

McPhedran, S., & Baker, J. (2012). Suicide prevention and method restriction: Evaluating the impact of limiting access to lethal means among young Australians. *Archives of Suicide Research, 16*(2), 135–146. doi:10.1080/13811118.2012.667330

McPheeters, M. L., Warren, Z., Sathe, N., Bruzek, J. L., Krishnaswami, S., Jerome, R. N., & Veenstra-Vanderweele, J. (2011). A systematic review of medical treatments for children with autism spectrum disorders. *Pediatrics, 127*(5), e1312–e1321. doi:10.1542/peds.2011-0427

McWilliams, N. (2011). The Psychodynamic Diagnostic Manual: An effort to compensate for the limitations of descriptive psychiatric diagnosis. *Journal of Personality Assessment, 93*(2), 112–122. doi:10.1080/00223891.2011.542709

Mead, M. (1974). On Freud's view of female psychology. In J. Strouse (Ed.), *Women and analysis: Dialogues on psychoanalytic views of femininity* (pp. 95–106). New York, NY: Dell.

Mealey, L. (1995). The sociobiology of sociopathy: An integrated evolutionary model. *Behavioral and Brain Sciences, 18*(3), 523–599. doi:10.1017/S0140525X00039595

Mealey, L. (2000). Anorexia: A 'losing' strategy? *Human Nature, 11*(1), 105–116. doi:10.1007/s12110-000-1005-3

Meana, M. (2012). *Sexual dysfunction in women*. Cambridge, MA: Hogrefe.

Medco. (2011). *America's state of mind*. Retrieved from http://apps.who.int/medicinedocs/en/d/Js19032en/

Meehan, K. B., & Levy, K. N. (2015). Personality disorders. In P. Luyten, L. C. Mayes, P. Fonagy, M. Target, & S. J. Blatt (Eds.), *Handbook of psychodynamic approaches to psychopathology* (pp. 311–333). New York, NY: Guilford Press.

Mehta, D., & Binder, E. B. (2012). Gene × environment vulnerability factors for PTSD: The HPA-axis. *Neuropharmacology, 62*(2), 654–662. doi:10.1016/j.neuropharm.2011.03.009

Mehta, U. M., Thirthalli, J., Kumar, C. N., Kumar, J. K., & Gangadhar, B. N. (2014). Negative symptoms mediate the influence of theory of mind on functional status in schizophrenia. *Social Psychiatry and Psychiatric Epidemiology, 49*(7), 1151–1156. doi:10.1007/s00127-013-0804-x

Mellor, D., McCabe, M., Ricciardelli, L., & Merino, M. E. (2008). Body dissatisfaction and body change behaviors in Chile: The role of sociocultural factors. *Body Image, 5*(2), 205–215. doi:http://dx.doi.org/10.1016/j.bodyim.2008.01.004

Mellor, D., McCabe, M., Ricciardelli, L., Yeow, J., Daliza, N., & Hapidzal, N. F. b. M. (2009). Sociocultural influences on body dissatisfaction and body change behaviors among Malaysian adolescents. *Body Image, 6*(2), 121–128. doi:http://dx.doi.org/10.1016/j.bodyim.2008.11.003

Meloni, E. G., Gillis, T. E., Manoukian, J., & Kaufman, M. J. (2014). Xenon impairs reconsolidation of fear memories in a rat model of post-traumatic stress disorder (PTSD). *PLOS One, 9*(8), e106189–e106189. doi:10.1371/journal.pone.0106189

Melville, J. D., & Naimark, D. (2002). Punishing the insane: The verdict of guilty but mentally ill. *Journal of the American Academy of Psychiatry and the Law, 30*(4), 553–555.

Memorandum of understanding on conversion therapy in the UK. (2015, November). Retrieved from https://www.psychotherapy.org.uk/wp-content/uploads/2016/09/Memorandum-of-understanding-on-conversion-therapy.pdf

Meneghelli, A., Alpi, A., Pafumi, N., Patelli, G., Preti, A., & Cocchi, A. (2011). Expressed emotion in first-episode schizophrenia and in ultra high-risk patients: Results from the Programma2000 (Milan, Italy). *Psychiatry Research, 189*(3), 331–338. doi:http://dx.doi.org/10.1016/j.psychres.2011.03.021

Meng, X., & D'Arcy, C. (2012). Education and dementia in the context of the cognitive reserve hypothesis: A systematic review with meta-analyses and qualitative analyses. *PLOS One, 7*(6), e38268. doi:10.1371/journal.pone.0038268

Meng, Y., Deng, W., Wang, H., Guo, W., Li, T., Lam, C., & Lin, X. (2014). Reward pathway dysfunction in gambling disorder: A meta-analysis of functional magnetic resonance imaging studies. *Behavioural Brain Research*, *275*, 243–251. doi:10.1016/j.bbr.2014.08.057

Mennin, D. S. (2004). Emotion regulation therapy for generalized anxiety disorder. *Clinical Psychology & Psychotherapy*, *11*(1), 17–29. doi:10.1002/cpp.389

Menninger, J. A. (2001). Involuntary treatment: Hospitalization and medications. In J. L. Jacobson & A. M. Jacobson (Eds.), Psychiatric Secrets (2nd ed., pp. 477–484). Philadelphia, PA: Hanley & Belfus. Retrieved from http://www.brown.edu/Courses/BI_278/Other/Clerkship/Didactics/Readings/INVOLUNTARY%20TREATMENT.pdf

Mennis, J., & Stahler, G. J. (2016). Racial and ethnic disparities in outpatient substance use disorder treatment episode completion for different substances. *Journal of Substance Abuse Treatment*, *63*, 25–33. doi:10.1016/j.jsat.2015.12.007

Mental Health Coordinating Council. (2015, January 30). MHCC Mental Health Rights Manual: Chapter 3 Section B: Specific rights in relation to medical treatment. Retrieved from http://mhrm.mhcc.org.au/chapter-3/3b.aspx

Mental Health Cop. (2013, September 22). Unfitness to plead. Retrieved from https://mentalhealthcop.wordpress.com/2013/09/22/unfitness-to-plead/

Menzies, L., Chamberlain, S. R., Laird, A. R., Thelen, S. M., Sahakian, B. J., & Bullmore, E. T. (2008). Integrating evidence from neuroimaging and neuropsychological studies of obsessive-compulsive disorder: The orbitofronto-striatal model revisited. *Neuroscience & Biobehavioral Reviews*, *32*(3), 525–549. doi:http://dx.doi.org/10.1016/j.neubiorev.2007.09.005

Meredith, S. E., & Dallery, J. (2013). Investigating group contingencies to promote brief abstinence from cigarette smoking. *Experimental and Clinical Psychopharmacology*, *21*(2), 144–154. doi:10.1037/a0031707

Merenda, P. F. (1987). Toward a four-factor theory of temperament and/or personality. *Journal of Personality Assessment*, *51*(3), 367–374. doi:10.1207/s15327752jpa5103_4

Merikangas, K. R., Jin, R., He, J.-P., Kessler, R. C., Lee, S., Sampson, N. A., ... Zarkov, Z. (2011). Prevalence and correlates of bipolar spectrum disorder in the World Mental Health Survey Initiative. *Archives of General Psychiatry*, *68*(3), 241–251. doi:10.1001/archgenpsychiatry.2011.12

Merriam-Webster Dictionary. (n.d.). Nomenclature. Retrieved from http://www.merriam-webster.com/dictionary/nomenclature

Messer, S. B. (2001). Introduction to the special issue on assimilative integration. *Journal of Psychotherapy Integration*, *11*(1), 1–4. doi:10.1023/A:1026619423048

Messer, S. B., & Abbass, A. A. (2010). Evidence-based psychodynamic therapy with personality disorders. In J. J. Magnavita (Ed.), *Evidence-based treatment of personality dysfunction: Principles, methods, and processes* (pp. 79–111). Washington, DC: American Psychological Association.

Meston, C. M., & Bradford, A. (2007). Sexual dysfunctions in women. *Annual Review of Clinical Psychology*, *3*, 233–256. doi:10.1146/annurev.clinpsy.3.022806.091507

Meyer, U. (2013). Developmental neuroinflammation and schizophrenia. *Progress in Neuro-Psychopharmacology & Biological Psychiatry*, *42*, 20–34. doi:10.1016/j.pnpbp.2011.11.003

Michaels, J. J. (1939). Enuresis—A method for its study and treatment: O. H. Mowrer and Willie Mae Mowrer: A critique. *American Journal of Orthopsychiatry*, *9*(3), 629–634. doi:10.1111/j.1939-0025.1939.tb05632.x

Michopoulos, V., & Jovanovic, T. (2015). Chronic inflammation: A new therapeutic target for post-traumatic stress disorder? *The Lancet Psychiatry*, *2*(11), 954–955. doi:10.1016/S2215-0366(15)00355-7

Middeldorp, C. M., Hammerschlag, A. R., Ouwens, K. G., Groen-Blokhuis, M. M., St. Pourcain, B., Greven, C. U., ... Boomsma, D. I. (2016). A genome-wide association meta-analysis of attention-deficit/hyperactivity disorder symptoms in population-based pediatric cohorts. *Journal of the American Academy of Child & Adolescent Psychiatry*, *55*(10), 896–905.e896. doi:http://dx.doi.org/10.1016/j.jaac.2016.05.025

Mignot, E. J. M. (2012). A practical guide to the therapy of narcolepsy and hypersomnia syndromes. *Neurotherapeutics*, *9*(4), 739–752. doi:10.1007/s13311-012-0150-9

Mihura, J. L., Meyer, G. J., Dumitrascu, N., & Bombel, G. (2013). The validity of individual Rorschach variables: Systematic reviews and meta-analyses of the comprehensive system. *Psychological Bulletin*, *139*(3), 548–605. doi:10.1037/a0029406

Mikhailova, O. (2005). Suicide in psychoanalysis. *Psychoanalytic Social Work*, *12*(2), 19–45. doi:10.1300/J032v12n02_02

Miklowitz, D. J. (2008). Adjunctive psychotherapy for bipolar disorder: State of the evidence. *The American Journal of Psychiatry*, *165*(11), 1408–1419. doi:10.1176/appi.ajp.2008.08040488

Miklowitz, D. J., Schneck, C. D., George, E. L., Taylor, D. O., Sugar, C. A., Birmaher, B., ... Axelson, D. A. (2014). Pharmacotherapy and family-focused treatment for adolescents with bipolar I and II disorders: A 2-year randomized trial. *The American Journal of Psychiatry*, *171*(6), 658–667. doi:10.1176/appi.ajp.2014.13081130

Miller, A. L., & Smith, H. L. (2008). Adolescent non-suicidal self-injurious behavior: The latest epidemic to assess and treat. *Applied and Preventive Psychology*, *12*(4), 178–188. doi:http://dx.doi.org/10.1016/j.appsy.2008.05.003

Miller, B. J., Buckley, P., Seabolt, W., Mellor, A., & Kirkpatrick, B. (2011). Meta-analysis of cytokine alterations in schizophrenia: Clinical status and antipsychotic effects. *Biological Psychiatry*, *70*(7), 663–671. doi:http://dx.doi.org/10.1016/j.biopsych.2011.04.013

Miller, B. J., Culpepper, N., Rapaport, M. H., & Buckley, P. (2013). Prenatal inflammation and neurodevelopment in schizophrenia: A review of human studies. *Progress in Neuro-Psychopharmacology & Biological Psychiatry*, *42*, 92–100. doi:10.1016/j.pnpbp.2012.03.010

Miller, B. J., Gassama, B., Sebastian, D., Buckley, P., & Mellor, A. (2013). Meta-analysis of lymphocytes in schizophrenia: Clinical status and antipsychotic effects. *Biological Psychiatry*, *73*(10), 993–999. doi:http://dx.doi.org/10.1016/j.biopsych.2012.09.007

Miller, D., & Hanson, A. (2016). *Committed: The battle over involuntary psychiatric care.* Baltimore, MD: Johns Hopkins University Press.

Miller, F. G., & Rosenstein, D. L. (2006). The nature and power of the placebo effect. *Journal of Clinical Epidemiology*, *59*(4), 331–335. doi:https://doi.org/10.1016/j.jclinepi.2005.12.001

Miller, J. S. (2004). The Child Abuse Potential (CAP) Inventory. In M. J. Hilsenroth & D. L. Segal (Eds.), *Comprehensive handbook of psychological assessment: Vol. 2. Personality assessment* (pp. 237–246). Hoboken, NJ: John Wiley.

Miller, M. W. (2003). Personality and the etiology and expression of PTSD: A three-factor model perspective. *Clinical Psychology: Science and Practice*, *10*(4), 373–393. doi:10.1093/clipsy/bpg040

Miller, M. W., Wolf, E. J., & Keane, T. M. (2014). Posttraumatic stress disorder in DSM-5: New criteria and controversies. *Clinical Psychology: Science and Practice*, *21*(3), 208–220. doi:10.1111/cpsp.12070

Miller, M. W., Wolf, E. J., Reardon, A., Greene, A., Ofrat, S., & McInerney, S. (2012). Personality and the latent structure of PTSD comorbidity. *Journal of Anxiety Disorders*, *26*(5), 599–607. doi:10.1016/j.janxdis.2012.02.016

Miller, O. H., Moran, J. T., & Hall, B. J. (2016). Two cellular hypotheses explaining the initiation of ketamine's antidepressant actions: Direct inhibition and disinhibition. *Neuropharmacology*, *100*, 17–26. doi:http://dx.doi.org/10.1016/j.neuropharm.2015.07.028

Miller, R. B. (2015). *Not so abnormal psychology.* Washington, DC: American Psychological Association.

Miller, V. M., Racine, R., & Zalcman, S. S. (2014). Neuroimmune mechanisms in autism. In A. W. Kusnecov & H. Anisman (Eds.), *The Wiley-Blackwell handbook of psychoneuroimmunology* (pp. 425–447). Chichester, UK: Wiley-Blackwell.

Miller, W. R., & Rollnick, S. (1991). *Motivational interviewing: Preparing people to change addictive behavior.* New York, NY: Guilford Press.

Miller, W. R., & Rollnick, S. (2002). *Motivational interviewing: Preparing people for change.* New York, NY: Guilford Press.

Miller, W. R., & Wilbourne, P. L. (2002). Mesa Grande: A methodological analysis of clinical trials of treatment for alcohol use disorders. *Addiction*, *97*(3), 265–277. doi:10.1046/j.1360-0443.2002.00019.x

Miller, W. R., Brown, J. M., Simpson, T. L., Handmaker, N. S., Bien, T. H., Luckie, L. F., ... Tonigan, J. S. (1995). What works? A methodological analysis of the alcohol treatment outcome literature. In R. K. Hester & W. R. Miller (Eds.), *Handbook of alcoholism treatment approaches: Effective alternatives* (2nd ed., pp. 12–44). Needham Heights, MA: Allyn & Bacon.

Millichap, J. G., & Yee, M. M. (2012). The diet factor in attention-deficit/hyperactivity disorder. *Pediatrics, 129*(2), 330–337. doi:10.1542/peds.2011-2199

Milling, L. S., & Breen, A. (2003). Mediation and moderation of hypnotic and cognitive-behavioural pain reduction. *Contemporary Hypnosis, 20*(2), 81–97. doi:10.1002/ch.268

Milling, L. S., Levine, M. R., & Meunier, S. A. (2003). Hypnotic enhancement of cognitive-behavioral interventions for pain: An analogue treatment study. *Health Psychology, 22*(4), 406–413. doi:10.1037/0278-6133.22.4.406

Millon, T. (2004). *Masters of the mind: Exploring the story of mental illness from ancient times to the new millenium.* Hoboken, NJ: John Wiley.

Mineka, S., & Öhman, A. (2002). Phobias and preparedness: The selective, automatic, and encapsulated nature of fear. *Biological Psychiatry, 52*(10), 927–937. doi:10.1016/S0006-3223(02)01669-4

Minuchin, S. (1974). *Families and family therapy.* Cambridge, MA: Harvard University Press.

Minuchin, S., Baker, L., Rosman, B. L., Liebman, R., Milman, L., & Todd, T. C. (1975). A conceptual model of psychosomatic illness in children: Family organization and family therapy. *Archives of General Psychiatry, 32*(8), 1031–1038. doi:10.1001/archpsyc.1975.01760260095008

Minuchin, S., Rosman, B. L., & Baker, L. (1978). *Psychosomatic families: Anorexia nervosa in context.* Oxford, UK: Harvard University Press.

Mischel, W. (1973). Toward a cognitive social learning reconceptualization of personality. *Psychological Review, 80*(4), 252–283. doi:10.1037/h0035002

Mischel, W. (2009). From Personality and Assessment (1968) to Personality Science, 2009. *Journal of Research in Personality, 43*(2), 282–290. doi:10.1016/j.jrp.2008.12.037

Mischel, W., & Shoda, Y. (1995). A cognitive-affective system theory of personality: Reconceptualizing situations, dispositions, dynamics, and invariance in personality structure. *Psychological Review, 102*(2), 246–268. doi:10.1037/0033-295X.102.2.246

Mishne, J. M. (1993). Primary nocturnal enuresis: A psychodynamic clinical perspective. *Child & Adolescent Social Work Journal, 10*(6), 469–495. doi:10.1007/BF00757431

Mishori, R., & McHale, C. (2014). Pica: an age-old eating disorder that's often missed. *The Journal of Family Practice, 63*(7), E1–E4.

Missori, P., Currà, A., Paris, H. S., Peschillo, S., Fattapposta, F., Paolini, S., & Domenicucci, M. (2015). Reconstruction of skull defects in the Middle Ages and Renaissance. *The Neuroscientist, 21*(3), 322–328. doi:10.1177/1073858414559252

Mitchell, A. M., Sakraida, T. J., & Kameg, K. (2003). Critical incident stress debriefing: implications for best practice. *Disaster Management & Response: DMR: An Official Publication Of The Emergency Nurses Association, 1*(2), 46–51.

Mitchell, G. (2015). Bertalanffy's general systems theory. Retrieved from http://www.mind-development.eu/systems.html

Mitchell, J. E., Agras, S., & Wonderlich, S. (2007). Treatment of bulimia nervosa: Where are we and where are we going? *International Journal of Eating Disorders, 40*(2), 95–101. doi:10.1002/eat.20343

Mitchell, J. E., Roerig, J., & Steffen, K. (2013). Biological therapies for eating disorders. *International Journal of Eating Disorders, 46*(5), 470–477. doi:10.1002/eat.22104

Mitchell, J. T. (1983). When disaster strikes... the critical incident stress debriefing process. *JEMS: A Journal Of Emergency Medical Services, 8*(1), 36–39.

Mitchell, J. T., Benson, J. W., Knouse, L. E., Kimbrel, N. A., & Anastopoulos, A. D. (2013). Are negative automatic thoughts associated with ADHD in adulthood? *Cognitive Therapy and Research, 37*(4), 851–859. doi:10.1007/s10608-013-9525-4

Mitchell, M. D., Gehrman, P., Perlis, M., & Umscheid, C. A. (2012). Comparative effectiveness of cognitive behavioral therapy for insomnia: A systematic review. *BMC Family Practice, 13*, 40–40. doi:10.1186/1471-2296-13-40

Mitchell, R. H. B., & Goldstein, B. I. (2014). Inflammation in children and adolescents with neuropsychiatric disorders: A systematic review. *Journal of the American Academy of Child & Adolescent Psychiatry, 53*(3), 274–296. doi:10.1016/j.jaac.2013.11.013

Mittal, D., Drummond, K. L., Blevins, D., Curran, G., Corrigan, P., & Sullivan, G. (2013). Stigma associated with PTSD: Perceptions of treatment seeking combat veterans. *Psychiatric Rehabilitation Journal, 36*(2), 86–92. doi:10.1037/h0094976

Miziou, S., Tsitsipa, E., Moysidou, S., Karavelas, V., Dimelis, D., Polyzoidou, V., & Fountoulakis, K. N. (2015). Psychosocial treatment and interventions for bipolar disorder: A systematic review. *Annals of General Psychiatry, 14*. doi:10.1186/s12991-015-0057-z

Moane, G. (2014). Liberation psychology, feminism, and social justice psychology. In C. V. Johnson, H. L. Friedman, J. Diaz, Z. Franco, & B. K. Nastasi (Eds.), *The Praeger handbook of social justice and psychology: Vol. 1. Fundamental issues and special populations* (pp. 115–132). Santa Barbara, CA: Praeger/ABC-CLIO.

The 'Model Penal Code' test for legal insanity. (n.d.). Retrieved from http://criminal.findlaw.com/criminal-procedure/the-model-penal-code-test-for-legal-insanity.html

Modestin, J. (1992). Multiple personality disorder in Switzerland. *The American Journal of Psychiatry, 149*(1), 88–92.

Modi, R. R., Camacho, M., & Valerio, J. (2014). Confusional arousals, sleep terrors, and sleepwalking. *Sleep Medicine Clinics, 9*(4), 537–551.

Möhler, H. (2013). Differential roles of GABA receptors in anxiety. In D. S. Charney, J. D. Buxbaum, P. Sklar, & E. J. Nestler (Eds.), *Neurobiology of mental illness* (4th ed., pp. 567–579). New York, NY: Oxford University Press.

Moldin, S. O. (2000). Gender and schizophrenia: An overview. In E. Frank (Ed.), *Gender and its effects on psychopathology* (pp. 169–186). Arlington, VA: American Psychiatric Publishing.

Moleiro, C., & Pinto, N. (2015). Sexual orientation and gender identity: Review of concepts, controversies and their relation to psychopathology classification systems. *Frontiers In Psychology, 6.*

Moll, K., Kunze, S., Neuhoff, N., Bruder, J., & Schulte-Körne, G. (2014). Specific learning disorder: Prevalence and gender differences. *PLOS One, 9*(7).

Monahan, J., & Shah, S. A. (1989). Dangerousness and commitment of the mentally disordered in the United States. *Schizophrenia Bulletin, 15*(4), 541–553. doi:10.1093/schbul/15.4.541

Moncrieff, J. (2009). A critique of the dopamine hypothesis of schizophrenia and psychosis. *Harvard Review of Psychiatry, 17*(3), 214–225. doi:10.1080/10673220902979896

Moncrieff-Boyd, J. (2016). Anorexia nervosa (apepsia hysterica, anorexia hysterica), Sir William Gull, 1873. *Advances in Eating Disorders: Theory, Research and Practice, 4*(1), 112–117. doi:10.1080/21662630.2015.1079694

Mondelli, V., & Howes, O. (2014). Inflammation: Its role in schizophrenia and the potential anti-inflammatory effects of antipsychotics. *Psychopharmacology, 231*(2), 317–318. doi:10.1007/s00213-013-3383-3

Mondimore, F. M., Fuller, G. A., & DePaulo, J. R., Jr. (2003). Drug combinations for mania. *Journal of Clinical Psychiatry, 64*(Suppl5), 25–31.

Mondorf, Y., Abu-Owaimer, M., Gaab, M. R., & Oertel, J. M. K. (2009). Chronic subdural hematoma--craniotomy versus burr hole trepanation. *British Journal of Neurosurgery, 23*(6), 612–616. doi:10.3109/02688690903370297

Monk, G., Winslade, J., Crocket, K., & Epston, D. (Eds.). (1997). *Narrative therapy in practice: The archaeology of hope.* San Francisco, CA: Jossey-Bass.

Monson, C. M., Macdonald, A., Fredman, S. J., Schumm, J. A., & Taft, C. (2014). Empirically supported couple and family therapies for PTSD. In M. J. Friedman, T. M. Keane, & P. A. Resick (Eds.), *Handbook of PTSD: Science and practice* (2nd ed., pp. 451–465). New York, NY: Guilford Press.

Monti, P. M., & O'Leary, T. A. (1999). Coping and social skills training for alcohol and cocaine dependence. *Psychiatric Clinics of North America, 22*(2), 447–470. doi:10.1016/S0193-953X(05)70086-1

Monti, P. M., Gulliver, S. B., & Myers, M. G. (1994). Social skills training for alcoholics: Assessment and treatment. *Alcohol and Alcoholism, 29*(6), 627–637.

Moore, D. (2014). Reflections on the enduring value of critical scholarship. *Drug and Alcohol Review, 33*(6), 577–580. doi:10.1111/dar.12190

Moore, D., Aveyard, P., Connock, M., Wang, D., Fry-Smith, A., & Barton, P. (2009). Effectiveness and safety of nicotine replacement therapy assisted reduction to stop smoking: Systematic review and meta-analysis. *BMJ: British Medical Journal, 338*(7699), 9–9.

Moral treatment in America's lunatic asylums. (1976). *Hospital & Community Psychiatry, 27*(7), 468–470.

Moran, M. (2012, March 2). DSM-5 emphasizes diagnostic reliability. Retrieved from http://psychnews.psychiatryonline.org/doi/10.1176/pn.47.5.psychnews_47_5_1-a

Moreno, C., Laje, G., Blanco, C., Jiang, H., Schmidt, A. B., & Olfson, M. (2007). National trends in the outpatient diagnosis and treatment of bipolar disorder in youth. *Archives of General Psychiatry, 64*(9), 1032–1039. doi:10.1001/archpsyc.64.9.1032

Moreno, J. L., Kurita, M., Holloway, T., López, J., Cadagan, R., Martínez-Sobrido, L., ... González-Maeso, J. (2011). Maternal influenza viral infection causes schizophrenia-like alterations of 5-HT$_2$A and mGlu$_2$ receptors in the adult offspring. *The Journal of Neuroscience, 31*(5), 1863–1872. doi:10.1523/JNEUROSCI.4230-10.2011

Moretti, R. J., & Rossini, E. D. (2004). The Thematic Apperception Test (TAT). In M. J. Hilsenroth & D. L. Segal (Eds.), *Comprehensive handbook of psychological assessment: Vol. 2. Personality assessment* (pp. 356–371). Hoboken, NJ: John Wiley.

Morey, L. C., Skodol, A. E., & Oldham, J. M. (2014). Clinician judgments of clinical utility: A comparison of DSM-IV-TR personality disorders and the alternative model for DSM-5 personality disorders. *Journal of Abnormal Psychology, 123*(2), 398–405. doi:10.1037/a0036481

Morey, L. C., Warner, M. B., & Boggs, C. D. (2002). Gender bias in the personality disorders criteria: An investigation of five bias indicators. *Journal of Psychopathology and Behavioral Assessment, 24*(1), 55–65. doi:10.1023/A:1014005308914

Morey, R. A., Gold, A. L., LaBar, K. S., Beall, S. K., Brown, V. M., Haswell, C. C., ... McCarthy, G. (2012). Amygdala volume changes in posttraumatic stress disorder in a large case-controlled veterans group. *JAMA Psychiatry, 69*(11), 1169–1178.

Morgan, J. D., Laungani, P., & Palmer, S. (2009). *Death and bereavement around the world: Vol. 5. Reflective essays.* Amityville, NY: Baywood Publishing.

Morishita, T., Fayad, S. M., Higuchi, M., Nestor, K. A., & Foote, K. D. (2014). Deep brain stimulation for treatment-resistant depression: Systematic review of clinical outcomes. *Neurotherapeutics, 11*(3), 475–484. doi:10.1007/s13311-014-0282-1

Morris, S. E., & Cuthbert, B. N. (2012). Research Domain Criteria: Cognitive systems, neural circuits, and dimensions of behavior. *Dialogues in Clinical Neuroscience, 14*(1), 29–37.

Morrison, A. P. (2001). Cognitive-behavioral therapy. In K. T. Mueser & D. V. Jeste (Eds.), *Clinical handbook of schizophrenia* (pp. 226–239). New York, NY: Guilford Press.

Morrison, A. P., Shryane, N., Fowler, D., Birchwood, M., Gumley, A. I., Taylor, H. E., ... Bentall, R. P. (2015). Negative cognition, affect, metacognition and dimensions of paranoia in people at ultra-high risk of psychosis: A multi-level modelling analysis. *Psychological Medicine, 45*(12), 2675–2684. doi:10.1017/S0033291715000689

Morrison, M. (2015). Growth hormone, enhancement and the pharmaceuticalisation of short stature. *Social Science & Medicine, 131*, 305–312. doi:10.1016/j.socscimed.2014.10.015

Morrow, S. L. (2005). Quality and trustworthiness in qualitative research in counseling psychology. *Journal of Counseling Psychology, 52*(2), 250–260. doi:10.1037/0022-0167.52.2.250

Morrow, S. L., & Beckstead, A. L. (2004). Conversion therapies for same-sex attracted clients in religious conflict: Context, predisposing factors, experiences, and implications for therapy. *The Counseling Psychologist, 32*, 641–650. doi:10.1177/0011000004268877

Morrow, S. L., Castañeda-Sound, C. L., & Abrams, E. M. (2012). Counseling psychology research methods: Qualitative approaches. In N. A. Fouad, J. A. Carter, & L. M. Subich (Eds.), *APA handbook of counseling psychology: Vol. 1. Theories, research, and methods* (pp. 93–117). Washington, DC: American Psychological Association.

Morrow, S. L., Hawxhurst, D. M., Montes de Vegas, A. Y., Abousleman, T. M., & Castañeda, C. L. (2006). Toward a radical feminist multicultural therapy: Renewing a commitment to activism. In R. L. Toporek, L. H. Gerstein, N. Fouad, G. Roysircar, & T. Israel (Eds.), *Handbook for social justice in counseling psychology: Leadership, vision, and action* (pp. 231–247). Thousand Oaks, CA: Sage.

Mortimer, A. M., Singh, P., Shepherd, C. J., & Puthiryackal, J. (2010). Clozapine for treatment-resistant schizophrenia: National Institute of Clinical Excellence (NICE) guidance in the real world. *Clinical Schizophrenia & Related Psychoses, 4*(1), 49–55. doi:10.3371/CSRP.4.1.4

Mosher, L. R. (1991). Soteria: A therapeutic community for psychotic persons. *International Journal of Therapeutic Communities, 12*(1), 53–67.

Mosher, L. R. (1999). Soteria and other alternatives to acute psychiatric hospitalization: A personal and professional review. *Journal of Nervous and Mental Disease, 187*(3), 142–149. doi:10.1097/00005053-199903000-00003

Mosher, L. R., Menn, A., & Matthews, S. M. (1975). Soteria: Evaluation of a home-based treatment for schizophrenia. *American Journal of Orthopsychiatry, 45*(3), 455–467. doi:10.1111/j.1939-0025.1975.tb02556.x

Mosher, L. R., Vallone, R., & Menn, A. (1995). The treatment of acute psychosis without neuroleptics: Six-week psychopathology outcome data from the Soteria project. *International Journal of Social Psychiatry, 41*(3), 157–173. doi:10.1177/002076409504100301

Mosher, L., Gosden, R., & Beder, S. (2013). Drug companies and "schizophrenia": Unbridled capitalism meets madness. In J. Read & J. Dillon (Eds.), *Models of madness: Psychological, social and biological approaches to psychosis* (2nd ed., pp. 125–139). London, UK: Routledge.

Mosley, P. E., Marsh, R., & Carter, A. (2015). Deep brain stimulation for depression: Scientific issues and future directions. *Australian and New Zealand Journal of Psychiatry.*

Moss, D. (2015). The roots and genealogy of humanistic psychology. In K. J. Schneider, J. F. Pierson, & J. F. T. Bugental (Eds.), *The handbook of humanistic psychology: Theory, research, and practice* (2nd ed., pp. 3–18). Thousand Oaks, CA: SAGE Publications.

Mossello, E., & Ballini, E. (2012). Management of patients with Alzheimer's disease: Pharmacological treatment and quality of life. *Therapeutic Advances In Chronic Disease, 3*(4), 183–193. doi:10.1177/2040622312452387

Mossman, D., Noffsinger, S. G., Ash, P., Frierson, R. L., Gerbasi, J., Hackett, M., ... Zonana, H. V. (2007). AAPL Practice Guideline for the Forensic Psychiatric Evaluation of Competence to Stand Trial. *Journal of the American Academy of Psychiatry and the Law Online, 35*(Supplement 4), S3–S72.

Motlagh, M. G., Fernandez, T. V., & Leckman, J. F. (2012). Genetics of Tourette syndrome and related disorders. In J. I. Nurnberger, Jr. & W. H. Berrettini (Eds.), *Principles of psychiatric genetics* (pp. 336–346). New York, NY: Cambridge University Press.

Moul, C., Dobson-Stone, C., Brennan, J., Hawes, D., & Dadds, M. (2013). An exploration of the serotonin system in antisocial boys with high levels of callous-unemotional traits. *PLOS One, 8*(2), e56619-e56619. doi:10.1371/journal.pone.0056619

Moul, C., Dobson-Stone, C., Brennan, J., Hawes, D. J., & Dadds, M. R. (2015). Serotonin 1B receptor gene (HTR1B) methylation as a risk factor for callous-unemotional traits in antisocial boys. *PLOS One, 10*(5), e0126903–e0126903. doi:10.1371/journal.pone.0126903

Moursy, E. E. S., Kamel, N. F., & Kaseem, A. F. (2014). Combined laser acupuncture and desmopressin for treating resistant cases of monosymptomatic nocturnal enuresis: A randomized comparative study. *Scandinavian Journal of Urology, 48*(6), 559–564. doi:10.3109/21681805.2014.922609

Mowrer, O. H. (1939). A stimulus-response analysis of anxiety and its role as a reinforcing agent. *Psychological Review, 46*(6), 553–565. doi:10.1037/h0054288

Mowrer, O. H. (1947). On the dual nature of learning—a re-interpretation of 'conditioning' and 'problem-solving'. *Harvard Educational Review, 17*, 102–148.

Mowrer, O. H., & Mowrer, W. M. (1938). Enuresis—A method for its study and treatment. *American Journal of Orthopsychiatry, 8*(3), 436–459. doi:10.1111/j.1939-0025.1938.tb06395.x

Moynihan, J. A., & Santiago, F. M. (2007). Brain behavior and immunity: Twenty years of T cells. *Brain, Behavior, and Immunity, 21*(7), 872–880. doi:10.1016/j.bbi.2007.06.010

Mucic, D., & Hilty, D. M. (2016). *e-Mental health.* Cham, Switzerland: Springer International Publishing.

Mudathikundan, F., Chao, O., & Forrester, A. (2014). Mental health and fitness to plead proposals in England and Wales. *International Journal of Law and Psychiatry, 37*(2), 135–141. doi:10.1016/j.ijlp.2013.11.008

Mueller, A., Mitchell, J. E., Peterson, L. A., Faber, R. J., Steffen, K. J., Crosby, R. D., & Claes, L. (2011). Depression, materialism, and excessive Internet use in relation to compulsive buying. *Comprehensive Psychiatry, 52*(4), 420–424. doi:10.1016/j.comppsych.2010.09.001

Mueller, B., Ahnert, P., Burkhardt, J., Brauer, J., Czepezauer, I., Quente, E., ... Kirsten, H. (2014). Genetic risk variants for dyslexia on chromosome 18 in a German cohort. *Genes, Brain & Behavior, 13*(3), 350–356. doi:10.1111/gbb.12118

Mueser, K. T., Gingerich, S., Addington, J., Brunette, M. F., Cather, C., Gottlieb, J. D., ... Penn, D. L. (2014). *The NAVIGATE team members' guide.* Retrieved from http://navigateconsultants.org/materials/

Muesser, K. T. (1998). Cognitive behavioral treatment of schizophrenia. In V. E. Caballo (Ed.), *International handbook of cognitive and behavioural treatments for psychological disorders* (pp. 551–570). Oxford, UK: Pergamon.

Mugisha, J., Muyinda, H., Wandiembe, P., & Kinyanda, E. (2015). Prevalence and factors associated with posttraumatic stress disorder seven years after the conflict in three districts in northern Uganda (The Wayo-Nero Study). *BMC Psychiatry, 15.*

Mulder, R. T., Horwood, J., Tyrer, P., Carter, J., & Joyce, P. R. (2016). Validating the proposed ICD-11 domains. *Personality and Mental Health, 10*(2), 84–95. doi:10.1002/pmh.1336

Mulia, N., & Karriker-Jaffe, K. J. (2012). Interactive influences of neighborhood and individual socioeconomic status on alcohol consumption and problems. *Alcohol and Alcoholism, 47*(2), 178–186. doi:10.1093/alcalc/agr168

Mulick, P. S., Landes, S. J., & Kanter, J. W. (2011). Contextual behavior therapies in the treatment of PTSD: A review. *International Journal of Behavioral Consultation and Therapy, 7*(1), 23–31. doi:10.1037/h0100923

Müller, N. (2014). Immunology of schizophrenia. *Neuroimmunomodulation, 21*(2-3), 109-116. doi:10.1159/000356538

Müller-Vahl, K. R., Cath, D. C., Cavanna, A. E., Dehning, S., Porta, M., Robertson, M. M., & Visser-Vandewalle, V. (2011). European clinical guidelines for Tourette syndrome and other tic disorders. Part IV: Deep brain stimulation. *European Child & Adolescent Psychiatry, 20*(4), 209–217. doi:10.1007/s00787-011-0166-4

Mullins-Sweatt, S. N., Bernstein, D. P., & Widiger, T. A. (2012). Retention or deletion of personality disorder diagnoses for DSM-5: An expert consensus approach. *Journal of Personality Disorders, 26*(5), 689–703.

Mulloy, A., Lang, R., O'Reilly, M., Sigafoos, J., Lancioni, G., & Rispoli, M. (2010). Gluten-free and casein-free diets in the treatment of autism spectrum disorders: A systematic review. *Research in Autism Spectrum Disorders, 4*(3), 328–339. doi:10.1016/j.rasd.2009.10.008

Mulloy, A., Lang, R., O'Reilly, M., Sigafoos, J., Lancioni, G., & Rispoli, M. (2011). Addendum to 'gluten-free and casein-free diets in treatment of autism spectrum disorders: A systematic review'. *Research in Autism Spectrum Disorders, 5*(1), 86–88. doi:10.1016/j.rasd.2010.07.004

Mundo, E., Zanoni, S., & Altamura, A. C. (2006). Genetic Issues in obsessive-compulsive disorder and related disorders. *Psychiatric Annals, 36*(7), 495–512.

Munn-Chernoff, M. A., & Baker, J. H. (2016). A primer on the genetics of comorbid eating disorders and substance use disorders. *European Eating Disorders Review, 24*(2), 91–100. doi:10.1002/erv.2424

Munn-Chernoff, M. A., Duncan, A. E., Grant, J. D., Wade, T. D., Agrawal, A., Bucholz, K. K., ... Heath, A. C. (2013). A twin study of alcohol dependence, binge eating, and compensatory behaviors. *Journal of Studies on Alcohol and Drugs, 74*(5), 664–673.

Munn-Chernoff, M. A., McQueen, M. B., Stetler, G. L., Haberstick, B. C., Rhee, S. H., Sobik, L. E., ... Stallings, M. C. (2012). Examining associations between disordered eating and serotonin transporter gene polymorphisms. *International Journal of Eating Disorders, 45*(4), 556–561. doi:10.1002/eat.22001

Murakami, J. M., Essayli, J. H., & Latner, J. D. (2016). The relative stigmatization of eating disorders and obesity in males and females. *Appetite, 102*, 77–82. doi:10.1016/j.appet.2016.02.027

Murphy, D., & Joseph, S. (2016). Person-centered therapy: Past, present, and future orientations. In D. J. Cain, K. Keenan, & S. Rubin (Eds.), *Humanistic psychotherapies: Handbook of research and practice* (2nd ed., pp. 185–218). Washington, DC: American Psychological Association.

Murphy, D., & Woolfolk, R. L. (2000). The harmful dysfunction analysis of mental disorder. *Philosophy, Psychiatry, & Psychology, 7*(4), 241–252.

Murphy, D., Hunt, E., Luzon, O., & Greenberg, N. (2014). Exploring positive pathways to care for members of the UK Armed Forces receiving treatment for PTSD: a qualitative study. *European Journal of Psychotraumatology, 5.* doi:10.3402/ejpt.v5.21759

Murphy, J., & Zlomke, K. R. (2016). A behavioral parent-training intervention for a child with avoidant/restrictive food intake disorder. *Clinical Practice in Pediatric Psychology, 4*(1), 23–34. doi:10.1037/cpp0000128

Murphy, J. F. A. (2011). Fallout of the enterocolitis, autism, MMR vaccine paper. *Irish Medical Journal, 104*(2), 36–37.

Murphy, R., Straebler, S., Basden, S., Cooper, Z., & Fairburn, C. G. (2012). Interpersonal psychotherapy for eating disorders. *Clinical Psychology & Psychotherapy, 19*(2), 150–158. doi:10.1002/cpp.1780

Murphy, S., Russell, L., & Waller, G. (2005). Integrated psychodynamic therapy for bulimia nervosa and binge eating disorder: Theory, practice and preliminary findings. *European Eating Disorders Review, 13*(6), 383–391. doi:10.1002/erv.672

Murray, R. M., & Lewis, S. W. (1987). Is schizophrenia a neurodevelopmental disorder? *British Medical Journal, 295*, 681–682.

Musazzi, L., Treccani, G., & Popoli, M. (2012). Glutamate hypothesis of depression and its consequences for antidepressant treatments. *Expert Review of Neurotherapeutics, 12*(10), 1169–1172. doi:10.1586/ern.12.96

Myers, K., & Vander Stoep, A. (2017). i-therapy: Asynchronous telehealth expands access to mental health care and challenges tenets of the therapeutic process. *Journal of the American Academy of Child & Adolescent Psychiatry, 56*(1), 5–7. doi:10.1016/j.jaac.2016.11.001

Myers, L. L., & Wiman, A. M. (2014). Binge eating disorder: A review of a new DSM diagnosis. *Research on Social Work Practice, 24*(1), 86–95. doi:10.1177/1049731513507755

Myers, T. A., & Crowther, J. H. (2007). Sociocultural pressures, thin-ideal internalization, self-objectification, and body dissatisfaction: Could feminist beliefs be a moderating factor? *Body Image, 4*(3), 296–308. doi:http://dx.doi.org/10.1016/j.bodyim.2007.04.001

Nabar, K. K. (2009). *Individualistic ideology as contained in the 'Diagnostic & Statistical Manual of Mental Disorders-Fourth Edition-Text Revision' personality disorders: A relational-cultural critique.* (Doctoral dissertation, The Chicago School of Professional Psychology). Retrieved from https://libdatabase.newpaltz.edu/login?url=http://search.ebscohost.com/login.aspx?direct=true&db=psyh&AN=2011-99060-226&site=ehost-live

Nadkarni, A., & Santhouse, A. (2012). Diagnostic and Statistical Manual of Mental Disorders (DSM): A culture bound syndrome? *Asian Journal of Psychiatry, 5*(1), 118–119. doi:10.1016/j.ajp.2012.01.002

Nagar, S., Mehta, S., Bhatara, V., & Aparasu, R. (2010). Health care consequences of Black-box warnings for antidepressants in the United States and Canada. *Research in Social & Administrative Pharmacy, 6*(1), 78–84. doi:10.1016/j.sapharm.2009.02.005

Nair, N. P., & Sharma, M. (1989). Neurochemical and receptor theories of depression. *Psychiatric Journal of the University of Ottawa, 14*(2), 328–341.

Najjar, S., Pearlman, D. M., Alper, K., Najjar, A., & Devinsky, O. (2013). Neuroinflammation and psychiatric illness. *Journal of Neuroinflammation, 10*(1), 816. doi:10.1186/1742-2094-10-43

Naken, C. (2009). *The addicitve personality: Understanding the addictive process and compulsive behavior* (2nd ed.). Center City, MN: Hazelden.

NAMI. (n.d.). About NAMI. Retrieved from https://www.nami.org/About-NAMI

NAMI Southern Arizona. (n.d.). What is mental illness: Mental illness facts. Retrieved from http://www.namisa.org/what-is-mental-illness--types-of-mental-disorders.html

Nanke, A., & Rief, W. (2004). Biofeedback in somatoform disorders and related syndromes. *Current Opinion in Psychiatry, 17*(2), 133–138. doi:10.1097/00001504-200403000-00011

Narayan, U. (1998). Essence of culture and a sense of history: A feminist critique of cultural essentialism. *Hypatia, 13*, 86–106.

Narrow, W. E., Clarke, D. E., Kuramoto, S. J., Kraemer, H. C., Kupfer, D. J., Greiner, L., & Regier, D. A. (2013). DSM-5 field trials in the United States and Canada, part III: Development and reliability testing of a cross-cutting symptom assessment for DSM-5. *The American Journal of Psychiatry, 170*(1), 71–82. doi:10.1176/appi.ajp.2012.12071000

Nash, J., & Nutt, D. (2007). Psychopharmacology of anxiety. *Psychiatry, 6*(4), 143–148. doi:http://dx.doi.org/10.1016/j.mppsy.2007.02.001

Natha, F., & Daiches, A. (2014). The effectiveness of EMDR in reducing psychological distress in survivors of natural disasters: A review. *Journal of EMDR Practice and Research, 8*(3), 157–170. doi:10.1891/1933-3196.8.3.157

Nathan, P. E. (1988). The addictive personality is the behavior of the addict. *Journal of Consulting and Clinical Psychology, 56*(2), 183–188. doi:10.1037/0022-006X.56.2.183

National Center for Complementary and Integrative Health. (2013, September). St. John's wort and depression: In depth. Retrieved from https://nccih.nih.gov/health/stjohnswort/sjw-and-depression.htm

National Center for Transgender Equality. (2015). Transgender terminology. Retrieved from http://www.transequality.org/issues/resources/transgender-terminology

National Clinical Guideline Centre. (2010). *Nocturnal enuresis: The management of bedwetting in children and young people.* London, UK: National Clinical Guideline Centre. Retrieved from https://www.ncbi.nlm.nih.gov/books/NBK62712/pdf/Bookshelf_NBK62712.pdf

National Collaborating Centre for Mental Health. (2005). *Post-traumatic stress disorder: The management of PTSD in adults and children in primary and secondary care.* London, UK: Gaskell and the British Psychological Society.

National Collaborating Centre for Mental Health. (2011). *Common mental health disorders: Identification and pathways to care.* Leicester (UK): British Psychological Society & The Royal College of Psychiatrists.

National Institute for Health and Care Excellence. (2013). *Autism spectrum disorder in under 19s: Support and management.* Retrieved from https://www.nice.org.uk/guidance/cg170/chapter/1-Recommendations#interventions-for-behaviour-that-challenges

National Institute of General Medical Sciences. (2015). Circadian rhythms fact sheet. Retrieved from http://www.nigms.nih.gov/Education/Pages/Factsheet_CircadianRhythms.aspx

National Institute of Health. (n.d.-a). What are common symptoms of Down syndrome? Retrieved from https://www.nichd.nih.gov/health/topics/down/conditioninfo/Pages/symptoms.aspx

National Institute of Health. (n.d.-b). What are the symptoms of fragile X syndrome? Retrieved from https://www.nichd.nih.gov/health/topics/fragilex/conditioninfo/Pages/commonsymptoms.aspx

National Institute on Alcohol Abuse and Alcoholism. (1999). Are women more vulnerable to alcohol's effects? Retrieved from https://pubs.niaaa.nih.gov/publications/aa46.htm

National Institute on Drug Abuse. (2016, June). What is cocaine? Retrieved from https://www.drugabuse.gov/publications/drugfacts/cocaine

National Institute on Drug Abuse. (2017, April). Is marijuana a gateway drug? Retrieved from https://www.drugabuse.gov/publications/research-reports/marijuana/marijuana-gateway-drug

National Sleep Foundation. (n.d.-a). Aging and sleep. Retrieved from https://sleepfoundation.org/sleep-topics/aging-and-sleep

National Sleep Foundation. (n.d.-b). REM sleep behavior disorder. Retrieved from https://sleepfoundation.org/sleep-disorders-problems/rem-behavior-disorder

National Sleep Foundation. (n.d.-c). What happens when you sleep? Retrieved from https://sleepfoundation.org/how-sleep-works/what-happens-when-you-sleep

Nedim, U. (2015, January 20). The mental illness defence in criminal trials. Retrieved from http://nswcourts.com.au/articles/the-mental-illness-defence-in-criminal-trials/

Nehls, N. (1998). Borderline personality disorder: Gender stereotypes, stigma, and limited system of care. *Issues in Mental Health Nursing, 19*(2), 97–112. doi:10.1080/016128498249105

Neimeyer, G. J., Taylor, J. M., Wear, D. M., & Buyukgoze-Kavas, A. (2011). How special are the specialties? Workplace settings in counseling and clinical psychology in the United States. *Counselling Psychology Quarterly, 24*(1), 43–53.

Neimeyer, R. A. (1983). Toward a personal construct conceptualization of depression and suicide. *Death Education, 7*(2–3), 127–173. doi:10.1080/07481188308252160

Neimeyer, R. A. (2001a). The language of loss: Grief therapy as a process of meaning reconstruction. In R. A. Neimeyer (Ed.), *Meaning reconstruction and the experience of loss.* (pp. 261–292). Washington, DC: American Psychological Association.

Neimeyer, R. A. (Ed.) (2001b). *Meaning reconstruction and the experience of loss.* Washington, DC: American Psychological Association.

Neimeyer, R. A. (2005). Complicated grief and the quest for meaning: A constructivist contribution. *Omega: Journal of Death and Dying, 52*(1), 37–52. doi:10.2190/EQL1-LN3V-KNYR-18TF

Neimeyer, R. A. (2009). *Constructivist psychotherapy: Distinctive features.* London, UK: Routledge.

Neimeyer, R. A., & Mahoney, M. J. (Eds.). (1995). *Constructivism in psychotherapy.* Washington, DC: American Psychological Association.

Neimeyer, R. A., & Raskin, J. D. (Eds.). (2000). *Constructions of disorder: Meaning-making frameworks for psychotherapy.* Washington, DC: American Psychological Association.

Neimeyer, R. A., Klass, D., & Dennis, M. R. (2014). A social constructionist account of grief: Loss and the narration of meaning. *Death Studies, 38*(8), 485–498. doi:10.1080/07481187.2014.913454

Nelson, B. (2014). Attenuated psychosis syndrome: Don't jump the gun. *Psychopathology, 47*(5), 292–296. doi:10.1159/000365291

Nelson, H. D., Humphrey, L. L., Nygren, P., Teutsch, S. M., & Allan, J. D. (2002). Postmenopausal hormone replacement therapy: scientific review. *JAMA: Journal of the American Medical Association, 288*(7), 872–881.

Neng, J. M. B., & Weck, F. (2015). Attribution of somatic symptoms in hypochondriasis. *Clinical Psychology & Psychotherapy, 22*(2), 116–124. doi:10.1002/cpp.1871

Neria, Y., Nandi, A., & Galea, S. (2008). Post-traumatic stress disorder following disasters: A systematic review. *Psychological Medicine, 38*(4), 467–480. doi:10.1017/S0033291707001353

Nesse, R. M. (1994). An evolutionary perspective on substance abuse. *Ethology & Sociobiology, 15*(5–6), 339–348. doi:10.1016/0162-3095(94)90007-8

Nesse, R. M. (2000). Is depression an adaptation? *Archives of General Psychiatry, 57*(1), 14–20. doi:10.1001/archpsyc.57.1.14

Nesse, R. M. (2004). Cliff-edged fitness functions and the persistence of schizophrenia. *Behavioral and Brain Sciences, 27*, 862–863.

Nesse, R. M. (2005a). An evolutionary framework for understanding grief. In D. Carr & R. M. Nesse (Eds.), *Spousal bereavement in late life* (pp. 195–226). New York, NY: Springer.

Nesse, R. M. (2005b). Evolutionary psychology and mental health. In D. M. Buss (Ed.), *The handbook of evolutionary psychology* (pp. 903–927). Hoboken, NJ: John Wiley.

Nesse, R. M., & Berridge, K. C. (1997). Psychoactive drug use in evolutionary perspective. *Science, 278*(5335), 63–66. doi:10.1126/science.278.5335.63

Nestler, E. J., & Malenka, R. C. (2004). The addicted brain. *Scientific American, 290*(3), 78–85.

Nettle, D. (2004). Evolutionary origins of depression: a review and reformulation. *Journal of Affective Disorders, 81*(2), 91–102. doi:http://dx.doi.org/10.1016/j.jad.2003.08.009

Nettle, D. (2006). The evolution of personality variation in humans and other animals. *American Psychologist, 61*(6), 622–631. doi:10.1037/0003-066X.61.6.622

Neuhaus, E., Beauchaine, T. P., & Bernier, R. (2010). Neurobiological correlates of social functioning in autism. *Clinical Psychology Review, 30*(6), 733–748. doi:http://dx.doi.org/10.1016/j.cpr.2010.05.007

Neumann, I. D. (2008). Brain oxytocin: A key regulator of emotional and social behaviours in both females and males. *Journal of Neuroendocrinology, 20*(6), 858–865. doi:10.1111/j.1365-2826.2008.01726.x

Nevels, R. M., Dehon, E. E., Alexander, K., & Gontkovsky, S. T. (2010). Psychopharmacology of aggression in children and adolescents with primary neuropsychiatric disorders: A review of current and potentially promising treatment options. *Experimental and Clinical Psychopharmacology, 18*(2), 184–201. doi:10.1037/a0018059

Nevéus, T. (2011). Nocturnal enuresis—theoretic background and practical guidelines. *Pediatric Nephrology, 26*(8), 1207–1214. doi:10.1007/s00467-011-1762-8

Nevéus, T., Läckgren, G., Tuvemo, T., Hetta, J., Hjälmås, K., & Stenberg, A. (2000). Enuresis—background and treatment. *Scandinavian Journal of Urology and Nephrology. Supplementum*(206), 1–44.

Newman, I., Leader, G., Chen, J. L., & Mannion, A. (2015). An analysis of challenging behavior, comorbid psychopathology, and attention-deficit/hyperactivity disorder in Fragile X syndrome. *Research in Developmental Disabilities, 38*, 7–17. doi:10.1016/j.ridd.2014.11.003

Newman, J. B. (2013). Heart disease: From psychosocial to pathophysiological to treatment with biofeedback—An overview. *Biofeedback, 41*(1), 39–42.

Newman, M. G., Llera, S. J., Erickson, T. M., Przeworski, A., & Castonguay, L. G. (2013). Worry and generalized anxiety disorder: A review and theoretical synthesis of evidence on nature, etiology, mechanisms, and treatment. *Annual Review of Clinical Psychology, 9*, 275–297. doi:10.1146/annurev-clinpsy-050212-185544

Newman-Toker, J. (2000). Risperidone in anorexia nervosa. *Journal of the American Academy of Child & Adolescent Psychiatry, 39*(8), 941–942. doi:10.1097/00004583-200008000-00002

Newton-Howes, G., Weaver, T., & Tyrer, P. (2008). Attitudes of staff towards patients with personality disorder in community mental health teams. *Australian and New Zealand Journal of Psychiatry, 42*(7), 572–577. doi:10.1080/00048670802119739

Nezu, A. M., & Nezu, C. M. (2008). The 'devil is in the details': Recognizing and dealing with threats to validity in randomized controlled trials. In A. M. Nezu & C. M. Nezu (Eds.), *Evidence-based outcome research: A practical guide to conducting randomized controlled trials for psychosocial interventions* (pp. 3–24). New York, NY: Oxford University Press.

Ng, B.-Y. (1999). Hysteria: A cross-cultural comparison of its origins and history. *History of Psychiatry, 10*(39, Pt 3), 287–301. doi:10.1177/0957154X9901003901

Ni, X., Chan, K., Bulgin, N., Sicard, T., Bismil, R., McMain, S., & Kennedy, J. L. (2006). Association between serotonin transporter gene and borderline personality disorder. *Journal of Psychiatric Research, 40*(5), 448–453. doi:10.1016/j.jpsychires.2006.03.010

Ni, X., Chan, D., Chan, K., McMain, S., & Kennedy, J. L. (2009). Serotonin genes and gene–gene interactions in borderline personality disorder in a matched case-control study. *Progress in Neuro-Psychopharmacology and Biological Psychiatry, 33*(1), 128–133. doi:http://dx.doi.org/10.1016/j.pnpbp.2008.10.022

Nicholls, L. (2008). Putting the new view classification scheme to an empirical test. *Feminism & Psychology, 18*(4), 515–526. doi:10.1177/0959353508096180

Nichols, C. (2009). Is there an evolutionary advantage of schizophrenia? *Personality and Individual Differences, 46*(8), 832–838. doi:http://dx.doi.org/10.1016/j.paid.2009.01.013

Nickel, M., Cangoez, B., Bachler, E., Muehlbacher, M., Lojewski, N., Mueller-Rabe, N., ... Nickel, C. (2006). Bioenergetic exercises in inpatient treatment of Turkish immigrants with chronic somatoform disorders: A randomized, controlled study. *Journal of Psychosomatic Research, 61*(4), 507–513. doi:10.1016/j.jpsychores.2006.01.004

Nicki, A. (2016). Borderline personality disorder, discrimination, and survivors of chronic childhood trauma. *International Journal of Feminist Approaches to Bioethics, 9*(1), 218–245.

Nicolini, H., Arnold, P., Nestadt, G., Lanzagorta, N., & Kennedy, J. L. (2009). Overview of genetics and obsessive-compulsive disorder. *Psychiatry Research, 170*(1), 7–14. doi:10.1016/j.psychres.2008.10.011

Nielsen, J., Jensen, S. O. W., Friis, R. B., Valentin, J. B., & Correll, C. U. (2015). Comparative effectiveness of risperidone long-acting injectable vs first-generation antipsychotic long-acting injectables in schizophrenia: Results from a nationwide, retrospective inception cohort study. *Schizophrenia Bulletin, 41*(3), 627–636. doi:10.1093/schbul/sbu128

Nigg, J. T. (2013). Attention deficits and hyperactivity–impulsivity: What have we learned, what next? *Development and Psychopathology, 25*(4, Pt 2), 1489–1503. doi:10.1017/S0954579413000734

Nigg, J. T., Lewis, K., Edinger, T., & Falk, M. (2012). Meta-analysis of attention-deficit/hyperactivity disorder or attention-deficit/hyperactivity disorder symptoms, restriction diet, and synthetic food color additives. *Journal of the American Academy of Child & Adolescent Psychiatry, 51*(1), 86–97. doi:10.1016/j.jaac.2011.10.015

Nijenhuis, E. R. S., & den Boer, J. A. (2009). Psychobiology of traumatization and trauma-related structural dissociation of the personality. In P. F. Dell & J. A. O'Neil (Eds.), *Dissociation and the dissociative disorders: DSM-V and beyond* (pp. 337–365). New York, NY: Routledge.

Nijenhuis, E. R. S., & van der Hart, O. (2011). Dissociation in trauma: A new definition and comparison with previous formulations. *Journal of Trauma & Dissociation, 12*(4), 416–445. doi:10.1080/15299732.2011.570592

Nikolas, M., Markon, K., & Tranel, D. (2016). Psychopathology: A neurobiological perspective. In J. E. Maddux & B. A. Winstead (Eds.), *Psychopathology: Foundations for a contemporary understanding* (4th ed., pp. 27–58). New York, NY: Routledge.

Nilsson, A. (2014). A non-reductive science of personality, character, and well-being must take the person's worldview into account. *Frontiers In Psychology, 5*.

Nissen, L. B. (2007). Reclaiming futures: Communities helping teens overcome drugs, alcohol and crime—A new practice framework for juvenile justice. *Journal of Psychoactive Drugs, 39*(1), 51-58. doi:10.1080/02791072.2007.10399864

Nissen, L. B. (2014, August). Strengthening a social justice lens for addictions practice: Exploration, reflections, possibilities, and a challenge to promote recovery among the most vulnerable.

Nissen, L. B., & Merrigan, D. (2011). The development and evolution of reclaiming futures at the ten-year mark: Reflections and recommendations. *Children and Youth Services Review, 33*(Suppl 1), S9–S15. doi:10.1016/j.childyouth.2011.06.007

Nissen, L. B., & Pearce, J. (2011). Exploring the implementation of justice-based alcohol and drug intervention strategies with juvenile offenders: Reclaiming Futures, enhanced adolescent substance abuse treatment, and juvenile drug courts. *Children and Youth Services Review, 33*(Suppl 1), S60–S65. doi:10.1016/j.childyouth.2011.06.014

Niznikiewicz, M. A., Kubicki, M., & Shenton, M. E. (2003). Recent structural and functional imaging findings in schizophrenia. *Current Opinion in Psychiatry, 16*(2), 123–147. doi:10.1097/00001504-200303000-00002

Nobre, P. J., & Pinto-Gouveia, J. (2006). Dysfunctional sexual beliefs as vulnerability factors for sexual dysfunction. *Journal of Sex Research, 43*(1), 68–75. doi:10.1080/00224490609552300

Nock, M. K., Hwang, I., Sampson, N. A., & Kessler, R. C. (2010). Mental disorders, comorbidity and suicidal behavior: Results from the National Comorbidity Survey replication. *Molecular Psychiatry, 15*(8), 868–876. doi:10.1038/mp.2009.29

Norberg, J. (2010). *The historical foundations of conduct disorders: Historical context, theoretical explanations, and interventions.* (Master's thesis), University of Oslo, Oslow, Norway.

Norbury, C. F. (2014). Practitioner Review: Social (pragmatic) communication disorder conceptualization, evidence and clinical implications. *Journal of Child Psychology and Psychiatry, 55*(3), 204–216. doi:10.1111/jcpp.12154

Norcross, J. C. (2000). Clinical versus counseling psychology: What's the diff? *Eye on Psi Chi, 5*(1). Retrieved from https://www.psichi.org/?051EyeFall00bNorcros

Norcross, J. C., Beutler, L. E., & Levant, R. F. (Eds.). (2006). *Evidence-based practices in mental health: Debate and dialogue on the fundamental questions.* Washington, DC: American Psychological Association.

Nordahl, H. M., & Nysæter, T. E. (2005). Schema therapy for patients with borderline personality disorder: A single case series. *Journal of Behavior Therapy and Experimental Psychiatry, 36*(3), 254–264. doi:10.1016/j.jbtep.2005.05.007

Nordqvist, J. (2015, November 9). What is rapid eye movement sleep? What is REM? *Medical News Today.*

Norman, J. (2004). Gender bias in the diagnosis and treatment of depression. *International Journal of Mental Health, 33*(2), 32–43.

Norton, A. R., Abbott, M. J., Norberg, M. M., & Hunt, C. (2015). A systematic review of mindfulness and acceptance-based treatments for social anxiety disorder. *Journal of Clinical Psychology, 71*(4), 283–301. doi:10.1002/jclp.22144

Nosyk, B., Marsh, D. C., Sun, H., Schechter, M. T., & Anis, A. H. (2010). Trends in methadone maintenance treatment participation, retention, and compliance to dosing guidelines in British Columbia, Canada: 1996–2006. *Journal of Substance Abuse Treatment, 39*(1), 22–31. doi:10.1016/j.jsat.2010.03.008

Nova, E., Samartín, S., Gómez, S., Morandé, G., & Marcos, A. (2002). The adaptive response of the immune system to the particular malnutrition of eating disorders. *European Journal of Clinical Nutrition, 56 Suppl 3*, S34–S37.

Novais, F., Araújo, A., & Godinho, P. (2015). Historical roots of histrionic personality disorder. *Frontiers In Psychology, 6*.

Novellino, M. (2012). The shadow and the demon: The psychodynamics of nightmares. *Transactional Analysis Journal, 42*(4), 277–284. doi:10.1177/036215371204200406

Nowak, D. A., & Fink, G. R. (2009). Psychogenic movement disorders: Aetiology, phenomenology, neuroanatomical correlates and therapeutic approaches. NeuroImage, 47(3), 1015–1025. doi:http://dx.doi.org/10.1016/j.neuroimage.2009.04.082

Nowak, M., Gawęda, A., Jelonek, I., & Janas-Kozik, M. (2013). The disruptive behavior disorders and the coexisting deficits in the context of theories describing family relations. Archives of Psychiatry and Psychotherapy, 15(1), 61–65.

Nuss, P. (2015). Anxiety disorders and GABA neurotransmission: A disturbance of modulation. Neuropsychiatric Disease and Treatment, 11.

Nussbaum, M. C. (1997). Constructing love, desire, and care. In M. C. Nussbaum & D. M. Estlund (Eds.), Sex, preference, and family: Essays on law and nature (pp. 17–43). New York, NY: Oxford University Press.

Nutt, D. J., Lingford-Hughes, A., Erritzoe, D., & Stokes, P. R. A. (2015). The dopamine theory of addiction: 40 years of highs and lows. Nature Reviews Neuroscience, 16(5), 305–312. doi:10.1038/nrn3939

Nutt, D., Argyropoulos, S., Hood, S., & Potokar, J. (2006). Generalized anxiety disorder: A comorbid disease. European Neuropsychopharmacology, 16, Supplement 2, S109–S118. doi:http://dx.doi.org/10.1016/j.euroneuro.2006.04.003

Nydegger, R. (2013). Somatoform disorders. In T. G. Plante (Ed.), Abnormal psychology across the ages: Vol. 2. Disorders and treatments (pp. 49–65). Santa Barbara, CA: Praeger/ABC-CLIO.

Nye, C., Vanryckeghem, M., Schwartz, J. B., Herder, C., Turner, H. M., III, & Howard, C. (2013). Behavioral stuttering interventions for children and adolescents: A systematic review and meta-analysis. Journal of Speech, Language, and Hearing Research, 56(3), 921–932. doi:10.1044/1092-4388(2012/12-0036)

Nylund, D., & Corsiglia, V. (1996). From deficits to special abilities: Working narratively with children labeled 'ADHD'. In M. F. Hoyt (Ed.), Constructive therapies (Vol. 2, pp. 163–183). New York, NY: Guilford Press.

Nysæter, T. E., & Nordahl, H. M. (2008). Principles and clinical application of schema therapy for patients with borderline personality disorder. Nordic Psychology, 60(3), 249–263. doi:10.1027/1901-2276.60.3.249

O'Brian, S., Iverach, L., Jones, M., Onslow, M., Packman, A., & Menzies, R. (2013). Effectiveness of the Lidcombe Program for early stuttering in Australian community clinics. International Journal of Speech-Language Pathology, 15(6), 593–603. doi:10.3109/17549507.2013.783112

O'Brien, A. J., McKenna, B. G., & Kydd, R. R. (2009). Compulsory community mental health treatment: Literature review. International Journal of Nursing Studies, 46(9), 1245–1255. doi:10.1016/j.ijnurstu.2009.02.006

O'Connell, B., & Dowling, M. (2014). Dialectical behaviour therapy (DBT) in the treatment of borderline personality disorder. Journal of Psychiatric and Mental Health Nursing, 21(6), 518–525. doi:10.1111/jpm.12116

O'Dea, J. A., & Dibley, M. J. (2014). Prevalence of obesity, overweight and thinness in Australian children and adolescents by socioeconomic status and ethnic/cultural group in 2006 and 2012. International Journal of Public Health, 59(5), 819–828. doi:10.1007/s00038-014-0605-3

O'Driscoll, C., Heary, C., Hennessy, E., & McKeague, L. (2012). Explicit and implicit stigma towards peers with mental health problems in childhood and adolescence. Journal of Child Psychology and Psychiatry, 53(10), 1054–1062. doi:10.1111/j.1469-7610.2012.02580.x

O'Hara, C. B., Campbell, I. C., & Schmidt, U. (2015). A reward-centred model of anorexia nervosa: A focussed narrative review of the neurological and psychophysiological literature. Neuroscience and Biobehavioral Reviews, 52, 131–152. doi:10.1016/j.neubiorev.2015.02.012

O'Leary, A. (1990). Stress, emotion, and human immune function. Psychological Bulletin, 108(3), 363–382. doi:10.1037/0033-2909.108.3.363

O'Loughlin, P. (2007). Is it harm reduction—or harm continuation? Journal of Global Drug Policy and Practice, 1(2). Retrieved from http://www.globaldrugpolicy.org/Issues/Vol%201%20Issue%202/Is%20it%20Harm%20Reduction.pdf

O'Malley, K. J., Cook, K. F., Price, M. D., Wildes, K. R., Hurdle, J. F., & Ashton, C. M. (2005). Measuring diagnoses: ICD code accuracy. Health Services Research, 40(5,part2), 1620–1639. doi:10.1111/j.1475-6773.2005.00444.x

O'Reilly, R. (2004). Why are community treatment orders controversial? The Canadian Journal of Psychiatry/La Revue Canadienne De Psychiatrie, 49(9), 579–584.

O'Rourke, J. A., Scharf, J. M., Yu, D., & Pauls, D. L. (2009). The genetics of Tourette syndrome: A review. Journal of Psychosomatic Research, 67(6), 533–545. doi:10.1016/j.jpsychores.2009.06.006

O'Shaughnessy, R. J. (2007). AAPL practice guideline for the forensic psychiatric evaluation of competence to stand trial: A Canadian legal perspective. Journal of the American Academy of Psychiatry and the Law, 35(4), 505–508.

Oaks, D. (2006). The Evolution of the Consumer Movement: Comment. Psychiatric Services, 57(8), 1212–1212. doi:10.1176/appi.ps.57.8.1212

Oberling, P., Rocha, B., di Scala, G., & Sandner, G. (1993). Evidence for state-dependent retrieval in conditioned place aversion. Behavioral & Neural Biology, 60(1), 27–32. doi:10.1016/0163-1047(93)90677-A

Oberndorfer, T. A., Frank, G. K. W., Simmons, A. N., Wagner, A., McCurdy, D., Fudge, J. L., … Kaye, W. H. (2013). Altered insula response to sweet taste processing after recovery from anorexia and bulimia nervosa. The American Journal of Psychiatry, 170(10), 1143–1151. doi:10.1176/appi.ajp.2013.11111745

Obiols, J. E. (2012). DSM 5: Precedents, present and prospects. International Journal of Clinical and Health Psychology, 12(2), 281–290.

Oblak, A. L., Gibbs, T. T., & Blatt, G. J. (2010). Decreased GABAB receptors in the cingulate cortex and fusiform gyrus in autism. Journal of Neurochemistry, 114(5), 1414–1423.

Oblak, A. L., Gibbs, T. T., & Blatt, G. J. (2011). Reduced GABAA receptors and benzodiazepine binding sites in the posterior cingulate cortex and fusiform gyrus in autism. Brain Research, 1380, 218–228. doi:10.1016/j.brainres.2010.09.021

Ochberg, F. (2014, March–April). An injury, not a disorder. Military Review, 96–99.

Oei, T. P. S., & Hashing, P. A. (2013). Alcohol use disorders. In P. M. Miller, S. A. Ball, M. E. Bates, A. W. Blume, K. M. Kampman, D. J. Kavanagh, M. E. Larimer, N. M. Petry, & P. De Witte (Eds.), Comprehensive addictive behaviors and disorders: Vol. 1. Principles of addiction (pp. 647–655). San Diego, CA: Elsevier Academic Press.

Offman, A., & Kleinplatz, P. J. (2004). Does PMDD belong in the DSM? Challenging the medicalization of women's bodies. Canadian Journal of Human Sexuality, 13(1), 17–27.

Ogden, C. L., Carroll, M. D., Fryar, C. D., & Flegal, K. M. (2015). Prevalence of obesity among adults and youth: United States, 2011–2014. NCHS Data Brief(219), 1-8.

Ogden, G. (2001). The taming of the screw: Reflections on 'A New View of women's sexual problems.'. Women & Therapy, 24(1–2), 17–21. doi:10.1300/J015v24n01_03

Ogden, S. P., & Simmonds, J. G. (2014). Psychologists' and counsellors' perspectives on prolonged grief disorder and its inclusion in diagnostic manuals. Counselling & Psychotherapy Research, 14(3), 212–219. doi:10.1080/14733145.2013.790456

Ogrodniczuk, J. S., & Oliffe, J. L. (2011). Men and depression. Canadian Family Physician, 57(2), 153–155.

Oh, H., Yang, L. H., Anglin, D. M., & DeVylder, J. E. (2014). Perceived discrimination and psychotic experiences across multiple ethnic groups in the United States. Schizophrenia Research, 157(1–3), 259–265. doi:10.1016/j.schres.2014.04.036

Ohan, J. L., Visser, T. A. W., Moss, R. G., & Allen, N. B. (2013). Parents' stigmatizing attitudes toward psychiatric labels for ADHD and depression. Psychiatric Services, 64(12), 1270–1273. doi:10.1176/appi.ps.201200578

Ohtani, A., Suzuki, T., Takeuchi, H., & Uchida, H. (2015). Language barriers and access to psychiatric care: A systematic review. Psychiatric Services, 66(8), 798–805. doi:10.1176/appi.ps.201400351

Olatunji, B. O., Davis, M. L., Powers, M. B., & Smits, J. A. J. (2013). Cognitive-behavioral therapy for obsessive-compulsive disorder: A meta-analysis of treatment outcome and moderators. Journal of Psychiatric Research, 47(1), 33–41. doi:http://dx.doi.org/10.1016/j.jpsychires.2012.08.020

Olatunji, B. O., Kauffman, B. Y., Meltzer, S., Davis, M. L., Smits, J. A. J., & Powers, M. B. (2014). Cognitive-behavioral therapy for hypochondriasis/health anxiety: A meta-analysis of treatment outcome and moderators. Behaviour Research and Therapy, 58, 65–74. doi:10.1016/j.brat.2014.05.002

Olff, M., Güzelcan, Y., de Vries, G.-J., Assies, J., & Gersons, B. P. R. (2006). HPA- and HPT-axis alterations in chronic posttraumatic stress disorder. Psychoneuroendocrinology, 31(10), 1220–1230. doi:http://dx.doi.org/10.1016/j.psyneuen.2006.09.003

Olfman, S. (2012). Drugging our children: A culture that has lost its compass. In S. Olfman & B. D. Robbins (Eds.), *Drugging our children: How profiteers are pushing antipsychotics on our youngest, and what we can do to stop it* (pp. 35–49). Santa Barbara, CA: Praeger/ABC-CLIO.

Oliva, F., Versino, E., Gammino, L., Colombi, N., Ostacoli, L., Carletto, S., ... Picci, R. L. (2016). Type D personality and essential hypertension in primary care: A cross-sectional observational study within a cohort of patients visiting general practitioners. *Journal of Nervous and Mental Disease, 204*(1), 43–48. doi:10.1097/NMD.0000000000000421

Ollendick, T. H., Alvarez, H. K., & Greene, R. W. (2004). Behavioral assessment: History of underlying concepts. In S. N. Haynes & E. M. Heiby (Eds.), *Comprehensive handbook of psychological assessment: Vol. 3. Behavioral assessment* (pp. 19–34). Hoboken, NJ: John Wiley.

Olmsted, D., & Blaxill, M. (2016). Leo Kanner's mention of 1938 in his report on autism refers to his first patient. *Journal of Autism & Developmental Disorders, 46*(1), 340–341. doi:10.1007/s10803-015-2541-3

Olsen, G. (2012). The marketing of madness and psychotropic drugs to children. In S. Olfman & B. D. Robbins (Eds.), *Drugging our children: How profiteers are pushing antipsychotics on our youngest, and what we can do to stop it.* (pp. 52–77). Santa Barbara, CA: Praeger/ABC-CLIO.

Oltmanns, T. F., & Powers, A. D. (2012). Gender and personality disorders. In T. A. Widiger (Ed.), *The Oxford handbook of personality disorders* (pp. 206–218). New York, NY: Oxford University Press.

Olver, M. E., & Wong, S. C. P. (2013). Treatment programs for high risk sexual offenders: Program and offender characteristics, attrition, treatment change and recidivism. *Aggression and Violent Behavior, 18*(5), 579–591. doi:10.1016/j.avb.2013.06.002

Online Etymology Dictionary. (n.d.). Diagnosis. Retrieved from http://www.etymonline.com/index.php?term=diagnosis

Oosterhuis, H. (2012). Sexual modernity in the works of Richard von Krafft-Ebing and Albert Moll. *Medical History, 56*(2), 133–155. doi:10.1017/mdh.2011.30

OPD Task Force (2007). *Operationalized psychodynamic diagnosis OPD2: Manual of diagnosis and treatment planning.* Cambridge, MA: Hogrefe.

Opris, I., & Casanova, M. F. (2014). Prefrontal cortical minicolumn: From executive control to disrupted cognitive processing. *Brain: A Journal of Neurology, 137*(7), 1863–1875. doi:10.1093/brain/awt359

Oquendo, M. A., & Baca-Garcia, E. (2014). Suicidal behavior disorder as a diagnostic entity in the DSM-5 classification system: Advantages outweigh limitations. *World Psychiatry, 13*(2), 128–130. doi:10.1002/wps.20116

Oquendo, M. A., Sullivan, G. M., Sudol, K., Baca-Garcia, E., Stanley, B. H., Sublette, M. E., & Mann, J. J. (2014). Toward a biosignature for suicide. *The American Journal of Psychiatry, 171*(12), 1259–1277. doi:10.1176/appi.ajp.2014.14020194

Oren, E., & Solomon, R. (2012). EMDR therapy: An overview of its development and mechanisms of action. *European Review of Applied Psychology/Revue Européenne de Psychologie Appliquée, 62*(4), 197–203. doi:10.1016/j.erap.2012.08.005

Organisation for Economic Co-operation and Development (OECD). (2012). *Health at a Glance: Europe 2012.* Paris, France and Washington, DC: Organisation for Co-operation and Development.

Organisation for Economic Co-operation and Development (OECD). (2015). *Health at a Glance 2015: OECD Indicators.* OECD Publishing, Paris. http://dx.doi.org/10.1787/health_glance-2015-en

Ornstein, R. M., Rosen, D. S., Mammel, K. A., Callahan, S. T., Forman, S., Jay, M. S., ... Walsh, B. T. (2013). Distribution of eating disorders in children and adolescents using the proposed DSM-5 criteria for feeding and eating disorders. *Journal of Adolescent Health, 53*(2), 303–305. doi:http://dx.doi.org/10.1016/j.jadohealth.2013.03.025

Orsillo, S. M., & Batten, S. V. (2005). Acceptance and commitment therapy in the treatment of posttraumatic stress disorder. *Behavior Modification, 29*(1), 95–129. doi:10.1177/0145445504270876

Osheroff v. Chestnut Lodge, 490 A.2d 720 (Court of Special Appeals of Maryland 1985).

Osório, C., Jones, N., Fertout, M., & Greenberg, N. (2013). Perceptions of stigma and barriers to care among UK military personnel deployed to Afghanistan and Iraq. *Anxiety, Stress & Coping: An International Journal, 26*(5), 539–557. doi:10.1080/10615806.2012.725470

Öst, L.-G., Havnen, A., Hansen, B., & Kvale, G. (2015). Cognitive behavioral treatments of obsessive–compulsive disorder. A systematic review and meta-analysis of studies published 1993–2014. *Clinical Psychology Review, 40,* 156–169. doi:10.1016/j.cpr.2015.06.003

Otasowie, J., Castells, X., Ehimare, U. P., & Smith, C. H. (2014). Tricyclic antidepressants for attention deficit hyperactivity disorder (ADHD) in children and adolescents. *Cochrane Database of Systematic Reviews*(9), CD006997. doi:10.1002/14651858.CD006997.pub2

Otero-López, J. M., & Villardefrancos, E. (2013). Materialism and addictive buying in women: The mediating role of anxiety and depression. *Psychological Reports, 113*(1), 328–344. doi:10.2466/18.02.PR0.113x11z9

Otto, M. W., & Miklowitz, D. J. (2004). The role and impact of psychotherapy in the management of bipolar disorder. *CNS Spectrums, 9*(11), 27–32.

Overmier, J. B., & Seligman, M. E. (1967). Effects of inescapable shock upon subsequent escape and avoidance responding. *Journal of Comparative and Physiological Psychology, 63*(1), 28–33. doi:10.1037/h0024166

Owens, J. A., Palermo, T. M., & Rosen, C. L. (2002). Overview of current management of sleep disturbances in children: II—Behavioral interventions. *Current Therapeutic Research, 63*(SupplB), B38–B52. doi:10.1016/S0011-393X(02)80102-3

Ozkiris, A., Essizoglu, A., Gulec, G., & Aksaray, G. (2015). The relationship between insight and the level of expressed emotion in patients with obsessive–compulsive disorder. *Nordic Journal of Psychiatry, 69*(3), 204–209. doi:10.3109/08039488.2014.959996

Paaver, M., Kurrikoff, T., Nordquist, N., Oreland, L., & Harro, J. (2008). The effect of 5-HTT gene promoter polymorphism on impulsivity depends on family relations in girls. *Progress in Neuro-Psychopharmacology and Biological Psychiatry, 32*(5), 1263–1268. doi:http://dx.doi.org/10.1016/j.pnpbp.2008.03.021

Pace, T. W. W., & Heim, C. M. (2011). A short review on the psychoneuroimmunology of posttraumatic stress disorder: from risk factors to medical comorbidities. *Brain, Behavior, and Immunity, 25*(1), 6–13. doi:10.1016/j.bbi.2010.10.003

Pack, M. J. (2013). Critical incident stress management: A review of the literature with implications for social work. *International Social Work, 56*(5), 608–627. doi:10.1177/0020872811435371

Packard, M. G., & Teather, L. A. (1999). Dissociation of multiple memory systems by posttraining intracerebral injections of glutamate. *Psychobiology, 27*(1), 40–50.

Packer, S. (2013). A belated obituary: Raphael J. Osheroff, MD. *Psychiatric Times.* Retrieved from http://www.psychiatrictimes.com/blog/belated-obituary-raphael-j-osheroff-md

Packman, A., Onslow, M., Webber, M., Harrison, E., Arnott, S., Bridgman, K., ... Lloyd, W. (2014, January). The Lidcombe Program treatment guide.

Paclawskyj, T. R., Matson, J. L., Rush, K. S., Smalls, Y., & Vollmer, T. R. (2000). Questions about behavioral function (QABF):: A behavioral checklist for functional assessment of aberrant behavior. *Research in Developmental Disabilities, 21*(3), 223–229. doi:https://doi.org/10.1016/S0891-4222(00)00036-6

Padesky, C. A. (1993). *Socratic questioning: Changing minds or guiding discovery?* Paper presented at the European Congress of Behavioural and Cognitive Therapies, London, UK. Retrieved from http://padesky.com/newpad/wp-content/uploads/2012/11/socquest.pdf

Pagano, M. E., Friend, K. B., Tonigan, J. S., & Stout, R. L. (2004). Helping Other Alcoholics in Alcoholics Anonymous and Drinking Outcomes: Findings from Project MATCH. *Journal of Studies on Alcohol, 65*(6), 766–773.

Pai, A., Suris, A., & North, C. (2017). Posttraumatic stress disorder in the DSM-5: Controversy, change, and conceptual considerations. *Behavioral Sciences, 7*(1), 7.

Pais, S. (2009). A systemic approach to the treatment of dissociative identity disorder. *Journal of Family Psychotherapy, 20*(1), 72–88. doi:10.1080/08975350802716566

Palamar, J. J., Halkitis, P. N., & Kiang, M. V. (2013). Perceived public stigma and stigmatization in explaining lifetime illicit drug use among emerging adults. *Addiction Research & Theory, 21*(6), 516–525. doi:10.3109/16066359.2012.762508

Palermo, G. B. (2015). Dusky is here to stay—For now. *International Journal of Offender Therapy and Comparative Criminology, 59*(14), 1503–1504. doi:10.1177/0306624X15616656

Palis, J., Rossopoulos, E., & Triarhou, L. C. (1985). The Hippocratic concept of hysteria: A translation of the original texts. *Integrative Psychiatry*, 3(3), 226–228.

Palmen, A., Didden, R., & Lang, R. (2012). A systematic review of behavioral intervention research on adaptive skill building in high-functioning young adults with autism spectrum disorder. *Research in Autism Spectrum Disorders*, 6(2), 602–617. doi:10.1016/j.rasd.2011.10.001

Palmer, B. W. (2006). Informed consent for schizophrenia research: What is an investigator (or IRB) to do? *Behavioral Sciences & the Law*, 24(4), 447–452. doi:10.1002/bsl.695

Palmer, C. A., & Hazelrigg, M. (2000). The guilty but mentally ill verdict: A review and conceptual analysis of intent and impact. *Journal of the American Academy of Psychiatry and the Law*, 28(1), 47–54.

Panepinto, A. R., Uschold, C. C., Olandese, M., & Linn, B. K. (2015). Beyond borderline personality disorder: Dialectical behavior therapy in a college counseling center. *Journal of College Student Psychotherapy*, 29(3), 211–226. doi:10.1080/87568225.2015.1045782

Panos, P. T., Jackson, J. W., Hasan, O., & Panos, A. (2014). Meta-analysis and systematic review assessing the efficacy of Dialectical Behavior Therapy (DBT). *Research on Social Work Practice*, 24(2), 213–223. doi:10.1177/1049731513503047

Panossian, A., Hamm, R., Wikman, G., & Efferth, T. (2014). Mechanism of action of Rhodiola, salidroside, tyrosol and triandrin in isolated neuroglial cells: An interactive pathway analysis of the downstream effects using RNA microarray data. *Phytomedicine*, 21(11), 1325–1348. doi:http://dx.doi.org/10.1016/j.phymed.2014.07.008

Paone, T. R., & Douma, K. B. (2009). Child-centered play therapy with a seven-year-old boy diagnosed with intermittent explosive disorder. *International Journal of Play Therapy*, 18(1), 31–44. doi:10.1037/a0013938

Papanastasiou, E., Stone, J. M., & Shergill, S. (2013). When the drugs don't work: The potential of glutamatergic antipsychotics in schizophrenia. *The British Journal of Psychiatry*, 202(2), 91–93. doi:10.1192/bjp.bp.112.110999

Papiasvili, E. D., & Mayers, L. A. (2013). Perceptions, thoughts, and attitudes in the Middle Ages. In T. G. Plante (Ed.), *Abnormal psychology across the ages: Vol. 1. History and conceptualizations* (pp. 15–31). Santa Barbara, CA: Praeger/ABC-CLIO.

Parens, E., & Johnston, J. (2010). Controversies concerning the diagnosis and treatment of bipolar disorder in children. *Child and Adolescent Psychiatry and Mental Health*, 4. doi:10.1186/1753-2000-4-9

Paris, J. (2007). Why psychiatrists are reluctant to diagnose: borderline personality disorder. *Psychiatry*, 4(1), 35–39.

Paris, J. (2011). Pharmacological treatments for personality disorders. *International Review of Psychiatry*, 23(3), 303–309. doi:10.3109/09540261.2011.586993

Paris, J. (2012). The rise and fall of dissociative identity disorder. *Journal of Nervous and Mental Disease*, 200(12), 1076–1079. doi:10.1097/NMD.0b013e318275d285

Paris, J. (2014). After DSM-5: Where does personality disorder research go from here? *Harvard Review of Psychiatry*, 22(4), 216–221. doi:10.1097/HRP.0000000000000041

Paris, J. (2015). *The intelligent clinician's guide to the DSM-5* (2nd ed.). Oxford, UK: Oxford University Press.

Paris, J., Bhat, V., & Thombs, B. (2015). Is adult attention-deficit hyperactivity disorder being overdiagnosed? *The Canadian Journal of Psychiatry/La Revue Canadienne De Psychiatrie*, 60(7), 324–328.

Pariyadath, V., Paulus, M. P., & Stein, E. A. (2013). Brain, reward, and drug addiction. In D. S. Charney, J. D. Buxbaum, P. Sklar, & E. J. Nestler (Eds.), *Neurobiology of mental illness* (4th ed., pp. 732–741). New York, NY: Oxford University Press.

Park, C. L., & Lechner, S. C. (2006). Measurement issues in assessing growth following stressful life experiences. In L. G. Calhoun & R. G. Tedeschi (Eds.), *Handbook of posttraumatic growth: Research and practice* (pp. 47–67). Mahwah, NJ: Lawrence Erlbaum.

Park, C. L., Cohen, L. H., & Murch, R. L. (1996). Assessment and prediction of stress-related growth. *Journal of Personality*, 64(1), 71–105. doi:10.1111/j.1467-6494.1996.tb00815.x

Park, H. R., Lee, J. M., Moon, H. E., Lee, D. S., Kim, B.-N., Kim, J., ... Paek, S. H. (2016). A short review on the current understanding of autism spectrum disorders. *Experimental Neurobiology*, 25(1), 1–13. doi:10.5607/en.2016.25.1.1

Park, R. J., Godier, L. R., & Cowdrey, F. A. (2014). Hungry for reward: How can neuroscience inform the development of treatment for Anorexia Nervosa? *Behaviour Research and Therapy*, 62, 47–59. doi:http://dx.doi.org/10.1016/j.brat.2014.07.007

Park, S., & Lee, M. (2014). Successful electroconvulsive therapy and improvement of negative symptoms in refractory schizophrenia with clozapine-induced seizures: A case report. *Psychiatria Danubina*, 26(4), 360–362.

Park, S., & Schepp, K. G. (2015). A systematic review of research on children of alcoholics: Their inherent resilience and vulnerability. *Journal of Child and Family Studies*, 24(5), 1222–1231. doi:10.1007/s10826-014-9930-7

Parker, K. J., Garner, J. P., Libove, R. A., Hyde, S. A., Hornbeak, K. B., Carson, D. S., ... Hardan, A. Y. (2014). Plasma oxytocin concentrations and OXTR polymorphisms predict social impairments in children with and without autism spectrum disorder. *Proceedings of the National Academy of Sciences*, 111(33), 12258–12263. doi:10.1073/pnas.1402236111

Parry, H. (2016, April 14). 'Let's find out the truth': Robert de Niro says autistic son changed 'overnight' after MMR jab as he says he regrets pulling anti-vaccination movie from Tribeca Film Festival. *The Daily Mail*. Retrieved from http://www.dailymail.co.uk/news/article-3537962/Let-s-truth-Robert-Niro-says-autistic-son-changed-overnight-MMR-jab-insists-isn-t-anti-vaccine-just-pro-safe-vaccines.html

Parry, M. S. (2006). Dorothea Dix (1802–1887). *American Journal of Public Health*, 96(4), 624–625. http://doi.org/10.2105/AJPH.2005.079152

Parry-Jones, B. (1994). Merycism or rumination disorder: A historical investigation and current assessment. *The British Journal of Psychiatry*, 165(3), 303–314. doi:10.1192/bjp.165.3.303

Parry-Jones, B., & Parry-Jones, W. L. (1992). Pica: symptom or eating disorder? A historical assessment. *The British Journal of Psychiatry*, 160, 341–354.

Parsons, A. (1970). Is the Oedipus complex universal? In W. Muensterberger (Ed.), *Man and his culture* (pp. 331–385). New York, NY: Taplinger Publishing.

Paschou, P. (2013). The genetic basis of Gilles de la Tourette Syndrome. *Neuroscience and Biobehavioral Reviews*, 37(6), 1026–1039. doi:10.1016/j.neubiorev.2013.01.016

Pascual, J. C., Soler, J., Barrachina, J., Campins, M. J., Alvarez, E., Pérez, V., ... Baiget, M. (2008). Failure to detect an association between the serotonin transporter gene and borderline personality disorder. *Journal of Psychiatric Research*, 42(1), 87–88. doi:10.1016/j.jpsychires.2006.10.005

Passos, I. C., Vasconcelos-Moreno, M. P., Costa, L. G., Kunz, M., Brietzke, E., Quevedo, J., ... Kauer-Sant'Anna, M. (2015). Inflammatory markers in post-traumatic stress disorder: A systematic review, meta-analysis, and meta-regression. *The Lancet Psychiatry*, 2(11), 1002–1012. doi:10.1016/S2215-0366(15)00309-0

Patil, T., & Giordano, J. (2010). On the ontological assumptions of the medical model of psychiatry: Philosophical considerations and pragmatic tasks. *Philosophy, Ethics, and Humanities in Medicine*, 5.

Patriquin, M. A., Bauer, I. E., Soares, J. C., Graham, D. P., & Nielsen, D. A. (2015). Addiction pharmacogenetics: A systematic review of the genetic variation of the dopaminergic system. *Psychiatric Genetics*, 25(5), 181–193. doi:10.1097/YPG.0000000000000095

Patten, S. B. (2015). Medical models and metaphors for depression. *Epidemiology and Psychiatric Sciences*, 24(4), 303–308. doi:10.1017/S2045796015000153

Pauls, D. L. (2012). The genetics of obsessive-compulsive disorder: Current status. In J. Zohar (Ed.), *Obsessive compulsive disorder: Current science and clinical practice* (pp. 277–299). Chichester, UK: Wiley-Blackwell.

Pauls, D. L., Fernandez, T. V., Mathews, C. A., State, M. W., & Scharf, J. M. (2014). The inheritance of tourette disorder: A review. *Journal of Obsessive-Compulsive and Related Disorders*, 3(4), 380–385. doi:10.1016/j.jocrd.2014.06.003

Pearce, J. M. S. (2004). Richard Morton: Origins of Anorexia nervosa. *European Neurology*, 52(4), 191–192. doi:10.1159/000082033

Pearce, N. (2012). Classification of epidemiological study designs. *International Journal of Epidemiology*, 41(2), 393–397. doi:doi: 10.1093/ije/dys049

Pearl, D., & Schrollinger, E. (1999). Acupuncture: Its use in medicine. *The Western Journal of Medicine*, 171(3), 176–180.

Pearson, D. G. (2012). Contextual representations increase analogue traumatic intrusions: Evidence against a dual-representation account of peri-traumatic processing. *Journal of Behavior Therapy and Experimental Psychiatry*, 43(4), 1026–1031. doi:10.1016/j.jbtep.2012.04.002

Pearson, D. G. (2014). Are C-reps contextual representations? A reply to Brewin and Burgess. *Journal of Behavior Therapy and Experimental Psychiatry, 45*(1), 220–222. doi:10.1016/j.jbtep.2013.07.010

Pearson, D. G., Ross, F. D. C., & Webster, V. L. (2012). The importance of context: Evidence that contextual representations increase intrusive memories. *Journal of Behavior Therapy and Experimental Psychiatry, 43*(1), 573–580. doi:10.1016/j.jbtep.2011.07.009

Pedersen, N. L., & Fiske, A. (2010). Genetic influences on suicide and nonfatal suicidal behavior: Twin study findings. *European Psychiatry, 25*(5), 264–267. doi:10.1016/j.eurpsy.2009.12.008

Pedersen, W., & Bakken, A. (2016). Urban landscapes of adolescent substance use. *Acta Sociologica, 59*(2), 131–150. doi:10.1177/0001699315625448

Peele, S. (1989). *Diseasing of America: Addiction treatment out of control.* Boston, MA: Houghton Mifflin.

Pelham, W. E., Burrows-MacLean, L., Gnagy, E. M., Fabiano, G. A., Coles, E. K., Wymbs, B. T., ... Waschbusch, D. A. (2014). A dose-ranging study of behavioral and pharmacological treatment in social settings for children with ADHD. *Journal of Abnormal Child Psychology, 42*(6), 1019–1031. doi:10.1007/s10802-013-9843-8

Pelham, W. E., Fabiano, G. A., Waxmonsky, J. G., Greiner, A. R., Gnagu, E. M., Pelham III, W. E., ... Murphy, S. A. (2016). Treatment sequencing for childhood ADHD: A multiple-randomization study of adaptive medication and behavioral interventions. *Journal of Clinical Child & Adolescent Psychology, 45*(4), 396-415 doi:10.1080/15374416.2015.1105138

Pemment, J. (2013). Psychopathy versus sociopathy: Why the distinction has become crucial. *Aggression and Violent Behavior, 18*(5), 458–461. doi:http://dx.doi.org/10.1016/j.avb.2013.07.001

Peñas-Lledó, E. M., Dorado, P., Agüera, Z., Gratacós, M., Estivill, X., Fernández-Aranda, F., & Llerena, A. (2012). CYP2D6 polymorphism in patients with eating disorders. *The Pharmacogenomics Journal, 12*(2), 173–175. doi:10.1038/tpj.2010.78

Pérez-López, F. R., Chedraui, P., Pérez-Roncero, G., López-Baena, M. T., & Cuadros-López, J. L. (2009). Premenstrual syndrome and premenstrual dysphoric disorder: Symptoms and cluster influences. *The Open Psychiatry Journal, 3.*

Perez-Rodriguez, M. M., New, A. S., & Siever, L. J. (2013). The neurobiology of personality disorders: The shift to DSM-5. In D. S. Charney, J. D. Buxbaum, P. Sklar, & E. J. Nestler (Eds.), *Neurobiology of mental illness* (4th ed., pp. 1089–1102). New York, NY: Oxford University Press.

Peris, T. S., Sugar, C. A., Bergman, R. L., Chang, S., Langley, A., & Piacentini, J. (2012). Family factors predict treatment outcome for pediatric obsessive-compulsive disorder. *Journal of Consulting and Clinical Psychology, 80*(2), 255–263. doi:10.1037/a0027084

Peris, T. S., Yadegar, M., Asarnow, J. R., & Piacentini, J. (2012). Pediatric obsessive compulsive disorder: Family climate as a predictor of treatment outcome. *Journal of Obsessive-Compulsive and Related Disorders, 1*(4), 267–273. doi:10.1016/j.jocrd.2012.07.003

Perkins, B. R., & Rouanzoin, C. C. (2002). A critical evaluation of current views regarding eye movement desensitization and reprocessing (EMDR): Clarifying points of confusion. *Journal of Clinical Psychology, 58*(1), 77–97. doi:10.1002/jclp.1130

Perkins, K. M., & Cross, W. E., Jr. (2014). False consciousness and the maintenance of injustice. In C. V. Johnson, H. L. Friedman, J. Diaz, Z. Franco, & B. K. Nastasi (Eds.), *The Praeger handbook of social justice and psychology: Vol. 1. Fundamental issues and special populations* (pp. 97–114). Santa Barbara, CA: Praeger.

Perlin, M. L. (2017a). "God said to Abraham/kill me a son": Why the insanity defense and the incompetency status are compatible with and required by the Convention on the Rights of Persons with Disabilities and basic principles of therapeutic jurisprudence. *American Criminal Law Review, 54*(2), 477–519.

Perlin, M. L. (2017b). The insanity defense: Nine myths that will not go away. In M. D. White (Ed.), *The insanity defense: Multidisciplinary views on Its history, trends, and controversies* (pp. 3–22). Santa Barbara, CA: Praeger.

Perlis, R. H. (2015). The emerging genetics of bipolar disorder. In A. Yildiz, P. Ruiz, & C. B. Nemeroff (Eds.), *The bipolar book: History, neurobiology, and treatment* (pp. 181–188). New York, NY: Oxford University Press.

Perloff, R. M. (2014). Social media effects on young women's body image concerns: Theoretical perspectives and an agenda for research. *Sex Roles, 71*(11–12), 363–377. doi:10.1007/s11199-014-0384-6

Perrin, N., Sayer, L., & While, A. (2015). The efficacy of alarm therapy versus desmopressin therapy in the treatment of primary mono-symptomatic nocturnal enuresis: A systematic review. *Primary Health Care Research and Development, 16*(1), 21–31. doi:10.1017/S146342361300042X

Perry, Y., Werner-Seidler, A., Calear, A. L., & Christensen, H. (2016). Web-based and mobile suicide prevention interventions for young people: A systematic review. *Journal of the Canadian Academy of Child and Adolescent Psychiatry/Journal de l'Académie canadienne de psychiatrie de l'enfant et de l'adolescent, 25*(2), 73–79.

Persico, A. M., & Napolioni, V. (2013). Autism genetics. *Behavioural Brain Research, 251,* 95–112. doi:10.1016/j.bbr.2013.06.012

Pertusa, A., Fullana, M. A., Singh, S., Alonso, P., Menchón, J. M., & Mataix-Cols, D. (2008). Compulsive hoarding: OCD symptom, distinct clinical syndrome, or both? *The American Journal of Psychiatry, 165*(10), 1289–1298. doi:10.1176/appi.ajp.2008.07111730

Peselow, E. D., Pizano, D. R., & IsHak, W. W. (2015). Maintenance treatment for obsessive-compulsive disorder: Findings from a naturalistic setting. *Annals of Clinical Psychiatry, 27*(1), 25–32.

Peters, B. M. (2013). Evolutionary psychology: Neglecting neurobiology in defining the mind. *Theory & Psychology, 23*(3), 305–322. doi:10.1177/0959354313480269

Petersen, L., Sørensen, T. I. A., Andersen, P. K., Mortensen, P. B., & Hawton, K. (2014). Genetic and familial environmental effects on suicide attempts: A study of Danish adoptees and their biological and adoptive siblings. *Journal of Affective Disorders, 155,* 273–277. doi:10.1016/j.jad.2013.11.012

Peterson, B. S. (2015). Research Domain Criteria (RDoC): A new psychiatric nosology whose time has not yet come. *Journal of Child Psychology and Psychiatry, 56*(7), 719–722. doi:10.1111/jcpp.12439

Petrides, G., Malur, C., Braga, R. J., Bailine, S. H., Schooler, N. R., Malhotra, A. K., ... Mendelowitz, A. (2015). Electroconvulsive therapy augmentation in clozapine-resistant schizophrenia: A prospective, randomized study. *The American Journal of Psychiatry, 172*(1), 52–58. doi:10.1176/appi.ajp.2014.13060787

Petry, N. M. (2016a). *Behavioral addictions: DSM-5® and beyond.* New York, NY: Oxford University Press.

Petry, N. M. (2016b). Gambling disorder: The first officially recognized behavioral addiction. In N. M. Petry (Ed.), *Behavioral addictions: DSM-5® and beyond.* (pp. 7–41). New York, NY: Oxford University Press.

Petry, N. M. (2016c). Introduction to behavioral addictions. In N. M. Petry (Ed.), *Behavioral addictions: DSM-5® and beyond* (pp. 1–5). New York, NY: Oxford University Press.

Petry, N. M., & O'Brien, C. P. (2013). Internet gaming disorder and the DSM-5. *Addiction, 108*(7), 1186–1187. doi:10.1111/add.12162

Petry, N. M., Rehbein, F., Gentile, D. A., Lemmens, J. S., Rumpf, H. J., Mößle, T., ... O'Brien, C. P. (2014). Moving Internet gaming disorder forward: A reply. *Addiction, 109*(9), 1412−1413. doi:10.1111/add.12653

Petry, N. M., Rehbein, F., Gentile, D. A., Lemmens, J. S., Rumpf, H. J., Mößle, T., ... O'Brien, C. P. (2014). An international consensus for assessing internet gaming disorder using the new DSM-5 approach. *Addiction, 109*(9), 1399–1406. doi:10.1111/add.12457

Petry, N. M., Weinstock, J., Morasco, B. J., & Ledgerwood, D. M. (2009). Brief motivational interventions for college student problem gamblers. *Addiction, 104*(9), 1569–1578. doi:10.1111/j.1360-0443.2009.02652.x

Pfaus, J. G. (2009). Pathways of sexual desire. *Journal of Sexual Medicine, 6*(6), 1506–1533. doi:10.1111/j.1743-6109.2009.01309.x

Phillipou, A., Rossell, S. L., & Castle, D. J. (2014). The neurobiology of anorexia nervosa: A systematic review. *Australian and New Zealand Journal of Psychiatry, 48*(2), 128–152. doi:10.1177/0004867413509693

Phillips, D. P. (1974). The influence of suggestion on suicide: Substantive and theoretical implications of the Werther effect. *American Sociological Review, 39*(3), 340–354. doi:10.2307/2094294

Phillips, L. A. (2013). Stigma and substance use disorders: Research, implications, and potential solutions. In A. M. Columbus (Ed.), *Advances in psychology research* (Vol. 96, pp. 287–295). Hauppauge, NY: Nova Biomedical Books.

Phillips, L. A., & Shaw, A. (2013). Substance use more stigmatized than smoking and obesity. *Journal of Substance Use, 18*(4), 247–253. doi: 10.3109/14659891.2012.661516

Phillips, R. D. (2010). How firm is our foundation? Current play therapy research. *International Journal of Play Therapy, 19*(1), 13–25. doi:10.1037/a0017340

Phillips, S. M. (2002). Free to speak: Clarifying the legacy of the witch hunts. *Journal of Psychology and Christianity, 21*(1), 29–41.

Pickup, G. J., & Frith, C. D. (2001). Theory of mind impairments in schizophrenia: Symptomatology, severity and specificity. *Psychological Medicine, 31*(2), 207–220. doi:10.1017/S0033291701003385

Pieper, S., Out, D., Bakermans-Kranenburg, M. J., & van Ijzendoorn, M. H. (2011). Behavioral and molecular genetics of dissociation: The role of the serotonin transporter gene promoter polymorphism (5-HTTLPR). *Journal of Traumatic Stress, 24*(4), 373–380. doi:10.1002/jts.20659

Pies, R. W. (2014). The bereavement exclusion and DSM-5: An update and commentary. *Innovations in Clinical Neuroscience, 11*(7–8), 19–22.

Pietrzak, R. H., Gallezot, J.-D., Ding, Y.-S., Henry, S., Potenza, M. N., Southwick, S. M., … Neumeister, A. (2013). Association of posttraumatic stress disorder with reduced in vivo norepinephrine transporter availability in the locus coeruleus. *JAMA Psychiatry, 70*(11), 1199–1205. doi:10.1001/jamapsychiatry.2013.399

Pike, K. M., Dunne, P. E., & Addai, E. (2013). Expanding the boundaries: reconfiguring the demographics of the "typical" eating disordered patient. *Current Psychiatry Reports, 15*(11), 411–411. doi:10.1007/s11920-013-0411-2

Pilc, A., Wierońska, J. M., & Skolnick, P. (2013). Glutamate-based antidepressants: Preclinical psychopharmacology. *Biological Psychiatry, 73*(12), 1125–1132. doi:10.1016/j.biopsych.2013.01.021

Pilkington, K., Boshnakova, A., & Richardson, J. (2006). St John's wort for depression: Time for a different perspective? *Complementary Therapies in Medicine, 14*(4), 268–281. doi:http://dx.doi.org/10.1016/j.ctim.2006.01.003

Pilon, M., Montplaisir, J., & Zadra, A. (2008). Precipitating factors of somnambulism: Impact of sleep deprivation and forced arousals. *Neurology, 70*(24), 2284–2290. doi:10.1212/01.wnl.0000304082.49839.86

Pincott, J. (2012, March 13). Slips of the tongue. *Psychology Today.* Retrieved from https://www.psychologytoday.com/articles/201203/slips-the-tongue

Pinel, J. P. J., Assanand, S., & Lehman, D. R. (2000). Hunger, eating, and ill health. *American Psychologist, 55*(10), 1105–1116. doi:10.1037/0003-066X.55.10.1105

Piotrowska, P. J., Stride, C. B., Croft, S. E., & Rowe, R. (2015). Socioeconomic status and antisocial behaviour among children and adolescents: A systematic review and meta-analysis. *Clinical Psychology Review, 35*, 47–55. doi:10.1016/j.cpr.2014.11.003

Piper, A., & Merskey, H. (2004a). The persistence of folly: A critical examination of dissociative identity disorder. Part I. The excesses of an improbable concept. *The Canadian Journal of Psychiatry/La Revue Canadienne De Psychiatrie, 49*(9), 592–600.

Piper, A., & Merskey, H. (2004b). The persistence of folly: Critical examination of dissociative identity disorder. Part II. The defence and decline of multiple personality or dissociative identity disorder. *The Canadian Journal of Psychiatry/La Revue Canadienne De Psychiatrie, 49*(10), 678–683.

Piquet-Pessôa, M., Ferreira, G. M., Melca, I. A., & Fontenelle, L. F. (2014). DSM-5 and the decision not to include sex, shopping or stealing as addictions. *Current Addiction Reports, 1*(3), 172–176. doi:10.1007/s40429-014-0027-6

Pithers, W. D., Kashima, K. M., Cumming, G. F., Beal, L. S., & Buell, M. M. (1988). Relapse prevention of sexual aggression. *Annals of the New York Academy of Sciences, 528*(1), 244–260. doi:10.1111/j.1749-6632.1988.tb50868.x

Pittenger, C., & Bloch, M. H. (2014). Pharmacological treatment of obsessive-compulsive disorder. *Psychiatric Clinics of North America, 37*(3), 375–391. doi:10.1016/j.psc.2014.05.006

Pittenger, C., Bloch, M. H., & Williams, K. (2011). Glutamate abnormalities in obsessive compulsive disorder: neurobiology, pathophysiology, and treatment. *Pharmacology & Therapeutics, 132*(3), 314–332. doi:10.1016/j.pharmthera.2011.09.006

Platt, J. J., & Husband, S. D. (1993). An overview of problem-solving and social skills approaches in substance abuse treatment. *Psychotherapy: Theory, Research, Practice, Training, 30*(2), 276–283. doi:10.1037/0033-3204.30.2.276

Platt, J., Keyes, K. M., & Koenen, K. C. (2014). Size of the social network versus quality of social support: Which is more protective against PTSD? *Social Psychiatry and Psychiatric Epidemiology, 49*(8), 1279–1286. doi:10.1007/s00127-013-0798-4

Plaud, J. J., & Holm, J. E. (1998). Sexual dysfunctions. In J. J. Plaud & G. H. Eifert (Eds.), *From behavior theory to behavior therapy* (pp. 136–151). Needham Heights, MA: Allyn & Bacon.

Plaut, V. L. (1983). Punishment versus treatment of the guilty but mentally ill. *Journal of Criminal Law & Criminology, 74*(2), 428–456. doi:10.2307/1143083

Ploeger, A., & Galis, F. (2011). Evolutionary approaches to autism—an overview and integration. *Mcgill Journal Of Medicine: MJM: An International Forum For The Advancement Of Medical Sciences By Students, 13*(2), 38–38.

Ploog, D. W. (2003). The place of the Triune Brain in psychiatry. *Physiology & Behavior, 79*(3), 487–493. doi:10.1016/S0031-9384(03)00154-9

Polańska, K., Jurewicz, J., & Hanke, W. (2012). Exposure to environmental and lifestyle factors and attention-deficit/hyperactivity disorder in children—A review of epidemiological studies. *International Journal of Occupational Medicine and Environmental Health, 25*(4), 330–355. doi:10.2478/S13382-012-0048-0

Polaschek, D. L. L. (2012). An appraisal of the risk-need-responsivity (RNR) model of offender rehabilitation and its application in correctional treatment. *Legal and Criminological Psychology, 17*(1), 1–17. doi:10.1111/j.2044-8333.2011.02038.x

Pole, N., Best, S. R., Metzler, T., & Marmar, C. R. (2005). Why are Hispanics at greater risk for PTSD? *Cultural Diversity and Ethnic Minority Psychology, 11*(2), 144–161. doi:10.1037/1099-9809.11.2.144

Polimeni, J., Reiss, J. P., & Sareen, J. (2005). Could obsessive-compulsive disorder have originated as a group-selected adaptive trait in traditional societies? *Medical Hypotheses, 65*(4), 655–664.

Pollack, R. (1997). *The creation of Dr. B: A biography of Bruno Bettelheim.* New York, NY: Simon & Schuster.

Pollak, J. (1987). Obsessive-compulsive personality: Theoretical and clinical perspectives and recent research findings. *Journal of Personality Disorders, 1*(3), 248–262. doi:10.1521/pedi.1987.1.3.248

Pomerantz, J. M. (2007). Glutamate hypofunction and schizophrenia: A new theory. *Drug Benefit Trends, 19*(7), 290–291.

Pope, H. G., Jr., Barry, S., Bodkin, A., & Hudson, J. I. (2006). Tracking scientific interest in the dissociative disorders: A study of scientific publication output 1984–2003. *Psychotherapy and Psychosomatics, 75*(1), 19–24. doi:10.1159/000089223

Pope, H. G., Jr., Oliva, P. S., Hudson, J. I., Bodkin, J. A., & Gruber, A. J. (1999). Attitudes toward DSM-IV dissociative disorders diagnoses among board-certified American psychiatrists. *The American Journal of Psychiatry, 156*(2), 321–323.

Popolo, R., Dimaggio, G., Luther, L., Vinci, G., Salvatore, G., & Lysaker, P. H. (2016). Theory of mind in schizophrenia: Associations with clinical and cognitive insight controlling for levels of psychopathology. *Journal of Nervous and Mental Disease, 204*(3), 240–243. doi:10.1097/NMD.0000000000000454

Popovic, D., Scott, J., & Colom, F. (2015). Cognitive behavioral therapy and psychoeducation. In A. Yildiz, P. Ruiz, & C. B. Nemeroff (Eds.), *The bipolar book: History, neurobiology, and treatment* (pp. 435–444). New York, NY: Oxford University Press.

Popper, C. W. (1997). Antidepressants in the treatment of attention-deficit/hyperactivity disorder. *Journal of Clinical Psychiatry, 58*(Suppl 14), 14–29.

Popper, H. (1977). Pathologic aspects of cirrhosis. A review. *The American Journal of Pathology, 87*(1), 228–264.

Porter, J. S., & Risler, E. (2014). The new alternative DSM-5 model for personality disorders: Issues and controversies. *Research on Social Work Practice, 24*(1), 50–56. doi:10.1177/1049731513500348

Porter, R. (2002). *Madness: A brief history.* Oxford, UK: Oxford University Press.

Portnow, L. H., Vaillancourt, D. E., & Okun, M. S. (2013). The history of cerebral PET scanning: From physiology to cutting-edge technology. *Neurology, 80*(10), 952–956. doi:10.1212/WNL.0b013e318285c135

Post, R. M., Altshuler, L., Kupka, R., McElroy, S., Frye, M. A., Rowe, M., … Nolen, W. A. (2014). More pernicious course of bipolar disorder in the United States than in many European countries: Implications for policy and treatment. *Journal of Affective Disorders, 160*, 27–33. doi:10.1016/j.jad.2014.02.006

Potegal, M. (2012). Temporal and frontal lobe initiation and regulation of the top-down escalation of anger and aggression. *Behavioural Brain Research, 231*(2), 386–395. doi:10.1016/j.bbr.2011.10.049

Potvin, S., Stip, E., Sepehry, A. A., Gendron, A., Bah, R., & Kouassi, E. (2008). Inflammatory cytokine alterations in schizophrenia: A systematic quantitative review. *Biological Psychiatry, 63*(8), 801–808. doi:10.1016/j.biopsych.2007.09.024

Poulakou-Rebelakou, E., Tsiamis, C., Panteleakos, G., & Ploumpidis, D. (2009). Lycanthropy in Byzantine times (AD 330–1453). *History of Psychiatry, 20*(4), 468–479. doi:10.1177/0957154X08338337

Poulsen, S., Lunn, S., Daniel, S. I. F., Folke, S., Mathiesen, B. B., Katznelson, H., & Fairburn, C. G. (2014). A randomized controlled trial of psychoanalytic psychotherapy or cognitive-behavioral therapy for bulimia nervosa. *The American Journal of Psychiatry, 171*(1), 109–116. doi:10.1176/appi.ajp.2013.12121511

Power, M. (2013). CBT for depression. In M. Power (Ed.), *The Wiley-Blackwell handbook of mood disorders* (2nd ed., pp. 173–191). Chichester, UK: Wiley-Blackwell.

Powers, P. S., & Bruty, H. (2009). Pharmacotherapy for eating disorders and obesity. *Child and Adolescent Psychiatric Clinics of North America, 18*(1), 175–187. doi:10.1016/j.chc.2008.07.009

Poznyak, V. (2014). *Alcohol use disorders: Their status in the draft ICD-11*. Paper presented at the Alcoholism: Clinical and Experimental Research.

Pratt, L. A., Brody, D. J., & Gu, Q. (2017, August). Antidepressant use among persons aged 12 and over: United States, 2011–2014. *NCHS Data Brief* (No. 283). Retrieved from https://www.cdc.gov/nchs/products/databriefs/db283.htm

Prescott, C. A., & Gottesman, I. I. (1993). Genetically mediated vulnerability to schizophrenia. *Psychiatric Clinics of North America, 16*(2), 245–267.

Pressman, D. L., & Bonanno, G. A. (2007). With whom do we grieve? Social and cultural determinants of grief processing in the United States and China. *Journal of Social and Personal Relationships, 24*(5), 729–746. doi:10.1177/0265407507081458

Preti, A., Melis, M., Siddi, S., Vellante, M., Doneddu, G., & Fadda, R. (2014). Oxytocin and autism: A systematic review of randomized controlled trials. *Journal of Child and Adolescent Psychopharmacology, 24*(2), 54–68. doi:10.1089/cap.2013.0040

Prichard, J. C. (1835). *A treatise on insanity and other disorders affecting the mind*. London, UK: Sherwood, Gilbert, and Piper.

Pridmore, S. (2000). Substitution of rapid transcranial magnetic stimulation treatments for electroconvulsive therapy treatments in a course of electroconvulsive therapy. *Depression and Anxiety, 12*(3), 118–123.

Pridmore, S. (2011). Medicalisation of suicide. *The Malaysian Journal of Medical Sciences, 18*(4), 78–83.

Priebe, S., Bhatti, N., Barnicot, K., Bremner, S., Gaglia, A., Katsakou, C., ... Zinkler, M. (2012). Effectiveness and cost-effectiveness of dialectical behaviour therapy for self-harming patients with personality disorder: A pragmatic randomised controlled trial. *Psychotherapy and Psychosomatics, 81*(6), 356–365. doi:10.1159/000338897

Priest, J. B. (2013). Emotionally focused therapy as treatment for couples with generalized anxiety disorder and relationship distress. *Journal of Couple & Relationship Therapy, 12*(1), 22–37. doi:10.1080/15332691.2013.749763

Priest, J. B. (2015). A Bowen family systems model of generalized anxiety disorder and romantic relationship distress. *Journal of Marital and Family Therapy, 41*(3), 340–353. doi:10.1111/jmft.12063

Prilleltensky, I. (1999). Critical psychology foundations for the promotion of mental health. *Annual Review of Critical Psychology, 1*(100–118).

Prilleltensky, I., Dokecki, P., Frieden, G., & Ota Wang, V. (2007). Counseling for wellness and justice: Foundations and ethical dilmmas. In E. Aldarondo (Ed.), *Advancing social justice through clinical practice* (pp. 19–42). Mahwah, NJ: Lawrence Erlbaum.

Pringsheim, T., Hirsch, L., Gardner, D., & Gorman, D. A. (2015a). The pharmacological management of oppositional behaviour, conduct problems, and aggression in children and adolescents with attention-deficit hyperactivity disorder, oppositional defiant disorder, and conduct disorder: A systematic review and meta-analysis. Part 1: Psychostimulants, alpha-2 agonists, and atomoxetine. *The Canadian Journal of Psychiatry / La Revue Canadienne De Psychiatrie, 60*(2), 42–51.

Pringsheim, T., Hirsch, L., Gardner, D., & Gorman, D. A. (2015b). The pharmacological management of oppositional behaviour, conduct problems, and aggression in children and adolescents with attention-deficit hyperactivity disorder, oppositional defiant disorder, and conduct disorder: A systematic review and meta-analysis. Part 2: Antipsychotics and traditional mood stabilizers. *The Canadian Journal of Psychiatry/ La Revue Canadienne De Psychiatrie, 60*(2), 52–61.

Prochaska, J. O., DiClemente, C. C., & Norcross, J. C. (1992). In search of how people change: Applications to addictive behaviors. *American Psychologist, 47*(9), 1102–1114. doi:10.1037/0003-066X.47.9.1102

Proctor, A., & Bianchi, M. T. (2012). Clinical pharmacology in sleep medicine. *ISRN Pharmacology, 2012*, 914168–914168. doi:10.5402/2012/914168

Protinsky, H., & Dillard, C. (1983). Enuresis: A family therapy model. *Psychotherapy: Theory, Research & Practice, 20*(1), 81–89. doi:10.1037/h0088482

Prouty, G. (1994). *Theoretical evolutions in person-centered/experiential therapy*. Westport, CT: Praeger.

Prouty, G. (2002). Humanistic psychotherapy for people with schizophrenia. In D. J. Cain (Ed.), *Humanistic psychotherapies: Handbook of research and practice* (pp. 579–601). Washington, DC: American Psychological Association.

Przepiorka, A. M., Blachnio, A., St. Louis, K. O., & Wozniak, T. (2013). Public attitudes toward stuttering in Poland. *International Journal of Language & Communication Disorders, 48*(6), 703–714. doi:10.1111/1460-6984.12041

Przeworski, A., Zoellner, L. A., Franklin, M. E., Garcia, A., Freeman, J., March, J. S., & Foa, E. B. (2012). Maternal and child expressed emotion as predictors of treatment response in pediatric obsessive–compulsive disorder. *Child Psychiatry and Human Development, 43*(3), 337–353. doi:10.1007/s10578-011-0268-8

Puente, A. N., & Mitchell, J. T. (2016). Cognitive-behavioral therapy for adult ADHD: A case study of multi-method assessment of executive functioning in clinical practice and manualized treatment adaptation. *Clinical Case Studies, 15*(3), 198–211. doi:10.1177/1534650115614098

Pulkki-Råback, L., Ahola, K., Elovainio, M., Kivimäki, M., Hintsanen, M., Isometsä, E., ... Virtanen, M. (2012). Socio-economic position and mental disorders in a working-age Finnish population: The Health 2000 Study. *European Journal of Public Health, 22*(3), 327–332. doi:10.1093/eurpub/ckr127

Pull, C. B. (2013). Too few or too many? Reactions to removing versus retaining specific personality disorders in DSM-5. *Current Opinion in Psychiatry, 26*(1), 73–78. doi:10.1097/YCO.0b013e32835b2cb5

Punja, S., Shamseer, L., Hartling, L., Urichuk, L., Vandermeer, B., Nikles, J., & Vohra, S. (2016). Amphetamines for attention deficit hyperactivity disorder (ADHD) in children and adolescents. *Cochrane Database of Systematic Reviews, 2*, CD009996. doi:10.1002/14651858.CD009996.pub2

Qian, J., Hu, Q., Wan, Y., Li, T., Wu, M., Ren, Z., & Yu, D. (2013). Prevalence of eating disorders in the general population: A systematic review. *Shanghai Archives of Psychiatry, 25*(4), 212–222.

Quinn, A. (2011). A person-centered approach to the treatment of borderline personality disorder. *Journal of Humanistic Psychology, 51*(4), 465–491. doi:10.1177/0022167811399764

Quinn, M., & Lynch, A. (2016). Is ADHD a 'real' disorder? *Support for Learning, 31*(1), 59–70. doi:10.1111/1467-9604.12114

Quist, J. F., & Kennedy, J. L. (2001). Genetics of childhood disorders: XXIII. ADHD, part 7: The serotonin system. *Journal of the American Academy of Child & Adolescent Psychiatry, 40*(2), 253–256. doi:10.1097/00004583-200102000-00022

Qureshi, N. A., & Al-Bedah, A. M. (2013). Mood disorders and complementary and alternative medicine: A literature review. *Neuropsychiatric Disease and Treatment, 9*.

Radulescu, E., Ganeshan, B., Shergill, S. S., Medford, N., Chatwin, C., Young, R. C. D., & Critchley, H. D. (2014). Grey-matter texture abnormalities and reduced hippocampal volume are distinguishing features of schizophrenia. *Psychiatry Research: Neuroimaging, 223*(3), 179–186. doi:10.1016/j.pscychresns.2014.05.014

Raevuori, A., Haukka, J., Vaarala, O., Suvisaari, J. M., Gissler, M., Grainger, M., ... Suokas, J. T. (2014). The increased risk for autoimmune diseases in patients with eating disorders. *PLOS One, 9*(8), e104845–e104845. doi:10.1371/journal.pone.0104845

Rafalovich, A. (2004). *Framing ADHD children: A critical examination of the history, discourse, and everyday experience of attention deficit/ hyperactivity disorder*. Lanham, MD: Lexington Books.

Raftery-Helmer, J. N., Moore, P. S., Coyne, L., & Reed, K. P. (2016). Changing problematic parent–child interaction in child anxiety disorders: The promise of Acceptance and Commitment Therapy (ACT). *Journal of Contextual Behavioral Science, 5*(1), 64–69. doi:10.1016/j.jcbs.2015.08.002

Raghavan, R., Riley, A., Caruso, D. M., Hong, X., Wang2, G., Ajao, B., ... Wang, X. (2016). *Maternal plasma folate, Vitamin B12 levels and multivitamin supplement during pregnancy and risk of autism spectrum disorders in the Boston Birth Cohort*. Paper presented at the 2016 International Meeting for Autism Research, Baltimore, MD, US. https://imfar.confex.com/imfar/2016/webprogram/Paper22533.html

Raguram, R., & Weiss, M. (2004). Stigma and somatisation. *The British Journal of Psychiatry, 185*(2), 174–174. doi:10.1192/bjp.185.2.174

Raguram, R., Weiss, M. G., Channabasavanna, S. M., & Devins, G. M. (1996). Stigma, depression, and somatization in South India. *The American Journal of Psychiatry, 153*(8), 1043–1049.

Rais, M., Cahn, W., Schnack, H. G., Pol, H. E. H., Kahn, R. S., & van Haren, N. E. M. (2012). Brain volume reductions in medication-naive patients with schizophrenia in relation to intelligence quotient. *Psychological Medicine, 42*(9), 1847–1856. doi:10.1017/S0033291712000098

Raising Children Network. (2016, July 19). About sleep. Retrieved from http://raisingchildren.net.au/articles/sleep_the_hows_and_whys.html

Ramirez-Bermudez, J. (2012). Alzheimer's disease: Critical notes on the history of a medical concept. *Archives of Medical Research, 43*(8), 595–599. doi:10.1016/j.arcmed.2012.11.008

Ramnani, N., & Owen, A. M. (2004). Anterior prefrontal cortex: Insights into function from anatomy and neuroimaging. *Nature Reviews Neuroscience, 5*(3), 184–194. doi:10.1038/nrn1343

Ramo, D. E., Grov, C., & Parsons, J. T. (2013). Ecstasy/MDMA. In P. M. Miller, S. A. Ball, M. E. Bates, A. W. Blume, K. M. Kampman, D. J. Kavanagh, M. E. Larimer, N. M. Petry, & P. De Witte (Eds.), *Comprehensive addictive behaviors and disorders: Vol. 1. Principles of addiction* (pp. 711–721). San Diego, CA: Elsevier Academic Press.

Ramsay, J. R. (2010). CBT for adult ADHD: Adaptations and hypothesized mechanisms of change. *Journal of Cognitive Psychotherapy, 24*(1), 37–45. doi:10.1891/0889-8391.24.1.37

Ramsay, J. R. (2017). The relevance of cognitive distortions in the psychosocial treatment of adult ADHD. *Professional Psychology: Research and Practice, 48*(1), 62–69. doi:10.1037/pro0000101

Ramsay, M. C., & Reynolds, C. R. (2004). Relations between intelligence and achievement tests. In G. Goldstein & S. R. Beers (Eds.), *Comprehensive handbook of psychological assessment: Vol. 1. Intellectual and neuropsychological assessment* (pp. 25–50). Hoboken, NJ: John Wiley.

Randløv, C., Mehlsen, J., Thomsen, C. F., Hedman, C., von Fircks, H., & Winther, K. (2006). The efficacy of St. John's Wort in patients with minor depressive symptoms or dysthymia – a double-blind placebo-controlled study. *Phytomedicine, 13*(4), 215–221. doi:http://dx.doi.org/10.1016/j.phymed.2005.11.006

Range, L. M., Campbell, C., Kovac, S. H., Marion-Jones, M., & Aldridge, H. (2002). No-suicide contracts: An overview and recommendations. *Death Studies, 26*(1), 51–74. doi:10.1080/07481180210147

Ranta, K., Kaltiala-Heino, R., Pelkonen, M., & Marttunen, M. (2009). Associations between peer victimization, self-reported depression and social phobia among adolescents: The role of comorbidity. *Journal of Adolescence, 32*(1), 77–93. doi:http://dx.doi.org/10.1016/j.adolescence.2007.11.005

Rao, N. P., Venkatasubramanian, G., Ravi, V., Kalmady, S., Cherian, A., & Yc, J. R. (2015). Plasma cytokine abnormalities in drug-naïve, comorbidity-free obsessive-compulsive disorder. *Psychiatry Research, 229*(3), 949–952. doi:10.1016/j.psychres.2015.07.009

Rao, T. S. S., & Andrade, C. (2011). The MMR vaccine and autism: Sensation, refutation, retraction, and fraud. *Indian Journal of Psychiatry, 53*(2), 95–96. doi:10.4103/0019-5545.82529

Rapp, C., Walter, A., Studerus, E., Bugra, H., Tamagni, C., Röthlisberger, M., ... Riecher-Rössler, A. (2013). Cannabis use and brain structural alterations of the cingulate cortex in early psychosis. *Psychiatry Research: Neuroimaging, 214*(2), 102–108. doi:10.1016/j.pscychresns.2013.06.006

Rash, C. J., & Petry, N. M. (2014). Psychological treatments for gambling disorder. *Psychology Research and Behavior Management, 7.*

Raskin, J. D. (2013). Can evolutionary theory help us define mental disorder? Retrieved from https://www.saybrook.edu/newexistentialists/posts/01-04-13

Raskin, J. D. (2014). A critical look at social justice ideology in counseling and psychotherapy. In C. V. Johnson, H. L. Friedman, J. Diaz, Z. Franco, & B. K. Nastasi (Eds.), *The Praeger handbook of social justice and psychology: Vol. 1. Fundamental issues and special populations* (pp. 51–64). Santa Barbara, CA: Praeger.

Raskin, J. D., & Bridges, S. K. (Eds.). (2008). *Studies in meaning 3: Constructivist psychotherapy in the real world.* New York, NY: Pace University Press.

Rasmussen, S. A. (1993). Genetic studies of obsessive-compulsive disorder. *Annals of Clinical Psychiatry, 5*(4), 241–247. doi:10.3109/10401239309148823

Rauch, S., & Foa, E. (2006). Emotional processing theory (EPT) and exposure therapy for PTSD. *Journal of Contemporary Psychotherapy, 36*(2), 61–65. doi:10.1007/s10879-006-9008-y

Rauch, S. A. M., Eftekhari, A., & Ruzek, J. I. (2012). Review of exposure therapy: a gold standard for PTSD treatment. *Journal of Rehabilitation Research and Development, 49*(5), 679–687.

Raven, M., & Parry, P. (2012). Psychotropic marketing practices and problems: Implications for DSM-5. *Journal of Nervous and Mental Disease, 200*(6), 512–516.

Ravindran, A. V., Balneaves, L. G., Faulkner, G., Ortiz, A., McIntosh, D., Morehouse, R. L., ... Parikh, S. V. (2016). Canadian Network for Mood and Anxiety Treatments (CANMAT) 2016 clinical guidelines for the management of adults with major depressive disorder: Section 5. Complementary and alternative medicine treatments. *The Canadian Journal of Psychiatry / La Revue Canadienne De Psychiatrie, 61*(9), 576–587. doi:10.1177/0706743716660290

Ray, D. C., & Jayne, K. M. (2016). Humanistic psychotherapy with children. In D. J. Cain, K. Keenan, & S. Rubin (Eds.), *Humanistic psychotherapies: Handbook of research and practice* (2nd ed., pp. 387–417). Washington, DC: American Psychological Association.

Ray, D. C., Armstrong, S. A., Balkin, R. S., & Jayne, K. M. (2015). Child-centered play therapy in the schools: Review and meta-analysis. *Psychology in the Schools, 52*(2), 107–123. doi:10.1002/pits.21798

Ray, D. C., Blanco, P. J., Sullivan, J. M., & Holliman, R. (2009). An exploratory study of child-centered play therapy with aggressive children. *International Journal of Play Therapy, 18*(3), 162–175. doi:10.1037/a0014742

Ray, D. C., Lee, K. R., Meany-Walen, K. K., Carlson, S. E., Carnes-Holt, K. L., & Ware, J. N. (2013). Use of toys in child-centered play therapy. *International Journal of Play Therapy, 22*(1), 43–57. doi:10.1037/a0031430

Ray, D. C., Schottelkorb, A., & Tsai, M.-H. (2007). Play therapy with children exhibiting symptoms of attention deficit hyperactivity disorder. *International Journal of Play Therapy, 16*(2), 95–111. doi:10.1037/1555-6824.16.2.95

Ray, D. C., Sullivan, J. M., & Carlson, S. E. (2012). Relational intervention: Child-centered play therapy with children on the autism spectrum. In L. Gallo-Lopez & L. C. Rubin (Eds.), *Play-based interventions for children and adolescents with autism spectrum disorders* (pp. 159–175). New York, NY: Routledge.

Read, J. (2013). Does "schizophrenia" exist? Reliability and validity. In J. Read & J. Dillon (Eds.), *Models of madness: Psychological, social and biological approaches to psychosis* (2nd ed., pp. 47–61). London, UK: Routledge.

Read, J., & Dillon, J. (Eds.). (2013). *Models of madness: Psychological, social and biological approaches to psychosis* (2nd ed.). London, UK: Routledge.

Reay, B., Attwood, N., & Gooder, C. (2013). Inventing sex: The short history of sex addiction. *Sexuality & Culture: An Interdisciplinary Quarterly, 17*(1), 1–19. doi:10.1007/s12119-012-9136-3

Redondo, R. L., Kim, J., Arons, A. L., Ramirez, S., Liu, X., & Tonegawa, S. (2014). Bidirectional switch of the valence associated with a hippocampal contextual memory engram. *Nature, 513*(7518), 426–430. doi:10.1038/nature13725

Reed, G. M. (2010). Toward ICD-11: Improving the clinical utility of WHO's international classification of mental disorders. *Professional Psychology: Research and Practice, 41*, 457–464. doi:19.1037/a0021701

Reed, G. M., Drescher, J., Krueger, R. B., Atalla, E., Cochran, S. D., First, M. B., ... Saxena, S. (2016). Disorders related to sexuality and gender identity in the ICD-11: Revising the ICD-10 classification based on current scientific evidence, best clinical practices, and human rights considerations. *World Psychiatry, 15*(3), 205–221. doi:10.1002/wps.20354

Reed, M. D., & Findling, R. L. (2002). Overview of current management of sleep disturbances in children: I—Pharmacotherapy. *Current Therapeutic Research, 63*(SuppIB), B18–B37. doi:10.1016/S0011-393X(02)80101-1

Reed, P., Vile, R., Osborne, L. A., Romano, M., & Truzoli, R. (2015). Problematic Internet usage and immune function. *PLOS One, 10*(8).

References for intention not to retain Neurasthenia for ICD-11. (2015, January 13). Retrieved from https://dxrevisionwatch.com/2015/01/13/references-for-intention-not-to-retain-neurasthenia-for-icd-11/

Regier, D. A., Narrow, W. E., Clarke, D. E., Kraemer, H. C., Kuramoto, S. J., Kuhl, E. A., & Kupfer, D. J. (2013). DSM-5 field trials in the United States and Canada, part II: Test-retest reliability of selected categorical diagnoses. *The American Journal of Psychiatry, 170*(1), 59–70. doi:10.1176/appi.ajp.2012.12070999

Rehbein, F., Kühn, S., Rumpf, H.-J., & Petry, N. M. (2016). Internet gaming disorder: A new behavioral addiction. In N. M. Petry (Ed.), *Behavioral addictions: DSM-5® and beyond.* (pp. 43–69). New York, NY: Oxford University Press.

Rehm, J., Taylor, B., Mohapatra, S., Irving, H., Baliunas, D., Patra, J., & Roerecke, M. (2010). Alcohol as a risk factor for liver cirrhosis: a systematic review and meta-analysis. *Drug and Alcohol Review, 29*(4), 437–445. doi:10.1111/j.1465-3362.2009.00153.x

Reich, W. (1945). *Character analysis* (V. R. Carfagno, Trans. M. Higgins & C. M. Raphael Eds. 3rd ed.). New York, NY: Farar, Straus and Giroux.

Reichborn-Kjennerud, T. (2010). The genetic epidemiology of personality disorders. *Dialogues in Clinical Neuroscience, 12*(1), 103–114.

Reichborn-Kjennerud, T., Czajkowski, N., Neale, M. C., Ørstavik, R. E., Torgersen, S., Tambs, K., ... Kendler, K. S. (2007). Genetic and environmental influences on dimensional representations of DSM-IV cluster C personality disorders: A population-based multivariate twin study. *Psychological Medicine, 37*(5), 645–653. doi:10.1017/S0033291706009548

Reid, R. C., Carpenter, B. N., Hook, J. N., Garos, S., Manning, J. C., Gilliland, R., ... Fong, T. (2012). Report of findings in a DSM-5 field trial for hypersexual disorder. *Journal of Sexual Medicine, 9*(11), 2868–2877. doi:10.1111/j.1743-6109.2012.02936.x

Reilly-Harrington, N. A., Roberts, S., & Sylvia, L. G. (2015). Family-focused therapy, interpersonal and social rhythm therapy, and dialectical behavioral therapy. In A. Yildiz, P. Ruiz, & C. B. Nemeroff (Eds.), *The bipolar book: History, neurobiology, and treatment* (pp. 445–453). New York, NY: Oxford University Press.

Reinares, M., Sánchez-Moreno, J., & Fountoulakis, K. N. (2014). Psychosocial interventions in bipolar disorder: What, for whom, and when. *Journal of Affective Disorders, 156*, 46–55. doi:10.1016/j.jad.2013.12.017

Reinders, A. A. T. S. (2008). Cross-examining dissociative identity disorder: Neuroimaging and etiology on trial. *Neurocase, 14*(1), 44–53. doi:10.1080/13554790801992768

Reinecke, M. A., & Freeman, A. (2003). Cognitive therapy. In A. S. Gurman & S. B. Messer (Eds.), *Essential psychotherapies: Theory and practice* (2nd ed., pp. 224–271). New York, NY: Guilford.

Reininghaus, U., Craig, T. K. J., Fisher, H. L., Hutchinson, G., Fearon, P., Morgan, K., ... Morgan, C. (2010). Ethnic identity, perceptions of disadvantage, and psychosis: Findings from the ÆSOP study. *Schizophrenia Research, 124*(1–3), 43–48. doi:10.1016/j.schres.2010.08.038

Reininghaus, U., Priebe, S., & Bentall, R. P. (2013). Testing the psychopathology of psychosis: Evidence for a general psychosis dimension. *Schizophrenia Bulletin, 39*(4), 884–895. doi:10.1093/schbul/sbr182

Reis, S., & Grenyer, B. F. S. (2002). Pathways to anaclitic and introjective depression. *Psychology and Psychotherapy: Theory, Research and Practice, 75*(4), 445–459. doi:10.1348/147608302321151934

Reitan, R. M., & Wolfson, D. (2004). Theoretical, methodological, and validational bases of the Halstead-Reitan Neuropsychological Test Battery. In G. Goldstein & S. R. Beers (Eds.), *Comprehensive handbook of psychological assessment: Vol. 1. Intellectual and neuropsychological assessment* (pp. 105–131). Hoboken, NJ: John Wiley.

Resick, P. A., & Schnicke, M. K. (1992). Cognitive processing therapy for sexual assault victims. *Journal of Consulting and Clinical Psychology, 60*(5), 748–756. doi:10.1037/0022-006X.60.5.748

Retraction—Ileal-lymphoid-nodular hyperplasia, non-specific colitis, and pervasive developmental disorder in children. (2010). *The Lancet, 375*(9713), 445–445. doi:10.1016/S0140-6736(10)60175-4

Reynaud, E., Guedj, E., Trousselard, M., El Khoury-Malhame, M., Zendjidjian, X., Fakra, E., ... Khalfa, S. (2015). Acute stress disorder modifies cerebral activity of amygdala and prefrontal cortex. *Cognitive Neuroscience, 6*(1), 39–43. doi:10.1080/17588928.2014.996212

Reynolds, T., Winegard, B. M., Baumeister, R. F., & Maner, J. K. (2015). The long goodbye: A test of grief as a social signal. *Evolutionary Behavioral Sciences, 9*(1), 20–42. doi:10.1037/ebs0000032

Ricciardelli, L. A., McCabe, M. P., Williams, R. J., & Thompson, J. K. (2007). The role of ethnicity and culture in body image and disordered eating among males. *Clinical Psychology Review, 27*(5), 582–606. doi:http://dx.doi.org/10.1016/j.cpr.2007.01.016

Richard Freiherr von Krafft-Ebing. (2008). *New World Encyclopedia*: Retrieved from http://www.newworldencyclopedia.org/p/index.php?title=Richard_Freiherr_von_Krafft-Ebing&oldid=680959

Richards, D. G. (1990). Dissociation and transformation. *Journal of Humanistic Psychology, 30*(3), 54–83. doi:10.1177/0022167890303004

Richardson, F. C., & Manaster, G. J. (2003). Social interest, emotional well-being, and the quest for civil society. *The Journal of Individual Psychology, 59*(2), 123–135.

Rief, W., Pilger, F., Ihle, D., Verkerkd, R., Scharpe, S., & Maes, M. (2004). Psychobiological aspects of somatoform disorders: Contributions of monoaminergic transmitter systems. *Neuropsychobiology, 49*(1), 24–29. doi:10.1159/000075335

Riemann, D., Spiegelhalder, K., Feige, B., Voderholzer, U., Berger, M., Perlis, M., & Nissen, C. (2010). The hyperarousal model of insomnia: A review of the concept and its evidence. *Sleep Medicine Reviews, 14*(1), 19–31. doi:10.1016/j.smrv.2009.04.002

Rigler, T., Manor, I., Kalansky, A., Shorer, Z., Noyman, I., & Sadaka, Y. (2016). New DSM-5 criteria for ADHD—Does it matter? *Comprehensive Psychiatry, 68*, 56–59. doi:10.1016/j.comppsych.2016.03.008

Rigter, H., Henderson, C. E., Pelc, I., Tossmann, P., Phan, O., Hendriks, V., ... Rowe, C. L. (2013). Multidimensional family therapy lowers the rate of cannabis dependence in adolescents: A randomised controlled trial in Western European outpatient settings. *Drug and Alcohol Dependence, 130*(1–3), 85–93. doi:10.1016/j.drugalcdep.2012.10.013

Rigter, H., Pelc, I., Tossmann, P., Phan, O., Grichting, E., Hendriks, V., & Rowe, C. (2010). INCANT: A transnational randomized trial of Multidimensional Family Therapy versus treatment as usual for adolescents with cannabis use disorder. *BMC Psychiatry, 10*. doi:10.1186/1471-244X-10-28

Rimland, B. (1964). *Infantile autism: The syndrome and its implications for a neural theory of behavior.* New York, NY: Appleton-Century-Crofts.

Ringuette, E. L. (1982). Double binds, schizophrenics, and psychological theory: Letters from mothers of schizophrenic and nonschizophrenic patients. *Psychological Reports, 51*(3, Pt 1), 693–694. doi:10.2466/pr0.1982.51.3.693

Ripke, S., O'Dushlaine, C., Chambert, K., Moran, J. L., Kähler, A. K., Akterin, S., ... Sullivan, P. F. (2013). Genome-wide association analysis identifies 13 new risk loci for schizophrenia. *Nature Genetics, 45*(10), 1150–1159. doi:10.1038/ng.2742

Ripoll, L. H., Triebwasser, J., & Siever, L. J. (2011). Evidence-based pharmacotherapy for personality disorders. *International Journal of Neuropsychopharmacology, 14*(9), 1257–1288. doi:10.1017/S1461145711000071

Rissmiller, D. J., & Rissmiller, J. H. (2006). Evolution of the antipsychiatry movement into mental health consumerism. *Psychiatric Services, 57*(6), 863–866. doi:10.1176/appi.ps.57.6.863

Ritvo, P., Lewis, M. D., Irvine, J., Brown, L., Matthew, A., & Shaw, B. F. (2003). The application of cognitive-behavioral therapy in the treatment of substance abuse. *Primary Psychiatry, 10*(5), 72–77.

Rizvi, S., & Zaretsky, A. E. (2007). Psychotherapy through the phases of bipolar disorder: Evidence for general efficacy and differential effects. *Journal of Clinical Psychology, 63*(5), 491–506. doi:10.1002/jclp.20370

ROAD. (n.d.). Retrieved from https://www.google.com/url?sa=t&rct=j&q=&esrc=s&source=web&cd=10&ved=0ahUKEwi16ejMt9TVAhWK7iYKHSfsATgQFghTMAk&url=http%3A%2F%2Fnned.net%2Fdocs-general%2FROAD.doc&usg=AFQjCNG405DS-T4KSX6_pO_OsTRmLSuRRg

ROAD* Reaching out about depression. (n.d.). Retrieved from https://www.cctvcambridge.org/node/4559

Robbins, B. D., Kamens, S. R., & Elkins, D. N. (2017). DSM-5 reform efforts by the Society for Humanistic Psychology. *Journal of Humanistic Psychology,* Advance online publication. doi:10.1177/0022167817698617

Roberto, C. A., Mayer, L. E., Brickman, A. M., Barnes, A., Muraskin, J., Yeung, L. K., ... Stern, Y. (2011). Brain tissue volume changes following weight gain in adults with anorexia nervosa. *International Journal of Eating Disorders, 44*. doi:10.1002/eat.20840

Roberts, M. C., & Evans, S. C. (2013). Using the *International Classification of Diseases* system (*ICD-10*). In G. P. Koocher, J. C. Norcross, & B. A. Greene (Eds.), *Psychologists' desk reference* (3rd ed., pp. 71–76). Oxford, UK: Oxford University Press.

Roberts, N. P., Roberts, P. A., Jones, N., & Bisson, J. I. (2015). Psychological interventions for post-traumatic stress disorder and comorbid substance use disorder: A systematic review and meta-analysis. *Clinical Psychology Review, 38*, 25–38. doi:10.1016/j.cpr.2015.02.007

Robertson, C. E., Ratai, E.-M., & Kanwisher, N. (2016). Reduced GABAergic action in the autistic brain. *Current Biology, 26*(1), 80–85. doi:10.1016/j.cub.2015.11.019

Robertson, M. M., Cavanna, A. E., & Eapen, V. (2015). Gilles de la Tourette syndrome and disruptive behavior disorders: Prevalence, associations, and explanation of the relationships. *The Journal of Neuropsychiatry and Clinical Neurosciences, 27*(1), 33–41. doi:10.1176/appi.neuropsych.13050112

Robins, E., & Guze, S. B. (1970). Establishment of diagnostic validity in psychiatric illness: Its application to schizophrenia. *The American Journal of Psychiatry, 126*(7), 983–986.

Robinson, A. L., Dolhanty, J., & Greenberg, L. (2015). Emotion-focused family therapy for eating disorders in children and adolescents. *Clinical Psychology & Psychotherapy, 22*(1), 75–82. doi:10.1002/cpp.1861

Robinson, A. L., McCague, E. A., & Whissell, C. (2014). 'That chair work thing was great': A pilot study of group-based emotion-focused therapy for anxiety and depression. *Person-Centered and Experiential Psychotherapies, 13*(4), 263–277. doi:10.1080/14779757.2014.910131

Robinson, D. N. (1996). *Wild beasts & idle humours: The insanity defense from antiquity to the present.* Cambridge, MA: Harvard University Press.

Robinson, J., Cox, G., Bailey, E., Hetrick, S., Rodrigues, M., Fisher, S., & Herrman, H. (2016). Social media and suicide prevention: A systematic review. *Early Intervention in Psychiatry, 10*(2), 103–121. doi:10.1111/eip.12229

Robinson, J. S., Larson, C. L., & Cahill, S. P. (2014). Relations between resilience, positive and negative emotionality, and symptoms of anxiety and depression. *Psychological Trauma: Theory, Research, Practice, and Policy, 6*(Suppl 1), S92–S98. doi:10.1037/a0033733

Robinson, T. E., & Berridge, K. C. (1993). The neural basis of drug craving: An incentive-sensitization theory of addiction. *Brain Research. Brain Research Reviews, 18*(3), 247–291.

Roehrig, J. P., & McLean, C. P. (2010). A comparison of stigma toward eating disorders versus depression. *International Journal of Eating Disorders, 43*(7), 671–674. doi:10.1002/eat.20760

Roessner, V., Plessen, K. J., Rothenberger, A., Ludolph, A. G., Rizzo, R., Skov, L., ... Hoekstra, P. J. (2011). European clinical guidelines for Tourette syndrome and other tic disorders. Part II: Pharmacological treatment. *European Child & Adolescent Psychiatry, 20*(4), 173–196. doi:10.1007/s00787-011-0163-7

Roessner, V., Schoenefeld, K., Buse, J., Bender, S., Ehrlich, S., & Münchau, A. (2013). Pharmacological treatment of tic disorders and Tourette Syndrome. *Neuropharmacology, 68*, 143–149. doi:10.1016/j.neuropharm.2012.05.043

Rogalin, M. T., & Nencini, A. (2015). Consequences of the 'Attention-Deficit/Hyperactivity Disorder' (ADHD) diagnosis. An investigation with education professionals. *Psychological Studies, 60*(1), 41–49. doi:10.1007/s12646-014-0288-0

Rogers, B., Stratton, P., Victor, J., Kennedy, B., & Andres, M. (1992). Chronic regurgitation among persons with mental retardation: A need for combined medical and interdisciplinary strategies. *American Journal on Mental Retardation, 96*(5), 522–527.

Rogers, C. R. (1951). *Client-centered therapy.* London, UK: Constable.

Rogers, C. R. (1959). A theory of therapy, personality, and interpersonal relationships, as developed in the client-centered framework. In S. Koch (Ed.), *Psychology: A study of science: Vol. 3. Formulations of the person and the social contact* (pp. 184–256). New York, NY: McGraw-Hill.

Rogers, C. R. (1961). *On becoming a person.* Boston, MA: Houghton Mifflin.

Rogers, C. R. (1967). *The therapeutic relationship and its impact: A study of psychotherapy with schizophrenics.* Oxford, UK: University of Wisconsin Press.

Rogers, J. R., & Soyka, K. M. (2004). 'One size fits all': An existential-constructivist perspective on the crisis intervention approach with suicidal individuals. *Journal of Contemporary Psychotherapy, 34*(1), 7–22. doi:10.1023/B:JOCP.0000010910.74165.3a

Rogers, J. R., Bromley, J. L., McNally, C. J., & Lester, D. (2007). Content analysis of suicide notes as a test of the motivational component of the existential-constructivist model of suicide. *Journal of Counseling & Development, 85*(2), 182–188. doi:10.1002/j.1556-6678.2007.tb00461.x

Rogers, T. P., Blackwood, N. J., Farnham, F., Pickup, G. J., & Watts, M. J. (2008). Fitness to plead and competence to stand trial: A systematic review of the constructs and their application. *Journal of Forensic Psychiatry & Psychology, 19*(4), 576–596. doi:10.1080/14789940801947909

Rohlof, H. G., Knipscheer, J. W., & Kleber, R. J. (2014). Somatization in refugees: A review. *Social Psychiatry and Psychiatric Epidemiology, 49*(11), 1793–1804. doi:10.1007/s00127-014-0877-1

Röhricht, F. (2009). Body oriented psychotherapy. The state of the art in empirical research and evidence-based practice: A clinical perspective. *Body, Movement and Dance in Psychotherapy, 4*(2), 135–156. doi:10.1080/17432970902857263

Röhricht, F. (2015). Body psychotherapy for the treatment of severe mental disorders—An overview. *Body, Movement and Dance in Psychotherapy, 10*(1), 51–67. doi:10.1080/17432979.2014.962093

Roiser, J. P., Stephan, K. E., den Ouden, H. E. M., Barnes, T. R. E., Friston, K. J., & Joyce, E. M. (2009). Do patients with schizophrenia exhibit aberrant salience? *Psychological Medicine, 39*(2), 199–209. doi:10.1017/S0033291708003863

Rolf, C. (2006). From M'Naghten to Yates – Transformation of the insanity defense in the United States – Is it still viable? *Rivier College Online Academic Journal, 2*(1). Retrieved from https://www.rivier.edu/journal/ROAJ-2006-Spring/J41-ROLF.pdf

Rolka, E. J., & Silverman, M. J. (2015). A systematic review of music and dyslexia. *The Arts in Psychotherapy, 46*, 24–32. doi:10.1016/j.aip.2015.09.002

Roll, J. M. (2007). Contingency management: An evidence-based component of methamphetamine use disorder treatments. *Addiction, 102*(Suppl 1), 114–120. doi:10.1111/j.1360-0443.2006.01774.x

Rollins, D. A. (2007). *Gender and ethnicity referral bias for ADHD: The school's view.* (67), ProQuest Information & Learning, US. Retrieved from https://libdatabase.newpaltz.edu/login?url=http://search.ebscohost.com/login.aspx?direct=true&db=psyh&AN=2007-99003-002&site=ehost-live Available from EBSCOhost psyh database

Rolls, G. (2015). *Classic case studies in psychology* (3rd ed.). London, UK: Routledge.

Ronald, A., & Hoekstra, R. (2014). Progress in understanding the causes of autism spectrum disorders and autistic traits: Twin studies from 1977 to the present day. In S. H. Rhee & A. Ronald (Eds.), *Behavior genetics of psychopathology* (pp. 33–65). New York, NY: Springer Science + Business Media.

Ronningstam, E. (2011). Psychoanalytic theories on narcissism and narcissistic personality. In W. K. Campbell & J. D. Miller (Eds.), *The handbook of narcissism and narcissistic personality disorder: Theoretical approaches, empirical findings, and treatments.* (pp. 41–55). Hoboken, NJ: John Wiley.

Root, M. P. P. (1992). Reconstructing the impact of trauma on personality. In L. S. Brown & M. Ballou (Eds.), *Personality and psychopathology: Feminist reappraisals* (pp. 229–265). New York, NY: Guilford Press.

Root, T. L., Thornton, L. M., Lindroos, A. K., Stunkard, A. J., Lichtenstein, P., Pedersen, N. L., ... Bulik, C. M. (2010). Shared and unique genetic and environmental influences on binge eating and night eating: A Swedish twin study. *Eating Behaviors, 11*(2), 92–98. doi:10.1016/j.eatbeh.2009.10.004

Rosa, P. G. P., Schaufelberger, M. S., Uchida, R. R., Duran, F. L. S., Lappin, J. M., Menezes, P. R., ... Busatto, G. F. (2010). Lateral ventricle differences between first-episode schizophrenia and first-episode psychotic bipolar disorder: A population-based morphometric MRI study. *The World Journal of Biological Psychiatry, 11*(7-8), 873–887. doi:10.3109/15622975.2010.486042

Rose, S. C., Bisson, J., & Churchill, R. (2002). Psychological debriefing for preventing post traumatic stress disorder (PTSD). *Cochrane Database of Systematic Reviews, 2002*(2), 1–49. doi:10.1002/14651858.CD000560

Rosen, G. M., & Lilienfeld, S. O. (2008). Posttraumatic stress disorder: An empirical evaluation of core assumptions. *Clinical Psychology Review, 28*(5), 837–868. doi:10.1016/j.cpr.2007.12.002

Rosen, K. H. (1998). The family roots of aggression and violence: A life span perspective. In L. L'Abate (Ed.), *Family psychopathology: The relational roots of dysfunctional behavior* (pp. 333–357). New York, NY: Guilford Press.

Rosenbaum, B., Harder, S., Knudsen, P., Køster, A., Lajer, M., Lindhardt, A., ... Winther, G. (2012). Supportive psychodynamic psychotherapy versus treatment as usual for first-episode psychosis: Two-year outcome. *Psychiatry: Interpersonal and Biological Processes, 75*(4), 331–341. doi:10.1521/psyc.2012.75.4.331

Rosenberg, H., & Davis, A. K. (2014). Differences in the acceptability of non-abstinence goals by type of drug among American substance abuse clinicians. *Journal of Substance Abuse Treatment, 46*(2), 214–218. doi:10.1016/j.jsat.2013.07.005

Rosenberg, H., & Melville, J. (2005). Controlled drinking and controlled drug use as outcome goals in British treatment services. *Addiction Research & Theory, 13*(1), 85–92. doi:10.1080/16066350412331314894

Rosenberg, N., Bloch, M., Ben Avi, I., Rouach, V., Schreiber, S., Stern, N., & Greenman, Y. (2013). Cortisol response and desire to binge following psychological stress: Comparison between obese subjects with and without binge eating disorder. *Psychiatry Research, 208*(2), 156–161. doi:http://dx.doi.org/10.1016/j.psychres.2012.09.050

Rosenberg, R. E., Law, J. K., Yenokyan, G., McGready, J., Kaufmann, W. E., & Law, P. A. (2009). Characteristics and concordance of autism spectrum disorders among 277 twin pairs. *Archives of Pediatrics & Adolescent Medicine, 163*(10), 907–914. doi:10.1001/archpediatrics.2009.98

Rosenblat, J. D., Brietzke, E., Mansur, R. B., Maruschak, N. A., Lee, Y., & McIntyre, R. S. (2015). Inflammation as a neurobiological substrate of cognitive impairment in bipolar disorder: Evidence, pathophysiology and treatment implications. *Journal of Affective Disorders, 188*, 149–159. doi:http://dx.doi.org/10.1016/j.jad.2015.08.058

Rosenblatt, P. C. (2008). Grief across cultures: A review and research agenda. In M. S. Stroebe, R. O. Hansson, H. Schut, & W. Stroebe (Eds.), *Handbook of bereavement research and practice: Advances in theory and intervention* (pp. 207–222). Washington, DC: American Psychological Association.

Rosenblum, A., Marsch, L. A., Joseph, H., & Portenoy, R. K. (2008). Opioids and the treatment of chronic pain: Controversies, current status, and future directions. *Experimental and Clinical Psychopharmacology, 16*(5), 405–416. doi:10.1037/a0013628

Rosenhan, D. L. (1973). On being sane in insane places. *Science, 179*(4070), 250–258. doi:10.1126/science.179.4070.250

Rosenheck, R. (2013). Second generation antipsychotics: Evolution of scientific knowledge or uncovering fraud. *Epidemiology and Psychiatric Sciences, 22*(3), 235–237. doi:10.1017/S2045796012000662

Rosenman, R. H. (1991). Type A behavior pattern and coronary heart disease: The hostility factor? *Stress Medicine, 7*(4), 245–253. doi:10.1002/smi.2460070407

Rosenman, R. H., & Friedman, M. (1961). Association of specific behavior pattern in women with blood and cardiovascular findings. *Circulation, 24*, 1173–1184. doi:10.1161/01.CIR.24.5.1173

Rosenthal, R. J., & Rugle, L. J. (1994). A psychodynamic approach to the treatment of pathological gambling: Part I. Achieving abstinence. *Journal of Gambling Studies, 10*(1), 21–42. doi:10.1007/BF02109777

Roshanaei-Moghaddam, B., Pauly, M. C., Atkins, D. C., Baldwin, S. A., Stein, M. B., & Roy-Byrne, P. (2011). Relative effects of CBT and pharmacotherapy in depression versus anxiety: Is medication somewhat better for depression, and CBT somewhat better for anxiety? *Depression and Anxiety, 28*(7), 560–567. doi:10.1002/da.20829

Rosin, H. (2014, March). Letting go of Asperger's. *The Atlantic*.

Ross, C. A. (1991). Epidemiology of multiple personality disorder and dissociation. *Psychiatric Clinics of North America, 14*(3), 503–517.

Ross, C. A. (2006). Overestimates of the genetic contribution to eating disorders. *Ethical Human Psychology and Psychiatry, 8*(2), 123–131. doi:10.1891/ehpp.8.2.123

Ross, C. A. (2008). Dissociative schizophrenia. In A. Moskowitz, I. Schäfer, & M. J. Dorahy (Eds.), *Psychosis, trauma and dissociation: Emerging perspectives on severe psychopathology* (pp. 281–294). Chichester, UK: Wiley-Blackwell.

Ross, C. A. (2009). Errors of logic and scholarship concerning dissociative identity disorder. *Journal of Child Sexual Abuse: Research, Treatment, & Program Innovations for Victims, Survivors, & Offenders, 18*(2), 221–231. doi:10.1080/10538710902743982

Ross, C. A. (2013a). Biology and genetics in DSM-5. *Ethical Human Psychology and Psychiatry, 15*(3), 195–198. doi:10.1891/1559-4343.15.3.195

Ross, C. A. (2013b). 'The rise and persistence of dissociative identity disorder': Comment. *Journal of Trauma & Dissociation, 14*(5), 584–588. doi:10.1080/15299732.2013.785464

Ross, C. A. (2014). The equal environments assumption in schizophrenia genetics. *Psychosis: Psychological, Social and Integrative Approaches, 6*(2), 189–191. doi:10.1080/17522439.2013.773365

Ross, C. A. (2015). Commentary: Problems with the sexual disorders sections of DSM-5. *Journal of Child Sexual Abuse, 24*(2), 195–201. doi:10.1080/10538712.2015.997411

Ross, C. A., & Goldner, E. M. (2009). Stigma, negative attitudes and discrimination towards mental illness within the nursing profession: A review of the literature. *Journal of Psychiatric and Mental Health Nursing, 16*(6), 558–567. doi:10.1111/j.1365-2850.2009.01399.x

Ross, D. M. (1984). Thought-stopping: A coping strategy for impending feared events. *Issues in Comprehensive Pediatric Nursing, 7*(2–3), 83–89. doi:10.3109/01460868409009046

Ross, M. J., & Berger, R. S. (1996). Effects of stress inoculation training on athletes' postsurgical pain and rehabilitation after orthopedic injury. *Journal of Consulting and Clinical Psychology, 64*(2), 406–410. doi:10.1037/0022-006X.64.2.406

Ross, M. W., Daneback, K., & Månsson, S.-A. (2012). Fluid versus fixed: A new perspective on bisexuality as a fluid sexual orientation beyond gender. *Journal of Bisexuality, 12*(4), 449–460. doi:10.1080/15299716.2012.702609

Ross, S. (2008). Ketamine and addiction. *Primary Psychiatry, 15*(9), 61–69.

Rossetti, C., Halfon, O., & Boutrel, B. (2014). Controversies about a common etiology for eating and mood disorders. *Frontiers In Psychology, 5*.

Rossi, G., Balottin, U., Rossi, M., Chiappedi, M., Fazzi, E., & Lanzi, G. (2007). Pharmacological treatment of anorexia nervosa: A retrospective study in preadolescents and adolescents. *Clinical Pediatrics, 46*(9), 806–811. doi:10.1177/0009922807303929

Rossignol, D. A., & Frye, R. E. (2012). A review of research trends in physiological abnormalities in autism spectrum disorders: Immune dysregulation, inflammation, oxidative stress, mitochondrial dysfunction and environmental toxicant exposures. *Molecular Psychiatry, 17*(4), 389–401. doi:10.1038/mp.2011.165

Rossini, E. D., & Moretti, R. J. (1997). Thematic Apperception Test (TAT) interpretation: Practice recommendations from a survey of clinical psychology doctoral programs accredited by the American Psychological Association. *Professional Psychology: Research and Practice, 28*(4), 393–398. doi:10.1037/0735-7028.28.4.393

Rossow, I., Felix, L., Keating, P., & McCambridge, J. (2016). Parental drinking and adverse outcomes in children: A scoping review of cohort studies. *Drug and Alcohol Review, 35*(4), 397–405. doi:10.1111/dar.12319

Rousseau, J. J. (1810). On suicide. Retrieved from http://www.sophia-project.org/uploads/1/3/9/5/13955288/rousseau_suicide.pdf

Rousseau, S., Grietens, H., Vanderfaeillie, J., Ceulemans, E., Hoppenbrouwers, K., Desoete, A., & Van Leeuwen, K. (2014). The distinction of 'psychosomatogenic family types' based on parents' self reported questionnaire information: A cluster analysis. *Families, Systems, & Health, 32*(2), 207–218. doi:10.1037/fsh0000031

Roussos, P., & Siever, L. J. (2012). Neurobiological contributions. In T. A. Widiger (Ed.), *The Oxford handbook of personality disorders* (pp. 299–324). New York, NY: Oxford University Press.

Rowan, K., McAlpine, D., & Blewett, L. (2013). Access and cost barriers to mental health care by insurance status, 1999 to 2010. *Health Affairs, 32*(10), 1723–1730. doi:10.1377/hlthaff.2013.0133

Rowe, C., Liddle, H. A., McClintic, K., & Quille, T. J. (2002). Integrative treatment development: Multidimensional family therapy for adolescent substance abuse. In F. W. Kaslow (Ed.), *Comprehensive handbook of psychotherapy: Integrative/eclectic* (Vol. 4, pp. 133–161). Hoboken, NJ: John Wiley.

Rowe, C. L. (2012). Family therapy for drug abuse: Review and updates 2003–2010. *Journal of Marital and Family Therapy, 38*(1), 59–81. doi:10.1111/j.1752-0606.2011.00280.x

Rowland, D. L. (2012). *Sexual dysfunction in men.* Cambridge, MA: Hogrefe.

Roy, A. K., Lopes, V., & Klein, R. G. (2014). Disruptive mood dysregulation disorder: A new diagnostic approach to chronic irritability in youth. *The American Journal of Psychiatry, 171*(9), 918–924.

Roy, A., Roy, A., & Roy, M. (2012). The human rights of women with intellectual disability. *Journal of the Royal Society of Medicine, 105*(9), 384–389. doi:10.1258/jrsm.2012.110303

Roy, M. J., Costanzo, M. E., Blair, J. R., & Rizzo, A. A. (2014). Compelling evidence that exposure therapy for PTSD normalizes brain function. *Annual Review of CyberTherapy and Telemedicine, 12*, 61–65.

Roy-Byrne, P. P., Craske, M. G., & Stein, M. B. (2006). Panic disorder. *The Lancet, 368*(9540), 1023–1032. doi:10.1016/S0140-6736(06)69418-X

Rubio, J. S., Krieger, M. A., Finney, E. J., & Coker, K. L. (2014). A review of the relationship between sociocultural factors and juvenile psychopathy. *Aggression and Violent Behavior, 19*(1), 23–31. doi:10.1016/j.avb.2013.11.001

Rudd, M. D., Mandrusiak, M., & Joiner, T. E., Jr. (2006). The case against no-suicide contracts: The commitment to treatment statement as a practice alternative. *Journal of Clinical Psychology, 62*(2), 243–251. doi:10.1002/jclp.20227

Rudy, B. M., Storch, E. A., & Lewin, A. B. (2015). When families won't play ball: A case example of the effect of family accommodation on anxiety symptoms and treatment. *Journal of Child and Family Studies, 24*(7), 2070–2078. doi:10.1007/s10826-014-0008-3

Rudy, L. J. (2017, January 31). Asperger syndrome is no longer an official diagnosis, but no one cares. Retrieved from https://www.verywell.com/does-asperger-syndrome-still-exist-259944

Ruiz, M. T., & Verbrugge, L. M. (1997). A two way view of gender bias in medicine. *Journal of Epidemiology and Community Health, 51*(2), 106–109.

Rush, A. J., & Beck, A. T. (1978). Cognitive therapy of depression and suicide. *American Journal of Psychotherapy, 32*(2), 201–219.

Rush, A. J., Trivedi, M. H., Wisniewski, S. R., Nierenberg, A. A., Stewart, J. W., Warden, D., ... Fava, M. (2006). Acute and longer-term outcomes in depressed outpatients requiring one or several treatment steps: A STAR*D report. *The American Journal of Psychiatry, 163*(11), 1905–1917. doi:10.1176/appi.ajp.163.11.1905

Rush, B. (1823). *An inquiry into the effects of ardent spirits on the human body and mind* (8th ed.). Boston, MA: James Loring. (Original work published 1784)

Russ, T. C., Stamatakis, E., Hamer, M., Starr, J. M., Kivimäki, M., & Batty, G. D. (2013). Socioeconomic status as a risk factor for dementia death: individual participant meta-analysis of 86 508 men and women from the UK. *The British Journal of Psychiatry, 203*(1), 10–17. doi:10.1192/bjp.bp.112.119479

Russell, G. (1979). Bulimia nervosa: An ominous variant of anorexia nervosa. *Psychological Medicine, 9*(3), 429–448. doi:10.1017/S0033291700031974

Russell, G. F. M. (2004). Invited article: Thoughts on the 25th anniversary of bulimia nervosa. *European Eating Disorders Review, 12*(3), 139–152. doi:10.1002/erv.575

Russell, G., Rodgers, L. R., Ukoumunne, O. C., & Ford, T. (2014). Prevalence of parent-reported ASD and ADHD in the UK: Findings from the Millennium Cohort Study. *Journal of Autism and Developmental Disorders, 44*(1), 31–40. doi:10.1007/s10803-013-1849-0

Rutherford, A. (2003). Skinner Boxes for Psychotics: Operant Conditioning at Metropolitan State Hospital. *The Behavior Analyst, 26*(2), 267–279.

Rutten, A. (2014). A person-centred approach to counselling clients with autistic process. In P. Pearce & L. Sommerbeck (Eds.), *Person-centred practice at the difficult edge* (pp. 74–87). Ross-on-Wye, UK: PCCS Books.

Ryan, B. P. (2004). Contingency management and stuttering in children. *The Behavior Analyst Today, 5*(2), 144–150. doi:10.1037/h0100026

Ryan, F., O'Dwyer, M., & Leahy, M. M. (2015). Separating the problem and the person: Insights from narrative therapy with people who stutter. *Topics in Language Disorders, 35*(3), 267–274. doi:10.1097/TLD.0000000000000062

Ryan, N. S., Rossor, M. N., & Fox, N. C. (2015). Alzheimer's disease in the 100 years since Alzheimer's death. *Brain: A Journal of Neurology, 138*(Pt 12), 3816–3821. doi:10.1093/brain/awv316

Rybarczyk, B., Lund, H. G., Garroway, A. M., & Mack, L. (2013). Cognitive behavioral therapy for insomnia in older adults: Background, evidence, and overview of treatment protocol. *Clinical Gerontologist: The Journal of Aging and Mental Health, 36*(1), 70–93. doi:10.1080/07317115.2012.731478

Saah, T. (2005). The evolutionary origins and significance of drug addiction. *Harm Reduction Journal, 2*, 8–8. doi:10.1186/1477-7517-2-8

Sacher, J., Neumann, J., Fünfstück, T., Soliman, A., Villringer, A., & Schroeter, M. L. (2012). Mapping the depressed brain: A meta-analysis of structural and functional alterations in major depressive disorder. *Journal of Affective Disorders, 140*(2), 142–148. doi:http://dx.doi.org/10.1016/j.jad.2011.08.001

Sadler, J. Z., & Agich, G. J. (1995). Diseases, functions, values, and psychiatric classification. *Philosophy, Psychiatry, & Psychology, 2*(3), 219–231.

Saeed, S. A., Johnson, T. L., Bagga, M., & Glass, O. (2016). Training residents in the use of telepsychiatry: Review of the literature and a proposed elective. *Psychiatric Quarterly.* doi:10.1007/s11126-016-9470-y

Saks, E. R. (2003). Involuntary outpatient commitment. *Psychology, Public Policy, and Law, 9*(1–2), 94–106. doi:10.1037/1076-8971.9.1-2.94

Sala, M., Perez, J., Soloff, P., di Nemi, S. U., Caverzasi, E., Soares, J. C., & Brambilla, P. (2004). Stress and hippocampal abnormalities in psychiatric disorders. *European Neuropsychopharmacology, 14*(5), 393–405. doi:10.1016/j.euroneuro.2003.12.005

Salamone, J. D., & Correa, M. (2013). Dopamine and food addiction: Lexicon badly needed. *Biological Psychiatry, 73*(9), e15–e24. doi:http://dx.doi.org/10.1016/j.biopsych.2012.09.027

Salcedo, S., Gold, A. K., Sheikh, S., Marcus, P. H., Nierenberg, A. A., Deckersbach, T., & Sylvia, L. G. (2016). Empirically supported psychosocial interventions for bipolar disorder: Current state of the research. *Journal of Affective Disorders, 201*, 203–214. doi:10.1016/j.jad.2016.05.018

Salkovskis, P. M. (1985). Obsessional-compulsive problems: A cognitive-behavioural analysis. *Behaviour Research and Therapy, 23*(5), 571–583. doi:10.1016/0005-7967(85)90105-6

Salkovskis, P. M. (2007). Cognitive-behavioural treatment for panic. *Psychiatry, 6*(5), 193–197. doi:http://dx.doi.org/10.1016/j.mppsy.2007.03.002

Salmon, C., & Crawford, C. (2012). When intersexual conflict leads to intrasexual competition: The reproductive suppression hypothesis. In T. K. Shackleford & A. T. Goetz (Eds.), *The Oxford handbook of sexual conflict in humans* (pp. 134–147). New York, NY: Oxford University Press.

Salmon, C., Crawford, C., Dane, L., & Zuberbier, O. (2008). Ancestral mechanisms in modern environments: Impact of competition and stressors on body image and dieting behavior. *Human Nature, 19*(1), 103–117. doi:10.1007/s12110-008-9030-8

Salmon, M. A. (1975). An historical account of nocturnal enuresis and its treatment. *Proceedings of The Royal Society of Medicine, 68*(7), 443–445.

Salomon, C., & Hamilton, B. (2014). Antipsychotic discontinuation syndromes: A narrative review of the evidence and its integration into Australian mental health nursing textbooks. *International Journal of Mental Health Nursing, 23*(1), 69–78. doi:10.1111/j.1447-0349.2012.00889.x

Salomon, R. M., Miller, H. L., Krystal, J. H., Heninger, G. R., & Charney, D. S. (1997). Lack of behavioral effects of monoamine depletion in healthy subjects. *Biological Psychiatry, 41*(1), 58–64. doi:10.1016/0006-3223(95)00670-2

Salomonsson, B. (2004). Some psychoanalytic viewpoints on neuropsychiatric disorders in children. *The International Journal of Psychoanalysis, 85*(1), 117–136. doi:10.1516/BQYA-14CN-LA29-C4H8

Salomonsson, B. (2011). Psychoanalytic conceptualizations of the internal object in an ADHD child. *Journal of Infant, Child & Adolescent Psychotherapy, 10*(1), 87–102. doi:10.1080/15289168.2011.575711

Salter, K., Beamish, W., & Davies, M. (2016). The effects of child-centered play therapy (CCPT) on the social and emotional growth of young Australian children with autism. *International Journal of Play Therapy, 25*(2), 78–90. doi:10.1037/pla0000012

Salvatore, J. E., & Dick, D. M. (2016). Genetic influences on conduct disorder. *Neuroscience and Biobehavioral Reviews.* doi:10.1016/j.neubiorev.2016.06.034

Samek, D. R., & Hicks, B. M. (2014). Externalizing disorders and environmental risk: Mechanisms of gene-environment interplay and strategies for intervention. *Clinical Practice, 11*(5), 537–547. doi:10.2217/CPR.14.47

Samokhvalov, A. V., & Rehm, J. (2013). Heroin addiction. In P. M. Miller, S. A. Ball, M. E. Bates, A. W. Blume, K. M. Kampman, D. J. Kavanagh, M. E. Larimer, N. M. Petry, & P. De Witte (Eds.), *Comprehensive addictive behaviors and disorders: Vol. 1. Principles of addiction* (pp. 657–667). San Diego, CA: Elsevier Academic Press.

Samuel, D. B. (2015). A review of the agreement between clinicians' personality disorder diagnoses and those from other methods and sources. *Clinical Psychology: Science and Practice, 22*(1), 1–19. doi:10.1111/cpsp.12088

Samuel, D. B., & Griffin, S. A. (2015). A critical evaluation of retaining personality categories and types. In S. K. Huprich (Ed.), *Personality disorders: Toward theoretical and empirical integration in diagnosis and assessment* (pp. 43–62). Washington, DC: American Psychological Association.

Sanacora, G., Frye, M. A., McDonald, W., Mathew, S. J., Turner, M. S., Schatzberg, A. F., ... Nemeroff, C. B. (2017). A consensus statement on the use of ketamine in the treatment of mood disorders. *JAMA Psychiatry.* doi:10.1001/jamapsychiatry.2017.0080

Sanacora, G., Treccani, G., & Popoli, M. (2012). Towards a glutamate hypothesis of depression: An emerging frontier of neuropsychopharmacology for mood disorders. *Neuropharmacology, 62*(1), 63–77. doi:10.1016/j.neuropharm.2011.07.036

Sanders, J. J., Roose, R. J., Lubrano, M. C., & Lucan, S. C. (2013). Meaning and methadone: Patient perceptions of methadone dose and a model to promote adherence to maintenance treatment. *Journal of Addiction Medicine, 7*(5), 307–313. doi:10.1097/ADM.0b013e318297021e

Sanders, J. L. (2011). A distinct language and a historic pendulum: The evolution of the Diagnostic and Statistical Manual of Mental Disorders. *Archives of Psychiatric Nursing, 25*(6), 394–403.

Sanders, L. (2018, January 2). Marijuana legalization 2018: Which states might consider cannabis laws this year? *Newsweek.* Retrieved from http://www.newsweek.com/marijuana-legalization-2018-which-states-will-consider-cannabis-laws-year-755282

Sanger, D. J. (2004). The pharmacology and mechanisms of action of new generation, non-benzodiazepine hypnotic agents. *CNS Drugs, 18 Suppl 1,* 9.

Sansone, R. A., & Sansone, L. A. (2009). The families of borderline patients: The psychological environment revisited. *Psychiatry, 6*(2), 19–24.

Santa Ana, E. J., Saladin, M. E., Back, S. E., Waldrop, A. E., Spratt, E. G., McRae, A. L., ... Brady, K. T. (2006). PTSD and the HPA axis: Differences in response to the cold pressor task among individuals with child vs. adult trauma. *Psychoneuroendocrinology, 31*(4), 501–509. doi:http://dx.doi.org/10.1016/j.psyneuen.2005.11.009

Sapolsky, R. M. (2000). Glucocorticoids and hippocampal atrophy in neuropsychiatric disorders. *Archives of General Psychiatry, 57*(10), 925–935. doi:10.1001/archpsyc.57.10.925

Sar, V. (2011). Epidemiology of dissociative disorders: An overview. *Epidemiology Research International,* 1–8. doi:10.1155/2011/404538

Şar, V. (2014). The many faces of dissociation: Opportunities for innovative research in psychiatry. *Clinical Psychopharmacology and Neuroscience, 12*(3), 171–179. doi:10.9758/cpn.2014.12.3.171

Şar, V., Akyüz, G., & Doğan, O. (2007). Prevalence of dissociative disorders among women in the general population. *Psychiatry Research, 149*(1–3), 169–176. doi:10.1016/j.psychres.2006.01.005

Sar, V., Önder, C., Kilincaslan, A., Zoroglu, S. S., & Alyanak, B. (2014). Dissociative identity disorder among adolescents: Prevalence in a university psychiatric outpatient unit. *Journal of Trauma & Dissociation, 15*(4), 402–419. doi:10.1080/15299732.2013.864748

Sar, V., Unal, S. N., & Ozturk, E. (2007). Frontal and occipital perfusion changes in dissociative identity disorder. *Psychiatry Research: Neuroimaging, 156*(3), 217–223. doi:http://dx.doi.org/10.1016/j.pscychresns.2006.12.017

Sarchiapone, M., Mandelli, L., Iosue, M., Andrisano, C., & Roy, A. (2011). Controlling access to suicide means. *International Journal of Environmental Research And Public Health, 8*(12), 4550–4562. doi:10.3390/ijerph8124550

Sarkar, D., Jung, M. K., & Wang, H. J. (2015). Alcohol and the immune system. *Alcohol Research: Current Reviews, 37*(2), 153–155.

Sarteschi, C. M. (2014). Randomized controlled trials of psychopharmacological interventions of children and adolescents with conduct disorder: A descriptive analysis. *Journal of Evidence-Based Social Work, 11*(4), 350–359. doi:10.1080/10911359.2014.897105

Sartre, J.-P. (2007). *Existentialism is a humanism* (C. Macomber, Trans.). New Haven, CT: Yale University Press. (Original work published 1947)

Sas, J. P. (2004). Theories of intelligence: Issues and applications. In G. Goldstein & S. R. Beers (Eds.), *Comprehensive handbook of psychological assessment: Vol. 1. Intellectual and neuropsychological assessment* (pp. 5–23). Hoboken, NJ: John Wiley.

Sayo, A., Jennings, R. G., & Van Horn, J. D. (2012). Study factors influencing ventricular enlargement in schizophrenia: A 20 year follow-up meta-analysis. *NeuroImage, 59*(1), 154–167. doi:10.1016/j.neuroimage.2011.07.011

Sbarra, D. A., Emery, R. E., Beam, C. R., & Ocker, B. L. (2014). Marital dissolution and major depression in midlife: A propensity score analysis. *Clinical Psychological Science, 2*(3), 249–257. doi:10.1177/2167702613498727

Schäfer, A., Vaitl, D., & Schienle, A. (2010). Regional grey matter volume abnormalities in bulimia nervosa and binge-eating disorder. *NeuroImage, 50*(2), 639–643. doi:10.1016/j.neuroimage.2009.12.063

Schäfer, M., & Quiring, O. (2015). The press coverage of celebrity suicide and the development of suicide frequencies in Germany. *Health Communication, 30*(11), 1149–1158. doi:10.1080/10410236.2014.923273

Schaffer, M., Jeglic, E. L., Moster, A., & Wnuk, D. (2010). Cognitive-behavioral therapy in the treatment management of sex offenders. *Journal of Cognitive Psychotherapy, 24*(2), 92–103. doi:10.1891/0889-8391.24.2.92

Schaler, J. A. (2000). *Addiction is a choice.* Chicago, IL: Open Court Publishing.

Schaler, J. A. (2002, October 2). Addiction is a choice. *Psychiatric Times.* Retrieved from http://www.psychiatrictimes.com/addiction/addiction-choice

Scharf, M. B., Pravda, M. F., Jennings, S. W., Kauffman, R., & Ringel, J. (1987). Childhood enuresis: A comprehensive treatment program. *Psychiatric Clinics of North America, 10*(4), 655–666.

Schaub, M. P., Henderson, C. E., Pelc, I., Tossmann, P., Phan, O., Hendriks, V., ... Rigter, H. (2014). Multidimensional family therapy decreases the rate of externalising behavioural disorder symptoms in cannabis abusing adolescents: Outcomes of the INCANT trial. *BMC Psychiatry, 14.* doi:10.1186/1471-244X-14-26

Scheff, T. J. (1984). *Being mentally ill: A sociological theory* (2nd ed.). New York, NY: Aldine de Gruyter.

Scher, L. M., Knudsen, P., & Leamon, M. (2014). Somatic symptom and related disorders. In R. E. Hales, S. C. Yudofsky, & L. W. Roberts (Eds.), *The American Psychiatric Publishing textbook of psychiatry* (6th ed., pp. 531–556). Arlington, VA: American Psychiatric Publishing.

Schiavi, R. C., Theilgaard, A., Owen, D. R., & White, D. (1988). Sex chromosome anomalies, hormones, and sexuality. *Archives of General Psychiatry, 45*(1), 19–24. doi:10.1001/archpsyc.1988.01800250023004

Schimmenti, A., Di Carlo, G., Passanisi, A., & Caretti, V. (2015). Abuse in childhood and psychopathic traits in a sample of violent offenders. *Psychological Trauma: Theory, Research, Practice and Policy, 7*(4), 340–347. doi:10.1037/tra0000023

Schlaepfer, T. E., Bewernick, B. H., Kayser, S., Mädler, B., & Coenen, V. A. (2013). Rapid effects of deep brain stimulation for treatment-resistant major depression. *Biological Psychiatry, 73*(12), 1204–1212. doi:http://dx.doi.org/10.1016/j.biopsych.2013.01.034

Schmajuk, N. A. (2001). Hippocampal dysfunction in schizophrenia. *Hippocampus, 11*(5), 599–613. doi:10.1002/hipo.1074

Schmidt, N. B., & Lerew, D. R. (1998). Prospective evaluation of psychological risk factors as predictors of functional impairment during acute stress. *Journal of Occupational Rehabilitation, 8*(3), 199–212. doi:10.1023/A:1021378523582

Schmidt, U. (2015). A plea for symptom-based research in psychiatry. *European Journal of Psychotraumatology, 6.*

Schmidt, U., Oldershaw, A., Jichi, F., Sternheim, L., Startup, H., McIntosh, V., ... Treasure, J. (2012). Out-patient psychological therapies for adults with anorexia nervosa: Randomised controlled trial. *The British Journal of Psychiatry, 201*(5), 392–399. doi:10.1192/bjp.bp.112.112078

Schneider, H. J., Pickel, J., & Stalla, G. K. (2006). Typical female 2nd-4th finger length (2D:4D) ratios in male-to-female transsexuals—possible implications for prenatal androgen exposure. *Psychoneuroendocrinology, 31*(2), 265–269. doi:10.1016/j.psyneuen.2005.07.005

Schneider, M. R., DelBello, M. P., McNamara, R. K., Strakowski, S. M., & Adler, C. M. (2012). Neuroprogression in bipolar disorder. *Bipolar Disorders, 14*(4), 356–374. doi:10.1111/j.1399-5618.2012.01024.x

Schniering, C. A., & Rapee, R. M. (1997). A test of the cognitive model of panic: Primed lexical decision in panic disorder. *Journal of Anxiety Disorders, 11*(6), 557–571. doi:http://dx.doi.org/10.1016/S0887-6185(97)00029-7

Schnoll, R., Burshteyn, D., & Cea-Aravena, J. (2003). Nutrition in the treatment of attention-deficit hyperactivity disorder: A neglected but important aspect. *Applied Psychophysiology and Biofeedback, 28*(1), 63–75. doi:10.1023/A:1022321017467

Schnoll, R. A., Goren, A., Annunziata, K., & Suaya, J. A. (2013). The prevalence, predictors and associated health outcomes of high nicotine dependence using three measures among US smokers. *Addiction, 108*(11), 1989–2000. doi:10.1111/add.12285

Schoeneman, T. J. (1984). The mentally ill witch in textbooks of abnormal psychology: Current status and implications of a fallacy. *Professional Psychology: Research and Practice, 15*(3), 299–314. doi:10.1037/0735-7028.15.3.299

Schofield, H. (2012, April 2). France's autism treatment 'shame'. Retrieved from http://www.bbc.com/news/magazine-17583123

Scholz, U., Doña, B. G., Sud, S., & Schwarzer, R. (2002). Is general self-efficacy a universal construct? Psychometric findings from 25 countries. *European Journal of Psychological Assessment, 18*(3), 242–251. doi:10.1027//1015-5759.18.3.242

School Psychologist Files. (n.d.). Understanding test scores.

Schöttle, D., Huber, C. G., Bock, T., & Meyer, T. D. (2011). Psychotherapy for bipolar disorder: A review of the most recent studies. *Current Opinion in Psychiatry, 24*(6), 549–555.

Schreiber, L. R. N., Odlaug, B. L., & Grant, J. E. (2013). The overlap between binge eating disorder and substance use disorders: Diagnosis and neurobiology. *Journal of Behavioral Addictions, 2*(4), 191–198. doi:10.1556/JBA.2.2013.015

Schreier, H. A. (1990). OCD and tricyclics. *Journal of the American Academy of Child & Adolescent Psychiatry, 29*(4), 668–669. doi:10.1097/00004583-199007000-00027

Schrijvers, D. L., Bollen, J., & Sabbe, B. G. C. (2012). The gender paradox in suicidal behavior and its impact on the suicidal process. *Journal of Affective Disorders, 138*(1-2), 19-26. doi:10.1016/j.jad.2011.03.050

Schröder, A., Heider, J., Zaby, A., & Göllner, R. (2013). Cognitive behavioral therapy versus progressive muscle relaxation training for multiple somatoform symptoms: Results of a randomized controlled trial. *Cognitive Therapy and Research, 37*(2), 296–306. doi:10.1007/s10608-012-9474-3

Schug, R. A., & Fradella, H. F. (2015). *Mental illness and crime.* Los Angeles, CA: SAGE Publications.

Schuham, A. I. (1967). The double-bind hypothesis a decade later. *Psychological Bulletin, 68*(6), 409–416. doi:10.1037/h0020188

Schulpen, T. W. (1997). The burden of nocturnal enuresis. *Acta Paediatrica, 86*(9), 981–984.

Schultze-Florey, C. R., Martínez-Maza, O., Magpantay, L., Breen, E. C., Irwin, M. R., Gündel, H., & O'Connor, M.-F. (2012). When grief makes you sick: Bereavement induced systemic inflammation is a question of genotype. *Brain, Behavior, and Immunity, 26*(7), 1066–1071. doi:http://dx.doi.org/10.1016/j.bbi.2012.06.009

Schulze, T. G., Alda, M., Adli, M., Akula, N., Ardau, R., Bui, E. T., ... McMahon, F. J. (2010). The International Consortium on Lithium Genetics (ConLiGen): An initiative by the NIMH and IGSLI to study the genetic basis of response to lithium treatment. *Neuropsychobiology, 62*(1), 72–78. doi:10.1159/000314708

Schumacher, J., Kristensen, A. S., Wendland, J. R., Nöthen, M. M., Mors, O., & McMahon, F. J. (2011). The genetics of panic disorder. *Journal of Medical Genetics, 48*(6), 361–368. doi:10.1136/jmg.2010.086876

Schwannauer, M. (2013). Cognitive behavioral therapy for bipolar affective disorders. In M. Power (Ed.), *The Wiley-Blackwell handbook of mood disorders* (2nd ed., pp. 361–381). Chichester, UK: Wiley-Blackwell.

Schwartz, C. (2015, July 23). A neuroscientist argues that everybody is misunderstanding fear and anxiety. *New York Magazine.* Retrieved from http://nymag.com/scienceofus/2015/07/everybody-misunderstanding-fear-and-anxiety.html

Schwarz, A. (2016). *ADHD nation: Children, doctors, Big Pharma, and the making of an American epidemic.* New York, NY: Scribner/Simon & Schuster.

Schwarz, A., & Cohen, S. (2013, March 31). A.D.H.D. seen in 11% of U.S. children as diagnoses rise. *The New York Times.* Retrieved from http://www.nytimes.com/2013/04/01/health/more-diagnoses-of-hyperactivity-causing-concern.html?_r=0

Schwitzgebel, R. K. (1974). The right to effctive mental treatment. *California Law Review, 62*(3), 936–956. doi:10.15779/Z385J2N

Scott, G. N. (2012). Which plants contain caffeine? Retrieved from http://www.medscape.com/viewarticle/780334

Scott, N., Hanstock, T. L., & Patterson-Kane, L. (2013). Using narrative therapy to treat eating disorder not otherwise specified. *Clinical Case Studies, 12*(4), 307–321.

Scully, D., & Marolla, J. (1985). 'Riding the bull at Gilley's': Convicted rapists describe the rewards of rape. *Social Problems, 32*(3), 251–263. doi:10.1525/sp.1985.32.3.03a00070

Scutti, S. (2014). What is the difference between transsexual and transgender? Facebook's new version of 'it's complicated'. Retrieved from http://www.medicaldaily.com/what-difference-between-transsexual-and-transgender-facebooks-new-version-its-complicated-271389

Seabrook, J. A., Gorodzinsky, F., & Freedman, S. (2005). Treatment of primary nocturnal enuresis: A randomized clinical trial comparing hypnotherapy and alarm therapy. *Paediatrics & Child Health, 10*(10), 609–610.

Searight, H. R., Rottnek, F., & Abby, S. L. (2001). Conduct disorder: Diagnosis and treatment in primary care. *American Family Physician, 63*(8), 1579–1589. Retrieved from http://www.aafp.org/afp/2001/0415/p1579.html#sec-7

Searles, H. F. (2013). Scorn, disillusionment and adoration in the psychotherapy of schizophrenia. *Psychoanalytic Review, 100*(2), 338–359.

Secades-Villa, R., García-Rodríguez, O., López-Núñez, C., Alonso-Pérez, F., & Fernández-Hermida, J. R. (2014). Contingency management for smoking cessation among treatment-seeking patients in a community setting. *Drug and Alcohol Dependence, 140,* 63–68. doi:10.1016/j.drugalcdep.2014.03.030

Sederer, L. I. (2013, August 6). The right to treatment and the right to refuse treatment. Retrieved from http://careforyourmind.org/the-right-to-treatment-and-the-right-to-refuse-treatment/

Seedat, S., Stein, D. J., & Carey, P. D. (2005). Post-traumatic stress disorder in women: Epidemiological and treatment issues. *CNS Drugs, 19*(5), 411–427. doi:10.2165/00023210-200519050-00004

Seeman, M. V. (2011a). Canada: Psychosis in the immigrant Caribbean population. *International Journal of Social Psychiatry, 57*(5), 462–470. doi:10.1177/0020764010365979

Seeman, M. V. (2011b). Sleepwalking, a possible side effect of antipsychotic medication. *Psychiatric Quarterly, 82*(1), 59–67. doi:10.1007/s11126-010-9149-8

Seeman, M. V., & Seeman, P. (2014). Is schizophrenia a dopamine supersensitivity psychotic reaction? *Progress in Neuro-Psychopharmacology & Biological Psychiatry, 48,* 155–160. doi:10.1016/j.pnpbp.2013.10.003

Seeman, P. (2009). Glutamate and dopamine components in schizophrenia. *Journal of Psychiatry & Neuroscience, 34*(2), 143–149.

Seeman, P. (2011). All roads to schizophrenia lead to dopamine supersensitivity and elevated dopamine D2High receptors. *CNS Neuroscience & Therapeutics, 17*(2), 118–132. doi:10.1111/j.1755-5949.2010.00162.x

Seeman, P. (2013). Schizophrenia and dopamine receptors. *European Neuropsychopharmacology, 23*(9), 999–1009. doi:http://dx.doi.org/10.1016/j.euroneuro.2013.06.005

Segal, D. L., & Coolidge, F. L. (2004). Objective assessment of personality and psychopathology: An overview. In M. J. Hilsenroth & D. L. Segal (Eds.), *Comprehensive handbook of psychological assessment: Vol. 2. Personality assessment* (pp. 3–13). Hoboken, NJ: John Wiley.

Segal, Z. V., Teasdale, J. D., & Williams, J. M. G. (2004). Mindfulness-based cognitive therapy: Theoretical rationale and empirical status. In S. C. Hayes, V. M. Follette, & M. M. Linehan (Eds.), *Mindfulness and acceptance: Expanding the cognitive-behavioral tradition* (pp. 45–65). New York, NY: Guilford Press.

Segal, Z. V., Williams, J. M. G., & Teasdale, J. D. (2013). *Mindfulness-based cognitive therapy for depression* (2nd ed.). New York, NY: Guilford Press.

Segerstrom, S. C., & Miller, G. E. (2004). Psychological stress and the human immune system: A meta-analytic study of 30 years of inquiry. *Psychological Bulletin, 130*(4), 601–630. doi:10.1037/0033-2909.130.4.601

Segraves, R. T., & Balon, R. (2014). Antidepressant-induced sexual dysfunction in men. *Pharmacology Biochemistry and Behavior, 121*, 132–137. doi:http://dx.doi.org/10.1016/j.pbb.2013.11.003

Seikkula, J., & Olson, M. E. (2003). The open dialogue approach to acute psychosis: Its poetics and micropolitics. *Family Process, 42*(3), 403–418. doi:10.1111/j.1545-5300.2003.00403.x

Seikkula, J., Aaltonen, J., Alakare, B., Haarakangas, K., Keränen, J., & Lehtinen, K. (2006). Five-year experience of first-episode nonaffective psychosis in open-dialogue approach: Treatment principles, follow-up outcomes, and two case studies. *Psychotherapy Research, 16*(2), 214–228. doi:10.1080/10503300500268490

Seikkula, J., Alakare, B., & Aaltonen, J. (2001a). Open dialogue in psychosis I: An introduction and case illustration. *Journal of Constructivist Psychology, 14*(4), 247–265. doi:10.1080/107205301750433397

Seikkula, J., Alakare, B., & Aaltonen, J. (2001b). Open dialogue in psychosis II: A comparison of good and poor outcome cases. *Journal of Constructivist Psychology, 14*(4), 267–284. doi:10.1080/107205301750433405

Seikkula, J., Alakare, B., & Aaltonen, J. (2011). The comprehensive open-dialogue approach in Western Lapland: II. Long-term stability of acute psychosis outcomes in advanced community care. *Psychosis: Psychological, Social and Integrative Approaches, 3*(3), 192–204. doi:10.1080/17522439.2011.595819

Selby, E. A., Kranzler, A., Fehling, K. B., & Panza, E. (2015). Nonsuicidal self-injury disorder: The path to diagnostic validity and final obstacles. *Clinical Psychology Review, 38*, 79–91. doi:10.1016/j.cpr.2015.03.003

Seligman, L., & Reichenberg, L. W. (2007). *Selecting effective treatments*. San Francisco, CA, US: Jossey-Bass.

Seligman, M. E. P. (1971). Phobias and preparedness. *Behavior Therapy, 2*(3), 307–320. doi:http://dx.doi.org/10.1016/S0005-7894(71)80064-3

Seligman, M. E., & Maier, S. F. (1967). Failure to escape traumatic shock. *Journal of Experimental Psychology, 74*(1), 1–9. doi:10.1037/h0024514

Seligman, M. E., Maier, S. F., & Geer, J. H. (1968). Alleviation of learned helplessness in the dog. *Journal of Abnormal Psychology, 73*(3, Pt.1), 256–262. doi:10.1037/h0025831

Selimbegović, L., & Chatard, A. (2015). Single exposure to disclaimers on airbrushed thin ideal images increases negative thought accessibility. *Body Image, 12*, 1–5. doi:10.1016/j.bodyim.2014.08.012

Selvaggi, G., & Bellringer, J. (2011). Gender reassignment surgery: an overview. *Nature Reviews. Urology, 8*(5), 274–282. doi:10.1038/nrurol.2011.46

Selye, H. (1950). Stress and the general adaptation syndrome. *British Medical Journal, 1*(4667), 1383–1392.

Sempértegui, G. A., Karreman, A., Arntz, A., & Bekker, M. H. J. (2013). Schema therapy for borderline personality disorder: A comprehensive review of its empirical foundations, effectiveness and implementation possibilities. *Clinical Psychology Review, 33*(3), 426–447. doi:10.1016/j.cpr.2012.11.006

Sennott, S. L. (2011). Gender disorder as gender oppression: A transfeminist approach to rethinking the pathologization of gender non-conformity. *Women & Therapy, 34*(1–2), 93–113. doi:10.1080/02703149.2010.532683

Sensiba, D., & Franklin, C. (2015). Family interventions for combat-related posttraumatic stress disorder: A review for practitioners. *Best Practices in Mental Health: An International Journal, 11*(2), 47–59.

Sepúlveda, A. R., & Calado, M. (2012). Westernization: The role of mass media on body image and eating disorders. In I. Jauregui-Lobera (Ed.), Relevant topics in eating disorders (pp. 47–64). Rijeka, Croatia: InTech. Retrieved from http://www.intechopen.com/books/relevant-topics-in-eating-disorders/westernization-the-role-of-mass-media-on-body-image-and-eating-disorders. doi:10.5772/31307

Servais, L. M., & Saunders, S. M. (2007). Clinical psychologists' perceptions of persons with mental illness. *Professional Psychology: Research and Practice, 38*(2), 214–219. doi:10.1037/0735-7028.38.2.214

Setterberg, S. R., Ernst, M., Rao, U., Campbell, M., Carlson, G. A., Shaffer, D., & Staghezza, B. M. (1991). Child psychiatrists' views of DSM-III—R: A survey of usage and opinions. *Journal of the American Academy of Child & Adolescent Psychiatry, 30*(4), 652–658. doi:10.1097/00004583-199107000-00019

Settle, E. C., Jr. (1998). Antidepressant drugs: Disturbing and potentially dangerous adverse effects. *Journal of Clinical Psychiatry, 59*(Suppl 16), 25–30.

Severance, E. G., Yolken, R. H., & Eaton, W. W. (2016). Autoimmune diseases, gastrointestinal disorders and the microbiome in schizophrenia: More than a gut feeling. *Schizophrenia Research, 176*(1), 23–35. doi:10.1016/j.schres.2014.06.027

Sewell, K. W., & Williams, A. M. (2001). Construing stress: A constructivist therapeutic approach to posttraumatic stress reactions. In R. A. Neimeyer (Ed.), *Meaning reconstruction and the experience of loss* (pp. 293–310). Washington, DC: American Psychological Association.

Sguazzin, C. M. G., Key, B. L., Rowa, K., Bieling, P. J., & McCabe, R. E. (2017). Mindfulness-based cognitive therapy for residual symptoms in obsessive-compulsive disorder: A qualitative analysis. *Mindfulness, 8*(1), 190–203. doi:10.1007/s12671-016-0592-y

Shafter, R. (1989). Women and madness: A social historical perspective. *Issues in Ego Psychology, 12*(1), 77–82.

Shah, A. (2012). Making fitness to plead fit for purpose. *International Journal of Criminology and Sociology, 1*, 176–197.

Shah, A. A., & Han, J. Y. (2015). Anxiety. *CONTINUUM: Lifelong Learning in Neurology, 21*(3), 772–782.

Shahab, L., Brose, L. S., & West, R. (2013). Novel delivery systems for nicotine replacement therapy as an aid to smoking cessation and for harm reduction: Rationale, and evidence for advantages over existing systems. *CNS Drugs, 27*(12), 1007–1019. doi:10.1007/s40263-013-0116-4

Shahar, B. (2014). Emotion-focused therapy for the treatment of social anxiety: An overview of the model and a case description. *Clinical Psychology & Psychotherapy, 21*(6), 536–547.

Shahar, B., Bar-Kalifa, E., & Alon, E. (2017). Emotion-focused therapy for social anxiety disorder: Results from a multiple-baseline study. *Journal of Consulting and Clinical Psychology, 85*(3), 238–249. doi:10.1037/ccp0000166

Shahar, B., Carlin, E. R., Engle, D. E., Hegde, J., Szepsenwol, O., & Arkowitz, H. (2012). A pilot investigation of emotion-focused two-chair dialogue intervention for self-criticism. *Clinical Psychology & Psychotherapy, 19*(6), 496–507. doi:10.1002/cpp.762

Shalev, R. S., Manor, O., Kerem, B., Ayali, M., Badichi, N., Friedlander, Y., & Gross-Tsur, V. (2001). Developmental dyscalculia is a familial learning disability. *Journal of Learning Disabilities, 34*(1), 59–65. doi:10.1177/002221940103400105

Shaner, A., Miller, G., & Mintz, J. (2008). Autism as the low-fitness extreme of a parentally selected fitness indicator. *Human Nature, 19*(4), 389–413. doi:10.1007/s12110-008-9049-x

Shapira, B. E., & Dahlen, P. (2010). Therapeutic treatment protocol for enuresis using an enuresis alarm. *Journal of Counseling & Development, 88*(2), 246–252. doi:10.1002/j.1556-6678.2010.tb00017.x

Shapiro, E. (2012). EMDR and early psychological intervention following trauma. *Revue Européenne de Psychologie Appliquée/European Review of Applied Psychology, 62*(4), 241–251. doi:http://dx.doi.org/10.1016/j.erap.2012.09.003

Shapiro, F. (2012). EMDR therapy: An overview of current and future research. *Revue Européenne de Psychologie Appliquée/European Review of Applied Psychology, 62*(4), 193–195. doi:http://dx.doi.org/10.1016/j.erap.2012.09.005

Shapiro, J. R., Berkman, N. D., Brownley, K. A., Sedway, J. A., Lohr, K. N., & Bulik, C. M. (2007). Bulimia nervosa treatment: A systematic review of randomized controlled trials. *International Journal of Eating Disorders, 40*(4), 321–336. doi:10.1002/eat.20372

Sharma, M., & Branscum, P. (2010). Is Alcoholics Anonymous effective? *Journal of Alcohol and Drug Education, 54*(3), 3–6.

Sharp, R. A., Phillips, K. J., & Mudford, O. C. (2012). Comparisons of interventions for rumination maintained by automatic reinforcement. *Research in Autism Spectrum Disorders, 6*(3), 1107–1112. doi:http://dx.doi.org/10.1016/j.rasd.2012.03.002

Sharpley, C. F. (2010). A review of the neurobiological effects of psychotherapy for depression. *Psychotherapy: Theory, Research, Practice, Training, 47*(4), 603–615. doi:10.1037/a0021177

Shaw, Z. A., & Coffey, B. J. (2014). Tics and Tourette syndrome. *Psychiatric Clinics of North America, 37*(3), 269–286. doi:10.1016/j.psc.2014.05.001

Shaywitz, S. E., & Shaywitz, B. A. (2005). Dyslexia (specific reading disability). *Biological Psychiatry, 57*(11), 1301–1309. doi:http://dx.doi.org/10.1016/j.biopsych.2005.01.043

Shea, M. T., McDevitt-Murphy, M., Ready, D. J., & Schnurr, P. P. (2009). Group therapy. In E. B. Foa, T. M. Keane, M. J. Friedman, & J. A. Cohen (Eds.), *Effective treatments for PTSD: Practice guidelines from the International Society for Traumatic Stress Studies* (2nd ed., pp. 306–326). New York, NY: Guilford Press.

Shean, G. D. (2004). *Understanding and treating schizophrenia: Contemporary research, theory, and practice.* New York, NY: Haworth Clinical Practice Press.

Shear, M. K., & Mulhare, E. (2008). Complicated grief. *Psychiatric Annals, 38*(10), 662–670. doi:10.3928/00485713-20081001-10

Shear, M. K., Simon, N., Wall, M., Zisook, S., Neimeyer, R., Duan, N., ... Keshaviah, A. (2011). Complicated grief and related bereavement issues for DSM-5. *Depression and Anxiety, 28*(2), 103–117. doi:10.1002/da.20780

Sheline, Y. I. (2003). Neuroimaging studies of mood disorder effects on the brain. *Biological Psychiatry, 54*(3), 338–352. doi:10.1016/S0006-3223(03)00347-0

Shelley-Tremblay, J. F., & Rosén, L. A. (1996). Attention deficit hyperactivity disorder: An evolutionary perspective. *The Journal of Genetic Psychology: Research and Theory on Human Development, 157*(4), 443–453. doi:10.1080/00221325.1996.9914877

Shepard, P. D. (2014). Basic science, RDoC, and Schizophrenia Bulletin. *Schizophrenia Bulletin, 40*(4), 717–718. doi:10.1093/schbul/sbu077

Sherer, M., Maddux, J. E., Mercandante, B., Prentice-Dunn, S., Jacobs, B., & Rogers, R. W. (1982). The self-efficacy scale: Construction and validation. *Psychological Reports, 51*(2), 663–671.

Sherin, J. E., & Nemeroff, C. B. (2011). Post-traumatic stress disorder: The neurobiological impact of psychological trauma. *Dialogues in Clinical Neuroscience, 13*(3), 263–278.

Sherkow, S. P., Harrison, A. M., & Singletary, W. M. (2014). *Autism spectrum disorder: Perspectives from psychoanalysis and neuroscience.* Lanham, MD: Jason Aronson.

Sherman, J. A. (2001). Evolutionary origin of bipolar disorder (EOBD). *Psycoloquy, 12*(28). Retrieved from http://www.cogsci.ecs.soton.ac.uk/cgi/psyc/newpsy?article=12.028&submit=View+Article

Sherman, J. A. (2012). Evolutionary origin of bipolar disorder-revised: EOBD-R. *Medical Hypotheses, 78*(1), 113–122. doi:http://dx.doi.org/10.1016/j.mehy.2011.10.005

Shibata, H., Yamamoto, K., Sun, Z., Oka, A., Inoko, H., Arinami, T., ... Fukumaki, Y. (2013). Genome-wide association study of schizophrenia using microsatellite markers in the Japanese population. *Psychiatric Genetics, 23*(3), 117–123. doi:10.1097/YPG.0b013e32835fe4f1

Shifrer, D., Muller, C., & Callahan, R. (2011). Disproportionality and learning disabilities: Parsing apart race, socioeconomic status, and language. *Journal of Learning Disabilities, 44*(3), 246–257. doi:10.1177/0022219410374236

Shimada-Sugimoto, M., Otowa, T., & Hettema, J. M. (2015). Genetics of anxiety disorders: Genetic epidemiological and molecular studies in humans. *Psychiatry and Clinical Neurosciences, 69*(7), 388–401. doi:10.1111/pcn.12291

Shin, L. M., Rauch, S. L., & Pitman, R. K. (2006). Amygdala, medial prefrontal cortex, and hippocampal function in PTSD. *Annals of the New York Academy of Sciences, 1071,* 67–79.

Shin, L. M., Wright, C. I., Cannistraro, P. A., Wedig, M. M., McMullin, K., Martis, B., ... Rauch, S. L. (2005). A functional magnetic resonance imaging study of amygdala and medial prefrontal cortex responses to overtly presented fearful faces in posttraumatic stress disorder. *Archives of General Psychiatry, 62*(3), 273–281. doi:10.1001/archpsyc.62.3.273

Shneidman, E. S. (1981a). Orientations toward death: Subintentioned death and indirect suicide. *Suicide and Life-Threatening Behavior, 11*(4), 232–253. doi:10.1111/j.1943-278X.1981.tb01004.x

Shneidman, E. S. (1981b). Suicide. *Suicide and Life-Threatening Behavior, 11*(4), 198–220. doi:10.1111/j.1943-278X.1981.tb01002.x

Shneidman, E. S. (1985). *Definition of suicide.* New York, NY: John Wiley.

Shneidman, E. S. (1993). Commentary: Suicide as psychache. *Journal of Nervous and Mental Disease, 181*(3), 145–147. doi:10.1097/00005053-199303000-00001

Shneidman, E. S. (1998). Further reflections on suicide and psychache. *Suicide and Life-Threatening Behavior, 28*(3), 245–250.

Shorter, E. (1997). *A history of psychiatry: From the era of the asylum to the age of Prozac.* New York, NY: John Wiley.

Shorter, E. (2007). The doctrine of the two depressions in historical perspective. *Acta Psychiatrica Scandinavica, 115*(Suppl433), 5–13. doi:10.1111/j.1600-0447.2007.00957.x

Shorter, E. (2009). *Before Prozac: The troubled history of mood disorders in psychiatry.* New York, NY: Oxford University Press.

Shorter, E. (2013). The history of DSM. In J. Paris & J. Phillips (Eds.), *Making the DSM-5* (pp. 3–19). New York, NY: Springer.

Shumaker, D. (2012). An existential-integrative treatment of anxious and depressed adolescents. *Journal of Humanistic Psychology, 52*(4), 375–400. doi:10.1177/0022167811422947

Shuster, E. (1997). Fifty years later: The significance of the Nuremberg Code. *The New England Journal of Medicine, 337*(20), 1436–1440. doi:10.1056/nejm199711133372006

Sibbald, B., & Roland, M. (1998). Understanding controlled trials: Why are randomised controlled trials important? *BMJ: British Medical Journal, 316*(7126), 201. doi:10.1136/bmj.316.7126.201

Sibley, M. H., Waxmonsky, J. G., Robb, J. A., & Pelham, W. E. (2013). Implications of changes for the field: ADHD. *Journal of Learning Disabilities, 46*(1), 34–42. doi:10.1177/0022219412464350

Sibrava, N. J., & Borkovec, T. D. (2006). The cognitive avoidance theory of worry. In G. C. L. Davey & A. Wells (Eds.), *Worry and its psychological disorders: Theory, assessment and treatment* (pp. 239–256). Hoboken, NJ: Wiley Publishing.

Siderowf, A., Pontecorvo, M. J., Shill, H. A., Mintun, M. A., Arora, A., Joshi, A. D., ... Sabbagh, M. N. (2014). PET imaging of amyloid with florbetapir F 18 and PET imaging of dopamine degeneration with 18F-AV-133 (florbenazine) in patients with Alzheimer's disease and Lewy body disorders. *BMC Neurology, 14.*

Siekmeier, P. J., & vanMaanen, D. P. (2014). Dopaminergic contributions to hippocampal pathophysiology in schizophrenia: A computational study. *Neuropsychopharmacology, 39*(7), 1713–1721. doi:10.1038/npp.2014.19

Siever, L. J., & Davis, K. L. (2004). The pathophysiology of schizophrenia disorders: Perspectives from the spectrum. *The American Journal of Psychiatry, 161*(3), 398–413. doi:10.1176/appi.ajp.161.3.398

Siever, L. J., & Weinstein, L. N. (2009). The neurobiology of personality disorders: Implications for psychoanalysis. *Journal of the American Psychoanalytic Association, 57*(2), 361–398. doi:10.1177/0003065109333502

Sikes, C., & Sikes, V. (2003). EMDR: Why the controversy? *Traumatology, 9*(3), 169–182. doi:10.1177/153476560300900304

Silberman, E. K., Putnam, F. W., Weingartner, H., Braun, B. G., & Post, R. M. (1985). Dissociative states in multiple personality disorder: A quantitative study. *Psychiatry Research, 15*(4), 253–260. doi:10.1016/0165-1781(85)90062-9

Silberman, S. (2015). *NeuroTribes: The legacy of autism and the future of neurodiversity.* New York, NY: Avery.

Silk, K. R., & Feurino, L., III. (2012). Psychopharmacology of personality disorders. In T. A. Widiger (Ed.), *The Oxford handbook of personality disorders* (pp. 713–726). New York, NY: Oxford University Press.

Silver, A.-L. S., & Stedman, L. (2009). United States of America: Psychodynamic developments, 1940s to the present. In Y. O. Alanen, M. González de Chávez, A.-L. S. Silver, & B. Martindale (Eds.), *Psychotherapeutic approaches to schizophrenic psychoses* (pp. 67–77). London, UK: Routledge.

Silverman, J. A. (1987). Robert Whytt, 1714–1766: Eighteenth century limner of anorexia nervosa and bulimia: An essay. *International Journal of Eating Disorders, 6*(1), 143–146. doi:10.1002/1098-108X(198701)6:1<143::AID-EAT2260060116>3.0.CO;2-I

Silverman, J. A. (1989). Louis-Victor Marcé, 1828–1864: Anorexia nervosa's forgotten man. *Psychological Medicine, 19*(4), 833–835. doi:10.1017/S0033291700005547

Simon, A. E., Riecher-Rössler, A., Lang, U. E., & Borgwardt, S. (2013). The attenuated psychosis syndrome in DSM-5. *Schizophrenia Research, 151*(1–3), 295. doi:http://dx.doi.org/10.1016/j.schres.2013.09.019

Simon, N. M. (2013). Treating complicated grief. *JAMA: Journal of the American Medical Association, 310*(4), 416–423. doi:10.1001/jama.2013.8614

Simon, R. J., & Ahn-Redding, H. (2006). *The insanity defense, the world over*. Lanham, MD: Rowman & Littlefield.

Simon, S. S., Cordás, T. A., & Bottino, C. M. C. (2015). Cognitive behavioral therapies in older adults with depression and cognitive deficits: A systematic review. *International Journal of Geriatric Psychiatry, 30*(3), 223–233. doi:10.1002/gps.4239

Simonds, L. M., & Thorpe, S. J. (2003). Attitudes toward obsessive-compulsive disorders: An experimental investigation. *Social Psychiatry and Psychiatric Epidemiology, 38*(6), 331–336.

Simone, S., & Fulero, S. M. (2005). Tarasoff and the duty to protect. *Journal of Aggression, Maltreatment & Trauma, 11*(1–2), 145–168. doi:10.1300/J146v11n01_12

Simpson, H. B. (2012). The RDoC project: A new paradigm for investigating the pathophysiology of anxiety. *Depression and Anxiety, 29*(4), 251–252. doi:10.1002/da.21935

Simpson, H. B., Foa, E. B., Liebowitz, M. R., Ledley, D. R., Huppert, J. D., Cahill, S., ... Petkova, E. (2008). A randomized, controlled trial of cognitive-behavioral therapy for augmenting pharmacotherapy in obsessive-compulsive disorder. *The American Journal of Psychiatry, 165*(5), 621–630. doi:10.1176/appi.ajp.2007.07091440

Sinason, V., & Silver, A.-L. S. (2008). Treating dissociative and psychotic disorders psychodynamically. In A. Moskowitz, I. Schäfer, & M. J. Dorahy (Eds.), *Psychosis, trauma and dissociation: Emerging perspectives on severe psychopathology* (pp. 239–253). Chichester, UK: Wiley-Blackwell.

Singh, A. A., & Burnes, T. R. (2010). Shifting the counselor role from gatekeeping to advocacy: Ten strategies for using the Competencies for counseling with transgender clients for individual and social change. *Journal of LGBT Issues in Counseling, 4*(3–4), 241–255. doi:10.1080/15538605.2010.525455

Singh, A. A., & dickey, l. m. (2016). Implementing the APA guidelines on psychological practice with transgender and gender nonconforming people: A call to action to the field of psychology. *Psychology of Sexual Orientation and Gender Diversity, 3*(2), 195–200. doi:10.1037/sgd0000179

Singh, I. (2003). Boys will be boys: Fathers' perspectives on ADHD symptoms, diagnosis, and drug treatment. *Harvard Review of Psychiatry, 11*(6), 308–316. doi:10.1080/714044393

Singh, I. (2004). Doing their jobs: Mothering with Ritalin in a culture of mother-blame. *Social Science & Medicine, 59*(6), 1193–1205. doi:10.1016/j.socscimed.2004.01.011

Singh, N., & Reece, J. (2014). Psychotherapy, pharmacotherapy, and their combination for adolescents with major depressive disorder: A meta-analysis. *The Australian Educational and Developmental Psychologist, 31*(1), 47–65. doi:10.1017/edp.2013.20

Sinke, C., Halpern, J. H., Zedler, M., Neufeld, J., Emrich, H. M., & Passie, T. (2012). Genuine and drug-induced synesthesia: A comparison. *Consciousness and Cognition, 21*(3), 1419–1434. doi:10.1016/j.concog.2012.03.009

Sinyor, M. (2012). Evolutionary approach highly informative but should not be overstated. *The Canadian Journal of Psychiatry / La Revue Canadienne De Psychiatrie, 57*(5), 336–336.

Sirri, L., & Fava, G. A. (2014). Clinical manifestations of hypochondriasis and related conditions. In V. Starcevic & R. Noyes, Jr. (Eds.), *Hypochondriasis and health anxiety: A guide for clinicians* (pp. 8–27). New York, NY: Oxford University Press.

Skinner, B. F. (1954). A new method for the experimental analysis of the behavior of psychotic patients. *Journal of Nervous and Mental Disease, 120*, 403–406.

Skinner, B. F. (1985). Cognitive science and behaviourism. *British Journal of Psychology, 76*(3), 291–301. doi:10.1111/j.2044-8295.1985.tb01953.x

Skinner, B. F. (1987). Whatever happened to psychology as the science of behavior? *American Psychologist, 42*(8), 780–786. doi:10.1037/0003-066X.42.8.780

Skinner, B. F. (1990). Can psychology be a science of mind? *American Psychologist, 45*(11), 1206–1210. doi:10.1037/0003-066X.45.11.1206

Skodol, A. E., & Krueger, R. F. (2013). Can the classification of personality disorders be based on behavior genetics? A comment on South and DeYoung (2013). *Personality Disorders: Theory, Research, and Treatment, 4*(3), 286–288. doi:10.1037/per0000003

Skodol, A. E., Bender, D. S., Gunderson, J. G., & Oldham, J. M. (2014). Personality disorders. In R. E. Hales, S. C. Yudofsky, & L. W. Roberts (Eds.), *The American Psychiatric Publishing textbook of psychiatry* (6th ed., pp. 851–894). Arlington, VA: American Psychiatric Publishing.

Skodol, A. E., Morey, L. C., Bender, D. S., & Oldham, J. M. (2015). The alternative DSM-5 model for personality disorders: A clinical application. *The American Journal of Psychiatry, 172*(7), 606–613. doi:10.1176/appi.ajp.2015.14101220

Skolnick, P., Popik, P., & Trullas, R. (2009). Glutamate-based antidepressants: 20 years on. *Trends in Pharmacological Sciences, 30*(11), 563–569. doi:10.1016/j.tips.2009.09.002

Skre, I., Onstad, S., Torgersen, S., Lygren, S., & Kringlen, E. (1993). A twin study of DSM-III–R anxiety disorders. *Acta Psychiatrica Scandinavica, 88*(2), 85–92. doi:10.1111/j.1600-0447.1993.tb03419.x

Slater, A., Tiggemann, M., Firth, B., & Hawkins, K. (2012). Reality check: An experimental investigation of the addition of warning labels to fashion magazine images on women's mood and body dissatisfaction. *Journal of Social and Clinical Psychology, 31*(2), 105–122. doi:10.1521/jscp.2012.31.2.105

Sleeter, C. E. (1986). Learning Disabilities: The Social Construction of a Special Education Category. *Exceptional Children, 53*(1), 46–54.

Sloan, D. M., Bovin, M. J., & Schnurr, P. P. (2012). Review of group treatment for PTSD. *Journal of Rehabilitation Research and Development, 49*(5), 689–701.

Slof-Op 't Landt, M. C. T., Meulenbelt, I., Bartels, M., Suchiman, E., Middeldorp, C. M., Houwing-Duistermaat, J. J., ... Slagboom, P. E. (2011). Association study in eating disorders: TPH2 associates with anorexia nervosa and self-induced vomiting. *Genes, Brain, And Behavior, 10*(2), 236–243. doi:10.1111/j.1601-183X.2010.00660.x

Slof-Op 't Landt, M. C. T., van Furth, E. F., Meulenbelt, I., Bartels, M., Hottenga, J. J., Slagboom, P. E., & Boomsma, D. I. (2014). Association study of the estrogen receptor I gene (ESR1) in anorexia nervosa and eating disorders: no replication found. *The International Journal Of Eating Disorders, 47*(2), 211–214. doi:10.1002/eat.22228

Slof-Op't Landt, M. C. T., Bartels, M., Middeldorp, C. M., van Beijsterveldt, C. E. M., Slagboom, P. E., Boomsma, D. I., ... Meulenbelt, I. (2013). Genetic variation at the TPH2 gene influences impulsivity in addition to eating disorders. *Behavior Genetics, 43*(1), 24–33. doi:10.1007/s10519-012-9569-3

Slotkin, T. A. (2013). Maternal smoking and conduct disorder in the offspring. *JAMA Psychiatry, 70*(9), 901–902. doi:10.1001/jamapsychiatry.2013.1951

Smedslund, G., C., B. R., Hammerstrøm, K. T., Steiro, A., Leiknes, K. A., Dahl, H. M., & Karlsen, K. (2011). Motivational interviewing for substance abuse (Review). *Cochrane Database of Systematic Reviews, 2011*(5), 1–130. doi:10.1002/14651858.CD008063.pub2

Šmigelskas, K., Žemaitienė, N., Julkunen, J., & Kauhanen, J. (2015). Type A behavior pattern is not a predictor of premature mortality. *International Journal of Behavioral Medicine, 22*(2), 161–169. doi:10.1007/s12529-014-9435-1

Smith, A. P. (2013). Caffeine and caffeinated energy drinks. In P. M. Miller, S. A. Ball, M. E. Bates, A. W. Blume, K. M. Kampman, D. J. Kavanagh, M. E. Larimer, N. M. Petry, & P. De Witte (Eds.), *Comprehensive addictive behaviors and disorders: Vol. 1. Principles of addiction* (pp. 777–785). San Diego, CA: Elsevier Academic Press.

Smith, C. B. R. (2010). Socio-spatial stigmatization and the contested space of addiction treatment: Remapping strategies of opposition to the disorder of drugs. *Social Science & Medicine, 70*(6), 859–866. doi:10.1016/j.socscimed.2009.10.033

Smith, D. (2012, August 24). It's still the 'age of anxiety.' Or is it? *The New York Times*. Retrieved from http://opinionator.blogs.nytimes.com/2012/01/14/its-still-the-age-of-anxiety-or-is-it/?_r=0

Smith, D. D. (2007, updated April 14, 2014). Emotional or behavioral disorders defined. Retrieved from http://www.education.com/reference/article/emotional-behavioral-disorders-defined/

Smith, D. E. (2016). Marijuana: A fifty-year personal addiction medicine perspective. *Journal of Psychoactive Drugs, 48*(1), 3–10. doi:10.1080/02791072.2015.1116720

Smith, D. G., & Robbins, T. W. (2013). The neurobiological underpinnings of obesity and binge eating: A rationale for adopting the food addiction model. *Biological Psychiatry, 73*(9), 804–810. doi:http://dx.doi.org/10.1016/j.biopsych.2012.08.026

Smith, E. S., Junger, J., Derntl, B., & Habel, U. (2015). The transsexual brain—A review of findings on the neural basis of transsexualism. *Neuroscience and Biobehavioral Reviews, 59*, 251–266. doi:10.1016/j.neubiorev.2015.09.008

Smith, H., Fox, J. R. E., & Trayner, P. (2015). The lived experiences of individuals with Tourette syndrome or tic disorders: A meta-synthesis of qualitative studies. *British Journal of Psychology, 106*(4), 609–634. doi:10.1111/bjop.12118

Smith, I. C., Reichow, B., & Volkmar, F. R. (2015). The effects of DSM-5 criteria on number of individuals diagnosed with autism spectrum disorder: A systematic review. *Journal of Autism and Developmental Disorders, 45*(8), 2541–2552. doi:10.1007/s10803-015-2423-8

Smith, J. J., & Graden, J. L. (1998). Fetal alcohol syndrome. In L. Phelps (Ed.), *Health-related disorders in children and adolescents: A guidebook for understanding and educating* (pp. 291–298). Washington, DC: American Psychological Association.

Smith, M. (2011). *An alternative history of hyperactivity: Food additives and the Feingold Diet.* New Brunswick, NJ: Rutgers University Press.

Smith, M. (2012). *Hyperactive: The controversial history of ADHD.* London, UK: Reaktion Books.

Smith, M. L., & Glass, G. V. (1987). *Research and evaluation in education and the social sciences.* Englewood Cliffs, NJ: Prentice-Hall.

Smith, S. D., Reynolds, C. A., & Rovnak, A. (2009). A critical analysis of the social advocacy movement in counseling. *Journal of Counseling & Development, 87*(4), 483–491. doi:10.1002/j.1556-6678.2009.tb00133.x

Smith, T. (2001). Discrete trial training in the treatment of autism. *Focus on Autism and Other Developmental Disabilities, 16*(2), 86–92. doi:10.1177/108835760101600204

Smith, T., & Iadarola, S. (2015). Evidence base update for autism spectrum disorder. *Journal of Clinical Child and Adolescent Psychology, 44*(6), 897–922. doi:10.1080/15374416.2015.1077448

Smith-Bell, M., & Winslade, W. J. (1994). Privacy, confidentiality, and privilege in psychotherapeutic relationships. *American Journal of Orthopsychiatry, 64*(2), 180–193. doi:10.1037/h0079520

Snowling, M. J., & Hulme, C. (2012). Interventions for children's language and literacy difficulties. *International Journal of Language & Communication Disorders, 47*(1), 27–34. doi:10.1111/j.1460-6984.2011.00081.x

Sobell, M. B., & Sobell, L. C. (1995). Controlled drinking after 25 years: How important was the great debate? *Addiction, 90*(9), 1149–1153. doi:10.1111/j.1360-0443.1995.tb01077.x

Socarides, C. W. (1989). *Homosexuality: Psychoanalytic therapy.* Northvale, NJ: Aronson. (Original work published 1978)

Social Solutions. (2016, June 14). Top 5 barriers to mental healthcare access. Retrieved from http://www.socialsolutions.com/blog/barriers-to-mental-healthcare-access/

Society of Counseling Psychology. (2014). What is counseling psychology? Retrieved from http://www.div17.org/about/what-is-counseling-psychology/

Sockol, L. E. (2015). A systematic review of the efficacy of cognitive behavioral therapy for treating and preventing perinatal depression. *Journal of Affective Disorders, 177*, 7–21. doi:10.1016/j.jad.2015.01.052

Sofuoglu, M., & Sewell, R. A. (2009). Norepinephrine and stimulant addiction. *Addiction Biology, 14*(2), 119–129. doi:10.1111/j.1369-1600.2008.00138.x

Soh, N., Walter, G., Robertson, M., & Malhi, G. S. (2010). Charles Lasègue (1816–1883): Beyond anorexie hystérique. *Acta Neuropsychiatrica, 22*(6), 300–301. doi:10.1111/j.1601-5215.2010.00499.x

Soloff, P. H., Chiappetta, L., Mason, N. S., Becker, C., & Price, J. C. (2014). Effects of serotonin-2A receptor binding and gender on personality traits and suicidal behavior in borderline personality disorder. *Psychiatry Research, 222*(3), 140–148. doi:10.1016/j.pscychresns.2014.03.008

Solomon, R. M., & Rando, T. A. (2007). Utilization of EMDR in the treatment of grief and mourning. *Journal of EMDR Practice and Research, 1*(2), 109–117. doi:10.1891/1933-3196.1.2.109

Somashekar, B., Jainer, A., & Wuntakal, B. (2013). Psychopharmacotherapy of somatic symptoms disorders. *International Review of Psychiatry, 25*(1), 107–115. doi:10.3109/09540261.2012.729758

Sonuga-Barke, E. J. S., Brandeis, D., Cortese, S., Daley, D., Ferrin, M., Holtmann, M., ... Sergeant, J. (2013). Nonpharmacological interventions for ADHD: Systematic review and meta-analyses of randomized controlled trials of dietary and psychological treatments. *The American Journal of Psychiatry, 170*(3), 275–289. doi:10.1176/appi.ajp.2012.12070991

South, S. C. (2015). Biological bases of personality disorders. In S. K. Huprich (Ed.), *Personality disorders: Toward theoretical and empirical integration in diagnosis and assessment* (pp. 163–201). Washington, DC: American Psychological Association.

South, S. C., & DeYoung, N. J. (2013a). Behavior genetics of personality disorders: Informing classification and conceptualization in DSM-5. *Personality Disorders: Theory, Research, and Treatment, 4*(3), 270–283. doi:10.1037/a0026255

South, S. C., & DeYoung, N. J. (2013b). The remaining road to classifying personality pathology in the DSM-5: What behavior genetics can add. *Personality Disorders: Theory, Research, and Treatment, 4*(3), 291–292. doi:10.1037/per0000005

Southwick, S. M., Paige, S., Morgan, C. A., 3rd, Bremner, J. D., Krystal, J. H., & Charney, D. S. (1999). Neurotransmitter alterations in PTSD: catecholamines and serotonin. *Seminars in Clinical Neuropsychiatry, 4*(4), 242–248.

Souza, T., & Spates, C. R. (2008). Treatment of PTSD and substance abuse comorbidity. *The Behavior Analyst Today, 9*(1), 11–26. doi:10.1037/h0100643

Spain, D., Sin, J., Chalder, T., Murphy, D., & Happé, F. (2015). Cognitive behaviour therapy for adults with autism spectrum disorders and psychiatric co-morbidity: A review. *Research in Autism Spectrum Disorders, 9*, 151–162. doi:10.1016/j.rasd.2014.10.019

Sparks, J. A. (2002). Taking a stand: An adolescent girl's resistance to medication. *Journal of Marital and Family Therapy, 28*(1), 27–38. doi:10.1111/j.1752-0606.2002.tb01169.x

Sparks, J. A., & Duncan, B. L. (2012). Pediatric antipsychotics: A call for ethical care. In S. Olfman & B. D. Robbins (Eds.), *Drugging our children: How profiteers are pushing antipsychotics on our youngest, and what we can do to stop it* (pp. 81–98). Santa Barbara, CA: Praeger/ABC-CLIO.

Sparks, J. A., & Duncan, B. L. (2013). Outside the black box: Re-assessing pediatric antidepressant prescription. *Journal of the Canadian Academy of Child and Adolescent Psychiatry/Journal de l'Académie canadienne de psychiatrie de l'enfant et de l'adolescent, 22*(3), 240–246.

Sparrow, E. P., & Erhardt, D. (2014). *Essentials of ADHD assessment for children and adolescents.* Hoboken, NJ: John Wiley.

Spence, R., Roberts, A., Ariti, C., & Bardsley, M. (2014). *Focus on: Antidepressant prescribing: Trends in the prescribing of antidepressants in primary care.* Retrieved from http://nuffield.dh.bytemark.co.uk/sites/files/nuffield/publication/140528_qualitywatch_focus_on_antidepressant_prescribing.pdf

Spermon, D., Darlington, Y., & Gibney, P. (2010). Psychodynamic psychotherapy for complex trauma: Targets, focus, applications, and outcomes. *Psychology Research and Behavior Management, 3.*

Sperry, L. (2011). Family therapy with personality-disordered individuals and families: Understanding and treating the borderline family. *The Journal of Individual Psychology, 67*(3), 222–231.

Sperry, L. (2016). *Handbook of diagnosis and treatment of DSM-5 personality disorders* (3rd ed.). New York, NY: Routledge.

Spettigue, W., & Henderson, K. A. (2004). Eating disorders and the role of the media. *Canadian Child and Adolescent Psychiatry Review, 13*(1), 16–19.

Spiegel, D., Lewis-Fernández, R., Lanius, R., Vermetten, E., Simeon, D., & Friedman, M. (2013). Dissociative disorders in DSM-5. *Annual Review of Clinical Psychology, 9*, 299–326. doi:10.1146/annurev-clinpsy-050212-185531

Spiegelhalder, K., Regen, W., Nanovska, S., Baglioni, C., & Riemann, D. (2013). Comorbid sleep disorders in neuropsychiatric disorders across the life cycle. *Current Psychiatry Reports, 15*(6), 364–364. doi:10.1007/s11920-013-0364-5

Spielberger, C. D., & Reheiser, E. C. (2004). Measuring anxiety, anger, depression, and curiosity as emotional states and personality states with the STAI, STAXI, and STPI. In M. J. Hilsenroth & D. L. Segal (Eds.), *Comprehensive handbook of psychological assessment: Vol. 2. Personality assessment* (pp. 70–86). Hoboken, NJ: John Wiley.

Spillers, J. L. H., Sensui, L. M., & Linton, K. F. (2014). Concerns about identity and services among people with autism and Asperger's regarding DSM-5 changes. *Journal of Social Work in Disability & Rehabilitation, 13*(3), 247–260. doi:10.1080/1536710X.2014.912186

Spitzer, R. L. (1975). On pseudoscience in science, logic in remission, and psychiatric diagnosis: A critique of Rosenhan's 'On being sane in insane places'. *Journal of Abnormal Psychology, 84*(5), 442–452. doi:10.1037/h0077124

Spitzer, R. L. (1976). More on pseudoscience in science and the case for psychiatric diagnosis. *Archives of General Psychiatry, 33*(4), 459–470. doi:10.1001/archpsyc.1976.01770040029007

Spitzer, R. L., Kroenke, K., Williams, J. B. W., & Löwe, B. (2006). A brief measure for assessing generalized anxiety disorder: The GAD-7. *Archives of Internal Medicine, 166*(10), 1092–1097. doi:10.1001/archinte.166.10.1092

Spitzer, R. L., Williams, J. B. W., & Endicott, J. (2012). Standards for DSM-5 reliability. *The American Journal of Psychiatry, 169*(5), 537–537.

Sprich, S. E., Knouse, L. E., Cooper-Vince, C., Burbridge, J., & Safren, S. A. (2010). Description and demonstration of CBT for ADHD in adults. *Cognitive and Behavioral Practice, 17*(1), 9–15. doi:10.1016/j.cbpra.2009.09.002

Sreevatsa, A. (2012, August 4). A short history of the insanity defence. Retrieved from http://blog.mylaw.net/a-short-history-of-the-insanity-defence/

St. Louis, K. O., Sønsterud, H., Junuzović-Žunić, L., Tomaiuoli, D., Del Gado, F., Caparelli, E., ... Węsierska, M. (2016). Public attitudes toward stuttering in Europe: Within-country and between-country comparisons. *Journal of Communication Disorders, 62*, 115–130. doi:10.1016/j.jcomdis.2016.05.010

Stack, L. (2016). Malta outlaws "conversion therapy," a first in Europe. *The New York Times.* Retrieved from https://www.nytimes.com/2016/12/07/world/europe/malta-outlaws-conversion-therapy-transgender-rights.html?_r=2

Stack, S., & Scourfield, J. (2015). Recency of divorce, depression, and suicide risk. *Journal of Family Issues, 36*(6), 695–715. doi:10.1177/0192513X13494824

Stahl, S. M., Grady, M. M., Moret, C., & Briley, M. (2005). SNRIs: The pharmacology, clinical efficacy, and tolerability in comparison with other classes of antidepressants. *CNS Spectrums, 10*(9), 732–747.

Stahl, S. M., Sommer, B., & Allers, K. A. (2011). Multifunctional pharmacology of flibanserin: Possible mechanism of therapeutic action in hypoactive sexual desire disorder. *Journal of Sexual Medicine, 8*(1), 15–27. doi:10.1111/j.1743-6109.2010.02032.x

Stallman, H. M. (2008). *University Stress Scale.* Brisbane: Queensland University of Technology.

Stallman, H. M., & Hurst, C. P. (2016). The University Stress Scale: Measuring domains and extent of stress in university students. *Australian Psychologist, 51*(2), 128–134. doi:10.1111/ap.12127

Stam, H. J. (1987). The psychology of control: A textual critique. In H. J. Stam, T. B. Rogers, & K. J. Gergen (Eds.), *The analysis of psychological theory: Metapsychological perspectives* (pp. 131–156). Washington, DC: Hemisphere Publishing.

Stams, G. J. J. M. (2015). From criminogenic risk to rehabilitation: Is there a need for a culturally sensitive approach? *International Journal of Offender Therapy and Comparative Criminology, 59*(12), 1263–1266. doi:10.1177/0306624X15608829

Stander, V. A., Thomsen, C. J., & Highfill-McRoy, R. M. (2014). Etiology of depression comorbidity in combat-related PTSD: A review of the literature. *Clinical Psychology Review, 34*(2), 87–98. doi:10.1016/j.cpr.2013.12.002

Staniloiu, A., & Markowitsch, H. J. (2014). Dissociative amnesia. *The Lancet Psychiatry, 1*(3), 226–241. doi:10.1016/S2215-0366(14)70279-2

Staniute, M., Brozaitiene, J., Burkauskas, J., Kazukauskiene, N., Mickuviene, N., & Bunevicius, R. (2015). Type D personality, mental distress, social support and health-related quality of life in coronary artery disease patients with heart failure: a longitudinal observational study. *Health and Quality of Life Outcomes, 13*, 1–1. doi:10.1186/s12955-014-0204-2

Stanley, B., Brown, G., Brent, D. A., Wells, K., Poling, K., Curry, J., ... Hughes, J. (2009). Cognitive-behavioral therapy for suicide prevention (CBT-SP): Treatment model, feasibility, and acceptability. *Journal of the American Academy of Child & Adolescent Psychiatry, 48*(10), 1005–1013. doi:10.1097/CHI.0b013e3181b5dbfe

Stanley, C. M., & Raskin, J. D. (2002). Abnormality: Does it define us or do we define it? In J. D. Raskin & S. K. Bridges (Eds.), *Studies in meaning: Exploring constructivist psychology* (pp. 123–142). New York, NY: Pace University Press.

Stansfeld, S. A., Clark, C., Rodger, B., Caldwell, T., & Power, C. (2008). Childhood and adulthood socio-economic position and midlife depressive and anxiety disorders. *The British Journal of Psychiatry, 192*(2), 152–153. doi:10.1192/bjp.bp.107.043208

Stebbins, M. B., & Corcoran, J. (2015). Pediatric bipolar disorder: The child psychiatrist perspective. *Child & Adolescent Social Work Journal.* doi:10.1007/s10560-015-0411-7

Steckler, T., & Risbrough, V. (2012). Pharmacological treatment of PTSD—Established and new approaches. *Neuropharmacology, 62*(2), 617–627. doi:10.1016/j.neuropharm.2011.06.012

Steenkamp, M. M., Litz, B. T., Hoge, C. W., & Marmar, C. R. (2015). Psychotherapy for military-related PTSD: A review of randomized clinical trials. *JAMA: Journal of the American Medical Association, 314*(5), 489–500. doi:10.1001/jama.2015.8370

Stefánsdóttir, G. V. (2014). Sterilisation and women with intellectual disability in Iceland. *Journal of Intellectual and Developmental Disability, 39*(2), 188–197. doi:10.3109/13668250.2014.899327

Steffen, E. (2013). Both 'being with' and 'doing to': Borderline personality disorder and the integration of humanistic values in contemporary therapy practice. *Counselling Psychology Review, 28*(1), 64–71.

Steffen, K. J., Roerig, J. L., & Mitchell, J. E. (2014). Pharmacological treatment of eating disorders. In G. O. Gabbard (Ed.), *Gabbard's treatments of psychiatric disorders* (5th ed., pp. 549–559). Arlington, VA: American Psychiatric Publishing.

Stein, D. J. (1997). Sociopathy: Adaptation, abnormality, or both? *Behavioral and Brain Sciences, 20*(3), 531–532. doi:10.1017/S0140525X97231511

Stein, D. J., & Bouwer, C. (1997). A neuro-evolutionary approach to the anxiety disorders. *Journal of Anxiety Disorders, 11*(4), 409–429. doi:10.1016/S0887-6185(97)00019-4

Stein, D. J., & Nesse, R. M. (2011). Threat detection, precautionary responses, and anxiety disorders. *Neuroscience and Biobehavioral Reviews, 35*(4), 1075–1079. doi:10.1016/j.neubiorev.2010.11.012

Stein, D. J., & Williams, D. (2010). Cultural and social aspects of anxiety disorders. In D. J. Stein, E. Hollander, & B. O. Rothbaum (Eds.), *Textbook of anxiety disorders* (2nd ed., pp. 717–729). Arlington, VA: American Psychiatric Publishing.

Stein, D. J., Lund, C., & Nesse, R. M. (2013). Classification systems in psychiatry: Diagnosis and global mental health in the era of DSM-5 and ICD-11. *Current Opinion in Psychiatry, 5*, 493–497. doi:10.1097/YCO.0b013e3283642dfd

Stein, D., Lilenfeld, L. R., Plotnicov, K., Pollice, C., Rao, R., Strober, M., & Kaye, W. H. (1999). Familial aggregation of eating disorders: results from a controlled family study of bulimia nervosa. *The International Journal Of Eating Disorders, 26*(2), 211–215.

Stein, M. B., Chen, C.-Y., Ursano, R. J., Cai, T., Gelernter, J., Heeringa, S. G., ... Smoller, J. (2016). Genome-wide association studies of posttraumatic stress disorder in 2 cohorts of US Army soldiers. *JAMA Psychiatry, 73*(7), 695–704. doi:10.1001/jamapsychiatry.2016.0350

Steinberg, M., & Lyketsos, C. G. (2012). Atypical antipsychotic use in patients with dementia: Managing safety concerns. *The American Journal of Psychiatry, 169*(9), 900–906. doi:10.1176/appi.ajp.2012.12030342

Steinberg, P. (2012, January 31). Asperger's history of overdiagnosis. *The New York Times.* Retrieved from http://www.nytimes.com/2012/02/01/opinion/aspergers-history-of-over-diagnosis.html

Steinert, C., Hofmann, M., Kruse, J., & Leichsenring, F. (2014). Relapse rates after psychotherapy for depression – stable long-term effects? A meta-analysis. *Journal of Affective Disorders, 168*, 107–118. doi:http://dx.doi.org/10.1016/j.jad.2014.06.043

Steinert, C., Munder, T., Rabung, S., Hoyer, J., & Leichsenring, F. (2017). Psychodynamic therapy: As efficacious as other empirically supported treatments? A meta-analysis testing equivalence of outcomes. *The American Journal of Psychiatry,* appi.ajp.2017.17010057. doi:10.1176/appi.ajp.2017.17010057

Steinglass, J., Mayer, L., & Attia, E. (2016). Treatment of restrictive eating and low-weight conditions, including anorexia nervosa and avoidant/restrictive food intake disorder. In B. T. Walsh, E. Attia, D. R. Glasofer, & R. Sysko (Eds.), *Handbook of assessment and treatment of eating disorders* (pp. 259–277). Arlington, VA: American Psychiatric Publishing.

Steinglass, J. E., Sysko, R., Glasofer, D., Albano, A. M., Simpson, H. B., & Walsh, B. T. (2011). Rationale for the application of exposure response prevention to the treatment of anorexia nervosa. *The International Journal Of Eating Disorders, 44*(2), 134–141. doi:10.1002/eat.20784

Steinmetz, K. (2010, July 2). AA around the world. *Time.*

Steketee, G., & Chambless, D. L. (2001). Does expressed emotion predict behaviour therapy outcome at follow-up for obsessive-compulsive disorder and agoraphobia? *Clinical Psychology & Psychotherapy, 8*(6), 389–399. doi:10.1002/cpp.307

Stepp, S. D., Lazarus, S. A., & Byrd, A. L. (2016). A systematic review of risk factors prospectively associated with borderline personality disorder: Taking stock and moving forward. *Personality Disorders: Theory, Research, and Treatment, 7*(4), 316–323. doi:10.1037/per0000186

Stern, D. B. (2009). Dissociation and unformulated experience: A psychoanalytic model of mind. In P. F. Dell & J. A. O'Neil (Eds.), *Dissociation and the dissociative disorders: DSM-V and beyond* (pp. 653–663). New York, NY: Routledge.

Stern, P. (2010). Paraphilic coercive disorder in the DSM: The right diagnosis for the right reasons. *Archives of Sexual Behavior, 39*(6), 1443–1447. doi:10.1007/s10508-010-9645-9

Stevenson, J., Buitelaar, J., Cortese, S., Ferrin, M., Konofal, E., Lecendreux, M., ... Sonuga-Barke, E. (2014). Research review: The role of diet in the treatment of attention-deficit/hyperactivity disorder – An appraisal of the evidence on efficacy and recommendations on the design of future studies. *Journal of Child Psychology and Psychiatry, 55*(5), 416–427. doi:10.1111/jcpp.12215

Stewart, A. (2018, June 18). WHO to unveil all-electronic ICD-11, over a decade in the making: 6 details. *Becker's ASC REview.* Retrieved from https://www.beckersasc.com/asc-coding-billing-and-collections/who-to-unveil-all-electronic-icd-11-over-a-decade-in-the-making-6-details.html

Stewart, R., Das, M., Ardagh, M., Deely, J. M., Dodd, S., Bartholomew, N., ... Than, M. (2014). The impact of alcohol-related presentations on a New Zealand hospital emergency department. *The New Zealand Medical Journal, 127*(1401), 23–39.

Stiegler, L. N. (2005). Understanding pica behavior: A review for clinical and education professionals. *Focus on Autism and Other Developmental Disabilities, 20*(1), 27–38. doi:10.1177/10883576050200010301

Still, G. F. (2006). Some abnormal psychical conditions in children: Excerpts from three lectures. *Journal of Attention Disorders, 10*(2), 126–136. doi:10.1177/1087054706288114

Stinneford, J. F. (2006). Incapacitation through maiming: Chemical castration, the Eighth Amendment, and the denial of human dignity. *University of Saint Thomas Law Journal, 3*(3), 559–599. Retrieved from http://ir.stthomas.edu/ustlj/vol3/iss3/10/

Stitzer, M., & Petry, N. (2006). Contingency management for treatment of substance abuse. *Annual Review of Clinical Psychology, 2*, 411–434. doi:10.1146/annurev.clinpsy.2.022305.095219

Stitzer, M. L., Iguchi, M. Y., Kidorf, M., & Bigelow, G. E. (1993). Contingency management in methadone treatment: The case for positive incentives. *NIDA Research Monograph, 137*, 19–36.

Stoffers, J., Völlm, B. A., Rücker, G., Timmer, A., Huband, N., & Lieb, K. (2010). Pharmacological interventions for borderline personality disorder. *Cochrane Database of Systematic Reviews*(6), CD005653. doi:10.1002/14651858.CD005653.pub2

Stoffers, J. M., Völlm, B. A., Rücker, G., Timmer, A., Huband, N., & Lieb, K. (2012). Psychological therapies for people with borderline personality disorder (Review). *Cochrane Database of Systematic Reviews, 2012*(2), 1–255. doi:10.1002/14651858.CD005652

Stokin, G. B., Krell-Roesch, J., Petersen, R. C., & Geda, Y. E. (2015). Mild neurocognitive disorder: An old wine in a new bottle. *Harvard Review of Psychiatry, 23*(5), 368–376. doi:10.1097/HRP.0000000000000084

Stoléru, S., & Mouras, H. (2007). Brain functional imaging studies of sexual desire and arousal in human males. In E. Janssen (Ed.), *The psychophysiology of sex* (pp. 3–34). Bloomington, IN: Indiana University Press.

Stoléru, S., Fonteille, V., Cornélis, C., Joyal, C., & Moulier, V. (2012). Functional neuroimaging studies of sexual arousal and orgasm in healthy men and women: A review and meta-analysis. *Neuroscience and Biobehavioral Reviews, 36*(6), 1481–1509. doi:10.1016/j.neubiorev.2012.03.006

Stoller, R. J. (1985). *Observing the erotic imagination.* New Haven, CT: Yale University Press.

Stoller, R. J. (1986). *Perversion: The erotic form of hatred.* London, UK: Karnac. (Original work published 1975)

Stone, A. A. (1975). *Mental health and law: A system in transition.* (DHEW Publication No. ADM). Washington, DC: Government Printing Office.

Stone, A. A. (1990). Law, science, and psychiatric malpractice: A response to Klerman's indictment of psychoanalytic psychiatry. *The American Journal of Psychiatry, 147*(4), 419–427. doi:10.1176/ajp.147.4.419

Stone, J. M. (2011). Glutamatergic antipsychotic drugs: a new dawn in the treatment of schizophrenia? *Therapeutic Advances In Psychopharmacology, 1*(1), 5–18. doi:10.1177/2045125311400779

Stone, J. M., Morrison, P. D., & Pilowsky, L. S. (2007). Glutamate and dopamine dysregulation in schizophrenia—A synthesis and selective review. *Journal of Psychopharmacology, 21*(4), 440–452. doi:10.1177/0269881106073126

Stone, J., Colyer, M., Feltbower, S., Carson, A., & Sharpe, M. (2004). Psychosomatic': A systematic review of its meaning in newspaper articles. *Psychosomatics: Journal of Consultation and Liaison Psychiatry, 45*(4), 287–290. doi:10.1176/appi.psy.45.4.287

Stone, J., Smyth, R., Carson, A., Warlow, C., & Sharpe, M. (2006). La belle indifférence in conversion symptoms and hysteria. *The British Journal of Psychiatry, 188*(3), 204–209.

Stone, M. H. (2010). History of anxiety disorders. In D. J. Stein, E. Hollander, & B. O. Rothbaum (Eds.), *Textbook of anxiety disorders* (2nd ed., pp. 3–15). Arlington, VA: American Psychiatric Publishing.

Stonecipher, A., Galang, R., & Black, J. (2006). Psychotropic discontinuation symptoms: A case of withdrawal neuroleptic malignant syndrome. *General Hospital Psychiatry, 28*(6), 541–543. doi:10.1016/j.genhosppsych.2006.07.007

Storebø, O. J., Ramstad, E., Krogh, H. B., Nilausen, T. D., Skoog, M., Holmskov, M., ... Gluud, C. (2015). Methylphenidate for children and adolescents with attention deficit hyperactivity disorder (ADHD). *Cochrane Database of Systematic Reviews, 2015*(11), 1–774. doi:10.1002/14651858.CD009885.pub2

Storebø, O. J., Skoog, M., Damm, D., Thomsen, P. H., Simonsen, E., & Gluud, C. (2011). Social skills training for Attention Deficit Hyperactivity Disorder (ADHD) in children aged 5 to 18 years. *Cochrane Database of Systematic Reviews*(12), CD008223. doi:10.1002/14651858.CD008223.pub2

Stork, E. (2013). A competent competency standard: Should it require a mental disease or defect? *Columbia Human Rights Law Review, 44*(3), 927–969.

Strain, J. J., & Diefenbacher, A. (2008). The adjustment disorders: The conundrums of the diagnoses. *Comprehensive Psychiatry, 49*(2), 121–130. doi:10.1016/j.comppsych.2007.10.002

Strain, J. J., & Friedman, M. J. (2011). Considering adjustment disorders as stress response syndromes for DSM-5. *Depression and Anxiety, 28*(9), 818–823. doi:10.1002/da.20782

Strauss, C., Hale, L., & Stobie, B. (2015). A meta-analytic review of the relationship between family accommodation and OCD symptom severity. *Journal of Anxiety Disorders, 33*, 95–102. doi:10.1016/j.janxdis.2015.05.006

Straussner, S. L. A., & Attia, P. R. (2002). Women's addiction and treatment through a historical lens. In S. L. A. Straussner & S. Brown (Eds.), *The handbook of addiction treatment for women* (pp. 3–25). San Francisco, CA: Jossey-Bass.

Strawbridge, R., Young, A. H., & Cleare, A. J. (2017). Biomarkers for depression: Recent insights, current challenges and future prospects. *Neuropsychiatric Disease and Treatment, 13*, 1245–1262. doi:10.2147/NDT.S114542

Striegel-Moore, R. H., & Franko, D. L. (2008). Should binge eating disorder be included in the DSM-V? A critical review of the state of the evidence. *Annual Review of Clinical Psychology, 4*, 305–324. doi:10.1146/annurev.clinpsy.4.022007.141149

Striegel-Moore, R. H., Silberstein, L. R., & Rodin, J. (1986). Toward an understanding of risk factors for bulimia. *American Psychologist, 41*(3), 246–263. doi:10.1037/0003-066X.41.3.246

Strober, M., Freeman, R., Lampert, C., Diamond, J., & Kaye, W. (2000). Controlled family study of anorexia nervosa and bulimia nervosa: Evidence of shared liability and transmission of partial syndromes. *The American Journal of Psychiatry, 157*(3), 393–401. doi:10.1176/appi.ajp.157.3.393

Stroebe, M., Schut, H., & Boerner, K. (2017). Cautioning health-care professionals: Bereaved persons are misguided through the stages of grief. *Omega: Journal of Death and Dying, 74*(4), 455–473. doi:10.1177/0030222817691870

Stroebe, M., Schut, H., & Stroebe, W. (2007). Health outcomes of bereavement. *The Lancet, 370*(9603), 1960–1973. doi:10.1016/S0140-6736(07)61816-9

Stroebe, W., Schut, H., & Stroebe, M. S. (2005). Grief work, disclosure and counseling: Do they help the bereaved? *Clinical Psychology Review, 25*(4), 395–414. doi:10.1016/j.cpr.2005.01.004

Strosahl, K. D., & Linehan, M. M. (1986). Basic issues in behavioral assessment. In A. R. Ciminero, K. S. Calhoun, & H. E. Adams (Eds.), *Handbook of behavioral assessment* (2nd ed., pp. 12–46). New York, NY: John Wiley.

Strupp, H. H. (1986). Review of Psychotherapy of schizophrenia: The treatment of choice. *Psychoanalytic Psychology, 3*(4), 385–388. doi:10.1037/h0085112

Struyk, R. (2018, January 4). Marijuana legalization by the numbers. Retrieved from http://www.cnn.com/2018/01/04/politics/marijuana-legalization-by-the-numbers/index.html

Stubnya, G., Nagy, Z., Lammers, C.-H., Rihmer, Z., & Bitter, I. (2010). Deinstitutionalization in Europe: Two recent examples from Germany and Hungary. *Psychiatria Danubina, 22*(3), 406–412.

Stuebing, K. K., Fletcher, J. M., LeDoux, J. M., Lyon, G. R., Shaywitz, S. E., & Shaywitz, B. A. (2002). Validity of IQ-discrepancy classifications of reading disabilities: A meta-analysis. *American Educational Research Journal, 39*(2), 469–518. doi:10.3102/00028312039002469

Sturges, J. W. (2013). Biological views. In T. G. Plante (Ed.), *Abnormal psychology across the ages: Vol. 1. History and conceptualizations* (pp. 187–200). Santa Barbara, CA: Praeger/ABC-CLIO.

Sturmey, P. (2009). Behavioral activation is an evidence-based treatment for depression. *Behavior Modification, 33*(6), 818–829. doi:10.1177/0145445509350094

Subcommittee on Energy Conservation and Power. (1986). *American nuclear guinea pigs: Three decades of radiation experiments on U.S. citizens.* Washington, DC: U.S. Government Printing Office Retrieved from http://contentdm.library.unr.edu/cdm/singleitem/collection/conghear/id/102#metajump

Subedi, B. (2014). Right to treatment. In E. Ford & M. Rotter (Eds.), Landmark cases in forensic psychiatry (pp. 51–53). New York, NY: Oxford University Press.

Suchan, B., Busch, M., Schulte, D., Gronemeyer, D., Herpertz, S., & Vocks, S. (2010). Reduction of gray matter density in the extrastriate body area in women with anorexia nervosa. *Behavioural Brain Research, 206.* doi:10.1016/j.bbr.2009.08.035

Sudak, D. M. (2011). *Combining CBT and medication.* Hoboken, NJ: John Wiley.

Sugarman, A. (2006). Attention deficit hyperactivity disorder and trauma. *The International Journal of Psychoanalysis, 87,* 237–241.

Sugranyes, G., de la Serna, E., Romero, S., Sanchez-Gistau, V., Calvo, A., Moreno, D., ... Castro-Fornieles, J. (2015). Gray matter volume decrease distinguishes schizophrenia from bipolar offspring during childhood and adolescence. *Journal of the American Academy of Child & Adolescent Psychiatry, 54*(8), 677–684. doi:10.1016/j.jaac.2015.05.003

Suh, J. J., Ruffins, S., Robins, C. E., Albanese, M. J., & Khantzian, E. J. (2008). Self-medication hypothesis: Connecting affective experience and drug choice. *Psychoanalytic Psychology, 25*(3), 518–532. doi:10.1037/0736-9735.25.3.518

Sukhodolsky, D. G., Bloch, M. H., Panza, K. E., & Reichow, B. (2013). Cognitive-behavioral therapy for anxiety in children with high-functioning autism: A meta-analysis. *Pediatrics, 132*(5), e1341–e1350. doi:10.1542/peds.2013-1193

Sullivan, H. S. (1962). *Schizophrenia as a human process.* New York, NY: Norton.

Sullivan, S., Bentall, R. P., Fernyhough, C., Pearson, R. M., & Zammit, S. (2013). Cognitive styles and psychotic experiences in a community sample. *PLOS One, 8*(11).

Sulzer, S. H. (2015). Does "difficult patient" status contribute to de facto demedicalization? The case of borderline personality disorder. *Social Science & Medicine, 142,* 82–89. doi:http://dx.doi.org/10.1016/j.socscimed.2015.08.008

Sumathipala, A. (2007). What is the evidence for the efficacy of treatments for somatoform disorders? A critical review of previous intervention studies. *Psychosomatic Medicine, 69*(9), 889–900. doi:10.1097/PSY.0b013e31815b5cf6

Summers, A., & Rosenbaum, B. (2013). Psychodynamic psychotherapy for psychosis: Empirical evidence. In J. Read & J. Dillon (Eds.), *Models of madness: Psychological, social and biological approaches to psychosis* (2nd ed., pp. 336–344). New York, NY: Routledge.

Sungur, M. Z., & Gunduz, A. (2013). Critiques and challenges to old and recently proposed American Psychiatric Association's website DSM 5 diagnostic criteria for sexual dysfunctions. *Klinik Psikofarmakoloji Bülteni / Bulletin of Clinical Psychopharmacology, 23*(1), 113–128. doi:10.5455/bcp.20130416063859

Sungur, M. Z., & Gündüz, A. (2014). A comparison of DSM-IV-TR and DSM-5 definitions for sexual dysfunctions: Critiques and challenges. *Journal of Sexual Medicine, 11*(2), 364–373. doi:10.1111/jsm.12379

Sussman, S., & Ames, S. L. (2008). *Drug abuse: Concepts, prevention, and cessation.* New York, NY: Cambridge University Press.

Suzuki, T., Griffin, S. A., & Samuel, D. B. (2016). Capturing the DSM-5 alternative personality disorder model traits in the five-factor model's nomological net. *Journal of Personality.* doi:10.1111/jopy.12235

Swales, M., Heard, H. L., & Williams, M. G. (2000). Linehan's Dialectical Behaviour Therapy (DBT) for borderline personality disorder: Overview and adaptation. *Journal of Mental Health, 9*(1), 7–23. doi:10.1080/09638230016921

Swami, V. (2015). Cultural influences on body size ideals: Unpacking the impact of Westernization and modernization. *European Psychologist, 20*(1), 44–51. doi:10.1027/1016-9040/a000150

Swartz, H. A. (2014). Family-focused therapy study raises new questions. *The American Journal of Psychiatry, 171*(6), 603–606. doi:10.1176/appi.ajp.2014.14020217

Swartz, H. A., Frank, E., Frankel, D. R., Novick, P., & Houck, P. (2009). Psychotherapy as monotherapy for the treatment of bipolar II depression: A proof of concept study. *Bipolar Disorders, 11*(1), 89–94. doi:10.1111/j.1399-5618.2008.00629.x

Swartz, H. A., Levenson, J. C., & Frank, E. (2012). Psychotherapy for bipolar II disorder: The role of interpersonal and social rhythm therapy. *Professional Psychology: Research and Practice, 43*(2), 145–153. doi:10.1037/a0027671

Swartz, J. R., Knodt, A. R., Radtke, S. R., & Hariri, A. R. (2015). A neural biomarker of psychological vulnerability to future life stress. *Neuron, 85*(3), 505–511. doi:10.1016/j.neuron.2014.12.055

Swayze, V. W., II. (1995). Frontal leukotomy and related psychosurgical procedures in the era before antipsychotics (1935–1954): A historical overview. *The American Journal of Psychiatry, 152*(4), 505–515.

Sweezy, M., & Ziskind, E. L. (2013). *Internal family systems therapy: New dimensions.* New York, NY: Routledge.

Swenson, C. C., Henggeler, S. W., Taylor, I. S., & Addison, O. W. (2005). *Multisystemic therapy and neighrhoos partnerships: Reducing adolescent violence and substance abuse.* New York, NY: Guilford Press.

Sykes, J. (2015). New York "Parachute" programme for people with acute mental distress lands in the UK. *The Guardian.* Retrieved from http://www.theguardian.com/society/2015/oct/20/parachute-therapy-psychosis-new-york-uk

Szabo, G., & Saha, B. (2015). Alcohol's effect on host defense. *Alcohol Research: Current Reviews, 37*(2), 159–170.

Szalavitz, M. (2015). No more addictive personality. *Nature, 522*(7557), S48–S49. doi:10.1038/522S48a

Szasz, T. S. (1963). *Law, liberty and psychiatry: An inquiry into the social uses of mental health practices.* New York, NY: Macmillan.

Szasz, T. S. (1974). *The myth of mental illness: Foundations of a theory of personal conduct* (Rev. ed.). New York, NY: Harper & Row.

Szasz, T. (1986). The case against suicide prevention. *American Psychologist, 41*(7), 806–812. doi:10.1037/0003-066X.41.7.806

Szasz, T. (1987). *Insanity: The idea and its consequences.* New York, NY: John Wiley.

Szasz, T. (1991a). *Ideology and insanity: Essays on the psychiatric dehumanization of man.* Syracuse, NY: Syracuse University Press. (Original work published 1970)

Szasz, T. (1991b). The medicalization of sex. *Journal of Humanistic Psychology, 31*(3), 34–42. doi:10.1177/0022167891313007

Szasz, T. (1994). *Cruel compassion: Psychiatric control of society's unwanted.* Oxford, UK: John Wiley.

Szasz, T. (1999). *Fatal freedom: The ethics and politics of suicide.* Westport, CT: Praeger Publishers/Greenwood Publishing Group.

Szasz, T. (2004). *Schizophrenia: The sacred symbol of psychiarty.* Syracuse, NY: Syracuse University Press. (Original work published 1976)

Szasz, T. (2010, October). The medicalization of suicide. *The Freeman, 8,* 13–14.

Szasz, T. (2011). *Suicide prohibition: The shame of medicine.* Syracuse, NY: Syracuse University Press.

Tabet, N., & Feldman, H. (2003). Ibuprofen for Alzheimer's disease. *Cochrane Database of Systematic Reviews, 2003*(2). doi:10.1002/14651858.CD004031

Tadić, A., Baskaya, Ö., Victor, A., Lieb, K., Höppner, W., & Dahmen, N. (2008). Association analysis of SCN9A gene variants with borderline personality disorder. *Journal of Psychiatric Research, 43*(2), 155–163. doi:http://dx.doi.org/10.1016/j.jpsychires.2008.03.006

Tait, R. C., & Chibnall, J. T. (2014). Racial/ethnic disparities in the assessment and treatment of pain: Psychosocial perspectives. *American Psychologist, 69*(2), 131–141. doi:10.1037/a0035204

Tal, J. Z., & Primeau, M. (2015). Circadian rhythms, sleep, and their treatment impact. In A. Yildiz, P. Ruiz, & C. B. Nemeroff (Eds.), *The bipolar book: History, neurobiology, and treatment* (pp. 127–135). New York, NY: Oxford University Press.

Talbot, K., & Wang, H.-Y. (2014). The nature, significance, and glucagon-like peptide-1 analog treatment of brain insulin resistance in Alzheimer's disease. *Alzheimer's & Dementia, 10*(1, Suppl), S12–S25. doi:10.1016/j.jalz.2013.12.007

Tam-Tham, H., Cepoiu-Martin, M., Ronksley, P. E., Maxwell, C. J., & Hemmelgarn, B. R. (2013). Dementia case management and risk of long-term care placement: A systematic review and meta-analysis. *International Journal of Geriatric Psychiatry, 28*(9), 889–902. doi:10.1002/gps.3906

Tan, G., Rintala, D. H., Jensen, M. P., Fukui, T., Smith, D., & Williams, W. (2015). A randomized controlled trial of hypnosis compared with biofeedback for adults with chronic low back pain. *European Journal of Pain, 19*(2), 271–280. doi:10.1002/ejp.545

Tan, K. R., Rudolph, U., & Lüscher, C. (2011). Hooked on benzodiazepines: GABAA receptor subtypes and addiction. *Trends in Neurosciences, 34*(4), 188–197. doi:http://dx.doi.org/10.1016/j.tins.2011.01.004

Tan, S.-Y., & Wong, T. K. (2012). Existential therapy: Empirical evidence and clinical applications from a Christian perspective. *Journal of Psychology and Christianity, 31*(3), 272–277.

Tandon, R., Gaebel, W., Barch, D. M., Bustillo, J., Gur, R. E., Heckers, S., ... Carpenter, W. (2013). Definition and description of schizophrenia in the DSM-5. *Schizophrenia Research, 150*(1), 3–10. doi:10.1016/j.schres.2013.05.028

Tandon, R., Keshavan, M. S., & Nasrallah, H. A. (2008). Schizophrenia, "Just the Facts" What we know in 2008. 2. Epidemiology and etiology. *Schizophrenia Research, 102*(1–3), 1–18. doi:http://dx.doi.org/10.1016/j.schres.2008.04.011

Tandon, R., Nasrallah, H. A., & Keshavan, M. S. (2010). Schizophrenia, "Just the Facts" 5. Treatment and prevention past, present, and future. *Schizophrenia Research, 122*(1–3), 1–23. doi:http://dx.doi.org/10.1016/j.schres.2010.05.025

Taniai, H., Nishiyama, T., Miyachi, T., Imaeda, M., & Sumi, S. (2008). Genetic influences on the broad spectrum of autism: Study of proband-ascertained twins. *American Journal of Medical Genetics Part B: Neuropsychiatric Genetics, 147B*(6), 844–849. doi:10.1002/ajmg.b.30740

Tanofsky-Kraff, M., & Wilfley, D. E. (2010). Interpersonal psychotherapy for bulimia nervosa and binge-eating disorder. In C. M. Grilo & J. E. Mitchell (Eds.), *The treatment of eating disorders: A clinical handbook* (pp. 271–293). New York, NY: Guilford Press.

Tarasoff v. Regents of the University of California, 529 P.2d 553 (Cal. 1974).

Tarrier, N., Sommerfield, C., & Pilgrim, H. (1999). Relatives' expressed emotion (EE) and PTSD treatment outcome. *Psychological Medicine, 29*(4), 801–811. doi:10.1017/S0033291799008569

Tarver, J., Daley, D., & Sayal, K. (2014). Attention-deficit hyperactivity disorder (ADHD): An updated review of the essential facts. *Child: Care, Health and Development, 40*(6), 762–774. doi:10.1111/cch.12139

Tasca, C., Rapetti, M., Carta, M. G., & Fadda, B. (2012). Women and hysteria in the history of mental health. *Clinical Practice and Epidemiology in Mental Health, 8.* doi:10.2174/1745017901208010110

Tateno, A., Sakayori, T., Kawashima, Y., Higuchi, M., Suhara, T., Mizumura, S., ... Okubo, Y. (2015). Comparison of imaging biomarkers for Alzheimer's disease: Amyloid imaging with [18F]florbetapir positron emission tomography and magnetic resonance imaging voxel-based analysis for entorhinal cortex atrophy. *International Journal of Geriatric Psychiatry, 30*(5), 505–513. doi:10.1002/gps.4173

Taylor, C., & Nutt, D. (2004). Anxiolytics. *Psychiatry, 3*(7), 17–21. doi:http://dx.doi.org/10.1383/psyt.3.7.17.42874

Taylor, D. J., & Pruiksma, K. E. (2014). Cognitive and behavioural therapy for insomnia (CBT-I) in psychiatric populations: A systematic review. *International Review of Psychiatry, 26*(2), 205–213. doi:10.3109/09540261.2014.902808

Taylor, L. E., Swerdfeger, A. L., & Eslick, G. D. (2014). Vaccines are not associated with autism: An evidence-based meta-analysis of case-control and cohort studies. *Vaccine, 32*(29), 3623–3629. doi:http://dx.doi.org/10.1016/j.vaccine.2014.04.085

Taylor, S. (2013). Molecular genetics of obsessive-compulsive disorder: A comprehensive meta-analysis of genetic association studies. *Molecular Psychiatry, 18*(7), 799–805. doi:10.1038/mp.2012.76

Taylor, S., Abramowitz, J. S., McKay, D., & Asmundson, G. J. G. (2010). Anxious traits and temperaments. In D. J. Stein, E. Hollander, & B. O. Rothbaum (Eds.), *Textbook of anxiety disorders* (2nd ed., pp. 73–86). Arlington, VA: American Psychiatric Publishing.

Teachman, B. A., Marker, C. D., & Clerkin, E. M. (2010). Catastrophic misinterpretations as a predictor of symptom change during treatment for panic disorder. *Journal of Consulting and Clinical Psychology, 78*(6), 964–973. doi:10.1037/a0021067

Teasdale, J. D. (2004). Mindfulness-based cognitive therapy. In J. Yiend (Ed.), *Cognition, emotion and psychopathology: Theoretical, empirical and clinical directions* (pp. 270–289). New York, NY: Cambridge University Press.

Tedeschi, R. G., & Calhoun, L. G. (1996). The Posttraumatic Growth Inventory: Measuring the positive legacy of trauma. *Journal of Traumatic Stress, 9*(3), 455–472. doi:10.1002/jts.2490090305

Tedeschi, R. G., & Calhoun, L. G. (2004). Posttraumatic growth: Conceptual foundations and empirical evidence. *Psychological Inquiry, 15*(1), 1–18. doi:10.1207/s15327965pli1501_01

TedX Talks. (2013, May 23). Depression is a disease of civilization: Stephen Ilardi at TEDxEmory [Video file]. Retrieved from https://www.youtube.com/watch?v=drv3BP0Fdi8

Tehrani, N. (2004). *Workplace trauma: Concepts, assessments, and interventions.* New York, NY: Brunner-Routledge.

Teive, H. A. G., Germiniani, F. M. B., Munhoz, R. P., & de Paola, L. (2014). 126 hysterical years—The contribution of Charcot. *Arquivos de Neuro-Psiquiatria, 72*(8), 636–639. doi:10.1590/0004-282X20140068

Telles-Correia, D., & Marques, J. G. (2015). Melancholia before the twentieth century: Fear and sorrow or partial insanity? *Frontiers In Psychology, 6.* Retrieved from doi:10.3389/fpsyg.2015.00081

Tenbergen, G., Wittfoth, M., Frieling, H., Ponseti, J., Walter, M., Walter, H., ... Kruger, T. H. C. (2015). The neurobiology and psychology of pedophilia: Recent advances and challenges. *Frontiers In Human Neuroscience, 9,* 344–344. doi:10.3389/fnhum.2015.00344

Tenhula, W. N., & Bellack, A. S. (2008). Social skills training. In K. T. Mueser & D. V. Jeste (Eds.), *Clinical handbook of schizophrenia* (pp. 240–248). New York, NY: Guilford Press.

ter Kuile, M. M., Both, S., & van Lankveld, J. J. D. M. (2010). Cognitive behavioral therapy for sexual dysfunctions in women. *Psychiatric Clinics of North America, 33*(3), 595–610. doi:10.1016/j.psc.2010.04.010

Testa, M., & West, S. G. (2010). Civil commitment in the United States. *Psychiatry, 7*(10), 30–40.

Teusch, L., Böhme, H., Finke, J., & Gastpar, M. (2001). Effects of client-centered psychotherapy for personality disorders alone and in combination with psychopharmacological treatment. *Psychotherapy and Psychosomatics, 70*(6), 328–336. doi:10.1159/000056273

Thagaard, M. S., Faraone, S. V., Sonuga-Barke, E. J., & Østergaard, S. D. (2016). Empirical tests of natural selection-based evolutionary accounts of ADHD: A systematic review. *Acta Neuropsychiatrica, 28*(5), 249–256. doi:10.1017/neu.2016.14

Thapar, A., & Cooper, M. (2016). Attention deficit hyperactivity disorder. *The Lancet, 387*(10024), 1240–1250. doi:10.1016/S0140-6736(15)00238-X

Thapar, A., Cooper, M., Eyre, O., & Langley, K. (2013). What have we learnt about the causes of ADHD? *Journal of Child Psychology and Psychiatry, 54*(1), 3–16. doi:10.1111/j.1469-7610.2012.02611.x

Thibaut, F. (2012). Pharmacological treatment of paraphilias. *Israeli Journal of Psychiatry, 49*(4), 297–305. Retrieved from http://doctorsonly.co.il/wp-content/uploads/2013/03/09_-Pharmacological-treatment.pdf

Thibodeau, R., & Finley, J. R. (2016). On associative stigma: Implicit and explicit evaluations of a mother of a child with autism spectrum disorder. *Journal of Child and Family Studies.* doi:10.1007/s10826-016-0615-2

Thomas, J. J., Eddy, K. T., Murray, H. B., Tromp, M. D. P., Hartmann, A. S., Stone, M. T., ... Becker, A. E. (2015). The impact of revised DSM-5 criteria on the relative distribution and inter-rater reliability of eating disorder diagnoses in a residential treatment setting. *Psychiatry Research, 229*(1–2), 517–523. doi:10.1016/j.psychres.2015.06.017

Thomas, J. J., Koh, K. A., Eddy, K. T., Hartmann, A. S., Murray, H. B., Gorman, M. J., ... Becker, A. E. (2014). Do DSM-5 eating disorder criteria overpathologize normative eating patterns among individuals with obesity? *Journal of Obesity,* 1–8. Retrieved from http://dx.doi.org/10.1155/2014/320803

Thomas, K. M., Hopwood, C. J., Donnellan, M. B., Wright, A. G. C., Sanislow, C. A., McDevitt-Murphy, M. E., ... Morey, L. C. (2014). Personality heterogeneity in PTSD: Distinct temperament and interpersonal typologies. *Psychological Assessment, 26*(1), 23–34. doi:10.1037/a0034318

Thomas, M. (2009, Spring). Expanded liability for psychiatrists: *Tarasoff* gone crazy? *Journal of Mental Health Law,* 45–56.

Thomas, N. (2015). What's really wrong with cognitive behavioral therapy for psychosis? *Frontiers In Psychology, 6.*

Thomas, S. P. (2011). Open-dialogue therapy: Can a Finnish approach work elsewhere? *Issues in Mental Health Nursing, 32*(10), 613–613. doi:10.3109/01612840.2011.608314

Thompson, D. F., Ramos, C. L., & Willett, J. K. (2014). Psychopathy: Clinical features, developmental basis and therapeutic challenges. *Journal of Clinical Pharmacy and Therapeutics, 39*(5), 485–495. doi:10.1111/jcpt.12182

Thompson, M. (2011). The disappearing "disorder": Why PTSD is becoming PTS. *Time.* Retrieved from http://nation.time.com/2011/06/05/the-disappearing-disorder-why-ptsd-is-becoming-pts/

Thompson, R. H., & Borrero, J. C. (2011). Direct observation. In W. W. Fisher, C. C. Piazza, & H. S. Roane (Eds.), *Handbook of applied behavior analysis* (pp. 191–205). New York, NY: Guilford Press.

Thompson-Hollands, J., Edson, A., Tompson, M. C., & Comer, J. S. (2014). Family involvement in the psychological treatment of obsessive-compulsive disorder: A meta-analysis. *Journal of Family Psychology, 28*(3), 287–298. doi:10.1037/a0036709

Thornicroft, G. (1994). The NHS and Community Care Act,1990. *Psychiatric Bulletin, 18,* 13–17.

Thornton, D. (2010). Evidence regarding the need for a diagnostic category for a coercive paraphilia. *Archives of Sexual Behavior, 39*(2), 411–418. doi:10.1007/s10508-009-9583-6

Thurber, S. (2016). Childhood enuresis: Current diagnostic formulations, salient findings, and effective treatment modalities. *Archives of Psychiatric Nursing.* doi:10.1016/j.apnu.2016.11.005

Thurgood, S. L., McNeill, A., Clark-Carter, D., & Brose, L. S. (2016). A systematic review of smoking cessation interventions for adults in substance abuse treatment or recovery. *Nicotine & Tobacco Research, 18*(5), 993–1001. doi:10.1093/ntr/ntv127

Tiefer, L. (1991). Historical, scientific, clinical and feminist criticisms of 'the human sexual response cycle' model. *Annual Review of Sex Research, 2,* 1–23.

Tiefer, L. (2001). A new view of women's sexual problems: Why new? Why now? *Journal of Sex Research, 38*(2), 89–96. doi:10.1080/00224490109552075

Tiefer, L. (2002). Beyond the medical model of women's sexual problems: A campaign to resist the promotion of 'female sexual dysfunction'. *Sexual and Relationship Therapy, 17*(2), 127–135. doi:10.1080/14681990220121248

Tiefer, L. (2003). Female sexual dysfunction (FSD): Witnessing social construction in action. *Sexualities, Evolution & Gender, 5*(1), 33–36. doi:10.1080/14616660310001594962

Tiefer, L. (2006). Sex therapy as a humanistic enterprise. *Sexual and Relationship Therapy, 21*(3), 359–375. doi:10.1080/14681990600740723

Tiefer, L. (2010). Activism on the medicalization of sex and female genital cosmetic surgery by the New View Campaign in the United States. *Reproductive Health Matters, 18*(35), 56–63. doi:10.1016/S0968-8080(10)35493-0

Tienari, P. J., & Wynne, L. C. (1994). Adoption studies of schizophrenia. *Annals of Medicine, 26*(4), 233–237. doi:10.3109/07853899409147896

Tienari, P. J., Wahlberg, K.-E., & Wynne, L. C. (2006). Finnish adoption study of schizophrenia: Implications for family interventions. *Families, Systems, & Health, 24*(4), 442–451. doi:10.1037/1091-7527.24.4.442

Tieu, M. (2010, March). Understanding the nature of drug addiction. *Bioethics Research Notes, 22,* 7–11.

Tiggemann, M. (2013). Objectification theory: Of relevance for eating disorder researchers and clinicians? *Clinical Psychologist, 17*(2), 35–45. doi:10.1111/cp.12010

Tiggemann, M., Slater, A., Bury, B., Hawkins, K., & Firth, B. (2013). Disclaimer labels on fashion magazine advertisements: Effects on social comparison and body dissatisfaction. *Body Image, 10*(1), 45–53. doi:10.1016/j.bodyim.2012.08.001

Timimi, S. (2004). A critique of the international consensus statement on ADHD. *Clinical Child and Family Psychology Review, 7*(1), 59–63. doi:10.1023/B:CCFP.0000020192.49298.7a

Timimi, S. (2015). Attention deficit hyperactivity disorder is an example of bad medicine. *Australian and New Zealand Journal of Psychiatry, 49*(6), 575–576. doi:10.1177/0004867415580820

Timimi, S., & Leo, J. (Eds.). (2009). *Rethinking ADHD: From brain to culture.* Basingstoke, UK: Palgrave Macmillan.

Timimi, S., & Taylor, E. (2003). ADHD is best understood as a cultural construct. *The British Journal of Psychiatry, 184*(1), 8.

Timm, J. C. (2013). PTSD is not a disorder, says Medal of Honor winner. *MSNBC.* Retrieved from http://www.msnbc.com/morning-joe/ptsd-not-disorder-says-medal-honor

Timulak, L., & McElvaney, J. (2016). Emotion-focused therapy for generalized anxiety disorder: An overview of the model. *Journal of Contemporary Psychotherapy, 46,* 41–52. doi:10.1007/s10879-015-9310-7

Ting, J. T., & Feng, G. (2008). Glutamatergic Synaptic Dysfunction and Obsessive-Compulsive Disorder. *Current Chemical Genomics, 2,* 62–75.

Titova, O. E., Hjorth, O. C., Schiöth, H. B., & Brooks, S. J. (2013). Anorexia nervosa is linked to reduced brain structure in reward and somatosensory regions: a meta-analysis of VBM studies. *BMC Psychiatry, 13*(1), 1–11. doi:10.1186/1471-244x-13-110

Tokita, K., Yamaji, T., & Hashimoto, K. (2012). Roles of glutamate signaling in preclinical and/or mechanistic models of depression. *Pharmacology Biochemistry and Behavior, 100*(4), 688–704. doi:http://dx.doi.org/10.1016/j.pbb.2011.04.016

Tolin, D. F. (2010). Is cognitive–behavioral therapy more effective than other therapies? A meta-analytic review. *Clinical Psychology Review, 30*(6), 710–720. doi:10.1016/j.cpr.2010.05.003

Tolin, D. F., & Foa, E. B. (2008). Sex differences in trauma and posttraumatic stress disorder: A quantitative review of 25 years of research. *Psychological Trauma: Theory, Research, Practice, and Policy, S*(1), 37–85. doi:10.1037/1942-9681.S.1.37

Tolin, D. F., Frost, R. O., Steketee, G., & Muroff, J. (2015). Cognitive behavioral therapy for hoarding disorder: A meta-analysis. *Depression and Anxiety, 32*(3), 158–166. doi:10.1002/da.22327

Tomasik, J., Rahmoune, H., Guest, P. C., & Bahn, S. (2016). Neuroimmune biomarkers in schizophrenia. *Schizophrenia Research, 176*(1), 3–13. doi:10.1016/j.schres.2014.07.025

Tomassini, C., Juel, K., Holm, N. V., Skytthe, A., & Christensen, K. (2003). Risk of suicide in twins: 51 year follow up study. *BMJ: British Medical Journal, 327*(7411), 373–374. doi:10.1136/bmj.327.7411.373

Tomic, N. (2011). Treating nocturnal enuresis with direct and indirect suggestions by using hypnosis. *Australian Journal of Clinical Hypnotherapy and Hypnosis, 32*(1), 26–39.

Tomlinson, M. F., Brown, M., & Hoaken, P. N. S. (2016). Recreational drug use and human aggressive behavior: A comprehensive review since 2003. *Aggression and Violent Behavior, 27,* 9–29. doi:10.1016/j.avb.2016.02.004

Tomlinson, W. C. (2006). Freud and psychogenic movement disorders. In M. Hallett, C. R. Cloninger, S. Fahn, J. Jankovic, A. E. Lang, & S. C. Yudofsky (Eds.), *Psychogenic movement disorders: Neurology and neuropsychiatry* (pp. 14–19). Philadelphia, PA: Lippincott Williams & Wilkins.

Toneatto, T. (2013). Gambling. In P. M. Miller, S. A. Ball, M. E. Bates, A. W. Blume, K. M. Kampman, D. J. Kavanagh, M. E. Larimer, N. M. Petry, & P. De Witte (Eds.), *Comprehensive addictive behaviors and disorders: Vol. 1. Principles of addiction* (pp. 797–807). San Diego, CA: Elsevier Academic Press.

Toodayan, N. (2016). Professor Alois Alzheimer (1864–1915): Lest we forget. *Journal of Clinical Neuroscience, 31,* 47–55. doi:10.1016/j.jocn.2015.12.032

Toplak, M. E., Connors, L., Shuster, J., Knezevic, B., & Parks, S. (2008). Review of cognitive, cognitive-behavioral, and neural-based interventions for attention-deficit/hyperactivity disorder (ADHD). *Clinical Psychology Review, 28*(5), 801–823. doi:10.1016/j.cpr.2007.10.008

Toporek, R. L., & Williams, R. A. (2006). Ethics and professional issues related to the practice of social justice in counseling psychology. In R. L. Toporek, L. H. Gerstein, N. Fouad, G. Roysircar, & T. Israel (Eds.), *Handbook for social justice in counseling psychology: Leadership, vision, and action* (pp. 17–34). Thousand Oaks, CA: Sage.

Torgersen, S. (1983). Genetic factors in anxiety disorders. *Archives of General Psychiatry, 40*(10), 1085–1089.

Torgersen, S. (1986). Genetics of somatoform disorders. *Archives of General Psychiatry, 43*(5), 502–505. doi:10.1001/archpsyc.1986.01800050108014

Torgersen, S., Lygren, S., Øien, P. A., Skre, I., Onstad, S., Edvardsen, J., ... Kringlen, E. (2000). A twin study of personality disorders. *Comprehensive Psychiatry, 41*(6), 416–425. doi:10.1053/comp.2000.16560

Torok, M., Calear, A., Shand, F., & Christensen, H. (2016). A systematic review of mass media campaigns for suicide prevention: Understanding their efficacy and the mechanisms needed for successful behavioral and literacy change. *Suicide and Life-Threatening Behavior.* doi:10.1111/sltb.12324

Torrey, E. F. (1992). Are we overestimating the genetic contribution to schizophrenia? *Schizophrenia Bulletin, 18*(2), 159–170.

Torrey, E. F. (2013). *Surviving schizophrenia: A family manual* (6th ed.). New York, NY: Harper Collins.

Torrey, E. F. (2014). *American psychosis: How the federal government destroyed the mental illness treatment system*. New York, NY: Oxford University Press.

Torrey, E. F., Simmons, W., & Yolken, R. H. (2015). Is childhood cat ownership a risk factor for schizophrenia later in life? *Schizophrenia Research, 165*(1), 1–2. doi:10.1016/j.schres.2015.03.036

Town, J. M., & Driessen, E. (2013). Emerging evidence for intensive short-term dynamic psychotherapy with personality disorders and somatic disorders. *Psychiatric Annals, 43*(11), 502–507. doi:10.3928/00485713-20131105-05

Town, J. M., Abbass, A., & Bernier, D. (2013). Effectiveness and cost effectiveness of Davanloo's Intensive Short-Term Dynamic Psychotherapy: Does unlocking the unconscious make a difference? *American Journal of Psychotherapy, 67*(1), 89–108.

Trace, S. E., Baker, J. H., Peñas-Lledó, E., & Bulik, C. M. (2013). The genetics of eating disorders. *Annual Review of Clinical Psychology, 9*, 589–620. doi:10.1146/annurev-clinpsy-050212-185546

Trace, S. E., Thornton, L. M., Root, T. L., Mazzeo, S. E., Lichtenstein, P., Pedersen, N. L., & Bulik, C. M. (2012). Effects of reducing the frequency and duration criteria for binge eating on lifetime prevalence of bulimia nervosa and binge eating disorder: Implications for DSM-5. *International Journal of Eating Disorders, 45*(4), 531–536. doi:10.1002/eat.20955

Tran, K., Moulton, K., Santesso, N., & Rabb, D. (2016). Cognitive processing therapy for post-traumatic stress disorder: A systematic review and meta-analysis: Canadian Agency for Drugs and Technologies in Health, Ottawa (ON).

Treadway, M. T., & Pizzagalli, D. A. (2014). Imaging the pathophysiology of major depressive disorder—from localist models to circuit-based analysis. *Biology of Mood & Anxiety Disorders, 4*, 5–5. doi:10.1186/2045-5380-4-5

Tretteteig, S., Vatne, S., & Rokstad, A. M. M. (2016). The influence of day care centres for people with dementia on family caregivers: An integrative review of the literature. *Aging & Mental Health, 20*(5), 450–462. doi:10.1080/13607863.2015.1023765

Trimble, M. R., & George, M. S. (2010). *Biological psychiatry* (3rd ed.). Chichester, UK: John Wiley.

Tripp, G., & Wickens, J. R. (2008). Dopamine transfer deficit: A neurobiological theory of altered reinforcement mechanisms in ADHD. *Journal of Child Psychology and Psychiatry, 49*(7), 691–704. doi:10.1111/j.1469-7610.2007.01851.x

Tristano, A. G. (2009). The impact of rheumatic diseases on sexual function. *Rheumatology International, 29*(8), 853–860. doi:10.1007/s00296-009-0850-6

Tristano, A. G. (2014). Impact of rheumatoid arthritis on sexual function. *World Journal of Orthopedics, 5*(2), 107–111. doi:10.5312/wjo.v5.i2.107

Trivedi, M. H., Rush, A. J., Wisniewski, S. R., Nierenberg, A. A., Warden, D., Ritz, L., ... Fava, M. (2006). Evaluation of Outcomes With Citalopram for Depression Using Measurement-Based Care in STAR*D: Implications for Clinical Practice. *The American Journal of Psychiatry, 163*(1), 28–40. doi:10.1176/appi.ajp.163.1.28

Trower, P., Casey, A., & Dryden, W. (1988). *Cognitive-behavioural counselling in action*. London, UK: Sage.

Trull, T. J. (2012). The Five-Factor Model of personality disorder and DSM-5. *Journal of Personality, 80*(6), 1697–1720. doi:10.1111/j.1467-6494.2012.00771.x

Trull, T. J., Jahng, S., Tomko, R. L., Wood, P. K., & Sher, K. J. (2010). Revised NESARC personality disorder diagnoses: Gender, prevalence, and comorbidity with substance dependence disorders. *Journal of Personality Disorders, 24*(4), 412–426. doi:10.1521/pedi.2010.24.4.412

Trull, T. J., Scheiderer, E. M., & Tomko, R. L. (2012). Axis II comorbidity. In T. A. Widiger (Ed.), *The Oxford handbook of personality disorders* (pp. 219–236). New York, NY: Oxford University Press.

Tsai, J.-D., Wang, I. C., Chen, H.-J., Sheu, J.-N., Li, T.-C., Tsai, H. J., & Wei, C.-C. (2017). Trend of nocturnal enuresis in children with attention deficit/hyperactivity disorder: a nationwide population-based study in Taiwan. *Journal of Investigative Medicine, 65*, 370–375. doi:10.1136/jim-2016-000223

Tsesis, A. (2011). Due process in civil commitments. *Washington and Lee Law Review, 68*, 253–307.

Tsoi, D. T. Y., Hunter, M. D., & Woodruff, P. W. R. (2008). History, aetiology, and symptomatology of schizophrenia. *Psychiatry, 7*(10), 404–409. doi:http://dx.doi.org/10.1016/j.mppsy.2008.07.010

Tsuang, M. T., Van Os, J., Tandon, R., Barch, D. M., Bustillo, J., Gaebel, W., ... Carpenter, W. (2013). Attenuated psychosis syndrome in DSM-5. *Schizophrenia Research, 150*(1), 31–35. doi:http://dx.doi.org/10.1016/j.schres.2013.05.004

Tueth, M. J. (1995). Schizophrenia: Emil Kraepelin, Adolph Meyer, and beyond. *The Journal of Emergency Medicine, 13*(6), 805–809. doi:http://dx.doi.org/10.1016/0736-4679(95)02022-5

Tufford, L., & Newman, P. (2012). Bracketing in qualitative research. *Qualitative Social Work: Research and Practice, 11*(1), 80–96. doi:10.1177/1473325010368316

Turecki, G., & Brent, D. A. (2016). Suicide and suicidal behaviour. *The Lancet, 387*(10024), 1227–1239. doi:10.1016/S0140-6736(15)00234-2

Turna, J., Grosman Kaplan, K., Anglin, R., & Van Ameringen, M. (2016). 'What's bugging the gut in OCD?' A review of the gut microbiome in obsessive–compulsive disorder. *Depression and Anxiety, 33*(3), 171–178. doi:10.1002/da.22454

Turner, R. M. (2000). Naturalistic evaluation of dialectical behavior therapy-oriented treatment for borderline personality disorder. *Cognitive and Behavioral Practice, 7*(4), 413–419. doi:10.1016/S1077-7229(00)80052-8

Twenge, J. M. (2011). Narcissism and culture. In W. K. Campbell & J. D. Miller (Eds.), *The handbook of narcissism and narcissistic personality disorder: Theoretical approaches, empirical findings, and treatments* (pp. 202–209). Hoboken, NJ: John Wiley.

Twenge, J. M. (2017, September). Have smartphones destroyed a generation? *The Atlantic*. Retrieved from https://www.theatlantic.com/magazine/archive/2017/09/has-the-smartphone-destroyed-a-generation/534198/

Twombly, J. H. (2013). Integrating IFS with phase-oriented treatment of clients with dissociative disorder. In M. Sweezy & E. L. Ziskind (Eds.), *Internal family systems therapy: New dimensions* (pp. 72–89). New York, NY: Routledge.

Tyrer, P. (2012). Diagnostic and Statistical Manual of Mental Disorders: A classification of personality disorders that has had its day. *Clinical Psychology & Psychotherapy, 19*(5), 372–374. doi:10.1002/cpp.1810

Tyrer, P., & Silk, K. R. (2011). A comparison of UK and US guidelines for drug treatment in borderline personality disorder. *International Review of Psychiatry, 23*(4), 388–394. doi:10.3109/09540261.2011.606540

Tyrer, P., Crawford, M., Sanatinia, R., Tyrer, H., Cooper, S., Muller-Pollard, C., ... Weich, S. (2014). Preliminary studies of the ICD-11 classification of personality disorder in practice. *Personality and Mental Health, 8*(4), 254–263. doi:10.1002/pmh.1275

Tyrer, P., Reed, G. M., & Crawford, M. J. (2015). Classification, assessment, prevalence, and effect of personality disorder. *The Lancet, 385*(9969), 717–726. doi:10.1016/S0140-6736(14)61995-4

Tyrrell, J., Melzer, D., Henley, W., Galloway, T. S., & Osborne, N. J. (2013). Associations between socioeconomic status and environmental toxicant concentrations in adults in the USA: NHANES 2001-2010. *Environment International, 59*, 328–335. doi:10.1016/j.envint.2013.06.017

Uchiyama, T., Kurosawa, M., & Inaba, Y. (2007). MMR-vaccine and regression in autism spectrum disorders: Negative results presented from Japan. *Journal of Autism and Developmental Disorders, 37*(2), 210–217. doi:10.1007/s10803-006-0157-3

Uddin, M., & Diwadkar, V. A. (2014). Inflammation and psychopathology: What we now know, and what we need to know. *Social Psychiatry and Psychiatric Epidemiology, 49*(10), 1537–1539. doi:10.1007/s00127-014-0934-9

Uher, R., & Rutter, M. (2012). Classification of feeding and eating disorders: Review of evidence and proposals for ICD-11. *World Psychiatry, 11*(2), 80–92.

Uher, R., Payne, J. L., Pavlova, B., & Perlis, R. H. (2014). Major depressive disorder in DSM-5: Implications for clinical practice and research of changes from DSM-IV. *Depression and Anxiety, 31*(6), 459–471. doi:10.1002/da.22217

Ung, D., Selles, R., Small, B. J., & Storch, E. A. (2015). A systematic review and meta-analysis of cognitive-behavioral therapy for anxiety in youth with high-functioning autism spectrum disorders. *Child Psychiatry and Human Development, 46*(4), 533–547. doi:10.1007/s10578-014-0494-y

Unis, A. S., Cook, E. H., Vincent, J. G., Gjerde, D. K., Perry, B. D., Mason, C., & Mitchell, J. (1997). Platelet serotonin measures in adolescents with conduct disorder. *Biological Psychiatry, 42*(7), 553–559. doi:10.1016/S0006-3223(96)00465-9

United Nations General Assembly. (2006, December 13). Convention on the Rights of Persons with Disabilities. Retrieved from http://www.un-documents.net/a61r106.htm

United Nations Office on Drugs and Crime. (2016). World Drug Report 2016. Retrieved from http://www.unodc.org/wdr2016/

United States v. Dusky, 295 F.2d 743 (1961).

Uphouse, L. (2014). Pharmacology of serotonin and female sexual behavior. *Pharmacology Biochemistry and Behavior*, 121, 31–42. doi:http://dx.doi.org/10.1016/j.pbb.2013.11.008

Ussher, J. M. (2011). *The madness of women: Myth and experience*. London, UK: Routledge.

Ussher, J. M. (2013). Diagnosing difficult women and pathologising femininity: Gender bias in psychiatric nosology. *Feminism & Psychology*, 23(1), 63–69. doi:10.1177/0959353512467968

Vadermeersch, P. (1994). "Les mythes d'origine" in the history of psychiatry. In M. S. Micale & R. Porter (Eds.), *Discovering the history of psychiatry* (pp. 219–231). New York, NY: Oxford University Press.

Vahia, I. V., & Cohen, C. I. (2008). Psychopathology. In K. T. Mueser & D. V. Jeste (Eds.), *Clinical handbook of schizophrenia* (pp. 82–90). New York, NY: Guilford Press.

Valenstein, E. S. (1998). *Blaming the brain: The truth about drugs and mental health*. New York, NY: The Free Press.

Vallerand, I. A., Kalenchuk, A. L., & McLennan, J. D. (2014). Behavioural treatment recommendations in clinical practice guidelines for attention-deficit/hyperactivity disorder: A scoping review. *Child and Adolescent Mental Health*, 19(4), 251–258. doi:10.1111/camh.12062

van Beijsterveldt, C. E. M., Hudziak, J. J., & Boomsma, D. I. (2006). Genetic and environmental influences on cross-gender behavior and relation to behavior problems: A study of Dutch twins at ages 7 and 10 years. *Archives of Sexual Behavior*, 35(6), 647–658. doi:10.1007/s10508-006-9072-0

van Bilsen, H. (2013). *Cognitive behaviour therapy in the real world: Back to basics*. London, UK: Karnac Books.

van Boekel, L. C., Brouwers, E. P. M., van Weeghel, J., & Garretsen, H. F. L. (2015). Comparing stigmatising attitudes towards people with substance use disorders between the general public, GPs, mental health and addiction specialists and clients. *International Journal of Social Psychiatry*, 61(6), 539–549. doi:10.1177/0020764014562051

van den Anker, L., Dalhuisen, L., & Stokkel, M. (2011). Fitness to stand trial: A general principle of European criminal law? *Utrecht Law Review*, 7(3), 120–136.

van den Bosch, L. M. C., Koeter, M. W. J., Stijnen, T., Verheul, R., & van den Brink, W. (2005). Sustained efficacy of dialectical behaviour therapy for borderline personality disorder. *Behaviour Research and Therapy*, 43(9), 1231–1241. doi:10.1016/j.brat.2004.09.008

van den Heuvel, O. A., Mataix-Cols, D., Zwitser, G., Cath, D. C., van der Werf, Y. D., Groenewegen, H. J., ... Veltman, D. J. (2011). Common limbic and frontal-striatal disturbances in patients with obsessive compulsive disorder, panic disorder and hypochondriasis. *Psychological Medicine*, 41(11), 2399–2410. doi:10.1017/S0033291711000535

van den Heuvel, O. A., Remijnse, P. L., Mataix-Cols, D., Vrenken, H., Groenewegen, H. J., Uylings, H. B. M., ... Veltman, D. J. (2009). The major symptom dimensions of obsessive-compulsive disorder are mediated by partially distinct neural systems. *Brain: A Journal of Neurology*, 132(4), 853–868. doi:10.1093/brain/awn267

van den Heuvel, O. A., Veale, D., & Stein, D. J. (2014). Hypochondriasis: Considerations for ICD-11. *Revista Brasileira de Psiquiatria*, 36, 21–27.

van der Feltz-Cornelis, C. M., & van Dyck, R. (1997). The notion of somatization: An artefact of the conceptualization of body and mind. *Psychotherapy and Psychosomatics*, 66(3), 117–127. doi:10.1159/000289121

van der Hart, O., & Horst, R. (1989). The dissociation theory of Pierre Janet. *Journal of Traumatic Stress*, 2(4), 397–412. doi:10.1002/jts.2490020405

van der Kolk, B. A. (2007). The history of trauma in psychiatry. In M. J. Friedman, T. M. Keane, & P. A. Resick (Eds.), *Handbook of PTSD: Science and practice* (pp. 19–36). New York, NY: Guilford Press.

van der Stel, J. (2015). Evolution of mental health and addiction care systems in Europe. In G. Dom & F. Moggi (Eds.), *Co-occurring addictive and psychiatric disorders: A practice-based handbook from a European perspective* (pp. 13–26). New York, NY: Springer-Verlag Publishing.

van der Stouwe, T., Asscher, J. J., Stams, G. J. J. M., Deković, M., & van der Laan, P. H. (2014). The effectiveness of multisystemic therapy (MST): A meta-analysis. *Clinical Psychology Review*, 34(6), 468–481. doi:10.1016/j.cpr.2014.06.006

van Deurzen, E. (2012). *Existential counselling and psychotherapy in practice* (3rd ed.). London, UK: SAGE Publications.

van Dijk, M., Benninga, M. A., Grootenhuis, M. A., Nieuwenhuizen, A.-M. O., & Last, B. F. (2007). Chronic childhood constipation: a review of the literature and the introduction of a protocolized behavioral intervention program. *Patient Education and Counseling*, 67(1–2), 63–77.

van Egmond, J. J. (2003). The multiple meanings of secondary gain. *The American Journal of Psychoanalysis*, 63(2), 137–147. doi:10.1023/A:1024027131335

van Emmerik, A. A. P., Kamphuis, J. H., Hulsbosch, A. M., & Emmelkamp, P. M. G. (2002). Single session debriefing after psychological trauma: A meta-analysis. *The Lancet*, 360(9335), 766–771. doi:10.1016/S0140-6736(02)09897-5

van Erp, T. G. M., Greve, D. N., Rasmussen, J., Turner, J., Calhoun, V. D., Young, S., ... Potkin, S. G. (2014). A multi-scanner study of subcortical brain volume abnormalities in schizophrenia. *Psychiatry Research: Neuroimaging*, 222(1–2), 10–16. doi:10.1016/j.pscychresns.2014.02.011

van Heeringen, C., Bijttebier, S., & Godfrin, K. (2011). Suicidal brains: A review of functional and structural brain studies in association with suicidal behaviour. *Neuroscience and Biobehavioral Reviews*, 35(3), 688–698. doi:10.1016/j.neubiorev.2010.08.007

Van Hoecke, E., Baeyens, D., Walle, J. V., Hoebeke, P., & Roeyers, H. (2003). Socioeconomic status as a common factor underlying the association between enuresis and psychopathology. *Journal of Developmental and Behavioral Pediatrics*, 24(2), 109–114. doi:10.1097/00004703-200304000-00006

van Lankveld, J. J. D. M., ter Kuile, M. M., de Groot, H. E., Melles, R., Nefs, J., & Zandbergen, M. (2006). Cognitive-behavioral therapy for women with lifelong vaginismus: A randomized waiting-list controlled trial of efficacy. *Journal of Consulting and Clinical Psychology*, 74(1), 168–178. doi:10.1037/0022-006X.74.1.168

van Minnen, A., Hendriks, L., & Olff, M. (2010). When do trauma experts choose exposure therapy for PTSD patients? A controlled study of therapist and patient factors. *Behaviour Research and Therapy*, 48(4), 312–320. doi:10.1016/j.brat.2009.12.003

van Os, J. (2009a). A salience dysregulation syndrome. *The British Journal of Psychiatry*, 194(2), 101–103. doi:10.1192/bjp.bp.108.054254

van Os, J. (2009b). 'Salience syndrome' replaces 'schizophrenia' in DSM-V and ICD-11: Psychiatry's evidence-based entry into the 21st century? *Acta Psychiatrica Scandinavica*, 120(5), 363–372. doi:10.1111/j.1600-0447.2009.01456.x

van Os, J., Rutten, B. P., Myin-Germeys, I., Delespaul, P., Viechtbauer, W., van Zelst, C., ... Baudin, G. e. a. (2014). Identifying gene-environment interactions in schizophrenia: Contemporary challenges for integrated, large-scale investigations. *Schizophrenia Bulletin*, 40(4), 729–736. doi:10.1093/schbul/sbu069

Van Rensburg, G. (2015). The adapted open dialogue approach. In A. Meaden & A. Fox (Eds.), *Innovations in psychosocial interventions for psychosis: Working with the hard to reach* (pp. 5–21). New York, NY: Routledge.

van Steensel, F. J. A., & Bögels, S. M. (2015). CBT for anxiety disorders in children with and without autism spectrum disorders. *Journal of Consulting and Clinical Psychology*, 83(3), 512–523. doi:10.1037/a0039108

van Wijngaarden, E., Thurston, S. W., Myers, G. J., Harrington, D., Cory-Slechta, D. A., Strain, J. J., ... Davidson, P. W. (2017). Methyl mercury exposure and neurodevelopmental outcomes in the Seychelles Child Development Study main cohort at age 22 and 24 years. *Neurotoxicology and Teratology*, 59, 35–42. doi:10.1016/j.ntt.2016.10.011

Vance, S. R., Cohen-Kettenis, P. T., Drescher, J., Meyer-Bahlburg, H. F. L., Pfäfflin, F., & Zucker, K. J. (2010). Opinions about the DSM gender identity disorder diagnosis: Results from an international survey administered to organizations concerned with the welfare of transgender people. *International Journal of Transgenderism*, 12(1), 1–14. doi:10.1080/15532731003749087

Vande Voort, J. L., He, J.-P., Jameson, N. D., & Merikangas, K. R. (2014). Impact of the DSM-5 attention-deficit/hyperactivity disorder age-of-onset criterion in the US adolescent population. *Journal of the American Academy of Child & Adolescent Psychiatry*, 53(7), 736–744. doi:10.1016/j.jaac.2014.03.005

Vandereycken, W., & Van Deth, R. (1990). A tribute to Lasègue's description of anorexia nervosa (1873), with completion of its English translation. *The British Journal of Psychiatry, 157*, 902–908. doi:10.1192/bjp.157.6.902

VanFleet, R., Sywulak, A. E., & Sniscak, C. C. (2010). *Child-centered play therapy*. New York, NY: Guilford Press.

Vanheule, S., Desmet, M., Meganck, R., Inslegers, R., Willemsen, J., De Schryver, M., & Devisch, I. (2014). Reliability in psychiatric diagnosis with the DSM: Old wine in new barrels. *Psychotherapy and Psychosomatics, 83*(5), 313–314. doi:10.1159/000358809

Varghese, F. P., & Brown, E. S. (2001). The hypothalamic-pituitary-adrenal axis in major depressive disorder: A brief primer for primary care physicians. *Primary Care Companion to the Journal of Clinical Psychiatry, 3*(4), 151–155.

Varley, C. K. (2001). Sudden death related to selected tricyclic antidepressants in children: epidemiology, mechanisms and clinical implications. *Paediatric Drugs, 3*(8), 613–627.

Vartanian, L. R., & Porter, A. M. (2016). Weight stigma and eating behavior: A review of the literature. *Appetite, 102*, 3–14. doi:10.1016/j.appet.2016.01.034

Vassend, O., Røysamb, E., & Nielsen, C. S. (2012). Neuroticism and self-reported somatic health: A twin study. *Psychology & Health, 27*(1), 1–12. doi:10.1080/08870446.2010.540665

Vatne, S., & Holmes, C. (2006). Limit setting in mental health: Historical factors and suggestions as to its rationale. *Journal of Psychiatric and Mental Health Nursing, 13*(5), 588–597.

Vatz, R. E., & Weinberg, L. S. (Eds.). (1983). *Thomas Szasz: Primary values and major contentions*. Buffalo, NY: Prometheus Books.

Veale, J. F., Clarke, D. E., & Lomax, T. C. (2010). Biological and psychosocial correlates of adult gender-variant identities: A review. *Personality and Individual Differences, 48*(4), 357–366. doi:10.1016/j.paid.2009.09.018

Veijola, J., Guo, J. Y., Moilanen, J. S., Jääskeläinen, E., Miettunen, J., Kyllönen, M., ... Murray, G. K. (2014). Longitudinal changes in total brain volume in schizophrenia: Relation to symptom severity, cognition and antipsychotic medication. *PLOS One, 9*(7).

Velikonja, T., Fisher, H. L., Mason, O., & Johnson, S. (2015). Childhood trauma and schizotypy: A systematic literature review. *Psychological Medicine, 45*(5), 947–963. doi:10.1017/S0033291714002086

Veling, W., & Susser, E. (2011). Migration and psychotic disorders. *Expert Review of Neurotherapeutics, 11*(1), 65–76. doi:10.1586/ern.10.91

Veling, W., Susser, E., Selten, J. P., & Hoek, H. W. (2015). Social disorganization of neighborhoods and incidence of psychotic disorders: A 7-year first-contact incidence study. *Psychological Medicine, 45*(9), 1789–1798. doi:10.1017/S0033291714002682

Veltman, A., & Chaimowitz, G. (2014). Mental health care for people who identify as lesbian, gay, bisexual, transgender, and (or) queer. *The Canadian Journal of Psychiatry / La Revue Canadienne De Psychiatrie, 59*(11), 1–7 (insert).

Verdellen, C., van de Griendt, J., Hartmann, A., & Murphy, T. (2011). European clinical guidelines for Tourette Syndrome and other tic disorders. Part III: Behavioural and psychosocial interventions. *European Child & Adolescent Psychiatry, 20*(4), 197–207. doi:10.1007/s00787-011-0167-3

Verheul, R. (2012). Personality disorder proposal for DSM-5: A heroic and innovative but nevertheless fundamentally flawed attempt to improve DSM-IV. *Clinical Psychology & Psychotherapy, 19*(5), 369–371. doi:10.1002/cpp.1809

Verheul, R., & Herbrink, M. (2007). The efficacy of various modalities of psychotherapy for personality disorders: A systematic review of the evidence and clinical recommendations. *International Review of Psychiatry, 19*(1), 25–38. doi:10.1080/09540260601095399

Verhoeff, B. (2013). Autism in flux: A history of the concept from Leo Kanner to DSM-5. *History of Psychiatry, 24*(4), 442–458. doi:10.1177/0957154X13500584

Verhulst, B., Neale, M. C., & Kendler, K. S. (2015). The heritability of alcohol use disorders: A meta-analysis of twin and adoption studies. *Psychological Medicine, 45*(5), 1061–1072. doi:10.1017/S0033291714002165

Vermetten, E., Schmahl, C., Lindner, S., Loewenstein, R. J., & Bremner, J. D. (2006). Hippocampal and amygdalar volumes in dissociative identity disorder. *The American Journal of Psychiatry, 163*(4), 630–636. doi:10.1176/appi.ajp.163.4.630

Vernberg, E. M., Steinberg, A. M., Jacobs, A. K., Brymer, M. J., Watson, P. J., Osofsky, J. D., ... Ruzek, J. I. (2008). Innovations in disaster mental health: Psychological first aid. *Professional Psychology: Research and Practice, 39*(4), 381–388. doi:10.1037/a0012663

Vesga-López, O., Schneier, F. R., Wang, S., Heimberg, R. G., Liu, S.-M., Hasin, D. S., & Blanco, C. (2008). Gender differences in generalized anxiety disorder: Results from the national epidemiologic survey on alcohol and related conditions (NESARC). *Journal of Clinical Psychiatry, 69*(10), 1606–1616. doi:10.4088/JCP.v69n1011

Vespia, K. M. (2009). Culture and psychotic disorders. In S. Eshun & R. A. R. Gurung (Eds.), *Culture and mental health: Sociocultural influences, theory, and practice* (pp. 245–272). Chichester, UK: Wiley-Blackwell.

Veysey, S. (2014). People with a borderline personality disorder diagnosis describe discriminatory experiences. *Kōtuitui: New Zealand Journal of Social Sciences Online, 9*(1), 20–35. doi:10.1080/1177083X.2013.871303

Vialou, V., Bagot, R. C., Cahill, M. E., Ferguson, D., Robison, A. J., Dietz, D. M., ... Nestler, E. J. (2014). Prefrontal cortical circuit for depression- and anxiety-related behaviors mediated by cholecystokinin: Role of ΔFosB. *The Journal of Neuroscience, 34*(11), 3878–3887. doi:10.1523/JNEUROSCI.1787-13.2014

Vicario, C. M. (2013). Altered insula response to sweet taste processing in recovered anorexia and bulimia nervosa: A matter of disgust sensitivity? *The American Journal of Psychiatry, 170*(12), 1497–1497. doi:10.1176/appi.ajp.2013.13060748

Vickers, A. J., & de Craen, A. J. (2000). Why use placebos in clinical trials? A narrative review of the methodological literature. *Journal of Clinical Epidemiology, 53*(2), 157–161.

Viding, E., McCrory, E., & Seara-Cardoso, A. (2014). Psychopathy. *Current Biology, 24*(18), R871–R874. doi:http://dx.doi.org/10.1016/j.cub.2014.06.055

Villarreal, G., Hamilton, D. A., Petropoulos, H., Driscoll, I., Rowland, L. M., Griego, J. A., ... Brooks, W. M. (2002). Reduced hippocampal volume and total white matter volume in posttraumatic stress disorder. *Biological Psychiatry, 52*(2), 119–125. doi:10.1016/S0006-3223(02)01359-8

Viney, W., & Bartsch, L. (1984). Dorothea Lynde Dix: Positive or negative influence on the development of treatment for the mentally ill. *The Social Science Journal, 21*(2), 71–82.

Virta, M., Salakari, A., Antila, M., Chydenius, E., Partinen, M., Kaski, M., ... Iivanainen, M. (2010). Short cognitive behavioral therapy and cognitive training for adults with ADHD—A randomized controlled pilot study. *Neuropsychiatric Disease and Treatment, 6*(1).

Vismara, L. A., & Rogers, S. J. (2010). Behavioral treatments in autism spectrum disorder: What do we know? *Annual Review of Clinical Psychology, 6*, 447–468. doi:10.1146/annurev.clinpsy.121208.131151

Visser, J., & Jehan, Z. (2009). ADHD: A scientific fact or a factual opinion? A critique of the veracity of attention deficit hyperactivity disorder. *Emotional & Behavioural Difficulties, 14*(2), 127–140. doi:10.1080/13632750902921930

Visser, S., & Bouman, T. K. (2001). The treatment of hypochondriasis: exposure plus response prevention vs cognitive therapy. *Behaviour Research and Therapy, 39*(4), 423–442. doi:http://dx.doi.org/10.1016/S0005-7967(00)00022-X

Vitola, E. S., Bau, C. H. D., Salum, G. A., Horta, B. L., Quevedo, L., Barros, F. C., ... Grevet, E. H. (2017). Exploring DSM-5 ADHD criteria beyond young adulthood: Phenomenology, psychometric properties and prevalence in a large three-decade birth cohort. *Psychological Medicine, 47*(4), 744–754. doi:10.1017/S0033291716002853

Vogel, E. A., Rose, J. P., Roberts, L. R., & Eckles, K. (2014). Social comparison, social media, and self-esteem. *Psychology of Popular Media Culture, 3*(4), 206–222. doi:10.1037/ppm0000047

Voland, E., & Voland, R. (1989). Evolutionary biology and psychiatry: The case of anorexia nervosa. *Ethology & Sociobiology, 10*(4), 223–240. doi:10.1016/0162-3095(89)90001-0

Volkmar, F. R., & Cohen, D. J. (1991). Comorbid association of autism and schizophrenia. *The American Journal of Psychiatry, 148*(12), 1705–1707. doi:10.1176/ajp.148.12.1705

Volkmar, F. R., & McPartland, J. C. (2014). From Kanner to DSM-5: Autism as an evolving diagnostic concept. *Annual Review of Clinical Psychology, 10*, 193–212. doi:10.1146/annurev-clinpsy-032813-153710

Volkow, N. D., & Koob, G. (2015). Brain disease model of addiction: Why is it so controversial? *The Lancet Psychiatry, 2*(8), 677–679. doi:10.1016/S2215-0366(15)00236-9

Volkow, N. D., Wang, G.-J., Fowler, J. S., & Tomasi, D. (2012). Addiction circuitry in the human brain. *Annual Review of Pharmacology and Toxicology, 52*, 321–336. doi:10.1146/annurev-pharmtox-010611-134625

Volkow, N. D., Wang, G.-J., Kollins, S. H., Wigal, T. L., Newcorn, J. H., Telang, F., ... Swanson, J. M. (2009). Evaluating dopamine reward pathway in ADHD: Clinical implications. *JAMA: Journal of the American Medical Association, 302*(10), 1084–1091. doi:10.1001/jama.2009.1308

Volkow, N. D., Wang, G.-J., Tomasi, D., & Baler, R. D. (2013). The addictive dimensionality of obesity. *Biological Psychiatry, 73*(9), 811–818. doi:http://dx.doi.org/10.1016/j.biopsych.2012.12.020

von Bertalanffy, L. (1969). General systems theory and psychiatry–an overview. In W. Gray, F. J. Duhl, & N. D. Rizzo (Eds.), *General systems theory and psychiatry* (pp. 33–46). Boston, MA: Little, Brown and Company.

von Gontard, A. (2013). The impact of DSM-5 and guidelines for assessment and treatment of elimination disorders. *European Child & Adolescent Psychiatry, 22*(Suppl 1), 61–67. doi:10.1007/s00787-012-0363-9

von Gontard, A., & Equit, M. (2015). Comorbidity of ADHD and incontinence in children. *European Child & Adolescent Psychiatry, 24*(2), 127–140. doi:10.1007/s00787-014-0577-0

von Gontard, A., Heron, J., & Joinson, C. (2011). Family history of nocturnal enuresis and urinary incontinence: Results from a large epidemiological study. *The Journal of Urology, 185*(6), 2303–2307. doi:http://dx.doi.org/10.1016/j.juro.2011.02.040

von Gontard, A., Hollmann, E., Eiberg, H., Benden, B., Rittig, S., & Lehmkuhl, G. (1997). Clinical enuresis phenotypes in familial nocturnal enuresis. *Scandinavian Journal of Urology and Nephrology. Supplementum, 183*, 11–16.

von Gontard, A., Schaumburg, H., Hollmann, E., Eiberg, H., & Rittig, S. (2001). The genetics of enuresis: A review. *The Journal of Urology, 166*(6), 2438–2443.

von Polier, G. G., Meng, H., Lambert, M., Strauss, M., Zarotti, G., Karle, M., ... Schimmelmann, B. G. (2014). Patterns and correlates of expressed emotion, perceived criticism, and rearing style in first admitted early-onset schizophrenia spectrum disorders. *Journal of Nervous and Mental Disease, 202*(11), 783–787. doi:10.1097/NMD.0000000000000209

Vos, J., Craig, M., & Cooper, M. (2015). Existential therapies: A meta-analysis of their effects on psychological outcomes. *Journal of Consulting and Clinical Psychology, 83*(1), 115–128. doi:10.1037/a0037167

Voyer, D. (2014, October 10). Sexing the autistic brain: Extreme male? Retrieved from https://www.psychologytoday.com/blog/perceptual-asymmetries/201410/sexing-the-autistic-brain-extreme-male

Wachbroit, R. (2001). Understanding the genetics-of-violence controversy. In D. Wasserman & R. Wachbroit (Eds.), *Genetics and criminal behavior* (pp. 25–46). New York, NY: Cambridge University Press.

Wade, T. D., Gordon, S., Medland, S., Bulik, C. M., Heath, A. C., Montgomery, G. W., & Martin, N. G. (2013). Genetic variants associated with disordered eating. *The International Journal Of Eating Disorders, 46*(6), 594–608. doi:10.1002/eat.22133

Wade, T. D., Tiggemann, M., Bulik, C. M., Fairburn, C. G., Wray, N. R., & Martin, N. G. (2008). Shared temperament risk factors for anorexia nervosa: A twin study. *Psychosomatic Medicine, 70*(2), 239–244. doi:10.1097/PSY.0b013e31815c40f1

Wagner, S., Baskaya, Ö., Lieb, K., Dahmen, N., & Tadić, A. (2009). The 5-HTTLPR Polymorphism modulates the association of serious life events (SLE) and impulsivity in patients with Borderline Personality Disorder. *Journal of Psychiatric Research, 43*(13), 1067–1072. doi:http://dx.doi.org/10.1016/j.jpsychires.2009.03.004

Wakefield, A. J., Murch, S. H., Anthony, A., Linnell, J., Casson, D. M., Malik, M., ... Walker-Smith, J. A. (1998). RETRACTED: Ileal-lymphoid-nodular hyperplasia, non-specific colitis, and pervasive developmental disorder in children. *The Lancet, 351*(9103), 637–641.

Wakefield, J. C. (1992). The concept of mental disorder: On the boundary between biological facts and social values. *American Psychologist, 47*, 373–388.

Wakefield, J. C. (1999). Evolutionary versus prototype analyses of the concept of disorder. *Journal of Abnormal Psychology, 108*, 374–399.

Wakefield, J. C. (2006). Is behaviorism becoming a pseudo-science?: Power versus scientific rationality in the eclipse of token economies by biological psychiatry in the treatment of schizophrenia. *Behavior and Social Issues, 15*(2), 202–221.

Wakefield, J. C. (2011). DSM-5 proposed diagnostic criteria for sexual paraphilias: Tensions between diagnostic validity and forensic utility. *International Journal of Law and Psychiatry, 34*(3), 195–209. doi:10.1016/j.ijlp.2011.04.012

Wakefield, J. C. (2012). The DSM-5's proposed new categories of sexual disorder: The problem of false positives in sexual diagnosis. *Clinical Social Work Journal, 40*(2), 213–223. doi:10.1007/s10615-011-0353-2

Wakefield, J. C. (2013a). DSM-5: An overview of changes and controversies. *Clinical Social Work Journal, 41*(2), 139–154. doi:10.1007/s10615-013-0445-2

Wakefield, J. C. (2013b). The DSM-5 debate over the bereavement exclusion: Psychiatric diagnosis and the future of empirically supported treatment. *Clinical Psychology Review, 33*(7), 825–845. doi:http://dx.doi.org/10.1016/j.cpr.2013.03.007

Wakefield, J. C. (2015). DSM-5 substance use disorder: How conceptual missteps weakened the foundations of the addictive disorders field. *Acta Psychiatrica Scandinavica, 132*(5), 327–334. doi:10.1111/acps.12446

Wakefield, J. C., & First, M. B. (2012). Validity of the bereavement exclusion to major depression: does the empirical evidence support the proposal to eliminate the exclusion in DSM-5? *World Psychiatry, 11*(1), 3-10.

Wakefield, J. C., & First, M. B. (2013). Diagnostic validity and the definition of mental disorder: A program for conceptually advancing psychiatry. *The Canadian Journal of Psychiatry / La Revue Canadienne De Psychiatrie, 58*(12), 653–655.

Walker, D. D., Walton, T. O., Neighbors, C., Kaysen, D., Mbilinyi, L., Darnell, J., ... Roffman, R. A. (2016). Randomized trial of motivational interviewing plus feedback for soldiers with untreated alcohol abuse. *Journal of Consulting and Clinical Psychology*. doi:10.1037/ccp0000148

Walker, J. S., Coleman, D., Lee, J., Squire, P. N., & Friesen, B. J. (2008). Children's stigmatization of childhood depression and ADHD: Magnitude and demographic variation in a national sample. *Journal of the American Academy of Child & Adolescent Psychiatry, 47*(8), 912–920. doi:10.1097/CHI.0b013e318179961a

Wallace, D., & Cooper, J. (2015). Update on the management of post-traumatic stress disorder. *Australian Prescriber, 38*(2), 55–59.

Waller, J. (2009). A forgotten plague: Making sense of dancing mania. *The Lancet, 373*(9664), 624–625. doi:10.1016/S0140-6736(09)60386-X

Waller, N. G., & Ross, C. A. (1997). The prevalence and biometric structure of pathological dissociation in the general population: Taxometric and behavior genetic findings. *Journal of Abnormal Psychology, 106*(4), 499–510. doi:10.1037/0021-843X.106.4.499

Wallerstein, R. S. (2011). The Psychodynamic Diagnostic Manual (PDM): Rationale, conception, and structure. *Journal of the American Psychoanalytic Association, 59*(1), 153–164. doi:10.1177/0003065111402330

Wallien, M. S. C., Zucker, K. J., Steensma, T. D., & Cohen-Kettenis, P. T. (2008). 2D:4D finger-length ratios in children and adults with gender identity order. *Hormones and Behavior, 54*(3), 450–454. doi:10.1016/j.yhbeh.2008.05.002

Wallis, J. (2012). Looking back: This fascinating and fatal disease. *The Psychologist, 25*, 790–791.

Walsh, C. G., Ribeiro, J. D., & Franklin, J. C. (2017). Predicting risk of suicide attempts over time through machine learning. *Clinical Psychological Science, 5*(3), 457–469. doi:10.1177/2167702617691560

Walsh, Z., Shea, M. T., Yen, S., Ansell, E. B., Grilo, C. M., McGlashan, T. H., ... Gunderson, J. G. (2013). Socioeconomic-status and mental health in a personality disorder sample: The importance of neighborhood factors. *Journal of Personality Disorders, 27*(6), 820–831. doi:10.1521/pedi_2012_26_061

Walton, J. S., & Chou, S. (2015). The effectiveness of psychological treatment for reducing recidivism in child molesters: A systematic review of randomized and nonrandomized studies. *Trauma, Violence, & Abuse, 16*(4), 401–417. doi:10.1177/1524838014537905

Waltz, M. (2013). *Autism: A social and medical history*. Basingstoke, UK: Palgrave Macmillan.

Waltz, M. M. (2015). Mothers and autism: The evolution of a discourse of blame. *AMA Journal of Ethics, 17*(4), 353–358.

Wampold, B. E., & Imel, Z. E. (2015). *The great psychotherapy debate: The evidence for what makes psychotherapy work* (2nd ed.). New York, NY: Routledge.

Wang, M.-Y., Wang, S.-Y., & Tsai, P.-S. (2005). Cognitive behavioural therapy for primary insomnia: A systematic review. *Journal of Advanced Nursing, 50*(5), 553–564. doi:10.1111/j.1365-2648.2005.03433.x

Wang, Y.-C., Chen, S.-K., & Lin, C.-M. (2010). Breaking the drug addiction cycle is not easy in ketamine abusers. *International Journal of Urology, 17*(5), 496; author reply 497. doi:10.1111/j.1442-2042.2010.02491.x

Ward, R. J., Lallemand, F., & de Witte, P. (2014). Influence of adolescent heavy session drinking on the systemic and brain innate immune system. *Alcohol and Alcoholism, 49*(2), 193–197. doi:10.1093/alcalc/agu002

Ward, T., & Brown, M. (2004). The Good Lives Model and conceptual issues in offender rehabilitation. *Psychology, Crime & Law, 10*(3), 243–257. doi:10.1080/10683160410001662744

Ward, T., & Marshall, W. L. (2004). Good lives, aetiology and the rehabilitation of sex offenders: A bridging theory. *Journal of Sexual Aggression, 10*(2), 153–169. doi:10.1080/13552600412331290102

Ward, T., & Stewart, C. (2003). Criminogenic needs and human needs: A theoretical model. *Psychology, Crime & Law, 9*(2), 125–143. doi:10.1080/1068316031000116247

Ward, T., Mann, R. E., & Gannon, T. A. (2007). The good lives model of offender rehabilitation: Clinical implications. *Aggression and Violent Behavior, 12*(1), 87–107. doi:10.1016/j.avb.2006.03.004

Warner, M. (2014). Client processes at the difficult edge. In P. Pearce & L. Sommerbeck (Eds.), *Person-centred practice at the difficult edge* (pp. 121-137). Ross-on-Wye, England: PCCS Books.

Warner, M. S. (1998). A client-centered approach to therapeutic work with dissociated and fragile process. In L. S. Greenberg, J. C. Watson, & G. Lietaer (Eds.), *Handbook of experiential psychotherapy* (pp. 368–387). New York, NY: Guilford Press.

Warner, M. S. (2013). Difficult client process. In M. Cooper, M. O'Hara, P. F. Schmid, & A. C. Bohart (Eds.), *The handbook of person-centred psychotherapy and counselling* (2nd ed., pp. 343–358). New York, NY: Palgrave Macmillan.

Waschbusch, D. A., & Waxmonsky, J. G. (2015). Empirically supported, promising, and unsupported treatments for attention-deficit/hyperactivity disorder. In S. O. Lilienfeld, S. J. Lynn, & J. M. Lohr (Eds.), *Science and pseudoscience in clinical psychology* (2nd ed., pp. 391–430). New York, NY: Guilford Press.

Wasser, S. K., & Barash, D. P. (1983). Reproductive suppression among female mammals: Implications for biomedicine and sexual selection theory. *The Quarterly Review of Biology, 58*(4), 513–538.

Wasserman, S., de Mamani, A. W., & Suro, G. (2012). Shame and guilt/self-blame as predictors of expressed emotion in family members of patients with schizophrenia. *Psychiatry Research, 196*(1), 27–31. doi:http://dx.doi.org/10.1016/j.psychres.2011.08.009

Waters, E., Posada, G., Crowell, J., & Keng-ling, L. (1993). Is attachment theory ready to contribute to our understanding of disruptive behavior problems? *Development and Psychopathology, 5*(1–2), 215–224. doi:10.1017/S0954579400004351

Watson, D. C. (2015). Materialism and the five-factor model of personality: A facet-level analysis. *North American Journal of Psychology, 17*(1), 133–150.

Watson, H. J., Allen, K., Fursland, A., Byrne, S. M., & Nathan, P. R. (2012). Does enhanced cognitive behaviour therapy for eating disorders improve quality of life? *European Eating Disorders Review, 20*(5), 393–399. doi:10.1002/erv.2186

Watson, J. B., & Rayner, R. (1920). Conditioned emotional reactions. *Journal of Experimental Psychology, 3*(1), 1–14. doi:10.1037/h0069608

Watson, P. J., & Andrews, P. W. (2002). Toward a revised evolutionary adaptationist analysis of depression: The social navigation hypothesis. *Journal of Affective Disorders, 72*(1), 1–14. doi:10.1016/S0165-0327(01)00459-1

Weber, J., & Czarnetzki, A. (2001). Trepanationen im frühen Mittelalter im Südwesten von Deutschland – Indikationen, Komplikationen und Outcome [Trepanations from the early medieval period of southwestern Germany – Indications, complications and outcome]. *Central European Neurosurgery, 62*(1), 10–14. doi:10.1055/s-2001-16333

Weber, M., Davis, K., & McPhie, L. (2006). Narrative therapy, eating disorders and groups: Enhancing outcomes in rural NSW. *Australian Social Work, 59*(4), 391–405. doi:10.1080/03124070600985970

Weck, F., Gropalis, M., Hiller, W., & Bleichhardt, G. (2015). Effectiveness of cognitive-behavioral group therapy for patients with hypochondriasis (health anxiety). *Journal of Anxiety Disorders, 30*, 1–7. doi:http://dx.doi.org/10.1016/j.janxdis.2014.12.012

Weeks, G. R., & Gambescia, N. (2015). Couple therapy and sexual problems. In A. S. Gurman, J. L. Lebow, & D. K. Snyder (Eds.), *Clinical handbook of couple therapy* (5th ed., pp. 635–656). New York, NY: Guilford Press.

Weinberger, D. R. (1987). Implications of normal brain development for the pathogenesis of schizophrenia. *Archives of General Psychiatry, 44*(7), 660–669.

Weiner, B. (1975). 'On being sane in insane places': A process (attributional) analysis and critique. *Journal of Abnormal Psychology, 84*(5), 433-441. doi:10.1037/h0077126

Weiner, D. B. (1994). "Le gest de Pinel": The history of a psychiatric myth. In M. S. Micale & R. Porter (Eds.), *Discovering the history of psychiatry* (pp. 232–247). New York, NY: Oxford University Press.

Weiner, I. B. (2004). Rorschach assessment: Current status. In M. J. Hilsenroth & D. L. Segal (Eds.), *Comprehensive handbook of psychological assessment: Vol. 2. Personality assessment* (pp. 343–355). Hoboken, NJ: John Wiley.

Weiner, L., & Avery-Clark, C. (2014). Sensate focus: Clarifying the Masters and Johnson's model. *Sexual and Relationship Therapy, 29*(3), 307–319. doi:10.1080/14681994.2014.892920

Weiner, M. W., Veitch, D. P., Aisen, P. S., Beckett, L. A., Cairns, N. J., Cedarbaum, J., ... Trojanowski, J. Q. (2015). 2014 update of the Alzheimer's disease neuroimaging initiative: A review of papers published since its inception. *Alzheimer's & Dementia, 11*(6), e1–e120. doi:10.1016/j.jalz.2014.11.001

Weingarden, H., & Renshaw, K. D. (2015). Shame in the obsessive compulsive related disorders: A conceptual review. *Journal of Affective Disorders, 171*, 74–84. doi:10.1016/j.jad.2014.09.010

Weingarten, C. P., & Strauman, T. J. (2015). Neuroimaging for psychotherapy research: Current trends. *Psychotherapy Research, 25*(2), 185–213. doi:10.1080/10503307.2014.883088

Weinshenker, D., & Schroeder, J. P. (2007). There and back again: A tale of norepinephrine and drug addiction. *Neuropsychopharmacology, 32*(7), 1433–1451. doi:10.1038/sj.npp.1301263

Weiss, A. (2001). The no-suicide contract: Possibilities and pitfalls. *American Journal of Psychotherapy, 55*(3), 414–419.

Weiss, M., Murray, C., Wasdell, M., Greenfield, B., Giles, L., & Hechtman, L. (2012). A randomized controlled trial of CBT therapy for adults with ADHD with and without medication. *BMC Psychiatry, 12.* doi:10.1186/1471-244X-12-30

Weiss, R. (2016, July 15). Can therapists "officially" diagnose sexual addiction? Retrieved from https://blogs.psychcentral.com/sex/2016/07/%E2%80%A8%E2%80%A8%E2%80%A8can-therapists-officially-diagnose-sexual-addiction/

Weiss, T., Skelton, K., Phifer, J., Jovanovic, T., Gillespie, C. F., Smith, A., ... Ressler, K. J. (2011). Posttraumatic stress disorder is a risk factor for metabolic syndrome in an impoverished urban population. *General Hospital Psychiatry, 33*(2), 135–142. doi:http://dx.doi.org/10.1016/j.genhosppsych.2011.01.002

Welch, S., Klassen, C., Borisova, O., & Clothier, H. (2013). The DSM-5 controversies: How should psychologists respond. *Canadian Psychology / Psychologie Canadienne, 3*, 166–175. doi:10.1037/a0033841

Wells, A. (1995). Meta-cognition and worry: A cognitive model of generalized anxiety disorder. *Behavioural and Cognitive Psychotherapy, 23*(3), 301–320. doi:10.1017/S1352465800015897

Wells, A. (2010). Metacognitive theory and therapy for worry and generalized anxiety disorder: Review and status. *Journal of Experimental Psychopathology, 1*(1), 133–145. doi:10.5127/jep.007910

Wells, M. C., Glickauf-Hughes, C., & Buzzell, V. (1990). Treating obsessive-compulsive personalities in psychodynamic/interpersonal group therapy. *Psychotherapy: Theory, Research, Practice, Training, 27*(3), 366–379. doi:10.1037/0033-3204.27.3.366

Wender, P. H., Rosenthal, D., Kety, S. S., Schulsinger, F., & Welner, J. (1974). Crossfostering: A research strategy for clarifying the role of genetic and experiential factors in the etiology of schizophrenia. *Archives of General Psychiatry, 30*(1), 121–128. doi:10.1001/archpsyc.1974.01760070097016

Wenthur, C. J. (2016). Classics in chemical neuroscience: Methylphenidate. *ACS Chemical Neuroscience, 7*(8), 1030–1040. doi:10.1021/acschemneuro.6b00199

Wenzel, A., & Beck, A. T. (2008). A cognitive model of suicidal behavior: Theory and treatment. *Applied and Preventive Psychology, 12*(4), 189–201. doi:http://dx.doi.org/10.1016/j.appsy.2008.05.001

Werneke, U., Ott, M., Renberg, E. S., Taylor, D., & Stegmayr, B. (2012). A decision analysis of long-term lithium treatment and the risk of renal failure. *Acta Psychiatrica Scandinavica, 126*(3), 186–197. doi:10.1111/j.1600-0447.2012.01847.x

Westermeyer, J. (2005). Historical and social context of psychoactive substance use disorders. In R. J. Frances, S. I. Miller, & A. H. Mack (Eds.), *Clinical textbook of addictive disorders* (3rd ed., pp. 16–34). New York, NY: Guilford Press.

Westermeyer, J. (2013). Historical understandings of addiction. In P. M. Miller, S. A. Ball, M. E. Bates, A. W. Blume, K. M. Kampman, D. J. Kavanagh, M. E. Larimer, N. M. Petry, & P. De Witte (Eds.), *Comprehensive addictive behaviors and disorders: Vol. 1. Principles of addiction* (pp. 3–12). San Diego, CA: Elsevier Academic Press.

Wettstein, R. M. (1999). The right to refuse psychiatric treatment. *Psychiatric Clinics of North America, 22*(1), 173–182. doi:10.1016/S0193-953X(05)70067-8

Whaley, A. L. (2004). Paranoia in African-American men receiving inpatient psychiatric treatment. *Journal of the American Academy of Psychiatry and the Law, 32*(3), 282–290.

Wheeler, A. C., Raspa, M., Bishop, E., & Bailey, D. B. (2016). Aggression in fragile X syndrome. *Journal of Intellectual Disability Research, 60*(2), 113–125. doi:10.1111/jir.12238

Whitaker, R. (2002). *Mad in America: Bad science, bad medicine, and the enduring mistreatment of the mentally ill.* Cambridge, MA: Perseus Publishing.

Whitaker, R. (2012). Weighing the evidence: What science has to say about prescribing atypical antipsychotics to children. In S. Olfman & B. D. Robbins (Eds.), *Drugging our children: How profiteers are pushing antipsychotics on our youngest, and what we can do to stop it* (pp. 3–16). Santa Barbara, CA: Praeger/ABC-CLIO.

Whitaker, R. (2017). Psychiatry under the influence. In J. Davies (Ed.), *The sedated society: The causes and harms of our psychiatric drug epidemic* (pp. 163–188). New York, NY: Palgrave Macmillan.

Whitaker, R., & Cosgrove, L. (2015). *Psychiatry under the influence: Institutional corruption, social injury, and prescriptions for reform.* New York, NY: Palgrave Macmillan.

White, M., & Epston, D. (1990). *Narrative means to therapeutic ends.* New York, NY: Norton.

White, W. L. (2007). *Substance abuse versus substance dependence: Implications for management of the DUI offender.* Briefing Paper for the Administrative Office of the Illinois Courts and the Illinois Secretary of State. Retrieved from http://www.williamwhitepapers.com/pr/Abuse%26dependencepaperFinal5-30-2007.pdf

Whitehead, P. R., Ward, T., & Collie, R. M. (2007). Time for a change: Applying the Good Lives Model of rehabilitation to a high-risk violent offender. *International Journal of Offender Therapy and Comparative Criminology, 51*(5), 578–598. doi:10.1177/0306624X06296236

Whitehouse, A. J. O. (2016). Commentary: Are we expecting too much from the extreme male brain theory of autism? A reflection on Kung et al. (2016). *Journal of Child Psychology and Psychiatry, and Allied Disciplines, 57*(12), 1463–1464. doi:10.1111/jcpp.12628

Whiteley, P. (2015). Nutritional management of (some) autism: A case for gluten- and casein-free diets? *The Proceedings of The Nutrition Society, 74*(3), 202–207. doi:10.1017/S0029665114001475

Whiteley, P., Haracopos, D., Knivsberg, A.-M., Reichelt, K. L., Parlar, S., Jacobsen, J., ... Shattock, P. (2010). The ScanBrit randomized controlled, single-blind study of a gluten- and casein-free dietary intervention for children with autism spectrum disorders. *Nutritional Neuroscience, 13*(2), 87–100. doi:10.1179/147683010X12611460763922

Whitely, M. (2015). Attention deficit hyperactive disorder diagnosis continues to fail the reliability and validity tests. *Australian and New Zealand Journal of Psychiatry, 49*(6), 497–498. doi:10.1177/0004867415579921

Whiteside, S. P., Port, J. D., & Abramowitz, J. S. (2004). A meta-analysis of functional neuroimaging in obsessive-compulsive disorder. *Psychiatry Research: Neuroimaging, 132*(1), 69–79. doi:10.1016/j.pscychresns.2004.07.001

WHO Advisory Group. (1980). The dependence potential of thebaine. *Bulletin on Narcotics, 32*(1), 45–54.

Widener, A. J. (1998). Beyond Ritalin: The importance of therapeutic work with parents and children diagnosed ADD/ADHD. *Journal of Child Psychotherapy, 24*(2), 267–281. doi:10.1080/00754179808414817

Widiger, T. A. (2011). The DSM-5 dimensional model of personality disorder: Rationale and empirical support. *Journal of Personality Disorders, 25*(2), 222–234. doi:10.1521/pedi.2011.25.2.222

Widiger, T. A. (2013). A postmortem and future look at the personality disorders in DSM-5. *Personality Disorders, 4*(4), 382–387. doi:10.1037/per0000030

Widiger, T. A. (2015). Assessment of DSM-5 personality disorder. *Journal of Personality Assessment, 97*(5), 456–466. doi:10.1080/00223891.2015.1041142

Widiger, T. A. (2016). Classification and diagnosis: Historical development and contemporary issues. In J. E. Maddux & B. A. Winstead (Eds.), *Psychopathology: Foundations for a contemporary understanding* (4th ed., pp. 97–110). New York, NY: Roultedge.

Widiger, T. A., & Costa, P. T., Jr. (2012). Integrating normal and abnormal personality structure: the Five-Factor Model. *Journal of Personality, 80*(6), 1471–1506. doi:10.1111/j.1467-6494.2012.00776.x

Widiger, T. A., & Presnall, J. R. (2013). Clinical application of the Five-Factor Model. *Journal of Personality, 81*(6), 515–527. doi:10.1111/jopy.12004

Widiger, T. A., Samuel, D. B., Mullins-Sweatt, S., Gore, W. L., & Crego, C. (2012). An integration of normal and abnormal personality structure: The Five-Factor Model. In T. A. Widiger (Ed.), *The Oxford handbook of personality disorders* (pp. 82–107). New York, NY: Oxford University Press.

Wiener, J., Malone, M., Varma, A., Markel, C., Biondic, D., Tannock, R., & Humphries, T. (2012). Children's perceptions of their ADHD symptoms: Positive illusions, attributions, and stigma. *Canadian Journal of School Psychology, 27*(3), 217–242. doi:10.1177/0829573512451972

Wignall, E. L., Dickson, J. M., Vaughan, P., Farrow, T. F. D., Wilkinson, I. D., Hunter, M. D., & Woodruff, P. W. R. (2004). Smaller hippocampal volume in patients with recent-onset posttraumatic stress disorder. *Biological Psychiatry, 56*(11), 832–836. doi:10.1016/j.biopsych.2004.09.015

Wilchens, R. A. (1997). *Read my lips: Sexual subversion and the end of gender.* Ithaca, NY: Firebrand Books.

Wilens, T. E., Adler, L. A., Adams, J., Sgambati, S., Rotrosen, J., Sawtelle, R., ... Fusillo, S. (2008). Misuse and diversion of stimulants prescribed for ADHD: A systematic review of the literature. *Journal of the American Academy of Child & Adolescent Psychiatry, 47*(1), 21–31. doi:http://dx.doi.org/10.1097/chi.0b013e31815a56f1

Wiles, N. J., Thomas, L., Turner, N., Garfield, K., Kounali, D., Campbell, J., ... Hollinghurst, S. (2016). Long-term effectiveness and cost-effectiveness of cognitive behavioural therapy as an adjunct to pharmacotherapy for treatment-resistant depression in primary care: follow-up of the CoBalT randomised controlled trial. *The Lancet Psychiatry.* doi:10.1016/S2215-0366(15)00495-2

Wilhelm, K. A. (2009). Men and depression. *Australian Family Physician, 38*(3), 102–105.

Wilkinson, P. (2013). Non-suicidal self-injury. *European Child & Adolescent Psychiatry, 22*(Suppl 1), 75–79. doi:10.1007/s00787-012-0365-7

Wilkinson, P., & Goodyer, I. (2011). Non-suicidal self-injury. *European Child & Adolescent Psychiatry, 20*(2), 103–108. doi:10.1007/s00787-010-0156-y

Wille, S. (1994). Primary nocturnal enuresis in children. Background and treatment. *Scandinavian Journal of Urology and Nephrology. Supplementum, 156,* 1–48.

Williams, D. R., Yu, Y., Jackson, J. S., & Anderson, N. B. (1997). Racial differences in physical and mental health: Socio-economic status, stress and discrimination. *Journal of Health Psychology, 2*(3), 335–351. doi:10.1177/135910539700200305

Williams, M. T., Davis, D. M., Powers, M., & Weissflog, L. O. (2014). Current trends in prescribing medications for obsessive-compulsive disorder: Best practices and new research. *Directions in Psychiatry, 34*(4), 247–259.

Williams, R. A., Mamotte, C. D. S., & Burnett, J. R. (2008). Phenylketonuria: An inborn error of phenylalanine metabolism. *The Clinical Biochemist Reviews, 29*(1), 31–41.

Williams, S. L. (2016). Anxiety disorders, obsessive-compulsive, and related disorders. In J. E. Maddux & B. A. Winstead (Eds.), *Psychopathology: Foundations for a contemporary understanding* (4th ed., pp. 141–161). New York, NY: Routledge.

Williams, S. P. (2001). Reaching the hard to reach: Implications of the New View of women's sexual problems. *Women & Therapy, 24*(1–2), 39–42.

Williamson, J., Goldman, J., & Marder, K. S. (2009). Genetic aspects of Alzheimer disease. *The Neurologist, 15*(2), 80–86. doi:10.1097/NRL.0b013e318187e76b

Williamson, J. B., Heilman, K. M., Porges, E. C., Lamb, D. G., & Porges, S. W. (2013). A possible mechanism for PTSD symptoms in patients with traumatic brain injury: central autonomic network disruption. *Frontiers In Neuroengineering, 6*, 13–13. doi:10.3389/fneng.2013.00013

Willick, M. S. (2001). Psychoanalysis and schizophrenia: A cautionary tale. *Journal of the American Psychoanalytic Association, 49*(1), 27–56. doi:10.1177/00030651010490012001

Wilson, C. E., Gillan, N., Spain, D., Robertson, D., Roberts, G., Murphy, C. M., ... Murphy, D. G. M. (2013). Comparison of ICD-10R, DSM-IV-TR and DSM-5 in an adult autism spectrum disorder diagnostic clinic. *Journal of Autism and Developmental Disorders, 43*(11), 2515–2525. doi:10.1007/s10803-013-1799-6

Wilson, K. G., & Roberts, M. (2002). Core principles in acceptance and commitment therapy: An application to anorexia. *Cognitive and Behavioral Practice, 9*(3), 237–243. doi:10.1016/S1077-7229(02)80054-2

Wilson, S. T., Stanley, B., Brent, D. A., Oquendo, M. A., Huang, Y., & Mann, J. J. (2009). The tryptophan hydroxylase-1 A218C polymorphism is associated with diagnosis, but not suicidal behavior, in borderline personality disorder. *American Journal Of Medical Genetics. Part B, Neuropsychiatric Genetics: The Official Publication Of The International Society Of Psychiatric Genetics, 150B*(2), 202–208. doi:10.1002/ajmg.b.30788

Wimalawansa, S. J. (2014). Mechanisms of developing post-traumatic stress disorder: New targets for drug development and other potential interventions. *CNS & Neurological Disorders Drug Targets, 13*(5), 807–816.

Wing, L. (1981). Asperger's syndrome: A clinical account. *Psychological Medicine, 11*(1), 115–129. doi:10.1017/S0033291700053332

Winokur, A. (2015). The relationship between sleep disturbances and psychiatric disorders: Introduction and overview. *Psychiatric Clinics of North America, 38*(4), 603–614. doi:10.1016/j.psc.2015.07.001

Winstead, B. A., & Sanchez, J. (2016). The role of gender, race, and class in psychopathology. In J. E. Maddux & B. A. Winstead (Eds.), *Psychopathology: Foundations for a contemporary understanding* (4th ed., pp. 76–96). New York, NY: Routledge.

Winstock, A. R., Lintzeris, N., & Lea, T. (2011). 'Should I stay or should I go?' Coming off methadone and buprenorphine treatment. *International Journal of Drug Policy, 22*(1), 77–81. doi:10.1016/j.drugpo.2010.08.001

Winstock, A. R., Mitcheson, L., Gillatt, D. A., & Cottrell, A. M. (2012). The prevalence and natural history of urinary symptoms among recreational ketamine users. *BJU International, 110*(11), 1762–1766. doi:10.1111/j.1464-410X.2012.11028.x

Winston, T. (2012). Psychodynamic approaches to eating disorders. In J. Fox & K. Goss (Eds.), *Eating and its disorders* (pp. 244–259). Chichester, UK: Wiley-Blackwell.

Winters, N. (2013). Whether to break confidentiality: An ethical dilemma. *Journal of Emergency Nursing, 39*(3), 233–235. doi:10.1016/j.jen.2012.03.003

Wirth-Cauchon, J. (2000). A dangerous symbolic mobility: Narratives of borderline personality disorder. In D. Fee (Ed.), *Pathology and the postmodern: Mental illness as discourse and experience* (pp. 141–162). London, UK: Sage.

Wise, M. S., Arand, D. L., Auger, R. R., Brooks, S. N., & Watson, N. F. (2007). Treatment of narcolepsy and other hypersomnias of central origin: An American Academy of Sleep Medicine review. *Sleep: Journal of Sleep and Sleep Disorders Research, 30*(12), 1712–1727.

Wise, R. A. (2013). Dual roles of dopamine in food and drug seeking: The drive-reward paradox. *Biological Psychiatry, 73*(9), 819–826. doi:http://dx.doi.org/10.1016/j.biopsych.2012.09.001

Wise, R. A., & Rompré, P.-P. (1989). Brain dopamine and reward. *Annual Review of Psychology, 40*, 191–225. doi:10.1146/annurev.ps.40.020189.001203

Witkiewitz, K., & Marlatt, G. A. (2006). Overview of harm reduction treatments for alcohol problems. *International Journal of Drug Policy, 17*(4), 285–294. doi:http://dx.doi.org/10.1016/j.drugpo.2006.03.005

Witkiewitz, K., & Marlatt, G. A. (2004). Relapse prevention for alcohol and drug problems: That was Zen, this Is Tao. *American Psychologist, 59*(4), 224–235. doi:10.1037/0003-066X.59.4.224

Witthöft, M., Basfeld, C., Steinhoff, M., & Gerlach, A. L. (2012). Can't suppress this feeling: Automatic negative evaluations of somatosensory stimuli are related to the experience of somatic symptom distress. *Emotion, 12*(3), 640–649. doi:10.1037/a0024924

Wittouck, C., Van Autreve, S., De Jaegere, E., Portzky, G., & van Heeringen, K. (2011). The prevention and treatment of complicated grief: A meta-analysis. *Clinical Psychology Review, 31*(1), 69–78. doi:10.1016/j.cpr.2010.09.005

Wolf, E. J., Rasmusson, A. M., Mitchell, K. S., Logue, M. W., Baldwin, C. T., & Miller, M. W. (2014). A genome-wide association study of clinical symptoms of dissociation in a trauma-exposed sample. *Depression and Anxiety, 31*(4), 352–360. doi:10.1002/da.22260

Wolf, N. J., & Hopko, D. R. (2008). Psychosocial and pharmacological interventions for depressed adults in primary care: A critical review. *Clinical Psychology Review, 28*(1), 131–161. doi:10.1016/j.cpr.2007.04.004

Wolff, M., Alsobrook, J. P., II, & Pauls, D. L. (2000). Genetic aspects of obsessive-compulsive disorder. *Psychiatric Clinics of North America, 23*(3), 535–544. doi:10.1016/S0193-953X(05)70179-9

Wolff, S. (2004). The history of autism. *European Child & Adolescent Psychiatry, 13*(4), 201–208. doi:10.1007/s00787-004-0363-5

Woloshin, S., & Schwartz, L. M. (2016). US Food and Drug Administration approval of flibanserin: Even the score does not add up. *JAMA Internal Medicine, 176*(4), 439–442. doi:10.1001/jamainternmed.2016.0073

Wolpe, J. (1958). *Psychotherapy by reciprocal inhibition.* Stanford, CA: Stanford University Press.

Wolpe, J. (1961). The systematic desensitization treatment of neuroses. *Journal of Nervous and Mental Disease, 132*, 189–203. doi:10.1097/00005053-196103000-00001

Wolz, R., Schwarz, A. J., Yu, P., Cole, P. E., Rueckert, D., Jack, C. R., Jr., ... Hill, D. (2014). Robustness of automated hippocampal volumetry across magnetic resonance field strengths and repeat images. *Alzheimer's & Dementia, 10*(4), 430–438. doi:10.1016/j.jalz.2013.09.014

Wong, L. C., Huang, H.-L., Weng, W.-C., Jong, Y.-J., Yin, Y.-J., Chen, H.-A., ... Ho, S.-Y. (2016). Increased risk of epilepsy in children with Tourette syndrome: A population-based case-control study. *Research in Developmental Disabilities, 51–52*, 181–187. doi:10.1016/j.ridd.2015.10.005

Wong, S. E. (2006). Behavior analysis of psychotic disorders: Scientific dead end or casualty of the mental health political economy? *Behavior and Social Issues, 15*(2), 152–177.

Wong, S. E. (2014). A critique of the diagnostic construct schizophrenia. *Research on Social Work Practice, 24*(1), 132–141.

Wong, S. Y. S., Yip, B. H. K., Mak, W. W. S., Mercer, S., Cheung, E. Y. L., Ling, C. Y. M., ... Ma, H. S. W. (2016). Mindfulness-based cognitive therapy v. group psychoeducation for people with generalised anxiety disorder: Randomised controlled trial. *The British Journal of Psychiatry, 209*(1), 68–75. doi:10.1192/bjp.bp.115.166124

Wood, H. (2003, Summer). Psychoanalytic theories of perversion reformulated. *Reformulation*, 26–31.

Wood, J. J., Ehrenreich-May, J., Alessandri, M., Fujii, C., Renno, P., Laugeson, E., ... Storch, E. A. (2015). Cognitive behavioral therapy for early adolescents with autism spectrum disorders and clinical anxiety: A randomized, controlled trial. *Behavior Therapy, 46*(1), 7–19. doi:10.1016/j.beth.2014.01.002

Wood, J. M., & Lilienfeld, S. O. (1999). The Rorschach Inkblot Test: A case of overstatement? *Assessment, 6*(4), 341–351. doi:10.1177/107319119900600405

Wood, J. M., Garb, H. N., Nezworski, M. T., Lilienfeld, S. O., & Duke, M. C. (2015). A second look at the validity of widely used Rorschach indices: Comment on Mihura, Meyer, Dumitrascu, and Bombel (2013). *Psychological Bulletin, 141*(1), 236–249. doi:10.1037/a0036005

Wood, J. M., Lilienfeld, S. O., Nezworski, M. T., Garb, H. N., Allen, K. H., & Wildermuth, J. L. (2010). Validity of Rorschach Inkblot scores for discriminating psychopaths from nonpsychopaths in forensic populations: A meta-analysis. *Psychological Assessment, 22*(2), 336–349. doi:10.1037/a0018998

Wood, J. M., Nezworski, M. T., Garb, H. N., & Lilienfeld, S. O. (2001). The misperception of psychopathology: Problems with norms of the Comprehensive System for the Rorschach. *Clinical Psychology: Science and Practice, 8*(3), 350–373. doi:10.1093/clipsy/8.3.350

Wood, L., Birtel, M., Alsawy, S., Pyle, M., & Morrison, A. (2014). Public perceptions of stigma towards people with schizophrenia, depression, and anxiety. *Psychiatry Research, 220*(1–2), 604–608. doi:10.1016/j.psychres.2014.07.012

Wood, M. J. M., Molassiotis, A., & Payne, S. (2011). What research evidence is there for the use of art therapy in the management of symptoms in adults with cancer? A systematic review. *Psycho-Oncology, 20*(2), 135–145. doi:10.1002/pon.1722

Woods, B., Aguirre, E., Spector, A. E., & Orrell, M. (2012). Cognitive stimulation to improve cognitive functioning in people with dementia. *Cochrane Database of Systematic Reviews, 2012*(2), CD005562. doi:10.1002/14651858. CD005562.pub2

Woody, J. D. (2011). Sexual addiction/hypersexuality and the DSM: Update and practice guidance for social workers. *Journal of Social Work Practice in the Addictions, 11*(4), 301–320. doi:10.1080/153325 6X.2011.619926

Woolfolk, R. L., & Allen, L. A. (2012). Cognitive behavioral therapy for somatoform disorders. In I. R. De Oliveira (Ed.), *Standard and innovative strategies in cognitive behavior therapy* (pp. 117–144). Rijeka, Croatia: InTech. Retrieved from http://cdn.intechopen.com/pdfs/31827/InTech-Cognitive_behavioral_therapy_for_somatoform_disorders.pdf

Woollaston, K., & Hixenbaugh, P. (2008). 'Destructive whirlwind': Nurses' perceptions of patients diagnosed with borderline personality disorder. *Journal of Psychiatric and Mental Health Nursing, 15*(9), 703–709. doi:10.1111/j.1365-2850.2008.01275.x

Woon, F. L., Sood, S., & Hedges, D. W. (2010). Hippocampal volume deficits associated with exposure to psychological trauma and posttraumatic stress disorder in adults: A meta-analysis. *Progress in Neuro-Psychopharmacology & Biological Psychiatry, 34*(7), 1181–1188. doi:10.1016/j.pnpbp.2010.06.016

Working Group for A New View of Women's Sexual Problems. (2001). A New View of women's sexual problems. *Women & Therapy, 24*(1–2), 1–8.

World Association of Sexual Health. (2014). *Declaration of sexual rights* (rev. ed.). Retrieved from http://www.worldsexology.org/resources/declaration-of-sexual-rights/

World Health Organization. (1992). The ICD-10 classification of mental and behavioural disorders. Retrieved from http://www.who.int/classifications/icd/en/bluebook.pdf

World Health Organization. (2010). ATLAS on substance use (2010): Resources for the prevention and treatment of substance use disorders. Retrieved from http://www.who.int/substance_abuse/publications/Media/en/

World Health Organization. (2014). *Preventing suicide: A global imperative.* Retrieved from http://www.who.int/mental_health/suicide-prevention/world_report_2014/en/

World Health Organization. (2015). WHO International Advisory Group for the revision of ICD-10 Mental and behavioural disorders. Retrieved from http://www.who.int/classifications/icd/TagMH/en/

World Health Organization. (2017, March 22). ICD-11 beta draft. Retrieved from http://apps.who.int/classifications/icd11/browse/l-m/en

World Health Organization. (2018a, January 5). 06 Mental, behavioural or neurodevelopmental disorders. Retrieved from https://icd.who.int/browse11/l-m/en#/http%3a%2f%2fid.who.int%2ficd%2fentity%2f334423054

World Health Organization. (2018b, January). Gaming disorder. Retrieved from http://www.who.int/features/qa/gaming-disorder/en/

World Health Organization. (n.d.). Cocaine. Retrieved from http://www.who.int/substance_abuse/facts/cocaine/en/

World Medical Association. (2013). Declaration of Helsinki ethical principles for medical research involving human subjects. *JAMA: Journal of the American Medical Association, 310*(20), 2191–2194. doi:10.1001/jama.2013.281053

Worley, S. (2014). Conduct disorder: Pathologizing the normal? In C. Perring & L. A. Wells (Eds.), *Diagnostic dilemmas in child and adolescent psychiatry: Philosophical perspectives* (pp. 182–208). New York, NY: Oxford University Press.

Woywodt, A., & Kiss, A. (2002). Geophagia: the history of earth-eating. *Journal of the Royal Society of Medicine, 95*(3), 143–146.

Wray, M., Colen, C., & Pescosolido, B. (2010). The sociology of suicide. *Annual Review of Sociology, 37*, 505–528. doi:10.1146/annurev-soc-081309-150058

Wright, D., & Abrahams, D. (2015). An investigation into the effectiveness of Dynamic Interpersonal Therapy (DIT) as a treatment for depression and anxiety in IAPT. *Psychoanalytic Psychotherapy, 29*(2), 160–170. doi:10.1080/02668734.2015.1035740

Wright, K. (2013). Psychological theories of and therapies for bipolar disorder. In M. Power (Ed.), *The Wiley-Blackwell handbook of mood disorders* (2nd ed., pp. 325–342). Chichester, UK: Wiley-Blackwell.

Wright, K., Haigh, K., & McKeown, M. (2007). Reclaiming the humanity in personality disorder. *International Journal of Mental Health Nursing, 16*(4), 236–246. doi:10.1111/j.1447-0349.2007.00480.x

Wright, M. J., Jr. (2015). Legalizing marijuana for medical purposes will increase risk of long-term, deleterious consequences for adolescents. *Drug and Alcohol Dependence, 149*, 298–303. doi:10.1016/j.drugalcdep.2015.01.005

Wu, J., Xiao, H., Sun, H., Zou, L., & Zhu, L.-Q. (2012). Role of dopamine receptors in ADHD: A systematic meta-analysis. *Molecular Neurobiology, 45*(3), 605–620. doi:10.1007/s12035-012-8278-5

Wu, K., Hanna, G. L., Rosenberg, D. R., & Arnold, P. D. (2012). The role of glutamate signaling in the pathogenesis and treatment of obsessive–compulsive disorder. *Pharmacology, Biochemistry and Behavior, 100*(4), 726–735. doi:10.1016/j.pbb.2011.10.007

Wu, S., Ding, Y., Wu, F., Li, R., Xie, G., Hou, J., & Mao, P. (2015). Family history of autoimmune diseases is associated with an increased risk of autism in children: A systematic review and meta-analysis. *Neuroscience and Biobehavioral Reviews, 55*, 322–332. doi:10.1016/j.neubiorev.2015.05.004

Wyatt v. Stickney, 325 F.Supp. 781 (United States District Court, M. D. Alabama 1971).

Wyatt, W. J., & Midkiff, D. M. (2006). Biological psychiatry: A practice in search of a science. *Behavior and Social Issues, 15*(2), 132–151.

Wylie, K., & Malik, F. (2009). Review of drug treatment for female sexual dysfunction. *International Journal of STD & AIDS, 20*(10), 671–674. doi:10.1258/ijsa.2009.009206

Xiang, Y. T., Ungvari, G. S., Correll, C. U., Chiu, H. F. K., Lai, K. Y. C., Wang, C. Y., ... Shinfuku, N. (2015). Use of electroconvulsive therapy for Asian patients with schizophrenia (2001–2009): Trends and correlates. *Psychiatry and Clinical Neurosciences, 69*(8), 489–496. doi:10.1111/pcn.12283

Xu, W., Tan, L., Wang, H.-F., Tan, M.-S., Tan, L., Li, J.-Q., ... Yu, J.-T. (2016). Education and risk of dementia: Dose-response meta-analysis of prospective cohort studies. *Molecular Neurobiology, 53*(5), 3113–3123. doi:10.1007/s12035-015-9211-5

Xu, X., Mellor, D., Kiehne, M., Ricciardelli, L. A., McCabe, M. P., & Xu, Y. (2010). Body dissatisfaction, engagement in body change behaviors and sociocultural influences on body image among Chinese adolescents. *Body Image, 7*(2), 156–164. doi:http://dx.doi.org/10.1016/j.bodyim.2009.11.003

Xu, Y., Schneier, F., Heimberg, R. G., Princisvalle, K., Liebowitz, M. R., Wang, S., & Blanco, C. (2012). Gender differences in social anxiety disorder: Results from the national epidemiologic sample on alcohol and related conditions. *Journal of Anxiety Disorders, 26*(1), 12–19. doi:http://dx.doi.org/10.1016/j.janxdis.2011.08.006

Xue, C., Ge, Y., Tang, B., Liu, Y., Kang, P., Wang, M., & Zhang, L. (2015). A meta-analysis of risk factors for combat-related PTSD among military personnel and veterans. *PLOS One, 10*(3).

Yaffe, K., Falvey, C., Harris, T. B., Newman, A., Satterfield, S., Koster, A., ... Simonsick, E. (2013). Effect of socioeconomic disparities on incidence of dementia among biracial older adults: Prospective study. *BMJ: British Medical Journal, 347*. doi:10.1136/bmj.f7051

Yairi, E., Ambrose, N., & Cox, N. (1996). Genetics of stuttering: A critical review. *Journal of Speech & Hearing Research, 39*(4), 771–784. doi:10.1044/jshr.3904.771

Yakovenko, I., Quigley, L., Hemmelgarn, B. R., Hodgins, D. C., & Ronksley, P. (2015). The efficacy of motivational interviewing for disordered gambling: Systematic review and meta-analysis. *Addictive Behaviors, 43*, 72–82. doi:10.1016/j.addbeh.2014.12.011

Yalom, I. D. (1980). *Existential psychotherapy.* New York, NY: Basic Books.

Yan, J., Aliev, F., Webb, B. T., Kendler, K. S., Williamson, V. S., Edenberg, H. J., ... Dick, D. M. (2014). Using genetic information from candidate gene and genome-wide association studies in risk prediction for alcohol dependence. *Addiction Biology, 19*(4), 708–721. doi:10.1111/adb.12035

Yang, C., Hao, Z., Zhu, C., Guo, Q., Mu, D., & Zhang, L. (2016). Interventions for tic disorders: An overview of systematic reviews and meta analyses. *Neuroscience and Biobehavioral Reviews, 63*, 239–255. doi:10.1016/j.neubiorev.2015.12.013

Yang, E. V., & Glaser, R. (2002). Stress-induced immunomodulation and the implications for health. *International Immunopharmacology, 2*(2–3), 315–324. doi:http://dx.doi.org/10.1016/S1567-5769(01)00182-5

Yang, M., Kavi, V., Wang, W., Wu, Z., & Hao, W. (2012). The association of 5-HTR2A-1438A/G, COMTVal158Met, MAOA-LPR, DATVNTR and 5-HTTVNTR gene polymorphisms and antisocial personality disorder in male heroin-dependent Chinese subjects. *Progress in Neuro-Psychopharmacology & Biological Psychiatry, 36*(2), 282–289. doi:10.1016/j.pnpbp.2011.11.009

Yang, M., Mamy, J., Wang, Q., Liao, Y.-H., Seewoobudul, V., Xiao, S.-Y., & Hao, W. (2014). The association of 5-HTR2A-1438A/G, COMTVal158Met, MAOA-LPR, DATVNTR and 5-HTTVNTR gene polymorphisms and borderline personality disorder in female heroin-dependent Chinese subjects. *Progress in Neuro-Psychopharmacology and Biological Psychiatry, 50,* 74–82. doi:http://dx.doi.org/10.1016/j.pnpbp.2013.12.005

Yang, Y., & Raine, A. (2009). Prefrontal structural and functional brain imaging findings in antisocial, violent, and psychopathic individuals: A meta-analysis. *Psychiatry Research: Neuroimaging, 174*(2), 81–88. doi:10.1016/j.pscychresns.2009.03.012

Yang, Y., Zhang, J., Ma, D., Zhang, M., Hu, S., Shao, J., & Gong, C.-X. (2013). Subcutaneous administration of liraglutide ameliorates Alzheimer-associated tau hyperphosphorylation in rats with type 2 diabetes. *Journal of Alzheimer's Disease, 37*(3), 637–648.

Yarmohammadian, M. H., Raeisi, A. R., Tavakoli, N., & Nansa, L. G. (2010). Medical record information disclosure laws and policies among selected countries; a comparative study. *Journal of Research in Medical Sciences, 15*(3), 140–149.

Yatawara, C. J., Einfeld, S. L., Hickie, I. B., Davenport, T. A., & Guastella, A. J. (2016). The effect of oxytocin nasal spray on social interaction deficits observed in young children with autism: A randomized clinical crossover trial. *Mol Psychiatry, 21*(9), 1225–1231. doi:10.1038/mp.2015.162

Yates, A., Edman, J., & Aruguete, M. (2004). Ethnic differences in BMI and body/self-dissatisfaction among Whites, Asian subgroups, Pacific Islanders, and African-Americans. *Journal of Adolescent Health, 34*(4), 300–307. doi:http://dx.doi.org/10.1016/j.jadohealth.2003.07.014

Yau, Y. H. C., & Potenza, M. N. (2015). Gambling disorder and other behavioral addictions: Recognition and treatment. *Harvard Review of Psychiatry, 23*(2), 134–146. doi:10.1097/HRP.0000000000000051

Yen, L.-L., Patrick, W. K., & Chie, W.-C. (1996). Comparison of relaxation techniques, routine blood pressure measurements, and self-learning packages in hypertension control. *Preventive Medicine: An International Journal Devoted to Practice and Theory, 25*(3), 339–345. doi:10.1006/pmed.1996.0064

Yeo, R. A., Arden, R., & Jung, R. E. (2011). Alzheimer's disease and intelligence. *Current Alzheimer Research, 8*(4), 345–353. doi:10.2174/156720511795745276

Yeomans, F. E., & Diamond, D. (2010). Transference-focused psychotherapy and borderline personality disorder. In J. F. Clarkin, P. Fonagy, & G. O. Gabbard (Eds.), *Psychodynamic psychotherapy for personality disorders: A clinical handbook* (pp. 209–238). Arlington, VA: American Psychiatric Publishing.

Yeomans, F. E., Clarkin, J. F., & Kernberg, O. F. (2015). *Transference-focused psychotherapy for borderline personality disorder: A clinical guide.* Arlington, VA: American Psychiatric Publishing.

Yildirim, B. O., & Derksen, J. J. L. (2013). Systematic review, structural analysis, and new theoretical perspectives on the role of serotonin and associated genes in the etiology of psychopathy and sociopathy. *Neuroscience and Biobehavioral Reviews, 37*(7), 1254–1296. doi:10.1016/j.neubiorev.2013.04.009

Yin, R. K. (2014). *Case study research: Design and methods.* Thousand Oaks, CA: SAGE Publications.

Yip, A. G., & Carpenter, L. L. (2010). Transcranial magnetic stimulation for medication-resistant depression. *Journal of Clinical Psychiatry, 71*(4), 502–503. doi:10.4088/JCP.10ac06054blu

Yoosefi Looyeh, M., Kamali, K., & Shafieian, R. (2012). An exploratory study of the effectiveness of group narrative therapy on the school behavior of girls with attention-deficit/hyperactivity symptoms. *Archives of Psychiatric Nursing, 26*(5), 404–410. doi:10.1016/j.apnu.2012.01.001

Yosephine, L. (2016, February 24). Indonesian psychiatrists label LGBT as mental disorders. *The Jakarta Post.* Retrieved from http://www.thejakartapost.com/news/2016/02/24/indonesian-psychiatrists-label-lgbt-mental-disorders.html

Yoshiyama, Y., Lee, V. M. Y., & Trojanowski, J. Q. (2013). Therapeutic strategies for tau mediated neurodegeneration. *Journal of Neurology, Neurosurgery & Psychiatry, 84*(7), 784–795. doi:10.1136/jnnp-2012-303144

Young, A. H., & Hammond, J. M. (2007). Lithium in mood disorders: Increasing evidence base, declining use? *The British Journal of Psychiatry, 191*(6), 474–476. doi:10.1192/bjp.bp.107.043133

Young, B. H., & Blake, D. D. (1999). *Group treatments for post-traumatic stress disorder.* Philadelphia, PA: Brunner/Mazel.

Young, G. (2014). PTSD, endophenotypes, the RDoC, and the DSM-5. *Psychological Injury and Law, 7*(1), 75–91. doi:10.1007/s12207-014-9187-x

Young, J. E. (1999). *Cognitive therapy for personality disorders: A schema-focused approach* (3rd ed.). Sarasota, FL: Professional Resource Press/Professional Resource Exchange.

Young, J. E., Klosko, J. S., & Weishaar, M. E. (2003). *Schema therapy: A practitioner's guide.* New York, NY: Guilford Press.

Young, J. J., Bruno, D., & Pomara, N. (2014). A review of the relationship between proinflammatory cytokines and major depressive disorder. *Journal of Affective Disorders, 169,* 15–20. doi:10.1016/j.jad.2014.07.032

Young, R. L., & Rodi, M. L. (2014). Redefining autism spectrum disorder using DSM-5: The implications of the proposed DSM-5 criteria for autism spectrum disorders. *Journal of Autism and Developmental Disorders, 44*(4), 758–765. doi:10.1007/s10803-013-1927-3

Younggren, J. N., & Harris, E. A. (2008). Can you keep a secret? Confidentiality in psychotherapy. *Journal of Clinical Psychology, 64*(5), 589–600. doi:10.1002/jclp.20480

Younis, A. A., & Moselhy, H. F. (2009). Lycanthropy alive in Babylon: The existence of archetype. *Acta Psychiatrica Scandinavica, 119*(2), 161–164. doi:10.1111/j.1600-0447.2008.01321.x

Yousry Elnazer, H., & Baldwin, D. S. (2014). Investigation of cortisol levels in patients with anxiety disorders: A structured review. In C. M. Pariante & M. D. Lapiz-Bluhm (Eds.), *Behavioral neurobiology of stress-related disorders* (Vol. 18, pp. 191–216). New York, NY: Springer-Verlag Publishing.

Yu, C.-J., Du, J.-C., Chiou, H.-C., Feng, C.-C., Chung, M.-Y., Yang, W., ... Chen, M.-L. (2016). Sugar-sweetened beverage consumption is adversely associated with childhood attention deficit/hyperactivity disorder. *International Journal of Environmental Research And Public Health, 13*(7). doi:10.3390/ijerph13070678

Yüce, M., Uçar, F., & Nur Say, G. (2015). Comorbid conditions in child and adolescent patients diagnosed with attention deficit/hyperactivity disorder. In J. M. Norvilitis (Ed.), *ADHD—New directions in diagnosis and treatment* (pp. 109–164). Rijeka, Croatia: InTech.

Yufik, A. (2005). Revisiting the Tarasoff decision: Risk assessment and liability in clinical and forensic practice. *American Journal of Forensic Psychology, 23*(4), 5–21.

Yüksel, C., McCarthy, J., Shinn, A., Pfaff, D. L., Baker, J. T., Heckers, S., ... Öngür, D. (2012). Gray matter volume in schizophrenia and bipolar disorder with psychotic features. *Schizophrenia Research, 138*(2–3), 177–182. doi:http://dx.doi.org/10.1016/j.schres.2012.03.003

Yung, A. R., Woods, S. W., Ruhrmann, S., Addington, J., Schultze-Lutter, F., Cornblatt, B. A., ... McGlashan, T. H. (2012). Whither the attenuated psychosis syndrome? *Schizophrenia Bulletin, 38*(6), 1130–1134. doi:10.1093/schbul/sbs108

Yuodelis-Flores, C., & Ries, R. K. (2015). Addiction and suicide: A review. *The American Journal on Addictions, 24*(2), 98–104. doi:10.1111/ajad.12185

Zachar, P. (2009). Psychiatric comorbidity: More than a Kuhnian anomaly. *Philosophy, Psychiatry, & Psychology, 16*(1), 13–22. doi:10.1353/ppp.0.0212

Zachar, P. (2011). The clinical nature of personality disorders: Answering the neo-Szaszian critique. *Philosophy, Psychiatry, & Psychology, 18*(3), 191–202. doi:10.1353/ppp.2011.0038

Zachar, P., & Kendler, K. S. (2012). The removal of Pluto from the class of planets and homosexuality from the class of psychiatric disorders: A comparison. *Philosophy, Ethics, and Humanities in Medicine, 7*(4). Retrieved from http://www.peh-med.com/content/7/1/4

Zachar, P., & Potter, N. N. (2010a). Personality disorders: Moral or medical kinds—Or both? *Philosophy, Psychiatry, & Psychology, 17*(2), 101–117. doi:10.1353/ppp.0.0290

Zachar, P., & Potter, N. N. (2010b). Valid moral appraisals and valid personality disorders. *Philosophy, Psychiatry, & Psychology, 17*(2), 131–142. doi:10.1353/ppp.0.0296

Zachar, P., Krueger, R. F., & Kendler, K. S. (2016). Personality disorder in DSM-5: An oral history. *Psychological Medicine, 46*(1), 1–10. doi:10.1017/S0033291715001543

Zadra, A., Desautels, A., Petit, D., & Montplaisir, J. (2013). Somnambulism: Clinical aspects and pathophysiological hypotheses. *The Lancet Neurology, 12*(3), 285–294. doi:10.1016/S1474-4422(12)70322-8

Zafiropoulou, M., & Pappa, E. (2002). The role of preparedness and social environment in developing social phobia. *Psychology: The Journal of the Hellenic Psychological Society, 9*(3), 365–377.

Zajac, K., Randall, J., & Swenson, C. C. (2015). Multisystemic therapy for externalizing youth. *Child and Adolescent Psychiatric Clinics of North America, 24*(3), 601–616. doi:10.1016/j.chc.2015.02.007

Zakowski, S. G., McAllister, C. G., Deal, M., & Baum, A. (1992). Stress, reactivity, and immune function in healthy men. *Health Psychology, 11*(4), 223–232. doi:10.1037/0278-6133.11.4.223

Zalta, A. K., & Foa, E. B. (2012). Exposure therapy: Promoting emotional processing of pathological anxiety. In W. T. O'Donohue & J. E. Fisher (Eds.), *Cognitive behavior therapy: Core principles for practice* (pp. 75–104). Hoboken, NJ: John Wiley.

Zanos, P., Piantadosi, S. C., Wu, H.-Q., Pribut, H. J., Dell, M. J., Can, A., ... Gould, T. D. (2015). The prodrug 4-chlorokynurenine causes ketamine-like antidepressant effects, but not side effects, by NMDA/glycineB-site inhibition. *The Journal of Pharmacology and Experimental Therapeutics, 355*(1), 76–85. doi:10.1124/jpet.115.225664

Zaroff, C. M., Davis, J. M., Chio, P. H., & Madhavan, D. (2012). Somatic presentations of distress in China. *Australian and New Zealand Journal of Psychiatry, 46*(11), 1053–1057.

Zerbe, K. J. (2010). Psychodynamic therapy for eating disorders. In C. M. Grilo & J. E. Mitchell (Eds.), *The treatment of eating disorders: A clinical handbook* (pp. 339–358). New York, NY: Guilford Press.

Zerbo, O., Qian, Y., Yoshida, C., Grether, J. K., Van de Water, J., & Croen, L. A. (2015). Maternal infection during pregnancy and autism spectrum disorders. *Journal of Autism and Developmental Disorders, 45*(12), 4015–4025. doi:10.1007/s10803-013-2016-3

Zetterqvist, M. (2015). The DSM-5 diagnosis of nonsuicidal self-injury disorder: A review of the empirical literature. *Child and Adolescent Psychiatry and Mental Health, 9*.

Zhang, J., Sheerin, C., Mandel, H., Banducci, A. N., Myrick, H., Acierno, R., ... Wang, Z. (2014). Variation in SLC1A1 is related to combat-related posttraumatic stress disorder. *Journal of Anxiety Disorders, 28*(8), 902–907. doi:10.1016/j.janxdis.2014.09.013

Zhao, L. N., Lu, L., Chew, L. Y., & Mu, Y. (2014). Alzheimer's disease—a panorama glimpse. *International Journal of Molecular Sciences, 15*(7), 12631–12650. doi:10.3390/ijms150712631

Zhao, X., & Dawson, J. (2014). The new Chinese mental health law. *Psychiatry, Psychology and Law, 21*(5), 669–686. doi:10.1080/13218719.2014.882248

Zheng, W., Li, X. B., Xiang, Y. Q., Zhong, B. L., Chiu, H. F. K., Ungvari, G. S., ... Xiang, Y. T. (2016). Aripiprazole for Tourette's syndrome: A systematic review and meta-analysis. *Human Psychopharmacology: Clinical and Experimental, 31*(1), 11–18. doi:10.1002/hup.2498

Zhou, J., Wang, X., Li, L., Cao, X., Xu, L., & Sun, Y. (2006). Plasma serotonin levels in young violent offenders: Aggressive responding and personality correlates. *Progress in Neuro-Psychopharmacology & Biological Psychiatry, 30*(8), 1435–1441. doi:10.1016/j.pnpbp.2006.05.021

Zhou, K., & Zhuang, G. (2014). Retention in methadone maintenance treatment in mainland China, 2004–2012: A literature review. *Addictive Behaviors, 39*(1), 22–29. doi:10.1016/j.addbeh.2013.09.001

Zhu, J., Weiss, L. G., Prifitera, A., & Coalson, D. (2004). The Weschler Intelligence Scales for children and adults. In G. Goldstein & S. R. Beers (Eds.), *Comprehensive handbook of psychological assessment: Vol. 1. Intellectual and neuropsychological assessment* (pp. 51–75). Hoboken, NJ: John Wiley.

Zhu, X., Yao, S., Dere, J., Zhou, B., Yang, J., & Ryder, A. G. (2014). The cultural shaping of social anxiety: Concerns about causing distress to others in Han Chinese and Euro-Canadian outpatients. *Journal of Social and Clinical Psychology, 33*(10), 906–917. doi:10.1521/jscp.2014.33.10.906

Zilboorg, G. (1941). *A history of medical psychology*. New York, NY: Norton.

Zimmerman, M. (1994). Diagnosing personality disorders: A review of issues and research models. *Archives of General Psychiatry, 51*(3), 225–245. doi:10.1001/archpsyc.1994.03950030061006

Zipfel, S., Wild, B., Groß, G., Friederich, H.-C., Teufel, M., Schellberg, D., ... Herzog, W. (2014). Focal psychodynamic therapy, cognitive behaviour therapy, and optimised treatment as usual in outpatients with anorexia nervosa (ANTOP study): Randomised controlled trial. *The Lancet, 383*(9912), 127–137. doi:10.1016/S0140-6736(13)61746-8

Zipursky, R. B., Reilly, T. J., & Murray, R. M. (2013). The myth of schizophrenia as a progressive brain disease. *Schizophrenia Bulletin, 39*(6), 1363–1372. doi:10.1093/schbul/sbs135

Zoellner, L. A., Rothbaum, B. O., & Feeny, N. C. (2011). PTSD not an anxiety disorder? DSM committee proposal turns back the hands of time. *Depression and Anxiety, 28*(10), 853–856. doi:10.1002/da.20899

Zoellner, T., & Maercker, A. (2006a). Posttraumatic growth and psychotherapy. In L. G. Calhoun & R. G. Tedeschi (Eds.), *Handbook of posttraumatic growth: Research & practice* (pp. 334–354). Mahwah, NJ: Lawrence Erlbaum.

Zoellner, T., & Maercker, A. (2006b). Posttraumatic growth in clinical psychology—A critical review and introduction of a two component model. *Clinical Psychology Review, 26*(5), 626–653. doi:10.1016/j.cpr.2006.01.008

Zorn, J. V., Schür, R. R., Boks, M. P., Kahn, R. S., Joëls, M., & Vinkers, C. H. (2017). Cortisol stress reactivity across psychiatric disorders: A systematic review and meta-analysis. *Psychoneuroendocrinology, 77*, 25–36. doi:10.1016/j.psyneuen.2016.11.036

Zung, W. W. (1971). A rating instrument for anxiety disorders. *Psychosomatics: Journal of Consultation and Liaison Psychiatry, 12*(6), 371–379. doi:10.1016/S0033-3182(71)71479-0

NAME INDEX

Page numbers in **bold** indicate tables and in *italic* indicate figures.

SUBJECT INDEX

/////////////////////////////

Page numbers in **bold** indicate tables and in *italic* indicate figures.

4P model of case formulation 84

12-step programs 365, 379–381, **379**

A

B

C

D

E

F

family-based treatment (FBT) 307–308
family studies 293
family systems therapies 307–308
gender and 303–305
genetic marker studies 293–294
genetic perspectives 293–294
genome-wide association (GWA) studies 294
heritability estimates 293
historical perspectives 287–288, 296
humanistic perspectives 301
immune system perspectives 295–296
interpersonal therapy (IPT) 297–298
media and 303–306
narrative therapy 301
night eating syndrome 286
obesity 286, 292, 295, 306, 307
object relations therapy 297
objectification theory 304
oral impregnation theory 287–288, 296
orthorexia nervosa 286–287
overcorrection therapy 299
pica 284
prevalence rates 283
psychodynamic perspectives 287–288, 296–298
psychosomatic families 307
purging 282
purging disorder 286
reproductive suppression hypothesis 294–295
reward pathway disturbances 292
rumination disorder 285
self-objectification 304
serotonin and 288, 289

sexual competition hypothesis 294
socioeconomic status and 306
specialist supportive clinical management (SSCM) 302
stigma 306–307
systems perspectives 307–308
twin studies 293
ventricle size and brain volume 292–293
Western ideal of thinness and 302–303
feeding disorder of infancy and early childhood 284
Feingold Diet 450
female orgasmic disorder 316, 317
female sexual arousal dysfunction 315–316
female sexual interest/arousal disorder 315, 316
feminist therapy 61–62
fentanyl 355
fetal alcohol syndrome (FAS) 351
fetishism/fetishistic disorder 319
fetishistic transvestism/transvestic disorder 319
FFT see family-focused therapy (FFT)
"Fidgety Philip" story 432
fight or flight response 225
fighter theory 440
financial barriers to care 517–518
first-generation antipsychotics 114–115, **114**
First World War 222
fitness 38–39
fitness to plead 523–524
five-stage theory of grief 214–215

fixation 44
flashbacks 216
flibanserin 327–328
flooding and response prevention 51, 199
fluoxetine 150, 188, 223, 290
fluvoxamine 188
fMRI see functional magnetic resonance imaging (fMRI)
food additives hypothesis 450
Food and Drug Administration (FDA), US 11–12
food exposure for anorexia 298
formal thought disorder 105
formulation 83–85
4P model of case formulation 84
compared to diagnosis 83
evaluating 85, **85**
integrative evidence-based case formulation 83–84
using interviews in 95
fragile process 411–412
Fragile X syndrome 476
free association 45–46
free will vs. determinism 522–523
freedom 203
frequency-dependent selection hypothesis 403–404
Freudian slips 45–46
frontal lobe 36, 36, 157
frotteurism/frotteuristic disorder 319
functional analysis 98
functional analysis interview (FAI) 98
functional magnetic resonance imaging (fMRI) 101
functional relaxation 270

G

GABA see gamma-aminobutyric acid (GABA)
GAD see generalized anxiety disorder (GAD)
galantamine 493
gambling disorders 362–363, 366, 372
gaming disorder 362, 363
gamma-aminobutyric acid (GABA) 36, 186–187, 350, 356, 437, 463
gamma-hydroxybutyrate (GHB) 463
GAS see general adaptation syndrome (GAS)
gatekeeping 340
gay people 312
GBMI see guilty but mentally ill (GBMI)
Geel, Belgium 16
gender
anxiety and 205–207
defined 311–312
dementia and 495
depression and 171–172
eating problems and 303–305
muscle dysmorphia 304–305
personality disorders and 414–415
PTSD and 238
self-objectification 304
suicide and 500–501, 508
see also sexual problems and gender issues
gender conformity 311
gender dysphoria/incongruence 320, 321, 322–323
brain chemistry perspectives 329

brain structure and function perspectives 330
cross-sex hormonal treatment 329
genetic perspectives 331
medicalization of 332
prenatal sex hormones 329
sex reassignment surgery **314**, 329
gender expression 311–312
gender identity 311–313
gender identity disorder of childhood 321
gender incongruence see gender dysphoria/incongruence
gender nonconformity 311
gender reassignment surgery see sex reassignment surgery
general adaptation syndrome (GAS) 213
general paresis 39
generalized anxiety disorder (GAD) **73**, **74–75**, 181, 185
see also anxiety disorders
genes 37–38
genetic marker studies
dissociation complaints 259
enuresis 467
feeding and eating problems 293–294
psychosis 119, **119**
genetic perspectives 37–38, 37
Alzheimer's disease 492–493
anxiety disorders 190

attention-deficit/hyperactivity disorder (ADHD) 439
autism 439
bereavement and grief 226
communication disorders 486–487
dementia 492–493
disruptive behavior issues 439
dissociation complaints 259
Down syndrome 476
elimination disorders 467
feeding and eating problems 293–294
Fragile X syndrome 476
gender dysphoria/incongruence 331
intellectual disabilities 475–476
learning disorders 476
mood problems 159–160
motor problems 481
obsessions and compulsions 191
personality disorders 402–403
phenylketonuria (PKU) 475–476
psychosis 116–119
schizophrenia 116–119
sexual problems and gender issues 330–331
somatic complaints 260
stuttering 486–487
substance use and addiction 369
suicide 504
Tourette's disorder 481
trauma and stress disorders 226

H

suicide 506–507
  trauma and stress disorders 235–236
  see also person-centered therapy
hunter-farmer theory 439
hydrocortisone 225
hydrotherapy 112
hyperkinetic conduct disorder 424, 425

hypersexual disorder 322
hypersomnia 457, 462
hypnosis 257, 471
hypoactive sexual desire dysfunction 315–316
hypochondriacal disorder 253
hypochondriasis 253

hypomanic episodes 140–141
hypothalamic-pituitary-adrenal (HPA) axis 158, 225, 258, 263, 292, 495, 504
hypothalamus 225, 291–292, 330
hypotheses 23
hysteria 13, 256–257
hysterical neurosis 221

I

iatrogenic conditions 255, 261, 271–272
ICD-11 model of personality disorders 395–397
id 43, 44, *44*
identification with the aggressor 334
identified patients 63
identity alteration 246
identity confusion 246
idiopathic illnesses 11–12
idiopathic short stature (ISS) 11–12
IFS *see* internal family systems therapy (IFS)
ignorance 4
illness anxiety disorder 253
illness model of drug addiction 364–365
imaginal exposure 200, 230
imipramine **436**
immune system perspectives 39
  anxiety disorders 193
  attention-deficit/hyperactivity disorder (ADHD) 440
  autism 440–441
  bereavement and grief 227
  disruptive behavior issues 440
  feeding and eating problems 295–296
  mood problems 161
  motor problems 481
  obsessions and compulsions 193
  personality disorders 404
  psychosis 121–122
  schizophrenia 121–122
  sexual problems and gender issues 331
  somatic complaints 261–263
  stress 261–263
  substance use and addiction 370
  suicide 504
  trauma and stress disorders 227
in vivo exposure 200, 230–231
in vivo food exposure 298
inauthenticity 58
incentive-sensitization theory 365–366
incidence rates 8, 23
incongruence 57
independent variables 23–24
indolamines 36
indoleamine hallucinogens 355
industrialization 148
inequality 23
  anxiety disorders and 205
  feeding and eating problems and 306
  intellectual disabilities and 477–478
  mood problems and 171
  posttraumatic stress disorder (PTSD) and 238
  psychosis and 129
  schizophrenia and 129
  sleep disorders and 465

inflammatory hypothesis
  anxiety disorders 193
  attention-deficit/hyperactivity disorder (ADHD) 440
  autism 440
  bereavement and grief 227
  mood problems 161
  obsessions and compulsions 193
  personality disorders 404
  posttraumatic stress disorder (PTSD) 227
  psychosis 121–122
  substance use and addiction 370
informed consent 514
inhalant-related disorders **360**, **361–362**
inhibitory learning 201–202
insanity 519
insanity defense 519–523
Insanity Defense Reform Act (IDRA), US 521
insomnia 455, 457, 459
  drugs for 463
  hyperarousal theory of 462
insula 189
insulin coma therapy 19, 112
integrated sociodevelopmental-cognitive model of schizophrenia 135, *136*
integrative behavioral couples therap 243
integrative evidence-based case formulation 83–84
intellectual disabilities
  cognitive-behavioral therapy (CBT) 477
  cross-cultural and social justice perspectives 477–478
  Down syndrome 476
  DSM and *ICD* perspectives 472
  Fragile X syndrome 476
  genetic perspectives 475–476
  group homes 478
  historical perspectives 475
  illnesses and brain injuries 476
  involuntary sterilization 475
  phenylketonuria (PKU) 475–476
  pregnancy and childbirth problems 476
  prevalence rates 472
  socioeconomic inequality and 477–478
intelligence 100
intelligence quotient (IQ) 100, 472, 474
intelligence tests 100, 472
intensive short-term dynamic psychotherapy (ISTDP) 408
intentionality 30
intermediate beliefs 53
intermittent explosive disorder **80**, 423–424, 436
internal dysfunction 6, 7
internal family systems therapy (IFS) 273–274

internal validity 25
internalized homophobia 312
internalizing behaviors 421
International Classification of Diseases (ICD) 70–83
  acute and transient psychotic disorder (ATPD) 108
  acute stress reaction 217–218
  adjustment disorders 218, 220
  agoraphobia 180–181, 185
  anankastic personality disorder 392
  anorexia nervosa 280, 282–283, 285
  anxiety disorders **73**, **74**, 178–182, 184–185
  anxious (avoidant) personality disorder 391–392
  autism-related diagnoses 425–427, 430–431
  avoidant/restrictive food intake disorder (ARFID) 283–284
  binge-eating disorder (BED) 283, 286
  bipolar affective disorder 142
  bodily distress disorder 251–252
  body dysmorphic disorder (BDD) 183, 184
  bulimia nervosa 282–283, 285
  categorical vs. dimensional diagnosis 110, 386–387, 397–398
  coercive sexual sadism disorder 333
  communication disorders 485–486
  compared to *PDM* 85–86
  conduct disorder (CD) 422–423
  culture and 80
  cyclothymic disorder 143
  definition of mental disorder 72–73
  delusional disorder 107–108
  dementia 489–491
  dependent personality disorder 392
  depersonalization/derealization disorder **248**, 249
  depressive episodes 139–140
  developmental language disorder with impairment of mainly pragmatic language 427, 428
  diagnostic codes 75
  diagnostic guidelines 73, **73**, **74**
  disruptive behavior issues 421–425, 428–430
  dissocial personality disorder 388–389
  dissociation complaints 247–251, **248**, 255
  dissociative amnesia 248–249, **248**
  dissociative disorders of movement and sensation 252
  dissociative fugue 248–249, **248**
  dissociative identity disorder (DID) **248**, 249–251, 255

J

K

L

M

N

O

OARS 375
obesity 286, 292, 295, 306, 307
object relations therapy 47–48
    feeding and eating problems 297
    personality disorders 407–408
    schizophrenia 123
objective tests 95
objective/universal/legal views 12
observational learning 197
obsessions and compulsions 176–211
    accommodation 209
    augmenting agents 188
    behavioral perspectives 198
    body dysmorphic disorder (BDD)
        183, 184
    brain chemistry perspectives 188–189
    brain structure and function
        perspectives 189–190
    cognitive-behavioral therapy (CBT)
        188, 196, 198–201, 204
    cognitive perspectives 198–199
    compulsions defined 177
    consumer and service-user perspectives
        207–208
    drugs for 188
    DSM and ICD perspectives 182–184
    evolutionary perspectives 192–193
    excoriation (skin-picking disorder)
        183, 184
    exposure plus response prevention 199
    expressed emotion and 208–209
    genetic perspectives 191
    glutamate hypothesis of OCD
        188–189
    group selection theory of OCD 192
    gut-brain axis 193
    heritability estimates 191
    historical perspectives 185–186
    hoarding disorder 183, 184
    humanistic perspectives 203
    immune system perspectives 193
    inflammatory hypothesis 193
    insecure attachments and 195
    logotherapy 203
    malfunctioning mental mechanisms
        192
    obsessions defined 177
    obsessive-compulsive disorder (OCD)
        182–183
    prevalence rates 183
    psychodynamic perspectives 194, 195
    stigma 207
    systems perspectives 208–209
    thought stopping 200
    trichotillomania (hair-pulling disorder)
        183, 184
obsessive-compulsive disorder (OCD)
    182–183, 392
    see also obsessions and compulsions
obsessive-compulsive personality disorder
    (OCPD) 392, **409**
obsessive trait complex hypothesis 404
occipital lobe 36, 36
OCD see obsessive-compulsive
    disorder (OCD)
OCPD see obsessive-compulsive
    personality disorder (OCPD)
ODD see oppositional defiant
    disorder (ODD)
odd or eccentric personality disorders
    387–388
Oedipus complex 45
olanzapine 290, 352
olfactory aversion 336
onanism 8–9
Open Dialogue 133–134
openness 385
operant conditioning 50–51, 267, 335
opioid antagonists 257
opioid blockers 367
opioid-related disorders **360**, **361–362**
opioids 354–355, 367–368
opium 354
oppositional defiant disorder (ODD)
    89, 422–423, 429–430
opralalia 479
oral impregnation 287–288, 296
oral stage 44
orbitofrontal cortex 37, 329, 504
orexin 462, 463
orexin-receptor antagonists 463
organismic valuing process 57
organizational injustice 465
orgasmic dysfunction 316, 317
orthorexia nervosa 286–287
outpatient civil commitment 525–526
outpatient services 20
overcorrection 299
oxybutynin 468
oxycodone 354
oxytocin 437

P

P-Axis (Personality Syndromes) 86,
    86–87, **88**
palilialia 479
PANDAS hypothesis 481
panic attacks 179
panic disorder 179–180, 185
    catastrophic misinterpretation
        model of 197–198
    cognitive perspectives 197–198
    cultural differences 204–205
    genetic perspectives 190
    see also anxiety disorders
paranoid personality disorder 387, **409**
paraphilias
    drugs for 328–329
    heritability estimates 331
paraphilias and paraphilic
    disorders 318–319
    aversion therapies 335–336
    behavioral perspectives 334–336
    brain chemistry perspectives 328–329
    brain structure and function
        perspectives 330
    cognitive-behavioral therapy (CBT)
        336–337
    effectiveness of psychological
        therapies 338–339
    genetic perspectives 331
    as hostile fantasies 333–334
    medicalization of 332–333
    psychodynamic perspectives 333–334
paraphilic coercive disorder (PCD) 332–333
parasomnias 458–459, 462
parasuicidal behavior 390, 501
parasympathetic nervous
    system (PNS) 225
parens patriae 525
parent management training 243
parietal cortex 258, 329, 438
parietal lobe 36, 36
paroxetine 223, 224
participant modeling 200
participants 24
pathogens 39
pathological gambling 362
pathological grief see prolonged
    grief disorder
patriarchy 61
PCD see paraphilic coercive disorder (PCD)
PCP see phencyclidine (PCP)
PDD see persistent depressive
    disorder (PDD)
PDM see Psychodynamic Diagnostic
    Manual (PDM)
PECS see Picture Exchange
    Communication System (PECS)
pedophilia/pedophilic disorder 319
pelvic floor rehabilitation 335
penis envy 45, 333
pentazocine 355
Perceived Stress Scale (PSS) 214
perceptual system, psychosis and 120
persecution 15
persecutory delusions 104
persistent (chronic) motor or vocal tic
    disorder 479, 480
persistent complex bereavement disorder
    219, 220–221
    consumer and service-user perspectives
        241
    drugs for 224
    exposure therapies 231
    genetic perspectives 226
    psychodynamic perspectives 230
    stigma 241
persistent depressive disorder (PDD)
    143–144, 145–146
persistent grief see prolonged grief
    disorder
person-centered therapy 56–57
    anxiety disorders 202
    autism 446
    dissociation complaints 269–270
    formulation 83
    mood problems 169
    personality disorders 411–412
    psychosis 127

Q

R

S